Lecture Notes in Computer Science   12224

More information about this series at http://www.springer.com/series/7407

Shuvendu K. Lahiri · Chao Wang (Eds.)

Computer Aided Verification

32nd International Conference, CAV 2020
Los Angeles, CA, USA, July 21–24, 2020
Proceedings, Part I

 Springer

Editors
Shuvendu K. Lahiri
Microsoft Research Lab
Redmond, WA, USA

Chao Wang
University of Southern California
Los Angeles, CA, USA

ISSN 0302-9743   ISSN 1611-3349   (electronic)
Lecture Notes in Computer Science
ISBN 978-3-030-53287-1   ISBN 978-3-030-53288-8   (eBook)
https://doi.org/10.1007/978-3-030-53288-8

LNCS Sublibrary: SL1 – Theoretical Computer Science and General Issues

This Springer imprint is published by the registered company Springer Nature Switzerland AG
The registered company address is: Gewerbestrasse 11, 6330 Cham, Switzerland

Preface

It was our privilege to serve as the program chairs for CAV 2020, the 32nd International Conference on Computer-Aided Verification. CAV 2020 was held as a virtual conference during July 21–24, 2020. The tutorial day was on July 20, 2020, and the pre-conference workshops were held during July 19–20, 2020. Due to the coronavirus disease (COVID-19) outbreak, all events took place online.

CAV is an annual conference dedicated to the advancement of the theory and practice of computer-aided formal analysis methods for hardware and software systems. The primary focus of CAV is to extend the frontiers of verification techniques by expanding to new domains such as security, quantum computing, and machine learning. This puts CAV at the cutting edge of formal methods research, and this year's program is a reflection of this commitment.

CAV 2020 received a very high number of submissions (240). We accepted 18 tool papers, 4 case studies, and 43 regular papers, which amounts to an acceptance rate of roughly 27%. The accepted papers cover a wide spectrum of topics, from theoretical results to applications of formal methods. These papers apply or extend formal methods to a wide range of domains such as concurrency, machine learning, and industrially deployed systems. The program featured invited talks by David Dill (Calibra) and Pushmeet Kohli (Google DeepMind) as well as invited tutorials by Tevfik Bultan (University of California, Santa Barbara) and Sriram Sankaranarayanan (University of Colorado at Boulder). Furthermore, we continued the tradition of Logic Lounge, a series of discussions on computer science topics targeting a general audience.

In addition to the main conference, CAV 2020 hosted the following workshops: Numerical Software Verification (NSV), Verified Software: Theories, Tools, and Experiments (VSTTE), Verification of Neural Networks (VNN), Democratizing Software Verification, Synthesis (SYNT), Program Equivalence and Relational Reasoning (PERR), Formal Methods for ML-Enabled Autonomous Systems (FoMLAS), Formal Methods for Blockchains (FMBC), and Verification Mentoring Workshop (VMW).

Organizing a flagship conference like CAV requires a great deal of effort from the community. The Program Committee (PC) for CAV 2020 consisted of 85 members – a committee of this size ensures that each member has to review a reasonable number of papers in the allotted time. In all, the committee members wrote over 960 reviews while investing significant effort to maintain and ensure the high quality of the conference program. We are grateful to the CAV 2020 PC for their outstanding efforts in evaluating the submissions and making sure that each paper got a fair chance. Like last year's CAV, we made the artifact evaluation mandatory for tool paper submissions and optional but encouraged for the rest of the accepted papers. The Artifact Evaluation Committee consisted of 40 reviewers who put in significant effort to evaluate each artifact. The goal of this process was to provide constructive feedback to tool developers and help make the research published in CAV more reproducible. The Artifact

Evaluation Committee was generally quite impressed by the quality of the artifacts, and, in fact, all accepted tools passed the artifact evaluation. Among the accepted regular papers, 67% of the authors submitted an artifact, and 76% of these artifacts passed the evaluation. We are also very grateful to the Artifact Evaluation Committee for their hard work and dedication in evaluating the submitted artifacts. The evaluation and selection process involved thorough online PC discussions using the EasyChair conference management system, resulting in more than 2,000 comments.

CAV 2020 would not have been possible without the tremendous help we received from several individuals, and we would like to thank everyone who helped make CAV 2020 a success. First, we would like to thank Xinyu Wang and He Zhu for chairing the Artifact Evaluation Committee and Jyotirmoy Deshmukh for local arrangements. We also thank Zvonimir Rakamaric for chairing the workshop organization, Clark Barrett for managing sponsorship, Thomas Wies for arranging student fellowships, and Yakir Vizel for handling publicity. We also thank Roopsha Samanta for chairing the Mentoring Committee. Last but not least, we would like to thank members of the CAV Steering Committee (Kenneth McMillan, Aarti Gupta, Orna Grumberg, and Daniel Kroening) for helping us with several important aspects of organizing CAV 2020.

We hope that you will find the proceedings of CAV 2020 scientifically interesting and thought-provoking!

June 2020   Shuvendu K. Lahiri
                                                                              Chao Wang

Organization

Program Chairs

Shuvendu K. Lahiri	Microsoft Research, USA
Chao Wang	University of Southern California, USA

Workshop Chair

Zvonimir Rakamaric	University of Utah, USA

Sponsorship Chair

Clark Barrett	Stanford University, USA

Publicity Chair

Yakir Vizel	Technion - Israel Institute of Technology, Israel

Fellowship Chair

Thomas Wies	New York University, USA

Local Arrangements Chair

Jyotirmoy Deshmukh	University of Southern California, USA

Program Committee

Aws Albarghouthi	University of Wisconsin-Madison, USA
Jade Alglave	University College London, UK
Christel Baier	Technical University of Dresden, Germany
Gogul Balakrishnan	Google, USA
Sorav Bansal	India Institute of Technology, Delhi, India
Gilles Barthe	Max Planck Institute, Germany
Josh Berdine	Facebook, UK
Per Bjesse	Synopsys, USA
Sam Blackshear	Calibra, USA
Roderick Bloem	Graz University of Technology, Austria
Borzoo Bonakdarpour	Iowa State University, USA
Ahmed Bouajjani	Paris Diderot University, France
Tevfik Bultan	University of California, Santa Barbara, USA
Pavol Cerny	Vienna University of Technology, Austria

Krishna S	India Institute of Technology, Bombay, India
Sriram Sankaranarayanan	University of Colorado at Boulder, USA
Natarajan Shankar	SRI International, USA
Natasha Sharygina	University of Lugano, Switzerland
Sharon Shoham	Tel Aviv University, Israel
Alexandra Silva	University College London, UK
Anna Slobodova	Centaur Technology, USA
Fabio Somenzi	University of Colorado at Boulder, USA
Fu Song	ShanghaiTech University, China
Aditya Thakur	University of California, Davis, USA
Ashish Tiwari	Microsoft, USA
Aaron Tomb	Galois, Inc., USA
Ashutosh Trivedi	University of Colorado at Boulder, USA
Caterina Urban	Inria, France
Niki Vazou	IMDEA, Spain
Margus Veanes	Microsoft, USA
Yakir Vizel	Technion - Israel Institute of Technology, Israel
Xinyu Wang	University of Michigan, USA
Georg Weissenbacher	Vienna University of Technology, Austria
Fei Xie	Portland State University, USA
Jin Yang	Intel, USA
Naijun Zhan	Chinese Academy of Sciences, China
He Zhu	Rutgers University, USA

Artifact Evaluation Committee

Xinyu Wang (Co-chair)	University of Michigan, USA
He Zhu (Co-chair)	Rutgers University, USA
Angello Astorga	University of Illinois at Urbana-Champaign, USA
Subarno Banerjee	University of Michigan, USA
Martin Blicha	University of Lugano, Switzerland
Brandon Bohrer	Carnegie Mellon University, USA
Jose Cambronero	Massachusetts Institute of Technology, USA
Joonwon Choi	Massachusetts Institute of Technology, USA
Norine Coenen	Saarland University, Germany
Katherine Cordwell	Carnegie Mellon University, USA
Chuchu Fan	Massachusetts Institute of Technology, USA
Yotam Feldman	Tel Aviv University, Israel
Timon Gehr	ETH Zurich, Switzerland
Aman Goel	University of Michigan, USA
Chih-Duo Hong	University of Oxford, UK
Bo-Yuan Huang	Princeton University, USA
Jeevana Priya Inala	Massachusetts Institute of Technology, USA
Samuel Kaufman	University of Washington, USA
Ratan Lal	Kansas State University, USA
Stella Lau	Massachusetts Institute of Technology, USA

Juneyoung Lee	Seoul National University, South Korea
Enrico Magnago	Fondazione Bruno Kessler, Italy
Umang Mathur	University of Illinois at Urbana-Champaign, USA
Jedidiah McClurg	Colorado School of Mines, USA
Sam Merten	Ohio University, USA
Luan Nguyen	University of Pennsylvania, USA
Aina Niemetz	Stanford University, USA
Shankara Pailoor	The University of Texas at Austin, USA
Brandon Paulsen	University of Southern California, USA
Mouhammad Sakr	Saarland University, Germany
Daniel Selsam	Microsoft Research, USA
Jiasi Shen	Massachusetts Institute of Technology, USA
Xujie Si	University of Pennsylvania, USA
Gagandeep Singh	ETH Zurich, Switzerland
Abhinav Verma	Rice University, USA
Di Wang	Carnegie Mellon University, USA
Yuepeng Wang	The University of Texas at Austin, USA
Guannan Wei	Purdue University, USA
Zikang Xiong	Purdue University, USA
Klaus von Gleissenthall	University of California, San Diego, USA

Mentoring Workshop Chair

Roopsha Samanta	Purdue University, USA

Steering Committee

Kenneth McMillan	Microsoft Research, USA
Aarti Gupta	Princeton University, USA
Orna Grumberg	Technion - Israel Institute of Technology, Israel
Daniel Kroening	University of Oxford, UK

Additional Reviewers

Shaull Almagor	Antti Hyvarinen
Sepideh Asadi	Matteo Marescotti
Angello Astorga	Rodrigo Ottoni
Brandon Bohrer	Junkil Park
Vincent Cheval	Sean Regisford
Javier Esparza	David Sanan
Marie Farrell	Aritra Sengupta
Grigory Fedyukovich	Sadegh Soudjani
Jerome Feret	Tim Zakian
James Hamil	

Contents – Part I

Concurrency

Hardware Verification and Decision Procedures

Hybrid and Dynamic Systems

Contents – Part II

Stochastic Systems

Synthesis

AI Verification

NNV: The Neural Network Verification Tool for Deep Neural Networks and Learning-Enabled Cyber-Physical Systems

Hoang-Dung Tran[1,2], Xiaodong Yang[1], Diego Manzanas Lopez[1],
Patrick Musau[1], Luan Viet Nguyen[3], Weiming Xiang[5], Stanley Bak[4],
and Taylor T. Johnson[1(✉)]

[1] University of Nebraska, Lincoln, USA
taylor.johnson@vanderbilt.edu
[2] Vanderbilt University, Nashville, USA
[3] University of Dayton, Dayton, USA
[4] Stony Brook University, Stony Brook, USA
[5] Augusta University, Augusta, USA

Abstract. This paper presents the Neural Network Verification (NNV) software tool, a set-based verification framework for deep neural networks (DNNs) and learning-enabled cyber-physical systems (CPS). The crux of NNV is a collection of reachability algorithms that make use of a variety of set representations, such as polyhedra, star sets, zonotopes, and abstract-domain representations. NNV supports both exact (sound and complete) and over-approximate (sound) reachability algorithms for verifying safety and robustness properties of feed-forward neural networks (FFNNs) with various activation functions. For learning-enabled CPS, such as closed-loop control systems incorporating neural networks, NNV provides exact and over-approximate reachability analysis schemes for linear plant models and FFNN controllers with piecewise-linear activation functions, such as ReLUs. For similar neural network control systems (NNCS) that instead have nonlinear plant models, NNV supports over-approximate analysis by combining the star set analysis used for FFNN controllers with zonotope-based analysis for nonlinear plant dynamics building on CORA. We evaluate NNV using two real-world case studies: the first is safety verification of ACAS Xu networks, and the second deals with the safety verification of a deep learning-based adaptive cruise control system.

The material presented in this paper is based upon work supported by the Defense Advanced Research Projects Agency (DARPA) through contract number FA8750-18-C-0089, the National Science Foundation (NSF) under grant numbers SHF 1910017 and FMitF 1918450, and the Air Force Office of Scientific Research (AFOSR) through award numbers FA9550-18-1-0122 and FA9550-19-1-0288. The U.S. Government is authorized to reproduce and distribute reprints for Government purposes notwithstanding any copyright notation thereon. Any opinions, finding, and conclusions or recommendations expressed in this material are those of the author(s) and do not necessarily reflect the views of AFOSR, DARPA, or NSF.

© The Author(s) 2020
S. K. Lahiri and C. Wang (Eds.): CAV 2020, LNCS 12224, pp. 3–17, 2020.
https://doi.org/10.1007/978-3-030-53288-8_1

Keywords: Neural networks · Machine learning · Cyber-physical systems · Verification · Autonomy

1   Introduction

Deep neural networks (DNNs) have quickly become one of the most widely used tools for dealing with complex and challenging problems in numerous domains, such as image classification [10,16,25], function approximation, and natural language translation [11,18]. Recently, DNNs have been used in safety-critical cyber-physical systems (CPS), such as autonomous vehicles [8,9,52] and air traffic collision avoidance systems [21]. Although utilizing DNNs in safety-critical applications can demonstrate considerable performance benefits, assuring the safety and robustness of these systems is challenging because DNNs possess complex non-linear characteristics. Moreover, it has been demonstrated that their behavior can be unpredictable due to slight perturbations in their inputs (i.e., adversarial perturbations) [36].

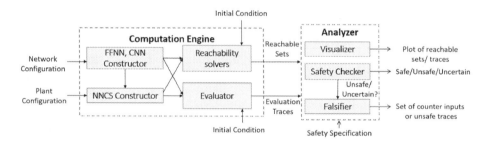

Fig. 1. An overview of NNV and its major modules and components.

In this paper, we introduce the NNV (**N**eural **N**etwork **V**erification) tool, which is a software framework that performs set-based verification for DNNs and learning-enabled CPS, known colloquially as neural network control systems (NNCS) as shown in Fig. 2[1]. NNV provides a set of reachability algorithms that can compute both the exact and over-approximate reachable sets of DNNs and NNCSs using a variety of set representations such as polyhedra [40,53–56], star sets [29,38,39,41], zonotopes [32], and abstract domain representations [33]. The reachable set obtained from NNV contains all possible states of a DNN from bounded input sets or of a NNCS from sets of initial states of a plant model. NNV declares a DNN or a NNCS to be safe if, and only if, their reachable sets do not violate safety properties (i.e., have a non-empty intersection with any state satisfying the negation of the safety property). If a safety property is violated,

---

[1] The source code for NNV is publicly available: https://github.com/verivital/nnv/. A CodeOcean capsule [43] is also available: https://doi.org/10.24433/CO.0221760. v1.

Table 1. Overview of major features available in NNV. Links refer to relevant files/-classes in the NNV codebase. BN refers to batch normalization layers, FC to fully-connected layers, AvgPool to average pooling layers, Conv to convolutional layers, and MaxPool to max pooling layers.

Feature	Exact analysis	Over-approximate analysis
Components	FFNN, CNN, NNCS	FFNN, CNN, NNCS
Plant dynamics (for NNCS)	Linear ODE	Linear ODE, Nonlinear ODE
Discrete/Continuous (for NNCS)	Discrete Time	Discrete Time, Continuous Time
Activation functions	ReLU, Satlin	ReLU, Satlin, Sigmoid, Tanh
CNN Layers	MaxPool, Conv, BN, AvgPool, FC	MaxPool, Conv, BN, AvgPool, FC
Reachability methods	Star, Polyhedron, ImageStar	Star, Zonotope, Abstract-domain, ImageStar
Reachable set/Flow-pipe Visualization	Yes	Yes
Parallel computing	Yes	Partially supported
Safety verification	Yes	Yes
Falsification	Yes	Yes
Robustness verification (for FFNN/CNN)	Yes	Yes
Counterexample generation	Yes	Yes

NNV can construct a complete set of counter-examples demonstrating the set of all possible unsafe initial inputs and states by using the star-based exact reachability algorithm [38,41]. To speed up computation, NNV uses parallel computing, as the majority of the reachability algorithms in NNV are more efficient when executed on multi-core platforms and clusters.

NNV has been successfully applied to safety verification and robustness analysis of several real-world DNNs, primarily feedforward neural networks (FFNNs) and convolutional neural networks (CNNs), as well as learning-enabled CPS. To highlight NNV's capabilities, we present brief experimental results from two case studies. The first compares methods for safety verification of the ACAS Xu networks [21], and the second presents safety verification of a learning-based adaptive cruise control (ACC) system.

2   Overview and Features

NNV is an object-oriented toolbox written in Matlab, which was chosen in part due to the prevalence of Matlab/Simulink in the design of CPS. NNV uses the MPT toolbox [26] for polytope-based reachability analysis and visualization [40], and makes use of CORA [3] for zonotope-based reachability analysis of nonlinear plant models [38]. NNV also utilizes the Neural Network Model Transformation Tool (NNMT) for transforming neural network models from Keras and Tensorflow into Matlab using the Open Neural Network Exchange (ONNX) format, and the Hybrid Systems Model Transformation and Translation tool (HyST) [5]

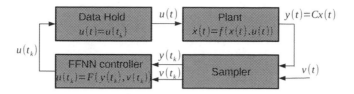

Fig. 2. Architecture of a typical neural network control system (NNCS).

for plant configuration. NNV makes use of YALMIP [27] for some optimization problems and MatConvNet [46] for some CNN operations.

The NNV toolbox contains two main modules: a *computation engine* and an *analyzer*, shown in Fig. 1. The computation engine module consists of four sub-components: 1) the *FFNN constructor*, 2) the *NNCS constructor*, 3) *the reachability solvers*, and 4) *the evaluator*. The FFNN constructor takes a network configuration file as an input and generates a FFNN object. The NNCS constructor takes the FFNN object and the plant configuration, which describes the dynamics of a system, as inputs and then creates an NNCS object. Depending on the application, either the FFNN (or NNCS) object will be fed into a reachability solver to compute the reachable set of the FFNN (or NNCS) from a given initial set of states. Then, the obtained reachable set will be passed to the analyzer module. The analyzer module consists of three subcomponents: 1) a *visualizer*, 2) a *safety checker*, and 3) a *falsifier*. The visualizer can be called to plot the obtained reachable set. Given a safety specification, the safety checker can reason about the safety of the FFNN or NNCS with respect to the specification. When an exact (sound and complete) reachability solver is used, such as the star-based solver, the safety checker can return either "safe," or "unsafe" along with a set of counterexamples. When an over-approximate (sound) reachability solver is used, such as the zonotope-based scheme or the approximate star-based solvers, the safety checker can return either "safe" or "*uncertain*" (unknown). In this case, the falsifier automatically calls the evaluator to generate simulation traces to find a counterexample. If the falsifier can find a counterexample, then NNV returns unsafe. Otherwise, it returns unknown. Table 1 shows a summary of the major features of NNV.

3   Set Representations and Reachability Algorithms

NNV implements a set of reachability algorithms for *sequential* FFNNs and CNNs, as well as NNCS with FFNN controllers as shown in Fig. 2. The reachable set of a sequential FFNN is computed layer-by-layer. The output reachable set of a layer is the input set of the next layer in the network.

3.1   Polyhedron [40]

The polyhedron reachability algorithm computes the exact polyhedron reachable set of a FFNN with ReLU activation functions. The exact reachability computation of layer L in a FFNN is done as follows. First, we construct the affine mapping $\bar{I}$ of the input polyhedron set I, using the weight matrix W and the bias vector b, i.e., $\bar{I} = W \times I + b$. Then, the exact reachable set of the layer R_L is constructed by executing a sequence of stepReLU operations, i.e., $R_L = stepReLU_n(stepReLU_{n-1}(\cdots (stepReLU_1(\bar{I}))))$. Since a $stepReLU$ operation can split a polyhedron into two new polyhedra, the exact reachable set of a layer in a FFNN is usually a union of polyhedra. The polyhedron reachability algorithm is computationally expensive because computing affine mappings with polyhedra is costly. Additionally, when computing the reachable set, the polyhedron approach extensively uses the expensive conversion between the H-representation and the V-representation. These are the main drawbacks that limit the scalability of the polyhedron approach. Despite that, we extend the polyhedron reachability algorithm for NNCSs with FFNN controllers. However, the propagation of polyhedra in NNCS may lead to a large degree of conservativeness in the computed reachable set [38].

3.2   Star Set [38, 41] (code)

The star set is an efficient set representation for simulation-based verification of large linear systems [6, 7, 42] where the superposition property of a linear system can be exploited in the analysis. It has been shown in [41] that the star set is also suitable for reachability analysis of FFNNs. In contrast to polyhedra, the affine mapping and intersection with a half space of a star set is more easily computed. NNV implements an enhanced version of the exact and over-approximate reachability algorithms for FFNNs proposed in [41] by minimizing the number of LP optimization problems that need to be solved in the computation. The exact algorithm that makes use of star sets is similar to the polyhedron method that makes use of $stepReLU$ operations. However, it is much faster and more scalable than the polyhedron method because of the advantage that star sets have in affine mapping and intersection. The approximate algorithm obtains an over-approximation of the exact reachable set by approximating the exact reachable set after applying an activation function, e.g., ReLU, Tanh, Sigmoid. We refer readers to [41] for a detailed discussion of star-set reachability algorithms for FFNNs.

We note that NNV implements enhanced versions of earlier star-based reachability algorithms [41]. Particularly, we minimize the number of linear programming (LP) optimization problems that must be solved in order to construct the reachable set of a FFNN by quickly estimating the ranges of all of the states in the star set using only the ranges of the predicate variables. Additionally, the extensions of the star reachability algorithms to NNCS with linear plant models can eliminate the explosion of conservativeness in the polyhedron method [38,39]. The reason behind this is that in star sets, the relationship between the plant state variables and the control inputs is preserved in the computation since they are defined by a unique set of predicate variables. We refer readers to [38,39] for a detailed discussion of the extensions of the star-based reachability algorithms for NNCSs with linear/nonlinear plant models.

3.3 Zonotope [32] (code)

NNV implements the zonotope reachability algorithms proposed in [32] for FFNNs. Similar to the over-approximate algorithm using star sets, the zonotope algorithm computes an over-approximation of the exact reachable set of a FFNN. Although the zonotope reachability algorithm is very fast and scalable, it produces a very conservative reachable set in comparison to the star set method as shown in [41]. Consequently, zonotope-based reachability algorithms are usually only more efficient for very small input sets. As an example it can be more suitable for robustness certification.

3.4 Abstract Domain [33]

NNV implements the abstract domain reachability algorithm proposed in [33] for FFNNs. NNV's abstract domain reachability algorithm specifies an abstract domain as a star set and estimates the *over-approximate ranges* of the states based on the ranges of the new introduced predicate variables. We note that better ranges of the states can be computed by solving LP optimization. However, better ranges come with more computation time.

3.5 ImageStar Set [37] (code)

NNV recently introduced a new set representation called the ImageStar for use in the verification of deep convolutional neural networks (CNNs). Briefly, the ImageStar is a generalization of the star set where the anchor and generator vectors are replaced by multi-channel images. The ImageStar is efficient in the analysis of convolutional layers, average pooling layers, and fully connected layers, whereas max pooling layers and ReLU layers consume most of the computation time. NNV implements exact and over-approximate reachability algorithms using the ImageStar for serial CNNs. In short, using the ImageStar, we can analyze the robustness under adversarial attacks of the real-world VGG16 and VGG19 deep perception networks [31] that consist of >100 million parameters [37].

4 Evaluation

The experiments presented in this section were performed on a desktop with the following configuration: Intel Core i7-6700 CPU @ 3.4 GHz 8 core Processor, 64 GB Memory, and 64-bit Ubuntu 16.04.3 LTS OS.

4.1 Safety Verification of ACAS Xu Networks

We evaluate NNV in comparison to Reluplex [22], Marabou [23], and ReluVal [49], by considering the verification of safety property ϕ_3 and ϕ_4 of the ACAS Xu neural networks [21] for all 45 networks.[2] All the experiments were done using 4 cores for computation. The results are summarized in Table 2 where (SAT) denotes the networks are safe, (UNSAT) is unsafe, and (UNK) is unknown. We note that (UNK) may occur due to the conservativeness of the reachability analysis scheme. Detailed verification results are presented in the appendix of the extended version of this paper [44]. For a fast comparison with other tools, we also tested a subset of the inputs for Property 1–4 on all the 45 networks. We note that the polyhedron method [40] achieves a timeout on most of networks, and therefore, we neglect this method in the comparison.

Verification Time. For property ϕ_3, NNV's exact-star method is about 20.7× faster than Reluplex, 14.2× faster than Marabou, 81.6× faster than Marabou-DnC (i.e., divide and conquer method). The approximate star method is 547× faster than Reluplex, 374× faster than Marabou, 2151× faster than Marabou-DnC, and 8× faster than ReluVal. For property ϕ_4, NNV's exact-star method is 25.3× faster than Reluplex, 18.0× faster than Marabou, 53.4× faster than Marabou-DnC, while the approximate star method is 625× faster than Reluplex, 445× faster than Marabou, 1321× faster than Marabou-DnC.

Table 2. Verification results of ACAS Xu networks.

ACAS XU ϕ_3	SAT	UNSAT	UNK	TIMEOUT			TIME(s)
				1 h	2 h	10 h	
Reluplex	3	42	0	2	0	0	28454
Marabou	3	42	0	1	0	0	19466
Marabou DnC	3	42	0	3	3	1	111880
ReluVal	3	42	0	0	0	0	416
Zonotope	0	2	43	0	0	0	3
Abstract Domain	0	0	45	0	0	0	8
NNV Exact Star	3	42	0	0	0	0	1371
NNV Appr. Star	0	29	16	0	0	0	52
ACAS XU ϕ_4							
Reluplex	3	42	0	0	0	0	11880
Marabou	3	42	0	0	0	0	8470
Marabou DnC	3	42	0	2	2	0	25110
ReluVal	3	42	0	0	0	0	27
Zonotope	0	1	44	0	0	0	5
Abstract Domain	0	0	45	0	0	0	7
NNV Exact Star	3	42	0	0	0	0	470
NNV Appr. Star	0	32	13	0	0	0	19

---

[2] We omit properties ϕ_1 and ϕ_2 for space and due to their long runtimes, but they can be reproduced in the artifact.

Conservativeness. The approximate star method is much less conservative than the zonotope and abstract domain methods. This is illustrated since it can verify more networks than the zonotope and abstract domain methods, and is because it obtains a tighter over-approximate reachable set. For property ϕ_3, the zonotope and abstract domain methods can prove safety of 2/45 networks, (4.44%) and 0/45 networks, (0%) respectively, while NNV's approximate star method can prove safety of 29/45 networks, (64.4%). For property ϕ_4, the zonotope and abstract domain method can prove safety of 1/45 networks, (2.22%) and 0/45 networks, (0.00%) respectively while the approximate star method can prove safety of 32/45, (71.11%).

4.2   Safety Verification of Adaptive Cruise Control System

To illustrate how NNV can be used to verify/falsify safety properties of learning-enabled CPS, we analyze a learning-based ACC system [1,38], in which the ego (following) vehicle has a radar sensor to measure the distance to the lead vehicle in the same lane, D_{rel}, as well as the relative velocity of the lead vehicle, V_{rel}. The ego vehicle has two control modes. In speed control mode, it travels at a driver-specified set speed $V_{set} = 30$, and in spacing control mode, it maintains a safe distance from the lead vehicle, D_{safe}. We train a neural network with 5 layers of 20 neurons per layer with ReLU activation functions to control the ego vehicle using a control period of 0.1 s.

We investigate safety of the learning-based ACC system with two types of plant dynamics: 1) a discrete linear plant, and 2) a nonlinear continuous plant governed by the following differential equations:

$$\dot{x}_{lead}(t) = v_{lead}(t), \quad \dot{v}_{lead}(t) = \gamma_{lead}, \quad \dot{\gamma}_{lead}(t) = -2\gamma_{lead}(t) + 2a_{lead} - \mu v_{lead}^2(t),$$
$$\dot{x}_{ego}(t) = v_{ego}(t), \quad \dot{v}_{ego}(t) = \gamma_{ego}, \quad \dot{\gamma}_{ego}(t) = -2\gamma_{ego}(t) + 2a_{ego} - \mu v_{ego}^2(t),$$

where $x_{lead}(x_{ego})$, $v_{lead}(v_{ego})$ and $\gamma_{lead}(\gamma_{ego})$ are the position, velocity and acceleration of the lead (ego) vehicle respectively. $a_{lead}(a_{ego})$ is the acceleration control input applied to the lead (ego) vehicle, and $\mu = 0.0001$ is a friction parameter. To obtain a discrete linear model of the plant, we let $\mu = 0$ and discretize the corresponding linear continuous model using a zero-order hold on the inputs with a sample time of 0.1 s (i.e., the control period).

Verification Problem. The scenario we are interested in is when the two vehicles are operating at a safe distance between them and the ego vehicle is in speed control mode. In this state the lead vehicle driver suddenly decelerates with $a_{lead} = -5$ to reduce the speed. We want to verify if the neural network controller on the ego vehicle will decelerate to maintain a safe distance between the two vehicles. To guarantee safety, we require that $D_{rel} = x_{lead} - x_{ego} \geq D_{safe} = D_{default} + T_{gap} \times v_{ego}$ where $T_{gap} = 1.4$ s and $D_{default} = 10$. Our analysis investigates whether the safety requirement holds during the 5 s after the lead vehicle decelerates. We consider safety of the system under the following initial conditions: $x_{lead}(0) \in [90, 92]$, $v_{lead}(0) \in [20, 30]$, $\gamma_{lead}(0) = \gamma_{ego}(0) = 0$, $v_{ego}(0) \in [30, 30.5]$, and $x_{ego} \in [30, 31]$.

Table 3. Verification results for ACC system with different plant models, where VT is the verification time (in seconds).

v_lead(0)	Linear plant		Nonlinear plant	
	Safety	$VT(s)$	*Safety*	$VT(s)$
[29, 30]	SAFE	9.60	UNSAFE	346.62
[28, 29]	SAFE	9.45	UNSAFE	277.50
[27, 28]	SAFE	9.82	UNSAFE	289.70
[26, 27]	UNSAFE	17.80	UNSAFE	315.60
[25, 26]	UNSAFE	19.24	UNSAFE	305.56
[24, 25]	UNSAFE	18.12	UNSAFE	372.00

Verification Results. For linear dynamics, NNV can compute both the exact and over-approximate reachable sets of the ACC system in bounded time steps, while for nonlinear dynamics, NNV constructs an over-approximation of the reachable sets. The verification results for linear and nonlinear models using the over-approximate star method are presented in Table 3, which shows that safety of the ACC system depends on the initial velocity of the lead vehicle. When the initial velocity of the lead vehicle is smaller than $27\,(m/s)$, the ACC system with the discrete plant model is unsafe. Using the exact star method, NNV can construct a *complete* set of counter-example inputs. When the over-approximate star method is used, if there is a potential safety violation, NNV simulates the system with 1000 random inputs from the input set to find counter examples. If a counterexample is found, the system is *UNSAFE*, otherwise, NNV returns a safety result of *UNKNOWN*. Figure 3 visualizes the reachable sets of the relative distance D_{rel} between two vehicles versus the required safe distance D_{safe} over time for two cases of initial velocities of the lead vehicle: $v_{lead}(0) \in [29, 30]$ and $v_{lead}(0) \in [24, 25]$. We can see that in the first case, $D_{ref} \geq D_{safe}$ for all 50 time steps stating that the system is safe. In the second case, $D_{ref} < D_{safe}$ in some control steps, so the system is unsafe. NNV supports a *reachLive* method to perform analysis and reachable set visualization on-the-fly to help the user observe the behavior of the system during verification.

The verification results for the ACC system with the nonlinear model are all *UNSAFE*, which is surprising. Since the neural network controller of the ACC system was trained with the linear model, it works quite well for the linear model. However, when a small friction term is added to the linear model to form a nonlinear model, the neural network controller's performance, in terms of safety, is significantly reduced. This problem raises an important issue in training neural network controllers using simulation data, and these schemes may not work in real systems since there is always a mismatch between the plant model in the simulation engine and the real system.

Verification Times. As shown in Table 3, the approximate analysis of the ACC system with discrete linear plant model is fast and can be done in 84 s. NNV

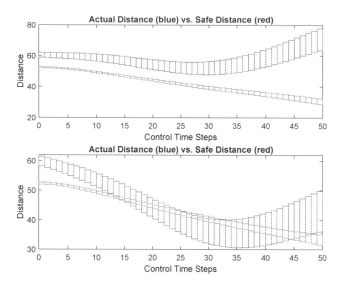

Fig. 3. Two scenarios of the ACC system. In the first (top) scenario ($v_{lead}(0) \in$ [29, 30] m/s), safety is guaranteed, $D_{rel} \geq D_{safe}$. In the second scenario (bottom) ($v_{lead}(0) \in$ [24, 25] m/s), safety is violated since $D_{ref} < D_{safe}$ in some control steps.

also supports exact analysis, but is computationally expensive as it constructs all reachable states. Because there are splits in the reachable sets of the neural network controller, the number of star sets in the reachable set of the plant increases quickly over time [38]. In contrast, the over-approximate method computes the interval hull of all reachable sets at each time step, and maintains a single reachable set of the plant throughout the computation. This makes the over-approximate method faster than the exact method. In terms of plant models, the nonlinear model requires more computation time than the linear one. As shown in Table 3, the verification for the linear model using the over-approximate method is 22.7× faster on average than of the nonlinear model.

5   Related Work

NNV was inspired by recent work in the emerging fields of neural network and machine learning verification. For the "open-loop" verification problem (verification of DNNs), many efficient techniques have been proposed, such as SMT-based methods [22,23,30], mixed-integer linear programming methods [14,24,28], set-based methods [4,17,32,33,48,50,53,57], and optimization methods [51,58]. For the "closed-loop" verification problem (NCCS verification), we note that the Verisig approach [20] is efficient for NNCS with nonlinear plants and with Sigmoid and Tanh activation functions. Additionally, the recent regressive polynomial rule inference approach [34] is efficient for safety verification of NNCS with nonlinear plant models and ReLU activation functions. The satisfiability modulo convex (SMC) approach [35] is also promising for NNCS with discrete linear plants, as it provides both soundness and completeness guarantees. ReachNN [19] is a recent approach that can efficiently control the conservativeness in the reachability analysis of NNCS with nonlinear plants and ReLU, Sigmoid, and Tanh activation functions in the controller. In [54], a novel simulation-guided approach has been developed to reduce significantly the computation cost for verification of NNCS. In other learning-enabled systems, falsification and testing-based approaches [12,13,45] have shown a significant promise in enhancing the safety of systems where perception components and neural networks interact with the physical world. Finally, there is significant related work in the domain of safe reinforcement learning [2,15,47,59], and combining guarantees from NNV with those provided in these methods would be interesting to explore.

6   Conclusions

We presented NNV, a software tool for the verification of DNNs and learning-enabled CPS. NNV provides a collection of reachability algorithms that can be used to verify safety (and robustness) of real-world DNNs, as well as learning-enabled CPS, such as the ACC case study. For closed-loop systems, NNV can compute the exact and over-approximate reachable sets of a NNCS with linear plant models. For NNCS with nonlinear plants, NNV computes an over-approximate reachable set and uses it to verify safety, but can also automatically falsify the system to find counterexamples.

References

1. Model Predictive Control Toolbox. The MathWorks Inc., Natick, Massachusetts (2019). https://www.mathworks.com/help/mpc/ug/adaptive-cruise-control-using-model-predictive-controller.html
2. Alshiekh, M., Bloem, R., Ehlers, R., Könighofer, B., Niekum, S., Topcu, U.: Safe reinforcement learning via shielding. In: Thirty-Second AAAI Conference on Artificial Intelligence (2018)
3. Althoff, M.: An introduction to cora 2015. In: Proceedings of the Workshop on Applied Verification for Continuous and Hybrid Systems (2015)
4. Anderson, G., Pailoor, S., Dillig, I., Chaudhuri, S.: Optimization and abstraction: A synergistic approach for analyzing neural network robustness. In: Proceedings of the 40th ACM SIGPLAN Conference on Programming Language Design and Implementation, PLDI 2019, pp. 731–744. Association for Computing Machinery, New York (2019)
5. Bak, S., Bogomolov, S., Johnson, T.T.: Hyst: a source transformation and translation tool for hybrid automaton models. In: Proceedings of the 18th International Conference on Hybrid Systems: Computation and Control, pp. 128–133. ACM (2015)
6. Bak, S., Duggirala, P.S.: Simulation-equivalent reachability of large linear systems with inputs. In: Majumdar, R., Kunčak, V. (eds.) CAV 2017. LNCS, vol. 10426, pp. 401–420. Springer, Cham (2017). https://doi.org/10.1007/978-3-319-63387-9_20

7. Bak, S., Tran, H.D., Johnson, T.T.: Numerical verification of affine systems with up to a billion dimensions. In: Proceedings of the 22nd ACM International Conference on Hybrid Systems: Computation and Control, pp. 23–32. ACM (2019)
8. Bojarski, M., et al.: End to end learning for self-driving cars (2016). arXiv preprint arXiv:1604.07316
9. Chen, C., Seff, A., Kornhauser, A., Xiao, J.: Deepdriving: Learning affordance for direct perception in autonomous driving. In: Proceedings of the IEEE International Conference on Computer Vision, pp. 2722–2730 (2015)
10. Cireşan, D., Meier, U., Schmidhuber, J.: Multi-column deep neural networks for image classification (2012). arXiv preprint arXiv:1202.2745
11. Collobert, R., Weston, J.: A unified architecture for natural language processing: Deep neural networks with multitask learning. In: Proceedings of the 25th International Conference on Machine Learning, pp. 160–167. ACM (2008)
12. Dreossi, T., Donzé, A., Seshia, S.A.: Compositional falsification of cyber-physical systems with machine learning components. In: NASA Formal Methods Symposium, pp. 357–372. Springer (2017)
13. Dreossi, T., et al.: VERIFAI: A toolkit for the formal design and analysis of artificial intelligence-based systems. In: Dillig, I., Tasiran, S. (eds.) CAV 2019. LNCS, vol. 11561, pp. 432–442. Springer, Cham (2019). https://doi.org/10.1007/978-3-030-25540-4_25
14. Dutta, S., Jha, S., Sanakaranarayanan, S., Tiwari, A.: Output range analysis for deep neural networks (2017). arXiv preprint arXiv:1709.09130
15. Fulton, N., Platzer, A.: Verifiably safe off-model reinforcement learning. In: Vojnar, T., Zhang, L. (eds.) TACAS 2019. LNCS, vol. 11427, pp. 413–430. Springer, Cham (2019). https://doi.org/10.1007/978-3-030-17462-0_28
16. Gatys, L.A., Ecker, A.S., Bethge, M.: Image style transfer using convolutional neural networks. In: Proceedings of the IEEE Conference on Computer Vision and Pattern Recognition, pp. 2414–2423 (2016)
17. Gehr, T., Mirman, M., Drachsler-Cohen, D., Tsankov, P., Chaudhuri, S., Vechev, M.: Ai 2: Safety and robustness certification of neural networks with abstract interpretation. In: 2018 IEEE Symposium on Security and Privacy (SP) (2018)
18. Goldberg, Y.: A primer on neural network models for natural language processing. J. Artif. Intell. Res. **57**, 345–420 (2016)
19. Huang, C., Fan, J., Li, W., Chen, X., Zhu, Q.: Reachnn: Reachability analysis of neural-network controlled systems (2019). arXiv preprint arXiv:1906.10654
20. Ivanov, R., Weimer, J., Alur, R., Pappas, G.J., Lee, I.: Verisig: verifying safety properties of hybrid systems with neural network controllers. In: Hybrid Systems: Computation and Control (HSCC) (2019)
21. Julian, K.D., Lopez, J., Brush, J.S., Owen, M.P., Kochenderfer, M.J.: Policy compression for aircraft collision avoidance systems. In: 2016 IEEE/AIAA 35th Digital Avionics Systems Conference (DASC), pp. 1–10. IEEE (2016)
22. Katz, G., Barrett, C., Dill, D.L., Julian, K., Kochenderfer, M.J.: Reluplex: An efficient SMT solver for verifying deep neural networks. In: Majumdar, R., Kunčak, V. (eds.) CAV 2017. LNCS, vol. 10426, pp. 97–117. Springer, Cham (2017). https://doi.org/10.1007/978-3-319-63387-9_5
23. Katz, G., et al.: The marabou framework for verification and analysis of deep neural networks. In: Dillig, I., Tasiran, S. (eds.) CAV 2019. LNCS, vol. 11561, pp. 443–452. Springer, Cham (2019). https://doi.org/10.1007/978-3-030-25540-4_26
24. Kouvaros, P., Lomuscio, A.: Formal verification of cnn-based perception systems (2018). arXiv preprint arXiv:1811.11373

25. Krizhevsky, A., Sutskever, I., Hinton, G.E.: Imagenet classification with deep convolutional neural networks. In: Advances in Neural Information Processing Systems, pp. 1097–1105 (2012)
26. Kvasnica, M., Grieder, P., Baotić, M., Morari, M.: Multi-parametric toolbox (MPT). In: Alur, R., Pappas, G.J. (eds.) HSCC 2004. LNCS, vol. 2993, pp. 448–462. Springer, Heidelberg (2004). https://doi.org/10.1007/978-3-540-24743-2_30
27. Löfberg, J.: Yalmip : A toolbox for modeling and optimization in MATLAB. In: Proceedings of the CACSD Conference,Taipei, Taiwan (2004). http://users.isy.liu.se/johanl/yalmip
28. Lomuscio, A., Maganti, L.: An approach to reachability analysis for feed-forward relu neural networks (2017). arXiv preprint arXiv:1706.07351
29. Lopez, D.M., Musau, P., Tran, H.D., Johnson, T.T.: Verification of closed-loop systems with neural network controllers. In: Frehse, G., Althoff, M. (eds.) ARCH19, 6th International Workshop on Applied Verification of Continuous and Hybrid Systems, EPiC Series in Computing, vol. 61, pp. 201–210. EasyChair (2019)
30. Pulina, L., Tacchella, A.: An abstraction-refinement approach to verification of artificial neural networks. In: Touili, T., Cook, B., Jackson, P. (eds.) CAV 2010. LNCS, vol. 6174, pp. 243–257. Springer, Heidelberg (2010). https://doi.org/10.1007/978-3-642-14295-6_24
31. Simonyan, K., Zisserman, A.: Very deep convolutional networks for large-scale image recognition (2014). arXiv preprint arXiv:1409.1556
32. Singh, G., Gehr, T., Mirman, M., Püschel, M., Vechev, M.: Fast and effective robustness certification. In: Advances in Neural Information Processing Systems, pp. 10825–10836 (2018)
33. Singh, G., Gehr, T., Püschel, M., Vechev, M.: An abstract domain for certifying neural networks. Proc. ACM Program. Lang. **3**(POPL), 1–30 (2019). Article 41
34. Dutta, S., Chen, X., Sankaranarayanan, S.: Reachability analysis for neural feedback systems using regressive polynomial rule inference. In: Hybrid Systems: Computation and Control (HSCC) (2019)
35. Sun, X., Khedr, H., Shoukry, Y.: Formal verification of neural network controlled autonomous systems. In: Hybrid Systems: Computation and Control (HSCC) (2019)
36. Szegedy, C., et al.: Intriguing properties of neural networks (2013). arXiv preprint arXiv:1312.6199
37. Tran, H.D., Bak, S., Xiang, W., Johnson, T.T.: Verification of deep convolutional neural networks using imagestars. In: 32nd International Conference on Computer-Aided Verification (CAV). Springer (2020)
38. Tran, H.D., Cei, F., Lopez, D.M., Johnson, T.T., Koutsoukos, X.: Safety verification of cyber-physical systems with reinforcement learning control. In: ACM SIGBED International Conference on Embedded Software (EMSOFT 2019). ACM (2019)
39. Tran, H.D., Cei, F., Lopez, D.M., Johnson, T.T., Koutsoukos, X.: Safety verification of cyber-physical systems with reinforcement learning control (July 2019)
40. Tran, H.D., et al.: Parallelizable reachability analysis algorithms for feed-forward neural networks. In: 7th International Conference on Formal Methods in Software Engineering (FormaliSE2019), Montreal, Canada (2019)
41. Tran, H.D., et al.: Star-based reachability analysis for deep neural networks. In: 23rd International Symposium on Formal Methods, FM 2019. Springer International Publishing (2019)

42. Tran, H.D., Nguyen, L.V., Hamilton, N., Xiang, W., Johnson, T.T.: Reachability analysis for high-index linear differential algebraic equations (daes). In: 17th International Conference on Formal Modeling and Analysis of Timed Systems (FORMATS 2019). Springer International Publishing (2019)

43. Tran, H.D., et al.: NNV: The neural network verification tool for deep neural networks and learning-enabled cyber-physical systems (CodeOcean Capsule) (2020). https://doi.org/10.24433/CO.0221760.v1

44. Tran, H.D., et al.: NNV: The neural network verification tool for deep neural networks and learning-enabled cyber-physical systems (2020). arXiv preprint arXiv:2004.05519

45. Tuncali, C.E., Fainekos, G., Ito, H., Kapinski, J.: Simulation-based adversarial test generation for autonomous vehicles with machine learning components (2018). arXiv preprint arXiv:1804.06760

46. Vedaldi, A., Lenc, K.: Matconvnet: Convolutional neural networks for matlab. In: Proceedings of the 23rd ACM International Conference on Multimedia, pp. 689–692. ACM (2015)

47. Verma, A., Murali, V., Singh, R., Kohli, P., Chaudhuri, S.: Programmatically interpretable reinforcement learning. In: Dy, J., Krause, A. (eds.) Proceedings of the 35th International Conference on Machine Learning, Proceedings of Machine Learning Research, PMLR, 10–15 Jul 2018, vol. 80, pp. 5045–5054 (2018)

48. Wang, S., Pei, K., Whitehouse, J., Yang, J., Jana, S.: Efficient formal safety analysis of neural networks. In: Advances in Neural Information Processing Systems, pp. 6369–6379 (2018)

49. Wang, S., Pei, K., Whitehouse, J., Yang, J., Jana, S.: Formal security analysis of neural networks using symbolic intervals. In: 27th USENIX Security Symposium (USENIX Security 18). USENIX Association, Baltimore (2018)

50. Wang, S., Pei, K., Whitehouse, J., Yang, J., Jana, S.: Formal security analysis of neural networks using symbolic intervals (2018). arXiv preprint arXiv:1804.10829

51. Weng, T.W., et al.: Towards fast computation of certified robustness for relu networks (2018). arXiv preprint arXiv:1804.09699

52. Wu, B., Iandola, F.N., Jin, P.H., Keutzer, K.: Squeezedet: Unified, small, low power fully convolutional neural networks for real-time object detection for autonomous driving. In: CVPR Workshops, pp. 446–454 (2017)

53. Xiang, W., Tran, H.D., Johnson, T.T.: Output reachable set estimation and verification for multilayer neural networks. IEEE Trans. Neural Netw. Learn. Syst. **29**(11), 5777–5783 (2018)

54. Xiang, W., Tran, H.D., Yang, X., Johnson, T.T.: Reachable set estimation for neural network control systems: A simulation-guided approach. IEEE Trans. Neural Netw. Learn. Syst. 1–10 (2020)

55. Xiang, W., Tran, H.D., Johnson, T.T.: Reachable set computation and safety verification for neural networks with relu activations (2017). arXiv preprint arXiv:1712.08163

56. Xiang, W., Tran, H.D., Johnson, T.T.: Specification-guided safety verification for feedforward neural networks. In: AAAI Spring Symposium on Verification of Neural Networks (2019)

57. Yang, X., Tran, H.D., Xiang, W., Johnson, T.: Reachability analysis for feedforward neural networks using face lattices (2020). arXiv preprint arXiv:2003.01226

58. Zhang, H., Weng, T.W., Chen, P.Y., Hsieh, C.J., Daniel, L.: Efficient neural network robustness certification with general activation functions. In: Advances in Neural Information Processing Systems, pp. 4944–4953 (2018)
59. Zhu, H., Xiong, Z., Magill, S., Jagannathan, S.: An inductive synthesis framework for verifiable reinforcement learning. In: Proceedings of the 40th ACM SIGPLAN Conference on Programming Language Design and Implementation, PLDI 2019, pp. 686–701. Association for Computing Machinery, New York (2019)

Verification of Deep Convolutional Neural Networks Using ImageStars

Hoang-Dung Tran[1,2], Stanley Bak[3], Weiming Xiang[4],
and Taylor T. Johnson[2(✉)]

[1] University of Nebraska, Lincoln, USA
[2] Vanderbilt University, Nashville, USA
taylor.johnson@vanderbilt.edu
[3] Stony Brook University, Stony Brook, USA
[4] Augusta University, Augusta, USA

Abstract. Convolutional Neural Networks (CNN) have redefined state-of-the-art in many real-world applications, such as facial recognition, image classification, human pose estimation, and semantic segmentation. Despite their success, CNNs are vulnerable to adversarial attacks, where slight changes to their inputs may lead to sharp changes in their output in even well-trained networks. Set-based analysis methods can detect or prove the absence of bounded adversarial attacks, which can then be used to evaluate the effectiveness of neural network training methodology. Unfortunately, existing verification approaches have limited scalability in terms of the size of networks that can be analyzed. In this paper, we describe a set-based framework that successfully deals with real-world CNNs, such as VGG16 and VGG19, that have high accuracy on ImageNet. Our approach is based on a new set representation called the ImageStar, which enables efficient exact and over-approximative analysis of CNNs. ImageStars perform efficient set-based analysis by combining operations on concrete images with linear programming (LP). Our approach is implemented in a tool called NNV, and can verify the robustness of VGG networks with respect to a small set of input states, derived from adversarial attacks, such as the DeepFool attack. The experimental results show that our approach is less conservative and faster than existing zonotope and polytope methods.

Keywords: Neural networks · Reachability analysis · Machine learning · Computer vision

The material presented in this paper is based upon work supported in part by the Defense Advanced Research Projects Agency (DARPA) through contract number FA8750-18-C-0089, the National Science Foundation (NSF) under grant numbers SHF 1910017 and FMitF 1918450, and the Air Force Office of Scientific Research (AFOSR) through award numbers FA9550-18-1-0122 and FA9550-19-1-0288. The U.S. Government is authorized to reproduce and distribute reprints for Government purposes notwithstanding any copyright notation thereon. Any opinions, finding, and conclusions or recommendations expressed in this material are those of the author(s) and do not necessarily reflect the views of AFOSR, DARPA, or NSF. An extended version of this paper with appendices is available [33].

S. K. Lahiri and C. Wang (Eds.): CAV 2020, LNCS 12224, pp. 18–42, 2020.
https://doi.org/10.1007/978-3-030-53288-8_2

1   Introduction

Convolutional neural networks (CNN) have rapidly accelerated progress in computer vision with many practical applications such as face recognition [19], image classification [18], document analysis [21] and semantic segmentation. Recently, it has been shown that CNNs are vulnerable to adversarial attacks, where a well-trained CNN can be fooled into producing errant predictions due to tiny changes in their inputs [9]. Many applications such as autonomous driving seek to leverage the power of CNNs. However due the opaque nature of these models there are reservations about using in safety-critical applications. Thus, there is an urgent need for formally evaluating the robustness of a trained CNN.

Formal verification of deep neural networks (DNNs) has recently become an important topic. The majority of existing approaches focus on verifying safety and robustness properties of feedforward neural networks (FNN) with the Rectified Linear Unit activation function (ReLU). These approaches include: mixed-integer linear programming (MILP) [5,17,23], satisfiability (SAT) and satisfiability modulo theory (SMT) techniques [7,15], optimization [6,11,22,42,44,51], and geometric reachability [29,30,36,37,41,43,45,47,48,50]. Adjacent to these methods are property inference techniques for DNNs, which are also an important and interesting research area being investigated [10]. In a similar fashion, the problem of verifying safety of cyber-physical systems (CPS) with learning-enabled neural network components with imperfect plant models and sensing information has recently attracted significant attention due to their real world applications [1,12–14,24,31,32,35,46,49]. This research area views the safety verification problem in a holistic manner by considering safety of the entire system where learning-enabled components interact with the physical world.

Although numerous tools and methods have been proposed for neural network verification, only a handful of methods can deal with CNNs [2,16,17,27, 29,30]. Moreover, in the aforementioned techniques, only one [27] can deal with real-world CNNs, such as VGGNet [28]. Their approach makes used of the concept of the L_0 distance between two images. Their optimization-based approach computes a tight bound on the number of pixels that may be changed in an image without affecting the classification result of the network. It can also efficiently generate adversarial examples that can be used to improve the robustness of network. In a similar manner, this paper seeks to verify robustness of real-world deep CNNs. Thus, we develop a set-based analysis method through the use of the *ImageStar*, a new set representation that can represent an infinite family of images. As an example, this representation can be used to represent a set of images distorted by an adversarial attack. Using the ImageStar, we develop both exact and over-approximate reachability algorithms to construct reachable sets that contain all the possible outputs of a CNN under an adversarial attack. These reachable sets are then used to reason about the overall robustness of the network. When a CNN violates a robustness property, our exact reachability scheme can construct a *set of concrete adversarial examples*. Our approach differs from [27] in two primary ways. First, our method does not provide robustness guarantees for a network in terms of the number of pixels that are allowed to be changed (in terms of L_0 distance). Instead, we prove the robustness of the network on images that are attacked by disturbances bounded by arbitrary linear constraints. Second, our approach relies on reachable set computation of a network corresponding to a bounded input set, as opposed to an optimization-based approach. We implement these methods in the NNV tool [39] and compare with the zonotope method used in DeepZ [29] and the polytope method used in DeepPoly [30]. The experimental results indicate our method is less conservative and faster than existing approaches when verifying robustness of CNNs.

The main contributions of the paper include the following. First is the ImageStar set representation, which is an efficient representation for reachability analysis of CNNs. Second are exact and over-approximate reachability algorithms for constructing reachable sets and verifying robustness of CNNs. Third is the implementation of the ImageStar representation and reachability algorithms in NNV [39]. Fourth is a rigorous evaluation and comparison of proposed approaches, such as zonotope and polytope methods on different CNNs.

2   Problem Formulation

The reachability problem for CNNs is the task of analyzing a trained CNN with respect to some perturbed input set in order to construct a set containing all possible outputs of the network. In this paper, we consider the reachability of a CNN $\mathcal{N}$ that consists of a series of layers L that may include convolutional layers, fully connected layers, max-pooling layers, average pooling layers, and ReLU activation layers. Mathematically, we define a CNN with n layers as $\mathcal{N} = \{L_i\}, i = 1, 2, \ldots, n$. The reachability of the CNN $\mathcal{N}$ is defined based on the concept of *reachable sets*.

Definition 1 (Reachable set of a CNN). *An (output) reachable set $\mathcal{R}_\mathcal{N}$ of a CNN $\mathcal{N} = \{L_i\}, i = 1, 2, \ldots, n$ corresponding to a linear input set $\mathcal{I}$ is defined incrementally as:*

$$\mathcal{R}_{L_1} \triangleq \{y_1 \mid y_1 = L_1(x), \ x \in \mathcal{I}\},$$
$$\mathcal{R}_{L_2} \triangleq \{y_2 \mid y_2 = L_2(y_1), \ y_1 \in \mathcal{R}_{L_1}\},$$
$$\vdots$$
$$\mathcal{R}_\mathcal{N} = \mathcal{R}_{L_n} \triangleq \{y_n \mid y_n = L_{n-1}(y_{n-1}), \ y_{n-1} \in \mathcal{R}_{L_{n-1}}\},$$

where $L_i(\cdot)$ is a function representing the operation of the ith layer.

The definition shows that the reachable set of the CNN $\mathcal{N}$ can be constructed *layer-by-layer*. The core computation is constructing the reachable set of each layer L_i defined by a specific operation, i.e., convolution, affine mapping, max pooling, average pooling, or ReLU.

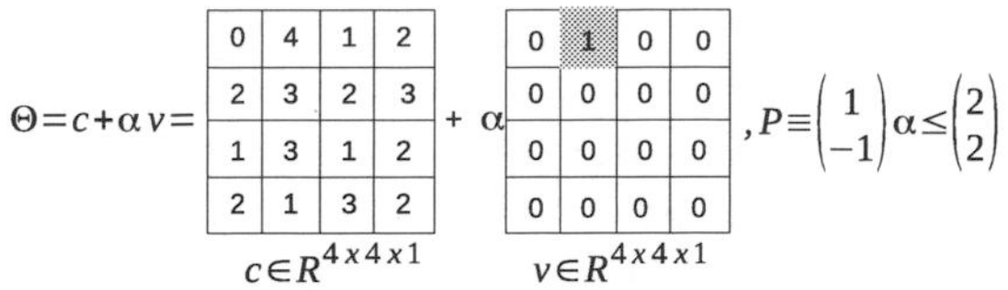

$$\Theta = c + \alpha v = \begin{array}{|c|c|c|c|}\hline 0 & 4 & 1 & 2 \\\hline 2 & 3 & 2 & 3 \\\hline 1 & 3 & 1 & 2 \\\hline 2 & 1 & 3 & 2 \\\hline\end{array} + \alpha \begin{array}{|c|c|c|c|}\hline 0 & 1 & 0 & 0 \\\hline 0 & 0 & 0 & 0 \\\hline 0 & 0 & 0 & 0 \\\hline 0 & 0 & 0 & 0 \\\hline\end{array}, P \equiv \begin{pmatrix} 1 \\ -1 \end{pmatrix} \alpha \leq \begin{pmatrix} 2 \\ 2 \end{pmatrix}$$

$$c \in R^{4 \times 4 \times 1} \qquad v \in R^{4 \times 4 \times 1}$$

Fig. 1. An example of an ImageStar.

3 ImageStar

Definition 2. *An **ImageStar** Θ is a tuple $\langle c, V, P \rangle$ where $c \in \mathbb{R}^{h \times w \times nc}$ is the anchor image, $V = \{v_1, v_2, \cdots, v_m\}$ is a set of m images in $\mathbb{R}^{h \times w \times nc}$ called generator images, $P : \mathbb{R}^m \to \{\top, \bot\}$ is a predicate, and h, w, nc are the height, width, and number of channels of the images, respectively. The generator images are arranged to form the ImageStar's $h \times w \times nc \times m$ basis array. The set of images represented by the ImageStar is:*

$$[\![\Theta]\!] = \{x \mid x = c + \Sigma_{i=1}^m (\alpha_i v_i) \text{ such that } P(\alpha_1, \cdots, \alpha_m) = \top\}.$$

Sometimes we will refer to both the tuple Θ and the set of states $[\![\Theta]\!]$ as Θ. In this work, we restrict the predicates to be a conjunction of linear constraints, $P(\alpha) \triangleq C\alpha \leq d$ where, for p linear constraints, $C \in \mathbb{R}^{p \times m}$, α is the vector of m-variables, i.e., $\alpha = [\alpha_1, \cdots, \alpha_m]^T$, and $d \in \mathbb{R}^{p \times 1}$. A ImageStar is an empty set if and only if $P(\alpha)$ is empty.

Example 1 (ImageStar). A $4 \times 4 \times 1$ gray image with a bounded disturbance $b \in [-2, 2]$ applied on the pixel of the position $(1, 2, 1)$ can be described as an ImageStar depicted in Fig. 1.

Remark 1. An ImageStar is an extension of the generalized star set recently defined in [3,4,37,38]. In a generalized star set, the anchor and the generators are vectors, while in an ImageStar, the anchor and generators are images with multiple channels. We will later show that the ImageStar is a very efficient representation for the reachability analysis of convolutional layers, fully connected layers, and average pooling layers.

Proposition 1 (Affine mapping of an ImageStar). *An affine mapping of an ImageStar $\Theta = \langle c, V, P \rangle$ with a scale factor γ and an offset image β is another ImageStar $\Theta' = \langle c', V', P' \rangle$ in which the new anchor, generators and predicate are as follows:*

$$c' = \gamma \times c + \beta, \quad V' = \gamma \times V, \quad P' \equiv P.$$

Note that, the scale factor γ can be a scalar or a vector containing scalar scale factors in which each factor is used to scale one channel in the ImageStar.

4   Reachability of CNN Using ImageStars

In this section, we present the reachable set computation for the convolutional, average pooling, fully connected, batch normalization, max pooling, and ReLU layers with respect to an input set consisting of an ImageStar.

4.1   Reachability of a Convolutional Layer

We consider a two-dimensional convolutional layer with following parameters: the weights $W_{Conv2d} \in \mathbb{R}^{h_f \times w_f \times nc \times nf}$, the bias $b_{Conv2d} \in \mathbb{R}^{1 \times 1 \times nf}$, the padding size P, the stride S, and the dilation factor D where h_f, w_f, nc are the height, width, and the number of channels of the filters in the layer respectively. Additionally, nf is the number of filters. The reachability of a convolutional layer is given in the following lemma.

Lemma 1. *The reachable set of a convolutional layer with an ImageStar input set $\mathcal{I} = \langle c, V, P \rangle$ is another ImageStar $\mathcal{I}' = \langle c', V', P \rangle$ where $c' = Convol(c)$ is the convolution operation applied to the anchor image, $V' = \{v'_1, \ldots, v'_m\}, v'_i = ConvolZeroBias(v_i)$ is the convolution operation with zero bias applied to the generator images, i.e., only using the weights of the layer.*

Proof. Any image in the ImageStar input set is a *linear* combination of the center and basis images. For any filter in the layer, the convolution operation applied to the input image performs local element-wise multiplication of a local matrix (of all channels) containing the values of the local pixels of the image and the weights of the filter and then combine the result with the bias to get the output for that local region. Due to the linearity of the input image, we can perform the convolution operation with the bias on the center and the convolution operation with zero bias on the basis images and then combine the result to get the output image.

Example 2 (Reachable set of a convolutional layer). The reachable set of a convolutional layer with single 2×2 filter and the ImageStar input set in Example 1 is described in Fig. 2, where the weights and the bias of the filter are $W = \begin{bmatrix} 1 & 1 \\ -1 & 0 \end{bmatrix}$, $b = -1$ respectively, the stride is $S = [2\ 2]$, the padding size is $P = [0\ 0\ 0\ 0]$ and the dilation factor is $D = [1\ 1]$.

4.2   Reachability of an Average Pooling Layer

The reachability of an average pooling layer with pooling size PS, padding size P, and stride S is given below, with its proof similar to that of the convolutional layer.

Lemma 2. *The reachable set of a average pooling layer with an ImageStar input set $\mathcal{I} = \langle c, V, P \rangle$ is another ImageStar $\mathcal{I}' = \langle c', V', P \rangle$ where $c' = average(c)$, $V' = \{v'_1, \ldots, v'_m\}, v'_i = average(v_i)$, $average(\cdot)$ is the average pooling operation applied to the anchor and generator images.*

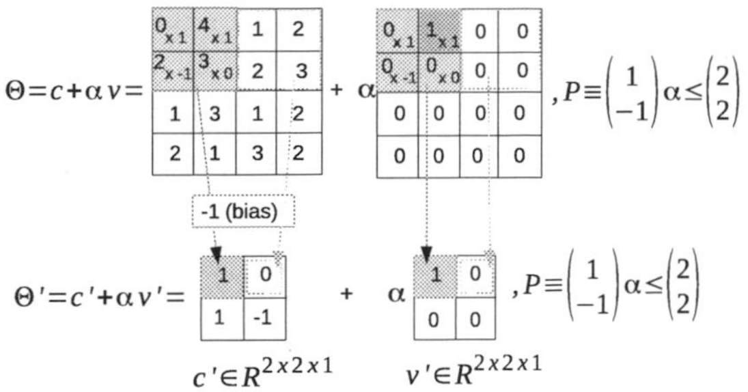

$$\Theta = c + \alpha v = \begin{array}{|c|c|c|c|} \hline 0_{\times 1} & 4_{\times 1} & 1 & 2 \\ \hline 2_{\times -1} & 3_{\times 0} & 2 & 3 \\ \hline 1 & 3 & 1 & 2 \\ \hline 2 & 1 & 3 & 2 \\ \hline \end{array} + \alpha \begin{array}{|c|c|c|c|} \hline 0_{\times 1} & 1_{\times 1} & 0 & 0 \\ \hline 0_{\times -1} & 0_{\times 0} & 0 & 0 \\ \hline 0 & 0 & 0 & 0 \\ \hline 0 & 0 & 0 & 0 \\ \hline \end{array} , P \equiv \binom{1}{-1} \alpha \leq \binom{2}{2}$$

$$\boxed{-1 \text{ (bias)}}$$

$$\Theta' = c' + \alpha v' = \begin{array}{|c|c|} \hline 1 & 0 \\ \hline 1 & -1 \\ \hline \end{array} + \alpha \begin{array}{|c|c|} \hline 1 & 0 \\ \hline 0 & 0 \\ \hline \end{array} , P \equiv \binom{1}{-1} \alpha \leq \binom{2}{2}$$

$$c' \in R^{2 \times 2 \times 1} \qquad v' \in R^{2 \times 2 \times 1}$$

Fig. 2. Reachability of convolutional layer using ImageStar.

Example 3 (Reachable set of an average pooling layer). The reachable set of an 2×2 average pooling layer with padding size $P = [0\ 0\ 0\ 0]$, stride $S = [2\ 2]$, and an ImageStar input set given by Example 1 is shown in Fig. 3.

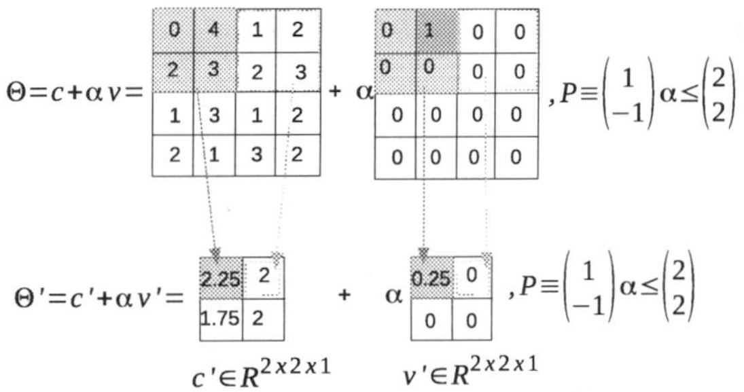

$$\Theta = c + \alpha v = \begin{array}{|c|c|c|c|} \hline 0 & 4 & 1 & 2 \\ \hline 2 & 3 & 2 & 3 \\ \hline 1 & 3 & 1 & 2 \\ \hline 2 & 1 & 3 & 2 \\ \hline \end{array} + \alpha \begin{array}{|c|c|c|c|} \hline 0 & 1 & 0 & 0 \\ \hline 0 & 0 & 0 & 0 \\ \hline 0 & 0 & 0 & 0 \\ \hline 0 & 0 & 0 & 0 \\ \hline \end{array} , P \equiv \binom{1}{-1} \alpha \leq \binom{2}{2}$$

$$\Theta' = c' + \alpha v' = \begin{array}{|c|c|} \hline 2.25 & 2 \\ \hline 1.75 & 2 \\ \hline \end{array} + \alpha \begin{array}{|c|c|} \hline 0.25 & 0 \\ \hline 0 & 0 \\ \hline \end{array} , P \equiv \binom{1}{-1} \alpha \leq \binom{2}{2}$$

$$c' \in R^{2 \times 2 \times 1} \qquad v' \in R^{2 \times 2 \times 1}$$

Fig. 3. Reachability of average pooling layer using ImageStar.

4.3 Reachability of a Fully Connected Layer

The reachability of a fully connected layer is stated in the following lemma.

Lemma 3. *Given a two-dimensional fully connected layer with weight $W_{fc} \in \mathbb{R}^{n_{fc} \times m_{fc}}$, bias $b_{fc} \in \mathbb{R}^{n_{fc}}$, and an ImageStar input set $\mathcal{I} = \langle c, V, P \rangle$, the reachable set of the layer is another ImageStar $\mathcal{I}' = \langle c', V', P \rangle$ where $c' = W * \bar{c} + b$, $V' = \{v'_1, \ldots, v'_m\}$, $v'_i = W_{fc} * \bar{v}_i$, $\bar{c}(\bar{v}_i) = reshape(c(v_i), [m_{fc}, 1])$. Note that it is required for consistency between the ImageStar and the weight matrix that $m_{fc} = h \times w \times nc$, where h, w, nc are the height, width and number of channels of the ImageStar.*

Proof. Similar to the convolutional layer and the average pooling layer, for any image in the ImageStar input set, the fully connected layer performs an affine mapping of the input image which is a linear combination of the center and the basis images of the ImageStar. Due to the linearity, the affine mapping of the input image can be decomposed into the affine mapping of the center image and the affine mapping without the bias of the basis images. The final result is the sum of the individual affine maps.

4.4 Reachability of a Batch Normalization Layer

In the prediction phase, a batch normalization layer normalizes each input channel x_i using the mean μ and variance σ^2 over the full training set. Then the batch normalization layer further shifts and scales the activations using the offset β and the scale factor γ that are learnable parameters. The formula for normalization is as follows:

$$\bar{x}_i = \frac{x_i - \mu}{\sqrt{\sigma^2 + \epsilon}}, \quad y_i = \gamma \bar{x}_i + \beta,$$

where ϵ is a used to prevent division by zero. The batch normalization layer can be described as a tuple $\mathcal{B} = \langle \mu, \sigma^2, \epsilon, \gamma, \beta \rangle$. The reachability of a batch normalization layer with an ImageStar input set is given in the following lemma.

Lemma 4. *The reachable set of a batch normalization layer* $\mathcal{B} = \langle \mu, \sigma^2, \epsilon, \gamma, \beta \rangle$ *with an ImageStar input set* $\mathcal{I} = \langle c, V, P \rangle$ *is another ImageStar* $\mathcal{I}' = \langle c', V', P' \rangle$ *where:*

$$c' = \frac{\gamma}{\sqrt{\sigma^2 + \epsilon}} c + \beta - \frac{\gamma}{\sqrt{\sigma^2 + \epsilon}} \mu, \quad V' = \frac{\gamma}{\sqrt{\sigma^2 + \epsilon}} V, \quad P' \equiv P.$$

The reachable set of a batch normalization layer can be obtained in a straightforward fashion using two affine mappings of the ImageStar input set.

4.5 Reachability of a Max Pooling Layer

Reachability of max pooling layer with an ImageStar input set is challenging because the value of each pixel in an image in the ImageStar depends on the predicate variables α_i. Therefore, the local max point when applying max-pooling operation may change with the values of the predicate variables. In this section, we investigate the exact reachability and over-approximate reachability of a max pooling layer with an ImageStar input set. The first obtains the exact reachable set while the second constructs an over-approximate reachable set.

Exact Reachability of a Max Pooling Layer. The central idea in the exact analysis of the max-pooling layer is finding a set of *local max point candidates* when we apply the max pooling operation on the image. We consider the max pooling operation on the ImageStar in Example 1 with a pool size of 2×2, a padding size of $P = [0\ 0\ 0\ 0]$, and a stride $S = [2\ 2]$ to clarify the exact analysis step-by-step. First, the max-pooling operation is applied on 4 local

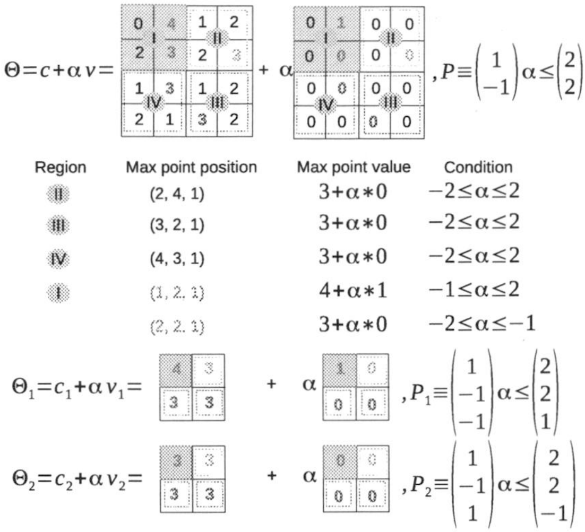

Fig. 4. Exact reachability of max pooling layer using ImageStars.

regions I, II, III, IV, as shown in Fig. 4. The local regions II, III, IV have only one *max point candidate* whic is the pixel that has the maximum value in the region. It is interesting to note that region I has two max point candidates at the positions $(1, 2, 1)$ and $(2, 2, 1)$ and these candidates correspond to different conditions of the predicate variable α. For example, the pixel at the position $(1, 2, 1)$ is the max point if and only if $4 + \alpha \times 1 \geq 3 + \alpha \times 0$. Note that with $-2 \leq \alpha \leq 2$, we always have $4 + \alpha * 1 \geq 2 + \alpha \times 0 \geq 0 + \alpha \times 0$. Since the local region I has two max point candidates, and other regions have only one, the exact reachable set of the max-pooling layer is the union of two new ImageStars Θ_1 and Θ_2. In the first reachable set Θ_1, the max point of the region I is $(1, 2, 1)$ with an additional constraint on the predicate variable $\alpha \geq -1$. For the second reachable set Θ_2, the max point of the region I is $(2, 2, 1)$ with an additional constraint on the predicate variable $\alpha \leq -1$. One can see that from a single ImageStar input set, the output reachable set of the max-pooling layer is split into two new ImageStars. Therefore, the number of ImageStars in the reachable set of the max-pooling layer may grow quickly if each local region has more than one max point candidates. The worst-case complexity of the number of ImageStars in the exact reachable set of the max-pooling layer is given in Lemma 5. The exact reachability algorithm is presented in the Appendix of the extended version of this paper [33].

Lemma 5. *The worst-case complexity of the number of ImageStars in the exact reachability of the max pooling layer is $\mathcal{O}(((p_1 \times p_2)^{h \times w})^{nc})$ where $[h, w, nc]$ is the size of the ImageStar output sets, and $[p_1, p_2]$ is the size of the max-pooling layer.*

Proof. An image in the ImageStar output set has $h \times w$ pixels in each channel. For each pixel, in the worst case, there are $p_1 \times p_2$ candidates. Therefore, the number of ImageStars in the output set in the worst case is $\mathcal{O}(((p_1 \times p_2)^{h \times w})^{nc})$.

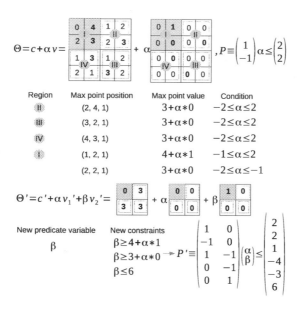

Fig. 5. Over-approximate reachability of max pooling layer using ImageStar.

Finding a set of local max point candidates is the core computation in the exact reachability of max-pooling layer. To optimize this computation, we divide the search for the local max point candidates into two steps. The first one is to estimate the ranges of all pixels in the ImageStar input set. We can solve $h_I \times w_I \times nc$ linear programming optimizations to find the exact ranges of these pixels, where $[h_I, w_I, nc]$ is the size of the input set. However, unfortunately this is a time-consuming computation. For example, *if a single linear optimization can be done in* 0.01 s, *for an ImageStar of the size* $224 \times 224 \times 32$, *we need about* 10 h *to find the ranges of all pixels*. To overcome this bottleneck, we quickly estimate the ranges using only the ranges of the predicate variables to get rid of a vast amount of non-max-point candidates. In the second step, we solve a much smaller number of LP optimizations to determine the exact set of the local max point candidates and then construct the ImageStar output set based on these candidates.

Lemma 5 shows that the number of ImageStars in the exact reachability analysis of a max-pooling layer may grow exponentially. To overcome this problem, we propose the following over-approximate reachability method.

Over-Approximate Reachability of a Max Pooling Layer. The central idea of the over-approximate analysis of the max-pooling layer is that if a local region has more than one max point candidates, we introduce a *new predicate variable* standing for the max point of that region. We revisit the example introduced earlier in the exact analysis to clarify this idea. Since the first local region I has two max point candidates, we introduce new predicate variable β to represent the max point of this region by adding three new constraints: 1) $\beta \geq 4+\alpha*1$, i.e., β must be equal or larger than the value of the first candidate ; 2) $\beta \geq 3+\alpha*0$, i.e., β must be equal or larger than the value of the second candidate; 3) $\beta \leq 6$, i.e., β must be equal or smaller than the upper bound of the pixels values in the region. With the new predicate variable, a single over-approximate reachable set Θ' can be constructed in Fig. 5. The approximate reachability algorithm is presented in the Appendix of the extended version of this paper [33].

Lemma 6. *The worst-case complexity of the new predicate variables introduced in the over-approximate analysis is $\mathcal{O}(h \times w \times nc)$ where $[h, w, nc]$ is the size of the ImageStar output set.*

4.6   Reachability of a ReLU Layer

Similar to max-pooling layer, the reachability analysis of a ReLU layer is also challenging because the value of each pixel in an ImageStar may be smaller than zero or larger than zero depending on the values of the predicate variables ($ReLU(x) = max(0, x)$). In this section, we investigate the exact and over-approximate reachability algorithms for a ReLU layer with an ImageStar input set. The techniques we use in this section are adapted from in [37].

Exact Reachability of a ReLU Layer. The central idea of the exact analysis of a ReLU layer with an ImageStar input set is performing a sequence of *stepReLU operations* over all pixels of the ImageStar input set. Mathematically, the exact reachable set of a ReLU layer L can be computed as follows.

$$\mathcal{R}_L = stepReLU_N(stepReLU_{N-1}(\ldots(stepReLU_1(\mathcal{I})))),$$

where N is the total number of pixels in the ImageStar input set $\mathcal{I}$. The $stepReLU_i$ operation determines whether or not a split occurs at the ith pixel. If the pixel value is larger than zero, then the output value of that pixel remains the same. If the pixel value is smaller than zero than the output value of that pixel is reset to be zero. The challenge is that the pixel value depends on the predicate variables. Therefore, there is the case that the pixel value may be negative or positive with *an extra condition* on the predicate variables. In this case, we split the input set into two *intermediate* ImageStar reachable sets and apply the ReLU law on each intermediate reach set. An example of the stepReLU operation on an ImageStar is illustrated in Fig. 6. The value of the first pixel value $-1 + \alpha$ would be larger than zero if $\alpha \leq 1$, and in this case we have $ReLU(-1+\alpha) = -1+\alpha$. If $\alpha <= 1$, then $ReLU(-1+\alpha) = 0+\alpha \times 0$. Therefore,

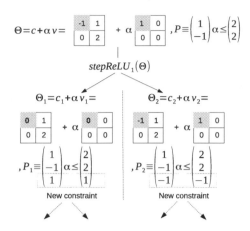

Fig. 6. stepReLU operation on an ImageStar.

the first stepReLU operation produces two intermediate reachable sets Θ_1 and Θ_2, as shown in the figure. The number of ImageStars in the exact reachable set of a ReLU layer increases quickly along with the number of splits in the analysis, as stated in the following lemma.

Lemma 7. *The worst-case complexity of the number of ImageStars in the exact analysis of a ReLU layer is $\mathcal{O}(2^N)$, where N is the number of pixels in the ImageStar input set.*

Proof. There are $h \times w \times nc$ local regions in the approximate analysis. In the worst case, we need to introduce a new variable for each region. Therefore, the worst case complexity of new predicate variables introduced is $\mathcal{O}(h \times w \times nc)$.

Similar to [37], to control the explosion in the number of ImageStars in the exact reachable set of a ReLU layer, we propose an over-approximate reachability algorithm in the following.

Over-Approximate Reachability of a ReLU Layer. The idea behind the over-approximate reachability of ReLU layer is replacing the stepReLU operation at each pixel in the ImageStar input set by an *approxStepReLU* operation. At each pixel where a split occurs, we introduce a new predicate variable to over-approximate the result of the stepReLU operation at that pixel. An example of the overStepReLU operation on an ImageStar is depicted in Fig. 7 in which the first pixel of the input set has the ranges of $[l_1 = -3, u_1 = 1]$ indicating that a split occurs at this pixel. To avoid this split, we introduce a new predicate variable β to over-approximate the exact intermediate reachable set (i.e., two blue segments in the figure) by a triangle. This triangle is determined by three constraints: 1) $\beta \geq 0$ (the $ReLU(x) \geq 0$ for any x); 2) $\beta \geq -1+\alpha$ ($ReLU(x) \geq x$ for any x); 3) $\beta \leq 0.5+0.25\alpha$ (upper bound of the new predicate variable). Using

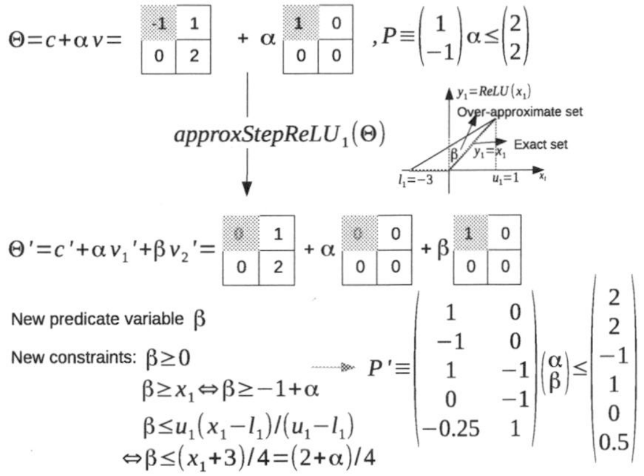

$$\Theta = c + \alpha v = \begin{array}{|c|c|} \hline -1 & 1 \\ \hline 0 & 2 \\ \hline \end{array} + \alpha \begin{array}{|c|c|} \hline 1 & 0 \\ \hline 0 & 0 \\ \hline \end{array} \;,\; P \equiv \left(\begin{array}{c} 1 \\ -1 \end{array} \right) \alpha \le \left(\begin{array}{c} 2 \\ 2 \end{array} \right)$$

$$approxStepReLU_1(\Theta)$$

$y_1 = ReLU(x_1)$
Over-approximate set
$\beta \quad y_1 = x_1$ Exact set
$l_1 = -3$ $u_1 = 1$

$$\Theta' = c' + \alpha v_1' + \beta v_2' = \begin{array}{|c|c|} \hline 0 & 1 \\ \hline 0 & 2 \\ \hline \end{array} + \alpha \begin{array}{|c|c|} \hline 0 & 0 \\ \hline 0 & 0 \\ \hline \end{array} + \beta \begin{array}{|c|c|} \hline 1 & 0 \\ \hline 0 & 0 \\ \hline \end{array}$$

New predicate variable β

New constraints: $\beta \ge 0$

$\beta \ge x_1 \Leftrightarrow \beta \ge -1 + \alpha$

$\beta \le u_1(x_1 - l_1)/(u_1 - l_1)$

$\Leftrightarrow \beta \le (x_1 + 3)/4 = (2 + \alpha)/4$

$$\longrightarrow P' \equiv \begin{pmatrix} 1 & 0 \\ -1 & 0 \\ 1 & -1 \\ 0 & -1 \\ -0.25 & 1 \end{pmatrix} \begin{pmatrix} \alpha \\ \beta \end{pmatrix} \le \begin{pmatrix} 2 \\ 2 \\ -1 \\ 1 \\ 0 \\ 0.5 \end{pmatrix}$$

Fig. 7. approxStepReLU operation on an ImageStar.

this over-approximation, a single intermediate reachable set Θ' is produced as shown in the figure. After performing a sequence of approxStepReLU operations, we obtain a single over-approximate ImageStar reachable set for the ReLU layer. However, the number of predicate variables and the number of constraints in the obtained reachable set increase.

Lemma 8. *The worst case complexity of the increment of predicate variables and constraints is $\mathcal{O}(N)$ and $\mathcal{O}(3 \times N)$ respectively, where N is the number of pixels in the ImageStar input set.*

Proof. In the worst case, splits occur at all N pixels in the ImageStar input set. In this case, we need to introduce N new predicate variables to over-approximate the exact intermediate reachable set. For each new predicate variable, we add 3 new constraints.

One can see that determining where splits occur is crucial in the exact and over-approximate analysis of a ReLU layer. To do this, we need to know the ranges of all pixels in the ImageStar input set. However, as mentioned earlier, the computation of the exact range is expensive. To reduce the computation cost, we first use the estimated ranges of all pixels to remove a vast amount of non-splitting pixels. Then, we compute exact ranges for the pixels where splits may occur to compute the exact or over-approximate reachable set of the layer.

4.7   Reachabilty Algorithm and Parallelization

We have presented the core ideas for reachability analysis of different types of layers in a CNN. The reachable set of a CNN is constructed layer-by-layer in which the output reachable set of the previous layer is the input for the next layer. For the convolutional layer, average pooling layer and fully connected layer, we always can compute efficiently the exact reachable set of each layer.

Algorithm 1. Reachability analysis for a CNN.

Input: $\mathcal{N} = \{L_i\}_1^n$, $\mathcal{I}$, *scheme* ('exact' or 'approx')
Output: $R_{\mathcal{N}}$
  1: **procedure** $R_{\mathcal{N}}$ = REACH($\mathcal{N}, \mathcal{I}, scheme$)
  2:     $In = \mathcal{I}$
  3:     **parfor** $i = 1 : n$ **do** $In = L_i.reach(In, scheme)$
  4:     **end parfor**
  5:     $R_{\mathcal{N}} = In$

For the max pooling layer and ReLU layer, we can compute both the exact and the over-approximate reachable sets. However, the number of ImageStars in the exact reachable set may grow quickly. Therefore, *in the exact analysis, a layer may receive multiple input sets which can be handled in parallel to speed up the computation time.* The reachability algorithm for a CNN is summarized in Algorithm 1. The detailed implementation of the reachability algorithm for each layer can be found in NNV [34,39].

5 Evaluation

The proposed reachability algorithms are implemented in NNV [39], a tool for verification of deep neural networks and learning-enabled CPS. NNV utilizes core functions in MatConvNet [40] for the analysis of several layers. The evaluation of our approach consists of two parts. First, we evaluate robustness verification of deep neural networks in comparison to zonotope [29] and polytope methods [30] that are re-implemented in NNV. Second, we evaluate the scalability of our approach and the DeepPoly polytope method using real-world image classifiers, VGG16, and VGG19 [28]. The experiments are done on a computer with following configurations: Intel Core i7-6700 CPU @ 3.4GHz × 8 Processor, 62.8 GiB Memory, Ubuntu 18.04.1 LTS OS.[1] Lastly, we present a comparison with ERAN-DeepZ method on their *ConvMaxPool* network trained on the CIFAR-10 data set in the Appendix of the extended version of this paper [33].

5.1   Robustness Verification of MNIST Classification Networks

We compare our approach with the zonotope and polytope methods in two aspects including verification time and conservativeness of the results. To do that, we train 3 CNNs in small, medium, and large architectures with $98\%, 99.7\%$, and 99.9% accuracy, respectively, using the MNIST data set consisting of 60000 images of handwritten digits with a resolution of 28×28 pixels [20]. The network architectures are given in the Appendix of the extended version of this paper [33].

---

[1] Comparison code is available in the NNV repository: https://github.com/verivital/nnv/tree/cav2020imagestar/code/nnv/examples/Submission/CAV2020_ImageStar and as a CodeOcean capsule [34]: https://doi.org/10.24433/CO.3351375.v1.

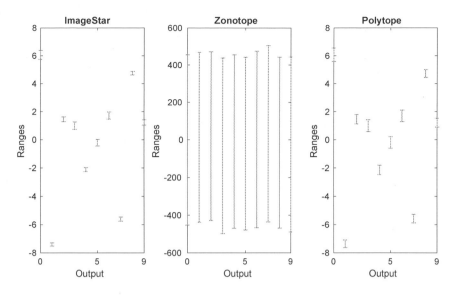

Fig. 8. Example output ranges of the small MNIST classification network using different approaches.

The networks classify images into ten classes: $0, 1, \ldots, 9$. The classified output is the index of the dimension that has maximum value, i.e., the argmax across the 10 outputs. We evaluate the robustness of the network under the well-known brightening attack used in [8]. The idea of a brightening attack is that we can change the value of some pixels independently in the image to make it brighter or darker to fool the network, to misclassify the image. In this case study, we darken a pixel of an image if its value x_i (between 0 and 255) is larger than a threshold d, i.e., $x_i \geq d$. Mathematically, we reduce the value of that pixel x_i to the new value x_i' such that $0 \leq x_i' \leq \delta \times x_i$.

The robustness verification is done as follows. We select 100 images that are correctly classified by the networks and perform the brightening attack on these, which are then used to evaluate the robustness of the networks. A network is robust to an input set if, for any *attacked* image, this is correctly classified by the network. We note that the input set contains an infinite number of images. Therefore, to prove the robustness of the network to the input set, we first compute the output set containing all possible output vectors of the network using reachability analysis. Then, we prove that in the output set, the correctly classified output always has the maximum value compared with other outputs. Note that we can neglect the *softmax* and *classoutput* layers of the networks in the analysis since we only need to know the maximum output in the output set of the last fully connected layer in the networks to prove the robustness of the network.

We are interested in the percentage of the number of input sets that a network is provably robust and the verification times of different approaches under different values of d and θ. When d is small, the number of pixels in the image that are attacked is large and vice versa. For example, the average number of pixels attacked (computed on 100 cases) corresponding to $d = 250$, 245 and 240 are 15, 21 and 25 respectively. The value of δ dictates the size of the input set that can be created by a specific attack. Stated differently it dictates the range in which the value of a pixel can be changed. For example, if $d = 250$ and $\delta = 0.01$, the value of an attacked pixel many range from 0 to 2.55.

Table 1. Verification results of the small MNIST CNN.

| | Robustness results (in Percent) | | | | | |
| | $\delta = 0.005$ | | $\delta = 0.01$ | | $\delta = 0.015$ | |
	Polytope	*ImageStar*	*Polytope*	*ImageStar*	*Polytope*	*ImageStar*
$d = 250$	86.00	87.00	84.00	87.00	83.00	87.00
$d = 245$	77.00	78.00	72.00	78.00	70.00	77.00
$d = 240$	72.00	73.00	67.00	72.00	65.00	71.00
	Verification times (in Seconds)					
$d = 250$	11.24	16.28	18.26	28.19	26.42	53.43
$d = 245$	14.84	19.44	24.96	40.76	38.94	85.97
$d = 240$	18.29	25.77	33.59	64.10	54.23	118.58

Table 2. Verification results of the medium MNIST CNN.

| | Robustness results (in Percent) | | | | | |
| | $\delta = 0.005$ | | $\delta = 0.01$ | | $\delta = 0.015$ | |
	Polytope	*ImageStar*	*Polytope*	*ImageStar*	*Polytope*	*ImageStar*
$d = 250$	86.00	99.00	73.00	99.00	65.00	99.00
$d = 245$	74.00	95.00	58.00	95.00	46.00	95.00
$d = 240$	69.00	90.00	49.00	89.00	38.00	88.00
	Verification times (in Seconds)					
$d = 250$	213.86	52.09	627.14	257.12	1215.86	749.41
$d = 245$	232.81	68.98	931.28	295.54	2061.98	1168.31
$d = 240$	301.58	102.61	1451.39	705.03	3148.16	2461.89

The experiments show that using the zonotope method, we cannot prove the robustness of any network. The reason is that the zonotope method obtains very conservative reachable sets. Figure 8 illustrates the ranges of the outputs computed by our ImageStar (approximate scheme), the zonotope and polytope approaches when we attack a digit 0 image with brightening attack in which $d = 250$ and $\delta = 0.05$. One can see that, using ImageStar and polytope method, we can prove that the output corresponding to the digit 0 is the one that has a maximum value, which means that the network is robust in this case. However, the zonotope method produces very large output ranges that cannot be used to prove the robustness of the network. The figure also shows that our ImageStar method produces tighter ranges than the polytope method, which means our result is less conservative than the one obtained by the polytope method. We note that the zonotope method is very time-consuming. It needs 93 s to compute the reachable set of the network in this case, while the polytope method only needs 0.3 s, and our approximate ImageStar method needs 0.74 s. The main reason is that the zonotope method introduces many new variables when constructing the reachable set of the network, which results in the increase in both computation time and conservativeness.

Table 3. Verification results of the large MNIST CNN.

	Robustness results (in Percent)					
	$\delta = 0.005$		$\delta = 0.01$		$\delta = 0.015$	
	Polytope	*ImageStar*	*Polytope*	*ImageStar*	*Polytope*	*ImageStar*
$d = 250$	90.00	99.00	83.00	99.00	*MemErr*	99.00
$d = 245$	91.00	100.00	75.00	100.00	*MemErr*	100.00
$d = 240$	81.00	99.00	*MemErr*	99.00	*MemErr*	99.00
	Verification times (in Seconds)					
$d = 250$	917.23	67.45	5221.39	231.67	*MemErr*	488.69
$d = 245$	1420.58	104.71	6491.00	353.02	*MemErr*	1052.87
$d = 240$	1872.16	123.37	*MemErr*	476.67	*MemErr*	1522.50

The comparison of the polytope and our ImageStar method is given in Tables 1, 2, and 3. The tables show that in all networks, our method is less conservative than the polytope approach since the number of cases that our approach can prove the robustness of the network is larger than the one proved by the polytope method. For example, for the small network, for $d = 240$ and $\delta = 0.015$, we can prove 71 cases while the polytope method can prove 65 cases. Importantly, the number of cases proved by DeepPoly reduces quickly when the network becomes larger. For example, for the case that $d = 240$ and $\delta = 0.015$, the polytope method is able to prove the robustness of the medium network for 38 cases while our approach can prove 88 cases. This is because the polytope method becomes more and more conservative when the network or the input set is large. The tables show that the polytope method is faster than our ImageStar method on the small network. However, it is slower than the ImageStar method on any larger networks in all cases. Notably, for the large network, the ImageStar approach is significantly faster than the polytope approach, 16.65 times faster in average. The results also show that the polytope approach may run into memory problem for some large input sets.

Table 4. Verification results of VGG networks.

	VGG16				VGG19			
Robustness results (in percentage)	$\delta = 10^{-7}$		$\delta = 2 \times 10^{-7}$		$\delta = 10^{-7}$		$\delta = 2 \times 10^{-7}$	
	$Polytope$	$ImageStar$	$Polytope$	$ImageStar$	$Polytope$	$ImageStar$	$Polytope$	$ImageStar$
$l = 0.96$	85.00	85.00	85.00	85.00	100.00	100.00	100.00	100.00
$l = 0.97$	85.00	85.00	85.00	85.00	100.00	100.00	100.00	100.00
$l = 0.98$	85.00	85.00	85.00	85.00	95.00	95.00	95.00	95.00
Verification times (in Seconds)								
$l = 0.96$	319.04	318.60	327.61	319.93	320.91	314.14	885.07	339.30
$l = 0.97$	324.93	323.41	317.27	324.90	315.84	315.27	319.67	314.58
$l = 0.98$	315.54	315.26	468.59	332.92	320.53	320.44	325.92	317.95

5.2   Robustness Verification of VGG16 and VGG19

In this section, we evaluate the polytope and ImageStar methods on real-world CNNs, the VGG16 and VGG19 classification networks [28]. We use Foolbox [26] to generate the well-known DeepFool adversarial attacks [25] on a set of 20 bell pepper images. From an original image ori_im, Foolbox generates an adversarial image adv_im that can fool the network. The difference between two images is defined by $diff\_im = adv\_im - ori\_im$. We want to verify if we apply $(l + \delta)$ percent of the attack on the original image, whether or not the network classifies the disturbed images correctly. The set of disturbed images can be represented as an ImageStar as follows $disb\_im = ori\_im + (l + \delta) \times diff\_im$, where l is the percentage of the attack at which we want to verify the robustness of the network, and δ is a small perturbation around l, i.e., $0 \leq \delta \leq \delta_{max}$. Intuitively, l describes how close we are to the attack, and the perturbation δ represents the size of the input set.

Table 4 shows the verification results of VGG16 and VGG19 with different levels of the DeepFool attack. The networks are robust if they classify correctly the set of disturbed images $disb\_im$ as bell peppers. To guarantee the robustness of the networks, the output corresponding to the bell pepper label (index 946) needs to be the maximum output compared with others. The table shows that with a small input set, small δ, the polytope and ImageStar can prove robustness of VGG16 and VGG19 in a reasonable amount of time. Notably, the verification times as well as the robustness results of the polytope and ImageStar methods are similar when they deal with small input sets except for two cases where ImageStar is faster than the polytope method. It is interesting to note that according to the verification results for the VGG and MNIST networks, deep networks may be more robust than shall ow networks.

5.3   Exact Analysis vs. Approximate Analysis

We compare our ImageStar approximate scheme with the zonotope and poly-tope approximation methods, and investigate the performance of the ImageStar

Table 5. Verification results of the VGG16 and VGG19 in which VT is the verification time (in seconds) using the ImageStar exact and approximate schemes.

l	δ_{max}	VGG16				VGG19			
		Exact		Approximate		Exact		Approximate	
		Robust	VT	Robust	VT	Robust	VT	Robust	VT
50%	10^{-7}	Yes	64.56226	Yes	60.10607	Yes	234.11977	Yes	72.08723
	2×10^{-7}	Yes	63.88826	Yes	59.48936	Yes	1769.69313	Yes	196.93728
80%	10^{-7}	Yes	64.92889	Yes	60.31394	Yes	67.11730	Yes	63.33389
	2×10^{-7}	Yes	64.20910	Yes	59.77254	Yes	174.55983	Yes	200.89500
95%	10^{-7}	Yes	67.64783	Yes	59.89077	Yes	73.13642	Yes	67.56389
	2×10^{-7}	Yes	63.83538	Yes	59.23282	Yes	146.16172	Yes	121.91447
97%	10^{-7}	Yes	64.30362	Yes	59.79876	Yes	77.25398	Yes	64.43168
	2×10^{-7}	Yes	64.06285	Yes	61.23296	Yes	121.70296	Yes	107.17331
98%	10^{-7}	Yes	64.06183	Yes	59.89959	No	67.68139	Unkown	64.47035
	2×10^{-7}	Yes	64.01997	Yes	59.77469	No	205.00939	Unknown	107.42679
98.999%	10^{-7}	Yes	64.24773	Yes	60.22833	No	71.90568	Unknown	68.25916
	2×10^{-7}	Yes	63.67108	Yes	59.69298	No	106.84492	Unknown	101.04668

exact scheme compared to the approximate one. To illustrate the advantages and disadvantages of the exact scheme and approximate scheme, we consider the robustness verification of VGG16 and VGG19 on a single ImageStar input set created by an adversarial attack on a bell pepper image. The verification results are presented in Table 5. The table shows that for a small perturbation δ, the exact and over-approximate analysis can prove the robustness of the VGG16 around some specific levels of attack in approximately one minute. We can intuitively verify the robustness of the VGG networks via visualization of their output ranges. An example of the output ranges of VGG19 for the case of $l = 0.95\%, \delta_{max} = 2 \times 10^{-7}$ is depicted in Fig. 9. One can see from the figure that the output of the index 946 corresponding to the bell pepper label is always the maximum one compared with others, which proves that VGG19 is robust in this case. From the table, it is interesting that VGG19 is not robust if we apply $\geq 98\%$ of the attack. Notably, the exact analysis can give us correct answers with a counter-example set in this case. However, the over-approximate analysis cannot prove that VGG19 is not robust since its obtained reachable set is an over-approximation of the exact one. Therefore, it may be the case that the over-approximate reachable set violates the robustness property because of its conservativeness. A counter-example generated by the exact analysis method is depicted in Fig. 10 in which the disturbed image is classified as strawberry instead of bell pepper since the strawberry output is larger than the bell pepper output in this case.

To optimize the verification time, it is important to know the times consumed by each type of layer in the reachability analysis step. Figure 11 described the total reachability times of the convolutional layers, fully connected layers, max pooling layers and ReLU layers in the VGG19 with 50% attack and 10^{-7} perturbation. As shown in the figure, the reachable set computation in the convo-

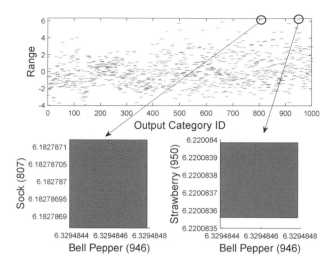

Fig. 9. Exact ranges of VGG19 show that VGG19 correctly classifies the input image as a bell pepper.

lutional layers and fully connected layers can be done very quickly, which shows the advantages of the ImageStar data structure. Notably, the total reachability time is dominated by the time of computing the reachable set for 5 max pooling layers and 18 ReLU layers. This is because the computation in these layers concerns solving a large number of linear programing (LP) optimization problems such as finding lower bound and upper bound, and checking max point candidates. Therefore, to optimize the computation time, we need to minimize the number of LP problems in the future.

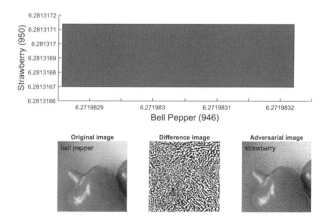

Fig. 10. A counter-example shows that VGG19 misclassifies the input image as a strawberry instead of a bell pepper.

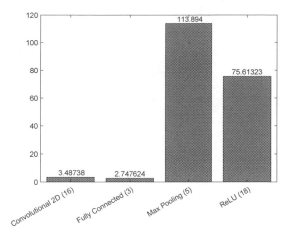

Fig. 11. Total reachability time of each type of layer in VGG19, where the max pooling and ReLU layers dominate the total reachability time.

6   Discussion

When we apply our approach on large networks, it has been shown that the size of the input set is the most important factor that influences the performance of verification approaches. However, this important issue has not been emphasized in the existing literature. Most of existing approaches focus on the size of the network that they can analyze. We hypothesize that existing methods (including the methods in this paper) scalable to large networks are only so for small input sets. When the input set is large, it causes three major problems in the analysis, which are explosions of 1) computation time; 2) memory usage; and 3) conservativeness. In the exact analysis method, a large input set causes more splits in the max-pooling and ReLU layers. A single ImageStar may split into many new ImageStars after these layers, which leads to explosion in the number of ImageStars in the reachable set as shown in Fig. 12. Therefore, it requires more memory to handle the new ImageStars and more time for the computation. One may think that the over-approximate method can overcome this challenge since it obtains only one ImageStar at each layer and at the cost of conservativeness of the result. An over-approximate method does usually help reduce the computation time, as shown in the experimental results. However, it is not necessarily efficient in terms of memory consumption. The reason is, if there is a split, it introduces a new predicate variable and new generator. If the number of generators and the dimensions of the ImageStar are large, it requires a massive amount of memory to store the over-approximate reachable set. For instance, if there are 100 splits in the first ReLU layer of VGG19, the second convolutional layer will receive an ImageStar of size $224 \times 224 \times 64$ with 100 generators. To store this ImageStar with double precision, we need approximately 2.4 GB of memory. In practice, the dimensions of the ImageStars obtained in the first several convolutional layers are usually large. Therefore, if splitting happens in these layers, we may run out of memory. We see that existing approaches, such as those using zonotopes and polytopes, also face the same challenges. Additionally, the conservativeness of an over-approximate reachable set is a crucial factor in evaluating an over-approximation approach. Therefore, the exact analysis still plays an essential role in the analysis of neural networks since it helps to evaluate the conservativeness of the over-approximation approaches.

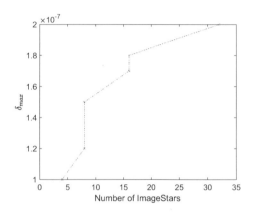

Fig. 12. Number of ImageStars in exact analysis increases with input size.

7   Conclusion

We have presented a new set-based method for robustness verification of deep CNNs using ImageStars. The core of this method are exact and over-approximate reachability algorithms for ImageStar input sets. The experiments show that our approach is less conservative than recent zonotope and polytope approaches. It is also faster than existing approaches when dealing with deep networks. Notably, our approach can be applied to verify the robustness of real-world CNNs with small perturbed input sets. It can also compute the exact reachable set and visualize the exact output range of deep CNNs, and the analysis can speed up significantly with parallel computing. We have found and shown the size of the input set to be an important factor that impacts the performance of reachability algorithms. Future work includes improving the method to deal with larger input sets and optimizing the memory and time complexity of our computations.

References

1. Akintunde, M.E., Botoeva, E., Kouvaros, P., Lomuscio, A.: Formal verification of neural agents in non-deterministic environments. In: Autonomous Agents and Multi-Agent Systems, May 2020

2. Anderson, G., Pailoor, S., Dillig, I., Chaudhuri, S.: Optimization and abstraction: a synergistic approach for analyzing neural network robustness. In: Proceedings of the 40th ACM SIGPLAN Conference on Programming Language Design and Implementation PLDI 2019, pp. 731–744. Association for Computing Machinery, New York (2019)
3. Bak, S., Duggirala, P.S.: Simulation-Equivalent reachability of large linear systems with inputs. In: Majumdar, R., Kunčak, V. (eds.) CAV 2017. LNCS, vol. 10426, pp. 401–420. Springer, Cham (2017). https://doi.org/10.1007/978-3-319-63387-9_20
4. Bak, S., Tran, H.D., Johnson, T.T.: Numerical verification of affine systems with up to a billion dimensions. In: Proceedings of the 22nd ACM International Conference on Hybrid Systems: Computation and Control, pp. 23–32. ACM (2019)
5. Dutta, S., Jha, S., Sanakaranarayanan, S., Tiwari, A.: Output range analysis for deep neural networks (2017). arXiv preprint arXiv:1709.09130
6. Dvijotham, K., Stanforth, R., Gowal, S., Mann, T.A., Kohli, P.: A dual approach to scalable verification of deep networks. In: UAI, pp. 550–559 (2018)
7. Ehlers, R.: Formal verification of piece-wise linear feed-forward neural networks. In: D'Souza, D., Narayan Kumar, K. (eds.) ATVA 2017. LNCS, vol. 10482, pp. 269–286. Springer, Cham (2017). https://doi.org/10.1007/978-3-319-68167-2_19
8. Gehr, T., Mirman, M., Drachsler-Cohen, D., Tsankov, P., Chaudhuri, S., Vechev, M.: Ai2: safety and robustness certification of neural networks with abstract interpretation. In: 2018 IEEE Symposium on Security and Privacy (SP), pp. 3–18. IEEE (2018)
9. Goodfellow, I.J., Shlens, J., Szegedy, C.: Explaining and harnessing adversarial examples (2014). arXiv preprint arXiv:1412.6572
10. Gopinath, D., Converse, H., Pasareanu, C., Taly, A.: Property inference for deep neural networks. In: 2019 34th IEEE/ACM International Conference on Automated Software Engineering (ASE), pp. 797–809, November 2019
11. Hein, M., Andriushchenko, M.: Formal guarantees on the robustness of a classifier against adversarial manipulation. In: Advances in Neural Information Processing Systems, pp. 2266–2276 (2017)
12. Huang, C., Fan, J., Li, W., Chen, X., Zhu, Q.: Reachnn: reachability analysis of neural-network controlled systems. ACM Trans. Embed. Comput. Syst. (TECS) 18(5s), 1–22 (2019)
13. Ivanov, R., Carpenter, T.J., Weimer, J., Alur, R., Pappas, G.J., Lee, I.: Case study: verifying the safety of an autonomous racing car with a neural network controller. In: Proceedings of the 23rd International Conference on Hybrid Systems: Computation and Control, pp. 1–7 (2020)
14. Ivanov, R., Weimer, J., Alur, R., Pappas, G.J., Lee, I.: Verisig: verifying safety properties of hybrid systems with neural network controllers. In: Hybrid Systems: Computation and Control (HSCC) (2019)
15. Katz, G., Barrett, C., Dill, D.L., Julian, K., Kochenderfer, M.J.: Reluplex: an efficient SMT solver for verifying deep neural networks. In: Majumdar, R., Kunčak, V. (eds.) CAV 2017. LNCS, vol. 10426, pp. 97–117. Springer, Cham (2017). https://doi.org/10.1007/978-3-319-63387-9_5
16. Katz, G.: The marabou framework for verification and analysis of deep neural networks. In: Dillig, I., Tasiran, S. (eds.) CAV 2019. LNCS, vol. 11561, pp. 443–452. Springer, Cham (2019). https://doi.org/10.1007/978-3-030-25540-4_26
17. Kouvaros, P., Lomuscio, A.: Formal verification of CNN-based perception systems (2018). arXiv preprint arXiv:1811.11373

18. Krizhevsky, A., Sutskever, I., Hinton, G.E.: Imagenet classification with deep convolutional neural networks. In: Advances in neural information processing systems, pp. 1097–1105 (2012)
19. Lawrence, S., Giles, C.L., Tsoi, A.C., Back, A.D.: Face recognition: a convolutional neural-network approach. IEEE Trans. Neural Netw. 8(1), 98–113 (1997)
20. LeCun, Y.: The MNIST database of handwritten digits (1998). http://yann.lecun.com/exdb/mnist/
21. LeCun, Y., Bottou, L., Bengio, Y., Haffner, P., et al.: Gradient-based learning applied to document recognition. Proc. IEEE 86(11), 2278–2324 (1998)
22. Lin, W., et al.: Robustness verification of classification deep neural networks via linear programming. In: Proceedings of the IEEE Conference on Computer Vision and Pattern Recognition. pp. 11418–11427 (2019)
23. Lomuscio, A., Maganti, L.: An approach to reachability analysis for feed-forward relu neural networks (2017). arXiv preprint arXiv:1706.07351
24. Lopez, D.M., Musau, P., Tran, H.D., Johnson, T.T.: Verification of closed-loop systems with neural network controllers. In: Frehse, G., Althoff, M. (eds.) ARCH19. 6th International Workshop on Applied Verification of Continuous and Hybrid Systems. EPiC Series in Computing, vol. 61, pp. 201–210. EasyChair, April 2019
25. Moosavi-Dezfooli, S.M., Fawzi, A., Frossard, P.: Deepfool: a simple and accurate method to fool deep neural networks. In: Proceedings of the IEEE Conference on Computer Vision and Pattern Recognition, pp. 2574–2582 (2016)
26. Rauber, J., Brendel, W., Bethge, M.: Foolbox v0. 8.0: A python toolbox to benchmark the robustness of machine learning models, 5 (2017). arXiv preprint arXiv:1707.04131
27. Ruan, W., Wu, M., Sun, Y., Huang, X., Kroening, D., Kwiatkowska, M.: Global robustness evaluation of deep neural networks with provable guarantees for the L_0 norm (2018). arXiv preprint arXiv:1804.05805
28. Simonyan, K., Zisserman, A.: Very deep convolutional networks for large-scale image recognition (2014). arXiv preprint arXiv:1409.1556
29. Singh, G., Gehr, T., Mirman, M., Püschel, M., Vechev, M.: Fast and effective robustness certification. In: Advances in Neural Information Processing Systems, pp. 10825–10836 (2018)
30. Singh, G., Gehr, T., Püschel, M., Vechev, M.: An abstract domain for certifying neural networks. In: Proceedings of the ACM on Programming Languages 3(POPL), 41 (2019)
31. Dutta, S., Chen, X., Sankaranarayanan, S.: Reachability analysis for neural feedback systems using regressive polynomial rule inference. In: Hybrid Systems: Computation and Control (HSCC) (2019)
32. Sun, X., Khedr, H., Shoukry, Y.: Formal verification of neural network controlled autonomous systems. In: Hybrid Systems: Computation and Control (HSCC) (2019)
33. Tran, H.D., Bak, S., Xiang, W., Johnson, T.T.: Verification of deep convolutional neural networks using imagestars (2020). arXiv preprint arXiv:2004.05511
34. Tran, H.D., Bak, S., Xiang, W., Johnson, T.T.: Verification of deep convolutional neural networks using imagestars (CodeOcean Capsule), May 2020. https://doi.org/10.24433/CO.3351375.v1
35. Tran, H.D., Cei, F., Lopez, D.M., Johnson, T.T., Koutsoukos, X.: Safety verification of cyber-physical systems with reinforcement learning control. In: ACM SIGBED International Conference on Embedded Software (EMSOFT 2019). ACM, October 2019

36. Tran, H.D., et al.: Parallelizable reachability analysis algorithms for feed-forward neural networks. In: 7th International Conference on Formal Methods in Software Engineering (FormaliSE 2019), Montreal, Canada (2019)

37. Tran, H.D., et al.: Star-based reachability analysis of deep neural networks. In: ter Beek, M.H., McIver, A., Oliveira, J.N. (eds.) FM 2019. LNCS, vol. 11800, pp. 670–686. Springer, Cham (2019). https://doi.org/10.1007/978-3-030-30942-8_39

38. Tran, H.-D., Nguyen, L.V., Hamilton, N., Xiang, W., Johnson, T.T.: Reachability analysis for high-index linear differential algebraic equations. In: André, É., Stoelinga, M. (eds.) FORMATS 2019. LNCS, vol. 11750, pp. 160–177. Springer, Cham (2019). https://doi.org/10.1007/978-3-030-29662-9_10

39. Tran, H.D., et al.: NNV: The neural network verification tool for deep neural networks and learning-enabled cyber-physical systems. In: 32nd International Conference on Computer-Aided Verification (CAV), July 2020

40. Vedaldi, A., Lenc, K.: Matconvnet: convolutional neural networks for matlab. In: Proceedings of the 23rd ACM international conference on Multimedia, pp. 689–692. ACM (2015)

41. Wang, S., Pei, K., Whitehouse, J., Yang, J., Jana, S.: Formal security analysis of neural networks using symbolic intervals (2018). arXiv preprint arXiv:1804.10829

42. Weng, T.W., et al.: Towards fast computation of certified robustness for relu networks (2018). arXiv preprint arXiv:1804.09699

43. Wong, E., Kolter, J.Z.: Provable defenses against adversarial examples via the convex outer adversarial polytope (2017). arXiv preprint arXiv:1711.00851

44. Wu, M., Wicker, M., Ruan, W., Huang, X., Kwiatkowska, M.: A game-basedapproximate verification of deep neural networks with provable guarantees. Theor. Comput. Sci. (2019)

45. Xiang, W., Tran, H.D., Johnson, T.T.: Output reachable set estimation and verification for multilayer neural networks. IEEE Trans. Neural Netw. Learn. Syst. **29**(11), 5777–5783 (2018)

46. Xiang, W., Tran, H.D., Yang, X., Johnson, T.T.: Reachable set estimation for neural network control systems: A simulation-guided approach. IEEE Transactions on Neural Networks and Learning Systems, pp. 1–10 (2020)

47. Xiang, W., Tran, H.D., Johnson, T.T.: Reachable set computation and safety verification for neural networks with relu activations (2017). arXiv preprint arXiv:1712.08163

48. Xiang, W., Tran, H.D., Johnson, T.T.: Specification-guided safety verification for feedforward neural networks. In: AAAI Spring Symposium on Verification of Neural Networks (2019)

49. Xiang, W., Tran, H.D., Rosenfeld, J.A., Johnson, T.T.: Reachable set estimation and safety verification for piecewise linear systems with neural network controllers. arXiv preprint arXiv:1802.06981 (2018)

50. Yang, X., Tran, H.D., Xiang, W., Johnson, T.T.: Reachability analysis for feedforward neural networks using face lattices (2020). https://arxiv.org/abs/2003.01226

51. Zhang, H., Weng, T.W., Chen, P.Y., Hsieh, C.J., Daniel, L.: Efficient neural network robustness certification with general activation functions. In: Advances in Neural Information Processing Systems, pp. 4944–4953 (2018)

An Abstraction-Based Framework for Neural Network Verification

Yizhak Yisrael Elboher[1], Justin Gottschlich[2], and Guy Katz[1(✉)]

[1] The Hebrew University of Jerusalem, Jerusalem, Israel
{yizhak.elboher,g.katz}@mail.huji.ac.il
[2] Intel Labs, Santa Clara, USA
justin.gottschlich@intel.com

Abstract. Deep neural networks are increasingly being used as controllers for safety-critical systems. Because neural networks are opaque, certifying their correctness is a significant challenge. To address this issue, several neural network verification approaches have recently been proposed. However, these approaches afford limited scalability, and applying them to large networks can be challenging. In this paper, we propose a framework that can enhance neural network verification techniques by using over-approximation to reduce the size of the network—thus making it more amenable to verification. We perform the approximation such that if the property holds for the smaller (abstract) network, it holds for the original as well. The over-approximation may be too coarse, in which case the underlying verification tool might return a spurious counterexample. Under such conditions, we perform counterexample-guided refinement to adjust the approximation, and then repeat the process. Our approach is orthogonal to, and can be integrated with, many existing verification techniques. For evaluation purposes, we integrate it with the recently proposed Marabou framework, and observe a significant improvement in Marabou's performance. Our experiments demonstrate the great potential of our approach for verifying larger neural networks.

1 Introduction

Machine programming (MP), the automatic generation of software, is showing early signs of fundamentally transforming the way software is developed [15]. A key ingredient employed by MP is the *deep neural network* (DNN), which has emerged as an effective means to semi-autonomously implement many complex software systems. DNNs are artifacts produced by *machine learning*: a user provides examples of how a system should behave, and a machine learning algorithm generalizes these examples into a DNN capable of correctly handling inputs that it had not seen before. Systems with DNN components have obtained unprecedented results in fields such as image recognition [24], game playing [33], natural language processing [16], computer networks [28], and many others, often surpassing the results obtained by similar systems that have been carefully hand-crafted. It seems evident that this trend will increase and intensify, and that DNN components will be deployed in various safety-critical systems [3,19].

© The Author(s) 2020
S. K. Lahiri and C. Wang (Eds.): CAV 2020, LNCS 12224, pp. 43–65, 2020.
https://doi.org/10.1007/978-3-030-53288-8_3

DNNs are appealing in that (in some cases) they are easier to create than handcrafted software, while still achieving excellent results. However, their usage also raises a challenge when it comes to certification. Undesired behavior has been observed in many state-of-the-art DNNs. For example, in many cases slight perturbations to correctly handled inputs can cause severe errors [26, 35]. Because many practices for improving the reliability of hand-crafted code have yet to be successfully applied to DNNs (e.g., code reviews, coding guidelines, etc.), it remains unclear how to overcome the opacity of DNNs, which may limit our ability to certify them before they are deployed.

To mitigate this, the formal methods community has begun developing techniques for the formal verification of DNNs (e.g., [10, 17, 20, 37]). These techniques can automatically prove that a DNN always satisfies a prescribed property. Unfortunately, the DNN verification problem is computationally difficult (e.g., NP-complete, even for simple specifications and networks [20]), and becomes exponentially more difficult as network sizes increase. Thus, despite recent advances in DNN verification techniques, network sizes remain a severely limiting factor.

In this work, we propose a technique by which the scalability of many existing verification techniques can be significantly increased. The idea is to apply the well-established notion of *abstraction and refinement* [6]: replace a network N that is to be verified with a much smaller, *abstract* network, $\bar{N}$, and then verify this $\bar{N}$. Because $\bar{N}$ is smaller it can be verified more efficiently; and it is constructed in such a way that if it satisfies the specification, the original network N also satisfies it. In the case that $\bar{N}$ does not satisfy the specification, the verification procedure provides a counterexample x. This x may be a true counterexample demonstrating that the original network N violates the specification, or it may be *spurious*. If x is spurious, the network $\bar{N}$ is *refined* to make it more accurate (and slightly larger), and then the process is repeated. A particularly useful variant of this approach is to use the spurious x to guide the refinement process, so that the refinement step rules out x as a counterexample. This variant, known as *counterexample-guided abstraction refinement* (*CEGAR*) [6], has been successfully applied in many verification contexts.

As part of our technique we propose a method for abstracting and refining neural networks. Our basic abstraction step *merges* two neurons into one, thus reducing the overall number of neurons by one. This basic step can be repeated numerous times, significantly reducing the network size. Conversely, refinement is performed by splitting a previously merged neuron in two, increasing the network size but making it more closely resemble the original. A key point is that not all pairs of neurons can be merged, as this could result in a network that is smaller but is not an over-approximation of the original. We resolve this by first transforming the original network into an equivalent network where each node belongs to one of four classes, determined by its edge weights and its effect on the network's output; merging neurons from the same class can then be done safely. The actual choice of which neurons to merge or split is performed heuristically. We propose and discuss several possible heuristics.

For evaluation purposes, we implemented our approach as a Python framework that wraps the Marabou verification tool [22]. We then used our framework to verify properties of the Airborne Collision Avoidance System (ACAS Xu) set of benchmarks [20]. Our results strongly demonstrate the potential usefulness of abstraction in enhancing existing verification schemes: specifically, in most cases the abstraction-enhanced Marabou significantly outperformed the original. Further, in most cases the properties in question could indeed be shown to hold or not hold for the original DNN by verifying a small, abstract version thereof.

To summarize, our contributions are: (i) we propose a general framework for over-approximating and refining DNNs; (ii) we propose several heuristics for abstraction and refinement, to be used within our general framework; and (iii) we provide an implementation of our technique that integrates with the Marabou verification tool and use it for evaluation. Our code is available online [9].

The rest of this paper is organized as follows. In Sect. 2, we provide a brief background on neural networks and their verification. In Sect. 3, we describe our general framework for abstracting an refining DNNs. In Sect. 4, we discuss how to apply these abstraction and refinement steps as part of a CEGAR procedure, followed by an evaluation in Sect. 5. In Sect. 6, we discuss related work, and we conclude in Sect. 7.

2 Background

2.1 Neural Networks

A neural network consists of an *input layer*, an *output layer*, and one or more intermediate layers called *hidden layers*. Each layer is a collection of nodes, called *neurons*. Each neuron is connected to other neurons by one or more directed edges. In a feedforward neural network, the neurons in the first layer receive input data that sets their initial values. The remaining neurons calculate their values using the weighted values of the neurons that they are connected to through edges from the preceding layer (see Fig. 1). The output layer provides the resulting value of the DNN for a given input.

There are many types of DNNs, which may differ in the way their neuron values are computed. Typically, a neuron is evaluated by first computing a weighted sum of the preceding layer's neuron values according to the edge weights, and then applying an activation function to this weighted sum [13]. We focus here on the Rectified Linear Unit (ReLU) activation function [29], given as $\text{ReLU}(x) = \max(0, x)$. Thus, if the weighted sum computation yields a positive value, it is kept; and otherwise, it is replaced by zero.

More formally, given a DNN N, we use n to denote the number of layers of N. We denote the number of nodes of layer i by s_i. Layers 1 and n are the input and output layers, respectively. Layers $2, \ldots, n - 1$ are the hidden layers. We denote the value of the j-th node of layer i by $v_{i,j}$, and denote the column vector $[v_{i,1}, \ldots, v_{i,s_i}]^T$ as V_i.

Evaluating N is performed by calculating V_n for a given input assignment V_1. This is done by sequentially computing V_i for $i = 2, 3, \ldots, n$, each time using

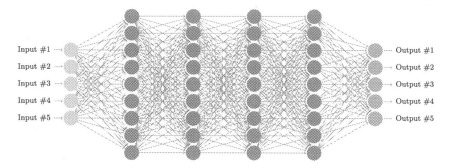

Fig. 1. A fully connected, feedforward DNN with 5 input nodes (in orange), 5 output nodes (in purple), and 4 hidden layers containing a total of 36 hidden nodes (in blue). Each edge is associated with a weight value (not depicted). (Color figure online)

the values of V_{i-1} to compute weighted sums, and then applying the ReLU activation functions. Specifically, layer i (for $i > 1$) is associated with a weight matrix W_i of size $s_i \times s_{i-1}$ and a bias vector B_i of size s_i. If i is a hidden layer, its values are given by $V_i = \text{ReLU}(W_i V_{i-1} + B_i)$, where the ReLUs are applied element-wise; and the output layer is given by $V_n = W_n V_{n-1} + B_n$ (ReLUs are not applied). Without loss of generality, in the rest of the paper we assume that all bias values are 0, and can be ignored. This rule is applied repeatedly once for each layer, until V_n is eventually computed.

We will sometimes use the notation $w(v_{i,j}, v_{i+1,k})$ to refer to the entry of W_{i+1} that represents the weight of the edge between neuron j of layer i and neuron k of layer $i + 1$. We will also refer to such an edge as an *outgoing edge* for $v_{i,j}$, and as an *incoming edge* for $v_{i+1,k}$.

As part of our abstraction framework, we will sometimes need to consider a *suffix* of a DNN, in which the first layers of the DNN are omitted. For $1 < i < n$, we use $N^{[i]}$ to denote the DNN comprised of layers $i, i + 1, \ldots, n$ of the original network. The sizes and weights of the remaining layers are unchanged, and layer i of N is treated as the input layer of $N^{[i]}$.

Figure 2 depicts a small neural network. The network has $n = 3$ layers, of sizes $s_1 = 1, s_2 = 2$ and $s_3 = 1$. Its weights are $w(v_{1,1}, v_{2,1}) = 1$, $w(v_{1,1}, v_{2,2}) = -1$, $w(v_{2,1}, v_{3,1}) = 1$ and $w(v_{2,2}, v_{3,1}) = 2$. For input $v_{1,1} = 3$, node $v_{2,1}$ evaluates to 3 and node $v_{2,2}$ evaluates to 0, due to the ReLU activation function. The output node $v_{3,1}$ then evaluates to 3.

2.2   Neural Network Verification

DNN verification amounts to answering the following question: given a DNN N, which maps input vector x to output vector y, and predicates P and Q, does there exist an input x_0 such that $P(x_0)$ and $Q(N(x_0))$ both hold? In other words, the verification process determines whether there exists a particular input that meets the input criterion P, and that is mapped to an output that meets the

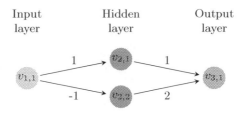

Fig. 2. A simple feedforward neural network.

output criterion Q. We refer to $\langle N, P, Q \rangle$ as the *verification query*. As is usual in verification, Q represents the *negation* of the desired property. Thus, if the query is *unsatisfiable* (UNSAT), the property holds; and if it is *satisfiable* (SAT), then x_0 constitutes a counterexample to the property in question.

Different verification approaches may differ in (i) the kinds of neural networks they allow (specifically, the kinds of activation functions in use); (ii) the kinds of input properties; and (iii) the kinds of output properties. For simplicity, we focus on networks that employ the ReLU activation function. In addition, our input properties will be conjunctions of linear constraints on the input values. Finally, we will assume that our networks have a single output node y, and that the output property is $y > c$ for a given constant c. We stress that these restrictions are for the sake of simplicity. Many properties of interest, including those with arbitrary Boolean structure and involving multiple neurons, can be reduced into the above single-output setting by adding a few neurons that encode the Boolean structure [20,32]; see Fig. 3 for an example. The number of neurons to be added is typically negligible when compared to the size of the DNN. In particular, this is true for the ACAS Xu family of benchmarks [20], and also for adversarial robustness queries that use the L_∞ or the L_1 norm as a distance metric [5,14,21]. Additionally, other piecewise-linear activation functions, such as max-pooling layers, can also be encoded using ReLUs [5].

Several techniques have been proposed for solving the aforementioned verification problem in recent years (Sect. 6 includes a brief overview). Our abstraction technique is designed to be compatible with most of these techniques, by simplifying the network being verified, as we describe next.

3   Network Abstraction and Refinement

Because the complexity of verifying a neural network is strongly connected to its size [20], our goal is to transform a verification query $\varphi_1 = \langle N, P, Q \rangle$ into query $\varphi_2 = \langle \bar{N}, P, Q \rangle$, such that the abstract network $\bar{N}$ is significantly smaller than N (notice that properties P and Q remain unchanged). We will construct $\bar{N}$ so that it is an over-approximation of N, meaning that if φ_2 is UNSAT then φ_1 is also UNSAT. More specifically, since our DNNs have a single output, we can regard $N(x)$ and $\bar{N}(x)$ as real values for every input x. To guarantee that φ_2 over-approximates φ_1, we will make sure that for every x, $N(x) \leq \bar{N}(x)$; and

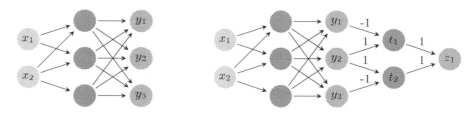

Fig. 3. Reducing a complex property to the $y > 0$ form. For the network on the left hand side, suppose we wish to examine the property $y_2 > y_1 \vee y_2 > y_3$, which is a property that involves multiple outputs and includes a disjunction. We do this (right hand side network) by adding two neurons, t_1 and t_2, such that $t_1 = \text{ReLU}(y_2 - y_1)$ and $t_2 = \text{ReLU}(y_2 - y_3)$. Thus, $t_1 > 0$ if and only if the first disjunct, $y_2 > y_1$, holds; and $t_2 > 0$ if and only if the second disjunct, $y_2 > y_3$, holds. Finally, we add a neuron z_1 such that $z_1 = t_1 + t_2$. It holds that $z_1 > 0$ if and only if $t_1 > 0 \vee t_2 > 0$. Thus, we have reduced the complex property into an equivalent property in the desired form.

thus, $\bar{N}(x) \leq c \implies N(x) \leq c$. Because our output properties always have the form $N(x) > c$, it is indeed the case that if φ_2 is UNSAT, i.e. $\bar{N}(x) \leq c$ for all x, then $N(x) \leq c$ for all x and so φ_1 is also UNSAT. We now propose a framework for generating various $\bar{N}$s with this property.

3.1 Abstraction

We seek to define an abstraction operator that removes a single neuron from the network, by merging it with another neuron. To do this, we will first transform N into an equivalent network, whose neurons have properties that will facilitate their merging. Equivalent here means that for every input vector, both networks produce the exact same output. First, each hidden neuron $v_{i,j}$ of our transformed network will be classified as either a pos neuron or a neg neuron. A neuron is pos if all the weights on its outgoing edges are positive, and is neg if all those weights are negative. Second, orthogonally to the pos/neg classification, each hidden neuron will also be classified as either an inc neuron or a dec neuron. $v_{i,j}$ is an inc neuron of N if, when we look at $N^{[i]}$ (where $v_{i,j}$ is an input neuron), increasing the value of $v_{i,j}$ increases the value of the network's output. Formally, $v_{i,j}$ is inc if for every two input vectors x_1 and x_2 where $x_1[k] = x_2[k]$ for $k \neq j$ and $x_1[j] > x_2[j]$, it holds that $N^{[i]}(x_1) > N^{[i]}(x_2)$. A dec neuron is defined symmetrically, so that *decreasing* the value of $x[j]$ *increases* the output. We first describe this transformation (an illustration of which appears in Fig. 4), and later we explain how it fits into our abstraction framework.

Our first step is to transform N into a new network, N', in which every hidden neuron is classified as pos or neg. This transformation is done by replacing each hidden neuron v_{i_j} with two neurons, $v_{i,j}^+$ and $v_{i,j}^-$, which are respectively pos and neg. Both $v_{i,j}^+$ an $v_{i,j}^-$ retain a copy of all incoming edges of the original $v_{i,j}$; however, $v_{i,j}^+$ retains just the outgoing edges with positive weights, and $v_{i,j}^-$ retains just those with negative weights. Outgoing edges with negative weights are removed from $v_{i,j}^+$ by setting their weights to 0, and the same is done for outgoing edges with positive weights for $v_{i,j}^-$. Formally, for every neuron $v_{i-1,p}$,

$$w'(v_{i-1,p}, v_{i,j}^+) = w(v_{i-1,p}, v_{i,j}), \qquad w'(v_{i-1,p}, v_{i,j}^-) = w(v_{i-1,p}, v_{i,j})$$

where w' represents the weights in the new network N'. Also, for every neuron $v_{i+1,q}$

$$w'(v_{i,j}^+, v_{i+1,q}) = \begin{cases} w(v_{i,j}, v_{i+1,q}) & w(v_{i,j}, v_{i+1,q}) \geq 0 \\ 0 & \text{otherwise} \end{cases}$$

and

$$w'(v_{i,j}^-, v_{i+1,q}) = \begin{cases} w(v_{i,j}, v_{i+1,q}) & w(v_{i,j}, v_{i+1,q}) \leq 0 \\ 0 & \text{otherwise} \end{cases}$$

(see Fig. 4). This operation is performed once for every hidden neuron of N, resulting in a network N' that is roughly double the size of N. Observe that N' is indeed equivalent to N, i.e. their outputs are always identical.

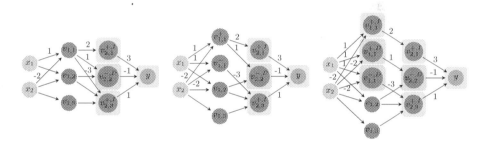

Fig. 4. Classifying neurons as pos/neg and inc/dec. In the initial network (left), the neurons of the second hidden layer are already classified: $^+$ and $^-$ superscripts indicate pos and neg neurons, respectively; the ^{I} superscript and green background indicate inc, and the ^{D} superscript and red background indicate dec. Classifying node $v_{1,1}$ is done by first splitting it into two nodes $v_{1,1}^+$ and $v_{1,1}^-$ (middle). Both nodes have identical incoming edges, but the outgoing edges of $v_{1,1}$ are partitioned between them, according to the sign of each edge's weight. In the last network (right), $v_{1,1}^+$ is split once more, into an inc node with outgoing edges only to other inc nodes, and a dec node with outgoing edges only to other dec nodes. Node $v_{1,1}$ is thus transformed into three nodes, each of which can finally be classified as inc or dec. Notice that in the worst case, each node is split into four nodes, although for $v_{1,1}$ three nodes were enough.

Our second step is to alter N' further, into a new network N'', where every hidden neuron is either inc or dec (in addition to already being pos or neg). Generating N'' from N' is performed by traversing the layers of N' backwards, each time handling a single layer and possibly doubling its number of neurons:

– Initial step: the output layer has a single neuron, y. This neuron is an inc node, because increasing its value will increase the network's output value.

– Iterative step: observe layer i, and suppose the nodes of layer $i + 1$ have already been partitioned into inc and dec nodes. Observe a neuron $v_{i,j}^+$ in layer i which is marked pos (the case for neg is symmetrical). We replace $v_{i,j}^+$ with two neurons $v_{i,j}^{+,I}$ and $v_{i,j}^{+,D}$, which are inc and dec, respectively. Both new neurons retain a copy of all incoming edges of $v_{i,j}^+$; however, $v_{i,j}^{+,I}$ retains only outgoing edges that lead to inc nodes, and $v_{i,j}^{+,D}$ retains only outgoing edges that lead to dec nodes. Thus, for every $v_{i-1,p}$ and $v_{i+1,q}$,

$$w''(v_{i-1,p}, v_{i,j}^{+,I}) = w'(v_{i-1,p}, v_{i,j}^+), \qquad w''(v_{i-1,p}, v_{i,j}^{+,D}) = w'(v_{i-1,p}, v_{i,j}^+)$$

$$w''(v_{i,j}^{+,I}, v_{i+1,q}) = \begin{cases} w'(v_{i,j}^+, v_{i+1,q}) & \text{if } v_{i+1,q} \text{ is inc} \\ 0 & \text{otherwise} \end{cases}$$

$$w''(v_{i,j}^{+,D}, v_{i+1,q}) = \begin{cases} w'(v_{i,j}^+, v_{i+1,q}) & \text{if } v_{i+1,q} \text{ is dec} \\ 0 & \text{otherwise} \end{cases}$$

where w'' represents the weights in the new network N''. We perform this step for each neuron in layer i, resulting in neurons that are each classified as either inc or dec.

To understand the intuition behind this classification, recall that by our assumption all hidden nodes use the ReLU activation function, which is monotonically increasing. Because $v_{i,j}^+$ is pos, all its outgoing edges have positive weights, and so if its assignment was to increase (decrease), the assignments of all nodes to which it is connected in the following layer would also increase (decrease). Thus, we split $v_{i,j}^+$ in two, and make sure one copy, $v_{i,j}^{+,I}$, is only connected to nodes that need to increase (inc nodes), and that the other copy, $v_{i,j}^{+,D}$, is only connected to nodes that need to decrease (dec nodes). This ensures that $v_{i,j}^{+,I}$ is itself inc, and that $v_{i,j}^{+,D}$ is dec. Also, both $v_{i,j}^{+,I}$ and $v_{i,j}^{+,D}$ remain pos nodes, because their outgoing edges all have positive weights.

When this procedure terminates, N'' is equivalent to N', and so also to N; and N'' is roughly double the size of N', and roughly four times the size of N. Both transformation steps are only performed for hidden neurons, whereas the input and output neurons remain unchanged. This is summarized by the following lemma:

Lemma 1. *Any DNN N can be transformed into an equivalent network N'' where each hidden neuron is pos or neg, and also inc or dec, by increasing its number of neurons by a factor of at most 4.*

Using Lemma 1, we can assume without loss of generality that the DNN nodes in our input query φ_1 are each marked as pos/neg and as inc/dec. We are now ready to construct the over-approximation network $\bar{N}$. We do this by specifying an abstract operator that merges a pair of neurons in the network (thus reducing network size by one), and can be applied multiple times. The only restrictions are that the two neurons being merged need to be from the same hidden layer, and must share the same pos/neg and inc/dec attributes. Consequently, applying abstract to saturation will result in a network with at most 4 neurons in each hidden layer, which over-approximates the original network. This, of course, would be an immense reduction in the number of neurons for most reasonable input networks.

The abstract operator's behavior depends on the attributes of the neurons being merged. For simplicity, we will focus on the $\langle \texttt{pos}, \texttt{inc} \rangle$ case. Let $v_{i,j}$, $v_{i,k}$ be two hidden neurons of layer i, both classified as $\langle \texttt{pos}, \texttt{inc} \rangle$. Because layer i is hidden, we know that layers $i+1$ and $i-1$ are defined. Let $v_{i-1,p}$ and $v_{i+1,q}$ denote arbitrary neurons in the preceding and succeeding layer, respectively. We construct a network $\bar{N}$ that is identical to N, except that: (i) nodes $v_{i,j}$ and $v_{i,k}$ are removed and replaced with a new single node, $v_{i,t}$; and (ii) all edges that touched nodes $v_{i,j}$ or $v_{i,k}$ are removed, and other edges are untouched. Finally, we add new incoming and outgoing edges for the new node $v_{i,t}$ as follows:

- Incoming edges: $\bar{w}(v_{i-1,p}, v_{i,t}) = \max\{w(v_{i-1,p}, v_{i,j}), w(v_{i-1,p}, v_{i,k})\}$
- Outgoing edges: $\bar{w}(v_{i,t}, v_{i+1,q}) = w(v_{i,j}, v_{i+1,q}) + w(v_{i,k}, v_{i+1,q})$

where $\bar{w}$ represents the weights in the new network $\bar{N}$. An illustrative example appears in Fig. 5. Intuitively, this definition of abstract seeks to ensure that the new node $v_{i,t}$ always contributes more to the network's output than the two original nodes $v_{i,j}$ and $v_{i,k}$—so that the new network produces a larger output than the original for every input. By the way we defined the incoming edges of the new neuron $v_{i,t}$, we are guaranteed that for every input x passed into both N and $\bar{N}$, the value assigned to $v_{i,t}$ in $\bar{N}$ is greater than the values assigned to both $v_{i,j}$ and $v_{i,k}$ in the original network. This works to our advantage, because $v_{i,j}$ and $v_{i,k}$ were both inc—so increasing their values increases the output value. By our definition of the outgoing edges, the values of any inc nodes in layer $i+1$ increase in $\bar{N}$ compared to N, and those of any dec nodes decrease. By definition, this means that the network's overall output increases.

The abstraction operation for the $\langle \texttt{neg}, \texttt{inc} \rangle$ case is identical to the one described above. For the remaining two cases, i.e. $\langle \texttt{pos}, \texttt{dec} \rangle$ and $\langle \texttt{neg}, \texttt{dec} \rangle$, the max operator in the definition is replaced with a min operator.

The next lemma (proof omitted due to lack of space) justifies the use of our abstraction step, and can be applied once per each application of abstract:

Lemma 2. *Let $\bar{N}$ be derived from N by a single application of* abstract. *For every x, it holds that $\bar{N}(x) \geq N(x)$.*

3.2 Refinement

The aforementioned abstract operator reduces network size by merging neurons, but at the cost of accuracy: whereas for some input x_0 the original network returns $N(x_0) = 3$, the over-approximation network $\bar{N}$ created by abstract might return $\bar{N}(x_0) = 5$. If our goal is prove that it is never the case that $N(x) > 10$, this over-approximation may be adequate: we can prove that always

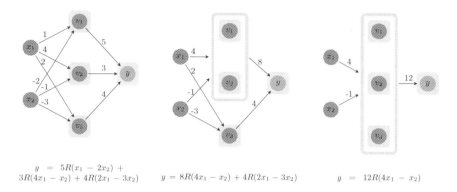

$$y = 5R(x_1 - 2x_2) + 3R(4x_1 - x_2) + 4R(2x_1 - 3x_2)$$

$$y = 8R(4x_1 - x_2) + 4R(2x_1 - 3x_2)$$

$$y = 12R(4x_1 - x_2)$$

Fig. 5. Using `abstract` to merge $\langle$pos, inc$\rangle$ nodes. Initially (left), the three nodes v_1, v_2 and v_3 are separate. Next (middle), `abstract` merges v_1 and v_2 into a single node. For the edge between x_1 and the new abstract node we pick the weight 4, which is the maximal weight among edges from x_1 to v_1 and v_2. Likewise, the edge between x_2 and the abstract node has weight -1. The outgoing edge from the abstract node to y has weight 8, which is the sum of the weights of edges from v_1 and v_2 to y. Next, `abstract` is applied again to merge v_3 with the abstract node, and the weights are adjusted accordingly (right). With every abstraction, the value of y (given as a formula at the bottom of each DNN, where R represents the ReLU operator) increases. For example, to see that $12R(4x_1 - x_2) \geq 8R(4x_1 - x_2) + 4R(2x_1 - 3x_2)$, it is enough to see that $4R(4x_1 - x_2) \geq 4R(2x_1 - 3x_2)$, which holds because ReLU is a monotonically increasing function and x_1 and x_2 are non-negative (being, themselves, the output of ReLU nodes).

$\bar{N}(x) \leq 10$, and this will be enough. However, if our goal is to prove that it is never the case that $N(x) > 4$, the over-approximation is inadequate: it is possible that the property holds for N, but because $\bar{N}(x_0) = 5 > 4$, our verification procedure will return x_0 as a *spurious counterexample* (a counterexample for $\bar{N}$ that is not a counterexample for N). In order to handle this situation, we define a *refinement operator*, `refine`, that is the inverse of `abstract`: it transforms $\bar{N}$ into yet another over-approximation, $\bar{N}'$, with the property that for every x, $N(x) \leq \bar{N}'(x) \leq \bar{N}(x)$. If $\bar{N}'(x_0) = 3.5$, it might be a suitable over-approximation for showing that never $N(x) > 4$. In this section we define the `refine` operator, and in Sect. 4 we explain how to use `abstract` and `refine` as part of a CEGAR-based verification scheme.

Recall that `abstract` merges together a couple of neurons that share the same attributes. After a series of applications of `abstract`, each hidden layer i of the resulting network can be regarded as a partitioning of hidden layer i of the original network, where each partition contains original, *concrete* neurons that share the same attributes. In the abstract network, each partition is represented by a single, *abstract* neuron. The weights on the incoming and outgoing edges of this abstract neuron are determined according to the definition of the `abstract` operator. For example, in the case of an abstract neuron $\bar{v}$ that represents a set of concrete neurons $\{v_1, \ldots, v_n\}$ all with attributes $\langle \text{pos}, \text{inc} \rangle$, the weight of each incoming edge to $\bar{v}$ is given by

$$\bar{w}(u, v) = \max(w(u, v_1), \ldots, w(u, v_n))$$

where u represents a neuron that has not been abstracted yet, and w is the weight function of the original network. The key point here is that the order of abstract operations that merged $v_1, \ldots, v_n$ does not matter—but rather, only the fact that they are now grouped together determines the abstract network's weights. The following corollary, which is a direct result of Lemma 2, establishes this connection between sequences of abstract applications and partitions:

Corollary 1. *Let N be a DNN where each hidden neuron is labeled as pos/neg and inc/dec, and let $\mathcal{P}$ be a partitioning of the hidden neurons of N, that only groups together hidden neurons from the same layer that share the same labels. Then N and $\mathcal{P}$ give rise to an abstract neural network $\bar{N}$, which is obtained by performing a series of abstract operations that group together neurons according to the partitions of $\mathcal{P}$. This $\bar{N}$ is an over-approximation of N.*

We now define a refine operation that is, in a sense, the inverse of abstract. refine takes as input a DNN $\bar{N}$ that was generated from N via a sequence of abstract operations, and splits a neuron from $\bar{N}$ in two. Formally, the operator receives the original network N, the partitioning $\mathcal{P}$, and a finer partition $\mathcal{P}'$ that is obtained from $\mathcal{P}$ by splitting a single class in two. The operator then returns a new abstract network, $\bar{N}'$, that is the abstraction of N according to $\mathcal{P}'$.

Due to Corollary 1, and because $\bar{N}$ returned by refine corresponds to a partition $\mathcal{P}'$ of the hidden neurons of N, it is straightforward to show that $\bar{N}$ is indeed an over-approximation of N. The other useful property that we require is the following:

Lemma 3. *Let $\bar{N}$ be an abstraction of N, and let $\bar{N}'$ be a network obtained from $\bar{N}$ by applying a single refine step. Then for every input x it holds that $\bar{N}(x) \geq \bar{N}'(x) \geq N(x)$.*

The second part of the inequality, $\bar{N}'(x) \geq N(x)$ holds because $\bar{N}'$ is an over-approximation of N (Corollary 1). The first part of the inequality, $\bar{N}(x) \geq \bar{N}'(x)$, follows from the fact that $\bar{N}(x)$ can be obtained from $\bar{N}'(x)$ by a single application of abstract.

In practice, in order to support the refinement of an abstract DNN, we maintain the current partitioning, i.e. the mapping from concrete neurons to the abstract neurons that represent them. Then, when an abstract neuron is selected for refinement (according to some heuristic, such as the one we propose in Sect. 4), we adjust the mapping and use it to compute the weights of the edges that touch the affected neuron.

4   A CEGAR-Based Approach

In Sect. 3 we defined the `abstract` operator that reduces network size at the cost of reducing network accuracy, and its inverse `refine` operator that increases network size and restores accuracy. Together with a black-box verification procedure *Verify* that can dispatch queries of the form $\varphi = \langle N, P, Q \rangle$, these components now allow us to design an abstraction-refinement algorithm for DNN verification, given as Algorithm 1 (we assume that all hidden neurons in the input network have already been marked `pos`/`neg` and `inc`/`dec`).

Algorithm 1. Abstraction-based DNN Verification(N, P, Q)

1: Use `abstract` to generate an initial over-approximation $\bar{N}$ of N
2: **if** *Verify*($\bar{N}, P, Q$) is `UNSAT` **then**
3:      return `UNSAT`
4: **else**
5:      Extract counterexample c
6:      **if** c is a counterexample for N **then**
7:          return `SAT`
8:      **else**
9:          Use `refine` to refine $\bar{N}$ into $\bar{N}'$
10:         $\bar{N} \leftarrow \bar{N}'$
11:         Goto step 2
12:     **end if**
13: **end if**

Because $\bar{N}$ is obtained via applications of `abstract` and `refine`, the soundness of the underlying *Verify* procedure, together with Lemmas 2 and 3, guarantees the soundness of Algorithm 1. Further, the algorithm always terminates: this is the case because all the `abstract` steps are performed first, followed by a sequence of `refine` steps. Because no additional `abstract` operations are performed beyond Step 1, after finitely many `refine` steps $\bar{N}$ will become identical to N, at which point no spurious counterexample will be found, and the algorithm will terminate with either `SAT` or `UNSAT`. Of course, termination is only guaranteed when the underlying *Verify* procedure is guaranteed to terminate.

There are two steps in the algorithm that we intentionally left ambiguous: Step 1, where the initial over-approximation is computed, and Step 9, where the current abstraction is refined due to the discovery of a spurious counterexample. The motivation was to make Algorithm 1 general, and allow it to be customized by plugging in different heuristics for performing Steps 1 and 9, which may depend on the problem at hand. Below we propose a few such heuristics.

4.1   Generating an Initial Abstraction

The most naïve way to generate the initial abstraction is to apply the `abstract` operator to saturation. As previously discussed, `abstract` can merge together any pair of hidden neurons from a given layer that share the same attributes. Since there are four possible attribute combinations, this will result in each hidden layer of the network having four neurons or fewer. This method, which we refer to as *abstraction to saturation*, produces the smallest abstract networks possible. The downside is that, in some case, these networks might be too coarse, and might require multiple rounds of refinement before a SAT or UNSAT answer can be reached.

A different heuristic for producing abstractions that may require fewer refinement steps is as follows. First, we select a finite set of input points, $X = \{x_1, \ldots, x_n\}$, all of which satisfy the input property P. These points can be generated randomly, or according to some coverage criterion of the input space. The points of X are then used as indicators in estimating when the abstraction has become too coarse: after every abstraction step, we check whether the property still holds for $x_1, \ldots, x_n$, and stop abstracting if this is not the case. The exact technique, which we refer to as *indicator-guided abstraction*, appears in Algorithm 2, which is used to perform Step 1 of Algorithm 1.

Algorithm 2. Indicator-Guided Abstraction(N, P, Q, X)

1: $\bar{N} \leftarrow N$
2: **while** $\forall x \in X$. $\bar{N}(x)$ satisfies Q and there are still neurons that can be merged **do**
3:     $\Delta \leftarrow \infty$, bestPair $\leftarrow \bot$
4:     **for** every pair of hidden neurons $v_{i,j}, v_{i,k}$ with identical attributes **do**
5:         m $\leftarrow 0$
6:         **for** every node $v_{i-1,p}$ **do**
7:             a $\leftarrow \bar{w}(v_{i-1,p}, v_{i,j})$, b $\leftarrow \bar{w}(v_{i-1,p}, v_{i,k})$
8:             **if** $|a - b| >$ m **then**
9:                 m $\leftarrow |a - b|$
10:            **end if**
11:        **end for**
12:        **if** m $< \Delta$ **then**
13:            $\Delta \leftarrow$ m, bestPair $\leftarrow \langle v_{i,j}, v_{i,k} \rangle$
14:        **end if**
15:    **end for**
16:    Use abstract to merge the nodes of bestPair, store the result in $\bar{N}$
17: **end while**
18: **return** $\bar{N}$

Another point that is addressed by Algorithm 2, besides how many rounds of abstraction should be performed, is which pair of neurons should be merged in every application of abstract. This, too, is determined heuristically. Since any pair of neurons that we pick will result in the same reduction in network size, our strategy is to prefer neurons that will result in a more accurate approximation. Inaccuracies are caused by the max and min operators within the abstract operator: e.g., in the case of max, every pair of incoming edges with weights a, b are replaced by a single edge with weight $\max(a, b)$. Our strategy here is to merge the pair of neurons for which the *maximal* value of $|a - b|$ (over all incoming edges with weights a and b) is *minimal*. Intuitively, this leads to $\max(a, b)$ being close to both a and b—which, in turn, leads to an over-approximation network that is smaller than the original, but is close to it weight-wise. We point out that although repeatedly exploring all pairs (line 4) may appear costly, in our experiments the time cost of this step was negligible compared to that of the verification queries that followed. Still, if this step happens to become a bottleneck, it is possible to adjust the algorithm to heuristically sample just some of the pairs, and pick the best pair among those considered—without harming the algorithm's soundness.

As a small example, consider the network depicted on the left hand side of Fig. 5. This network has three pairs of neurons that can be merged using abstract (any subset of $\{v_1, v_2, v_3\}$). Consider the pair v_1, v_2: the maximal value of $|a - b|$ for these neurons is $\max(|1 - 4)|, |(-2) - (-1)|) = 3$. For pair v_1, v_3, the maximal value is 1; and for pair v_2, v_3 the maximal value is 2. According to the strategy described in Algorithm 2, we would first choose to apply abstract on the pair with the minimal maximal value, i.e. on the pair v_1, v_3.

4.2   Performing the Refinement Step

A refinement step is performed when a spurious counterexample x has been found, indicating that the abstract network is too coarse. In other words, our abstraction steps, and specifically the max and min operators that were used to select edge weights for the abstract neurons, have resulted in the abstract network's output being too great for input x, and we now need to reduce it. Thus, our refinement strategies are aimed at applying refine in a way that will result in a significant reduction to the abstract network's output. We note that there may be multiple options for applying refine, on different nodes, such that any of them would remove the spurious counterexample x from the abstract network. In addition, it is not guaranteed that it is possible to remove x with a single application of refine, and multiple consecutive applications may be required.

One heuristic approach for refinement follows the well-studied notion of counterexample-guided abstraction refinement [6]. Specifically, we leverage the spurious counterexample x in order to identify a concrete neuron v, which is currently mapped into an abstract neuron $\bar{v}$, such that splitting v away from $\bar{v}$ might rule out counterexample x. To do this, we evaluate the original network on x and compute the value of v (we denote this value by $v(x)$), and then do the same for $\bar{v}$ in the abstract network (value denoted $\bar{v}(x)$). Intuitively, a neuron pair $\langle v, \bar{v} \rangle$ for which the difference $|v(x) - \bar{v}(x)|$ is significant makes a good candidate for a refinement operation that will split v away from $\bar{v}$.

In addition to considering $v(x)$ and $\bar{v}(x)$, we propose to also consider the weights of the incoming edges of v and $\bar{v}$. When these weights differ significantly, this could indicate that $\bar{v}$ is too coarse an approximation for v, and should be refined. We argue that by combining these two criteria—edge weight difference between v and $\bar{v}$, which is a property of the current abstraction, together with the difference between $v(x)$ and $\bar{v}(x)$, which is a property of the specific input x, we can identify abstract neurons that have contributed significantly to x being a spurious counterexample.

The refinement heuristic is formally defined in Algorithm 3. The algorithm traverses the original neurons, looks for the edge weight times assignment value that has changed the most as a result of the current abstraction, and then performs refinement on the neuron at the end of that edge. As was the case with Algorithm 2, if considering all possible nodes turns out to be too costly, it is possible to adjust the algorithm to explore only some of the nodes, and pick the best one among those considered—without jeopardizing the algorithm's soundness.

Algorithm 3. Counterexample-Guided Refinement$(N, \bar{N}, x)$

1: bestNeuron $\leftarrow \perp$, $m \leftarrow 0$
2: **for** each concrete neuron $v_{i,j}$ of N mapped into abstract neuron $\bar{v}_{i,j'}$ of $\bar{N}$ **do**
3:     **for** each concrete neuron $v_{i-1,k}$ of N mapped into abstract neuron $\bar{v}_{i-1,k'}$ of $\bar{N}$ **do**
4:         **if** $|w(v_{i-1,k}, v_{i,j}) - \bar{w}(\bar{v}_{i-1,k'}, \bar{v}_{i,j'})| \cdot |v_{i,j}(x) - \bar{v}_{i,j'}(x)| > m$ **then**
5:             $m \leftarrow |w(v_{i-1,k}, v_{i,j}) - \bar{w}(\bar{v}_{i-1,k'}, \bar{v}_{i,j'})| \cdot |v_{i,j}(x) - \bar{v}_{i,j'}(x)|$
6:             bestNeuron $\leftarrow v_{i,j}$
7:         **end if**
8:     **end for**
9: **end for**
10: Use `refine` to split bestNeuron from its abstract neuron

As an example, let us use Algorithm 3 to choose a refinement step for the right hand side network of Fig. 5, for a spurious counterexample $\langle x_1, x_2 \rangle = \langle 1, 0 \rangle$. For this input, the original neurons' evaluation is $v_1 = 1, v_2 = 4$ and $v_3 = 2$, whereas the abstract neuron that represents them evaluates to 4. Suppose v_1 is considered first. In the abstract network, $\bar{w}(x_1, \bar{v}_1) = 4$ and $\bar{w}(x_2, \bar{v}_1) = -1$; whereas in the original network, $w(x_1, v_1) = 1$ and $w(x_2, v_1) = -2$. Thus, the largest value m computed for v_1 is $|w(x_1, v_1) - \bar{w}(x_1, \bar{v}_1)| \cdot |4 - 1| = 3 \cdot 3 = 9$. This value of m is larger than the one computed for v_2 (0) and for v_3 (4), and so v_1 is selected for the refinement step. After this step is performed, v_2 and v_3 are still mapped to a single abstract neuron, whereas v_1 is mapped to a separate neuron in the abstract network.

5   Implementation and Evaluation

Our implementation of the abstraction-refinement framework includes modules that read a DNN in the NNet format [19] and a property to be verified, create an initial abstract DNN as described in Sect. 4, invoke a black-box verification engine, and perform refinement as described in Sect. 4. The process terminates when the underlying engine returns either UNSAT, or an assignment that is a true counterexample for the original network. For experimentation purposes, we integrated our framework with the Marabou DNN verification engine [22]. Our implementation and benchmarks are publicly available online [9].

Our experiments included verifying several properties of the 45 ACAS Xu DNNs for airborne collision avoidance [19,20]. ACAS Xu is a system designed to produce horizontal turning advisories for an unmanned aircraft (the *ownship*), with the purpose of preventing a collision with another nearby aircraft (the *intruder*). The ACAS Xu system receive as input sensor readings, indicating the location of the intruder relative to the ownship, the speeds of the two aircraft, and their directions

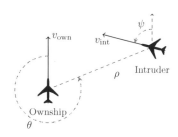

Fig. 6. (From [20]) An illustration of the sensor readings passed as input to the ACAS Xu DNNs.

(see Fig. 6). Based on these readings, it selects one of 45 DNNs, to which the readings are then passed as input. The selected DNN then assigns scores to five output neurons, each representing a possible turning advisory: strong left, weak left, strong right, weak right, or clear-of-conflict (the latter indicating that it is safe to continue along the current trajectory). The neuron with the *lowest* score represents the selected advisory. We verified several properties of these DNNs based on the list of properties that appeared in [20]—specifically focusing on properties that ensure that the DNNs always advise clear-of-conflict for distant intruders, and that they are robust to (i.e., do not change their advisories in the presence of) small input perturbations.

Each of the ACAS Xu DNNs has 300 hidden nodes spread across 6 hidden layers, leading to 1200 neurons when the transformation from Sect. 3.1 is applied. In our experiments we set out to check whether the abstraction-based approach could indeed prove properties of the ACAS Xu networks on abstract networks that had significantly fewer neurons than the original ones. In addition, we wished to compare the proposed approaches for generating initial abstractions (the abstraction to saturation approach versus the indicator-guided abstraction described in Algorithm 2), in order to identify an optimal configuration for our tool. Finally, once the optimal configuration has been identified, we used it to compare our tool's performance to that of vanilla Marabou. The results are described next.

Figure 7 depicts a comparison of the two approaches for generating initial abstractions: the abstraction to saturation scheme (x axis), and the indicator-guided abstraction scheme described in Algorithm 2 (y axis). Each experiment included running our tool twice on the same benchmark (network and property), with an identical configuration except for the initial abstraction being used. The plot depicts the total time (log-scale, in seconds, with a 20-h timeout) spent by Marabou solving verification queries as part of the abstraction-refinement procedure. It shows that, in contrast to our intuition, abstraction to saturation almost always outperforms the indicator-guided approach. This is perhaps due to the fact that, although it might entail additional rounds of refinement, the abstraction to saturation approach tends to produce coarse verification queries that are easily solved by Marabou, resulting in an overall improved performance. We thus conclude that, at least in the ACAS Xu case, the abstraction to saturation approach is superior to that of indicator-guided abstraction.

This experiment also confirms that properties can indeed be proved on abstract networks that are significantly smaller than the original—i.e., despite the initial 4x increase in network size due to the preprocessing phase, the final abstract network on which our abstraction-enhanced approach could solve the query was usually substantially smaller than the original network. Specifically, among the abstraction to saturation experiments that terminated, the final network on which the property was shown to be SAT or UNSAT had an average size of 268.8 nodes, compared to the original 310—a 13% reduction. Because DNN verification becomes exponentially more difficult as the network size increases, this reduction is highly beneficial.

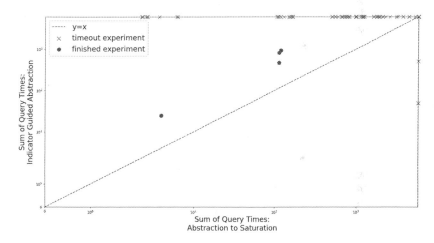

Fig. 7. Generating initial abstractions using abstraction to saturation and indicator-guided abstraction.

Next, we compared our abstraction-enhanced Marabou (in abstraction to saturation mode) to the vanilla version. The plot in Fig. 8 compares the total query solving time of vanilla Marabou (y axis) to that of our approach (x axis). We ran the tools on 90 ACAS Xu benchmarks (2 properties, checked on each of the 45 networks), with a 20-h timeout. We observe that the abstraction-enhanced version significantly outperforms vanilla Marabou on average—often solving queries orders-of-magnitude more quickly, and timing out on fewer benchmarks. Specifically, the abstraction-enhanced version solved 58 instances, versus 35 solved by Marabou. Further, over the instances solved by both tools, the abstraction-enhanced version had a total query median runtime of 1045 s, versus 63671 s for Marabou. Interestingly, the average size of the abstract networks for which our tool was able to solve the query was 385 nodes—which is an increase compared to the original 310 nodes. However, the improved runtimes demonstrate that although these networks were slightly larger, they were still much easier to verify, presumably because many of the network's original neurons remained abstracted away.

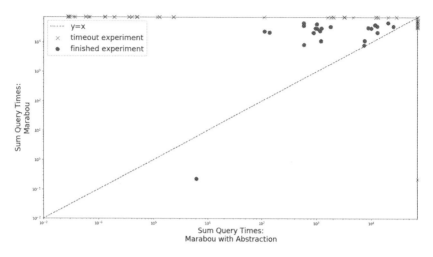

Fig. 8. Comparing the run time (in seconds, logscale) of vanilla Marabou and the abstraction-enhanced version on the ACAS Xu benchmarks.

Finally, we used our abstraction-enhanced Marabou to verify *adversarial robustness* properties [35]. Intuitively, an adversarial robustness property states that slight input perturbations cannot cause sudden spikes in the network's output. This is desirable because such sudden spikes can lead to misclassification of inputs. Unlike the ACAS Xu domain-specific properties [20], whose formulation required input from human experts, adversarial robustness is a *universal property*, desirable for every DNN. Consequently it is easier to formulate, and has received much attention (e.g., [2,10,20,36]).

In order to formulate adversarial robustness properties for the ACAS Xu networks, we randomly sampled the ACAS Xu DNNs to identify input points where the selected output advisory, indicated by an output neuron y_i, received a much lower score than the second-best advisory, y_j (recall that the advisory with the lowest score is selected). For such an input point x_0, we then posed the verification query: does there exist a point x that is close to x_0, but for which y_j receives a lower score than y_i? Or, more formally: $(\|x - x_0\|_{L_\infty} \leq \delta) \wedge (y_j \leq y_i)$. If this query is SAT then there exists an input x whose distance to x_0 is at most δ, but for which the network assigns a better (lower) score to advisory y_j than to y_i. However, if this query is UNSAT, no such point x exists. Because we select point x_0 such that y_i is initially much smaller than y_j, we expect the query to be UNSAT for small values of δ.

For each of the 45 ACAS Xu networks, we created robustness queries for 20 distinct input points—producing a total of 900 verification queries (we arbitrarily set $\delta = 0.1$). For each of these queries we compared the runtime of vanilla Marabou to that of our abstraction-enhanced version (with a 20-h timeout). The results are depicted in Fig. 9. Vanilla Marabou was able to solve more instances—893 out of 900, versus 805 that the abstraction-enhanced version was able to solve. However, on the vast majority of the remaining experiments, the abstraction-enhanced version was significantly faster, with a total query median runtime of only 0.026 s versus 15.07 s in the vanilla version (over the 805 benchmarks solved by both tools). This impressive 99% improvement in performance highlights the usefulness of our approach also in the context of adversarial robustness. In addition, over the solved benchmarks, the average size of the abstract networks for which our tool was able to solve the query was 104.4 nodes, versus 310 nodes in each of the original networks—a 66% reduction in size. This reinforces our statement that, in many cases, DNNs contain a great deal of unneeded neurons, which can safely be removed by the abstraction process for the purpose of verification.

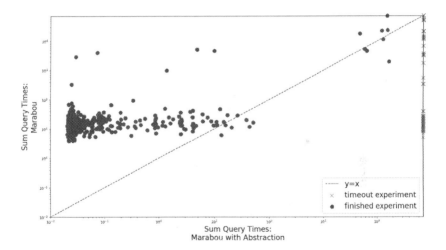

Fig. 9. Comparing the run time (seconds, logscale) of vanilla Marabou and the abstraction-enhanced version on the ACAS Xu adversarial robustness properties.

6 Related Work

In recent years, multiple schemes have been proposed for the verification of neural networks. These include SMT-based approaches, such as Marabou [22,23], Reluplex [20], DLV [17] and others; approaches based on formulating the problem as a mixed integer linear programming instance (e.g., [4,7,8,36]); approaches that use sophisticated symbolic interval propagation [37], or abstract interpretation [10]; and others (e.g., [1,18,25,27,30,38,39]). These approaches have been applied in a variety of tasks, such as measuring adversarial robustness [2,17], neural network simplification [11], neural network modification [12], and many others (e.g., [23,34]). Our approach can be integrated with any sound and complete solver as its engine, and then applied towards any of the aforementioned tasks. Incomplete solvers could also be used and might afford better performance, but this could result in our approach also becoming incomplete.

Some existing DNN verification techniques incorporate abstraction elements. In [31], the authors use abstraction to over-approximate the Sigmoid activation function with a collection of rectangles. If the abstract verification query they produce is UNSAT, then so is the original. When a spurious counterexample is found, an arbitrary refinement step is performed. The authors report limited scalability, tackling only networks with a few dozen neurons. Abstraction techniques also appear in the AI2 approach [10], but there it is the input property and reachable regions that are over-approximated, as opposed to the DNN itself. Combining this kind of input-focused abstraction with our network-focused abstraction is an interesting avenue for future work.

7 Conclusion

With deep neural networks becoming widespread and with their forthcoming integration into safety-critical systems, there is an urgent need for scalable techniques to verify and reason about them. However, the size of these networks poses a serious challenge. Abstraction-based techniques can mitigate this difficulty, by replacing networks with smaller versions thereof to be verified, without compromising the soundness of the verification procedure. The abstraction-based approach we have proposed here can provide a significant reduction in network size, thus boosting the performance of existing verification technology.

In the future, we plan to continue this work along several axes. First, we intend to investigate refinement heuristics that can split an abstract neuron into two arbitrary sized neurons. In addition, we will investigate abstraction schemes for networks that use additional activation functions, beyond ReLUs. Finally, we plan to make our abstraction scheme parallelizable, allowing users to use multiple worker nodes to explore different combinations of abstraction and refinement steps, hopefully leading to faster convergence.

Acknowledgements. We thank the anonymous reviewers for their insightful comments. This project was partially supported by grants from the Binational Science Foundation (2017662) and the Israel Science Foundation (683/18).

References

1. Anderson, G., Pailoor, S., Dillig, I., Chaudhuri, S.: Optimization and abstraction: a synergistic approach for analyzing neural network robustness. In: Proceedings 40th ACM SIGPLAN Conference on Programming Language Design and Implementation (PLDI), pp. 731–744 (2019)
2. Bastani, O., Ioannou, Y., Lampropoulos, L., Vytiniotis, D., Nori, A., Criminisi, A.: Measuring neural net robustness with constraints. In: Proceedings 30th Conference on Neural Information Processing Systems (NIPS) (2016)
3. Bojarski, M., et al.: End to end learning for self-driving cars. Technical report (2016). http://arxiv.org/abs/1604.07316
4. Bunel, R., Turkaslan, I., Torr, P., Kohli, P., Kumar, M.: Piecewise linear neural network verification: a comparative study. Technical report (2017). https://arxiv.org/abs/1711.00455v1
5. Carlini, N., Katz, G., Barrett, C., Dill, D.: Provably minimally-distorted adversarial examples. Technical report (2017). https://arxiv.org/abs/1709.10207
6. Clarke, E., Grumberg, O., Jha, S., Lu, Y., Veith, H.: Counterexample-guided abstraction refinement. In: Proceedings 12th Internation Conference on Computer Aided Verification (CAV), pp. 154–169 (2010)
7. Dutta, S., Jha, S., Sanakaranarayanan, S., Tiwari, A.: Output range analysis for deep neural networks. In: Proceedings 10th NASA Formal Methods Symposium (NFM), pp. 121–138 (2018)
8. Ehlers, R.: Formal verification of piece-wise linear feed-forward neural networks. In: Proceedings 15th Internatioanl Symposium on Automated Technology for Verification and Analysis (ATVA), pp. 269–286 (2017)
9. Elboher, Y.Y., Gottschlich, J., Katz, G.: An abstraction-based framework for neural network verification: proof-of-concept implementation (2020). https://drive.google.com/file/d/1KCh0vOgcOR2pSbGRdbtAQTmoMHAFC2Vs/view
10. Gehr, T., Mirman, M., Drachsler-Cohen, D., Tsankov, E., Chaudhuri, S., Vechev, M.: AI2: safety and robustness certification of neural networks with abstract interpretation. In: Proceedings 39th IEEE Symposium on Security and Privacy (S&P) (2018)
11. Gokulanathan, S., Feldsher, A., Malca, A., Barrett, C., Katz, G.: Simplifying neural networks using formal verification. In: Proceedings 12th NASA Formal Methods Symposium (NFM) (2020)
12. Goldberger, B., Adi, Y., Keshet, J., Katz, G.: Minimal modifications of deep neural networks using verification. In: Proceedings 23rd International Conference on Logic for Programming, Artificial Intelligence and Reasoning (LPAR) (2020)
13. Goodfellow, I., Bengio, Y., Courville, A.: Deep Learning. MIT Press, Cambridge (2016)
14. Gopinath, D., Katz, G., Păsăreanu, C.S., Barrett, C.: DeepSafe: a data-driven approach for assessing robustness of neural networks. In: Lahiri, S.K., Wang, C. (eds.) ATVA 2018. LNCS, vol. 11138, pp. 3–19. Springer, Cham (2018). https://doi.org/10.1007/978-3-030-01090-4_1
15. Gottschlich, J., et al.: The three pillars of machine programming. In: Proceedings 2nd ACM SIGPLAN Internatioanl Workshop on Machine Learning and Programming Languages (MALP), pp. 69–80 (2018)
16. Hinton, G., et al.: Deep neural networks for acoustic modeling in speech recognition: the shared views of four research groups. IEEE Signal Proces. Mag. **29**(6), 82–97 (2012)

17. Huang, X., Kwiatkowska, M., Wang, S., Wu, M.: Safety verification of deep neural networks. In: Majumdar, R., Kunčak, V. (eds.) CAV 2017. LNCS, vol. 10426, pp. 3–29. Springer, Cham (2017). https://doi.org/10.1007/978-3-319-63387-9_1
18. Jacoby, Y., Barrett, C., Katz, G.: Verifying recurrent neural networks using invariant inference. Technical report (2020). http://arxiv.org/abs/2004.02462
19. Julian, K., Lopez, J., Brush, J., Owen, M., Kochenderfer, M.: Policy compression for aircraft collision avoidance systems. In: Proceedings 35th Digital Avionics Systems Conference (DASC), pp. 1–10 (2016)
20. Katz, G., Barrett, C., Dill, D.L., Julian, K., Kochenderfer, M.J.: Reluplex: an efficient SMT solver for verifying deep neural networks. In: Majumdar, R., Kunčak, V. (eds.) CAV 2017. LNCS, vol. 10426, pp. 97–117. Springer, Cham (2017). https://doi.org/10.1007/978-3-319-63387-9_5
21. Katz, G., Barrett, C., Dill, D., Julian, K., Kochenderfer, M.: Towards proving the adversarial robustness of deep neural networks. In: Proceedings 1st Workshop on Formal Verification of Autonomous Vehicles (FVAV), pp. 19–26 (2017)
22. Katz, G., et al.: The marabou framework for verification and analysis of deep neural networks. In: Dillig, I., Tasiran, S. (eds.) CAV 2019. LNCS, vol. 11561, pp. 443–452. Springer, Cham (2019). https://doi.org/10.1007/978-3-030-25540-4_26
23. Kazak, Y., Barrett, C., Katz, G., Schapira, M.: Verifying deep-RL-driven systems. In: Proceedings 1st ACM SIGCOMM Workshop on Network Meets AI & ML (NetAI) (2019)
24. Krizhevsky, A., Sutskever, I., Hinton, G.: ImageNet classification with deep convolutional neural networks. In: Advances in Neural Information Processing Systems, pp. 1097–1105 (2012)
25. Kuper, L., Katz, G., Gottschlich, J., Julian, K., Barrett, C., Kochenderfer, M.: Toward scalable verification for safety-critical deep networks. Technical report (2018). https://arxiv.org/abs/1801.05950
26. Kurakin, A., Goodfellow, I., Bengio, S.: Adversarial examples in the physical world. Technical report (2016). http://arxiv.org/abs/1607.02533
27. Lomuscio, A., Maganti, L.: An approach to reachability analysis for feed-forward ReLU neural networks. Technical report (2017). https://arxiv.org/abs/1706.07351
28. Mao, H., Netravali, R., Alizadeh, M.: Neural adaptive video streaming with Pensieve. In: Proceedings Conference of the ACM Special Interest Group on Data Communication (SIGCOMM), pp. 197–210 (2017)
29. Nair, V., Hinton, G.: Rectified linear units improve restricted boltzmann machines. In: Proceedings 27th International Conference on Machine Learning (ICML), pp. 807–814 (2010)
30. Narodytska, N., Kasiviswanathan, S., Ryzhyk, L., Sagiv, M., Walsh, T.: Verifying properties of binarized deep neural networks. Technical report (2017). http://arxiv.org/abs/1709.06662
31. Pulina, L., Tacchella, A.: An abstraction-refinement approach to verification of artificial neural networks. In: Touili, T., Cook, B., Jackson, P. (eds.) CAV 2010. LNCS, vol. 6174, pp. 243–257. Springer, Heidelberg (2010). https://doi.org/10.1007/978-3-642-14295-6_24
32. Ruan, W., Huang, X., Kwiatkowska, M.: Reachability analysis of deep neural networks with provable guarantees. In: Proceedings 27th International Joint Conference on Artificial Intelligence (IJACI), pp. 2651–2659 (2018)
33. Silver, D., et al.: Mastering the game of go with deep neural networks and tree search. Nature **529**(7587), 484–489 (2016)

34. Sun, X., Khedr, H., Shoukry, Y.: Formal verification of neural network controlled autonomous systems. In: Proceedings 22nd ACM International Conference on Hybrid Systems: Computation and Control (HSCC) (2019)
35. Szegedy, C., et al.: Intriguing properties of neural networks. Technical report (2013). http://arxiv.org/abs/1312.6199
36. Tjeng, V., Xiao, K., Tedrake, R.: Evaluating robustness of neural networks with mixed integer programming. In: Proceedings 7th International Conference on Learning Representations (ICLR) (2019)
37. Wang, S., Pei, K., Whitehouse, J., Yang, J., Jana, S.: Formal security analysis of neural networks using symbolic intervals. In: Proceedings 27th USENIX Security Symposium (2018)
38. Wu, H., et al.: Parallelization techniques for verifying neural networks. Technical report (2020). https://arxiv.org/abs/2004.08440
39. Xiang, W., Tran, H.-D., Johnson, T.: Output reachable set estimation and verification for multilayer neural networks. IEEE Trans. Neural Networks Learn. Syst. (TNNLS) **99**, 1–7 (2018)

Improved Geometric Path Enumeration for Verifying ReLU Neural Networks

Stanley Bak[1]([✉]), Hoang-Dung Tran[2,3],
Kerianne Hobbs[4,5],
and Taylor T. Johnson[3]

[1] Stony Brook University, Stony Brook, USA
stanleybak@gmail.com
[2] University of Nebraska, Lincoln, USA
[3] Vanderbilt University, Nashville, USA
[4] Air Force Research Laboratory, Wright-Patterson Air Force Base, USA
[5] Georgia Institute of Technology, Atlanta, USA

Abstract. Neural networks provide quick approximations to complex functions, and have been increasingly used in perception as well as control tasks. For use in mission-critical and safety-critical applications, however, it is important to be able to analyze what a neural network can and cannot do. For feed-forward neural networks with ReLU activation functions, although exact analysis is NP-complete, recently-proposed verification methods can sometimes succeed.

The main practical problem with neural network verification is excessive analysis runtime. Even on small networks, tools that are theoretically complete can sometimes run for days without producing a result. In this paper, we work to address the runtime problem by improving upon a recently-proposed geometric path enumeration method. Through a series of optimizations, several of which are new algorithmic improvements, we demonstrate significant speed improvement of exact analysis on the well-studied ACAS Xu benchmarks, sometimes hundreds of times faster than the original implementation. On more difficult benchmark instances, our optimized approach is often the fastest, even outperforming inexact methods that leverage overapproximation and refinement.

1 Introduction

Neural networks have surged in popularity due to their ability to learn complex function approximations from data. This ability has led to their proposed application in perception and control decision systems, which are sometimes safety-critical. For use in safety-critical applications, it is important to prove properties about neural networks rather than treating them as black-box components.

S. K. Lahiri and C. Wang (Eds.): CAV 2020, LNCS 12224, pp. 66–96, 2020.
https://doi.org/10.1007/978-3-030-53288-8_4

A recent method [24] based on path enumeration and geometric set propagation has shown that exact analysis can be practical for piecewise linear neural networks. This includes networks with fully-connected layers, convolutional layers, average and max pooling layers, and neurons with ReLU activation functions. Here, we focus on fully-connected layers with ReLU activation functions. The verification problem in this method is presented in terms of input/output properties of the neural network. The method works by taking the input set of states and performing a set-based execution of the neural network. Due to the linear nature of the set representation and the piecewise linear nature of the ReLU activation function, the set may need to be split after each neuron is executed, so that the output after the final layer is a collection of sets that can each be checked for intersection with an unsafe set.

Since the formal verification problem we are addressing has been shown to be NP-Complete [13], we instead focus on improving practical scalability. This requires us to choose a set of benchmarks for evaluation. For this, we focus on properties from the well-studied ACAS Xu system [13]. This contains a mix of safe and unsafe instances, where the original verification times measured from seconds to days, including some unsolved instances.

The main contributions of this paper are:

- several new speed improvements to the path enumeration method, along with correctness justifications, that are each systematically evaluated;
- the first verification method that verifies all 180 benchmark instances from ACAS Xu properties 1–4, each in under 10 min on a standard laptop;
- a comparison with other recent tools, including Marabou, Neurify, NNV, and ERAN, where our method is often the fastest and over 100x faster than the original path enumeration method implementation in NNV.

This paper first reviews background related to neural networks, the path enumeration verification approach, and the ACAS Xu benchmarks in Sect. 2. Next, Sect. 3 analyzes several algorithmic optimizations to the basic procedure, and systematically evaluates each optimization's effect on the execution times of the ACAS Xu benchmarks. A comparison with other tools is provided in Sect. 4, followed by review of related work in Sect. 5 and a conclusion.

2 Background

We now review the neural network verification problem (Sect. 2.1), the basic geometric path enumeration algorithm (Sect. 2.2), important spatial data structures (Sect. 2.3), and the ACAS Xu benchmarks (Sect. 2.4).

2.1 Neural Networks and Verification

In this work, we focus our attention on fully-connected, feedforward neural networks with ReLU activation functions. A neural network computes a function $\mathsf{NN} : \mathbb{R}^{n_i} \to \mathbb{R}^{n_o}$, where n_i is the number of inputs and n_o is the number of outputs. A neural network consists of k layers, where each layer i is defined with a weight matrix W_i and a bias vector b_i. Given an input point $y_0 \in \mathbb{R}^{n_i}$, a neural network will compute an output point $y_k \in \mathbb{R}^{n_o}$ as follows:

$$x^{(1)} = W_1 y_0 + b_1, \quad y_1 = f(x^{(1)})$$
$$x^{(2)} = W_2 y_1 + b_2, \quad y_2 = f(x^{(2)})$$
$$\vdots$$
$$x^{(k)} = W_k y_{k-1} + b_k, \quad y_k = f(x^{(k)})$$

We call y_{i-1} and y_i the input and output of the i-th layer, respectively, and $x^{(i)}$ the intermediate values at layer i. The vector-function f is defined using a so-called *activation function*, that is applied element-wise to the vector of intermediate values at each layer. We focus on the popular rectified linear unit (ReLU) activation function, $\mathsf{ReLU}(x) = \max(x, 0)$.

For this computation definition to make sense, the sizes of the weights matrices and bias vectors are restricted. The first layer must accept n_i-dimensional inputs, the final layer must produce n_o-dimensional outputs, and the intermediate layers must have weights and biases that have sizes compatible with their immediate neighbors, in the sense of matrix/vector multiplication and addition. The number of neurons (sometimes called hidden units) at layer i is defined as the number of elements in the layer's output vector y_i.

Definition 1 (Output Range). *Given a neural network that computes the function* NN *and an input set* $\mathcal{I} \subseteq \mathbb{R}^{n_i}$, *the* **output range** *is the set of possible outputs of the network, when executed from a point inside the input set,* $\mathsf{Range}(\mathsf{NN}, \mathcal{I}) = \{y_k \mid y_k = \mathsf{NN}(y_0),\ y_0 \in \mathcal{I}\}$.

Computing the output range is one way to solve the verification problem.

Definition 2 (Verification Problem for Neural Networks). *Given a neural network that computes the function* NN, *an input set* $\mathcal{I} \subseteq \mathbb{R}^{n_i}$, *and an unsafe set* $\mathcal{U} \subseteq \mathbb{R}^{n_o}$, *the* **verification problem for neural networks** *is to check if* $\mathsf{Range}(\mathsf{NN}, \mathcal{I}) \cap \mathcal{U} = \emptyset$.

If verification is impossible, we would also prefer to generate a counterexample $y_0 \in \mathcal{I}$ where $y_k = \mathsf{NN}(y_0)$ and $y_k \in \mathcal{U}$, although not all tools do this. We also further assume in this work that the input and unsafe sets are defined with linear constraints, $\mathcal{I} = \{x \mid A_i x \leq b_i, x \in \mathbb{R}^{n_i}\}$, and $\mathcal{U} = \{x \mid A_u x \leq b_u, x \in \mathbb{R}^{n_o}\}$.

2.2   Basic Geometric Path Enumeration Algorithm

Given enough time, the output range of a neural network can be computed exactly using a recently-proposed geometric path enumeration approach [24].

```
   input  : Input Set: I, Unsafe Set: U
   output: Verification Result (safe or unsafe)
 1 s ← ⟨layer:0, neuron:None, θ : convert(I)⟩ // computation-state tuple
 2 W ← List() // initialize waiting list
 3 W.put(s)
 4 result ← safe
 5 while result = safe and ¬W.empty() do
 6 │   s ← W.pop()
 7 │   result ← step(s,W,U) // updates W, given in Algorithm 2
 8 end
 9 return result
```

Algorithm 1: High-level neural-network path enumeration algorithm.

The general strategy is to execute the neural network with *sets* instead of points. A *spatial data structure* is used to represent the input set of states, and this set is propagated through each layer of the neural network, computing the set of possible intermediate values and then the set of possible outputs repeatedly until the output of the final layer is computed. In this context, a spatial data structure represents some subset of states in a Euclidean space $\mathbb{R}^n$, where the number of dimensions n is the number of neurons in one of the layers of the network, and may change as the set is propagated layer by layer. An example spatial data structure could be a polytope defined using a finite set of half-spaces (linear constraints), although as explained later this is not the most efficient choice. Section 2.3 will discuss spatial data structures in more detail.

The high-level verification method is shown in Algorithm 1, where functions in red are custom to the spatial data structure being used. The convert function (line 1) converts the input set I from linear constraints to the desired spatial data structure, and stores it in the θ element of s, where s is called a *computation-state tuple*. A neuron value of None in the tuple indicates that next operation should be an affine transformation. The computation-state tuple is then put into a waiting list (line 3), which stores tuples that need further processing. The step function (line 7) propagates the set θ by a single neuron in a single layer of the network, and is elaborated on in the next paragraph. This function can modify W, possibly inserting one or more computation-state tuples, although always at a point further along in the network (with a larger layer number or neuron index), which ensures eventual termination of the loop. This function will also check if the set, after being fully propagated through the network, intersects the unsafe set. In this case, step will return unsafe, which causes the while loop to immediately terminate since the result is known.

The step function propagates the set of states θ by one neuron, and is shown in Algorithm 2. The intermediate values are computed from the input set of each layer by calling affine_transformation (line 12). For the current neuron index n, the algorithm will check if the input to the ReLU activation function, dimension n of the set θ, is always positive (or zero), always negative, or can be either positive or negative. This is done by the get_sign function (line 21), which

---

input : Computation-State Tuple: s, Waiting List: $\mathcal{W}$, Unsafe Set: $\mathcal{U}$
output: Safe so far? (safe or unsafe)

```
 1  if s.neuron = None then
 2  │   // finished with the previous layer
 3  │   if s.layer = k then
 4  │   │   // finished with all layers
 5  │   │   if s.θ.has_intersection(U) = ∅  then
 6  │   │   │   return safe
 7  │   │   else
 8  │   │   │   return unsafe // alternatively, return counterexample here
 9  │   │   end
10  │   else
11  │   │   s.layer ← s.layer + 1
12  │   │   s.θ.affine_transformation(W_{s.layer}, b_{s.layer})
13  │   │   s.neuron ← 1
14  │   end
15  end
16  n ← s.neuron
17  s.neuron ← n + 1
18  if s.neuron > size(b_{s.layer}) then
19  │   s.neuron ← None // n is the last neuron in the current layer
20  end
21  switch get_sign(s, n)  do
22  │   case pos do
23  │   │   // do nothing
24  │   case neg do
25  │   │   s.θ.project_to_zero(n)
26  │   case posneg do
27  │   │   t ← ⟨s.layer, s.neuron, s.θ⟩ // deep copy s
28  │   │   s.θ.add_constraint(n, ≥, 0) // split on positive case
29  │   │   t.θ.add_constraint(n, ≤, 0) // split on negative case
30  │   │   t.θ.project_to_zero(n)
31  │   │   W.put(t)
32  end
33  W.put(s)
34  return safe // safe so far
```

Algorithm 2: Pseudocode for step function, which propagates a set through the network by one neuron.

returns pos, neg, or posneg, respectively. In the first two cases, the current dimension n of the set is left alone or assigned to zero (using the project_to_zero method), to reflect the semantics of the ReLU activation function when the input is positive or negative, respectively. In the third case, the set is split into two sets along linear constraint where the input to the activation function equals zero. In the case where the input to the activation function is less than zero, the value of dimension n is projected to zero, reflecting the semantics of the ReLU activation function. The splitting is done using the add_constraint method of the spatial data structure, which takes three arguments: n, sign, and val. This method intersects the set with the linear condition that the n-th dimension is, depending on sign, greater than, less than, and/or equal to val. Once the set has been propagated through the whole network, it is checked for intersection with the unsafe set (line 5), using the has_intersection method.

This enumeration algorithm has been shown to be sound and complete [24]. However, for this strategy to work in practice, the spatial data structure used to store θ must support certain operations *efficiently*. These are denoted in red in Algorithms 1 and 2: convert, has_intersection, affine_transformation, get_sign, project_to_zero, and add_constraint. Polytopes represented with half-spaces, for example, do not have a known efficient way to compute general affine transformations in high dimensions. Instead, linear star sets [4] will be used, which are a spatial data structure that support all the required operations efficiently and without overapproximation error. These will be elaborated on more in the next subsection.

In this work, we focus on optimizations to the presented algorithm that increase its practical scalability, while exploring the same set of paths. The most important factor that we do not control and influences whether this can succeed is the number of paths that exist. Each output set that gets checked for intersection with the unsafe set corresponds to a unique *path* through the network, where the path is defined by the sign of each element of the intermediate values vector at each layer. The algorithm enumerates every path of the network for a given input set. An upper bound on this is 2^N, where N is the total number of neurons in all the layers of the network. For many practical verification problem instances, however, the actual number of unique paths is significantly smaller than the upper bound.

2.3 Spatial Data Structures

Using the correct spatial data structure (set representation in this context) is important to the efficiency of Algorithm 1 and 2, as well as some of our optimizations. Here we review two important spatial data structures, zonotopes and (linear) star sets.

Zonotopes. A *zonotope* is an affine transformation of the $[-1,1]^p$ box. Zonotopes have been used for efficient analysis of hybrid systems [8] as well as more recently to verify neural networks using overapproximations [7,21]. Zonotopes can be described mathematically as $Z = (c, G)$, where the *center* c is an n-dimensional vector and *generator matrix* G is an $n \times p$ matrix. The columns of G are sometimes referred to as *generators* of the zonotope, and we write these as $g_1, \ldots, g_p$. A zonotope Z encodes a set of states as:

$$Z = \left\{ x \in \mathbb{R}^n \mid x = c + G\alpha, \ \alpha \in [-1,1]^p \right\} \tag{1}$$

The two most important properties of zonotopes for the purposes of verification are that they are efficient for (i) affine transformation, and (ii) optimization.

An affine transformation of an n-dimensional point x to a q-dimensional space is defined with a $q \times n$ matrix A and q-dimensional vector b so that the transformed point is $x' = Ax + b$. An affine transformation of every point in an n-dimensional set of points described by a zonotope $Z = (c, G)$ is easily computed as $Z' = (Ac + b, AG)$. Note this uses standard matrix operations which scale polynomially with the dimension of A, and are especially efficient if the number of generators is small. In the verification problem, the number of generators, p, corresponds to the degrees of freedom needed to encode the input set of states. In ACAS Xu system, for example, there are 5 inputs, and so the input set can be encoded with 5 generators. In contrast, affine transformations of polytopes require converting between a half-space and vertex representation, which is slow.

The second efficient operation for zonotopes is optimization in some direction vector v. Given a zonotope $Z = (c, G)$ and a direction v to maximize, the point $x^* \in Z$ that maximizes the dot product $v \cdot x^*$ can be obtained as a simple summation $x^* = c + \sum_{i=1}^{p} x_i^*$, where each x_i^* is given as:

$$x_i^* = \begin{cases} v_i, & \text{if } v_i \cdot g_i \geq -v_i \cdot g_i \\ -v_i, & \text{otherwise} \end{cases} \tag{2}$$

Star Sets. A (linear) *star set* is another spatial data structure that generalizes a zonotope. A star set is an affine transformation of an arbitrary p-dimensional polytope. Mathematically, a star set S is a 3-tuple, (c, G, P), where c and G are the same as with a zonotope, and P is a half-space polytope in p dimensions. A star set S encodes a set of states (compare with Eq. 1):

$$S = \{x \in \mathbb{R}^n \mid x = c + G\alpha, \ \alpha \in P\} \tag{3}$$

A star set can encode any zonotope by letting P be the $[-1, 1]^p$ box. Star sets can also encode more general sets than zonotopes by using a more complex polytope P. A triangle, for example, can be encoded as a star set by setting P to be a triangle, using the origin as c and the identity matrix as V. This cannot be encoded with zonotopes, as they must be centrally symmetric. In Algorithm 1 on line 1, the `convert` function produces the input star set (c, G, P) from input polytope $\mathcal{I}$ setting c to the zero vector, G to the identity matrix, and P to $\mathcal{I}$.

Affine transformations by a $q \times n$ matrix A and q-dimensional vector b of a star set S can be computed efficiently similar to a zonotope: $S' = (Ac + b, AG, P)$.

Optimization in some direction v is slightly less efficient than with a zonotope, and can be done using linear programming (LP). To find a point $x^* \in S$ that maximizes the dot product $v \cdot x^*$, we convert the optimization direction v to the initial space $w = (vG)^T$, find a point $\alpha^* \in P$ that maximizes w using LP, and then convert α^* back to the n-dimensional space $x^* = c + G\alpha^*$.

Star sets, unlike zonotopes, also efficiently support half-space intersection operations by adding constraints to the star set's polytope. Given a star set $S = (c, G, P)$ and an n-dimensional half-space $dx \leq \mathsf{e}$ defined by vector d and scalar e, we convert this to a p-dimensional half-space as follows:

$$(dG)\alpha \leq \mathsf{e} - dc \tag{4}$$

The star set after intersection is then $S' = (c, G, P')$, where the half-space polytope P' is the same as P, with one additional constraint given by Eq. 4.

2.4   ACAS Xu Benchmarks

Since the verification problem for neural networks is NP-Complete, we know exact analysis methods cannot work well in all instances. In order to evaluate improvements, therefore, we must focus on a set of benchmarks.

In this work, we choose to focus on the Airborne Collision System X Unmanned (ACAS Xu) set of neural network verification benchmarks [13]. As these benchmarks have been widely-used for evaluation in other publications, and some authors have even made their tools available publicly, using these allows us to provide a common comparison point with other methods later in Sect. 4.

ACAS Xu is a flight-tested aircraft system designed to avoid midair collisions of unmanned aircraft by issuing horizontal maneuver advisories [17]. The system was designed using a partially observable Markov decision process that resulted in a 2 GB lookup table which mapped states to commands. This mapping was compressed to 3 MB using 45 neural networks (two of the inputs were discretized and are used to choose the applicable network) [12]. Since the compression is not exact, the verification step checks if the system still functions correctly.

Each network contains five inputs that get set to the current the aircraft state, and five outputs that determine the current advisory. The network has six ReLU layers with 50 neurons each, for a total of 300 neurons. Ten properties were originally defined, encoding things like, if the aircraft are approaching each other head-on, a turn command will be advised (property 3). The formal definition of all the properties encoded as linear constraints is available in the appendix of the original work [13].

3   Improvements

We now systematically explore several improvements to the exact path enumeration verification method from Sect. 2.2. For each proposed improvement, we compare the run-time on the ACAS Xu system with and without the change. We focus on properties 1–4. Although originally these were measured on a subset of the 45 networks [13], the same authors later used all the networks to check these properties [14], which is what we will do here. Each verification instance is run with a 10 min timeout, so that the maximum time needed to test a single method, if a timeout is encountered on each of the 180 benchmarks, is 30 h. Later, in Sect. 4, we will compare the most optimized method with other verification tools and the other ACAS Xu properties. Unless indicated otherwise, our experiments were performed on a Laptop platform with Ubuntu Linux 18.04, 32 GB RAM and an Intel Xeon E-2176M CPU running at 2.7 GHz with 6 physical cores (12 virtual cores with hyperthreading). The full data measurements summarized in this section are provided in Appendix C.

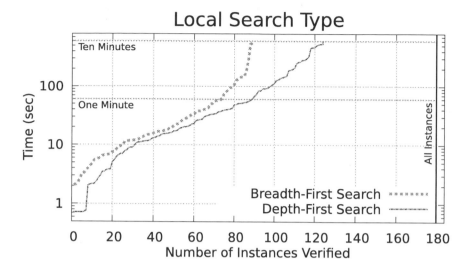

Fig. 1. Depth-first search outperforms breadth-first search.

3.1   Local Search Type (DFS vs BFS)

Algorithm 1 uses a waiting list to store the computation-state tuples, which are popped off one at a time and passed to the step function. This need not strictly be a list, but is rather a collection of computation-state tuples, and we can consider changing the order states are popped to explore the state space with different strategies. If the possible paths through the neural network are viewed as a tree, two well-known strategies for tree traversal that can be considered are depth-first search (DFS) and breadth-first search (BFS). A DFS search can be performed popping the computation-state tuple with the largest (layer, neuron) pair, whereas a BFS search is done by popping the tuple with the smallest (layer, neuron) pair.

The original path enumeration with star set approach [24] describes a layer-by-layer exploration strategy, which is closer to a BFS search. Finite-state machine model-checking methods, however, more often use DFS search.

We compare the two approaches in Fig. 1, which summarizes the execution of all 180 benchmarks. Here, the y-axis is a timeout in seconds, and the x-axis is the number of benchmarks verified within that time. Within the ten minute timeout, around 90 benchmarks can be successfully verified with BFS, and 120 with DFS[1]. Notice that the y-axis is log scale, so that differences in runtimes between easy and hard benchmark instances are both visible.

As can be seen in the figure, the DFS strategy is superior. This is primarily due to unsafe instances of the benchmarks, where DFS can often quickly find an unsafe execution and exit the high-level loop, whereas BFS first iterates through

---

[1] The DFS method solves every benchmark that can be solved with BFS. Appendix C contains the complete results.

all the layers and neurons (DFS explores deep paths, which sometimes are quickly found to be unsafe). In the cases where the system was safe, both approaches took similar time. Another known advantage of DFS search is that the memory needed to store the waiting list is significantly smaller, which can be a factor for the benchmarks with a large number of paths.

Correctness Justification: Both DFS and BFS explore the same sets of states, just in a different order.

3.2   Bounds for Splitting

Using DFS search, we consider other improvements. The original path enumeration publication mentions the following optimization:

> "... to minimize the number of [operations] and computation time, we first determine the ranges of all states in the input set which can be done efficiently by solving ... linear programming problems." [24]

An evaluation of the improvement is not provided, so we investigate this here. The optimization is referring to the implementation of the `get_sign` function on line 21 of Algorithm 2. The `get_sign`(s, n) function takes as input a computation-state tuple s with spatial data structure θ (a star set) and a dimension number n. It returns pos, neg, or posneg, depending on whether value of dimension n, which we call x_n, in set θ can be positive (or zero), negative or both. Our baseline implementation, which we refer to as Copy, determines the output of `get_sign` by creating two copies of the passed-in star set, intersecting them with the condition that $x_n \leq 0$ or $x_n \geq 0$, and then checking each star set for feasibility, done using linear programming (LP). In the second version, which we call Bounds, the passed-in star set is instead minimized and maximized in the direction of x_n, to determine the possible signs. While Copy incurs overhead from creating copies and adding intersections, Bounds does extra work by computing the minimum and maximum which are not really needed (we only need the possible signs of x_n).

A comparison of the optimizations on the ACAS Xu benchmarks are shown in Fig. 2 by comparing Copy to Bounds, we confirm the original paper's claim that Bounds is faster.

Correctness Justification: If θ intersected with $x_n \leq 0$ is feasible, then the minimum value of x_n in θ will be less than or equal to zero and vice versa. Similar for the maximum case.

3.3   Fewer LPs with Concrete Simulations

We next consider strategies to determine the possible signs of a neuron's output with fewer LP calls, which we call *prefiltering*. Consider a modification of the Bounds optimization, where rather than computing both the upper and lower bound of x_n, we first compute the lower bound and check if its value is positive.

If this is the case, we know get_sign should return pos, and we do not need to compute the upper bound. We could, alternatively, first compute the upper bound and check if its value is negative. If there is no branching and we guess the correct side to check, only a single LP needs to be solved instead of two.

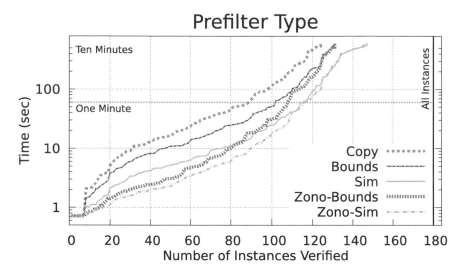

Fig. 2. Prefilter optimizations improve performance by rejecting branches without LP solving. The Zono-Sim method works best.

We can do even better than guessing by tracking extra information in the computation-state tuple. We add a simulation field to s, which contains a concrete value in the set of states θ. This is initialized to any point in the input set $\mathcal{I}$, which can be obtained using LP, or using the center point if the input states are a box. When get_sign returns posneg and the set is split (line 27 in Algorithm 2), the optimization point x^* that proved a split was possible is used as the value of simulation in the new set. Also, when an affine transformation of the set is computed (line 12 in Algorithm 2), or when the set is projected to zero, simulation must also be modified by the same transformation.

With a concrete value of x_n available in simulation, we use its sign to decide whether to first check the upper or lower bound of dimension n in θ. If the nth element of simulation is positive, for example, we first compute the lower bound. If this is positive (or zero), then get_sign can return pos. If the lower bound is negative, then we can immediately return posneg without solving another LP, since the simulation serves as a witness that x_n can also be positive. Only when the simulation value of x_n is zero do we need to solve two LPs.

We call this method Sim in Fig. 2. This is shown to be generally faster than the previous methods, as the overhead to track simulations is small compared with the gains of solving fewer LPs.

Correctness Justification: If the lower bound of x_n is greater than zero, than its upper bound will be also be greater than zero and pos is the correct output. If the lower bound is less than zero and the nth element of simulation is greater than zero, than the upper bound will also be positive, since it must be greater than or equal to the value in the simulation (simulation is always a point in the set θ), and so posneg is correct. Similar for the opposite case.

3.4   Zonotope Prefilter

We can further reduce LP solving by using a zonotope. In each computation-state tuple s, we add a zonotope field z that overapproximates θ, so that $\theta \subseteq z$. In the ACAS Xu benchmarks (and most current benchmarks for verification of NNs), the input set of states is provided as interval values on each input, which is a box and can be used to initialize the zonotope. Otherwise, LPs can be solved to compute box bounds on the input set to serve as an initial value. During the affine transformation of θ (line 12 in Algorithm 2), the zonotope also gets the same transformation applied. Cases where θ gets projected to zero are also affine transformations and can be exactly computed with the zonotope z. The only unsupported operation in the algorithm for zonotopes is add_constraint, used during the splitting operation (lines 28–29 in Algorithm 2). We skip these operations for the zonotope, which is why z is an overapproximation of θ.

With a zonotope overapproximation z available during get_sign, we can sometimes reduce the number of LPs to zero. Computing the minimum and maximum of the n-th dimension of z is an optimization problem over zonotopes, which recall from Sect. 2.3 can be done efficiently as a simple summation. If the n-th dimension of z is completely positive or negative, we can return pos or neg immediately. Otherwise, if both positive and negative values are possible in the zonotope, we fall back to LP solving on θ to compute the possible signs. This can be done either by computing both bounds, which we call Zono-Bounds or with the simulation optimization from before, which we call Zono-Sim. The performance of the methods are shown in Fig. 2. The Zonotope-Sim method performs the fastest, verifying about 145 benchmarks in under 10 min and demonstrating that reduction in LP solving is worth the extra bookkeeping.

Correctness Justification: Rejecting branches without LP solving is justified by the fact that z is an overapproximation of θ. This is initially true, as if the input set is a box then $z = \theta$ and otherwise z is the box overapproximation of θ. This is also true for every operation other than add_constraint, as these are exact for zonotopes. Finally, it is also true when add_constraint operation is skipped on z, as adding constraints can only reduce the size of the set θ. If $\theta \subseteq z$, every smaller set θ' will also be a subset of z by transitivity, $\theta' \subseteq \theta \subseteq z$, and so an overapproximation is maintained by ignoring these operations with z. Finally, if the n-th dimension of an overapproximation of θ is strictly positive (or negative), the n-th dimension of θ will also be strictly positive (or negative).

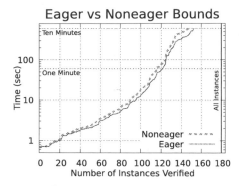

Fig. 3. Computing neuron output bounds eagerly improves speed.

Fig. 4. Zonotope domain contraction improves overall performance.

3.5 Eager Bounds Computation

The step function shown in Algorithm 2 computes the sign of x_n for the current neuron n. An alternative approach is to compute the possible signs for every neuron's output in the current layer immediately after the affine transformation on line 12. These bounds can be saved in the computation-state tuple s and then accessed by get_sign. The potential advantage is that, if a split is determined as impossible for some neuron n, and a split occurs at some earlier neuron $i < n$, then the split will also be impossible for neuron n in both of the sets resulting from the earlier split at neuron i. In this way, computing the bounds once for neuron n is sufficient in the parent set, as opposed to computing the bounds twice, in each of the two children sets resulting from the split. The benefit can be even more drastic if there are multiple splits before neuron n is processed, where potentially an exponential number of bounds computations can be skipped due to a single computation in the parent. On the other hand, if a split is possible, we will have computed more bounds than we needed, as we will do the computation once in the parent and then once again in each of the children. Furthermore, this method incurs additional storage overhead for the bounds, as well as copy-time overhead when computation-state tuples are deep copied on line 27. Experiments are important to check if the benefits outweigh the costs.

The modified algorithm, which we call Eager, will use the zonotope prefilter and simulation as before to compute the bounds, but this will be done immediately after the affine transformation on line 12. Further, when a split occurs along neuron n in the posneg case, the bounds also get recomputed in the two children for the remaining neurons in the layer, starting at the next neuron $n+1$. Neurons where a split was already rejected do not have their bounds recomputed. This algorithm is compared with the previous approach, called Noneager. In Fig. 3, we see eager computation of bounds slightly improves performance.

Correctness Justification: When sets are split in the posneg case in Algorithm 2, each child's θ is a subset of the parent's θ. Thus, the upper and lower bound of the output of each neuron n can only move inward. Thus, if the parent's bounds for some neuron are strictly positive (or negative), then the two childrens' bounds will match the parent's and do not need to be recomputed.

3.6 Zonotope Contraction

The accuracy of the zonotope prefilters is important, as large overapproximation error will lead to the computed overapproximation range of x_n in zonotope z always overlapping zero, and thus performance similar to the Sim method. This effect is observed near the top of the curves in Fig. 2.

In order to improve accuracy, we propose a zonotope domain contraction approach, where the size of the zonotope set z is reduced while still maintaining an overapproximation of the exact star set θ. As discussed before, computing exact intersections of zonotopes is generally impossible when splitting (lines 28–29 in Algorithm 2). However, we can lower our expectations and instead consider other ways to reduce the size of zonotope z while maintaining $\theta \subseteq z$.

To do this, we use a slightly different definition of a zonotope, which we refer to as an *offset zonotope*. Instead of an affine transformation of the $[-1, 1]^p$ box, an offset zonotope is an affine transformation of an arbitrary box, $[l_1, u_1] \times \ldots \times [l_p, u_p]$, where each upper bound u_i is greater than or equal to the lower bound l_i. As this corresponds to an affine transformation of the $[-1, 1]^p$ box, offset zonotopes are equally expressive as ordinary zonotopes. Optimization over offset zonotopes can also be done using a simple summation, but instead of using Eq. 2, we use the following modified equation:

$$x_i^* = \begin{cases} u_i v_i, & \text{if } u_i v_i \cdot g_i \geq l_i v_i \cdot g_i \\ l_i v_i, & \text{otherwise} \end{cases} \tag{5}$$

Using offset zonotopes allows for some memory savings in the algorithm. The initial zonotope can be created using a zero vector as the zonotope center and the identity matrix as the generator matrix, the same as the initial input star set. In fact, with this approach, since the affine transformations being applied to the zonotope z and star set θ are identical, the centers and generator matrices will always remain the same, so that we only need to store one copy of these.

Beyond memory savings, with offset zonotopes we can consider ways to reduce the zonotope's overapproximation error when adding constraints to θ. The proposed computations are done after splitting (lines 28–29 in Algorithm 2), each time an extra constraint gets added to the star set's polytope P. The new linear constraint in the output space ($x_n \leq 0$ or $x_n \geq 0$) is transformed to a linear constraint in the initial space using Eq. 4. We then try to contract the size of the zonotope's box domain by increasing each l_i and reducing each u_i, while still maintaining an overapproximation of the intersection. We consider two ways to do this which we call Contract-LP and Contract-Simple.

In Contract-LP, linear programming is used to adjust each l_i and u_i. Since the affine transformations for the star set θ and the zonotope z are the same, z is an overapproximation if and only if the star set's polytope P is a subset of z's initial

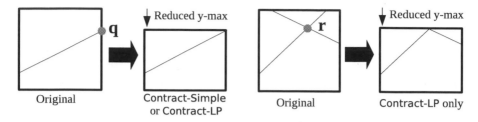

Fig. 5. Both Contract-Simple and Contract-LP can find point q to contract a zonotope's initial box (left), but only Contract-LP can find point r (right), as it requires reasoning with multiple linear constraints.

domain box $[l_1, u_1] \times \ldots \times [l_p, u_p]$. Thus, we can compute tight box bounds on P using linear programming, and using this box as the offset zonotope's initial domain box. This will be the smallest box that is possible for the current affine transformation while still maintaining an overapproximation. This approach, however, requires solving $2p$ linear programs, which may be expensive.

Another approach is possible without invoking LP, which we call Contract-Simple. Contract-Simple overapproximates the intersection by considering only the new linear constraint. This is a problem of finding the smallest box that contains the intersection of an initial box and a single halfspace, which can be solved geometrically without LP solving (see Appendix A for an algorithm).

Since Contract-Simple only considers a single constraint, it can be less accurate than Contract-LP. An illustration of the two methods is given in Fig. 5, where the initial domain is a two-dimensional box. The thin lines are the linear constraints that were added to θ, where all points below these lines are in the corresponding halfspaces. On the left, both Contract-Simple and Contract-LP can reduce the upper bound in the y direction by finding the point q, which lies at the intersection of one side of the original box domain and the new linear constraint. On the right, two constraints were added to the star θ (after two split operations), and they both must be considered at the same time to find point r to be able to reduce the upper bound in the y direction. In this case, only Contract-LP will succeed, as Contract-Simple works with only a single linear constraint at a time, and intersecting the original box with each of the constraints individually does not change its size.

Comparing the performance of the methods in Fig. 4, we see that the less-accurate but faster Contract-Simple works best for the ACAS Xu benchmarks. We expect both methods to take longer when the input set has more dimensions, but especially Contract-LP since it requires solving two LPs for every dimension.

Correctness Justification: The domain contraction procedures reduces the size of zonotope z while maintaining an overapproximation of the star set θ. This can be seen since the affine transformations in z and θ are always the same, and every point in the star set's initial input polytope P is also a point in the initial box domain of z. Since an overapproximation of θ is maintained, it is still sound to use z when determining the possible signs of a neuron's output.

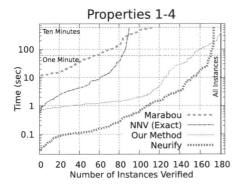

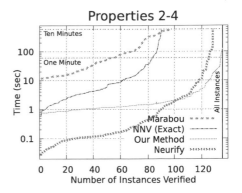

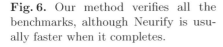

Fig. 6. Our method verifies all the benchmarks, although Neurify is usually faster when it completes.

Fig. 7. Without property 1, our approach is generally fastest when the runtime exceeds two seconds.

4 Evaluation with Other Tools

We next compare the optimized implementation with other neural network verification tools. Our optimizations are part of the exact analysis mode of the NNENUM tool available at https://github.com/stanleybak/nnenum. The artifact evaluation package for our measurements here is online at http://stanleybak.com/papers/bak2020cav_repeatability.zip.

We evaluate with the fully optimized method, using DFS local search, Zono-Sim prefilter, Eager bounds, Contract-Simple zonotope domain contraction. Further, we use a parallelized version of the algorithm, where the details of the parallalization are provided in Appendix B. With a 12-thread implementation (one for each core on our evaluation system), the algorithm can now verify all 180 ACAS Xu benchmarks from properties 1–4 within the 10 min timeout. All measurements are done on our Laptop system, with hardware as described in the first paragraph of Sect. 3. The complete measurement data summarized here is available in Appendix D.

ACAS Xu Properties 1–4. We compare our method with Marabou [14] Neurify [26], and NNV [25]. Marabou is the newer, faster version of the Reluplex algorithm [13], where a Simplex-based LP solver is modified with special ReLU pivots[2]. Neurify is the newer, 20x faster version of the ReluVal algorithm [27], which does interval-based overapproximation, and splits intervals based on gradient information, ensuring the overapproximation error cannot cause to an incorrect result. NNV is the original Matlab implementation of the path enumeration method with star sets, available online at https://github.com/verivital/nnv. The verification result is consistent between the methods, which is a good sanity check for implementation correctness.

---

[2] For Marabou, we used the faster parallel divide-and-conquer mode with arguments as suggested in the paper [14]: `--dnc --initial-divides=4 --initial-timeout=5 --num-online-divides=4 --timeout-factor=1.5 --num-workers=12`.

Table 1. Tool runtime (secs) for ACAS Xu properties 5–10.

Property	Net	Result	Our method	ERAN	Neurify	NNV exact	Marabou
5	1-1	SAFE	13	–	12	671	1969
6.1	1-1	SAFE	67	–	3	6230	12425
6.2	1-1	SAFE	76	–	1	7612	17755
7	1-9	UNSAFE	5948	–	804	–	–
8	2-9	UNSAFE	.7	–	64	–	–
9	3-3	SAFE	88	318	393	12576	15235
10	4-5	SAFE	12	–	1	457	2795

The comparison on ACAS Xu benchmarks on properties 1–4 is shown in Fig. 6. Our method is the only approach able to analyze all 180 benchmarks in less than 10 min, and outperforms both Marabou and NNV.

The comparison with Neurify is more complicated. In Fig. 6, Neurify was faster (when it finished) on all but the largest instances. One advantage of Neurify compared with the other tools is that if the unsafe set is very far away from the possible outputs of a neural network, it can prove safety quickly with a very coarse overapproximation. Path enumeration methods, on the other hand, explore all paths regardless of the distance to the unsafe set. This is especially relevant for ACAS Xu property 1, where the system is unsafe if the first output, clear-of-conflict, is greater than 1500 whereas, for example on network 1-1, this output is always smaller than 1. The meaning of this property is also strange: the absolute value of a specific output is irrelevant, as relative values are used to select the current advisory. Neurify is admittedly the clear winner for all the networks with this property.

When this property is excluded and instead only the more difficult properties 2–4 are considered (Fig. 7), a different trend emerges. Here, our method outperforms Neurify when analysis takes more than about two seconds, which we believe is an encouraging result. Further, part of the reason why Neurify can be very quick on the easier benchmarks (with runtime less than two seconds) is that our implementation incurs a startup delay of about 0.6 s simply to start the Python process and begin executing our script, by which time the C++-based Neurify can verify 80 benchmarks. We believe the more interesting cases are when the runtimes are large, and we outperform Neurify in these cases.

Finally, we compare with using single-set overapproximations for analysis. NNV provides an approximate-star method, where rather splitting, a single star set is used to overapproximate the result of ReLU operations. While fast when it succeeds, this strategy can only verify 68 of the 180 benchmarks. Furthermore, the benchmarks it verified were also quickly checked with exact path enumeration. Of the 68 verified benchmarks, the largest performance difference was property 3 with network 3-3, which took 3.1 s with exact enumeration and 1.2 s with single-set overapproximation. For these ACAS Xu benchmarks, overapproximation using a single set does not provide much benefit.

Other ACAS Xu Properties. Another recently proposed and well received analysis method is presented in the elegant framework of abstract interpretation using zonotopes, in tools such as AI^2 [7] or DeepZ [21]. These methods are single-set overapproximation methods, similar to the approximate-star method in NNV, but with strictly more error (see Fig. 2 in the NNV paper [24] and the associated discussion). As these methods have more error than approximate-star, and since approximate-star could only verify 68 of the 180 benchmarks, we do not expect these methods to work well on the ACAS Xu system.

However, a recent extension to these methods has been proposed where the overapproximation is augmented with MILP solving [22] to provide complete analysis. This has been implemented in the ERAN tool, publicly available at https://github.com/eth-sri/eran. According to current version of the README, ERAN currently only supports property 9 of ACAS Xu, so we were unable to try this method on the other ACAS Xu networks or properties. Verifying property 9 uses a hard-coded custom strategy of first partitioning the input space into 6300 regions and analyzing these individually. This problem-specific parameter presents a problem for fair timing comparison, as the time needed to find the splitting parameter value of 6300 is unknown and does not get measured.

Ignoring this issue, we ran a comparison on property 9 and network 3-3, the only network where the property applies. A runtime comparison for ERAN^3 and the other tools is shown in Table 1. Surprisingly, our enumeration method significantly outperforms the overapproximation and refinement approaches both in Neurify and ERAN on this benchmark. Notice, however, that the original enumeration method in NNV is much slower than our method (about 150x slower in this case). Without the optimizations from this work, one would reach the opposite conclusion about which type of method works better for this benchmark. Both NNV and our method, however, report exploring the same number of paths, 338600 on this system.

For completeness, Table 1 also includes the other original ACAS Xu properties, which were each defined over a single network^4. Both our method and Neurify completed all the benchmarks, although neither was best in all cases. Property 7 is particularly interesting, since the input set is the entire input space, so the number of path is very large. Hundreds of millions of paths were explored before finding a case where the property was violated.

5   Related Work

As the interest in neural networks has surged, so has research in their verification. We review some notable results here, although recent surveys may provide more

---

^{3} For ACAS Xu analysis, we used the following arguments provided by the ERAN authors: `--domain deepzono --dataset acasxu --complete True`.
^{4} Property 6's input set was a disjunction of two boxes which we split into two cases.

a thorough overview [15,28]. Verification approaches for NNs can broadly be characterized into geometric techniques, SMT methods, and MILP approaches.

Geometric approaches, like this work, propagate sets of states layer by layer. This can be done with polytopes [6,29] using libraries like the multi-parametric toolbox (MPT) [10], although certain operations do not scale well, in particular, affine transformation. Other approaches use geometric methods to bound the range of a neural network. These include AI^2 [7] and DeepZ [21] which propagate zonotopes through networks and are presented in the framework of abstract interpretation. ReluVal [27] and Neurify [26] also fall into this category, using interval symbolic methods to create overapproximations, followed by a refinement strategy based on symbolic gradient information. Some of these implementations are also sound with respect to floating-point rounding errors, which we have not considered here, mostly for lack of an LP solver that is both fast and does outward rounding. Other NN verification tools such as Reluplex, Marabou, ERAN, and NNV also use numeric LP solving. Another performance difference is that we used the free GLPK library for LP solving and some other tools used the commercial Gurobi optimizer, which is likely faster. Other refinement approaches partition the input space to detect adversarial examples [11], compute maximum sensitivity for verification [30], or perform refinement based on optimization shadow prices [20].

Mixed integer-linear programming (MILP) solvers can be used to exactly encode the reachable set of states through a ReLU network using the big-M trick to encode the possible branches [16,23]. This introduces a new boolean variables for each neuron, which may limit scalability. The MILP approach has also been combined with a local search [5] that uses gradient information to speed up the search process.

SMT approaches include the Reluplex [13] and Marabou [14], which modify the Simplex linear programming algorithm by splitting nodes into two, which are linked by the semantics of a ReLU. The search process is modified with updates that fix the ReLU semantics for the node pairs. Another tool, Planet, combines the MILP approach with SAT solving and linear overapproximation [6].

Here, we focused on input/output properties of the neural network, given as linear constraints. This formulation can check for adversarial examples [9] in image classification within some L_∞ norm of a base image, which are essentially box input sets. Other more meaningful semantic image perturbations such as rotations, color shifting, and lighting adjustments can also be converted into input/output set verification problems [19].

6   Conclusions

One of the major successes of formal verification is the development of fast model checking algorithms. When talking about how improvements to model checking algorithms came about, Ken McMillan noted:

> "Engineering matters: you can't properly evaluate a technique without an efficient implementation." [18]

With this in mind, we have strived to improve the practical efficiency of the complete path-enumeration method for neural network verification. Although the geometric path-enumeration method has been proposed before, we have shown that, by a sequence of optimizations, the method's scalability can be improved by orders of magnitude.

One limitation is that we have focused on the ACAS Xu benchmarks. Although there is a risk of overfitting our optimizations to the benchmarks being considered, we believe these benchmarks are fairly general in that they contain a mix of safe and unsafe instances, where the original verification times varied from seconds to days. In particular, we believe these networks are similar to others being used in control tasks, in terms of number of inputs and network size. Further, practical considerations prevent us from considering too many more benchmarks; our measurements already need over five days to run.

Unreported here, we were also able to run the implementation on larger perception networks to analyze L_∞ perturbation properties, networks with thousands of neurons and hundreds of inputs, which succeeds when the perturbation is sufficiently small. However, we believe path enumeration is the wrong approach for those systems, as the number of paths quickly becomes too large to enumerate. Instead, overapproximation and refinement methods would likely work best, and evaluating optimizations for these methods may be done in future work. One interpretation of the results presented here is that overapproximation and refinement methods still have significant room for improvement, as it is sometimes faster to explicitly enumerate benchmarks with millions of paths.

Many of the tools we have compared against also support more complicated network structures, with different layer types and nonlinear activation functions, whereas we only focused on the subclass of networks with ReLUs and fully-connected layers. We believe that this is an important enough subclass of neural networks that the results are still meaningful. Once the neural network verification community is more mature, we expect a standard input format and a set of categorized benchmarks will arise, similar to what has happened in the SMT [2], software verification [3], and hybrid systems [1] communities.

Acknowledgment. The material presented in this paper is based upon work supported by the National Science Foundation (NSF) under grant numbers SHF 1910017 and FMitF 1918450, the Air Force Office of Scientific Research (AFOSR) through contract numbers FA9550-18-1-0122 and FA9550-19-1-0288, the Air Force Research Laboratory (AFRL) under prime contract FA8650-15-D-2516 and the Defense Advanced Research Projects Agency (DARPA) through contract number FA8750-18-C-0089. The U.S. Government is authorized to reproduce and distribute reprints for Government purposes notwithstanding any copyright notation thereon. The views and conclusions contained herein are those of the authors and should not be interpreted as necessarily representing the official policies or endorsements, either expressed or implied, of the AFOSR, DARPA, or NSF. Any opinions, finding, and conclusions or recommendations expressed in this material are those of the author(s) and do not necessarily reflect the views of the United States Air Force.

A   Box Bounds Algorithm for Box-Halfspace Intersection

The problem of computing the box bounds of an intersection of an initial box and a single halfspace can be computed without LP. Consider a p-dimensional initial box defined with lower and upper bounds $[l_1, u_1] \times \ldots \times [l_p, u_p]$. Call the constraint defining the halfspace $f\alpha \leq g$, where α is a p-dimensional vector of variables, f is a p-dimensional vector with entries $f_1, \ldots, f_p$, and g is a scalar.

Based on the signs of the signs of $f_1, \ldots, f_p$, we first find the vertex v^* in the box that minimizes the dot product $f \cdot v^*$. This can be done by choosing the ith element of v^* as:

$$v_i^* = \begin{cases} l_i, & \text{if } f_i \geq 0 \\ u_i, & \text{otherwise} \end{cases} \tag{6}$$

If $f \cdot v^* > g$, then the intersection is the empty set. Otherwise, we attempt to contract in each of the p dimensions one-by-one.

For dimension i, if the lower bound was used to define v_i^*, then we attempt to decrease u_i. If the upper bound was used to define v_i^*, then we attempt to increase l_i. This is done by finding the point on the edge of the box which intersects the halfspace (point q in Fig. 5). Without loss of generality, assume the lower bound of dimension i defined v_i^*. The intersection point q is given by $(v_1^*, v_2^*, \ldots x, \ldots v_p^*)$, where value of the ith coordinate, x, can be determined from the single-variable equation $q \cdot f = g$. If f_i was zero, then this equation has no solution, and we cannot contract in this dimension (the half-space and the box edge where q must lie do not intersect). Otherwise, if we solve for x and find $x < u_i$, then we reduce u_i, setting it to x. The process repeats for every other dimension.

B   Parallelization

The proposed approach can be parallelized in many ways. Here, we propose and evaluate a work-stealing strategy, where each thread maintains a local set of computation-state tuples and runs the high-level algorithm. Periodically, the number of tuples in each local set are communicated using a shared data structure, and if some worker thread has no work remaining, the other threads will push some of their local computation-state tuples to a shared global queue.

For this evaluation, we used the usual system setup described in the first paragraph of Sect. 3, which we label Laptop. In addition, to see the effect of more cores, we rented a c5.metal EC2 instance from Amazon Web Services, which we refer to as AWS Server. This setup ran Ubuntu 18.08, and included a dual Intel(R) Xeon(R) Platinum 8275CL processor running at 3.0 GHz, with a total of 48 physical cores (96 with hyperthreading) and 384 GB of main memory.

To evaluate parallelism, we needed to use a benchmark with sufficient difficulty where computation time dominates. For this, we chose ACAS Xu network

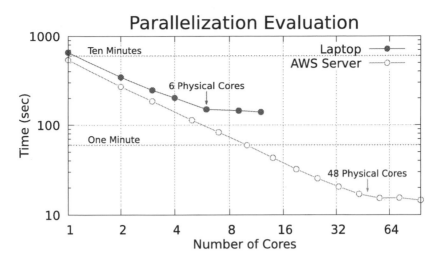

Fig. 8. Doubling the number of cores roughly halves the computation time, up to the physical core count on each platform.

4-2 with specification 2. In an earlier ACAS Xu evaluation [14], this property timed out (>55 min) or ran out of memory for every tool analyzed. The single-threaded runtime on the Laptop platform with our enumeration approach was 655 s (about 11 min), which enumerated 484555 paths in the network.

An evaluation where we adjusted the number of cores available to the computation process for each of the two platforms is shown in Fig. 8. The AWS Server platform was faster than the Laptop setup and, with all the cores being used, could enumerate the same 484555 paths in about 15 s. The linear trend on the log-log graph shows continuous improvement as more cores are added, up to the physical-core limit on each platform. The gains from hyperthreading are comparatively smaller. Even using all the cores, about 90% of the computation time was in the step function, as opposed to managing shared state. With more cores, further improvement through additional parallelization is likely possible.

Correctness Justification: Parallelization explores the same set of states, just in a different order.

C   Full Optimization Data

See Table 2.

Table 2. Runtimes (sec) for each optimization. Dashes (—) are timeouts (10 min).

Prop	Net	Result	BFS	Copy	Bound	Sim	Zono-B	Zono-S	Eager	Con-LP	Con-Sim	Par
1	1-1	SAFE	—	—	399	166	359	159	129	65	50	10
1	1-2	SAFE	—	—	467	206	416	191	154	76	57	12
1	1-3	SAFE	—	—	—	485	—	496	375	197	163	32
1	1-4	SAFE	—	—	—	558	—	538	407	271	177	36
1	1-5	SAFE	—	—	—	492	—	491	360	215	138	30
1	1-6	SAFE	—	—	—	—	—	—	—	—	445	95
1	1-7	SAFE	—	—	539	250	518	259	190	113	78	17
1	1-8	SAFE	—	—	—	409	—	434	287	188	128	27
1	1-9	SAFE	—	—	—	476	—	446	324	221	132	29
1	2-1	SAFE	—	—	—	—	—	—	523	343	216	47
1	2-2	SAFE	—	—	—	—	—	—	—	—	599	119
1	2-3	SAFE	—	—	—	—	—	—	564	332	227	47
1	2-4	SAFE	—	—	—	383	—	412	272	193	120	27
1	2-5	SAFE	—	—	—	—	—	—	—	—	—	188
1	2-6	SAFE	—	—	—	—	—	—	—	517	400	82
1	2-7	SAFE	—	—	—	—	—	—	—	—	—	195
1	2-8	SAFE	—	—	—	—	—	—	—	—	—	163
1	2-9	SAFE	—	—	—	—	—	—	—	—	—	271
1	3-1	SAFE	—	—	—	—	—	—	438	411	263	57
1	3-2	SAFE	—	—	—	—	—	—	521	308	214	46
1	3-3	SAFE	—	—	—	—	—	—	—	596	390	84
1	3-4	SAFE	—	—	—	442	—	438	323	221	141	30
1	3-5	SAFE	—	—	—	—	—	—	—	—	401	86
1	3-6	SAFE	—	—	—	—	—	—	—	—	—	297
1	3-7	SAFE	—	—	—	—	—	—	—	—	—	155
1	3-8	SAFE	—	—	—	—	—	—	—	—	—	141
1	3-9	SAFE	—	—	—	—	—	—	—	—	507	107
1	4-1	SAFE	—	—	—	—	—	—	—	—	517	107
1	4-2	SAFE	—	—	—	—	—	—	—	—	568	124
1	4-3	SAFE	—	—	—	537	—	508	396	233	160	34
1	4-4	SAFE	—	—	—	523	—	584	365	245	155	34
1	4-5	SAFE	—	—	—	—	—	—	—	—	573	119
1	4-6	SAFE	—	—	—	—	—	—	—	—	—	408
1	4-7	SAFE	—	—	—	—	—	—	—	—	—	195
1	4-8	SAFE	—	—	—	—	—	—	—	—	—	131
1	4-9	SAFE	—	—	—	—	—	—	—	—	—	304
1	5-1	SAFE	—	—	—	—	—	—	482	322	232	48
1	5-2	SAFE	—	—	—	—	—	—	—	426	303	64
1	5-3	SAFE	—	—	—	508	—	498	366	214	143	32
1	5-4	SAFE	—	—	—	305	—	289	211	136	98	21
1	5-5	SAFE	—	—	—	—	—	—	—	368	264	57
1	5-6	SAFE	—	—	—	—	—	—	—	—	—	176
1	5-7	SAFE	—	—	—	—	—	—	—	—	474	97
1	5-8	SAFE	—	—	—	—	—	—	—	—	—	153
1	5-9	SAFE	—	—	—	—	—	—	—	—	—	161
2	1-1	SAFE	—	—	404	159	368	165	128	67	46	10
2	1-2	UNSAFE	—	58	24	11	23	12	9	5	4	1
2	1-3	UNSAFE	—	463	192	74	177	78	58	32	26	21
2	1-4	UNSAFE	—	31	15	6	13	6	5	4	3	1
2	1-5	UNSAFE	—	4	2	1	1	1	1	.8	.8	1
2	1-6	UNSAFE	—	—	—	517	—	579	373	260	175	19
2	1-7	SAFE	—	—	557	234	520	255	193	111	79	17
2	1-8	SAFE	—	—	—	403	—	399	297	184	126	27
2	1-9	SAFE	—	—	—	431	—	472	317	206	136	29
2	2-1	UNSAFE	—	92	39	18	37	18	13	7	5	.9
2	2-2	UNSAFE	—	.7	.7	.7	.7	.7	.7	.7	.7	.8
2	2-3	UNSAFE	—	8	4	2	4	2	2	1	1	1
2	2-4	UNSAFE	—	4	2	1	2	1	1	1	.9	.9
2	2-5	UNSAFE	—	37	17	8	18	8	6	3	3	1
2	2-6	UNSAFE	—	284	146	58	144	65	48	25	18	8

(*continued*)

Table 2. (continued)

Prop	Net	Result	BFS	Copy	Bound	Sim	Zono-B	Zono-S	Eager	Con-LP	Con-Sim	Par
2	2-7	UNSAFE	—	506	250	85	256	96	78	43	30	.9
2	2-8	UNSAFE	—	51	26	10	24	10	9	5	4	2
2	2-9	UNSAFE	—	—	—	291	—	320	242	132	94	2
2	3-1	UNSAFE	—	190	68	31	50	24	20	12	9	4
2	3-2	UNSAFE	—	250	88	38	96	44	27	19	14	1
2	3-3	SAFE	—	—	—	—	—	—	—	590	409	83
2	3-4	UNSAFE	—	197	106	41	97	42	32	18	13	.9
2	3-5	UNSAFE	—	67	34	14	32	15	11	6	5	.9
2	3-6	UNSAFE	—	27	10	5	11	5	5	3	2	5
2	3-7	UNSAFE	—	49	25	11	25	12	9	5	4	1
2	3-8	UNSAFE	—	266	112	42	114	50	32	20	15	2
2	3-9	UNSAFE	—	20	11	5	10	5	4	2	2	2
2	4-1	UNSAFE	—	115	45	19	40	20	14	8	7	5
2	4-2	SAFE	—	—	—	—	—	—	—	—	597	125
2	4-3	UNSAFE	—	2	1	1	2	1	.9	.8	.8	.9
2	4-4	UNSAFE	—	39	17	7	19	8	6	4	3	2
2	4-5	UNSAFE	—	470	239	97	200	94	71	34	27	2
2	4-6	UNSAFE	—	139	64	25	71	28	22	11	9	2
2	4-7	UNSAFE	—	461	215	93	210	93	65	35	27	1
2	4-8	UNSAFE	—	322	162	60	163	67	49	22	16	.9
2	4-9	UNSAFE	—	—	390	164	413	180	121	73	56	5
2	5-1	UNSAFE	—	32	15	7	15	8	6	3	3	.9
2	5-2	UNSAFE	—	91	39	18	30	16	12	6	6	1
2	5-3	UNSAFE	—	—	—	460	—	487	316	201	141	24
2	5-4	UNSAFE	—	2	1	1	1	1	.9	.8	.8	.9
2	5-5	UNSAFE	—	261	107	48	111	46	36	19	14	2
2	5-6	UNSAFE	—	208	102	41	95	41	30	15	10	2
2	5-7	UNSAFE	—	107	52	21	53	22	18	8	7	2
2	5-8	UNSAFE	—	302	161	63	160	67	50	27	19	1
2	5-9	UNSAFE	—	—	477	189	472	218	163	81	61	1
3	1-1	SAFE	561	526	232	116	125	80	58	103	58	12
3	1-2	SAFE	534	533	233	116	104	65	50	64	43	9
3	1-3	SAFE	143	147	75	35	30	20	15	19	14	4
3	1-4	SAFE	77	73	40	19	8	6	5	7	5	2
3	1-5	SAFE	88	84	42	21	10	7	6	8	6	2
3	1-6	SAFE	21	22	12	6	3	3	2	3	2	1
3	1-7	SAFE	8	.7	.7	.7	.7	.7	.7	.7	.7	.8
3	1-8	UNSAFE	6	.7	.7	.7	.7	.7	.7	.7	.7	.8
3	1-9	UNSAFE	4	.7	.7	.7	.7	.7	.7	.7	.7	.8
3	2-1	SAFE	147	142	75	34	31	21	16	24	14	4
3	2-2	SAFE	59	55	30	14	12	8	6	10	6	2
3	2-3	SAFE	108	101	50	25	19	12	9	14	9	3
3	2-4	SAFE	6	6	4	2	1	1	1	1	1	1
3	2-5	SAFE	33	33	18	9	4	4	3	4	3	1
3	2-6	SAFE	5	5	4	2	1	1	1	1	.9	1
3	2-7	SAFE	17	16	11	5	3	2	2	2	2	1
3	2-8	SAFE	6	6	5	2	1	1	1	1	1	1
3	2-9	SAFE	4	4	3	2	.9	.9	.8	1	.9	.9
3	3-1	SAFE	57	53	25	12	11	7	5	9	6	2
3	3-2	SAFE	578	537	226	117	93	53	40	59	36	8
3	3-3	SAFE	128	128	65	31	22	14	11	13	11	3
3	3-4	SAFE	27	26	16	7	5	4	3	4	2	1
3	3-5	SAFE	16	16	10	5	2	2	2	2	2	1
3	3-6	SAFE	31	33	20	10	5	4	3	3	3	1
3	3-7	SAFE	2	2	2	1	.8	.8	.7	.8	.8	.8
3	3-8	SAFE	12	12	8	4	2	2	1	2	1	1
3	3-9	SAFE	16	15	10	5	3	2	2	2	2	1
3	4-1	SAFE	18	18	11	5	5	3	2	4	3	1
3	4-2	SAFE	189	187	88	43	44	24	19	25	16	4
3	4-3	SAFE	282	283	136	63	64	35	29	32	24	5
3	4-4	SAFE	12	11	7	4	2	1	1	2	1	1
3	4-5	SAFE	4	4	3	2	1	1	.9	1	.9	1
3	4-6	SAFE	33	34	20	10	7	5	4	4	3	1
3	4-7	SAFE	15	15	11	5	2	2	2	2	2	1
3	4-8	SAFE	11	12	8	4	2	1	1	2	1	1
3	4-9	SAFE	12	11	8	4	2	2	2	2	1	1
3	5-1	SAFE	97	91	50	25	19	12	9	14	9	3
3	5-2	SAFE	18	19	11	6	5	3	2	4	2	1

(continued)

Table 2. (*continued*)

Prop	Net	Result	BFS	Copy	Bound	Sim	Zono-B	Zono-S	Eager	Con-LP	Con-Sim	Par
3	5-3	SAFE	22	23	12	6	5	3	3	4	3	1
3	5-4	SAFE	11	11	7	4	2	2	1	2	1	1
3	5-5	SAFE	15	14	10	5	2	2	2	2	2	1
3	5-6	SAFE	23	21	14	7	3	3	2	3	2	1
3	5-7	SAFE	2	2	2	1	.8	.8	.7	.8	.7	.8
3	5-8	SAFE	37	38	24	10	6	4	4	5	3	1
3	5-9	SAFE	2	2	2	1	.9	.8	.7	.8	.8	.8
4	1-1	SAFE	149	150	72	34	33	22	16	23	16	4
4	1-2	SAFE	135	130	52	27	21	15	12	16	11	3
4	1-3	SAFE	95	96	44	23	18	12	10	13	9	3
4	1-4	SAFE	12	11	7	4	2	2	2	2	2	1
4	1-5	SAFE	81	84	42	20	12	9	8	9	7	2
4	1-6	SAFE	41	37	20	11	7	5	4	6	4	2
4	1-7	UNSAFE	6	.7	.7	.7	.7	.7	.7	.7	.7	.8
4	1-8	UNSAFE	7	.8	.7	.7	.7	.7	.7	.7	.7	.8
4	1-9	UNSAFE	5	.7	.7	.7	.7	.7	.7	.7	.7	.8
4	2-1	SAFE	38	41	21	11	7	5	5	7	4	2
4	2-2	SAFE	50	51	27	13	8	6	5	6	4	2
4	2-3	SAFE	9	9	6	3	2	2	2	2	1	1
4	2-4	SAFE	8	9	5	3	2	2	1	2	1	1
4	2-5	SAFE	28	27	14	7	6	4	4	4	3	1
4	2-6	SAFE	15	15	9	5	3	2	2	2	2	1
4	2-7	SAFE	7	7	5	3	1	1	1	1	1	1
4	2-8	SAFE	40	43	25	11	5	4	3	4	3	1
4	2-9	SAFE	3	3	3	2	.9	.9	.9	.9	.9	.9
4	3-1	SAFE	56	52	27	13	7	6	5	6	5	2
4	3-2	SAFE	63	61	31	15	12	9	7	11	7	2
4	3-3	SAFE	10	9	6	3	2	2	2	2	2	1
4	3-4	SAFE	12	12	7	3	2	2	2	2	2	1
4	3-5	SAFE	38	40	22	10	8	6	4	5	4	2
4	3-6	SAFE	20	20	12	6	3	3	2	3	2	1
4	3-7	SAFE	17	17	11	5	3	2	2	2	2	1
4	3-8	SAFE	7	7	5	2	2	2	1	1	1	1
4	3-9	SAFE	51	48	29	13	7	5	5	5	4	2
4	4-1	SAFE	7	7	5	3	2	1	1	2	1	1
4	4-2	SAFE	14	14	8	5	3	2	2	2	2	1
4	4-3	SAFE	26	27	14	8	5	4	3	5	3	1
4	4-4	SAFE	20	20	11	6	3	2	2	2	2	1
4	4-5	SAFE	17	16	9	5	3	2	2	2	2	1
4	4-6	SAFE	30	30	15	7	5	3	3	4	3	1
4	4-7	SAFE	3	3	2	1	1	.9	.9	.9	.8	.8
4	4-8	SAFE	24	23	16	7	4	3	2	3	2	1
4	4-9	SAFE	43	40	24	12	5	4	4	4	4	2
4	5-1	SAFE	57	53	26	14	10	7	6	8	5	2
4	5-2	SAFE	38	34	17	9	7	4	4	5	4	2
4	5-3	SAFE	14	13	8	4	3	2	2	3	2	1
4	5-4	SAFE	13	13	8	4	2	2	2	2	2	1
4	5-5	SAFE	17	17	11	6	3	3	2	2	2	1
4	5-6	SAFE	10	10	6	3	2	2	2	2	1	1
4	5-7	SAFE	3	3	2	1	.9	.8	.8	.9	.8	.8
4	5-8	SAFE	8	8	6	3	2	1	1	1	1	1
4	5-9	SAFE	14	13	8	4	2	2	2	2	2	1

D   Full Tool Comparison Data

This section contains the complete data measured in the optimization improvements from Sect. 3 (Table 3).

Table 3. Runtimes (sec) for each tool. Dashes (—) are timeouts (10 min).

Prop	Net	Result	Marabou	NNV Exact	Our Method	Neurify
1	1-1	SAFE	95	—	10	.1
1	1-2	SAFE	168	—	12	.2
1	1-3	SAFE	—	—	32	1
1	1-4	SAFE	—	—	36	2
1	1-5	SAFE	119	—	30	.2
1	1-6	SAFE	110	—	95	.2
1	1-7	SAFE	63	—	17	.1
1	1-8	SAFE	56	—	27	.1
1	1-9	SAFE	43	—	29	.1
1	2-1	SAFE	—	—	47	.6
1	2-2	SAFE	—	—	119	1
1	2-3	SAFE	—	—	47	1
1	2-4	SAFE	294	—	27	.5
1	2-5	SAFE	—	—	188	4
1	2-6	SAFE	—	—	82	3
1	2-7	SAFE	—	—	195	11
1	2-8	SAFE	—	—	163	3
1	2-9	SAFE	—	—	271	8
1	3-1	SAFE	—	—	57	.4
1	3-2	SAFE	—	—	46	.7
1	3-3	SAFE	521	—	84	1
1	3-4	SAFE	510	—	30	.6
1	3-5	SAFE	—	—	86	2
1	3-6	SAFE	—	—	297	28
1	3-7	SAFE	—	—	155	12
1	3-8	SAFE	—	—	141	8
1	3-9	SAFE	—	—	107	11
1	4-1	SAFE	—	—	107	16
1	4-2	SAFE	—	—	124	3
1	4-3	SAFE	—	—	34	1
1	4-4	SAFE	387	—	34	.7
1	4-5	SAFE	—	—	119	3
1	4-6	SAFE	—	—	408	22
1	4-7	SAFE	—	—	195	23
1	4-8	SAFE	—	—	131	47
1	4-9	SAFE	—	—	304	21
1	5-1	SAFE	353	—	48	.4
1	5-2	SAFE	522	—	64	.7
1	5-3	SAFE	128	—	32	.2
1	5-4	SAFE	574	—	21	.4
1	5-5	SAFE	—	—	57	1
1	5-6	SAFE	—	—	176	15
1	5-7	SAFE	—	—	97	3
1	5-8	SAFE	—	—	153	16
1	5-9	SAFE	—	—	161	8
2	1-1	SAFE	—	—	10	.6
2	1-2	UNSAFE	254	—	1	3
2	1-3	UNSAFE	—	—	21	11
2	1-4	UNSAFE	—	—	1	10
2	1-5	UNSAFE	—	—	1	—
2	1-6	UNSAFE	—	—	19	52
2	1-7	SAFE	—	—	17	6
2	1-8	SAFE	—	—	27	23
2	1-9	SAFE	—	—	29	11
2	2-1	UNSAFE	59	—	.9	.1

(*continued*)

Table 3. (*continued*)

Prop	Net	Result	Marabou	NNV Exact	Our Method	Neurify
2	2-2	UNSAFE	—	—	.8	.1
2	2-3	UNSAFE	549	—	1	.1
2	2-4	UNSAFE	18	—	.9	.1
2	2-5	UNSAFE	547	—	1	.1
2	2-6	UNSAFE	—	—	8	.1
2	2-7	UNSAFE	24	—	.9	.1
2	2-8	UNSAFE	102	—	2	.1
2	2-9	UNSAFE	—	—	**2**	—
2	3-1	UNSAFE	97	—	4	.1
2	3-2	UNSAFE	345	—	1	—
2	3-3	SAFE	—	—	**83**	—
2	3-4	UNSAFE	—	—	.9	.1
2	3-5	UNSAFE	319	—	.9	.1
2	3-6	UNSAFE	471	—	5	.1
2	3-7	UNSAFE	—	—	1	—
2	3-8	UNSAFE	—	—	2	.1
2	3-9	UNSAFE	457	—	2	.1
2	4-1	UNSAFE	—	—	5	**.2**
2	4-2	SAFE	—	—	**125**	—
2	4-3	UNSAFE	566	—	.9	.1
2	4-4	UNSAFE	288	—	2	.1
2	4-5	UNSAFE	—	—	2	.1
2	4-6	UNSAFE	419	—	2	.1
2	4-7	UNSAFE	—	—	1	.1
2	4-8	UNSAFE	336	—	.9	.1
2	4-9	UNSAFE	—	—	**5**	45
2	5-1	UNSAFE	119	—	.9	.1
2	5-2	UNSAFE	24	—	1	.1
2	5-3	UNSAFE	—	—	**24**	—
2	5-4	UNSAFE	360	—	.9	.1
2	5-5	UNSAFE	278	—	2	.1
2	5-6	UNSAFE	547	—	2	.1
2	5-7	UNSAFE	17	—	2	.1
2	5-8	UNSAFE	246	—	1	.1
2	5-9	UNSAFE	47	—	1	.1
3	1-1	SAFE	—	564	**12**	104
3	1-2	SAFE	—	283	9	**2**
3	1-3	SAFE	—	58	4	**3**
3	1-4	SAFE	342	12	2	**.3**
3	1-5	SAFE	520	17	2	**.2**
3	1-6	SAFE	43	4	1	**.1**
3	1-7	UNSAFE	12	2	.8	**.1**
3	1-8	UNSAFE	12	2	.8	**.1**
3	1-9	UNSAFE	12	1	.8	**.05**
3	2-1	SAFE	—	70	**4**	21
3	2-2	SAFE	—	23	**2**	8
3	2-3	SAFE	—	39	**3**	3
3	2-4	SAFE	15	2	1	**.5**
3	2-5	SAFE	18	7	1	**.4**
3	2-6	SAFE	15	1	1	**.04**
3	2-7	SAFE	16	4	1	**.3**
3	2-8	SAFE	15	2	1	**.1**
3	2-9	SAFE	13	1	.9	**.03**
3	3-1	SAFE	406	21	**2**	3
3	3-2	SAFE	—	247	8	**6**
3	3-3	SAFE	—	35	3	**.2**
3	3-4	SAFE	47	8	1	**.4**
3	3-5	SAFE	15	4	**1**	5
3	3-6	SAFE	390	7	**1**	151
3	3-7	SAFE	13	.9	.8	**.1**
3	3-8	SAFE	36	3	**1**	4
3	3-9	SAFE	45	4	**1**	3
3	4-1	SAFE	—	8	**1**	8
3	4-2	SAFE	—	88	**4**	97
3	4-3	SAFE	—	130	5	**2**
3	4-4	SAFE	14	2	1	**.1**
3	4-5	SAFE	14	1	1	**.1**
3	4-6	SAFE	102	11	1	**.2**

(*continued*)

Table 3. (*continued*)

Prop	Net	Result	Marabou	NNV Exact	Our Method	Neurify
3	4-7	SAFE	96	3	1	**.6**
3	4-8	SAFE	85	2	**1**	2
3	4-9	SAFE	33	3	1	**.1**
3	5-1	SAFE	—	35	**3**	21
3	5-2	SAFE	—	8	**1**	2
3	5-3	SAFE	146	8	1	**.2**
3	5-4	SAFE	17	3	1	**.2**
3	5-5	SAFE	24	4	1	**.5**
3	5-6	SAFE	88	5	1	**.9**
3	5-7	SAFE	14	.6	.8	**.04**
3	5-8	SAFE	43	9	**1**	.1
3	5-9	SAFE	14	.9	.8	**.1**
4	1-1	SAFE	—	82	4	**1**
4	1-2	SAFE	—	50	3	**1**
4	1-3	SAFE	—	36	3	**.4**
4	1-4	SAFE	105	3	1	**.2**
4	1-5	SAFE	504	24	2	**.4**
4	1-6	SAFE	89	12	2	**.2**
4	1-7	UNSAFE	12	2	.8	**.1**
4	1-8	UNSAFE	12	2	.8	**.1**
4	1-9	UNSAFE	12	2	.8	**.1**
4	2-1	SAFE	171	14	2	**.8**
4	2-2	SAFE	520	14	**2**	2
4	2-3	SAFE	77	3	1	**.8**
4	2-4	SAFE	23	3	1	**.2**
4	2-5	SAFE	61	11	1	**.4**
4	2-6	SAFE	90	5	1	**.3**
4	2-7	SAFE	14	2	1	**.1**
4	2-8	SAFE	43	8	1	**.1**
4	2-9	SAFE	13	1	.9	**.03**
4	3-1	SAFE	—	13	2	**1**
4	3-2	SAFE	134	27	2	**.4**
4	3-3	SAFE	21	4	1	**.1**
4	3-4	SAFE	20	4	1	**.2**
4	3-5	SAFE	59	15	2	**1**
4	3-6	SAFE	66	5	**1**	2
4	3-7	SAFE	16	4	1	**.3**
4	3-8	SAFE	29	3	1	**.3**
4	3-9	SAFE	63	12	2	**1**
4	4-1	SAFE	78	3	**1**	3
4	4-2	SAFE	60	5	**1**	2
4	4-3	SAFE	134	10	**1**	1
4	4-4	SAFE	41	5	**1**	1
4	4-5	SAFE	62	4	**1**	2
4	4-6	SAFE	14	8	1	**.04**
4	4-7	SAFE	21	1	.8	**.2**
4	4-8	SAFE	37	6	**1**	.2
4	4-9	SAFE	25	8	2	**.1**
4	5-1	SAFE	339	19	**2**	3
4	5-2	SAFE	51	12	2	**.5**
4	5-3	SAFE	52	5	1	**.2**
4	5-4	SAFE	31	4	1	**.2**
4	5-5	SAFE	49	5	1	**.6**
4	5-6	SAFE	76	3	1	**.3**
4	5-7	SAFE	14	1	.8	**.04**
4	5-8	SAFE	31	3	1	**.1**
4	5-9	SAFE	26	3	1	**.1**

References

1. Althoff, M., et al.: ARCH-COMP19 category report: continuous and hybrid systems with linear continuous dynamics. In: ARCH 2019, 6th International Workshop on Applied Verification of Continuous and Hybrid Systems, pp. 14–40 (2019)

2. Barrett, C., Stump, A., Tinelli, C., et al.: The SMT-LIB standard: version 2.0. In: Proceedings of the 8th International Workshop on Satisfiability Modulo Theories (Edinburgh, England), vol. 13, p. 14 (2010)

3. Beyer, D.: Competition on software verification. In: Flanagan, C., König, B. (eds.) TACAS 2012. LNCS, vol. 7214, pp. 504–524. Springer, Heidelberg (2012). https://doi.org/10.1007/978-3-642-28756-5_38

4. Duggirala, P.S., Viswanathan, M.: Parsimonious, simulation based verification of linear systems. In: Chaudhuri, S., Farzan, A. (eds.) CAV 2016. LNCS, vol. 9779, pp. 477–494. Springer, Cham (2016). https://doi.org/10.1007/978-3-319-41528-4_26

5. Dutta, S., Jha, S., Sankaranarayanan, S., Tiwari, A.: Output range analysis for deep feedforward neural networks. In: Dutle, A., Muñoz, C., Narkawicz, A. (eds.) NFM 2018. LNCS, vol. 10811, pp. 121–138. Springer, Cham (2018). https://doi.org/10.1007/978-3-319-77935-5_9

6. Ehlers, R.: Formal verification of piece-wise linear feed-forward neural networks. In: D'Souza, D., Narayan Kumar, K. (eds.) ATVA 2017. LNCS, vol. 10482, pp. 269–286. Springer, Cham (2017). https://doi.org/10.1007/978-3-319-68167-2_19

7. Gehr, T., Mirman, M., Drachsler-Cohen, D., Tsankov, P., Chaudhuri, S., Vechev, M.: AI^2: safety and robustness certification of neural networks with abstract interpretation. In: 2018 IEEE Symposium on Security and Privacy (SP), pp. 3–18. IEEE (2018)

8. Girard, A.: Reachability of uncertain linear systems using zonotopes. In: Morari, M., Thiele, L. (eds.) HSCC 2005. LNCS, vol. 3414, pp. 291–305. Springer, Heidelberg (2005). https://doi.org/10.1007/978-3-540-31954-2_19

9. Goodfellow, I.J., Shlens, J., Szegedy, C.: Explaining and harnessing adversarial examples. arXiv preprint arXiv:1412.6572 (2014)

10. Herceg, M., Kvasnica, M., Jones, C.N., Morari, M.: Multi-parametric toolbox 3.0. In: 2013 European Control Conference (ECC), pp. 502–510. IEEE (2013)

11. Huang, X., Kwiatkowska, M., Wang, S., Wu, M.: Safety verification of deep neural networks. In: Majumdar, R., Kunčak, V. (eds.) CAV 2017. LNCS, vol. 10426, pp. 3–29. Springer, Cham (2017). https://doi.org/10.1007/978-3-319-63387-9_1

12. Julian, K.D., Lopez, J., Brush, J.S., Owen, M.P., Kochenderfer, M.J.: Policy compression for aircraft collision avoidance systems. In: 2016 IEEE/AIAA 35th Digital Avionics Systems Conference (DASC), pp. 1–10. IEEE (2016)

13. Katz, G., Barrett, C., Dill, D.L., Julian, K., Kochenderfer, M.J.: Reluplex: an efficient SMT solver for verifying deep neural networks. In: Majumdar, R., Kunčak, V. (eds.) CAV 2017. LNCS, vol. 10426, pp. 97–117. Springer, Cham (2017). https://doi.org/10.1007/978-3-319-63387-9_5

14. Katz, G., et al.: The Marabou framework for verification and analysis of deep neural networks. In: Dillig, I., Tasiran, S. (eds.) CAV 2019. LNCS, vol. 11561, pp. 443–452. Springer, Cham (2019). https://doi.org/10.1007/978-3-030-25540-4_26

15. Liu, C., Arnon, T., Lazarus, C., Barrett, C., Kochenderfer, M.J.: Algorithms for verifying deep neural networks. arXiv preprint arXiv:1903.06758 (2019)

16. Lomuscio, A., Maganti, L.: An approach to reachability analysis for feed-forward ReLU neural networks. arXiv preprint arXiv:1706.07351 (2017)

17. Marston, M., Baca, G.: ACAS-Xu initial self-separation flight tests (2015). http://hdl.handle.net/2060/20150008347
18. McMillan, K.: A perspective on formal verification. In: David Dill @ 60 Workshop, colocated with CAV (2017)
19. Mohapatra, J., Chen, P.-Y., Liu, S., Daniel, L., et al.: Towards verifying robustness of neural networks against semantic perturbations. arXiv preprint arXiv:1912.09533 (2019)
20. Royo, V.R., Calandra, R., Stipanovic, D.M., Tomlin, C.: Fast neural network verification via shadow prices. arXiv preprint arXiv:1902.07247 (2019)
21. Singh, G., Gehr, T., Mirman, M., Püschel, M., Vechev, M.: Fast and effective robustness certification. In: Advances in Neural Information Processing Systems, pp. 10802–10813 (2018)
22. Singh, G., Gehr, T., Püschel, M., Vechev, M.: Boosting robustness certification of neural networks. In: International Conference on Learning Representations (ICLR 2019) (2019)
23. Tjeng, V., Xiao, K., Tedrake, R.: Evaluating robustness of neural networks with mixed integer programming. arXiv preprint arXiv:1711.07356 (2017)
24. Tran, H.-D., et al.: Star-based reachability analysis of deep neural networks. In: ter Beek, M.H., McIver, A., Oliveira, J.N. (eds.) FM 2019. LNCS, vol. 11800, pp. 670–686. Springer, Cham (2019). https://doi.org/10.1007/978-3-030-30942-8_39
25. Tran, H.-D., et al.: NNV: the neural network verification tool for deep neural networks and learning-enabled cyber-physical systems. In: Lahiri, S.K., Wang, C. (eds.) CAV 2020. LNCS, vol. 12224, pp. 3–17. Springer, Cham (2020)
26. Wang, S., Pei, K., Whitehouse, J., Yang, J., Jana, S.: Efficient formal safety analysis of neural networks. In: Advances in Neural Information Processing Systems, pp. 6367–6377 (2018)
27. Wang, S., Pei, K., Whitehouse, J., Yang, J., Jana, S.: Formal security analysis of neural networks using symbolic intervals. In: 27th USENIX Security Symposium, pp. 1599–1614 (2018)
28. Xiang, W., et al.: Verification for machine learning, autonomy, and neural networks survey. arXiv preprint arXiv:1810.01989 (2018)
29. Xiang, W., Tran, H.-D., Johnson, T.T.: Reachable set computation and safety verification for neural networks with ReLU activations. arXiv preprint arXiv:1712.08163 (2017)
30. Xiang, W., Tran, H.-D., Johnson, T.T.: Output reachable set estimation and verification for multilayer neural networks. IEEE Trans. Neural Netw. Learn. Syst. **29**(11), 5777–5783 (2018)

Systematic Generation of Diverse Benchmarks for DNN Verification

Dong Xu[✉], David Shriver, Matthew B. Dwyer,
and Sebastian Elbaum

University of Virginia,
Charlottesville, VA 22904, USA
{dx3yy,dls2fc,matthewbdwyer,
selbaum}@virginia.edu

Abstract. The field of verification has advanced due to the interplay of theoretical development and empirical evaluation. Benchmarks play an important role in this by supporting the assessment of the state-of-the-art and comparison of alternative verification approaches. Recent years have witnessed significant developments in the verification of deep neural networks, but diverse benchmarks representing the range of verification problems in this domain do not yet exist. This paper describes a neural network verification benchmark generator, GDVB, that systematically varies aspects of problems in the benchmark that influence verifier performance. Through a series of studies, we illustrate how GDVB can assist in advancing the sub-field of neural network verification by more efficiently providing richer and less biased sets of verification problems.

Keywords: Neural network · Verification · Benchmark · Covering array

1 Motivation

Advances in machine learning have enabled training of deep neural networks (DNN) that are capable of realizing complex functions that rival or exceed the performance of human-built software, e.g., [27,32,41]. This success has led system developers to deploy, or consider deployment of, DNN models in critical systems, e.g., [12,39,53]. Consequently, the verification of correctness properties of DNNs has become a key challenge to assuring autonomous systems, and the research community has risen to this challenge. In the three years since Katz et al. [30] presented RELUPLEX at CAV 2017, researchers have published more than 20 DNN verification approaches supporting different properties and DNN architectures and spanning a range of algorithmic approaches [9,13,14,18–20,22,29–31,36,45,46,50,56,59–63]. While DNN verification has its own unique challenges, it is also a recent example in the long-history of domain-specific verification research, e.g., for hardware [25], software [17], real-time systems [58], and cryptographic protocols [40], and can benefit from the experience of these communities.

S. K. Lahiri and C. Wang (Eds.): CAV 2020, LNCS 12224, pp. 97–121, 2020.
https://doi.org/10.1007/978-3-030-53288-8_5

A key lesson learned by the community is that despite the fact that verification emphasizes the development of theoretical and algorithmic techniques, *advances in verification research often arise from understanding how different algorithmic and implementation approaches compare* – a process that requires empirical study. Empirical study in verification is common, but unlike many other fields of computer science, for decades it has organized *verification tool competitions* that serve as a regular and long-running form of community-driven empirical study. Researchers tracked the progress of SMT solvers over a span of 6 years at these community-driven empirical studies and found that repeatedly "a certain solver presents a key idea that improves the performance in a particular division, and this idea is implemented by most solvers" in the following year [7]. Enabling the type of comparative studies that drive such advances requires *verification benchmarks* – a fact that the verification community has recognized for at least 25 years, e.g., [8, 10, 33, 43, 55].

Benchmarking in verification has evolved in response to the demands of empirical study within the field, e.g., [1–4], to support two objectives: (A1) *assessment of the state-of-the-art* and (A2) *comparison of alternative approaches*. In support of these, the verification community has favored benchmarks that: (R1) **are diverse in structure and difficulty**; (R2) **represent verifier use cases**; and (R3) **evolve as verification technology advances**.

The verification benchmarking and competition literature suggests that these requirements are widely accepted. For example, the TPTP benchmark's stated goals include R1 ("contains problems varying in difficulty"), R2 ("spans a diversity of subject matters"), and R3 ("is up-to-date", "provides a mechanism for adding new problems") [54]. Moreover, these requirements are promoted, either explicitly or implicitly, by many of the regularly held verification competitions. To meet R1 and R2 SAT competitions construct benchmarks that include problems from six different domains: software, hardware, A.I, obstruction, combinatorial challenges, and theorem proving [4]. SAT competitions since 2017 have instituted a *bring your own benchmarks* policy that requires verifier developers to submit 20 new benchmarks with at least 10 that are "not too easy" or "too hard" – which helps to address R1 and R3. SMT competitions have used selection criteria that are biased towards these same requirements, e.g., "balancing the difficulty of benchmarks" [7].

Verification competitions have undoubtedly been a positive force for developing high-quality verification benchmarks, but prior to their existence researchers were forced to develop their own "benchmarks" – a collection of verification problems on which they evaluate their techniques and perhaps others. This is the situation that the subfield of *DNN verification* finds itself in.

The risk in letting technique developers choose their own benchmark is selection bias – that the selected problems do not represent a broad or important population of problems. For example, if an SMT benchmark were selected based on the constraints generated by symbolic execution tools they would be structurally biased, consisting only of conjunctive formula. As another example, if a SAT benchmark were generated randomly it is likely that a large portion of the benchmark would not represent realistic use cases.

Good benchmarks are expensive to develop, e.g., [11], but they are an invaluable resource for advancing a research community. When well designed they seek to balance requirements R1-R3 and to support a fair and accurate assessment of the state-of-the-art and comparison between alternative algorithmic and implementation approaches. This paper reports on GDVB, the first *framework for systematic Generation of DNN Verification problem Benchmarks*, that meets the de-facto requirements for verification benchmarks, R1–R3, in order to support objectives A1–A2 for the rapidly evolving field of DNN verification.

GDVB takes a **generative** approach to benchmark development – an approach that has risen in popularity in recent years [5,35,64]. Unlike, other generative benchmark approaches GDVB seeks to systematically cover variations in verification problems that are known to influence verifier performance. Towards that end, GDVB is parameterized by: (1) a set of *factors* known to influence the performance of DNN verifiers; (2) a *coverage* goal that determines the combination of factors that should be reflected in the benchmark; and (3) a *seed* verification problem from which a set of variant problems are generated. From these parameters, it computes a constrained mixed-level covering array [15] defining a set of factor-value tuples. Each tuple defines how the seed verification problem can be transformed to give rise to a verification problem capable of exposing performance variation in a DNN verifier.

As a benchmark generator GDVB naturally meets requirement R3. By starting from a seed network representing a DNN verification use case, GDVB is guaranteed to meet R2. As we discuss in Sect. 4, the use of factors allows GDVB to produce systematically diverse verification problems both in terms of structure and difficulty in order to meet requirement R1. Moreover, GDVB offers the potential to reduce selection bias in performing evaluations of DNN verifiers, since it assures coverage of a space of performance related factors. Finally, GDVB is designed to support the rapidly evolving field of DNN verifiers by allowing the generation of benchmarks, e.g., from new seeds as verifiers improve, as new performance factors are identified, and to target challenge problems in different DNN domains, e.g., regression models for autonomous UAV navigation [39,53].

The contributions of this paper are: identification of the need for unbiased and diverse benchmarks for DNN verification; a study of factors that affect the performance of DNN verification tools (Sect. 3); the specification of a verification benchmark as the solution to a constrained mixed-level covering array problem (Sect. 4); the GDVB algorithm for computing a benchmark from a verification problem by transforming the neural network and correctness specification (Sect. 4.3); the evaluation of GDVB on multiple state-of-the-art DNN verifiers using different seed verification problems that demonstrates how GDVB results can support the evaluation of DNN verifiers (Sect. 5); and the GDVB tool.

2   Background and Related Wok

Deep Neural Networks (DNN). A DNN is trained to accurately approximate a target function, $f : \mathbb{R}^d \to \mathbb{R}^r$. A network, $n : \mathbb{R}^d \to \mathbb{R}^r$, is comprised of a graph of L hidden layers, $l_1, \ldots, l_L$, along with an input layer, $l_{in} = l_0$, and output layer, $l_{out} = l_{L+1}$. Each hidden layer defines an independent function, where their composition when applied to the output of l_{in} generates values in l_{out} that define the network output.

Hidden layers are, generally, comprised of a set of *neurons* that accumulate a weighted sum of their inputs from the prior layer and then apply an *activation function* to determine how to non-linearly scale that sum to compute the output from the layer. A variety of different activation functions have been explored in the literature, including: rectified linear units (ReLU), sigmoid, and tanh.

The design of a DNN involves choosing an appropriate set of *layer types*, e.g., convolutional, maxpooling, fully-connected, the instantiation of those layers, e.g., the number of neurons, the specific activation function, and the definition of how layers are interconnected. Together these comprise the DNN *architecture* [23].

Networks are trained using a variety of algorithmic strategies with the goal of minimizing the loss in the approximation of the learned function relative to some proxy for f, e.g., labeled training data. The training process is stochastic, e.g., initial weight values are randomized, which leads to variation in n even when architecture, training algorithm, and training data are fixed.

Section 3 reveals how DNN architecture can influence verification performance.

DNN Specifications. Given a network $n : \mathbb{R}^d \to \mathbb{R}^r$, a property, ϕ, defines a set of constraints over the inputs, ϕ_x, and an associated set of constraints over the outputs, ϕ_y. Verification of n seeks to prove: $\forall \boldsymbol{x} \in \mathbb{R}^d : \phi_x(\boldsymbol{x}) \Rightarrow \phi_y(\mathbf{N}(x))$ where $\mathbf{N}(x)$ is running the neural network n with input x.

Specifying behavioral properties of DNNs is challenging and is an active area of research [24]. In [30], a set of 188 purely conjunctive properties, of the form described above, were defined for a simple neural network, with 7 inputs, encoding of a rule set for autonomous aircraft collision avoidance (ACAS). In [44,59,60], properties expressing output range invariants were used, for example, that the steering angle never exceeded an absolute value of $30°$. Much of the work on DNN verification has focused on local robustness properties [50–52], which state that for a selected target input the output of the network is invariant for other inputs within a specified distance of the target.

Section 3 reveals how the specification can influence verification performance.

DNN Verification Methods and Tools. There are a variety of different algorithmic and implementation approaches taken to verifying the validity of a DNN with respect to a stated correctness property.

Definition 1. *A DNN verification problem,* $\langle n, \phi \rangle$, *is comprised of a DNN, n, and a property specification, ϕ. The outcome of a verification problem for a DNN verifier indicates whether $n \models \phi$ is valid, invalid, or unknown – indicating that the problem cannot be determined to be either valid or invalid.*

A recent DNN verification survey [37], classifies approaches as being based on reachability, optimization, and search algorithms – or their combination. Reachability methods begin with a symbolic encoding of an input set and compute, for each layer, a symbolic encoding of the output set. They vary in the symbolic encodings used, e.g., intervals, polyhedra, and in the degree of overapproximation they introduce [22,46,50,63]. Optimization methods formulate verification as an optimization problem whose solution implies the validity of ϕ [9,19,38,45,56,62]. Search methods work in combination with reachability and optimization, by decomposing the input space to formulate verification sub-problems that are discharged by the above techniques [13,14,18,20,29,30,59–61].

In this paper, we use implementations of the following verifiers: ERAN [50], BaB [14], Neurify [59], Planet [20], and ReLuplex [30].

Verification Benchmarking. We covered the broad landscape of work on benchmark development for verification in (Sect. 1). There have been efforts to develop benchmarks within a variety of different verification problem domains, e.g. hardware [25], software [17], real-time systems [58], cryptographic protocols [40], and for different encodings of verification problems, e.g., model checking [33], SAT [4], SMT [8], and theorem proving [55].

In recent work on DNN verification, researchers have shared collections of examples that, in a sense, serve as informal benchmarks and permit comparative evaluation, e.g. [30,50]. While valuable, these examples were not intended to, and do not, comprise a benchmark meeting requirements R1–R3. To our knowledge, GDVB is the first approach to achieving those goals for DNN verification.

For several years, the SAT community has been exploring scalable benchmarks, e.g., [21,35]. For instance, to explore conflict-driven clause learning (CDCL) SAT solver performance, Elffers et al. [21] used crafted parameterized benchmarks that can be scaled with respect to different factors that may influence performance. We conduct a similar domain analysis of factors, but focus on the landscape of DNN verification algorithms developed to date. Like this line of work, GDVB advocates a scalable approach to benchmark generation. As described in Sect. 4, GDVB starts with seed problems that are challenging for current verifiers and "scales them down", but it can also be applied to start with easier seed problems and "scale them up" as more typical of the prior work on scalable benchmarking.

Verification Benchmark Ranking. The verification community has explored a variety of ranking schemes for assessing the cost-effectiveness of techniques. A key challenge is that verification techniques vary not only in their cost, e.g., time to produce a verification result, but also in their accuracy, e.g., whether they produce an *unknown* result. For example, SAT competitions have employed a range of scoring models, e.g., purse-based ranking, *solution-count ranking* (SCR), careful ranking, and penalized average runtime (PAR2) [6]. SCR, which counts the number of solved problem instances and uses verification time as a tie breaker [57], is the scoring system of choice [1,4]. In Sect. 5, we report DNN verifier performance using both SCR and PAR2 scoring systems.

Covering Arrays. In Sect. 3 we explore factors that influence DNN verifier performance. Studying all their combinations would be cost prohibitive, so we consider weaker notions of coverage.

A covering array defines a systematic method for testing how combinations of parameter values influence system performance [16]. A covering array is an $N \times k$ array. The k columns represent *factors* that may influence performance and cells can take on v *levels* – defining settings for factors. The N rows of the array define combinations of factor-levels. Arrays are defined to achieve a *strength* of the coverage, t. $t = 2$ defines pairwise strength, which means that all pairs of levels for all factors are present in some row of the covering array.

We require a richer form of covering array that permits the number of levels to vary with different factors, i.e., a mixed-level covering array (MCA), and that can constrain specified factor-level combinations, e.g., by forbidding their inclusion in the MCA. By modeling each factor as a variable and its levels as the domain of the variable, one can express constraints as propositional logic formulae over equality terms; if the levels are ordered then richer underlying theories can be applied. A constrained-MCA defines an MCA that is consistent with a given constraint, C.

Definition 2. *Constrained Mixed-level Covering Array (Definition 2.9 from [15])*
$CMCA(N; t, k, (|v_1|, |v_2|, ..., |v_k|), C)$ *is an $N \times k$ array on $|v|$ symbols, where* $|v| = \sum_{i=0}^{k} |v_i|$, *with the following properties: 1) Each column $i(1 \leq i \leq k)$ contains only elements from a set S_i of size $|v_i|$, 2) the rows of each $N \times t$ subarray cover all t-tuples of values from the t columns at least one time, and 3) all rows are models of C.*

Transforming Neural Networks. The GDVB approach manipulates factors that influence DNN verifier performance to construct a diverse benchmark. For DNN construction, we leverage a recent approach, R4V [47], that given an original DNN and an architectural specification automates the transformation of the DNN and uses distillation [28] to train it to closely match the test accuracy of the original DNN. R4V transformation specifications can be written to change a number of architectural parameters of a network including: the input dimension, the range of values for each input dimension, the number of layers, the number of neurons per layer, the number of convolutional kernels, and the stride and padding of a convolutional layer.

3   Identifying Factors that Influence Verifier Performance

As discussed in Sect. 1 the verification community has acted to create policies that incentivize *diverse* benchmarks. Diversity is desirable in a benchmark
because it (a) demonstrates the range of applicability of a verification technology
and (b) exposes performance variation within and across verification technologies. Consider, that the SMT competition benchmark selection process seeks
to "include equal numbers of satisfiable and unsatisfiable benchmarks at different levels of difficulty" [7]. This is due to the fact that the SMT community
understands that the satisfiability or unsatisfiability of a benchmark problem is
a factor that influences verifier performance[1].

GDVB seeks to make factors influencing verifier performance explicit and to
manipulate them to generate a diverse benchmark. To determine an initial set of
factors for DNN verifiers we began with an analysis of the literature, which identified several candidate factors, and then conducted a targeted and exploratory
factor study to identify whether *manipulating a factor could influence some
performance measure of some DNN verifier*. This study only aims to identify
such factors and does not seek to characterize the complex relationship between
factors and DNN verifier performance; for example, we do not aim to capture
a comprehensive set of factors, assess the independence of or relations between
factors, or rank factors in terms of their degree of influence. A richer and more
detailed factor study might further improve the utility of GDVB, but we leave
such a study to future work.

3.1   Potential Factors

Relatively few published papers on DNN verification explicitly discuss the factors that influence performance, but nearly all of them present metrics on the
verification problems they solved.

Evaluation results for RELUPLEX present data on verifier outcome and solve
time for local robustness properties that vary in the input center point and
radius [30]; most subsequent papers report similar property variation. Evaluation
results for ROBUSTVERIFIER present a study of varying the number of layers in
the DNN and its impact on verifier performance [36]. Evaluation results for
ERAN present performance variations across a range of networks varying in
the number of layers, layer types, and neurons [22,50–52]. Bunel et al. [14] were
the first that we are aware of to explicitly vary factors of DNN verification
problems. They found that the performance varied with input dimension, number
of neurons per layer, and number of layers across a set of 6 different DNN
verifiers. All of the other papers published on DNN verification in recent years
have used verification problems that varied, in an ad-hoc fashion, over a subset
of the above factors.

---

[1] Since unsatisfiability requires the consideration of all possible variable assignments
which generally is more costly than finding a single satisfiable assignment.

3.2   Exploratory Factor Study

As in other verification domains, DNN verifier performance is multi-faceted. In our study, we consider both verification time and accuracy. We say that the result of a verification problem is *accurate* if a verifier determines conclusively that the problem is *valid* or *invalid*, result as opposed to *unknown*[2].

We study factors associated with both properties and DNNs. Based on the literature analysis, we identified 2 factors related to the correctness property: *scale* and *translation*. Scaling a property involves increasing the size of the input

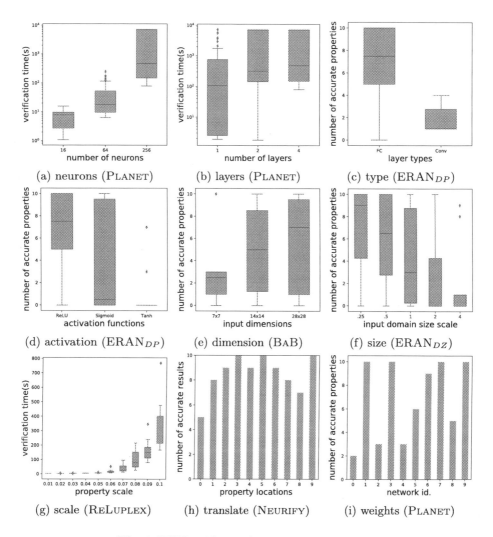

Fig. 1. DNN verifier performance across factors

---

[2] We cross-check accurate results with multiple verifiers.

domain which will involve *more DNN behavior* in verification. Translating a property involves moving it to a different location in the input domain which will involve *different DNN behavior* in verification. For robustness properties, scaling and translation involve changing the radius and center point of the hypercube describing the input space under verification. One might wonder whether rotation of a property can influence verification performance. For robustness properties, this seems unlikely given their symmetry, but it could be a factor for more irregular input regions – we leave this for future work.

Based on the literature analysis, we identified 4 factors related to the DNN: number of *neurons*, number of *layers*, the *type* of layers, the input *dimension*. We conjectured that an additional 3 factors might impact verifier performance: the type of *activation* function, the input domain *size*, and the learned *weights*.

Our exploratory factor study is opportunistic in that we seek to find a verification problem for which manipulation of a selected factor exhibits performance variation. Towards this end, we conducted a series of trials where we vary a factor hypothesized to influence verification performance, while holding all other factors constant and report the results in Fig. 1. We studied variations of networks for the MNIST task and considered local robustness properties since these were well-supported across a range of different verifiers. We used different verifiers across the study: RELUPLEX, PLANET, NEURIFY, BAB, ERAN with the DeepPoly (DP) and DeepZono (DZ) abstract domains. We now briefly describe the trials and then summarize the outcome.

Number of Neurons: The architecture of the DNN was fixed, with 4 fully-connected layers using ReLU activation functions, and the total number of neurons was varied (16, 64, 256) – they were spread evenly across layers. Each network is trained 10 times and verified on 100 local robustness properties. Figure 1(a) plots the number of neurons versus verification time for PLANET. **Verification time can increase with the number of neurons.**

Number of Layers: We use the same context as for the neuron factor study, except that we fixed the number of neurons at 256 and vary the number of layers (1, 2, 4). Figure 1(b) plots the number of layers versus verification time for PLANET. **Verification time can increase with the number of layers.**

Layer Types: We use a pair of two-layer neural networks, with the same number of neurons, where one has a fully-connected layer and the other a convolutional layer. Each network is trained 10 times and verified on 10 local robustness properties. Figure 1(c) plots layer type versus the number of properties for which accurate results are produced using $ERAN_{DP}$. **Verification accuracy can vary with layer type.**

Activation Function: We use the fully-connected network from the layer types study, we generated three networks by altering the activation function to use sigmoid and tanh. The training setup and properties remain the same as in the previous trial. Figure 1(d) plots the activation function versus the number of properties for which accurate results are produced using $ERAN_{DP}$. **Verification accuracy can vary with activation function.**

Input Dimension: We use 3 architectures that differ only in their input dimension which is scaled $(\frac{1}{16}, \frac{1}{4}, 1)$ relative on the original problem. The training setup and properties are from the layer type study. Figure 1(e) plots the input dimension versus the number of properties for which accurate results are produced using BAB. **Verification accuracy can increase with increasing input dimension.**

Input Size: We use 5 architectures that differ only in the range of values of their inputs which are scaled ($\frac{1}{4}, \frac{1}{2}, 1, 2, 4$) based on the original problem. The training setup and properties are from the layer type study. Figure 1(f) plots the input size versus the number of properties for which accurate results are produced using ERAN$_{DZ}$. **Verification accuracy can decrease with increasing input domain size.**

Property Scale: We use a single-layer network and reuse the training setup and properties from the layer type study. We scale the properties ($0.01 - 0.1$) to generate verification problems. Figure 1(g) plots property scaling versus the verification time using RELUPLEX. **Verification time can increase with increasing property scale.**

Property Translation: We replicated the property scale study, but held the scale fixed and translated the center point of the local robustness property to 10 other locations. Figure 1(h) plots the number of DNNs for each of the 10 translated properties for which accurate results could be produced using NEURIFY. **Verification accuracy can vary with property translation.**

Network Weights: Building of the property studies, we explore the verification of 10 scaled property variants across the same network trained 10 times with different initial weights. Figure 1(i) plots the number of accurate properties for which the results could be produced using PLANET. **Verification accuracy can vary with the learned weights of the network.**

Exploraty Study Findings. Varying the factors studied influences the performance of different DNN verifiers differently – in terms of time or accuracy. For example, we found that: varying input dimension impacts BAB's accuracy, but not RELUPLEX's; varying input domain size impacts ERAN$_{DZ}$'s accuracy, but not NEURIFY's; and varying property scale impacts RELUPLEX's verification time, but not NEURIFY's.

This study provides a starting set of viable factors that can be used to parameterize the GDVB approach to produce verification problem benchmarks in which those factors are systematically varied. Futhermore, as we discuss in Sect. 4, GDVB generative process allows for us to accommodate information about new factors that might be revealed in future factor studies.

4   The GDVB Approach

The goal of GDVB is to meet requirements R1–R3 by producing a *factor diverse* benchmark that (a) reflects aspects of the complexity encoded in a real verification problem that acts as a seed for generation $\langle n_s, \phi_s \rangle$, (b) varies aspects of the problem that are related to verifier performance, (c) accounts for interactions among those factors, and (d) is comprised only of well-defined verification problems.

Rather than synthesize random verification problems, we seed the generation process in order to generate a benchmark that reflects the complexity of the seed problem. This permits benchmarks to be generated to reflect the challenges present in different DNN problem sub-domains.

Factors, like those described in Sect. 3, may interact; changes to one factor may mask or amplify DNN verifier performance changes arising from another. Exploring all combinations of factors is expensive, but by using covering arrays we can systematically explore interactions among factors. Accounting for such interactions helps to produce a benchmark that is *less biased* than one that only covers individual factor variations.

Not all combinations of factors are possible. For example, if one reduces the number of layers in a network to 0, then it is not possible to preserve the number of neurons in the original network. Thus, benchmark generation must take into account constraints among factors to ensure that only well-defined problems are included in a benchmark.

4.1 Factor Diverse Benchmarks

Consider a set of factors, F, with a set of levels, L_f, for each factor, $f \in F$; we refer to L_f as the *level set* of f. For a verification problem, p, let $l(p)$ be the set of factor levels corresponding to the problem. A benchmark, B, is a set of verification problems and we can denote the factor levels for the benchmark as $l(B) = \{l(p) \mid p \in B\}$.

The simplest form of diversity for a benchmark is requiring that all individual factor levels be present in at least one verification problem, $\forall f \in F : \forall l \in L_f : \exists p \subset l(B) : l \subset p$. However, this diversity fails to account for interactions among factors. The simplest form of interaction-sensitive diversity considers pairs of factors, but as we discuss below our approach generalizes to any arity of factor-level coverage.

For a pair of factors, $f, f' \in F$, the Cartesian product of their level sets defines the set of all pairwise combinations of their levels. Across all factors the set of such pairs is $pairs(F) = \{(l, l') \mid f, f' \in F \wedge f \neq f' \wedge l \in L_f \wedge l' \in L_{f'}\}$. A *pairwise diverse benchmark* is one in which

$$\forall(x, y) \in pairs(F) : \exists p \in l(B) : (x, y) \in \{(x', y') \mid x' \in p \wedge y' \in p\}$$

Constraints on allowable combinations of factors serve to restrict a benchmark. A pairwise exclusion constraint, $\gamma(F) \subseteq pairs(F)$, requires that

$$\forall(x, y) \in \gamma(F) : \forall p \in l(B) : \neg(x \in p \wedge y \in p)$$

We write γ when F is understood from the context.

The arity of factor-level coverage and exclusion constraints can vary independently. It is common for factor-level coverage to be uniform and to generalize it to t-way coverage, i.e., to require coverage of the elements of the Cartesian product of the level sets of t factors. On the other hand, as observed in prior work [15], constraints generally involve a mix of arity. To denote this generality we define $\Gamma \subseteq \bigcup_i \gamma_i$ where γ_i defines the set of possible i-way exclusion constraints.

Example. Consider the DAVE-2 DNN which accepts 100 by 100 color images and infers an output indicating the steering angle [12]. DAVE-2 is comprised of 5 convolutional layers with 55296, 17424, 3888, 3136, and 1600 neurons, respectively, followed by 4 fully connected layers with 1164, 100, 50, and 10 neurons, respectively. All 82668 neurons use ReLU activations. One can define a local robustness property for DAVE-2 as

$$\phi = \forall \boldsymbol{x} \in i \pm 0.02 : \|\text{DAVE-2}(\boldsymbol{x}) - \text{DAVE-2}(i)\| \leq 5$$

which states that for a given an input image, i, all inputs within a distance of 0.02 will result in an inferred steering angle within $5°$ of the angle for i. These yield the verification problem $\langle \text{DAVE-2}, \phi \rangle$.

Consider factors for the number of neurons, number of convolutional layers, and number of fully-connected layers; a tuple $(\#neuron, \#conv, \#fc)$ represents levels for these factors. For each factor consider two percentage levels: 100% and 50%. A neuron factor level of 50% indicates that a version of DAVE-2 with 41334 neurons is required. In the absence of constraints, an example pairwise factor diverse benchmark for $\langle \text{DAVE-2}, \phi \rangle$ consists of the following four verification problems: (100%, 100%, 100%), (100%, 50%, 50%), (50%, 100%, 50%), and (50%, 50%, 100%). The property ϕ is constant across the benchmark.

4.2   From Factor Covering Arrays to Verification Problems

Given a set of factors, $F = \{f_1, f_2, \ldots, f_{|F|}\}$, and levels, L_{f_i}, a t-way factor diverse benchmark of k verification problems is specified by

$$CMCA(|F|; t, k, (|L_{f_1}|, |L_{f_2}|, \ldots, |L_{f_{|F|}}|), \Gamma)$$

Each element in this mixed level covering array specifies how to construct a verification problem in the benchmark from the seed problem.

Levels are operationalized as transformations on verification problems. We assume a sufficient set of transformations, Δ, such that a verification problem can be transformed into a form that achieves any level of any factor

$$\forall f \in F : \forall l_f \in L_f : \exists \delta \in \Delta : l_f \in l(\delta(\langle n_s, \phi_s \rangle))$$

The definition of Δ and L_i must be coordinated to achieve this property.

A per-factor transformation $\delta \in \Delta$ may impact a single component of a verification problem, e.g., reducing the number of neurons in a DNN does not impact the property, or both components, e.g., the input dimension impacts the DNN and the property by transforming the input data domain. The set of all transformations Δ defines the set of verification problems that can be produced by application of a set of per-factor transformations to the seed problem,

$$\Delta(\langle n_s, \phi_s \rangle) = \{\langle n, \phi \rangle \mid \langle n, \phi \rangle = \delta_{f_1} \circ \delta_{f_2} \ldots \circ \delta_{f_{|F|}}(\langle n_s, \phi_s \rangle) \wedge \delta_i \in \Delta\}$$

The set of all possible factor level combinations is $\Pi_{f \in F} L_f$, i.e., the product of all of the per-factor levels. The set of t-way factor level combinations is

$$c_t = \{c | a \in \Pi_{f \in F} L_f \wedge c \subseteq a \wedge |c| = t\}$$

allowing for the interpretation of $|F|$-tuples as sets.

Definition 3. *Given a set of factors F, with associated factor levels L_f, a t-way factor diverse benchmark, B, for a seed problem $\langle n_s, \phi_s \rangle$ with exclusion constraints Γ is defined by the following: (1) $B \subseteq \Delta(\langle n_s, \phi_s \rangle)$; (2) $\forall \langle n, \phi \rangle \in B :$ $\forall \gamma \in \Gamma : \gamma \not\subseteq l(\langle n, \phi \rangle)$; and (3) $\forall c \in c_t - \Gamma : \exists \langle n, \phi \rangle \in B : c \subseteq l(\langle n, \phi \rangle)$*

4.3   Generating Benchmarks

GDVB is defined in Algorithm 1. We use existing techniques, e.g. Automated Combinatorial Testing for Software (ACTS) [34], for generating a CMCA for constraints specified as logical formulae where factors are variables and levels are values for those variables. A CMCA is a set of k-tuples. Each such tuple defines the target level for each factor for a problem in the generated benchmark. Those levels are used to transform the given seed verification problem and the resultant problem is accumulated in the benchmark.

Algorithm 1: GDVB($\langle n_s, \phi_s \rangle, F, \Gamma, t$) Algorithm

---
    Data: a seed problem $\langle n_s, \phi_s \rangle$, a set of factors F and constraints Γ, a coverage
          goal t
    Result: A benchmark of DNN verification problems B
1   $C \leftarrow \text{GENCMCA}(F, \Gamma, t)$
2   $B \leftarrow \emptyset$
3   **for** $c \in C$ **do**
4 | $B \leftarrow B \cup \text{TRANSFORM}(\langle n_s, \phi_s \rangle, c)$
5   **end**

TRANSFORM uses different approaches to transform the seed DNN and the property. DNN transformation builds on an approach called R4V that automates architectural transformations to DNNs by scaling (1) the number of neurons in a fully connected layer, (2) the number of kernels in a convolutional layer, (3) the input dimension, or (4) the range of values within an input dimension [47]. The first 3 of these require changes to the structure of the DNN and the last two require changes to the training data, e.g., reshaping, renormalizing. R4V ensures that the network is well-defined after transformation. TRANSFORM maps factor-levels to per-layer scale parameters for R4V.

R4V permits the training of a network using network distillation which we find advantageous for GDVB because: it accelerates the training process, and it drives training to match the accuracy of the problem DNN to that of n_s, which reduces variation in accuracy across B. We adapt R4V so that after each training epoch, the learned DNN weights and the validation accuracy is recorded. When training finishes, we select the weights associated with the highest validation accuracy. Training is performed using the training data and hyperparameters for n_s.

Whereas R4V can be used to directly manipulate DNN architecture related factors, it can only indirectly affect the learned weights. To address this, we adopt the approach taken throughout the machine learning literature – train a network on multiple initial seeds and report performance across seeds. Thus, each DNN in B is trained multiple times, thereby producing a benchmark comprised of $s * |B|$ verification problems, where is the desired number of seeds.

DNN Transformation Example. Consider this element of the CMCA described above: $\langle (50\%, 100\%, 50\%), \phi \rangle$, applied to DAVE-2. TRANSFORM would compute that 50% of the fully connected layers should be present in the resultant DNN and randomly select 2 of the 4 layers to scale by 0. The fully-connected layers are chosen at random, since the layer count factor does not consider layer ordering. If we consider the case where the layers with 100 and 50 neurons are dropped, this will eliminate 150 neurons. The other transformation required is to reduce the number of neurons by half. To do that all remaining layers will be scaled by $\frac{82668 * 0.5 - 150}{82688} = 0.498$.

Property transformation builds on a domain-specific language (DSL) for specifying DNN correctness properties defined by the *deep neural network verification framework* (DNNV) [48]. Specifications in this Python-based DSL are parametric and TRANSFORM maps factor-levels to those parameters. For example, Fig. 2 defines the parametric local robustness property ϕ that is centered at the image stored at "path/to/image", has radius 0.02, and can be translated and scaled through parameters t and s, respectively.

Restricting factors to levels that are supported by TRANSFORM and using CMCA algorithms that meet Definition 2 ensures that GDVB produces a solution that meets Definition 3.

```
N=Network("N")
s=Parameter("s",float,
            default=1.0)
e=0.02*s
x=Image("path/to/image")
t=np.load(Parameter("t",
    str,
    "path/to/zeros.npy"))
x=x+t
Forall(x_,
  Implies(
  (x-e)<x_<(x+e),
  abs(N(x_)-N(x)) <= 5
)
```

Fig. 2. Parametric property ϕ

4.4   An Instantiation of GDVB

We developed an instance of GDVB[3] that supports a set of factors informed by the results of the study in Sect. 3, *percentage-based levels* for those factors, and a

---

[3] https://github.com/edwardxu0/GDVB.

set of constraints that restrict benchmark problems to those that are non-trivial and that can be efficiently trained.

Our instantiation of GDVB supports the following factors: the total number of neurons in the DNN (**neu**), the number of fully-connected layers (**fc**), the number of convolutional layers (**conv**), the dimension of the DNN input (**idm**), the size of each DNN input dimension (**ids**), the scale of the property (**scl**), and the translation of the property (**trn**). We do not support an activation function factor because only ERAN support non-ReLU activations and, thus, using them would render other verifiers inapplicable for large portions generated benchmarks.

We use quintile factor levels, {20%, 40%, 60%, 80%, 100%}, for factors neu, idm, ids, and scl. To permit the elimination of layer types we extend these levels with an additional quintile, 0%, for fc and conv. For trn, we select a set of five translations that shift the property to be centered on a different instance of the training data; unlike the above levels this level is unordered.

Our instantiation of GDVB exclusion constraints for DAVE-2 are as follows: (1) $fc = 0 \land conv = 0$, (2) $conv = 0 \land neu \geq 20$, (3) $conv = 0 \land idm \geq 80$, and (4) $conv = 100 \land idm = 20$. The first of these requires that some layer be present. The second and third are related to the blowup in the size of fully-connected layers that results from dropping all convolutional layers which makes training difficult; limiting the total number of neurons and the reduction input dimension mitigates this. The fourth constraint ensures that the input dimension reduction results in a meaningful network; without it the dimensionality reduction achieved by sequences of convolutional layers yields an invalid network, i.e., the input to some layer is smaller than the kernel size.

These constraints were developed iteratively based on feedback from the R4V tool, which reports when TRANSFORM has specified an invalid DNN, and when training failed to closely approximate the accuracy of the seed network.

We note that this instance of GDVB is flexible in that it permits the customization of levels, as we demonstrate in the next section, to generate a benchmark that focuses on variation in a subset of factors. More generally, GDVB can easily be extended to support additional factors and levels for which an instance of TRANSFORM can be defined. We expect that GDVB will evolve in this way as studies of DNN verifiers are performed.

5   GDVB in Use

In this section we showcase the potential uses of GDVB across a series of artifacts and verifiers, while highlighting the challenges it helps to systematically address.

5.1   Setup

Our evaluation applies GDVB to two seed networks: MNIST$_{ConvBig}$ and DAVE-2. We selected MNIST$_{ConvBig}$ because it is one of the largest networks in

ERAN's evaluation [50]; it includes 4 convolutional layers and 3 fully connected layers with 48,074 neurons and 1,974,762 parameters. We selected DAVE-2 to illustrate the application of GDVB to a larger network that has been the subject of other DNN analysis [42]; it has 5 convolutional layers and 5 fully connected layers with 82,669 neurons and 2,116,983 parameters.

Table 1 lists the 9 verifiers we selected for our study. This list includes the most well-known verifiers and verification algorithms. We also select variations of some verification approaches. We use Branch-and-Bound (BAB), as well as a variation of Branch-and-Bound with Smart-Branching (BABSB). Additionally, we evaluate the ERAN verifier with 4 available abstract domains: DeepZono (ERAN$_{DZ}$), DeepPoly (ERAN$_{DP}$), RefineZono (ERAN$_{RZ}$), and RefinePoly (ERAN$_{RP}$).

Table 1. Verifiers used in GDVB study

Verifier	Algorithm
RELUPLEX [30]	Search-optimization
PLANET [20]	Search-optimization
BAB [14]	Search-optimization
BABSB [14]	Search-optimization
NEURIFY[a] [59]	Optimization
ERAN$_{DZ}$ [50]	Reachability
ERAN$_{DP}$ [51]	Reachability
ERAN$_{RZ}$ [52]	Reachability
ERAN$_{RP}$ [49]	Reachability

[a]We use the version of NEURIFY provided in DNNV [48], which is modified to be applicable to a wide range of problems, whereas the original version was hard-coded to a particular verification problem [59].

To evaluate verifier performance, we use the *solution-count ranking* (SCR) [57], which counts the number of properties that returned accurate verification results. Additionally, we measured the *penalized average runtime* (PAR2) [6], which is computed as the sum of the verification times for *sat* and *unsat* results and twice time limit for all other verification results.

Table 2. Mean & variance of SCR and PAR2 scores across benchmarks. (The darker and lighter gray boxes indicate the best and second best results.)

Verifier	MNIST$_{ConvBig}$		DAVE-2	
	SCR	PAR2	SCR	PAR2
ERAN$_{DZ}$	11.40 ± 0.49	$18,126.80 \pm 488.27$	7.20 ± 1.94	$24,496.20 \pm 1,176.59$
ERAN$_{DP}$	21.00 ± 0.89	$9,206.00 \pm 806.70$	18.40 ± 2.15	$17,443.00 \pm 1,344.65$
ERAN$_{RZ}$	10.20 ± 0.40	$19,252.60 \pm 343.66$	5.80 ± 2.14	$25,236.60 \pm 1,253.90$
ERAN$_{RP}$	12.60 ± 1.02	$16,981.40 \pm 930.71$	10.20 ± 1.83	$22,250.60 \pm 1,186.44$
NEURIFY	22.00 ± 1.10	$8,636.20 \pm 1,008.63$	19.20 ± 2.56	$17,247.80 \pm 1,397.05$
PLANET	7.00 ± 0.63	$23,145.60 \pm 468.18$	3.40 ± 1.62	$27,268.60 \pm 775.56$
BAB	0.20 ± 0.40	$28,689.80 \pm 220.40$	0.00 ± 0.00	$28,800.00 \pm 0.00$
BABSB	0.00 ± 0.00	$28,800.00 \pm 0.00$	0.00 ± 0.00	$28,800.00 \pm 0.00$
RELUPLEX	3.20 ± 0.40	$25,757.80 \pm 381.40$	4.40 ± 1.02	$26,023.60 \pm 635.90$

All training and verification took place under CentOS Linux 7. R4V transformation and distillation jobs ran on NVIDIA 1080Ti GPUs. Verification jobs were limited to 4 h and ran on 2.3 GHz and 2.2 GHz Xeon processors with 64 GB of memory, for DAVE-2 and MNIST$_{ConvBig}$, respectively.

5.2   Comparing Verifiers Across a Range of Challenges

Consider the use case where a researcher is attempting to compare a new verifier (e.g., a new algorithm, a revised implementation, an extension to an existing approach) against existing verifiers. As shown earlier, for such comparison to be meaningful, many factors must be considered and properly explored. Given a seed network, a property, a set of factors, and a coverage goal, GDVB can generate a benchmark that helps to reduce bias in conducting such an evaluation.

For this use case we consider seed networks and local robustness properties similar to those from the ERAN$_{DZ}$ study [50] for the MNIST$_{ConvBig}$ verification problem and local robustness properties based on those from the NEURIFY study [59] for the DAVE-2 verification problem. We run an instance of GDVB using the factors and levels described in Sect. 4.4, a coverage strength of 2, and train 5 versions of each network to account for stochastic weight variation. The total time to generate and train GDVB (MNIST$_{ConvBig}$, ...) was 24.3 h and the resulting 30 verification problems took 401.8 h to run across all 9 verifiers. For GDVB (DAVE-2, ...) 44 verification problems were generated with training and verification times of 158.2 h and 772.4 h, respectively. CMCA generation took less than a minute for both problems. Each problem in the benchmark must be trained and verified in sequence, but across problems they can be parallelized. We exploited this to reduce the cost of running the benchmarks to 4.9 h for MNIST$_{ConvBig}$ and 7.9 h for DAVE-2. We measured the SCR and PAR2 score for the nine verifiers across the benchmarks.

The results are shown in Table 2. Since the SCR and PAR2 score trends are the same we depict just SCR in Fig. 3. Boxplots show the SCR scores for a verifier across all the generated problems; variation in plots arises from the 5 trained versions of the networks for each problem. For each box, the middle line represent the median, the box-bounds are the first and third quartiles, and the whiskers represent minimal and maximal values.

The plot for MNIST$_{ConvBig}$ on the left of Fig. 3 shows that **the GDVB benchmark with the MNIST$_{ConvBig}$ seed is able to identify considerable performance variation across verifiers**, with ERAN$_{DP}$ and NEURIFY accurately verifying a median of over 20 properties, the rest of the ERAN-variants verifying between 10 and 13 properties, and the remaining tools verifying between 0 and 8 properties. The results are consistent when we employ DAVE-2 as the seed network, with **marked differences among groups of verifiers** although the generated problems turned out to be more challenging across all verifiers. ERAN$_{DP}$ and NEURIFY, the top performers, can verify less than half of the generated problems. Verifiers like BAB were unable to verify any problem derived from DAVE-2 because of the complexity of the seed problem. This point highlights the need for benchmarks to evolve with networks that incorporate emerging technology, and also GDVB's ability to automatically generate a benchmark from different seeds to address that need.

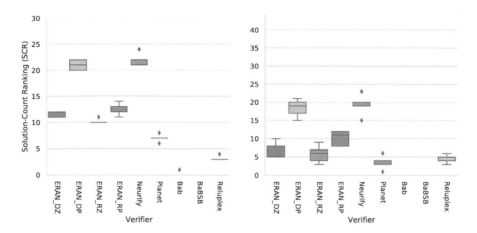

Fig. 3. SCR score for nine verifiers on GDVB benchmarks with MNIST$_{ConvBig}$ (left) and DAVE-2 (right) seeds

Now, understanding the overall performance of a family of verifiers is useful but it is likely just the first step for a researcher to understand under what conditions a verifier excels or struggles. When such conditions correspond to the factors manipulated by GDVB, then they are readily available for further analysis. One analysis may consist of simply plotting the data across its multiple dimensions. We do so in the form of radar-charts for DAVE-2 in Fig. 4 and for MNIST$_{ConvBig}$ in Fig. 5[4]. Since the observations we can gather from both networks are similar, we just discuss DAVE-2 in detail. Each chart includes six axes representing a factor scaled between 0 and 1. The solid lines link the maximum values across factors that were accurately verified while the dotted lines link the median values across factors.

The shape of the lines in the radar plots clearly show that the **verification problems generated by GDVB reveal unique patterns across the verifiers**. For example, the RELUPLEX plot indicates that it can do well verifying networks with multiple fully connected (fc) layers but is challenged by larger networks (neu) and those with convolutional layers (conv). Comparing multiple charts also reveals some interesting trade-offs. For example, for smaller networks with just fully connected layers, the medians seem to indicate that RELUPLEX is better than PLANET. However, when a network incorporates convolutional layers or a larger number of neurons, PLANET appears to outperform RELUPLEX.

Looking across charts can also pinpoint specific improvements resulting from tool extensions or revisions. For example, the median line of ERAN$_{RZ}$ indicates that it was not as effective in handling verification problems with a larger number of layers as its predecessor ERAN$_{DZ}$; the same trend holds for the pair ERAN$_{RP}$ and ERAN$_{DP}$. We note that a more restrictive benchmark that is biased towards fewer fully connected layers might not reveal such differences.

---

[4] We do not plot BABSB as its performance was identical to BAB.

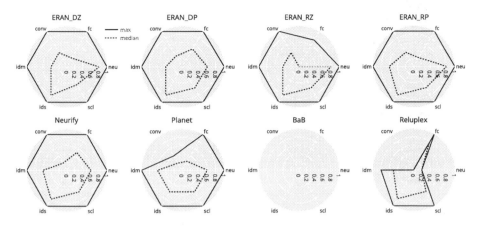

Fig. 4. DAVE-2: radar plot with maximum (solid) and median (dotted) values

GDVB offers the opportunity to investigate such differences even further by generating targeted verification problems for a subset of factors hypothesized to be culprits of those differences. For example, GDVB could generate additional verification problems with a number of fully connected layers between 60% and 80% of the total, while keeping the other factors constant, to refine the understanding of the differences between $ERAN_{RZ}$ and $ERAN_{DZ}$.

This study illustrates how GDVB benchmarks support the exploration of verifier performance, lowering the burden on researchers to manually prepare tens to hundreds of verification problems, and reducing the opportunities for bias.

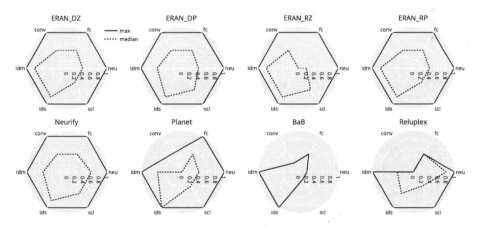

Fig. 5. MNIST$_{ConvBig}$: radar plot with maximum (solid) and median (dotted) values

5.3   GDVB and Benchmark Requirements R1–R3

As explained in Sect. 1, benchmarking in verification seeks to develop benchmarks that are: diverse; representative of real use cases; and reactive to new technologies. The previous sections have provided evidence of how, through its generative nature, GDVB is reactive to new advances in technology included in the seed network. We have also seen the high degree of parameterization GDVB offers including for setting a seed network from which realistic attributes are inherited in the generated verification problems. In this section we want to illustrate how GDVB addresses the diversity requirement.

To depict diversity we use the parallel coordinate graph in Fig. 6. Each vertical line corresponds to a factor, and the markers in each vertical line corresponds to an explored level. Each verification problem is a polyline that connects the factors' levels explored by it. The two sets of lines correspond to the verification problems included in the DAVE-2 benchmark published with NEURIFY [59], which is a downsized version of the full DAVE-2 DNN, and the benchmark produced by GDVB (DAVE-2, ...). Each factor in the plot is normalized by dividing by the maximum value for the factor.

Figure 6 shows that the NEURIFY's DAVE-2 has a large number of neurons, inputs, and dimensions. Yet, it provides very limited coverage of all the factor levels that may affect verification performance. In contrast, GDVB provides a systematic exploration of the factors levels that can affect verifier performance making it much less biased – especially to the numbers of layers in the verification problems, and the combination of those factor levels.

The parallel plot for GDVB benchmark with the $MNIST_{ConvBig}$ seed (not shown for space reasons), depicts a similar trend in terms of systematic exploration of diversity, but since $MNIST_{ConvBig}$ is simpler than DAVE-2, the generated benchmark is correspondingly simpler. This points to the need to identify representative and challenging seeds when parameterizing GDVB. GDVB is fully capable of accomodating factor levels that exceed 100% of a seed network, which is a means of pushing verifiers to the limits of their abilities.

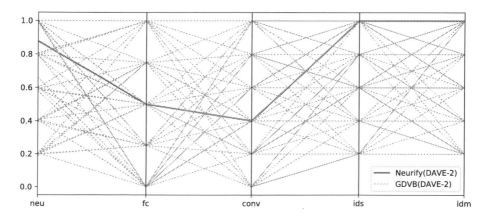

Fig. 6. Diversity explored across factor levels

We note that excluding factors or levels can yield a systematically generated benchmark that is unable to characterize differences between verifiers, or worse, misleads such a characterization by emphasizing certain factors while overlooking others. For example, not exploring different network sizes or exploring networks sizes under 1000 neurons will render similar scores across many DNN verifiers that are differentiated by more comprehensive benchmarks. In applying GDVB, we suggest selecting as many factors as we know may matter, starting from a challenging seed problem, and incrementally refining the levels as needed to focus benchmark results to differentiate verifier performance.

6 Conclusion

The increasing adoption of DNNs has led to a surge in research on DNN verification techniques. Benchmarks to assess these emerging techniques, however, are costly to develop, often lack in diversity and do not represent the population of real evolving DNNs. To address this challenge, we have introduced GDVB, a framework for systematically generating DNN verification problems seeded in complex, real-world networks, ensuring that benchmarks are derived from real problems. GDVB is parameterizable by the factors that may influence verification performance and thereby supports scalable benchmarking. A preliminary study, using 9 DNN verifiers, demonstrates how GDVB can support the assessment of the state-of-the-art.

We plan to conduct broader studies of verifier performance using GDVB, and we encourate other researchers to use and contribute to it. There are many directions to explore in identifying new factors that influence performance, e.g., the impact of quantization and model compression approaches [26]. Work in this direction promises to deepen the community's understanding and lead to advances in DNN verification.

Acknowledgements. This material is based in part upon work supported by the National Science Foundation under grant numbers 1901769 and 1900676, by the U.S. Army Research Office under grant number W911NF-19-1-0054.

References

1. 14th International Satisfiability Modulo Theories Competition. https://smt-comp. github.io/2019/
2. Competition on Software Verification. https://sv-comp.sosy-lab.org/2019/
3. Hardware Model Checking Competition. http://fmv.jku.at/hwmcc19/index.html
4. The International Satisfiability Competitions. http://www.satcompetition.org/
5. Amendola, G., Ricca, F., Truszczynski, M.: A generator of hard 2QBF formulas and ASP programs. In: 16th International Conference on Principles of Knowledge Representation and Reasoning (2018)
6. Balint, A., Belov, A., Järvisalo, M., Sinz, C.: Overview and analysis of the SAT challenge 2012 solver competition. Artif. Intell. **223**, 120–155 (2015)

7. Barrett, C., Deters, M., De Moura, L., Oliveras, A., Stump, A.: 6 years of SMT-COMP. J. Autom. Reasoning **50**(3), 243–277 (2013)
8. Barrett, C., Stump, A., Tinelli, C.: The SMT-LIB standard: version 2.0, vol. 13, p. 14 (2010)
9. Bastani, O., Ioannou, Y., Lampropoulos, L., Vytiniotis, D., Nori, A.V., Criminisi, A.: Measuring neural net robustness with constraints. In: Proceedings of the 30th International Conference on Neural Information Processing Systems, pp. 2621–2629 (2016)
10. Beyer, D., Löwe, S., Wendler, P.: Reliable benchmarking: requirements and solutions. Int. J. Softw. Tools Technol. Transfer **21**(1), 1–29 (2019)
11. Blackburn, S.M., et al.: The DaCapo benchmarks: Java benchmarking development and analysis. In: Proceedings of the 21st Annual ACM SIGPLAN Conference on Object-Oriented Programming Systems, Languages, and Applications, pp. 169–190 (2006)
12. Bojarski, M., et al.: End to end learning for self-driving cars. CoRR (2016)
13. Boopathy, A., Weng, T.W., Chen, P.Y., Liu, S., Daniel, L.: CNN-Cert: an efficient framework for certifying robustness of convolutional neural networks. In: Association for the Advancement of Artificial Intelligence, January 2019
14. Bunel, R., Turkaslan, I., Torr, P.H., Kohli, P., Kumar, M.P.: A unified view of piecewise linear neural network verification. In: Proceedings of the 32nd International Conference on Neural Information Processing Systems, pp. 4795–4804 (2018)
15. Cohen, M.B., Dwyer, M.B., Shi, J.: Constructing interaction test suites for highly-configurable systems in the presence of constraints: a greedy approach. IEEE Trans. Softw. Eng. **34**(5), 633–650 (2008)
16. Cohen, M.B., Gibbons, P.B., Mugridge, W.B., Colbourn, C.J.: Constructing test suites for interaction testing. In: 25th International Conference on Software Engineering, pp. 38–48, May 2003
17. D'silva, V., Kroening, D., Weissenbacher, G.: A survey of automated techniques for formal software verification. IEEE Trans. Comput.-Aided Des. Integr. Circuits Syst. **27**(7), 1165–1178 (2008)
18. Dutta, S., Jha, S., Sankaranarayanan, S., Tiwari, A.: Output range analysis for deep feedforward neural networks. In: NASA Formal Methods Symposium, pp. 121–138 (2018)
19. Dvijotham, K., Stanforth, R., Gowal, S., Mann, T., Kohli, P.: A dual approach to scalable verification of deep networks. In: Proceedings of the 34th Conference Annual Conference on Uncertainty in Artificial Intelligence, pp. 162–171 (2018)
20. Ehlers, R.: Formal verification of piece-wise linear feed-forward neural networks. In: D'Souza, D., Narayan Kumar, K. (eds.) ATVA 2017. LNCS, vol. 10482, pp. 269–286. Springer, Cham (2017). https://doi.org/10.1007/978-3-319-68167-2_19
21. Elffers, J., Giráldez-Cru, J., Gocht, S., Nordström, J., Simon, L.: Seeking practical CDCL insights from theoretical SAT benchmarks. In: International Joint Conferences on Artificial Intelligence, pp. 1300–1308 (2018)
22. Gehr, T., Mirman, M., Drachsler-Cohen, D., Tsankov, P., Chaudhuri, S., Vechev, M.: AI2: safety and robustness certification of neural networks with abstract interpretation. In: IEEE Symposium on Security and Privacy, pp. 3–18, May 2018
23. Goodfellow, I., Bengio, Y., Courville, A.: Deep Learning, vol. 1. MIT Press, Cambridge (2016)
24. Gopinath, D., Converse, H., Pasareanu, C.S., Taly, A.: Property inference for deep neural networks. In: 34th IEEE/ACM International Conference on Automated Software Engineering, pp. 797–809 (2019)

25. Gupta, A.: Formal hardware verification methods: a survey. In: Kurshan, R. (ed.) Computer Aided Verification, pp. 5–92. Springer, Boston (1992). https://doi.org/10.1007/978-1-4615-3556-0_2
26. Han, S., Mao, H., Dally, W.J.: Deep compression: compressing deep neural networks with pruning, trained quantization and Huffman coding (2015)
27. Hinton, G., et al.: Deep neural networks for acoustic modeling in speech recognition: the shared views of four research groups. IEEE Signal Process. Mag. **29**(6), 82–97 (2012)
28. Hinton, G., Vinyals, O., Dean, J.: Distilling the knowledge in a neural network. In: NIPS Deep Learning and Representation Learning Workshop (2015)
29. Huang, X., Kwiatkowska, M., Wang, S., Wu, M.: Safety verification of deep neural networks. In: Majumdar, R., Kunčak, V. (eds.) CAV 2017. LNCS, vol. 10426, pp. 3–29. Springer, Cham (2017). https://doi.org/10.1007/978-3-319-63387-9_1
30. Katz, G., Barrett, C., Dill, D.L., Julian, K., Kochenderfer, M.J.: Reluplex: an efficient SMT solver for verifying deep neural networks. In: Majumdar, R., Kunčak, V. (eds.) CAV 2017. LNCS, vol. 10426, pp. 97–117. Springer, Cham (2017). https://doi.org/10.1007/978-3-319-63387-9_5
31. Katz, G., et al.: The Marabou framework for verification and analysis of deep neural networks. In: Dillig, I., Tasiran, S. (eds.) CAV 2019. LNCS, vol. 11561, pp. 443–452. Springer, Cham (2019). https://doi.org/10.1007/978-3-030-25540-4_26
32. Krizhevsky, A., Sutskever, I., Hinton, G.E.: ImageNet classification with deep convolutional neural networks. In: Advances in Neural Information Processing Systems 25: Proceedings of the 26th Annual Conference on Neural Information Processing Systems 2012, pp. 1106–1114 (2012)
33. Kropf, T.: Benchmark-circuits for hardware-verification. In: Kumar, R., Kropf, T. (eds.) TPCD 1994. LNCS, vol. 901, pp. 1–12. Springer, Heidelberg (1995). https://doi.org/10.1007/3-540-59047-1_39
34. Kuhn, R., Kacker, R.: Automated Combinatorial Testing for Software. https://csrc.nist.gov/projects/automated-combinatorial-testing-for-software
35. Lauria, M., Elffers, J., Nordström, J., Vinyals, M.: CNFgen: a generator of crafted benchmarks. In: Gaspers, S., Walsh, T. (eds.) SAT 2017. LNCS, vol. 10491, pp. 464–473. Springer, Cham (2017). https://doi.org/10.1007/978-3-319-66263-3_30
36. Lin, W., et al.: Robustness verification of classification deep neural networks via linear programming. In: Proceedings of the IEEE Conference on Computer Vision and Pattern Recognition, pp. 11418–11427 (2019)
37. Liu, C., Arnon, T., Lazarus, C., Barrett, C., Kochenderfer, M.J.: Algorithms for verifying deep neural networks. CoRR (2019)
38. Lomuscio, A., Maganti, L.: An approach to reachability analysis for feed-forward ReLU neural networks. CoRR (2017)
39. Loquercio, A., Maqueda, A.I., Blanco, C.R.D., Scaramuzza, D.: DroNet: learning to fly by driving. IEEE Robot. Autom. Lett. **3**, 1088–1095 (2018)
40. Meadows, C.A., Meadows, C.A.: Formal verification of cryptographic protocols: a survey. In: Pieprzyk, J., Safavi-Naini, R. (eds.) ASIACRYPT 1994. LNCS, vol. 917, pp. 133–150. Springer, Heidelberg (1995). https://doi.org/10.1007/BFb0000430
41. Mnih, V., et al.: Human-level control through deep reinforcement learning. Nature **518**(7540), 529–533 (2015)
42. Pei, K., Cao, Y., Yang, J., Jana, S.: DeepXplore: automated whitebox testing of deep learning systems. In: Proceedings of the 26th Symposium on Operating Systems Principles, pp. 1–18 (2017)

43. Pelánek, R.: BEEM: benchmarks for explicit model checkers. In: Bošnački, D., Edelkamp, S. (eds.) SPIN 2007. LNCS, vol. 4595, pp. 263–267. Springer, Heidelberg (2007). https://doi.org/10.1007/978-3-540-73370-6_17
44. Pulina, L., Tacchella, A.: An abstraction-refinement approach to verification of artificial neural networks. In: Touili, T., Cook, B., Jackson, P. (eds.) CAV 2010. LNCS, vol. 6174, pp. 243–257. Springer, Heidelberg (2010). https://doi.org/10.1007/978-3-642-14295-6_24
45. Raghunathan, A., Steinhardt, J., Liang, P.: Certified defenses against adversarial examples. In: The International Conference on Learning Representations (2018)
46. Ruan, W., Huang, X., Kwiatkowska, M.: Reachability analysis of deep neural networks with provable guarantees. In: International Joint Conferences on Artificial Intelligence, pp. 2651–2659 (2018)
47. Shriver, D., Xu, D., Elbaum, S.G., Dwyer, M.B.: Refactoring neural networks for verification. CoRR (2019)
48. Shriver, D.L.: Deep Neural Network Verification Toolbox. https://github.com/dlshriver/DNNV
49. Singh, G., Ganvir, R., Püschel, M., Vechev, M.: Beyond the single neuron convex barrier for neural network certification. In: Wallach, H., Larochelle, H., Beygelzimer, A., d'Alché-Buc, F., Fox, E., Garnett, R. (eds.) Advances in Neural Information Processing Systems 32, pp. 15072–15083 (2019)
50. Singh, G., Gehr, T., Mirman, M., Püschel, M., Vechev, M.: Fast and effective robustness certification. In: Bengio, S., Wallach, H., Larochelle, H., Grauman, K., Cesa-Bianchi, N., Garnett, R. (eds.) Advances in Neural Information Processing Systems 31, pp. 10802–10813 (2018)
51. Singh, G., Gehr, T., Püschel, M., Vechev, M.: An abstract domain for certifying neural networks. Proc. ACM Program. Lang. **3**, article no. 41 (2019)
52. Singh, G., Gehr, T., Püschel, M., Vechev, M.: Boosting robustness certification of neural networks. In: Proceedings of the International Conference on Learning Representations (2019)
53. Smolyanskiy, N., Kamenev, A., Smith, J., Birchfield, S.: Toward low-flying autonomous MAV trail navigation using deep neural networks for environmental awareness. In: IEEE/RSJ International Conference on Intelligent Robots and Systems, pp. 4241–4247, September 2017
54. Sutcliffe, G.: The TPTP problem library and associated infrastructure. J. Autom. Reasoning **43**(4), 337–362 (2009)
55. Sutcliffe, G., Suttner, C.: The TPTP problem library. J. Autom. Reasoning **21**(2), 177–203 (1998)
56. Tjeng, V., Xiao, K.Y., Tedrake, R.: Evaluating robustness of neural networks with mixed integer programming. In: International Conference on Learning Representations (2019)
57. Gelder, A.: Careful ranking of multiple solvers with timeouts and ties. In: Sakallah, K.A., Simon, L. (eds.) SAT 2011. LNCS, vol. 6695, pp. 317–328. Springer, Heidelberg (2011). https://doi.org/10.1007/978-3-642-21581-0_25
58. Wang, F.: Formal verification of timed systems: a survey and perspective. Proc. IEEE **92**(8), 1283–1305 (2004)
59. Wang, S., Pei, K., Whitehouse, J., Yang, J., Jana, S.: Efficient formal safety analysis of neural networks. In: Advances in Neural Information Processing Systems, pp. 6367–6377 (2018)
60. Wang, S., Pei, K., Whitehouse, J., Yang, J., Jana, S.: Formal security analysis of neural networks using symbolic intervals. In: USENIX Security Symposium, pp. 1599–1614 (2018)

61. Weng, T., et al.: Towards fast computation of certified robustness for ReLU networks. In: International Conference on Machine Learning, Proceedings of Machine Learning Research, vol. 80, pp. 5273–5282 (2018)
62. Wong, E., Kolter, J.Z.: Provable defenses against adversarial examples via the convex outer adversarial polytope. In: International Conference on Machine Learning, Proceedings of Machine Learning Research, vol. 80, pp. 5283–5292 (2018)
63. Xiang, W., Tran, H., Johnson, T.T.: Output reachable set estimation and verification for multilayer neural networks. IEEE Trans. Neural Netw. Learn. Syst. **29**(11), 5777–5783 (2018)
64. You, J., Wu, H., Barrett, C., Ramanujan, R., Leskovec, J.: G2SAT: learning to generate SAT formulas. In: Advances in Neural Information Processing Systems, pp. 10552–10563 (2019)

Formal Analysis and Redesign of a Neural Network-Based Aircraft Taxiing System with VERIFAI

Daniel J. Fremont[1,2]($\boxtimes$), Johnathan Chiu[2], Dragos D. Margineantu[3],
Denis Osipychev[3], and Sanjit A. Seshia[2]

[1] University of California, Santa Cruz, USA
dfremont@ucsc.edu
[2] University of California, Berkeley, USA
[3] Boeing Research & Technology, Seattle, USA

Abstract. We demonstrate a unified approach to rigorous design of safety-critical autonomous systems using the VERIFAI toolkit for formal analysis of AI-based systems. VERIFAI provides an integrated toolchain for tasks spanning the design process, including modeling, falsification, debugging, and ML component retraining. We evaluate all of these applications in an industrial case study on an experimental autonomous aircraft taxiing system developed by Boeing, which uses a neural network to track the centerline of a runway. We define runway scenarios using the SCENIC probabilistic programming language, and use them to drive tests in the X-Plane flight simulator. We first perform falsification, automatically finding environment conditions causing the system to violate its specification by deviating significantly from the centerline (or even leaving the runway entirely). Next, we use counterexample analysis to identify distinct failure cases, and confirm their root causes with specialized testing. Finally, we use the results of falsification and debugging to retrain the network, eliminating several failure cases and improving the overall performance of the closed-loop system.

Keywords: Falsification · Automated testing · Debugging · Simulation · Autonomous systems · Machine learning

1   Introduction

The expanding use of machine learning (ML) in safety-critical applications has led to an urgent need for rigorous design methodologies that can ensure the reliability of systems with ML components [15,17]. Such a methodology would need to provide tools for *modeling* the system, its requirements, and its environment, *analyzing* a design to find failure cases, *debugging* such cases, and finally *synthesizing* improved designs.

The VERIFAI toolkit [1] provides a unified framework for all of these design tasks, based on a simple paradigm: simulation driven by formal models and

© The Author(s) 2020
S. K. Lahiri and C. Wang (Eds.): CAV 2020, LNCS 12224, pp. 122–134, 2020.
https://doi.org/10.1007/978-3-030-53288-8_6

specifications. The top-level architecture of VERIFAI is shown in Fig. 1. We first define an *abstract feature space* describing the environments and system configurations of interest, either by explicitly defining parameter ranges or using the SCENIC probabilistic environment modeling language [6]. VERIFAI then generates concrete tests by searching this space, using a variety of algorithms ranging from random sampling to global optimization techniques. Finally, we simulate the system for each test, monitoring the satisfaction or violation of a system-level specification; the results of each test are used to guide further search, and any violations are recorded in a table for automated analysis (e.g. clustering) or visualization. This architecture enables a wide range of use cases, including falsification, fuzz testing, debugging, data augmentation, and parameter synthesis; Dreossi et al. [1] demonstrated all of these applications individually through several small case studies.

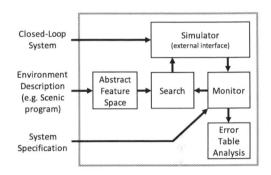

Fig. 1. Architecture of VERIFAI.

In this paper, we provide an *integrated* case study, applying VERIFAI to a complete design flow for a large, realistic system from industry: TaxiNet, an experimental autonomous aircraft taxiing system developed by Boeing for the DARPA Assured Autonomy project. This system uses a neural network to estimate the aircraft's position from a camera image; a controller then steers the plane to track the centerline of the runway. The main requirement for TaxiNet, provided by Boeing, is that it keep the plane within 1.5 m of the centerline; we formalized this as a specification in Metric Temporal Logic (MTL) [11]. Verifying this specification is difficult, as the neural network must be able to handle the wide range of images resulting from different lighting conditions, changes in runway geometry, and other disturbances such as tire marks on the runway.

Our case study illustrates a complete iteration of the design flow for TaxiNet, analyzing and debugging an existing version of the system to inform an improved design. Specifically, we demonstrate:

1. Modeling the environment of the aircraft using the SCENIC language.
2. Falsifying an initial version of TaxiNet, finding environment conditions under which the aircraft significantly deviates from the centerline.
3. Analyzing counterexamples to identify distinct failure cases and diagnose potential root causes.
4. Testing the system in a targeted way to confirm these root causes.
5. Designing a new version of the system by retraining the neural network based on the results of falsification and debugging.
6. Validating that the new system eliminates some of the failure cases in the original system and has higher overall performance.

Following the procedure above, we were able to find several scenarios where TaxiNet exhibited unsafe behavior. For example, we found the system could not properly handle intersections between runways. More interestingly, we found that TaxiNet could get confused when the shadow of the plane was visible, which only occurred during certain times of day and weather conditions. We stress that these types of failure cases are meaningful counterexamples that could easily arise in the real world, unlike pixel-level adversarial examples [8]; we are able to find such cases because VERIFAI searches through a space of *semantic* parameters [3]. Furthermore, these counterexamples are *system-level*, demonstrating undesired behavior from the complete system rather than simply its ML component. Finally, our work differs from other works on validation of cyber-physical systems with ML components (e.g. [19]) in that we address a broader range of design tasks (including debugging and retraining as well as testing) and also allow designers to *guide* search by encoding domain knowledge using SCENIC.

For our case study, we extend VERIFAI in two ways. First, we interface the toolkit to the X-Plane flight simulator [12] in order to run closed-loop simulations of the entire system, with X-Plane rendering the camera images and simulating the aircraft dynamics. More importantly, we extend the SCENIC language to allow it to be used in combination with VERIFAI's active sampling techniques. Previously, as in any probabilistic programming language, a SCENIC program defined a fixed distribution [6]; while adequate for modeling particular scenarios, this is incompatible with active sampling, where we change how tests are generated over time in response to feedback from earlier tests. To reconcile these two approaches, we extend SCENIC with *parameters* that are assigned by an external sampler. This allows us to continue to use SCENIC's convenient syntax for modeling, while now being able to use not only random sampling but optimization or other algorithms to search the parameter space.

Adding parameters to SCENIC enables important new applications. For example, in the design flow we described above, after finding through testing some rare event which causes a failure, we need to generate a dataset of such failures in order to retrain the ML component. Naïvely, we would have to manually write a new SCENIC program whose distribution was concentrated on these rare events (as was done in [6]). With parameters, we can simply take the generic SCENIC program we used for the initial testing, and use VERIFAI's cross-entropy sampler [1,14] to automatically converge to such a distribution [16]. Alternatively, if we have an intuition about where a failure case may lie, we can use SCENIC to encode this domain knowledge as a *prior* for cross-entropy sampling, helping the latter to find failures more quickly.

In summary, the novel contributions of this paper are:

- The first demonstration on an industrial case study of an integrated toolchain for falsification, debugging, and retraining of ML-based autonomous systems.
- An interface between VERIFAI and the X-Plane flight simulator.

– An extension of the SCENIC language with parameters, and a demonstration using it in conjunction with cross-entropy sampling to learn a SCENIC program encoding the distribution of failure cases.

We begin in Sect. 2 with a discussion of our extension of SCENIC with parameters and our X-Plane interface. Section 3 presents the experimental setup and results of our case study, and we close in Sect. 4 with some conclusions and directions for future work.

2   Extensions of VERIFAI

SCENIC *with Parameters*. To enable search algorithms other than random sampling to be used with SCENIC we extend the language with a concept of *external parameters* assigned by an *external sampler*. A SCENIC program can specify an external sampler to use; this sampler will define the allowed types of parameters, which can then be used in the program in place of any distribution. The default external sampler provides access to the VERIFAI samplers and defines parameter types corresponding to VERIFAI's continuous and discrete ranges. Thus for example one could write a SCENIC program which picks the colors of two cars randomly according to some realistic distribution, but chooses the distance between them using VERIFAI's Bayesian Optimization sampler.

The semantics of external parameters is simple: when sampling from a SCENIC program, the external sampler is first queried to provide values for all the parameters; the program is then equivalent to one without parameters, and can be sampled as usual[1].

X-Plane Interface. Our interface between X-Plane and VERIFAI uses the latter's client-server architecture for communicating with simulators. The server runs inside VERIFAI, taking each generated feature vector and sending it to the client. The client runs inside X-Plane and calls its APIs to set up and execute the test, reporting back information needed to monitor the specifications. For our client, we used X-Plane Connect [18], an X-Plane plugin providing access to X-Plane's "datarefs". These are named values which represent simulator state, e.g., positions of aircraft and weather conditions. Our interface exposes all datarefs to SCENIC, allowing arbitrary distributions to be placed on them. We also set up the SCENIC coordinate system to be aligned with the runway, performing the appropriate conversions to set the raw position datarefs.

3   TaxiNet Case Study

3.1   Experimental Setup

TaxiNet's neural network estimates the aircraft's position from a camera image; the camera is mounted on the right wing and faces forward. Example images are

---

[1] One complication arises because SCENIC uses rejection sampling to enforce constraints: if a sample is rejected, what value should be returned to active samplers that expect feedback, e.g. a cross-entropy sampler? By default we return a special value indicating a rejection occurred.

shown in Fig. 2. From such an image, the network estimates the *cross-track error (CTE)*, the left-right offset of the plane from the centerline, and the *heading error (HE)*, the angular offset of the plane from directly down the centerline. These estimates are fed into a handwritten controller which outputs (the equivalent of) a steering angle for the plane.

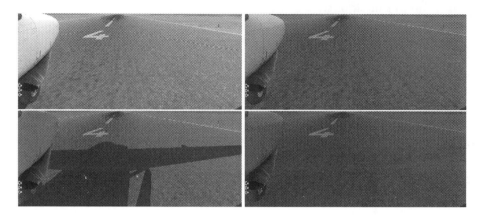

Fig. 2. Example input images to TaxiNet, rendered in X-Plane. Left/right = clear/cloudy weather. Top/bottom = 12 pm/4 pm.

The Boeing team provided the Berkeley team with an initial version of Taxi-Net without describing which images were used to train it. In this way, the Berkeley team were not aware in advance of potential gaps in the training set and corresponding potential failure cases[2]. For retraining experiments, the same sizes of training and validation sets were used as for the original model, as well as identical training hyperparameters.

The semantic feature space defined by our SCENIC programs and searched by VERIFAI was 6-dimensional, made up of the following parameters[3]:

- the initial position and orientation of the aircraft (in 2D, on the runway);
- the type of clouds, out of 6 discrete options ranging from clear to stormy;
- the amount of rain, as a percentage, and
- the time of day.

---

[2] After drawing conclusions from initial runs of all the experiments, the Berkeley team were informed of the training parameters and trained their own version of TaxiNet locally, repeating the experiments. This was done in order to ensure that minor differences in the training/testing platforms at Boeing and Berkeley did not affect the results (which was in fact qualitatively the case). All numerical results and graphs use data from this second round of experiments.

[3] We originally had additional parameters controlling the position and appearance of a tire mark superimposed on the runway (using a custom X-Plane plugin to do such rendering), but deleted the tire mark for simplicity after experiments showed its effect on TaxiNet was negligible.

Given values for these parameters from VerifAI, the test protocol we used in all of our experiments was identical: we set up the initial condition described by the parameters, then simulated TaxiNet controlling the plane for 30 s.

The main requirement for TaxiNet provided by Boeing was that it should always track the centerline of the runway to within 1.5 m. For many of our experiments we created a greater variety of test scenarios by allowing the plane to start up to 8 m off of the centerline: in such cases we required that the plane approach within 1.5 m of the centerline within 10 s and then stay there for the remainder of the simulation. We formalized these two specifications as MTL formulas φ_{always} and $\varphi_{\text{eventually}}$ respectively:

$$\varphi_{\text{always}} = \Box(\text{CTE} \leq 1.5) \qquad \varphi_{\text{eventually}} = \Diamond_{[0,10]}\Box(\text{CTE} \leq 1.5)$$

While both of these specifications are true/false properties, VerifAI uses a continuous quantity ρ called the *robustness* of an MTL formula [4]. Its crucial property is that $\rho \geq 0$ when the formula is satisfied, while $\rho \leq 0$ when the formula is violated, so that ρ provides a metric of *how close* the system is to violating the property. The exact definition of ρ is not important here, but as an illustration, for φ_{always} it is (the negation of) the greatest deviation beyond the allowed 1.5 m achieved over the whole simulation.

For additional experimental results, see the Appendix of the full version [5].

3.2   Falsification

In our first experiment, we searched for conditions in the nominal operating regime of TaxiNet which cause it to violate $\varphi_{\text{eventually}}$. To do this, we wrote a SCENIC program $\mathcal{S}_{\text{falsif}}$ modeling that regime, shown in Fig. 3. We first place a uniform distribution on time of day between 6 am and 6 pm local time (approximate daylight hours). Next, we determine the weather. Since only some of the cloud types are compatible with rain, we put a joint distribution on them: with probability 2/3, there is no rain, and any cloud type is equally likely; otherwise, there is a uniform amount of rain between 25% and 100%[4], and we allow only cloud types consistent with rain. Finally, we position the plane uniformly up to 8 m left or right of the centerline, up to 2000 m down the runway, and up to 30° off of the centerline. These ranges ensured that (1) the plane began on the runway and stayed on it for the entire simulation when tracking succeeded, and (2) it was always possible to reach the centerline within 10 s and so satisfy $\varphi_{\text{eventually}}$.

---

[4] The 25% lower bound is because we observed that X-Plane seemed to only render rain at all when the rain fraction was around that value or higher.

```
# Time of day: from 6 am to 6 pm. (+8 to get GMT, as used by X-Plane)
param zulu_time = ((6, 18) + 8) * 60 * 60

# Rain: 1/3 of the time. Clouds: rain requires types 3-5; otherwise 0-5.
clouds_and_rain = Options({
    tuple([Uniform(0, 1, 2, 3, 4, 5), 0]): 2,   # no rain
    tuple([Uniform(3, 4, 5), (0.25, 1)]): 1      # 25% to 100% rain
})
param cloud_type = clouds_and_rain[0], rain_percent = clouds_and_rain[1]

# Plane: up to 8 m left/right, 2000 m down the runway, 30° left/right.
ego = Plane at (-8, 8) @ (0, 2000),
             facing (-30, 30) deg
```

Fig. 3. Generic SCENIC program S_{falsif} used for falsification and retraining.

However, it was quite easy to find falsifying initial conditions within this scenario. We simulated over 4,000 runs randomly sampled from S_{falsif}, and found many counterexamples: in only 55% of the runs did TaxiNet satisfy $\varphi_{eventually}$, and in 9.1% of runs, the plane left the runway entirely. This showed that TaxiNet's behavior was problematic, but did not explain *why*. To answer that question, we analyzed the data VERIFAI collected during falsification, as we explain next.

3.3   Error Analysis and Debugging

VERIFAI builds a table which stores for each run the point sampled from the abstract feature space and the resulting robustness value ρ (see Sect. 3.1) for the specification. The table is compatible with the *pandas* data science library [13], making visualization easy. While VERIFAI contains algorithms for automatic analysis of the table (e.g., clustering and Principal Component Analysis), we do not use them here since the parameter space was low-dimensional enough to identify failure cases by direct visualization.

We began by plotting TaxiNet's performance as a function of each of the parameters in our falsification scenario. Several parameters had a large impact on performance:

- **Time of day:** Figure 4 plots ρ vs. time of day, each orange dot representing a run during falsification; the red line is their median, using 30-min bins (ignore the blue dots for now). Note the strong time-dependence: for example, TaxiNet works well in the late morning (almost all runs having $\rho > 0$ and so satisfying $\varphi_{eventually}$) but consistently fails to track the centerline in the early morning.
- **Clouds:** Figure 5 shows the median performance curves (as in Fig. 4) for 3 of X-Plane's cloud types: no clouds, moderate "overcast" clouds, and dark "stratus" clouds. Notice that at 8 am TaxiNet performs much worse with stratus clouds than no clouds, while at 2 pm the situation is reversed. Performance also varies quite irregularly when there are no clouds — we will analyze why this is the case shortly.

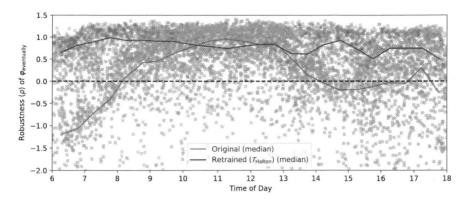

Fig. 4. Performance of TaxiNet as a function of time of day, before and after retraining. (Color figure online)

- **Distance along the runway:** The green data in Fig. 6 show performance as a function of how far down the runway the plane starts (ignore the orange/purple data for now). TaxiNet behaves similarly along the whole length of the runway, except around 1350–1500 m, where it veers completely off of the runway ($\rho \approx -30$). Consulting the airport map, we find that another runway intersects the one we tested with at approximately 1450 m. Images from the simulations show that at this intersection, both the centerline and edge markings of our test runway are obscured.

These visualizations identify several problematic behaviors of TaxiNet: consistently poor performance in the early morning, irregular performance at certain times depending on clouds, and an inability to handle runway intersections. The first and last of these are easy to explain as being due to dim lighting and obscured runway markings. The cloud issue is less clear, but VERIFAI can help us to debug it and identify the root cause.

Inspecting Fig. 5 again, observe that performance at 2–3 pm with no clouds is poor. This is surprising, since under these conditions the runway image is bright and clear; the brightness itself is not the problem, since TaxiNet does very well at the brightest time, noon. However, comparing images from a range of times, we noticed another difference: shortly after noon, the plane's shadow enters the frame, and moves across the image over the course of the afternoon. Furthermore, the shadow is far less visible under cloudy conditions (see Fig. 2). Thus, we hypothesized that TaxiNet might be confused by the strong shadows appearing in the afternoon when there are no clouds.

To test this hypothesis, we wrote a new SCENIC scenario with no clouds, varying only the time of day; we used VERIFAI's Halton sampler [9] to get an even spread of times with relatively few samples. We then ran two experiments: one with our usual test protocol, and one where we disabled the rendering of shadows in X-Plane. The results are shown in Fig. 7: as expected, in the normal run there are strong fluctuations in performance during the afternoon, as the

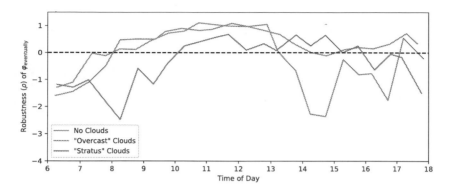

Fig. 5. Median TaxiNet performance by time of day, for different cloud types. (For clarity, individual runs are not shown as dots in this figure.)

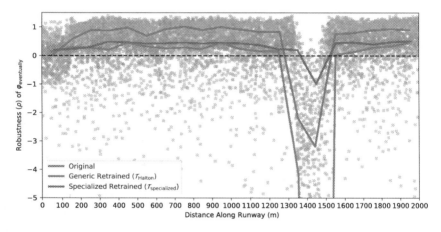

Fig. 6. TaxiNet performance by distance along the runway. Solid lines are medians. The lowest median value for original TaxiNet clipped by the bottom of the chart is −32. (Color figure online)

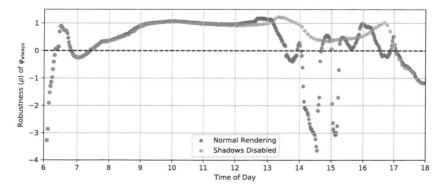

Fig. 7. TaxiNet performance (with fixed plane position) by time of day, with and without shadows.

shadow is moving across the image; with shadows disabled, the fluctuations disappear. This confirms that shadows are a root cause of TaxiNet's irregular performance in the afternoon.

Figures 4 and 6 show that there are failures even at favorable times and runway positions. We diagnosed several additional factors leading to such cases, such as starting at an extreme angle or further away from the centerline; see the Appendix [5] for details.

Finally, we can use VERIFAI for fault localization, identifying which part of the system is responsible for an undesired behavior. TaxiNet's main components are the neural network used for perception and the steering controller: we can test which is in error by replacing the network with ground truth CTE and HE values and testing the counterexamples we found above again. Doing this, we found that the system always satisfied $\varphi_{\text{eventually}}$; therefore, all the failure cases were due to mispredictions by the neural network. Next, we use VERIFAI to retrain the network and improve its predictions.

3.4   Retraining

The easiest approach to retraining using VERIFAI is simply to generate a new generic training set using the falsification scenario $\mathcal{S}_{\text{falsif}}$ from Fig. 3, which deliberately includes a wide variety of different positions, lighting conditions, and so forth. We sampled new configurations from the scenario, capturing a single image from each, to form new training and validation sets with the same sizes as for original TaxiNet. We used these to train a new version of TaxiNet, $\mathcal{T}_{\text{generic}}$, and evaluated it as in the previous section, obtaining much better overall performance: out of approximately 4,000 runs, 82% satisfied $\varphi_{\text{eventually}}$, and only 3.9% left the runway (compared to 55% and 9.1% before). A variant of $\mathcal{T}_{\text{generic}}$ using VERIFAI's Halton sampler, $\mathcal{T}_{\text{Halton}}$, was even more robust, satisfying $\varphi_{\text{eventually}}$ in 83% of runs and leaving the runway in only 0.6% (a 15× improvement over the original model). Furthermore, retraining successfully eliminated the undesired behaviors caused by time-of-day and cloud dependence: the blue data in Fig. 4 shows the retrained model's performance is consistent across the entire day, and in fact this is the case for each cloud type individually.

However, this naïve retraining did not eliminate all failure cases: the orange data in Fig. 6 shows that $\mathcal{T}_{\text{Halton}}$ still does not handle the runway intersection well. To address this issue, we used a second approach to retraining: overrepresenting the failure cases of interest in the training set using a specialized SCENIC scenario [6].

We altered $\mathcal{S}_{\text{falsif}}$ as shown in Fig. 8, increasing the probability of the plane starting 1200–1600 m along the runway, a range which brackets the intersection; we also emphasized the range 0–400 m, since Fig. 6 shows the model also has difficulty at the start of the runway. We trained a specialized model $\mathcal{T}_{\text{specialized}}$ using training data from this scenario together with the validation set from $\mathcal{T}_{\text{generic}}$. The new model had even better overall performance than $\mathcal{T}_{\text{Halton}}$, with 86% of runs satisfying $\varphi_{\text{eventually}}$ and 0.5% leaving the runway. This is because performance near the intersection is significantly improved, as shown by the purple data in Fig. 6; however, while the plane rarely leaves the runway completely, it still typically deviates several meters from the centerline. Furthermore, performance is worse than $\mathcal{T}_{\text{generic}}$ and $\mathcal{T}_{\text{Halton}}$ over the rest of the runway, suggesting that larger training sets might be necessary for further performance improvements.

While in this case it was straightforward to write the SCENIC program in Fig. 8 by hand, we can also *learn* such a program automatically: starting from $\mathcal{S}_{\text{falsif}}$ (Fig. 3), we use cross-entropy sampling to move the distribution towards failure cases. Applying this procedure to $\mathcal{T}_{\text{generic}}$ for around 1200 runs, VERIFAI indeed converged to a distribution concentrated on failures. For example, the distribution of distances along the runway gave ~79% probability to the range 1400–1600 m, 16% to 1200–1400 m, and 5%

```
rd = Options({
  (0, 400): 0.35,      # 0.2
  (400, 1200): 0.1,    # 0.4
  (1200, 1600): 0.5,   # 0.2
  (1600, 2000): 0.05   # 0.2
})
ego = Plane at (-8, 8) @ rd
```

Fig. 8. Position distribution emphasizing the runway beginning and intersection. Probabilities corresponding to the original scenario (Fig. 3) shown in comments.

to 0–200, with all other distances getting only ~1% in total. Referring back to Fig. 6, we see that these ranges exactly pick out where $\mathcal{T}_{\text{Halton}}$ (and $\mathcal{T}_{\text{generic}}$) has the worst performance.

Finally, we also experimented with a third approach to retraining, namely augmenting the existing training and validation sets with additional data rather than generating completely new data as we did above. The augmentation data can come from counterexamples from falsification [2], from a handwritten SCENIC scenario, or from a failure scenario learned as we saw above. However, we were not able to achieve better performance using such iterative retraining approaches than simply generating a larger training set from scratch, so we defer discussion of these experiments to the Appendix [5].

4   Conclusion

In this paper, we demonstrated VERIFAI as an integrated toolchain useful throughout the design process for a realistic, industrial autonomous system. We were able to find multiple failure cases, diagnose them, and in some cases fix them through retraining. We interfaced VERIFAI to the X-Plane flight simulator, and extended the SCENIC language with external parameters, allowing the combination of probabilistic programming and active sampling techniques. These extensions are publicly available [1, 7].

While we were able to improve TaxiNet's rate of satisfying its specification from 55% to 86%, a 14% failure rate is clearly not good enough for a safety-critical system (noting of course that TaxiNet is a simple prototype not intended for deployment). In future work, we plan to explore a variety of ways we might further improve performance, including repeating our falsify-debug-retrain loop (which we only showed a single iteration of), increasing the size of the training set, and choosing a more complex neural network architecture. We also plan to further automate error analysis, building on clustering and other techniques (e.g., [10]) available with VERIFAI and SCENIC, and to incorporate white-box reasoning techniques to improve the efficiency of search.

Acknowledgments. The authors are grateful to Forrest Laine and Tyler Staudinger for assistance with the experiments and TaxiNet, to Ankush Desai for suggesting using SCENIC as a prior for cross-entropy sampling, and to the anonymous reviewers.

This work was supported in part by NSF grants 1545126 (VeHICaL), 1646208, 1739816, and 1837132, the DARPA BRASS (FA8750-16-C0043) and Assured Autonomy programs, Toyota under the iCyPhy center, and Berkeley Deep Drive.

References

1. Dreossi, T., et al.: VERIFAI: a toolkit for the formal design and analysis of artificial intelligence-based systems. In: Dillig, I., Tasiran, S. (eds.) CAV 2019. LNCS, vol. 11561, pp. 432–442. Springer, Cham (2019). https://doi.org/10.1007/978-3-030-25540-4_25

2. Dreossi, T., Ghosh, S., Yue, X., Keutzer, K., Sangiovanni-Vincentelli, A.L., Seshia, S.A.: Counterexample-guided data augmentation. In: 27th International Joint Conference on Artificial Intelligence (IJCAI), pp. 2071–2078, July 2018. https://doi.org/10.24963/ijcai.2018/286

3. Dreossi, T., Jha, S., Seshia, S.A.: Semantic adversarial deep learning. In: Chockler, H., Weissenbacher, G. (eds.) CAV 2018. LNCS, vol. 10981, pp. 3–26. Springer, Cham (2018). https://doi.org/10.1007/978-3-319-96145-3_1

4. Fainekos, G.E., Pappas, G.J.: Robustness of temporal logic specifications. In: Havelund, K., Núñez, M., Roşu, G., Wolff, B. (eds.) Formal Approaches to Software Testing and Runtime Verification, pp. 178–192. Springer, Berlin (2006)

5. Fremont, D.J., Chiu, J., Margineantu, D.D., Osipychev, D., Seshia, S.A.: Formal analysis and redesign of a neural network-based aircraft taxiing system with VerifAI (2020). https://arxiv.org/abs/2005.07173

6. Fremont, D.J., Dreossi, T., Ghosh, S., Yue, X., Sangiovanni-Vincentelli, A.L., Seshia, S.A.: Scenic: a language for scenario specification and scene generation. In: 40th ACM SIGPLAN Conference on Programming Language Design and Implementation (PLDI), pp. 63–78 (2019). https://doi.org/10.1145/3314221.3314633

7. Fremont, D.J., Dreossi, T., Ghosh, S., Yue, X., Sangiovanni-Vincentelli, A.L., Seshia, S.A.: Scenic: a language for scenario specification and scene generation (2019). https://github.com/BerkeleyLearnVerify/Scenic

8. Goodfellow, I.J., Shlens, J., Szegedy, C.: Explaining and harnessing adversarial examples. CoRR (2014). http://arxiv.org/abs/1412.6572

9. Halton, J.H.: On the efficiency of certain quasi-random sequences of points in evaluating multi-dimensional integrals. Numer. Math. **2**(1), 84–90 (1960). https://doi.org/10.1007/BF01386213

10. Kim, E., Gopinath, D., Pasareanu, C.S., Seshia, S.A.: A programmatic and semantic approach to explaining and debugging neural network based object detectors. In: Proceedings of the IEEE Conference on Computer Vision and Pattern Recognition (CVPR) (2020)

11. Koymans, R.: Specifying real-time properties with metric temporal logic. Real-Time Syst. **2**(4), 255–299 (1990)

12. Laminar Research: X-Plane 11 (2019). https://www.x-plane.com/

13. McKinney, W.: Data structures for statistical computing in python. In: van der Walt, S., Millman, J. (eds.) 9th Python in Science Conference, pp. 51–56 (2010). https://pandas.pydata.org/
14. Rubinstein, R.Y., Kroese, D.P.: The Cross-Entropy Method: A Unified Approach to Combinatorial Optimization, Monte-Carlo Simulation, and Machine Learning. Springer, New York (2004). https://doi.org/10.1007/978-1-4757-4321-0
15. Russell, S., Dewey, D., Tegmark, M.: Research priorities for robust and beneficial artificial intelligence. AI Mag. **36**(4), 105–114 (2015). https://doi.org/10.1609/aimag.v36i4.2577
16. Sankaranarayanan, S., Fainekos, G.E.: Falsification of temporal properties of hybrid systems using the cross-entropy method. In: Hybrid Systems: Computation and Control (part of CPS Week 2012), HSCC 2012, Beijing, China, April 17–19, 2012, pp. 125–134 (2012). https://doi.org/10.1145/2185632.2185653,
17. Seshia, S.A., Sadigh, D., Sastry, S.S.: Towards Verified Artificial Intelligence. CoRR (2016). http://arxiv.org/abs/1606.08514
18. Teubert, C., Watkins, J.: The X-Plane Connect Toolbox (2019). https://github.com/nasa/XPlaneConnect
19. Tian, Y., Pei, K., Jana, S., Ray, B.: Deeptest: automated testing of deep-neural-network-driven autonomous cars. In: Proceedings of the 40th International Conference on Software Engineering, ICSE 2018, pp. 303–314. Association for Computing Machinery, New York (2018). https://doi.org/10.1145/3180155.3180220

Blockchain and Security

The Move Prover

Jingyi Emma Zhong[1], Kevin Cheang[2], Shaz Qadeer[3], Wolfgang Grieskamp[3], Sam Blackshear[4], Junkil Park[4], Yoni Zohar[1], Clark Barrett[1(✉)], and David L. Dill[4]

[1] Stanford University, Stanford, USA
barrett@cs.stanford.edu
[2] UC Berkeley, Berkeley, USA
[3] Novi, Seattle, WA, USA
[4] Novi, Menlo Park, CA, USA

Abstract. The Libra blockchain is designed to store billions of dollars in assets, so the security of code that executes transactions is important. The Libra blockchain has a new language for implementing transactions, called "Move." This paper describes the Move Prover, an automatic formal verification system for Move. We overview the unique features of the Move language and then describe the architecture of the Prover, including the language for formal specification and the translation to the Boogie intermediate verification language.

Keywords: Libra · Blockchain · Smart contracts · Formal verification

1 Introduction

The ability to implement arbitrary transactions on a blockchain via so-called *smart contracts* has led to an explosion in innovative services in systems such as Ethereum [41]. Unfortunately, bugs in smart contracts have led to massive amounts of funds being stolen or made inaccessible [5,15]. In retrospect, the source of these disasters is fairly obvious: smart contracts operate without a safety net. A fundamental requirement for blockchains is that transactions be automatic and irreversible. Unlike traditional financial applications, there is little opportunity for humans to oversee or intervene in transactions. Indeed, the design of the blockchain is intended to prevent human involvement. The resulting potential havoc that can be caused by a bug in a smart contract makes it essential for these contracts to be correct, without vulnerabilities. Not surprisingly, there is great interest in formal verification and other advanced testing methods for smart contracts, and several verification systems already exist or are under development.

This work was supported by the Stanford Center for Blockchain Research and Novi, a Facebook subsidiary whose goal is to provide financial services that let people participate in the Libra network. The Libra Association manages the Libra network and is an independent, not-for-profit membership organization, headquartered in Geneva, Switzerland.

© The Author(s) 2020
S. K. Lahiri and C. Wang (Eds.): CAV 2020, LNCS 12224, pp. 137–150, 2020.
https://doi.org/10.1007/978-3-030-53288-8_7

The Libra blockchain [3,38] is designed to be a foundation for supporting financial services for billions of people around the world. If successful, it could store and manage assets worth billions of dollars, with correspondingly stringent security requirements. The code that modifies the state of the blockchain is especially important. The architecture of the Libra blockchain requires that all such modifications be performed by the Move [12] virtual machine, which executes the well-defined Move instruction set. This architecture means that verification efforts can focus on the correctness of bytecode programs implementing smart contracts, including formally verifying those programs.

Contributions

In this paper, we describe a specification language and formal verification system for Move. If a programmer writes functional correctness properties for a procedure, the Move Prover tool can automatically verify it. Although many similar Floyd-Hoare verifiers exist, widespread adoption has been a challenge because conventional software is large, complex, and uses language features that present difficulties for even the simplest verification tasks. However, we are hopeful that the Move Prover will be used by the majority of Move programmers. There are three reasons for this optimism. First, the Move language has been designed to support verification. Second, we are building a culture of specification from the beginning: each Move module used by the Libra blockchain is being written with an accompanying formal specification. Finally, we are working to make the Move Prover as precise, fast, and user-friendly as possible.

The Move language, the Move Prover, Move programs, and their specifications, have been evolving rapidly, so this description necessarily represents a snapshot of the project at a particular time. However, we expect most of the changes to be improvements and extensions to the basics described here. In the remainder of this paper, we will:

1. Present a brief overview of Move and explain the language design decisions that facilitate verification (Sect. 2);
2. Describe how the Move Prover toolchain is implemented (Sect. 3);
3. Explain the model used to represent Move programs (Sect. 4);
4. Define the Move specification language and give examples of useful properties it can encode (Sect. 5); and
5. Demonstrate that the Move Prover can verify important aspects of the Libra core modules (Sect. 6).

2   Background: The Move Language

Move [12] is an executable bytecode language for writing smart contracts and custom transaction logic. Contracts in Move are written as *modules* that contain record types and procedures. Records in modules may either be struct or *resource* types—the most novel feature of Move. A resource type has linear [17] semantics, meaning that resources cannot be created, copied, or destroyed except by

```
module LibraCoin {
  resource struct T { value: u64 }

  public fun join(coin: &mut LibraCoin::T, to_consume: LibraCoin::T) {
    let   T { value } = to_consume; // MoveLoc(1); Unpack
    let c_value_ref = &mut coin.value; // MoveLoc(0); MutBorrowField<value>; StLoc(0)
    *c_value_ref = *c_value_ref + value; // CopyLoc(0); ReadRef; Add; MoveLoc(0); WriteRef
    return; // Ret
  }
}
```

Fig. 1. A Move module with its bytecode representation in comments.

procedures in its declaring module. Resources allow programmers to encode safe, yet customizable assets that cannot be accidentally (or intentionally) copied or destroyed by code outside the module.

Move is minimal in comparison to most conventional programming languages. The only types besides records are primitives (Booleans, unsigned integers, addresses), vectors, and references (which must be labeled as mutable or immutable, similar to Rust [30]). Records can contain primitives and other records, but not references. Control-flow constructs can be encoded via jumps to static labels in the bytecode.

Move programs execute in the context of a blockchain with modules and resources published under *account addresses*. To interact with the blockchain, a programmer can write a Move *transaction script*, a single-procedure program similar to a main procedure in a conventional language, that invokes procedures of published modules. This script is then packaged into a cryptographically signed transaction that is executed by validators in the Libra blockchain. As in Ethereum, transaction execution is *metered*, meaning that computational resources (or "gas") used when a Move program is executed are measured and must be paid for by the submitter of a transaction (though we note that the Move Prover does not yet reason about gas usage).

Verification-Friendly Design. There are several aspects of Move's design that facilitate verification. The first is limited interaction with the environment: to ensure deterministic execution, the language can only read data from the global blockchain state or the current transaction (no file or network I/O). Second, many features that are challenging for verification are absent from Move: concurrency, higher-order functions, exceptions, sub-typing, and dynamic dispatch. The absence of the last feature is particularly notable because it is present in Ethereum bytecode and has contributed to subtle *re-entrancy* bugs (e.g., [14]). Third, Move has built-in safe arithmetic: overflows and underflows are detected during execution and result in a transaction abort. Finally, many common errors are prevented by the Move *bytecode verifier* (not to be confused with the Move Prover), a static analyzer that checks each bytecode program before execution (similar to the JVM [26] or CLR [31] bytecode verifier). The bytecode verifier ensures that:

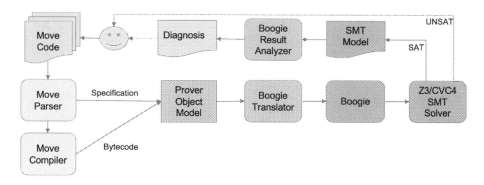

Fig. 2. The Move Prover architecture.

1. Procedures and struct declarations are well-typed (e.g., linearity of resources)
2. Dependent modules and procedure targets exist (i.e., static linking)
3. Module dependencies are acyclic
4. The operand stack height is the same at the beginning and end of each basic block
5. A procedure can only touch stack locations belonging to callers via a reference passed to the callee
6. The global and local memory are always tree-shaped
7. There are no dangling references
8. A mutable reference has exclusive access to its referent

Because these checks are run on every Move bytecode program, the prover can rely on them in its own reasoning. Note that this would not be true if the checks were performed by a source language compiler, since bad bytecode programs could be created by compiler bugs or by writing programs directly in the executable bytecode representation.

Limited Aliasing. In the rest of this section, we present an example that explains the memory-related invariants enforced by the Move bytecode verifier (6–8 above). The example in Fig. 1 is written in the Move source language, which can be directly compiled to the Move bytecode representation shown in the comments (note that the Move Prover analyzes the bytecode itself). The join procedure accepts two arguments: coin of type &**mut** LibraCoin::T (a mutable reference to a LibraCoin::T value stored elsewhere) and to_consume of type LibraCoin::T (an *owned* LibraCoin::T value). The purpose of this procedure is to destroy the LibraCoin::T resource stored in to_consume and add its value to the LibraCoin::T resource referenced by coin. The first line of the procedure performs the destruction by "unpacking" to_consume (placing the program value bound to its field into the program variable value), and the next two lines read the current value of c_value_ref and update it.

The careful reader might wonder: what will happen if c_value_ref is a reference to to_consume? In a C-like language, the first line would make `c_value_ref` into a dangling reference, which would lead to a memory error when it is subsequently used. Fortunately, the Move bytecode verifier ensures that this cannot happen. An owned value like `to_consume` can only be moved (either onto the operand stack or into global storage) if there are no outstanding references to the value. In addition, the bytecode verifier guarantees that no mutable reference can be an ancestor or descendant of another (mutable or immutable) reference in the same local or global data tree. This is a very strong restriction! It ensures that procedure formals that can be mutated (mutable references or owned values) point to disjoint memory locations. For example, an additional formal of type `&`**`mut`** **`u64`** in the code above could not point into the memory of the other formals. Formals that are immutable references may alias with each other, but not with mutable references or owned values. This means it is impossible for an update to a reference to affect the value retrieved by a simultaneously existing reference. These restrictions on the structure of memory enable greatly simplified reasoning about aliased mutable data, a significant challenge for verification in conventional languages.

3   Tool Overview

Figure 2 shows the architecture of the Move Prover. The prover takes as input Move source code annotated with specifications. The overall workflow consists of several steps. First, the specifications are extracted from the annotated code, and the Move source code is compiled into Move bytecode. Next, all stack operations are removed from the bytecode and replaced with operations on local variables, and the stackless bytecode is abstracted into a prover object model. Along a separate path, the specifications are parsed and added to the prover object model. The finalized model is translated to a program in the Boogie *intermediate verification language (IVL)* [23,24].

The Boogie program is handed to the Boogie verification system, which generates an SMT formula in the SMT-LIB format [10]. This can then be checked using an SMT solver such as Z3 [32] or CVC4 [9]. If the result of this check is UNSAT, then the specification holds, which is reported to the user. Otherwise, a countermodel is obtained from the SMT-solver, which gets translated back to Boogie. Boogie produces a Boogie-level error report, and this result is analyzed and transformed into a source-level diagnosis that is given back to the user. Using this diagnosis, the user can refine the implementation and/or specification and start the process again.

The prover is written in Rust and can be found in the `language/move-prover` directory in the Libra repository on GitHub [25].[1] We describe the Boogie model and the specification language in more detail in the following sections.

---

[1] This paper reflects the state of the Move Prover at github commit https://github.com/libra/libra/tree/6798b1cd50ac7d524d3e494783910b3d7e827eef.

4   Boogie Model

Boogie IVL is a simple imperative programming language that supports local and global variables, branching and loops, and procedures and procedure calls. Boogie is designed for verification, so it also supports pre- and post-conditions, loop invariants, and global axioms. Boogie programs are not executable; instead, they are provided as input to the Boogie verification system, which applies a verification strategy to generate verification conditions (as SMT formulas) [8]. If all of the verification conditions hold, then each procedure ensures its post-conditions, under the assumption that its pre-conditions hold. The variable types supported by Boogie IVL match the sorts supported by SMT solvers, e.g., Booleans, integers, arrays, bitvectors, and datatypes. This makes the translation of Boogie verification conditions into SMT formulas fairly transparent. Boogie is used as a back-end for a wide variety of verification tools. The general strategy is to model the semantics of a source language in Boogie. Then, programs and specifications in the source language can be translated into Boogie IVL and checked using the Boogie verification system. For more details about Boogie, we refer the reader to [1,7,23,24].

Following this pattern, we built a Boogie model for Move bytecode programs. A few highlights of the model are shown in Fig. 3 and described below. For a detailed understanding of the model, we refer the reader to the full Boogie model, which can be found in the Libra repository at `language/move-prover/src/prelude.bpl` and to a formalization of the core Move bytecode language described in [13].

As mentioned above, in Move, a data value is either a primitive value (e.g., Boolean, integer, address), a struct (i.e. a record) containing one or more data values, or a vector of data values. Data values are represented in Boogie as the `Value` datatype, with one constructor for each primitive type, plus a *vector* constructor (containing one field: a finite array of `Value`), used to model both vectors and structs.

Because Move supports generic functions (i.e. type-parameterized functions), we define a similar Boogie datatype for types called `TypeValue` (not shown). A type-parameterized function can then be represented as a Boogie procedure whose initial arguments are of type `TypeValue` (for the type parameters) and whose data arguments are of type `Value` (regardless of their actual Move type). The bytecode verifier ensures type-correctness, so we do not check that types are used correctly, but rather assume this is the case (by using Boogie `assume` statements as needed).

The `Value` and `ValueArray` datatypes are mutually recursive, and thus a `Value` can be thought of as a finite tree. A primitive `Value` is a leaf node of the tree, while a struct or vector `Value` is an internal node. A position within the tree can be uniquely identified by a *path*, which is a sequence of integers. A path specifies a node of the tree by starting at the root node and then following children according to the indices in the path. We model paths as finite arrays (also shown in Fig. 3). This simplifies the specification that two trees are disjoint, which is a necessary precondition in some smart contract functions.

```
type {:datatype} Value;
function {:constructor} Boolean(b: bool): Value;
function {:constructor} Integer(i: int): Value;
function {:constructor} Address(a: int): Value;
function {:constructor} Vector(v: ValueArray): Value;

type {:datatype} ValueArray;
function {:constructor} ValueArray(v: [int]Value, l: int): ValueArray;

type {:datatype} Path;
function {:constructor} Path(p: [int]int, size: int): Path;

type {:datatype} Location;
function {:constructor} Global(t: TypeValue, a: int): Location;
function {:constructor} Local(i: int): Location;

type {:datatype} Reference;
function {:constructor} Reference(l: Location, p: Path): Reference;

type {:datatype} Memory;
function {:constructor} Memory(domain: [Location]bool, contents: [Location]Value): Memory;
var $m : Memory;
```

Fig. 3. Highlights of the Boogie model for the Move Prover. The `type {:datatype}` syntax is used to declare a new datatype, and the `function {:constructor}` syntax is used to declare datatype constructors with their selectors. An array indexed by type `T` containing elements of type `V` is denoted in Boogie as `[T]V`.

A `Value` can be stored in either local or global state, and references to data in either are allowed as local variables. For simplicity and uniformity, we have a single memory object which is a map from `Location` to `Value` (because memory is a partial function, it also contains a map from `Location` to `bool`, which indicates whether a particular location is present in memory). A `Location` is either global (indexed by an account address and a type) or local (indexed by an integer). References are then represented as a pair consisting of a location and a path. To model reading from or writing to a reference, the global memory is accessed along the reference's path. Note that this is done by enumerating cases up to the maximum possible path depth (based on the data structures in the modules being verified).[2]

Finally, each bytecode instruction is modeled as a procedure modifying local or global state in Boogie. A bytecode program is then translated to a sequence of procedure calls, with `goto` statements handling control-flow.

---

[2] As with most verification approaches based on generating verification conditions, verifying recursive procedures or loops in Boogie requires writing loop invariants, which can be difficult and may also introduce quantifiers, making the problem harder for the underlying SMT solver. We have avoided this so far by relying on bounded iteration, but our roadmap includes full handling of recursion and loops via loop invariants.

```
public fun pay_from_sender(payee: address, amount: u64) acquires T
{
  Transaction::assert(payee != Transaction::sender(), 1);  // new!

  if (!exists<T>(payee)) {
    Self::create_account(payee);
  };
  Self::deposit(
    payee,
    Self::withdraw_from_sender(amount),
  );
}

spec fun pay_from_sender {
// ... omitted aborts_ifs ...
  aborts_if amount == 0;
  aborts_if global<T>(sender()).balance.value < amount;
  ensures exists<T>(payee);
  ensures global<T>(sender()).balance.value
      == old(global<T>(sender()).balance.value) - amount;
}
```

Fig. 4. A simplified version of an example where verification led to an insight about a function. Without the `assert` marked "new," the specification fails to hold if `payee` and `sender` are the same, as explained in Sect. 6.

5   Specifications

The Move Prover has a basic specification language for individual functions. Specifications include classical Floyd-Hoare pre-conditions, post-conditions, and a new condition specifying when a function aborts. (We are expanding this functionality to include ghost variables and global invariants for modules.) These conditions are separated from the actual code, in "spec blocks," which are linked by name to the structure or function being specified, or to the containing module. Specifications never affect the execution of a module. A simplified example based on verifying a real Libra module appears in Fig. 4.

Pre-conditions and post-conditions are standard. Pre-conditions are introduced by the reserved word `requires` and post-conditions are introduced by `ensures`, and each is followed by a Boolean expression, in a syntax that is very similar to Move, which includes the usual relational and arithmetic operators, record field access, etc. A sub-expression after `ensures` can be enclosed in `old(...)`, causing the expression to be evaluated using the variable values in the program state immediately after entry to the function, instead of using the program state just before exit from the function. Move functions can return multiple values, so the expressions `return_1`, `return_2`, etc. represent those return values.

Formal verifiers for conventional programming languages treat run-time errors as bugs to be reported. However, as in most smart contract languages, performing an undefined operation in Move, such as division by zero, cancels the entire transaction with no effect on the state except the consumption of some currency to pay for the computational resources consumed by the code that was executed before the error occurred. In Libra, this event is called an *abort*. Aborts are not necessarily run-time errors in Move. They are the standard way to handle illegal transactions, such as trying to perform an operation that is not authorized by the sender of the transaction.

Instead of treating all possible abort conditions as bugs, the Move Prover allows the user to specify the conditions under which a function is expected to abort. This type of specification is introduced by the reserved word `aborts_if`, which is followed by the same kind of expressions that can appear after `requires`. When `aborts_if` P appears in the specification of a function, the Move Prover requires that the function aborts if and only if P holds. If multiple `aborts_if` conditions are specified, there is an error unless the function aborts if and only if the disjunction of all their conditions holds. (This current semantics of `aborts_if` is subject to change.)

There are two expressions that are specific to the Libra blockchain. The expression `exists<M::T>(A)` is true iff there is an instance of the type T from module M appearing under account A in the global state tree. In the example of Fig. 4, the first post-condition asserts that the payee account exists after a payment transaction (the payee account might not exist before the payment, in which case it is created). The expression `global<M::T>(A)` represents the value of type T from module M stored at account A. In the example, this construct accesses the balance values of the sender (the payer), to make sure that the balance covers the payment, and to assert that the payer account balance has decreased by the payment amount if the payment is successful.

Specification Translation. Specifications are translated into `requires` and `ensures` statements in Boogie and combined with the prelude (the Boogie model, see Sect. 4) and the translated Move bytecode for the program.

A global Boolean variable `$abort_flag` is introduced and assumed to be `false` at the beginning of each procedure. The Boogie code for each instruction sets this flag to `true` for conditions that cause abort, such as undefined operations or failures of explicit Move `assert` statements.

The specification translator combines, using logical disjunction, the conditions of all `aborts_if` statements into a single expression (called `condition` here), which is translated into the Boogie specifications `ensures condition ==> $abort_flag` and `ensures !condition ==> !$abort_flag`.

6   Evaluation

In this section, we report on our experience using the Move Prover. We first demonstrate that it can successfully be used on core modules in the Libra codebase.

Verifying Core Modules. We wrote specifications for all of the functions (25/25) in the Libra module and most of the functions (34/38) in the LibraAccount module (4 functions use features that are not yet supported: non-linear arithmetic and referencing data in the spec that does not appear in the code).[3] These are core modules of the Libra system, and their correct execution is crucial. The Move Prover was able to prove all of these specifications in under a minute, as shown below. The modules with their specifications are available in the Move Prover source tree.[4] The Libra and LibraAccount modules comprise nearly 1300 lines (including specifications). The total size of the generated Boogie files is a little over 14,000 lines, and the generated SMT files are around 52,000 lines. Writing these specifications was quite natural, thanks to the tree-based memory model and to the support for type-generics. Experiments were run on a machine with an Intel Core i9 processor with 8 cores @2.4 GHz and 32 GB RAM, running macOS Catalina.

Move Module	LoC	Boogie LoC	SMT LoC	Functions	Verified	Runtime
Libra	420	3875	11,688	25	25	2.99 s
LibraAccount	867	10,362	40293	38	34	46.66 s

Impact of Move Prover. The Move Prover is co-developed with the Move language itself (which is relatively stable) to ensure that contracts remain correct as the entire toolset evolves. The prover is used in continuous integration, and is beginning to be used to verify contracts in production. As of this writing, the Move Prover hasn't exposed any serious bugs. However, it has had an impact on how we understand code. An example is a function called `pay_from_sender` (a version with some specifications and comments omitted appears in Fig. 4). This function simply pays money from the account of the sender (who signed the transaction) to `payee`. In a previous version of the function, the Prover reported errors for two of the "obvious" specification properties shown. The first specification says that the function always aborts when paying zero Libra, because `deposit` aborts unless the amount is positive. However, in the earlier version, `create_account` handled the payment to deposit the amount in the account when the account did not yet exist, and that payment was allowed to be zero, violating the specification. The function was rewritten as it appears now, so that the same deposit code is called regardless of whether the payee account was newly created. The last specification says that the payer's account decreases by `amount` after a successful payment. This condition was violated when the payer and payee were the same, resulting in no decrease. Adding an assert (marked "new!" in the figure) to abort in that useless case makes the specification simpler.

---

[3] Two additional functions in LibraAccount are "native" which means that they are built-in and don't have any Move code. These are modeled directly in Boogie and are not included in the count here.

[4] To reproduce, run `cargo run -- -s . -- <libra|libra_account>.move` from `tests/sources/stdlib/modules` in the `move-prover` source tree.

7   Related Work

The only other formal verification framework for Move that we are aware of is described in [36], where a high-level approach and some case studies are described, but no implementation details are provided.

The closest work in the literature has been done in the context of verification of solidity smart contracts using Boogie. VERISOL [22] is one tool which formally verifies solidity smart contracts via a translation to Boogie. Its specification language is designed for the specific context of application policies, but general specifications can be given by using solidity assertions. SOLC-VERIFY [19, 20] also uses Boogie to perform formal verification for solidity. It includes an annotation-based specification language and supports a larger feature-set of solidity than VERISOL. Interestingly, the formalization of the solidity persistent memory model presented in [20] is similar to our tree-based memory model for Move, though they were developed independently. One novelty of our model in comparison to theirs is its ability to handle generic functions as discussed in Sect. 4 (generics are supported in Move but not in solidity). Both VERISOL and SOLC-VERIFY target contracts written in solidity, and not in the Ethereum bytecode. In contrast, the Move Prover operates on the Move bytecode.

The solidity compiler itself includes a formal verification framework that works via a direct translation to SMT [2]. Several other tools have focused on specific vulnerability patterns, rather than user-defined specifications [16, 28, 34, 40]. Other theoretical foundations have also been employed for the verification of solidity smart contracts. These include the $\mathbb{K}$ framework [35] (see, e.g., [21]), F* [29] (see, e.g., [11, 18]), and proof assistants such as Coq [37] (see, e.g., [42, 43]).

Formal verification of Rust [30] programs is also related to the Move Prover, as Move's type system has similar characteristics to Rust [30]. Prusti [4] is a tool that leverages Rust's type system information to verify Rust programs. It is based on a higher-level intermediate framework called Viper [33] (that internally uses Boogie in some scenarios). Other verification efforts for Rust employ a translation to LLVM and then leverage LLVM-based verification techniques (see, e.g., [6, 27, 39]).

8   Conclusion

In this paper, we introduced the Move Prover, a formal verification tool designed to be an integral part of the process of smart contract development for the Libra platform. Though our initial experience with the Move Prover is positive, there are many avenues for future work that we plan to pursue.

As Move continues to evolve, we expect that some constructs may be easier and more efficient to model by using custom SMT constructs. An example of this is the built-in vector type. Our current model requires the use of quantifiers to compare two vector objects. However, an SMT theory of sequences could be used to model vectors without needing to use quantifiers to define equality. We plan to investigate the use of richer (and possibly custom) SMT theories in our model.

The specifications we have written so far are *local* in the sense that they deal with only a single execution of a single Move function. However, some properties of the Libra blockchain are inherently *global* in nature, such as the fact that the total amount of currency should remain constant. We plan to investigate techniques for creating and checking such global specifications.

The current Prover is still in a prototype phase. But the goal is for it to be a product that is usable by everyone who is writing contracts for the Libra platform. We expect that there will be many challenges in producing a user-friendly, industrial-strength tool, but we also look forward to a future where formal specification and verification is a routine part of the development process for Move modules on the Libra blockchain.

References

1. Boogie. https://github.com/boogie-org/boogie
2. Alt, L., Reitwiessner, C.: SMT-based verification of solidity smart contracts. In: Margaria, T., Steffen, B. (eds.) ISoLA 2018. LNCS, vol. 11247, pp. 376–388. Springer, Cham (2018). https://doi.org/10.1007/978-3-030-03427-6_28
3. Amsden, Z., et al.: The Libra Blockchain (2019). https://developers.libra.org/docs/the-libra-blockchain-paper
4. Astrauskas, V., Müller, P., Poli, F., Summers, A.J.: Leveraging rust types for modular specification and verification. PACMPL 3(OOPSLA), 147:1–147:30 (2019)
5. Atzei, N., Bartoletti, M., Cimoli, T.: A survey of attacks on ethereum smart contracts (SoK). In: Maffei, M., Ryan, M. (eds.) POST 2017. LNCS, vol. 10204, pp. 164–186. Springer, Heidelberg (2017). https://doi.org/10.1007/978-3-662-54455-6_8
6. Baranowski, M., He, S., Rakamarić, Z.: Verifying rust programs with SMACK. In: Lahiri, S.K., Wang, C. (eds.) ATVA 2018. LNCS, vol. 11138, pp. 528–535. Springer, Cham (2018). https://doi.org/10.1007/978-3-030-01090-4_32
7. Barnett, M., Chang, B.-Y.E., DeLine, R., Jacobs, B., Leino, K.R.M.: Boogie: a modular reusable verifier for object-oriented programs. In: de Boer, F.S., Bonsangue, M.M., Graf, S., de Roever, W.-P. (eds.) FMCO 2005. LNCS, vol. 4111, pp. 364–387. Springer, Heidelberg (2006). https://doi.org/10.1007/11804192_17
8. Barnett, M., Leino, K.R.M.: Weakest-precondition of unstructured programs. In: Proceedings of the 6th ACM SIGPLAN-SIGSOFT Workshop on Program Analysis for Software Tools and Engineering, pp. 82–87. Association for Computing Machinery, New York (2005). https://doi.org/10.1145/1108792.1108813
9. Barrett, C., et al.: CVC4. In: Gopalakrishnan, G., Qadeer, S. (eds.) CAV 2011. LNCS, vol. 6806, pp. 171–177. Springer, Heidelberg (2011). https://doi.org/10.1007/978-3-642-22110-1_14
10. Barrett, C., Stump, A., Tinelli, C.: The SMT-LIB standard: version 2.0. In: Gupta, A., Kroening, D. (eds.) Proceedings of the 8th International Workshop on Satisfiability Modulo Theories, Edinburgh, UK (2010)
11. Bhargavan, K., et al.: Formal verification of smart contracts: short paper. In: PLAS@CCS, pp. 91–96. ACM (2016)
12. Blackshear, S., et al.: Move: A language with programmable resources (2019). https://developers.libra.org/docs/move-paper
13. Blackshear, S., et al.: Resources: A safe language abstraction for money (2020). https://arxiv.org/abs/2004.05106

14. Buterin, V.: Critical update re DAO (2016). https://ethereum.github.io/blog/2016/06/17/critical-update-re-dao-vulnerability
15. Chen, H., Pendleton, M., Njilla, L., Xu, S.: A survey on Ethereum systems security: vulnerabilities, attacks and defenses. CoRR abs/1908.04507 (2019)
16. ConsenSys: Mythril Classic: Security analysis tool for Ethereum smart contracts. https://github.com/skylightcyber/mythril-classic
17. Girard, J.: Linear logic. Theor. Comput. Sci. **50**(1), 1–101 (1987)
18. Grishchenko, I., Maffei, M., Schneidewind, C.: A semantic framework for the security analysis of Ethereum smart contracts. In: Bauer, L., Küsters, R. (eds.) POST 2018. LNCS, vol. 10804, pp. 243–269. Springer, Cham (2018). https://doi.org/10.1007/978-3-319-89722-6_10
19. Hajdu, Á., Jovanovic, D.: solc-verify: A modular verifier for solidity smart contracts. CoRR abs/1907.04262 (2019)
20. Hajdu, Á., Jovanović, D.: SMT-friendly formalization of the solidity memory model. ESOP 2020. LNCS, vol. 12075, pp. 224–250. Springer, Cham (2020). https://doi.org/10.1007/978-3-030-44914-8_9
21. Hildenbrandt, E., et al.: KEVM: a complete formal semantics of the Ethereum virtual machine. In: CSF, pp. 204–217. IEEE Computer Society (2018)
22. Lahiri, S.K., Chen, S., Wang, Y., Dillig, I.: Formal specification and verification of smart contracts for azure blockchain. CoRR abs/1812.08829 (2018)
23. Leino, K.R.M.: This is boogie 2 (2008). https://www.microsoft.com/en-us/research/publication/this-is-boogie-2-2/, manuscript KRML 178
24. Leino, K.R.M., Rümmer, P.: A polymorphic intermediate verification language: design and logical encoding. In: Esparza, J., Majumdar, R. (eds.) TACAS 2010. LNCS, vol. 6015, pp. 312–327. Springer, Heidelberg (2010). https://doi.org/10.1007/978-3-642-12002-2_26
25. Libra. https://github.com/libra/libra
26. Lindholm, T., Yellin, F.: The Java Virtual Machine Specification. Addison-Wesley, Reading (1997)
27. Lindner, M., Aparicius, J., Lindgren, P.: No panic! verification of rust programs by symbolic execution. In: INDIN, pp. 108–114. IEEE (2018)
28. Luu, L., Chu, D., Olickel, H., Saxena, P., Hobor, A.: Making smart contracts smarter. In: ACM Conference on Computer and Communications Security, pp. 254–269. ACM (2016)
29. Maillard, K., et al.: Dijkstra monads for all. In: 24th ACM SIGPLAN International Conference on Functional Programming (ICFP) (2019). https://arxiv.org/abs/1903.01237
30. Matsakis, N.D., Klock II, F.S.: The rust language. Ada Lett. **34**(3), 103–104 (2014). https://doi.org/10.1145/2692956.2663188
31. Meijer, E., Wa, R., Gough, J.: Technical overview of the common language runtime (2000)
32. de Moura, L., Bjørner, N.: Z3: an efficient SMT solver. In: Ramakrishnan, C.R., Rehof, J. (eds.) TACAS 2008. LNCS, vol. 4963, pp. 337–340. Springer, Heidelberg (2008). https://doi.org/10.1007/978-3-540-78800-3_24
33. Müller, P., Schwerhoff, M., Summers, A.J.: Viper: a verification infrastructure for permission-based reasoning. In: Dependable Software Systems Engineering, NATO Science for Peace and Security Series - D: Information and Communication Security, vol. 50, pp. 104–125. IOS Press (2017)
34. Nikolic, I., Kolluri, A., Sergey, I., Saxena, P., Hobor, A.: Finding the greedy, prodigal, and suicidal contracts at scale. In: ACSAC, pp. 653–663. ACM (2018)

35. Rosu, G., Serbanuta, T.: An overview of the K semantic framework. J. Log. Algebr. Program. **79**(6), 397–434 (2010)
36. Synthetic Minds Blog: Verifying smart contracts in the move language (2019). https://synthetic-minds.com/pages/blog/blog-2019-09-11.html
37. The Coq development team: The coq proof assistant reference manual version 8.9 (2019). https://coq.inria.fr/distrib/current/refman/
38. The Libra Association: An Introduction to Libra (2019). https://libra.org/en-us/whitepaper
39. Toman, J., Pernsteiner, S., Torlak, E.: Crust: a bounded verifier for rust (N). In: ASE, pp. 75–80. IEEE Computer Society (2015)
40. Tsankov, P., Dan, A.M., Drachsler-Cohen, D., Gervais, A., Bünzli, F., Vechev, M.T.: Securify: practical security analysis of smart contracts. In: ACM Conference on Computer and Communications Security, pp. 67–82. ACM (2018)
41. Wood, G.: Ethereum: a secure decentralised generalised transaction ledger (2014). https://ethereum.github.io/yellowpaper/paper.pdf
42. Yang, Z., Lei, H.: Formal process virtual machine for smart contracts verification. CoRR abs/1805.00808 (2018)
43. Yang, Z., Lei, H.: Fether: an extensible definitional interpreter for smart-contract verifications in Coq. IEEE Access **7**, 37770–37791 (2019)

End-to-End Formal Verification
of Ethereum 2.0 Deposit Smart Contract

Daejun Park[1]([✉])[iD], Yi Zhang[1,2], and Grigore Rosu[1,2]

[1] Runtime Verification, Inc., Urbana, IL, USA
daejun.park@runtimeverification.com
[2] University of Illinois at Urbana-Champaign, Urbana, IL, USA
{yzhng173,grosu}@illinois.edu

Abstract. We report our experience in the formal verification of the
deposit smart contract, whose correctness is critical for the security
of Ethereum 2.0, a new Proof-of-Stake protocol for the Ethereum
blockchain. The deposit contract implements an incremental Merkle tree
algorithm whose correctness is highly nontrivial, and had not been proved
before. We have verified the correctness of the compiled bytecode of the
deposit contract to avoid the need to trust the underlying compiler. We
found several critical issues of the deposit contract during the verification
process, some of which were due to subtle hidden bugs of the compiler.

1 Introduction

The deposit smart contract [14] is a gateway to join Ethereum 2.0 [15] that is
a new sharded Proof-of-Stake (PoS) protocol which at its early stage, lives in
parallel with the existing Proof-of-Work (PoW) chain, called Ethereum 1.x chain.
Validators drive the entire PoS chain, called Beacon chain, of Ethereum 2.0. To
be a validator, one needs to deposit a certain amount of Ether, as a "stake", by
sending a transaction (over the Ethereum 1.x network) to the deposit contract.
The deposit contract records the history of deposits, and locks all the deposits
in the Ethereum 1.x chain, which can be later claimed at the Beacon chain of
Ethereum 2.0.[1] Note that the deposit contract is a one-way function; one can
move her funds from Ethereum 1.x to Ethereum 2.0, but not vice versa.

The deposit contract, written in Vyper [19], employs the Merkle tree [30] data
structure to efficiently store the deposit history, where the tree is *dynamically*
updated (i.e., leaf nodes are incrementally added in order from left to right)
whenever a new deposit is received. The Merkle tree employed in this contract
is very large: it has height 32, so it can store up to 2^{32} deposits. Since the size
of the Merkle tree is huge, it is not practical to reconstruct the whole tree every
time a new deposit is received.

To reduce both time and space complexity, thus saving the gas[2] cost significantly, the contract implements an *incremental Merkle tree algorithm* [6]. The

---

[1] This deposit process will change at a later stage.
[2] In Ethereum, gas refers to the fee to execute a transaction or a smart contract on
the blockchain. The amount of gas fee depends on the size of the payloads.

© The Author(s) 2020
S. K. Lahiri and C. Wang (Eds.): CAV 2020, LNCS 12224, pp. 151–164, 2020.
https://doi.org/10.1007/978-3-030-53288-8_8

incremental algorithm enjoys $O(h)$ time and space complexity to reconstruct (more precisely, compute the root of) a Merkle tree of height h, while a naive algorithm would require $O(2^h)$ time or space complexity. The efficient incremental algorithm, however, leads to the deposit contract implementation being unintuitive, and makes it non-trivial to ensure its correctness. The correctness of the deposit contract, however, is critical for the security of Ethereum 2.0, since it is a gateway for becoming a validator. Considering the utmost importance of the deposit contract for the Ethereum blockchain, formal verification is demanded to ultimately guarantee its correctness.

In this paper, we present our formal verification of the deposit contract.[3] The scope of verification is to ensure the correctness of the contract bytecode within a single transaction, without considering transaction-level or off-chain behaviors. We take the compiled bytecode as the verification target to avoid the need to trust the compiler.[4]

We adopt a refinement-based verification approach. Specifically, our verification effort consists of the following two tasks:

– Verify that the incremental Merkle tree algorithm implemented in the deposit contract is *correct* w.r.t. the original full-construction algorithm.
– Verify that the compiled bytecode is *correctly generated* from the source code of the deposit contract.

Intuitively, the first task amounts to ensuring the correctness of the contract source code, while the second task amounts to ensuring the compiled bytecode being a sound refinement of the source code (i.e., translation validation of the compiler). This refinement-based approach allows us to avoid reasoning about the complex algorithmic details, especially specifying and verifying loop invariants, directly at the bytecode level. This separation of concerns helped us to save a significant amount of verification effort. See Sect. 1.1 for more details.

Challenges. Formally verifying the deposit contract was challenging. First, the algorithm employed in the contract is sophisticated and its correctness is not straightforward to prove. Indeed, we found a critical bug in the algorithm implementation which had been not detected by existing tests (Sect. 3.1).

Second, we had to take the compiled bytecode as the verification target, which is much larger (consisting of ~3,000 instructions) and more complex than the source code. The source-code-level verification was not accepted by the customer for the end-to-end correctness guarantee, especially considering the fact that the compiler is not mature enough [11]. Indeed, we found several new critical bugs in the compiler during the formal verification process (Sect. 3.2).

Third, we had to consider not only the functional correctness, but also security properties of the contract. That is, we had to identify the behaviors of the contract in exceptional cases, and check if they are exploitable. We found a bug of the contract in case that it receives invalid inputs (Sect. 3.3).

---

[3] This was done as part of a contract funded by the Ethereum Foundation [16].
[4] Indeed, we found several new critical bugs [41–44] of the Vyper compiler in the process of formal verification. See Sect. 3 for more details.

Finally, we had to take into account potential future changes in the Ethereum blockchain system (called hard-forks). That is, we had to verify that the compiled bytecode will work not only in the current system, but also in any future version of the system that employs a different gas fee schedule. Considering such potential changes of the system required us to generalize the semantics of bytecode execution. We also found a bug regarding that (Sect. 3.4).

1.1   Our Refinement-Based Verification Approach

We illustrate our refinement-based formal verification approach used in the deposit contract verification. We present our approach using the K framework and its verification infrastructure [46,52,55], but it can be applied to other program verification frameworks.

Let us consider a sum program that computes the summation from 1 to n:

```
int sum(int n) { int s = 0; int i = 1;
                 while(i <= n) { s = s + i; i = i + 1; } return s; }
```

Given this program, we first manually write an abstract model of the program in the K framework [52]. Such a K model is essentially a state transition system of the program, and can be written as follows:

```
rule: sum(n) ⇒ loop(s: 0, i: 1, n: n)
rule: loop(s: s, i: i, n: n) ⇒ loop(s: s + i, i: i + 1, n: n) when i ≤ n
rule: loop(s: s, i: i, n: n) ⇒ return(s) when i > n
```

These transition rules correspond to the initialization, the while loop, and the return statement, respectively. The indexed tuple (s: s, i: i, n: n) represents the state of the program variables s, i, and n.[5]

Then, given the abstract model, we specify the functional correctness property in reachability logic [54], as follows:

```
claim: sum(n) ⇒ return(n(n+1)/2) when n > 0
```

This reachability claim says that sum(n) will eventually return $\frac{n(n+1)}{2}$ in all possible execution paths, if n is positive. We verify this specification using the K reachability logic theorem prover [55], which requires us only to provide the following loop invariant:[6]

```
invariant: loop(s: i(i−1)/2, i: i, n: n) ⇒ return(n(n+1)/2) when 0 < i ≤ n + 1
```

Once we prove the desired property of the abstract model, we manually refine the model to a bytecode specification, by translating each transition rule of the abstract model into a reachability claim at the bytecode level, as follows:

---

[5] Note that this abstract model can be also automatically derived by instantiating the language semantics with the particular program, if a formal semantics of the language is available (in the K framework).

[6] The loop invariants in reachability logic mentioned here look different from those in Hoare logic. See the comparison between the two logic proof systems in [55, Section 4]. These loop invariants can be also seen as transition invariants [48].

```
claim: evm(pc: pc_begin, calldata: #bytes(32, n), stack: [], ...)
    ⇒ evm(pc: pc_loophead, stack: [0, 1, n], ...)
claim: evm(pc: pc_loophead, stack: [s, i, n], ...)
    ⇒ evm(pc: pc_loophead, stack: [s+i, i+1, n], ...) when i ≤ n
claim: evm(pc: pc_loophead, stack: [s, i, n], ...)
    ⇒ evm(pc: pc_end, stack: [], output: #bytes(32, s), ...) when i > n
```

Here, the indexed tuple evm(pc:_, calldata:_, stack:_, output:_) represents (part of) the Ethereum Virtual Machine (EVM) state, and #bytes(N, V) denotes a sequence of N bytes of the two's complement representation of V.

We verify this bytecode specification against the compiled bytecode using the same K reachability theorem prover [46,55]. Note that no loop invariant is needed in this bytecode verification, since each reachability claim involves only a bounded number of execution steps—specifically, the second claim involves only a single iteration of the loop.

Then, we manually prove the soundness of the refinement, which can be stated as follows: *for any EVM states σ_1 and σ_2, if $\sigma_1 \Rightarrow \sigma_2$, then $\alpha(\sigma_1) \Rightarrow \alpha(\sigma_2)$*, where the abstraction function α is defined as follows:

```
α(evm(pc: pc_begin, calldata: #bytes(32, n), stack: [], ...)) = sum(n)
α(evm(pc: pc_loophead, stack: [s, i, n], ...)) = loop(s: s, i: i, n: n)
α(evm(pc: pc_end, stack: [], output: #bytes(32, s), ...)) = return(s)
```

Putting all the results together, we finally conclude that the compiled bytecode will return #bytes($32, \frac{n(n+1)}{2}$).

Note that the abstract model and the compiler are *not* in the trust base, thanks to the refinement, while the K reachability logic theorem prover [46,55] and the formal semantics of EVM [24] are.

2 Formal Verification of the Deposit Contract

Following the refinement-based approach illustrated in Sect. 1.1, we first formalized the main business logic of the deposit contract (i.e., the incremental Merkle tree algorithm), and proved its correctness. Then we refined the formal model into a bytecode specification, and verified the compiled bytecode of the deposit contract against the refined specification. From these, we concluded the correctness of the deposit contract bytecode.

2.1 Incremental Merkle Tree Algorithm

We briefly describe the incremental Merkle tree algorithm of the deposit contract. Due to space limitations, we omit the formalization of the algorithm and the formal proof of the correctness, and refer the readers to our companion technical report [45] for the full details.

A Merkle tree [30] is a perfect binary tree [34] where leaf nodes store the hash of data, and non-leaf nodes store the hash of their children. A *partial Merkle tree*

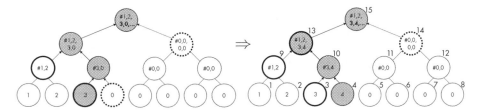

Fig. 1. Illustration of the incremental Merkle tree algorithm. Node numbers are labeled in the upper-right corner of each node.

up-to m is a Merkle tree whose first (leftmost) m leaves are filled with data hashes and the other leaves are empty and filled with zeros. The incremental Merkle tree algorithm takes as input a partial Merkle tree up-to m and a new data hash, and inserts the new data hash into the $(m+1)^{\text{th}}$ leaf, resulting in a partial Merkle tree up-to $m+1$.

Figure 1 illustrates the algorithm, showing how the given partial Merkle tree up-to 3 (shown in the left) is updated to the resulting partial Merkle tree up-to 4 (in the right) when a new data hash is inserted into the 4th leaf node. The key idea of the algorithm is that only the path from the new leaf to the root (i.e., the gray nodes) needs to be computed (hence linear-time), and moreover the path can be computed by using only the left (i.e., node 3 and node 9) or right (i.e., node 14) sibling of each node in the path, which are only nodes that the algorithm maintains (hence linear-space). Refer to [45] for the full details.

2.2   Bytecode Verification of the Deposit Contract

Now we present the formal verification of the compiled bytecode of the deposit contract. The bytecode verification ensures that the compiled bytecode is a sound refinement of the source code. This rules out the need to trust the compiler.

As illustrated in Sect. 1.1, we first manually refined the abstract model (in which we proved the algorithm correctness) to the bytecode specification. For the refinement, we consulted the ABI interface standard [13] (to identify, e.g., `calldata` and `output` in the illustrating example of Sect. 1.1), as well as the bytecode (to identify, e.g., the pc and `stack` information).[7] Then, we used the KEVM verifier [46] to verify the compiled bytecode against the refined specification. We adopted the KEVM verifier to reason about all possible corner-case behaviors of the compiled bytecode, especially those introduced by certain unintuitive and questionable aspects of the underlying Ethereum Virtual Machine (EVM) [60]. This was possible because the KEVM verifier is derived from a complete formal semantics of the EVM, called KEVM [24]. Our formal specification and verification artifacts are publicly available at [50].

---

[7] However, we want to note that the Vyper compiler can be augmented to extract such information, which can automate the refinement process to a certain extent. We leave that as future work.

Let us elaborate on specific low-level behaviors verified against the bytecode. In addition to executing the incremental Merkle tree algorithm, most of the functions perform certain additional low-level tasks, and we verified that such tasks are correctly performed. Specifically, for example, given deposit data,[8] the `deposit` function computes its 32-byte hash (called Merkleization) according to the SimpleSerialize (SSZ) specification [18]. The leaves of the Merkle tree store only the computed hashes instead of the original deposit data. The `deposit` function also emits a `DepositEvent` log that contains the original deposit data, where the log message needs to be encoded as a byte sequence following the contract event ABI specification [13]. Other low-level operations performed by those functions that we verified include: correct zero-padding for the 32-byte alignment, correct conversions from big-endian to little-endian, input bytes of the SHA2-256 hash function being correctly constructed, and return values being correctly serialized to byte sequences according to the ABI specification [13].

We also verified a liveness property that the contract is always able to accept a new (valid) deposit as long as a sufficient amount of gas is provided. This liveness is not trivial since it needs to hold even in any future hard-fork where the gas fee schedule is changed. Indeed, we found a bug that violates the liveness. See Sect. 3.4 for more details.

Our formal specification includes both positive and negative behaviors. The positive behaviors describe the desired behaviors of the contracts in a legitimate input state. The negative behaviors, on the other hand, describe how the contracts handle exceptional cases (e.g., when benign users feed invalid inputs by mistake, or malicious users feed crafted inputs to take advantage of the contracts). The negative behaviors are mostly related to security properties.

For the full specification of the verified bytecode behaviors, refer to [49].

3   Findings and Lessons Learned

In the course of our formal verification effort, we found subtle bugs [35–37] of the deposit contract, as well as a couple of refactoring suggestions [38–40] that can improve the code readability and reduce the gas cost. The subtle bugs of the deposit contract are partly due to bugs of the Vyper compiler [41–44] that we newly found (and reported to the Vyper team) in the verification process.

Below we elaborate on the bugs we found and lessons we learned along the way. We note that all the bugs of the deposit contract have been reported, confirmed, and properly fixed in the latest version (v0.11.2).

3.1   Maximum Number of Deposits

In the original version of the contract that we were asked to verify, a bug is triggered when all of the leaf nodes of a Merkle tree are filled with deposit

---

[8] Each deposit data consists of the public key, the withdrawal credentials, the deposit amount, and the signature of the deposit owner.

data, in which case the contract (specifically, the get_deposit_root function) incorrectly computes the root hash of a tree, returning the zero root hash (i.e., the root hash of an empty Merkle tree) regardless of the content of leaf nodes. For example, suppose that we have a Merkle tree of height 2, which has four leaf nodes, and every leaf node is filled with certain deposit data, say v_1, v_2, v_3, and v_4, respectively. Then, while the correct root hash of the tree is $\mathsf{hash}(\mathsf{hash}(v_1, v_2), \mathsf{hash}(v_3, v_4))$, the get_deposit_root function returns $\mathsf{hash}(\mathsf{hash}(0, 0), \mathsf{hash}(0, 0))$, which is incorrect.

Due to the complex logic of the code, it is non-trivial to properly fix this bug without significantly rewriting the code, and thus we suggested a workaround that simply forces to never fill the last leaf node, i.e., accepting only $2^h - 1$ deposits at most, where h is the height of a tree. We note that, however, it is infeasible in practice to trigger this buggy behavior in the current setting, since the minimum deposit amount is 1 Ether and the total supply of Ether is less than 130M which is much smaller than 2^{32}, thus it is not feasible to fill all the leaves of a tree of height 32. Nevertheless, this bug has been fixed by the contract developers as we suggested, since the contract may be used in other settings in which the buggy behavior can be triggered and an exploit may be possible. Refer to [37] for more details.

We also want to note that this bug was quite subtle to catch. Indeed, we had initially thought that the original code was correct until we failed to write a formal proof of the correctness theorem. The failure of our initial attempt to prove the correctness led us to identify a missing premise that was needed for the theorem to hold, from which we could find the buggy behavior scenario, and suggested the bugfix. This experience reconfirms the importance of formal verification. Although we were not "lucky" to find this bug when we had eyeball-reviewed the code, which is all traditional security auditors do, the formal verification process thoroughly guided and even "forced" us to find it eventually.

3.2 ABI Standard Conformance of get_deposit_count Function

In the previous version, the get_deposit_count function does not conform to the ABI standard [13], where its return value contains incorrect zero-padding [35], due to a Vyper compiler bug [41]. Specifically, in the buggy version of the compiled bytecode, the get_deposit_count function, whose return type is bytes[8], returns a byte sequence of length 96, where the last byte is 0x20 while it should be 0x00. According to the ABI specification [13], the last 24 bytes must be all zero, serving as zero-pad for the 32-byte alignment. Thus the return value does not conform to the ABI standard. This is problematic because any contract (written in either Solidity or Vyper) that calls to (the buggy version of) the deposit contract, expecting that the deposit_count function conforms to the ABI standard, could have misbehaved.[9]

---

[9] The returned byte sequence, including the incorrect last byte, is copied to the caller's memory. If the caller reuses the last byte assuming that it is zero, the garbage value will be passed around, which may break the business logic of the caller.

This buggy behavior is mainly due to a subtle Vyper compiler bug [41] that fails to correctly compile a function whose return type is bytes[n] where $n < 16$. This leads to the compiled function returning a byte sequence with insufficient zero-padding as mentioned above, failing to conform to the ABI standard.

We note that this bug could not have been detected if we did not take the bytecode as the verification target. This reconfirms that the bytecode-level verification is critical to ensure the ultimate correctness (unless we formally verify the underlying compiler), because we cannot (and should not) trust the compiler.

3.3   Checking Well-Formedness of Calldata

The calldata decoding process in the previous version of the compiled bytecode does not have sufficient runtime-checks for the well-formedness of calldata. As such, it fails to detect certain ill-formed calldata, causing invalid deposit data to be put into the Merkle tree. This is problematic especially when clients make mistakes and send deposit transactions with incorrectly encoded calldata, which may result in losing their deposit fund.

Specifically, we found a counter-example ill-formed calldata whose size (196 bytes) is much less than that of well-formed calldata (356 bytes). The problem, however, is that the deposit function does *not* reject the ill-formed calldata, but simply inserts certain invalid (garbage) deposit data in the Merkle tree. Since the invalid deposit data cannot pass the signature validation later, no one can claim the deposited fund associated with this, and the deposit owner loses the fund. Note that this happens even though the deposit function employs assertions at the beginning of the function that ensures the size of each of the arguments is correct, which turned out to not work as expected.

This problem would not exist if the Vyper compiler thoroughly generated runtime checks to ensure the well-formedness of calldata.[10] However, since it was not trivial to fix the compiler to generate such runtime checks, we suggested several ways to improve the deposit contract source code to prevent this behavior without fixing the compiler. After careful discussion with the deposit contract development team, we together decided to employ a checksum-based approach where the deposit function takes as an additional input a checksum for the deposit data, and rejects any ill-formed calldata using the checksum. The checksum-based approach is the least intrusive and the most gas-efficient of all the suggested fixes. For more details of other suggested fixes, refer to [36].

We note that this issue was found when we were verifying the negative behaviors of the deposit contract. This shows the importance of having the formal specification to include not only positive but also negative behaviors.

---

[10] The compiler developers failed to consider the case when the given calldata is not correctly encoded. For example, while the header of calldata contains offsets (i.e., pointers) to the positions of data elements, it could be the case that certain offsets are beyond the calldata range. In that case, the calldata can be accessed outside its bounds, due to the missing runtime-checks.

3.4   Liveness

As mentioned in Sect. 2.2, the previous version of the deposit contract fails to satisfy a liveness property in that it may not be able to accept a new deposit, even if it is valid, in a certain future hard-fork that updates the gas fee schedule. This was mainly due to another subtle Vyper compiler bug [44] that generates bytecode where a hard-coded amount of gas is supplied when calling to certain precompiled contracts. Although this hard-coded amount of gas is sufficient in the current hard-fork (code-named Istanbul [17]), it may not be sufficient in a certain future hard-fork that increases the gas fee schedule of the precompiled contracts. In such a future hard-fork, the previous version of the deposit contract will always fail due to the out-of-gas exception, regardless of how much gas is initially supplied. Refer to [44] for more details.

We admit that we could not find this issue until the deposit contract development team carefully reviewed and discussed with us the formal specification [49] of the bytecode. Initially, we considered only the behaviors of the bytecode in the current hard-fork, without identifying the requirement that the contract bytecode should work in any future hard-fork. We identified the missing requirement, and found this liveness issue, at a very late stage of the formal verification process, which delayed the completion of formal verification.

This experience essentially illustrates the well-known problem caused by the gap between the intended behaviors (that typically exists only informally) by developers, and the formal specification written by verification engineers. To reduce this gap, the two groups should work closely together, or ideally, developers should write their own specifications in the first place. For the former, the formal verification process should involve developers more frequently. For the latter, the formal verification tools should become much easier to use without requiring advanced knowledge of formal methods. We leave both as future work.

3.5   Discussion

Verification Effort. The net effort for formal verification took 7 person-weeks (excluding various discussions with developers, reporting bugs and following-up, especially for compiler bugs, etc.), where the algorithm correctness proof took 2 person-weeks, and the bytecode verification took 5 person-weeks. This includes the time spent on writing specifications as well. The bytecode specification consists of ~1,000 LOC (excluding comments), in addition to auxiliary lemmas consisting of ~200 LOC. The size of the source code is ~100 LOC, and the number of instructions in the compiled bytecode is ~3,000.

Trust Base. The validity of the bytecode verification result assumes the correctness of the bytecode specification and the KEVM verifier. The algorithm correctness proof is partially mechanized—only the proof of major lemmas are mechanized in the K framework. The non-mechanized proofs are included in our trust base. The Vyper compiler is *not* in the trust base.

Continuous Verification. The verification target contract was a moving target. Even if the contract code had been frozen before starting the formal verification process, the code (both source code or bytecode) was updated in the middle of the verification process, to fix bugs found during the process. Indeed, we found several bugs in both the contract and the compiler, and each time we found a bug, we had to re-verify the newly compiled bytecode that fixes the bug. Here the problem was the overhead of re-verification. About 20% of the bytecode verification effort was spent on re-verification.

The re-verification overhead could have been reduced by automatically adjusting formal specifications to updated bytecode, and/or making specifications as independent of the specific details of the bytecode as possible. For example, the current bytecode specification employs specific program-counter (PC) values to refer to some specific positions of the bytecode, especially when specifying loop invariants. Most of such PC values need to be updated whenever the bytecode is modified. The re-verification overhead could have been reduced by automatically updating such PC values, or even having the specification refer to specific positions without using PC values. We leave this as future work.

4 Related Work

Static Analysis and Verification of Smart Contracts. There have been proposed many static analysis tools [5,10,20,25,28,29,32,57,58] that are designed to automatically detect a certain fixed set of bugs and vulnerabilities of smart contracts, at the cost of generality and expressiveness. VerX [47] can verify past-time linear temporal properties over multiple runs of smart contracts, but it requires the target contracts to be effectively loop-free.

There also have been proposed verification tools that allow us to specify and verify arbitrary functional correctness and/or security properties, such as [3,22] based on the F* proof assistant [1,56] based on Isabelle/HOL [33], the KEVM verifier [46] based on the K framework [52], and VeriSol [27] based on Boogie [2]. The KEVM verifier has also been used to verify high-profile and challenging smart contracts [51], including a multi-signature wallet called Gnosis Safe [21], a decentralized token exchange called Uniswap [59], and a partial consensus mechanism called Casper FFG [7].

Verification of Systems Software. There are many success stories of formal verification of systems software, from OS kernels [23,26,31], to file systems [8,53], to cryptographic code [4]. While most of the verified systems code is either synthesized from specifications, or implemented (or adjusted) to be verification-friendly, there also exist efforts [9,12] to verify actual production code as is. Such efforts are necessary especially when the production code is highly performance-critical and/or existing development processes are hard to change to help produce verification-friendly code. The deposit contract we verified was given to us at the code-frozen stage, and also performance-critical (especially in terms of the gas cost), and thus we took and verified the given production-ready code as is, without any modification except for fixing bugs.

References

1. Amani, S., Bégel, M., Bortin, M., Staples, M.: Towards verifying Ethereum smart contract bytecode in Isabelle/hol. In: Proceedings of the 7th ACM International Conference on Certified Programs and Proofs, CPP 2018 (2018)
2. Barnett, M., Chang, B.E., DeLine, R., Jacobs, B., Leino, K.R.M.: Boogie: a modular reusable verifier for object-oriented programs. In: 4th International Symposium on Formal Methods for Components and Objects, FMCO 2005, Amsterdam, The Netherlands, November 1–4, 2005, Revised Lectures (2005)
3. Bhargavan, K., et al.: Formal verification of smart contracts: Short paper. In: Proceedings of the 2016 ACM Workshop on Programming Languages and Analysis for Security, PLAS 2016 (2016)
4. Bond, B., et al.: Vale: verifying high-performance cryptographic assembly code. In: 26th USENIX Security Symposium, USENIX Security 2017, Vancouver, BC, Canada, August 16–18, 2017 (2017)
5. Brent, L., et al.: Vandal: a scalable security analysis framework for smart contracts. CoRR abs/1809.03981 (2018)
6. Buterin, V.: Progressive Merkle Tree. https://github.com/ethereum/research/blob/master/beacon_chain_impl/progressive_merkle_tree.py
7. Buterin, V., Griffith, V.: Casper the friendly finality gadget. CoRR abs/1710.09437 (2017)
8. Chen, H., Ziegler, D., Chajed, T., Chlipala, A., Kaashoek, M.F., Zeldovich, N.: Using crash hoare logic for certifying the FSCQ file system. In: Proceedings of the 25th Symposium on Operating Systems Principles, SOSP 2015, Monterey, CA, USA, October 4–7, 2015 (2015)
9. Chudnov, A., et al.: Continuous formal verification of Amazon s2n. In: Chockler, H., Weissenbacher, G. (eds.) CAV 2018. LNCS, vol. 10982, pp. 430–446. Springer, Cham (2018). https://doi.org/10.1007/978-3-319-96142-2_26
10. ConsenSys Diligence: MythX. https://mythx.io/
11. ConsenSys Diligence: Vyper Security Review. https://diligence.consensys.net/audits/2019/10/vyper/
12. Cook, B., Khazem, K., Kroening, D., Tasiran, S., Tautschnig, M., Tuttle, M.R.: Model checking boot code from AWS data centers. In: Chockler, H., Weissenbacher, G. (eds.) CAV 2018. LNCS, vol. 10982, pp. 467–486. Springer, Cham (2018). https://doi.org/10.1007/978-3-319-96142-2_28
13. Ethereum Foundation: Contract ABI Specification. https://solidity.readthedocs.io/en/v0.6.1/abi-spec.html
14. Ethereum Foundation: Ethereum 2.0 Deposit Contract. https://github.com/ethereum/eth2.0-specs/blob/v0.11.2/deposit_contract/contracts/validator_registration.vy
15. Ethereum Foundation: Ethereum 2.0 Specifications. https://github.com/ethereum/eth2.0-specs
16. Ethereum Foundation: Ethereum Foundation Spring 2019 Update. https://blog.ethereum.org/2019/05/21/ethereum-foundation-spring-2019-update/
17. Ethereum Foundation: Hardfork Meta: Istanbul. https://github.com/ethereum/EIPs/blob/master/EIPS/eip-1679.md
18. Ethereum Foundation: SimpleSerialize (SSZ). https://github.com/ethereum/eth2.0-specs/tree/dev/ssz
19. Ethereum Foundation: Vyper. https://vyper.readthedocs.io

20. Feist, J., Grieco, G., Groce, A.: Slither: a static analysis framework for smart contracts. In: Proceedings of the 2nd International Workshop on Emerging Trends in Software Engineering for Blockchain, WETSEB@ICSE 2019, Montreal, QC, Canada, May 27, 2019 (2019)
21. Gnosis Ltd.: Gnosis Safe. https://safe.gnosis.io/
22. Grishchenko, I., Maffei, M., Schneidewind, C.: A semantic framework for the security analysis of Ethereum smart contracts. In: Proceedings of the 7th International Conference on Principles of Security and Trust, POST 2018 (2018)
23. Gu, R., et al.: Certikos: an extensible architecture for building certified concurrent OS kernels. In: 12th USENIX Symposium on Operating Systems Design and Implementation, OSDI 2016, Savannah, GA, USA, November 2–4, 2016 (2016)
24. Hildenbrandt, E., et al.: KEVM: a complete semantics of the Ethereum virtual machine. In: Proceedings of the 31st IEEE Computer Security Foundations Symposium, CSF 2018 (2018)
25. Kalra, S., Goel, S., Dhawan, M., Sharma, S.: ZEUS: analyzing safety of smart contracts. In: Proceedings of the 25th Annual Network and Distributed System Security Symposium, NDSS 2018 (2018)
26. Klein, G., et al.: seL4: formal verification of an OS kernel. In: Proceedings of the 22nd ACM Symposium on Operating Systems Principles 2009, SOSP 2009, Big Sky, Montana, USA, October 11–14, 2009 (2009)
27. Lahiri, S.K., Chen, S., Wang, Y., Dillig, I.: Formal specification and verification of smart contracts for azure blockchain. CoRR abs/1812.08829 (2018)
28. Luu, L., Chu, D.H., Olickel, H., Saxena, P., Hobor, A.: Making smart contracts smarter. In: Proceedings of the 2016 ACM SIGSAC Conference on Computer and Communications Security, CCS 2016 (2016)
29. Marescotti, M., Blicha, M., Hyvärinen, A.E.J., Asadi, S., Sharygina, N.: Computing exact worst-case gas consumption for smart contracts. In: Margaria, T., Steffen, B. (eds.) ISoLA 2018. LNCS, vol. 11247, pp. 450–465. Springer, Cham (2018). https://doi.org/10.1007/978-3-030-03427-6_33
30. Merkle, R.C.: A digital signature based on a conventional encryption function. In: Pomerance, C. (ed.) CRYPTO 1987. LNCS, vol. 293, pp. 369–378. Springer, Heidelberg (1988). https://doi.org/10.1007/3-540-48184-2_32
31. Nelson, L., et al.: Hyperkernel: push-button verification of an OS kernel. In: Proceedings of the 26th Symposium on Operating Systems Principles, Shanghai, China, October 28–31, 2017 (2017)
32. Nikolic, I., Kolluri, A., Sergey, I., Saxena, P., Hobor, A.: Finding the greedy, prodigal, and suicidal contracts at scale. In: Proceedings of the 34th Annual Computer Security Applications Conference, ACSAC 2018, San Juan, PR, USA, December 03–07, 2018 (2018)
33. Nipkow, T., Wenzel, M., Paulson, L.C. (eds.): Isabelle/HOL- A Proof Assistant for Higher-Order Logic. LNCS, vol. 2283. Springer, Heidelberg (2002). https://doi.org/10.1007/3-540-45949-9
34. NIST: Perfect Binary Tree. https://xlinux.nist.gov/dads/HTML/perfectBinaryTree.html
35. Park, D.: Ethereum 2.0 deposit contract issue 1341: non ABI-standard return value of get_deposit_count of deposit contract. https://github.com/ethereum/eth2.0-specs/issues/1341
36. Park, D.: Ethereum 2.0 deposit contract issue 1357: Ill-formed call data to deposit contract can add invalid deposit data. https://github.com/ethereum/eth2.0-specs/issues/1357

37. Park, D.: Ethereum 2.0 deposit contract issue 26: maximum deposit count. https://github.com/ethereum/deposit_contract/issues/26
38. Park, D.: Ethereum 2.0 deposit contract issue 27: redundant assignment in init(). https://github.com/ethereum/deposit_contract/issues/27
39. Park, D.: Ethereum 2.0 deposit contract issue 28: loop fusion optimization. https://github.com/ethereum/deposit_contract/issues/28
40. Park, D.: Ethereum 2.0 deposit contract issue 38: a refactoring suggestion for the loop of deposit(). https://github.com/ethereum/deposit_contract/issues/38
41. Park, D.: Vyper Issue 1563: Insufficient zero-padding bug for functions returning byte arrays of size < 16. https://github.com/vyperlang/vyper/issues/1563
42. Park, D.: Vyper Issue 1599: Off-by-one error in zero_pad(). https://github.com/vyperlang/vyper/issues/1599
43. Park, D.: Vyper Issue 1610: Non-semantics-preserving refactoring for zero_pad(). https://github.com/vyperlang/vyper/issues/1610
44. Park, D.: Vyper Issue 1761: Potentially insufficient gas stipend for precompiled contract calls. https://github.com/vyperlang/vyper/issues/1761
45. Park, D., Zhang, Y:, Rosu, G.: End-to-End Formal Verification of Ethereum 2.0 Deposit Smart Contract. http://hdl.handle.net/2142/107129
46. Park, D., Zhang, Y., Saxena, M., Daian, P., Roşu, G.: A formal verification tool for Ethereum VM Bytecode. In: Proceedings of the 26th ACM Joint European Software Engineering Conference and Symposium on the Foundations of Software Engineering, ESEC/FSE 2018 (2018)
47. Permenev, A., Dimitrov, D., Tsankov, P., Drachsler-Cohen, D., Vechev, M.: VerX: Safety Verification of Smart Contracts. https://files.sri.inf.ethz.ch/website/papers/sp20-verx.pdf
48. Podelski, A., Rybalchenko, A.: Transition invariants. In: Proceedings of the 19th Annual IEEE Symposium on Logic in Computer Science, LICS 2004 (2004)
49. Runtime Verification Inc.: Bytecode Behavior Specification of Ethereum 2.0 Deposit Contract. https://github.com/runtimeverification/verified-smart-contracts/blob/master/deposit/bytecode-verification/deposit-spec.ini.md
50. Runtime Verification Inc.: Formal Verification of Ethereum 2.0 Deposit Contract. https://github.com/runtimeverification/verified-smart-contracts/tree/master/deposit
51. Runtime Verification Inc.: Formally Verified Smart Contracts. https://github.com/runtimeverification/verified-smart-contracts
52. Serbanuta, T., Arusoaie, A., Lazar, D., Ellison, C., Lucanu, D., Rosu, G.: The K primer (version 3.3). Electr. Notes Theor. Comput. Sci. **304**, 57–80 (2014)
53. Sigurbjarnarson, H., Bornholt, J., Torlak, E., Wang, X.: Push-button verification of file systems via crash refinement. In: 12th USENIX Symposium on Operating Systems Design and Implementation, OSDI 2016, Savannah, GA, USA, November 2–4, 2016 (2016)
54. Stefanescu, A., Ciobaca, S., Mereuta, R., Moore, B.M., Serbanuta, T., Rosu, G.: All-Path Reachability Logic. Logical Methods in Computer Science **15**(2), (2019)
55. Stefanescu, A., Park, D., Yuwen, S., Li, Y., Rosu, G.: Semantics-based program verifiers for all languages. In: Proceedings of the 2016 ACM SIGPLAN International Conference on Object-Oriented Programming, Systems, Languages, and Applications, OOPSLA 2016 (2016)
56. Swamy, N., et al.: Dependent types and multi-monadic effects in F. In: Proceedings of the 43rd Annual ACM SIGPLAN-SIGACT Symposium on Principles of Programming Languages, POPL 2016, St. Petersburg, FL, USA, January 20–22, 2016 (2016)

57. Tikhomirov, S., Voskresenskaya, E., Ivanitskiy, I., Takhaviev, R., Marchenko, E., Alexandrov, Y.: Smartcheck: static analysis of Ethereum smart contracts. In: 1st IEEE/ACM International Workshop on Emerging Trends in Software Engineering for Blockchain, WETSEB@ICSE 2018, Gothenburg, Sweden, May 27–June 3, 2018 (2018)
58. Tsankov, P., Dan, A.M., Drachsler-Cohen, D., Gervais, A., Bünzli, F., Vechev, M.T.: Securify: practical security analysis of smart contracts. In: Proceedings of the 2018 ACM SIGSAC Conference on Computer and Communications Security, CCS 2018, Toronto, ON, Canada, October 15–19, 2018 (2018)
59. Uniswap: Uniswap Exchange Protocol. https://uniswap.io/
60. Wood, G.: Ethereum: A Secure Decentralised Generalised Transaction Ledger. https://ethereum.github.io/yellowpaper/paper.pdf

Stratified Abstraction of Access Control Policies

John Backes, Ulises Berrueco, Tyler Bray, Daniel Brim, Byron Cook,
Andrew Gacek(✉), Ranjit Jhala, Kasper Luckow, Sean McLaughlin,
Madhav Menon, Daniel Peebles, Ujjwal Pugalia, Neha Rungta,
Cole Schlesinger, Adam Schodde, Anvesh Tanuku, Carsten Varming,
and Deepa Viswanathan

Amazon Web Services, Seattle, USA
gacek@amazon.com

Abstract. The shift to cloud-based APIs has made application security
critically depend on understanding and reasoning about *policies* that regulate access to cloud resources. We present *stratified predicate abstraction*, a new approach that summarizes complex security policies into a
compact set of positive and declarative statements that precisely state
who has access to a resource. We have implemented stratified abstraction and deployed it as the engine powering AWS's IAM Access Analyzer
service, and hence, demonstrate how formal methods and SMT can be
used for security policy *explanation*.

1 Introduction

A growing number of developers are using cloud-based implementations of basic
resources like associative arrays, encryption, storage, queuing, and event-driven
execution, to engineer client applications. For example, millions of Amazon Web
Services (AWS) customers use cloud APIs like Amazon SQS for queues, Amazon
S3 for storage, AWS KMS for crypto key management, Amazon DynamoDB for
associative arrays, and AWS Lambda for executing functions in a pure virtualized
environment. This shift to the cloud has made application security critically
depend upon deeply understanding and reasoning about *policies* that regulate
how different principals are allowed to access cloud resources. AWS users, for
example, configure principals in the Identity and Access Management (IAM)
service. The users define which requests are allowed access via *resource policies*
which allow some resources to be purposefully shared with the entire internet,
while restricting access to others to limited sets of identities.

The IAM policy language has many features that are essential to allow users
to build a wide array of possible applications. Some of these features make reasoning about policies challenging. First, individual policy elements can use regular
expressions, negation, and conditionals. Second, the policy elements can interact with each other in subtle ways that make the net effect of a policy unclear.
Previously, we developed ZELKOVA [2], a tool that encodes policies as logical

© The Author(s) 2020
S. K. Lahiri and C. Wang (Eds.): CAV 2020, LNCS 12224, pp. 165–176, 2020.
https://doi.org/10.1007/978-3-030-53288-8_9

formulas and then uses SMT solvers [3,8] to answer questions about policies, *e.g.* whether a particular policy is *correct*, too strict, or too permissive. While ZELKOVA can be queried to *explore* the properties of policies *e.g.* whether some resource is "publicly" accessible, our experience shows that formal policy analysis remains challenging as users must have sufficient technical sophistication to realize the criteria important to them *and* be able to formalize the above as ZELKOVA queries.

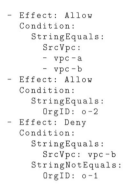

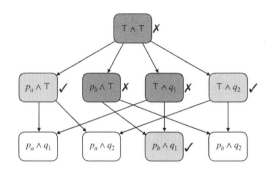

Fig. 1. An example AWS policy   **Fig. 2.** Stratified abstraction search tree

In this paper, we present a new approach to help users understand whether their policy is correct, by *abstracting* the policy into a compact set of positive and declarative statements that precisely summarize *who* has access to a resource. Users can review the summary to decide whether the policy grants access according to their intentions. The key challenge to computing such summaries is the combinatorial blowup in the number of possible requests, which comprise the combination of user name and account, identifiers, hostnames, IP addresses and so on. Our key insight is that we can make summarization tractable via *stratified predicate abstraction*, which allows us to collapse many equivalent (concrete) requests into a single (abstract) *finding*. To this end, we introduce a new algorithm for computing stratified abstractions of policies, yielding a set of findings that are *sound*, *i.e.* which include all possible requests that can be granted access, and *precise*, *i.e.* where the findings are as specific as possible.

We have implemented stratified abstraction and deployed it as the engine powering AWS's recently launched IAM Access Analyzer service, which helps users reason about the semantics of their policy configurations. We present an empirical evaluation of our method over a large set of real-world IAM policies. We show that IAM Access Analyzer generates a sound, precise, and *compact* set of findings for complex policies, taking less than a second per finding. Thus, our results show how key ideas like SMT solving and predicate abstraction [1,5], can be used not just to *verify* computing systems, but to precisely *explain* their behavior to users.

2   Overview

AWS access control policies specify *who* has access to a given resource, via a set of `Allow` and `Deny` statements that grant and prohibit access, respectively. Figure 1 shows a simplified policy specifying access to a particular resource. This policy uses conditions based on which network (known as a VPC) the request originated from and which organizational Amazon customer (referred to by an Org ID) made the request. The first statement *allows* access to any request whose `SrcVpc` is either `vpc-a` *or* `vpc-b`. The second statement *allows* access to any request whose `OrgId` is `o-2`. However, the third statement *denies* access from `vpc-b` *unless* the `OrgId` is `o-1`.

Crucially, for each request, access is granted only if: (a) *some* `Allow` statement matches the request, and (b) *none* of the `Deny` statements match the request. Consequently, it can be quite tricky to determine what accesses are allowed by a given policy. First, individual statements can use regular expressions, negation, and conditionals. Second, to know the effect of an allow statement, one must consider all possible deny statements that can *overlap* with it, *i.e.* can refer to the same request as the allow. Thus, policy verification is not *compositional*, in that we cannot determine if a policy is "correct" simply by *locally* checking that each statement is "correct". Instead, we require a *global* verification mechanism, that simultaneously considers all the statements and their subtle interactions, to determine if a policy grants only the intended access.

As policies organically grow and become more complex and baroque, the ultimate question that users have is: "is my policy correct?" Of course, this *specification* problem has bedeviled formal methods from the day they were invented. In our context: how does the security analyst know whether the policy is, in fact not too strict or too permissive? Zelkova [2] is already used by users of Amazon's Simple Storage Service (S3) to determine whether any of their "data buckets" are *publicly* accessible. More generally, the AWS Config service provides templated Zelkova checks that can be filled in by users to validate their policies. Some advanced users even use the Zelkova service directly, asking their own questions about policies. While all of the above are useful, formal policies and formal analysis remains difficult to use, as the user must have sufficient technical sophistication to: (1) *intuit* the criteria important to them, (2) *formalize* the above in the query language of Zelkova, and (3) *interpret* the results returned by the tool. Ultimately, to answer "is this policy correct?", the tool must *help the user understand* what "correct" means in their particular context.

2.1   Approach

The core contribution of this work is to change the question from *"is this policy correct?"* to *"who has access?"*. The response to the former is a Boolean while the response to the latter is a set of *findings*. There are several key requirements that findings must meet to be useful in the context of analyzing security policies and answering the question *"who has access?"*.

J. Backes et al.

Sound. Users need confidence that findings *summarize* a policy. In particular, we must ensure that *every* access allowed by the policy is represented by *some* finding. This over-approximation crucially enables compositional reasoning about the policy: if a user deems that *each* finding is safe, then she may rest assured that the *entire* policy is safe.

Precise. Users require that findings be *specific*. A finding of "everybody has access" is a sound and over-approximate summary of every policy, but is only useful if the policy allows everyone access. Instead, we want findings that adhere closely to the accesses allowed by the policy, and do not report false-alarms that say certain identities have access when that is not, in fact, the case.

Compact. Users require that the set of findings be *small*. For example, we could simply *enumerate* all the different kinds of requests that have access, but such a list would typically be far too large to manually inspect. Instead, we require that the findings be a compact representation of who has access, while still ensuring soundness and precision.

Example. For example, the policy in Fig. 1 can be summarized through a set of three findings, that say that access is granted to a request iff:

- Its `SrcVpc` is `vpc-a`, *or*,
- Its `OrgId` is `o-2`, or,
- Its `SrcVpc` is `vpc-b` *and* its `OrgId` is `o-1`.

The findings are sound as no other requests are granted access. The findings are precise as in each case, there are requests matching the conditions that are granted access.[1] Finally, the findings compactly summarize the policy in three positive statements declaring *who* has access.

2.2 Solution: Computing Findings via Stratified Abstraction

Next, we describe an informal overview of our algorithm for computing the findings, by building it up in three stages.

1: Concrete Enumeration. One approach to synthesize findings would be to (1) *enumerate* possible requests, (2) *query* ZELKOVA to filter out the requests that do not have access, and (3) *return* the remainder as findings. Such an approach is guaranteed to be both sound and precise. However, real-world policies comprise many fields, each of which have many possible values. For example, there are 10^{12} (currently) possible AWS account numbers and 2^{128} possible IPv6 addresses. Enumerating all possible requests is computationally *intractable*, and even if it were, the resulting set of findings is far too large and hence *useless*.

2: Predicate Abstraction. We tackle the problem of summarizing the super-astronomical request-space by using *predicate abstraction*. Specifically, we make a syntactic pass over the policy to extract the set of constants that are used to constrain access, and we use those constants to generate a family of predicates

---

[1] The finding "`OrgId` is `o-2`" also includes some requests that are not allowed, *e.g.* when `SrcVpc` is `vpc-b`.

whose conjunctions compactly describe partitions of the space of all requests. For example, from the policy in Fig. 1 we would extract the following predicates

$$p_a \doteq \mathsf{SrcVpc} = \mathsf{vpc\text{-}a}, \; p_b \doteq \mathsf{SrcVpc} = \mathsf{vpc\text{-}b}, \; p_\star \doteq \mathsf{SrcVpc} = \star,$$
$$q_1 \doteq \mathsf{OrgId} = \mathsf{o\text{-}1}, \qquad q_2 \doteq \mathsf{OrgId} = \mathsf{o\text{-}2}, \qquad q_\star \doteq \mathsf{OrgId} = \star.$$

The first row has three predicates describing the possible value of the `SrcVpc` of the request: that it equals `vpc-a` or `vpc-b` or some value other than `vpc-a` and `vpc-b`. Similarly, the second row has three predicates describing the value of the `OrgId` of the request: that it equals `o-1` or `o-2` or some value other than `o-1` and `o-2`.

We can compute findings by enumerating all the *cubes* generated by the above predicates, and querying ZELKOVA to determine if the policy allows access to the requests described by the cube. For example, the above predicates would generate the cubes shown in Fig. 3. We omit trivially inconsistent cubes like $p_a \wedge p_b$ which correspond to the empty set of requests. Next to each cube, we show the result of querying ZELKOVA to determine whether the policy allows access to the requests described by the cube: ✓(resp. ✗) indicates requests are allowed (resp. denied).

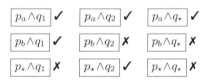

Fig. 3. Cubes generated by the predicates $p_a, p_b, p_\star, q_1, q_2, q_\star$ generated from the policy in Fig. 1 and the result of querying ZELKOVA to check if the requests corresponding to each cube are granted access by the policy.

Finally, we can translate each *allowed* cube into a finding, yielding five findings. While this set of findings is sound and precise, it suffers in two ways. First, real-world policies have many different fields, and hence, enumerating-and-querying each cube can be quite slow. Second, the result is not compact. The same information is more succinctly captured by the set of three findings in Sect. 2.1 which, for example, collapses the three findings in the top row to a single finding, "`SrcVpc` is `vpc-a`."

3: Stratified Abstraction. The chief difficulty with enumerating all the cubes *greedily* is that we end up eagerly *splitting-cases* on the values of fields when that may not be required. For example, in Fig. 3, we split cases on the possible value of `OrgId` even though it is irrelevant when `SrcVpc` is `vpc-a`. This observation points the way to a new algorithm where we *lazily* generate the cubes as follows. Our algorithm maintains a *worklist* of minimally refined cubes. At each step, we (1) ask ZELKOVA if the cube allows an access that is not covered by any of its refinements, (2) if so, we add it to the set of findings; and (3) if not, we refine the cube "point-wise" along the values of each field individually and add the results to the worklist. The above process is illustrated in Fig. 2.

- **Level 1.** The worklist is initialized with $\top \wedge \top$ which represents the cube where we *don't care* about the value of either SrcVpc or OrgId, *i.e.* which represents *every* possible request. ZELKOVA determines that every access allowed by this cube and by the policy are covered by one of the refinements of this cube (the second level of the tree). Thus this $\top \wedge \top$ finding is not essential, and we can find more precise findings. We indicate this by the red shade and the ✗. Next, we *refine* the above cube point-wise, by considering the two sub-cubes $p_a \wedge \top$ and $p_b \wedge \top$ which respectively represent the requests where SrcVpc is either vpc-a or vpc-b (and OrgId could be any value), and, the two sub-cubes $\top \wedge q_1$ and $\top \wedge q_2$ which respectively represent the requests where OrgId is either o-1 or o-2 (and SrcVpc could be any value). These refined cubes are added to the worklist and considered in turn.
- **Level 2.** ZELKOVA determines that there are requests allowed by $p_a \wedge \top$ and $\top \wedge q_2$ which are not covered by any of their refinements, hence those are shaded green and have a ✓. However, ZELKOVA rejects $p_b \wedge \top$ and $\top \wedge q_1$ as anything allowed by them is allowed by one of their refinements. Now we further refine the rejected cubes, but can *omit* considering the cubes $p_a \wedge q_1$, $p_a \wedge q_2$ and $p_b \wedge q_2$ in the unshaded boxes, as each of those is covered or subsumed by one of the two accepted cubes.
- **Level 3.** Hence, we issue one last ZELKOVA query for $p_b \wedge q_1$ which indeed allows a request which is not covered by any of its refinements (as it has none). Finally, we gather the set of accepted cubes, *i.e.* those in the green shaded boxes, and translate those to the findings described in Sect. 2.1.

3   Algorithm

Next, we formalize our algorithm for computing policy summaries and show how it yields findings that are sound and precise. In Sect. 4 we demonstrate how our algorithm yields compact results for real-world policies..

3.1   Policies and Findings

Requests. Let $K = \{k_1, \ldots, k_n\}$ be a set of *keys*. Let $V_k = \{v_1, \ldots\}$ be a (possibly infinite) set of *values* for the key k. A *request* r a mapping from keys k to values in V_k. For example, the request r_1 maps the keys Principal, SrcIP, and OrgID as:

$$r_1 = \{\text{Principal} \mapsto 123 : \text{user/A}, \ \text{SrcIP} \mapsto 192.0.2.3, \ \text{OrgID} \mapsto \text{o-1}\}$$

Policies. A *policy* is a predicate on requests $p : r \rightarrow Bool$. The *denotation* of a policy p is the set of requests it allows:

$$\gamma(p) \doteq \{r \mid p(r) = True\}$$

Predicates. A *predicate* is a map $\phi : V_k \rightarrow Bool$. The *denotation* of a predicate is the set of values that satisfy the predicate:

$$\gamma(\phi) \doteq \{v \mid \phi(v) = True\}$$

We define a partial order on predicates, $\phi_1 \preceq \phi_2$ iff $\gamma(\phi_1) \subseteq \gamma(\phi_2)$. For example:

$$\phi_{123}(v) \doteq \text{``}v \text{ is a principal in account 123''}$$
$$\phi_{ua}(v) \doteq \text{``}v \text{ is user-a in account 123''}$$
$$\phi_{ub}(v) \doteq \text{``}v \text{ is user-b in account 123''}$$

Here we have $\phi_{ua} \preceq \phi_{123}$ and $\phi_{ub} \preceq \phi_{123}$ because users are a type of principal. The set of predicates must always contain $\top$ and must have the following property: for all ϕ_1, ϕ_2 either $\phi_1 \preceq \phi_2$, $\phi_2 \preceq \phi_1$, or $\gamma(\phi_1) \cap \gamma(\phi_2) = \emptyset$. This ensures the set of predicates for a given key can be tree-ordered.

Findings. A *finding* σ is a map from keys K to predicates Φ. The *denotation* of a finding σ is the set of requests where each key k is mapped to a value v in the denotation of $\sigma(k)$:

$$\gamma(\sigma) \doteq \{r \mid \forall k.r(k) \in \gamma(\sigma(k))\}$$

We represent a finite set of findings as $\Sigma = \{\sigma_1, \ldots, \sigma_n\}$. The *denotation* of a set of findings is the union of the denotations the findings:

$$\gamma(\{\sigma_1, \ldots, \sigma_n\}) \doteq \gamma(\sigma_1) \cup \cdots \cup \gamma(\sigma_n)$$

3.2   Properties

Next, we formalize the key desirable properties of findings, *i.e.* that they be sound, precise, and compact, as *coverage*, *irreducibility*, and *minimality* respectively.

Coverage. A set of findings Σ *covers* a policy p if $\gamma(p) \subseteq \gamma(\Sigma)$. For example, the set Σ_1 containing the two findings

$$\Sigma_1 \doteq \{[\mathsf{SrcVpc} \mapsto p_a, \mathsf{OrgID} \mapsto \top], [\mathsf{SrcVpc} \mapsto \top, \mathsf{OrgID} \mapsto q_2]\}$$

corresponding to the green boxes on level 2 of Fig. 2, *does not* cover the policy from Fig. 1, as it excludes the request whose SrcVpc is vpc-b and OrgID is o-1. However, Σ_2 below *does* cover the policy as it includes all requests that are granted access.

$$\Sigma_2 \doteq \Sigma_1 \cup \{[\mathsf{SrcVpc} \mapsto p_b, \mathsf{OrgID} \mapsto q_1]\}$$

Reducibility. A finding σ refines another finding σ', written $\sigma \sqsubseteq \sigma'$ if *for each* key k we have $\sigma(k) \preceq \sigma'(k)$. A finding σ refines a set of findings Σ, written

$\sigma \sqsubseteq \Sigma$ if σ refines *some* $\sigma' \in \Sigma$. Note that $\sigma \sqsubseteq \sigma'$ implies $\gamma(\sigma) \subseteq \gamma(\sigma')$. We say that a finding σ is *irreducible* for a policy p if

$$\exists r \in \gamma(p) \cap \gamma(\sigma). \ \forall \sigma' \sqsubset \sigma. \ r \notin \gamma(\sigma').$$

That is, σ is irreducible if it contains some request that is excluded by all its proper refinements. For example, the finding $[\mathsf{SrcVpc} \mapsto p_a, \mathsf{OrgID} \mapsto \top]$ is irreducible as it contains a request $[\mathsf{SrcVpc} \mapsto \mathsf{vpc\text{-}a}, \mathsf{OrgID} \mapsto \mathsf{o\text{-}3}]$ that is excluded by its refinements $[\mathsf{SrcVpc} \mapsto p_a, \mathsf{OrgID} \mapsto q_1]$ and $[\mathsf{SrcVpc} \mapsto p_a, \mathsf{OrgID} \mapsto q_2]$. Note that irreducibility is inherently tied to the available predicates, Φ.

Minimality. A set of findings Σ is *minimal* if the denotation of each $\Sigma' \subset \Sigma$ is strictly contained in the denotation of Σ. For example, the set

$$\{[\mathsf{SrcVpc} \mapsto p_a, \mathsf{OrgID} \mapsto \top], [\mathsf{SrcVpc} \mapsto p_a, \mathsf{OrgID} \mapsto q_1]\}$$

is *not* minimal as the subset containing just the first finding denotes the same set of requests, but, the set containing either finding individually *is* minimal.

3.3   Algorithm

Given a policy p and a finite set of partially ordered predicates Φ, our goal is to produce a minimal covering of p comprising only irreducible findings.

Access Oracle. Our algorithm is built using an *access oracle* that takes as input a policy p and a finding σ and returns Some iff some request described by σ is allowed by p, and None otherwise.

$$\mathsf{CanAccess}(p, \sigma) = \begin{cases} \mathsf{Some} & \text{if } \gamma(\sigma) \cap \gamma(p) \neq \emptyset \\ \mathsf{None} & \text{if } \gamma(\sigma) \cap \gamma(p) = \emptyset \end{cases}$$

```
def AccessSummary(p:P) -> [Σ]:
    σ⊤ = λk→⊤
    wkl = queue([σ⊤])
    res = []
    while wkl≠∅:
        σ = wkl.deque()
        if CanAccess(p,Reduce(σ)) == Some:
            res += [σ]
        else:
            wkl += [σ'|σ'∈Refine(σ), σ'⋢res]
    return res
```

Fig. 4. Algorithm to compute a minimal set of irreducible findings that cover policy p.

Dominators. We define the *immediately dominates* set of $\phi \in \Phi$ as the set of elements strictly smaller than ϕ but unrelated to each other:

$$\mathsf{idom}(\phi) \doteq \{\phi' \mid \phi' \prec \phi \text{ and } \forall \phi''. \neg(\phi' \prec \phi'' \prec \phi)\}$$

Reducing a Finding. The procedure ReducePred (resp. Reduce) takes as input a predicate ϕ (resp. finding σ) and strengthens it to *exclude* all the requests that are covered by the refinements of ϕ (resp. σ):

```
def  ReducePred(φ:Φ)  ->  Φ:              def  Reduce(σ:Σ)  ->  Σ:
    φ₁,...,φₙ  =  idom(φ)                     σ'  =  λk → ReducePred(σ(k))
    return  φ ∧ ¬φ₁ ∧ ··· ∧ ¬φₙ              return  σ'
```

Intuitively, Reduce allows us to determine if a finding is irreducible.

Lemma 1. σ *is irreducible iff* $\gamma(\mathsf{Reduce}(\sigma)) \cap \gamma(p) \neq \emptyset$.

Refining a Finding. The procedure Refine takes as input a finding σ and returns the set of findings obtainable by *individually* refining one value of σ.

```
def  Refine(σ:Σ)  ->  [Σ]:
    return  [σ[k ↦ φ']  |  k ∈ K,  φ' ∈ idom(σ(k))]
```

If a finding σ is reducible, we will use Refine to *split* it into more precise findings.

Lemma 2. *Let* σ *be reducible for* p. *Then* $\gamma(\sigma) \cap \gamma(p) = \gamma(\mathsf{Refine}(\sigma)) \cap \gamma(p)$.

Summarizing Access. The procedure AccessSummary (Fig. 4) takes as input a policy p and returns a minimal set of irreducible findings *res* that covers p. The procedure maintains a queue *wkl* comprising a *frontier* of findings that are to be explored. The queue is initialized with the trivial finding $\sigma_\top$ that maps each key to $\top$. It then iteratively picks an element from the queue, checks if it is an irreducible finding, and if so, adds it to the result set *res*. If not, it computes the finding's refinements and adds those to *wkl*. The process repeats till the queue is empty. The algorithm maintains three loop invariants: (1) *wkl* $\cup$ *res* covers p; (2) Each finding in *res* is irreducible; (3) *res* is minimal. Consequently, the algorithm terminates with a minimal set of irreducible findings that covers p. Note, the worklist is a queue so that if $\sigma_1 \sqsubset \sigma_2$ the algorithm will consider σ_2 before σ_1.

Theorem 1. *Let* $\Sigma = \mathsf{AccessSummary}(p)$. *Then (1)* Σ *covers* p, *(2) each* $\sigma \in \Sigma$ *is irreducible, and (3)* Σ *is minimal.*

4   Implementation and Evaluation

The algorithm AccessSummary is implemented in the IAM Access Analyzer feature launched on Dec 2, 2019 [10]. The ZELKOVA tool [2] is used as the access oracle for the algorithm. Access Analyzer monitors the relevant resource policies in an account and re-runs the algorithm on any changes. Findings are presented to the user through a web console and through APIs. Users can *archive* findings that represent intended access to the resource. For unintended findings, Access Analyzer links to the relevant policy that users can edit to remove that access. Access Analyzer will automatically run on the changed policy and any findings that are no longer relevant will be set to a *resolved* state. By monitoring any existing or new *active* findings, users can ensure their polices grant only the intended access.

Evaluation Metrics. We evaluate our algorithm along two dimensions: (1) "how efficient is the algorithm at generating findings?" and (2) "how effective are the generated findings at simplifying the complexity of a policy?". As our algorithm solves a new problem, we do not have an external basis for comparison. Instead, we compare the algorithm against the state space it operates over. To this end, for each policy, we define the following measures:

- **size** is the size of the set of all possible findings for the policy.
- **findings** is the number of findings produced by the algorithm.
- **queries** is the number of SMT queries made by the algorithm.
- **runtime** is the total runtime of the algorithm.

Note that **findings** ≤ **queries** ≤ **size**, as each query generates at most one finding and we query each possible finding at most once.

Benchmarks. We randomly selected 1,387 policies from a corpus of in-use policies. As we are interested primarily in difficult policies, we filtered out all policies that had **size** less than 10. That left 165 policies. Each policy was evaluated on a 2.5 GHz Intel Core i7 with 16 GB of RAM. The runtime per finding (**runtime/findings**) was less than 430ms for all policies except one outlier at 2,267 ms. The 165 policies ranged in size from 56 to 810 lines of pretty-printed JSON with a median size of 91 lines.

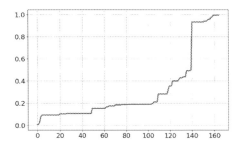 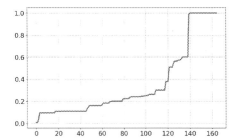

Fig. 5. Actual findings vs. search space   **Fig. 6.** Actual queries vs. search space

Results. Figures 5 and 6 show the number of findings and queries, respectively, compared to the overall search space. Both graphs are sorted to be monotonic, *i.e.* the *x*-axes are different. Figure 5 shows to what degree the findings simplify the policy, with smaller numbers being better. This measure will always be between 0 and 1 since 0 ≤ **findings** ≤ **size**. We see that 85% of policies achieve a ratio of 0.5 or better, and 64% achieve a ratio of 0.2 or better. Figure 6 shows how efficient the algorithm is in exploring its state space, with smaller numbers being better. This measure is between 0 and 1 as 0 ≤ **queries** ≤ **size**. The algorithm explores the entire search space for only 15% of the policies, with a median ratio of 0.22.

5   Related Work

The majority of tools available for access policy analysis are based on log analysis or syntactic pattern matching, which are both imprecise (*i.e.* fail to account for the complex logic in AWS policies) and unsound (*i.e.* fail to check for all requests) and hence, can take months to discover that resources are susceptible to potentially unintended access. Most formal methods based work has focused on securing individual pieces of cloud infrastructure via low-level proofs of software correctness *e.g.* Ironclad [6]. Cloud Contracts [4] are requirements over network access control lists and routing tables. Cloud Contracts are verified using the SecGuru tool [7] that compares network connectivity policies using the SMT theory of bit vectors. In contrast, our work answers a larger question about the entire enterprise-level security posture using a series of ZELKOVA queries [2]. The Fireman system [11] shows how to use Binary Decision Diagrams to analyze access control lists (ACL) in firewall configurations. The ACL configuration language is more restricted than IAM's and the tool is limited to a fixed set of queries about which accesses (packets) are allowed. Most closely related to our work is the Margrave system [9] which encodes firewall policies as propositional logic formulas, and then use SAT solvers to answer queries about the policies. Margrave introduces the notion of *scenario finding*, and shows how to produce an exhaustive set of scenarios that *witness* the queried behavior. The IAM policy language is significantly richer, and hence, enumerating scenarios is computationally intractable, which led us to the develop stratified abstraction as a means of summarizing policy semantics, thereby providing analysts comprehensive visibility into the accessibility of resources, helping detect misconfigurations, and ensuring that updates indeed fix the potential for unintended accesses.

References

1. Agerwala, T., Misra, J.: Assertion graphs for verifying and synthesizing programs. Technical report, University of Texas at Austin, USA (1978)
2. Backes, J., et al.: Semantic-based automated reasoning for AWS access policies using SMT. In: 2018 Formal Methods in Computer Aided Design (FMCAD), pp. 1–9. IEEE (2018)
3. Barrett, C., et al.: CVC4. In: Gopalakrishnan, G., Qadeer, S. (eds.) CAV 2011. LNCS, vol. 6806, pp. 171–177. Springer, Heidelberg (2011). https://doi.org/10.1007/978-3-642-22110-1_14
4. Bjørner, N., Jayaraman, K.: Checking cloud contracts in microsoft azure. In: Natarajan, R., Barua, G., Patra, M.R. (eds.) ICDCIT 2015. LNCS, vol. 8956, pp. 21–32. Springer, Cham (2015). https://doi.org/10.1007/978-3-319-14977-6_2
5. Grumberg, O. (ed.): CAV 1997. LNCS, vol. 1254. Springer, Heidelberg (1997). https://doi.org/10.1007/3-540-63166-6
6. Hawblitzel, C., et al.: Ironclad apps: end-to-end security via automated full-system verification. OSDI **14**, 165–181 (2014)
7. Jayaraman, K., Bjorner, N., Outhred, G., Kaufman, C.: Automated analysis and debugging of network connectivity policies. Technical report MSR-TR-2014-102, Microsoft Research (2014)

8. de Moura, L., Bjørner, N.: Z3: an efficient SMT solver. In: Ramakrishnan, C.R., Rehof, J. (eds.) TACAS 2008. LNCS, vol. 4963, pp. 337–340. Springer, Heidelberg (2008). https://doi.org/10.1007/978-3-540-78800-3_24

9. Nelson, T., Barratt, C., Dougherty, D.J., Fisler, K., Krishnamurthi, S.: The margrave tool for firewall analysis. In: Proceedings of the 24th International Conference on Large Installation System Administration, LISA 2010, pp. 1–8. USENIX Association, USA (2010)

10. West, B.: AWS news blog, December 2019. https://aws.amazon.com/blogs/aws/identify-unintended-resource-access-with-aws-identity-and-access-management-iam-access-analyzer/

11. Yuan, L., Mai, J., Su, Z., Chen, H., Chuah, C., Mohapatra, P.: FIREMAN: a toolkit for firewall modeling and analysis. In: 2006 IEEE Symposium on Security and Privacy (S&P 2006), Berkeley, California, USA, May 21–24, pp. 199–213 (2006). https://doi.org/10.1109/SP.2006.16

Synthesis of Super-Optimized Smart Contracts Using Max-SMT

Elvira Albert[1,2], Pablo Gordillo[2(✉)], Albert Rubio[1,2],
and Maria A. Schett[3]

[1] Instituto de Tecnología del Conocimiento,
Madrid, Spain
[2] Complutense University of Madrid,
Madrid, Spain
pabgordi@ucm.es
[3] University College London, London, U.K.

Abstract. With the advent of smart contracts that execute on the blockchain ecosystem, a new mode of reasoning is required for developers that must pay meticulous attention to the *gas* spent by their smart contracts, as well as for optimization tools that must be capable of effectively reducing the gas required by the smart contracts. Super-optimization is a technique which attempts to find the best translation of a block of code by trying all possible sequences of instructions that produce the same result. This paper presents a novel approach for super-optimization of smart contracts based on Max-SMT which is split into two main phases: (i) the extraction of a *stack functional specification* from the basic blocks of the smart contract, which is simplified using rules that capture the semantics of the arithmetic, bit-wise, relational operations, etc. (ii) the *synthesis of optimized blocks* which, by means of an efficient Max-SMT encoding, finds the bytecode blocks with minimal gas cost whose stack functional specification is equal (modulo commutativity) to the extracted one. Our experimental results are very promising: we are able to optimize 55.41 % of the blocks, and prove that 34.28 % were already optimal, for more than 61 000 blocks from the most called 2500 Ethereum contracts.

1 Introduction

Open-source software that leverages on the blockchain ecosystem is known as *smart contract*. Smart contracts are not necessarily restricted to the classical concept of contracts, but can be any kind of program that executes on a blockchain or distributed ledger. A smart contract can be regarded as a collection of secured stored functions whose execution and effects (e.g., the transfer of some value between parties) cannot be manipulated. This is because all records of the transactions must be stored on a public and decentralized blockchain that avoids the

This work was funded partially by the Spanish MCIU, AEI and FEDER (EU) projects RTI2018-094403-B-C31 and RTI2018-094403-B-C33, by the CM project P2018/TCS-4314 and by the UCM CT27/16-CT28/16 grant.

S. K. Lahiri and C. Wang (Eds.): CAV 2020, LNCS 12224, pp. 177–200, 2020.
https://doi.org/10.1007/978-3-030-53288-8_10

pitfalls of centralization. While Bitcoin [21] paved the way for cryptocurrencies and for the popularity of the blockchain technology, Ethereum [25] showed the full potential of blockchains by allowing developers to run their decentralized applications on top of their platform. The Ethereum Virtual Machine (EVM) is capable of running smart contracts coded by Ethereum developers that have the potential of replacing all sorts of legal, financial and social agreements, e.g., can be used to fulfill employment contracts, execute bets and wagers, etc.

On the Ethereum blockchain platform, as well as in other emerging blockchains equipped with a smart contract programming language (e.g., Tezos [1], Zilliqa [24], Facebook's Libra [23]), *gas* refers to the fee, or pricing value, required to successfully conduct a transaction or to execute a smart contract. Gas is priced in a sub-unit of the cryptocurrency—in Ethereum in *gwei*, a sub-unit of its *Ether* cryptocurrency. The EVM specification [25] provides the *gas model*, i.e., a precise definition of the gas consumption for each EVM bytecode instruction. The EVM is a simple stack-based architecture: computation on the EVM is done using a stack-based bytecode language; the word size of the machine is 256-bits (32-bytes), and this is also the size of a stack item. The proposer of a transaction allots an amount of gas (known as gas limit) to carry out the execution. If the transaction exceeds the allotted gas limit, an *out-of-gas* exception is raised, interrupting the current execution. The rationale of gas metering is three-fold: first, a gas-metered execution puts a cap on the number of operations that a transaction can execute and prevents attacks based on non-terminating executions; second, paying for gas at the moment of creating the transaction does not allow the proposer to waste other parties' (aka *miners*) computational resources; third, gas fees discourage users to overuse replicated *storage*, which is an expensive and valuable resource in a blockchain-based consensus system.

Optimization of smart contracts has thus a clear optimization target: gas usage, as both computational and storage costs are accounted within the gas cost of each of the EVM instructions. Indeed, reducing gas costs of smart contracts is a problem of utmost relevance in the blockchain ecosystem, as there are normally between half a million and a million transactions a day. The cost of a transaction in Ethereum ranges from cents to few dollars, except in certain peak periods that has been ten or a hundred times more. In order to provide an idea of the impact of gas saving techniques, we have estimated that the money spent in transactions (excluding the intrinsic gas cost) from 2017 to 2019 is around 157 Million dollars[1]. Thus, optimizing programs in an energy-saving way is essential in general, but it is even more so in the blockchain ecosystem. The Solidity[2] documentation [13], and posterior documents (e.g., [9,19]), identify gas-costly patterns and propose replacements with gas-efficient ones. Adopting these guidelines requires a deep understanding of EVM instructions and the gas consumption for the different operations. Compilers for Solidity also try to optimize the bytecode for minimizing its gas consumption (e.g., the flag optimize of the

---

[1] The data is taken from [3] using the gas spent by transactions and the average *gwei* and Ether exchange rate per day.

[2] It is the most popular programming language for writing Ethereum smart contracts.

`solc` compiler optimizes storage of large constants and the `dispatch` routine, with the goal of saving gas).

Even when the guidelines are followed and the optimize flag is used, the compiled EVM code is not always as efficient as desired. Super-optimization [17] is a technique proposed over 30 years ago which attempts to find the best translation of a block of code using exhaustive search to try all possible sequences of instructions that produce the same result. As an exhaustive search problem, it is computationally extremely demanding. The work in [15] proposed the idea of "unbounded" super-optimization that consists in shifting the *search* for the target program into the solver. Recently, unbounded super-optimization has been applied to Ethereum bytecode [20] for *basic block* optimization (i.e., optimizations are made inside a basic block formed by a sequence of instructions without any JUMP operation in the middle). The experimental results in [20] confirm the extreme computational demands of the technique (e.g., the tool times out in 92% of the blocks used in their evaluation). This is a severe limitation for the use of the technique, and the problem of finding the optimal code for an EVM block still remains very challenging. The complexity stems mainly from three sources: First, the problem is expressed in the theory of bit-vector arithmetic with bit-width size of 256, which is a challenging width size for most SMT solvers. Second, expressing the problem involves an exists-forall quantification, since we want to find an assignment of instructions that works for all values in the initial stack. Third, since we look for the gas-optimal code, the problem is not a satisfaction problem but rather an optimization problem.

Contributions. This paper proposes a novel method for gas optimization of smart contracts which is based on synthesizing optimized EVM blocks using Max-SMT. The main novel features that distinguish our work from previous approaches, that attack the same or a similar problem [15,20], are:

1. *Stack functional specification.* Our method takes as input an EVM bytecode and first obtains from it a stack functional specification (SFS) of the input and output operational stacks for each of the blocks of the control-flow graph (CFG) for the bytecode by using symbolic execution. The SFS determines thus the target stack that the block has to compute and is simplified using a set of rules that capture a great part of the semantics of the arithmetic, bit-wise, relational, etc., EVM operations which are relevant for gas optimization.
2. *Synthesis problem using SMT.* We approach optimization as a synthesis problem in which an SMT solver is used to synthesize optimal EVM bytecode which, for the input stack given in the functional specification, produces the target stack determined by the specification. We present a very efficient encoding that, in contrast to the previous attempts, uses only existential quantification in a very simple fragment of integer arithmetic. According to our evaluation, its simplicity greatly improves the performance of the SMT solvers while accuracy is kept as we cover the main possible optimizations. Importantly, only the semantics of the stack operations (PUSH, DUP, SWAP, etc.) is encoded, while all other operations are treated as uninterpreted functions.

3. *Use of Max-SMT.* We encode the optimization problem using Max-SMT, by adding soft constraints that encode the gas cost of the selected instructions, by adding the needed weights. This allows us to take advantage of the features given by recent Max-SMT optimizers that can improve the search.

4. *Experiments.* We report on syrup, an implementation of our approach, and evaluate it on (i) the same data set used for evaluating the tool ebso from [20] and, (ii) on 128 of the most called contracts on the Ethereum blockchain. Our results are very promising: while ebso timed out in 92.12 % of the blocks in (i), we only time out in 8.64 % and obtain gains that are two orders of magnitude larger than ebso. These results show that we have found the right balance between what is optimized by means of symbolic execution and symbolic simplification using rules and what is encoded as a Max-SMT problem. Moreover, for set (ii), we obtain gas savings of 0.59% of the total gas. Assuming that these savings are uniformly distributed, it would amount nearly to 1 Million dollars from 2017 to 2019.

While the purpose of superoptimization is to optimize at the level of basic blocks (intra-block), our approach to synthesize EVM code from a given SFS can be applied also in a richer optimization framework that enables the optimization of multiple basic blocks (inter-block). For this purpose, the framework should be extended to include branching instructions (which in the SMT encoding can be handled with uninterpreted functions as well) and, besides, additional components would be required, e.g., in the context of EVM we would need to resolve the jumping addresses, and to ensure that there are no additional incoming jumps to intermediate blocks that are being merged by the optimizer. Inter-block optimization is especially interesting in the context of smart contracts to gain storage-related gas, since the optimizations that can be achieved locally for the storage are quite limited as explained in Sect. 6.

```
1  pragma solidity ^0.4.25;               1   JUMPDEST    10  DUP4     19  POP
2  contract addExp{                        2   PUSH1 0x00  11  DUP6     20  POP
3    function ae(uint x3, uint x2, uint x1, 3   DUP1        12  ADD      21  POP
4      uint x0) returns (uint){            4   PUSH1 0x00  13  SWAP1    22  SWAP5
5      uint x = x3+x2;                      5   DUP6        14  POP      23  SWAP4
6      uint y = x1+x0;                      6   DUP8        15  DUP1     24  POP
7      return x**y;   //EXP operation       7   ADD         16  DUP3     25  POP
8    }                                      8   SWAP2       17  EXP      26  POP
9  }                                        9   POP         18  SWAP3    27  POP
                                                                         28  JUMP
```

Fig. 1. Solidity code (left). Under-optimized EVM bytecode using solc (right).

2   Overview: Optimal Bytecode as a Synthesis Problem

This section provides a general overview of our method for synthesizing super-optimized smart contracts from given EVM bytecode. We use the motivating example in Fig. 1 whose Solidity source code contract appears to the left and the EVM bytecode generated by the `solc` compiler appears to the right. Solidity is an object-oriented, high-level language that is statically typed, supports inheritance, libraries and user-defined types, among other features. It is designed to target the EVM. As it can be observed in the example the EVM bytecodes that operate on the stack (i.e., `DUP`, `SWAP`, `ADD`, `AND`, etc.) are standard operators. In the following, we refer as *stack operations* only to `DUP`, `PUSH`, `SWAP` and `POP`, which modify the stack without performing computations. The EVM has also bytecodes to access persistent data stored in the contract's storage (`SLOAD` and `SSTORE`), to access data stored in the local memory (`MLOAD` and `MSTORE`), bytecodes that jump to a different code address location (`JUMP`, `JUMPI`), bytecodes for calling a function on a different contract (`CALL`, `DELEGATECALL`, `CALLCODE` and `CALLSTATIC`), to write a log (`LOG`), to access information about the blockchain and transaction (`GAS`, `CALLER`, `BLOCKHASH`, etc.) and copy information related to an external call (`CODECOPY`, `RETURNDATACOPY`, etc.). However, as we explain in the coming sections, our approach is based on optimizing the operations that modify the stack as we have a great coverage of all potential bytecode optimizations while we still remain scalable, i.e., we do not optimize those bytecodes whose effects are not reflected in the stack, e.g., `MSTORE`, `SSTORE`, `LOG1` or `EXTCODECOPY`. The gas consumed by this bytecode (excluding the `JUMPDEST` and `JUMP` opcodes that cannot be optimized and are thus not accounted in the examples) is 76. As specified in [25], the operations from the so-called *base* family (like `POP`) have cost 2, the operators from the *verylow* family (like `PUSH`, `SWAP`, `ADD`) cost 3, operators from the *low* family (like `MUL`, `DIV`) cost 5, and so on.

2.1 Extracting Stack Functional Specifications from EVM Bytecode

Our method takes as input the set of blocks that make up the control flow graph (CFG) of the bytecode. The first step is, for each of the blocks, to extract from it a *stack functional specification* (SFS) from which the super-optimized bytecode will be synthesized. The SFS is a functional description of the initial stack when entering the block and the final stack after executing the block, which instead of using bytecode instructions to determine how the final stack is computed, is defined by means of *symbolic first-order terms* over the initial stack elements. The SFS for our running example is shown in Fig. 2. As can be observed, it consists of an initial stack shown at the left which simply determines what the size of the input stack to the block is and assigns a symbolic variable as identifier to each stack position (e.g., the initial stack contains five elements named $x_0, \ldots, x_4$); while the output stack

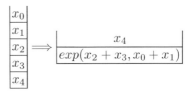

Fig. 2. Initial and final stack

contains two elements: x_4 at the top, and the symbolic term $exp(x_2 + x_3, x_0 + x_1)$ at the bottom. The output stack is obtained by symbolic execution of the bytecodes that operate on the stack, as it will be formalized in Sect. 3. The resulting expressions are then optimized by means of simplification rules based on the semantics of the non-stack operations (e.g., the neutral elements, double negations or idempotent operations are removed, operations on constants performed). This captures a relevant part of the semantics of the non-stack operators.

2.2   The Synthesis Problem

This section hints on how the generated bytecode will be, and on that the synthesis of optimal bytecode from the specification is challenging.

Example 1. From the SFS in Fig. 2, we know that we have to compute $x_0 + x_1$ and $x_2 + x_3$, but we have to decide which summation we compute first. On the left, we have the best bytecode (together with the stack evolution) when we first compute $x_2 + x_3$ and on the right when we first compute $x_0 + x_1$. Computing first one subexpression or the other has an impact on the consumed gas, since the bytecode on the left has a gas cost of 31 and the bytecode on the right has a gas cost of 25, which is indeed the optimum.

SWAP3	$[x_3, x_1, x_2, x_0, x_4]$		
SWAP1	$[x_1, x_3, x_2, x_0, x_4]$	ADD	$[x_0 + x_1, x_2, x_3, x_4]$
SWAP2	$[x_2, x_3, x_1, x_0, x_4]$	SWAP2	$[x_3, x_2, x_0 + x_1, x_4]$
ADD	$[x_2 + x_3, x_1, x_0, x_4]$	ADD	$[x_3 + x_2, x_0 + x_1, x_4]$
SWAP2	$[x_0, x_1, x_2 + x_3, x_4]$	SWAP1	$[x_0 + x_1, x_3 + x_2, x_4]$
ADD	$[x_0 + x_1, x_2 + x_3, x_4]$	EXP	$[(x_0 + x_1) \ast\ast (x_2 + x_3), x_4]$
EXP	$[(x_0 + x_1) \ast\ast (x_2 + x_3), x_4]$	SWAP1	$[x_4, (x_0 + x_1) \ast\ast (x_2 + x_3)]$
SWAP1	$[x_4, (x_0 + x_1) \ast\ast (x_2 + x_3)]$		

Both codes are far better than the original generated bytecode whose gas cost was 76. Besides, note that the cost of the two additions and the exponentiation is in total 16 (that necessarily has to remain), which means that the optimal code has used only 9 units of gas for the rest while the original code needed 60 units.

The next example shows that the optimal code is obtained when the subterms of the exponential are computed in the other order (compared to the previous example). Hence, an exhaustive search of all possibilities (with its associated computational demands) must be carried out to find the optimum.

Example 2. Let us now consider a slight variation of the previous example in which the functional specification is $[x_0, x_1, x_2, x_3] \implies [x_3, (x_0 + x_1) \ast\ast (x_0 + x_2)]$. Now, on the left-hand side we have the best bytecode (together with the stack evolution) when we compute first $x_0 + x_2$ and on the right-hand side we have the best bytecode when we compute first $x_0 + x_1$.

DUP1	$[x_0, x_0, x_1, x_2, x_3]$
SWAP3	$[x_2, x_0, x_1, x_0, x_3]$
ADD	$[x_2 + x_0, x_1, x_0, x_3]$
SWAP2	$[x_0, x_1, x_2 + x_0, x_3]$
ADD	$[x_0 + x_1, x_2 + x_0, x_3]$
EXP	$[(x_0 + x_1) ** (x_2 + x_0), x_3]$
SWAP1	$[x_3, (x_0 + x_1) ** (x_2 + x_0)]$

DUP1	$[x_0, x_0, x_1, x_2, x_3]$
SWAP2	$[x_1, x_0, x_0, x_2, x_3]$
ADD	$[x_1 + x_0, x_0, x_2, x_3]$
SWAP2	$[x_2, x_0, x_1 + x_0, x_3]$
ADD	$[x_2 + x_0, x_1 + x_0, x_3]$
SWAP1	$[x_1 + x_0, x_2 + x_0, x_3]$
EXP	$[(x_1 + x_0) ** (x_2 + x_0), x_3]$
SWAP1	$[x_3, (x_1 + x_0) ** (x_2 + x_0)]$

In this case the bytecode on the left has a gas cost of 28, which is indeed the optimum, and the bytecode on the right has a gas cost of 31. The original bytecode generated by solc has gas cost 74, so again the improvement is huge.

Both examples show that, in principle, even if we have the functional specification that guides the search, we have to exhaustively try all possible ways to obtain it, if we want to ensure that we have found the optimal bytecode.

2.3   Characteristics of Our SMT Encoding of the Synthesis Problem

Our approach to super-optimize blocks is based on restricting the problem in such a way that we have both a great coverage of most EVM code optimizations and we can propose an encoding in a simple theory where an SMT solver can perform efficiently. To this end, the key point is to handle all non-stack operations, like ADD, SUB, AND, OR, LT, as *uninterpreted bytecodes*. This allows us to simplify the encoding in two directions. First, by considering them as uninterpreted bytecodes we can avoid reasoning on the theory of bit-vectors with width 256. Second, and even more important, this allows us to express the problem in the existentially quantified fragment, avoiding the exists/forall alternation:

1. We start from the SFS by introducing fresh variables abstracting out all terms built with uninterpreted functions, in such a way that every fresh variable represents a term $f(a_1, \ldots, a_n)$, where every a_i is either a (256 bit) numeric value, a fresh variable, or an initial stack variable. We also have sharing by having a single variable for every term, e.g., $(x_0+1) ** (x_0+1)$, where x_0 is the top of the initial stack, is abstracted into $y_0 = \text{EXP}_\text{U}(y_1, y_1)$ and $y_1 = \text{ADD}_\text{U}(x_0, 1)$, where y_0 and y_1 are fresh variables and EXP_U and ADD_U are the uninterpreted bytecodes for exponentiation and addition, respectively.
2. Now, in order to avoid universal quantification, we take advantage of the fact that only values from 0 to $2^{256} - 1$ can be introduced in the stack by a PUSH opcode and hence only this range can appear in the SFS. Therefore, if we assign values from 2^{256} on to fresh variables and initial stack variables we avoid the confusion between themselves and all other values in the problem.

After these two key observations have been made, we fix the maximal number n of opcodes and highest size h of the stack that is allowed in a solution. This can be bound by analyzing the original code generated by the compiler. From this, we roughly encode the problem using variables $o_0, \ldots, o_{n-1}$ to express the operations of our code (together with variables $p_0, \ldots, p_{n-1}$ that encode the value

$0 \leq p_i \leq 2^{256} - 1$ added to the stack when o_i is a PUSH), variables $s_0^i, \ldots, s_{h-1}^i$ to encode the contents of the stack before executing the operation o_i, where s_0^i is the top of the stack (we also use some Boolean variables to express the active part of the stack). Using this, we can encode the behavior of all stack operations: POP, PUSH, DUP, SWAP for all its versions (like DUP1, DUP2, . . .). For the uninterpreted bytecodes f_u, we basically add for every abstraction $y = f_u(a_1, \ldots, a_m)$ assertions stating that if we have $a_1, \ldots, a_m$ at the top of the stack at step i (i.e., $s_0^i, \ldots, s_{m-1}^i$) and we take the operation f in o_i then in step $i + 1$ we have $y, s_m^i, \ldots$ on the top of the stack. Again, as all fresh variables and initial stack variables have been replaced by values form 2^{256} on, there is no confusion with all other values.

As a final remark, we have also encoded the commutativity property of uninterpreted bytecodes representing the ADD, MUL, AND, OR, etc. This can be easily made by considering that the arguments can occur at the top of the stack in the two possible orders. Other properties like associativity are more difficult to encode and are left for future developments.

2.4   Optimal Synthesis Using Max-SMT

The last key element is how we encode the optimization problem of finding the bytecode with minimal gas cost. First, let us describe which notion of optimality we are considering. Our problem is defined as, given an SFS in which all occurring bytecodes there are considered uninterpreted and maybe commutative, we have to provide the bytecode with minimal gas cost whose SFS is equal modulo commutativity to the given one. From the encoding we have described in the previous section, we know that every solution to the SMT problem will have the same SFS as the given one. Hence, we only need to find the solution with minimal gas cost. In [20], this was made by implementing a loop on top of the SMT solving process which was calling the solver asking every time for a better solution in terms of gas, which was also encoded in the SMT problem. Such approach cannot be easily implemented in an incremental way using the SMT solver as a black box without the corresponding performance penalty.

Alternatively, we propose to encode the problem as a Max-SMT problem and hence, we can easily use any Max-SMT optimizer, like Z3 [12], Barcelogic [7] or (Opti)MathSAT [11], as a black box with an important gain in efficiency. The Max-SMT encoding adds to the previously defined SMT encoding some soft constraints, indicating which is the cost associated to choosing every family of operators. As mentioned, choosing an operator from the *base* family has cost 2, from the *verylow* 3, and so on. Then, the optimal solution is the solution that minimizes this cost, which can be obtained with a Max-SMT optimizer.

29	SSTORE	35	DUP2	41	DUP1		
30	SWAP1	36	MSTORE	42	SWAP2	47	PUSH1 0x01
31	DUP5	37	PUSH1 0x20	43	SUB	48	SWAP2
32	SWAP1	38	ADD	44	SWAP1	49	SWAP1
33	MLOAD	39	PUSH1 0x40	45	LOG2	50	POP
34	SWAP1	40	MLOAD	46	POP	51	JUMP

Block 1		Block 2		Block 3	

30	SWAP1						
31	DUP5	37	PUSH1 0x20	41	DUP1	46	POP
32	SWAP1	38	ADD	42	SWAP2	47	PUSH1 0x01
33	MLOAD	39	PUSH1 0x40	43	SUB	48	SWAP2
34	SWAP1	40	MLOAD	44	SWAP1	49	SWAP1
35	DUP2					50	POP

Fig. 3. CFG block of a real smart contract (top), and blocks generated to build the functional description of the EVM bytecode (bottom)

3 Stack Functional Specification from EVM Bytecode

The starting point of our work is the CFG of the EVM bytecode to be optimized. There are already a number of tools (e.g., ETHIR [6], Madmax [14], Mythril [18] or Rattle [4]) that are able to compute the CFG from the bytecode of a given smart contract. Therefore, we do not need to formalize, neither to implement, this initial CFG generation step. Since there are bytecode instructions that we do not optimize, for each of the blocks of the provided CFG, we first perform a further block-partitioning that splits a basic block into the sub-blocks that will be optimized by our method as defined below. A basic block is defined as a sequence of EVM instructions without any JUMP bytecode.

Definition 1 (block-partitioning). *Given a basic block* $B = [b_0, b_1, ..., b_n]$, *we define its block-partitioning as follows:*

$$blocks(B) = \left\{ B_i \equiv b_i, \ldots, b_j \; \middle| \; \begin{array}{l} (\forall k.i < k < j, b_k \notin Jump \cup Terminal \cup Split \cup \\ \{JUMPDEST\}) \wedge (\ i{=}0 \vee b_{i-1} \in Split \cup \{JUMPDEST\} \ ) \wedge \\ (\ j{=}n \vee b_{j+1} \in Jump \cup Split \cup Terminal \ ) \end{array} \right\}$$

where

$$Jump = \{JUMP, JUMPI\}$$
$$Terminal = \{RETURN, REVERT, STOP, INVALID\}$$
$$Split = \{SSTORE, MSTORE, LOGX, CALLDATACOPY, CODECOPY, EXTCODECOPY,$$
$$RETURNDATACOPY\}$$

As it can be observed, the bytecodes whose effects are not reflected on the stack induce the partitioning and are omitted in the fragmented sub-blocks. These include the bytecodes that modify the memory, the storage or record a log, that belong to the *Split* set. Figure 3 shows a CFG block at the top and the blocks generated to build the functional description at the bottom. The original CFG block contains the bytecodes SSTORE, MSTORE and LOG2. Thus, it is split into three different blocks that do not contain these bytecodes.

$$(1)\ \tau(\mathcal{S}, \texttt{PUSHX}\ A) = [A \mid \mathcal{S}]$$
$$(2)\quad \tau(\mathcal{S}, \texttt{DUPX}) = [\mathcal{S}[0] \mid \mathcal{S}]$$
$$(3)\quad \tau(\mathcal{S}, \texttt{SWAPX}) = temp = \mathcal{S}[0], \mathcal{S}[0] = \mathcal{S}[X], \mathcal{S}[X] = temp$$
$$(4)\quad \tau(\mathcal{S}, \texttt{POP}) = \mathcal{S}.remove(0)$$
$$(5)\quad \tau(\mathcal{S}, \texttt{OP}) = [\texttt{OP}(\mathcal{S}[0], ..., \mathcal{S}[\delta - 1]) \mid \mathcal{S}[\delta : n]\ ]$$

Fig. 4. Symbolic execution of the instructions that operate on the stack

Once we have the partitioned blocks from the CFG, we aim at obtaining a functional description of the output stack (i.e., the stack after executing the sequence of bytecodes in the block) using symbolic execution for each of the partitioned blocks. As the stack is empty before executing a transaction and the number of elements that each EVM bytecode consumes and produces is known, the size of the stack at the beginning of each block can be inferred statically. We can thus assume that the initial stack size is given within the CFG. A symbolic stack $\mathcal{S}$ is a list of size k that represents the state of the stack where the list position 0 corresponds to the top of the stack and $k - 1$ is the index of the bottom of the stack, such that $\mathcal{S}[i]$ is the symbolic value stored at the position i of the stack. Initially, the input stack maps each index to a symbolic variable s_i.

The symbolic execution of each bytecode is defined using the transfer function τ described in Fig. 4 which takes an input stack and a bytecode and returns the output stack as follows: (1) the PUSHX bytecode stores at the top of the stack the value A, (2) DUPX duplicates the element stored at position X-1 to the top of the stack, (3) SWAPX exchanges the values stored at the top of the stack with the one stored at position X, (4) POP deletes the value stored in the top of the stack (using the list operation $remove$ to delete the element at the given position), (5) OP represents all other EVM bytecodes that operate with the stack (arithmetic and bit-wise operations among others). In that case, τ creates a symbolic expression that is a functor with the same name as the original EVM bytecode and as arguments the symbolic expressions stored in the stack elements that it consumes. Here, δ stands for the number of elements that the EVM bytecode OP gets from the stack. Now, the SFS can be defined using the function τ as follows.

Definition 2 (SFS). *Given a block B with an initial size of the stack k, the initial state of the stack $\mathcal{S}_0$ stores at each position $i \in \{0, ..., k - 1\}$ a symbolic variable s_i. Then, the transfer function τ is extended to the block B, denoted by $\tau(B)$, as: $[s_0, \ldots, s_{k-1}]$ if B is empty; and $\tau(\tau(B'), o)$ if B has o as last operation and B' is the resulting block without o. The SFS of B is $\mathcal{S}_0 \implies \mathcal{S} = \tau(B)$.*

Example 3. Consider the block formed by the EVM bytecode shown in Fig. 1, starting with the bytecode at program point 2 (pp2 for short) and finishing with the bytecode at pp27. Before executing the block symbolically, the initial stack is $\mathcal{S}_0 = [s_0, s_1, s_2, s_3, s_4]$ and $k = 5$. After applying the transfer function τ, we obtain the following results at the next selected program points:

$pp2:\ \tau(\mathcal{S}, \text{PUSH1 0X00}) = [0, s_0, s_1, s_2, s_3, s_4]$

$pp3:\ \tau(\mathcal{S}, \text{DUP1}) = [0, 0, s_0, s_1, s_2, s_3, s_4]$

$pp5:\ \tau(\mathcal{S}, \text{DUP6}) = [s_2, 0, 0, 0, s_0, s_1, s_2, s_3, s_4]$

$pp6:\ \tau(\mathcal{S}, \text{DUP8}) = [s_3, s_2, 0, 0, 0, s_0, s_1, s_2, s_3, s_4]$

$pp7:\ \tau(\mathcal{S}, \text{ADD}) = [\text{ADD}(s_3, s_2), 0, 0, 0, s_0, s_1, s_2, s_3, s_4]$

$pp8:\ \tau(\mathcal{S}, \text{SWAP2}) = [0, 0, \text{ADD}(s_3, s_2), 0, s_0, s_1, s_2, s_3, s_4]$

$pp9:\ \tau(\mathcal{S}, \text{POP}) = [0, \text{ADD}(s_3, s_2), 0, s_0, s_1, s_2, s_3, s_4]$

$pp15:\ \tau(\mathcal{S}, \text{DUP1}) = [\text{ADD}(s_1, s_0), \text{ADD}(s_1, s_0), \text{ADD}(s_3, s_2), 0, s_0, s_1, s_2, s_3, s_4]$

$pp16:\ \tau(\mathcal{S}, \text{DUP3}) = [\text{ADD}(s_3, s_2), \text{ADD}(s_1, s_0), \text{ADD}(s_1, s_0), \text{ADD}(s_3, s_2), 0, s_0, s_1, s_2, s_3, s_4]$

$pp17:\ \tau(\mathcal{S}, \text{EXP}) = [\text{EXP}(\text{ADD}(s_3, s_2), \text{ADD}(s_1, s_0)), \text{ADD}(s_1, s_0), \text{ADD}(s_3, s_2), s_0, s_1, s_2, s_3, s_4]$

$pp27:\ \tau(\mathcal{S}, \text{POP}) = [s_4, \text{EXP}(\text{ADD}(s_3, s_2), \text{ADD}(s_1, s_0))]$

Thus, altogether, the output stack of the SFS given by τ for the block in Fig. 1 is $\mathcal{S} = [s_4, \text{EXP}(\text{ADD}(s_3, s_2), \text{ADD}(s_1, s_0))]$. For example, we can see that τ updates the stack inserting a 0 in the top of the stack at pp2. At pp8, it swaps the element in the top of the stack ($\text{ADD}(s_3, s_2)$) with the element stored at position 2 (0). It generates a symbolic expression to represent the addition at pp7 with the values stored in the position of the stack that it consumes. At pp17 it generates a new symbolic expression $\text{EXP}(\text{ADD}(s_3, s_2), \text{ADD}(s_1, s_0))$ to represent the exponentiation of the two elements stored in the top of the stack. Note that in this case these elements are also symbolic expressions of the two previous additions symbolically executed before.

Finally, we capture optimizations based on the semantics of the arithmetic and bit-wise operations, by applying simplification rules on the SFS of the block before we proceed to generate the optimized code. This simplification besides reducing the number of operations includes other notions of simplification as well. The easiest examples are the application of simplification rules like with the units of every operation, or with the idempotence of bit-wise Boolean operators.

4   Optimal Synthesis Using Max-SMT

This section describes our Max-SMT encoding. We start by preprocessing the SFS into an abstract form that is convenient for the encoding in Sect. 4.1. Next, Sect. 4.2 describes a key element of our encoding: the stack model. Sect. 4.3 presents the complete encoding of the problem and Sect. 4.4 how to obtain the optimized EVM blocks from the model obtained by the SMT solver. Finally, Sect. 4.5 describes the optimization problem. The SFS and the encoding generated for the example shown in Fig. 1 are available at https://github.com/mariaschett/syrup-backend/tree/master/examples/cav2020.

4.1   Abstracting Uninterpreted Functions

Before we apply our encoding, we need to abstract all (sub)expressions occurring in the SFS, by introducing new fresh variables $s_k, s_{k+1}, \ldots$ that start after the last stack variable in the initial stack $[s_0, \ldots, s_{k-1}]$ (of size k). In this process we have a mapping from fresh variables to shallow expressions of depth one, i.e., built with a function symbol and variables or constants as arguments. Here we introduce the *minimal* number of fresh variables that allow us to describe the SFS using only shallow expressions. By minimal, we mean that we use the same variable if some subterm occurs more than once (we also take into account commutativity properties to avoid creating unnecessary fresh variables). Finally if an uninterpreted function occurs more than once, we add a subscript from 0 on to distinguish them. As a result we have that the *abstracted SFS* is defined by a stack S containing only stack variables, fresh variables or constants (in $\{0, \ldots, 2^{256} - 1\}$) and a map M from fresh variables to shallow terms formed by an uninterpreted function (maybe with subscript) applied to stack variables, fresh variables or constants (in $\{0, \ldots, 2^{256} - 1\}$). Besides, we note that the *abstracted SFS* generated is equivalent to first-order A-normal form with shearing. Trivially, all positions in the stack in the SFS and the abstracted SFS are equal when the map is fully applied to remove all fresh variables and the subscripts are removed. Moreover, we have that every uninterpreted function of the SFS has a fresh variable assigned in the map and all function symbols in the map are different.

Example 4. The abstraction of the SFS $[s_4, \mathtt{EXP}(\mathtt{ADD}(s_3, s_2), \mathtt{ADD}(s_1, s_0))]$ shown in Example 3 needs three fresh variables s_5, s_6 and s_7. Then, the abstracted SFS is the stack $S = [s_4, s_7]$ and the mapping M is defined as $\{s_5 \mapsto \mathtt{ADD}_0(s_3, s_2), s_6 \mapsto \mathtt{ADD}_1(s_1, s_0), s_7 \mapsto \mathtt{EXP}(s_5, s_6)\}$.

4.2   Modeling the Stack

A key element in our encoding is the representation of the stack and the elements it contains. As mentioned in Sect. 2.3, a first observation is that in our approach we will only have in the stack constants in the domain $\{0, \ldots, 2^{256} - 1\}$ (we do not care if they represent a negative number or not, as they are handled simply as 256-bit words), initial stack variables $s_0, \ldots, s_{k-1}$ and fresh variables $s_k, \ldots, s_v$. In order to distinguish between constants and the variables s_i, we assign to every variable s_i, with $i \in \{0, \ldots, v\}$, the constant $2^{256} + i$. Now, for instance, we can establish that a PUSH operation can only introduce a constant in $\{0, \ldots, 2^{256} - 1\}$ and that fresh variables s_i can only be introduced by uninterpreted functions if the appropriate arguments are in the stack (see below). The rest of stack operations, like DUP or SWAP, just duplicate or move whatever is in the stack. Since in our encoding we will use the variables $s_0, \ldots, s_v$, as they are part of the SFS, we have a first constraint assigning the constant values to all these variables (this could be done as well with a *let* expression).

$$S_V = \bigwedge_{0 \leqslant i < v} s_i = 2^{256} + i$$

Let us now show how we model the stack along the execution of the instructions. First, we have to fix a bound on the number of operations b_o and the size of the stack b_s. We can apply different heuristics to this end though considering the initial number of operations and the maximum number of stack elements involved in the block are sound bounds. We have to express a stack of b_s positions after executing j operations with $j \in \{0, \ldots, b_o\}$. To this end, on the one hand, we use existentially quantified variables $x_{i,j} \in \mathbb{Z}$ with $i \in \{0, \ldots, b_s - 1\}$ and $j \in \{0, \ldots, b_o\}$ to express the word at position i of the stack after executing the first j operations of the code, where $x_{0,j}$ encodes the word on the top of the stack. On the other hand to complete the modeling we introduce propositional variables $u_{i,j}$ with $i \in \{0, \ldots, b_s - 1\}$ and $j \in \{0, \ldots, b_o\}$, to denote the *utilization* of the stack (i.e., the words that the stack currently holds). Here, $u_{i,j}$ indicates that the word at position i of the stack after executing the first j operations exists or not.

Additionally, to simplify the next definitions we have the following parameterized constraint that, given an instruction step j with $0 < j \leq b_o$, two stack positions α and β and a shift amount $\delta \in \mathbb{Z}$, with $0 \leq \alpha$, $0 \leq \alpha + \delta$, $\beta < b_s$ and $\beta + \delta < b_s$, imposes that the stack after executing $j + 1$ instructions between positions α and β is the same as the stack after executing the j instruction but with a shift of δ (they are moved up if negative and moved down otherwise).

$$Move(j, \alpha, \beta, \delta) = \bigwedge_{\alpha \leq i \leq \beta} u_{i+\delta,j+1} = u_{i,j} \ \wedge \ x_{i+\delta,j+1} = x_{i,j}$$

4.3 Encoding of Instructions

Let $\mathcal{I}$ be the set of instructions occurring in our problem. The set $\mathcal{I}$ is split in three subsets $\mathcal{I}_C \uplus \mathcal{I}_U \uplus \mathcal{I}_S$, where:

- $\mathcal{I}_C$ contains the commutative uninterpreted functions occurring in the map M of the abstracted SFS,
- $\mathcal{I}_U$ contains the non-commutative uninterpreted functions occurring in M,
- $\mathcal{I}_S$ contains the stack operations: PUSH, that introduces an up to 32-bytes item on top of the stack; POP that removes the top of the stack; DUPk, with $k \in \{1, \ldots, 16\}$ that copies the $k-1$ element of the stack on top of the stack; SWAPk, with $k \in \{1, \ldots, 16\}$ that swaps the top of the stack with the k element of the stack; and an extra operation NOP that does nothing.

Note that, although in EVM there are 32 different PUSH instructions depending on the amount of bytes needed to express the item, in our context this distinction is unnecessary, since we can decide afterwards which PUSH do we need by checking in the obtained solution which is the value to be pushed. Also, the operations DUPk in $\mathcal{I}_S$ are reduced to only those with $k < b_s$ (otherwise we go beyond the maximal size of the stack) and, similarly, the operations SWAPk in $\mathcal{I}_S$ are reduced to only those with $k < b_s$.

Let θ be a mapping from the set of instructions in $\mathcal{I}$ to consecutive different non-negative integers in $\{0, \ldots, m_\iota\}$, where $m_\iota + 1$ is the cardinality of $\mathcal{I}$. In order to encode the selected instructions at every step, we introduce the existentially quantified variables $t_j \in \{0, \ldots, m_\iota\}$, with $j \in \{0, \ldots, b_o - 1\}$ where for every instruction $\iota \in \mathcal{I}$, if $t_j = \theta(\iota)$ then we have that the operation executed at step j is ι. Additionally, we introduce associated existentially quantified variables $a_j \in \{0, \ldots, 2^{256} - 1\}$, with $j \in \{0, \ldots, b_o - 1\}$, to express the value pushed at the top of the stack when $t_j = \theta(\text{PUSH})$ (otherwise the value of a_j is meaningless).

Encoding the Stack Operations. First we show how we encode the effect of choosing in t_j one of the operations in $\mathcal{I}_S$ that does not depend on the particular (abstracted) SFS we are considering. The following parameterized constraints show this effect:

$$C_{\text{PUSH}}(j) = t_j = \theta(\text{PUSH}) \Rightarrow 0 \leq a_j < 2^{256} \wedge \neg u_{b_s-1,j} \wedge u_{0,j+1} \wedge x_{0,j+1} = a_j \wedge$$
$$Move(j, 0, b_s - 2, 1)$$
$$C_{\text{DUP}k}(j) = t_j = \theta(\text{DUP}k) \Rightarrow \neg u_{b_s-1,j} \wedge u_{k-1,j} \wedge u_{0,j+1} \wedge x_{0,j+1} = x_{k-1,j} \wedge$$
$$Move(j, 0, b_s - 2, 1)$$
$$C_{\text{SWAP}k}(j) = t_j = \theta(\text{SWAP}k) \Rightarrow u_{k,j} \wedge u_{0,j+1} \wedge x_{0,j+1} = x_{k,j} \wedge u_{k,j+1} \wedge$$
$$x_{k,j+1} = x_{0,j} \wedge Move(j, 1, k - 1, 0) \wedge$$
$$Move(j, k + 1, b_s - 1, 0)$$
$$C_{\text{POP}}(j) = t_j = \theta(\text{POP}) \Rightarrow u_{0,j} \wedge \neg u_{b_s-1,j+1} \wedge Move(j, 1, b_s - 1, -1)$$
$$C_{\text{NOP}}(j) = t_j = \theta(\text{NOP}) \Rightarrow Move(j, 0, b_s - 1, 0)$$

Notice that the stack before executing the instruction t_j is given in the variables $x_{0,j}, \ldots, x_{b_s-1,j}$ and $u_{0,j}, \ldots, u_{b_s-1,j}$, while the stack after executing t_j is given in $x_{0,j+1}, \ldots, x_{b_s-1,j+1}$ and $u_{0,j+1}, \ldots, u_{b_s-1,j+1}$.

In order to avoid redundant solutions (with NOP in intermediate steps), we have to add as well a constraint stating that once we choose NOP as instruction t_j we can only choose NOP for the following instructions $t_{j+1}, t_{j+2} \ldots$:

$$C_{\text{fromNOP}} = \bigwedge_{0 \leq j < b_o - 1} t_j = \theta(\text{NOP}) \Rightarrow t_{j+1} = \theta(\text{NOP})$$

Encoding the Uninterpreted Operations. The encoding of the uninterpreted operations comes from the map M of the abstracted SFS. First of all, note that, every function f occurs only once in M (since subscripts are introduced) and for every $r \mapsto f(o_0, \ldots, o_{n-1})$ in M we have that $f \in \mathcal{I}_C \uplus \mathcal{I}_U$, r is a fresh variable, and $o_0, \ldots, o_{n-1}$ are either initial stack variables, fresh variables or constants. Note also that if $f \in \mathcal{I}_C$ then $n = 2$. Therefore, we define in the encoding the effect of choosing in t_j the uninterpreted function f with $r \mapsto f(o_0, \ldots, o_{n-1})$ in M, as an operation that takes its arguments $o_0, \ldots, o_{n-1}$ from the stack and places its result r in the stack (where o_0 must be at the top of the stack).

$$C_U(j, f) = t_j = \theta(f) \Rightarrow \bigwedge_{0 \leq i \leq n-1}(u_{i,j} \wedge x_{i,j} = o_i) \wedge u_{0,j+1} \wedge x_{0,j+1} = r \wedge$$
$$Move(j, n, min(b_s - 2 + n, b_s - 1), 1 - n) \wedge$$
$$\bigwedge_{b_s-n+1 \leq i \leq b_s-1} \neg u_{i,j+1}$$
$$\text{where } f \in \mathcal{I}_U \text{ and } r \mapsto f(o_0, \ldots, o_{n-1}) \in M$$

Now for the commutative functions the only difference is that we know that $n = 2$ and that we can find the arguments in any of both orders in the stack:

$$C_C(j, f) = t_j = \theta(f) \Rightarrow u_{0,j} \wedge u_{1,j} \wedge$$
$$((x_{0,j} = o_0 \wedge x_{1,j} = o_1) \vee (x_{0,j} = o_1 \wedge x_{1,j} = o_0)) \wedge$$
$$u_{0,j+1} \wedge x_{0,j+1} = r \wedge Move(j, 2, b_s - 1, -1) \wedge \neg u_{b_s-1,j}$$
$$\text{where } f \in \mathcal{I}_C \text{ and } r \mapsto f(o_0, o_1) \in M$$

Finding the Target Program. We assign to every $\iota \in \mathcal{I}$ an integer. Then, $t_j \in \mathbb{Z}$ encodes the chosen instruction at position j in the target program for $0 \leqslant j < b_o$. To encode the selection of an instruction for every t_j, we have the following constraint:

$$C_{\mathcal{I}} = C_{\texttt{fromNOP}} \wedge \bigwedge_{0 \leqslant j < b_o} 0 \leq t_j \leq m_\iota \wedge$$
$$C_{\texttt{PUSH}}(j) \wedge C_{\texttt{DUP}k}(j) \wedge C_{\texttt{SWAP}k}(j) \wedge C_{\texttt{POP}}(j) \wedge$$
$$C_{\texttt{NOP}}(j) \wedge \bigwedge_{f \in \mathcal{I}_U} C_U(j, f) \wedge \bigwedge_{f \in \mathcal{I}_C} C_C(j, f))$$

Complete Encoding. Let us conclude our encoding by defining the formula C_{SFS} that states the whole problem of finding an EVM block for a given initial stack $[s_0, \ldots, s_{k-1}]$ and abstracted SFS with final stack $[f_0, \ldots, f_{w-1}]$ and map M. Hence, we introduce a constraint B to describe how the stack at the beginning is and a constraint E to describe how the stack at the end is and combine all the constraints defined above to express C_{SFS}.

$$B = \bigwedge_{0 \leqslant \alpha < k} (u_{\alpha,0} \wedge x_{\alpha,0} = s_\alpha) \wedge \bigwedge_{k \leqslant \beta \leqslant b_s - 1} \neg u_{\beta,0}$$
$$E = \bigwedge_{0 \leqslant \alpha < w} (u_{\alpha,b_o} \wedge x_{\alpha,b_o} = f_\alpha) \wedge \bigwedge_{w \leqslant \beta \leqslant b_s - 1} \neg u_{\beta,b_o}$$
$$C_{SFS} = S_V \wedge C_{\mathcal{I}} \wedge B \wedge E$$

Finally, let us mention that the performance of the used SMT solvers greatly improves when the following (redundant) constraint, which states that all functions in $\mathcal{I}_U \uplus \mathcal{I}_C$ should be eventually used, is added: $\bigwedge_{\iota \in \mathcal{I}_U \uplus \mathcal{I}_C} \bigvee_{0 \leqslant j < b_o} t_j = \theta(\iota)$

Empirical evidence shows, that this constraint helps the solver to establish optimality, and removing it increases the time-outs and time taken by roughly 50%. On the other hand, adding the similar constraint that all functions in $\mathcal{I}_U \uplus \mathcal{I}_C$ are used at most once, while also helping the solvers to show optimality for already optimal blocks, the performance for finding optimizations decreases by a similar rate. As the latter is our main motivation, we did not include the constraint.

4.4 From Models to EVM Blocks

The following definition shows how we can extract a concrete set of operations from a model for the formula C_{SFS} that computes the given SFS.

Definition 3. *Given a model σ for C_{SFS} we have that $block(\sigma)$ is defined as the sequence of EVM operations $o_0, \ldots, o_f$ where f is the largest $j \in \{0, \ldots, b_o - 1\}$ such that $t_j \neq \theta(\texttt{NOP})$. Now for all $\alpha \in \{0, \ldots, f\}$ the operation o_α is taken as*

1. *$o_\alpha = \texttt{PUSH}k \ a_\alpha$ if $t_\alpha = \theta(\texttt{PUSH})$ and a_α can be represented with k bytes.*
2. *$o_\alpha = \iota$ if $t_\alpha = \theta(\iota)$ where $\iota \in \mathcal{I}_S \setminus \{\texttt{PUSH}\}$*
3. *$o_\alpha = \iota$ if $t_\alpha = \theta(\iota)$ where $\iota \in \mathcal{I}_U \uplus \mathcal{I}_C$ and ι has no subscript.*
4. *$o_\alpha = \iota$ if $t_\alpha = \theta(\iota_l)$ where $\iota_l \in \mathcal{I}_U \uplus \mathcal{I}_C$ and has subscript l.*

The following result easily follows from the construction of C_{SFS}.

Theorem 1 (soundness). *Given an SFS and values for b_o and b_s, we have that if σ is a model for C_{SFS} obtained from the abstracted SFS then $block(\sigma)$ computes the given SFS.*

4.5   Optimization Using Max-SMT

Now that we know that every model of C_{SFS} provides a block that computes the SFS, we want to obtain the optimal solution. Since the cost of the solution can be expressed in terms of the cost of every of the instructions we select in all t_j, we will introduce soft constraints expressing the cost of every selection. A (partial weighted) Max-SMT problem is an optimization problem where we have an SMT formula which establishes the *hard constraints* of the problem and a set of pairs $\{[C_1, \omega_1], \ldots, [C_m, \omega_m]\}$, where each C_i is an SMT clause and ω_i is its weight, that establishes the *soft constraints*. In this context, the optimization problem consists in finding the model that satisfies the hard constraints and minimizes the sum of the weights of the falsified soft constraints. Our approach to find the optimal code is by encoding the problem as a Max-SMT optimization problem, where we add to the SMT formula C_{SFS} which defines our *hard constraints* a set of *soft constraints* such that sum of the weights of the falsified soft constraints coincides with the cost (in terms of gas) of the operations taken in every step. Therefore the optimal solution to the Max-SMT problem coincides with the optimal solution in terms of gas cost.

In the EVM, every operation has an associated gas cost, which in general is constant, but in some few cases may depend on the particular arguments it is applied to or on the state of the blockchain. All these operations that are non-constant are considered as uninterpreted, and hence we cannot change the operands on which they are applied. Therefore, omitting the non-constant part cannot affect which is the optimal solution. Thanks to this, we can split our set of instructions $\mathcal{I}$ in $p + 1$ disjoint sets $W_0 \uplus \ldots \uplus W_p$ where all instructions in W_i have the same constant cost cost_i, and such that the costs are strictly increasing, i.e., $\mathsf{cost}_0 = 0$ and $\mathsf{cost}_{i-1} < \mathsf{cost}_i$ for all $i \in \{1, \ldots, p\}$.

In the following we describe the encoding we have chosen for the weighted clauses (we have tried other slightly simpler alternatives but, in general, they behave worse). Let $w_i = \mathsf{cost}_i - \mathsf{cost}_{i-1}$ for $i \in \{1, \ldots, p\}$. Hence, we have that $w_i > 0$ and, moreover, $\mathsf{cost}_i = \Sigma_{1 \leqslant \alpha \leqslant i} w_\alpha$ for $i \in \{1, \ldots, p\}$. Then, our Max-SMT problem O_{SFS} is obtained adding to C_{SFS} the following soft constraints

$$O_{SFS} = C_{SFS} \wedge \bigwedge_{0 \leqslant j < b_o} \bigwedge_{1 \leqslant i \leqslant p} [\bigvee_{\iota \in W_0 \uplus \ldots \uplus W_{i-1}} t_j = \theta(\iota) , w_i]$$

Therefore, if the selected instruction at step j is ι (i.e. $t_j = \theta(\iota)$) for some $\iota \in W_i$ then we accumulate the weight w_α of all soft clauses with $\alpha \in \{1, \ldots, i\}$, which as said sums cost_i, and hence we accumulate the cost of executing the instruction ι. From this fact, our optimality theorem follows.

Theorem 2 (optimality). *Given an SFS P and values for b_o and b_s, we have that if σ is the optimal solution for the weighted Max-SMT problem O_{SFS} obtained from the abstracted SFS of P, then $block(\sigma)$ is the optimal code that has an SFS equal to P modulo commutativity.*

5   Experimental Evaluation

This section presents the results of our evaluation using syrup, the SYnthesizeR of sUPer-optimized smart contracts that implements our approach. Our tool syrup uses ETHIR [6] to generate the CFGs of the analyzed contracts and Z3 [12] version 4.8.7, Barcelogic [7], and MathSAT [11] version 1.6.3 (namely its optimality framework OptiMathSAT), as SMT solvers. We refer by s-Z3, s-Bar, s-OMS, to the results of using syrup with the respective solvers. Experiments have been performed on a cluster with Intel Xeon Gold 6126 CPUs at 2.60 GHz, 2 GB of memory and timeout of 15 min, running CentOS Linux 7.6. The main components of syrup are implemented in Python and OCaml. The backend of syrup generating SMT constraints from a SFS is open-source and can be found at github.com/mariaschett/syrup-backend. Our tool accepts smart contracts written in versions of Solidity up to 0.4.25 and EVM bytecode v1.8.18, namely the three new EVM bytecodes (SHL, SHR and SAR) introduced from the Solidity compiler version 0.5.0 are not handled yet by ETHIR. Our experimental setup consists of two groups of benchmarks:

(i) In order to compare with the existing tool ebso, we use the same data set (and the results for ebso) from [20]: the blocks of the 2500 most called contracts deployed on the Ethereum blockchain[3] after removing the duplicates and the blocks which are only different in the arguments of PUSH by abstracting to word size 4 bit. This results in a data set of 61 217 blocks.

(ii) A more realistic setting in which we analyze the 150 most called contracts[4] queried from the Ethereum blockchain and removing those of the versions not supported, resulting in 128. As the dates in which the contracts are fetched are different, not all 128 contracts are included in setup (i), indeed, the intersection are 106 contracts (besides there might be updated versions). This setting is more realistic since the analysis is performed at the contract-level (without removing any duplicates or similar blocks) and allows us to gather statistics to assess the gains at the level of the deployed contracts.

We note that analyzing the most called contracts corresponds to the most relevant case study as, according to [16], many Ethereum contracts are not used.

5.1   Comparison with ebso (setup I)

As seen in Definition. 1, we split the 61 217 blocks on certain bytecodes that are not optimized, leading to a total of 72 450. For comparison, we merge the split blocks back together. The next table shows the results of optimizing the 61 217 blocks by ebso (first column), and by syrup for every solver (next columns). In column s-All, we use the 3 solvers as a single framework in syrup that yields the best solution returned by any of the solvers (in parenthesis we show percentages).

---

[3] Up to Ethereum blockchain block number 7 300 000 until 2019-03-04 01:22:15 UTC.
[4] Up to Ethereum blockchain block number 9 193 265 until 2019-12-31 23:59:45 UTC.

	ebso	s-Z3	s-Bar	s-OMS	s-All
A	3882 (6.34%)	20 636 (33.71%)	20 783 (33.95%)	20 973 (34.26%)	20 988 (34.28%)
O	393 (0.64%)	25 922 (42.34%)	26 458 (43.22%)	28 063 (45.84%)	28 195 (46.06%)
B	550 (0.90%)	6288 (10.27%)	3051 (4.98%)	5293 (8.65%)	5726 (9.35%)
N	n/a	1933 (3.16%)	563 (0.92%)	837 (1.37%)	1020 (1.67%)
T	56 392 (92.12%)	6438 (10.52%)	10 362 (16.93%)	6051 (9.88%)	5288 (8.64%)
G	27 726	1 188 311	1 003 717	1 272 381	1 309 875
S	Not avail	13 710 904.75	13 141 046.21	12 239 980.85	10 948 011.57

Row **A** shows the number of blocks that were *A*lready optimal, i.e., those that cannot be optimized because they already consume the minimal amount of gas and ebso/syrup find bytecode with the same consumption. Row **O** contains the number of blocks that have been optimized and the found solution has been proven to be *O*ptimal, i.e., the one that consumes the minimum amount of gas needed to obtain the SFS provided. The solvers used are able to provide the best solution found until the timeout is reached. Row **B** contains the number of blocks that have been optimized into a *B*etter solution that consumes less gas but it is not shown to be the optimum. Row **N** shows the number of blocks that have *N*ot been optimized and not proven to be optimal, i.e., the solution found is the original one but there may exist a better one. Row **T** contains the number of blocks for which no model could be found when the *T*imeout was reached. Row **G** contains the accumulated *G*as savings for all optimized blocks. Importantly, the real savings would be larger if the optimized blocks are part of a loop and hence might be executed multiple times. Row **S** shows the time in *S*econds in which each setting analyzes all the blocks.

Let us first compare the results by ebso and our best results when using the portfolio of solvers in s-All. It is clear from the figures that syrup significantly outperforms ebso on the number of blocks handled (while ebso times out in 92.12 % of the blocks, we only timeout in 8.64 %) and on the overall gas gains (two orders of magnitude larger). For the analyzed blocks (i.e., those that do not timeout), the percentages of syrup for number of optimized into better blocks, into optimal blocks, and those proven to be already optimal, are much larger than those of ebso. We now discuss how the gains for the blocks that ebso can analyze compare to the gains by syrup. In particular, if missing part of the semantics of the uninterpreted instructions and the SSTORE bytecode significantly affects the gains. Out of 943 examples, where ebso found an optimization, in 46 cases syrup proved optimality w.r.t. the SFS and saved 348 gas but saved less gas than ebso (total 10 514 gas). The source of this gain is the SSTORE bytecode: there are two blocks where ebso saves 5000 each, because it realizes that we read from a key in storage to then store the value back unchanged. As we discuss in Sect. 7, our framework naturally extends to handle this storage optimization. However, in nearly all of 393 cases, where ebso found an optimal solution—in 378 cases—syrup saves as much as ebso amounting to 2670 gas. That is, the additional semantics did not improve savings. Furthermore, in 43 cases out of 943, the semantics did impede ebso's performance so that syrup found a better result with 597 gas versus 440 of ebso. Therefore, we can conclude that syrup is far more scalable and precise than ebso, the cases in which syrup optimizes less than ebso are seldom and can be naturally handled in the future. Moreover, they are offset by the cases where syrup did find an optimization, whereas ebso did not.

Finally, we can see that MathSAT is the solver that shows the best performance: It proves optimality of 34.26 % and optimizes 54.49 % of the blocks (c.f. Sect. 5.3). Regarding analysis time, the global figure is not reported in [20]. In syrup, by accumulating the time of all four scenarios (s-X) and using the 900 s timeout of ebso, we analyze the whole data set in about 3042 h. We note that, by considering the solvers as a portfolio, we reduce the analysis time as when an optimal solution is found, the execution of the other two solvers is stopped. However, for the other cases, we take the highest time taken by the solvers as we need to know all solutions in order to keep the best one and provide an answer.

5.2 Analysis of the Most Called Contracts with Gas Savings (setup Ii)

For our second setup, syrup produces the following results for the 46 966 blocks of the 128 (most called) smart contracts:

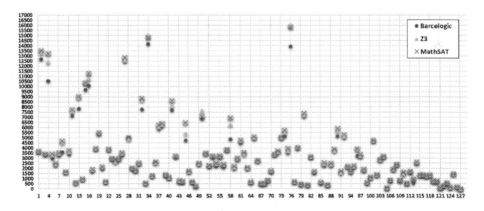

Fig. 5. Gas saved per contract in the 128 most called smart contracts

	s-Z3	s-Bar	s-OMS	s-All
A	30 846 (65.68%)	30 923 (65.84%)	30 971 (65.94%)	30 974 (65.95%)
O	13 102 (27.9%)	13 240 (28.19%)	13 586 (28.93%)	13 606 (28.97%)
B	933 (1.98%)	510 (1.09%)	746 (1.59%)	801 (1.71%)
N	695 (1.48%)	95 (0.2%)	295 (0.63%)	467 (0.99%)
T	1390 (2.96%)	2198 (4.68%)	1368 (2.91%)	1118 (2.38%)
G	438 483	406 086	437 165	443 248
S	2 919 830.35	2 682 469.58	2 413 612.39	2 378 446.26

As before, MathSAT is the solver that shows the best performance: It proves optimality of 65.94% and optimizes 30.52% of the blocks. The overall gas savings in **G** amount to 0.73% of the total gas which, assuming a uniform distribution of this saving among the contracts, amounts to around a million dollars from 2017 to 2019 (see Sect. 1 for details on this estimations). Moreover, we have calculated that the 64% of the saved gas is due to the simplification rules and the 36% to the Max-SMT optimization, which shows that both parts are highly relevant in our results. For this data set, we additionally display in Fig. 5 the amount of gas saved for each contract. The X-axis corresponds to each of the 128 analyzed contracts and the Y-axis corresponds to the amount of gas saved when using each solver. In general the gains obtained by the different solvers are quite aligned. On average, each contract saves 3425.65 units of gas using Z3, 3172.55 using Barcelogic and 3415.35 using MathSAT. However, we can observe that the gains are dispersed w.r.t. the mean, and there are big differences in the savings obtained for each of the contracts (the standard deviation is 2798.19 for Z3, 2664.05 for Barcelogic and 2889.01 for MathSAT). The biggest amount of gas optimized in all contracts is 18 989 gas using Z3, 18 704 using Barcelogic and 19 205 using MathSAT. In the case of this contract, MathSAT optimizes 706 blocks out of 1910, and the highest amount of gas optimized is 162 though the most common amount of gas optimized is 3 (in 165 blocks). The highest amount of gas optimized per block in all contracts is 481. Finally, we have analyzed the impact of our optimization on the function `transfer` of the AirdropToken smart contract, that has been called around 520 000 times. For this function, which has no loops, syrup saves 832 units of gas per call. From the number of calls per day (obtained from [2]), we estimate a total saving (just for this function) of 2815 $.

5.3   Comparison of SMT Solvers in Precision and Time

Figure 6 aims at providing some data to compare the accuracy and efficiency of the process using the three SMT solvers. The table to the left shows in: **Unique** the number of blocks that are uniquely optimized by the corresponding solver, in **UOptim** the number of blocks that are proven to be optimal uniquely by one solver, and **+GSave** the number of blocks for which one solver has strictly more gains that the others. The suffixes 1 and 2 refer to the data set in Sects. 5.1 and

	s-Z3	s-Bar	s-OMS
Unique1	608	73	925
UOPtim1	22	108	1296
+GSave1	694	634	4286
Unique2	238	6	234
UOPtim2	6	14	237
+GSave2	107	79	563

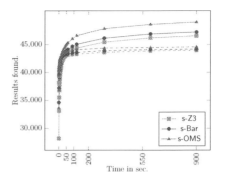

Fig. 6. Comparison of SMT Solvers

5.2, resp., excluding all timeouts. In both data sets, MathSAT uniquely finds a result, uniquely shows the block optimal, or finds the best gain for the large majority. But clearly, in both data sets, every solver was needed to get the best possible solution in every category. The plot to the right of Fig. 6 displays the amount of blocks (Y-axis) that are solved in the corresponding amount of time (X-axis). Dashed lines correspond to data set 1 and plain lines to 2. We can see that for data set (i) within 10 s, nearly 89% of the results were found. For data set (ii) this is even more pronounced, after 10 s around 95% were found, with around 90% already being available after 1 s. The analysis shows that most results can be found very fast and thus our optimizer could be invoked during the compilation of a smart contract without adding a large overhead to compilation.

6   Related Work

There are currently two automated approaches to gas optimization of Ethereum smart contracts. (i) First, the closest to ours is blockchain superoptimization [20], whose goal is the same as ours: find the gas-optimal block of code for each of the blocks in the CFG of the smart contract. While the approach of [20] would not be applicable within a compiler (e.g., it times out in 92.12 % of the blocks used in their experimental evaluation), our optimization tool performs very efficiently (e.g., we have seen that 89% of the blocks are optimized in less than 10 s). The reasons for our efficiency are indeed the fundamental differences with [20]: (1) we use the SFS to solve the optimization problem efficiently as a synthesis problem in which the semantic optimizations are carried out within the SFS part, (2) we do not encode the semantics of the arithmetic and bit-vector operations in the SMT problem, as [20] does, what allows us to express the problem using only existential quantification, (3) we use Max-SMT to solve the optimization problem. The basis for ebso is in [15], where the description of an encoding of unbounded superoptimization with the idea to shift the search for optimal program to the SMT solver is first found. (ii) Second, the system GASOL [5] incorporates also an automatic optimization for storage operations that consists in replacing accesses to the storage (i.e., bytecodes SSTORE and SLOAD) by equivalent accesses to memory locations (i.e., bytecodes MSTORE and MLOAD), when a static analysis identifies that it is sound and efficient doing such transformation. This optimization is not intra-block, as done in supercompilation, therefore it is not achievable by our approach as it involves modifying multiple blocks, and also requires an analysis that identifies the patterns and the soundness of the transformation. On the other hand, GASOL is not able to make the intra-block optimizations that we are achieving. Therefore, the optimizations in GASOL are orthogonal (and complementary) to those achievable by means of superoptimization.

There is work also focused on identifying gas expensive patterns: (1) the work in [9] identifies 7 expensive patterns on Solidity contracts and proposes optimizations for them. However, there is no tool in [9] that carries out these optimizations automatically; (2) The work in [10] identifies 24 anti-patterns, e.g. [OP,POP] optimizes to POP. Again, there is not automation and those patterns are manually identified. There is recent work that experimentally proves that the gas model for some EVM instructions is not correctly aligned with respect to the observed computational costs in real experiments [26], and that these misalignments can lead to gas-related attacks [22]. Our work is parametric on the gas model used, and new adjustments in the gas model of Ethereum are integrated in our optimizer by just updating the cost for the corresponding modified instructions in our implementation. Finally, the tool TOAST [8] also superoptimizes machine code. Although applied to different settings, the performance of syrup is significantly better and the notions of optimality used are different (sequence length and gas-usage respectively).

7   Conclusions and Future Work

We have presented a novel method for gas super-optimization of smart contracts that combines symbolic execution with an effective Max-SMT encoding. Our focus is on the stack operations because these bytecode operations allow for multiple reorderings, simplifications, and cover the major part of the potential optimizations; while reading and/or writing on memory or storage can be seldom optimized (unless the same value is written, or read, consecutively). In spite of this, the same methodology we have formalized for the stack could be extended to optimize the memory and storage bytecode operations. Basically, the symbolic execution phase would extract a functional specification also for memory and for storage that would be analogous to our SFS and that could include storage-related optimizations (e.g., detecting unnecessary storage). The SMT encoding for these operations would be similar to ours but, for soundness, would have to maintain the order among the memory and storage accesses. It is part of our future work to implement also the super-optimizations for memory and storage and experimentally evaluate if there is significant gain. We also plan to extend the SMT encoding to include information gained from the original program such as the original cost. Currently, in roughly 0.05% of the blocks of Sect. 5.2, syrup synthesizes a more expensive solution.

References

1. The Michelson Language. https://www.michelson-lang.com
2. Bloxy (2018). https://bloxy.info
3. Etherscan (2018). https://etherscan.io
4. Rattle - An EVM Binary Static Analysis Framework (2018). https://github.com/crytic/rattle
5. Albert, E., Correas, J., Gordillo, P., Román-Díez, G., Rubio, A.: GASOL: gas analysis and optimization for ethereum smart contracts. TACAS 2020. LNCS, vol. 12079, pp. 118–125. Springer, Cham (2020). https://doi.org/10.1007/978-3-030-45237-7_7
6. Albert, E., Gordillo, P., Livshits, B., Rubio, A., Sergey, I.: ETHIR: a framework for high-level analysis of ethereum bytecode. In: Lahiri, S.K., Wang, C. (eds.) ATVA 2018. LNCS, vol. 11138, pp. 513–520. Springer, Cham (2018). https://doi.org/10.1007/978-3-030-01090-4_30
7. Bofill, M., Nieuwenhuis, R., Oliveras, A., Rodríguez-Carbonell, E., Rubio, A.: The barcelogic SMT solver. In: Gupta, A., Malik, S. (eds.) CAV 2008. LNCS, vol. 5123, pp. 294–298. Springer, Heidelberg (2008). https://doi.org/10.1007/978-3-540-70545-1_27
8. Brain, M., Crick, T., De Vos, M., Fitch, J.: TOAST: applying answer set programming to superoptimisation. In: Etalle, S., Truszczyński, M. (eds.) ICLP 2006. LNCS, vol. 4079, pp. 270–284. Springer, Heidelberg (2006). https://doi.org/10.1007/11799573_21
9. Chen, T., Li, X., Luo, X., Zhang, X.: Under-optimized smart contracts devour your money. In SANER, pp. 442–446. IEEE Computer Society (2017)
10. Chen, T., et al.: Towards saving money in using smart contracts. In: Proceedings of the 40th International Conference on Software Engineering: New Ideas and Emerging Results, ICSE (NIER) 2018, Gothenburg, Sweden, 27 May–03 June 2018, pp. 81–84 (2018)
11. Cimatti, A., Griggio, A., Schaafsma, B.J., Sebastiani, R.: The MathSAT5 SMT solver. In: Piterman, N., Smolka, S.A. (eds.) TACAS 2013. LNCS, vol. 7795, pp. 93–107. Springer, Heidelberg (2013). https://doi.org/10.1007/978-3-642-36742-7_7
12. de Moura, L., Bjørner, N.: Z3: an efficient SMT solver. In: Ramakrishnan, C.R., Rehof, J. (eds.) TACAS 2008. LNCS, vol. 4963, pp. 337–340. Springer, Heidelberg (2008). https://doi.org/10.1007/978-3-540-78800-3_24
13. Ethereum. Solidity (2018). https://solidity.readthedocs.io
14. Grech, N., Kong, M., Jurisevic, A., Brent, L., Scholz, B., Smaragdakis, Y.: Madmax: surviving out-of-gas conditions in ethereum smart contracts. PACMPL 2(OOPSLA), 116:1–116:27 (2018)
15. Jangda, A., Yorsh, G.: Unbounded superoptimization. In: Proceedings of the 2017 ACM SIGPLAN International Symposium on New Ideas, New Paradigms, and Reflections on Programming and Software, Onward! 2017, Vancouver, BC, Canada, 23–27 October 2017, pp. 78–88 (2017)
16. Kiffer, L., Levin, D., Mislove, A.: Analyzing ethereum's contract topology. In: Proceedings of the Internet Measurement Conference 2018, IMC 2018, pp. 494–499 (2018)
17. Massalin, H.: Superoptimizer - a look at the smallest program. In: Proceedings of the Second International Conference on Architectural Support for Programming Languages and Operating Systems (ASPLOS II), pp. 122–126 (1987)

18. Mueller, B.: Smashing ethereum smart contracts for fun and real profit. In: The 9th annual HITB Security Conference (2018)
19. Mukhopadhyay, M.: Ethereum Smart Contract Development. Packt publishing, Birmingham (2018)
20. Mesnard, F., Stuckey, P.J. (eds.): LOPSTR 2018. LNCS, vol. 11408. Springer, Cham (2019). https://doi.org/10.1007/978-3-030-13838-7
21. Nakamoto, S.: Bitcoin: a peer-to-peer electronic cash system (2008)
22. Pérez, D., Livshits, B.: Broken metre: attacking resource metering in EVM (2019). CoRR, abs/1909.07220
23. Dill, D.L., et al.: Move: A language with programmablere sources. Technical report (2019). https://developers.libra.org/docs/state-machine-replication-paper
24. Sergey, I., Nagaraj, V., Johannsen, J., Kumar, A., Trunov, A., Hao, K.C.G.: Safer smart contract programming with Scilla. In: 34th ACM SIGPLAN Conference on Object-Oriented Programming Systems, Languages and Applications (OOPSLA 2019) (2019)
25. Wood, G.: Ethereum: a secure decentralised generalised transaction ledger (2019)
26. Yang, R., Murray, T., Rimba, P., Parampalli, U.: Empirically analyzing ethereum's gas mechanism. In 2019 IEEE European Symposium on Security and Privacy Workshops, EuroS&P Workshops 2019, Stockholm, Sweden, 17–19 June 2019, pp. 310–319 (2019)

Verification of Quantitative Hyperproperties Using Trace Enumeration Relations

Shubham Sahai[1]([✉])(iD), Pramod Subramanyan[1](iD),
and Rohit Sinha[2](iD)

[1] Indian Institute of Technology,
Kanpur, India
{ssahai,spramod}@cse.iitk.ac.in
[2] Visa Research, Palo Alto, USA

Abstract. Many important cryptographic primitives offer probabilistic guarantees of security that can be specified as quantitative hyperproperties; these are specifications that stipulate the existence of a certain number of traces in the system satisfying certain constraints. Verification of such hyperproperties is extremely challenging because they involve simultaneous reasoning about an unbounded number of different traces. In this paper, we introduce a technique for verifying quantitative hyperproperties based on the notion of trace enumeration relations. These relations allow us to reduce the problem of trace-counting into one of model-counting of formulas in first-order logic. We also introduce a set of inference rules for machine-checked reasoning about the number of satisfying solutions to first-order formulas (aka model counting). Putting these two components together enables semi-automated verification of quantitative hyperproperties on infinite-state systems. We use our methodology to prove confidentiality of access patterns in Path ORAMs of unbounded size, soundness of a simple interactive zero-knowledge proof protocol as well as other applications of quantitative hyperproperties studied in past work.

1 Introduction

Recent years have seen significant progress in automated and semi-automated techniques for the verification of security requirements of computer systems [4, 10,16,19,30,47,50,55]. Much of this progress has built on the theory of *hyperproperties* [21], and these have been used extensively in analysis of whether systems satisfy secure information flow properties [1,2,6,8,15,28,35,37,39,49,57] such as observational determinism [41,55] and non-interference [32]. Unfortunately, the security specification of several important security primitives cannot be captured by secure information flow properties like observational determinism. In particular, observational determinism and non-interference are not applicable when reasoning about algorithms that offer probabilistic – as opposed to deterministic – guarantees of confidentiality and integrity. Prominent examples

© The Author(s) 2020
S. K. Lahiri and C. Wang (Eds.): CAV 2020, LNCS 12224, pp. 201–224, 2020.
https://doi.org/10.1007/978-3-030-53288-8_11

of security primitives offering probabilistic guarantees include Path ORAM [48] and various zero-knowledge proof protocols.

A promising direction for the verification of such protocols are the class of quantitative hyperproperties [29], one example of which is deniability [12,14]. Deniability states that for every infinitely-long sequence of observations that an adversary makes, there are (exponentially) many different secrets that could have resulted in exactly these observations. Therefore, the adversary learns very little about the secrets in an execution from a particular sequence of observations.

How does one prove a quantitative hyperproperty like deniability? Suppose our goal is to show that for every trace of adversary observations, there exist 2^n traces with the same observations but different secrets. Here n is a parameter of the system, e.g., the length of a password in bits. One option, first suggested by Yasuoka and Terauchi [54] and recently revisited by Finkbeiner, Hahn, and Torfah [29], is to consider the following k-trace property, where $k = 2^n + 1$.

$$\forall \pi_0. \; \exists \pi_1, \pi_2, \ldots, \pi_{2^n}.$$

$$\left(\bigwedge_{j=1}^{2^n} obs(\pi_0) = obs(\pi_j) \right) \wedge \left(\bigwedge_{j=1}^{2^n} \bigwedge_{k=1}^{2^n} (j \neq k) \Rightarrow secret(\pi_j) \neq secret(\pi_k) \right)$$

The property states that for every trace of the system, there must exist 2^n other traces with identical observations and pairwise different secrets. In the above, $\pi_0, \pi_1, \ldots$ represent trace variables, $obs(\pi_j)$ refers to the trace of adversary observations projected from the trace π_j, while $secret(\pi_j)$ refers to the trace of secret values in the trace π_j. There are at least three problems with the verification of the above property. First, the size of this property grows exponentially with n; verification needs to reason about 2^n traces simultaneously and is not scalable. The second problem is quantifier alternation. Even if we could somehow reason about 2^n traces, we have to show that *for every* trace π_0, there *exist* 2^n other traces satisfying the above condition. The third problem is that the above technique does not work for *symbolic* bounds. While it is possible – at least in principle – to use the above construction by picking a specific value of n, say 16, to show that 2^{16} traces exist that satisfy deniability, we would like to show that the property holds for all n, where n is a state variable or parameter of the transition system. Capturing the dependence of the trace-count bound on parameters, such as n, is important because it shows that the attacker has to work exponentially harder as n increases. Such general proofs are not possible by reduction to a k-trace property because the construction requires k be bounded.

Recent work by Finkbeiner, Hahn, and Torfah [29] has made significant progress in addressing the first two problems by showing a reduction from k-trace property checking into the problem of maximum model counting [31]. However, their technique still produces a propositional formula whose size grows exponentially in the size of the quantitative hyperproperty. Further, model counting itself is a computationally hard problem that is known to be #P-complete, and maximum model counting is even harder. As a result, their technique does not scale well and times out on the verification of an 8-bit leakage bound for an 8-bit password. Finally, their method does not support symbolic bounds, and therefore cannot be used to verify parametric systems; we verify several examples of such systems in this paper (e.g., Path ORAM [48] of symbolic size).

In this work, we propose a new technique for quantitative hyperproperty verification that addresses each of the above problems. Our approach is based on the following insights. First, instead of trying to count the number of traces that have the same observations and different inputs, we instead show injectivity/surjectivity from satisfying assignments of a first-order formula to traces of a transition system. This allows us to bound the number of traces satisfying the quantitative hyperproperty by the number of satisfying solutions to this formula. We introduce the notion of a trace enumeration relation to formalize this relation between the first-order formula and traces of the transition system. An important advantage of the above reduction is that proving the validity of a trace enumeration relation is only a hyperproperty – not a quantitative hyperproperty.

Next, we develop a novel technique to bound the number of satisfiable solutions to a first-order logic formula, which is of independent interest. While this is a hard problem, we exploit the fact that our formulas have a significant amount of structure. We introduce a set of inference rules inspired by ideas from enumerative combinatorics [13,52,56]. These rules allow us to bound the number of satisfying assignments to a formula by making only satisfiability queries.

In summary, our techniques can prove quantitative hyperproperties with symbolic bounds on parametric infinite-state systems. We demonstrate their utility by verifying representative quantitative hyperproperties of diverse applications.

Contributions

1. We introduce a specification language for quantitative hyperproperties (QHPs) over symbolic transition systems and define formal satisfaction semantics for this language. Our specification language is more expressive than past work on QHP specification because it allows the bound to be a first-order formula over the state variables of the transition system.
2. We provide several examples of QHPs relevant to security verification. We identify a new class of QHPs, referred to as soundness hyperproperties, applicable to protocols that provide statistical guarantees of integrity.
3. We propose a novel semi-automated verification methodology for proving that a system satisfies a QHP. Our methodology applies to properties that involve a single instance of quantifier alternation and works by reducing the problem of QHP verification to that of checking non-quantitative hyperproperties over two and three traces of the system and counting satisfiable solutions to a formula in first-order logic.
4. We introduce a set of inference rules for bounding the number of satisfiable solutions to a first-order logic formula, using only satisfiability queries.
5. We demonstrate the applicability of our specification language and verification methodology by providing proofs of security for Path ORAM, soundness of a simple zero-knowledge protocol, as well as examples taken from prior work on quantitative security specifications. We show that our verification

methodology scales to larger systems than could be handled in prior work. To the best of our knowledge, our work is the first machine-checked proof of confidentiality of the access patterns in Path ORAM.

2   Motivating Example

In this section, we first introduce the model of transition systems used in this paper. We then discuss quantitative hyperproperty (QHP) specification and verification for our running example – a simple zero-knowledge puzzle.

2.1   Preliminaries

Let $FOL(\mathcal{T})$ denote first-order logic modulo a theory $\mathcal{T}$. The theory $\mathcal{T}$ is assumed to be multi-sorted, includes the theory of linear integer arithmetic (LIA), and contains the $=$ relation. Let $\Sigma_{\mathcal{T}}$ be the theory $\mathcal{T}$'s signature: the set consisting of the constant, function, and predicate symbols in the theory. We say that a formula is a $\Sigma_{\mathcal{T}}$-formula if it consists of the symbols in $\Sigma_{\mathcal{T}}$ along with variables, logical connectives, and quantifiers. We only consider theories which are such that the set of satisfying assignments for any $\Sigma_{\mathcal{T}}$-formula is a countable set.[1]

For every variable x, we will assume there exists a unique variable x', which we refer to as the primed version of x. We will use X, Y, and Z to denote sets of variables. Given a set of variables X, we will use X' to refer to the set consisting of the primed version of each variable in X, that is $X' = \{x' \mid x \in X\}$. Similarly X_1, X_2, etc. are sets consisting of new variables defined as follows: $X_1 = \{x_1 \mid x \in X\}$ and $X_2 = \{x_2 \mid x \in X\}$. We will use $F(X)$ to denote the application of a function or predicate symbol F on the variables in the set X. A satisfying assignment σ to the formula $F(X)$ is written as $\sigma \models F(X)$. Given a formula $F(X)$ and a satisfying assignment σ to this formula, we will denote the valuation of the variable $x \in X$ in the assignment σ as $\sigma(x)$. We will abuse notation in two ways and also write $\sigma(X)$ to refer to a map from the variables $x \in X$ to their assignments in σ. We will also write $\sigma(G(X))$ to denote the valuation of the term $G(X)$ under the assignment σ.

The number of satisfiable assignments for the variables in the set X to a formula $F(X, Y)$ as a function of the variables Y will be denoted by $\#X . F(X, Y)$. $\#X . F(X, Y)$ is the function $\lambda Y . |\{\sigma(X) \mid \sigma \models F(X, \mathrm{Y})\}|$ evaluated at Y; $|S|$ is the cardinality of the set S. For example, consider the predicate $f(i, n) \doteq (0 \leq i < 2n)$. In this case, $\#i . f(i, n) = \max(0, 2n)$, meaning that for a given value of $n > 0$, there are $2n$ satisfying assignments to i.

Definition 1 (Transition System). *A transition system M is defined as the tuple $M = \langle X, Init(X), Tx(X, X') \rangle$. X is a finite set of (uninterpreted) constants that represents the state variables of the transition system. Init and Tx are $\Sigma_{\mathcal{T}}$-formulas representing the initial states and the transition relation, respectively.*

---

[1] Our experiments mostly use the AUFLIA theory which allows arrays, uninterpreted functions, and linear integer arithmetic.

Init is defined over the signature $\Sigma_T \cup X$. Tx is over the signature $\Sigma_T \cup X \cup X'$; X represents the pre-state of the transition and X' represents its post-state.

A state of the system is an assignment to the variables in X. We use $\sigma^0, \sigma^1, \sigma^2$ etc. to represent states. A trace of the system M is an infinite sequence of states $\tau = \sigma^0 \sigma^1 \sigma^2 \ldots \sigma^i \ldots$ such that $Init(\sigma^0)$ is valid and for all $i \geq 0$, $Tx(\sigma^i, \sigma^{i+1})$ is valid; in order to keep notation uncluttered, we will often drop the ≥ 0 qualifier when referring to trace indices. We assume that every state of the transition system has a successor: for all σ there exists some σ' such that $Tx(\sigma, \sigma')$ is valid, ensuring every run of the system is infinite. We will represent traces by τ, τ_1, τ_2, etc. Given a trace τ, we refer to its ith element by τ^i. If $\tau = \sigma^0 \sigma^1 \ldots$, then $\tau^0 = \sigma^0$ and $\tau^1 = \sigma^1$. The notation $\tau^{[i,\infty]}$ refers to the suffix of trace τ starting at index i. The set of all traces of the system M is denoted by Φ_M. Given a state σ and a variable $x \in X$, $\sigma(x)$ is the valuation of x in the state σ.

2.2   Motivating Example: Zero-Knowledge Hats

Zero-knowledge (Z-K) proofs are constructions involving two parties: *a prover* and *a verifier*, where the prover's goal is to convince the verifier about the veracity of a given statement without revealing any additional information. We motivate the need for quantitative hyperproperty verification using a Z-K puzzle.

Puzzle Overview: Consider the following scenario. Peggy has a pair of otherwise identical hats of different colors (say, yellow and green). She wants to convince Victor, who is yellow-green color blind, that the hats are of different colors, without revealing the colors of the hats. This problem can be solved using the following interactive protocol. Peggy gives both hats to Victor, and Victor randomly chooses a hat behind a curtain and shows it to Peggy. Next, he goes back behind the curtain and uniformly randomly chooses if he wants to switch the hat or not. He now appears in front of Peggy and asks: "Did I switch?"

If the hats are really of different colors, Peggy will be able to answer correctly with probability 1. If Peggy is cheating – the hats are in fact of the same color – her best strategy is to guess, and with probability 0.5 she will answer incorrectly. If the interaction is repeated k-times, Peggy will be caught with probability $1 - 2^{-k}$. The interaction between Peggy and Victor only reveals the fact that Peggy can detect a switch and not the color of the hat, making this zero-knowledge.

Verification Objectives: A zero-knowledge proof must satisfy three properties: *completeness* (an honest prover should be able to convince an honest verifier of a true statement), *soundness* (a cheating prover can convince an honest verifier with negligible probability) and *zero-knowledge* (no information apart from the veracity of the statement should be revealed). Completeness is a standard trace property, while zero-knowledge is the 2-safety property of indistinguishability. Consequently, the main challenge in automated verification of the zero-knowledge protocol described above is that of soundness. In this section, we discuss its specification and verification using quantitative hyperproperties.

$$
\begin{array}{ll}
X & \doteq \{\mathsf{C}, \mathsf{P}, \mathsf{S}, i, \mathsf{R}\} \\
Init(X) & \doteq (\forall i.\ 0 \leq \mathsf{C}[i] \leq 1) \wedge (\forall i.\ 0 \leq \mathsf{P}[i] \leq 1) \wedge \mathsf{S} \wedge (i = 1) \wedge (\mathsf{R} > 0) \\
Tx(X, X') & \doteq (\mathsf{C}' = \mathsf{C}) \wedge (\mathsf{P}' = \mathsf{P}) \wedge (\mathsf{R}' = \mathsf{R}) \wedge \big(\mathsf{S}' = \big(\mathsf{S} \wedge (\mathsf{C}[i] = \mathsf{P}[i])\big)\big) \wedge \\
& \quad\ i' = \min(i + 1, \mathsf{R})
\end{array}
$$

Fig. 1. Transition system model of the example protocol.

Soundness as a Quantitative Hyperproperty: Consider the transition system $M = \langle X, Init(X), Tx(X, X') \rangle$, shown in Fig. 1, representing this protocol. The variable R is a *parameter* of the system and refers to the number of rounds of the protocol. C and P are boolean arrays representing the challenges from the verifier to the prover, and the responses from the prover to the verifier, respectively. i is the current round, and S is a boolean flag that corresponds to whether the zero-knowledge proof has succeeded. C and P are initialized non-deterministically to model the fact that the verifier chooses their challenges randomly, and a cheating prover's best strategy is guessing. While a cheating prover can use any strategy, if the challenges are indistinguishable to her, then the best strategy is to sample responses from a uniform distribution.

Soundness is captured by the following quantitative hyperproperty (QHP):

$$
\forall \pi_0.\#\pi_1\colon \mathbf{F}\,(\delta_{\pi_j,\pi_k}).\ \mathbf{G}\,(\psi_{\pi_0,\pi_1}) \geq 2^{\mathsf{R}} - 1 \tag{1}
$$

We will provide formal satisfaction semantics for QHPs in Sect. 3. For now, we informally describe its meaning. The term $\#\pi_1\colon \mathbf{F}\,(\delta_{\pi_j,\pi_k}).\ \mathbf{G}\,(\psi_{\pi_0,\pi_1}) \geq 2^{\mathsf{R}} - 1$ introduces a counting quantifier which stipulates the existence of at least $2^{\mathsf{R}} - 1$ traces satisfying certain conditions: (i) these traces must all be pairwise-different, where difference is defined by satisfaction of the formula $\mathbf{F}\,(\delta_{\pi_j,\pi_k})$ and (ii) all of these traces must be related to trace π_0 by the relation $\mathbf{G}\,(\psi_{\pi_0,\pi_1})$.

The state predicates δ and ψ are defined as follows.

$$
\begin{aligned}
\delta(\sigma_1, \sigma_2) &\doteq \sigma_1(\mathsf{P}[i]) \neq \sigma_2(\mathsf{P}[i]) \\
\psi(\sigma_1, \sigma_2) &\doteq \big(\sigma_1((i = \mathsf{R}) \Rightarrow \mathsf{S}) \Rightarrow \sigma_2((i = \mathsf{R}) \Rightarrow \neg\mathsf{S})\big) \quad \wedge \\
&\quad\ \big(\sigma_1(\mathsf{C}) = \sigma_2(\mathsf{C}) \wedge \sigma_1(\mathsf{R}) = \sigma_2(\mathsf{R})\big)
\end{aligned}
$$

The requirement imposed by δ is that Peggy's responses be different at some step i for every pair of traces captured by the counting quantifier. ψ says that if trace π_0 is a trace where Peggy's cheating succeeds (i.e., $\mathsf{S} = true$ when $i = \mathsf{R}$), then in all traces captured by π_1, the challenges and number of rounds are the same as π_0 but Peggy's cheating is detected by Victor (i.e., $\mathsf{S} = false$ when $i = \mathsf{R}$). These requirements are illustrated in Fig. 2(b).

The QHP requires that for every trace in which a cheating prover succeeds in tricking the verifier for a given trace of challenges, there are $2^{\mathsf{R}} - 1$ other traces with the same challenges in which the prover's cheating is detected. Even though soundness is a probabilistic property over the distribution of the system's traces, it can be reduced to counting (and thus specified as a QHP) because each execution trace is sampled uniformly from a finite set. Therefore, if the QHP is satisfied, Peggy's probability of successful cheating is upper-bounded by 2^{-R}.

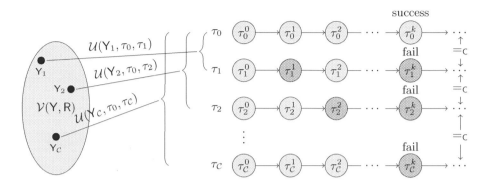

(a) Trace enumeration predicates.   (b) Traces in the soundness QHP.

Fig. 2. Using trace enumeration predicates to verify the soundness QHP.

2.3 Solution Outline

To prove a QHP of the form $\forall \pi_0.\ \#\pi_1 : \Delta_{\pi_j, \pi_k}.\ \varphi \lhd N(Z)$, we construct a *trace enumeration predicate* $\mathcal{V}(Y, Z)$ and show an injective/bijective mapping from assignments to Y in $\mathcal{V}(Y, Z)$ and traces of the system. This allows us to prove $\forall \pi_0.\ \#\pi_1 : \Delta_{\pi_j, \pi_k}.\ \varphi \lhd \#Y.\ \mathcal{V}(Y, Z)$. This part of the proof relies on the notion of a trace enumeration relation (Sect. 4). In the next step, we show that $\#Y.\ \mathcal{V}(Y, Z) \lhd N(Z)$ using the inference rules presented in Sect. 5. We now describe these steps in the context of the motivating example.

Verification of Soundness for the Z-K Hats Puzzle: Property 1 is illustrated in Fig. 2(b). τ_0 is a trace where the Z-K proof succeeds, while the proof fails for the set of traces $\Phi_C = \{\tau_1, \tau_2, \ldots, \tau_C\}$. The red states show the particular step of the proof in which an incorrect response is given by the prover, and each of these steps as well as their associated prover responses are pairwise different. The QHP is satisfied if $|\Phi_C| \geq 2^R - 1$ for every $\tau_0 \in \Phi_M$, where $R = \tau_0^0(R)$.

The first step in our methodology is to construct a parameterized relation, called a trace enumeration relation, $\mathcal{U}(Y, \tau_0, \tau_1)$. This relates τ_0 to each trace in the set Φ_C and is parameterized by Y. For every value of the parameter Y, $\mathcal{U}$ relates a trace in which the proof succeeds (τ_0) to a trace in which the proof fails (τ_1). For every trace τ_0 in which the proof succeeds, the set $\{\tau_1 \mid \exists Y.\ \mathcal{U}(Y, \tau_0, \tau_1)\}$ corresponds to the set of traces with the same challenges and the same number of rounds, but with failed proofs of knowledge. Note this is a subset of Φ_C.

Next, we construct a predicate $\mathcal{V}(Y, R)$ which defines valid assignments to $\mathcal{V}$ for a particular value of R. For a particular R, consider the set: $\{\sigma(Y) \mid \sigma \models$

$\mathcal{V}(\mathsf{Y}, \mathsf{R})\}$. Suppose we are able to show that the relation $\mathcal{U}$ is injective in Y and τ_0 for assignments to Y drawn from this set, then we can lower-bound the size of $\Phi_\mathcal{C}$ by the size of this set. In other words, we have reduced the problem of trace counting to the problem of counting assignments to $\mathcal{V}(\mathsf{Y}, \mathsf{R})$.

Precisely stated, using $\mathcal{V}$ and $\mathcal{U}$, we show the following.

1. For every trace τ_0, and every assignment Y_i satisfying $\mathcal{V}(\mathsf{Y}_i, \tau_0^0(\mathsf{R}))$, there exists a corresponding trace τ_i that satisfies both $\mathcal{U}(\mathsf{Y}_i, \tau_0, \tau_i)$ and $\psi(\tau_0, \tau_i)$. (Note $\tau_0^0(\mathsf{R})$ refers to the valuation of R in the initial state of τ_0.)
2. Given two different satisfying assignments to $\mathcal{V}$ for a particular value of R, say Y_j and Y_k, the corresponding traces τ_j and τ_k are guaranteed to have different prover responses; in other words, the traces satisfy $\delta(\tau_j, \tau_k)$.

The above two properties, illustrated in Fig. 2(a), imply there is an injective mapping from satisfying assignments of $\mathcal{V}(\mathsf{Y}, \mathsf{R})$ to traces in $\Phi_\mathcal{C}$. Therefore, the number of traces in $\Phi_\mathcal{C}$ can be lower bounded by the number of satisfying assignments to Y in $\mathcal{V}(\mathsf{Y}, \mathsf{R})$, i.e. $\#\mathsf{Y}. \mathcal{V}(\mathsf{Y}, \mathsf{R})$. We have reduced the difficult problem of counting traces into a slightly easier problem of counting satisfying assignments to a $FOL(\mathcal{T})$ formula.

The final step is to bound $\#\mathsf{Y}. \mathcal{V}(\mathsf{Y}, \mathsf{R})$. For example, one well-known idea from enumerative combinatorics is that if a set A is the union of disjoint sets B and C, then $|A| = |B| + |C|$. Translated to model counting, the above can be written as $\#X. F(X, Y) = \#X. G(X, Y) + \#X. H(X, Y)$ if $F(X, Y) \Leftrightarrow G(X, Y) \vee H(X, Y)$ is valid and $G(X, Y) \wedge H(X, Y)$ is unsat.[2] We present a set of inference rules in Sect. 5 that build on this and related ideas. These inference rules allow us derive a machine-checked proof of the bound $\#\mathsf{Y}. \mathcal{V}(\mathsf{Y}, \mathsf{R}) \geq 2^\mathsf{K} - 1$, thus completing the proof of Property 1 for the Z-K hats puzzle.

3 Overview of Quantitative Hyperproperties

This section introduces a logic for the specification of quantitative hyperproperties over symbolic transition systems. We present satisfaction semantics for this logic and then discuss its applications in security verification.

$$
\begin{aligned}
\psi &::= \forall \pi.\ \psi \mid \#\pi{:}\Delta_{\pi_j, \pi_k}.\ \psi \vartriangleleft N(Z) \mid \varphi \\
\varphi &::= \mathcal{P}_{\pi_1, \pi_2, \ldots, \pi_k} \mid \neg\varphi \mid \varphi \vee \varphi \mid \varphi\,\mathbf{U}\,\varphi \mid \mathbf{X}\,\varphi \\
\vartriangleleft &::= \leq \mid = \mid \geq
\end{aligned}
$$

Fig. 3. Grammar of Quantitative HyperLTL.

---

[2] We note there is an implied universal quantifier here. To be precise, we must write $\forall Y. \#X. F(X, Y) = \#X. G(X, Y) + \#X. H(X, Y)$.

3.1 Quantitative Hyperproperties

Figure 3 shows the syntax of Quantitative HyperLTL, our extension of Hyper-LTL [30] that allows specification of quantitative hyperproperties over symbolic transition systems. There are two noteworthy differences from the presentation of HyperLTL in [30]. The first is the predicate $\mathcal{P}_{\pi_1,\pi_2,...,\pi_k}$. This refers to a k-ary state predicate $\mathcal{P}$ that is applied to the first element of each trace in the subscript. These are analogous to atomic propositions in presentations that use Kripke structures and are defined as k-ary state predicates to capture relational properties over traces of the transition system. For example, consider the predicate $\mathcal{P}(\sigma_0,\sigma_1) \doteq (input(\sigma_0) = input(\sigma_1))$. Given this definition, a system M with exactly two traces $\Phi_M = \{\tau_1, \tau_2\}$ satisfies the HyperLTL formula $\forall \pi_1, \pi_2.\ \mathcal{P}_{\pi_1,\pi_2}$ iff $input(\tau_1^0) = input(\tau_2^0)$. This hyperproperty requires that the input in the initial state of the system be deterministically initialized.

The second difference is the new *counting quantifier*: $\#\pi\colon \Delta_{\pi_j,\pi_k}.\ \psi \triangleleft N(Z)$.[3] Δ_{π_j,π_k} is an unquantified HyperLTL formula over two "fresh" trace variables π_j and π_k that encodes when two traces are considered different. ψ is another (possibly-quantified) HyperLTL formula. The operator $\triangleleft$ can be $\leq$, $=$, or $\geq$. $N(Z)$ is an integer-sorted term in $FOL(\mathcal{T})$ over the variables in the set Z, $Z \subset X$ where X is the set of state variables of the transition system under consideration. Z typically refers to the subset of the state variables that define the parameters of the transition system; e.g. $Z = \{R\}$ for the Z-K proof transition system in Fig. 1, the number of blocks in a model of Path ORAM, the size of an array, etc. Typically, the variables in the set Z do not change after initialization. Informally stated, the counting quantifier is satisfied if a maximally large set $\Phi_C \subseteq \Phi$, satisfying the two conditions below, has cardinality $\triangleleft$ *count* where *count* is the valuation of $N(Z)$ in the initial state of every trace in Φ_C. Those conditions are: (i) each of the traces in Φ_C are pairwise different as defined by satisfaction of Δ_{π_j,π_k}, and (ii) every trace in this set satisfies the HyperLTL formula ψ.

The remaining operators are standard, so we do not discuss them further and instead provide formal satisfaction semantics.

Satisfaction Semantics of Quantitative HyperLTL The validity judgement of a property φ by a set of traces Φ is defined with respect to a trace assignment $\Pi\ :\ Vars \rightarrow \Phi$. Here, $Vars$ is the set of trace variables. We use $\pi, \pi_1, \pi_2, \ldots$ to refer to trace variables.[4] The partial function Π is a mapping from trace variables to traces. We use the notation $\Pi[\pi \mapsto \tau]$ to refer to a trace assignment that is identical to Π except for the trace variable π which now maps to the trace τ. We write $\Pi \models_\Phi \psi$ if the set of traces Φ satisfies the property ψ under the trace assignment Π. We will drop the subscript Φ from $\models_\Phi$ if it is clear from the context or irrelevant. The notation $\Pi^{[i,\infty]}$ is an abbreviation

---

[3] A counting quantifier over Kripke structures was introduced by Finkbeiner et al. [29]. Our definition is slightly different and a detailed comparison is deferred to Sect. 7.

[4] Note the distinction between trace variables denoted by π_1, π_2, etc. and traces which are denoted by τ_1, τ_2, etc.

for the new trace assignment obtained by taking the suffix starting from index i of every trace in Π: $\Pi^{[i,\infty]}(\pi) = \Pi(\pi)^{[i,\infty]}$ for every trace $\pi \in dom(\Pi)$ where $dom(\Pi)$ is the domain of Π. We write $\Pi \not\models_{\Phi} \psi$ when $\Pi \models_{\Phi} \psi$ is not satisfied. Satisfaction rules for HyperLTL formulas are shown in Fig. 4.

$\Pi \models_{\Phi} \forall \pi.\ \psi$	iff for all $\tau \in \Phi$: $\Pi[\pi \mapsto \tau] \models_{\Phi} \psi$
$\Pi \models_{\Phi} \#\pi{:}\Delta_{\pi_j,\pi_k}.\ \psi \lhd N(Z)$	iff $|\Phi_{\mathcal{C}}| = 0 \Rightarrow 0 \lhd N(Z)$ is valid, and
	$\quad |\Phi_{\mathcal{C}}| > 0 \Rightarrow \forall \tau \in \Phi_{\mathcal{C}}.\ |\Phi_{\mathcal{C}}| \lhd \tau^0(N(Z))$, where,
	$\quad \Phi_{\mathcal{C}} \subseteq \Phi$ is a maximally large set such that:
	$\quad \forall \tau_j, \tau_k \in \Phi_{\mathcal{C}}.$
	$\quad\quad \tau_j \neq \tau_k \Leftrightarrow \{\pi_j \mapsto \tau_j, \pi_k \mapsto \tau_k\} \models \Delta_{\pi_j,\pi_k}$
	$\quad$ and, $\forall \tau \in \Phi_{\mathcal{C}}.\ \Pi[\pi \mapsto \tau] \models_{\Phi} \psi$
$\Pi \models_{\Phi} \mathcal{P}_{\pi_1,\dots,\pi_k}$	iff $\mathcal{P}(\Pi(\pi_1)^0, \dots, \Pi(\pi_k)^0)$ is valid
$\Pi \models_{\Phi} \neg\psi$	iff $\Pi \not\models_{\Phi} \psi$
$\Pi \models_{\Phi} \psi \vee \varphi$	iff $\Pi \models_{\Phi} \psi$ or $\Pi \models_{\Phi} \varphi$
$\Pi \models_{\Phi} \mathbf{X}\,\varphi$	iff $\Pi^{[1,\infty]} \models_{\Phi} \varphi$
$\Pi \models_{\Phi} \varphi\,\mathbf{U}\,\psi$	iff there exists $j \geq 0$: $\Pi^{[j,\infty]} \models_{\Phi} \psi$
	and for all $0 \leq i < j$: $\Pi^{[i,\infty]} \models_{\Phi} \varphi$

Fig. 4. Satisfaction semantics for Quantitative HyperLTL formulas over symbolic transition systems.

Definition 2 (Quantitative HyperLTL Satisfaction). *We say that the transition system M satisfies the property ψ, denoted by $M \models \psi$ if the empty trace assignment $\emptyset$ satisfies formula ψ for the set of traces Φ_M, that is $\emptyset \models_{\Phi_M} \psi$.*

Additional Operators: The above showed the minimal set of operators required in Quantitative HyperLTL. The rest of this paper will use the other standard operators such as $\wedge$ (conjunction), $\Rightarrow$ (implication), $\mathbf{F}$ (future/eventually) and $\mathbf{G}$ (globally/always) which can be defined in terms of the operators in Fig. 3.

Well-Defined Formulas: In order for the semantics of Quantified HyperLTL to be meaningful, we need certain semantic restrictions on the structure of QHPs.

Definition 3 (Well-defined QHPs). *An instance of a counting quantifier $\#\pi$: $\Delta_{\pi_j,\pi_k}.\ \varphi \lhd N(Z)$ is said to be well-defined if:*

1. *$\neg\Delta_{\pi_j,\pi_k}$ is an equivalence relation over the set of all traces Φ, and*
2. *In every set of the traces $\Phi_{\mathcal{C}}$ captured by the counting quantifier in the semantics shown in Fig. 4, the term $N(Z)$ has the same valuation for all initial states: $\forall \tau_i, \tau_j \in \Phi_{\mathcal{C}}.\ \tau_i^0(N(Z)) = \tau_j^0(N(Z))$.*

A Quantified HyperLTL formula is said to be well-defined if every instance of a counting quantifier in the formula is well-defined.

Example 1 (Well-defined QHPs). The QHPs presented in the rest of this paper are all well-defined, so here we give an example of a QHP that is *not* well-defined. Consider this variant of Property 1: $\forall \pi_0. \# \pi_1: true.$ $\mathbf{G}\left(\psi_{\pi_0,\pi_1}\right) \geq 2^{\mathsf{R}} - 1$. This is not a well-defined QHP because Δ_{π_j,π_k} in the counting quantifier is simply *true*, and its negation is not an equivalence relation over the set of traces.

Note that condition (1) in the definition above affects Δ_{π_j,π_k} while condition (2) places a restriction on φ. The former condition prevents double-counting of traces, while the latter ensures that the trace count is unambiguous.

The properties in our experiments require only syntactic checks to verify well-definedness. Specifically, Δ_{π_j,π_k} is always of the form $\mathbf{F}\left(\mathcal{P}_{\pi_j,\pi_k}\right)$ where $\mathcal{P}$ is of the form $\mathcal{P}(\sigma_1,\sigma_2) \doteq f(\sigma_1) \neq f(\sigma_2)$. The negation of this is obviously an equivalence relation over the set of all traces. Secondly, our QHPs are of the form $\forall \pi_0.$ $\# \pi_1: \Delta_{\pi_j,\pi_k}.$ $\varphi \lhd N(Z)$ where φ enforces equality of the variables in Z between the traces π_0 and π_1. These two features guarantee well-definedness. In the rest of this paper, we only consider well-defined QHPs.

3.2   Applications of QHPs in Security Specification

Deniability: Our first example of a quantitative hyperproperty is deniability. Suppose $obs(\sigma)$ is a term that corresponds to the adversary observable part of the state σ, while $secret(\sigma)$ corresponds to the secret component of the state σ. Deniability is satisfied when every trace of adversary observations can be generated by at least $N(Z)$ different secrets. For this, we define $\delta(\sigma_1,\sigma_2) \doteq secret(\sigma_1) \neq secret(\sigma_2)$ and $\approx^O (\sigma_1,\sigma_2) \doteq obs(\sigma_1) = obs(\sigma_2)$.

$$\forall \pi_0. \# \pi_1: \mathbf{F}\left(\delta_{\pi_j,\pi_k}\right). \ \mathbf{G}\left(\approx^O_{\pi_0,\pi_1}\right) \geq N(Z)$$

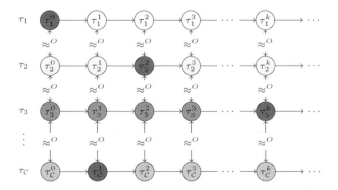

Fig. 5. Illustrating deniability.

Figure 5 illustrates deniability. It shows a set of traces $\Phi_C := \{\tau_1, \tau_2, \ldots, \tau_C\}$; the circles represent the states in each trace and the secret values are shown by color of the circle. For these traces, every pair of corresponding states have the same observations: represented by $\approx^O$, and every distinct pair of traces differ in the secrets. Deniability is satisfied if $|\Phi_C| \geq N(Z)$. Satisfaction implies that every trace of adversary observations has at least $N(Z)$ counterparts with identical observations but different values of $secret(\sigma)$. If we can show in a system satisfying deniability that each trace of secrets is equiprobable and $N(Z)$ grows exponentially in some parameters of the system, then we can conclude that the system satisfies computational indistinguishability. Deniability can capture probabilistic notions of confidentiality, such as confidentiality of Path ORAM.

Soundness: While deniability encodes a form of confidentiality, soundness is its dual in the context of integrity. One example of soundness was given in Sect. 2.2 for the Z-K hats puzzle. Soundness is generally applicable to protocols that offer probabilistic integrity guarantees. For instance, many interactive challenge-response protocols consist of repeated rounds such that if the prover succeeds in all rounds, the verifier can be convinced with a high probability that the prover is not cheating. This can be viewed as a QHP stating that for every trace in which a dishonest prover tricks a verifier into accepting an invalid proof, there are at least $N(Z)$ other traces with different prover responses in which the cheating is detected. As usual, we require that traces be uniformly sampled from a finite set in order to state soundness as a QHP.

Soundness is stated as $\forall \pi_0. \# \pi_1 \colon \mathbf{F}\left(\delta_{\pi_j, \pi_k}\right). \ \mathbf{G}\left(\psi_{\pi_0, \pi_1}\right) \ \geq \ N(Z)$. The relation δ is defined as two states having different prover responses. ψ requires the challenge-response protocol to fail in π_1 if it succeeded in π_0 and also that the system parameters (the variables in Z) be identical between π_0 and π_1.

Summarizing QHP Specification: These examples demonstrate that QHPs have important applications in security verification. They capture probabilistic notions of both confidentiality and integrity. In particular, the following form of QHPs consisting of a single quantifier alternation seems especially relevant for security verification: $\forall \pi_0. \ \# \pi_1 \colon \Delta_{\pi_j, \pi_k}. \ \varphi \ \lhd \ N(Z)$. Each of the examples of quantitative hyperproperties discussed in the previous subsection – deniability, soundness, as well as others like quantitative non-interference [46,54] fit in this template. Therefore, in the rest of this paper, we focus on developing scalable verification techniques for QHPs that follow this template.

4   Trace Enumerations

This section introduces the notion of a trace enumeration, which is a technique that allows us to reduce the problem of counting traces to that of counting satisfiable assignments to a formula in $FOL(\mathcal{T})$.

4.1   Trace Enumeration Relations

We now formalize injective trace enumerations, which allow us to lower-bound the number of traces captured by a counting quantifier in a QHP.

Definition 4 (Injective Trace Enumeration). *Let us consider a transition system $M = \langle X, Init(X), Tx(X, X') \rangle$ and the relation $\mathcal{U}(Y, \tau_1, \tau_2)$ where Y is a set of variables disjoint from X, τ_1 and τ_2 are traces of this transition system. Let $\forall \pi_0.\ \#\pi_1 \colon \Delta_{\pi_j, \pi_k}.\ \varphi \geq N(Z)$ be a QHP where $Z \subset X$. Suppose $\mathcal{V}(Y, Z)$ is a predicate over the variables in Y and Z. We say that the pair $\mathcal{V}(Y, Z)$ and $\mathcal{U}(Y, \tau_1, \tau_2)$ form an injective trace enumeration of the system M for the QHP $\forall \pi_0.\ \#\pi_1 \colon \Delta_{\pi_j, \pi_k}.\ \varphi \geq N(Z)$ iff the following conditions are satisfied:*

1. *For every trace τ_0 in Φ_M and every satisfying assignment (Y, Z) for the predicate $\mathcal{V}(Y, Z)$, there exists a trace $\tau_1 \in \Phi_M$ which is related to the trace τ_0 as per the relation $\mathcal{U}$ via this same assignment to Y. Further, the pair τ_0 and τ_1 satisfy the property φ and the valuation of the variables in Z in the initial state of τ_1 is equal to Z.*

$$\forall \tau_0 \in \Phi_M, Y, Z.\ \mathcal{V}(Y, Z) \Rightarrow \tag{2}$$
$$\left(\exists \tau_1 \in \Phi_M.\ \mathcal{U}(Y, \tau_0, \tau_1) \wedge \{\pi_0 \mapsto \tau_0, \pi_1 \mapsto \tau_1\} \models \varphi \wedge \tau_1^0(Z) = Z \right)$$

2. *Different assignments to the variables in Y for the formula $\mathcal{V}(Y, Z)$ enumerate different traces in $\mathcal{U}(Y, \tau_0, \tau_1)$, where "different" means satisfaction of Δ_{π_j, π_k}.*

$$\forall \tau_0, \tau_1, \tau_2 \in \Phi_M, Y_1, Y_2, Z. \tag{3}$$
$$\mathcal{V}(Y_1, Z) \wedge \mathcal{V}(Y_2, Z) \wedge Y_1 \neq Y_2 \qquad\qquad \Rightarrow$$
$$\mathcal{U}(Y_1, \tau_0, \tau_1) \wedge \mathcal{U}(Y_2, \tau_0, \tau_2) \wedge \tau_1^0(Z) = Z \wedge \tau_2^0(Z) = Z \qquad \Rightarrow$$
$$\{\pi_j \mapsto \tau_1, \pi_k \mapsto \tau_2\} \models \Delta_{\pi_j, \pi_k}$$

If $\mathcal{V}$ and $\mathcal{U}$ form an injective trace enumeration M for the property $\forall \pi_0.\ \#\pi_1 \colon \Delta_{\pi_j, \pi_k}.\ \varphi \geq N(Z)$, then for every trace τ_0, there exist at least as many traces satisfying the counting quantifier as there are satisfying assignments to Y in $\mathcal{V}(Y, Z)$. This is made precise in the following lemma.

Lemma 1. *[Trace Count Lower-Bound] If $\mathcal{V}(Y, Z)$ and $\mathcal{U}(Y, \tau_1, \tau_2)$ form an injective trace enumeration of the system M for the QHP $\forall \pi_0.\ \#\pi_1 \colon \Delta_{\pi_j, \pi_k}.\ \varphi \geq N(Z)$ and if $\#Y. \mathcal{V}(Y, Z)$ is finite for all assignments to Z, then $M \models \forall \pi_0.\#\pi_1 \colon \Delta_{\pi_j, \pi_k}.\ \varphi \geq \#Y. \mathcal{V}(Y, Z)$.*

Example 2 (Injective Trace Enumeration). Let $\mathsf{P}_0[1], \ldots, \mathsf{P}_0[\mathsf{R}]$ be a trace of correct responses for some particular sequence of challenges for our running example. Consider the array $\mathsf{Y}[1], \mathsf{Y}[2], \ldots, \mathsf{Y}[\mathsf{R}]$ where each $\mathsf{Y}[j] \in \{0, 1\}$. Y is a boolean array of size R, and $\mathsf{Y}[i] = 1$ means that the prover gives an incorrect response to the challenge in round i. We can define the predicate $\mathcal{V}$ as follows.

$$\mathcal{V}(Y, R) \doteq \left(\exists i.\ 1 \leq i \leq R \wedge Y[i] \neq 0 \right) \wedge \left(\forall i.\ (i < 1 \vee i > R) \Rightarrow Y[i] = 0 \right) \tag{4}$$

The above definition ensures that at least one response is incorrect. Notice that for every assignment to Y except the assignment of all zeros, the trace of responses defined by $\forall j.\ \mathsf{P}_1[j] = \mathsf{P}_0[j] \oplus \mathsf{Y}[j]$ (where $\oplus$ is exclusive or) corresponds to a valid trace of the system and satisfies the counting quantifier in Property 1. Specifically, every such response from the prover is incorrect and will result in the protocol failing. We can use the above facts to define the relation $\mathcal{U}$ as follows:

$$\mathcal{U}(\mathsf{Y}, \tau_1, \tau_2) \doteq \left(\forall j.\ \tau_1^0(\mathsf{P}[j]) = \tau_2^0(\mathsf{P}[j]) \oplus \mathsf{Y}[j]\right) \qquad\qquad \wedge \quad (5)$$
$$\tau_1^0(\mathsf{C}) = \tau_2^0(\mathsf{C}) \wedge \tau_1^0(\mathsf{R}) = \tau_2^0(\mathsf{R}) \wedge (\tau_1^\mathsf{R}(S) \Rightarrow \neg \tau_2^\mathsf{R}(S))$$

The pair $\mathcal{V}$ and $\mathcal{U}$ form an injective trace enumeration for the system M (defined in Fig. 1) for the Property 1. This is because different Y's will result in different prover responses for the same challenges. By Lemma 1, we can conclude that Property 1 is satisfied if $\#Y.\ \mathcal{V}(\mathsf{Y}, \mathsf{R}) \geq 2^\mathsf{R} - 1$.

Analogous to injective trace enumerations, it is also possible to define surjective trace enumerations that upper-bound the number of traces captured by a counting quantifier. Details of surjective trace enumerations are presented in the extended version of the paper [43].

5   Model Counting

As discussed in the previous section, trace enumeration relations can bound the number of satisfying traces in a QHP. Given a QHP $\forall \pi_0.\ \#\pi_1 \colon \Delta_{\pi_j, \pi_k}.\ \varphi \lhd N(Z)$, appropriate trace enumeration predicates $\mathcal{V}(Y, Z)$ and $\mathcal{U}$ can be used to derive that $\forall \pi_0.\ \#\pi_1 \colon \Delta_{\pi_j, \pi_k}.\ \varphi \lhd \#Y.\ \mathcal{V}(Y, Z)$. The final step in our verification methodology is to show validity of $\#Y.\ \mathcal{V}(Y, Z) \lhd N(Z)$. To that end, this section discusses our novel technique for model counting.

5.1   Model Counting via SMT Solving

Our approach borrows ideas from enumerative combinatorics [13,52,56] and introduces the inference rules shown in Fig. 6 to reason about model counts for formulas in $FOL(\mathcal{T})$. Each of the conclusions in the inference rules is a statement involving model counts of $FOL(\mathcal{T})$ formulas, while each of the premises is a formula in $FOL(\mathcal{T})$ that *does not involve model counts* and can, therefore, be checked using SAT/SMT solvers. Most of the rules are straightforward, and we do not describe them due to space constraints. The three interesting rules – *Injectivity*, *Ind*$_\leq$ and *Ind*$_\geq$ – are discussed below.

Injectivity: This rule is based on the following idea from enumerative combinatorics. Suppose we have two sets A and B. We can show that $|A| \leq |B|$ if there exists an injective function from A to B. Translating this to model counts, the set A in the rule corresponds to satisfying assignments to $f(X)$, B corresponds to satisfying assignments to $g(Y)$ and $\mathscr{F}$ is the injective witness function.

$Ind_\geq$ and $Ind_\leq$: Suppose the formulas $f(X, n)$ and $g(Y, n)$ are parameterized by the integer variable n. If an injective witness function $\mathscr{G}(X, Y, n)$ is able to "lift" satisfying assignments of $f(X_n, n)$ and $g(Y_n, n)$ into a satisfying assignment of $f(X_{n+1}, n + 1)$, then we can conclude that the number of satisfying assignments to $f(X, n + 1)$ are at least as many as the product of the number of satisfying assignments to $f(X, n)$ and $g(Y, n)$. *$Ind_\leq$* is the surjective version of this rule. It applies when a satisfying assignment to $f(X_{n+1}, n + 1)$ can be "lowered" into satisfying assignments to $f(X_n, n)$ and $g(Y_n, n)$ where the values of X_n and Y_n are given by the witness functions $\mathscr{H}_x$ and $\mathscr{H}_y$ respectively.

$$\overline{(\#i.\, a \leq i < b) \;=\; \max(b - a, 0)} \; \textit{Range} \qquad \overline{\#Y.\, f(X) \;\geq\; 0} \; \textit{Positive}$$

$$\frac{\bigwedge_{i=1}^{c} f(X_i) \wedge distinct(X_1, \ldots, X_c) \text{ is sat}}{\#X.\, f(X) \;\geq\; c} \; \textit{ConstLB}$$

$$\frac{\bigwedge_{i=1}^{c} f(X_i) \wedge distinct(X_1, \ldots, X_c) \text{ is unsat}}{\#X.\, f(X) \;<\; c} \; \textit{ConstUB}$$

$$\frac{f(X, Y) \Rightarrow g(X, Y)}{\#X.\, f(X, Y) \;\leq\; \#X.\, g(X, Y)} \; \textit{UB}$$

$$\frac{h(X, Y) \Leftrightarrow f(X) \wedge g(Y)}{\#X \cup Y.\, h(X, Y) \;\leq\; \#X.\, f(X) \times \#Y.\, g(Y)} \; \textit{AndUB}$$

$$\frac{f(X) \Rightarrow g(\mathscr{F}(X)) \quad \big(f(X_1) \wedge f(X_2) \wedge X_1 \neq X_2\big) \Rightarrow \mathscr{F}(X_1) \neq \mathscr{F}(X_2)}{\#X.\, f(X) \;\leq\; \#Y.\, g(Y)} \; \textit{Injectivity}$$

$$\frac{h(X, Y) \Leftrightarrow f(X) \wedge g(Y) \quad X \cap Y = \emptyset}{\#X \cup Y.\, h(X, Y) \;=\; \#X.\, f(X) \times \#Y.\, g(Y)} \; \textit{Disjoint}$$

$$\frac{f(X, Y) \Leftrightarrow g(X, Y) \vee h(X, Y)}{\#X.\, f(X, Y) \;=\; \#X.\, g(X, Y) + \#X.\, h(X, Y) - \#X.\big(g(X, Y) \wedge h(X, Y)\big)} \; \textit{Or}$$

$$\frac{\big(f(X, n) \wedge g(Y, n)\big) \Rightarrow f(\mathscr{G}(X, Y, n), n + 1) \quad (X_1 \neq X_2 \vee Y_1 \neq Y_2) \Rightarrow \mathscr{G}(X_1, Y_1, n) \neq \mathscr{G}(X_2, Y_2, n)}{\#X.\, f(X, n + 1) \;\geq\; \#X.\, f(X, n) \times \#Y.\, g(Y, n)} \; \textit{Ind}_\geq$$

$$\frac{f(X, n + 1) \Rightarrow \big(f(\mathscr{H}_x(X, n + 1), n) \wedge g(\mathscr{H}_y(X, n + 1), n)\big) \quad X_1 \neq X_2 \Rightarrow \big(\mathscr{H}_x(X_1, n) \neq \mathscr{H}_x(X_2, n) \vee \mathscr{H}_y(Y_1, n) \neq \mathscr{H}_y(Y_2, n)\big)}{\#X.\, f(X, n + 1) \;\leq\; \#X.\, f(X, n) \times \#Y.\, g(Y, n)} \; \textit{Ind}_\leq$$

Fig. 6. Model counting proof rules. Unless otherwise specified, premises are satisfied when the formula is valid. Conclusions have an implicit universal quantifier.

5.2   Model Counting in the Motivating Example

The definition of the predicate $\mathcal{V}$ in the motivating example is shown below.

$$\mathcal{V}(\mathsf{Y},\mathsf{R}) \doteq \left(\exists i.\ 1 \leq i \leq \mathsf{R} \wedge \mathsf{Y}[i] \neq 0\right) \wedge \left(\forall i.\ ((i < 1 \vee i > \mathsf{R}) \Rightarrow \mathsf{Y}[i] = 0)\right)$$

Our task is to show $\#\mathsf{Y}.\,\mathcal{V}(\mathsf{Y},\mathsf{R}) = 2^{\mathsf{R}} - 1$. Recall that Y is an array of binary values (i.e. the integers 0 and 1) and consider the following predicates: $\mathcal{V}_f(\mathsf{Y},\mathsf{R}) \doteq \left(\forall i.\ (i < 1 \vee i > \mathsf{R}) \Rightarrow \mathsf{Y}[i] = 0\right)$, $\mathcal{V}_1(\mathsf{Y},\mathsf{R}) \doteq \left(\forall i.\ \mathsf{Y}[i] = 0\right)$ and $\mathcal{W}(i) \doteq 0 \leq i < 2$. Using these definitions, the proof is as follows.

1. $(ConstUB,\ Positive)$ $\#\mathsf{Y}.\,\mathcal{V}_f(\mathsf{Y},\mathsf{R}) \wedge \mathcal{V}_1(\mathsf{Y},\mathsf{R}) = 1$.
2. (Or) $\#\mathsf{Y}.\,\mathcal{V}_f(\mathsf{Y},\mathsf{R}) = \#\mathsf{Y}.\,\mathcal{V}(\mathsf{Y},\mathsf{R}) + \#\mathsf{Y}.\,\mathcal{V}_1(\mathsf{Y},\mathsf{R})$.
3. $(ConstLB,\ ConstUB)$ $\#\mathsf{Y}.\,\mathcal{V}_1(\mathsf{Y},\mathsf{R}) = 1$.
4. $(ConstLB,\ ConstUB)$ $\#\mathsf{Y}.\,\mathcal{V}_f(\mathsf{Y},1) = 2$.
5. $(Ind_\leq)$: $\#\mathsf{Y}.\,\mathcal{V}_f(\mathsf{Y},\mathsf{R}) \leq \#i.\,\mathcal{W}(i) \times \#\mathsf{Y}.\,\mathcal{V}_f(\mathsf{Y},\mathsf{R}-1)$.
6. $(Ind_\geq)$: $\#\mathsf{Y}.\,\mathcal{V}_f(\mathsf{Y},\mathsf{R}) \geq \#i.\,\mathcal{W}(i) \times \#\mathsf{Y}.\,\mathcal{V}_f(\mathsf{Y},\mathsf{R}-1)$.
7. $(Range)$: $\#i.\,\mathcal{W}(i) = 2$.
8. $(4 - 7)$ imply that $\#\mathsf{Y}.\,\mathcal{V}_f(\mathsf{Y},\mathsf{R}) = 2 \times \#\mathsf{Y}.\,\mathcal{V}_f(\mathsf{Y},\mathsf{R}-1)$, $\#\mathsf{Y}.\,\mathcal{V}_f(\mathsf{Y},1) = 2$, this means $\#\mathsf{Y}.\,\mathcal{V}_f(\mathsf{Y},\mathsf{R}) = 2^{\mathsf{R}}$.
9. $(2, 3, 8)$ imply that $\#\mathsf{Y}.\,\mathcal{V}(\mathsf{Y},\mathsf{R}) = 2^{\mathsf{R}} - 1$.

In step 5, the witness function is $\mathcal{G}(\mathsf{Y},\mathsf{R},i) \doteq \mathsf{Y}[\mathsf{R}+1 \mapsto i]$, while in step 6, they are $\mathcal{H}_{\langle \mathsf{Y},\mathsf{R}\rangle}(\mathsf{Y},\mathsf{R}+1) \doteq \langle \mathsf{Y}[\mathsf{R}+1 \mapsto 0],\mathsf{R}\rangle$ and $\mathcal{H}_i(\mathsf{Y},\mathsf{R}+1) \doteq (\mathsf{Y}[\mathsf{R}+1]).^{5}$ Note steps 8 and 9 are automatically discharged by the SMT solver.

6   Experimental Results and Discussion

In this section, we present an experimental evaluation of the use of trace enumerations for the verification of quantitative hyperproperties.

6.1   Methodology

We studied five systems with varying complexity and QHPs. These were modeled in the UCLID5 modeling and verification framework [44,51], which uses the Z3 SMT solver (v4.8.6) [23] to discharge the proof obligations. The experiments were run on an Intel i7-4770 CPU @ 3.40 GHz with 8 cores and 32 GB RAM.

The verification conditions are currently manually generated from the models, but automation of this is straightforward and ongoing. The k-trace properties were proven using self-composition [9,10] and induction. A number of strengthening invariants had to be specified manually for the inductive proofs. Many of the invariants are relational *and* quantified and, therefore, difficult to infer algorithmically. We note that recent work has made progress toward automated inference of quantified invariants [27,36].

---

[5] The notation $arr[i \mapsto v]$ denotes an array that is identical to arr except for index i which contains v.

6.2   Overview of Results

Due to limited space, we only provide a brief description of our benchmarks for evaluation and refer the interested reader to the extended version of our paper [43] for a more detailed discussion. We have also made the models and associated proof scripts available at [25]. A brief overview of the case studies follows.

Table 1. Verification results of models.

Benchmark	Hyperproperty	Model LoC	Proof LoC	Num. Annot	Verif. Time
Electronic purse [7]	Deniability	46	93	9	3.92 s
Password checker [29]	Quantitative non-interference	59	100	10	4.69 s
F-Y array shuffle	Quantitative information flow	86	195	96	7.38 s
ZK hats (Sect. 2.2)	Soundness	91	191	36	6.34 s
Path ORAM [48]	Deniability	587	209	142	9.74 s

1. **Electronic Purse.** We model an electronic purse, with a secret initial balance, proposed by Backes et al. [7]. A fixed amount is debited from the purse until the balance is insufficient for the next transaction. We prove a deniability property: there is a sufficient number of traces with identical attacker observations but different initial balances.
2. **Password Checker.** We model the password checker from Finkbeiner et al. [29], but we allow passwords of unbounded length n. We prove quantitative non-interference: information leakage to an attacker is $\leq n$ bits.
3. **Array Shuffle.** We implement a variant of the Fisher-Yates shuffle. We chose this because producing random permutations of an array is an important component of certain cryptographic protocols (e.g., Ring ORAM [40]). We prove a quantitative information flow property stating that all possible permutations are indeed generated by the shuffling algorithm.
4. **ZK Hats.** We prove soundness of the zero-knowledge protocol in Sect. 2.
5. **Path ORAM.** Discussed in Sect. 6.3.

The properties we prove on these models and the results of our evaluation are presented in Table 1 which shows the size of each model, the number of lines of proof code (this is the code for self-composition, property specification, etc.), the number of verification annotations (invariants and procedure pre-/post-conditions) and the verification time for each example. Once the auxiliary strengthening invariants are specified, the verification completes within a few seconds. This suggests that the methodology can scale to larger models, and even implementations. The main challenge in the application of the methodology is the construction of the trace enumeration relations, associated witness functions, and the specification of strengthening invariants. Each of these requires application-specific insight. Since most of our enumerations and invariants are quantified, some of the proofs also required tweaking the SMT solver's configuration options (e.g. turning off model-based quantifier instantiation in Z3).

6.3 Deniability of Path ORAM

In this section, we discuss our main case study: the application of trace enumerations for verifying deniability of server access patterns in Path ORAM [48], a practical variant of Oblivious RAM (ORAM) [33]. ORAMs refer to a class of algorithms that allow a client with a small amount of storage to store/load a large amount of data on an untrusted server while concealing the client access pattern from the server. Path ORAM stores encrypted data on the server in an augmented binary tree format. Each node stores Z data blocks, referred to as *buckets* of size Z. Additionally, the client has a small amount of local storage called the *stash*. The client maintains a secret mapping called the *position map* to keep track of the path where a data block is stored on the server. Each entry in the position map maps a client address to a leaf on the server. Path ORAM maintains the invariant that every block is stored somewhere along the path from the root to the leaf node that the block is mapped to by the position map.

Deniability of Server Access Patterns in Path ORAM: We formulate security of access patterns in Path ORAM as a deniability property stating that for every infinitely-long trace of server accesses, there are $(\mathsf{numBlks} - 1)!$ traces of client accesses with identical server observations but different client requests.

$$\forall \pi_0. \ \#\pi_1 : \mathbf{F}\left(\delta_{\pi_j, \pi_k}\right). \ \mathbf{G}\left(\psi_{\pi_0, \pi_1}\right) \ \geq \ (\mathsf{numBlks} - 1)! \qquad (6)$$

The binary predicate δ imposes the requirement that the client's request are different in each of the traces captured by the counting quantifier, and the condition in ψ states that all the traces captured by the counting quantifier have the same observable access pattern as π_0.

Verification of Deniability in Path ORAM: To verify the QHP stated in Eq. 6, for every trace of server accesses we need to generate $(\mathsf{numBlks} - 1)!$ traces of client requests that produce the same server access.

Suppose we have Path ORAM (a) that is initialized with some position map. Now consider the Path ORAM (b) with the same number of blocks, but with an initial position map that is a derangement of the position map of (a).[6] The key insight is that ORAM (b) can simulate an identical server access pattern as ORAM (a) by appropriately choosing a different client request that maps to the same leaf that is being accessed by (a) and then updating the position map identically as (a). This is shown in Fig. 7, which shows two Path ORAMs that produce identical server access patterns but service different client requests.

---

[6] A **derangement** of a set is a permutation of the elements of the set such that no element appears in its original position.

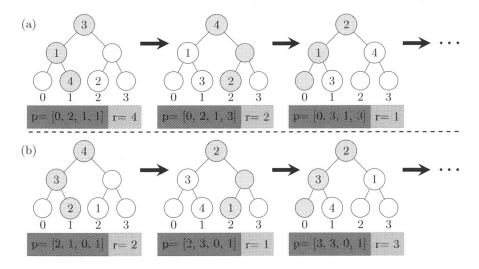

Fig. 7. Path ORAMs satisfying the counting quantifier of Eq. 6, where, p represents the position map indexed from 1 and r is the client's request.

The above insight leads to a trace enumeration where two traces are related via $\mathcal{U}$ if their position maps are derangements of each other, the client accesses are permuted as per the derangement while all other parameters of the ORAM are identical. We use this to prove Property 6. Further details are given in [43].

7   Related Work

Hyperproperties: Research into secure information flow started with the seminal work of Denning and Denning [24], Goguen and Meseguer [32] and Rushby [42]. The self-composition construction for the verification of secure information flow was introduced by Barthe et al. [10]. Clarkson and Schneider [21] introduced the class of specifications called hyperproperties. Clarkson and colleagues also introduced HyperLTL and HyperCTL* [19], which are temporal logics for specifying hyperproperties, while verification algorithms for these were introduced by Finkbeiner and colleagues in [30]. Cartesian Hoare Logic [47] was introduced by Sousa and Dillig and enables the specification and verification of hyperproperties over programs as opposed to transition systems. A number of subsequent efforts have studied hyperproperties in the context of program verification [5,26,45,53].

Quantitative Information Flow: Quantitative hyperproperties build on the rich literature of quantitative information flow (QIF) [3,17,20,34,46]. The QIF problem is to quantify (or bound) the number of bits of secret information that is attacker-observable. Certain notions of QIF can be expressed as QHPs. It is important to note QHPs can express security specifications (e.g., soundness) that are not QIF. Yasuoka and Terauchi studied QIF from a theoretical perspective and showed that it could be expressed as hypersafety and hyperliveness [54]. Approaches based on QIF measures such as min-entropy [46], Shannon entropy [18] etc. have also been applied in the context of static analysis [38].

Quantitative Hyperproperties: Quantitative Cartesian Hoare Logic (QCHL) enables verification of certain quantitative properties of programs [16]. QHPs are more expressive than QCHL, the latter counts events within a trace (e.g. memory accesses), while QHPs count the number of traces satisfying certain conditions.

The most closely related work to ours is of Finkbeiner et al. [29] who introduced Quantitative HyperLTL over Kripke structures. They also introduced a verification algorithm for this logic that is based on maximum model counting. However, their algorithm does not scale to reasonable-sized systems, and experiments from their paper show that the approach times out when checking an 8-bit leak in a password checker (using 8-bit passwords). We differ from their work in three important ways. First, our properties are defined over symbolic transition systems rather than Kripke structures. This allows modeling and verification of QHPs over infinite-state systems. Second, our bounds are symbolic, which enables us to express bounds as functions of transition system parameters. Finally, our definition of Quantitative HyperLTL is also more expressive. It is not possible to convert our QHPs into (non-quantitative) HyperLTL formulas with k-traces for any fixed value of k.

Verification of ORAMs: In concurrent work with ours, Barthe et al. [11] and Darais et al. [22] have introduced specialized mechanisms to prove security of ORAMs. Barthe et al. [11] introduced a probabilistic separation logic (PSL) that (among other things) can be used to reason about the security of ORAMs. Unlike QHPs, PSL does not permit quantitative reasoning about probabilities of events and also does not (yet) support machine-checked reasoning. Darais et al. [22] introduce a type system that enforces obliviousness; they use this type system to implement a tree-based ORAM. Note that QHPs can express specifications other than obliviousness, and obliviousness need not necessarily be a QHP.

8   Conclusion

Quantitative hyperproperties are a powerful class of specifications that stipulate the existence of a certain number of traces satisfying certain constraints. Many important security guarantees, especially those involving probabilistic guarantees of security, can be expressed as quantitative hyperproperties. Unfortunately, verification of quantitative hyperproperties is a challenging problem because these specifications require simultaneous reasoning about a large number of traces of a system. In this paper, we introduced a specification language, satisfaction semantics, and a verification methodology for quantitative hyperproperties. Our verification methodology is based on reducing the problem of counting traces into that of counting the number of assignments that satisfy a first-order logic formula. Our methodology enables security verification of many interesting security protocols that were previously out of reach, including confidentiality of access pattern accesses in Path ORAM.

Acknowledgements. We sincerely thank the anonymous reviewers for their insightful comments, which helped improve this paper. This work was supported in part by the Semiconductor Research Corporation under Task 2854 and the Science and Engineering Research Board of India, a unit of the Department of Science and Technology, Government of India.

References

1. Almeida, J.B., Barbosa, M., Barthe, G., Dupressoir, F.: Verifiable side-channel security of cryptographic implementations: constant-time MEE-CBC. In: Peyrin, T. (ed.) FSE 2016. LNCS, vol. 9783, pp. 163–184. Springer, Heidelberg (2016). https://doi.org/10.1007/978-3-662-52993-5_9
2. Almeida, J.B., Barbosa, M., Barthe, G., Dupressoir, F., Emmi, M.: Verifying constant-time implementations. In: 25th USENIX Security Symposium, USENIX Security, pp. 53–70 (2016)
3. Alvim, M.S., Andrés, M.E., Palamidessi, C.: Quantitative information flow in interactive systems. J. Comput. Secur. **20**(1), 3–50 (2012)
4. Antonopoulos, T., Gazzillo, P., Hicks, M., Koskinen, E., Terauchi, T., Wei, S.: Decomposition instead of self-composition for proving the absence of timing channels. In: PLDI, pp. 362–375 (2017)
5. Antonopoulos, T., Gazzillo, P., Hicks, M., Koskinen, E., Terauchi, T., Wei, S.: Decomposition instead of self-composition for proving the absence of timing channels. In: Proceedings of the 38th ACM SIGPLAN Conference on Programming Language Design and Implementation, PLDI 2017, New York, NY, USA, pp. 362–375. ACM (2017)
6. Almeida, J.B., Barbosa, M., Pinto, J.S., Vieira, B.: Formal verification of side-channel countermeasures using self-composition. Sci. Comput. Program. **78**(7), 796–812 (2013)
7. Backes, M., Kopf, B., Rybalchenko, A.: Automatic discovery and quantification of information leaks. In: Proceedings of the 2009 30th IEEE Symposium on Security and Privacy, SP 2009, Washington, DC, USA, pp. 141–153. IEEE Computer Society (2009)
8. Barthe, G., Betarte, G., Campo, J., Luna, C., Pichardie, D.: System-level noninterference for constant-time cryptography. In: Proceedings of the 2014 ACM SIGSAC Conference on Computer and Communications Security, pp. 1267–1279. ACM (2014)
9. Barthe, G., Crespo, J.M., Kunz, C.: Relational verification using product programs. In: Butler, M., Schulte, W. (eds.) FM 2011. LNCS, vol. 6664, pp. 200–214. Springer, Heidelberg (2011). https://doi.org/10.1007/978-3-642-21437-0_17
10. Barthe, G., D'Argenio, P.R., Rezk, T.: Secure information flow by self-composition. In: 17th IEEE Computer Security Foundations Workshop (CSFW-17), pp. 100–114 (2004)
11. Barthe, G., Hsu, J., Liao, K.: A probabilistic separation logic. In: Proceedings of ACM Programming Language, vol. 4, no. POPL, December 2019
12. Bindschaedler, V., Shokri, R., Gunter, C.A.: Plausible deniability for privacy-preserving data synthesis. In: Proceedings of the VLDB Endowment, vol. 10, no. 5, pp. 481–492 (2017)

13. Björner, A., Stanley, R.P.: A Combinatorial Miscellany. L'Enseignement mathématique (2010)
14. Chakraborti, A., Chen, C., Sion, R.: Datalair: efficient block storage with plausible deniability against multi-snapshot adversaries. In: Proceedings on Privacy Enhancing Technologies, vol. 2017, no. 3, pp. 179–197 (2017)
15. Cheang, K., Rasmussen, C., Seshia, S., Subramanyan, P.: A formal approach to secure speculation. In: 2019 IEEE 32nd Computer Security Foundations Symposium (CSF), pp. 288–28815, June 2019
16. Chen, J., Feng, Y., Dillig, I.: Precise detection of side-channel vulnerabilities using quantitative cartesian hoare logic. In: Proceedings of the 2017 ACM SIGSAC Conference on Computer and Communications Security, CCS 2017, New York, NY, USA, pp. 875–890. ACM (2017)
17. Clark, D., Hunt, S., Malacaria, P.: Quantitative information flow, relations and polymorphic types. J. Logic Comput. **15**(2), 181–199 (2005)
18. Clark, D., Hunt, S., Malacaria, P.: A static analysis for quantifying information flow in a simple imperative language. J. Comput. Secur. **15**(3), 321–371 (2007)
19. Clarkson, M.R., Finkbeiner, B., Koleini, M., Micinski, K.K., Rabe, M.N., Sánchez, C.: Temporal logics for hyperproperties. In: Abadi, M., Kremer, S. (eds.) POST 2014. LNCS, vol. 8414, pp. 265–284. Springer, Heidelberg (2014). https://doi.org/10.1007/978-3-642-54792-8_15
20. Clarkson, M.R., Myers, A.C., Schneider, F.B.: Belief in information flow. In: 18th IEEE Computer Security Foundations Workshop (CSFW 2005), pp. 31–45. IEEE (2005)
21. Clarkson, M.R., Schneider, F.B.: Hyperproperties. J. Comput. Secur. **18**(6), 1157–1210 (2010)
22. Darais, D., Sweet, I., Liu, C., Hicks, M.: A language for probabilistically oblivious computation. In: Proceedings of ACM Programming Language, vol. 4, no. POPL, December 2019
23. De Moura, L., Bjørner, N.: Z3: an efficient SMT solver. In: Tools and Algorithms for the Construction and Analysis of Systems (2008)
24. Denning, D.E., Denning, P.J.: Certification of programs for secure information flow. Commun. ACM **20**(7), 504–513 (1977)
25. Experiments: Models and Proof Scripts for the paper Verification of Quantitative Hyperproperties Using Trace Enumeration Relations (2020). https://github.com/ssahai/CAV-2020-benchmarks
26. Farzan, A., Vandikas, A.: Automated hypersafety verification. In: Computer Aided Verification - 31st International Conference, CAV 2019, New York City, NY, USA, 15–18 July 2019, Proceedings, Part I, pp. 200–218 (2019)
27. Fedyukovich, G., Prabhu, S., Madhukar, K., Gupta, A.: Quantified invariants via syntax-guided synthesis. In: Dillig, I., Tasiran, S. (eds.) CAV 2019. LNCS, vol. 11561, pp. 259–277. Springer, Cham (2019). https://doi.org/10.1007/978-3-030-25540-4_14
28. Ferraiuolo, A., Xu, R., Zhang, D., Myers, A.C., Suh, G.E.: Verification of a practical hardware security architecture through static information flow analysis. In: Proceedings of the Twenty-Second International Conference on Architectural Support for Programming Languages and Operating Systems, ASPLOS 2017, Xi'an, China, 8–12 April 2017, pp. 555–568 (2017)
29. Finkbeiner, B., Hahn, C., Torfah, H.: Model checking quantitative hyperproperties. In: Computer Aided Verification - 30th International Conference, CAV 2018, Held as Part of the Federated Logic Conference, FloC 2018, Oxford, UK, 14–17 July 2018, Proceedings, Part I, pp. 144–163 (2018)

30. Finkbeiner, B., Rabe, M.N., Sánchez, C.: Algorithms for model checking Hyper-LTL and HyperCTL*. In: Kroening, D., Păsăreanu, C.S. (eds.) CAV 2015. LNCS, vol. 9206, pp. 30–48. Springer, Cham (2015). https://doi.org/10.1007/978-3-319-21690-4_3

31. Fremont, D.J., Rabe, M.N., Seshia, S.A.: Maximum model counting. In: Thirty-First AAAI Conference on Artificial Intelligence (2017)

32. Goguen, J.A., Meseguer, J.: Security policies and security models. In: 1982 IEEE Symposium on Security and Privacy, Oakland, CA, USA, 26–28 April 1982, pp. 11–20 (1982)

33. Goldreich, O., Ostrovsky, R.: Software protection and simulation on oblivious rams. J. ACM **43**(3), 431–473 (1996)

34. James, W., Gray, I.I.I.: Toward a mathematical foundation for information flow security. J.Comput. Secur. **1**(3–4), 255–294 (1992)

35. Guarnieri, M., Morales, B.J.F., Reineke, J., Sánchez, A.: SPECTECTOR: principled detection of speculative information flows. CoRR, abs/1812.08639 (2018)

36. Gurfinkel, A., Shoham, S., Vizel, Y.: Quantifiers on demand. In: Lahiri, S.K., Wang, C. (eds.) ATVA 2018. LNCS, vol. 11138, pp. 248–266. Springer, Cham (2018). https://doi.org/10.1007/978-3-030-01090-4_15

37. Hawblitzel, C., et al.: Ironclad apps: end-to-end security via automated full-system verification. In: Proceedings of the 11th USENIX Conference on Operating Systems Design and Implementation, pp. 165–181 (2014)

38. Köpf, B., Mauborgne, L., Ochoa, M.: Automatic quantification of cache side-channels. In: International Conference on Computer Aided Verification, pp. 564–580. Springer, Heidelberg (2012). https://doi.org/10.1007/978-3-642-31424-7_40

39. Muduli, S.K., Subramanyan, P., Ray, S.: Verification of authenticated firmware loaders. In: Proceedings of Formal Methods in Computer-Aided Design. IEEE (2019)

40. Ren, L., et al.: Constants count: practical improvements to oblivious RAM. In: 24th USENIX Security Symposium (USENIX Security 15), Washington, D.C., pp. 415–430, August 2015. USENIX Association (2015)

41. Roscoe, A.W.: CSP and determinism in security modelling. In: Proceedings of the 1995 IEEE Symposium on Security and Privacy, Oakland, California, USA, 8–10 May 1995, pp. 114–127 (1995)

42. Rushby, J.M.: Proof of separability: a verification technique for a class of a security kernels. In: International Symposium on Programming, 5th Colloquium, Torino, Italy, 6–8 April 1982, Proceedings, pp. 352–367 (1982)

43. Sahai, S., Subramanyan, P., Sinha, R.: Verification of quantitative hyperproperties using trace enumeration relations. arXiv e-prints arXiv:abs/2005.04606, May 2020

44. Seshia, S.A., Subramanyan, P.: Uclid 5: integrating modeling, verification, synthesis and learning. In: Proceedings of the 16th ACM-IEEE International Conference on Formal Methods and Models for System Design (MEMOCODE), October 2018

45. Shemer, R., Gurfinkel, A., Shoham, S., Vizel, Y.: Property directed self composition. In: Dillig, I., Tasiran, S. (eds.) CAV 2019. LNCS, vol. 11561, pp. 161–179. Springer, Cham (2019). https://doi.org/10.1007/978-3-030-25540-4_9

46. Smith, G.: On the foundations of quantitative information flow. In: de Alfaro, L. (ed.) FoSSaCS 2009. LNCS, vol. 5504, pp. 288–302. Springer, Heidelberg (2009). https://doi.org/10.1007/978-3-642-00596-1_21

47. Sousa, M., Dillig, I.: Cartesian hoare logic for verifying k-safety properties. In: Proceedings of the 37th ACM SIGPLAN Conference on Programming Language Design and Implementation, PLDI 2016, New York, NY, USA, pp. 57–69. ACM (2016)

48. Stefanov, E., et al.: Path ORAM: an extremely simple oblivious RAM protocol. In: 2013 ACM SIGSAC Conference on Computer and Communications Security, CCS 2013, Berlin, Germany, 4–8 November 2013, pp. 299–310 (2013)
49. Subramanyan, P., Sinha, R., Lebedev, I.A., Devadas, S., Seshia, S.A.: A formal foundation for secure remote execution of enclaves. In: Proceedings of the 2017 ACM SIGSAC Conference on Computer and Communications Security, CCS 2017, Dallas, TX, USA, 30 October–03 November 2017, pp. 2435–2450 (2017)
50. Terauchi, T., Aiken, A.: Secure information flow as a safety problem. In: Static Analysis, 12th International Symposium, SAS, Proceedings, pp. 352–367 (2005)
51. UCLID5 Verification and Synthesis System (2019). http://github.com/uclid-org/uclid/
52. Wilf, H.S.: Generatingfunctionology. AK Peters/CRC Press (2005)
53. Yang, W., Subramanyan, P., Vizel, Y., Gupta, A., Malik, S.: Lazy self-composition for security verification. In: Computer Aided Verification - 30th International Conference, CAV 2018, Oxford, UK, 14–17 July 2018, Proceedings (2018)
54. Yasuoka, H., Terauchi, T.: Quantitative information flow as safety and liveness hyperproperties. Theor. Comput. Sci. **538**, 167–182 (2014)
55. Zdancewic, S., Myers, A.C.: Observational determinism for concurrent program security. In: Proceedings of the 16th IEEE Computer Security Foundations Workshop, pp. 29–43. IEEE (2003)
56. Zeilberger, D.: Enumerative and algebraic combinatorics. In: The Princeton Companion to Mathematics, pp. 550–561. Princeton University Press (2010)
57. Zhang, D., Wang, Y., Edward Suh, G., Myers, A.C.: A hardware design language for timing-sensitive information-flow security. In: Proceedings of the Twentieth International Conference on Architectural Support for Programming Languages and Operating Systems, ASPLOS 2015, Istanbul, Turkey, 14–18 March 2015, pp. 503–516 (2015)

Validation of Abstract Side-Channel Models for Computer Architectures

Hamed Nemati[1], Pablo Buiras[2], Andreas Lindner[2(✉)], Roberto Guanciale[2], and Swen Jacobs[1]

[1] Helmholtz Center for Information Security (CISPA),
Saarbrücken, Germany
{hnnemati,jacobs}@cispa.saarland
[2] KTH Royal Institute of Technology,
Stockholm, Sweden
{buiras,andili,robertog}@kth.se

Abstract. Observational models make tractable the analysis of information flow properties by providing an abstraction of side channels. We introduce a methodology and a tool, Scam-V, to validate observational models for modern computer architectures. We combine symbolic execution, relational analysis, and different program generation techniques to generate experiments and validate the models. An experiment consists of a randomly generated program together with two inputs that are observationally equivalent according to the model under the test. Validation is done by checking indistinguishability of the two inputs on real hardware by executing the program and analyzing the side channel. We have evaluated our framework by validating models that abstract the data-cache side channel of a Raspberry Pi 3 board with a processor implementing the ARMv8-A architecture. Our results show that Scam-V can identify bugs in the implementation of the models and generate test programs which invalidate the models due to hidden microarchitectural behavior.

Keywords: Testing · Side channels · Information flow security · Model validation · Microarchitectures

1 Introduction

Information flow analysis that takes into account side channels is a topic of increasing relevance, as attacks that compromise confidentiality via different microarchitectural features and sophisticated side channels continue to emerge [2,27,28,31–33,40]. While there are information flow analyses that try to counter these threats [3,15], these approaches use models that abstract from many features of modern processors, like caches and pipelining, and their effects on channels that can be accessed by an attacker, like execution time and power consumption. Instead, these models [36] include explicit "observations" that become available to an attacker when the program is executed and that should overapproximate the information that can be observed on the real system.

© The Author(s) 2020
S. K. Lahiri and C. Wang (Eds.): CAV 2020, LNCS 12224, pp. 225–248, 2020.
https://doi.org/10.1007/978-3-030-53288-8_12

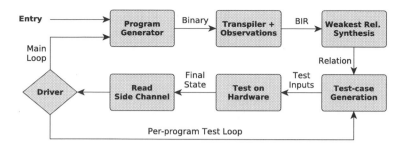

Fig. 1. Validation framework workflow

While abstract models are indispensable for automatic verification because of the complexity of modern microarchitectures, the amount of details hidden by these models makes it hard to trust that no information flow is missed, i.e., their soundness. Different implementations of the same architecture, as well as optimizations such as parallel and speculative execution, can introduce side channels that may be overlooked by the abstract models. This has been demonstrated by the recent Spectre attacks [32]: disregarding these microarchitectural features can lead to consider programs that leak information on modern CPUs as secure. Thus, it is essential to validate whether an abstract model adequately reflects all information flows introduced by the low-level features of a specific processor.

In this work, we introduce an approach that addresses this problem: we show how to validate observational models by comparing their outputs against the behavior of the real hardware in systematically generated experiments. In the following, we give an overview of our approach and this paper.

Our Contribution. We introduce Scam-V (Side Channel Abstract Model Validator), a framework for the automatic validation of abstract observational models. At a high level, Scam-V generates well-formed[1] random binaries and attempts to construct pairs of initial states such that runs of the binaries from these states are indistinguishable at the level of the model, but distinguishable on the real hardware. In essence, finding such counterexamples implies that the observational model is not sound, and leads to a potential vulnerability. Figure 1 illustrates the main workflow of Scam-V.

The first step of our workflow (described in Sect. 3) is the generation of a binary program for the given architecture, guided towards programs that trigger certain features of the architecture. The second step translates the program to the intermediate language BIR (described in Sect. 2.4) and annotates the result with observations according to the observational model under validation. This transpilation is provably correct with respect to the formal model of the ISA, i.e., the original binary program and the transpiled BIR program have the same effects on registers and memory. In step three we use symbolic execution to syn-

---

[1] Terminating programs which do not cause run-time exceptions and emit observations required by the analysis.

thesize the weakest relation on program states that guarantees indistinguishability in the observational model (Sect. 4). Through this relation, the observational model is used to drive the generation of *test cases* – pairs of states that satisfy the relation and can be used as inputs to the program (Sect. 5). Finally, we run the generated binary with different test cases on the real hardware, and compare the measurements on the side channel of the real processor. A description of this process together with general remarks on our framework implementation are in Sect. 6. Since the generated test cases satisfy the synthesized relation, soundness of the model would imply that the side-channel data on the real hardware cannot be distinguished either. Thus, a test case where we can distinguish the two runs on the hardware amounts to a counterexample that invalidates the observational model. After examining a given test case, the driver of the framework decides whether to generate more test cases for the same program, or to generate a new program.

We have implemented Scam-V in the HOL4 theorem prover[2] and have evaluated the framework on three observational models (introduced in Sect. 2.3) for the L1 data-cache of the ARMv8 processor on the Raspberry Pi 3 (Sect. 2.2). Our experiments (Sect. 7) led to the identification of model invalidating microarchitectural features as well as bugs in the ARMv8 ISA model and our observational extensions. This shows that many existing abstractions are substantially unsound.

Since our goal is to validate that observational models overapproximate hardware information flows, we do not attempt to identify practically exploitable vulnerabilities. Instead, our experiments attempt to validate these models in the worst case scenario for the victim. This consists of an attacker that can precisely identify the cache lines that have been evicted by the victim and that can minimize the noise of these measurements in the presence of background processes and interrupts.

2   Background

2.1   Observational Models

We briefly introduce the concepts of side channels, indistinguishability, observational models, and observational equivalence. For the rest of this section, consider a fixed program that runs on a fixed processor. We can model the program running on the processor by a transition system $M = \langle S, \rightarrow \rangle$, where S is a set of states and $\rightarrow \subseteq S \times S$ a transition relation. In automated verification, the state space of such a model usually reflects the possible values of program variables (or: registers of the processor), abstracting from low-level behavior of the processor, such as cache contents, electric currents, or real-time behavior. That is, for every state of the real system there is a state in the model that represents it, and a state of the model usually represents a set of states of the real system.

Then, a *side channel* is a trait of the real system that can be read from by an attacker and that is not modeled in M.

---

[2] https://hol-theorem-prover.org.

Definition 1 (Indistinguishability). *States r_1 and r_2 of the real system are* indistinguishable *if a real-world attacker is not able to distinguish executions from r_1 or r_2 by means of the side channel on the real hardware.*

Note that executions may be distinguishable even if they end in the same final state, e.g., if the attacker is able to measure execution time.

In order to verify resilience against attacks that use side channels, one option is to extend the model to include additional features of the real system and to formalize indistinguishability in terms of some variations of non-interference [25,26]. Unfortunately, it is infeasible to develop formal models that capture *all* side channels of a modern computer architecture. For instance, precisely determining execution time or power consumption of a program requires to deal with complex processor features such as cache hierarchies, cache replacement policies, speculative execution, branch prediction, or bus arbitration. Moreover, for some important parts of microarchitectures, their exact behavior may not even be public knowledge, e.g., the mechanism used to train the branch predictor. Additionally, information flow analyses cannot use the same types of overapproximations that are used for checking safety properties or analyzing worst-case execution time, e.g., the introduction of nondeterminism to cover all possible outcomes.

In order to handle this complexity, information flow analyses [3,15] use models designed to overapproximate information flow to channels in terms of system state observations. To this end, the model is extended with a set of possible observations O and we consider a transition relation $\rightarrow \subseteq S \times O \times S$, i.e., each transition produces an observation that captures the information that it potentially leaks to the attacker. We assume that the set O contains an *empty observation* $\perp$, and call a transition labeled with $\perp$ a *silent* transition. We call the resulting transition system an *observational model*. For instance, in case of a rudimentary cacheless processor, the execution time of a program depends only on the sequence of executed instructions. In this case, extending the model with observations that reveal the instructions is more convenient than producing a clock-accurate model of the system.

We use the operator $\circ$ for the sequential composition of observations. In particular, for a trace $\pi = s_0 \rightarrow^{o_1} s_1 \ldots \rightarrow^{o_n} s_n$ of the model, we write $o_1 \circ \ldots \circ o_n$ for the sequence of observations along π. We write $o_1 \circ \ldots \circ o_n \approx o'_1 \circ \ldots \circ o'_{n'}$ if the two sequences are equal after removing silent transitions. Comparing traces with observations leads to a notion of *observational equivalence*, defined as a relation on program states.

Definition 2 (Observational equivalence). *Traces $\pi = s_0 \rightarrow^{o_1} s_1 \ldots \rightarrow^{o_n} s_n$ and $\pi' = s'_0 \rightarrow^{o'_1} s'_1 \ldots \rightarrow^{o'_{n'}} s'_{n'}$ of an observational model M are* observationally equivalent *(written as $\pi \sim_M \pi'$) iff $o_1 \circ \ldots \circ o_n \approx o'_1 \circ \ldots \circ o'_{n'}$.*

States $s_1 \in S$ and $s_2 \in S$ are observationally equivalent, *denoted $s_1 \sim_M s_2$, iff for every possible trace π_1 of M that starts in s_1 there is a trace π_2 of M that starts in s_2 such that $\pi_1 \sim_M \pi_2$, and vice versa.*

Note that this notion is, in principle, different from the notion of *indistinguishability*. The overapproximation of information flows can lead to false positives: for example, execution of a program may require the same amount of time

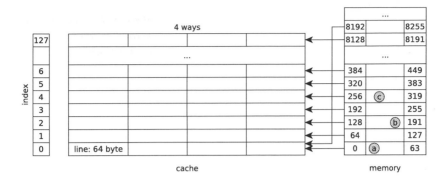

Fig. 2. L1 data-cache structure.

even if the sequences of executed instructions are different. A more severe concern is that these abstractions may overlook some flows of information due to the number of low-level details that are hidden. For instance, an observational model may not take into account that for some microcontrollers the number of clock cycles required for multiplication depends on the value of the operands.

The use of an abstract model to verify resilience against side-channel attacks relies on the assumption that observational equivalence entails indistinguishability for a real-world attacker on the real system:

Definition 3 (Soundness). *An observational model M is* sound *if whenever the model states s_1 and s_2 represent the real system states r_1 and r_2, respectively, then $s_1 \sim_M s_2$ entails indistinguishability of r_1 and r_2.*

2.2   The Evaluation Platform: Raspberry Pi 3

In order to evaluate our framework, we selected Raspberry Pi 3[3], which is a widely available ARMv8 embedded system. The platform's CPU is a Cortex-A53, which is an 8-stage pipelined processor with a 2-way superscalar and in-order execution pipeline. The CPU implements branch prediction, but it does not support speculative execution. This makes the CPU resilient against variations of Spectre attacks [5].

In the following, we focus on side channels that exploit the Level 1 (L1) data-cache of the system. The L1 data-cache is transparent for programmers. When the CPU needs to read a location in memory in case of a cache miss, it copies the data from memory into the cache for subsequent uses, tagging it with the memory location from which the data was read.

Data is transferred between memory and cache in blocks of 64 bytes, called cache lines. The L1 data-cache (Fig. 2) is physically indexed and physically tagged and is 4-way set associative: each memory location can be cached in four different entries in the cache—when a line is loaded, if all corresponding entries

---

[3] https://www.raspberrypi.org.

are occupied, the CPU uses a specific (and usually underspecified) replacement policy to decide which colliding line should be evicted. The whole L1 cache is 32KB in size, hence it has 128 cache sets (i.e. $32\,\text{KB}/64\,\text{B}/4$). Let a be a physical address, in the following we use $\text{off}(a)$ (i.e., least significant 6 bits), $\text{index}(a)$ (i.e., bits from 6 to 12), and $\text{tag}(a)$ (i.e., the remaining bits) to extract the cache offset, cache set index, and cache tag of the address.

The cache implements a prefetcher, for some configurable $k \in \mathbb{N}$: when it detects a sequence of k cache misses whose cache set indices are separated by a fixed stride, the prefetcher starts to fetch data in the background. For example, in Fig. 2, if $k = 3$ and the cache is initially empty then accessing addresses a, b, and c, whose cache lines are separated by a stride of 2, can cause the cache to prefetch the block $[384 \ldots 449]$.

2.3   Different Attacker and Observational Models

Attacks that exploit the L1 data-cache are usually classified in three categories: In *time-driven attacks* (e.g. [47]), the attacker measures the execution time of the victim and uses this knowledge to estimate the number of cache misses and hits of the victim; In *trace-driven attacks* (e.g. [1, 48]), the adversary can profile the cache activities during the execution of the victim and observe the cache effects of a particular operation performed by the victim; Finally, in *access-driven attacks* (e.g. [39, 46]), the attacker can only determine the cache sets modified after the execution of the victim has completed. A widely used approach to extract information via cache is Prime+Probe [40]: (1) the attacker reads its own memory, filling the cache with its data; (2) the victim is executed; (3) the attacker measures the time needed to access the data loaded at step (1): slow access means that the corresponding cache line has been evicted in step (2).

In the following we disregard time-driven attacks and trace-driven attacks: the former can be countered by normalizing the victim execution time; the latter can be countered by preventing victim preemption. Focusing on access-driven attacks leads to the following notion of indistinguishability:

Definition 4. *Real system states r_1 and r_2 are* indistinguishable *for access-driven attacks on the L1 data-cache iff executions starting in r_1 or r_2 modify the same cache sets.*

We remark that for multi-way caches, the need for models that overapproximate the information flow is critical since the replacement policies are seldom formally specified and a precise model of the channel is not possible. The following observational model attempts to overapproximate information flows for data-caches by relying on the fact that accessing two different addresses that only differ in their cache offset produces the same cache effects:

Definition 5. *The transition relation of the multi-way cache and pc observational model is $s \to^o_{mwc,pc} s'$, where $\to^o_{mwc,pc}$ models the execution of one single instruction, with $o \in \mathbb{N} \times ((\{rd, wt\} \times \mathbb{N} \times \mathbb{N}) \cup \bot)$. If $o = (pc, acc)$ then pc is the current program counter and $acc = (op, t, i)$ is the memory access performed* *by the instruction, where op is the memory operation, t is the cache tag and i is the cache set index corresponding to the address. If the instruction does not access the memory, then acc $=\perp$.*

Notice that by making the program counter observable, this model assumes that the attacker can infer the sequence of instructions executed by the program.

We introduce several relaxed models, representing different assumptions on the hardware behavior and attacker capability. Each relaxed model is obtained by projecting observations of Definition 5. Let α be a relaxed model and f_α the corresponding projection function, then $s \to_\alpha^{o'} s'$ iff exists o such that $f_\alpha(o) = o'$ and $s \to_{mwc,pc}^o s'$.

The following model assumes that the effects of instructions that do not interact with the data memory are not measurable, hence the attacker does not observe the program counter:

Definition 6. *The projection of the* multi-way cache observational model *is* $f_{mwc}((pc, acc)) = acc$.

On many processors, the replacement policy for a cache set does not depend on previous accesses performed to other cache sets. The resulting isolation among cache sets leads to the development of an efficient countermeasure against access-driven attacks: cache coloring [23,45]. This consists in partitioning the cache sets into multiple regions and ensuring that memory pages accessible by the adversary are mapped to a specific region of the cache. In this case, accesses to other regions do not affect the state of cache sets that an attacker can examine. Therefore these accesses are not observable. This assumption is captured by the following model:

Definition 7. *The projection of the* partitioned multi-way cache observational model *is* $f_{pmwc}((pc, acc)) = acc$ *if* $acc = (op, t, i)$ *and i belongs to the set of cache sets that are addressable by the attacker, and is* $\perp$ *otherwise.*

Notice that cache prefetching can violate soundness of this model, since accesses to the non-observable region of the cache may lead to prefetching addresses that lie in the observable part of the cache (see Sect. 7.2).

Finally, for direct-mapped caches, where each memory address is mapped to only one cache entry, the cache tag should not be observable if the attacker does not share memory with the victim:

Definition 8. *The projection of the* direct-mapped cache observational model *is* $f_{dc}((pc, (op, t, i))) = (op, i)$ *and* $f_{dc}((pc, \perp)) = \perp$.

Since the cache in Cortex-A53 is multi-way set associative, this model is not sound. For example, in a two-way set associative cache, accessing a, a and a, b, where both a and b have the same cache set index but different cache tags, may result in different cache states.

```
BIR program with observation
//b.eq 12
[10:CJMP Z 12 11]
//mul x1 x2 x3
[11:X1= X2*X3; JMP 12]
//ldr x2 {x1} +8
[12:OBS(sline(X1),[tag(X1),index(X1)]);
    X2= LOAD(M, X1);X1= X1+8;HALT]
```

Fig. 3. BIR transpilation example

2.4   Binary Intermediate Representation

To achieve a degree of hardware independence, we use the architecture-agnostic intermediate representation BIR [34]. It is an abstract assembly language with statements that work on memory, arithmetic expressions, and jumps. Figure 3 shows an example of code in a generic assembly language and its transpiled BIR code. This code performs a conditional jump to *l2* if **Z** holds, and otherwise it sets **X1** to the multiplication **X2** ∗ **X3**. Then, at *l2* it loads a word from memory at address **X1** into **X2**, and finally adds 8 to the pointer **X1**. BIR programs are organized into blocks, which consist of jump-free statements and end in either conditional jump (CJMP), unconditional jump (JMP), or HALT.

BIR also has explicit support for *observations*, which are produced by statements that evaluate a list of expressions in the current state. To account for expressive observational models, BIR allows conditional observation. The condition is represented by an expression attached to the observation statement. The observation itself happens only if this condition evaluates as true in the current state. The observations in Fig. 3 reflect a scenario where the data-cache has been partitioned: some lines are exclusively accessible by the victim (i.e. the program), some lines can be shared with the attacker. The statement OBS(sline(**X1**), [tag(**X1**), index(**X1**)]) for the load instruction consists of an observation condition (sline(**X1**)) and a list of expressions to observe ([tag(**X1**), index(**X1**)]). The function sline checks that the argument address is mapped in a shared line and therefore visible to the attacker. The functions tag and index extract the cache tag and set index in which the argument address is mapped. Binary programs can be translated to BIR via a process called *transpilation*. This transformation reuses formal models of the ISAs and generates a proof that certifies correctness of the translation by establishing a bisimulation between the two programs.

3   Program Generation

We base our validation of observational models on the execution of binary programs rather than higher-level code representations. This approach has the following benefits: (i) It obviates the necessity to trust compilers or reason about

```
                    Random program generator
        udiv x3, x16, x8
        cbnz x28, #12
        bics x14, x3, x26, ror #21
        ldrsb w4, [x24, x3]
        ldp x22, x14, [x3], #0xD0
```

Fig. 4. Example programs generated by the Scam-V random program generator.

Load generator	Load strides	Load seq. with branches
ldr x5, [x1, 4]	ldr x16, [x2, #0]	cmp x13, x3
ldr x0, x3	ldr x19, [x2, #64]	b.eq #0x14
ldr x2, [x9, 8]	ldr x1, [x2, #128]	ldr x6, #0x1DFA
	ldr x22, [x2, #192]	ldr x9, [x20]
	ldr x17, [x2, #256]	ldr x20, [x22, #8]
		b #0x10
		ldr x16, [x0, #16]
		ldr x16, #0x1BE8
		ldr x12, #0x17D5

Fig. 5. Example programs generated by Scam-V monadic program generators.

how their compilation affects side-channels. (ii) Implementation effort is reduced because most existing side-channel analysis approaches also operate on binary representations, which requires ISA models. (iii) This approach allows to find ISA model faults independently of the compilation. (iv) It enables a unified infrastructure to handle many different types of channels.

In Scam-V, we implemented two techniques to generate well-formed binaries: *random* program generation and *monadic* program generation. The random generator leverages the instruction encoding machinery from the existing HOL4 model of the ISA and produces arbitrary well-formed ARMv8 binaries, with the possibility to control the frequency of occurrences of each instruction class. The monadic generator is following a grammar-driven approach in the style of QuickCheck [13] that generates arbitrary programs that fit a specific pattern or template. The program templates can be defined in a modular, declarative style and are extensible. We use this approach to generate programs in a guided fashion, focusing on processor features that we want to exercise in order to validate a model, or those we suspect may lead to a counterexample. Figures 4 and 5 show some example programs generated by Scam-V, including straight-line programs that only do memory loads, programs that load from addresses in a stride pattern to trigger automatic prefetching, and programs with branches. More details on how the program generators work can be found in [38].

4   Synthesis of Weakest Relation

Synthesis of the weakest relation is based on standard symbolic execution techniques. We only cover the basic ideas of symbolic execution in the following and refer the reader to [30] for more details. We use $\mathbf{X}$ to range over symbols, and $\mathbf{c}$, $\mathbf{e}$, and $\mathbf{p}$ to range over symbolic expressions. A symbolic state σ consists of a concrete program counter i_σ, a path condition $\mathbf{p}_\sigma$, and a mapping $\mathbf{m}_\sigma$ from variables to symbolic expressions. We write $e(\sigma) = \mathbf{e}$ for the symbolic evaluation of the expression e in σ, and $\mathbf{e}(s)$ for the value obtained by substituting the symbols of the symbolic expression $\mathbf{e}$ with the values of the variables in s, where s is a concrete state.

Symbolic execution produces one terminating state[4] for each possible execution path: a terminating state is produced when HALT is encountered; the execution of CJMP c l_1 l_2 from state σ follows both branches using the path conditions $c(\sigma)$ and $\neg c(\sigma)$. Symbolic execution of the example in Fig. 3 produces the terminating states σ_1 and σ_2. For the first branch we have $\mathbf{p}_{\sigma_1} = \mathbf{Z}$ and $\mathbf{m}_{\sigma_1} = \{X_1 \to \mathbf{X}_1 + 8, X_2 \to \text{LOAD}(\mathbf{M}, \mathbf{X}_1)\}$ (we omit the variables that are not updated), and for the second branch $\mathbf{p}_{\sigma_2} = \neg\mathbf{Z}$ and $\mathbf{m}_{\sigma_2} = \{X_1 \to \mathbf{X}_2 * \mathbf{X}_3 + 8, X_2 \to \text{LOAD}(\mathbf{M}, \mathbf{X}_2 * \mathbf{X}_3)\}$.

We extend standard symbolic execution to handle observations. That is, we add to each symbolic state a list $\mathbf{l}_\sigma$, and the execution of OBS c $\vec{e}$ in σ appends the pair $(\mathbf{c}, \vec{\mathbf{e}})$ to $\mathbf{l}_\sigma$, where $\mathbf{c} = c(\sigma)$ and $\vec{\mathbf{e}}[i] = \vec{e}[i](\sigma)$ are the symbolic evaluation of the condition and expressions of the observation. For instance, in the example of Fig. 3 the list for the terminating states are

$$\mathbf{l}_{\sigma_1} = [(\text{sline}(\mathbf{X}_1), [\text{tag}(\mathbf{X}_1), \text{index}(\mathbf{X}_1)])]$$
$$\mathbf{l}_{\sigma_2} = [(\text{sline}(\mathbf{X}_2 * \mathbf{X}_3), [\text{tag}(\mathbf{X}_2 * \mathbf{X}_3), \text{index}(\mathbf{X}_2 * \mathbf{X}_3)])]$$

Let Σ be the set of terminating states produced by the symbolic execution, s be a concrete state, and $\sigma \in \Sigma$ be a symbolic state such that $\mathbf{p}_\sigma(s)$ holds, then executing the program from the initial state s produces the value $\mathbf{m}_\sigma(X)(s)$ for the variable X. Moreover, let $\mathbf{l}_\sigma = [(\mathbf{c}_1, \vec{\mathbf{e}}_1) \dots (\mathbf{c}_n, \vec{\mathbf{e}}_n)]$, then the generated observations are $(\mathbf{c}_1, \vec{\mathbf{e}}_1)(s) \circ \dots \circ (\mathbf{c}_n, \vec{\mathbf{e}}_n)(s)$, where $(\mathbf{c}_1, \vec{\mathbf{e}}_1)(s) = \vec{\mathbf{e}}_1(s)$ if $\mathbf{c}_1(s)$, and otherwise $\bot$ (i.e. observations are list of concrete values).

After computing Σ, we synthesize the observational equivalence relation (denoted by $\sim$) by ensuring that every possible pair of execution paths have equivalent lists of observations. Formally, $s_1 \sim s_2$ is equivalent to:

$$\bigwedge_{(\sigma_1, \sigma_2) \in \Sigma \times \Sigma} (\mathbf{p}_{\sigma_1}(s_1) \wedge \mathbf{p}_{\sigma_2}(s_2) \Rightarrow \mathbf{l}_{\sigma_1}(s_1) = \mathbf{l}_{\sigma_2}(s_2))$$

This synthesized relation implies the observational equivalence defined in Sect. 2 (Definition 2). In the example, the synthesized relation (after simplification) is as follows (notice that primed symbols represent variables of the second state and we omitted the symmetric cases):

---

[4] We consider only terminating programs.

$$\begin{matrix} s_1 = \\ \left\{\begin{array}{l} \mathbf{Z} = T \\ \mathbf{X}_1 = 130 \\ \mathbf{X}_2 = 123546 \\ \mathbf{X}_3 = 87465 \end{array}\right\} \end{matrix} \sim \begin{matrix} s_2 = \\ \left\{\begin{array}{l} \mathbf{Z} = F \\ \mathbf{X}_1 = 37846 \\ \mathbf{X}_2 = 2 \\ \mathbf{X}_3 = 64 \end{array}\right\} \end{matrix} \quad \begin{matrix} s'_1 = \\ \left\{\begin{array}{l} \mathbf{Z} = F \\ \mathbf{X}_1 = 3246 \\ \mathbf{X}_2 = 64 \\ \mathbf{X}_3 = 30 \end{array}\right\} \end{matrix} \sim \begin{matrix} s'_2 = \\ \left\{\begin{array}{l} \mathbf{Z} = F \\ \mathbf{X}_1 = 856 \\ \mathbf{X}_2 = 12 \\ \mathbf{X}_3 = 64 \end{array}\right\} \end{matrix}$$

Fig. 6. Example test cases when the first 10 cache sets are shared.

$$(\mathbf{Z} \wedge \mathbf{Z}') \Rightarrow$$
$$\left(\begin{array}{l} \texttt{sline}(\mathbf{X}_1) = \texttt{sline}(\mathbf{X'}_1) \wedge \\ \texttt{sline}(\mathbf{X}_1) \Rightarrow (\texttt{tag}(\mathbf{X}_1) = \texttt{tag}(\mathbf{X'}_1) \wedge \texttt{index}(\mathbf{X}_1) = \texttt{index}(\mathbf{X'}_1)) \end{array} \right) \wedge$$
$$(\mathbf{Z} \wedge \neg\mathbf{Z}') \Rightarrow$$
$$\left(\begin{array}{l} \texttt{sline}(\mathbf{X}_1) = \texttt{sline}(\mathbf{X'}_2 * \mathbf{X'}_3) \wedge \\ \texttt{sline}(\mathbf{X}_1) \Rightarrow (\texttt{tag}(\mathbf{X}_1) = \texttt{tag}(\mathbf{X'}_2 * \mathbf{X'}_3) \wedge \texttt{index}(\mathbf{X}_1) = \texttt{index}(\mathbf{X'}_2 * \mathbf{X'}_3)) \end{array} \right) \wedge$$
$$(\neg\mathbf{Z} \wedge \neg\mathbf{Z}') \Rightarrow$$
$$\left(\begin{array}{l} \texttt{sline}(\mathbf{X}_2 * \mathbf{X}_3) = \texttt{sline}(\mathbf{X'}_2 * \mathbf{X'}_3) \wedge \\ \texttt{sline}(\mathbf{X}_2 * \mathbf{X}_3) \Rightarrow (\texttt{tag}(\mathbf{X}_2 * \mathbf{X}_3) = \texttt{tag}(\mathbf{X'}_2 * \mathbf{X'}_3) \wedge \texttt{index}(\mathbf{X}_2 * \mathbf{X}_3) = \texttt{index}(\mathbf{X'}_2 * \mathbf{X'}_3)) \end{array} \right)$$

We recall that Raspberry Pi 3 has 128 cache sets and 64 bytes per line. Figure 6 shows two pairs of states that satisfy the relation, assuming only the first 10 cache sets are shared. States s_1 and s_2 lead the program to access the third cache set, while s'_1 and s'_2 lead the program to access cache sets that are not shared, therefore they generate no observations.

5   Test-Case Generation

A test case for a program P is a pair of initial states s_1, s_2 such that P produces the same observations when executed from either state, i.e., $s_1 \sim s_2$. The relation as described in Sect. 4 characterizes the space of observationally equivalent states, so a simple but naive approach to test-case generation consists in querying the SMT solver for a model of this relation. The model that results from the query gives us two concrete observationally equivalent values for the registers that affect the observations of the program, so at this point we could forward these to our testing infrastructure to perform the experiment on the hardware.

However, the size of an observational equivalence class can be enormous, because there are many variations to the initial states that cannot have effects on the channels available to the attacker. Choosing a satisfying assignment for the entire relation every time without any extra guidance risks producing many test cases that are too similar to each other, and thus unlikely to find counterexamples. For instance, the SMT solver may generate many variations of the test case (s_1, s_2) in Fig. 6 by iterating over all possible values for register X_2 of state s_1, even if the value of this register is immaterial for the observation.

In practice, we explore the space of observationally equivalent states in a more systematic manner. To this end, Scam-V supports two mechanisms to guide the selection of test cases: *path enumeration* and *term enumeration*. Path enumeration partitions the space according to the combination of symbolic execution paths that are taken, whereas term enumeration partitions the space according to the value of a user-supplied BIR expression. In both cases, the partitions are explored in round-robin fashion, choosing one test case from each partition in turn. To make the queries to the SMT solver more efficient, we only generate a fragment of the relation that corresponds to the partition under test.

Path Enumeration. Every time we have to generate a test case, we first select a pair $(\sigma_1, \sigma_2) \in \Sigma \times \Sigma$ of symbolic states as per Sect. 4, which identifies a pair of paths $(\mathbf{p}_{\sigma_1}, \mathbf{p}_{\sigma_2})$. The chosen paths vary in each iteration in order to achieve full path coverage. The query given to the SMT solver then becomes[5]

$$\mathbf{p}_{\sigma_1}(s_1) \wedge \mathbf{p}_{\sigma_2}(s_2) \wedge \mathbf{l}_{\sigma_1}(s_1) = \mathbf{l}_{\sigma_2}(s_2)$$

Since the meat of the relation is a conjunction of implications, this is a natural partitioning scheme that ensures all conjuncts are actually explored. Note that without this mechanism, the SMT solver could always choose states that only satisfy one and the same conjunct. To guide this process even further, the user can supply a *path guard*, which is a predicate on the space of paths. Any path not satisfying the guard is skipped, allowing the user to avoid exploring unwanted paths. For example, for the program in Fig. 3 we can use a path guard to force the test generation to select only paths that produce no observations: e.g., $(\mathbf{Z} \Rightarrow \neg\mathtt{sline}(\mathbf{X}_1)) \wedge (\neg\mathbf{Z} \Rightarrow \neg\mathtt{sline}(\mathbf{X}_2 * \mathbf{X}_3))$.

Term Enumeration. In addition to path enumeration, we can choose a BIR expression e that depends on the symbolic state, and a range R of values to enumerate. Every query also includes the conjuncts $e_{\sigma_1} = v_1 \wedge e_{\sigma_2} = v_2$ where $v_1, v_2 \in R$ and such that the v_i are chosen to achieve full coverage of $R \times R$. Term enumeration can be useful to introduce domain-specific partitions, provided that $R \times R$ is small enough. For example, this mechanism can be used to ensure that we explore addresses that cover all possible cache sets, if we set e to be a mask that extracts the cache set index bits of the address. For example, for the program in Fig. 3 we can use $\mathbf{Z} * \mathtt{index}(\mathbf{X}_1) + (1 - \mathbf{Z}) * \mathtt{index}(\mathbf{X}_2 * \mathbf{X}_3)$ to enumerate all combinations of accessed cache sets while respecting the paths.

6   Implementation

The implementation[6] of Scam-V is done in the HOL4 theorem prover using its meta-language, i.e., SML. Scam-V relies on the binary analysis platform HolBA for transpiling the binary code of test programs to the BIR representation. This

---

[5] Note that this is equivalent to taking a fragment of the observational equivalence relation, specifically the case when $\mathbf{p}_{\sigma_1}(s_1) \wedge \mathbf{p}_{\sigma_2}(s_2)$ holds.

[6] Our implementation of Scam-V is embedded in HolBA, which is available at https://github.com/kth-step/HolBA. Our extendable experimentation platform consists of several "EmbExp-*" repositories available at https://github.com/kth-step.

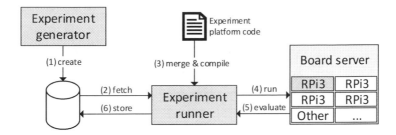

Fig. 7. Experiment handling design with numbered steps. This showcases the workflow for producing, preparing, executing and evaluating one experiment.

transpilation uses the existing HOL4 model of the ARMv8 architecture [16] for giving semantics to ARM programs. In order to validate the observational models of Sect. 2.3, we extended the transpilation process to inline observation statements into the resulting BIR program. These observations represent the observational power of the side channel. In order to compute possible execution paths of test programs and their corresponding observations, which are needed to synthesize the observational equivalence relation of Sect. 4, we implemented a symbolic execution engine in HOL4. All program generators from Sect. 3 as well as the weakest relation synthesis from Sect. 4 and the test-case generator from Sect. 5 are implemented as SML libraries in Scam-V. The latter uses the SMT solver Z3 [14] to generate test inputs. For conducting the experiments in this paper, we used Raspberry Pi 3 boards equipped with ARM Cortex-A53 processors implementing the ARMv8-A architecture.

The Scam-V pipeline generates programs and pairs of observationally equivalent initial states (test cases) for each program. Each combination of a program with one of its test cases is called an *experiment*. After generating experiments, we execute them on the processor implementation of interest to examine their effects on the side channel. Figure 7 depicts the life of a single experiment as goes through our experiment handling design. This consists of: (step 1) generating an experiment and storing it in a database, (step 2) retrieving the experiment from the database, (step 3) integrating it with *experiment-platform code* and compiling it into platform-compatible machine code, and (step 4–6) executing the generated binary on the real board, as well as finally receiving and storing the experiment result.

The experiment-platform code configures page tables to setup *cacheable* and *uncacheable* memory, clears the cache before every execution of the program, and inserts memory barriers around the experiment code. The platform executes in ARM TrustZone, which enables us to use privileged debug instructions to obtain the cache state directly for comparison after experiment execution.

The way in which we compare final cache states for distinguishability depends on the attacker and observational model in question. For multi-way cache, we say two states are *indistinguishable* if and only if for each valid entry in one state, there is a valid entry with the same cache tag in the corresponding cache set of the other state and vice versa. For the partitioned multi-way cache, we check the states in the same way, except we do it only for a subset of the cache sets (see Sect. 7.2 for details on the exact partition). For the direct-mapped cache, we compare how many valid cache lines there are in each set, disregarding the cache tags. These comparison functions have been chosen to match the attacker power of the relaxed models in Definitions 6, 7, and 8 respectively.

7 Results

Since the ARM-v8 experimentation platform runs as bare-metal code, there are no background processes or interrupts. Despite this fact, our measurements may contain noise due to other hardware components that share the same memory subsystem, such as the GPU, and because our experiments are not synchronized with the memory controller. In order to simplify repeatability of our experiments, we execute each experiment 10 times and check for discrepancies in the final state of the data cache. Unless all executions give the same result, this experiment is classified as *inconclusive* and excluded from further analysis.

7.1   Direct-Mapped Cache Observational Model

First, we want to make sure that Scam-V can invalidate unsound observational models in general. For this purpose, we generated experiments that use the model of Definition 8, i.e., for every memory access in BIR we observe the cache set index of the address of the access. We know that this is not a sound model for Raspberry Pi 3, because the platform uses a 4-way cache. Table 1.1 shows that both the random program generator and the monadic load generator uncovered counterexamples that invalidated this observational model.

7.2   Partitioned Cache Observational Model

Next, we consider the partitioned cache observational model from Definition 7. That is, we partition the L1 cache of the Raspberry Pi 3 into two contiguous regions and assume that the attacker has only access to the second region. Due to the prefetcher of Cortex-A53 we expect this model to be unsound and indeed we could invalidate it.

To this end, we generated experiments for two variations of the model. Variation A splits the cache at cache set 61, meaning that only cache sets 61–127 were considered accessible to the attacker. Variation B splits the cache at cache set 64 (the midpoint), such that cache sets 64–127 were considered visible. The following program is one of the counterexamples for variation A that have been discovered by Scam-V using the monadic program generator.

Program	Input 1	Input 2

`ldr x2,  [x10, #0]`
`ldr x20, [x10, #128]`
`ldr x17, [x10, #256]`
	`x10: 0x80100080`	`0x80100cc0`

Table 1. Invalidation of cache and faulty observational models.

(1.1)	Observations	Cache set index only (Definition 8)		
	Programs	Monadic load generator		Random program generator
	Experiments	39660		20872
	- Inconclusive	0		1
	- Counterexample	19		18
(1.2)	Experiment set	Variation A		Variation B
	Observations	Page unaligned cache partitioning (Definition 7)		Page aligned cache partitioning (Definition 7)
	Programs	Monadic stride generator		
	Experiments	36160		37843
	- Inconclusive	5426		6967
	- Counterexample	3460		0
(1.3)	Observations	Cache tag and set index (Definition 6)		
	Programs	Random program generator	Monadic generator	
			Loads	Previction
	Experiments	20256	23120	23290
	- Inconclusive	2	0	0
	- Counterexample	0	5	16
(1.4)	Observations	Cache tag and set index (Definition 6)		
	Programs	Random program generator		
	Experiments	22321		
	- Inconclusive	0		
	- Failure	308		

The counterexample exploits the fact that prefetching fills more lines than those loaded by the program, provided the memory accesses happen in a certain stride pattern. Thus, it essentially needs to have two properties: (i) two different starting addresses for the stride, a_1 and a_2, with a cache set index that is lower than 61 to avoid any observations in the model, and thus satisfying observational equivalence, and (ii) one of a_1 and a_2 is close enough to the partition boundary. In this case, automatic prefetching will continue to fill lines in subsequent sets, effectively crossing the boundary into the attacker-visible region.

In our experiments, we used a path guard to generate only states that produce only memory accesses to the region of the cache that is not visible by the attacker. Additionally, we used term enumeration to force successive test cases to start a stride on a different cache set and therefore cover the different cache set indices. Without this guidance, the tool could generate only experiments that affect the lower sets of the cache and never explore scenarios that affect the sets with indices closer to the split boundary.

For variation B, we have not found such a counterexample. The only difference is that the partition boundary is on line 64, which means that each partition fits exactly in a small page (4K). We conjecture that the prefetcher does not perform line fills across small page (4K) boundaries. This could be for performance reasons, as crossing a page boundary can involve a costly page walk if the next page is not in the TLB. If this is the case, it would seem that it is safe to use prefetching with a partitioned cache, provided the partitions are page-aligned. Table 1.2 summarizes our experiments for this model.

7.3   Multi-way Cache Observational Model

In the remaining experiments, we consider the model of Definition 6 and we assume that the attacker has access to the complete L1 cache. Even if we expected this model to be sound, our experiments (Table 1.3) identified several counterexamples. We comment on two classes of counterexamples below.

Previction. Some counterexamples are due to an undocumented behavior that we called "prevition" because it causes a cache line to be evicted before the corresponding cache set is full. The following program compares x0 and x1 and executes a sequence of three loads. In case of equality, fourteen nop are executed between the first two loads.

Program	Input 1	Input 2
cmp x0, x1	x0: 0x00000000	0x00000000
b.eq #0x14	x1: 0x00000000	0x00000001
ldr x9, [x2]	x2: 0x80100000	0x80100000
ldr x9, [x3]	x3: 0x80110000	0x80110000
ldr x9, [x4]	x4: 0x80120000	0x80120000
b #0x48		
ldr x9, [x2]		
nop {14 times}		
ldr x9, [x3]		
ldr x9, [x4]		

Input 1 and Input 2 are two states that exercise the two execution paths and have the same values for x2, x3 and x4, hence the two states are observationally equivalent. Notice that all memory loads access cache set 0. Since the cache is 4-way associative and the cache is initially empty, we expect no eviction to occur.

Executions starting in Input 2 behave as expected and terminate with the addresses of x2, x3, and x4 in the final cache state. However, the execution from Input 1 leads to a prevition, which causes the final cache state to only contain the addresses of x3 and x4. The address of x2 has been evicted even if the cache set is not full. Therefore the two states are distinguishable by the attacker. Our hypothesis is that the processor detects a short sequence of loads to the same cache set and anticipates more loads to the same cache set with no reuse of previously loaded values. It evicts the valid cache line in order to make space for more colliding lines. We note that these cache entries are not dirty and thus eviction is most likely a cheap operation. The execution of a nop sequence probably ensures that the first cache line fill is completed before the other addresses are accessed.

Offset-Dependent Behaviors. Our experiments identified further counterexamples that invalidate the observational model. In particular, the following counterexample also invalidates the observational model of Definition 5, where cache line offsets are not observable.

Program	Input 1	Input 2
ldr x6, [x0]	x0 : 0x80108000	0x80108000
ldr x9, [x3, #4]	x3 : 0x800FFFFC	0x800FFFFC
ldr x2, [x16]	x16: 0x80100020	0x80100000
ldr x16,[x22]	x22: 0x8011FFF8	0x8011FFF8
ldr x9, [x22,#8]		

This program consists of five consecutive load instructions. This program always produces five observations consisting of the cache tag and set index of the five addresses. Input 1 and Input 2 are observationally equivalent: they only differ for x16, which affects the address used for the third load, but the addresses 0x80100020 and 0x80100000 have the same cache tag and set index and only differ for the offset within the same cache line. However, these experiments lead to two distinguishable microarchitectural states. More specifically, execution from Input 1 results in the filling of cache set 0, where the addresses of registers x0, x3, x16 and x22 + 8 are present in the cache, while executions from Input 2 leads a cache state where the address of x0 is not in the cache and has been probably evicted. This effect can be the result of the interaction between cache previction and cache bank collision [9,40], whose behavior depends on the cache offset. Notice that cache bank collision is undocumented for ARM Cortex-A53. Tromer et al. [46] have shown that such offset-dependent behaviors can make insecure side-channel countermeasures for AES that rely on making accesses to memory blocks (rather than addresses) key-independent.

7.4   Problems in Model Implementations

Additionally to microarchitectural features that invalidate the formal models, our experiments identified bugs of the implementation of the models: (1) the formalization of the ARMv8 instruction set used by the transpiler and (2) the module that inserts BIR observation statements into the transpiled binary to capture the observations that can be made according to a given observational model. Table 1.4 reports problems identified by the random program generator. Some of these failing experiments result in distinguishable states while others result in run-time exceptions. In fact, if the model predicts wrong memory accesses for a program then our framework can generate test inputs that cause accesses to unmapped memory regions. The example program in Fig. 4 exhibits both problems when executed with appropriate inputs.

Missing Observations. The second step of our framework translates binary programs to BIR and adds observations to reflect the observational model under validation. In order to generate observations that correspond to memory loads, we syntactically analyze the right-hand side of BIR assignments. For instance, for line $l2$ in Fig. 3 we generate an observation that depends on variable X1 because the expression of assignment is LOAD(MEM, X1). This approach is problematic when a memory load is immaterial for the result of an instruction. For example, ldr xzr and ldr wzr instructions load from memory to a register that is constantly zero. The following program loads from x30 into xzr.

Program	Input 1	Input 2
ldr xzr, [x30]	x30: 0x80000040	0x800000038

The translation of this instruction is simply [JMP next_addr]: there is no assignment that loads from x30 because the register xzr remains zero. Therefore, our model generates no observations and any two input states are observationally equivalent. The ARM specification does not clarify that the microarchitecture can skip the immaterial memory load. Our experiments show that this is not the case and therefore our implementation of the model is not correct. In fact, the program accesses cache set $index(0x80000040) = 1$ for Input 1 and cache set $index(0x80000038) = 0$ for Input 2, which results in distinguishable states. Moreover, by not taking into account the memory access our framework generates some tests that set x30 to unmapped addresses and cause run-time exceptions.

Flaw in HOL4 ARMv8 ISA Model. Our tool has identified a bug of the HOL4 ARMv8 ISA model. This model has been used in several projects [8,17] as the basis for formal analysis and is used by our framework to transform ARM programs to BIR programs. Despite its wide adoption, we identified a problem in the semantics of instructions *Compare and Branch on Zero* (CBZ) and *Compare and Branch on Non-Zero* (CBNZ). These instructions implement a conditional jump based on the comparison of the input register with zero. While CBZ jumps in case of equality, CBNZ jumps in case of inequality. However, our tests identified that CBNZ wrongly behaves as CBZ in the HOL4 model.

8   Related Work

Hardware Models. Verification approaches that take into account the underlying hardware architecture have to rely on a formal model of that architecture. Commercial instruction set architectures (ISAs) are usually specified mostly in natural language, and their formalization is an active research direction. For example, Goel et al. [24] formalize the ISA of x86 in ACL2, Morrisett et al. [37] model the x86 architecture in the Coq theorem prover, and Sarkar et al. [42] provide a formal semantics of the x86 multiprocessor ISA in HOL. Moreover, domain-specific languages for ISAs have been developed, such as the L3 language [19], which has been used to model the ARMv7 architecture. As another example, Siewiorek et al. [44] proposed the *Instruction-Set Processor* language for formalizing the semantics of the instructions of a processor.

Processor Verification and Validation. To gain confidence in the correctness of a processor model, it needs to be verified or validated against the actual hardware. This problem has received considerable attention lately. There are white-box approaches such as the formal verification that a processor model matches a hardware design [10,18]. These approaches differ from ours in that they try to give a formal guarantee that a processor model is a valid abstraction of the actual hardware, and to achieve that they require the hardware to be accessible as a white box. More similar to ours are black-box approaches that validate an abstract model by randomly generated instructions or based on dynamic instrumentation [20,29]. Combinations of formal verification and testing approaches for hardware verification and validation have also been considered [11].

In contrast to our work, all of the approaches above are limited to functional correctness, and validation is limited to single-instruction test cases, which we show to be insufficient for information flow properties. Going beyond these restrictions is the work of Campbell and Stark [12], who generate sequences of instructions as test cases, and go beyond functional correctness by including timing properties. Still, neither their models nor their approach is suitable to identify violations of information flow properties.

Validating Information Flow Properties. To the best of our knowledge, we present the first automated approach to validate processor models with respect to information flow properties. To this end, we build on the seminal works of McLean [35] on non-interference, Roscoe [41] on observational determinism, and Barthe et al. [7] on self-composition as a method for proving information flow properties. Most closely related is the work by Balliu et al. [6] on *relational analysis* based on *observational determinism*.

These approaches are based on the different observational models that have been proposed in the literature. For example, the program counter security model [36] has been used when the execution time depends on the control flow of the victim. Extensions of this model also make observable data that can affect execution time of an instruction, or memory addresses accessed by the program to model timing differences due to caching [4].

Many analysis tools use these observational models. Ct-verif [3] implements a sound information flow analysis by proving observational equivalence constructing a product program. CacheAudit [15] quantifies information leakage by using abstract interpretation.

The risks of using unsound models for such analyses have been demonstrated by the recent Spectre attack family [32], which exploits speculation to leak data through caches. Several other architectural details require special caution when using abstract models, as some properties assumed by the models could be unmet. For instance, cache clean operations do not always clean residual state in implementations of replacement policies [21]. Furthermore, many processors do not provide sufficient means to close all leakage, e.g., shared state cannot be cleaned properly on a context switch [22]. Finally, it has been shown that fixes relying on too specific assumptions can be circumvented by modifying the attack [43], and that attacks are possible even against formally verified software if the underlying processor model is unsound [28]. For these reasons, validation of formal models by directly measuring the hardware is of great importance.

9   Concluding Remarks

We presented Scam-V, a framework for automatic validation of observational models of side channels. Scam-V uses a novel combination of symbolic execution, relational analysis, and observational models to generate experiments. We evaluated Scam-V on the ARM Cortex-A53 processor and we invalidated all models of Sect. 2.3, i.e., those with observations that are cache-line-offset-independent.

Our results are summarized as follows: (i) in case of cache partitioning, the attacker can discover victim accesses to the other cache partitions due to the automatic data prefetcher; (ii) the Cortex-A53 prefetcher seems to respect 4K page boundaries, like in some Intel processors; (iii) a mechanism of Cortex-A53, which we called previction, can leak the time between accesses to the same cache set; (iv) the cache state is affected by the cache line offset of the accesses, probably due to undocumented cache bank collisions like in some AMD processors; (v) the formal ARMv8 model had a flaw in the implementation of CBNZ; (vi) our implementation of the observational model had a flaw in case of loads into the constant zero register. Moreover, since the microarchitectural features that lead to these findings are also available on other ARMv8 cores, including some that are affected by Spectre (e.g. Cortex A57), it is likely that similar behaviors can be observed on these cores, and that more powerful observational models, including those that take into account Spectre-like effects, may also be unsound.

These promising results show that Scam-V can support the identification of undocumented and security-relevant features of processors (like results (ii), (iii), and (iv)) and discover problems in the formal models (like results (v) and (vi)). In addition, users can drive test-case generation to conveniently explore classes of programs that they suspect would lead to side-channel leakage (like in result (i)). This process is enabled by path and term enumeration techniques as well as custom program generators. Moreover, Scam-V can aid vendors to validate implementations with respect to desired side-channel specifications.

Given the lack of vendor communication regarding security-relevant processor features, validation of abstract side-channel models is of critical importance. As a future direction of work, we are planning to extend Scam-V for other architectures (e.g. ARM Cortex-M0 based microcontrollers), noisy side channels (e.g. time and power consumption), and other side channels (e.g. cache replacement state). Moreover, we are investigating approaches to automatically repair an unsound observational model starting from the counterexamples, e.g., by adding state observations. Finally, the theory in Sect. 4 can be used to develop a certifying tool for verifying observational determinism.

Acknowledgement. We thank Matthias Stockmayer for his contributions to the symbolic execution engine in this work. This work has been supported by the TrustFull project financed by the Swedish Foundation for Strategic Research, the KTH CERCES

Center for Resilient Critical Infrastructures financed by the Swedish Civil Contingencies Agency, as well as the German Federal Ministry of Education and Research (BMBF) through funding for the CISPA-Stanford Center for Cybersecurity (FKZ: 13N1S0762).

References

1. Acıiçmez, O., Koç, Ç.K.: Trace-driven cache attacks on AES (short paper). In: Ning, P., Qing, S., Li, N. (eds.) ICICS 2006. LNCS, vol. 4307, pp. 112–121. Springer, Heidelberg (2006). https://doi.org/10.1007/11935308_9

2. Acıiçmez, O., Koç, Ç.K., Seifert, J.-P.: Predicting secret keys via branch prediction. In: Abe, M. (ed.) CT-RSA 2007. LNCS, vol. 4377, pp. 225–242. Springer, Heidelberg (2006). https://doi.org/10.1007/11967668_15

3. Almeida, J.B., Barbosa, M., Barthe, G., Dupressoir, F., Emmi, M.: Verifying constant-time implementations. In: USENIX Security, pp. 53–70 (2016)

4. Almeida, J.B., Barbosa, M., Pinto, J.S., Vieira, B.: Formal verification of side-channel countermeasures using self-composition. Sci. Comput. Program. **78**(7), 796–812 (2013)

5. ARM Limited: Vulnerable ARM processors to Spectre attack. https://developer.arm.com/support/arm-security-updates/speculative-processor-vulnerability. Accessed 2019

6. Balliu, M., Dam, M., Guanciale, R.: Automating information flow analysis of low level code. In: Proceedings of the Conference on Computer and Communications Security, CCS, pp. 1080–1091 (2014)

7. Barthe, G., D'Argenio, P.R., Rezk, T.: Secure information flow by self-composition. Math. Struct. Comput. Sci. **21**(6), 1207–1252 (2011)

8. Baumann, C., Schwarz, O., Dam, M.: On the verification of system-level information flow properties for virtualized execution platforms. J. Cryptogr. Eng. **9**(3), 243–261 (2019). https://doi.org/10.1007/s13389-019-00216-4

9. Bernstein, D.J.: Cache-timing attacks on AES. Technical report (2005). http://cr.yp.to/antiforgery/cachetiming-20050414.pdf

10. Beyer, S., Jacobi, C., Kröning, D., Leinenbach, D., Paul, W.J.: Putting it all together – formal verification of the VAMP. Int. J. Softw. Tools Technol. Transfer **8**(4–5), 411–430 (2006). https://doi.org/10.1007/s10009-006-0204-6

11. Bhadra, J., Abadir, M.S., Wang, L.C., Ray, S.: A survey of hybrid techniques for functional verification. Des. Test Comput. **24**(2), 112–122 (2007)

12. Campbell, B., Stark, I.: Randomised testing of a microprocessor model using SMT-solver state generation. Sci. Comput. Program. **118**, 60–76 (2016)

13. Claessen, K., Hughes, J.: QuickCheck: a lightweight tool for random testing of Haskell programs. SIGPLAN Not. **35**(9), 268–279 (2000)

14. de Moura, L., Bjørner, N.: Z3: an efficient SMT solver. In: Ramakrishnan, C.R., Rehof, J. (eds.) TACAS 2008. LNCS, vol. 4963, pp. 337–340. Springer, Heidelberg (2008). https://doi.org/10.1007/978-3-540-78800-3_24

15. Doychev, G., Köpf, B., Mauborgne, L., Reineke, J.: CacheAudit: a tool for the static analysis of cache side channels. ACM Trans. Inf. Syst. Secur. **18**(1), 4:1–4:32 (2015)

16. Fox, A.: L3: A Specification Language for Instruction Set Architectures. https://acjf3.github.io/l3. Accessed 2019

17. Fox, A., Myreen, M.O., Tan, Y.K., Kumar, R.: Verified compilation of CakeML to multiple machine-code targets. In: Proceedings of the 6th ACM SIGPLAN Conference on Certified Programs and Proofs, CPP, pp. 125–137. Association for Computing Machinery, New York (2017)

18. Fox, A.: Formal specification and verification of ARM6. In: Basin, D., Wolff, B. (eds.) TPHOLs 2003. LNCS, vol. 2758, pp. 25–40. Springer, Heidelberg (2003). https://doi.org/10.1007/10930755_2

19. Fox, A.: Directions in ISA specification. In: Beringer, L., Felty, A. (eds.) ITP 2012. LNCS, vol. 7406, pp. 338–344. Springer, Heidelberg (2012). https://doi.org/10.1007/978-3-642-32347-8_23

20. Fox, A., Myreen, M.O.: A trustworthy monadic formalization of the ARMv7 instruction set architecture. In: Kaufmann, M., Paulson, L.C. (eds.) ITP 2010. LNCS, vol. 6172, pp. 243–258. Springer, Heidelberg (2010). https://doi.org/10.1007/978-3-642-14052-5_18

21. Ge, Q., Yarom, Y., Heiser, G.: Do hardware cache flushing operations actually meet our expectations. arXiv e-prints (2016)

22. Ge, Q., Yarom, Y., Li, F., Heiser, G.: Your processor leaks information-and there's nothing you can do about it. CoRR abs/1612.04474 (2017)

23. Godfrey, M.M., Zulkernine, M.: Preventing cache-based side-channel attacks in a cloud environment. IEEE Trans. Cloud Comput. **2**(4), 395–408 (2014)

24. Goel, S., Hunt Jr., W.A., Kaufmann, M., Ghosh, S.: Simulation and formal verification of x86 machine-code programs that make system calls. In: FMCAD, pp. 91–98. IEEE (2014)

25. Goguen, J.A., Meseguer, J.: Security policies and security models. In: IEEE Symposium on Security and Privacy, pp. 11–20. IEEE Computer Society (1982)

26. Goguen, J.A., Meseguer, J.: Unwinding and inference control. In: IEEE Symposium on Security and Privacy, pp. 75–87. IEEE Computer Society (1984)

27. Gruss, D., Maurice, C., Mangard, S.: Rowhammer.js: a remote software-induced fault attack in JavaScript. In: Caballero, J., Zurutuza, U., Rodríguez, R.J. (eds.) DIMVA 2016. LNCS, vol. 9721, pp. 300–321. Springer, Cham (2016). https://doi.org/10.1007/978-3-319-40667-1_15

28. Guanciale, R., Nemati, H., Baumann, C., Dam, M.: Cache storage channels: alias-driven attacks and verified countermeasures. In: IEEE Symposium on Security and Privacy, pp. 38–55. IEEE Computer Society (2016)

29. Hou, Z., Sanan, D., Tiu, A., Liu, Y., Hoa, K.C.: An executable formalisation of the SPARCv8 instruction set architecture: a case study for the LEON3 processor. In: Fitzgerald, J., Heitmeyer, C., Gnesi, S., Philippou, A. (eds.) FM 2016. LNCS, vol. 9995, pp. 388–405. Springer, Cham (2016). https://doi.org/10.1007/978-3-319-48989-6_24

30. King, J.C.: Symbolic execution and program testing. Commun. ACM **19**(7), 385–394 (1976)

31. Kocher, P.C.: Timing attacks on implementations of Diffie-Hellman, RSA, DSS, and other systems. In: Koblitz, N. (ed.) CRYPTO 1996. LNCS, vol. 1109, pp. 104–113. Springer, Heidelberg (1996). https://doi.org/10.1007/3-540-68697-5_9

32. Kocher, P., et al.: Spectre attacks: exploiting speculative execution. In: S&P (2019)

33. Kocher, P., Jaffe, J., Jun, B.: Differential power analysis. In: Wiener, M. (ed.) CRYPTO 1999. LNCS, vol. 1666, pp. 388–397. Springer, Heidelberg (1999). https://doi.org/10.1007/3-540-48405-1_25

34. Lindner, A., Guanciale, R., Metere, R.: TrABin: trustworthy analyses of binaries. Sci. Comput. Program. **174**, 72–89 (2019)

35. McLean, J.: Proving noninterference and functional correctness using traces. J. Comput. Secur. **1**(1), 37–58 (1992)
36. Molnar, D., Piotrowski, M., Schultz, D., Wagner, D.: The program counter security model: automatic detection and removal of control-flow side channel attacks. In: Won, D.H., Kim, S. (eds.) ICISC 2005. LNCS, vol. 3935, pp. 156–168. Springer, Heidelberg (2006). https://doi.org/10.1007/11734727_14
37. Morrisett, G., Tan, G., Tassarotti, J., Tristan, J., Gan, E.: RockSalt: better, faster, stronger SFI for the x86. In: PLDI, pp. 395–404. ACM (2012)
38. Nemati, H., Buiras, P., Lindner, A., Guanciale, R., Jacobs, S.: Validation of abstract side-channel models for computer architectures (2020). https://arxiv.org/abs/2005.05254
39. Neve, M., Seifert, J.-P.: Advances on access-driven cache attacks on AES. In: Biham, E., Youssef, A.M. (eds.) SAC 2006. LNCS, vol. 4356, pp. 147–162. Springer, Heidelberg (2007). https://doi.org/10.1007/978-3-540-74462-7_11
40. Osvik, D.A., Shamir, A., Tromer, E.: Cache attacks and countermeasures: the case of AES. In: Pointcheval, D. (ed.) CT-RSA 2006. LNCS, vol. 3860, pp. 1–20. Springer, Heidelberg (2006). https://doi.org/10.1007/11605805_1
41. Roscoe, A.W.: CSP and determinism in security modelling. In: IEEE Symposium on Security and Privacy, pp. 114–127. IEEE Computer Society (1995)
42. Sarkar, S., et al.: The semantics of x86-CC multiprocessor machine code. In: POPL, pp. 379–391. ACM (2009)
43. Schaik, S.V., Giuffrida, C., Bos, H., Razavi, K.: Malicious management unit: why stopping cache attacks in software is harder than you think. In: USENIX Security Symposium, pp. 937–954. USENIX Association (2018)
44. Siewiorek, D.P., Bell, G., Newell, A.C.: Computer Structures: Principles and Examples. McGraw-Hill Inc, New York (1982)
45. Taylor, G., Davies, P., Farmwald, M.: The TLB slice-a low-cost high-speed address translation mechanism. SIGARCH Comput. Archit. News **18**(2SI), 355–363 (1990)
46. Tromer, E., Osvik, D.A., Shamir, A.: Efficient cache attacks on AES, and countermeasures. J. Cryptol. **23**(1), 37–71 (2009). https://doi.org/10.1007/s00145-009-9049-y
47. Tsunoo, Y., Saito, T., Suzaki, T., Shigeri, M., Miyauchi, H.: Cryptanalysis of DES implemented on computers with cache. In: Walter, C.D., Koç, Ç.K., Paar, C. (eds.) CHES 2003. LNCS, vol. 2779, pp. 62–76. Springer, Heidelberg (2003). https://doi.org/10.1007/978-3-540-45238-6_6
48. Zhang, Y., Juels, A., Reiter, M.K., Ristenpart, T.: Cross-VM side channels and their use to extract private keys. In: Proceedings of the Conference on Computer and Communications Security, CCS, pp. 305–316. ACM (2012)

Concurrency

Semantics, Specification, and Bounded Verification of Concurrent Libraries in Replicated Systems

Kartik Nagar[1]([⊠]), Prasita Mukherjee[2], and Suresh Jagannathan[2]

[1] IIT Madras, Chennai, India
nagark@cse.iitm.ac.in
[2] Purdue University, West Lafayette, USA
mukher39@purdue.edu, suresh@cs.purdue.edu

Abstract. Geo-replicated systems provide a number of desirable properties such as globally low latency, high availability, scalability, and built-in fault tolerance. Unfortunately, programming correct applications on top of such systems has proven to be very challenging, in large part because of the weak consistency guarantees they offer. These complexities are exacerbated when we try to adapt existing highly-performant concurrent libraries developed for shared-memory environments to this setting. The use of these libraries, developed with performance and scalability in mind, is highly desirable. But, identifying a suitable notion of correctness to check their validity under a weakly consistent execution model has not been well-studied, in large part because it is problematic to naïvely transplant criteria such as linearizability that has a useful interpretation in a shared-memory context to a distributed one where the cost of imposing a (logical) global ordering on all actions is prohibitive. In this paper, we tackle these issues by proposing appropriate semantics and specifications for highly-concurrent libraries in a weakly-consistent, replicated setting. We use these specifications to develop a static analysis framework that can automatically detect correctness violations of library implementations parameterized with respect to the different consistency policies provided by the underlying system. We use our framework to analyze the behavior of a number of highly non-trivial library implementations of stacks, queues, and exchangers. Our results provide the first demonstration that automated correctness checking of concurrent libraries in a weakly geo-replicated setting is both feasible and practical.

1 Introduction

Geo-replicated systems maintain multiple copies of data at different locations and provide a number of attractive properties such as globally uniform low access-latency, always-on availability, fault tolerance, and improved scalability. Applications with a geo-distributed user base need to necessarily run on top of replicated systems to ensure fast and always-available service. On the other hand, due to concurrent updates at different replicas and the possibility of arbitrary

© The Author(s) 2020
S. K. Lahiri and C. Wang (Eds.): CAV 2020, LNCS 12224, pp. 251–274, 2020.
https://doi.org/10.1007/978-3-030-53288-8_13

re-ordering of updates by the underlying network, replicated systems typically guarantee a very weak form of consistency called *eventual consistency* [4], that only requires replicas which have received the same set of updates to exhibit the same state. Because this guarantee is often too weak to satisfy an application's correctness requirements, a number of (stronger) consistency policies have emerged in recent years; these policies offer session [39], causality [27] or transactional [13] guarantees, and constrain system behavior by imposing additional synchronization on actions. Nonetheless, writing correct applications in this environment using these policies remains a challenging problem.

Having a library of performant *and correct* data structure implementations developed with replication and geo-distribution in mind can significantly alleviate the problem of writing correct applications, as demonstrated by the availability of highly popular concurrent library implementations developed for shared-memory systems [21,33]. CRDTs [36] (Conflict-Free Replicated Data Types) offer an analog of such implementations for geo-replicated environments. However, using CRDTS to build useful data structure libraries is challenging because the strong requirements imposed by CRDTs (namely that all operations commute with each other) appears satisfiable only for simple objects such as sets, lists, or maps. Important data structures such as stacks, queues, or exchangers that serve as building blocks for many concurrent and distributed algorithms have eluded implementations using CRDTs. Even when a data structure can be expressed in this way, reasoning about its correctness is typically given in terms of non-standard criteria such as replicated data type specifications [12], convergence [31] or replication-aware linearizability [41], concepts that are likely to be difficult for programmers to grasp, especially when contrasted with well-established notions such as linearizability used to reason about shared-memory concurrency. This state of affairs has made it difficult to seamlessly adapt and exploit ongoing progress in the development of scalable and correct concurrent algorithms used in the shared-memory world to a geo-replicated setting.

In order to bridge this gap, we study how to *automatically transplant* concurrent library implementations developed for shared memory systems to replicated ones. Doing so would allow us to use carefully-crafted implementations which have been proven to run correctly in shared memory environments, thereby simplifying the task of building distributed replication-aware applications. However, realizing this goal poses a number of challenges, the most critical of which is the widely different memory consistency models used in the two domains: the eventually consistent memory model typically provided by a replicated system is significantly weaker than the sequential consistency guarantees offered by shared-memory. Consistency policies offering session, causal, or transactional guarantees must be additionally considered to facilitate correct behavior. This requires enriching the *semantics* of existing library implementations to take into account the consistency policy of the underlying replicated system. Furthermore, the *de facto* correctness criterion for concurrent library implementations is linearizability, which is clearly too restrictive to be directly applied to this much weaker setting, since it demands that any correct execution be equivalent to some sequential execution of a reference implementation. Such a requirement is problematic in a geo-replicated environment where the cost of coordination to enforce a global ordering of all actions is prohibitive. These observations are similar to those made by Raad et al. [34] who considered the applicability of linearizability in a weak memory context, a scenario that faces similar challenges to our own. To address these issues, we therefore consider alternative declarative specifications of data structures, based on axiomatic definitions [17], that are roughly equivalent to the guarantees provided by linearizability (and hence familiar to programmers), but suitably relaxed to take into account the weak behaviors admitted by replicated systems.

We then propose an automated approach to find bounded violations of these declarative specifications given an implementation and a consistency policy. Due to the non-deterministic nature of replicated systems, manifesting violations in actual executions requires (1) a specific combination of library methods to be called (2) with specific argument values and (3) a specific interaction of low-level read/write events. Indeed, existing approaches to checking application safety under weak consistency [24] potentially involve long (on the order of hours) and costly execution runs to offer meaningful assurance on application correctness given the large space of possible behaviors that can be exhibited.

In contrast to testing approaches, our analysis framework directly searches for an execution violating a specification, and in the process *constructs* the combination of library methods to be called as well as their argument values, and the low-level read/writes which can lead to the violation. Moreover, because our analysis is parametric in the choice of consistency policy, we can constrain the search for violating executions on-demand as per the chosen policy. We additionally show how our technique is capable of expressing complex correctness specifications of libraries (see Sect. 3.4) and how it can be used to automatically find violations in the face of this complexity. The analysis is sound in that it only reports actual violations. Notably, our experiments manifest a number of non-trivial and complex violating executions for realistic concurrent libraries which require intricate interaction with library methods. We were also able to analyse application behavior under different consistency policies, and in particular, were able to find the weakest consistency policy to eliminate a particular violation. Our analysis is based on developing an efficient encoding of the implementation, the consistency policy, and the correctness specification as first-order logic formulae which can be dispatched to off-the-shelf SMT solvers to find violations. Unlike random testing approaches, our technique is capable of identifying non-trivial subtle safety violations in the order of minutes, making it feasible to use not only for finding violations, but also for checking the feasibility of any proposed remediations. We make the following major contributions:

1. We propose a novel operational semantics for replicated systems parameterized under realistic consistency policies which can be used to describe executions of sophisticated concurrent library implementations.
2. We demonstrate how to adapt existing specification frameworks developed for concurrent libraries on shared memory systems to replicated systems with minimal changes.

3. We describe an automated bounded verification procedure to detect violations of such specifications for implementations intended to execute under a given consistency policy.
4. We catalog the results of applying our analysis on a number of well-studied implementations including stacks, queues and exchangers, on a commercial replicated store (Cassandra), demonstrating empirically that our correctness checking procedure is useful in practice.

The remainder of the paper is organized as follows. In the next section, we provide a motivating example to illustrate the challenges of reasoning about concurrent libraries in a weakly-consistent replicated environment. Section 3 formalizes the language used to write library implementations and the specifications that characterize their intended behavior. Section 4 describes our bounded verification procedure and provides details about how we encode extracted verification conditions. Section 5 describes experimental results and presents case studies to illustrate the effectiveness of our approach. Related work and conclusions are given in Sect. 6.

2   Illustrative Example

```
push(v){                              pop(v){
1:    n = New(Node);                      while(true){
2:    n.Val = v;                      6:      t = Top;
      while(true){                             if (t == NULL)
3:      t = Top;                                 return EMPTY;
4:      n.Next = t;                    7:      v = t.Val;
5:      if (CAS(Top, t, n))            8:      n = t.Next;
          break;                       9:      if (CAS(Top, t, n))
      }                                          return v;}
}                                         }
```

Fig. 1. Treiber Stack

In this section, we illustrate the various issues that arise when running standard concurrent library implementations on replicated systems. Figure 1 shows the implementation of a Treiber stack, suitably adapted to execute in a replicated environment. The Treiber stack provides two methods (push and pop) to clients, and stores the elements of the stack in a linked list, with the order of elements in the list corresponding to the order in which elements are pushed. Since replicated stores typically offer a database or a key-value store interface, we store the linked list as a table of type Node with columns Val and Next, where each row stores a node of the linked list, with Val storing the value and Next storing the id of the next node. Top contains the id of the Node row which is current top of the stack (Top is initialized with the special value NULL indicating an empty stack).

In Fig. 1, variables denoted by lower-case letters are assumed to be stored locally and are not replicated. New(Node) returns the id of a new row in the Node table. CAS(Top, t, n) is the typical Compare-And-Swap operation which atomically compares Top to t, and if it is equal to t then updates it to n[1].

Clients of concurrent libraries issue invocations of a data structure's methods, possibly at different replicas, with invocations being grouped together into *sessions*, with each session containing invocations issued by the same client. Whenever a method is invoked, the underlying implementation of the method is executed; we assume the various reads and writes per-

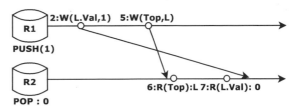

Fig. 2. An execution of Treiber Stack on a replicated store

formed by the method may possibly be executed at different replicas. All low-level operations performed by the same invocation are defined to be in the same session (i.e. the session of the parent invocation). Notice that the implementation stores data across a number of locations (e.g. Top or a cell in the Node table), each of which are operated independently through low-level read/write/CAS operations. The replicated store only guarantees eventual consistency, which means that the values stored at all locations eventually converge across all replicas. However, users expect the behavior of the library to conform to the specification of the stack data structure, regardless of when and how updates propagate across replicas.

Consider the following basic specification (adapted from the AddRem axiom in [17]), which simply says that any value returned by a POP operation must have been pushed by some PUSH operation in the execution; observe that the specification does not allude to any specific system-level issues related to replication or weak consistency:

$$\forall \gamma.\mathsf{meth}(\gamma) = \mathsf{POP} \ \wedge \ \mathsf{ret}(\gamma) \neq \mathsf{EMPTY} \ \Rightarrow \ \exists \gamma'.\mathsf{meth}(\gamma') = \mathsf{PUSH} \ \wedge \ \mathsf{arg}(\gamma') = \mathsf{ret}(\gamma)$$

Consider the execution shown in Fig. 2 that involves an invocation of PUSH(1) and POP from two different replicas. Among the many operations that the implementation of PUSH performs, we show only two write operations in the figure (along with line numbers referring to the implementation in Fig. 1), namely the write to the Val field of location L (L is the id of the new Node), and the write to Top as a result of the successful CAS. Similarly, for the POP operation, we show the read to Top, and then the read to the Val field. In the execution, the write to Top propagates from replica R1 to R2 before the read, but the write to

---

[1] CAS operations are typically supported in replicated systems by providing transactional guarantees to a group of operations; e.g., lightweight transaction support provided in Cassandra [26].

Val does not, so that POP sees that a new node has been pushed but does not read the value that was actually pushed, instead returning the initial value of the location, thus breaking the specification described above. Eventual consistency only guarantees that eventually, the write to Val will also be propagated to R2, which is not sufficient to guarantee the specification holds under all executions.

One way to avoid this counterexample would be to ensure that the write to Val field by PUSH is propagated to another replica before the write to Top, thus guaranteeing that it would be available to the read of Val by POP. Notice that the write to Val occurs before the write to Top in the same session, and hence we can use session guarantees to ensure the required behavior. In particular, under a *Monotonic Writes* (MW) consistency policy, writes are always propagated in their session order to all replicas [1]. However, MW is not sufficient by itself to eliminate the counterexample since the reads to Top and Val by POP may occur at different replicas, so that the read to Val may occur at a replica in which none of the writes by PUSH have propagated. Hence, we also need to have these operations execute under a *Monotonic Reads* (MR) consistency policy that mandates all writes witnessed by an operation will also be witnessed by later operations in the same session.[2]

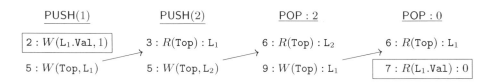

PUSH(1)   PUSH(2)   POP : 2   POP : 0

$2 : W(L_1.\text{Val}, 1)$ $3 : R(\text{Top}) : L_1$ $6 : R(\text{Top}) : L_2$ $6 : R(\text{Top}) : L_1$

$5 : W(\text{Top}, L_1)$ $5 : W(\text{Top}, L_2)$ $9 : W(\text{Top}) : L_1$ $7 : R(L_1.\text{Val}) : 0$

Fig. 3. A violation of AddRem by Treiber Stack under MW+MR

Hence, a combination of MW+MR prevents the counterexample in Fig. 2, but it is unfortunately not enough to guarantee the AddRem specification is correctly enforced. Consider the execution in Fig. 3 which involves four method invocations (2 Pushes and 2 Pops), where each invocation occurs on a different replica. Again, we only show some relevant low-level operations performed by these invocations, with arrows from write to read operations showing reads-from (rf) dependencies. In the execution, after the two pushes, 2 is stored on the top of stack at Node L_2. Thus, the first Pop operation returns 2 and sets the Top to point at L_1, which is then read by the second Pop. However, MW+MR only guarantees that all write operations performed by the first Pop will be witnessed by the second Pop. Hence, just like in Fig. 2, the second Pop operation may see the node at location L_1 but not the write to the Val field (which was performed by PUSH(1)), resulting in violation of the specification. To avoid this, it must be guaranteed that the write to L_1.Val by Push(1) must be visible to its read by the second Pop (depicted by the two boxes in Fig. 3). This can be guaranteed by the *Write Follows Read* (WFR) policy, which analogously to MW, ensures

---

[2] We formalize all consistency policies used in the paper in the next section.

that writes witnessed in a session are propagated to all replicas before writes of the session itself (as opposed to MW which only ensures that writes performed in a session are propagated in session order). We note that both the violations described above (along with their repairs) were automatically discovered using our proposed methods, which devised solutions significantly less expensive than imposing strong consistency (aka global coordination) on all accesses.

While MW+MR+WFR is required to ensure AddRem in a Treiber Stack, we found that weaker consistency policies (including *Eventual Consistency*) were sufficient for other properties and benchmarks (more details are provided in Sect. 5).

3   Semantics and Specifications

In this section, we define a simple language to write library implementations that is nonetheless powerful enough to express a number of real-world implementations. We then define an operational semantics to express executions of any implementation written in this language on top of a replicated store. A key feature of this operational semantics is that it is parametric in the consistency policies available to the store. Thus, instantiating the semantics with different consistency policy definitions allows us to reason about library behavior under replicated stores providing different consistency guarantees. Another important feature of the semantics is that it abstracts out low-level operational details such as the number of replicas, the specific manifestation of how message sends and receives are implemented, etc., and instead uses a succinct representation involving read and write events (and various binary relations among them) to capture salient characteristics sufficient to reason about library correctness with respect to consistency properties. The proposed semantics facilitates a bounded verification approach that is parametric in the consistency policy, and also matches very well with existing axiomatic approaches to specify correctness of library implementations in shared memory systems.

First, we define a simple imperative language in which implementations can be written:

$$v \in \texttt{LocalVar} \qquad \texttt{l} \in \texttt{Locations} \qquad n \in \mathbb{V}$$
$$\oplus \in \{+, -, \times, /\} \qquad \odot \in \{<, \leq, ==, >, \geq\} \qquad \circ \in \{\wedge, \vee\}$$
$$e := e \oplus e \mid v \mid n$$
$$b := b \circ b \mid e \odot e$$
$$c := v = e \mid v = \texttt{l} \mid \texttt{l} = e \mid \texttt{If } b \texttt{ then } c \texttt{ else } c$$
$$\mid c; c \mid \texttt{while } b \texttt{ do } c \mid v = \texttt{CAS}(\texttt{l}, e_1, e_2)$$
$$\mid \texttt{return } e \mid \texttt{return}$$

The only difference between standard shared-memory programs and those written in the above language is that read and write operations can now be performed on either Locations, which are replicated, or local variables which are not. As we saw in Sect. 2, replicated Locations can in general refer to any field in any table. Let $\mathbb{P}$ be the set of programs (c) generated using the above grammar. A **library** $L = (M, I)$ consists of a set of methods (M) and an implementation function $I : M \rightarrow \mathbb{P}$. For simplicity, we assume that each method takes as input one argument. Assume that $I(m)$ contains the free variable a that stores the input argument. Let $\mathbb{V}$ be the value domain for arguments and return values. We designate a special value $\perp \in \mathbb{V}$ for the cases where the argument or return value is empty.

The methods of a library implementation L can be invoked any number of times by multiple clients. Invocations from the same client are grouped together into **sessions**, where each session consists of a sequence of method invocations. Following standard terminology, given a set of sessions S, an interaction between clients and the library is expressed as a **history**, $h : S \rightarrow (M \times \mathbb{V})^*$, which simply associates a sequence of methods invocations to each session. An execution of the history corresponds to executing the library implementation of each method in the history on the replicated store. The store constrains the behavior of reads, writes and CAS operations to replicated `Locations` through its consistency policy.

We now formally define the operational semantics of a history on a replicated store that is parametric in a consistency policy Ψ. While the history only associates arguments with method invocations, executing it on the replicated store will give rise to an **abstract execution**, which will also associate return values with invocations, and whose correctness we are interested in checking. Given a history h, library L, and consistency policy Ψ, we define our semantics in terms of a labeled transition system (LTS) $\Omega_{h,L,\Psi} = (\Phi, \mathcal{E}, \rightarrow)$, where Φ denotes a set of states, $\mathcal{E}$ denotes a set of events (also used as labels) and $\rightarrow \subseteq \Phi \times \mathcal{E} \times \Phi$ defines a transition relation over states and events.

Each state in Φ is specified as a tuple $(\chi, h', \mu, \mathsf{c}, \alpha)$. χ denotes the replicated store state and consists of read/write/update events to `Locations` and various relations among them (described in detail later); $h' : S \rightarrow (M \times \mathbb{V})^*$ denotes the continuation of the history, i.e., the remaining history yet to be executed; $\mu : S \rightarrow (\texttt{LocalVar} \rightarrow \mathbb{V})$ denotes the local variables map for each session; $\mathsf{c} : S \rightarrow \mathbb{P}$ denotes the continuation of the current invocation for each session, i.e., the implementation of the current invocation for each session that is yet to be executed and α denotes the abstract execution. Each **event** $\sigma \in \mathcal{E}$ is a tuple (i, s, a), where i is a unique event-id, $s \in S$ is the session from which the event originated, and a is the action to the replicated store (either read $\mathsf{R}(l, n)$, write $\mathsf{W}(l, n)$ or update $\mathsf{U}(l, m, n)$). Given an event $\sigma = (i, s, a)$, $act(\sigma)$ denotes the action a, $loc(\sigma)$ denotes the location that is the subject of the action.

3.1   Language Semantics

To simplify the presentation, we decouple the semantics of the language from the semantics of the replicated store. The language is defined via a standard imperative semantics *except* that there are no constraints on reads to replicated locations (i.e., we do not mandate a specific replica that is targeted by the read), and every operation to a replicated location generates an event. These rules do not concern the replicated store state, and hence are of the form $(h_1, \mu_1, c_1, \alpha_1) \xrightarrow{\sigma} (h_2, \mu_2, c_2, \alpha_2)$ (i.e. omitting χ from Φ). We essentially pick any session and then execute the next operation from the current invocation in the session, or initiate the next invocation in the session if there is no invocation currently running. As an illustration, consider the following rule L-READ:

$$\frac{c(s) \equiv \mathsf{v} = \mathsf{l}; c' \quad \sigma = (\mathsf{i}, s, \mathsf{R}(l, n)) \quad \text{fresh i}}{(h', \mu, c, \alpha) \xrightarrow{\sigma} (h', \mu[s \to \mu(s)[\mathsf{v} \to n]], c[s \to c'], \alpha)}$$

The rule picks the next operation in session s which is a read operation to location l, and generates the read event σ reading value n from l. It updates the local variable v to this value, leaving the yet-to-be-executed history (h') and abstract execution (α) unchanged. Write statements (i.e. $\mathsf{l} = n$) generate write events $(\mathsf{W}(l, n))$, successful CAS statements (i.e. $\mathsf{v} = \mathtt{CAS}(\mathsf{l}, m, n)$) generate update events $(\mathsf{U}(l, m, n))$, and unsuccessful CAS generates read events $(\mathsf{R}(l, m'))$. The complete set of rules can be found in the technical report [32].

3.2   Abstract Execution Semantics

An **abstract execution** $\alpha = (\Gamma, \mathsf{so}_\Gamma)$ maintains a set of method invocation events in Γ and a session order relation so_Γ among these events. Each method invocation event $\gamma \in \Gamma$ is a tuple (i, m, a, r, s) where i is a unique event-id, $m \in M$ is a method of the library, $a, r \in V$ are the method argument and return values respectively and $s \in S$ is the session from which the method was called. We use the notation Γ^s for the subset of Γ which only contains method invocation events that originate in session s. The following rule (L-RETURN-VAL) describes the generation of a method invocation event, which occurs on encountering a **return** statement during execution, and which is added to the abstract execution.

$$\frac{c(s) \equiv \mathtt{return}\ e; c' \quad h'(s) = m(k) \cdot h'' \quad \llbracket e \rrbracket_{\mu(s)} = n}{\alpha = (\Gamma, \mathsf{so}_\Gamma) \quad \gamma = (i, m, k, n, s) \quad \alpha' = (\Gamma \cup \{\gamma\}, \mathsf{so}_\Gamma \cup \Gamma^s \times \{\gamma\})}{(h', \mu, c, \alpha) \to (h'[s \to h''], \mu, c[s \to \epsilon], \alpha')}$$

The rule updates the yet-to-be executed history h' by removing the current invocation $m(k)$ (since this invocation has now completed), updates the abstract execution α to now include the newly completed invocation, and updates the current invocation implementation to empty. Note that $\llbracket e \rrbracket_{\mu(s)}$ denotes the evaluation of the expression e under the local variable map $\mu(s)$. When the history h' becomes empty, i.e. there are no more method invocations to be executed, the abstract execution becomes complete and would include all method instances present in the original history h. Note that this rule does not generate any read/write/update event.

3.3   Replicated Store Semantics

The replicated store state $\chi = (\Sigma, \mathsf{vis}, \mathsf{ar}, \mathsf{so})$ consists of the set of replicated store events (Σ) and various relations on Σ. Events can either be read, write or update events, and depending on the type of event, Σ is partitioned into Σ_R, Σ_W and Σ_U. The visibility relation $\mathsf{vis} \subseteq \Sigma \times \Sigma$ denotes the events visible to an event and is used to determine the output of read events. The arbitration relation $\mathsf{ar} \subseteq (\Sigma_W \cup \Sigma_U) \times (\Sigma_W \cup \Sigma_U)$ provides a total ordering on write or update events to the same location. Finally, the session order relation $\mathsf{so} \subseteq \Sigma \times \Sigma$ provides a total ordering on events originating from the same session. All events generated by statements in the same method invocation would belong to the same session and hence would be related by so. We also define a happens-before relation $\mathsf{hb} = (\mathsf{vis} \cup \mathsf{so})^+$ in the usual way.

We use Ψ to refer to a consistency policy supported by the store. Ψ is a predicate on the store state, which must be maintained at every step of the execution. Ψ essentially controls the visibility relation on events based on session or happens-before order. The following table illustrates the various consistency policies that we consider in our work; all of these policies can be implementation without the need for global coordination [1].[3] (all σ_i belong to Σ):

Table 1. Axiomatic characterization of various weak consistency policies.

Consistency policy	$\Psi(\Sigma, \mathsf{vis}, \mathsf{ar}, \mathsf{so})$
Read Your Writes [39]	$\mathsf{so}(\sigma_1, \sigma_2) \Rightarrow \mathsf{vis}(\sigma_1, \sigma_2)$
Monotonic Writes [39]	$\mathsf{so}(\sigma_1, \sigma_2) \wedge \mathsf{vis}(\sigma_2, \sigma_3) \Rightarrow \mathsf{vis}(\sigma_1, \sigma_3)$
Monotonic Reads [39]	$\mathsf{vis}(\sigma_1, \sigma_2) \wedge \mathsf{so}(\sigma_2, \sigma_3) \Rightarrow \mathsf{vis}(\sigma_1, \sigma_3)$
Write Follow Read [39]	$\mathsf{vis}(\sigma_1, \sigma_2) \wedge \mathsf{so}(\sigma_2, \sigma_3) \wedge \mathsf{vis}(\sigma_3, \sigma_4) \Rightarrow \mathsf{vis}(\sigma_1, \sigma_4)$
Causal Visibility [27]	$\mathsf{hb}(\sigma_1, \sigma_2) \wedge \mathsf{vis}(\sigma_2, \sigma_3) \Rightarrow \mathsf{vis}(\sigma_1, \sigma_3)$
Causal Consistency [27]	$\mathsf{hb}(\sigma_1, \sigma_2) \Rightarrow \mathsf{vis}(\sigma_1, \sigma_2)$

As we saw earlier in Sect. 2, MonotonicWrites enforces the constraint that if an event is visible, then all events before it in session order must also be visible. MonotonicReads requires that if an event is visible, it will continue to remain visible to all operations later in the session. On the other hand, WriteFollowsRead enforces that all events visible to a prior event in a session will continue to remain visible to other events which witness a later event of the session.

We use the notation Σ^l to denote the subset of events pertaining to location l, and Σ^s to denote the subset of events of session s. Given a set of events Σ', $\mathsf{MAX}^1_{\mathsf{ar}}(\Sigma')$ denotes the maximal events in Σ' according to the relation ar which write to location 1. Given events $\sigma \in \Sigma^l_R$, $\sigma' \in \Sigma^l_W$, we define the *Reads-From* relation rf in terms of vis and ar relations as follows:

$$\mathsf{rf}(\sigma', \sigma) \Leftrightarrow \mathsf{vis}(\sigma', \sigma) \wedge \forall \sigma'' \in \Sigma^l.(\mathsf{vis}(\sigma'', \sigma) \wedge \sigma'' \neq \sigma) \Rightarrow \mathsf{ar}(\sigma'', \sigma')$$

---

[3] Note that the lack of any constraints (i.e. $\Psi = true$) corresponds to Strong Eventual Consistency [18]. Since we assume SEC, our definition of Causal Consistency corresponds to Causal Convergence (CCv) as defined by [8].

The rf relation essentially encodes the 'last writer wins' nature of the store, whereby the most recent visible write event according to ar becomes the event supplying the value available to subsequent reads. The replicated store state evolves by the addition of new events. On addition of a write/update event, the arbitration order is appropriately modified to ensure that it remains a total order on events targeting the same location. In addition, we also ensure causal arbitration [11] by enforcing that ar and hb do not disagree with each other. For update and read events, the values that these events read depend upon the most recent write event to the same location visible to the events, which in turn is controlled by the consistency policy. To elaborate, consider the rule R-CAS:

$$\frac{\begin{array}{c} \Sigma' \subseteq \Sigma \quad \sigma' \in \mathsf{MAX}^l_{\mathsf{ar}}(\Sigma') \quad \mathsf{ar} \subseteq \mathsf{ar}' \\ act(\sigma') = \mathsf{W}(l,m) \vee act(\sigma') = \mathsf{U}(l,\_,m) \quad \sigma = (i,s,U(l,m,n)) \quad \forall\tau \in \Sigma^l_U.\neg(\mathsf{rf}(\sigma',\tau)) \\ \mathsf{ar}' \text{ is a total order on } \Sigma^l_W \cup \Sigma^l_U \cup \{\sigma\} \quad \forall\sigma_1,\sigma_2.\neg(\mathsf{hb}(\sigma_1,\sigma_2) \wedge \mathsf{ar}'(\sigma_2,\sigma_1)) \\ vis' = vis \cup \Sigma' \times \{\sigma\} \quad so' = so \cup \Sigma^s \times \{\sigma\} \quad \Psi(\Sigma \cup \{\sigma\}, vis', \mathsf{ar}', so') \end{array}}{(\Sigma, vis, \mathsf{ar}, so) \xrightarrow{\sigma} (\Sigma \cup \{\sigma\}, vis', \mathsf{ar}', so')}$$

Here, we want to add a new update event to location l. First, an *arbitrary* subset (Σ') of events of Σ is selected. This step essentially corresponds to the creation of a new replica on which the events in Σ' have been applied. Then, we select the most recent write event (σ') from Σ' which ensures atomicity of the update event (and hence the CAS statement responsible for the update). In particular, we require that no other update event must have read from (rf) σ'. The value written by σ' (i.e. m) would be the read value of the update event. vis, so and ar are appropriately updated, and the new store state must satisfy the consistency policy Ψ, which in turn will govern the selection of the initial subset Σ'. The formal rules for read and write events can be found in [32].

Note that enforcing the above rule would in essence prohibit two CAS operations to be executed concurrently, and hence would establish a global ordering among the CAS operations. However, unlike in shared memory systems where this is sufficient to establish a global ordering among all operations thus ensuring linearizability, in replicated systems, this does not constrain the behavior of other read and write operations (as we saw in Sect. 2, and hence more constraints must be enforced through the consistency policy.

We can now combine the language, abstract execution, and replicated store rules to describe transitions of the LTS $\Omega_{h,L,\Psi}$, which simply requires the language rules and the replicated store rules to agree on the structure of all replicated store events:

$$\frac{(h', \mu, \mathsf{c}, \alpha) \xrightarrow{\sigma} (h'', \mu', \mathsf{c}', \alpha) \quad \chi \xrightarrow{\sigma} \chi'}{(\chi, h', \mu, \mathsf{c}, \alpha) \xrightarrow{\sigma} (\chi', h'', \mu', \mathsf{c}', \alpha)}$$

$$\frac{(h', \mu, \mathsf{c}, \alpha) \rightarrow (h'', \mu', \mathsf{c}', \alpha')}{(\chi, h', \mu, \mathsf{c}, \alpha) \rightarrow (\chi, h'', \mu', \mathsf{c}', \alpha')}$$

Example: Let us revisit the Treiber Stack and in particular the violating execution described in Fig. 2. The violating history consists of two sessions, with one session containing the invocation push(1) and another containing pop. The execution of push(1), following the language semantics, creates the events σ_1 and σ_2 such that $act(\sigma_1) = \mathsf{W}(L.\mathtt{Val}, 1)$ and $act(\sigma_2) = \mathsf{U}(\mathtt{Top}, \mathtt{NULL}, \mathsf{L})$ which are both added to the store state. The execution of pop generates the read event to Top, which following the store semantics picks the set $\Sigma' = \{\sigma_2\}$, resulting in read event σ_3 such that $act(\sigma_3) = \mathsf{R}(\mathtt{Top}, \mathsf{L})$. Under EC, the following read to L.Val by pop is unconstrained and hence simply picks $\Sigma' = \phi$, resulting in the event σ_4 such that $act(\sigma_4) = \mathsf{R}(L.\mathtt{Val}, 0)$ where 0 is the initial value. This results in violation of the AddRem specification.

Notice that $\mathsf{so}(\sigma_1, \sigma_2)$ and $\mathsf{vis}(\sigma_2, \sigma_3)$. Hence, under MW+MR, while generating the read event to L.Val by pop, the store must pick $\Sigma' = \{\sigma_1, \sigma_2\}$ to satisfy the axioms of MW+MR, so that the event must read the value 1, which prevents the violation from occurring.

3.4 Correctness Specification

Given an abstract execution obtained after executing a history on a replicated store under some consistency policy, how do we decide if it correctly obeys the semantics of the data structure implemented by the library? Linearization would require us to demonstrate a total order on all method invocations which would be admissible by a sequential reference implementation of the data structure. However, since the consistency model of a replicated system is substantially weaker than sequential consistency, it becomes necessary to also weaken correctness requirements [34,37]. We use the axiomatic specifications of data structure correctness as proposed by Emmi et al. [17], which are equivalent to standard linearizability, as our basis, and then weaken them systematically to adapt them to be useful in a replicated environment. Axiomatic specifications do not require a total order to be established on method invocations, do not refer back to a reference implementation, and also match the axiomatic, declarative nature of the semantics of the replicated store.

First, we define all abstract executions that can be generated given a library implementation, a history and a consistency policy. The initial state of the replicated store is assumed to be empty, i.e. $\chi_{\mathsf{Init}} = (\phi, \phi, \phi, \phi)$. Let h_ϵ be the empty history which associates an empty sequence (ϵ) of invocations to each session. Let $\mathsf{c}_{\mathsf{Init}}$ be the initial implementation state which simply associates the empty program ϵ to each session.

Definition 1. *Given a set of sessions S, a history h, a library implementation L and a consistency policy Ψ, the abstract executions generated by $\Omega_{h,L,\Psi}$ are defined as* $: [\![\Omega_{h,L,\Psi}]\!] = \{\Gamma \mid (\chi_{\mathsf{Init}}, h, (\phi, \phi), \mathsf{c}_{\mathsf{Init}}) \to^* (\_, h_\epsilon, \Gamma, \_)\}$

Thus, executing all invocations in the history under a given consistency policy and library implementation gives rise to the set of final abstract executions. Due to the non-deterministic nature of the semantics, multiple abstract executions could be generated. Correctness of an abstract execution is specified in terms of various **axioms** that it must obey. An implementation is correct under a consistency policy if for all possible histories, all final abstract executions generated by the implementation obey the axioms.

To illustrate, let us consider the Stack data structure. It has two methods $M = \{\text{Push}, \text{Pop}\}$. Given a method invocation event $\gamma = (i, m, a, r, s)$, we assume projection functions for all the respective components (e.g., m, a, and r). Further, we assume a match predicate relating two method invocation events defined thus:

$$\text{match}(\gamma_1, \gamma_2) \Leftrightarrow \text{m}(\gamma_1) = \text{Push} \wedge \text{m}(\gamma_2) = \text{Pop} \wedge \text{a}(\gamma_1) = \text{r}(\gamma_2)$$

Let EMPTY denote a special value signifying the empty return value (see, e.g. the Treiber Stack impl. in Fig. 1). Consider an abstract execution $\alpha = (\Gamma, \text{so}_\Gamma)$. We define the happens-before relation for method invocations as $\text{hb}_\Gamma = (\text{match} \cup \text{so}_\Gamma)^+$. Then, the correctness of α can be specified in terms of the following axioms:

- AddRem : $\forall \gamma \in \Gamma.\text{m}(\gamma) = \text{Pop} \wedge \text{r}(\gamma) \neq \text{EMPTY} \Rightarrow \exists \gamma' \in \Gamma.\text{match}(\gamma', \gamma)$
- Injective : $\forall \gamma_1, \gamma_2, \gamma_3 \in \Gamma.\text{match}(\gamma_1, \gamma_2) \wedge \text{match}(\gamma_1, \gamma_3) \Rightarrow \gamma_2 = \gamma_3$
- Empty : $\forall \gamma_1, \gamma_2, \gamma_3 \in \Gamma.\text{m}(\gamma_1) = \text{Pop} \wedge \text{r}(\gamma_1) = \text{EMPTY} \wedge \text{m}(\gamma_2) = \text{Push} \wedge$ $\text{hb}_\Gamma(\gamma_2, \gamma_1) \Rightarrow \exists \gamma_3 \in \Gamma.\text{match}(\gamma_2, \gamma_3)$
- LIFO $-$ 1 : $\forall \gamma_1, \gamma_2, \gamma_3 \in \Gamma.\text{m}(\gamma_1) = \text{Push} \wedge \text{match}(\gamma_2, \gamma_3) \wedge \text{hb}(\gamma_2, \gamma_1) \wedge$ $\text{hb}(\gamma_1, \gamma_3) \Rightarrow \exists \gamma_4 \in \Gamma.\text{match}(\gamma_1, \gamma_4)$
- LIFO $-$ 2 : $\forall \gamma_1, \gamma_2, \gamma_3, \gamma_4 \in \Gamma.\neg(\text{match}(\gamma_1, \gamma_4) \wedge \text{match}(\gamma_2, \gamma_3) \wedge \text{hb}(\gamma_2, \gamma_1) \wedge$ $\text{hb}(\gamma_3, \gamma_4) \wedge \text{hb}(\gamma_1, \gamma_3))$

These axioms follow from those given in [17], except that instead of using a linearization order as done in [17], we use a weaker happens-before hb_Γ order. It is also possible to use the even weaker session order so_Γ in place of hb_Γ. We have already seen the AddRem axiom in §2. The Injective axiom enforces that an element pushed onto the stack is not popped more than once[4]. The Empty axiom says that if a pop invocation (γ_1) returns EMPTY and if there is a push invocation (γ_2) that happens-before it, then γ_2 must be matched to another pop. This reflects the expected stack-like behavior from the point of view of a client who observes these invocations. The LIFO $-$ 1 property specifies that if a push invocation γ_2 happens-before another push invocation γ_1, with both of them happening-before a pop invocation γ_3, and if γ_2 is matched with γ_3, then to respect the LIFO order, γ_1 must also be matched (to some γ_4). LIFO $-$ 2 complements LIFO $-$ 1 by requiring that γ_3 cannot happen-before such a γ_4. The specifications for other data structures we have considered, including Queue and Exchanger can be found in [32].

4   Bounded Verification

We now present an automated bounded verification procedure capable of generating abstract executions that violate data structure correctness specifications

---

[4] Note that we assume all methods are called with distinct arguments.

under a given consistency policy. We take advantage of the axiomatic nature of both the semantics and specification and reduce the problem to that of checking the satisfiability of a collection of formulae in first-order logic (FOL), which can be dispatched to an off-the-shelf SMT solver. In particular, our strategy is to instantiate a bounded number of invocations (k) without specifying their method types, arguments, or session information, and instead leave it upto the solver to search efficiently among all histories of length k.

4.1   Vocabulary

Given a library $L = (\mathsf{M}, \mathsf{Impl})$, we first take each method implementation and unroll loops upto a constant bound[5], and give a label to each program statement that interacts with a replicated location (e.g. see the Treiber Stack impl. in Fig. 1). Let $\mathbb{L}$ denote this set of labels.

We use an uninterpreted, finite sort I to represent invocations in the history that we wish to construct, and then constrain this sort to contain only the distinct elements $\mathsf{INV}_1, \ldots, \mathsf{INV}_k$. In addition, we use uninterpreted sorts E and V to represent the set of replicated store events and values that are read or written by them. We define the function $\mathsf{meth} : \mathsf{I} \rightarrow \mathsf{M}$ to associate a method type with each invocation. We use an uninterpreted sort S to denote the set of sessions involved in the history. The function $\mathsf{sess} : \mathsf{I} \rightarrow \mathsf{S}$ associates a session with each invocation.

For each method $m \in \mathsf{M}$ and each program statement labeled n in the implementation $\mathsf{Impl}(m)$, we define the function $\mathsf{P}_{mn} : \mathsf{I} \rightarrow \mathsf{E}$ to associates the event generated by the program statement to an invocation. In addition, functions $\mathsf{arg}, \mathsf{ret} : \mathsf{I} \rightarrow \mathsf{V}$ associate the argument and return values to each invocation. For every local variable v used in a program, function $\rho_{\mathsf{v}} : \mathsf{I} \rightarrow \mathsf{V}$ denotes the value of the local variable in that invocation. The predicate $\mathsf{so}_\mathsf{I} : \mathsf{I} \times \mathsf{I} \rightarrow \mathbb{B}$ denotes the session order relation among invocation instances.

We define functions $\mathsf{loc}, \mathsf{rval}, \mathsf{wval} : \mathsf{E} \rightarrow \mathsf{V}$ to associate locations, values read and values written by events resp. We use the uninterpreted, finite sort $\mathbb{E}$ containing elements $\mathsf{R}, \mathsf{W}, \mathsf{U}$ to denote various event types. The function $\mathsf{Etype} : \mathsf{E} \rightarrow \mathbb{E}$ associates the type with each event. Finally, predicates $\mathsf{vis}, \mathsf{ar}, \mathsf{so}_\mathsf{E}, \mathsf{rf} : \mathsf{E} \times \mathsf{E} \rightarrow \mathbb{B}$ denote the visibility, arbitration, session order, and read-from relations resp. among events.

For every replicated location, we also instantiate a distinct value referring to the location. For example, for the Treiber Stack implementation (Fig. 1), we have distinct values for $\mathtt{Top}$ and for the $\mathtt{Val}$ and $\mathtt{Next}$ fields of each $\mathtt{New\ Node}$ generated by an invocation. Since the number of invocations is fixed (k), the number of such locations to be instantiated can also be pre-determined statically. We also define a function $\mathsf{Initval} : \mathsf{V} \rightarrow \mathsf{V}$ which fixes an initial value for every location, and assigns initial values to all locations used in the execution.

---

[5] Loops are typically only used to busy wait for a successful CAS operation in the applications we consider.

4.2 Implementation Constraints

We now describe constraints on the events imposed by the implementation. First, note that even though the set of functions $\{P_{mn} | m \in \mathbb{M}, n \in \mathbb{L}\}$ are defined for every invocation, an invocation i will only have a fixed method type meth(i), and hence will only generate events corresponding to program statements in the implementation of meth(i). We designate a special event $\perp : E$ and associate it for program statements of every other method type using the following constraint:

$$\forall i \in I \; \forall m \in \mathbb{M} \; \forall n \in \mathbb{L}. \; m \neq \mathsf{meth}(i) \Rightarrow P_{mn}(i) = \perp$$

For program statements in the implementation of meth(i), we add constraints for every statement based on its type. Note that loops have already been unrolled and for every statement labeled n in method m, we collect the conditionals of any if statement enclosing the statement and replace any local variable v used in those conditionals with the corresponding function $\rho_v(i)$ (for invocation i) to obtain the formulae $[\![\phi_{mn}]\!]$. To illustrate the constraints added for different types of statements, consider the rule for reads:

$$\frac{\mathsf{Impl}(m) : n : \; \mathtt{v = 1}}{\forall i \in I. \; (\mathsf{meth}(i) = m \wedge [\![\phi_{mn}]\!]_i) \Rightarrow (\mathsf{Etype}(P_{mn}(i)) = R \wedge \mathsf{loc}(P_{mn}(i)) = 1 \atop \wedge \mathsf{rval}(P_{mn}(i)) = \rho_v(i)}$$

The rule essentially specifies the constraint for statement labeled n in the implementation of method m if it is a read operation. The constraint appropriately sets the Etype, loc and rval functions of event $P_{mn}(i)$ for every invocation i, if the invocation has a method type of m and the enclosing if conditionals (if any) are satisfied. The rules for write and CAS statements are similar (they also set the wval function and additionally CAS also checks whether the value read is equal to its first argument) and can be found in [32]. In addition, we also relate adjacent events of the same invocation with the session order relation $\mathsf{so_E}$.

4.3 Abstract Execution Constraints

On encountering a return statement, we record the returned value using the following constraint:

$$\frac{\mathsf{Impl}(m) : n : \; \mathtt{return\ v}}{\forall i \in I. \; (\mathsf{meth}(i) = m \wedge [\![\phi_{mn}]\!]_i) \Rightarrow (\mathsf{ret}(i) = \rho_v(i) \wedge \mathsf{completed}(i))}$$

Apart from setting the ret value, we also use another unary predicate completed to encode that the invocation has completed and reached the return statement. This is needed because we are unrolling loops upto a fixed bound. Since we know the last program statement statically, if we encounter this statement without reaching return for an invocation, then completed will be set to false.

We also encode the constraint that the session order relation (so_I) among invocations of the same session is a total order. Finally, we also encode that if two invocations i_1 and i_2 are in session order ($so_I(i_1, i_2)$), then the last event of i_1 and the first event of i_2 are in event session order (so_E).

4.4   Replicated Store Constraints

We must also encode constraints ensuring that the semantics of the replicated store are preserved. First, we capture various properties of relations on events, viz. vis is anti-symmetric and irreflexive, ar among write events to the same location is a total order, vis and so_I do not clash with each other, ar does not clash with vis and so_I. All these constraints are implicitly enforced by the semantics of the replicated store, so that the state of the store reached after any number of execution steps must obey them.

The various consistency policies in Table 1 can be directly encoded using the relations defined in the vocabulary. We now turn to encoding the last-writer-wins nature of the data store, which relates the vis and ar relations with the read and write values (rval and wval) of the events.

$$\forall e_1, e_2 \in E.\mathsf{rf}(e_1, e_2) \Rightarrow \mathsf{vis}(e_1, e_2) \wedge \mathsf{wval}(e_1) = \mathsf{rval}(e_2) \wedge$$
$$\forall e_3 \in E_W^{\mathsf{loc}(e_2)}.(\mathsf{vis}(e_3, e_2) \Rightarrow e_3 = e_1 \vee \mathsf{ar}(e_3, e_1))$$

$$\forall e_1 \in E_R.(\forall e_2 \in E.\neg\mathsf{rf}(e_2, e_1)) \Rightarrow \mathsf{rval}(e_1) = \mathsf{Initval}(\mathsf{loc}(e_1))$$

In the above constraints, we use the notation E_W^l to indicate only those events that write to location l, and E_R for read events. The first constraint enforces the reads-from event to be the most recent visible event according to the arbitration order, and also constrains the read value. The second constraint disallows out-of-thin-air reads by enforcing that if there are no rf events, then the value read must be the initial value. As an optimization, while encoding this constraint in our tool, we enumerate all possible write events to the same location (which are guaranteed to be finite since we only have k invocations) in the antecedent, instead of the universal quantification used above.

For CAS operations which generate update events, we encode the constraint (as derived from the semantics rule R-CAS) that two update events should not read from the same event:

$$\forall e, e_1, e_2 \in E. \mathsf{Etype}(e_1) = U \wedge \mathsf{Etype}(e_2) = U \wedge \mathsf{rf}(e, e_1) \wedge \mathsf{rf}(e, e_2) \Rightarrow e_1 = e_2$$

4.5   Specification Constraints

The axioms of correctness for data structures only use an invocation's argument and return values, and the session order relation among invocations in the abstract execution. Thus, they can be directly encoded using our vocabulary. Given an axiom θ, we encode its negation to find histories which have abstract executions that violate the axiom.

For example, to find violations of the AddRem axiom, we add the following constraint:

$$\exists i_1 \in I.\ \mathsf{meth}(i_1) = \mathsf{POP} \wedge \mathsf{ret}(i_1) \neq \mathsf{EMPTY} \wedge \forall i_2 \in I.\ \neg\mathsf{match}(i_2, i_1)$$

where we use the predicate $\mathsf{match} : I \times I \to \mathbb{B}$ defined in a similar manner as in Sect. 3.4. This completes the entire description of our encoding.

Our main soundness result can be formalized thus[6]

Theorem 1. *Given a library implementation L, consistency policy Ψ and a correctness axiom θ, if the collection of formulae described above are satisfiable, then there exists a history h and an abstract execution $\Gamma \in [\![\Omega_{h,L,\Psi}]\!]$ which violates θ.*

5   Experimental Evaluation

Table 2. Consistency policies required for various implementations and specifications.

Benchmark	AddRem	Injective	Empty[SO]	Empty[HB]	FIFO-1/LIFO-1/Exchange	FIFO-2/LIFO-2	Max time (s)
2Lock Queue [29]	MW+MR	MW+MR +WFR	CC	CC	MW+MR	MW+MR	269
LockFree Queue [29]	MW+MR	EC	CC	CC	MW+MR	EC	152
HW Queue [22]	EC	EC	RMW	MW+MR +RMW	CC	MW+MR	61
Treiber Stack [40]	MW+MR +WFR	EC	CC	CC	MW+MR +WFR	EC	245
Elimination Stack [20]	MW+MR +WFR	EC	CC	CC	MW+MR +WFR	MW	65
Exchanger [20]	MW	EC	-NA-	-NA-	MW	-NA-	40

We have implemented our bounded verification procedure and applied it to a number of library implementations that have been widely-used in the world of shared-memory systems. We generate FOL formulae for each implementation as described in Sect. 4 and dispatch them to Z3 to determine their satisfiability. For queues, we have used the 2LockQueue, LockFree Queue and Herlihy and Wing (HW) Queue implementations, while for stacks, we have applied our approach on the Treiber and Elimination Stack implementations. The Elimination stack uses the exchanger implementation, and so we have also checked the correctness of the exchanger.

Since our analysis takes as input the bound on the number of invocations (k), the consistency policy, and the specification, we deploy the system as follows: For each implementation and specification pairing, we start with bound $k = 2$ and the weakest consistency policy (EC). If we do not find any violation, then we

---

[6] A Proof Sketch can be found in [32].

increase the bound by 1 and perform the analysis again. On the other hand, if we do find a violation, then by Theorem-1, we know that it is guaranteed to be an actual violation. We record its structure from the satisfiable model returned by Z3, and then increase the consistency policy to the next higher level. We continue this process until we exhaust our verification time budget (of 1 hour per benchmark implementation). Note that all the consistency policies that we consider can be arranged in a lattice [38] whereby the higher one goes up the lattice, the consistency policies become stronger, which means they allow only a subset of executions that are allowed by policies weaker than them. Our tool automatically traverses this lattice to find the weakest consistency policy at which no bounded violation is found.

Table 2 summarizes the results of this process. For each pair of benchmark implementation and correctness specification, it shows the weakest consistency policy at which we did not find any violations. This means that at every consistency policy weaker than the one specified in the table, violations were discovered. For each benchmark, we also note the maximum time needed to find a violation for any specification by Z3. Some specifications were discussed in §3.4, with Empty[SO] meaning we replace the relation hb_Γ with so_Γ in the specification; the correctness specifications for Queues and Exchangers are given in [32]. Across all benchmarks, we found that the longest history which violated any specification within the time bound considered consisted of 6 invocations.

To empirically validate our results, we also executed all the benchmarks at the appropriate consistency levels on Cassandra, a real-world replicated data store. We configured Cassandra with 3 replicas running on Amazon EC2 instances at different physical locations (all on the US East Coast). We randomly generated client invocations at all 3 replicas and ran each implementation for 4 h (on average 92000 invocations/benchmark). We collected the resulting traces and checked the specifications. We did not find any violation of the specifications, and surmise that violations, when they do occur, manifest in smaller executions that can be systematically checked by our analysis.

The results yield a number of interesting observations. First and foremost, note that even for the same benchmark, different correctness specifications require different consistency policies, ranging from the weakest, *Eventual Consistency*, (EC) to the strongest, *Causal Consistency*, (CC). This suggests that depending upon the requirements of the clients of the library, there is a trade-off between consistency and correctness that can be effectively explored. It has long been known that *Causal Consistency* incurs a performance penalty [3] due to expensive dependency tracking, significant metadata storage, and long wait times for all causally dependent data to arrive. A number of recent approaches [9,14,28] have looked at improving the performance of *Causal Consistency*, mainly by reducing the amount of dependent data required. Our experiments suggest that many important correctness properties of library implementations may not require CC, but would work correctly under weaker session guarantees or even EC. Note that as we discussed in Sect. 2, MW+MR only require all data to be propagated from the same session, while MW+MR+WFR requires data to be propagated across the entire causal chain.

Another interesting observation is that important properties such as Injective and FIFO/LIFO only require EC for most benchmarks. We also notice that for the same correctness specification, different benchmarks require different consistency policies, especially among the various Queue benchmarks. This illustrates that clients have flexibility in choosing an implementation, based on the properties that they need. For example, an HW queue can satisfy the AddRem specification at the weakest consistency policy (EC), but requires CC for FIFO-1, which can be satisfied using just session guarantees by both 2LockQueue and LockFree-Queue. No single queue implementation provides all correctness guarantees at the weakest consistency level. For stacks, the Elimination Stack and the Treiber Stack require the same consistency policies for every specification except LIFO-2, for which the Elimination Stack requires MW for the Exchange property of the underlying Exchanger to be satisfied. By analyzing violations, we also found that both the access pattern of different implementations as well as the semantics of the data structure (stack vs. queue) played a major role in determining how and if violations occur.

Note that even though we unroll loops upto a fixed bound, for all benchmarks except LockFree Queue, the unrolling factor does not matter because in every loop, every iteration except the last only performs read events, and the values read are only used in the same iteration. Hence, only the last iteration which performs a write/update event is relevant; unrolling the loop once is sufficient.

$$\textbf{push(1)} \qquad\qquad \textbf{push(3)} \qquad\qquad \textbf{pop} : 0$$

$$5 : U(\text{Top}, \text{NULL}, L_1) \qquad 5 : U(\text{Top}, L_2, L_3) \qquad 6 : R(\text{Top}, L_2)$$

$$\textbf{push(2)} \qquad\qquad \textbf{pop} : 3 \qquad\qquad 7 : R(L_2.\text{Val}, 0)$$

$$5 : U(\text{Top}, L_1, L_2) \qquad 9 : U(\text{Top}, L_3, L_2) \qquad 9 : U(\text{Top}, L_2, L_1)$$

$$\textbf{pop} : 1$$

$$6 : R(\text{Top}, L_1)$$

Fig. 4. A violation of LIFO $-$ 1 by Treiber Stack under MW+MR involving 6 invocations

In order to illustrate the complex violations automatically generated by our framework, consider the violation of LIFO-1 in the Treiber stack implementation under MW+MR in Fig. 4. Here, invocations in the same column are in the same session. Following the notation as used in the specification in Sect. 3.4, $\gamma_1 = \text{push}(2)$, $\gamma_2 = \text{push}(1)$, $\gamma_3 = \text{pop} : 1$. As a concrete violation of the specification, γ_2 happens before γ_1, but γ_3 returns the value pushed by γ_2 even though γ_1 is unmatched, thus disobeying the LIFO property. The reason behind this violation is that another pop operation (pop:0) is actually popping the element pushed by push(2), but it does not read the value 1 and instead reads the initial value 0 (thus also violating AddRem). As a result, the last pop operation in the leftmost session sees only the element 1 on the stack. We note that there is no violation of smaller length under MW+MR. By upgrading the consistency level to MW+MW+WFR, the violation is eliminated.

6   Related Work and Conclusion

Verifying applications under weak consistency has received significant attention in recent years. A number of efforts [2,19,23,25,38] have looked at the problem of verifying arbitrary safety invariants while others have considered verification with respect to distributed database applications and specific high-level transactional properties [5–7,10,30,35]. These results are orthogonal to the work described here, since neither consider the question of safely migrating performant concurrent libraries to a replicated environment.

More directly related are proposals to deal with the specification and verification of various properties of CRDTs [12,18,31,41,42]. CRDTs also offer a library interface to clients and have been implemented for various data structures such as set, list, map, etc. They follow a different system model than the library implementations that we have considered in our work, and typically do not require any form of synchronization. However, this requirement imposes stringent constraints on their design (for example, in an op-based CRDT, all operations have to commute with each other). We are not aware of any CRDT-like implementation of concurrent data structures such as Queue, Stack and Exchangers that we have considered here.

Prior works [18,31] have also developed automated or semi-automated approaches to verify the convergence of CRDTs, an important but fairly low-level property that does not shed much insight on the correctness of libraries built using them. High-level correctness specifications of CRDTs are either given in terms of abstract RDT specifications [12,42] or customized specification frameworks such as replication-aware linearizability [41]. Both of these specification styles are closer to linearizability, but since direct linearization of all operations an execution is not possible in a distributed environment, both approaches allow relaxations to help decide a linearization order. These relaxations typically take the form of allowing different per-invocation linearizations based on the type of the invocation and the visibility relation. This can lead to complicated specifications that can be substantially different from their shared-memory counterparts, complicating verification. In contrast, our axiomatic style also allows clients of the library to know exactly how the relaxations in a replicated environment will impact observable behavior. Finally, unlike other prior work, we develop a fully automated approach for bounded verification of library implementations.

There has also been recent interest in specifying and verifying concurrent library implementations for shared memory systems [16] and weak memory models [15,34]. While the specification style of weak memory models bears some superficial resemblance to that of weak consistency, the underlying system model is quite different, and weak consistency models allows relaxed behaviors which are not allowed by weak memory models. They also offer more fine-grained control than possible under weak memory given their ability to provide session-level as well as system-wide consistency guarantees to individual low-level operations. [34] proposes axiomatic specifications of libraries using happens-before and program orders. Our specifications, while similar in spirit, are more fine-grained and better suited to replicated systems.

To conclude, we tackle the problem of migrating concurrent library implementations from shared-memory systems to replicated, distributed ones. We define a sensible semantics for such implementations on a replicated store parametric in the consistency policy of the store and describe how to migrate the correctness specifications for such libraries with minimal changes. Our verification framework automatically finds bounded violations of these specifications. Parametericity of consistency policies in the analysis allows us to find the weakest policy that eliminates a discovered violation. Our experiments have demonstrated that the proposed framework is effective in finding non-trivial violations in a number of challenging and diverse benchmarks. We also find that the spectrum of weak consistency policies in replicated systems can be effectively explored to tradeoff correctness and performance.

Acknowledgments. We thank the anonymous reviewers for their insightful comments. This material is based upon work supported by the National Science Foundation under Grant No. CCF-SHF 1717741.

References

1. Bailis, P., Davidson, A., Fekete, A., Ghodsi, A., Hellerstein, J.M., Stoica, I.: Highly available transactions: virtues and limitations. PVLDB **7**(3), 181–192 (2013). https://doi.org/10.14778/2732232.2732237. http://www.vldb.org/pvldb/vol7/p181-bailis.pdf

2. Bailis, P., Fekete, A., Franklin, M.J., Ghodsi, A., Hellerstein, J.M., Stoica,I.: Coordination avoidance in database systems. PVLDB **8**(3), 185–196 (2014). https://doi.org/10.14778/2735508.2735509. http://www.vldb.org/pvldb/vol8/p185-bailis.pdf

3. Bailis, P., Fekete, A., Ghodsi, A., Hellerstein, J.M., Stoica, I.: The potential dangers of causal consistency and an explicit solution. In: ACM Symposium on Cloud Computing, SOCC 2012, San Jose, CA, USA, 14–17 October 2012, p. 22 (2012). https://doi.org/10.1145/2391229.2391251

4. Bailis, P., Ghodsi, A.: Eventual consistency today: limitations, extensions, and beyond. Commun. ACM **56**(5), 55–63 (2013). https://doi.org/10.1145/2447976.2447992

5. Beillahi, S.M., Bouajjani, A., Enea, C.: Checking robustness against snapshot isolation. In: Computer Aided Verification - 31st International Conference, CAV 2019, New York City, NY, USA, 15–18 July 2019, Proceedings, Part II, pp. 286–304 (2019). https://doi.org/10.1007/978-3-030-25543-5_17

6. Beillahi, S.M., Bouajjani, A., Enea, C.: Robustness against transactional causal consistency. In: 30th International Conference on Concurrency Theory, CONCUR 2019, Amsterdam, The Netherlands, 27–30 August 2019, pp. 30:1–30:18 (2019). https://doi.org/10.4230/LIPIcs.CONCUR.2019.30

7. Bernardi, G., Gotsman, A.: Robustness against consistency models with atomic visibility. In: 27th International Conference on Concurrency Theory, CONCUR 2016, Québec City, Canada, 23–26 August 2016, pp. 7:1–7:15 (2016). https://doi.org/10.4230/LIPIcs.CONCUR.2016.7

8. Bouajjani, A., Enea, C., Guerraoui, R., Hamza, J.: On verifying causal consistency. In: Castagna, G., Gordon, A.D. (eds.) Proceedings of the 44th ACM SIGPLAN Symposium on Principles of Programming Languages, POPL 2017, Paris, France, 18–20 January 2017, pp. 626–638. ACM (2017). http://dl.acm.org/citation.cfm?id=3009888

9. Bravo, M., Rodrigues, L.E.T., Roy, P.V.: Saturn: a distributed metadata service for causal consistency. In: Proceedings of the Twelfth European Conference on Computer Systems, EuroSys 2017, Belgrade, Serbia, 23–26 April 2017, pp. 111–126 (2017). https://doi.org/10.1145/3064176.3064210

10. Brutschy, L., Dimitrov, D., Müller, P., Vechev, M.T.: Static serializability analysis for causal consistency. In: Proceedings of the 39th ACM SIGPLAN Conference on Programming Language Design and Implementation, PLDI 2018, Philadelphia, PA, USA, 18–22 June 2018, pp. 90–104 (2018). https://doi.org/10.1145/3192366.3192415

11. Burckhardt, S.: Principles of eventual consistency. Found. Trends Program. Lang. **1**(1–2), 1–150 (2014). https://doi.org/10.1561/2500000011

12. Burckhardt, S., Gotsman, A., Yang, H., Zawirski, M.: Replicated data types: specification, verification, optimality. In: The 41st Annual ACM SIGPLAN-SIGACT Symposium on Principles of Programming Languages, POPL 2014, San Diego, CA, USA, 20–21 January 2014, pp. 271–284 (2014). https://doi.org/10.1145/2535838.2535848

13. Cerone, A., Bernardi, G., Gotsman, A.: A framework for transactional consistency models with atomic visibility. In: 26th International Conference on Concurrency Theory, CONCUR 2015, Madrid, Spain, 1.4 September 2015, pp. 58–71 (2015). https://doi.org/10.4230/LIPIcs.CONCUR.2015.58

14. Didona, D., Guerraoui, R., Wang, J., Zwaenepoel, W.: Causal consistency and latency optimality: friend or foe? PVLDB **11**(11), 1618–1632 (2018). https://doi.org/10.14778/3236187.3236210. http://www.vldb.org/pvldb/vol11/p1618-didona.pdf

15. Doherty, S., Dongol, B., Wehrheim, H., Derrick, J.: Making linearizability compositional for partially ordered executions. In: Integrated Formal Methods - 14th International Conference, IFM 2018, Maynooth, Ireland, 5–7 September 2018, Proceedings, pp. 110–129 (2018). https://doi.org/10.1007/978-3-319-98938-9_7

16. Emmi, M., Enea, C.: Weak-consistency specification via visibility relaxation. Proc. ACM Program. Lang. 3(POPL), 60:1–60:28 (2019). https://doi.org/10.1145/3290373

17. Emmi, M., Enea, C., Hamza, J.: Monitoring refinement via symbolic reasoning. In: Proceedings of the 36th ACM SIGPLAN Conference on Programming Language Design and Implementation, Portland, OR, USA, 15–17 June 2015, pp. 260–269 (2015). https://doi.org/10.1145/2737924.2737983

18. Gomes, V.B.F., Kleppmann, M., Mulligan, D.P., Beresford, A.R.: Verifying strong eventual consistency in distributed systems. PACMPL **1**(OOPSLA), 109:1–109:28 (2017). https://doi.org/10.1145/3133933

19. Gotsman, A., Yang, H., Ferreira, C., Najafzadeh, M., Shapiro, M.: 'cause i'm strong enough: reasoning about consistency choices in distributed systems. In: Proceedings of the 43rd Annual ACM SIGPLAN-SIGACT Symposium on Principles of Programming Languages, POPL 2016, St. Petersburg, FL, USA, 20–22 January 2016, pp. 371–384 (2016). https://doi.org/10.1145/2837614.2837625
20. Hendler, D., Shavit, N., Yerushalmi, L.: A scalable lock-free stack algorithm. In: SPAA 2004: Proceedings of the Sixteenth Annual ACM Symposium on Parallelism in Algorithms and Architectures, Barcelona, Spain, 27–30 June 2004, pp. 206–215 (2004). https://doi.org/10.1145/1007912.1007944
21. Herlihy, M., Shavit, N.: The Art of Multiprocessor Programming. Morgan Kaufmann Publishers Inc., San Francisco (2008)
22. Herlihy, M., Wing, J.M.: Linearizability: a correctness condition for concurrent objects. ACM Trans. Program. Lang. Syst. **12**(3), 463–492 (1990). https://doi.org/10.1145/78969.78972
23. Houshmand, F., Lesani, M.: Hamsaz: replication coordination analysis and synthesis. PACMPL **3**(POPL), 74:1–74:32 (2019). https://dl.acm.org/citation.cfm?id=3290387
24. Jepsen. https://jepsen.io. Accessed 27 Jan 2019
25. Kaki, G., Earanky, K., Sivaramakrishnan, K.C., Jagannathan, S.: Safe replication through bounded concurrency verification. PACMPL **2**(OOPSLA), 164:1–164:27 (2018). https://doi.org/10.1145/3276534
26. Lightweight transactions in cassandra. https://docs.datastax.com/en/cql/3.3/cql/cql_using/useInsertLWT.html. Accessed 2 Dec 2019
27. Lloyd, W., Freedman, M.J., Kaminsky, M., Andersen, D.G.: Don't settle for eventual: scalable causal consistency for wide-area storage with COPS. In: Proceedings of the 23rd ACM Symposium on Operating Systems Principles 2011, SOSP 2011, Cascais, Portugal, 23–26 October 2011, pp. 401–416 (2011). https://doi.org/10.1145/2043556.2043593
28. Mehdi, S.A., Littley, C., Crooks, N., Alvisi, L., Bronson, N., Lloyd, W.: I can't believe it's not causal! scalable causal consistency with no slowdown cascades. In: 14th USENIX Symposium on Networked Systems Design and Implementation, NSDI 2017, Boston, MA, USA, 27–29 March 2017, pp. 453–468 (2017). https://www.usenix.org/conference/nsdi17/technical-sessions/presentation/mehdi
29. Michael, M.M., Scott, M.L.: Simple, fast, and practical non-blocking and blocking concurrent queue algorithms. In: Proceedings of the Fifteenth Annual ACM Symposium on Principles of Distributed Computing, Philadelphia, Pennsylvania, USA, 23–26 May 1996, pp. 267–275 (1996). https://doi.org/10.1145/248052.248106
30. Nagar, K., Jagannathan, S.: Automated detection of serializability violations under weak consistency. In: 29th International Conference on Concurrency Theory, CONCUR 2018, Beijing, China, 4–7 September 2018, pp. 41:1–41:18 (2018). https://doi.org/10.4230/LIPIcs.CONCUR.2018.41
31. Nagar, K., Jagannathan, S.: Automated parameterized verification of CRDTs. In: Computer Aided Verification - 31st International Conference, CAV 2019, New York City, NY, USA, 15–18 July 2019, Proceedings, Part II, pp. 459–477 (2019). https://doi.org/10.1007/978-3-030-25543-5_26
32. Nagar, K., Mukherjee, P., Jagannathan, S.: Semantics, Specification and Bounded Verification of Concurrent Libraries in Replicated Systems (Extended Version). https://arxiv.org/abs/2004.10158
33. Peierls, T., Goetz, B., Bloch, J., Bowbeer, J., Lea, D., Holmes, D.: Java Concurrency in Practice. Addison-Wesley Professional, Reading (2005)

34. Raad, A., Doko, M., Rozic, L., Lahav, O., Vafeiadis, V.: On library correctness under weak memory consistency: specifying and verifying concurrent libraries under declarative consistency models. PACMPL **3**(POPL), 68:1–68:31 (2019). https://doi.org/10.1145/3290381

35. Rahmani, K., Nagar, K., Delaware, B., Jagannathan, S.: CLOTHO: directed test generation for weakly consistent database systems. PACMPL **3**(OOPSLA), 117:1–117:28 (2019). https://doi.org/10.1145/3360543

36. Shapiro, M., Preguiça, N., Baquero, C., Zawirski, M.: A comprehensive study of Convergent and Commutative Replicated Data Types. Technical report, RR-7506, INRIA, Inria - Centre Paris-Rocquencourt (2011)

37. Shavit, N.: Data structures in the multicore age. Commun. ACM **54**(3), 76–84 (2011). https://doi.org/10.1145/1897852.1897873

38. Sivaramakrishnan, K.C., Kaki, G., Jagannathan, S.: Declarative programming over eventually consistent data stores. In: Proceedings of the 36th ACM SIGPLAN Conference on Programming Language Design and Implementation, Portland, OR, USA, 15–17 June 2015, pp. 413–424 (2015). https://doi.org/10.1145/2737924.2737981

39. Terry, D.B., Demers, A.J., Petersen, K., Spreitzer, M., Theimer, M., Welch, B.B.: Session guarantees for weakly consistent replicated data. In: Proceedings of the Third International Conference on Parallel and Distributed Information Systems (PDIS 94), Austin, Texas, USA, 28–30 September 1994, pp. 140–149 (1994). https://doi.org/10.1109/PDIS.1994.331722

40. Treiber, R.K.: Systems programming: coping with parallelism. International Business Machines Incorporated, Thomas J. Watson Research (1986)

41. Wang, C., Enea, C., Mutluergil, S.O., Petri, G.: Replication-aware linearizability. In: Proceedings of the 40th ACM SIGPLAN Conference on Programming Language Design and Implementation, PLDI 2019, Phoenix, AZ, USA, 22–26 June 2019, pp. 980–993 (2019). https://doi.org/10.1145/3314221.3314617

42. Zeller, P., Bieniusa, A., Poetzsch-Heffter, A.: Formal specification and verification of CRDTs. In: Formal Techniques for Distributed Objects, Components, and Systems - 34th IFIP WG 6.1 International Conference, FORTE 2014, Held as Part of the 9th International Federated Conference on Distributed Computing Techniques, DisCoTec 2014, Berlin, Germany, 3–5 June 2014, Proceedings, pp. 33–48 (2014). https://doi.org/10.1007/978-3-662-43613-4_3

Refinement for Structured Concurrent Programs

Bernhard Kragl[1]($\boxtimes$) (iD), Shaz Qadeer[2], and Thomas A. Henzinger[1] (iD)

[1] IST Austria, Klosterneuburg, Austria
{bkragl,tah}@ist.ac.at
[2] Novi, Seattle, USA
shaz@fb.com

Abstract. This paper presents a foundation for refining concurrent programs with structured control flow. The verification problem is decomposed into subproblems that aid interactive program development, proof reuse, and automation. The formalization in this paper is the basis of a new design and implementation of the CIVL verifier.

1 Introduction

We present a solution to the problem of proving that no execution of a concurrent program leads to a failure. This problem is equivalent to proving an arbitrary safety property on the program. In *deductive verification*, a proof system decomposes this verification problem into a set of *proof obligations* (or *verification conditions*), and discharging these obligations implies the correctness of the program. At its core, any proof system depends on *inductive invariants*, and, in general, these have to be supplied manually. Inventing an inductive invariant is especially challenging for concurrent programs, since it has to capture complicated relationships over the entire program state, across all concurrent computations. Thus, the main practical obstacle to deductive verification is a suitable interaction mode for the programmer to invent and supply the necessary proof hints. This paper develops and implements a systematic conceptual framework for supplying these proof hints on a structured representation of the concurrent program, specifically eliminating the need to write complex invariants on the low-level encoding of the program as a flat transition system.

The CIVL verifier [18,25] addresses the aforementioned challenge by advocating *layered refinement over structured concurrent programs*. Instead of the monolithic approach that requires the programmer to prove the safety of a program $\mathcal{P}$ directly, CIVL allows the programmer to specify a chain of increasingly simpler programs $\mathcal{P} = \mathcal{P}_0, \mathcal{P}_1, \ldots, \mathcal{P}_n = \mathcal{P}'$ such that the safety of $\mathcal{P}_i$ implies the safety of $\mathcal{P}_{i-1}$ for all $i \in [1, n]$, thus transferring the safety obligation on $\mathcal{P}$ to $\mathcal{P}'$. The overall correctness of the program is established piecemeal by focusing on the invariant required for each refinement step separately. While the programmer does the creative work of specifying the chain of programs and the inductive

S. K. Lahiri and C. Wang (Eds.): CAV 2020, LNCS 12224, pp. 275–298, 2020.
https://doi.org/10.1007/978-3-030-53288-8_14

invariant justifying each link in the chain, the tool automatically constructs the verification conditions underlying each refinement step.

The core principle of a layered refinement proof in CIVL is *iterative program simplification* through two kinds of creative reasoning. First, the programmer must think about the primitive atomic actions used to specify a particular program $\mathcal{P}_i$ in the chain of programs. These atomic actions must be chosen to have useful commutativity properties which allow the tool to provably eliminate preemptions at many control locations in $\mathcal{P}_i$, thus creating large preemption-free execution fragments. Second, the programmer must think about the justification for the transformation of $\mathcal{P}_i$ into the next program $\mathcal{P}_{i+1}$. This transformation may be complex because (1) some of the variables in $\mathcal{P}_i$ may become irrelevant, (2) new variables may be needed for the primitive atomic actions in $\mathcal{P}_{i+1}$, and (3) the transformation may simplify complex control flow (branching, procedure calls, recursion, etc.) into a single step that executes an atomic action. This paper focuses on the necessary foundation and tool support for this second kind of creative reasoning.

We present our technique on an idealized yet general language RefPL, suitable for expressing structured parallelism, asynchronous computation, atomic actions of arbitrary granularity, and dynamically-scoped preemption-free code fragments. Using the design of RefPL and the formalization of its operational semantics, we present two technical contributions.

Our first contribution is a general proof rule for soundly abstracting a recursive RefPL program $\mathcal{P}$ into another RefPL program $\mathcal{P}'$ that hides subsets of global variables, local variables, procedures, and atomic actions in $\mathcal{P}$. Our proof rule goes beyond CIVL in two ways. First, it provides the capability to hide local variables of procedures, specifically parameters, in addition to global variables. This capability allows us to replace a procedure with an atomic action with a smaller interface by hiding the extra parameters. Refinement proofs are simplified because it becomes easy to introduce local snapshots of global variables needed for specifications, pass these snapshots around as parameters to procedures, and finally recover the original interface by hiding these extra parameters. Second, unlike CIVL our proof rule is capable of performing refinement proofs on arbitrarily recursive programs. Since hiding low-level details is the core principle of the layered refinement methodology, our proof rule contributes towards increasing the expressiveness of refinement proofs compared to CIVL.

Our proof rule depends on invariants that constrain the reachable states of the program. Our second contribution, an aid to our refinement rule but also independently useful, is a new specification idiom called *yield invariants*—named, parameterized, and interference-free invariants that can be called in parallel with ordinary procedures to soundly constrain the interference possible at yields within the called procedure. Since a yield invariant is named, its definition is separate from its invocation, thereby allowing proofs of interference-freedom to be performed once and reused for each call site. Since it is parameterized, it can be specialized to the needs of a call site by passing suitable input parameters.

Reasoning with yield invariants becomes difficult in concurrent programs when the absence of interference must be justified using facts referring to local variables of different procedures executing in different threads. The alternative of using global ghost variables that have the same information as local variables is theoretically possible but impossibly tedious. We observe that local proofs for many of these programming patterns can be achieved by exploiting *permissions* that are redistributed by atomic actions and otherwise passed around the program without duplication via input and output parameters of procedures. To track permissions, we enhance the interface of yield invariants, procedures, and atomic actions with annotations that satisfy a discipline enforced by a combination of linear typing [38] over procedure bodies and logical reasoning over the transitions of atomic actions.

The formalization in this paper is the basis of a new design and implementation of the CIVL verifier. We hope that CIVL will serve researchers as a viable platform for experimenting with optimizations and implementation decisions.

To summarize, this paper makes the following contributions:

- It presents a core language RefPL for expressing modular proofs of refinement over structured concurrent programs. The formulation of refinement for RefPL is general and allows the user to encode verification of an arbitrary safety property as refinement verification. Furthermore, RefPL enables the construction of layered proofs [25] of safety via iterated refinement.
- A refinement proof for RefPL is modular and decomposed along program syntax through the use of yield invariants. The interfaces to procedures, actions, and yield invariants exploit a linear typing discipline [38] that enhances local verification through the use of permissions.
- Finally, we present a robust implementation of the refinement rule and yield invariants in the CIVL verifier.

1.1 Related Work

Formal verification techniques based on stepwise refinement have long been advocated, in theory, for construction of verified programs (e.g., [5,35,36]). This paper takes its inspiration from TLA [28] and Event-B [3,4] which popularized refinement as an approach for reasoning about a concurrent program modeled as a transition system. Recent efforts [10,16,17] have developed support for development of verified programs atop the foundation of refinement over transition systems. Our work develops a foundation and tool support for refinement over structured concurrent programs rather than flat transition systems. We are encouraged by broad interest in the use of automatic program simplification [12,15] to reduce the complexity of reasoning about concurrent programs.

The technique of yield invariants is inspired by interference-free location invariants in the work of Owicki and Gries [34] and the rely specification in rely-guarantee reasoning [21]. Yield invariants attempt to import the reuse of rely specifications to location invariants. We introduce linear interfaces to encode permissions to address the practical concern of unwieldy ghost state. While permissions have been used before for encoding ownership in heap-manipulating programs [32], our encoding of permissions is different, applicable to any shared resource, and targeted specifically at noninterference reasoning.

There are other efforts to build practical verifiers for concurrent programs. Some verifiers focus on automation and target specific programming models and languages [7,11,20,29]. Our verifier is just as automated but capable of targeting a variety of programming models because of the foundation of atomic actions in RefPL. Other verifiers share our focus on expressiveness by providing general and certified metatheory [22] but are less automated; our verifier attempts to increase expressiveness without sacrificing automation. None of these aforementioned verifiers focus on refinement and layered proofs.

Our work bears a superficial resemblance to proof methods [8,23,37] for linearizability [19]. Our work targets the general problem of safety verification. Linearizability is a specific safety property to which our method is applicable.

2   Overview

In this section, we illustrate our contributions on a set of example programs. Section 2.1 presents yield invariants, Sect. 2.2 presents refinement, and Sect. 2.3 presents linear interfaces.

2.1   Yield Invariants

Figure 1 shows a simple RefPL program. The first column shows a global counter x, a procedure incr_x that increments x twice, and a yield invariant yield_x that characterizes the interference from other threads while a thread is executing incr_x. The increments of x on lines 4 and 6 are separated by a call to the yield invariant yield_x. RefPL provides a single call statement for calling any number (including zero) of procedures and yield invariants in parallel. The preserves specification on line 3 indicates that yield_x is both a precondition (usually indicated by requires) and a postcondition (usually indicated by ensures). In RefPL, each precondition of a procedure is a call to a yield invariant; all preconditions are called in parallel at procedure entry. Similarly, each postcondition is a call to a yield invariant; all postconditions are called in parallel at procedure exit.

This paper focuses on reasoning about cooperative semantics in which preemptions occur only at entry into a procedure, at a call during its execution, and at exit. The RefPL verifier proves the correctness of yield_x and incr_x modularly on these cooperative semantics. Specifically, the yield invariant yield_x is proved interference-free since the only operations in the program that modify x increment it. The procedure incr_x is proved by using the precondition of incr_x to establish the yield invariant at line 5 and then using the yield invariant to prove the postcondition at exit. This proof of incr_x depends on the observation that the input parameter _x of incr_x is passed as the argument to the three calls to yield_x: in the precondition, on line 5, and in the postcondition. The second

```
1   var x: int // ≥ 0              9   var y: int // ≥ 0              17  procedure incr_x_y()
                                                                      18    requires yield_x(0)
2   procedure incr_x(_x: int)      10  procedure incr_y(_y: int)      19    requires yield_y(0)
3     preserves yield_x(_x)        11    preserves yield_y(_y)        20    if (∗)
4     x := x + 1                   12    y := y + 1                   21      async incr_x_y()
5     call yield_x(_x)             13    call yield_y(_y)             22    call incr_x(0) || yield_y(0)
6     x := x + 1                   14    y := y + 1                   23    call incr_y(0) || yield_x(0)
                                                                      24    assert 0 ≤ x ∧ 0 ≤ y
7   invariant yield_x(_x: int)     15  invariant yield_y(_y: int)
8     _x ≤ x                       16    _y ≤ y
```

Fig. 1. Incrementing two separate counters to illustrate yield invariants.

column shows code similar to what we just discussed, except on global variable y, procedure incr_y, and yield invariant yield_y.

The third column show a procedure incr_x_y which uses recursion to create an unbounded number of concurrent threads. incr_x_y nondeterministically spawns a copy of itself on lines 20–21, calls procedures to increment x and y on lines 22–23, and asserts a safety property about x and y on line 24. Our verification goal is to prove that if a single instance of incr_x_y starts in a state that satisfies the initial constraints on x and y, indicated on lines 1 and 9 respectively, then the assertion on line 24 holds in every copy of incr_x_y.

The proof of procedure incr_x_y shows the modularity of yield invariants. First, notice that no new yield invariants are needed; the entire proof of incr_x_y is achieved by reusing yield_x and yield_y. Specifically, yield_x and yield_y are called in parallel with each other at entry, yield_y is called in parallel with incr_x at line 22, and yield_x is called in parallel with incr_y at line 23. Second, the arguments to yield_x and yield_y are specialized to match the constraints in the initial state and the assertions.

2.2   Refining Atomic Actions

Figure 2 shows a spin lock implementation and a client that uses the spin lock to atomically increment a shared counter. Procedure Acquire (lines 22–28) acquires the lock and procedure Release (lines 29–34) releases the lock. Both procedures use a primitive atomic action CAS (compare-and-swap) defined on lines 10–14 with two parameters—old_b and new_b. This action compares the value of a global variable b to old_b. If they are equal, b is set to new_b and true is returned, otherwise, b is not modified and false is returned. Acquire attempts to set b from false to true repeatedly via recursive call to itself (line 28) until it succeeds. Release sets b back to false from true.

Procedure Incr (lines 16–21) atomically increments the global variable count by acquiring the lock, reading count into a local variable t by calling Read (lines 35–39), writing t+1 back to count by calling Write (lines 40–43), and finally releasing the lock. We prove that Incr implements an atomic increment via a sequence of two refinement steps.

The first step abstracts the procedures Acquire, Release, Read, and Write into atomic actions AcquireSpec, ReleaseSpec, ReadSpec, and WriteSpec, respectively.

```
 1   // Concrete global variables      22   procedure Acquire(             44   action AcquireSpec(
 2   var b: bool // false              23     linear tid: Tid)             45     linear tid: Tid)
 3   var count: int                    24   refines AcquireSpec            46     assume l = None
                                       25   preserves LockInv()           47     l := Some(tid)
 4   // Abstract global variable       26     exec t := CAS(false, true)
 5   var l: Option⟨Tid⟩ // None        27     if (t) l := Some(tid)
                                       28     else call Acquire(tid)
 6   // Supporting invariant
 7   invariant LockInv()               29   procedure Release(             48   action ReleaseSpec(
 8     b ⟺ (l ≠ None)                  30     linear tid: Tid)             49     linear tid: Tid)
                                       31   refines ReleaseSpec           50     assert l = Some(tid)
 9   // Primitive actions              32   preserves LockInv()           51     l := None
10   action CAS(old_b, new_b: bool)    33     exec CAS(true, false)
11   returns (success: bool)           34     l := None
12     success := b = old_b
13     if (success)                    35   procedure Read(               52   action ReadSpec(
14       b := new_b                    36     linear tid: Tid)             53     linear tid: Tid)
                                       37   returns (v: int)              54   returns (v: int)
15   // Atomic increment               38   refines ReadSpec              55     assert l = Some(tid)
16   procedure Incr(linear tid: Tid)   39     v := count;                 56     v := count
17   preserves LockInv()
18     call Acquire(tid)               40   procedure Write(              57   action WriteSpec(
19     call t := Read(tid) || LockInv()  41     linear tid: Tid, v: int)  58     linear tid: Tid, v: int)
20     call Write(tid, t+1) || LockInv()  42   refines WriteSpec          59     assert l = Some(tid)
21     call Release(tid)               43     count := v;                 60     count := v
```

Fig. 2. Spin lock to illustrate refinement of atomic actions.

These atomic actions, defined in the third column of Fig. 2, provide an explicit specification of the locking protocol for accessing the shared variable count. The specification of these actions requires the introduction of (1) a local parameter tid containing the unique id of the thread executing the code, and (2) a global variable l whose value is either None when the lock is not held or Some(tid) when the lock is held by thread tid. The second step uses these atomic actions to abstract Incr to an atomic action that increments count by 1.

There are two challenges in the first refinement proof. First, the lock implementation is defined using the concrete Boolean variable b, whereas the lock specification is defined using the logical lock variable l. Second, the implementation of Acquire is recursive, which is technically challenging for refinement reasoning. The solution to the first problem is to *introduce* l and *hide* b during the refinement proof. To introduce l into the concrete program, it is updated appropriately when Acquire (line 27) and Release (line 34) complete successfully. Furthermore, the relationship between the variables b and l is captured by the yield invariant LockInv (lines 7–8) which is used in the precondition and postcondition of Acquire and Release. The solution to the second problem is a powerful rule for refinement reasoning, described in Sect. 4, which allows the recursive call to Acquire on line 28 to be replaced by a call to the specification AcquireSpec while modularly proving that the body of Acquire refines AcquireSpec.

To set up the second refinement proof, the procedure calls in the body of Incr are replaced by invocations of the corresponding abstract atomic actions (as shown on the right here). The rewritten body of Incr is preemption-free; a yield may occur only at the beginning or the end. This assumption is justified by a commutativity analy-

```
procedure Incr(linear tid: Tid)
refines IncrSpec
  exec AcquireSpec(tid)
  exec t := ReadSpec(tid)
  exec WriteSpec(tid, t+1)
  exec ReleaseSpec(tid)

action IncrSpec()
  count := count + 1
```

sis based on the observation that AcquireSpec is a right mover, ReleaseSpec is a left mover, and ReadSpec and WriteSpec are both movers [14]. Proving these mover types requires that the tid input parameters of two concurrent actions are distinct, which is specified by the *linear* annotation. In addition to encoding distinctness of values, linear variables can be used for encoding disjointness of permissions associated with values. We present an example illustrating permissions in Sect. 2.3 and a detailed technical description in Sect. 4.

For the prove that procedure Incr refines the action IncrSpec, which increments count atomically, we do not need the invariant LockInv anymore; in fact we do not need any invariant. Furthermore, the local parameter tid and the global variable l are no longer needed in the program and can be hidden. Hiding local variables is a novel feature of the refinement method described in this paper. The capability to introduce and subsequently hide global and local variables allows us to chain a sequence of refinement steps, localizing the use of variables to the parts of the proof that need them.

2.3   Linear Interfaces

Figure 3 shows a synchronization protocol extracted from a verified concurrent garbage collector [18]. There are N mutator threads (procedure Mutator on line 28) numbered from 1 to N, and one collector thread (procedure Collector on line 38) with ID 0. The protocol ensures that no mutator accesses memory (line 37) concurrently while the collector is doing a root scan (line 44) using barrier synchronization. Before the collector runs, it sets the Boolean variable barrierOn to true (line 40) and waits until the integer variable barrierCounter gets 0 (line 42). Before a mutator accesses memory, it reads barrierOn (line 31). If false, the mutator goes ahead. Otherwise, it signals to the collector by decrementing barrierCounter (line 34) and waits for barrierOn to be reset to false (line 36).

This example declares both global and local *linear variables* (specified by *linear*, *linear_in*, *linear_out*). Every linear variable—or more precisely, its current value—is assigned a set of *permissions* of type Perm according to the *collector functions* C1, C2, and C3. A linear integer i holds both Left(i) and Right(i), a set of integers holds the corresponding Left permissions, and a Perm value holds itself. Note that Perm is not special; any value can be a permission. For every program location we can compute the set of *available* linear variables. For example, when a mutator enters the barrier (line 34), i becomes *unavailable* because the permission Left(i) is transferred to the ghost variable mutatorsInBarrier. Then i becomes available again after exiting the barrier (line 36). Global linear variables (mutatorsInBarrier here) are always available. Parameterized by the linear collectors, our linearity framework establishes the generic invariant that all permissions across all available linear variables are disjoint. Now suppose that some mutator i is at line 37, where it holds both of its permissions and in particular Left(i), while the collector is at line 45, where mutatorsInBarrier holds all Left permissions and in particular Left(i). This situation is impossible, since the linearity feature of RefPL ensures that a duplication of permissions is impossible.

```
1   datatype Perm = Left(int) | Right(int)

2   function linear C1(i: int) = {Left(i), Right(i)}
3   function linear C2(ids: Set⟨int⟩) = {Left(i) | i ∈ ids}
4   function linear C3(p: Perm) = {p}

5   const N: int // positive
6   var barrierOn: bool // false
7   var barrierCounter: int // N
8   var linear mutatorsInBarrier: Set⟨int⟩ // ∅

9   // Primitive actions
10  action IsBarrierOn() returns (b: bool)
11    b := barrierOn

12  action EnterBarrier(linear_in i: int)
13  returns (linear_out p: Perm)
14    assert i ∈ [1..N]
15    mutatorsInBarrier := mutatorsInBarrier + {i}
16    barrierCounter := barrierCounter − 1
17    p := Right(i)

18  action WaitForBarrierRelease
19    (linear_in p: Perm, linear_out i: int)
20    assert p = Right(i) ∧ i ∈ mutatorsInBarrier
21    assume ¬barrierOn
22    mutatorsInBarrier := mutatorsInBarrier − {i}
23    barrierCounter := barrierCounter + 1

24  action SetBarrier(b: bool)
25    barrierOn := b

26  action WaitBarrier()
27    assume barrierCounter = 0
```

```
28  procedure Mutator(linear i: int)
29  requires i ∈ [1..N] preserves BarrierInv()
30    var b: bool, p: Perm
31    exec b := IsBarrierOn()
32    if (b)
33      call BarrierInv()
34      exec p := EnterBarrier(i)
35      call BarrierInv() || MutatorInv(p, i)
36      exec WaitForBarrierRelease(p, i)
37      // access memory here

38  procedure Collector(linear i: int)
39  requires i = 0 preserves BarrierInv()
40    exec SetBarrier(true)
41    call BarrierInv() || CollectorInv(i, false)
42    exec WaitBarrier()
43    call BarrierInv() || CollectorInv(i, true)
44    // do root scan here
45    assert mutatorsInBarrier = [1..N]
46    exec SetBarrier(false)

47  // Supporting invariants
48  invariant BarrierInv()
49    mutatorsInBarrier ⊆ [1..N] ∧
50    size(mutatorsInBarrier) + barrierCounter = N

51  invariant MutatorInv(linear p: Perm, i: int)
52    p = Right(i) ∧ i ∈ mutatorsInBarrier

53  invariant CollectorInv(linear i: int, done: bool)
54    i = 0 ∧ barrierOn ∧
55    (done ⟹ mutatorsInBarrier = [1..N])
```

Fig. 3. Barrier synchronization to illustrate linear interfaces.

The strength of linearity, which leads to a less tedious verification task, is that its invariant connects variables from different scopes, without the need to explicitly state (and prove) this invariant. The programmer only provides a linearity specification which is checked automatically (see Sect. 4). The resulting guarantees can then be assumed "for free". In contrast, even stating a corresponding invariant requires the introduction of auxiliary global variables and helper invariants to connect them to local variables.

3   RefPL: Syntax and Semantics

In this section we present RefPL, a core programming language which is carefully designed to be (1) a minimal yet general modeling language to express concurrent programs, (2) able to express invariants over program executions, and (3) suitable for expressing (refinement-based) program transformations. RefPL focuses on interfaces for modular verification, while abstracting from detailed expression syntax and types.

Syntax. Figure 4 (top panel) summarizes the syntax of RefPL. We assume sets of *names* which we use to name actions (A), procedures (P, Q), yield invariants (Y), and statement labels (λ). A set of *variables* is partitioned into *global* and *local variables*, and a *store* σ is a partial map from variables to *values*. We write $\sigma' \subseteq \sigma$ if σ is an extension of σ', $\sigma|_V$ for the restriction of σ to V, $\sigma[\sigma']$ for the store that is like σ' on $\mathrm{dom}(\sigma')$ and otherwise like σ, and $g \cdot \ell$ for the combination of a *global* and *local store*. A *program* consists of a finite set of global variables gs, a partial map as from action names to actions, and a partial map ps from procedure names to procedures. Both actions and procedures have an interface of *input variables* I and *output variables* O, and procedures have additional *local variables* L. A *(gated atomic) action* [13,26] consists of a *gate* ρ and a *transition relation* τ. The gate is a set of stores (i.e., a predicate) over $gs \cup I$. Executing the action in a state that does not satisfy the gate fails the execution. Otherwise, every transition $(\sigma, \sigma', \Omega)$ in τ describes a possible atomic state transition from σ (over $gs \cup I$) to σ' (over $gs \cup O$), together with the creation of new asynchronous threads according to a set of *pending asyncs* Ω; every pending async $(\ell, P) \in \Omega$ is turned into a new thread that executes procedure P with input store ℓ. A *procedure* consists of a *statement* s that is composed of standard control-flow commands and two call commands: `exec` to invoke actions and `call` for the parallel invocation of multiple procedures. Every entry in the invocation sequence of a `call` is called an *arm* of the call, and the *label* λ is used to attach specification information to the call. Parameter passing is expressed using an *input map* ι from the callee's formals I to the caller's actuals $I \cup O \cup L$, and an injective *output map* o from the callee's formals O to the caller's actuals $O \cup L$. Input variables are immutable, since they are not mapped to by output maps and the variables of a procedure are not modified anywhere else. Output and local variables of a procedure are initialized to the default value ❄. In RefPL, loops are modeled using recursion, and conditional statements are modeled using nondeterministic branching ($*$) and actions that assume the branching condition.

Type Checking. For a program we require that (1) the action name in an `exec` statement is in $\mathrm{dom}(as)$, (2) the procedure names in a `call` statement are in $\mathrm{dom}(ps)$, and the actual outputs of all arms are disjoint from each other and all actual inputs, and (3) for every pending async (ℓ, P) in the transition relation of an action in $\mathrm{img}(as)$, $P \in \mathrm{dom}(ps)$ and $\mathrm{dom}(\ell)$ contains all inputs of P.

Semantics. Figure 4 (bottom panel) presents the operational semantics of RefPL, a transition relation $\Rightarrow$ over *configurations* that consist of a global store over gs and a finite multiset of threads. Each thread is a tree (which generalizes a call stack); a `call` statement creates new leaf nodes (Lf) and blocks the caller in an internal node (Nd) until all arms of the parallel call finish. Each tree node contains a *frame* (P, ℓ, s) that represents the current state of a procedure P during execution: ℓ is the procedure's current local store and s is a statement that remains to be executed. In the definition of $\Rightarrow$ we use several evaluation contexts that have a unique hole •; filling the hole is denoted by $\cdot[\cdot]$. In particular, $SC[s]$ is a statement with s in evaluation position, and $PC[t]$ is a multiset of thread trees where t is a subtree in one of these trees. The operator $\circ$ means function or relation composition.

Atomic actions (invoked through the `exec` command) execute directly in the context of the caller; inline, if you will. If the current store does not satisfy the gate of an executed action, the execution stops in the *failure configuration* ↯. It is important to appreciate the generality of atomic actions. First, they can rep-

$$A \in \mathit{ActionName} \quad P, Q \in \mathit{ProcName} \quad Y \in \mathit{InvName} \quad \lambda \in \mathit{Label}$$

$$
\begin{aligned}
\mathit{Val} &\quad \ni \ \circledast & s \in \mathit{Stmt} &::= \ | \ \mathtt{skip} \ | \ s \,;\, s \ | \ s * s \\
v \in \mathit{Var} &= \mathit{GVar} \cup \mathit{LVar} & &\quad | \ \mathtt{call}_\lambda \ \overline{(P, \iota, o)} \ | \ \mathtt{exec}\,(A, \iota, o) \\
g \in \mathit{GStore} &= \mathit{GVar} \rightharpoonup \mathit{Val} & I, O, L &\in \ 2^{\mathit{LVar}} \\
\ell \in \mathit{LStore} &= \mathit{LVar} \rightharpoonup \mathit{Val} & \mathit{Action} &::= (I, O, \rho, \tau) \\
\sigma \in \mathit{Store} &= \mathit{Var} \rightharpoonup \mathit{Val} & \mathit{Proc} &::= (I, O, L, s) \\
\rho \in \mathit{Gate} &= 2^{\mathit{Store}} & gs &\in \ 2^{\mathit{GVar}} \\
\tau \in \mathit{Trans} &= 2^{\mathit{Store} \times \mathit{Store} \times \mathit{PASet}} & as &\in \ \mathit{ActionName} \rightharpoonup \mathit{Action} \\
\Omega \in \mathit{PASet} &= 2^{\mathit{LStore} \times \mathit{ProcName}} & ps &\in \ \mathit{ProcName} \rightharpoonup \mathit{Proc} \\
\iota, o \in \mathit{IOMap} &= \mathit{LVar} \rightharpoonup \mathit{LVar} & \mathcal{P} \in \mathit{Prog} &::= (gs, as, ps)
\end{aligned}
$$

$$
\begin{aligned}
\mathit{Inv} &::= (I, \rho) & lg &\in \ 2^{\mathit{GVar}} \\
\mathit{InvCall} &::= (Y, \iota) & li &\in \ (\mathit{ActionName} \cup \mathit{ProcName} \cup \mathit{InvName}) \\
ys &\in \ \mathit{InvName} \rightharpoonup \mathit{Inv} & &\quad \times \{\rhd, \lhd\} \rightharpoonup 2^{\mathit{LVar}} \\
\mathit{pre}, \mathit{post} &\in \ \mathit{ProcName} \rightharpoonup 2^{\mathit{InvCall}} & lo &\in \ (\mathit{ActionName} \cup \mathit{ProcName}) \rightharpoonup 2^{\mathit{LVar}} \\
\mathit{inv} &\in \ \mathit{Label} \rightharpoonup 2^{\mathit{InvCall}} & lc &\in \ \mathit{Val} \rightarrow 2^{\mathit{Val}} \\
\mathcal{Y} &::= (ys, \mathit{pre}, \mathit{post}, \mathit{inv}) & \mathcal{L} &::= (lg, li, lo, lc)
\end{aligned}
$$

$$
\begin{aligned}
\mathit{ref} &\in \ \mathit{ProcName} \rightharpoonup \mathit{ActionName} \\
\mathit{mark} &\in \ \mathit{Label} \rightharpoonup \{\square, \blacksquare\} \cup \mathbb{N} \\
\mathcal{R} &::= (\mathit{ref}, \mathit{mark})
\end{aligned}
$$

$$
\begin{aligned}
f &::= (P, \ell, s) & SC &::= \bullet_s \ | \ SC \,;\, s \\
t &::= \mathsf{Lf}\, f \ | \ \mathsf{Nd}\, f\, \overline{t} & TC &::= \bullet_t \ | \ \mathsf{Nd}\, f\, \overline{t}TC\overline{t} \\
\mathcal{T} &::= \{t, \dots, t\} & PC &::= \{TC\} \uplus \mathcal{T} \\
c &::= (g, \mathcal{T}) \ | \ \lightning & LC &::= PC[\mathsf{Lf}\,(P, \bullet_\ell, SC)]
\end{aligned}
$$

$$\text{for } ps(Q) = (I, O, L, s) \text{ let}$$
$$\mathit{init}(Q, \ell) = (Q, \ell|_I \cup [v \mapsto \circledast]_{v \in O \cup L}, s)$$

(call) $(g, PC[\mathsf{Lf}\,(P, \ell, SC[\mathtt{call}_\lambda\, \overline{(Q_i, \iota_i, o_i)}])]) \Rightarrow$
$\qquad (g, PC[\mathsf{Nd}\,(P, \ell, SC[\mathtt{call}_\lambda\, \overline{(Q_i, \iota_i, o_i)}])\ \overline{\mathsf{Lf}\,\mathit{init}(Q_i, \ell \circ \iota_i)}])$

(return) $(g, PC[\mathsf{Nd}\,(P, \ell, SC[\mathtt{call}_\lambda\, \overline{(Q_i, \iota_i, o_i)}])\ \overline{\mathsf{Lf}\,(Q_i, \ell_i, \mathtt{skip})}]) \Rightarrow$
$\qquad (g, PC[\mathsf{Lf}\,(P, \ell[\overline{\ell_i \circ o_i^{-1}}], SC[\mathtt{skip}])])$

(exec) $\dfrac{as(A) = (\_, \_, \rho, \tau) \quad \tilde{g} \subseteq g \quad (\tilde{g} \cdot (\ell \circ \iota), \hat{g} \cdot \hat{\ell}, \Omega) \in \rho \circ \tau}{}$
$\dfrac{g' = g[\hat{g}] \quad \ell' = \ell[\hat{\ell} \circ o^{-1}] \quad T' = \{\mathsf{Lf}\,\mathit{init}(Q, \ell'') \mid (\ell'', Q) \in \Omega\}}{(g, PC[\mathsf{Lf}\,(P, \ell, SC[\mathtt{exec}\,(A, \iota, o)])]) \Rightarrow (g', PC[\mathsf{Lf}\,(P, \ell', SC[\mathtt{skip}])] \uplus T')}$

(fail) $\dfrac{as(A) = (\_, \_, \rho, \_) \quad \neg \exists \tilde{g} \subseteq g : \tilde{g} \cdot (\ell \circ \iota) \in \rho}{(g, LC[\ell][\mathtt{exec}\,(A, \iota, o)]) \Rightarrow \lightning}$ **(choice)** $\dfrac{s' \in \{s_1, s_2\}}{(g, LC[\ell][s_1 * s_2]) \Rightarrow (g, LC[\ell][s'])}$

(skip) $(g, LC[\ell][\mathtt{skip}\,;\, s]) \Rightarrow (g, LC[\ell][s])$ **(stop)** $(g, \{\mathsf{Lf}\,(\_, \mathtt{skip})\} \uplus \mathcal{T}) \Rightarrow (g, \mathcal{T})$

Fig. 4. The programming language RefPL: syntax (top panel), proof annotations (middle panel), and operational semantics (bottom panel).

resent atomic operations at an arbitrary level of granularity, from fine-grained low-level operations (e.g., as implemented in hardware) to coarse-grained summaries (e.g., obtained as part of a layered proof). Second, the notion of pending asyncs subsumes the need for a dedicated asynchronous call statement, and enables advanced proof techniques for asynchronous programs [24,26]. Finally, all accesses to global variables are confined to atomic actions.

We distinguish between the *preemptive semantics* and the *cooperative semantics* of a program. The preemptive semantics $\Rightarrow$ defines the standard fine-grained behaviors of a concurrent program, where a context switch can happen at any time. A program should be proved correct under its preemptive semantics. However, for reasoning purposes we consider a cooperative semantics, where context switches only happen at procedure calls and returns. We call these locations *yields*. The justification for reducing reasoning about preemptive semantics to cooperative semantics is outside the scope of this paper (CIVL uses commutativity reasoning and a reduction argument).

A leaf node $\mathsf{Lf}(P, \_, s)$ is *yielding*, if it denotes the *entry* or *exit* of procedure P, i.e., if $ps(P) = (\_, \_, \_, s)$ or $s = \mathtt{skip}$. A configuration is *yielding* if all leaves are yielding, and *cooperative* if at most one leaf is not yielding. Then the cooperative semantics is given by restricting $\Rightarrow$ to cooperative configurations. Notice that the configuration after an $\mathtt{exec}$ might be non-yielding. Thus, under cooperative semantics the pending asyncs created by $\mathtt{exec}$ can only start executing once the caller reaches the next yield. We note that arbitrary yields can be modeled with "empty" parallel calls (i.e., a $\mathtt{call}$ with no arms).

A *yield-to-yield fragment* $\{P \mid \kappa_1\} \, \overline{e} \, \{\kappa_2\}$ of a procedure P is any sequence of $\mathtt{exec}$ statements $\overline{e}$ that forms a path in P from κ_1 to κ_2, where κ_1 and κ_2 are either $\mathtt{call}$ statements, $\perp$, or $\top$ ($\kappa_1 = \perp$ for procedure entries; $\kappa_2 = \top$ for procedure exits). For example, procedure Acquire in Fig. 2 has three yield-to-yield fragments: (A1) entry/successful CAS/then branch/exit, (A2) entry/failed CAS/call in the else branch, and (A3) call in the else branch/exit (i.e., an "empty" fragment). Let $Gate(\overline{e})$ be the set of stores from which executing $\overline{e}$ cannot fail, and let $Trans(\overline{e})$ be the set of tuples $(\sigma, \sigma', \Omega)$ where executing $\overline{e}$ from store σ can result in σ' with all created pending asyncs collected in Ω. We define a reduced transition relation $\Rrightarrow$ over yielding configurations, such that $c \Rrightarrow c'$ if and only if there are cooperative but non-yielding configurations $(c_i)_{1 \leq i \leq n \wedge n \geq 0}$ with $c \Rightarrow c_1 \Rightarrow \ldots \Rightarrow c_n \Rightarrow c'$. Thus, every step in $\Rrightarrow$ corresponds to the execution of a yield-to-yield fragment under cooperative semantics.

4   Abstracting **RefPL** Programs

This section presents a proof rule for transforming a concurrent program $\mathcal{P}$ into a concurrent program $\mathcal{P}'$ such that there is a simulation between the cooperative executions of $\mathcal{P}$ and $\mathcal{P}'$. The transformation comprises *variable hiding* ($\mathcal{P}'$ has fewer global and local variables than $\mathcal{P}$) and *procedure abstraction* (procedures in $\mathcal{P}$ are summarized to atomic actions in $\mathcal{P}'$). Our proof rule takes as input a *yield specification* $\mathcal{Y}$, a *linearity specification* $\mathcal{L}$, and a *refinement specification*

$\mathcal{R}$ (see Fig. 4), and decomposes the refinement verification problem as follows.

$$\frac{Linearity(\mathcal{P}, \mathcal{Y}, \mathcal{L}) \quad Safety(\mathcal{P}, \mathcal{Y}, \mathcal{L}) \quad Refinement(\mathcal{P}, \mathcal{Y}, \mathcal{L}, \mathcal{R}, \mathcal{P}')}{\mathcal{Y}, \mathcal{L}, \mathcal{R} \vdash \mathcal{P} \rightsquigarrow \mathcal{P}'}$$

The yield specification declares yield invariants and attaches them to program locations, and the linearity specification declares linear interfaces and sets up a permission discipline (Sect. 4.1). The *Linearity* judgment (Sect. 4.2) ensures that the linear interfaces of procedures, actions, and invariants in $\mathcal{P}$ are valid, which establishes a linear disjointness property. The *Safety* judgment (Sect. 4.3) ensures that preconditions, postconditions, and invariants in $\mathcal{P}$ are valid and interference-free, which captures reachability information in $\mathcal{P}$. Note that *Linearity* and *Safety* interact, as yield invariants can have a linear interface and safety checking assumes the guarantees of linearity checking. In our proof rule, the guarantees of *Linearity* (Lemma 1) and *Safety* (Lemma 2) establish the context for refinement checking. However, we stress that these guarantees are useful on their own, independent of refinement. The refinement specification (Sect. 4.4) declares how $\mathcal{P}$ is converted to $\mathcal{P}'$, and the *Refinement* judgment ensures that every execution of $\mathcal{P}$ is simulated by an execution of $\mathcal{P}'$ (Theorem 1). In Sect. 5 we show how all of our obligations are implemented in practice.

4.1   Yield Invariants and Linear Interfaces

RefPL supports *yield invariants* of the form (I, ρ), where I are input variables and ρ is a gate over $gs \cup I$. In a yield specification $\mathcal{Y} = (ys, pre, post, inv)$, the map ys assigns invariant names to yield invariants, such that invariants can be "invoked" by name—similar to actions and procedures—by supplying an input map ι. We will write φ and ψ for sets of such *invariant calls*, and $\sigma \models \varphi$ to denote that store σ satisfies φ, i.e., $g \cdot \ell \models \varphi \iff \forall (Y, \iota) \in \varphi \; \exists \hat{g} \subseteq g : \hat{g} \cdot (\ell \circ \iota) \in ys(Y).\rho$. Then invariant calls are assigned to program locations as follows: $pre(P)$ are the *preconditions* that must hold on entry to procedure P, $post(P)$ are the *postconditions* that must hold on exit from procedure P, and $inv(\lambda)$ are the invariants that must hold at calls labeled with λ. These are the yield locations in the cooperative semantics, under which we will show the invariants correct and stable under interference.

RefPL supports *linear permissions* to enhance local reasoning. The core idea of linearity is to identify a subset of *(linear) available variables* among all variables in all frames of a configuration. Every value stored in an available variable is mapped to a set of values called *permissions*, with the desired property that the values in available variables are mapped to disjoint permissions. This disjointness property can then be used as free assumption in other verification conditions.

In a linearity specification $\mathcal{L} = (lg, li, lo, lc)$, the *linear global variables* lg are a subset of gs, which are always available. For every action/procedure/invariant name X, $li(X, \triangleright)$ and $li(X, \triangleleft)$ are subsets of its input variables called *linear-in* and *linear-out*, respectively. The linear-ins expect to receive from an available actual parameter, while the linear-outs ensure that their actual parameter will be available upon return. An input variable can be both linear-in and linear-out (which we assume for all invariants). For every action/procedure name X, its *linear outputs* $lo(X)$ are a subset of its output variables, such that the receiving actual return parameters become available when X returns. For example, in Fig. 3 the global variable mutatorsInBarrier is linear, procedure Mutator and yield invariant CollectorInv have a linear (linear-in and linear-out) input i, action EnterBarrier has linear-in input i and linear output p, and WaitFor-BarrierRelease has a linear-in input p and linear-out input i. The permissions assigned to an available variable are determined by a *linear collector* function lc, which is a flexible mechanism to encode various permission disciplines. For convenience, we lift lc to collect all permissions of a set of variables V in store σ, i.e., $lc(\sigma, V) = \biguplus_{v \in V} lc(\sigma(v))$. A simple example of a collector function that expresses unique identifiers (as needed in Fig. 2) would return the singleton set $\{\mathsf{tid}\}$ for a thread identifier variable tid. Figure 3 shows a more advanced usage, where the definition of lc is split across the functions C1, C2, and C3 (see Sect. 2.3).

4.2 Linearity

Let us assign to every (sub)statement s in $\mathcal{P}$ a *linear type* $_{out}^{in}$, written as $s : _{out}^{in}$, where in/out is the set of local variables available directly before/after executing s. Based on the linear interfaces in li and lo, the most general linear types can be inferred, but for simplicity we assume all types to be given and define a type checker below. Since linear types annotate each program location with available variables, we can define the collection of linear permissions over a configuration $c = (g, \mathcal{T})$ as $lc(c) = lc(g, lg) \uplus \left(\biguplus_{(P, \ell, s : _{out}^{in})} lc(\ell, in) \right)$, where $(P, \ell, s : _{out}^{in})$ ranges over all frames in all nodes of $\mathcal{T}$. Then the *linear disjointness property* for a configuration c is $IsSet(lc(c))$, where $IsSet(\cdot)$ states that a multiset does not contain duplicates. We call such a configuration $\mathcal{L}$-*valid*. The $Linearity(\mathcal{P}, \mathcal{Y}, \mathcal{L})$ judgment comprises a semantic check on actions and a syntactic check on procedures, which ensures the preservation of the linear disjointness property as follows.

Lemma 1. *Let c be an $\mathcal{L}$-valid configuration of $\mathcal{P}$. If $c \Rightarrow c'$ then c' is $\mathcal{L}$-valid.*

Essentially, an execution starts with a set of permissions and redistributes these in every step. The permissions can stay the same or decrease, but never increase.

Linear Action Checking. All state updates (other than parameter passing) are confined to atomic actions. We need to ensure that the outgoing permissions of an action are always a subset of the incoming permissions. Thus, for every $A \in \mathrm{dom}(as)$ with $as(A) = (\_, \_, \rho, \tau)$ we check

$$(g \cdot \ell, g' \cdot \ell', \Omega) \in \rho \circ \tau \wedge inPerm = \big(lc(g, lg) \uplus lc(\ell, li(A, \rhd))\big) \wedge IsSet(inPerm) \implies$$

$$\Big(lc(g', lg) \uplus lc(\ell, li(A, \lhd)) \uplus lc(\ell', lo(A)) \uplus \big(\biguplus_{(\ell'', P) \in \Omega} lc(\ell'', li(P, \rhd))\big)\Big) \subseteq inPerm.$$

Starting with a set of permissions in the linear globals and linear-in inputs, the action can redistribute these permissions among the linear globals, its linear-out

$$\frac{out \subseteq in}{\texttt{skip} : {}^{in}_{out}} \qquad \frac{s_1 : {}^{in}_{out} \quad s_2 : {}^{out}_{out'}}{s_1 \,;\, s_2 : {}^{in}_{out'}} \qquad \frac{s_1 : {}^{in}_{out_1} \quad s_2 : {}^{in}_{out_2}}{s_1 \,*\, s_2 : {}^{in}_{out_1 \cap out_2}}$$

$$\frac{\iota(li(A, \rhd)) \subseteq in \quad out \subseteq \big(in \setminus \iota(li(A, \rhd))\big) \uplus \iota(li(A, \lhd)) \uplus o(lo(A))}{\texttt{exec}\,(A, \iota, o) : {}^{in}_{out}}$$

$$\frac{\big(\uplus_i \iota_i(li(P_i, \rhd))\big) \uplus \big(\uplus_{(Y, \iota) \in inv(\lambda)} \iota(li(Y, \rhd))\big) \subseteq in}{out \subseteq \big(in \setminus \uplus_i \iota_i(li(P_i, \rhd))\big) \uplus \big(\uplus_i \iota_i(li(P_i, \lhd))\big) \uplus \big(\uplus_i o_i(lo(P_i))\big)}{\texttt{call}_\lambda \,\overline{(P_i, \iota_i, o_i)} : {}^{in}_{out}}$$

Fig. 5. Linear type checking.

inputs and linear outputs, and the linear-ins of pending asyncs, but permissions cannot appear out of thin air. Notice that this check depends on the user-provided linear collector function lc. For example, consider action EnterBarrier in Fig. 3. The linear-in input i holds the permissions Left(i) and Right(i) on entry (cf. collector C1). By adding i to mutatorsInBarrier we hand over the permission Left(i) (cf. collector C2), and by the assignment to the linear output p we hand over the permission Right(i) (cf. collector C3). Thus, the set of permissions in mutatorsInBarrier and i before is the same as the permissions in mutatorsInBarrier and p after executing EnterBarrier.

Linear Type Checking. Now that we can trust the linear interfaces of actions, we need to ensure that the linear types in procedures "add up" w.r.t. control flow and parameter passing. For every $P \in dom(ps)$ with body $s : {}^{in}_{out}$ we require $in = li(P, \rhd)$, $out = li(P, \lhd) \cup lo(P)$, and a derivation of $s : {}^{in}_{out}$ according to the rules in Fig. 5, where $\iota(V)$ means $\uplus_{v \in V} \iota(v)$. For example, in procedure Mutator in Fig. 3 the linear input parameter i becomes unavailable at line 34, where it is passed as linear-in. However, this call makes the local variable p available, such that it can be passed as linear-in to the call on line 36. This call also passes i as linear-out input, which makes i available again on line 37.

4.3 Safety

In a yielding configuration $(g, \mathcal{T})$, every frame (P, ℓ, s) in $\mathcal{T}$ is associated with a set of invariant calls φ as follows: $\varphi = pre(P)$ if s is the entry of P, $\varphi = post(P)$ if s is $\texttt{skip}$ (the exit of P), or $\varphi = inv(\lambda)$ if s is blocked at a call labeled with λ. If $g \cdot \ell \models \varphi$ holds in every frame, then we call the configuration $\mathcal{Y}$-valid. To show that this property is preserved across the execution of a yield-to-yield fragment (i.e, a step in $\Rightarrow$), the $Safety(\mathcal{P}, \mathcal{Y}, \mathcal{L})$ judgment is decomposed into two kinds of procedure-modular verification conditions: (1) a *sequential check* which ensures that the next φ in the executing frame is established, and (2) a *noninterference check* which ensures that the φ's in all other frames are preserved. Both checks weave in linearity to enhance local reasoning.

Lemma 2. *Let c be an $\mathcal{L}$-valid, $\mathcal{Y}$-valid configuration of $\mathcal{P}$. If $c \Rightarrow c'$ then c' is $\mathcal{Y}$-valid.*

Floyd Packages. For convenience, let $pre(\kappa)$ be the set of all invariants and preconditions of a `call` statement κ (and $post(\kappa)$ analogously):

$$pre(\texttt{call}_\lambda\,\overline{(Q_i, \iota_i, o_i)}) = inv(\lambda) \cup \left(\bigcup_i \{(Y, \iota_i \circ \iota) \mid (Y, \iota) \in pre(Q_i)\} \right)$$

$$post(\texttt{call}_\lambda\,\overline{(Q_i, \iota_i, o_i)}) = inv(\lambda) \cup \left(\bigcup_i \{(Y, (\iota_i \cup o_i) \circ \iota) \mid (Y, \iota) \in post(Q_i)\} \right)$$

For every yield-to-yield fragment $\{P \mid \kappa_1\}\,\overline{e}\,\{\kappa_2\}$ of $P \in dom(ps)$ we define a *Floyd package* $\{P \mid \varphi \mid ll\}\,\overline{e}\,\{\psi\}$, which contains the invariants φ and linear available variables ll before, and the invariants ψ after the yield-to-yield fragment:

$$(\varphi, ll) = \begin{cases} (pre(P)\;\;,\, li(P, \rhd)) & \text{if } \kappa_1 = \bot \\ (post(\kappa_1)\,,\, out(\kappa_1)) & \text{if } \kappa_1 \neq \bot \end{cases}; \qquad \psi = \begin{cases} post(P) & \text{if } \kappa_2 = \top \\ pre(\kappa_2) & \text{if } \kappa_2 \neq \top \end{cases}.$$

Sequential Checking. For every Floyd package $\{P \mid \varphi \mid ll\}\,\overline{e}\,\{\psi\}$ we check

$$\begin{pmatrix} ① \; g \cdot \ell \models \varphi \\ ② \; (g \cdot \ell, g' \cdot \ell', \Omega) \in Trans(\overline{e}) \\ ③ \; IsSet(lc(g \cdot \ell, lg \cup ll)) \end{pmatrix} \implies \begin{pmatrix} ④ \; g' \cdot \ell' \models \psi \\ ⑤ \; \forall (\ell'', P) \in \Omega : g' \cdot \ell'' \models pre(P) \end{pmatrix}.$$

After ② executing $\overline{e}$ from a store with ③ disjoint permissions that ① satisfies φ, it must be the case that ④ ψ and ⑤ the preconditions of all created pending asyncs hold. Notice that we can assume all gates of atomic actions when executing $\overline{e}$. This is the case because yield invariants are not supposed to be strong enough to prove $\mathcal{P}$ safe. Their purpose is to establish the context for refinement checking.

Noninterference Checking. For every Floyd package $\{P \mid \varphi \mid ll\}\,\overline{e}\,\{\psi\}$ and every yield invariant $Y \in dom(ys)$ we check

$$\begin{pmatrix} ① \; g \cdot \ell \models \varphi \wedge g \cdot \ell' \models Y \\ ② \; (g \cdot \ell, g' \cdot \_, \_) \in Trans(\overline{e}) \\ ③ \; IsSet(lc(g \cdot \ell, lg \cup ll) \uplus lc(\ell', li(Y, \rhd))) \end{pmatrix} \implies ④ \; g' \cdot \ell' \models Y.$$

After ② executing $\overline{e}$ from a store with ③ disjoint permissions that ① satisfies both φ and Y, it must be the case that ④ Y still holds. A key ingredient that makes our yield invariants powerful is the possibility to pass parameters to them (ℓ' above, which is the same before and after executing $\overline{e}$), together with the possibility to give invariants a linear interface to include them in the disjointness assumption ③. The reuse of named, parameterized invariants that are inductive on their own facilitates ergonomic and modular proofs as well as a reduction in the number of noninterference checks compared to location invariants.

The example in Fig. 3 uses three yield invariants. BarrierInv states a global property on barrierCounter and mutatorsInBarrier, MutatorInv states a property of mutators on line 35, and CollectorInv states a property of the collector at lines 41 and 43 (notice the difference in the Boolean parameter). The linear parameters to both MutatorInv and CollectorInv are essential to prove their noninterference. For example, linearity discharges all noninterference obligations of CollectorInv w.r.t. yield-to-yield fragments in procedure Collector; there cannot be two different available variables i both holding thread identifier 0. CollectorInv is also stable across the yield-to-yield fragments in procedure Mutator: by linearity, we know that EnterBarrier cannot execute if mutatorsInBarrier holds all mutator identifiers, and WaitForBarrierRelease is blocked when barrierOn is true. As an example of a sequential check, observe that the invariants at line 41 together with barrierCounter = 0 from executing WaitBarrier imply the invariants at line 43, in particular that mutatorsInBarrier holds all mutator identifiers.

4.4   Refinement

Recall that the goal of our proof rule is to transform a program $\mathcal{P} = (gs, as, ps)$ into a program $\mathcal{P}' = (gs', as', ps')$. So far, we showed how the two judgments $Linearity(\mathcal{P}, \mathcal{Y}, \mathcal{L})$ and $Safety(\mathcal{P}, \mathcal{Y}, \mathcal{L})$ establish properties on executions of $\mathcal{P}$, using a linearity specification $\mathcal{L}$ and yield specification $\mathcal{Y}$. In the remainder of this section we show how the $Refinement(\mathcal{P}, \mathcal{Y}, \mathcal{L}, \mathcal{R}, \mathcal{P}')$ judgment ties together $\mathcal{P}$ and $\mathcal{P}'$ using a refinement specification $\mathcal{R}$.

Consider an execution step $c \Rightarrow c'$ of $\mathcal{P}$. We want to say that there is a representative step $\hat{c} \Rightarrow \hat{c}'$ in $\mathcal{P}'$. Representative means that $\hat{c}$ and $\hat{c}'$ are abstract representations of c and c', respectively. We capture this notion in an *abstraction mapping* α, which maps every concrete configuration of $\mathcal{P}$ to an abstract configuration of $\mathcal{P}'$. Then the meaning of the judgment $\mathcal{L}, \mathcal{Y}, \mathcal{R} \vdash \mathcal{P} \rightsquigarrow \mathcal{P}'$ derived by our proof rule is expressed in the following theorem.

Theorem 1. *Let c be an $\mathcal{L}$-valid, $\mathcal{Y}$-valid configuration of $\mathcal{P}$. (1) If $c \Rightarrow \frac{1}{2}$ then $\alpha(c) \Rightarrow \frac{1}{2}$. (2) If $c \Rightarrow c'$ then either $\alpha(c) = \alpha(c')$, $\alpha(c) \Rightarrow \alpha(c')$, or $\alpha(c) \Rightarrow \frac{1}{2}$.*

The safety of $\mathcal{P}'$ should imply the safety of $\mathcal{P}$. Thus, (1) states that any failure in $\mathcal{P}$ is preserved in $\mathcal{P}'$. And (2) states that every step in $\mathcal{P}$ is matched with a (potentially stuttering) step or failure in $\mathcal{P}'$. Hence, $\mathcal{P}'$ can fail "more often" than $\mathcal{P}$, but otherwise "behaves like" $\mathcal{P}$.

Refinement Specification. In a refinement specification $\mathcal{R} = (ref, mark)$, the *refinement mapping ref* is a partial map from dom(ps) to dom(as'). For every procedure $P \in$ dom(ref), we check that P is abstracted by action $A = ref(P)$. Since our refinement checks are procedure-modular, we require dom(ref) to be closed under calls in ps (not including pending asyncs). In general, P executes multiple yield-to-yield fragments and possibly calls other procedures, while A executes in a single atomic step. Thus we need to ensure that exactly one yield-to-yield fragment in P behaves like A, while all other fragments have no visible side effect. We use a *marking function mark* to identify where A should happen in P. For every call statement with label λ, $mark(\lambda)$ is either $\square$ ("before"), $\blacksquare$ ("after"), or the index $i \in \mathbb{N}$ of some arm of the call. This means that we are still before A when the call returns, that we are already after A when reaching the call, or that arm i establishes A, respectively. Naturally, procedure entry and exit are marked with $\square$ and $\blacksquare$, respectively. Then the marks along every path of P must match the regular expression $\square^+ \mathbb{N}? \blacksquare^+$, which distinguishes two cases. (M1) No call is marked with an index $i \in \mathbb{N}$. Then some yield-to-yield fragment switches from $\square$ to $\blacksquare$, which we will check to behave like A. All other yield-to-yield fragments and calls on the path must have no side effect. (M2) Some call is marked with index $i \in \mathbb{N}$. We will check that arm i of this call behaves like A, while all other calls and yield-to-yield fragments on the path must have no side effect. Since we check *mark* per path, there are in general multiple occurrences of (M1) and (M2).

In Fig. 2, the *ref* mapping is specified using the refines keyword. For example, procedure Acquire refines the atomic action AcquireSpec. The *mark* mapping is not explicitly specified, but we consider the call on line 28 to be marked with 1 (the index of its only arm). Then one path through Acquire is marked with $\square\blacksquare$ and the other one with $\square 1 \blacksquare$, both matching the regular expression above.

Program Rewriting. The program $\mathcal{P} = (gs, as, ps)$ is rewritten into $\mathcal{P}' = (gs', as', ps')$ as follows. First, global variables can be hidden, such that $gs' \subseteq gs$. Second, new atomic actions can be added (for new abstractions of procedures) and unreferenced ones removed, but for $A \in \mathrm{dom}(as) \cap \mathrm{dom}(as')$ we require $as'(A) = as(A)$. Recall that an action can execute in any program that contains the referenced global variables and procedures. Third, $\mathrm{dom}(ps') = \mathrm{dom}(ps)$ and we rewrite every $ps(P) = (I, O, L, s)$ into $ps'(P) = (I', O', L', s')$ as follows. Local variables can be hidden, such that $I' \subseteq I \wedge O' \subseteq O' \wedge L' \subseteq L$. If $P \notin \mathrm{dom}(ref)$, then s' is like s, except that call arms (Q, ι, o) with $ps'(Q) = (I_Q, O_Q, \_, \_)$ turn into $(Q, \iota|_{I_Q}, o|_{O_Q})$, with the requirement $\mathrm{img}(o) \cap (O' \cup L') = \mathrm{img}(o|_{O_Q})$ that formal and actual outputs can only be hidden together. We denote this rewriting of a statement by $\alpha(s)$. If $P \in \mathrm{dom}(ref)$, then $s' = \mathsf{exec}(ref(P), id(I'), id(O'))$, where $id(\cdot)$ is the identity mapping on a given set of variables. We denote this exec statement by $\alpha(P)$. Thus, procedures in $\mathrm{dom}(ref)$ remain in $\mathcal{P}'$, but with their bodies rewritten to a single exec to their abstraction. Clearly, the action interface $as' \circ ref(P) = (I', O', \_, \_)$ must match the procedure, and $L' = \varnothing$. Overall, $\mathcal{P}'$ must still typecheck, which ensures, e.g., that the remaining actuals in input/output maps were not hidden.

In the first refinement step of Sect. 2.2, where the procedures in the second column of Fig. 2 are abstracted to the atomic actions in the third column, the global variable b is hidden. In the second refinement step, where procedure Incr is abstracted to action IncrSpec, the input parameter tid and the global variable l are hidden. Notice that, in order to chain together these two refinement steps, we performed an auxiliary rewriting step in procedure Incr that converted `call` statements to `exec` statements. CIVL automatically performs this transformation as part of a refinement step, justified by a commutativity argument we explained in Sect. 2.2. However, this rewriting is not formalized as part of our refinement rule in this paper.

Skip Action. In the following we assume a special action *Skip* that has no inputs and outputs, does not modify global variables, and creates no pending asyncs. Formally, $as(Skip) = (\varnothing, \varnothing, \{\varepsilon\}, \{(\varepsilon, \varepsilon, \varnothing)\})$, where ε is the empty store. Observe that safety verification (i.e., showing that the failure configuration $\frac{1}{2}$ is unreachable) is a special case of refinement, where all global and local variables are hidden, and all procedures are abstracted to *Skip*.

Abstraction Mapping. Figure 6 defines the abstraction mapping α. In a given yielding configuration, we restrict the global store to gs' and drop all trees rooted in a node that refines *Skip*. The remaining nodes are traversed recursively, where frames with $P \notin \text{dom}(\text{ref})$ (nodes ● on the right) are rewritten as expected. The interesting case is for nodes with 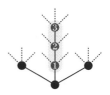 $P \in \text{dom}(\text{ref})$, like node ❶ on the right. In this case, ❶ is turned into a leave (cutting off the remaining subtree) whose statement is either $\alpha(P)$ (the single exec of $\text{ref}(P)$) or skip. Intuitively, to match the concrete steps of P (in ❶ and its subnodes), the abstract configuration first stutters at $\alpha(P)$, then transitions to skip when the effect of $\text{ref}(P)$ happens, and then stutters at skip until the return from ❶. The delicate part is to determine if $\text{ref}(P)$ happened and to compute the local store for the abstract configuration. This is done by the *early-return function* r. The function recurses on the unique path of marked arms in calls, ❶—❷—❸ in our example, and either returns □ (when "before $\text{ref}(P)$") or a local store ℓ (when "after $\text{ref}(P)$"). Suppose that ❶,❷,❸ have local stores ℓ_1, ℓ_2, ℓ_3, and that $r(❸) = \ell_3$. Then $r(❷)$ equals ℓ_2 updated with the return parameters from ℓ_3, say ℓ_2', and similarly $r(❶)$ equals ℓ_1 updated with the return parameters from ℓ_2', say ℓ_1', which is the local store for the abstract configuration. Thus, r performs "early" return parameter passing, even though we are still in the middle of executing procedures. To prove Theorem 1, our verification conditions below have to ensure that throughout subsequent concrete execution steps, $r(❶)$ remains ℓ_1'.

Refinement Packages. In a procedure $P \in \text{dom}(\text{ref})$, the effect of the abstract action $\text{ref}(P)$ can happen either in a yield-to-yield fragment directly in P, or nested inside another called procedure. To handle (potentially recursive) procedure calls during refinement, we decompose the problem into procedure-modular checks. Recall that the marking function *mark* identifies yield-to-yield fragments and call arms in P that should behave like the abstract action $\text{ref}(P)$. Conversely, all other yield-to-yield fragments and call arms should have no side effect, which is to say that they should behave like *Skip*. Hence we have a refinement obligation for *every* yield-to-yield fragment and *every* call arm in P, where refinement is either checked against $\text{ref}(P)$ or *Skip*. We capture all these refinement obligations uniformly in *refinement packages* of the form $\{P \mid \varphi \mid ll\}\, \overline{e}\, \{A\}$, where P is the procedure we check refinement for, φ is a set of invariant calls and ll a set of available variables we can assume, $\overline{e}$ is an exec sequence denoting the effect we check refinement for, and A is the action we check refinement against.

(R1) Refinement Packages for Yield-to-Yield Fragments. For every procedure $P \in \text{dom}(\text{ref})$ and yield-to-yield fragment $\{P \mid \kappa_1\}\, \overline{e}\, \{\kappa_2\}$ of P we define the refinement package $\{P \mid \varphi \mid ll\}\, \overline{e}\, \{A\}$ where φ and ll are defined the same as for Floyd packages, and $A = \text{ref}(P)$ if $\text{mark}(\kappa_1) = \square$ and $\text{mark}(\kappa_2) = \blacksquare$, or $A = \textit{Skip}$ otherwise. This case is rather straightforward. We proved the validity

Abstraction of configuration

$$\alpha((g, \mathcal{T})) = (g|_{gs'}, \{\alpha(t) \mid t \in \mathcal{T} \wedge root(t) = P \wedge ref(P) \neq Skip\})$$

Abstraction of thread tree

For the definitions of $o(s)$ and $o(P)$, see program rewriting.

$$\ell|_P = \ell|_{I \cup O \cup L} \quad \text{if } ps'(P) = (I, O, L, \_)$$

$$\alpha(\mathsf{Lf}\,(P, \ell, s)) = \mathsf{Lf}\,(P, \ell|_P, \alpha(s)) \qquad\qquad\qquad\qquad\qquad \text{if } P \notin dom(ref)$$

$$\alpha(\mathsf{Nd}\,(P, \ell, s)\,\,\overline{t}) = \mathsf{Nd}\,(P, \ell|_P, \alpha(s))\,\,\overline{\alpha(t)} \qquad\qquad\qquad\quad \text{if } P \notin dom(ref)$$

$$\alpha(\mathsf{Lf}\,(P, \ell, s)) = \mathsf{Lf}\,(P, \ell|_P, s') \qquad s' = \begin{cases} \alpha(P) \text{ if } s \neq \mathtt{skip} \\ \mathtt{skip} \text{ if } s = \mathtt{skip} \end{cases} \quad \text{if } P \in dom(ref)$$

$$\alpha(\underbrace{\mathsf{Nd}\,(P, \ell, \_)\,\_}_{t}) = \mathsf{Lf}\,(P, \ell'|_P, s')\,\,s', \ell' = \begin{cases} \alpha(P), \ell \quad\;\; \text{if } r(t) = \square \\ \mathtt{skip}, r(t) \text{ if } r(t) \neq \square \end{cases} \quad \text{if } P \in dom(ref)$$

Early-return computation

$$r(\mathsf{Lf}\,(P, \ell, s)) = \begin{cases} \square \text{ if } s \neq \mathtt{skip} \\ \ell \;\; \text{if } s = \mathtt{skip} \end{cases}$$

$$r(\mathsf{Nd}\,(P, \ell, SC[\mathtt{call}_\lambda\,\overline{(Q, \iota, o)}])\,\,\overline{t}) = \begin{cases} \square & \text{if } mark(\lambda) = \square \\ \ell & \text{if } mark(\lambda) = \blacksquare \\ \square & \text{if } mark(\lambda) = i \wedge r(t_i) = \square \\ \ell[r(t_i) \circ o_i^{-1}] & \text{if } mark(\lambda) = i \wedge r(t_i) \neq \square \end{cases}$$

Fig. 6. Abstraction mapping from configurations of $\mathcal{P}$ to configurations of $\mathcal{P}'$.

of φ and ll before the fragment, and need to check that the code $\overline{e}$ in the fragment behaves either like $ref(P)$ or $\mathtt{skip}$.

(R2) Refinement Packages for Call Arms. For every procedure $P \in dom(ref)$ and $\mathtt{call}_\lambda\,\overline{(Q_i, \iota_i, o_i)} : {}^{in}_{out}$ in P, let $\varphi = inv(\lambda)$ and $ll = in \setminus \bigcup_i \iota_i(li(Q_i, \rhd))$. At a call we know the validity of the invariants attached to the call and the availability of in minus the linear variables passed into the callees. Then for every arm (Q_i, ι_i, o_i), let $A_i = ref(P)$ if $mark(\lambda) = i$ or $A_i = Skip$ otherwise. Now the final missing ingredient for a refinement package $\{P \mid \varphi \mid ll\}\,\overline{e}\,\{A_i\}$ for every arm i is the effect $\overline{e}$ for which we check refinement against A_i. To obtain a modular check, our solution is to use the abstract action specification of the callee Q_i. Formally, $\overline{e} = \mathtt{exec}\,(B_i, \iota_i|_I, o_i|_O)$ for $B_i = ref(Q_i)$ with $as'(B_i) = (I, O, \_, \_)$. Recall that this is well-defined, since $dom(ref)$ is closed under calls. Notice that using the specification of a callee while checking the specification of a caller is akin to reasoning with procedure pre- and postconditions, where circular dependencies are resolved via induction on the nesting depth.

Recall (from the end of Sect. 3) that procedure Acquire in Fig. 2 has three yield-to-yield fragments: (A1), (A2), (A3). Each fragment induces an (R1)-type refinement package, where (A1) is checked against AcquireSpec, while both (A2) and (A3) are checked against *Skip*. Furthermore, the call on line 28 induces an (R2)-type refinement package against AcquireSpec.

Refinement Checking. The $Refinement(\mathcal{P}, \mathcal{Y}, \mathcal{L}, \mathcal{R}, \mathcal{P}')$ judgment requires every refinement package $\{P \mid \varphi \mid ll\} \overline{e} \{A\}$ to be discharged as follows. Let $e = \texttt{exec}\ (A, id(I), id(O))$ for $as'(A) = (I, O, \_, \_)$ be the abstract effect we check refinement against, let $V = gs' \cup I' \cup O'$ for $as' \circ ref(P) = (I', O', \_, \_)$ be the non-hidden variables in the scope of the refinement package, and check

$$
\left(
\begin{array}{l}
① \ g{\cdot}\ell \models \varphi \\
② \ IsSet(lc(g{\cdot}\ell, lg \cup ll))
\end{array}
\right)
\implies
\left(
\begin{array}{l}
① \ g{\cdot}\ell \in Gate(e) \implies g{\cdot}\ell \in Gate(\overline{e}) \\
② \ (g{\cdot}\ell, g'{\cdot}\ell', \Omega) \in Gate(e) \circ Trans(\overline{e}) \implies \\
\quad \exists \hat{g}{\cdot}\hat{\ell}, \hat{g}'{\cdot}\hat{\ell}' : (\hat{g}{\cdot}\hat{\ell}, \hat{g}'{\cdot}\hat{\ell}', \Omega|_{ref}) \in Trans(e) \\
\quad \wedge g{\cdot}\ell|_V = \hat{g}{\cdot}\hat{\ell}|_V \wedge g'{\cdot}\ell'|_V = \hat{g}'{\cdot}\hat{\ell}'|_V
\end{array}
\right)
$$

$$
\text{where}\ \Omega|_{ref} = \{(\ell, Q) \in \Omega \mid ref(Q) \neq Skip\}.
$$

We assume a store $g\ell$ that satisfies ① invariants and ② linear disjointness according to the refinement package. Then refinement consists of two parts, failure preservation and behavior preservation. First, ③ if $\overline{e}$ can fail in the concrete then e must also fail in the abstract. Second, ④ if e cannot fail in the abstract and $\overline{e}$ can transition to store $g'\ell'$ while creating pending asyncs Ω in the concrete, then there must be a matching transition of e in the abstract. Here matching means that e starts in a store $\hat{g}\hat{\ell}$ that agrees with $g\ell$ on the non-hidden variables V, ends in a store $\hat{g}'\hat{\ell}'$ that agrees with $g'\ell'$ on V, and creates the same pending asyncs except the ones to procedures abstracted to *Skip*.

5 Implementation

CIVL is a refinement-based verifier for concurrent programs built on top of the widely-used Boogie intermediate verification language. The Boogie [6] verifier provides infrastructure for compiling annotated sequential procedures into logical verification conditions whose validity is checked by a satisfiability-modulo-theories solver. CIVL is implemented as an extension of Boogie, which takes as input an annotated layered concurrent program [25] (in a language whose core is RefPL), performs concurrency-specific type checking and static analyses, and then encodes all the verification conditions of its proof rule into a standard sequential Boogie program. Thus, CIVL can be understood as a compiler that eliminates concurrency in a RefPL program by translating it down to a collection of sequential procedures, thus reusing the rest of the Boogie pipeline unchanged.

The open-source CIVL verifier is a stable tool which is part of the master branch [2] and public release [1] of Boogie. CIVL has over 100 regression tests comprising both realistic programs and microbenchmarks. There are many published papers [9,26,27,33,39] that describe nontrivial examples verified using CIVL, most written by researchers other than the developers of CIVL. The code in CIVL is extensible; entirely new tactics for rewriting concurrent programs have been added to it [24,26]. Finally, CIVL is designed for interactive program development. It is fast and provides several command-line flags to focus verification on parts of the program. CIVL has fine-grained error reporting including error traces, which attributes a verification failure to a particular check, local to a small part of the program. This helps the programmer to debug and iteratively improve both implementation and specification.

An early version of the CIVL verifier was reported by Hawblitzel et al. [18]. The implementation of the techniques described in this paper has been done as part of the new design and implementation of CIVL based on the framework of layered concurrent programs [25]. In the rest of this section, we will continue to use CIVL to refer to our new implementation. We now present an overview of the different parts of the verifier.

Type Checking. In addition to the standard type checking of a Boogie program, the CIVL type checker performs several extra checks. First, it checks that the layer specifications [25] on program elements such as global and local variables, atomic actions, and procedures are correct. Second, it checks using a dataflow analysis that it is sufficient to reason about the safety of cooperative semantics. This analysis exploits mover type [14] annotations on atomic actions to reason that yield-to-yield code fragments satisfy the requirements of Lipton reduction [30]. It also generates logical verification conditions whose validity guarantee the correctness of the mover annotations on atomic actions.

Linearity Checking. The CIVL linearity checker implements the method described in Sect. 4.2 in two parts. First, it creates for each atomic action a sequential procedure which verifies that the multiset of outgoing permissions is a subset of the multiset of incoming permissions. We use the generalized array theory [31] to encode multisets, and the *IsSet* constraint in particular. Second, it type checks each procedure to compute the set of available variables at each control location and to verify that linear interfaces of called procedures and atomic actions are used appropriately.

Safety Checking. The CIVL safety checker implements the method described in Sect. 4.3. Unlike the formal description which enumerates yield-to-yield code fragments, the implementation is efficient, encodes all code fragments in a RefPL procedure into a single sequential procedure with maximal sharing, and adds the safety checks by injecting instrumentation code and assertions into a cloned copy of the original procedure. To express the noninterference check, we add instrumentation variables that take snapshots of global and output variables at every yield. Furthermore, the generalized array theory is used here as well to record the pending asyncs created in a yield-to-yield code fragment, such that their preconditions can be checked.

Refinement Checking. The CIVL refinement checker implements the method described in Sect. 4.4. Similar to safety checking, the refinement checks are added as instrumentation to procedure copies. At every yield, snapshot variables (similar as for noninterference) are used to refer to the state at the previous yield when asserting the appropriate transition relation. CIVL computes a representation of the transition relation of an atomic actions as a logical formula from the user-provided representation as imperative code.

6 Conclusions

In this paper, we provide a foundation for refining structured concurrent programs and an implementation in the CIVL verifier. The contribution of this paper, and that of CIVL in general, is the capability to express *new proofs* with significant advantages for the programmer in terms of proof structuring, annotation effort, and tool performance.

Acknowledgments. Bernhard Kragl and Thomas A. Henzinger were supported by the Austrian Science Fund (FWF) under grant Z211-N23 (Wittgenstein Award).

References

1. Boogie (release). https://www.nuget.org/packages/Boogie
2. Boogie (source code). https://github.com/boogie-org/boogie
3. Abrial, J.: The B-Book: Assigning Programs to Meanings (1996). https://doi.org/10.1017/CBO9780511624162
4. Abrial, J., Butler, M.J., Hallerstede, S., Hoang, T.S., Mehta, F., Voisin, L.: Rodin: an open toolset for modelling and reasoning in Event-B. Int. J. Softw. Tools Technol. Transf. **12**(6) (2010). https://doi.org/10.1007/s10009-010-0145-y
5. Back, R., von Wright, J.: Refinement calculus: a systematic introduction. Graduate Texts Comput. Sci. (1998). https://doi.org/10.1007/978-1-4612-1674-2
6. Barnett, M., Chang, B.E., DeLine, R., Jacobs, B., Leino, K.R.M.: Boogie: a modular reusable verifier for object-oriented programs. In: FMCO (2005). https://doi.org/10.1007/11804192_17
7. Blom, S., Darabi, S., Huisman, M., Oortwijn, W.: The VerCors tool set: verification of parallel and concurrent software. In: IFM (2017). https://doi.org/10.1007/978-3-319-66845-1_7
8. Bouajjani, A., Emmi, M., Enea, C., Mutluergil, S.O.: Proving linearizability using forward simulations. In: CAV (2017). https://doi.org/10.1007/978-3-319-63390-9_28
9. Bouajjani, A., Enea, C., Mutluergil, S.O., Tasiran, S.: Reasoning about TSO programs using reduction and abstraction. In: CAV (2018). https://doi.org/10.1007/978-3-319-96142-2_21
10. Chajed, T., Kaashoek, M.F., Lampson, B.W., Zeldovich, N.: Verifying concurrent software using movers in CSPEC. In: OSDI (2018). https://www.usenix.org/conference/osdi18/presentation/chajed
11. Cohen, E., et al.: VCC: a practical system for verifying concurrent C. In: TPHOLs (2009). https://doi.org/10.1007/978-3-642-03359-9_2
12. Damian, A., Dragoi, C., Militaru, A., Widder, J.: Communication-closed asynchronous protocols. In: CAV (2019). https://doi.org/10.1007/978-3-030-25543-5_20
13. Elmas, T., Qadeer, S., Tasiran, S.: A calculus of atomic actions. In: POPL (2009). https://doi.org/10.1145/1480881.1480885
14. Flanagan, C., Qadeer, S.: A type and effect system for atomicity. In: PLDI (2003). https://doi.org/10.1145/781131.781169
15. von Gleissenthall, K., Kici, R.G., Bakst, A., Stefan, D., Jhala, R.: Pretend synchrony: synchronous verification of asynchronous distributed programs. In: POPL (2019). https://doi.org/10.1145/3290372

16. Gu, R., et al.: Certified concurrent abstraction layers. In: PLDI (2018). https://doi.org/10.1145/3192366.3192381
17. Hawblitzel, C., et al.: IronFleet: proving practical distributed systems correct. In: SOSP (2015). https://doi.org/10.1145/2815400.2815428
18. Hawblitzel, C., Petrank, E., Qadeer, S., Tasiran, S.: Automated and modular refinement reasoning for concurrent programs. In: CAV (2015). https://doi.org/10.1007/978-3-319-21668-3_26
19. Herlihy, M., Wing, J.M.: Linearizability: a correctness condition for concurrent objects. ACM Trans. Program. Lang. Syst. **12**(3) (1990). https://doi.org/10.1145/78969.78972
20. Jacobs, B., Smans, J., Philippaerts, P., Vogels, F., Penninckx, W., Piessens, F.: VeriFast: a powerful, sound, predictable, fast verifier for C and Java. In: NFM (2011). https://doi.org/10.1007/978-3-642-20398-5_4
21. Jones, C.B.: Specification and design of (parallel) programs. In: IFIP Congress (1983)
22. Jung, R., Krebbers, R., Jourdan, J., Bizjak, A., Birkedal, L., Dreyer, D.: Irisfrom the ground up: a modular foundation for higher-order concurrentseparation logic. J. Funct. Program. **28** (2018).https://doi.org/10.1017/S0956796818000151
23. Khyzha, A., Dodds, M., Gotsman, A., Parkinson, M.J.: Proving linearizability using partial orders. In: ESOP (2017). https://doi.org/10.1007/978-3-662-54434-1_24
24. Kragl, B., Enea, C., Henzinger, T.A., Mutluergil, S.O., Qadeer, S.: Inductive sequentialization of asynchronous programs. In: PLDI (2020). https://doi.org/10.1145/3385412.3385980
25. Kragl, B., Qadeer, S.: Layered concurrent programs. In: CAV (2018). https://doi.org/10.1007/978-3-319-96145-3_5
26. Kragl, B., Qadeer, S., Henzinger, T.A.: Synchronizing the asynchronous. In: CONCUR (2018). https://doi.org/10.4230/LIPIcs.CONCUR.2018.21
27. Krishna, S., Emmi, M., Enea, C., Jovanovic, D.: Verifying visibility-based weak consistency. In: ESOP (2020). https://doi.org/10.1007/978-3-030-44914-8_11
28. Lamport, L.: Specifying Systems, The TLA+ Language and Tools for Hardware and Software Engineers (2002)
29. Leino, K.R.M., Müller, P., Smans, J.: Verification of concurrent programs with Chalice. In: FOSAD (2009). https://doi.org/10.1007/978-3-642-03829-7_7
30. Lipton, R.J.: Reduction: a method of proving properties of parallel programs. Commun. ACM **18**(12) (1975). https://doi.org/10.1145/361227.361234
31. de Moura, L.M., Bjørner, N.: Generalized, efficient array decision procedures. In: FMCAD (2009). https://doi.org/10.1109/FMCAD.2009.5351142
32. Müller, P., Schwerhoff, M., Summers, A.J.: Viper: a verification infrastructure for permission-based reasoning. In: VMCAI (2016). https://doi.org/10.1007/978-3-662-49122-5_2
33. Mutluergil, S.O., Tasiran, S.: A mechanized refinement proof of the Chase–Lev deque using a proof system. Computing **101**(1), 59–74 (2018). https://doi.org/10.1007/s00607-018-0635-4
34. Owicki, S.S., Gries, D.: Verifying properties of parallel programs: an axiomatic approach. Commun. ACM **19**(5) (1976). https://doi.org/10.1145/360051.360224
35. de Roever, W.P., de Boer, F.S., Hannemann, U., Hooman, J., Lakhnech, Y., Poel,M., Zwiers, J.: Concurrency Verification: Introduction to Compositional and Noncompositional Methods. Cambridge Tracts in Theoretical Computer Science, vol. 54 (2001)

36. Schneider, F.B.: On concurrent programming. Graduate Texts Comput. Sci. (1997). https://doi.org/10.1007/978-1-4612-1830-2
37. Vafeiadis, V.: Automatically proving linearizability. In: CAV (2010). https://doi.org/10.1007/978-3-642-14295-6_40
38. Walker, D.: Substructural type systems. In: Pierce, B.C. (ed.) Advanced Topics in Types and Programming Languages, pp. 3–44. The MIT Press (2004). https://doi.org/10.7551/mitpress/1104.003.0003
39. Wilcox, J.R., Flanagan, C., Freund, S.N.: VerifiedFT: a verified, high-performance precise dynamic race detector. In: PPoPP (2018). https://doi.org/10.1145/3178487.3178514

Parameterized Verification of Systems with Global Synchronization and Guards

Nouraldin Jaber[1(✉)], Swen Jacobs[2], Christopher Wagner[1], Milind Kulkarni[1], and Roopsha Samanta[1]

[1] Purdue University, West Lafayette, USA
{njaber,wagne279,milind,roopsha}@purdue.edu
[2] CISPA Helmholtz Center for Information Security, Saarbrücken, Germany
jacobs@cispa.saarland

Abstract. Inspired by distributed applications that use consensus or other agreement protocols for global coordination, we define a new computational model for parameterized systems that is based on a general global synchronization primitive and allows for global transition guards. Our model generalizes many existing models in the literature, including broadcast protocols and guarded protocols. We show that reachability properties are decidable for systems without guards, and give sufficient conditions under which they remain decidable in the presence of guards. Furthermore, we investigate cutoffs for reachability properties and provide sufficient conditions for small cutoffs in a number of cases that are inspired by our target applications.

1 Introduction

Distributed applications are notoriously difficult to implement and reason about, primarily due to the combinatorial explosion of behaviors resulting from the interleaving of computation and communication. Naturally, they have received a lot of attention from the formal methods community to facilitate reasoning about correctness properties that are too complex to reason about informally or manually [3,7,14,15,34,36,42,46,50,52,55].

One of the main challenges in *fully automated* reasoning about a distributed system is *scalability* in a critical system parameter—the number of processes—with the epitome of success being *parameterized verification of correctness*—correctness that holds regardless of this parameter. Unfortunately, the parameterized verification problem is known to be undecidable even in very simple cases, for example, finite-state processes that pass a 2-valued token in a ring [54]. Hence, approaches for parameterized verification are divided into two groups: (i)

This research was partially supported by the National Science Foundation under Grant Nos. 1846327, 1908504, and 1919197 and by a grant from the Purdue Research Foundation. Any opinions, findings, and conclusions in this paper are those of the authors only and do not necessarily reflect the views of our sponsors.
N. Jaber and S. Jacobs—Joint first-authors.

S. K. Lahiri and C. Wang (Eds.): CAV 2020, LNCS 12224, pp. 299–323, 2020.
https://doi.org/10.1007/978-3-030-53288-8_15

ones that support a large class of systems, but only provide semi-decision procedures [1, 41] and (ii) ones that provide fully automatic decision procedures for a
well-defined class of systems, but need to carefully restrict this class of systems
to obtain such a strong result. While the former cannot provide any guarantee of
success, the latter are often not sufficiently general to model practical examples.

In this work, we target fully-automated parameterized verification for a significantly more general class of systems than addressed in prior work (cf. the
surveys [9, 21, 26]). Inspired by distributed applications that use consensus or
other *agreement protocols* for global coordination, we introduce *global synchronization protocols*, a new computational model for distributed systems that generalizes most of the existing models based on process synchronization, including
models based on pairwise rendezvous [32], asynchronous rendezvous [16], negotiation [27] and broadcasts [28]. We show that despite this generality, we can
still decide parameterized verification for safety properties. Going beyond that,
we show that under certain conditions, our model can be augmented with global
transition guards—which allow to model semaphore-based access control as well
as preconditions for global consensus-like coordination—while retaining decidability. This makes our model one of the most expressive models for which the
parameterized verification problem is still decidable. Furthermore, we present
several results on *cutoffs* for our model, i.e., the number of processes sufficient
to prove or disprove properties of a parameterized system. Inspired both by
the decision procedure and by negative examples that require large cutoffs, we
define sufficient conditions on systems in our computational model that make
small, practical cutoffs possible. Finally, we evaluate our approach on several
distributed applications, showing that they can indeed be modeled as global
synchronization protocols, and we illustrate the significance of our cutoff results
in the verification of these benchmarks.

Motivating Example. Our system model is inspired by applications that *use*
agreement protocols, like leader election or consensus, as building blocks to
achieve a more complex overall functionality. We are interested in a compositional verification setting where we *assume* that the agreement protocols have
been verified separately and want to *guarantee* the overall correctness of an
application without having to explicitly model and verify the agreement protocols within the application; in particular, we focus on a setting where verified
agreement protocols are encapsulated into an abstraction with precondition obligations and postcondition guarantees.

Thus, our system model needs to be able to incorporate such pre- and post-
conditions of agreement protocols. As a simple example, consider the smoke
detector application in Fig. 1 whose intended behavior is as follows. Upon detecting smoke, the processes coordinate to choose (up to) 2 processes to report the
smoke to the fire department. It uses different types of transitions, several of
which are popular in the literature and are supported by existing decidability
results: an *internal transition* (from state ENV to state ASK), a *broadcast* (on
action **Smoke**), and a *negotiation*, i.e., a synchronous transition of all processes

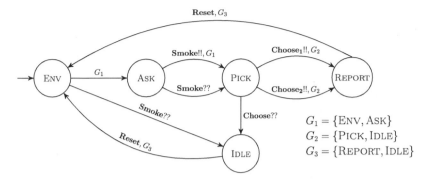

$G_1 = \{\text{ENV}, \text{ASK}\}$
$G_2 = \{\text{PICK}, \text{IDLE}\}$
$G_3 = \{\text{REPORT}, \text{IDLE}\}$

Fig. 1. A smoke detector process. The internal transition from initial state ENV to ASK models that a process detects smoke (an environment signal). A process that detected smoke can initiate a broadcast **Smoke**, moving all processes from ENV to IDLE and from ASK to PICK, where the transition **Choose** moves (up to) 2 processes to REPORT, and the rest from PICK to IDLE. Finally, all processes from REPORT and IDLE may move back to ENV in a synchronous transition with no dedicated sender. Transitions labeled with a set G_i can only be taken if all processes are in this set. The safety property for a distributed smoke detector based on this process is that at most 2 processes should report the fire.

with no distinguished sender (on action **Reset**). However, additionally our application requires that some transitions can only happen under certain conditions, given by guards G_i in transition labels. For example, action **Reset** should only be possible if all processes are in G_3, i.e., in states REPORT or IDLE. And most importantly, in state PICK we want the system to *agree* on (up to) 2 processes that move into state REPORT . This requires a novel type of transition that we have not found in existing literature, allowing two processes to take a distinguished role while all other processes are treated uniformly. To faithfully model agreement of processes, we also require a guard on this transition, since any agreement protocol is based on the assumption that all processes are ready (i.e., their local state satisfies some condition) before invocation of the protocol.

2   System Model: Global Synchronization Protocols

We present *global synchronization protocols* (GSPs), a formal system model that generalizes most of the existing synchronization-based models in the literature [16,27,28,32], including models based on rendezvous and broadcasts. In this model, each global transition synchronizes all processes, where an arbitrary number k of processes *act* as the senders of the transitions, while the remaining processes react uniformly as receivers. The model supports two basic types of transitions: (i) a *k-sender transition*, which *can fire* only if at least k processes are ready to act as senders, and *is fired* with exactly k processes acting as senders, and (ii) a *k-maximal transition*, which *can fire* if the number m of processes that are ready to act as senders is at least 1, and *is fired* with $min(m, k)$

processes acting as senders. Additionally, each transition can be equipped with a *global guard* that identifies a subset of the local state space. Then, a transition is *enabled* whenever it can fire and the local states of all processes are in the set identified by the transition guard.

We formalize these notions in the following, starting with the case without transition guards.

2.1 Global Synchronization Without Guards

Unguarded Processes. An *unguarded process* is a labeled transition system $P = \langle A, S, s_0, T \rangle$, where A is a set of *local actions*, S is a finite set of states, $s_0 \in S$ is the initial state, and $T \subseteq S \times A \times S$ is the transition relation. A is based on a set $\mathcal{A}$ of *global actions*, where each $a \in \mathcal{A}$ has an *arity* $k \geq 1$ and is either a *k-sender action* or a *k-maximal action*. For every global action $a \in \mathcal{A}$ with arity k, A contains *local actions* $a_1!!, \ldots, a_k!!, a??$. Actions $a_1!!, \ldots, a_k!!$ are called *sending actions* and $a??$ is called a *receiving action*.

A local transition from state s to state s' on sending action $\alpha \in A$ denoted $s \xrightarrow{\alpha} s'$ is called a *sending transition* (resp., *receiving transition*) if α is a sending action (resp., receiving action). We assume that receives are *deterministic*: for each state s and each receiving action $a??$, there is exactly one state s' with $s \xrightarrow{a??} s'$, and that sends are *unique*: for each sending action a_i there is exactly one pair of states s, s' with $s \xrightarrow{a_i!!} s'$.[1]

Example 1. If we ignore guards on transitions, the process in Fig. 1 is an unguarded process. Global action **Choose** has arity 2, and local sending transitions $\text{PICK} \xrightarrow{\textbf{Choose}_i!!} \text{REPORT}$ for $i \in \{1, 2\}$. One local receiving transition is $\text{PICK} \xrightarrow{\textbf{Choose}??} \text{IDLE}$, and all other receiving transitions on **Choose** are self-loops (not depicted).

Unguarded Systems. Given an unguarded process $P = \langle A, S, s_0, T \rangle$, we consider systems composed of n identical processes, and use a counter abstraction to efficiently represent global states, without loss of precision [25].[2]

That is, the parameterized global transition system is defined as $\mathcal{M}(n) = \langle \mathcal{A}, Q, \mathbf{q}_0, \rightarrow \rangle$, where $Q = \{0, \ldots, n\}^S$, i.e., a global state is a function $\mathbf{q} : S \rightarrow \{0, \ldots, n\}$. Assuming a fixed order on S, we will also use $\mathbf{q}$ as a vector of natural numbers. The initial state $\mathbf{q}_0$ is the state with $\mathbf{q}_0(s_0) = n$ and $\mathbf{q}_0(s) = 0$ for all $s \neq s_0$. Finally, we define the global transition relation $\rightarrow$, separated into the two different types of actions:

---

[1] Processes that do not satisfy the assumptions can easily be rewritten to satisfy them, e.g. by adding self-loops on any missing receive actions, and by renaming the actions of duplicate sending transitions (and adding corresponding receiving transitions).

[2] For presentation clarity, we do not explicitly consider an environment process in our model. All of our results extend to the case with an explicit environment process; see the extended version [38] for a justification.

k-sender Actions. A k-sender action $a \in \mathcal{A}$ with local sending transitions $s_i \xrightarrow{a_i!!} s'_i$ for $i \in \{1, \ldots, k\}$ can be fired from a global state $\mathbf{q}$ if there are k processes that can take these local transitions. Upon firing the action, each of the local transitions on actions $a_i!!$ is taken by exactly one process, and all other processes take a transition on action $a??$ to arrive in the new global state $\mathbf{q}'$. Formally, we assign to each k-sender action $a \in \mathcal{A}$ (i) a vector $\mathbf{v}_a \in Q$ containing the number of expected senders for each state $t \in S$: $\mathbf{v}_a(t) = |\{s \xrightarrow{a_i!!} s' \mid s = t\}|$, (ii) a vector $\mathbf{v}'_a$ containing the number of senders that will be in each state $t \in S$ after the transition: $\mathbf{v}'_a(t) = |\{s \xrightarrow{a_i!!} s' \mid s' = t\}|$, and (iii) a function $M_a : S \times S \to \{0,1\}$, where $M_a(s, s') = 1$ if there is a local transition $s \xrightarrow{a??} s'$, and $M_a(s, s') = 0$ otherwise. We also use M_a as a $|S| \times |S|$ matrix, called the *synchronization matrix* of action a.

Then, a transition from global state $\mathbf{q}$ on action a is possible if $\mathbf{q}(s_i) \geq \mathbf{v}_a(s_i)$ for all $i \in \{1, \ldots, k\}$, and the resulting global state can be computed as

$$\mathbf{q}' = M_a \cdot (\mathbf{q} - \mathbf{v}_a) + \mathbf{v}'_a,$$

and we write $\mathbf{q} \xrightarrow{a} \mathbf{q}'$. Intuitively, $\mathbf{q}'$ is obtained from $\mathbf{q}$ by "removing" the senders from their local start states, moving all the remaining (receiving) processes to their respective local destination states, and then adding the senders to their appropriate local destination states. Note that this representation relies on the assumption that sends are unique and receives are deterministic, which also implies that each column of a synchronization matrix M_a is a unit vector.

Example 2. Consider the process in Fig. 1. The synchronization matrix and vectors for action **Smoke** are shown below, with global states given in the order $\langle \text{Env}, \text{Ask}, \text{Idle}, \text{Pick}, \text{Report} \rangle$ (and abbreviated as $\langle \text{E}, \text{A}, \text{I}, \text{P}, \text{R} \rangle$). Notice, for instance, that the first column in $M_{\textbf{Smoke}}$ encodes the local receive transition $\text{Env} \xrightarrow{\textbf{Smoke}??} \text{Idle}$. The vector-pair $\mathbf{v}_{\textbf{Smoke}}$ and $\mathbf{v}'_{\textbf{Smoke}}$ encode the local send transition $\text{Ask} \xrightarrow{\textbf{Smoke}!!} \text{Pick}$. In particular, $\mathbf{v}_{\textbf{Smoke}}$ indicates that the sender starts in Ask and $\mathbf{v}'_{\textbf{Smoke}}$ indicates that the sender moves to Pick.

	$M_{\textbf{Smoke}}$						$\mathbf{v}_{\textbf{Smoke}}$		$\mathbf{v}'_{\textbf{Smoke}}$
	E	A	I	P	R				
E	0	0	0	0	0		E 0		E 0
A	0	0	0	0	0		A 1		A 0
I	1	0	1	0	0		I 0		I 0
P	0	1	0	1	0		P 0		P 1
R	0	0	0	0	1		R 0		R 0

Now, consider a global state $\langle 3, 2, 0, 0, 0 \rangle$ with three processes in Env and two in Ask. From this state, the transition $\langle 3, 2, 0, 0, 0 \rangle \xrightarrow{\textbf{Smoke}} \langle 0, 0, 3, 2, 0 \rangle$ is enabled (since there is at least 1 sender in Ask), where all three processes in Env act as receivers to move to Idle (according to the synchronization matrix $M_{\textbf{Smoke}}$), one process in Ask acts as the sender to move to Pick, and the other process in Ask acts as a receiver, also moving to Pick.

k-maximal Actions. A k-maximal action $a \in \mathcal{A}$ with local sending transitions $s_i \xrightarrow{a_i!!} s_i'$ for $i \in \{1, \ldots, k\}$ can be fired from a global state $\mathbf{q}$ if there is at least one process that can take one of these local transitions. Upon firing the action, for each state s_i with at least one local transition $s_i \xrightarrow{a_i!!} s_i'$, (i) if $\mathbf{q}(s_i) \geq \mathbf{v}_a(s_i)$ then each of the local transitions $s_i \xrightarrow{a_i!!} s_i'$ is taken by exactly one process, or, (ii) if $\mathbf{q}(s_i) < \mathbf{v}_a(s_i)$ then a total of $\mathbf{q}(s_i)$ of the local transitions $s_i \xrightarrow{a_i!!} s_i'$ are taken, each by exactly one process. All other processes take a transition on the receiving action $a??$ to arrive in the new global state $\mathbf{q}'$. Formally, we again assign to each action a vectors $\mathbf{v}_a, \mathbf{v}_a'$ and a synchronization matrix M_a, as above. If $\mathbf{q}(s_i) \geq \mathbf{v}_a(s_i)$ for all $i \in \{1, \ldots, k\}$, then these are used as defined above. For cases where this does not hold, we assign to the action an additional set of vector-pairs $(\mathbf{u}_a, \mathbf{u}_a')$ with different numbers of senders that actually participate, and $\mathbf{q}'$ is computed based on a vector-pair with the maximal number of senders that is supported by $\mathbf{q}$.

Example 3. The synchronization matrix and vectors for action **Choose** are shown below. Note that, if **Choose** is a 2-maximal action, then the vector-pair $(\mathbf{u}_{\text{Choose}}, \mathbf{u}_{\text{Choose}}')$ is used to model the case where only one sender is available to take the sending transition.

	M_{Choose}					$\mathbf{u}_{\text{Choose}}$	$\mathbf{u}_{\text{Choose}}'$	$\mathbf{v}_{\text{Choose}}$	$\mathbf{v}_{\text{Choose}}'$
	E	A	I	P	R				
E	1	0	0	0	0	0	0	0	0
A	0	1	0	0	0	0	0	0	0
I	0	0	1	1	0	0	0	0	0
P	0	0	0	0	0	1	0	2	0
R	0	0	0	0	1	0	1	0	2

Regardless of whether **Choose** is a 2-sender or a 2-maximal action, the global transition $\langle 0, 0, 1, 4, 0 \rangle \xrightarrow{\text{Choose}} \langle 0, 0, 3, 0, 2 \rangle$ is possible. In a state $\mathbf{q} = \langle 0, 0, 4, 1, 0 \rangle$, with 4 processes in IDLE and 1 in PICK, the **Choose** action will not be enabled if it is a 2-sender action because two sending processes are required (in PICK), but only one sender is available. However, if **Choose** is a 2-maximal action, then the global transition $\langle 0, 0, 4, 1, 0 \rangle \xrightarrow{\text{Choose}} \langle 0, 0, 4, 0, 1 \rangle$ is possible.

Runs, Reachability Properties. A *run* of system $\mathcal{M}(n)$ is a finite or infinite sequence of global states $\mathbf{q}_0 \mathbf{q}_1 \ldots$, where $\mathbf{q}_0$ is the initial state and $\mathbf{q}_i \xrightarrow{a} \mathbf{q}_{i+1}$ for all i. We say that a state $\mathbf{q}$ is *reachable* in $\mathcal{M}(n)$ if there is a run of $\mathcal{M}(n)$ that ends in $\mathbf{q}$. For a fixed $m \in \mathbb{N}$ and local state $s \in S$, let $\phi_m(s)$ be a property denoting the reachability of a global state $\mathbf{q}$ with $\mathbf{q}(s) \geq m$. If such a state is reachable in $\mathcal{M}(n)$, we write $\mathcal{M}(n) \models \phi_m(s)$.

Other Communication Primitives in the GSP Model. Note that most of the synchronization-based communication primitives from the literature are instances of k-sender transitions or k-maximal transitions: *broadcasts* [28] are simply 1-sender transitions, *internal transitions* are 1-sender transitions with $M_a = Id$ (the identity matrix), *pairwise rendezvous transitions* [32] are 2-sender transitions (denoting the sender and receiver of the rendezvous transition) with $M_a = Id$, *asynchronous rendezvous transitions* [16] are 2-maximal transitions with $M_a = Id$. *Negotiations* [27], i.e., a synchronous transition of all processes with no distinguished sender, can be modeled as a set of 1-sender transitions, where every local receiving transition $s \xrightarrow{a??} s'$ is paired with a sending transition $s \xrightarrow{a!!} s'$, allowing an arbitrary process to act as the sender. In addition to these, GSPs allow us to express many other natural synchronization primitives, e.g., summarizing the election of (up to) k leaders in a single step.

Finally, *disjunctive guards* [19], i.e., guards $G \subseteq S$ that require that there *exists* a process that is in some state $s \in G$, can be modeled by adding an auxiliary sending action $a_G!!$, and transitions $s \xrightarrow{a_G!!} M_a(s)$ for every $s \in G$, i.e., a process in some state $s \in G$ must exist to enable the transition, but apart from that this process acts like a receiver. Note that this works without adding a notion of guards to our model.

In what follows, we extend our model to allow *conjunctive guards*, i.e., guards that require that *all* processes are in some subset of the local state space.

2.2   Global Synchronization with Guards

Guarded Processes. A *guarded process* is a tuple $P_{GSP} = \langle A, S, s_0, T \rangle$, where all components are as before, except that now we have $T \subseteq S \times A \times \mathcal{P}(S) \times S$, i.e., transitions are additionally labeled with a subset of S, called a *guard*. A local transition from state s to state s' on action α with guard G will be denoted $s \xrightarrow{\alpha, G} s'$. We call a guard G *non-trivial* if $G \neq S$. Wlog, we assume that for any global action a, all local transitions based on a have the same guard.

Guarded Systems. Let the *support* of a global state $\mathbf{q}$ be $\mathsf{supp}(\mathbf{q}) = \{s \in S \mid \mathbf{q}(s) > 0\}$, i.e., the set of local states that appear at least once in $\mathbf{q}$. Then the semantics of a global transition on action a with guard G, denoted $\mathbf{q} \xrightarrow{a, G} \mathbf{q}'$, is as defined before, except that the transition is enabled only if $\mathsf{supp}(\mathbf{q}) \subseteq G$.

Example 4. Consider the global transitions introduced in Example 2, and recall that global states are given in the order $\langle \text{ENV}, \text{ASK}, \text{IDLE}, \text{PICK}, \text{REPORT} \rangle$. While the transition $\langle 0, 0, 1, 4, 0 \rangle \xrightarrow{\textbf{Reset}} \langle 1, 0, 0, 4, 0 \rangle$ would be possible in the unguarded model, the guard $G_3 = \{\text{REPORT}, \text{IDLE}\}$ on the **Reset** action disables this transition, as $\mathsf{supp}(\langle 0, 0, 1, 4, 0 \rangle) = \{\text{PICK}, \text{IDLE}\} \not\subseteq G_3$. Similarly, from $\mathbf{q} = \langle 1, 0, 1, 2, 0 \rangle$, while a transition on action **Choose** is enabled for unguarded processes, the guard $G_2 = \{\text{PICK}, \text{IDLE}\}$ on action **Choose** disables this transition, since $\mathsf{supp}(\langle 1, 0, 1, 2, 0 \rangle) \not\subseteq G_2$.

3   Parameterized Verification for GSPs Without Guards

In this section, instead of the parameterized system $\mathcal{M}(n)$, we consider an infinite-state system $\mathcal{M}_\infty$ that includes the behaviors of $\mathcal{M}(n)$ for every n: it initializes to $\mathcal{M}(n)$ for arbitrary $n \in \mathbb{N}$, and then behaves according to the semantics of a GSP of that size. We are interested in reachability properties $\phi_m(s)$, where $\mathcal{M}_\infty \models \phi_m(s)$ is equivalent to $\exists n. \ \mathcal{M}(n) \models \phi_m(s)$, i.e., we are considering a *parameterized reachability property* over all instances of $\mathcal{M}$.

We use this slightly different model in order to make use of the notion of *well-structured transition systems (WSTS)*, as defined by Finkel [30]: an infinite-state transition system that is equipped with a *well-quasi-order (WQO)* on its state space and has some additional properties. Finkel and Schnoebelen [31] have surveyed existing results on WSTSs and put them into a common framework.

We will show that, for a suitable WQO, $\mathcal{M}_\infty$ is a WSTS, and that this enables parameterized verification for reachability properties $\phi_m(s)$.

3.1   Compatibility and Effective Computability of Predecessors

For the following definitions, fix an infinite set of states Q and a transition relation $\rightarrow$. Moreover, let $\preceq$ be a WQO on Q, i.e., a reflexive and transitive relation such that, for any infinite sequence $\mathbf{q}_0, \mathbf{q}_1, \mathbf{q}_2, \ldots$ of states from Q, there exist indices $i < j$ with $\mathbf{q}_i \preceq \mathbf{q}_j$. In particular, $\preceq$ does not admit infinitely decreasing sequences or infinite anti-chains.

Compatibility. We say that $\preceq$ is *compatible* with $\rightarrow$ if for every $\mathbf{q}, \mathbf{q}', \mathbf{p} \subset Q$ with $\mathbf{q} \preceq \mathbf{p}$ and $\mathbf{q} \rightarrow \mathbf{q}'$ there exists $\mathbf{p}' \in Q$ with $\mathbf{q}' \preceq \mathbf{p}'$ and $\mathbf{p} \rightarrow^* \mathbf{p}'$. If the property also holds after replacing $\mathbf{p} \rightarrow^* \mathbf{p}'$ with $\mathbf{p} \rightarrow \mathbf{p}'$, then we say $\preceq$ is *strongly compatible* with $\rightarrow$.

Well-Structured Transition System. A transition system $(Q, \rightarrow)$ equipped with a WQO that is compatible with $\rightarrow$ is called a *well-structured transition system (WSTS)*.

Upwards-Closed Sets. For a (possibly infinite) subset $U \subseteq Q$, the *upwards closure* of U is the set $\uparrow U = \{\mathbf{p} \in Q \mid \exists \mathbf{q} \in U : \mathbf{q} \preceq \mathbf{p}\}$. A set U is *upwards closed* if $\uparrow U = U$. Every upwards closed set U has a finite *basis*: a finite set $B \subseteq U$ such that $\uparrow B = U$.

Effectively Computable Predecessors. For $U \subseteq Q$, let $Pred(U)$ denote the predecessor states of U with respect to $\rightarrow$. We say that we can *effectively compute Pred* if there exists an algorithm that computes a finite basis of $Pred(U)$ from any finite basis of any upwards-closed $U \subseteq Q$.

Theorem 1 ([31]). *In a WSTS with effectively computable Pred, reachability of any upwards-closed set is decidable.*

3.2   Decidability for Unguarded GSPs

We prove that any unguarded GSP is a WSTS with effectively computable $Pred$, which implies that reachability properties are decidable for GSPs. To this end, let $\preceq$ be the component-wise order on global state vectors $\mathbf{q}$, $\mathbf{p}$:

$$\mathbf{q} \preceq \mathbf{p} \text{ iff } \mathbf{q}(s) \leq \mathbf{p}(s) \text{ for all } s \in S.$$

Note that with respect to this WQO, the set of global states $\mathbf{q}$ with $\mathbf{q}(s) \geq m$ is an upwards-closed set, i.e., if we can decide reachability of upwards-closed sets, then we can decide reachability properties $\phi_m(s)$. Thus, decidability of checking $\mathcal{M}_\infty \models \phi_m(s)$ follows from the following theorem.

Theorem 2. *If $\mathcal{M}_\infty$ is based on an unguarded GSP process, then $\mathcal{M}_\infty$ equipped with $\preceq$ is a WSTS and we can effectively compute Pred.*

Proof. To prove that $\mathcal{M}_\infty$ is a WSTS, we show strong compatibility of transitions w.r.t. $\preceq$. We consider the following two cases separately: (i) k-sender transitions, and (ii) k-maximal transitions.

(i) For k-sender transitions, let $\mathbf{q} \preceq \mathbf{p}$ and $\mathbf{q} \xrightarrow{a} \mathbf{q}'$ for some k-sender action a. Then $\mathbf{q}' = M_a \cdot (\mathbf{q} - \mathbf{v}_a) + \mathbf{v}_a'$ for some synchronization matrix M_a and vectors $\mathbf{v}_a, \mathbf{v}_a'$ associated with action a. First observe that since $\mathbf{q} \preceq \mathbf{p}$, there is also a transition $\mathbf{p} \xrightarrow{a} \mathbf{p}' = M_a \cdot (\mathbf{p} - \mathbf{v}_a) + \mathbf{v}_a'$. Moreover, we have $M_a \cdot \mathbf{q} \preceq M_a \cdot \mathbf{p}$, and therefore $M_a \cdot (\mathbf{q} - \mathbf{v}_a) + \mathbf{v}_a' \preceq M_a \cdot (\mathbf{p} - \mathbf{v}_a) + \mathbf{v}_a'$, i.e., $\mathbf{q}' \preceq \mathbf{p}'$.

(ii) For k-maximal transitions, consider again $\mathbf{q} \preceq \mathbf{p}$ and $\mathbf{q} \xrightarrow{a} \mathbf{q}'$, where now a is a k-maximal action. Then $\mathbf{q}' = M_a \cdot (\mathbf{q} - \mathbf{u}_{a,\mathbf{q}}) + \mathbf{u}_{a,\mathbf{q}}'$ for some vectors $\mathbf{u}_{a,\mathbf{q}}, \mathbf{u}_{a,\mathbf{q}}'$ with $\sum_{s \in S} \mathbf{u}_{a,\mathbf{q}}(s) = \sum_{s \in S} \mathbf{u}_{a,\mathbf{q}}'(s) \leq k$. Again, first observe that since $\mathbf{q} \preceq \mathbf{p}$, a transition $\mathbf{p} \xrightarrow{a} \mathbf{p}'$ is enabled, where $\mathbf{p}' = M_a \cdot (\mathbf{p} - \mathbf{u}_{a,\mathbf{p}}) + \mathbf{u}_{a,\mathbf{p}}'$ and $\mathbf{u}_{a,\mathbf{p}}(s) \geq \mathbf{u}_{a,\mathbf{q}}(s)$, $\mathbf{u}_{a,\mathbf{p}}'(s) \geq \mathbf{u}_{a,\mathbf{q}}'(s)$ for all $s \in S$. Note that, for any $s \in S$, we can have $\mathbf{u}_{a,\mathbf{p}}(s) > \mathbf{u}_{a,\mathbf{q}}(s)$ only if $\mathbf{q}(s) - \mathbf{u}_{a,\mathbf{q}}(s) \leq 0$ and $\mathbf{p}(s) > \mathbf{q}(s)$. Furthermore, $\mathbf{u}_{a,\mathbf{p}}(s) - \mathbf{u}_{a,\mathbf{q}}(s) \leq \mathbf{p}(s) - \mathbf{q}(s)$. Therefore, we get $\mathbf{q} - \mathbf{u}_{a,\mathbf{q}} \preceq \mathbf{p} - \mathbf{u}_{a,\mathbf{p}}$, which implies $M_a \cdot (\mathbf{q} - \mathbf{u}_{a,\mathbf{q}}) \preceq M_a \cdot (\mathbf{p} - \mathbf{u}_{a,\mathbf{p}})$, and thus $M_a \cdot (\mathbf{q} - \mathbf{u}_{a,\mathbf{q}}) + \mathbf{u}_{a,\mathbf{q}}' \preceq M_a \cdot (\mathbf{p} - \mathbf{u}_{a,\mathbf{p}}) + \mathbf{u}_{a,\mathbf{p}}'$, i.e., $\mathbf{q}' \preceq \mathbf{p}'$.

Next, we prove that we can effectively compute the basis of $Pred(C)$, where $Pred(C)$ is the set of states from which a transition exists to a state in an upwards-closed set C, as follows:

(i) For a k-sender transition based on action a, any predecessor $\mathbf{q}$ in $Pred(C)$ must satisfy (i) $\mathbf{v}_a \preceq \mathbf{q}$, and (ii) $M_a \cdot (\mathbf{q} - \mathbf{v}_a) + \mathbf{v}_a' = \mathbf{q}'$, for some $\mathbf{q}' \in C$. The basis of $Pred(C)$ consists of the minimal elements (w.r.t. $\preceq$) that satisfy these conditions, and thus is computable.

(ii) For k-maximal transitions, the proof works in the same way, except that now we may have multiple possibilities of what a minimal predecessor could be, based on different subsets of the senders being present or not. Since this is always a finite case distinction, effective computability of $Pred$ is still guaranteed.   □

4   Parameterized Verification for GSPs with Guards

For GSPs with guards, compatibility under $\preceq$ in general does not hold, since for $\mathbf{q} \preceq \mathbf{p}$, a transition on action a that is enabled in $\mathbf{q}$ may not be enabled in $\mathbf{p}$. Furthermore, note that even strong restrictions on processes are unlikely to yield compatibility with respect to $\preceq$, since whenever $\mathsf{supp}(\mathbf{q}) \subseteq G$ for a non-trivial G, one can always find a $\mathbf{p}$ with $\mathbf{q} \preceq \mathbf{p}$ and $\mathsf{supp}(\mathbf{p}) \nsubseteq G$, disabling the action.

Therefore, we introduce a refined WQO, denoted $\trianglelefteq$, that is based on the semantics of guards, as well as sufficient conditions on the guarded process P, such that the system $\mathcal{M}_\infty$ is a WSTS and we can effectively compute $Pred$.

Let $\mathcal{G}$ be the set of guards that appear on transitions in P, and recall that $\mathsf{supp}(\mathbf{q}) = \{s \in S \mid \mathbf{q}(s) > 0\}$. Then we consider the following WQO[3]:

$$\mathbf{q} \trianglelefteq \mathbf{p} \text{ iff } (\mathbf{q} \preceq \mathbf{p} \wedge \forall G \in \mathcal{G} : (\mathsf{supp}(\mathbf{q}) \subseteq G \iff \mathsf{supp}(\mathbf{p}) \subseteq G)).$$

Intuitively, a global state $\mathbf{p}$ is considered greater than a global state $\mathbf{q}$ if $\mathbf{p}$ has at least as many processes as $\mathbf{q}$ in any given state, *and* for every transition $\mathbf{q} \xrightarrow{a} \mathbf{q}'$ that is enabled in $\mathbf{q}$, a transition on action a is also enabled in $\mathbf{p}$.

We will see that compatibility with respect to $\trianglelefteq$ can only be ensured under additional conditions, as formalized in the following.

4.1   Guard-Compatibility and Well-Behaved Processes

Strong Guard-Compatibility for k-Sender Actions. For a k-sender action a with local sending transitions $s_i \xrightarrow{a_i!!,G} s_i'$ for $i \in \{1, \dots, k\}$, let $\hat{s}$ be the set of all states s_i, $\hat{s}'$ the set of states s_i', and M_a the synchronization matrix. We say that action a is *strongly guard-compatible* if the following holds for all $G' \in \mathcal{G}$:

$$\hat{s}' \subseteq G' \Rightarrow \forall s \in G : M_a(s) \in G' \tag{C1}$$

Intuitively, if all senders move into a guard G', then also all receivers need to move into G'. This ensures that if G' is satisfied after the transition in a system of a given size, then it is satisfied after that transition in a system of any bigger size, because any additional receivers must also move into G'. Note that Condition (C1) always holds for trivial guards.

Strong Guard-Compatibility for k-Maximal Actions. For a k-maximal action a, the idea of the condition is the same as before, but it must be extended

---

[3] We show that $\trianglelefteq$ is a WQO by proving that every infinite sequence of global states $\mathbf{q}_1, \mathbf{q}_2, \dots$ contains $\mathbf{q}_i, \mathbf{q}_j$ with $i < j$ and $\mathbf{q}_i \trianglelefteq \mathbf{q}_j$. To this end, consider an arbitrary infinite sequence $\overline{\mathbf{q}} = \mathbf{q}_1, \mathbf{q}_2, \dots$. Then there is at least one set S of local states such that infinitely many $\mathbf{q}_i$ have $\mathsf{supp}(\mathbf{q}_i) = S$. Let $\overline{\mathbf{q}'}$ be the infinite subsequence of $\overline{\mathbf{q}}$ where all elements have $\mathsf{supp}(\mathbf{q}_i') = S$. Since $\preceq$ is a WQO, there exist $\mathbf{q}_i', \mathbf{q}_j'$ with $i < j$ and $\mathbf{q}_i' \preceq \mathbf{q}_j'$, and since $\mathsf{supp}(\mathbf{q}_i') = \mathsf{supp}(\mathbf{q}_j') = S$, we also get $\mathbf{q}_i' \trianglelefteq \mathbf{q}_j'$. Since $\mathbf{q}_i' = \mathbf{q}_k$ and $\mathbf{q}_j' = \mathbf{q}_l$ for some $k < l$, we get $\mathbf{q}_k \trianglelefteq \mathbf{q}_l$ for $k < l$, and thus $\trianglelefteq$ is a WQO.

to allow different subsets of the *potential* senders to act as *actual* senders in a given transition with action a. A simple approximation is that all senders must agree, for every $G \in \mathcal{G}$, on whether they enter G or not.

In the following, we formalize a notion that takes into account that transitions that only use a subset of the potential senders are only possible from certain global states, and that global states with different sets of actual senders may be incomparable with respect to $\trianglelefteq$, and therefore unproblematic for compatibility.

We write $t \triangleleft s$ if, for all guards $G \in \mathcal{G}$, $s \in G \Rightarrow t \in G$. Similarly, we write $t \triangleleft H$ for a set of states H if, for all guards $G \in \mathcal{G}$, $H \subseteq G \Rightarrow t \in G$.

Consider a k-maximal action a with local transitions $s_i \xrightarrow{a_i!!,G} s_i'$ for $i \in \{1, \ldots, k\}$ and synchronization matrix M_a. Let $R = G \setminus \{s_1, \ldots, s_k\}$ and let $\mathcal{G}'$ be the set of all guards $G_R \in \mathcal{G}$ such that $R \subseteq G_R$.

Then we say the action a is *strongly guard-compatible* if both of the following hold for all $G' \in \mathcal{G}$:

$$\left(\bigvee_{1 \leq i \leq k} s_i' \in G' \right) \Rightarrow (\forall s \in R : M_a(s) \in G') \tag{C2.1}$$

$$\bigwedge_{i,j \in \{1, \ldots, k\}} \left((s_i \triangleleft s_j \wedge s_j' \in G') \Rightarrow (s_i' \in G' \wedge M_a(s_i) \in G') \right) \tag{C2.2}$$

Intuitively, if one potential sender moves from a state s_j into a guard G', then every receiver from R must do the same, so that G' will be satisfied regardless of the number of receivers. This is also required for other senders and receivers from a state $s_i \notin R$, unless there exists a guard that is satisfied if s_j is occupied, but not if s_i is occupied, since that means that a global state where only s_j is occupied is incomparable (w.r.t. $\trianglelefteq$) to a state where also s_i is occupied, and therefore we do not care about compatibility of the transitions.

Note that for $k = 1$, the first condition (C2.1) instantiates to condition (C1) and the second condition (C2.2) is an empty conjunction, i.e., vacuously satisfied. This is to be expected, since semantically there is no difference between a 1-sender action and a 1-maximal action.

Example 5. We can see that actions **Smoke**, **Choose**, and **Reset** from our motivating example in Fig. 1 are strongly guard-compatible:

- **Smoke** is a 1-sender action with sending transition ASK $\xrightarrow{\textbf{Smoke}!!,\{\text{ENV. ASK}\}}$ PICK. The state PICK is only included in one non-trivial guard $G_2 = \{$PICK, IDLE$\}$. Since receiving transitions from $\{$ENV, ASK$\}$ end in $\{$PICK, IDLE$\} \subseteq G_2$, condition (C1) holds, so **Smoke** is strongly guard-compatible.

- Consider **Choose** with sending transitions PICK $\xrightarrow{\textbf{Choose}_i!!,\{\text{PICK,IDLE}\}}$ REPORT for $i \in \{1, 2\}$ as a 2-sender action. REPORT is only included in one non-trivial guard $G_3 = \{$REPORT, IDLE$\}$. Since the receiving transition from $\{$PICK$\}$ ends in IDLE $\in G_3$ as well, (C1) holds, so **Choose** is strongly guard-compatible.

- Consider **Choose** as a 2-maximal action. Again, REPORT is only included in one non-trivial guard $G_3 = \{\text{REPORT}, \text{IDLE}\}$. Since all senders and receivers start from PICK and end up in a state in G_3, conditions (C2.1) and (C2.2) hold and **Choose** is, again, strongly guard-compatible.
- **Reset** is a negotiation action. Recall that negotiations are modeled as a set of 1-sender actions, allowing for an arbitrary sender. Therefore, each of these broadcasts must satisfy (C1) for the negotiation to be guard-compatible. **Reset** is indeed strongly guard-compatible because all of its sending and receiving transitions end in ENV, meaning that when the action fires, all processes will move into a single state, ensuring that all guards will be uniformly enabled or disabled, regardless of the number of processes, which of them is the sender, or whether they begin in REPORT or IDLE.
- Finally, as stated in Sect. 2.1, the internal transition $\text{ENV} \xrightarrow{G_1} \text{ASK}$ can be modeled by a 1-sender action, say a, with a send transition $\text{ENV} \xrightarrow{a!!,G_1} \text{ASK}$ and self-loop receive transitions on all states. The sender ends up in one non-trivial guard $G_1 = \{\text{ENV}, \text{ASK}\}$. Since receiving transitions from $\{\text{ENV}, \text{ASK}\}$ end in $\{\text{ENV}, \text{ASK}\} \subseteq G_1$, condition (C1) holds, so a is strongly guard-compatible.

Refinement: Weak Guard-Compatibility. To support a larger class of systems, we show how one can relax the previous conditions, at the cost of making them more complex. The idea is that, instead of requiring that if the sender ends up in a guard then the receivers *immediately* end up in that guard after the transition, it is enough if the receivers *have a path* to a state in that guard. To avoid unnecessary complexity, we only consider paths of internal transitions.

If there exists a path of unguarded internal transitions from s to s', we write $s \rightsquigarrow s'$. Then, condition (C1) can be relaxed to

$$\hat{s}' \subseteq G' \Rightarrow \forall s \in G \colon \left(M_a(s) \in G' \vee \exists s' \in S \colon (s' \triangleleft \hat{s}' \wedge M_a(s) \rightsquigarrow s') \right). \qquad \text{(C1w)}$$

Actions that satisfy condition (C1w) are called *weakly guard-compatible*.

Remark. In a similar way, we can relax conditions (C2.1) and (C2.2). Furthermore, the path $\rightsquigarrow$ of internal transitions can be guarded, as long as the guards are sufficiently general to guarantee that these transitions can be taken. We refer the interested reader to the extended version [38] for more details.

Well-Behavedness. Based on guard-compatibility, we can now define the class of processes that will allow us to retain decidability of reachability properties in the parameterized system: We say that a process P is **well-behaved** if every action is (weakly) guard-compatible.

Note that unguarded processes are trivially well-behaved.

Example 6. Observing that all actions in the process depicted in Fig. 1 are (strongly) guard-compatible, it is clear that the process is **well-behaved**.

Well-Behaved Systems in the Literature. We want to point out that many systems studied in the literature are naturally well-behaved.

For example, Emerson and Kahlon [20] introduce a model for cache coherence protocols that is based on broadcast communication and guards. They show that many textbook protocols can be modeled under the following restrictions: (i) every state is assumed to have an unguarded internal transition to the initial state INIT, and (ii) the only conjunctive guard is {INIT}. Clearly, every action in a process that satisfies these conditions will also satisfy condition (C1w), and therefore well-behaved systems subsume and significantly generalize the types of protocols considered by Emerson and Kahlon.

Moreover, there has recently been much research on the verification of round-based distributed systems [14,34,37], where processes can move independently to some extent, with the restriction that transitions between rounds can only be done synchronously for all processes. When abstracting from certain features (e.g. fault-tolerance and process IDs), our model is well-suited to express such systems: guards can be used to restrict transitions to happen only in a certain round, and can furthermore model the "border" of a round that needs to be reached by all processes, such that they can jointly move to the next round.

Our example from Fig. 1 can also be seen as a round-based system: the first round includes states ENV, ASK, and upon taking the transition on **Smoke**, all processes move to the second round, which includes states PICK, IDLE. From there, on action **Choose** the system moves to the third round, which includes states REPORT, IDLE, and on action **Reset** back to the first round. Note that the states in different rounds are exactly the guards that are used in the transitions—or seen the other way around, guards induce a set of rounds on the local state space, and the guard-compatibility conditions ensure that processes move between these rounds in a systematic way.

While the rounds are very simple in this example, the technique is much more general and can be used to express many round-based systems, including those described in Sect. 6.

4.2 Decidability for Well-Behaved Guarded Processes

Based on the notion of well-behavedness, we can now obtain a decidability result that works in the presence of guards. The following theorem implies that parameterized verification for properties $\phi_m(s)$ is decidable for well-behaved processes.

Theorem 3. *If $\mathcal{M}_\infty$ is based on a well-behaved GSP process, then $\mathcal{M}_\infty$ is a WSTS and we can effectively compute Pred.*

Proof. To prove that $\mathcal{M}_\infty$ is a WSTS, we show compatibility of transitions w.r.t. $\trianglelefteq$, i.e., if $\mathbf{q} \trianglelefteq \mathbf{p}$ and $\mathbf{q} \to \mathbf{q}'$, then $\exists \mathbf{p}'$ with $\mathbf{q}' \trianglelefteq \mathbf{p}'$ and $\mathbf{p} \to^* \mathbf{p}'$. We consider two cases: (i) k-sender transitions, and (ii) k-maximal transitions.

(i) Suppose a is a k-sender action. Let $\mathbf{q} \xrightarrow{a,G} \mathbf{q}'$ be a transition and $\mathbf{q} \trianglelefteq \mathbf{p}$. Since $\mathbf{q} \trianglelefteq \mathbf{p}$ implies that $\mathsf{supp}(\mathbf{p}) \subseteq G$, we know that transition $\mathbf{p} \xrightarrow{a,G} \mathbf{p}'$ is possible, and by the proof of Theorem 2 we know that $\mathbf{q}' \preceq \mathbf{p}'$. To prove compatibility with respect to $\trianglelefteq$, it remains to show that $\forall G' \in \mathcal{G} : (\mathsf{supp}(\mathbf{q}') \subseteq G' \Rightarrow \mathsf{supp}(\mathbf{p}') \subseteq G')$.

First assume that condition (C1) holds. Then, let $G' \in \mathcal{G}$ be an arbitrary guard. By (C1), we either have $\hat{s} \not\subseteq G'$, in which case the desired condition is satisfied for G', or we have that $\forall s \in G: M_a(s) \in G'$, i.e., all potential receivers move into G'. Thus, we get $\mathsf{supp}(\mathbf{q}') \subseteq G'$ iff $\mathsf{supp}(\mathbf{p}') \subseteq G'$, satisfying the desired condition.

If instead of (C1) the action satisfies (C1w), the argument is the same, except that if necessary we use the internal transitions that are guaranteed to exist by the condition to arrive in a state $\mathbf{p}'$ with $\mathbf{q}' \preceq \mathbf{p}'$.

(ii) Suppose a is a k-maximal action with local transitions $s_i \xrightarrow{a_i!!,G} s_i'$ for $i \in \{1, \ldots, k\}$ and synchronization matrix M_a. By the proof of Theorem 2 we know that there exists a transition $\mathbf{p} \xrightarrow{a,G} \mathbf{p}'$ with $\mathbf{q}' \preceq \mathbf{p}'$, and it remains to show that $\forall G' \in \mathcal{G} : (\mathsf{supp}(\mathbf{q}') \subseteq G' \iff \mathsf{supp}(\mathbf{p}') \subseteq G')$.

Let $G' \in \mathcal{G}$ be an arbitrary guard, and assume the action is strongly guard-compatible. By condition (C2.1) we know that if there is a single local sending transition with $s_i' \in G'$, then all receivers will move into G'. So first suppose there is no such local transition: then G' cannot be satisfied in $\mathbf{q}'$ (since at least one sender must be present), and the desired property holds. Inversely, suppose there is such a local transition: then all processes that start in R will be mapped into G', so G' will be satisfied iff all remaining processes are mapped into G'. Now, suppose that *all* local transitions taken in $\mathbf{q} \xrightarrow{a,G} \mathbf{q}'$ are such that $s_i' \in G'$ (for otherwise $\mathbf{q}'$ does not satisfy G'). Since $\mathbf{q} \preceq \mathbf{p}$, there exists a transition $\mathbf{p} \xrightarrow{a,G} \mathbf{p}'$ such that the set of local transitions that are fired in $\mathbf{q} \xrightarrow{a,G} \mathbf{q}'$ is a subset of the local transitions that are fired in $\mathbf{p} \xrightarrow{a,G} \mathbf{p}'$. If all sending transitions taken in $\mathbf{p} \xrightarrow{a,G} \mathbf{p}'$ are also such that $s_i' \in G'$, then by conditions (C2.1) and (C2.2) the same will hold for all receiving transitions from $\mathbf{p}$, and therefore, $\mathsf{supp}(\mathbf{p}') \subseteq G'$. Thus, suppose there is a local transition $s_i \xrightarrow{a_i!!,G} s_i'$ that is taken in $\mathbf{p} \xrightarrow{a,G} \mathbf{p}'$, but not in $\mathbf{q} \xrightarrow{a,G} \mathbf{q}'$, and $s_i' \notin G'$. Let $s_j \xrightarrow{a_j!!,G} s_j'$ be an arbitrary local transition that is taken in $\mathbf{q} \xrightarrow{a,G} \mathbf{q}'$. Then by condition (C2.2), either there must be a guard $G'' \in \mathcal{G}$ with $s_i \notin G'' \wedge s_j \in G''$, contradicting the assumption that $\mathbf{q} \trianglelefteq \mathbf{p}$, or we have $s_j' \in G' \Rightarrow s_i' \in G' \wedge M_a(s_i) \in G'$, contradicting the assumption that $s_i' \notin G'$.

Again, if the action is weakly guard-compatible, the argument can be extended by using the paths of internal transitions, if necessary.

Effective computability of *Pred* follows from the proof of Theorem 2— the only difference is that we must consider the guards, i.e., a predecessor is only valid if it additionally satisfies the guard of the transition under consideration. $\square$

5   Cutoffs for GSPs

We investigate cutoff results for GSPs and their connection to the decidability results in Theorem 2 and 3. While the proofs of these theorems yield a decision procedure for parameterized verification, a cutoff result is more versatile as it reduces parameterized verification to a problem over a fixed number of processes, and under certain conditions can also be used for parameterized synthesis [39].

5.1   Definition and Basic Observations

A *cutoff* for a class of processes Π and a class of properties Φ is a number $c \in \mathbb{N}$ such that for every $P \in \Pi$ and $\phi \in \Phi$,

$$\mathcal{M}_\infty \models \phi \Leftrightarrow \mathcal{M}(c) \models \phi$$

We show how to obtain cutoffs for well-behaved GSPs that satisfy additional conditions, and for reachability properties of the form $\phi_m(s)$, based on observations from the proof of Theorem 2. While for any given parametrized system and any safety property a cutoff exists [45], a general cutoff, even if it can be computed, may be too large to be of practical value: it has been shown that for broadcast protocols the time complexity of checking reachability is non-primitive recursive in the size of the processes [51], and from the proof one can conclude that the same must hold for the size of cutoffs.

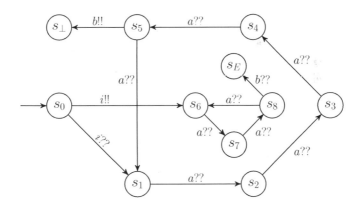

Fig. 2. Example witnessing quadratic cutoff. Not depicted are additional sending transitions on $a!!$ from every state in the outer cycle to $s_\perp$.

Example: Quadratic Cutoffs. Consider the (unguarded) process in Fig. 2. We are interested in a lower bound on the cutoff for this process, with respect to $\phi_1(s_E)$, i.e., reachability of s_E by at least one process. Note that to reach s_E, we need at least one process in s_8 and one in s_5 at the same time. From the initial state s_0, the only possible action is i, sending one process to s_6 in the inner cycle and all other processes to s_1 in the outer cycle. Then, the only way to make progress is action a, moving the process in the inner cycle to s_7, the sending process from s_1 to $s_\perp$ (sending transitions on a!! are not depicted in Fig. 2), and all other processes to s_2. After three further transitions on a, the outer processes are in s_5, where the sending transition on b!! could be fired, but the process in the inner cycle is in s_7, so additional transitions on a are required. Only after two additional rounds around the outer cycle we arrive in a state where both s_5 and s_8 are occupied, and we can take the final transition on b that takes one process into s_E. To arrive there, we took 16 transitions (one on i, 14 on a, and one on b), and by construction every process can only take one sending transition in a run. Thus, we need a system with at least 16 processes to have one of them reach s_E, and no smaller number can be a cutoff for $\phi_1(s_E)$.

To see that cutoffs grow at least quadratically, note that in similar examples where the inner and outer cycles consist of p_1 and p_2 states, respectively, and p_1 and p_2 are relatively prime, then we need $p_1 \cdot p_2 + 1$ processes to reach s_E.

5.2   Conditions for Small Cutoffs

We introduce sufficient conditions on processes that allow us to obtain small cutoffs. These conditions are inspired by our intended applications (see Sect. 6), and based on insights from the decision procedure in the proof of Theorem 2 and the example above. We observe that any $\mathbf{q} \in Pred(C)$ that reaches a state $\mathbf{q}' \in C$ through a k-sender action a must satisfy (i) $\mathbf{v}_a \preceq \mathbf{q}$, and (ii) $M_a \cdot (\mathbf{q} - \mathbf{v}_a) + \mathbf{v}'_a = \mathbf{q}'$. Thus, if there is $\mathbf{q}' \in C$ such that $\neg(\mathbf{v}_a \preceq \mathbf{q})$, we need to consider a predecessor $\mathbf{q}$ with $|\mathbf{q}| > |\mathbf{q}'|$. It is easy to see that this can only happen if $\mathbf{q}'$ contains processes in states that can be reached through a only through either a receiving transition, or a sending transition if $k > 1$. Thus, we want to avoid that states we are interested in are only reachable through such transitions.

We restrict our attention to specifications $\phi_m(s)$ and to cases where we can identify conditions on a GSP process P such that the cutoff for such specifications is $c = m$. If this is the case, then we say that reachability of s is *synchronization-independent* in P, and that the pair $\langle P, \phi_m(s) \rangle$ is **cutoff-amenable**.

We begin with a simple case, where systems are restricted to only internal transitions and negotiations (we defined in Sect. 2.1 how these are expressed in terms of 1-sender transitions).

Lemma 1. *Let $P = \langle A, S, s_0, T \rangle$ be a **well-behaved** GSP process such that all transitions are internal transitions or negotiations. Then reachability of s is synchronization-independent in P for every $s \in S$.*

Proof. To see this, first consider a system with $n > m$ processes, where eventually m of them reach s. We can simulate this run in a system with m processes by simply keeping the m processes that reach s, and removing all others. Similarly, if all processes in a system of size m eventually reach s, then we can simulate this run in a bigger system by adding processes that "follow" the internal transitions of the other processes such that always the same guards as in the original run will be satisfied. Well-behavedness ensures that this is always possible.   □

While we are in general not interested in systems that *only* communicate through internal transitions and negotiations, we can refine this observation based on the states we are interested in, and allow other types of communication.

To this end, define a transition of a process P to be *free* if it is (i) an internal transition, (ii) a sending transition of either a broadcast (i.e., a 1-sender action) or a k-maximal action, or (iii) a receiving transition $s \xrightarrow{a??,G} s'$ of a broadcast with matching sending transition $s \xrightarrow{a!!,G} s'$. Note that the latter includes negotiation transitions. A path from one state to another is *free* if all transitions on the path are free. The idea is that free transitions and paths are only restricted by guards (i.e., the *absence* of processes in certain states), but not by the *existence* of other processes in certain states (as, e.g., a 2-sender transition would be, since a sender depends on the presence of another sender to be able to fire the global transition and move along its own local transition).

Lemma 2. *Let $P = \langle A, S, s_0, T \rangle$ be a **well-behaved** GSP process, and $s \in S$ such that **all** paths from s_0 to s in P are free. Then reachability of s is synchronization-independent in P.*

Proof. The argument follows the same line as the one above for protocols with only internal transitions and negotiations, since the same transitions for existing processes are also possible if we can ensure that the same guards can be satisfied in the bigger system. Well-behavedness ensures that there is a run in the bigger system where the same guards are satisfied.   □

We require that all paths be free, since *existence* of a free path is not sufficient in general: if $m > 1$, then the first process that moves along that free path may force other processes to leave it (e.g., by taking a sending transition of a broadcast). However, this condition is still slightly restrictive, and can be relaxed.

Define a *simple* path as a path with no repeated states. We show that under additional conditions, it is enough to consider restrictions that are based on paths that are simple *and* free:

Lemma 3. *Let $P = \langle A, S, s_0, T \rangle$ be a **well-behaved** GSP process, $s \in S$, and let $\mathcal{F}$ be the set of simple free paths from s_0 to s. If for each send transition:*

1. *the transition does not appear in paths in $\mathcal{F}$ and the corresponding receiving transitions $s_s \xrightarrow{a??,G_a} s_d$ with $s_s \in p$ for some $p \in \mathcal{F}$ have $s_d = s_s$, or,*

2. *the transition appears in paths in $\mathcal{F}$ and the following holds for every corresponding receive transition $s_s \xrightarrow{a??,G_a} s_d$ where $s_s \in p$ for some $p \in \mathcal{F}$ and $s_d \notin p$ for any $p \in \mathcal{F}$: either (a) there exists an internal transition $s_s \to s'_d$ with $s'_d \in p$ for some $p \in \mathcal{F}$, or (b) all paths out of s_d lead back to a state s_f in a path in $\mathcal{F}$ and are free between s_d and s_f.*

then reachability of s is synchronization-independent in P.

Proof. First consider a run of a system that satisfies the above conditions, and has $n > m$ processes, where eventually m of them reach s. We can simulate this run in a system with m processes by keeping the m processes that reach s, and removing all others. Note that the sending transitions are on the same free simple path from which processes can diverge using the corresponding receiving or sending transitions, or they do not affect them at all. Hence, at least one of the senders is guaranteed to reach s. All other senders and receivers may diverge from a simple free path but are guaranteed a free path back to a state along a free path and hence, can reach s freely.

Now assume that all processes in a system of size m eventually reach s, then we can simulate this run in a bigger system by adding processes (that behave in the same way as an existing process). Note that, since any transition diverging from a free simple path can *only* be triggered by a sending transition on that same free path, it is impossible to add a sender that can make processes diverge and then not reach s after.   □

Example 7. In this example we show how Lemma 3 applies to the example in Fig. 1. Here s_0 is the Env state, s is the Report state, and the value of m is 3 (since the safety specification is: no more than 2 detectors can report the fire).

The set of simple free paths $\mathcal{F}$ is:

– Env $\rightarrow$ Ask $\xrightarrow{\textbf{Smoke!!}}$ Pick $\xrightarrow{\textbf{Choose}_i\textbf{!!}}$ Report for $i \in \{1,2\}$, and
– Env $\rightarrow$ Ask $\xrightarrow{\textbf{Smoke??}}$ Pick $\xrightarrow{\textbf{Choose}_i\textbf{!!}}$ Report for $i \in \{1,2\}$.

It is clear that all the sending transitions $\textbf{Smoke!!}, \textbf{Choose}_1\textbf{!!}, \textbf{Choose}_2\textbf{!!}$ appear only in $\mathcal{F}$. Furthermore, the corresponding broadcast-receive transitions satisfy the required conditions as follows:

– the transition Env $\xrightarrow{\textbf{Smoke??}}$ Idle satisfies condition (2a) because the internal transition Env $\rightarrow$ Ask exists in a path in $\mathcal{F}$.
– the transition Pick $\xrightarrow{\textbf{Choose??}}$ Idle satisfies condition (2b) since all paths out of Idle are free (namely, the negotiation transition Idle $\xrightarrow{\textbf{Reset}}$ Env) and lead back to a path in $\mathcal{F}$.

Since Lemma 3 holds, the reachability of s is synchronization-independent and the cutoff is 3.

Checking the Cutoff Conditions. Note that while the conditions in Lemma 3 seem complex, all our cutoff conditions can be checked on the process definition in polynomial time, making them well-suited for fully automatic verification.

6 Applications and Evaluation

To evaluate our approach, we consider several distributed applications that use agreement protocols like consensus or leader election, and that can be modeled as well-behaved systems that satisfy one of our cutoff lemmas:

- Chubby [11]: A distributed lock service for coarse-grained synchronization with an elected leader node that handles client messages.
- Distributed Smoke Detector (SD): A sensor network application that elects a subset of processes, who have detected smoke, to report to the authorities.
- Smoke Detector with Reset (SDR): A variant of SD that uses a "reset" signal to resume monitoring for smoke, thereby requiring infinite rounds of agreement. (this was our motivating example in Fig. 1)
- Distributed Mobile Robotics (DMR): Based on an existing benchmark [18], where a set of robots successively coordinate to create a motion plan.
- Distributed Key-Value Store (KVS) modeling a key-value store á la Redis [48].
- Small Aircraft Transportation System (SATS): The landing protocol of SATS proposed by NASA [53]. SATS aims to increase access to small airports without control towers by allowing aircrafts to coordinate with each other to operate safely upon entering the airport airspace.
- SATS^{++}: A variant of the SATS protocol where all processes communicate explicitly to determine subsets of aircrafts to coordinate the landing with.

In addition, we provide an experimental evaluation, based on related work [37] in which a new model—the CHOOSE model—that can be seen as a refinement of GSP, is proposed. The CHOOSE model extends a standard model of distributed systems [2,3] with a primitive that abstracts various types of distributed agreement protocols. The work further defines a mapping from the CHOOSE model to GSP that establishes a simulation equivalence between the two models, enabling interchange of safety verification and cutoff results between the two models.

Table 1. Performance of parameterized verification based on our cutoffs.

Benchmark	States	Cutoff	Verification time(s)
Chubby	9	2	0.12
SD	5	3	0.28
SDR	5	3	0.13
DMR	8	3	0.16
KVS	18	3	3.06
SATS	24	5	3.83
SATS^{++}	26	5	17.1

To make use of the ease of encoding the above benchmarks in the CHOOSE model and the ease of verification in the CHOOSE model using off-the-shelf model checkers, we illustrate the effect of our cutoff results on efficiency of verification in the CHOOSE model. For the benchmarks given above, Fig. 3 depicts the verification time as a function of the number of processes. Observe that verification time grows roughly exponentially with the number of processes. Moreover, verification for all the benchmarks timed out beyond 9 processes, for a timeout of 30 min. In contrast, in Table 1 all benchmarks have a cutoff of less than 6, and reasonable verification times.

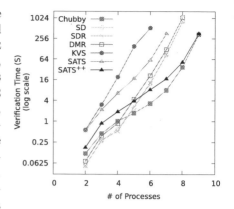

Fig. 3. Verification time as a function of the number of processes.

7   Related Work

Bodies of work that aim at automatically solving the parameterized verification problem (which is undecidable in the most general case [23,54]) take a large variety of different approaches [1,10,13,33,35,41,43,47,56], in most cases without a focus on decidability. In the following we consider the approaches that target decidability, with models closely related to our GSP model.

Models with Broadcasts and/or Global Guards. We want to enable reasoning about distributed systems, abstracting complex building blocks like agreement protocols by primitives that satisfy *assume-guarantee* specifications. To support parameterized reasoning for systems with such abstractions, one needs a model with (i) conjunctive guards to model the assumptions, and (ii) forms of synchronization that are sufficiently general to model the guarantees of those building blocks, i.e., generalizations of broadcast communication.

Esparza et al. [28] present a decidability result for safety properties of broadcast protocols, but without global guards. Their result is also based on a reduction to WSTSs, but we showed that the WQO presented in their work (corresponding to the WQO $\preceq$ in Sect. 3.2) is not suitable for systems with guards. We note that our GSP model subsumes the model of Esparza et al., and that our cutoff results also apply to their model (which had no previous cutoff results).

Other existing models either are not sufficiently general [19,20,22], or support a combination of broadcasts and conjunctive guards without restrictions [21], which makes safety undecidable. This highlights the significance of our result: we manage to find a model with conjunctive guards and global synchronization such that safety remains decidable.

Other Decidable Classes. One way to obtain decidability is to restrict the generality of the parameterized verification problem in various ways. Most results in this direction consider a fully connected network (a clique), either with rendezvous communication [5,32], local updates with global guards [6,19], or variants of these [16]. Some communication primitives have also been considered in more complex networks, for example token passing [4,12,24], or broadcasts [17]. Decidability results for systems that are composed of identical components have recently been surveyed by Bloem et al. [9] as well as Espazra et al. [26]. Several bodies of work attempt to identify cutoff bounds for different classes of distributed systems. For example, cutoffs have been obtained for cache coherence protocols [20], guarded protocols [19,21,40], consensus protocols [44], and self-stabilizing systems [8]. None of these approaches are sufficiently general to tackle the types of distributed applications we address.

Petri Nets and Vector Addition Systems. Also closely related to the parameterized verification problems we consider is the body of work on Petri nets and vector addition systems, surveyed e.g. by Esparza and Nielsen [29] or Reisig [49]. While some types of communication can faithfully be expressed in these systems, global synchronization in general cannot.

8   Conclusion

We introduced global synchronization protocols (GSP), a system model that generalizes many existing models supporting global synchronization such as broadcast synchronization, pairwise rendezvous, and asynchronous rendezvous. We identified sufficient conditions, summarized under our notion of well-behavedness, that ensure decidability of the parameterized verification problem even in the presence of global (conjunctive) transition guards. Finally, we investigated cutoffs for parameterized verification, and identified sufficient conditions under which small cutoffs exist.

In ongoing work, we are focusing on extensions of our cutoff results as well as a dedicated implementation of our decision procedure. In the near future, we plan to investigate sufficient conditions that enable support for the parameterized verification of liveness properties for GSPs, and intend to develop a domain-specific language for writing GSPs that are well-behaved by construction.

References

1. Abdulla, P., Haziza, F., Holik, L.: Parameterized Verification Through View Abstraction. Int. J. Softw. Tools Technol. Transfer **18**(5), 495–516 (2016)
2. Alur, R., Raghothaman, M., Stergiou, C., Tripakis, S., Udupa, A.: Automatic completion of distributed protocols with symmetry. In: Kroening, D., Păsăreanu, C.S. (eds.) CAV 2015. LNCS, vol. 9207, pp. 395–412. Springer, Cham (2015). https://doi.org/10.1007/978-3-319-21668-3_23

3. Alur, R., Tripakis, S.: Automatic synthesis of distributed protocols. SIGACT News **48**(1), 55–90 (2017)
4. Aminof, B., Jacobs, S., Khalimov, A., Rubin, S.: Parameterized model checking of token-passing systems. In: McMillan, K.L., Rival, X. (eds.) VMCAI 2014. LNCS, vol. 8318, pp. 262–281. Springer, Heidelberg (2014). https://doi.org/10.1007/978-3-642-54013-4_15
5. Aminof, B., Kotek, T., Rubin, S., Spegni, F., Veith, H.: Parameterized model checking of rendezvous systems. Distrib. Comput. **31**(3), 187–222 (2018)
6. Außerlechner, S., Jacobs, S., Khalimov, A.: Tight cutoffs for guarded protocols with fairness. In: Jobstmann, B., Leino, K.R.M. (eds.) VMCAI 2016. LNCS, vol. 9583, pp. 476–494. Springer, Heidelberg (2016). https://doi.org/10.1007/978-3-662-49122-5_23
7. Berkovits, I., Lazic, M., Losa, G., Padon, O., Shoham, S.: Verification of Threshold-Based Distributed Algorithms by Decomposition to Decidable Logics. In: International Conference on Computer Aided Verification (2019)
8. Bloem, R., Braud-Santoni, N., Jacobs, S.: Synthesis of self-stabilising and byzantine-resilient distributed systems. In: Chaudhuri, S., Farzan, A. (eds.) CAV 2016. LNCS, vol. 9779, pp. 157–176. Springer, Cham (2016). https://doi.org/10.1007/978-3-319-41528-4_9
9. Bloem, R., Jacobs, S., Khalimov, A., Konnov, I., Rubin, S., Veith, H., Widder, J.: Decidability of Parameterized Verification. Morgan & Claypool Publishers, Synthesis Lectures on Distributed Computing Theory (2015)
10. Bouajjani, A., Jonsson, B., Nilsson, M., Touili, T.: Regular model checking. In: Emerson, E.A., Sistla, A.P. (eds.) CAV 2000. LNCS, vol. 1855, pp. 403–418. Springer, Heidelberg (2000). https://doi.org/10.1007/10722167_31
11. Burrows, M.: The chubby lock service for loosely-coupled distributed systems. In: Proceedings of the 7th Symposium on Operating Systems Design and Implementation, pp. 335–350. USENIX Association (2006)
12. Clarke, E., Talupur, M., Touili, T., Veith, H.: Verification by network decomposition. In: Gardner, P., Yoshida, N. (eds.) CONCUR 2004. LNCS, vol. 3170, pp. 276–291. Springer, Heidelberg (2004). https://doi.org/10.1007/978-3-540-28644-8_18
13. Clarke, E., Talupur, M., Veith, H.: Environment abstraction for parameterized verification. In: Emerson, E.A., Namjoshi, K.S. (eds.) VMCAI 2006. LNCS, vol. 3855, pp. 126–141. Springer, Heidelberg (2005). https://doi.org/10.1007/11609773_9
14. Damian, A., Dragoi, C., Militaru, A., Widder, J.: Communication-closed Asynchronous Protocols. In: International Conference on Computer Aided Verification (2019)
15. Damm, W., Finkbeiner, B.: Automatic Compositional Synthesis of Distributed Systems. In: International Symposium on Formal Methods. pp. 179–193. Springer (2014)
16. Delzanno, G., Raskin, J., Begin, L.V.: Towards the Automated Verification of Multithreaded Java Programs. In: TACAS. Lecture Notes in Computer Science, vol. 2280, pp. 173–187. Springer (2002)
17. Delzanno, G., Sangnier, A., Traverso, R., Zavattaro, G.: On the Complexity of Parameterized Reachability in Reconfigurable Broadcast Networks. In: D'Souza, D., Kavitha, T., Radhakrishnan, J. (eds.) IARCS Annual Conference on Foundations of Software Technology and Theoretical Computer Science, FSTTCS 2012, Hyderabad, India, 15–17 December, 2012. LIPIcs, vol. 18, pp. 289–300. Schloss Dagstuhl - Leibniz-Zentrum fuer Informatik (2012)

18. Desai, A., Saha, I., Yang, J., Qadeer, S., Seshia, S.A.: DRONA: a framework for safe distributed mobile robotics. In: Proceedings of the 8th International Conference on Cyber-Physical Systems, ICCPS 2017, pp. 239–248. ACM (2017)

19. Emerson, E.A., Kahlon, V.: Reducing model checking of the many to the few. In: McAllester, D. (ed.) CADE 2000. LNCS (LNAI), vol. 1831, pp. 236–254. Springer, Heidelberg (2000). https://doi.org/10.1007/10721959_19

20. Emerson, E.A., Kahlon, V.: Exact and efficient verification of parameterized cache coherence protocols. In: Geist, D., Tronci, E. (eds.) CHARME 2003. LNCS, vol. 2860, pp. 247–262. Springer, Heidelberg (2003). https://doi.org/10.1007/978-3-540-39724-3_22

21. Emerson, E.A., Kahlon, V.: Model checking guarded protocols. In: Proceedings of the 18th IEEE Symposium on Logic in Computer Science (LICS 2003), Ottawa, Canada, 22–25 June 2003, pp. 361–370. IEEE Computer Society (2003)

22. Emerson, E.A., Kahlon, V.: Rapid parameterized model checking of snoopy cache coherence protocols. In: Garavel, H., Hatcliff, J. (eds.) TACAS 2003. LNCS, vol. 2619, pp. 144–159. Springer, Heidelberg (2003). https://doi.org/10.1007/3-540-36577-X_11

23. Emerson, E.A., Namjoshi, K.S.: Reasoning about rings. In: Proceedings of the 22nd ACM SIGPLAN-SIGACT Symposium on Principles of Programming Languages, POPL 1995, pp. 85–94. ACM (1995)

24. Emerson, E.A., Namjoshi, K.S.: On reasoning about rings. Int. J. Found. Comput. Sci. **14**(4), 527–550 (2003)

25. Emerson, E.A., Trefler, R.J.: From asymmetry to full symmetry: new techniques for symmetry reduction in model checking. In: Pierre, L., Kropf, T. (eds.) CHARME 1999. LNCS, vol. 1703, pp. 142–157. Springer, Heidelberg (1999). https://doi.org/10.1007/3-540-48153-2_12

26. Esparza, J.: Parameterized Verification of Crowds of Anonymous Processes. In: Esparza, J., Grumberg, O., Sickert, S. (eds.) Dependable Software Systems Engineering, NATO Science for Peace and Security Series - D: Information and Communication Security, vol. 45, pp. 59–71. IOS Press (2016)

27. Esparza, J., Desel, J.: On negotiation as concurrency primitive. In: D'Argenio, P.R., Melgratti, H. (eds.) CONCUR 2013. LNCS, vol. 8052, pp. 440–454. Springer, Heidelberg (2013). https://doi.org/10.1007/978-3-642-40184-8_31

28. Esparza, J., Finkel, A., Mayr, R.: On the verification of broadcast protocols. In: 14th Annual IEEE Symposium on Logic in Computer Science, Trento, Italy, 2–5 July 1999, pp. 352–359. IEEE Computer Society (1999)

29. Esparza, J., Nielsen, M.: Decidability issues for petri nets - a survey. Bull. EATCS **52**, 244–262 (1994)

30. Finkel, A.: A generalization of the procedure of karp and miller to well structured transition systems. In: Ottmann, T. (ed.) ICALP 1987. LNCS, vol. 267, pp. 499–508. Springer, Heidelberg (1987). https://doi.org/10.1007/3-540-18088-5_43

31. Finkel, A., Schnoebelen, P.: Well-structured transition systems everywhere!. Theor. Comput. Sci. **256**(1–2), 63–92 (2001)

32. German, S.M., Sistla, A.P.: Reasoning about systems with many processes. J. ACM **39**(3), 675–735 (1992)

33. Ghilardi, S., Ranise, S.: Backward reachability of array-based systems by SMT solving: termination and invariant synthesis. Logical Methods Comput. Sci. **6**(4), 1–48 (2010)

34. v. Gleissenthall, K., Kici, R.G., Bakst, A., Stefan, D., Jhala, R.: Pretend Synchrony: Synchronous Verification of Asynchronous Distributed Programs. Proc. ACM Program. Lang. 3(POPL), 59:1–59:30 (2019)

35. Gurfinkel, A., Shoham, S., Meshman, Y.: SMT-based verification of parameterized systems. In: SIGSOFT FSE, pp. 338–348. ACM (2016)
36. Hawblitzel, C., et al.: IronFleet: proving practical distributed systems correct. In: Proceedings of the 25th Symposium on Operating Systems Principles, SOSP 2015, pp. 1–17. ACM (2015)
37. Jaber, N., Jacobs, S., Wagner, C., Kulkarni, M., Samanta, R.: Parameterized Reasoning for Distributed Systems with Consensus. arXiv arXiv:2004.04613 (2020)
38. Jaber, N., Jacobs, S., Wagner, C., Kulkarni, M., Samanta, R.: Parameterized Verification of Systems with Global Synchronization and Guards (Extended Version). arXiv arXiv:2004.04896 (2020)
39. Jacobs, S., Bloem, R.: Parameterized synthesis. Logical Methods in Comput. Sci. **10**(1), 1–29 (2014)
40. Jacobs, S., Sakr, M.: Analyzing guarded protocols: better cutoffs, more systems, more expressivity. VMCAI 2018. LNCS, vol. 10747, pp. 247–268. Springer, Cham (2018). https://doi.org/10.1007/978-3-319-73721-8_12
41. Kaiser, A., Kroening, D., Wahl, T.: Dynamic cutoff detection in parameterized concurrent programs. In: Touili, T., Cook, B., Jackson, P. (eds.) CAV 2010. LNCS, vol. 6174, pp. 645–659. Springer, Heidelberg (2010). https://doi.org/10.1007/978-3-642-14295-6_55
42. Konnov, I., Lazić, M., Veith, H., Widder, J.: A short counterexample property for safety and liveness verification of fault-tolerant distributed algorithms. ACM SIGPLAN Not. **52**(1), 719–734 (2017)
43. Kurshan, R.P., McMillan, K.L.: A structural induction theorem for processes. Inf. Comput. **117**(1), 1–11 (1995)
44. Marić, O., Sprenger, C., Basin, D.: Cutoff bounds for consensus algorithms. In: Majumdar, R., Kunčak, V. (eds.) CAV 2017. LNCS, vol. 10427, pp. 217–237. Springer, Cham (2017). https://doi.org/10.1007/978-3-319-63390-9_12
45. Namjoshi, K.S.: Symmetry and completeness in the analysis of parameterized systems. In: Cook, B., Podelski, A. (eds.) VMCAI 2007. LNCS, vol. 4349, pp. 299–313. Springer, Heidelberg (2007). https://doi.org/10.1007/978-3-540-69738-1_22
46. Padon, O., McMillan, K.L., Panda, A., Sagiv, M., Shoham, S.: IVY: safety verification by interactive generalization. In: Proceedings of the 37th ACM SIGPLAN Conference on Programming Language Design and Implementation, PLDI 2016, pp. 614–630. ACM (2016)
47. Pnueli, A., Ruah, S., Zuck, L.: Automatic deductive verification with invisible invariants. In: Margaria, T., Yi, W. (eds.) TACAS 2001. LNCS, vol. 2031, pp. 82–97. Springer, Heidelberg (2001). https://doi.org/10.1007/3-540-45319-9_7
48. Redis. https://redis.io/
49. Reisig, W.: Understanding Petri Nets - Modeling Techniques, Analysis Methods,Case Studies. Springer (2013). https://doi.org/10.1007/978-3-642-33278-4
50. Scalas, A., Yoshida, N., Benussi, E.: Verifying message-passing programs with dependent behavioural types. In: Proceedings of the 40th ACM SIGPLAN Conference on Programming Language Design and Implementation, PLDI 2019, pp. 502–516. ACM (2019)
51. Schmitz, S., Schnoebelen, P.: The power of well-structured systems. In: D'Argenio, P.R., Melgratti, H. (eds.) CONCUR 2013. LNCS, vol. 8052, pp. 5–24. Springer, Heidelberg (2013). https://doi.org/10.1007/978-3-642-40184-8_2
52. Sergey, I., Wilcox, J.R., Tatlock, Z.: Programming and proving with distributed protocols. Proc. ACM Program. Lang. **2**(POPL), 28:1–28:30 (2017)
53. NASA - Small Aircraft Transportation System. https://www.nasa.gov/centers/langley/news/factsheets/SATS.html

54. Suzuki, I.: Proving properties of a ring of finite-state machines. Inf. Process. Lett. **28**(4), 213–214 (1988)
55. Wilcox, J.R., et al.: Verdi: a framework for implementing and formally verifying distributed systems. In: Proceedings of the 36th ACM SIGPLAN Conference on Programming Language Design and Implementation, PLDI 2015, pp. 357–368. ACM (2015)
56. Wolper, P., Lovinfosse, V.: Verifying properties of large sets of processes with network invariants. In: Sifakis, J. (ed.) CAV 1989. LNCS, vol. 407, pp. 68–80. Springer, Heidelberg (1990). https://doi.org/10.1007/3-540-52148-8_6

Hampa: Solver-Aided Recency-Aware Replication

Xiao Li$^{(\boxtimes)}$, Farzin Houshmand$^{(\boxtimes)}$,
and Mohsen Lesani$^{(\boxtimes)}$

University of California, Riverside, USA
{xli289,fhous001,lesani}@ucr.edu

Abstract. Replication is a common technique to build reliable and scalable systems. Traditional strong consistency maintains the same total order of operations across replicas. This total order is the source of multiple desirable consistency properties: integrity, convergence and recency. However, maintaining the total order has proven to inhibit availability and performance. Weaker notions exhibit responsiveness and scalability; however, they forfeit the total order and hence its favorable properties. This project revives these properties with as little coordination as possible. It presents a tool called Hampa that given a sequential object with the declaration of its integrity and recency requirements, automatically synthesizes a correct-by-construction replicated object that simultaneously guarantees the three properties. It features a relational object specification language and a syntax-directed analysis that infers optimum staleness bounds. Further, it defines coordination-avoidance conditions and the operational semantics of replicated systems that provably guarantees the three properties. It characterizes the computational power and presents a protocol for recency-aware objects. Hampa uses automatic solvers statically and embeds them in the runtime to dynamically decide the validity of coordination-avoidance conditions. The experiments show that recency-aware objects reduce coordination and response time.

1 Introduction

Replicated objects [12,13,23,32,45] are pervasively used for fault-tolerance, availability, responsiveness and scalability. They are used in diverse application areas [14,20–22,37,39,40,50,53] including embedded controllers, online services and game engines. However, coordinating the replicas has proven to be challenging. Strongly consistent replication, provided by consensus protocols such as Viewstamp [42], Paxos [34] and Raft [44], guarantees the same total order of operations across replicas. The total order simultaneously provides a hoard of favorable properties: integrity, convergence and recency. Replicas converge to the same state as the result of the same sequence of operations. Further, a propagated operation executes in the same state as the originating replica. Therefore, if an operation preserves the integrity properties [8] at the originating replica, it

This project was supported by the NSF grant #1942711.

S. K. Lahiri and C. Wang (Eds.): CAV 2020, LNCS 12224, pp. 324–349, 2020.
https://doi.org/10.1007/978-3-030-53288-8_16

will certainly preserve them in the other replicas as well. In addition, the lock-step execution keeps the replicas recent: an operations executes in all replicas before the next. Thus, replicas can be stale by at most one operation.

However, strong consistency may not be available and responsive during network failures or offline use. Further, its scalability is limited. The trade-off between strong consistency of replicated objects, and their availability and responsiveness is a famous dilemma [1,3,26–28]. Therefore, system designers opted for weaker notions of consistency such as eventual [4,15,17,19,24,25,48,52] and causal [2,13,33] consistency that can provide availability, responsiveness and scalability but lose the same total order of operations. Several projects [16,49,51] provide programming interfaces for weak consistency notions. Unfortunately, the large collection of subtle weak consistency notions is unintuitive to users. If the chosen notion is too weak, it can affect correctness, and if it is too strong, it may degrade scalability.

Therefore, researchers have recently provided high-level abstractions to shield the user from low-level complexities of weak consistency. These projects seem to be the steps towards reviving the same three pillars of consistency, i.e. integrity, convergence and recency, with as little coordination [7,35,47] as possible. CRDTs [48] revived convergence. If an object satisfies a few algebraic properties, its repli-cation can enjoy convergence even on top of eventual consistency. However, the replicas can experience states that violate the integrity properties. Therefore, follow-up projects revived the integrity property. CISE [29] and Soteria [41] present proof techniques to verify the integrity properties of a replicated object. Sieve [36], Indigo [10] and Hamsaz [30] translate the given high-level integrity properties to hybrid models. However, they are oblivious to state recency. The operations are eventually delivered to all replicas, however, they may be arbi-trarily delayed. Some updates may be delivered too late and expose the clients to stale data. On the other hand, at the expense of more communication, some updates may be immediately sent and delivered. However, applications may prefer to obtain more scalability and energy efficiency in return for bounded staleness. In fact, many applications such as ticketing, distributed sensors and network accounting can work with fairly recent data. Previous work such as TACT [55], TRAPP [43], FRACT [59], and PBS [9] considered staleness but did not address integrity and communication minimization. Further, they did not provide automatic analysis, decision and synthesis. In addition to convergence and integrity, this project, HAMPA, revives recency. Given a sequential object with the declaration of its integrity properties and recency requirements for its methods, it automatically synthesizes a correct-by-construction replicated object that guarantees integrity, convergence and recency while avoiding unnecessary coordination.

To capture object specifications from the user, we present a relational lan-guage and its denotational semantics. The language provides a complete set of relational operators to define the object methods and integrity properties, and allows the user to declare recency requirements for the return value of each method. Given a principled object specification, we present a syntax-directed analysis that infers optimum staleness bounds for each element of the state.

We present the conditions required to simultaneously preserve the three properties: convergence, integrity and recency. These conditions are used to define a novel operational semantics of replicated objects that provably preserve convergence, integrity and the inferred staleness bound. We observe that recency-awareness not only guarantees a limit on the staleness, but also allows buffering of calls and reduces the coordination required to preserve integrity.

We characterize the computational power of recency-aware replicated objects. We show that recency-aware objects have the same power as the perfect failure detector. We present a novel protocol for recency-aware replicated objects that implements the semantics. We use off-the-shelve SMT solvers both statically and embed them at runtime to decide the validity of coordination-avoidance conditions. We present a tool called HAMPA that given an object definition, analyzes the object and instantiates the protocol to synthesize replicated objects. Our experiments with the synthesized objects show that the staleness bound has an inverse relationship with the coordination and response time.

In summary, this paper presents the following contributions: (1) A relational object specification language that captures integrity and recency declarations, and its denotational semantics (Sect. 2). (2) The coordination conditions and the operational semantics of replicated systems that simultaneously preserve convergence, integrity and recency (Sects. 3 and 4). (3) A syntax-directed analysis that infers optimum staleness bounds for each element of the state (Sect. 5). (4) The characterization of the computational power and a protocol for recency-aware replicated objects, (Sect. 6). (5) The HAMPA replicated object synthesis tool and its experimental results (Sect. 7). All the proofs are available in the appendix [5].

2   Recency-Aware Relational Object Language

Language. Figure 1 shows our core relational language for object specification. An object is a record $\langle \Sigma, \mathcal{I}, \mathcal{M} \rangle$ that includes a state type Σ, an invariant $\mathcal{I}$ on the state, and a set of methods $\mathcal{M}$. The state can be a tuple of natural number Nat and relation Rel types. The invariant $\mathcal{I}$ is a boolean function on the state. A method m is a function from the parameter x and the pre-state $\langle x_1, .., x_n \rangle$ to a record of $\langle e_g, e_u, e_r \rangle$. The guard e_g is a boolean expression that captures the semantic preconditions of m such as conditions on the arguments. The expressions e_u and e_r are for the post-state and the return value. We use guard, update and retv as functions that extract elements of this record. For each method, the user declares an integer as the staleness bound ϵ for its return value. A method call c is a method applied to its argument i.e. it is a function from the current state to a record of $\langle e_g, e_u, e_r \rangle$.

An expression e is either a value v (that can be either a number n or a relation R), a variable denoted by x, an application of the operators $\{+, -, =, <, \&, !\}$ to operand expressions where $\&$ is the conjunction and and $!$ is the negation operator, a selection $\sigma_{\lambda \langle \overline{x} \rangle . e}(e')$ that binds the attributes of each element of the relation e' to the variables $\bar{x}$ and returns the elements that satisfy the condition e, a projection $\Pi_{\lambda\langle\bar{x}\rangle.\langle\bar{e}\rangle}(e')$ that for each element of the relation e', binds its attributes to the variables $\bar{x}$ and calculates a tuple of elements $\langle\bar{e}\rangle$ and returns the set of resulting tuples, a union $e \cup e'$ that results in a relation with elements of both of the relations e and e', a difference $e \setminus e'$ that results in a relation with the elements in the relation e that are not in the relation e', and the Cartesian product $e \times e'$ that results in a relation with pair elements where the first and second elements are in the relations e and e' respectively. The language supports a complete set of relational operators: any relational algebra expression can be expressed by a combination of them. Selection (σ), projection (π), union ($\cup$), difference ($\setminus$), product ($\times$) and renaming (ρ) are a complete set of operators. We note that since the language uses functions with argument names, a renaming operator is unnecessary. The update and join operations are defined as a syntactic sugar. The update operation $\mathcal{U}_{\lambda\langle\bar{x}\rangle.\langle e,\langle\bar{e'}\rangle\rangle}e''$ returns a relation that updates each element of e'' that satisfies the condition e to the tuple $\langle\bar{e'}\rangle$. The join $e_1 \bowtie_{\lambda\langle\bar{x_1},\bar{x_2}\rangle.e} e_2$ results in pairs of elements of e_1 and e_2 that satisfy the condition e.

$$o := \langle\Sigma, \mathcal{I}, \mathcal{M}\rangle \qquad \text{Object}$$
$$\Sigma := \langle T, .., T\rangle \qquad \text{State}$$
$$T := \mathsf{Nat} \mid \mathsf{Rel}$$
$$\mathcal{I} \qquad \text{Invariant}$$
$$\mathcal{M} := \overline{me} \qquad \text{Methods}$$
$$me := \mathsf{def} \ \epsilon \ m(x)(\langle x_1, .., x_n\rangle) \qquad \text{Method}$$
$$\langle e_g, e_u, e_r\rangle$$
$$e := \qquad\qquad \text{Expression}$$
$$v \qquad\qquad \text{Value}$$
$$\mid \ x \qquad\qquad \text{Variable}$$
$$\mid \ e+e \mid e-e \qquad \text{Math}$$
$$\mid \ e=e \mid e<e$$
$$\mid \ e \ \& \ e \mid !e$$
$$\mid \ \sigma_{\lambda\langle\bar{x}\rangle.e}(e) \qquad \text{Selection}$$
$$\mid \ \Pi_{\lambda\langle\bar{x}\rangle.\langle\bar{e}\rangle}(e') \qquad \text{Projection}$$
$$\mid \ e \cup e \qquad\qquad \text{Union}$$
$$\mid \ e \setminus e \qquad\qquad \text{Difference}$$
$$\mid \ e \times e \qquad\qquad \text{Product}$$
$$v := n \mid \mathsf{true} \mid \mathsf{false} \mid R \qquad \text{Value}$$

$$\mathcal{U}_{\lambda\langle\bar{x}\rangle.\langle e,\langle\bar{e'}\rangle\rangle}e'' := \qquad \text{Update}$$
$$\Pi_{\lambda\langle\bar{x}\rangle.\langle\bar{e'}\rangle} \ \sigma_{\lambda\langle\bar{x}\rangle.e} \ e'' \cup$$
$$\sigma_{\lambda\langle\bar{x}\rangle.\neg e}e''$$

$$e_1 \bowtie_{\lambda\langle\bar{x_1},\bar{x_2}\rangle.e} e_2 := \qquad \text{Join}$$
$$\sigma_{\lambda\langle\bar{x_1},\bar{x_2}\rangle.e}(e_1 \times e_2)$$

$$[\![v]\!] = v \qquad\qquad [\![x]\!] = \bot$$

$$[\![e \oplus e']\!] = [\![e]\!] \oplus [\![e']\!] \qquad [\![!e]\!] = ! [\![e]\!]$$

$$[\![\sigma_{\lambda\bar{x}.e'}(e)]\!] =$$
$$\{ t \mid t \in [\![e]\!] \ \wedge \ [\![e'[\bar{x} \mapsto t]]\!] = \mathsf{true} \}$$

$$[\![\Pi_{\lambda\langle\bar{x}\rangle.\langle\bar{e}\rangle}(e')]\!] =$$
$$\{ \langle [\![e[\bar{x} \mapsto t]]\!] \rangle \mid t \in [\![e']\!] \}$$

$$[\![e \cup e']\!] = [\![e]\!] \cup [\![e']\!]$$
$$[\![e \setminus e']\!] = [\![e]\!] \setminus [\![e']\!]$$
$$[\![e \times e']\!] = [\![e]\!] \times [\![e']\!]$$

Fig. 1. Syntax and semantics of the specification language

Semantics. Figure 1 presents a denotational semantics for expressions. The semantics for values, variables, and binary and unary operations is standard. The semantics of the selection expression $\sigma_{\lambda\langle\bar{x}\rangle.e'}(e)$ is the set of tuples t in the semantics of e such that substitution of the attributes $\bar{x}$ in e' with their corresponding values in t evaluates to true. The semantics of the projection

Class MovieBooking

Σ := let rs := Set $\mathbb{N} \times \mathbb{N}$ in   ▷ Reservation: user identifier and movie identifier

let ms := Set $\mathbb{N} \times \mathbb{N}$ in   ▷ Movie: movie identifier and available space

$\langle rs, ms \rangle$

$\mathcal{I}$:= $\lambda \langle rs, ms \rangle$. unique $(ms, \lambda \langle m, a \rangle.\ m)\ \wedge$

refIntegrity $(rs, \lambda \langle u, m \rangle.\ m, ms, \lambda \langle m, a \rangle.\ m)\ \wedge$

rowIntegrity $(ms, \lambda \langle m, a \rangle.\ a \geq 0)$

book$(\langle u, m \rangle)$:= 0 $\lambda \langle rs, ms \rangle$.

$\langle \langle u, m \rangle \notin rs,\quad \langle rs \cup \langle u, m \rangle,\ \mathcal{U}_{\lambda \langle m', a \rangle.\ \langle m' = m, \langle m, a-1 \rangle \rangle}\ ms \rangle,\quad \perp \rangle$

cancelBook$(\langle u, m \rangle)$:= 0 $\lambda \langle rs, ms \rangle$.

$\langle \text{True},\quad \langle rs \setminus \langle u, m \rangle,\ \mathcal{U}_{\lambda \langle m', a \rangle.\ \langle m' = m, \langle m, a+1 \rangle \rangle}\ ms \rangle,\quad \perp \rangle$

offScreen(m) := 0 $\lambda \langle rs, ms \rangle$.

$\langle \text{True},\quad \langle rs,\ ms \setminus \sigma_{\lambda \langle m', a \rangle.\ m' = m}\ ms \rangle,\quad \perp \rangle$

specialReserve$(\langle m, n \rangle)$:= 0 $\lambda \langle rs, ms \rangle$.

$\langle n > 0,\quad \langle rs,\ \mathcal{U}_{\lambda \langle m', a \rangle.\ \langle m' = m, \langle m, a-n \rangle \rangle}\ ms \rangle,\quad \perp \rangle$

increaseSpace$(\langle m, n \rangle)$:= 0 $\lambda \langle rs, ms \rangle$.

$\langle n > 0,\quad \langle rs,\ \mathcal{U}_{\lambda \langle m', a \rangle.\ \langle m' = m, \langle m, a+n \rangle \rangle}\ ms \rangle,\quad \perp \rangle$

querySpace(m) := ϵ_1 $\lambda \langle rs, ms \rangle$.

$\langle \text{True},\quad \langle rs, ms \rangle,\quad \Pi_{\lambda \langle m', a \rangle.\ \langle a \rangle}\ (\sigma_{\lambda \langle m', a \rangle.\ m' = m}\ ms) \rangle$

queryReservations(u) := ϵ_2 $\lambda \langle rs, ms \rangle$.

$\langle \text{True},\quad \langle rs, ms \rangle,\quad \Pi_{\lambda \langle u', m \rangle.\ \langle m \rangle}\ (\sigma_{\lambda \langle u', m \rangle.\ u' = u}\ rs) \rangle$

querySpaces(u) := ϵ_3 $\lambda \langle rs, ms \rangle$.

$\langle \text{True},\quad \langle rs, ms \rangle,\quad \Pi_{\lambda \langle u, m, m', a \rangle\ \langle m, a \rangle}\ (rs \bowtie_{\lambda \langle u, m \rangle, \langle m', a \rangle.\ m = m'}\ ms) \rangle$

Fig. 2. Movie booking use-case

expression $\Pi_{\lambda \langle \overline{x} \rangle.\langle \overline{e} \rangle}(e')$ is a set of tuples, one per each tuple t in the semantics of e': a tuple resulted from substituting $\overline{x}$ with t in the expressions $\overline{e}$ and evaluating them. The semantics of union, difference and product are standard from the set theory. We define the difference Δ between two values as follows: the difference between two natural numbers is the absolute value of their subtraction i.e. $\Delta(n, n') = |n - n'|$; the difference of two relations is the size of their symmetric difference i.e. $\Delta(R, R') = |R \setminus R'| + |R' \setminus R|$. We use delta δ to represents the staleness of a value that is the difference between the value and its target value. The delta for a completely recent (or exact) value is zero. For a call c, the weight weight(c) is a bound on the difference that the execution of c can make on the state of the object. In other words, for every call c, we have $\forall \sigma$. Let $\langle \_, \sigma', \_ \rangle := c(\sigma)$ in $\Delta(\sigma', \sigma) <$ weight(c).

Running Use-Case. Figure 2 shows the movie booking use-case. The state of the object is the two relations reservation rs and movie ms. The reservation relation rs stores the movies that the users have booked; it is the pairs of users u and movies m. The movie relation ms stores the number of available spaces for each movie; it is the pairs of movies m and spaces a. The integrity property $\mathcal{I}$ is a conjunction of three conditions: (1) The movie in ms should be unique. (2) The referential integrity requires that every movie in rs exists in ms. (3) The number of available spaces for every movie should be non-negative. The object provides five update methods and three query methods. Given a user u and a movie m, the method book adds the pair to rs and decrements the available spaces for m in ms. Similarly, the method cancelBook removes a reservation and increments available spaces. Given a movie m, the method offScreen removes the corresponding tuple from ms. Given a movie m and a number n, the method specialReserve subtracts n from the available spaces for m in ms. The dual method increaseSpace adds n to the spaces for m. Given a movie m, the method querySpace returns the number of available spaces for m. The method queryReservations returns the set of movies that the given user has booked. Given a user u, the method querySpaces returns the pairs of movies and their available spaces for the movies that u has booked. The staleness bound for the update methods is specified as 0. The returned none constant $\bot$ is always exact. The bound values ϵ_1, ϵ_2 and ϵ_3 of the query methods represent the number of tuples that are different between the current state and the pending stable state of the result relation.

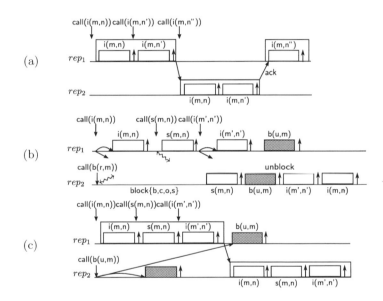

Fig. 3. (a) Buffering and coordination. Example execution (b) without and (c) with recency. $\downarrow$: request, $\uparrow$: indication, $\leadsto$: synchronization

To reduce communication, certain calls can be executed locally and buffered, and the buffer can be communicated to other replicas later. As an example, in Fig. 3(a), the first two calls to the method increaseSpace do not exceed the staleness bound for ms and can be buffered. However, the third call exceeds the bound and cannot be added to the buffer. Therefore, the buffer is flushed to other replicas and the third call is blocked until an acknowledgement for the delivery of the buffer is received. All the calls of the buffer can be sent in a single message and the acknowledgement for them can be sent in a single message as well.

Let us now consider the interaction of buffering with coordination. We will see that buffering (staleness) interestingly reduces the coordination required for the conflicts. (We will define conflicting calls that should be synchronized later in Sect. 3.) Fig. 3(b) and (c) show the same execution without and with buffering respectively. In Fig. 3(b), the first replica rep_1 executes the sequence of calls increaseSpace, specialReserve and increaseSpace. The method increaseSpace does not conflict with any other method; therefore, calls to it are simply broadcast. The method specialReserve conflicts with itself and the method book; therefore, the call to it goes through synchronization. The second replica rep_2 calls book that conflicts with four other methods. Hence, it should synchronize. (The synchronization reaches to other replicas, blocks calling the four methods, and propagates previous calls to those methods.) In this example, the conflicting specialReserve call in rep_1 should be propagated to rep_2 before the book call can be executed.

In Fig. 3(c), the recency bound allows the three calls of rep_1 to be buffered. Replicas use SMT solvers at runtime to check the validity of three properties for the buffers: all-$\mathcal{S}$-commutativity, invariant-sufficiency and let-$\mathcal{P}$-R-commutativity that we will formally define in Sect. 3. In this example, the buffer is invariant-sufficient if the number of spaces that the call specialReserve decrements is less than the number that the increaseSpace calls increment. Therefore, the buffer can be sent to other replicas without any additional synchronization; the invariant in the pre-state is sufficient for the invariant in its post-state. We note that the call specialReserve that previously went through synchronization does not need any synchronization inside the buffer. Further, the let-$\mathcal{P}$-R-commutativity property of the buffer guarantees that the book call will preserve the integrity after the buffer. Thus, the synchronization of the book call that previously waited for the specialReserve call does not need to wait anymore.

3   Coordination Conditions

In this section, we present the coordination conditions for replicated objects that preserve the three properties: convergence, integrity and recency. The state of the given sequential object is replicated across replicas. Clients can request method calls at every replica, and replicas coordinate the calls. *Convergence* is the safety property that when all pending updates are processed, the replicas converge to the same state. *Integrity* is the safety property that every method call is executed only on a state where the guard of the method and the invariant are satisfied. *Recency* is the safety property that bounds the difference between the state of a replica and its impending state after the pending calls are applied.

The state of each replica is initialized to the same state σ_0 that satisfies the invariant $\mathcal{I}$. The replica that accepts the request for a call from the user is called the originating replica of the call. We uniquely identify requests by identifiers r. We use the two maps call and orig that map request identifiers to the method call and originating replica respectively. The execution history of a replica is modeled as a permutation of a set of request identifiers. An execution x of a set of requests R is a bijective from positions $[0..|R| - 1]$ to R. We denote the range of x as $R(\mathsf{x})$. An execution x of R defines the total order $\prec_\mathsf{x}$ on R: A request r precedes another request r' in an execution x written as $r \prec_\mathsf{x} r'$ iff $\mathsf{x}^{-1}(r) < \mathsf{x}^{-1}(r')$. A replicated execution xs is a function from replicas $\mathcal{N}$ to executions. The post-state of each call at a replica is the result of applying the call to its pre-state.

We first revisit the coordination conditions for convergence and integrity [30], and then present coordination conditions for recency and their impact on the prior conditions.

Convergence. A replicated execution is convergent if the state of the replicas is the same after all the calls are propagated. Out of order delivery of method calls at different replicas can lead to divergence of their states. Method calls such as special reservation specialReserve and increasing space increaseSpace result in the same state if their order of execution is swapped. However, the resulting state of the two method calls book and cancelBook is dependent on their execution order. Therefore, they should synchronize.

Definition 1 (State-Commutativity and State-Conflict). *Two method calls c_1 and c_2 $\mathcal{S}$-commute, written as $c_1 \leftrightarrows_\mathcal{S} c_2$ iff for every state σ,* update$(c_2)($update$(c_1)(\sigma))$ = update$(c_1)($update$(c_2)(\sigma))$. *Otherwise, they $\mathcal{S}$-conflict, written as $c_1 \bowtie_\mathcal{S} c_2$.*

Integrity. The body of each method relies on the invariant in the pre-state. Further, methods have explicit guards that declare their pre-conditions. We say that a method call enjoys integrity at a state if the invariant and the guard of the method hold in that state.

Definition 2 (Integrity). *A method call c enjoys integrity in a state σ, written as* integrity(σ, c), *iff* guard$(c)(\sigma)$ *and* $\mathcal{I}(\sigma)$.

Method calls should be executed only in states that they have integrity in. The integrity condition is simply lifted to executions and replicated executions: An execution enjoys integrity iff every request in it enjoys integrity.

Definition 3 (Permissibility). *A method call c is permissible in a state σ, written as* $\mathcal{P}(\sigma, c)$, *iff* guard$(c)(\sigma)$ *and* $\mathcal{I}($update$(c)(\sigma))$.

In contrast to integrity that requires the invariant to hold in the pre-state, permissibility requires it to hold in the post-state. The post-state of a call is the pre-state of the next call in a replica. Further, the initial state is assumed to satisfy the invariant. Therefore, if every call is permissible in its pre-state, then every call enjoys integrity. By induction, permissibility leads to integrity.

To execute a method call, we check that it is permissible at its originating replica. Thus, we say that each method call is *locally permissible*. Otherwise, the call is aborted or delayed. Still, if the call is simply broadcast, it is not necessarily permissible when it arrives at other replicas. Some calls need coordination.

Conflict. There are calls such as increaseSpace that are always permissible as far as they are applied to a state that satisfies the invariant. Increasing the space cannot result in a missing or duplicate movie or a negative number for available spaces. Thus, if it is broadcast and executed on another replica, it is sufficient that the pre-state satisfies the invariant to preserve it in the post-state.

Definition 4 (Invariant-Sufficient). *A call c is invariant-sufficient iff for every state σ, if $\mathcal{I}(\sigma)$ then $\mathcal{P}(\sigma, c)$.*

However, not all calls are invariant-sufficient. For example, a book call may be permissible in a replica but may become impermissible in another when it is executed after an already executed offScreen call for the same movie. These two calls should synchronize to preserve integrity. Nonetheless, some pairs of calls such as offScreen and specialReserve do not affect each other's permissibility. (In the running example, specialReserve has no guards. After an offScreen call, it remains permissible as it doesn't find the movie and leaves the relation unchanged).

Definition 5 (Permissible-Right-Commutativity). *The call c_1 $\mathcal{P}$-R-commutes with the call c_2 written as $c_1 \rightarrow_{\mathcal{P}} c_2$ iff for every state σ, if $\mathcal{P}(\sigma, c_1)$ then $\mathcal{P}(\text{update}(c_2)(\sigma), c_1)$.*

If a call c_1 is invariant-sufficient or $\mathcal{P}$-R-commutes another call c_2, then the call c_1 will stay permissible when it is propagated and applied to another replica even if c_2 is executed before it in that replica.

Definition 6 (Permissible-Concur and Permissible-Conflict). *A call c_1 $\mathcal{P}$-concurs with a call c_2 iff c_1 is invariant-sufficient or $c_1 \rightarrow_{\mathcal{P}} c_2$. Otherwise, c_1 $\mathcal{P}$-conflicts with c_2.*

The call offScreen $\mathcal{P}$-concurs with the call specialReserve; however, the call book $\mathcal{P}$-conflicts with the call offScreen.

We say that two calls *concur* iff they both $\mathcal{S}$-commute and $\mathcal{P}$-concur with each other. Otherwise, we say they *conflict* and need synchronization.

Definition 7 (Concur and Conflict). *A pair of calls c_1 and c_2 concur iff they $\mathcal{S}$-commute and $\mathcal{P}$-concur with each other. Otherwise, they conflict $c_1 \bowtie c_2$.*

Dependency. As we saw above, invariant-sufficient method calls can always preserve the invariant. However, there are calls whose preservation of the invariant is dependent on the calls that have executed before them at that replica. For example, taking the movie off-screen offScreen is dependent on cancelling the last booking cancelBook. If offScreen is moved left before cancelBook, it can become impermissible. Nonetheless, taking a movie off-screen offScreen is independent of the previous special reservations specialReserve.

Definition 8 (Permissible-Left-Commutative). *A call c_2 $\mathcal{P}$-L-commutes a call c_1, written as $c_2 \leftarrow_{\mathcal{P}} c_1$ iff for every σ, if $\mathcal{P}(\text{update}(c_1)(\sigma), c_2)$ then $\mathcal{P}(\sigma, c_2)$.*

A call can avoid tracking dependencies to another call if the former is invariant-sufficient or $\mathcal{P}$-L-commutes with the latter.

Definition 9 (Independent and Dependent). *A call c_2 is independent of c_1, written as $c_2 \perp\!\!\!\perp c_1$, iff either c_2 is invariant-sufficient or $c_2 \leftarrow_{\mathcal{P}} c_1$. Otherwise, c_2 is dependent on c_1, written as $c_2 \not\perp\!\!\!\perp c_1$.*

If c_1 is executed before c_2 in the originating replica of c_2 and c_2 is dependent on c_1, then c_2 should be applied to other replicas only if c_1 is already applied.

Recency. Calls executed at a replica may be delayed in the network before they are executed in other replicas. Further, they may be buffered at the originating replica to reduce communication. The *pending* calls for a replica are the calls that have executed in other replicas but not at that replica yet. The staleness of a replica is the difference of its current state and its state after applying its pending calls. Given a bound ϵ, a replica is sufficiently recent if its staleness is less than ϵ. The calls that have originated in the current replica n but have not been received yet by another replica n' make the state of n' stale. To bound the staleness of n' by ϵ, the staleness imposed to n' by the calls originated by each of the other $|\mathcal{N}| - 1$ replicas should be bounded by $\epsilon/(|\mathcal{N}| - 1)$. The difference that these calls can make is bounded by the sum of their weights (defined in Sect. 2). The staleness bound can be evenly divided between the replicas. However, in general it can be distributed unevenly and even dynamically. In particular, replicas that tend to issue updates more often can get a larger share.

Given a recency bound, a buffering quota can be calculated for each replica and the recency bound can be preserved when calls are buffered. Buffering calls can reduce communication; however, it can affect the convergence and integrity properties. To preserve these properties a buffer should have three properties: all-state-commutativity, invariant-sufficiency and let-$\mathcal{P}$-R-commutativity. We consider each condition in turn.

Definition 10 (All-State-Commutative). *A call is all-$\mathcal{S}$-commutative if it is $\mathcal{S}$-commutative with respect to every call.*

The calls of the buffer are executed locally and are not synchronized with other replicas. Therefore, if the buffer is not all-$\mathcal{S}$-commutative, concurrent execution of $\mathcal{S}$-conflicting calls in other replicas can lead to divergence. Similarly, if the buffer is not invariant-sufficient, concurrent execution of $\mathcal{P}$-conflicting calls in other replicas can lead to impermissibility of the buffer when it is propagated and executed in other replicas. The buffer in Fig. 3(c) is all-$\mathcal{S}$-commutative: it includes increaseSpace and specialReserve calls that result in increasing or decreasing the space for movies; the result is $\mathcal{S}$-commutative with respect to all method calls. Further, it is invariant-sufficient if the net result of its calls is a non-negative addition to the space of each movie. For example, if the increaseSpace calls add s spaces and the specialReserve calls subtract s' spaces from the same movie where $s' \leq s$, then the net effect is adding spaces and the buffer is invariant-sufficient.

Definition 11 (Let-Permissible-Right-Commutative). *A call is let-$\mathcal{P}$-R-commutative if every call $\mathcal{P}$-R-commutes with it.*

Calls in other replicas are checked to be permissible with no knowledge of the buffered calls in the current replica. Let-$\mathcal{P}$-R-commutativity of the buffer of the current replica guarantees that the calls in other replicas will continue to be permissible once they are propagated and executed after the buffer in the current replica. The buffer in Fig. 3(c) is let-$\mathcal{P}$-R-commutative; it may only increase the number of spaces that cannot make any call impermissible.

4   Replicated System Semantics

In this section, we define the operational semantics of replicated objects where (1) the integrity property $\mathcal{I}$ on the state of each replica is always preserved, (2) replicas converge to the same state once all the calls are propagated, and (3) the staleness of each replica is always bounded by ϵ. The semantics declares the conditions for execution and propagation of method calls on the replicated object to guarantee the three properties. In particular, it represents the conditions for local buffering of method calls to avoid communication while preserving the recency of the other replicas. In Sect. 5, we will see a static analysis that infers staleness bounds for the state. In this section, the semantics preserves the inferred staleness bound ϵ for the state σ of the object. (For objects with multiple pieces of state, the staleness of each piece can be tracked separately.) The semantics strives to concisely define the conditions; we will present the protocols that implement these conditions in Sect. 6.

As Fig. 4 shows, the global state of the replicated system is represented as a world w that is a tuple of $\langle h, t, \mathsf{xs}, \mathsf{orig}, \mathsf{call} \rangle$. The hosts h is a mapping from replica identifiers $\mathcal{N}$ to the local state of replicas. Each call is assigned a unique request identifier r at the originating replica. The two maps call and orig keep a mapping from request identifiers to the call and the originating replica of the request respectively. The state of each replica is a statement $s \in S$, the state of the object $\sigma \in \Sigma$, and the identifier $r \in R$ of the current buffer. A statement s is either $x \leftarrow c; s'$ that is the sequence of a call c and another statement s', or the terminal statement skip. A call c is the application of a method m to an argument expression e. A call can also

$$
\begin{array}{rlll}
w & := & \langle h, t, \mathsf{xs}, \mathsf{orig}, \mathsf{call} \rangle & \text{World} \\
h & : & \mathcal{N} \mapsto S \times \Sigma \times R & \text{Hosts} \\
n & : & \mathcal{N} & \text{Replica nodes} \\
s : S & := & x \leftarrow c; s \mid \mathsf{skip} & \text{Statement} \\
c : C & := & m(e) \mid \mathsf{id} & \text{Call} \\
m & : & \mathcal{M} & \text{Method} \\
e & := & x \mid v & \text{Expression} \\
x & & & \text{Variable} \\
v & & & \text{Value} \\
\sigma & : & \Sigma & \text{Object State} \\
r & : & R & \text{Request} \\
t & : & \mathsf{Set}\ P & \text{Transit} \\
p : P & := & \langle n, r \rangle \mid \langle n, r^* \rangle & \text{Packet} \\
\mathsf{xs} & : & \mathcal{N} \mapsto \mathsf{List}\ R & \text{History} \\
\mathsf{orig} & : & R \mapsto \mathcal{N} & \text{Original node} \\
\mathsf{call} & : & R \mapsto C & \text{Request call} \\
w_0 & := & & \text{Init World} \\
\end{array}
$$

$$
\langle n \mapsto \langle s_n, \sigma_0, r_n \rangle_{n \in \mathcal{N}}, \emptyset, \emptyset,
$$
$$
[r_n \mapsto n]_{n \in \mathcal{N}}, [r_n \mapsto \mathsf{id}]_{n \in \mathcal{N}} \rangle
$$

Fig. 4. Operational semantics state

be the identity call id that leaves the state unchanged. (It is assumed that client statements do not make id calls.) The network t is the set of packets that are sent but not yet delivered. A packet p contains the identifier of the destination replica n and the request identifier r of the call. If a packet is transmitting a buffered call, it is decorated with an asterisk $*$. The history xs is a mapping from replica identifiers $\mathcal{N}$ to the list of request identifiers of the calls that are previously applied to that replica. The initial value of the world state is w_0 where each replica n hold its initial statement s_n, the initial state σ_0 of the object that satisfies the integrity property $\mathcal{I}$, and an empty buffer. Empty buffers are represented by mapping the buffer identifier r_n of each replica n to the identity call id.

Figure 5 presents the operational semantics. The rule CALL executes a method call c at a replica n. The call c can be executed if the following conditions hold. (1) To preserve integrity, the call c should be locally permissible $\mathcal{P}(\sigma, c)$ in the current state σ. (2) To preserve convergence and integrity, any pair of conflicting calls should have the same order across the replicas, a property that we call conflict-synchronization. Thus, to execute a new request r, the rule CALL requires the condition ConflictSyncInit: any call r' that is already executed in another replica n' and conflicts with the current call r should have been already executed in the current replica n. Otherwise, once the calls r and r' are propagated and executed on the other replicas, they will have different orders in the two replicas n and n'. (3) To preserve recency, this rule requires the condition InBound: the difference that the pending calls from the current replica n can make to the state of every other replica n' should be bounded by $\epsilon/(|\mathcal{N}| - 1)$. If the conditions above hold, a fresh identifier r is created for the call, the history xs and the maps orig and call are updated to reflect the new call, a packet is sent in the network t to every other replica, and the variable x is substituted with the returned value v of the call in the continuation statement s of the current replica.

The rule DELIVER delivers a call that has been sent to the current replica. It requires two conditions: conflict-synchronization and dependency-preservation. (1) Similar to the rule CALL, conflict-synchronization requires ConflictSync: if a conflicting call r' is executed before the received call r in another replica n', then r' should have been already executed before r in n as well. (2) To preserve integrity, the dependencies of calls should be preserved. Thus, the dependency-preservation condition DepPres requires that a call r originated from a replica n' is executed in the current replica n only if the calls r' that have been executed before r in n' and r is dependent on r' should have been already executed in n.

Recency-aware replication can be applied to any object, but it can improve performance when there are method calls that can be buffered. The rule CALLLOCAL executes a call but locally buffers it. Similar to the rule CALL, it first checks the local permissibility of the call c. Since a buffered call is not immediately coordinated with calls in other replicas, it should satisfy the three properties (that saw in Sect. 5) to make it concur with any call: (1) all-state-commutativity AllSComm, (2) invariant-sufficiency InvSuff, and (3) let-$\mathcal{P}$-Right-commutativity LetPRComm. The identifier of the current buffer is r; the current

CALL

$$\frac{\begin{array}{c} \mathcal{P}(\sigma, c) \qquad c(\sigma) = \langle \_, \sigma', v \rangle \\ \text{fresh } r \qquad \text{orig}' = \text{orig}[r \mapsto n] \\ \text{call}' = \text{call}[r \mapsto c] \\ \text{xs}' = \text{xs}[n \mapsto (\text{xs}(n) ::: r)] \\ \text{ConflictSyncInit}_{\langle \text{call}' \rangle}(\text{xs}', n, r) \\ \text{InBound}_{\langle \text{orig}', \text{call}' \rangle}(\text{xs}', n) \\ t' = t \cup \{\langle n', r \rangle \mid n' \in \mathcal{N} \setminus \{n\}\} \end{array}}{(h[n \mapsto (x \leftarrow c; s, \sigma, r')], t, \text{xs}, \text{orig}, \text{call})}$$

$$\xrightarrow{n, r, c}$$

$$(h[n \mapsto (s[x \mapsto v], \sigma', r')], t', \text{xs}', \text{orig}', \text{call}')$$

DELIVER

$$\frac{\begin{array}{c} \text{call}(r)(\sigma) = \langle \_, \sigma', \_ \rangle \\ \text{xs}' = \text{xs}[n \mapsto (\text{xs}(n) ::: r)] \\ \text{ConflictSync}_{\langle \text{call} \rangle}(\text{xs}', n, r) \\ \text{DepPres}_{\langle \text{orig}, \text{call} \rangle}(\text{xs}', n, r) \end{array}}{(h[n \mapsto (s, \sigma, r')], t \cup \{\langle n, r \rangle\}, \text{xs}, \text{orig}, \text{call})}$$

$$\xrightarrow{n, r, \text{call}(r)}$$

$$(h[n \mapsto (s, \sigma', r')], t, \text{xs}', \text{orig}, \text{call})$$

CALLLOCAL

$$\frac{\begin{array}{c} \mathcal{P}(\sigma, c) \qquad c(\sigma) = \langle \_, \sigma', v \rangle \\ c' = c \cdot \text{call}(r) \\ \text{AllSComm}(c) \\ \text{InvSuff}(c') \qquad \text{LetPRComm}(c') \\ \text{call}' = \text{call}[r \mapsto c'] \\ \text{xs}' = \begin{cases} \text{xs}[n \mapsto (\text{xs}(n) ::: r)] & \text{if call}(r) = \text{id} \\ \text{xs} & \text{else} \end{cases} \\ \text{InBound}_{\langle \text{orig}, \text{call}' \rangle}(\text{xs}', n) \end{array}}{(h[n \mapsto (x \leftarrow c; s, \sigma, r)], t, \text{xs}, \text{orig}, \text{call})}$$

$$\xrightarrow{n, r, c}$$

$$(h[n \mapsto (s[x \mapsto v], \sigma', r)], t, \text{xs}', \text{orig}, \text{call}')$$

SENDBUFFER

$$\frac{\begin{array}{c} \text{call}(r) \neq \text{id} \qquad \text{fresh } r' \\ \text{orig}' = \text{orig}[r' \mapsto n] \qquad \text{call}' = \text{call}[r' \mapsto \text{id}] \\ t' = t \cup \{\langle n', r^* \rangle \mid n' \in \mathcal{N} \setminus \{n\}\} \end{array}}{(h[n \mapsto (s, \sigma, r)], t, \text{xs}, \text{orig}, \text{call})}$$

$$\xrightarrow{}$$

$$(h[n \mapsto (s, \sigma, r')], t', \text{xs}, \text{orig}', \text{call}')$$

DELIVERBUFFER

$$\frac{\begin{array}{c} \text{call}(r)(\sigma) = \langle \_, \sigma', \_ \rangle \\ \text{xs}' = \text{xs}[n \mapsto (\text{xs}(n) ::: r)] \end{array}}{(h[n \mapsto (s, \sigma, r')], t \cup \{\langle n, r^* \rangle\}, \text{xs}, \text{orig}, \text{call})}$$

$$\xrightarrow{n, r, \text{call}(r)}$$

$$(h[n \mapsto (s, \sigma', r')], t, \text{xs}', \text{orig}, \text{call})$$

$$
\begin{aligned}
\text{id} &:= \lambda\sigma. \ \langle \text{True}, \sigma, \bot \rangle \\
\mathcal{P}(\sigma, c) &:= \text{Let } \langle g, \sigma', \_ \rangle := c(\sigma) \text{ in } (g = \text{true} \wedge \mathcal{I}(\sigma') = \text{true}) \\
\text{ConflictSyncInit}_{\langle \text{call} \rangle}(\text{xs}, n, r) &:= \forall n', r'. \ r' \in \text{xs}(n') \wedge \text{call}(r) \bowtie \text{call}(r') \rightarrow r' \in \text{xs}(n) \\
\text{ConflictSync}_{\langle \text{call} \rangle}(\text{xs}, n, r) &:= \forall n', r'. \ r' \prec_{\text{xs}(n')} r \wedge \text{call}(r) \bowtie \text{call}(r') \rightarrow r' \prec_{\text{xs}(n)} r \\
\text{DepPres}_{\langle \text{orig}, \text{call} \rangle}(\text{xs}, n, r) &:= \forall r'. \ r' \prec_{\text{xs}(\text{orig}(r))} r \wedge \text{call}(r) \not\Perp \text{call}(r') \rightarrow r' \in \text{xs}(n) \\
\text{AllSComm}(c) &:= \forall c'. \ c \leftrightarrows_S c' \\
\text{InvSuff}(c) &:= \forall \sigma. \ \mathcal{I}(\sigma) \rightarrow \mathcal{P}(\sigma, c) \\
\text{LetPRComm}(c) &:= \forall c'. \ c' \rightarrow_P c \\
\text{InBound}_{\langle \text{orig}, \text{call} \rangle}(\text{xs}, n) &:= \forall n'. \ \sum_{r \in \text{xs}(n) \setminus \text{xs}(n') \wedge \text{orig}(r) = n} \text{weight}(\text{call}(r)) < \frac{\epsilon}{|\mathcal{N}| - 1} \\
(c \cdot c')(\sigma) &:= \text{Let } \langle \_, \sigma', \_ \rangle := c'(\sigma) \text{ in } c(\sigma')
\end{aligned}
$$

Fig. 5. Replicated system semantics

call c is composed with the current buffered call $\text{call}(r)$ to result in a composed call c' for the updated buffer. The composition $\cdot$ of calls simply cascades their updates to the state. The all-state-commutativity condition is stated for single calls c (that implies the same condition for the composed call c' as well). This condition is required for the call c because there might be other calls delivered between the last buffered call and the currently buffered call c. The call c should state-commute past the calls in between. Further, as explained for the rule CALL, the condition InBound requires that the added staleness remains within bound. If the above conditions hold, the map call is updated with the new buffer call c', and the identifier r of the buffered call is added to the history xs, if the buffer was empty and the current call c is the first buffered call.

The rule SENDBUFFER sends the buffer to every other replica and resets the buffer. Packets transmitting buffers are decorated with an asterisk. The rule DELIVERBUFFER receives a packet containing a buffer. As we saw in the rule CALLLOCAL, buffers are checked to be invariant-sufficient in the originating replica. Therefore, on receiving a packet containing a buffer, in contrast to the rule DELIVER, the rule DELIVERBUFFER does not checks the dependency-preservationDepPres and the conflict-synchronization ConflictSync conditions.

The following lemmas state the three properties of the semantics. The following lemma states that once the buffers are flushed $\text{call}(r) = \text{call}(r') = \text{id}$ and the messages are delivered $l = \emptyset$, the replicas converge to the same state.

Lemma 1 (Convergence). *For all h, n, n', σ, σ', r and r', if $w_0 \longrightarrow^*$ $\langle h, \emptyset, \_, \_, \_ \rangle$ where $h(n) = \langle \_, \sigma, r \rangle$, $h(n') = \langle \_, \sigma', r' \rangle$ and $\text{call}(r) = \text{call}(r') = \text{id}$ then $\sigma = \sigma'$.*

The following lemma states that every call enjoys the integrity property.

Lemma 2 (Integrity). *For all h, n, r, c, w and σ, if $w_0 \longrightarrow^* \langle h, \_, \_, \_, \_ \rangle \xrightarrow{n, \_, c}$ w where $h(n) = \langle \_, \sigma, \_ \rangle$ then $\text{integrity}(\sigma, c)$.*

The staleness of a replica is the difference of its current state and its state after applying its pending calls from others (buffered calls and in transit calls). The following lemma states that the stateless of every replica is bounded by ϵ.

Lemma 3 (Recency). *For all h, h', n, s, σ and σ', if $w_0 \longrightarrow^* \langle h, \_, \_, \_, \_ \rangle$ $(\longrightarrow \cup \xrightarrow{n, \_, \_})^* \langle h', \_, \_, \_, \_ \rangle, h(n) = \langle s, \sigma, \_ \rangle$, and $h'(n) = \langle s, \sigma', \_ \rangle$ then $\Delta(\sigma', \sigma) < \epsilon$.*

5   Staleness Bound Inference and Optimization

In Sect. 4, we presented an operational semantics that preserves a given staleness bound for the state. The users declare the recency that they expect from the return value of each method of the object. The specified bounds for the methods can be used to infer the bounds for the elements of the state. In this section, given an object specification that includes recency declarations for the methods, we present a static analysis that infers optimum staleness bounds for each element of the state. We present a syntax-directed analysis that derives recency constraints between bound variables for the state elements. A solution to the constraints assigns a bound value to each state element such that if every state element keeps its staleness bound then the result of every method call respects the recency declaration of the method. The optimum solution maximizes the (weighted) sum of the bounds to increase buffered calls and hence decrease communication.

$$\delta := n \mid dx \mid \delta + \delta \mid \delta \times \delta \qquad \text{Bound}$$
$$C := \delta = \delta \mid \delta < \delta \mid C \wedge C \qquad \text{Constraints}$$

COBJ
$$\frac{me \triangleright C}{\langle \Sigma, \mathcal{I}, \overline{me} \rangle \triangleright \wedge \overline{C}}$$

CMET
$$\frac{\mathsf{free}(e_r) = \{x, \sigma_1, .., \sigma_n\} \qquad [x \mapsto 0, \sigma_1 \mapsto d\sigma_1, .., \sigma_n \mapsto d\sigma_n] \vdash e_r \triangleright \delta', C}{\mathsf{def}\ \delta\ m(x)(\langle \sigma_1, .., \sigma_n \rangle)\ \langle e_g, e_u, e_r \rangle \triangleright C \wedge (\delta' \leq \delta)}$$

CVAL
$$\Gamma \vdash v \triangleright 0, \emptyset$$

CVAR
$$\frac{(x \mapsto \delta) \in \Gamma}{\Gamma \vdash x \triangleright \delta, \emptyset}$$

COP
$$\frac{\Gamma \vdash e \triangleright \delta, C \qquad \Gamma \vdash e' \triangleright \delta', C' \qquad \oplus \in \{+, -, \cup, \backslash\}}{\Gamma \vdash e \oplus e' \triangleright \delta + \delta', C \wedge C'}$$

CBOP
$$\frac{\Gamma \vdash e \triangleright \delta, C \qquad \Gamma \vdash e' \triangleright \delta', C' \qquad \oplus \in \{=, <, \&\}}{\Gamma \vdash e \oplus e' \triangleright 0, C \wedge C' \wedge (\delta = 0 \wedge \delta' = 0)}$$

CSEL
$$\frac{\Gamma[x \mapsto 0] \vdash e \triangleright \delta, C \qquad \Gamma \vdash e' \triangleright \delta', C'}{\Gamma \vdash \sigma_{\lambda \overline{x}.e}(e') \triangleright \delta', C \wedge C' \wedge (\delta = 0)}$$

CPROJ
$$\frac{\Gamma \vdash e \triangleright \delta, C}{\Gamma \vdash \Pi_{\overline{x}}(e) \triangleright \delta, C}$$

CPROD
$$\frac{\Gamma \vdash e \triangleright \delta, C \qquad \Gamma \vdash e' \triangleright \delta', C'}{\Gamma \vdash e \times e' \triangleright \delta \times \delta', C \wedge C'}$$

Fig. 6. Bound constraint derivation

Figure 6 presents the constraint inference rules for the object language that we saw in Fig. 1. A delta bound δ is either a natural number n, a delta variable dx, or addition or multiplication of two deltas. A constraint C is equality or comparison of two deltas, or conjunction of two constraints. A delta environment Γ is a mapping from variables to delta variables or values. The judgements are of the following forms: the judgement $o \triangleright C$ states the bounding constraint C for the object o, the judgement $m \triangleright C$ states the constraint C for the method m, and the judgement $\Gamma \vdash e \triangleright \delta, C$ states that under the delta environment Γ, the staleness of the expression e is bounded by δ when the constraints C are satisfied. The rule COBJ states that the constraint for an object is the conjunction of the constraints for its methods. (We assume that the state variables passed to all the methods are renamed to the same variables $\langle \sigma_1, .., \sigma_n \rangle$.) The rule CMET infers the constraints for a method by first, inferring the constraints for its return expression under a delta environment where the argument is mapped to the delta value of zero (exactly recent) and the state variables σ_i are mapped to delta variables $d\sigma_i$ to be inferred, and second, bounding the return value. The rule CVAL assigns the delta value zero to values with no constraints. (Values are exact.) The rule CVAR retrieves the bindings for delta variables from the environment. The rule COP states that the delta for the result of the operators $\{+, -, \cup, \backslash\}$ is the sum of the delta of its operands. On the other hand, the rule CBOP requires the operands of the boolean operators $\{=, <, \&\}$ to be exact and states that the result is exact as well. We elide the similar rule for the unary negation operator !. The rule CSEL requires the selection condition to be exact and states that the delta of the resulting relation is the same as the input relation. In other words, the resulting relation is stale by the same number of elements as the input relation. Similarly, the rule CPROJ states that the delta of the resulting relation is the same as the input relation. On the other hand, the rule CPROD states that the delta for the resulting relation is the multiplication of the deltas for the input relations. In our running example, let us associate the bound variables drs and dms to rs and ms respectively. The constraint inferred for querySpace is $dms \leq \epsilon_2$, for queryReservations is $drs \leq \epsilon_1$, and for querySpace that involves the join operator (product and selection) is $drs \times dms \leq \epsilon_3$. More detailed explanation for these derivation is available in the appendix [5].

We now define the notion of sufficiently-recent states. Intuitively, a state is sufficiently-recent with respect to the target state if the difference of the return value of every method call on that state versus the target state is within the declared bound of the method.

Definition 12 (Sufficiently-recent State). *A state $\langle v_1, .., v_n \rangle$ is a sufficiently-recent state with respect to the target state $\langle v_1^*, .., v_n^* \rangle$ for an object o iff for every method* def ϵ $m(x)(\langle \sigma_1, .., \sigma_n \rangle)$ $\langle e_g, e_u, e_r \rangle$ *of o, and every argument v, let v_r be $\left[\!\left[e_r[x \mapsto v] \overline{[\sigma_i \mapsto v_i]} \right]\!\right]$ and v_r^* be $\left[\!\left[e_r[x \mapsto v] \overline{[\sigma_i \mapsto v_i^*]} \right]\!\right]$, we have $\Delta(v_r, v_r^*) \leq \epsilon$.*

The following lemma states that the bound inference presented in Fig. 6 is sound. In other words, if the inference derives the constraints C for an object, for any solution S of C, if the staleness of each state element σ_i of the object remains within the bound $S(d\sigma_i)$, then the state remains sufficiently-recent.

Lemma 4 (Soundness of Bound Inference). *Given an object o with the state variables $\langle \sigma_1, .., \sigma_n \rangle$, if $o \rhd C$ that is the constraints C (over the bound variables $\overline{d\sigma_i}$) are derived for o, and S is a solution for C, then for every pair of states $\sigma = \langle v_1, .., v_n \rangle$ and $\sigma^* = \langle v_1^*, .., v_n^* \rangle$, if $\Delta(v_i, v_i^*) < S(d\sigma_i)$ then o is sufficiently-recent for σ^*.*

There may be many solutions for the derived constraints, and hence, many sound state bounds that preserve the user-specified bounds for the object. However, solutions that allow more staleness (albeit appropriately bounded) are more favorable since they allow more buffered calls and require less communication. Thus, a candidate objective function to maximize is $d\sigma_1 + .. + d\sigma_n$. In other words, what are the largest delta bounds for the state elements that still preserve the recency specifications of the methods? This function gives the same weight to all the state elements; however, some may be updated more frequently. Let f_i be the relative update frequency of the state element σ_i. Frequencies can be obtained from historical logs or profiling. The objective function is defined as the following weighted sum $d\sigma_1/f_1 + .. + d\sigma_n/f_n$. More frequently updated state elements are given proportionally larger bounds. In our running example, let $\epsilon_1 = 3$, $\epsilon_2 = 4$, and $\epsilon_3 = 6$. If the update frequency of rs is twice as ms, the optimum solution is $drs = 3$ and $dms = 2$.

Definition 13 (Recency Bound Optimization). *Give an object o and the relative update frequency f_i of the state elements σ_i of o, if $o \rhd C$ then the optimum staleness bounds for o are the solution S of C that maximizes $d\sigma_1/f_1 + .. + d\sigma_n/f_n$.*

It is obvious that the objective function can be easily translated to a linear function by multiplying the least common denominator of the frequencies.

6   The Power and the Protocol of Recency-Aware Objects

Now, we show that recency-aware objects are stronger than the perfect failure detector abstraction [18] and present a protocol that implements recency-aware objects using perfect failure detectors. These two results show that recency-aware objects have the same computational power as the perfect failure detector.

The perfect failure detector abstraction $\mathcal{P}$ notifies processes about the crash of the other processes in a synchronous network. It has the following properties: Liveness: Every crashed process is eventually detected by all correct processes. Safety: No correct process is ever suspected by other processes. The recency-aware object $\mathcal{R}$ has the following liveness and safety properties. Liveness: If the user makes a request to a correct replica, it eventually responds. Safety: Executed calls that are yet pending for each correct replica is bounded. The following lemma states that $\mathcal{P}$ is reducible to $\mathcal{R}$ and also its opposite, $\mathcal{R}$ is reducible to $\mathcal{P}$.

```
RecencyAwareObject
    request : call(C)
    indication : ret(C, V) | aborted(C)
    Params :
        ε : Int
        SConf : Set[M]
    Using :
        rb : ReliableBroadcast
        pl : PerfectPointToPointLink
        pfd : Perfect Failure Detector
        bro : BasicRepObject
    State :
        σ : Σ = σ₀; buff = ∅; wq = ∅;
        up = N; p : N ↦ Set[C] = N → ∅

    request (call(c))    if (method(c) ∉ blocked(bro))
        if (¬P(σ, c))
            issue indication aborted(c)
        else
            if (method(c) ∉ SConf ∧
                InvSuff(buff) ∧ LetPRComm(buff))
                foreach (r ∈ up \ {self})
                    p'(r) ← ((p(r) \ {buff}) ∪ {c · buff})
                if (InBound(p'))
                    p ← p'
                    exec(c); buff ← c · buff
                else
                    issue request (rb, broadcast(buff(buff)))
                    insert(wq, c)
            else
```

```
            foreach (r ∈ up \ {self})
                p'(r) ← (p(r) ∪ {c})
            if (InBound(p'))
                p ← p'
                issue request(bro, call(c))
            else
                issue request (rb, broadcast(buff(buff)))
                insert(wq, c)
    indication crash(pfd, p)
        up ← up \ {p}
    fun InBound(p)
        foreach(n ∈ up)
            if (∑_{c'∈p(n)} weight(c') > ε/(N − 1))
                return False
        return True
    indication (rb, deliver(n, buff(buff)))
        if (self ≠ n)
            exec(buff)
            issue request (pl, send(n, ack(buff)))
    indication (pl, deliver(n, ack(c)))
        p ← p[n ↦ (p(n) \ {c})]
        foreach (c ∈ wq) issue request(call(c))
        wq ← ∅
    fun exec(c)
        σ ← update(c)(σ); v ← retv(c)(σ)
        issue indication ret(c, v)
    indication (bro, ret(c, v))
        issue request (pl, send(orig(c), ack(c)))
        issue indication ret(c, v)
```

Fig. 7. Recency-aware protocol

Lemma 5. $\mathcal{P} \preceq \mathcal{R} \wedge \mathcal{R} \preceq \mathcal{P}$.

For the proof of the first conjunct, consider two replicas rep_1 and rep_2. We show by contradiction that rep_1 will eventually know whether rep_2 has crashed. We assume the opposite. Consider an execution where rep_1 has already executed a set of requests R and receives another request r from the user, such that the pending set $R \cup \{r\}$ makes a difference in the state of rep_2 that pushes it out-of-bound. By the contradiction assumption, rep_1 is never informed when rep_2 crashes. Therefore, if rep_1 does not hear from rep_2, the following two scenarios are indistinguishable to rep_1. (S_1) The replica rep_2 has crashed. (S_2) The replica rep_2 is too slow. The replica rep_1 has the following two choices: (C_1) The replica rep_1 waits to hear from rep_2 about receiving a request in R before processing and responding to r. (C_2) The replica rep_1 processes and responds to r. If the protocol makes the choice C_1, it might be the scenario S_1 and then the liveness property is violated. If the protocol makes the choice C_2, it might be the scenario S_2 and then the recency bound for rep_2 is violated.

The second conjunct, directly follows from the protocol. We briefly describe the protocol in Fig. 7 that implements a recency-aware replicated object. The full description of the protocol is available in the appendix [5]. Given an object definition, the protocol benefits from both static and dynamic coordination analysis to guarantee convergence, integrity and recency. To reduce communication, replicas try to execute the calls locally while maintaining the staleness bound ϵ. Each replica keeps its locally executed calls in a buffer *buff* before they are broadcast. Replicas send an acknowledgement ack to the originating replica once they receive and execute a call or a buffer of calls. Each replica *rep* keeps a map called pending p from each replica rep' to the set of pending calls sent from *rep* to rep'. When a replica originates a call c, it adds c to its local pending set for each of the other replicas; once it receives an acknowledgement for c from a replica rep', it removes c from the set of pending calls for rep'. Each replica keeps the set of correct replicas *up*, and removes a replica from the set if the prefect failure detector *pfd* issues a crash event for that replica. A requested call can be executed only if it does not push the pending set for any correct replica out of the bound. Otherwise, it cannot be immediately executed and is kept in a waiting queue *wq* to be retried later, and further, the buffer is sent to the other replicas and is reset to accelerate the shrinking of the pending set. To decide whether a call can be executed locally, the conditions of the rule CALLLOCAL of the operational semantics (Sect. 4) are checked. The set of state-conflicting methods SConf that is statically calculated is consulted to check if the call is all-state-commutative. The validity of the two conditions invariant-sufficiency and let-$\mathcal{P}$-R-commutativity of the buffer (after the new call is added) are dynamically decided by a solver at run-time. If the conditions do not hold, the call is coordinated with other replicas using the basic blocking coordination protocol *bro* [30] that guarantees integrity and convergence but not recency.

7   Experimental Results

We have implemented the analysis and protocol as a synthesis tool called HAMPA. We applied it to two use-cases: the bank account use-case (with the withdraw, deposit and balance methods and the integrity property of non-negative balance) and the movie booking use-case (Fig. 2). The experiments show that as the staleness bound increases, the coordination overhead and response time of recency-aware objects is decreased. Further, recency-aware objects are twice as responsive as sequentially consistent counterparts.

Platform and Setup. The experiments are conducted on a cluster of 4 computing nodes. Each node has 2 AMD Opteron 6272 CPUs with a total 8 cores, 64GB ECC memory and 40Gbps InfiniBand network. JDK is openjdk version 1.8.0_222. We used the CVC4 [11] SMT solver v.1.7. Reported numbers are the arithmetic means of results from three repetitions on 4 replicas. In the experiments for the bank account use-case, all the calls are applied to the same account object and the amount is selected randomly in the range [10, 20]. For the movie use-case, we send requests for each movie identifier to the same replica. Further, we do not issue offScreen calls because taking a movie off-screen causes later method calls on the same movie to be aborted and thus, these methods are not fully exercised. This would significantly improve the response time. However, in practice, offScreen calls are rarely used. The movie and user IDs are chosen at random from six and a hundred unique IDs. In all the experiments, we execute 500 calls in millisecond intervals evenly distributed between 4 replicas.

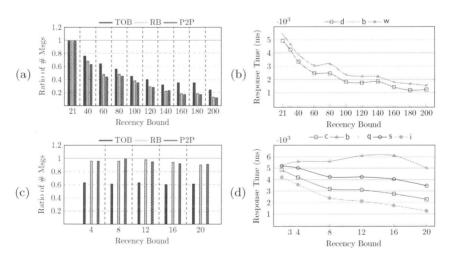

Fig. 8. Effect of recency on coordination load and response time. (a) and (b) show the bank account use-case. d, w, and b stand for deposit, withdraw and balance (with the frequencies of 75%, 25%, 5% in the workload respectively). (c) and (d) show the movie use-case. c, b, q, s, and i stand for cancelBook, book, querySpace, specialReserve, and increaseSpace (with frequencies 4%, 6%, 5%, 40% and 45%).

Measurements. We measure two comparison criteria: coordination load and response time. At the lower layers, the protocol reduces to three communication primitives: total-order-broadcast (TOB), reliable-broadcast (RB) and point-to-point links (P2P). To measure the coordination overhead, we separately count the number of different types of messages that replicas send during the execution of their requests. The response time for a call is the duration between the time that the client requests the call and the time that the user receives the return value.

We performed three experiments. In the first experiment, we study the effect of increasing the staleness bound on the coordination load. We report the ratio of the number of messages that the protocol sends for the bound under test over the number of messages that it sends for the base-line bound. (The base-line recency bound is the maximum weight of the calls. The baseline allows every single call to be buffered.) In the second experiment, we study the effect of increasing the staleness bound on the response time of each method. Finally, in the last experiment, we compare the response time of our protocol with the base-line recency, with the sequential consistency (SC). SC uses total-order broadcast for all the methods.

Assessment. Figure 8(a) and (c) show the effect of increasing the staleness bound on the coordination load for the two use-cases. As the staleness bound is increased, the ratio of the messages sent by RB, TOB and P2P decreases. Figure 8(a) (bank account), shows 88% decrease in the number of messages sent to RB when the bound is increased from 20 to 200. Likewise, the TOB and P2P ratios decrease by 78% and 90%, respectively. In Fig. 8(c) (movie booking), buffering helps to reduce TOB calls by 40% across the experiments. This decrease, however, unlike the bank account use-case, is steady over different bounds. This is because it is more difficult to "buffer" in the movie booking use-case. There are no S-conflicts in the bank account use-case and hence two out of two update methods can be buffered. However, S-conflicts in the movie use-case allow only 2 out of 4 update methods to be buffered: increaseSpace and specialReserve. Also, we observe that the number of RB and P2P messages decrease by at most 10%.

Figure 8(b) and (d) shows the effect of increasing the staleness bound on the response time for the two use-cases. In Fig. 8(b) (bank account), the response time of withdraw and deposit methods decrease by 71% and 75%, respectively when the staleness bound is increased from 20 to 200. The withdraw method is the least responsive method. The reason is that it has a self-conflict and requires synchronization if it cannot be buffered. In Fig. 8(d) (movie booking), we observe slight increase in response time for the book method while increasing the bound from 2 to 20. This is because the book operation cannot be buffered

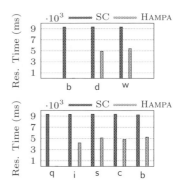

Fig. 9. Response time comparison between HAMPA and sequential consistency for each method type. Top: bank account, Bottom: movie booking use-case.

due to the S-conflict with other methods and has to be synchronized. On the other hand, the response time of the specialReserve method decreases by 33% when the bound is increased from 2 to 20. The reason is that it has a self-conflict and if it cannot be buffered, it should be synchronized by the TOB and TOB incurs a high coordination overhead. Therefore, as buffered calls increase and the use of TOB decreases, the response time is significantly improved. The response time of the increaseSpace method also benefits from recency awareness; it decreases by 72%. The methods book and cancelBook have conflicts. In the blocking protocol that HAMPA uses, the method book handles synchronization; therefore, the method cancelBook just broadcasts the request. As the recency bound is increased, the network is less crowded and therefore, the response time of cancelBook is decreased.

Figure 9 compares the response time of recency-aware objects with the baseline bound with the sequentially consistent objects. The SC protocol synchronizes all the calls and orders them with respect to each other. However, HAMPA minimizes coordination while preserving convergence, integrity and recency. We observe that the response time speedup is in average as high as 2× and 1.8× for the bank account and movie use-cases respectively. More experiments are available in the appendix [5]. In particular, they show that the runtime cost of SMT solving is only 0.2% to 1% of the average response time.

8   Related Work

Epsilon serializability [46] allows concurrent execution of updates with queries and bounds the difference of the inconsistent values that are observed in these executions and the consistent values that would be observed in a serializable execution. In contrast, HAMPA preserves the integrity of the state, bounds staleness, allows different orders in different replicas, and formally defines the difference for relational operators.

In TACT [54–58], operations return tentative values; they might be eventually reordered to preserve strong consistency. TACT bounds the numeric error between the tentative and final return values. The user specifies the granularity of the bounded object "conit" and the strength of the protocol. On the other hand in HAMPA, the states are final and enjoy integrity provided on top of weak consistency. Further, the staleness bound with respect to the pending future state is automatically optimized with static and dynamic analyses.

In AQuA [31], given a query and a staleness bound, the master server dynamically selects a recent enough server to service the query. Similarly, TRAPP [43] finds recent enough servers for different parts of data that are needed for the query. FRACS [59] allows operations to be buffered at replicas up to a given threshold. In contrast to HAMPA, these projects do not guarantee integrity and convergence, and do not automatically infer the staleness bounds. PIQL [6] bounds the number of key-value store operations for each query trading the precision of the result for performance. However, it does not consider the staleness of replicas.

To reduce synchronization, PBS [9] communicates with only a partial quorum of replicas to bring a total order to operations, and probabilistically bounds the staleness of the observed states. In contrast, HAMPA performs synchronization with full quorums but only for conflicting calls, and allows different orders for replicas. Further, it analyzes and synthesizes replicated objects and supports relational in addition to single-key operations.

The trade-off between consistency and latency presented as PACELC [1] aligns with our experiments. As the consistency decreases (staleness bound increases), the latency decreases (responsiveness increases). Warranties [38] and Homeostasis [17] allow local updates if they keep the validity of certain assertions. Although other replicas can rely on the validity of the assertions, the staleness of their state is not bounded. In contrast, HAMPA maintains a staleness bound. Further, it exploits weak consistency and guarantees convergence.

9   Conclusion

This paper presented a relational object specification language that captures the integrity and recency requirements of the object. It presented a syntax-directed analysis that given a specification, infers optimum staleness bounds. In addition, it presented the coordination avoidance conditions, operational semantics, a protocol and a synthesis tool for replicated systems that guarantee convergence, integrity and recency. The recency-aware protocol embeds a solver to decide whether coordination avoidance is safe and increases the responsiveness.

References

1. Abadi, D.: Consistency tradeoffs in modern distributed database system design. Computer 45(2) (2012)

2. Ahamad, M., Neiger, G., Burns, J.E., Kohli, P., Hutto, P.W.: Causal memory: definitions, implementation, and programming. Distrib. Comput. **9**(1), 37–49 (1995)
3. Alagappan, R., et al.: Protocol-aware recovery for consensus-based distributed storage. ACM Trans. Storage (TOS) **14**(3), 1–30 (2018)
4. Alglave, J., Cousot, P., Maranget, L.: Syntax and semantics of the weak consistency model specification language cat. arXiv preprint arXiv:1608.07531 (2016)
5. Appendix: Appendix. Attached at the paper (2020)
6. Armbrust, M., Curtis, K., Kraska, T., Fox, A., Franklin, M.J., Patterson, D.A.: PIQL: success-tolerant query processing in the cloud. Proc. VLDB Endow. **5**(3), 181–192 (2011)
7. Bailis, P., Fekete, A., Franklin, M.J., Ghodsi, A., Hellerstein, J.M., Stoica, I.: Coordination avoidance in database systems. Proc. VLDB Endow. **8**(3), 185–196 (2014). https://doi.org/10.14778/2735508.2735509
8. Bailis, P., Fekete, A., Franklin, M.J., Ghodsi, A., Hellerstein, J.M., Stoica, I.: Feral concurrency control: An empirical investigation of modern application integrity. In: Proceedings of the 2015 ACM SIGMOD International Conference on Management of Data, pp. 1327–1342. ACM (2015)
9. Bailis, P., Venkataraman, S., Franklin, M.J., Hellerstein, J.M., Stoica, I.: Probabilistically bounded staleness for practical partial quorums. Proc. VLDB Endow. **5**(8), 776–787 (2012)
10. Balegas, V., et al.: Putting consistency back into eventual consistency. In: Proceedings of the Tenth European Conference on Computer Systems, EuroSys 2015, pp. 6:1–6:16. ACM, New York (2015). https://doi.org/10.1145/2741948.2741972
11. Barrett, C.: CVC4. In: Gopalakrishnan, G., Qadeer, S. (eds.) CAV 2011. LNCS, vol. 6806, pp. 171–177. Springer, Heidelberg (2011). https://doi.org/10.1007/978-3-642-22110-1_14. http://www.cs.stanford.edu/ barrett/pubs/BCD+11.pdf
12. Belaramani, N., et al.: PRACTI replication. In: Proceedings NSDI (2006)
13. Birman, K.P.: Replication and fault-tolerance in the ISIS system. In: Proceedings SOSP (1985)
14. Bonakdarpour, B., Bozga, M., Jaber, M., Quilbeuf, J., Sifakis, J.: Automated conflict-free distributed implementation of component-based models. In: International Symposium on Industrial Embedded System (SIES), pp. 108–117. IEEE (2010)
15. Bouajjani, A., Enea, C., Hamza, J.: Verifying eventual consistency of optimistic replication systems. In: Proceedings POPL (2014)
16. Bouajjani, A., Enea, C., Mukund, M., Shenoy R., G., Suresh, S.P.: Formalizing and checking multilevel consistency. In: Beyer, D., Zufferey, D. (eds.) VMCAI 2020. LNCS, vol. 11990, pp. 379–400. Springer, Cham (2020). https://doi.org/10.1007/978-3-030-39322-9_18
17. Burckhardt, S., Gotsman, A., Yang, H., Zawirski, M.: Replicated data types: specification, verification, optimality. In: Proceedings POPL (2014)
18. Cachin, C., Guerraoui, R., Rodrigues, L.: Introduction to Reliable and Secure Distributed Programming, 2nd edn. Springer, Heidelberg (2011). https://doi.org/10.1007/978-3-642-15260-3 10.1007/978-3-642-15260-3
19. Clancy, K., Miller, H.: Monotonicity types for distributed dataflow. In: Proceedings of the Programming Models and Languages for Distributed Computing, p. 2. ACM (2017)
20. Cooper, B.F., et al.: PNUTS: Yahoo!'s hosted data serving platform. Proc. VLDB Endow. 1(2) (2008)
21. Corbett, J.C., et al.: Spanner: Google's globally distributed database. ACM Trans. Comput. Syst. **31**(3), 8:1–8:22 (2013). https://doi.org/10.1145/2491245

22. DeCandia, G., et al.: Dynamo: Amazon's highly available key-value store. In: Proceedings SOSP (2007)
23. Drăgoi, C., Henzinger, T.A., Zufferey, D.: PSYNC: a partially synchronous language for fault-tolerant distributed algorithms. ACM SIGPLAN Not. **51**(1), 400–415 (2016)
24. Emmi, M., Enea, C.: Monitoring weak consistency. In: Chockler, H., Weissenbacher, G. (eds.) CAV 2018. LNCS, vol. 10981, pp. 487–506. Springer, Cham (2018). https://doi.org/10.1007/978-3-319-96145-3_26
25. Emmi, M., Enea, C.: Weak-consistency specification via visibility relaxation. Proc. ACM Program. Lang. **3**(POPL), 1–28 (2019)
26. Fischer, M.J., Lynch, N.A., Paterson, M.S.: Impossibility of distributed consensus with one faulty process. J. ACM **32**(2), 374–382 (1985). https://doi.org/10.1145/3149.214121
27. Gilbert, S., Lynch, N.: Brewer's conjecture and the feasibility of consistent, available, partition-tolerant web services. SIGACT News **33**(2) (2002)
28. Gilbert, S., Lynch, N.A.: Perspectives on the CAP theorem. IEEE Comput. **45**(2), 30–36 (2012)
29. Gotsman, A., Yang, H., Ferreira, C., Najafzadeh, M., Shapiro, M.: cause i'm strong enough: reasoning about consistency choices in distributed systems. In: Proceedings of the 43rd Annual ACM SIGPLAN-SIGACT Symposium on Principles of Programming Languages, POPL 2016, pp. 371–384. ACM, New York (2016). https://doi.org/10.1145/2837614.2837625
30. Houshmand, F., Lesani, M.: Hamsaz: replication coordination analysis and synthesis. In: Proceedings of Annual ACM SIGPLAN-SIGACT Symposium on Principles of Programming Languages, POPL 2019. ACM, New York (2019)
31. Krishnamurthy, S., Sanders, W.H., Cukier, M.: An adaptive quality of service aware middleware for replicated services. IEEE Trans. Parallel Distrib. Syst. **14**(11), 1112–1125 (2003)
32. Ladin, R., Liskov, B., Shrira, L., Ghemawat, S.: Providing high availability using lazy replication. ACM Trans. Comput. Syst. **10**(4) (1992)
33. Lamport, L.: Time, clocks, and the ordering of events in a distributed system. Commun. ACM **21**(7) (1978)
34. Lamport, L.: The part-time parliament. ACM Trans. Comput. Syst. **16**(2) (1998)
35. Lewchenko, N.V., Radhakrishna, A., Gaonkar, A., Černý, P.: Conflict-aware replicated data types. arXiv preprint arXiv:1802.08733 (2018)
36. Li, C., Leitão, J.A., Clement, A., Preguica, N., Rodrigues, R., Vafeiadis, V.: Automating the choice of consistency levels in replicated systems. In: Proceedings of the 2014 USENIX Conference on USENIX Annual Technical Conference, USENIX ATC 2014, pp. 281–292. USENIX Association, Berkeley (2014). http://dl.acm.org/citation.cfm?id=2643634.2643664
37. Li, C., Porto, D., Clement, A., Gehrke, J., Preguica, N., Rodrigues, R.: Making geo-replicated systems fast as possible, consistent when necessary. In: Proceedings of the 10th USENIX Conference on Operating Systems Design and Implementation, OSDI 2012, pp. 265–278. USENIX Association, Berkeley (2012). http://dl.acm.org/citation.cfm?id=2387880.2387906
38. Liu, J., Magrino, T., Arden, O., George, M.D., Myers, A.C.: Warranties for faster strong consistency. In: Proceedings of the 11th USENIX Conference on Networked Systems Design and Implementation, NSDI 2014, pp. 503–517. USENIX Association, Berkeley (2014). http://dl.acm.org/citation.cfm?id=2616448.2616495

39. Lloyd, W., Freedman, M.J., Kaminsky, M., Andersen, D.G.: Don't settle for eventual: scalable causal consistency for wide-area storage with COPS. In: Proceedings SOSP (2011)
40. Lloyd, W., Freedman, M.J., Kaminsky, M., Andersen, D.G.: Stronger semantics for low-latency geo-replicated storage. In: Proceedings NSDI (2013)
41. Nair, S.S., Petri, G., Shapiro, M.: Proving the safety of highly-available distributed objects. ESOP 2020. LNCS, vol. 12075, pp. 544–571. Springer, Cham (2020). https://doi.org/10.1007/978-3-030-44914-8_20
42. Oki, B.M., Liskov, B.H.: Viewstamped replication: a new primary copy method to support highly-available distributed systems. In: Proceedings of the Seventh Annual ACM Symposium on Principles of Distributed Computing, PODC 1988, pp. 8–17. ACM, New York (1988). https://doi.org/10.1145/62546.62549
43. Olston, C., Widom, J.: Offering a precision-performance tradeoff for aggregation queries over replicated data. Technical report, Stanford (2000)
44. Ongaro, D., Ousterhout, J.: In search of an understandable consensus algorithm. In: Proceedings of the 2014 USENIX Conference on USENIX Annual Technical Conference, USENIX ATC 2014, pp. 305–320. USENIX Association, Berkeley (2014). http://dl.acm.org/citation.cfm?id=2643634.2643666
45. Petersen, K., Spreitzer, M.J., Terry, D.B., Theimer, M.M., Demers, A.J.: Flexible update propagation for weakly consistent replication. In: Proceedings SOSP (1997)
46. Ramamritham, K., Pu, C.: A formal characterization of epsilon serializability. IEEE Trans. Knowl. Data Eng. **7**(6), 997–1007 (1995)
47. Roy, S., et al.: The homeostasis protocol: Avoiding transaction coordination through program analysis. In: Proceedings of the 2015 ACM SIGMOD International Conference on Management of Data, SIGMOD 2015, pp. 1311–1326. ACM, New York (2015). https://doi.org/10.1145/2723372.2723720
48. Shapiro, M., Preguiça, N., Baquero, C., Zawirski, M.: A comprehensive study of convergent and commutative replicated data types, Technical report, RR-7506, INRIA (2011)
49. Sivaramakrishnan, K., Kaki, G., Jagannathan, S.: Declarative programming over eventually consistent data stores. In: Proceedings of the 36th ACM SIGPLAN Conference on Programming Language Design and Implementation, PLDI 2015, pp. 413–424. ACM, New York (2015). https://doi.org/10.1145/2737924.2737981
50. Sovran, Y., Power, R., Aguilera, M.K., Li, J.: Transactional storage for geo-replicated systems. In: Proceedings of the Twenty-Third ACM Symposium on Operating Systems Principles, SOSP 2011, pp. 385–400. ACM, New York (2011). https://doi.org/10.1145/2043556.2043592
51. Terry, D.B., Prabhakaran, V., Kotla, R., Balakrishnan, M., Aguilera, M.K., Abu-Libdeh, H.: Consistency-based service level agreements for cloud storage. In: Proceedings of the Twenty-Fourth ACM Symposium on Operating Systems Principles, SOSP 2013, pp. 309–324. ACM, New York (2013). https://doi.org/10.1145/2517349.2522731
52. Vogels, W.: Eventually consistent. ACM Queue **6**(6) (2008)
53. Wang, C., Enea, C., Mutluergil, S.O., Petri, G.: Replication-aware linearizability. In: Proceedings of the 40th ACM SIGPLAN Conference on Programming Language Design and Implementation, pp. 980–993 (2019)
54. Yu, H., Vahdat, A.: Design and evaluation of a continuous consistency model for replicated services. In: Proceedings of the 4th Conference on Symposium on Operating System Design & Implementation-Volume 4, p. 21. USENIX Association (2000)

55. Yu, H., Vahdat, A.: Efficient numerical error bounding for replicated network services. In: VLDB, pp. 123–133. Citeseer (2000)
56. Yu, H., Vahdat, A.: Combining generality and practicality in a conit-based continuous consistency model for wide-area replication. In: Proceedings 21st International Conference on Distributed Computing Systems, pp. 429–438. IEEE (2001)
57. Yu, H., Vahdat, A.: The costs and limits of availability for replicated services. In: ACM SIGOPS Operating Systems Review, vol. 35, pp. 29–42. ACM (2001)
58. Yu, H., Vahdat, A.: Minimal replication cost for availability. In: Proceedings of the Twenty-First Annual Symposium on Principles of Distributed Computing, pp. 98–107. ACM (2002)
59. Zhang, C., Zhang, Z.: Trading replication consistency for performance and availability: an adaptive approach. In: 23rd International Conference on Distributed Computing Systems, Proceedings, pp. 687–695. IEEE (2003)

Root Causing Linearizability Violations

Berk Çirisci[1], Constantin Enea[1(✉)], Azadeh Farzan[2],
and Suha Orhun Mutluergil[1]

[1] Université de Paris, CNRS, IRIF,
75013 Paris, France
{cirisci,cenea,mutluergil}@irif.fr
[2] University of Toronto, Toronto, Canada
azadeh@cs.toronto.edu

Abstract. Linearizability is the de facto correctness criterion for concurrent data type implementations. Violation of linearizability is witnessed by an error trace in which the outputs of individual operations do not match those of a sequential execution of the same operations. Extensive work has been done in discovering linearizability violations, but little work has been done in trying to provide useful hints to the programmer when a violation is discovered by a tester tool. In this paper, we propose an approach that identifies the root causes of linearizability errors in the form of code blocks whose atomicity is required to restore linearizability. The key insight of this paper is that the problem can be reduced to a simpler algorithmic problem of identifying minimal root causes of conflict serializability violation in an error trace combined with a heuristic for identifying which of these are more likely to be the true root cause of non-linearizability. We propose theoretical results outlining this reduction, and an algorithm to solve the simpler problem. We have implemented our approach and carried out several experiments on realistic concurrent data types demonstrating its efficiency.

1 Introduction

Efficient multithreaded programs typically rely on optimized implementations of common abstract data types (ADTs) like stacks, queues, sets, and maps [31], whose operations execute in parallel across processor cores to maximize performance [36]. Programming these concurrent objects correctly is tricky. Synchronization between operations must be minimized to reduce response time and increase throughput [23,36]. Yet this minimal amount of synchronization must also be adequate to ensure that operations behave as if they were executed atomically, one after the other, so that client programs can rely on the (sequential) ADT specification; this de-facto correctness criterion is known as *linearizability* [24]. These opposing requirements, along with the general challenge

This work is supported in part by the European Research Council (ERC) under the EU's Horizon 2020 research and innovation program (grant agreement No. 678177).

S. K. Lahiri and C. Wang (Eds.): CAV 2020, LNCS 12224, pp. 350–375, 2020.
https://doi.org/10.1007/978-3-030-53288-8_17

in reasoning about thread interleavings, make concurrent objects a ripe source of insidious programming errors [12,15,35].

Program properties like linearizability that are difficult to determine statically are typically substantiated by dynamic techniques like testing and runtime verification. While monitoring linearizability of an execution against an arbitrary ADT specification requires exponential time in general [20], there exist several efficient approaches for dealing with this problem that led to practical tools, e.g., [3,4,13,14,16,33,39,47]. Although these approaches are effective at identifying non-linearizable executions of a given object, they do not provide any hints or guidelines about the source of a non-linearizability error once one is found. If some sort of *root-cause* for non-linearizability can be identified, for example a minimal set of commands in the code that explain the error, then the usability of such testing tools will significantly increase for average programmers. Root-causing concurrency bugs in general is a difficult problem. It is easy enough to fix linearizability if one is willing to disregard or sacrifice performance measures, e.g., by enforcing coarse-grain atomic sections that span a whole method body. It is difficult to localize the problem to a degree that fixing it would not affect the otherwise correct behaviours of the ADT. Simplifying techniques, such as equating root causes with some limited set of "bad" patterns, e.g., a non-atomic section formed of two accesses to the same shared variable [10,28,38] have been used to provide efficient coarse approximations for root cause identifications.

In this paper, we present an approach for identifying non-linearizability root-causes in a given execution, which equates root causes with optimal repairs that rule out the non-linearizable execution and as few linearizable executions as possible (from a set of linearizable executions given as input). Our approach can be extended to a set of executions and therefore in the limit identify the root cause of the non-linearizability of an ADT as a whole. Sequential[1] executions of a concurrent object are linearizable, and therefore, linearizability bugs can always be ruled out by introducing one atomic section per each method in the ADT. Thus, focusing on atomic sections as repairs, there is a guarantee of existence of a repair in all scenarios. We emphasize the fact that our goal is to interpret such repairs as root-causes. Implementing these repairs in the context of a concrete concurrent object using synchronization primitives (eg., locks) is orthogonal and beyond the scope of this paper. Some solutions are proposed in [28,29,46].

As a first step, we investigate the problem of finding *all optimal repairs* in the form of sets of atomic sections that rule out a given (non-linearizable) execution. A repair is considered optimal when roughly, it allows a maximal number of interleavings. We identify a connection between this problem and *conflict serializability* [37], an atomicity condition originally introduced in the context of database transactions. In the context of concurrent programs, given a decomposition of the program's code into code blocks, an execution is conflict serializable

---

[1] An execution is called sequential when methods execute in isolation, one after another.

Shared variables:

```
range: integer initialized to 0
items: array of objects
       initialized to NULL

1 procedure push(x)
2   i := F&I(range);
3   items[i] := x
```

```
4 procedure pop()
5   t := range-1;
6   x := NULL;
7   for i := t downto 1 {
8       x := items[i];
9       items[i] := null;
10      if ( x != null ) break; }
11  return x;
```

Fig. 1. A non-linearizable concurrent stack.

if it is equivalent[2] to an execution in which all code blocks are executed in a sequential non-interleaved fashion. A repair that rules out a non-linearizable execution τ can be obtained using a decomposition of the set of events in τ into a set of blocks that we call intervals, such that τ is *not* conflict serializable with respect to this decomposition. Each interval will correspond to an atomic section in the repair (obtained by mapping events in the execution to statements in the code). A naive approach to compute all optimal repairs would enumerate all decompositions into intervals and check conflict-serializabiliy with respect to each one of them. Such an approach would be inefficient because the number of possible decompositions is exponential in both the number of events in the execution and the number of threads. We show that this problem is actually *polynomial time* assuming a fixed number of threads. This is quite non-trivial and requires a careful examination of the cyclic dependencies in non conflict-serializable executions. Assuming a fixed number of threads is not an obstacle in practice since recent work shows that most linearizability bugs can be caught with client programs with two threads only [12,15].

In general, there may exist multiple optimal repairs that rule out a non-linearizable execution. To identify which repairs are more likely to correspond to root-causes, we rely on a given set of *linearizable* executions. We rank the repairs depending on how many linearizable executions they disable, prioritizing those that exclude fewer linearizable executions. This is inspired by the hypothesis that cyclic memory accesses occurring in linearizable executions are harmless.

We evaluated this approach on several concurrent objects, which are variations of lock-based concurrent sets/maps from the Synchrobench repository [21]. We considered a set of non-linearizable implementations obtained by modifying the placement of the lock/unlock primitives, and applied a linearizability testing tool called Violat [14] to obtain client programs that admit non-linearizable executions. We applied our algorithms on the executions obtained by running these clients using Java Pathfinder [44]. Our results show that our approach is highly effective in identifying the precise root cause of linearizability violations since in every case, our tool precisely identifies the root cause of a violation that is discoverable by the client of the library used to produce the error traces.

---

[2] Two executions are equivalent if roughly, they are the same modulo reordering statements that do not access the same shared variable.

2   Overview

Figure 1 lists a variation of a concurrent stack introduced by Afek et al. [1]. The values pushed into the stack are stored into an unbounded array `items`; a shared variable `range` keeps the index of the first unused position in `items`. The `push` method stores the input in the array and it increments `range` using a call to an atomic fetch and increment (`F&I`) primitive. This primitive returns the current value of `range` while also incrementing it at the same time. The `pop` method reads `range` and then traverses the array backwards starting from the predecessor of this position, until it finds a position storing a non-null value. It also nullifies all the array cells encountered during this traversal. If it reaches the bottom of the array without finding non-null values, it returns that the stack is empty.

This concurrent stack is *not* linearizable as witnessed by the execution in Fig. 2. This is an execution of a client with three threads executing two `push` and two `pop` operations in total. The `push` in the first thread is interrupted by operations from the other two threads which makes both `pop` operations return the same value b. The execution is not linearizable because the value b was pushed only once and it cannot be returned by two different `pop` operations.

The root-cause of this violation is the non-atomicity of the statements at lines 8 and 9 of `pop`, reading `items[i]` and updating it to `null`. The stack is linearizable when the two statements are executed atomically (see [1]).

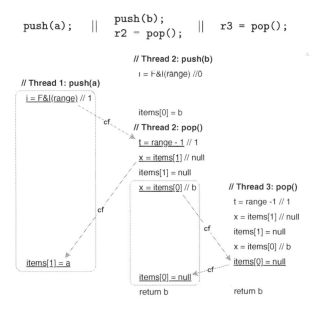

Fig. 2. A client program of the concurrent stack of Fig. 1 and one of its non-linearizable executions illustrate as a sequence of read/write events.

Our goal is to identify such root-causes. We start with a non-linearizable execution like the one in Fig. 2. The first step is to compute all optimal repairs in the form of atomic sections that disable the non-linearizable execution. There are two such optimal repairs for the execution in Fig. 2: (1) an atomic section containing the statements at lines 8 and 9 in pop (representing the root-cause), and (2) an atomic section that includes the two statements in the push method.

These repairs disable the execution because each pair of statements is interleaved with *conflicting*[3] memory accesses in that execution. This is illustrated by the boxes and the edges in Fig. 2 labeled by cf: the boxes include these two pairs of statements and the edges emphasize the order between conflicting memory accesses. In Sect. 5, we formalize this by leveraging the notion of conflict serializability. The execution is not conflict-serializable assuming any decomposition of the code in Fig. 1 into a set of code blocks (transactions) such that one of them contains one of these two pairs. These repairs are optimal because they consist of a single atomic section of minimal size (with just two statements). We formalize a generic notion of optimality in Sect. 4 through the introduction of an order relation between repairs, defined as component-wise inclusion of atomic sections and compute the minimal repairs w.r.t. this order.

At the end of the first phase, our approach produces a set of all such optimal (incomparable) repairs. To isolate one as the best candidate, we use a heuristic to rank the optimal repairs. The heuristic relies on the hypothesis that repairs which disable fewer linearizable executions are more likely to represent the best candidate for the true root-cause of a linearizability bug.

For instance, the client in Fig. 2 admits a linearizable execution where the first two threads are interleaved exactly as in Fig. 2 and where the pop in the third thread executes *after* the first two threads finished. This is linearizable because the pop in the third thread returns the value a written by the push in the first thread in items[1] (this is the first non-null array cell starting from the end). Focusing on the two optimal repairs mentioned above, enforcing only the atomic section in the push will disable this linearizable execution. The atomic section in the pop, which permits this execution, is ranked higher to indicate it as the more likely root-cause. This is the expected result for our example.

This ranking scheme can easily be extended to a set of linearizable executions. Given a set of linearizable executions, we rank optimal repairs by keeping track of how many of the linearizable executions each disables.

3   Preliminaries

We formalize executions of a concurrent object as sequences of events representing calling or returning from a method invocation (called *operation*), or an access (read or write) to a memory location. Then, we recall the notion of linearizability [24].

---

[3] As usual, two memory accesses are conflicting when they access the same variable and at least one of them is a write.

We fix arbitrary sets $\mathbb{M}$ and $\mathbb{V}$ of method names and parameter/return values. We fix an arbitrary set $\mathbb{O}$ of operation identifiers, and for given sets $\mathbb{M}$ and $\mathbb{V}$ of methods and values, we fix the sets $C = \{o.call\ m(v) : m \in \mathbb{M}, v \in \mathbb{V}, o \in \mathbb{O}\}$ and $R = \{o.ret\ v : v \in \mathbb{O}, o \in \mathbb{O}\}$ of *call actions* and *return actions*. Each call action $o.call\ m(v)$ combines a method $m \in \mathbb{M}$ and value $v \in \mathbb{V}$ with an *operation identifier* $o \in \mathbb{O}$. A return action $o.ret\ v$ combines an operation identifier $o \in \mathbb{O}$ with a value $v \in \mathbb{V}$. Operation identifiers are used to pair call and return actions. Also, let $\mathbb{L}$ be a set of (shared) memory locations and $A = \{o.rd(x), o.wr(x) : o \in \mathbb{O}, x \in \mathbb{L}\}$ the set of *read* and *write* actions. The operation identifier of an action a is denoted by $\mathsf{op}(a)$.

We fix an arbitrary set $\mathbb{T}$ of thread ids. An *event* is a tuple $\langle t, a \rangle$ formed of a thread id $t \in \mathbb{T}$ and an action a. A *trace* τ is a sequence of events satisfying standard well-formedness properties, e.g., the projection of τ on events of the same thread is a concatenation of sequences formed of a call action, followed by read/write actions with the same operation identifier, and a return action. Also, we assume that every atomic section (block) is interpreted as an *uninterrupted* sequence of events that correspond to the instructions in that atomic section.

We define two relations over the events in a trace τ: the *program order* relation po_τ relates any two events e_1 and e_2 of the same thread such that e_1 occurs before e_2 in τ, and the *conflict* relation cf_τ relates any two events e_1 and e_2 of different threads that access the same location, at least one of them being a write, such that e_1 occurs before e_2 in τ. We omit the subscript τ when the trace is understood from the context.

Two traces τ_1 and τ_2 are called *equivalent*, denoted by $\tau_1 \equiv \tau_2$, when $\mathsf{po}_{\tau_1} = \mathsf{po}_{\tau_2}$ and $\mathsf{cf}_{\tau_1} = \mathsf{cf}_{\tau_2}$. They are called po-*equivalent* when only $\mathsf{po}_{\tau_1} = \mathsf{po}_{\tau_2}$.

The projection of a trace τ over call and return actions is called a *history* and denoted by $h(\tau)$. A history is *sequential* when each call action c is immediately followed by a return action r with $\mathsf{op}(c) = \mathsf{op}(r)$. A *linearization* of a history h_1 is a sequential history h_2 that is a permutation of h_1 that preserves the order between return and call actions, i.e., a given return action occurs before a given call action in h_1 iff the same holds in h_2.

A *library* L is a set of traces[4]. A trace τ of a library L is *linearizable* if L contains some sequential trace whose history is a linearization of $h(\tau)$. A library is *linearizable* if all its traces are linearizable[5]. In the following, since *linearizability* is used as the main correctness criterion, a *bug* is a trace τ that is not linearizable.

---

[4] Intuitively, this corresponds to running a concrete library under a most general client that makes an arbitrary number of invocations from an arbitrary number of threads.

[5] Linearizability is typically defined with respect to a sequential ADT. Here, we take the simplifying assumption that the ADT is defined by the set of sequential histories of the library. This holds for all concurrent libraries that we are aware of.

356   B. Çirisci et al.

4   Linearizability Violations and Their Root Causes

Given a non-linearizable library, our goal is to identify the root cause of non-linearizability in the library code. Let us start by formally describing the state space of all such causes and state some properties of the space that will aid the understanding of our algorithm. First, our focus is on a specific category of causes, namely those that can be removed through the introduction of new atomic code blocks to the library code without any other code changes.

Definition 1 (Non-linearizability Root Cause). *For a non-linearizable library L, the root cause is formally identified by $\mathcal{R}$, a set of atomic blocks $\mathcal{A}$ such that L is linearizable with the addition of blocks from $\mathcal{A}$.*

Observe that the set of atomic blocks identified in Definition 1 can conceptually be viewed as blocks of code whose non-atomicity is the *root cause* of non-linearizability and their introduction would *repair* the library. For the rest of this paper, we use the two terminologies interchangeably since for this specific class, the two notions perfectly coincide. The immediate question that comes to mind is whether Definition 1 is general enough. Observe that since linearizability is fundamentally an atomicity type property for individual methods in a library, if every single method of the library is declared atomic at the code level, then the library is trivially linearizable. The only valid executions of the library are the linear (sequential) executions in this case. Therefore,

Remark 1. Every non-linearizable library can be made linearizable by adding atomic code blocks in $\mathcal{R}$ according to Definition 1.

Since there always is a trivial repair, one is interested in finding a *good* one. The quality of a repair is contingent on the amount of *parallelism* that the addition of the corresponding atomic blocks removes from the executions of an arbitrary client of the library. Generally, it is understood that the fewer the number of introduced atomic blocks and the shorter their length, the more permissive they will be in terms of the parallel executions of a client of this library. This motivates a simple formal subsumption relationship between repairs of a bug. We say an atomic code block b subsumes another atomic code block b', denoted as $b \sqsupseteq_c b'$, if and only if b' is contained within b.

Definition 2 (Repair Subsumption). *A repair $\mathcal{R}$ subsumes another repair $\mathcal{R}'$, we write $\mathcal{R} \sqsupseteq_c \mathcal{R}'$ if and only if for all atomic blocks $b' \in \mathcal{R}'$, there exists an atomic block $b \in \mathcal{R}$ such that $b \sqsupseteq_c b'$.*

It is easy to see that $\sqsupseteq_c$ is a partial order, and combined with the finite set of all possible program repairs gives rise to the concept of a set of optimal repairs, namely those that do not subsume any other repair. It can be lifted to sets of repairs in the natural way: $\mathbb{R} \sqsupseteq_c \mathbb{R}'$ iff $\forall \mathcal{R}' \in \mathbb{R}', \exists \mathcal{R} \in \mathbb{R} : \mathcal{R} \sqsupseteq_c \mathcal{R}'$.

Remark 2. The set of traces of a library L with a repair $\mathcal{R}$ is a superset of the set of traces of L with the repair $\mathcal{R}'$ if $\mathcal{R}' \sqsupseteq_c \mathcal{R}$.

This means that an optimal repair identification according to Definition 2 should lead to an optimal amount of parallelism in the library repaired by forcing the corresponding code blocks to execute atomically. The goal of our algorithm is to identify such a set of *optimal repairs*.

Now, let us turn our attention to an algorithmic setup to solve this problem. The non-linearizability of a library L is witnessed by a non-empty set of non-linearizable traces T. These are the concrete erroneous traces of (a client of) the library, for which we intend to identify the repair.

Note that if τ is a non-linearizable trace, then all the traces τ' that are equivalent to τ are also non-linearizable. Indeed, if τ' is equivalent to τ, then the values that are read in τ' are the same as in τ^6, which implies that the return values in τ' are the same as in τ, and therefore, τ' is non-linearizable when τ is.

Consider a conceptual oracle, $\mathcal{O}^L(T)$, that takes a set of non-linearizable traces of a library L and produces the set of all optimal repairs $\mathbb{R}$ such that each $\mathcal{R} \in \mathbb{R}$ excludes all the traces that are equivalent to those in T. Then the following iterative algorithm produces $\mathbb{R}$ for a library L:

1. Let $T = \emptyset$ and $\mathbb{R} = \emptyset$.
2. Check if L with the addition of atomic blocks from $\mathbb{R}$ is linearizable:
   - Yes? Return $\mathbb{R}$.
   - NO? Produce a set of non-linearizability witnesses T' and let $T = T \cup T'$.
3. Call $\mathcal{O}^L(T)$ and update the set of repairs $\mathbb{R}$ with the result.
4. Go to back to step 2.

Proposition 1. *The above algorithm produces an optimal set of repairs $\mathbb{R}$ that make its input library linearizable.*

It is easy to see that if oracle $\mathcal{O}^L(T)$ can be relied on to produce perfect results, then the algorithm satisfies a progress property in the sense that $\mathbb{R}_{k+1} \sqsupseteq_c \mathbb{R}_k$, where $\mathbb{R}_k$ is the value of $\mathbb{R}$ in the k-th iteration of the loop. Following Remark 1, this chain of increasingly stronger repairs is bounded by the specific repair in which every method of the library L has to be declared atomic. Therefore, the algorithm converges. The assumption of optimality for $\mathcal{O}^L(T)$ implies that on the iteration that the algorithm terminates, it will produce the optimal $\mathbb{R}$.

Note that in oracle $\mathcal{O}^L$, the focus shifts from identifying the source of error for the entire library to identifying the source of error in a specific set of non-linearizability witnesses. First, we propose a solution for implementing $\mathcal{O}^L$ for a singleton set, i.e. precisely one error trace, and later argue why the solution easily generalizes to finitely many error traces.

4.1   Repair Oracle Approximation

Given a trace τ as a violation of linearizability, we wish to implement $\mathcal{O}^L$ that takes a single trace τ and proposes an optimal set of repairs for it.

---

[6] We assume that program instructions are deterministic, which is usually the case.

Observe that if every trace of L is *conflict serializable* [37] (i.e., equivalent to a sequential trace), assuming method boundaries as transaction boundaries, then it is necessarily linearizable. Therefore, knowing that it is not linearizable, we can conclude that there exists some trace of L which is not serializable. Following the same line of reasoning, we can conclude that the error trace τ itself is not *conflict serializable*, for some choice of transaction boundaries. This observation is the basis of our solution for approximating repairs for non-linearizability through an oracle that is actively seeking to repair for non-serializability violations.

Definition 3 (Trace Eliminator). *For an error trace (a bug) τ, a set of atomic blocks $\mathcal{R}$ is called a* trace eliminator *if and only if every trace that is equivalent to τ is not a trace of the new library with the addition of blocks from $\mathcal{R}$.*

Any trace eliminator that removes τ as a valid trace of a client of the library L (and all the traces equivalent to τ), by amending the library for the conflict serializability violation, (indirectly) eliminates it as a witness to non-linearizability as well. Note that the universes of *trace eliminators* and *non-linearizability repairs* are the same set of objects, and therefore the subsumption relation $\sqsupseteq_c$ is well defined for trace eliminators, and the concept of optimality is similarly defined. Moreover, Definition 3 is agnostic to linearizability and can be interchangeably used for serializability repairs.

Theorem 1. $\mathcal{R}$ *is a trace eliminator for τ if and only if τ is not conflict serializable with transaction boundaries that subsume $\mathcal{R}$ (statements that are not included in the atomic sections from $\mathcal{R}$ are assumed to form singleton transactions).*

Proof. (Sketch) For the if direction, assume by contradiction that $\mathcal{R}$ is not a trace eliminator for τ. This implies that there exists a trace $\tau' \equiv \tau$ where the sequences of events corresponding to the atomic sections in $\mathcal{R}$ occur uninterrupted (not interleaved with other events). This is a direct contradiction to τ not being conflict serializable when transaction boundaries are defined precisely by the atomic sections in $\mathcal{R}$. For the only if direction, assume by contradiction that τ is conflict serializable. By definition, there is an equivalent trace τ' where the sequences of events corresponding to the atomic sections in $\mathcal{R}$ occur uninterrupted. Therefore, the library L' obtained by adding the atomic code blocks in $\mathcal{R}$ admits τ', which contradicts the fact that $\mathcal{R}$ is a trace eliminator for τ. $\square$

The relationship between the set of trace eliminators for τ and $\mathcal{O}^L(\tau)$ can be made precise. Since every trace eliminator is a linearizability repair by definition, but not necessarily an optimal one, we have:

Proposition 2. *Let $\mathcal{O}^L(\tau)$ represent the optimal set of repairs that eliminate τ as a witness to non-linearizability and $\mathbb{R}$ be the set of optimal trace eliminators for τ. We have $\mathbb{R} \supseteq \mathcal{O}^L(\tau)$.*

This is precisely why the set of trace eliminators safely overapproximates the set of linearizability repairs for a single trace. Note that Theorem 1 links any trace eliminator (a set of code blocks) to a collection of dynamic (runtime) transactions. It is fairly straightforward to see that given the latter as an input, the former can be inferred in a way that the dynamic transactions generated by the static code blocks are as close as possible to the input transaction boundaries, assuming no structural changes occur in the code. In Sect. 5, we discuss how an optimal set of dynamic transaction boundaries can be computed, which give rise to a set of optimal trace eliminators.

4.2   Generalization to Multiple Traces

If we have an implementation for an oracle $\mathcal{O}^L(\tau)$ that takes a single trace and produces the set of optimal trace eliminators for it, then the following algorithm implements an oracle for $\mathcal{O}^L(\{\tau_1, \ldots, \tau_n\})$ for any finite number of traces:

- Let $\mathbb{R} = \emptyset$.
- For each τ_i $(1 \leq i \leq n)$: let $\mathbb{R}_i = \mathcal{O}^L(\tau_i)$.
- Let $\mathbb{T} = \mathbb{R}_1 \times \cdots \times \mathbb{R}_n$.
- For each $\mathcal{T} \in \mathbb{T}$: let $\mathbb{R} = \mathbb{R} \cup \mathit{flatten}(\mathcal{T})$.
- For each $\mathcal{R} \in \mathbb{R}$: if $\exists \mathcal{R}' \in \mathbb{R}$ s.t. $\mathcal{R} \sqsupseteq_c \mathcal{R}'$ then $\mathbb{R} = \mathbb{R} - \{\mathcal{R}\}$.

where $\mathit{flatten}(\mathcal{T})$ basically takes the union of repairs suggested by individual components of $\mathcal{T}$ while merging any overlapping atomic blocks. Note that the ith component of $\mathcal{T}$ suggests an *optimal* trace eliminator for τ_i. If we want a tight combination of all such trace eliminators, we need the minimal set of atomic blocks that *covers* all atomic blocks suggested by each eliminator. Formally:

$$\mathit{flatten}(\langle \mathcal{R}_1, \ldots, \mathcal{R}_n \rangle) = \text{ smallest } \mathcal{R} \text{ wrt } \sqsupseteq_c \text{ st } \forall 1 \leq i \leq n: \; \mathcal{R} \sqsupseteq_c \mathcal{R}_i$$

we can then conclude:

Theorem 2. *If $\mathcal{O}^L(\tau)$ produces the optimal set of trace eliminators for trace τ, then the above algorithm correctly implements $\mathcal{O}^L(\{\tau_1, \ldots, \tau_n\})$, that is, it produces the optimal set of repairs for the set of error traces $\{\tau_1, \ldots, \tau_n\}$.*

5   Conflict-Serializability Repairs

In this section, we investigate the theoretical properties of conflict serializability repairs to provide a set up for an algorithm that implements the oracle $\mathcal{O}^L$ for a single input trace. The goal of this algorithm is to take a trace τ as an input and return the optimal trace eliminator for τ, under the assumption that τ witnesses the violation of linearizability.

5.1 Repairs and Conflict Cycles

We start by introducing a few formal definitions and some theoretical connections that will give rise to an algorithm for identifying an optimal set of atomic blocks that can eliminate a trace τ as a witness to violation of conflict serialiazability.

Definition 4 (Decompositions and Intervals). *A decomposition of a trace* τ *is an equivalence relation* D *over its set of events such that:*

- *D relates only events of the same operation, i.e. if $(e_1, e_2) \in D$, then $\mathsf{op}(e_1) = \mathsf{op}(e_2)$, and*
- *the equivalence classes of D are continuous sequences of events of the same operation, i.e., if $(e_1, e_3) \in D$ and $\{(e_1, e_2), (e_2, e_3)\} \subseteq \mathsf{po}_\tau$, then $\{(e_1, e_2), (e_2, e_3)\} \subseteq D$*

The equivalence classes of a decomposition D, *denoted by* $I_{\tau, D}$ *are called* inter-vals.

Observe that the relation $\sqsupseteq_c$ is well defined partial order over the universal all possible intervals (of all possible decompositions) of a trace τ.

Definition 5 (Interval Graphs). *Given a trace* τ, *and decomposition* D, *an interval graph is defined as* $G_{\tau, D} = (V, E)$ *where the set of vertexes* V *is the set of intervals of* D *and the set of edges* E *is defined as follows*

$$E = \{(i, i') \mid i \neq i' \wedge \exists e \in i, e' \in i' : (e, e') \in \mathsf{po}_\tau \cup \mathsf{cf}_\tau\}$$

Since, by definition, each edge in the interval graph is induced by an edge from either relation po_τ or cf_τ, but note both, we lift these relations over the sets of intervals in the natural way, that is:

$$(i, i') \in \mathsf{cf}_\tau^i \iff \exists e \in i, e' \in i' : e \neq e' \wedge (e, e') \in \mathsf{cf}_\tau$$
$$(i, i') \in \mathsf{po}_\tau^i \iff \exists e \in i, e' \in i' : e \neq e' \wedge (e, e') \in \mathsf{po}_\tau$$

Given an interval graph edge $(i, i') \in \mathsf{cf}_\tau^i \cup \mathsf{po}_\tau^i$, let

$$tre(i, i') = \{(e, e') \mid e \in i \wedge e' \in i' \wedge (e, e') \in \mathsf{cf}_\tau \cup \mathsf{po}_\tau\}$$

Figure 3 illustrates an interval graph. Node o_i : e_j denotes an event e_j of operation o_i. Events of the same thread are aligned vertically. We draw only cf_τ edges since the po_τ edges are implied by the vertical alignment of events. Non-singleton intervals of D are $i_1 = \{e_1, e_2, e_3, e_4\}$, $i_2 = \{e_5, e_6\}$ and $i_3 = \{e_7, e_8\}$. Singleton intervals are identified by the corresponding event identifiers. Edges among interval nodes correspond to cf_τ or po_τ. For instance, $(i_1, i_2) \in \mathsf{cf}_\tau^i$ since $(e_1, e_6) \in \mathsf{cf}_\tau$, $e_1 \in i_1$ and $e_6 \in i_2$. As an example for the function tre, we have $tre(i_2, i_3) = \{(e_5, e_7), (e_5, e_8), (e_6, e_7), (e_6, e_8)\}$ that consists of po_τ edges and $tre(i_3, i_1) = \{(e_8, e_3), (e_8, e_4)\}$ that consists of cf_τ edges.

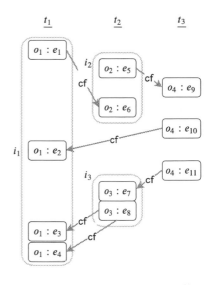

Fig. 3. An interval graph.

For the degenerate decomposition in which each event is an interval of size one by itself, the interval graph collapses into a *trace graph*, denoted by G_τ. Note that G_τ is acyclic since the relations po_τ and cf_τ are consistent with the order between the events in τ.

Intervals are closely related to the static notion of transactions and the induced transaction boundaries on traces. For example, in the decomposition in which the intervals coincide with the boundaries of transactions (e.g. method boundaries), it is straightforward to see that the interval graph becomes precisely the *conflict graph* [19] widely known in the conflict serializability literature. It is a known fact that a trace is conflict serializable if and only if its conflict graph is acyclic [37]. Since τ is not conflict serializable with respect to the boundaries of methods from L, we know the interval graph with those boundaries is cyclic.

With intervals set as single events, G_τ is acyclic, and with the intervals set at method boundaries, it is cyclic. The high level observation is that there exist a decomposition D in the middle of this spectrum, so to speak, such that $G_{\tau,D}$ is cyclic, but $G_{\tau,D'}$ for any $D \sqsupseteq_c D'$ is acyclic. In the following we will formally argue why such a decomposition D is at the centre of identification of serializability repairs.

A cycle in a graph is *simple* if only one vertex is repeated more than once.

Definition 6 (Critical Segment Sets). *Let D be a decomposition such that the interval graph $G_{\tau,D}$ is cyclic and $\alpha = i_0 \ldots i_{n-1} i_0$ be a simple cycle. Define*

$$edges(\alpha) = tre(i_0, i_1) \times tre(i_1, i_2) \times \cdots \times tre(i_{n-1}, i_0)$$
$$segs(\vec{e}) = \{[e_k^\odot, e_k^\otimes] \mid 0 \leq k \leq n-1 \wedge (e_k^\odot, e_{(k+1) \bmod n}^\otimes) = \vec{e}.k\}$$
$$critSegs(\vec{e}) = \{[e_k^\odot, e_k^\otimes] \in segs(\vec{e}) \mid (e_k^\odot, e_k^\otimes) \in \mathsf{po}_\tau\}$$
$$CritSegs(\alpha) = \{s \mid \exists \vec{e} \in edges(\alpha) : s = critSegs(\vec{e})\}$$

where the set CritSegs(α) is the set of all critical segments sets of cycle α.

Note that each cycle may induce several different segment sets, determined by $|edges(\alpha)|$. More importantly, each segment set includes at least one critical segment.

Lemma 1. *For any $\vec{e} \in edges(\alpha)$, we have critSegs($\vec{e}$) $\neq \emptyset$.*

Example 1. In Fig. 3, $\alpha_1 = i_1, i_2, i_3, i_1$ is a simple cycle. Included in $edges(\alpha)$ are the following three cycles and their corresponding segments:

$$\alpha_1^1 = \langle (e_1, e_6), (e_6, e_7)(e_8, e_3) \rangle \qquad segs(\alpha_1^1) = \{[e_1, e_3], [e_6, e_6], [e_8, e_7]\}$$
$$\alpha_1^2 = \langle (e_1, e_6), (e_6, e_7), (e_8, e_4) \rangle \qquad segs(\alpha_1^2) = \{[e_1, e_4], [e_6, e_6], [e_8, e_7]\}$$
$$\alpha_1^3 = \langle (e_1, e_6), (e_5, e_8), (e_8, e_3) \rangle \qquad segs(\alpha_1^3) = \{[e_1, e_3], [e_5, e_6], [e_8, e_8].\}$$

The critical segments for these are $critSegs(\alpha_1^1) = \{[e_1, e_3]\}$, $critSegs(\alpha_1^2) = \{[e_1, e_4]\}$ and $critSegs(\alpha_1^3) = \{[e_1, e_3], [e_5, e_6]\}$.

There is a direct connection between the notion of critical segment sets and conflict serializability repairs that the following lemma captures. A segment is called *uninterrupted* in a trace τ when all its events occur continuously one after another in τ without an interruption from events of another interval.

Lemma 2. *Let α be a cycle in some interval graph $G_{\tau,D}$ of trace τ which is not conflict serializable wrt to the decomposition D and $critSeg_\alpha \in CritSegs(\alpha)$. There does not exist trace τ' which is equivalent to τ in which all segments from $critSeg_\alpha$ are uninterrupted in τ'.*

The immediate corollary of Lemma 2 is that if one ensures the atomicity of the segments of events in $CritSegs(\alpha)$ by adding atomic blocks at the code level, then τ can no longer be an execution of the library. In other words, a set of such atomic code blocks is precisely a trace eliminator (Definition 3) for τ.

5.2   A Simple Algorithm

Lemma 2 and its corollary suggest a simple enumerative algorithm to discover the set of all trace eliminators for a buggy trace τ.

– Let $\mathbb{D}$ be the set of all decompositions of τ and $\mathbb{R} = \emptyset$.
– For each $D \in \mathbb{D}$:
  - Let $\mathbb{C}$ be the set of all simple cycles in $G_{\tau,D}$.
  - For each $\alpha \in \mathbb{C}$:
    * Let $\mathbb{S} = CritSegs(\alpha)$.
    * $\mathbb{R} = \mathbb{R} \cup \mathbb{S}$
– For each $\mathcal{R} \in \mathbb{R}$:
  - If $\exists \mathcal{R}' \in \mathbb{R} : \mathcal{R} \sqsupseteq_c \mathcal{R}'$ then $\mathbb{R} = \mathbb{R} - \{\mathcal{R}\}$.

Theorem 3. *The above algorithm produces the optimal set of trace eliminators for a buggy trace τ.*

This theorem is non-trivial, because the set of cycles considered are limited to simple cycles and an argument is required for why no optimal solution is missed as the result of this limitation. An important point is that any optimal trace eliminator $\mathcal{R}$ defines a decomposition D where the non-singleton intervals are precisely those defined by $\mathcal{R}$ such that $G_{\tau,D}$ contains a simple cycle α and the set of code blocks in $\mathcal{R}$ is a member of $CritSegs(\alpha)$. Note that the algorithm may end up producing non-ideal solutions in the first loop, and the proof of Theorem 3 relies on the argument that all such solutions will be filtered out by a proper solution that guarantees to exist and subsume them.

Example 2. The first loop of the above algorithm includes in $\mathbb{R}$ the trace eliminators induced by the critical segments mentioned in Example 1. After the last loop, however, only $critSegs(\alpha_1^1) = \{[e_1, e_3]\}$ will remain in $\mathbb{R}$ since the other two are subsumed by it.

The algorithm is obviously very inefficient. There are two levels of enumeration: all decompositions and all cycles of each decomposition. Assuming that there are $O(|\mathsf{po}_\tau|)$ events in an operation, then there are $O(2^{|\mathsf{po}_\tau|})$ different decompositions for it. Assuming that there are $O(|\mathbb{T}|)$ operations, we conclude that $|\mathbb{D}| = O(2^{|\mathsf{po}_\tau||\mathbb{T}|})$. There could be $O(2^{|E_\tau|})$ possible cycles for each decomposition where $E_\tau = \mathsf{po}_\tau \cup \mathsf{cf}_\tau$. Therefore, the first loop may generate $O(2^{2|E_\tau||\mathbb{T}|})$ many repairs. The last loop iterates over $\mathbb{R}$ and each repair takes $O(\mathbb{R})$ time. The algorithm operates in time $O(2^{4|E_\tau||\mathbb{T}|})$. It is exponential both in the size of threads set and the graph. There are many redundancies in the output of the first loop, however. These are exploited to propose an optimized version of this algorithm.

5.3   A Sound Optimization

Consider an arbitrary cycle α in the interval graph $G_{\tau,D}$. If we want to trace the cycle α over the trace graph G_τ, we would potentially need additional edges that would let us go against the program order inside some intervals that appear on α. Let us call the graph extended with such edges G_τ^D. Formally, G_τ^D includes all the nodes and edges from a trace graph and incorporates additional edges between the events of each interval of D to turn it into a *clique*[7] which is by definition a strongly connected and therefore accommodates the connectivity of any event of an interval to another event in it.

The converse also holds, that is, every *simple* cycle with at least one conflict edge in the G_τ^D with the aforementioned additional edges corresponds to a cycle in the interval graph $G_{\tau,D}$. Note that the inclusion of at least one conflict edge is essential, since every interval graph cycle always includes one such edge by default; since the program order relation is acyclic. Formally:

---

[7] A clique is a complete subgraph of a given graph.

Lemma 3. *For each simple cycle α of $G_{\tau,D}$, there exists a simple cycle α' of G_τ^D that contains at most two events from each interval in α.*

The above lemma can immediately be generalized. Consider the graph G_τ^M where M indicates the decomposition whose intervals coinciding with the library method boundaries. Since for any arbitrary decomposition D, we have $M \sqsupseteq_c D$, we can conclude that G_τ^M includes all possible additional edges that one may want to consider as part of a cycle in an arbitrary G_τ^D for an arbitrary decomposition D. Hence, the set of edges of G_τ^M is a superset of the set of edges of all graphs G_τ^D for all D. This immediately implies that the set of cycles of G_τ^M is the superset of the set of cycles of all such graphs. This fact, combined with Lemma 3 leads us to the new simplified algorithm below in place of the one in Sect. 5.2:

- Let $\mathbb{R} = \emptyset$.
- Let $\mathbb{C}'$ be the set of all simple cycles in G_τ^M.
- For each $\alpha \in \mathbb{C}$:
  - Let $\mathbb{S} = critSegs(\alpha)$.
  - $\mathbb{R} = \mathbb{R} \cup \mathbb{S}$
- For each $\mathcal{R} \in \mathbb{R}$:
  - If $\exists \mathcal{R}' \in \mathbb{R}: \mathcal{R} \sqsupseteq_c \mathcal{R}'$ then $\mathbb{R} = \mathbb{R} - \{\mathcal{R}\}$.

Note that we are slightly bending the definition of *critSegs* in the above algorithm, compared to the one given in Definition 6 since the input cycle there is formally a tuple, and here itis simply a list. The function is semantically the same, however and therefore we do not redefine it.

Observe that ever cycle of G_τ^M corresponds to a cycle in some graph G_τ^D for some decomposition D. This observation together with Lemma 3 and Theorem 3 implies the correctness of the above algorithm. Every cycle of every G_τ^D is covered by the algorithm, and conversely every cycle considered is valid.

We can simplify the above algorithm one step further by further limiting the set of cycles $\mathbb{C}'$ that need to be enumerated. In graph theory, a chord of a simple cycle is an edge connecting two vertices in the cycle which is not part the cycle.

Theorem 4. *The above algorithm produces the set of optimal trace eliminators for τ if $\mathbb{C}'$ is limited to the set of simple chordless cycles of G_τ^M.*

Theorem 4 makes a non-trivial and algorithmically subtle observation. Enumerating the set of all simple chordless cycles of G_τ^D is a much simpler algorithmic problem to solve compared to the initial one from Sect. 5.2. Lemma 3 supports part of this argument since it ensures that all repairs explored in the algorithm from Sect. 5.2 are also explored by the above algorithm. For Theorem 4 to hold, one needs to additionally argue that the cycles of G_τ^M do not produce any junk, that is, each cycle's critical segments correspond to a valid trace eliminator for τ. Also, as for simple cycles, $CritSegs(\alpha)$ for a cycle α subsumes $CritSegs(\alpha')$ for any chordless cycle α' included in α. In Sect. 6.1, we present an algorithm that solves the problem of enumerating all cycles in $\mathbb{C}'$ effectively.

6   Repair List Generation

In this section, we first start by giving a detailed algorithm that produces the set of all optimal trace eliminators. These repairs suggest incomparable optimal ways of removing an erroneous trace from the library. We then present a novel heuristic that orders this set into a list such that the the ones ranked higher in the list are more likely to correspond to something that a human programmer would identify (amongst the entire set) as the ideal repair.

6.1   Optimal Repairs Enumeration Algorithm

In this section, we present an algorithm for enumerating all simple chordless cycles in G_τ^M with at least one cf_τ edge, prove its correctness, and formally analyze its time complexity. The algorithm is the following:

- Let $\mathbb{C} = \emptyset$.
- For each sequence $\alpha = c_1, c_2, \ldots, c_n$ where $c_i \in \mathsf{cf}_\tau$ and $0 < n \leq |\mathbb{T}|$:
  - Let $c_i = (e_i^\otimes, e_i^\odot)$ for all $i \in [1, n]$.
  - If $(e_i^\odot, e_{(i \bmod n)+1}^\otimes) \in E_\tau^M \backslash \mathsf{cf}_\tau$ and $e_i^\odot \neq e_j^\odot$ s.t. $i, j \in [1, n]$ s.t. $i \neq j$:
    * $\mathbb{C} = \mathbb{C} \cup \{\alpha\}$

It enumerates all non-empty cf_τ sequences of length less than or equal to $|\mathbb{T}|$. If the sequence forms a valid simple cycle and visits each thread at most once (i.e. there are no two distinct conflict edges such that its end points are on the same thread), then it is added to the result set $\mathbb{C}$. Correctness of the algorithm relies on the following observation:

Lemma 4. *α is a chordless cycle of G_τ^D with at least one cf_τ edge if and only if α visits each thread at most once and it visits at least two threads.*

As a corollary of Lemma 4, we know that a chordless cycle could have at most $|\mathbb{T}|$ conflict edges. Otherwise, by the pigeon hole principle, at least two conflict edges end up in the same thread. Therefore, the algorithm can soundly enumerate only sequences of cf_τ edges of length less than or equal to $|\mathbb{T}|$. Moreover, the choice of cf_τ determines the rest of the edges in the cycle. Therefore, there are at most $O(|\mathsf{cf}_\tau|^{|\mathbb{T}|})$ chordless cycles with at least one cf_τ edge of a graph G_τ^D.

Note that, in general, the number of simple cycles can be exponential in the number of edges. This means that enumerating only chordless cycles reduces the size asymptotically. In other words, our proposed sound optimization of Sect. 5.3 is at the roof of the polynomial complexity results presented here.

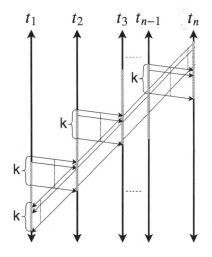

Fig. 4. G_τ^M with $|\mathsf{cf}_\tau|^{|\mathbb{T}|}$ chordless cycles. (Color figure online)

Interestingly, this upper bound is not loose. There is a class of traces parametrized by $|\mathbb{T}|$ such that the number of chordless cycles with at least one cf_τ edge is $|\mathsf{cf}_\tau|^{|\mathbb{T}|}$. Let $\mathbb{T} = \{t_1, \ldots, t_n\}$ be the set of threads and G_τ^M has k parallel conflict edges between t_i and $t_{(i \bmod n)+1}$ for all $i \in [1, n]$. Moreover, conflict edges that start from t_i is above the conflict edges that end at t_i in terms of program order. This graph is depicted in Fig. 4. To form a cycle, one needs to pick one of k edges between t_i and $t_{(i \bmod n)+1}$ for all $i \in [1, n]$. So, there are k^n cycles. Since $k = \frac{|\mathsf{cf}_\tau|}{|\mathbb{T}|}$, there are $\left(\frac{|\mathsf{cf}_\tau|}{|\mathbb{T}|}\right)^{|\mathbb{T}|}$ chordless cycles with a conflict edge. If we consider $|\mathbb{T}|$ as a constant, there are $\Omega(|\mathsf{cf}_\tau|^{|\mathbb{T}|})$ chordless cycles with at least one cf_τ edge. We are finally ready to state the main complexity result:

Theorem 5. *Above enumeration algorithm generates all chordless cycles with at least one cf_τ edge of G_τ^D in $O((|\mathsf{po}_\tau| + |\mathsf{cf}_\tau|)|\mathsf{cf}_\tau|^{|\mathbb{T}|})$ time.*

Proof. The loop enumerates all the cf_τ sequences of length at most $|\mathbb{T}|$ in $O(|\mathsf{cf}_\tau|^{|\mathbb{T}|})$ time. For each such sequence, it takes $O(|\mathsf{po}_\tau| + |\mathsf{cf}_\tau|)$ time to check whether this sequence forms a cycle (if each consecutive conflict edges are connected through a $E_\tau^M \backslash \mathsf{cf}_\tau$ edge) and whether it visits a thread more than once. As a consequence, the above bound holds. $\square$

Lastly, there may be as many optimal repairs as there are chordless cycles in G_τ^M. Consider the class of traces depicted in Fig. 4. Each chordless cycle with at least one cf_τ edge has exactly n critical segments (illustrated in red). Consider two distinct chordless cycles α_1 and α_2. There exists a thread t_i such that there is a different edge between t_i and $t_{(i \bmod n)+1}$ in α_1 compared to α_2. Without loss of generality, assume that the corresponding edge of α_1 has source and destination events that appear before the source and destination events of the corresponding edge of α_2 in program order (po_τ). Then, α_1 has a larger critical segment on t_i and smaller critical segment in $t_{(i \bmod n)+1}$ compared to α_2. Therefore, the neither critical segment subsumes the other. Therefore, each chordless cycle with at least one cf_τ edge produces an optimal repair.

This implies that the bound presented in Theorem 5, namely $O((|\mathsf{po}_\tau| + |\mathsf{cf}_\tau|)|\mathsf{cf}_\tau|^{|\mathbb{T}|})$, applies any other algorithm that outputs all optimal repairs.

6.2   Ranking Optimal Repairs

We argued through the example in Sect. 2 and a formal statement in Sect. 4.1 that not every eliminator of a buggy trace τ is an optimal root cause for non-linearizability. All that we know is that they are all optimal trace eliminators. As a heuristic to identify optimal linearizability repairs out of a set of trace eliminators, we rely on another input in the form of a set Γ of linearizable executions, and rank trace eliminators depending on how many linearizable traces from Γ they disable, giving preference to trace eliminators that disable fewer ones. This heuristic relies on an experimental hypothesis that there are harmless cyclic dependencies that occur in linearizable executions.

Given a buggy trace τ, and a set Γ of linearizable traces, we use the following algorithm to rank trace eliminators for τ:

- Let $\mathbb{R}$ be the set of optimal trace eliminators for τ
- For each $\mathcal{R} \in \mathbb{R}$:
  - Let $f(\mathcal{R}) = |\{\tau' \in \Gamma : \mathcal{R}$ is a trace eliminator for $\tau'\}|$
- Sort $\mathbb{R}$ in ascending order depending on $f(\mathcal{R})$ with $\mathcal{R} \in \mathbb{R}$.

Since the above algorithm is heuristic in nature, there are no theoretical guarantees for the optimality of its results. For instance, its effectiveness depends on the set of linearizable traces Γ given as input. We discuss the empirical aspects of the underlying hypothesis in more detail in Sect. 7.

7   Experimental Evaluation

We demonstrate the efficacy of our approach for computing linearizability root-causes on several variations of lock-based concurrent sets/maps from the Synchrobench repository [21]. We consider three libraries from this repository: two linked-list set implementations, with coarse-grain and fine-grain locking, respectively, and a map implementation based on an AVL tree overlapping with two singly-linked lists, and fine-grain locking. We define three non-linearizable variations for each library by shrinking one atomic section only in the `add` method, only in the `remove` method, or an atomic section in each of these two methods. For each non-linearizable variation, we use Violat [14] to randomly sample three library clients that admit non-linearizable traces[8]. We use Java Pathfinder [44] to extract all traces of each client, up to partial-order reduction, partitioning them into linearizable and non-linearizable traces. Traces are extracted as sequences of call/return events and read/write accesses to explicit memory addresses, associated to line numbers in the source code of each of the API methods. The latter is important for being able to map critical segments (which refer to events in a trace) to atomic code blocks in the source code.

In Table 1, we list some quantitative data about our benchmarks, the clients, and the non-linearizable variations identified by the line numbers of the modified atomic sections (the original libraries can be found in the Synchrobench repository). For instance, the first variation of RWLockCoarseGrainedListIntSet is obtained by shrinking the atomic section in the `add` method between lines [26, 32/35] to [32, 32/35] (there are two line numbers for the end of the atomic section because it ends with an `if` conditional).

For each non-linearizable trace τ of a client C, we compute the set of optimal trace eliminators for τ using the algorithm in Sect. 5.3 with the cycle enumeration described in Sect. 6.1. We then compute the ranking of these trace eliminators using as input the set of linearizable traces of C (the restriction to linearizable traces of the same client is only for convenience). Note that multiple trace eliminators can be ranked first since they disable exactly the same number of linearizable traces. Also, note that an optimal root-cause can disable a number

---

[8] These linearizability violations are quite rare. The frequencies reported by Violat in the context of a fixed client (when using standard testing) are in the order of $1/1000$.

Table 1. Benchmark data. Column **Lib.** shows the transformation on the atomic section(s) of the original library (we write atomic sections as pairs of line numbers in square brackets), **Client** shows the clients (we abbreviate the names of add, remove, and contains to a, r, and c, resp.), **Non-lin. Out.** shows an outcome (set of return values) witnessing for non-linearizability (true, false, and null are abbreviated to T, F, and N, resp.), **# bugs** and **#valid** give the number of non-linearizable and linearizable traces extracted using Java Pathfinder, respectively, **# ev.** and **# conf.** give the average number of events and conflict edges in these traces, **Total(s)** and **Tr. Elim(s)** give the clock time in seconds for applying our approach, the latter excluding the Java Pathfinder time for extracting traces.

RWLockCoarseGrainedListIntSet (119 LOC)

Id	Lib.	Client	Non-Lin Out.	# bugs	# valid	# ev.	# conf.	Total(s)	Tr. Elim.(s)
1	a: [26, 32/35] →[32, 32/35]	{c(1); r(1); a(1)} || {a(1)}	F, F, T, T	9	36	48	5	13	5
2		{a(0); a(1)} || {a(0)}	T, T, T	18	18	45	6	11	4
3		{a(0); a(0)} || {a(1)}	T, T, T	9	27	43	8	11	4
4	r: [47, 54/56] →[53, 54/56]	{a(0); a(0); r(0)} || {r(0)}	T, F, T, T	9	27	48	10	12	4
5		{a(0); a(0)} || {a(1); r(1)}	T, T, T, T	9	18	54	14	12	3
6		{r(0)} || {a(0); r(0)}	T, T, T	9	18	39	9	11	3
7	a: [26, 32/35] →[32, 32/35]	{a(0); r(0)} || {r(0); a(1)}	T, T, T, T / T, F, F, T	27	27	51	12	23	8
8	r: [47, 54/56]	{a(1); r(1)} || {a(0)}	T, F, T	9	27	41	6	11	4
9	→[53, 54/56]	{c(0); a(1); r(1); c(0)} || {r(1)}	F, T, T, F, T	9	18	57	11	12	3

OptimisticListSortedSetWaitFreeContains (193 LOC)

Id	Lib.	Client	Non-lin. Out.	# bugs	# valid	# ev.	# conf.	Total(s)	Tr. Elim.(s)
1	a: [51, 52/56] →[52, 52/56]	{a(0); a(0)} || {a(1)}	T, T, T	6	39	64	16	23	31
2		{a(0); a(1)} || {a(0)}	T, T, T	18	27	70	13	17	8
3		{a(0)} || {c(1); a(0)}	T, F, T	6	18	46	6	7	3
4	r: [78, 80/82] →[79, 80/82]	{c(0); a(1); r(1); c(0)} || {r(1)}	F, T, T, F, T	6	18	64	17	10	3
5		{a(0); r(0)} || {r(0); a(1)}	T, T, T, T	12	30	70	25	22	5
6		{a(0); a(0)} || {a(1); r(1)}	T, T, T, T	6	42	83	28	38	16
7	a: [51, 52/56]	{a(0); a(0); r(0)} || {r(0)}	T, F, T, T	6	27	65	17	18	6
8	→[52, 52/56]	{a(0)} || {a(0); r(1)}	T, T, F	9	18	58	9	12	5
9	r: [78, 80/82] →[79, 80/82]	{c(1); r(1); a(1)} || {a(1)}	F, F, T, T	6	36	59	8	11	5

LogicalOrderingAVL (1092 LOC)

Id	Lib	Client	Non-lin. Out.	# bugs	# valids	# ev.	# conf.	Total(s)	Tr. Elim.(s)
1	a: [267, 293] →[268, 269][271, 293]	{a(1,0)} || {a(1,1); r(1,1)}	1, N, T	6	51	99	11	131	24
2		{r(1,1); r(0,1)} || {a(1,1); a(1,0)}	T, F, N, 1	6	30	126	42	115	24
3		{r(0,0); r(1,0)} || {a(0,0); a(0,1)}	T, F, N, 0	6	30	126	42	100	22
4	r: [432, 454] →[433, 434][436, 445]	{a(1,0); a(0,0); r(0,0)} || {r(1,0)}	N, N, F, T	9	75	152	40	593	37
5		{a(1,0); r(1,0)} || {r(1,0)}	N, T, T	9	36	122	31	77	8
6		{a(0,1); r(0,1); r(0,0)} || {r(0,1)}	N, T, F, T	9	36	138	33	92	10
7	a: [267, 293] →[268, 269][271, 293]	{a(0,1); r(0,1)} || {a(0,0)}	N, T, 1	6	51	102	11	119	16
8		{r(1,0)} || {a(1,0); a(1,1); a(1,0)}	T, N, 0, N	9	39	137	41	53	19
9	r: [432, 454] →[433, 434][436, 445]	{r(1,0); a(0,1)} || {a(0,0); r(0,0)}	F, 0, N, T	6	51	117	17	171	26

of linearizable traces. This is true even for the ground truth repair (i.e. a repair that a human would identify trough manual inspection).

The results are presented in Table 2 and are self-explanatory. In the majority of cases, the first elements in this ranking are atomic sections which are precisely or very close to the expected results, i.e., atomic sections that belong to the original (error-free) version of the corresponding library. In some cases, the output of our approach is close, but not precisely the expected one. This is only due to the particular choice of the client used to generate the traces. In general, the quality of the produced repairs (compared to the ground truth) depends the types of behaviours of the library that the client exercises. However, if our tool

Table 2. Experimental data. Column **#res** gives the number of different results (sequences of trace eliminators) returned by our algorithm when applied on each of the non-linearizable traces of a client, and **Tr. Elim.** gives the first or the first two trace eliminators in the ranking obtained with our approach. For each trace eliminator we give the number of linearizable traces it disables (after →).

RWLockCoarseGrainedListIntSet

Id	Lib.	# res.	Tr. Elim.
1	a: [26, 32/35] →[32, 32/35]	1	[[27, 35]] → 0
2		1	[[27, 35]] → 0
3		1	[[27, 35]] → 18
4	r: [47, 54/56] →[53, 54/56]	1	[[48, 54]] → 0
5		1	[[48, 54]] → 9
6		1	[[48, 54]] → 9
7	a: [26, 32/35] →[32, 32/35]	2	[[48, 54]] → 0 ; [[27, 35]] → 0
8	r: [47, 54/56] →[53, 54/56]	1	[[27, 35]] → 9
9		1	[[48, 54]] → 0

OptimisticListSortedSetWaitFreeContains

Id	Lib.	# res.	Tr. Elim.
1	a: [51, 52/56] →[52, 52/56]	2	[[55, 56]] → 0 ; [[43, 44], [55, 56]] → 0
2		2	[[43, 51]] → 0 ; [[51, 56]] → 15
3		1	[[55, 56]] → 0
4		1	[[51, 56]] → 12
5	r: [78, 80/82] →[79, 80/82]	1	[[78, 80]] → 0
6		2	[[78, 80]] → 0 ; [[78, 80]] → 6
7	a: [51, 52/56] →[52, 52/56] r: [78, 80/82] →[79, 80/82]	1	[[43, 44], [55, 56]] → 0 ; [[78, 80]] → 6
8		2	[[78, 80]] → 0 ; [[51, 56]] → 12
9		1	[[55, 56]] → 0 ; [[51, 56]] → 27

LogicalOrderingAVL

Id	Lib.	#res	Tr. Elim.
1	a: [267, 293] →[268, 269][271, 293]	1	[[271, 279], [448, 451]] → 0 ; [[265, 271]] → 27
2		2	[[271, 279], [448, 451]] → 0 ; [[430, 436]] → 9 ; [[289, 290]] → 0 ; [[290, 293], [423, 430]] → 0
3		2	[[271, 279], [448, 451]] → 0 ; [[430, 436]] → 9 ; [[289, 290]] → 0 ; [[290, 293], [423, 430]] → 0
4		1	[[436, 445]] → 6 ; [[451, 454], [423 ,436]] → 15
5	r: [432, 454] →[433, 434][436, 445]	1	[[436, 451]] → 0
6		2	[[436, 450]] → 0 ; [[436, 450]] → 0 ; [[430, 436]] → 0
7	a: [267, 293] →[268, 269][271, 293] r: [432, 454] →[433, 434][436, 445]	1	[[271, 279], [448, 451]] → 0
8		1	[[271, 279], [448, 451]] → 0 ; [[430, 436]] → 30
9		1	[[271, 279], [448, 451]] → 0 ; [[265, 271]] → 27

ranks repair $\mathcal{R}$ first, in the context of a client C, then after repairing the library according to $\mathcal{R}$ the client C produces no linearizability violations.

The methods in the libraries OptimisticListSortedSetWaitFreeContains and LogicalOrderingAVL use optimistic concurrency, i.e., unbounded loops that restart when certain interferences are detected. This could potentially guide our heuristic in the wrong direction of giving the ground truth a lower rank. Indeed, a ground truth that concerns statements in the loop body could disable a large number of executions which only differ in the number of loop iterations. This, however, does not happen for small-size clients (like the ones used in our evaluation) since the number of invocations are bounded, which bounds the number of interferences and therefore the number of restarts.

Optimistic concurrency has the potential to mess with the heuristic, but this does not happen in small bounded clients as witnessed by our blah benchmark that does just fine.

To conclude, our empirical study demonstrates that given a good client (one that exercises the problems in the library properly), our approach is very effective in identifying the method at fault and the part of its code that is the root cause of the linearizability violation.

8   Related Work

Linearizability Violations. There is a large body of work on automatic detection of specific bugs such as data races, atomicity violations, e.g. [18,40,41,45]. The focus of this paper is on linearizability errors. Wing and Gong [47] proposed an exponential-time monitoring algorithm for linearizability, which was later optimized by Lowe [33] and by Horn and Kroening [25]; neither avoided exponential-time asymptotic complexity. Burckhardt et al. [4] and Burnim et al. [5] implement exponential-time monitoring algorithms in their tools for testing of concurrent objects in .NET and Java. Emmi and Enea [14,15] introduce the tool Violat (used in our experiments) for checking linearizability of Java objects.

Concurrency Errors. There have been various techniques for fault localization, error explanation, counterexample minimization and bug summarization for sequential programs. We restrict our attention to relevant works for concurrent programs. More relevant to our work are those that try to extract simple explanations (i.e. root causes) from concurrent error traces. In [30], the authors focus on shortening counterexamples in message-passing programs to a set of "crucial events" that are both necessary and sufficient to reach the bug. In [27], the authors introduce a heuristic to simplify concurrent error traces by reducing the number of context-switches. Tools that attempt to minimize the number of context switches, such as SimTrace [26] and Tinertia [27], are orthogonal to the approach presented in this paper. To gain efficiency and robustness, some works rely on simple patterns of bugs for detection and a simple family of matching fixes to remove them, e.g., [10,28,29,38]. Our work is set apart from these works by addressing linearizability (in contrast to simple atomicity violation patterns) as the correctness property of choice, and by being more systematic in the sense that it enumerates all trace eliminators for a given linearizability violation. We also present crisp results for the theoretical guarantees behind our approach and an analysis of the time complexity. Weeratunge et al. [46] use a set of good executions to derive an atomicity "specification", i.e., pairs of accesses that are atomic, and then enforce it using locks.

There is large body of work on synchronization synthesis [2,6–8,11,22,34,42, 43]. The approaches in [11,42] are based on inferring synchronization by constructing and exploring the entire product graph or tableaux corresponding to a concurrent program. A different group of approaches infer synchronization incrementally from traces [43] or generalizations of bad traces [7,8]. These techniques [7,8,43] also infer atomic sections but they do not focus on linearizability as the underlying correctness property but rather on assertion local violations. Several works investigate the problem of deriving an optimal lock placement given as input a program annotated with atomic sections, e.g., [9,17,48]. Afix [28] and ConcurrencySwapper [7] automatically fix concurrency-related errors. The latter uses error invariants to generalize a linear error trace to a partially ordered trace, which is then used to synthesize a fix.

Linearizability Repairs. Flint [32] is the only approach we know of that focuses on repairing non-linearizable libraries, but it has a very specific focus, namely fixing linearizability of composed map operations. It uses a different approach based on enumeration-based synthesis and it does not rely on concrete linearizability bugs.

References

1. Afek, Y., Gafni, E., Morrison, A.: Common2 extended to stacks and unbounded concurrency. Distrib. Comput. **20**(4), 239–252 (2007). https://doi.org/10.1007/s00446-007-0023-3
2. Bloem, R., Hofferek, G., Könighofer, B., Könighofer, R., Ausserlechner, S., Spork, R.: Synthesis of synchronization using uninterpreted functions. In: Formal Methods in Computer-Aided Design, FMCAD 2014, Lausanne, Switzerland, 21–24 October 2014, pp. 35–42. IEEE (2014). https://doi.org/10.1109/FMCAD.2014.6987593
3. Bouajjani, A., Emmi, M., Enea, C., Hamza, J.: Tractable refinement checking for concurrent objects. In: Rajamani, S.K., Walker, D. (eds.) Proceedings of the 42nd Annual ACM SIGPLAN-SIGACT Symposium on Principles of Programming Languages, POPL 2015, Mumbai, India, 15–17 January 2015, pp. 651–662. ACM (2015). https://doi.org/10.1145/2676726.2677002
4. Burckhardt, S., Dern, C., Musuvathi, M., Tan, R.: Line-up: a complete and automatic linearizability checker. In: Zorn, B.G., Aiken, A. (eds.) Proceedings of the 2010 ACM SIGPLAN Conference on Programming Language Design and Implementation, PLDI 2010, Toronto, Ontario, Canada, 5–10 June 2010, pp. 330–340. ACM (2010). https://doi.org/10.1145/1806596.1806634
5. Burnim, J., Necula, G.C., Sen, K.: Specifying and checking semantic atomicity for multithreaded programs. In: Gupta, R., Mowry, T.C. (eds.) Proceedings of the 16th International Conference on Architectural Support for Programming Languages and Operating Systems, ASPLOS 2011, Newport Beach, CA, USA, 5–11 March 2011, pp. 79–90. ACM (2011). https://doi.org/10.1145/1950365.1950377
6. Černý, P., et al.: From non-preemptive to preemptive scheduling using synchronization synthesis. In: Kroening, D., Păsăreanu, C.S. (eds.) CAV 2015. LNCS, vol. 9207, pp. 180–197. Springer, Cham (2015). https://doi.org/10.1007/978-3-319-21668-3_11
7. Černý, P., Henzinger, T.A., Radhakrishna, A., Ryzhyk, L., Tarrach, T.: Efficient synthesis for concurrency by semantics-preserving transformations. In: Sharygina, N., Veith, H. (eds.) CAV 2013. LNCS, vol. 8044, pp. 951–967. Springer, Heidelberg (2013). https://doi.org/10.1007/978-3-642-39799-8_68
8. Černý, P., Henzinger, T.A., Radhakrishna, A., Ryzhyk, L., Tarrach, T.: Regression-free synthesis for concurrency. In: Biere, A., Bloem, R. (eds.) CAV 2014. LNCS, vol. 8559, pp. 568–584. Springer, Cham (2014). https://doi.org/10.1007/978-3-319-08867-9_38
9. Cherem, S., Chilimbi, T.M., Gulwani, S.: Inferring locks for atomic sections. In: Gupta, R., Amarasinghe, S.P. (eds.) Proceedings of the ACM SIGPLAN 2008 Conference on Programming Language Design and Implementation, Tucson, AZ, USA, 7–13 June 2008, pp. 304–315. ACM (2008). https://doi.org/10.1145/1375581.1375619

10. Chew, L., Lie, D.: Kivati: fast detection and prevention of atomicity violations. In: Morin, C., Muller, G. (eds.) European Conference on Computer Systems, Proceedings of the 5th European Conference on Computer Systems, EuroSys 2010, Paris, France, 13–16 April 2010, pp. 307–320. ACM (2010). https://doi.org/10.1145/1755913.1755945

11. Clarke, E.M., Emerson, E.A.: Design and synthesis of synchronization skeletons using branching time temporal logic. In: Grumberg, O., Veith, H. (eds.) 25 Years of Model Checking. LNCS, vol. 5000, pp. 196–215. Springer, Heidelberg (2008). https://doi.org/10.1007/978-3-540-69850-0_12

12. Emmi, M., Enea, C.: Exposing non-atomic methods of concurrent objects. CoRR abs/1706.09305 (2017). http://arxiv.org/abs/1706.09305

13. Emmi, M., Enea, C.: Sound, complete, and tractable linearizability monitoring for concurrent collections. PACMPL 2(POPL), 25:1–25:27 (2018). https://doi.org/10.1145/3158113

14. Emmi, M., Enea, C.: Violat: generating tests of observational refinement for concurrent objects. In: Dillig, I., Tasiran, S. (eds.) CAV 2019. LNCS, vol. 11562, pp. 534–546. Springer, Cham (2019). https://doi.org/10.1007/978-3-030-25543-5_30

15. Emmi, M., Enea, C.: Weak-consistency specification via visibility relaxation. PACMPL 3(POPL), 60:1–60:28 (2019). https://doi.org/10.1145/3290373

16. Emmi, M., Enea, C., Hamza, J.: Monitoring refinement via symbolic reasoning. In: Grove, D., Blackburn, S. (eds.) Proceedings of the 36th ACM SIGPLAN Conference on Programming Language Design and Implementation, Portland, OR, USA, 15–17 June 2015, pp. 260–269. ACM (2015). https://doi.org/10.1145/2737924.2737983

17. Emmi, M., Fischer, J.S., Jhala, R., Majumdar, R.: Lock allocation. In: Hofmann, M., Felleisen, M. (eds.) Proceedings of the 34th ACM SIGPLAN-SIGACT Symposium on Principles of Programming Languages, POPL 2007, Nice, France, 17–19 January 2007, pp. 291–296. ACM (2007). https://doi.org/10.1145/1190216.1190260

18. Engler, D.R., Ashcraft, K.: Racerx: effective, static detection of race conditions and deadlocks. In: Scott, M.L., Peterson, L.L. (eds.) Proceedings of the 19th ACM Symposium on Operating Systems Principles 2003, SOSP 2003, Bolton Landing, NY, USA, 19–22 October 2003, pp. 237–252. ACM (2003). https://doi.org/10.1145/945445.945468

19. Farzan, A., Madhusudan, P.: Monitoring atomicity in concurrent programs. In: Gupta, A., Malik, S. (eds.) CAV 2008. LNCS, vol. 5123, pp. 52–65. Springer, Heidelberg (2008). https://doi.org/10.1007/978-3-540-70545-1_8

20. Gibbons, P.B., Korach, E.: Testing shared memories. SIAM J. Comput. 26(4), 1208–1244 (1997). https://doi.org/10.1137/S0097539794279614

21. Gramoli, V.: More than you ever wanted to know about synchronization: synchrobench, measuring the impact of the synchronization on concurrent algorithms. In: Cohen, A., Grove, D. (eds.) Proceedings of the 20th ACM SIGPLAN Symposium on Principles and Practice of Parallel Programming, PPoPP 2015, San Francisco, CA, USA, 7–11 February 2015, pp. 1–10. ACM (2015). https://doi.org/10.1145/2688500.2688501

22. Gupta, A., Henzinger, T.A., Radhakrishna, A., Samanta, R., Tarrach, T.: Succinct representation of concurrent trace sets. In: Rajamani, S.K., Walker, D. (eds.) Proceedings of the 42nd Annual ACM SIGPLAN-SIGACT Symposium on Principles of Programming Languages, POPL 2015, Mumbai, India, 15–17 January 2015, pp. 433–444. ACM (2015). https://doi.org/10.1145/2676726.2677008

23. Herlihy, M., Shavit, N.: The Art of Multiprocessor Programming. Morgan Kaufmann, Burlington (2008)
24. Herlihy, M., Wing, J.M.: Linearizability: a correctness condition for concurrent objects. ACM Trans. Program. Lang. Syst. **12**(3), 463–492 (1990). https://doi.org/10.1145/78969.78972
25. Horn, A., Kroening, D.: Faster linearizability checking via P-compositionality. In: Graf, S., Viswanathan, M. (eds.) FORTE 2015. LNCS, vol. 9039, pp. 50–65. Springer, Cham (2015). https://doi.org/10.1007/978-3-319-19195-9_4
26. Huang, J., Zhang, C.: An efficient static trace simplification technique for debugging concurrent programs. In: Yahav, E. (ed.) SAS 2011. LNCS, vol. 6887, pp. 163–179. Springer, Heidelberg (2011). https://doi.org/10.1007/978-3-642-23702-7_15
27. Jalbert, N., Sen, K.: A trace simplification technique for effective debugging of concurrent programs. In: Roman, G., van der Hoek, A. (eds.) Proceedings of the 18th ACM SIGSOFT International Symposium on Foundations of Software Engineering, 2010, Santa Fe, NM, USA, 7–11 November 2010, pp. 57–66. ACM (2010). https://doi.org/10.1145/1882291.1882302
28. Jin, G., Song, L., Zhang, W., Lu, S., Liblit, B.: Automated atomicity-violation fixing. In: Hall, M.W., Padua, D.A. (eds.) Proceedings of the 32nd ACM SIGPLAN Conference on Programming Language Design and Implementation, PLDI 2011, San Jose, CA, USA, 4–8 June 2011, pp. 389–400. ACM (2011). https://doi.org/10.1145/1993498.1993544
29. Jin, G., Zhang, W., Deng, D.: Automated concurrency-bug fixing. In: Thekkath, C., Vahdat, A. (eds.) 10th USENIX Symposium on Operating Systems Design and Implementation, OSDI 2012, Hollywood, CA, USA, 8–10 October 2012, pp. 221–236. USENIX Association (2012). https://www.usenix.org/conference/osdi12/technical-sessions/presentation/jin
30. Kashyap, S., Garg, V.K.: Producing short counterexamples using "crucial events". In: Gupta, A., Malik, S. (eds.) CAV 2008. LNCS, vol. 5123, pp. 491–503. Springer, Heidelberg (2008). https://doi.org/10.1007/978-3-540-70545-1_47
31. Liskov, B., Zilles, S.N.: Programming with abstract data types. SIGPLAN Not. **9**(4), 50–59 (1974)
32. Liu, P., Tripp, O., Zhang, X.: Flint: fixing linearizability violations. In: Black, A.P., Millstein, T.D. (eds.) Proceedings of the 2014 ACM International Conference on Object Oriented Programming Systems Languages & Applications, OOPSLA 2014, part of SPLASH 2014, Portland, OR, USA, 20–24 October 2014, pp. 543–560. ACM (2014). https://doi.org/10.1145/2660193.2660217
33. Lowe, G.: Testing for linearizability. Concurr. Comput.: Pract. Exper. **29**(4) (2017). https://doi.org/10.1002/cpe.3928
34. Manna, Z., Wolper, P.: Synthesis of communicating processes from temporal logic specifications. ACM Trans. Program. Lang. Syst. **6**(1), 68–93 (1984). https://doi.org/10.1145/357233.357237
35. Michael, M.M.: ABA prevention using single-word instructions. Technical report RC 23089, IBM Thomas J. Watson Research Center, January 2004
36. Moir, M., Shavit, N.: Concurrent data structures. In: Mehta, D.P., Sahni, S. (eds.) Handbook of Data Structures and Applications. Chapman and Hall/CRC (2004). https://doi.org/10.1201/9781420035179.ch47
37. Papadimitriou, C.H.: The serializability of concurrent database updates. J. ACM **26**(4), 631–653 (1979). https://doi.org/10.1145/322154.322158

38. Park, S., Lu, S., Zhou, Y.: Ctrigger: exposing atomicity violation bugs from their hiding places. In: Soffa, M.L., Irwin, M.J. (eds.) Proceedings of the 14th International Conference on Architectural Support for Programming Languages and Operating Systems, ASPLOS 2009, Washington, DC, USA, 7–11 March 2009, pp. 25–36. ACM (2009). https://doi.org/10.1145/1508244.1508249

39. Pradel, M., Gross, T.R.: Automatic testing of sequential and concurrent substitutability. In: Notkin, D., Cheng, B.H.C., Pohl, K. (eds.) 35th International Conference on Software Engineering, ICSE 2013, San Francisco, CA, USA, 18–26 May 2013, pp. 282–291. IEEE Computer Society (2013). https://doi.org/10.1109/ICSE.2013.6606574

40. Said, M., Wang, C., Yang, Z., Sakallah, K.: Generating data race witnesses by an SMT-based analysis. In: Bobaru, M., Havelund, K., Holzmann, G.J., Joshi, R. (eds.) NFM 2011. LNCS, vol. 6617, pp. 313–327. Springer, Heidelberg (2011). https://doi.org/10.1007/978-3-642-20398-5_23

41. Savage, S., Burrows, M., Nelson, G., Sobalvarro, P., Anderson, T.E.: Eraser: a dynamic data race detector for multithreaded programs. ACM Trans. Comput. Syst. **15**(4), 391–411 (1997). https://doi.org/10.1145/265924.265927

42. Vechev, M., Yahav, E., Yorsh, G.: Inferring synchronization under limited observability. In: Kowalewski, S., Philippou, A. (eds.) TACAS 2009. LNCS, vol. 5505, pp. 139–154. Springer, Heidelberg (2009). https://doi.org/10.1007/978-3-642-00768-2_13

43. Vechev, M.T., Yahav, E., Yorsh, G.: Abstraction-guided synthesis of synchronization. In: Hermenegildo, M.V., Palsberg, J. (eds.) Proceedings of the 37th ACM SIGPLAN-SIGACT Symposium on Principles of Programming Languages, POPL 2010, Madrid, Spain, 17–23 January 2010, pp. 327–338. ACM (2010). https://doi.org/10.1145/1706299.1706338

44. Visser, W., Pasareanu, C.S., Khurshid, S.: Test input generation with java pathfinder. In: Avrunin, G.S., Rothermel, G. (eds.) Proceedings of the ACM/SIGSOFT International Symposium on Software Testing and Analysis, ISSTA 2004, Boston, Massachusetts, USA, 11–14 July 2004, pp. 97–107. ACM (2004). https://doi.org/10.1145/1007512.1007526

45. Wang, C., Limaye, R., Ganai, M., Gupta, A.: Trace-based symbolic analysis for atomicity violations. In: Esparza, J., Majumdar, R. (eds.) TACAS 2010. LNCS, vol. 6015, pp. 328–342. Springer, Heidelberg (2010). https://doi.org/10.1007/978-3-642-12002-2_27

46. Weeratunge, D., Zhang, X., Jagannathan, S.: Accentuating the positive: atomicity inference and enforcement using correct executions. In: Lopes, C.V., Fisher, K. (eds.) Proceedings of the 26th Annual ACM SIGPLAN Conference on Object-Oriented Programming, Systems, Languages, and Applications, OOPSLA 2011, part of SPLASH 2011, Portland, OR, USA, 22–27 October 2011, pp. 19–34. ACM (2011). https://doi.org/10.1145/2048066.2048071

47. Wing, J.M., Gong, C.: Testing and verifying concurrent objects. J. Parallel Distrib. Comput. **17**(1–2), 164–182 (1993). https://doi.org/10.1006/jpdc.1993.1015

48. Zhang, Y., Sreedhar, V.C., Zhu, W., Sarkar, V., Gao, G.R.: Minimum lock assignment: a method for exploiting concurrency among critical sections. In: Amaral, J.N. (ed.) LCPC 2008. LNCS, vol. 5335, pp. 141–155. Springer, Heidelberg (2008). https://doi.org/10.1007/978-3-540-89740-8_10

Symbolic Partial-Order Execution
for Testing Multi-Threaded Programs

Daniel Schemmel[1]([✉])[iD], Julian Büning[1][iD], César Rodríguez[2,3],
David Laprell[1][iD], and Klaus Wehrle[1][iD]

[1] RWTH Aachen University, Aachen, Germany
{daniel.schemmel,julian.buening,david.laprell,
wehrle}@comsys.rwth-aachen.de
[2] Diffblue Ltd., Oxford, UK
[3] Université Paris 13, Sorbonne Paris Cité, CNRS,
Paris, France
cesar.rodriguez@lipn.fr

Abstract. We describe a technique for systematic testing of multi-threaded programs. We combine Quasi-Optimal Partial-Order Reduction, a state-of-the-art technique that tackles path explosion due to interleaving non-determinism, with symbolic execution to handle data non-determinism. Our technique iteratively and exhaustively finds all executions of the program. It represents program executions using partial orders and finds the next execution using an underlying unfolding semantics. We avoid the exploration of redundant program traces using cutoff events. We implemented our technique as an extension of KLEE and evaluated it on a set of large multi-threaded C programs. Our experiments found several previously undiscovered bugs and undefined behaviors in memcached and GNU sort, showing that the new method is capable of finding bugs in industrial-size benchmarks.

Keywords: Software testing · Symbolic Execution · Partial-Order Reduction

1 Introduction

Advances in formal testing and the increased availability of affordable concurrency have spawned two opposing trends: While it has become possible to analyze increasingly complex sequential programs in new and powerful ways, many projects are now embracing parallel processing to fully exploit modern hardware, thus raising the bar for practically useful formal testing. In order to make formal testing accessible to software developers working on parallel programs, two main problems need to be solved. Firstly, a significant portion of the API in concurrency libraries such as `libpthread` must be supported. Secondly, the analysis must be accessible to non-experts in formal verification. Currently, this niche is mostly occupied by manual and fuzz testing, oftentimes combined with dynamic concurrency checkers such as ThreadSanitizer [45] or Helgrind [2].

© The Author(s) 2020
S. K. Lahiri and C. Wang (Eds.): CAV 2020, LNCS 12224, pp. 376–400, 2020.
https://doi.org/10.1007/978-3-030-53288-8_18

Data non-determinism in sequential and concurrent programs, and scheduling non-determinism are two major sources of path explosion in program analysis. *Symbolic execution* [10,11,22,29,38] is a technique to reason about input data in sequential programs. It is capable of dealing with real-world programs. Partial-Order Reductions (PORs) [5,19,20,41] are a large family of techniques to explore a reduced number of thread interleavings without missing any relevant behavior.

In this paper we propose a technique that combines symbolic execution and a Quasi-Optimal POR [35]. In essence, our approach (1) runs the program using a symbolic executor, (2) builds a partial order representing the occurrence of POSIX threading synchronization primitives (library functions pthread_*) seen during that execution, (3) adds the partial order to an underlying tree-like, unfolding [32,41] data structure, (4) computes the first events of the next partial orders to explore, and (5) selects a new partial order to explore and starts again. We use cutoff events [32] to prune the exploration of different traces that reach the same state, thus natively dealing with non-terminating executions.

We implemented our technique as an extension of KLEE. During the evaluation of this prototype we found nine bugs (that we attribute to four root causes) in the production version of memcached. All of these bugs have since been confirmed by the memcached maintainers and are fixed as of version 1.5.21. Our tool handles a significant portion of the POSIX threading API [4], including barriers, mutexes and condition variables without being significantly harder to use than common fuzz testing tools.

The main challenge that our approach needs to address is that of scalability in the face of an enormous state space. We tackle this challenge by detecting whenever any two Mazurkiewicz traces reach the same program state to only further explore one of them. Additionally, we exploit the fact that data races on non-atomic variables cause undefined behavior in C [25, § 5.1.2.4/35], which means that any unsynchronized memory access is, strictly speaking, a bug. By adding a data race detection algorithm, we can thereby restrict thread scheduling decisions to synchronization primitives, such as operations on mutexes and condition variables, which significantly reduces the state space.

This work has three core contributions, the combination of which enables the analysis of real-world multi-threaded programs (see also Sect. 6 for related work):

1. A partial-order reduction algorithm capable of handling real-world POSIX programs that use an arbitrary amount of threads, mutexes and condition variables. Our algorithm continues analysis in the face of deadlocks.
2. A cutoff algorithm that recognizes whenever two Mazurkiewicz traces reach the same program state, as identified by its actual memory contents. This significantly prunes the search space and even enables the partial-order reduction to deal with non-terminating executions.
3. An implementation that finds real-world bugs.

We also present an extended, more in-depth version of this paper [42].

2 Overview

The technique proposed in this paper can be described as a process of 5 conceptual steps, each of which we describe in a section below:

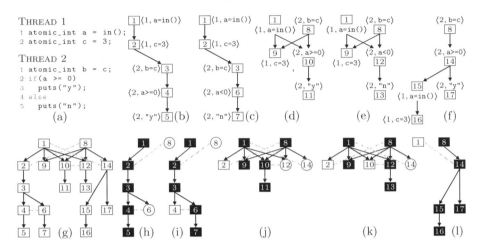

Fig. 1. A program (a) with its 5 partial-order runs (b–f), its unfolding (g) and the 5 steps used by our algorithm to visit the unfolding (h–l).

2.1 Sequential Executions

Consider the program shown in Fig. 1a. Assume that all variables are initially set to zero. The statement a = in() initializes variable a non-deterministically. A *run* of the program is a sequence of *actions*, i.e., pairs $\langle i, s \rangle$ where $i \in \mathbb{N}$ identifies a thread that executes a statement s. For instance, the sequence

$$\sigma_1 := \langle 1, \mathtt{a=in()} \rangle, \langle 1, \mathtt{c=3} \rangle, \langle 2, \mathtt{b=c} \rangle, \langle 2, \mathtt{a<0} \rangle, \langle 2, \mathtt{puts("n")} \rangle$$

is a run of Fig. 1a. This run represents all program paths where both statements of thread 1 run before the statements of thread 2, and where the statement a = in() initializes variable a to a negative number. In our notion of run, concurrency is represented explicitly (via thread identifiers) and data non-determinism is represented symbolically (via constraints on program variables). To keep things simple the example only has atomic integers (implicitly guarded by locks) instead of POSIX synchronization primitives.

2.2 Independence Between Actions and Partial-Order Runs

Many POR techniques use a notion called *independence* [20] to avoid exploring concurrent interleavings that lead to the same state. An independence relation associates pairs of actions that commute (running them in either order results in the same state). For illustration purposes, in Fig. 1 let us consider two actions as *dependent* iff either both of them belong to the same thread or one of them writes into a variable which is read/written by the other. Furthermore, two actions will be *independent* iff they are not dependent.

A sequential run of the program can be viewed as a partial order when we take into account the independence of actions. These partial orders are known as *dependency graphs* in Mazurkiewicz trace theory [31] and as *partial-order runs* in this paper. Figures 1b to 1f show all the partial-order runs of Fig. 1a. The partial-order run associated to the run σ_1 above is Fig. 1c. For

$$\sigma_2 := \langle 2, \mathtt{b=c} \rangle, \langle 2, \mathtt{a>=0} \rangle, \langle 1, \mathtt{a=in()} \rangle, \langle 2, \mathtt{puts("y")} \rangle, \langle 1, \mathtt{c=3} \rangle,$$

we get the partial order shown in Fig. 1f.

2.3   Unfolding: Merging the Partial Orders

An unfolding [16,32,37] is a tree-like structure that uses partial orders to represent concurrent executions and conflict relations to represent thread interference and data non-determinism. We can define unfolding semantics for programs in two conceptual steps: (1) identify isomorphic events that occur in different partial-order runs; (2) bind the partial orders together using a conflict relation.

Two events are *isomorphic* when they are structurally equivalent, i.e., they have the same label (run the same action) and their causal (i.e., happens-before) predecessors are (transitively) isomorphic. The number within every event in Figs. 1b to 1f identifies isomorphic events.

Isomorphic events from different partial orders can be merged together using a conflict relation for the un-merged parts of those partial orders. To understand why conflict is necessary, consider the set of events $C := \{1, 2\}$. It obviously represents part of a partial-order run (Fig. 1c, for instance). Similarly, events $C' := \{1, 8, 9\}$ represent (part of) a run. However, their union $C \cup C'$ does not represent any run, because (1) it does not describe what happens-before relation exists between the dependent actions of events 2 and 8, and (2) it executes the statement c=3 twice. Unfoldings fix this problem by introducing a *conflict* relation between events. Conflicts are to unfoldings what branches are to trees. If we declare that events 2 and 8 are in conflict, then any conflict-free (and causally-closed) subset of $C \cup C'$ is exactly one of the original partial orders. This lets us merge the common parts of multiple partial orders without losing track of the original partial orders.

Figure 1g represents the unfolding of the program (after merging all 5 partial-order runs). Conflicts between events are represented by dashed red lines. Each original partial order can be retrieved by taking a ($\subseteq$-maximal) set of events which is conflict-free (no two events in conflict are in the set) and causally closed (if you take some event, then also take all its causal predecessors).

For instance, the partial order in Fig. 1d can be retrieved by resolving the conflicts between events 1 vs. 14, 2 vs. 8, 10 vs. 12 in favor of, resp., 1, 8, 10.

Resolving in favor of 1 means that events 14 to 17 cannot be selected, because they causally succeed 14. Similarly, resolving in favor of 8 and 10 means that only events 9 and 11 remain eligible, which hold no conflicts among them—all other events are causal successors of either 2 or 12.

2.4   Exploring the Unfolding

Since the unfolding represents all runs of the program via a set of compactly-merged, prefix-sharing partial orders, enumerating all the behaviors of the program reduces to exploring all partial-order runs represented in its unfolding. Our algorithm iteratively enumerates all ⊆-maximal partial-order runs.

In simplified terms, it proceeds as follows. Initially we explore the black events shown in Fig. 1h, therefore exploring the run shown in Fig. 1b. We discover the next partial order by computing the so-called *conflicting extensions* of the current partial order. These are, intuitively, events in conflict with some event in our current partial order but such that all its causal predecessors are in our current partial order. In Fig. 1h these are shown in circles, events 8 and 6.

We now find the next partial order by (1) selecting a conflicting extension, say event 6, (2) removing all events in conflict with the selected extension and their causal successors, in this case events 4 and 5, and (3) expanding the partial order until it becomes maximal, thus exploring the partial order Fig. 1c, shown as the black events of Fig. 1i. Next we select event 8 (removing 2 and its causal successors) and explore the partial order Fig. 1d, shown as the black events of Fig. 1j. Note that this reveals two new conflicting extensions that were hidden until now, events 12 and 14 (hidden because 8 is a causal predecessor of them, but was not in our partial order). Selecting either of the two extensions makes the algorithm explore the last two partial orders.

2.5   Cutoff Events: Pruning the Unfolding

When the program has non-terminating runs, its unfolding will contain infinite partial orders and the algorithm above will not finish. To analyze non-terminating programs we use *cutoff events* [32]. In short, certain events do not need to be explored because they reach the same state as another event that has been already explored using a shorter (partial-order) run. Our algorithm prunes the unfolding at these cutoff events, thus handling terminating and non-terminating programs that repeatedly reach the same state.

3   Main Algorithm

This section formally describes the approach presented in this paper.

3.1 Programs, Actions, and Runs

Let $P := \langle T, \mathcal{L}, \mathcal{C} \rangle$ represent a (possibly non-terminating) multi-threaded POSIX
C program, where T is the set of statements, $\mathcal{L}$ is the set of POSIX mutexes
used in the program, and $\mathcal{C}$ is the set of condition variables. This is a deliberately simplified presentation of our program syntax, see [42] for full details. We
represent the behavior of each statement in P by an *action*, i.e., a pair $\langle i, b \rangle$ in
$A \subseteq \mathbb{N} \times B$, where $i \geq 1$ identifies the thread executing the statement and b is
the *effect* of the statement. We consider the following effects:

$$B := (\{\mathsf{loc}\} \times T) \cup (\{\mathsf{acq}, \mathsf{rel}\} \times \mathcal{L}) \cup (\{\mathsf{sig}\} \times \mathcal{C} \times \mathbb{N})$$
$$\cup (\{\mathsf{bro}\} \times \mathcal{C} \times 2^{\mathbb{N}}) \cup (\{\mathsf{w}_1, \mathsf{w}_2\} \times \mathcal{C} \times \mathcal{L})$$

Below we informally explain the intent of an effect and how actions of different
effects interleave with each other. In [42] we use *actions* and *effects* to define
labeled transition system semantics to P. Below we also (informally) define an
independence relation (see Sect. 2.2) between actions.

Local Actions. An action $\langle i, \langle \mathsf{loc}, t \rangle \rangle$ represents the execution of a *local* statement t from thread i, i.e., a statement which manipulates local variables. For
instance, the actions labeling events 1 and 3 in Fig. 2b are local actions. Note
that local actions do not interfere with actions of other threads. Consequently,
they are only dependent on actions of the same thread.

Mutex Lock/Unlock. Actions $\langle i, \langle \mathsf{acq}, l \rangle \rangle$ and $\langle i, \langle \mathsf{rel}, l \rangle \rangle$ respectively represent
that thread i locks or unlocks mutex $l \in \mathcal{L}$. The semantics of these actions cor-
respond to the so-called NORMAL mutexes in the POSIX standard [4]. Actions
of $\langle \mathsf{acq}, l \rangle$ or $\langle \mathsf{rel}, l \rangle$ effect are only dependent on actions whose effect is an operation on the same mutex l (acq, rel, w_1 or w_2, see below). For instance the action
of event 4 (rel) in Fig. 2b depends on the action of event 6 (acq).

Wait on Condition Variables. The occurrence of a pthread_cond_wait(c, l)
statement is represented by two separate actions of effect $\langle \mathsf{w}_1, c, l \rangle$ and $\langle \mathsf{w}_2, c, l \rangle$.
An action $\langle i, \langle \mathsf{w}_1, c, l \rangle \rangle$ represents that thread i has atomically released the lock l
and started waiting on condition variable c. An action $\langle i, \langle \mathsf{w}_2, c, l \rangle \rangle$ indicates
that thread i has been woken up by a *signal* or *broadcast* operation on c *and*
that it successfully re-acquired mutex l. For instance the action $\langle 1, \langle \mathsf{w}_1, c, m \rangle \rangle$ of
event 10 in Fig. 2c represents that thread 1 has released mutex m and is waiting
for c to be signaled. After the signal happens (event 12) the action $\langle 1, \langle \mathsf{w}_2, c, m \rangle \rangle$
of event 14 represents that thread 1 wakes up and re-acquires mutex m. An
action $\langle i, \langle \mathsf{w}_1, c, l \rangle \rangle$ is dependent on any action whose effect operates on mutex l
(acq, rel, w_1 or w_2) as well as signals directed to thread i ($\langle \mathsf{sig}, c, i \rangle$, see below),
lost signals ($\langle \mathsf{sig}, c, 0 \rangle$, see below), and any broadcast ($\langle \mathsf{bro}, c, W \rangle$ for any $W \subseteq \mathbb{N}$,
see below). Similarly, an action $\langle i, \langle \mathsf{w}_2, c, l \rangle \rangle$ is dependent on any action whose
effect operates on lock l as well as signals and broadcasts directed to thread i
(that is, either $\langle \mathsf{sig}, c, i \rangle$ or $\langle \mathsf{bro}, c, W \rangle$ when $i \in W$).

Signal/Broadcast on Condition Variables. An action $\langle i, \langle \text{sig}, c, j \rangle \rangle$, with $j \geq 0$ indicates that thread i executed a `pthread_cond_signal(c)` statement. If $j = 0$ then no thread was waiting on condition variable c, and the *signal* had no effect, as per the POSIX semantics. We refer to these as *lost signals*. Example: events 7 and 17 in Fig. 2b and 2d are labeled by lost signals. In both cases thread 1 was not waiting on the condition variable when the signal happened. However, when $j \geq 1$ the action represents that thread j wakes up by this signal. Whenever a signal wakes up a thread $j \geq 1$, we can always find a (unique) w_1 action of thread j that happened before the signal and a unique w_2 action in thread j that happens after the signal. For instance, event 12 in Fig. 2c signals thread 1, which went sleeping in the w_1 event 10 and wakes up in the w_2 event 14. Similarly, an action $\langle i, \langle \text{bro}, c, W \rangle \rangle$, with $W \subseteq \mathbb{N}$ indicates that thread i executed a `pthread_cond_broadcast(c)` statement and any thread j such that $j \in W$ was woken up. If $W = \emptyset$, then no thread was waiting on condition variable c (*lost broadcast*). Lost signals and broadcasts on c depend on any action of $\langle w_1, c, \cdot \rangle$ effect as well as any non-lost signal/broadcast on c. Non-lost signals and broadcasts on c that wake up thread j depend[1] on w_1 and w_2 actions of thread j as well as any signal/broadcast (lost or not) on the same condition variable.

A *run* of P is a sequence of actions in A^* which respects the constraints stated above for actions. For instance, a run for the program shown in Fig. 2a is the sequence of actions which labels *any* topological order of the events shown in any partial order in Fig. 2b to 2e. The sequence below,

$$\langle 1, \langle \text{loc}, \text{x=in}() \rangle \rangle, \langle 2, \langle \text{loc}, \text{y=1} \rangle \rangle, \langle 1, \langle \text{acq}, m \rangle \rangle,$$
$$\langle 1, \langle \text{loc}, \text{x>=0} \rangle \rangle, \langle 1, \langle \text{rel}, m \rangle \rangle, \langle 2, \langle \text{acq}, m \rangle \rangle$$

is a run of Fig. 2a. Naturally, if $\sigma \in A^*$ is a run, any prefix of σ is also a run. Runs explicitly represent concurrency, using thread identifiers, and symbolically represent data non-determinism, using constraints, as illustrated by the 1st and 4th actions of the run above. We let $runs(P)$ denote the set of all runs of P.

A *concrete state of* P is a tuple that represents, intuitively, the program counters of each thread, the values of all memory locations, the mutexes locked by each thread, and, for each condition variable, the set of threads waiting for it (see [42] for a formal definition). Since runs represent operations on symbolic data, they reach a symbolic state, which conceptually corresponds to a set of concrete states of P.

The *state of a run* σ, written $state(\sigma)$, is the set of all concrete states of P that are reachable when the program executes the run σ. For instance, the run σ' given above reaches a state consisting on all program states where y is 1, x is a non-negative number, thread 2 owns mutex m and its instruction pointer is at line 3, and thread 1 has finished. We let $reach(P) := \bigcup_{\sigma \in runs(P)} state(\sigma)$ denote the set of all *reachable states* of P.

---

[1] The formal definition is slightly more complex, see [42] for the details.

3.2 Independence

In the previous section, given an action $a \in A$ we informally defined the set of actions which are *dependent* on a, therefore indirectly defining an *independence relation*. We now show that this relation is a *valid independence* [19,41]. Intuitively, an independence relation is *valid* when every pair of actions it declares as independent can be executed in any order while still producing the same state.

Our independence relation is valid only for *data-race-free* programs. We say that P is *data-race-free* iff any two local actions $a := \langle i, \langle \mathsf{loc}, t \rangle \rangle$ and $a' := \langle i', \langle \mathsf{loc}, t' \rangle \rangle$ from different threads $(i \neq i')$ commute at every reachable state of P. See [42] for additional details. This ensures that local statements of different threads of P modify the memory without interfering each other.

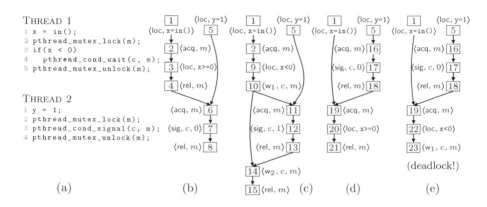

Fig. 2. A program and its four partial-order runs.

Theorem 1. *If P is data-race-free, then the independence relation defined in Sect. 3.1 is valid.*

Proof. See [42].

Our technique does not use data races as a source of thread interference for partial-order reduction. It will not explore two execution orders for the two statements that exhibit a data race. However, it can be used to detect and report data races found during the POR exploration, as we will see in Sect. 4.4.

3.3 Partial-Order Runs

A *labeled partial-order* (LPO) is a tuple $\langle X, <, h \rangle$ where X is a set of *events*, $< \subseteq X \times X$ is a *causality* (a.k.a., *happens-before*) relation, and $h \colon X \to A$ labels each event by an *action* in A.

A *partial-order run* of P is an LPO that represents a run of P without enforcing an order of execution on actions that are independent. All partial-order runs of Fig. 2a are shown in Fig. 2b to 2e.

Given a run σ of P, we obtain the corresponding partial-order run $\mathcal{E}_\sigma :=$ $\langle E, <, h \rangle$ by the following procedure: (1) initialize $\mathcal{E}_\sigma$ to be the only totally-ordered LPO that consists of $|\sigma|$ events where the i-th event is labeled by the i-th action of σ; (2) for every two events e, e' such that $e < e'$, remove the pair $\langle e, e' \rangle$ from $<$ if $h(e)$ is independent from $h(e')$; (3) restore transitivity in $<$ (i.e., if $e < e'$ and $e' < e''$, then add $\langle e, e'' \rangle$ to $<$). The resulting LPO is a partial-order run of P.

Furthermore, the originating run σ is an *interleaving* of $\mathcal{E}_\sigma$. Given some LPO $\mathcal{E} := \langle E, <, h \rangle$, an interleaving of $\mathcal{E}$ is the sequence that labels any topo-logical ordering of $\mathcal{E}$. Formally, it is any sequence $h(e_1), \ldots, h(e_n)$ such that $E = \{e_1, \ldots, e_n\}$ and $e_i < e_j \implies i < j$. We let $inter(\mathcal{E})$ denote the set of all interleavings of $\mathcal{E}$. Given a partial-order run $\mathcal{E}$ of P, the interleavings $inter(\mathcal{E})$ have two important properties: every interleaving in $inter(\mathcal{E})$ is a run of P, and any two interleavings $\sigma, \sigma' \in inter(\mathcal{E})$ reach the same state $state(\sigma) = state(\sigma')$.

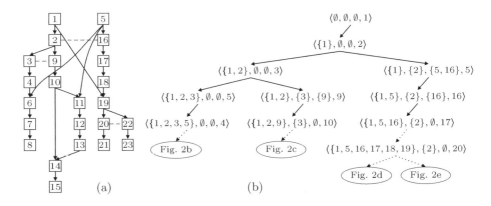

Fig. 3. (a): unfolding of the program in Fig. 2a; (b): its POR exploration tree.

3.4   Prime Event Structures

We use unfoldings to give semantics to multi-threaded programs. Unfoldings are Prime Event Structures [37], tree-like representations of system behavior that use partial orders to represent concurrent interaction.

Figure 3a depicts an unfolding of the program in Fig. 2a. The nodes are events and solid arrows represent causal dependencies: events 1 and 4 must fire before 8 can fire. The dotted line represents conflicts: 2 and 5 are not in conflict and may occur in any order, but 2 and 16 are in conflict and cannot occur in the same (partial-order) run.

Formally, a *Prime Event Structure* [37] (PES) is a tuple $\mathcal{E} := \langle E, <, \#, h \rangle$ with a set of events E, a causality relation $< \subseteq E \times E$, which is a strict partial order, a conflict relation $\# \subseteq E \times E$ that is symmetric and irreflexive, and a labeling function $h \colon E \to A$.

The *causes* of an event $\lceil e \rceil := \{e' \in E \colon e' < e\}$ are the least set of events that must fire before e can fire. A *configuration* of $\mathcal{E}$ is a finite set $C \subseteq E$ that is causally closed ($\lceil e \rceil \subseteq C$ for all $e \in C$), and conflict-free ($\neg(e \,\#\, e')$) for all $e, e' \in C$). We let $conf(\mathcal{E})$ denote the set of all configurations of $\mathcal{E}$. For any $e \in E$, the *local configuration* of e is defined as $[e] := \lceil e \rceil \cup \{e\}$. In Fig. 3a, the set $\{1, 2\}$ is a configuration, and in fact it is a local configuration, i.e., $[2] = \{1, 2\}$. The local configuration of event 6 is $\{1, 2, 3, 4, 5, 6\}$. Set $\{2, 5, 16\}$ is not a configuration, because it is neither causally closed (1 is missing) nor conflict-free (2 $\#$ 16).

3.5 Unfolding Semantics for Programs

Given a program P, in this section we define a PES $\mathcal{U}_P$ such that every configuration of $\mathcal{U}_P$ is a partial-order run of P.

Let $\mathcal{E}_1 := \langle E_1, <_1, h_1 \rangle, \ldots, \mathcal{E}_n := \langle E_n, <_n, h_n \rangle$ be the collection of all the partial-order runs of P. The events of $\mathcal{U}_P$ are the equivalence classes of the structural equality relation that we intuitively described in Sect. 2.3.

Two events are structurally equal iff their *canonical name* is the same. Given some event $e \in E_i$ in some partial-order run $\mathcal{E}_i$, the canonical name $cn(e)$ of e is the pair $\langle a, H \rangle$ where $a := h_i(e)$ is the executed action and $H := \{cn(e') \colon e' <_i e\}$ is the set of canonical names of those events that causally precede e in $\mathcal{E}_i$. Intuitively, canonical names indicate that action $h(e)$ runs after the (transitively canonicalized) partially-ordered history preceding e. For instance, in Fig. 3a for events 1 and 6 we have $cn(1) = \langle\langle 1, \langle \mathsf{loc}, \mathsf{a=in()} \rangle\rangle, \emptyset\rangle$, and $cn(6) = \langle\langle 2, \langle \mathsf{acq}, m \rangle\rangle, \{cn(1), cn(2), cn(3), cn(4), cn(5)\}\rangle$. Actually, the number within every event in Fig. 2b to 2e identifies (is in bijective correspondence with) its canonical name. Event 19 in Fig. 2d is the same event as event 19 in Fig. 2e because it fires the same action ($\langle 1, \langle \mathsf{acq}, m \rangle\rangle$) after the same causal history ($\{1, 5, 16, 17, 18\}$). Event 2 in Fig. 2c and 19 in Fig. 2d are *not* the same event because while $h(2) = h(19) = \langle 1, \langle \mathsf{acq}, m \rangle\rangle$ they have a different causal history ($\{1\}$ vs. $\{1, 5, 16, 17, 18\}$). Obviously events 4 and 6 in Fig. 2b are different because $h(4) \neq h(6)$. We can now define the *unfolding* of P as the only PES $\mathcal{U}_P := \langle E, <, \#, h \rangle$ such that

- $E := \{cn(e) \colon e \in E_1 \cup \ldots \cup E_n\}$ is the set of canonical names of all events;
- Relation $< \subseteq E \times E$ is the union $<_1 \cup \ldots \cup <_n$ of all happens-before relations;
- Any two events $e, e' \in E$ of $\mathcal{U}_P$ are in conflict, $e \,\#\, e'$, when $e \neq e'$, and $\neg(e < e')$, and $\neg(e' < e)$, and $h(e)$ is dependent on $h(e')$.

Figure 3a shows the unfolding produced by merging all 4 partial-order runs in Fig. 2b to 2e. Note that the configurations of $\mathcal{U}_P$ are partial-order runs of P. Furthermore, the $\subseteq$-maximal configurations are exactly the 4 originating partial orders. It is possible to prove that $\mathcal{U}_P$ is a semantics of P. In [42] we show that (1) $\mathcal{U}_P$ is uniquely defined, (2) any interleaving of any local configuration of $\mathcal{U}_P$ is a run of P, (3) for any run σ of P there is a configuration C of $\mathcal{U}_P$ such that $\sigma \in inter(C)$.

3.6   Conflicting Extensions

Our technique analyzes P by iteratively constructing (all) partial-order runs of P. In every iteration we need to find the next partial order to explore. We use the so-called *conflicting extensions* of a configuration to detect how to start a new partial-order run that has not been explored before.

Given a configuration C of $\mathcal{U}_P$, an *extension* of C is any event $e \in E \setminus C$ such that all the causal predecessors of e are in C. We denote the set of extensions of C as $ex(C) := \{e \in E : e \notin C \wedge \lceil e \rceil \subseteq C\}$. The *enabled* events of C are extensions that can form a larger configuration: $en(C) := \{e \in ex(C) : C \cup \{e\} \in conf(\mathcal{E})\}$. For instance, in Fig. 3a, the (local) configuration $[6]$ has 3 extensions, $ex([6]) = \{7, 9, 16\}$ of which, however, only event 7 is enabled: $en([6]) = \{7\}$. Event 19 is not an extension of $[6]$ because 18 is a causal predecessor of 19, but $18 \notin [6]$. A *conflicting extension* of C is an extension for which there is at least one $e' \in C$ such that $e \# e'$. The (local) configuration $[6]$ from our previous example has two conflicting extensions, events 9 and 16. A conflicting extension is, intuitively, an incompatible addition to the configuration C, an event e that cannot be executed together with C (without removing e' and its causal successors from C). We denote by $cex(C)$ the set of all conflicting extensions of C, which coincides with the set of all extensions that are not enabled: $cex(C) := ex(C) \setminus en(C)$.

Algorithm 1: Conflicting extensions for acq/w_2 events.

---

1 **Function** cex-acq-w2(e)
2   Assume that e is $\langle\langle i, \langle \mathsf{acq}, l \rangle\rangle, K\rangle$ or $\langle\langle i, \langle \mathsf{w_2}, c, l \rangle\rangle, K\rangle$
3      $R := \emptyset$
4      $e_t := $ last-of (K, i)
5   **if** $\mathit{effect}(e) = \langle \mathsf{acq}, l \rangle$ **then**
6 | $P := [e_t]$
7   **else**
8          $e_s := $ last-notify(e, c, i)
9          $P := [e_t] \cup [e_s]$
10     $e_m := $ last-lock(P, l)
11     $e_r := $ last-lock(K, l)
12   **if** $e_m = e_r$ **then return** R
13   **if** $e_m = \bot \vee \mathit{effect}(e_m) \in \{\langle \mathit{rel}, l \rangle, \langle \mathsf{w_1}, \cdot, l \rangle\}$ **then**
14 | Add $\langle h(e), P \rangle$ to R
15   **foreach** *event* $e' \in K \setminus (P \cup \{e_r\})$ **do**
16   **if** $\mathit{effect}(e') \in \{\langle \mathit{rel}, l \rangle, \langle \mathsf{w_1}, \cdot, l \rangle\}$ **then**
17 | Add $\langle h(e), P \cup [e'] \rangle$ to R
18   **return** R

Our technique discovers new conflicting extension events by trying to revert the causal order of certain events in C. Owing to space limitations we only explain how the algorithm handles events of acq and w_2 effect ([42] presents the remaining 4 procedures of the algorithm). Algorithm 1 shows the procedure that handles this case. It receives an event e of acq or w_2 effect (line 2). We build and return a set of conflicting extensions, stored in variable R. Events are added to R in line 14 and 17. Note that we define events using their canonical name. For instance, in line 14 we add a new event whose action is $h(e)$ and whose causal history is P. Note that we only create events that execute action $h(e)$. Conceptually speaking, the algorithm simply finds different causal histories (variables P and e') within the set $K = \lceil e \rceil$ to execute action $h(e)$.

Procedure last-of(C, i) returns the only $<$-maximal event of thread i in C; last-notify(e, c, i) returns the only immediate $<$-predecessor e' of e such that the effect of $h(e')$ is either $\langle \text{sig}, c, i \rangle$ or $\langle \text{bro}, c, S \rangle$ with $i \in S$; finally, procedure last-lock(C, l) returns the only $<$-maximal event that manipulates lock l in C (an event of effect acq, rel, w_1 or w_2), or $\bot$ if no such event exists. See [42] for additional details.

Algorithm 2: Main algorithm. See Sect. 3.7.

---

1 Global variables: $U := \emptyset$ (set of events of $\mathcal{U}_P$) and $N := \emptyset$ (set of tree nodes)

2 **Procedure** explore()
3   nod$(\emptyset, \emptyset, \emptyset)$
4   **repeat**
5   Select $n := \langle C, D, A, e \rangle$ from N
6   Add $cex(C)$ to U
7   **if** ena$(C) \subseteq D$ **then**
8        $\lfloor$ **continue**
9   **if** n *has no left child* **then**
10       $n' := $ nod$(C \cup \{e\}, D, A \setminus \{e\})$
11       $\lfloor$ Make n' the left child of n
12   **if** n *has no right child* **then**
13       $J := $ alt$(C, D \cup \{e\})$
14   **if** $J \neq \emptyset$ **then**
15         $n' := $ nod$(C, D \cup \{e\}, J \setminus C)$
16         $\lfloor$ Make n' the right child of n
17   **until** *fixed point (N is stable)*

18 **Function** nod(C, D, A)
19   **if** $A \neq \emptyset$ **then**
20      $\lfloor$ $e := $ select from ena$(C) \cap A$
21   **else**
22      $\lfloor$ $e := $ select from ena$(C) \setminus D$
23    $n := \langle C, D, A, e \rangle$
24   Add n to N
25    $\lfloor$ **return** n

26 **Function** ena(C)
27    $\lfloor$ **return** $\{e \in en(C) : \neg \text{cutoff}(e)\}$

28 **Function** alt(C, D)
29   Let e be some event in $D \cap en(C)$
30    $S := \{e' \in U : e' \# e \wedge \lceil e' \rceil \cap D = \emptyset\}$
31    $S := \{e' \in S : \lceil e' \rceil \cup C$ is a config.$\}$
32   **if** $S = \emptyset$ **then** **return** $\emptyset$
33   Select some event e' from S
34    $\lfloor$ **return** $\lceil e' \rceil$

3.7 Exploring the Unfolding

This section presents an algorithm that explores the state space of P by constructing all maximal configurations of $\mathcal{U}_P$. In essence, our procedure is an improved Quasi-Optimal POR algorithm [35], where the unfolding is not explored using a DFS traversal, but a user-defined search order. This enables us to build upon the preexisting exploration heuristics ("searchers") in KLEE rather than having to follow a strict DFS exploration of the unfolding.

Our algorithm explores one configuration of $\mathcal{U}_P$ at a time and organizes the exploration into a binary tree. Figure 3b shows the tree explored for the unfolding shown in Fig. 3a. A tree node is a tuple $n := \langle C, D, A, e \rangle$ that represents both the exploration of a configuration C of $\mathcal{U}_P$ and a choice to execute, or not, event $e \in en(C)$. Both D (for *disabled*) and A (for *add*) are sets of events.

The key insight of this tree is as follows. The subtree rooted at a given node n explores all configurations of $\mathcal{U}_P$ that include C and exclude D, with the following constraint: n's left subtree explores all configurations including event e and n's right subtree explores all configuration excluding e. Set A is used to guide the algorithm when exploring the right subtree. For instance, in Fig. 3b the subtree rooted at node $n := \langle \{1, 2\}, \emptyset, \emptyset, 3 \rangle$ explores all maximal configurations that contain events 1 and 2 (namely, those shown in Fig. 2b and 2c). The left subtree of n explores all configurations including $\{1, 2, 3\}$ (Fig. 2b) and the right subtree all of those including $\{1, 2\}$ but excluding 3 (Fig. 2c).

Algorithm 2 shows a simplified version of our algorithm. The complete version, in [42], specifies additional details including how nodes are selected for exploration and how they are removed from the tree. The algorithm constructs and stores the exploration tree in the variable N, and the set of currently known events of $\mathcal{U}_N$ in variable U. At the end of the exploration, U will store all events of $\mathcal{U}_N$ and the leafs of the exploration tree in N will correspond to the maximal configurations of $\mathcal{U}_N$.

The tree is constructed using a fixed-point loop (line 4) that repeats the following steps as long as they modify the tree: select a node $\langle C, D, A, e \rangle$ in the tree (line 5), extend U with the conflicting extensions of C (line 6), check if the configuration is $\subseteq$-maximal (line 7), in which case there is nothing left to do, then try to add a left (line 9) or right (line 12) child node.

The subtree rooted at the left child node will explore all configurations that include $C \cup \{e\}$ and exclude D (line 10); the right subtree will explore those including C and excluding $D \cup \{e\}$ (line 15), if any of them exists, which we detect by checking (line 14) if we found a so-called *alternative* [41].

An alternative is a set of events which witnesses the existence of some maximal configuration in $\mathcal{U}_P$ that extends C without including $D \cup \{e\}$. Computing such witness is an NP-complete problem, so we use an approximation called *k-partial alternatives* [35], which can be computed in P-time and works well in practice. Our procedure `alt` specifically computes 1-partial alternatives: it selects $k = 1$ event e from $D \cap en(C)$, searches for an event e' in conflict with e (we have added all known candidates in line 6, using the algorithms of Sect. 3.6) that can extend C (i.e., such that $C \cup [e']$ is a configuration), and returns it. When such an event e' is found (line 33), some events in its local configuration $[e']$ become the A-component of the right child node (line 15), and the leftmost branch rooted at that node will re-execute those events (as they will be selected in line 20), guiding the search towards the witnessed maximal configuration.

For instance, in Fig. 3b, assume that the algorithm has selected node $n = \langle\{1\}, \emptyset, \emptyset, 2\rangle$ at line 5 when event 16 is already in U. Then a call to $\mathtt{alt}(\{1\}, \{2\})$ is issued at line 13, event $e = 2$ is selected at line 29 and event $e' = 16$ gets selected at line 33, because $2 \# 16$ and $[16] \cup \{1\}$ is a configuration. As a result, node $n' = \langle\{1\}, \{2\}, \{5, 16\}, 5\rangle$ becomes the right child of n in line 15, and the leftmost branch rooted at n' adds $\{5, 16\}$ to C, leading to the maximal configuration Fig. 2d.

3.8   Cutoffs and Completeness

All interleavings of a given configuration always reach the same state, but interleavings of different configurations can also reach the same state. It is possible to exclude certain such redundant configurations from the exploration without making the algorithm incomplete, by using *cutoff* events [32].

Intuitively, an event is a cutoff if we have already visited another event that reaches the same state with a shorter execution. Formally, in Algorithm 2, line 27 we let $\mathtt{cutoff}(e)$ return *true* iff there is some $e' \in U$ such that $state([e]) = state([e'])$ and $|[e']| < |[e]|$. This makes Algorithm 2 ignore cutoff events and any event that causally succeeds them. Sect. 4.2 explains how to effectively implement the check $state([e]) = state([e'])$.

While cutoffs prevent the exploration of redundant configurations, the analysis is still complete: it is possible to prove that every state reachable via a configuration with cutoffs is also reachable via a configuration without cutoffs. Furthermore, cutoff events not only reduce the exploration of redundant configurations, but also force the algorithm to terminate for non-terminating programs that run on bounded memory.

Theorem 2 (Correctness).   *For any reachable state $s \in reach(P)$, Algorithm 2 explores a configuration C such that for some $C' \subseteq C$ it holds that $state(C') = s$. Furthermore, it terminates for any program P such that $reach(P)$ is finite.*

A proof sketch is available in [42]. Naturally, since Algorithm 2 explores $\mathcal{U}_P$, and $\mathcal{U}_P$ is an exact representation of all runs of P, then Algorithm 2 is also *sound*: any event constructed by the algorithm (added to set U) is associated with a real run of P.

4   Implementation

We implemented our approach on top of the symbolic execution engine KLEE [10], which was previously restricted to sequential programs. KLEE already provides a minimal POSIX support library that we extended to translate calls to pthread functions to their respective actions, enabling us to test real-world multi-threaded C programs. We also extended already available functionality to make it thread-safe, e.g., by implementing a global file system lock that ensures that concurrent reads from the same file descriptor do not result in unsafe behavior. The source code of our prototype is available at https://github.com/por-se/por-se.

4.1   Standby States

When a new alternative is explored, a symbolic execution state needs to be computed to match the new node in the POR tree. However, creating it from scratch requires too much time and keeping a symbolic execution state around for each node consumes significant amounts of memory. Instead of committing to either extreme, we store *standby states* at regular intervals along the exploration tree and, when necessary, replay the closest standby state. This way, significantly fewer states are kept in memory without letting the replaying of previously computed operations dominate the analysis either.

4.2   Hash-Based Cutoff Events

Schemmel et al. presented [43] an incremental hashing scheme to identify infinite loops during symbolic execution. The approach detects when the program under test can transition from any one state back to that same state. Their scheme computes *fragments* for small portions of the program state, which are then hashed individually, and combined into a compound hash by bitwise xor operations. This compound hash, called a *fingerprint*, uniquely (modulo hash collisions) identifies the whole state of the program under test. We adapt this scheme to provide hashes that identify the concurrent state of parallel programs.

To this end, we associate each configuration with a fingerprint that describes the whole state of the program at that point. For example, if the program state consists of two variables, $x = 3$ and $y = 5$, the fingerprint would be $fp = \text{hash}\,(\texttt{"x=3"}) \oplus \text{hash}\,(\texttt{"y=5"})$. When one fragment changes, e.g., from $x = 3$ to $x = 4$, the old fragment hash needs to be replaced with the new one. This operation can be performed as $fp' = fp \oplus \text{hash}\,(\texttt{"x=3"}) \oplus \text{hash}\,(\texttt{"x=4"})$ as the duplicate fragments for $x = 3$ will cancel out. To quickly compute the fingerprint of a configuration, we annotate each event with an xor of all of these update operations that were done on its thread. Computing the fingerprint of a configuration now only requires xor-ing the values from its thread-maximal events, which will ensure that all changes done to each variable are accounted for, and cancel out one another so that only the fragment for the last value remains.

Any two local configurations that have the same fingerprint represent the same program state; each variable, program counter, etc., has the same value. Thus, it is not necessary to continue exploring both—we have found a potential cutoff point, which the POR algorithm will treat accordingly (Sect. 3.8).

4.3   Deterministic and Repeatable Allocations

KLEE usually uses the system allocator to determine the addresses of objects allocated by the program under test. But it also provides a (more) deterministic mode, in which addresses are consumed in sequence from a large pre-allocated array. Since our hash-based cutoff computation uses memory address as part of the computation, using execution replays from standby states (Sect. 4.1) requires that we have fully repeatable memory allocation.

We tackle this problem by decoupling the addresses returned by the emulated system allocator in the program under test from the system allocator of KLEE itself. A new allocator requires a large amount of virtual memory in which it will perform its allocations. This large virtual memory mapping is not actually used unless an external function call is performed, in which case the relevant objects are temporarily copied into the region from the symbolic execution state for which the external function call is to be performed. Afterwards, the pages are marked for reclamation by the OS. This way, allocations done by different symbolic execution states return the same address to the program under test.

While a deterministic allocator by itself would be enough for providing deterministic allocation to sequential programs, parallel programs also require an allocation pattern that is independent of which sequentialization of the same partial order is chosen. We achieve this property by providing independent allocators for each thread (based on the thread id, thus ensuring that the same virtual memory mapping is reused for each instance of the same semantic thread). When an object is deallocated on a different thread than it was allocated on, its address only becomes available for reuse once the allocating thread has reached a point in its execution where it is causally dependent on the deallocation. Additionally, the thread ids that are used by our implementation are hierarchically defined: A new thread t that is the i-th thread started by its parent thread p has the thread id $t := (p, i)$, with the main thread being denoted as (1). This way, thread ids and the associated virtual memory mappings are independent of how the concurrent creation of multiple threads are sequentialized.

We have also included various optimizations that promote controlled reuse of addresses to increase the chance that a cutoff event (Sect. 4.2) is found, such as binning allocations by size, which reduces the chance that temporary allocations impact which addresses are returned for other allocations.

4.4   Data Race Detection

Our data race detection algorithm simply follows the happens-before relationships established by the POR. However, its implementation is complicated by the possibility of addresses becoming symbolic. Generally speaking, a symbolic address can potentially point to any and every byte in the whole address space, thus requiring frequent and large SMT queries to be solved.

To alleviate the quadratic blowup of possibly aliasing accesses, we exploit how KLEE performs memory accesses with symbolic addresses: The symbolic state is forked for every possible memory object that the access may refer to (and one additional time if the memory access may point to unallocated memory). Therefore, a symbolic memory access is already resolved to memory object granularity when it potentially participates in a data race. This drastically reduces the amount of possible data races without querying the SMT solver.

4.5   External Function Calls

When a program wants to call a function that is neither provided by the program itself nor by the runtime, KLEE will attempt to perform an *external function call* by moving the function arguments from the symbolic state to its own address space and attempting to call the function itself. While this support for uninterpreted functions is helpful for getting some results for programs which are not fully supported by KLEE's POSIX runtime, it is also inherently incomplete and not sound in the general case. Our prototype includes this option as well.

5   Experimental Evaluation

To explore the efficacy of the presented approach, we performed a series of experiments including both synthetic benchmarks from the SV-COMP [9] benchmark suite and real-world programs, namely, Memcached [3] and GNU sort [1]. We compare against Yogar-CBMC [49], which is the winner of the concurrency safety category of SV-COMP 2019 [9], and stands in for the family of bounded model checkers. As such, Yogar-CBMC is predestined to fare well in the artificial SV-COMP benchmarks, while our approach may demonstrate its strength in dealing with more complicated programs.

Table 1. Our prototype and Yogar-CBMC running SV-COMP benchmarks. Timeout set at 15 min with maximum memory usage of 15 GB. Columns are: T: true result, output matches expected verdict; F: false result, output does not match expected verdict; U: unknown result, tool yields no answer; Time: total time taken; RSS: maximum resident set size over all benchmarks.

Benchmark	Our tool					Yogar-CBMC				
	T	F	U	Time	RSS	T	F	U	Time	RSS
pthread	29	–	9	1:50:19	16 GB	29	–	9	0:31:21	948 MB
pthread-driver-races	16	1	4	1:03:08	6049 MB	21	–	–	0:00:12	72 MB

We ran the experiments on a cluster of multiple identical machines with dual Intel Xeon E5-2643 v4 CPUs and 256 GiB of RAM. We used a 4 h timeout and 200 GB maximum memory usage for real-world programs. We used a 15 min timeout and 15 GB maximum memory for individual SV-COMP benchmarks.

5.1   SV-COMP

We ran our tool and Yogar-CBMC on the "pthread" and "pthread-driver-races" benchmark suites in their newest (2020) incarnation. As expected, Table 1 shows that Yogar-CBMC clearly outperforms our tool for this specific set of benchmarks. Not only does Yogar-CBMC not miscategorize even a single benchmark, it does so quickly and without using a lot of memory. Our tool, in contrast, takes significantly more time and memory to analyze the target benchmarks. In fact, several benchmarks do not complete within the 15 min time frame and therefore cannot give a verdict for those.

The "pthread-driver-races" benchmark suite contains one benchmark that is marked as a failure for our tool in Table 1. For the relevant benchmark, a verdict of "target function unreachable" is expected, which we translate to mean "no data race occurs". However, the benchmark program constructs a pointer that may point to effectively any byte in memory, which, upon dereferencing it, leads to both, memory errors and data races (by virtue of the pointer also being able to touch another thread's stack). While we report this behavior for completeness sake, we attribute it to the adaptations made to fit the SV-COMP model to ours.

Preparation of Benchmark Suites. The SV-COMP benchmark suite does not only assume various kinds of special casing (e.g., functions whose name begins with __VERIFIER_atomic must be executed atomically), but also routinely violates the C standard by, for example, employing data races as a control flow mechanism [25, § 5.1.2.4/35]. Partially, this is because the analysis target is a question of reachability of a certain part of the benchmark program, not its correctness. We therefore attempted to guess the intention of the individual benchmarks, making variables atomic or leaving the data race in when it is the aim of the benchmark.

5.2   Memcached

Memcached [3] is an in-memory network object cache written in C. As it is a somewhat large project with a fairly significant state space, we were unable to analyze it completely, even though our prototype still found several bugs. Our attempts to run Yogar-CBMC did not succeed, as it reproducibly crashes.

Faults Detected. Our prototype found nine bugs in memcached 1.5.19, attributable to four different root causes, all of which where previously unknown. The first bug is a misuse of the pthread API, causing six mutexes and condition variables to be initialized twice, leading to undefined behavior. We reported[2] the issue, a fix is included in version 1.5.20. The second bug occurs during the initialization of memcached, where fields that will later be accessed in a thread-safe manner are sometimes accessed in a non-thread-safe manner, assuming that competing accesses are not yet possible. We reported[3] a mistake our tool found in the initialization order that invalidates the assumption that locking is not (yet) necessary on one field. A fix ships with memcached 1.5.21. For the third bug, memcached utilizes a maintenance thread to manage and resize its core hash table when necessary. Additionally, on another thread, a timer checks whether the maintenance thread should perform an expansion of the hash table. We

---

[2] https://github.com/memcached/memcached/pull/566.
[3] https://github.com/memcached/memcached/pull/575.

found[4] a data race between these two threads on a field that stores whether the maintenance thread has started expanding. This is fixed in version 1.5.20. The fourth and final issue is a data race on the stats_state storing execution statistics. We reported[5] this issue and a fix is included in version 1.5.21.

Experiment. We run our prototype on five different versions of memcached, the three releases 1.5.19, 1.5.20 and 1.5.21 plus variants of the earlier releases (1.5.19+ and 1.5.20+) which include patches for the two bugs we found during program initialization. Those variants are included to show performance when not restricted by inescapable errors very early in the program execution.

Table 2 shows clearly how the two initialization bugs may lead to very quick analyses—versions 1.5.19 and 1.5.20 are completely analyzed in 7 s each, while versions 1.5.19+, 1.5.20+ and 1.5.21 exhaust the memory budget of 200 GB. We have configured the experiment to stop the analysis once the memory limit is reached, although the analysis could continue in an incomplete manner by removing parts of the exploration frontier to free up memory. Even though the number of error paths in Table 2 differs between configurations, it is notable that each configuration can only reach exactly one of the bugs, as execution is arrested at that point. When not restricted to the program initialization, the analysis of memcached produces hundreds of thousands of events and retires hundreds of millions of instructions in less than 2 h.

Table 2. Our prototype analyzing various versions of memcached and GNU sort. Time-out set at 4 h with maximum memory usage of 200 GB. Columns are: RSS: maximum resident set size (swap space is not available); #I: number of instructions executed; Th: maximum number of threads active at the same time; Σ: total number of events in the explored unfolding; Mut: number of mutex lock/unlock events; CV: number of wait1/wait2/signal/broadcast events; λ: number of symbolic choices; Cut: number of events determined to be cutoffs; and the number of Finished Paths distinguish between normal termination of the program under test (Exit), detection of an error (Err) and being cut off (Cut).

Program					Th	Events					Finished Paths			Halt
	Version	LoC	Time	RSS	#I		Σ	Mut	CV	λ	Cut	Exit	Err	Cut	Reason
Memcached	1.5.19	31065	0:00:07	204 MB	23K	1	12	6	0	3	0	0	1	0	Finished
	1.5.19+	31051	1:33:42	208 GB	1.2B	6	331K	271K	60K	3	24K	0	41K	29K	Memory
	1.5.20	31093	0:00:07	197 MB	92K	2	24	16	0	3	0	0	1	0	Finished
	1.5.20+	31093	1:51:10	207 GB	228M	10	745K	742K	2.7K	5	882	0	1	2.6K	Memory
	1.5.21	31090	1:29:57	207 GB	546M	10	1.1M	1.1M	3.1K	3	558	0	0	2.6K	Memory
Sort	8.31	86596	0:24:29	23 GB	266M	2	1.8M	1.4M	269K	25K	58K	8.0K	4.9K	55K	Finished
	8.31+	86599	4:01:39	88 GB	1.0B	2	6.9M	5.8M	777K	276K	346K	6.3K		0	285K	Time

Our setup delivers a single symbolic packet to memcached followed by a concrete shutdown packet. As this packet can obviously only be processed once the

---

[4] https://github.com/memcached/memcached/pull/569.
[5] https://github.com/memcached/memcached/pull/573.

server is ready to process input, we observe symbolic choices only after program startup is complete. (Since our prototype builds on KLEE, note that it assumes a single symbolic choice during startup, without generating an additional path.)

5.3   GNU sort

GNU sort uses threads for speeding up the sorting of very large workloads. We reduced the minimum size of input required to trigger concurrent sorting to four lines to enable the analysis tools to actually trigger concurrent behavior. Nevertheless, we were unable to avoid crashing Yogar-CBMC on this input.

During analysis of GNU sort 8.31, our prototype detected a data race, that we manually verified, but were unable to trigger in a harmful manner. Table 2 shows two variants of GNU sort, the baseline version with eager parallelization (8.31) and a version with added locking to prevent the data race (8.31+).

Surprisingly, version 8.31 finishes the exploration, as all paths either exit, encounter the data race and are terminated or are cut off. By fixing the data race in version 8.31+, we make it possible for the exploration to continue beyond this point, which results in a full 4 h run that retires a full billion instructions while encountering almost seven million unique events.

6   Related Work

The body of work in *systematic concurrency testing* [5,6,19,21,23,35,41,47,50] is large. These approaches explore thread interleavings under a fixed program input. They prune the search space using context-bounding [34], increasingly sophisticated PORs [5–7,12,19,23,35,41], or random testing [13,50]. Our main difference with these techniques is that we handle input data.

Thread-modular abstract interpretation [18,30,33] and unfolding-based abstract interpretation [46] aim at proving safety rather than finding bugs. They use over-approximations to explore all behaviors, while we focus on testing and never produce false alarms. *Sequentialization* techniques [26,36,40] encode a multi-threaded program into a sequential one. While these encodings can be very effective for small programs [26] they grow quickly with large context bounds (5 or more, see [36]). However, some of the bugs found by our technique (Sect. 5) require many context switches to be reached.

Bounded-model checking [8,15,28,39,49] for multi-threaded programs encode multiple program paths into a single logic formula, while our technique encodes a single path. Their main disadvantage is that for very large programs, even constructing the multi-path formula can be extremely challenging, often producing an upfront failure and no result. Conversely, while our approach faces path explosion, it is always able to test some program paths.

Techniques like [17,27,44] operate on a data structure conceptually very similar to our unfolding. They track read/write operations to every variable, which becomes a liability on very large executions. In contrast, we only use POSIX synchronization primitives and compactly represent memory accesses to detect data races. Furthermore, they do not exploit anything similar to cutoff events for additional trace pruning.

Interpolation [14,48] and weakest preconditions [24] have been combined with POR and symbolic execution for *property-guided* analysis. These approaches are mostly complementary to PORs like our technique, as they eliminate a different class of redundant executions [24].

This work builds on top of previous work [35,41,46]. The main contributions w.r.t. those are: (1) we use symbolic execution instead of concurrency testing [35, 41] or abstract interpretation [46]; (2) we support condition variables, providing algorithms to compute conflicting extensions for them; and (3) here we use hash-based fingerprints to compute cutoff events, thus handling much more complex partial orders than the approach described in [46].

7   Conclusion

Our approach combines POR and symbolic execution to analyze programs w.r.t. both input (data) and concurrency non-determinism. We model a significant portion of the pthread API, including try-lock operations and robust mutexes. We introduce two techniques to cope with state-space explosion in real-world programs. We compute cutoff events by using efficiently-computed fingerprints that uniquely identify the total state of the program. We restrict scheduling to synchronization points and report data races as errors. Our experiments found previously unknown bugs in real-world software projects (memcached, GNU sort).

Acknowledgements. This research is supported in parts by the European Research Council (ERC) under the European Union's Horizon 2020 Research and Innovation Programme (grant agreement No. 647295 (SYMBIOSYS)).

References

1. GNU sort. https://www.gnu.org/software/coreutils/
2. Helgrind: A thread error detector. https://valgrind.org/docs/manual/hg-manual.html
3. Memcached. https://www.memcached.org/
4. IEEE Standard for Information Technology–Portable Operating System Interface (POSIX(R)) Base Specifications, Issue 7. Standard IEEE Std 1003.1-2017 (Revision of IEEE Std 1003.1-2008) (2018)
5. Abdulla, P., Aronis, S., Jonsson, B., Sagonas, K.: Optimal dynamic partial order reduction. In: Proceedings of the 41st ACM SIGPLAN-SIGACT Symposium on Principles of Programming Languages, POPL 14, San Diego, California, USA, pp. 373–384. Association for Computing Machinery, January 2014. https://doi.org/10.1145/2535838.2535845
6. Abdulla, P.A., Aronis, S., Atig, M.F., Jonsson, B., Leonardsson, C., Sagonas, K.: Stateless model checking for TSO and PSO. In: Baier, C., Tinelli, C. (eds.) TACAS 2015. LNCS, vol. 9035, pp. 353–367. Springer, Heidelberg (2015). https://doi.org/10.1007/978-3-662-46681-0_28

7. Albert, E., de la Banda, M.G., Gómez-Zamalloa, M., Isabel, M., Stuckey, P.J.: Optimal context-sensitive dynamic partial order reduction with observers. In: Proceedings of the 28th ACM SIGSOFT International Symposium on Software Testing and Analysis, ISSTA 2019, Beijing, China, pp. 352–362. Association for Computing Machinery, July 2019. https://doi.org/10.1145/3293882.3330565

8. Alglave, J., Kroening, D., Tautschnig, M.: Partial orders for efficient bounded model checking of concurrent software. In: Sharygina, N., Veith, H. (eds.) CAV 2013. LNCS, vol. 8044, pp. 141–157. Springer, Heidelberg (2013). https://doi.org/10.1007/978-3-642-39799-8_9

9. Beyer, D.: Automatic verification of C and Java programs: SV-COMP 2019. In: Beyer, D., Huisman, M., Kordon, F., Steffen, B. (eds.) TACAS 2019. LNCS, vol. 11429, pp. 133–155. Springer, Cham (2019). https://doi.org/10.1007/978-3-030-17502-3_9

10. Cadar, C., Dunbar, D., Engler, D.R.: KLEE: unassisted and automatic generation of high-coverage tests for complex systems programs. In: Proceedings of the 8th USENIX Symposium on Operating Systems Design and Implementation (OSDI 2008), vol. 8, pp. 209–224 (2008)

11. Cadar, C., Sen, K.: Symbolic execution for software testing: three decades later. Commun. ACM **56**(2), 82–90 (2013). https://doi.org/10.1145/2408776.2408795

12. Chalupa, M., Chatterjee, K., Pavlogiannis, A., Sinha, N., Vaidya, K.: Data-centric dynamic partial order reduction. In: Proceedings of the ACM on Programming Languages 2(POPL), pp. 31:1–31:30, December 2017. https://doi.org/10.1145/3158119

13. Chen, D., Jiang, Y., Xu, C., Ma, X., Lu, J.: Testing multithreaded programs via thread speed control. In: Proceedings of the 2018 26th ACM Joint Meeting on European Software Engineering Conference and Symposium on the Foundations of Software Engineering, ESEC/FSE 2018, Lake Buena Vista, FL, USA, pp. 15–25. Association for Computing Machinery, October 2018. https://doi.org/10.1145/3236024.3236077

14. Chu, D.-H., Jaffar, J.: A framework to synergize partial order reduction with state interpolation. In: Yahav, E. (ed.) HVC 2014. LNCS, vol. 8855, pp. 171–187. Springer, Cham (2014). https://doi.org/10.1007/978-3-319-13338-6_14

15. Cordeiro, L., Fischer, B.: Verifying multi-threaded software using SMT-based context-bounded model checking. In: 2011 33rd International Conference on Software Engineering (ICSE), pp. 331–340, May 2011. https://doi.org/10.1145/1985793.1985839

16. Esparza, J., Römer, S., Vogler, W.: An improvement of McMillan's unfolding algorithm. Form. Methods Syst. Des. **20**(3), 285–310 (2002). https://doi.org/10.1023/A:1014746130920

17. Farzan, A., Holzer, A., Razavi, N., Veith, H.: Con2colic testing. In: Proceedings of the 2013 9th Joint Meeting on Foundations of Software Engineering, ESEC/FSE 2013, Saint Petersburg, Russia, pp. 37–47. ACM (2013). https://doi.org/10.1145/2491411.2491453

18. Farzan, A., Madhusudan, P.: Causal dataflow analysis for concurrent programs. In: Grumberg, O., Huth, M. (eds.) TACAS 2007. LNCS, vol. 4424, pp. 102–116. Springer, Heidelberg (2007). https://doi.org/10.1007/978-3-540-71209-1_10

19. Flanagan, C., Godefroid, P.: Dynamic partial-order reduction for model checking software. In: Proceedings of the 32nd ACM SIGPLAN-SIGACT Symposium on Principles of Programming Languages, POPL 2005, Long Beach, California, USA, pp. 110–121. Association for Computing Machinery, January 2005. https://doi.org/10.1145/1040305.1040315

20. Godefroid, P. (ed.): Partial-Order Methods for the Verification of Concurrent Systems. LNCS, vol. 1032. Springer, Heidelberg (1996). https://doi.org/10.1007/3-540-60761-7
21. Godefroid, P.: Model checking for programming languages using VeriSoft. In: Proceedings of the 24th ACM SIGPLAN-SIGACT Symposium on Principles of Programming Languages, POPL 1997, Paris, France, pp. 174–186. Association for Computing Machinery, January 1997. https://doi.org/10.1145/263699.263717
22. Godefroid, P., Levin, M.Y., Molnar, D.: Automated whitebox fuzz testing. In: 16th Annual Network & Distributed System Security Symposium, pp. 151–166, February 2008
23. Gueta, G., Flanagan, C., Yahav, E., Sagiv, M.: Cartesian partial-order reduction. In: Bošnački, D., Edelkamp, S. (eds.) SPIN 2007. LNCS, vol. 4595, pp. 95–112. Springer, Heidelberg (2007). https://doi.org/10.1007/978-3-540-73370-6_8
24. Guo, S., Kusano, M., Wang, C., Yang, Z., Gupta, A.: Assertion guided symbolic execution of multithreaded programs. In: Proceedings of the 2015 10th Joint Meeting on Foundations of Software Engineering, ESEC/FSE 2015, Bergamo, Italy, pp. 854–865. Association for Computing Machinery, August 2015. https://doi.org/10.1145/2786805.2786841
25. International Organization for Standardization: Information technology — Programming languages — C. Standard ISO/IEC 9899:2018 (2018). https://www.iso.org/standard/74528.html
26. Inverso, O., Tomasco, E., Fischer, B., La Torre, S., Parlato, G.: Bounded model checking of multi-threaded C programs via lazy sequentialization. In: Biere, A., Bloem, R. (eds.) CAV 2014. LNCS, vol. 8559, pp. 585–602. Springer, Cham (2014). https://doi.org/10.1007/978-3-319-08867-9_39
27. Kähkönen, K., Saarikivi, O., Heljanko, K.: Unfolding based automated testing of multithreaded programs. Autom. Softw. Eng. **22**(4), 475–515 (2015). https://doi.org/10.1007/s10515-014-0150-6
28. Kahlon, V., Wang, C., Gupta, A.: Monotonic partial order reduction: an optimal symbolic partial order reduction technique. In: Bouajjani, A., Maler, O. (eds.) CAV 2009. LNCS, vol. 5643, pp. 398–413. Springer, Heidelberg (2009). https://doi.org/10.1007/978-3-642-02658-4_31
29. King, J.C.: Symbolic execution and program testing. Commun. ACM **19**(7), 385–394 (1976). https://doi.org/10.1145/360248.360252
30. Kusano, M., Wang, C.: Flow-sensitive composition of thread-modular abstract interpretation. In: Proceedings of the 2016 24th ACM SIGSOFT International Symposium on Foundations of Software Engineering, FSE 2016, Seattle, WA, USA, pp. 799–809. Association for Computing Machinery, November 2016. https://doi.org/10.1145/2950290.2950291
31. Mazurkiewicz, A.: Trace theory. In: Brauer, W., Reisig, W., Rozenberg, G. (eds.) ACPN 1986. LNCS, vol. 255, pp. 278–324. Springer, Heidelberg (1987). https://doi.org/10.1007/3-540-17906-2_30
32. McMillan, K.L.: Using unfoldings to avoid the state explosion problem in the verification of asynchronous circuits. In: von Bochmann, G., Probst, D.K. (eds.) CAV 1992. LNCS, vol. 663, pp. 164–177. Springer, Heidelberg (1993). https://doi.org/10.1007/3-540-56496-9_14
33. Miné, A.: Relational thread-modular static value analysis by abstract interpretation. In: McMillan, K.L., Rival, X. (eds.) VMCAI 2014. LNCS, vol. 8318, pp. 39–58. Springer, Heidelberg (2014). https://doi.org/10.1007/978-3-642-54013-4_3

34. Musuvathi, M., Qadeer, S.: Iterative context bounding for systematic testing of multithreaded programs. In: Proceedings of the 28th ACM SIGPLAN Conference on Programming Language Design and Implementation, PLDI 2007, San Diego, California, USA, pp. 446–455. Association for Computing Machinery, June 2007. https://doi.org/10.1145/1250734.1250785
35. Nguyen, H.T.T., Rodríguez, C., Sousa, M., Coti, C., Petrucci, L.: Quasi-optimal partial order reduction. In: Chockler, H., Weissenbacher, G. (eds.) CAV 2018. LNCS, vol. 10982, pp. 354–371. Springer, Cham (2018). https://doi.org/10.1007/978-3-319-96142-2_22
36. Nguyen, T.L., Schrammel, P., Fischer, B., La Torre, S., Parlato, G.: Parallel bug-finding in concurrent programs via reduced interleaving instances. In: Proceedings of the 32nd IEEE/ACM International Conference on Automated Software Engineering, ASE 2017, Urbana-Champaign, IL, USA, pp. 753–764. IEEE Press, October 2017. https://doi.org/10.1109/ASE.2017.8115686
37. Nielsen, M., Plotkin, G., Winskel, G.: Petri nets, event structures and domains, Part I. Theoret. Comput. Sci. **13**(1), 85–108 (1981)
38. Păsăreanu, C.S., Rungta, N.: Symbolic PathFinder: symbolic execution of Java bytecode. In: Proceedings of the IEEE/ACM International Conference on Automated Software Engineering, ASE 2010, Antwerp, Belgium, pp. 179–180. Association for Computing Machinery, September 2010. https://doi.org/10.1145/1858996.1859035
39. Prabhu, S., Schrammel, P., Srivas, M., Tautschnig, M., Yeolekar, A.: Concurrent program verification with invariant-guided underapproximation. In: D'Souza, D., Narayan Kumar, K. (eds.) ATVA 2017. LNCS, vol. 10482, pp. 241–248. Springer, Cham (2017). https://doi.org/10.1007/978-3-319-68167-2_17
40. Qadeer, S., Wu, D.: KISS: keep it simple and sequential. In: Proceedings of the ACM SIGPLAN 2004 Conference on Programming Language Design and Implementation, PLDI 2004, Washington DC, USA, pp. 14–24. Association for Computing Machinery, June 2004. https://doi.org/10.1145/996841.996845
41. Rodríguez, C., Sousa, M., Sharma, S., Kroening, D.: Unfolding-based partial order reduction. In: Aceto, L., Escrig, D.d.F. (eds.) 26th International Conference on Concurrency Theory (CONCUR 2015). Leibniz International Proceedings in Informatics (LIPIcs), vol. 42, pp. 456–469. Schloss Dagstuhl–Leibniz-Zentrum fuer Informatik, Dagstuhl (2015). https://doi.org/10.4230/LIPIcs.CONCUR.2015.456
42. Schemmel, D., Büning, J., Rodríguez, C., Laprell, D., Wehrle, K.: Symbolic partial-order execution for testing multi-threaded programs. arXiv:2005.06688 [cs], May 2020. https://arxiv.org/abs/2005.06688
43. Schemmel, D., Büning, J., Soria Dustmann, O., Noll, T., Wehrle, K.: Symbolic liveness analysis of real-world software. In: Chockler, H., Weissenbacher, G. (eds.) CAV 2018. LNCS, vol. 10982, pp. 447–466. Springer, Cham (2018). https://doi.org/10.1007/978-3-319-96142-2_27
44. Sen, K., Agha, G.: A race-detection and flipping algorithm for automated testing of multi-threaded programs. In: Bin, E., Ziv, A., Ur, S. (eds.) HVC 2006. LNCS, vol. 4383, pp. 166–182. Springer, Heidelberg (2007). https://doi.org/10.1007/978-3-540-70889-6_13
45. Serebryany, K., Iskhodzhanov, T.: ThreadSanitizer: data race detection in practice. In: Proceedings of the Workshop on Binary Instrumentation and Applications, WBIA 2009, New York, NY, USA, pp. 62–71. Association for Computing Machinery, December 2009. https://doi.org/10.1145/1791194.1791203

46. Sousa, M., Rodríguez, C., D'Silva, V., Kroening, D.: Abstract interpretation with unfoldings. In: Majumdar, R., Kunčak, V. (eds.) CAV 2017. LNCS, vol. 10427, pp. 197–216. Springer, Cham (2017). https://doi.org/10.1007/978-3-319-63390-9_11

47. Thomson, P., Donaldson, A.F., Betts, A.: Concurrency testing using controlled schedulers: an empirical study. ACM Trans. Parallel Comput. **2**(4), 23:1–23:37 (2016). https://doi.org/10.1145/2858651

48. Wachter, B., Kroening, D., Ouaknine, J.: Verifying multi-threaded software with impact. In: 2013 Formal Methods in Computer-Aided Design, pp. 210–217, October 2013. https://doi.org/10.1109/FMCAD.2013.6679412

49. Yin, L., Dong, W., Liu, W., Li, Y., Wang, J.: YOGAR-CBMC: CBMC with scheduling constraint based abstraction refinement. In: Beyer, D., Huisman, M. (eds.) TACAS 2018. LNCS, vol. 10806, pp. 422–426. Springer, Cham (2018). https://doi.org/10.1007/978-3-319-89963-3_25

50. Yu, J., Narayanasamy, S., Pereira, C., Pokam, G.: Maple: a coverage-driven testing tool for multithreaded programs. In: Proceedings of the 27th Annual ACM SIGPLAN Conference on Object-Oriented Programming, Systems, Languages, and Applications, OOPSLA 2012, Part of SPLASH 2012, OOPSLA 2012, Tucson, Arizona, USA, pp. 485–502. Association for Computing Machinery, October 2012. https://doi.org/10.1145/2384616.2384651

Hardware Verification and Decision Procedures

fault: A Python Embedded Domain-Specific Language for Metaprogramming Portable Hardware Verification Components

Lenny Truong[✉], Steven Herbst,
Rajsekhar Setaluri, Makai Mann, Ross Daly,
Keyi Zhang, Caleb Donovick, Daniel Stanley,
Mark Horowitz, Clark Barrett, and Pat Hanrahan

Stanford University, Stanford, CA 94305, USA
lenny@stanford.edu

Abstract. While hardware generators have drastically improved design productivity, they have introduced new challenges for the task of verification. To effectively cover the functionality of a sophisticated generator, verification engineers require tools that provide the flexibility of metaprogramming. However, flexibility alone is not enough; components must also be portable in order to encourage the proliferation of verification libraries as well as enable new methodologies. This paper introduces **fault**, a Python embedded hardware verification language that aims to empower design teams to realize the full potential of generators.

1 Introduction

The new golden age of computer architecture relies on advances in the design and implementation of computer-aided design (CAD) tools that enhance productivity [11,21]. While hardware generators have become much more powerful in recent years, the capabilities of verification tools have not improved at the same pace [12]. This paper introduces **fault**,[1] a domain-specific language (DSL) that aims to enable the construction of flexible and portable verification components, thus helping to realize the full potential of hardware generators.

Using flexible hardware generators [1,16] drastically improves the productivity of the hardware design process, but simultaneously increases verification cost. A *generator* is a program that consumes a set of parameters and produces a hardware module. The scope of the verification task grows with the capabilities of the generator, since more sophisticated generators can produce hardware with varying interfaces and behavior. To reduce the cost of attaining functional coverage of a generator, verification components must be as flexible as their design

---

[1] https://github.com/leonardt/fault.

© The Author(s) 2020
S. K. Lahiri and C. Wang (Eds.): CAV 2020, LNCS 12224, pp. 403–414, 2020.
https://doi.org/10.1007/978-3-030-53288-8_19

counterparts. To achieve flexibility, hardware verification languages must provide the metaprogramming facilities found in hardware construction languages [1].

However, flexibility alone is not enough to match the power of generators; verification tools must also enable the construction of portable components. Generators facilitate the development of hardware libraries and promote the integration of components from external sources. Underlying the utility of these libraries is the ability for components to be reused in a diverse set of environments. The dominance of commercial hardware verification tools with strict licensing requirements presents a challenge in the development of portable verification components. To encourage the proliferation of verification libraries, hardware verification languages must design for portability across verification tools. Design for portability will also promote innovation in tools by simplifying the adoption of new technologies, as well as enable new verification methodologies based on unified interfaces to multiple technologies.

This paper presents **fault**, a domain-specific language (DSL) embedded in Python designed to enable the flexible construction of portable verification components. As an embedded DSL, **fault** users can employ all of Python's rich metaprogramming capabilities in the description of verification components. Integration with **magma** [15], a hardware construction language embedded in Python, is an essential feature of **fault** that enables full introspection of the hardware circuit under test. By using a staged metaprogramming architecture, **fault** verification components are portable across a wide variety of open-source and commercial verification tools. A key benefit of this architecture is the ability to provide a unified interface to constrained random and formal verification, enabling engineers to reuse the same component in simulation and model checking environments. **fault** is actively used by academic and industrial teams to verify digital, mixed-signal, and analog designs for use in research and production chips. This paper demonstrates **fault**'s capabilities by evaluating the runtime performance of different tools on a variety of applications ranging in complexity from unit tests of a single module to integration tests of a complex design. These experiments leverage **fault**'s portability by reusing the same source input across separate trials for each target tool.

2   Design

We had three goals in designing **fault**: enable the construction of flexible test components through metaprogramming, provide portable abstractions that allow test component reuse across multiple target environments, and support direct integration with standard programming language features. The ability to metaprogram test components is a vital requirement for scaling verification efforts to cover the space of functionality utilized by hardware generators. Portability widens the target audience of a reusable component and enhances a design team's productivity by enabling simple migration to different technologies. Integration with a programming language enables design teams to leverage standard software patterns for reuse as well as feature-rich test automation frameworks.

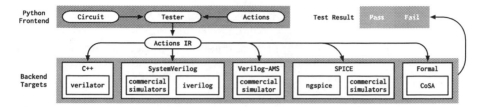

Fig. 1. Architectural overview of the **fault** testing system. In a Python program, the user constructs a `Tester` object with a **magma** `Circuit` and records a sequence of test `Actions`. The compiler uses the action sequence as an intermediate representation (IR). Backend targets lower the actions IR into a format compatible with the corresponding tool and provide an API to run the test and report the results.

Figure 1 provides an overview of the system architecture. **fault** is a DSL embedded in Python, a prolific dynamic language with rich support for metaprogramming and a large ecosystem of libraries. **fault** is designed to work with **magma** [15], a Python embedded hardware construction language which represents circuits as introspectable Python objects containing ports, connections, and instances of other circuits. While **fault** and **magma** separate the concerns of design and verification into separate DSLs, they are embedded in the same host language for simple interoperability. This multi-language design avoids the complexity of specifying and implementing a single general purpose language without sacrificing the benefits of tightly integrating design and verification code.

To construct **fault** test components, the user first instantiates a `Tester` object with a **magma** circuit as an argument. The user then records a sequence of test actions using an API provided by the `Tester` class. Here is an example of constructing a test for a 16-bit `Add` circuit:

```
tester = Tester(Add16)
tester.poke(Add16.in0, 3)
tester.poke(Add16.in1, 2)
tester.eval()
tester.expect(Add16.out, 5)
```

The `poke` action (method) sets an input value, the `eval` action triggers evaluation of the circuit (the effects of `poke` actions are not propagated until an `eval` action occurs), and the `expect` action asserts the value of an output. Attributes of the `Add16` object refer to circuit ports by name.

fault's design is based on the concept of staged metaprogramming [20]; the user writes a program that constructs another program to be executed in a subsequent stage. In **fault**, the first stage executes Python code to construct a test specification; the second stage invokes a target runtime that executes this specification. To run the test for the 16-bit `Add`, the user simply calls a method and provides the desired target:

```
tester.compile_and_run("verilator")
tester.compile_and_run("system-verilog", simulator="iverilog")
```

By applying staged metaprogramming, **fault** allows the user to leverage the full capabilities of the Python host language in the programmatic construction of test components. For example, a test can use a native `for` loop to construct a sequence of actions using the built-in random number library and integer type:

```
for _ in range(32):
    N = (1 << 16) - 1
    in0, in1 = random.randint(0, N), random.randint(0, N)
    tester.poke(Add16.in0, in0)
    tester.poke(Add16.in1, in1)
    tester.eval()
    tester.expect(Add16.out, (in0 + in1) & N)
```

Python `for` loops are executed during the first stage of computation and are effectively "unrolled" into a flat sequence of actions. Other control structures such as `while` loops, `if` statements, and function calls are handled similarly.

Python's object introspection capabilities greatly enhance the flexibility of **fault** tests. For example, the core logic of the above test can be generalized to support an arbitrary width `Add` circuit by inspecting the interface:

```
# compute max value based on port width (length)
N = (1 << len(Add.in0)) - 1
in0, in1 = random.randint(0, N), random.randint(0, N)
tester.poke(Add.in0, in0)
tester.poke(Add.in1, in1)
tester.eval()
tester.expect(Add.out, (in0 + in1) & N)
```

This ability to metaprogram components as a function of the design under test is an essential aspect of **fault**'s design. It allows the construction of generic components that can be reused across designs with varying interfaces and behavior.

fault's embedding in Python's class system provides an opportunity for reuse through inheritance. For example, a design team could subclass the generic `Tester` class and add a new method to perform an asynchronous reset sequence:

```
class ResetTester(Tester):
    def __init__(self, circuit, clock, reset_port):
        super().__init__(self, circuit, clock)
        self.reset_port = reset_port

    def reset(self):
        # asynchronous reset, negative edge
        self.poke(self.reset_port, 1)
        self.eval()
        self.poke(self.reset_port, 0)
        self.eval()
        self.poke(self.reset_port, 1)
        self.eval()
```

Combining inheritance with introspection, we can augment the the `ResetTester` to automatically discover the reset port by inspecting port types:

```
class AutoResetTester(ResetTester):
    def __init__(self, circuit, clock):
        # iterate over interface to find reset (assumes exactly one)
        for port in circuit.interface.ports.values():
            if isinstance(port, AsyncResetN):
                reset_port = port
        super().__init__(self, circuit, clock, reset_port)
```

2.1   Frontend: Tester API

fault's Python embedding is implemented by the `Tester` class which provides
various interfaces for recording test actions as well as methods for compiling and
running tests using a specific target. By using Python's class system to perform a
shallow embedding [5], **fault** avoids the complexity of processing abstract syntax
trees and simply uses Python's standard execution to construct test components.
As a result, programming in **fault** is much like programming with a standard
Python library. This design choice reduces the overhead of learning the DSL
and simplifies aspects of implementation such as error messages, but comes at
the cost of limited capabilities for describing control flow. The **fault** frontend
described in this paper focuses on implementation simplicity, but the system is
designed to be easily extended with new frontends using alternative embeddings.

Action Methods. The `Tester` class provides a low-level interface for
recording actions using methods. The basic action methods are `poke` (set
a port to a value), `expect` (assert a port equals a value), `step` (invert
the value of the clock), `peek` (read the value of a port), and `eval` (evaluate the circuit). The `peek` method returns an object containing a reference to the value of a circuit port in the current simulation state.
Using logical and arithmetic operators, the user can construct expressions
with this object and pass the result to other actions. For example, to
expect that the value of the port `O0` is equal to the inverse of the
value of port `O1`, the user would write `tester.expect(circuit.O0,`
`~tester.peek(circuit.O1))`. The `Tester` provides a `print` action to
display simulation runtime information included the peeked values.

Metaprogramming Control Flow. Notably absent from the basic method
interface described above are control flow abstractions. As noted before, standard
Python control structures such as loops and `if` statements are executed in the
first stage of computation as part of the metaprogram. However, there are cases
where the user intends to preserve the control structure in the generated code,
such as long-running loops that should not be unrolled at compile time or loops
that are conditioned on dynamic values from the circuit state. For example,
consider a `while` loop that executes until it receives a ready signal:

```
# Construct while loop conditioned on circuit.ready.
loop = tester._while(tester.peek(circuit.ready))
loop.expect(circuit.ready, 0) # executes inside loop
loop.step(2)                   # executes inside loop
# Check final state after loop has exited
tester.expect(circuit.count, expected_cycle_count)
```

This logic could not be encoded in the metaprogram, because the metaprogram is evaluated before the test is run, and thus does not know anything about the runtime state of the circuit. To capture this dynamic control flow, the `Tester` provides methods for inserting if-else statements, for loops, and while loops. Each of these methods returns a new instance of the current `Tester` object which provides the same API, allowing the user to record actions corresponding to the body of the control construct. The `Tester` class provides convenience functions for using these control structures to generate common patterns, such as wait_on, wait_until_low, and wait_until_posedge.

Attribute Interface. While the low-level method interface is useful for writing complex metaprograms, simple components are rather verbose to construct. To simplify the handling of basic actions like poke and peek, the `Tester` object exposes an interface for referring to circuit ports and internal signals using Python's object attribute syntax. For example, to poke the input port I of a circuit with value 1, one would write `tester.circuit.I = 1`. This interface supports referring to internal signals using a hierarchical syntax. For example, referring to port Q of an instance ff can be done with `tester.circuit.ff.Q`.

Assume/Guarantee. The `Tester` object provides methods for specifying assumptions and guarantees that are abstracted over constrained random and formal model checking runtime environments. An *assumption* is a constraint on input values, and a *guarantee* is an assertion on output values. Assumptions and guarantees are specified using Python lambda functions that return symbolic expressions referring to the input and output and ports of a circuit. For example, the guarantee lambda a, b, c: (c >= a) and (c >= b) states that the output c is always greater than or equal to the inputs a and b. Here is an example of verifying a simple ALU using the assume/guarantee interface:

```
# Configuration sequence for opcode register
tester.circuit.opcode_en = 1
tester.circuit.opcode = 0 # opcode for add (+)
tester.step(2)
tester.circuit.opcode_en = 0
tester.step(2)
# Verify add does not overflow
tester.circuit.a.assume(lambda a: a < BitVector[16](32768))
tester.circuit.b.assume(lambda b: b < BitVector[16](32768))
tester.circuit.c.guarantee(
    lambda a, b, c: (c >= a) and (c >= b)
)
```

Note that this example demonstrates the use of poke and step to initialize circuits not only for constrained random testing, but also for formal verification.

2.2 Actions IR

In using the `Tester` API, users construct a sequence of `Action` objects that are used as an intermediate representation (IR) for the compiler. Basic port action objects, such as `Poke` and `Expect`, simply store references to ports and values. Control flow action objects, such as `While` and `If`, contain sub-sequences of actions, resulting in a hierarchical data-structure similar to an abstract syntax tree. This view of the compiler internals reveals that the metaphor of *recording actions* is really an abstraction over the construction of program fragments.

2.3   Backend Targets

fault supports a variety of open-source and commercial backend targets for running tests. A target is responsible for consuming an action sequence, compiling it into a format compatible with the target runtime, and providing an API for invoking the runtime. Targets must also report the result of the test either by reading the exit code of running the process or processing the test output.

Verilog Simulation Targets. The **fault** compiler includes support for the open-source Verilog simulators **verilator** [17] and **iverilog** [22], plus three commercial simulators. To compile **fault** programs to a **verilator** test bench, the backend lowers the action sequence into a C++ program that interacts with the software simulation object produced by the **verilator** compiler. For **iverilog** and the commercial simulators, the backend lowers the action sequence into a SystemVerilog test bench that interacts with the test circuit through an `initial` block inside the top-level module. One useful aspect of the SystemVerilog backend is its handling of variations in the feature support of target simulators. For example, the commercial simulators use different commands for enabling waveform tracing and **iverilog** uses a non-standard API for interacting with files. Constrained random inputs are generated using rejection or SMT [9] sampling.

CoSA. The CoreIR Symbolic Analyzer (CoSA) is a solver-agnostic SMT-based hardware model checker [13]. **fault**'s CoSA target relies on **magma**'s ability to compile Python circuit descriptions to CoreIR [8], a hardware intermediate representation. CoreIR's formal semantics are based on finite-state machines and the SMT theory of fixed-size bitvectors [3]. **fault** action sequences are lowered into CoSA's custom explicit transition system format (ETS) and combined with the CoreIR representation of the circuit to produce a model. CoSA allows the user to specify assumptions and properties, providing a straightforward lowering of **fault** assumptions and guarantees.

SPICE. In addition to being able to test designs with Verilog simulators, **fault** supports analog and mixed-signal simulators. Compared to the traditional approach of maintaining separate implementations for digital and analog tests, this is a significantly easier way to write tests for mixed-signal circuits. Basic actions such as `poke` and `expect` are supported in the SPICE simulation mode, but they are implemented quite differently than they are in Verilog-based tests. Rather than emitting a sequential list of actions in an `initial` block, **fault**

compiles `poke` actions into piecewise-linear (PWL) waveforms. Other actions, such as `expect`, are implemented by post-processing the simulation data.

Verilog-AMS. For designs containing a mixture of SPICE and Verilog blocks, **fault** supports testing with a Verilog-AMS simulator. This mode is more similar to running SystemVerilog-based tests than SPICE-based tests. In particular, the test bench is implemented using a top-level SystemVerilog module, meaning that a wide range of actions are supported including loops and conditionals. This is a key benefit of using a Verilog-AMS simulator as opposed to a SPICE simulator.

3   Evaluation

To demonstrate **fault**'s capabilities, we evaluate the runtime performance of four different testing tasks from the domain of hardware verification. Each task highlights the utility of **fault**'s portability by reusing the same source input across separate trials of different targets. Due to licensing restrictions, we omit the name of the commercial simulators and replace them with a generic name. The code to reproduce these experiments is available in the artifact.[2] Each experiment involves at least one open-source simulator, but reproducing all the results requires access to commercial simulators.

CGRA Processing Element Unit Tests. To demonstrate the capability of **fault** as a tool for writing portable tests for digital verification, Fig. 2 reports the runtime performance of a subset of the **lassen** test suite. **lassen** [19] is an open-source implementation of a CGRA processing element that contains a large suite of unit tests using **fault**. Interestingly, we see comparable performance between **verilator** and **commercial simulator 1**, while **commercial simulator 2** is consistently ~5x slower than the others. One important property of the **lassen** test suite is that it generates a new test bench for each operation and input/output pair. This stresses a simulator's ability to efficiently handle incremental changes, since each invocation involves a new top-level test bench file, but an unchanged design under test.

Test	verilator	commercial sim 1	commercial sim 2
test_unsigned_binary	94.483	88.700	519.079
test_smult	31.439	28.668	170.115
test_fp_binary_op	104.117	91.878	571.759
test_stall	10.424	9.629	56.458

Fig. 2. Runtime (s) for unit tests of a CGRA processing element collected with a VM running on an Intel(R) Xeon(R) Silver 4214 CPU @ 2.20 GHz with 256 GB of RAM.

---

[2] https://github.com/leonardt/fault_artifact/blob/master/README.md.

SRAM Array. To demonstrate the capability of **fault** as a tool for writing portable tests for analog and mixed-signal verification, we used **OpenRAM** to generate a 16x16 SRAM and then ran a randomized readback test of the design with SPICE, Verilog-AMS, and SystemVerilog simulators. **OpenRAM** [10] is an open-source memory compiler that produces a SPICE netlist and Verilog model.

The results shown in Fig. 3a reveal two interesting trends. First, as expected, SPICE simulations of the array were significantly slower than Verilog simulations (100-1000x). Since **fault** allows the user to prototype tests with fast Verilog simulations, and then seamlessly switch to SPICE for signoff verification, our tool may reduce the latency in developing mixed-signal tests by orders of magnitude. Second, even for simulations of the same type, there was significant variation in the runtime of different simulators. SPICE simulation time varied by about 2x, while Verilog simulation time varied by about 10x. One of the advantages of using **fault** is that it is easy to switch between simulators to find the one that works best for a particular scenario.

Target	Simulator	Runtime (s)		Lines of Code (LoC)	
spice	ngspice	117.660		**fault**	136
spice	comm sim 1	199.868		Handwritten	
spice	comm sim 2	98.043		SPICE	223
system-verilog	iverilog	0.238			
system-verilog	comm sim 1	1.081		Handwritten	
system-verilog	comm sim 2	2.807		SystemVerilog	189
verilog-ams	comm sim 1	228.405		and Verilog-AMS	

(a) Runtime using a VM on an Intel(R) Xeon(R) CPU E5-2680 v4 @ 2.40GHz with 64GB of RAM.

(b) LoC for **fault** and language-specific implementations of the test.

Fig. 3. Results for OpenRAM 16x16 SRAM randomized readback test.

We also looked at the amount of human effort required to use **fault** to implement this test as compared to the traditional approach of writing separate testbenches for each simulation language. Since "human effort" is subjective, we used lines of code as a rough metric, as measured from handwritten implementations of the same test in SystemVerilog, Verilog-AMS, and SPICE. Figure 3b shows the results of this experiment: the **fault**-based approach used 136 LoC as compared to 412 LoC for the traditional approach, a reduction of 3.02x.

CGRA Integration Test Bench. To observe how **fault** scales to more complex testing tasks, we report numbers for an integration test of the Stanford Garnet CGRA [18]. This test generates an instance of the CGRA chip, runs a simulation that programs the chip for an image processing application, streams the input image data onto the chip, and streams the output image data to a file. The output is compared to a reference software model. Running the test took 232 min with the **verilator** target, 185 min with **commercial simulator 1**, and 221 min with **commercial simulator 2**. Leveraging the portability of **fault**-based tests could save up to 47 min in testing time. These results were collected using the same machine as the SRAM experiment (see Fig. 3a).

Unified Constrained Random and Formal. To demonstrate the utility of the assume/guarantee interface as a unified abstraction for constrained random and formal verification, we compared the runtime performance of using a constrained random target versus a formal model checker to verify the simple ALU property shown in Sect. 2.1. The first test evaluated the runtime performance of verifying correctness of the property on 100 constrained random inputs versus using a formal model checker. The formal model checker provided a complete proof of correctness using interpolation-based model checking [14] in 1.613 s, while constrained random verified 100 samples in 2.269 s (rejection sampling) and 2.799 s (SMT sampling). The second test injected a bug into the ALU by swapping the opcodes for addition and subtraction. The model checker found a counterexample in 1.154 s with bounded model checking [4], while constrained random failed in 2.947 s (rejection sampling) and 1.230 s (SMT sampling). In both cases the model checker was at least as fast as the constrained random equivalent while providing better coverage in the case of no bug. These results were collected using a MacBook Pro (13-in 2017, 4 Thunderbolt, macOS 10.15.2), with a 3.5 GHz Dual-Core Intel i7 CPU, and 16 GB RAM.

4   Related Work

Prior work has leveraged using a generic API to Verilog simulators to build portability into testing infrastructures. The **ChiselTest** library [2] and **cocotb** [7] provide this capability for Scala and Python respectively. Using a generic API offers many of the same advantages with regards to test portability, simplicity, and automation, but the lack of multi-stage execution limits the application to more diverse backend targets such as SPICE simulations and formal model checkers. However, because these libraries interact with the simulator directly, they do allow user code to immediately respond to the simulator state, enabling interactive debugging through the host language. **cocotb** also presents a coroutine abstraction that naturally models the concurrency found in hardware simulation. Future work could investigate using cocotb as a runtime target for **fault**'s frontend, enabling a similar concurrent, interactive style of testing. Another interesting avenue of work would be to extend **fault**'s backend targets to support lowering **cocotb**'s coroutine abstraction.

5   Conclusion

The ethos of **fault** is to enable the construction of flexible, portable test components that are simple to integrate and scale for testing complex applications.

The ability to metaprogram test components is essential for enabling verification teams to match the productivity of design teams using generators. **fault**'s portability enables teams to easily transition to different tools for different use cases, and enables the proliferation of reusable verification libraries that are applicable in a diverse set of tooling environments.

While **fault** has already demonstrated utility to design teams in academia and industry, there remains a bright future filled with opportunity to improve the system. Extending the assume/guarantee interface to support temporal properties/constraints and leverage compositional reasoning [6] is essential for scaling the approach to more complex systems. Adding concurrent programming abstractions such as coroutines are essential for capturing the common patterns used in the testing of parallel hardware. Using a deep embedding architecture could significantly improve the performance of generating **fault** test benches.

Funding. The authors would like to thank the DARPA DSSoC (FA8650-18-2-7861) and POSH (FA8650-18-2-7854) programs, the Stanford AHA and SystemX affiliates, Intel's Agile ISTC, the Hertz Foundation Fellowship, and the Stanford Graduate Fellowship for supporting this work.

References

1. Bachrach, J., et al.: Chisel: constructing hardware in a scala embedded language. In: 2012 DAC Design Automation Conference, pp. 1212–1221, June 2012. https://doi.org/10.1145/2228360.2228584
2. ucb bar: chisel-testers2 (2019). https://github.com/ucb-bar/chisel-testers2
3. Barrett, C., Fontaine, P., Tinelli, C.: The Satisfiability Modulo Theories Library (SMT-LIB). www.SMT-LIB.org(2016)
4. Biere, A., Cimatti, A., Clarke, E., Zhu, Y.: Symbolic model checking without BDDs. In: Cleaveland, W.R. (ed.) TACAS 1999. LNCS, vol. 1579, pp. 193–207. Springer, Heidelberg (1999). https://doi.org/10.1007/3-540-49059-0_14
5. Boulton, R.J., Gordon, A., Gordon, M.J.C., Harrison, J., Herbert, J., Tassel, J.V.: Experience with embedding hardware description languages in HOL. In: Proceedings of the IFIP TC10/WG 10.2 International Conference on Theorem Provers in Circuit Design: Theory, Practice and Experience, pp. 129–156. North-Holland Publishing Co., NLD (1992)
6. Clarke, E.M., Long, D.E., McMillan, K.L.: Compositional model checking. In: LICS, pp. 353–362. IEEE Computer Society (1989)
7. cocotb: cocotb (2019). https://github.com/cocotb/cocotb
8. Daly, R.: CoreIR: A simple LLVM-style hardware compiler (2017). https://github.com/rdaly525/coreir
9. Dutra, R., Bachrach, J., Sen, K.: SMTsampler: efficient stimulus generation from complex SMT constraints. In: 2018 IEEE/ACM International Conference on Computer-Aided Design (ICCAD), pp. 1–8. IEEE (2018)
10. Guthaus, M.R., Stine, J.E., Ataei, S., Chen, B., Wu, B., Sarwar, M.: OpenRAM: an open-source memory compiler. In: 2016 IEEE/ACM International Conference on Computer-Aided Design (ICCAD), pp. 1–6, November 2016. https://doi.org/10.1145/2966986.2980098

11. Hennessy, J.L., Patterson, D.A.: A new golden age for computer architecture. Commun. ACM **62**(2), 48–60 (2019). https://doi.org/10.1145/3282307
12. Lockhart, D., et al.: Experiences building edge TPU with chisel. In: 2018 Chisel Community Conference (CCC) (2018)
13. Mattarei, C., Mann, M., Barrett, C., Daly, R.G., Huff, D., Hanrahan, P.: CoSA: integrated verification for agile hardware design. In: 2018 Formal Methods in Computer Aided Design (FMCAD), pp. 1–5, October 2018. https://doi.org/10.23919/FMCAD.2018.8603014
14. McMillan, K.L.: Interpolation and SAT-based model checking. In: Hunt, W.A., Somenzi, F. (eds.) CAV 2003. LNCS, vol. 2725, pp. 1–13. Springer, Heidelberg (2003). https://doi.org/10.1007/978-3-540-45069-6_1
15. phanrahan: magma (2019). https://github.com/phanrahan/magma (2019)
16. Shacham, O., Azizi, O., Wachs, M., Richardson, S., Horowitz, M.: Rethinking digital design: why design must change. IEEE Micro **30**(6), 9–24 (2010). https://doi.org/10.1109/MM.2010.81
17. Snyder, W.: Verilator and systemperl. In: North American SystemC Users' Group, Design Automation Conference (2004)
18. StanfordAHA: Garnetflow (2019). https://github.com/StanfordAHA/GarnetFlow
19. StanfordAHA: lassen (2019). https://github.com/StanfordAHA/lassen
20. Taha, W., Sheard, T.: MetaML and multi-stage programming with explicit annotations. Theor. Comput. Sci. **248**(1–2), 211–242 (2000)
21. Truong, L., Hanrahan, P.: A golden age of hardware description languages: applying programming language techniques to improve design productivity. In: Lerner, B.S., Bodík, R., Krishnamurthi, S. (eds.) 3rd Summit on Advances in Programming Languages, SNAPL 2019, 16–17 May 2019, Providence, RI, USA. LIPIcs, vol. 136, pp. 7:1–7:21. Schloss Dagstuhl - Leibniz-Zentrum fuer Informatik (2019). https://doi.org/10.4230/LIPIcs.SNAPL.2019.7
22. Williams, S.: Icarus verilog (2006). http://iverilog.icarus.com

Nonlinear Craig Interpolant Generation

Ting Gan[1], Bican Xia[2(✉)], Bai Xue[3,4], Naijun Zhan[3,4(✉)],
and Liyun Dai[5]

[1] School of Computer Science, Wuhan University, Wuhan, China
ganting@whu.edu.cn
[2] LMAM, School of Mathematical Sciences, Peking University, Beijing, China
xbc@math.pku.edu.cn
[3] State Key Laboratory of Computer Science, Institute of Software, CAS,
Beijing, China
{xuebai,znj}@ios.ac.cn
[4] University of Chinese Academy of Sciences, Beijing, China
[5] RISE, School of Computer and Information Science, Southwest University,
Chongqing, China
dailiyun@swu.edu.cn

Abstract. Craig interpolant generation for non-linear theory and its combination with other theories are still in infancy, although interpolation-based techniques have become popular in the verification of programs and hybrid systems where non-linear expressions are very common. In this paper, we first prove that a polynomial interpolant of the form $h(\mathbf{x}) > 0$ exists for two mutually contradictory polynomial formulas $\phi(\mathbf{x}, \mathbf{y})$ and $\psi(\mathbf{x}, \mathbf{z})$, with the form $f_1 \geq 0 \wedge \cdots \wedge f_n \geq 0$, where f_i are polynomials in $\mathbf{x}, \mathbf{y}$ or $\mathbf{x}, \mathbf{z}$, and the quadratic module generated by f_i is Archimedean. Then, we show that synthesizing such interpolant can be reduced to solving a semi-definite programming problem (SDP). In addition, we propose a verification approach to assure the validity of the synthesized interpolant and consequently avoid the unsoundness caused by numerical error in SDP solving. Besides, we discuss how to generalize our approach to general semi-algebraic formulas. Finally, as an application, we demonstrate how to apply our approach to invariant generation in program verification.

Keywords: Craig interpolant · Archimedean condition · Semi-definite programming · Program verification · Sum of squares

1 Introduction

Interpolation-based techniques have become popular in recent years because of their inherently modular and local reasoning, which can scale up existing formal verification techniques like theorem proving, model-checking, abstract interpretation, and so on, while the scalability is the bottleneck of these techniques. The study of interpolation was pioneered by Krajíček [20] and Pudlák [30] in connection with theorem proving, by McMillan in connection with model-checking

© The Author(s) 2020
S. K. Lahiri and C. Wang (Eds.): CAV 2020, LNCS 12224, pp. 415–438, 2020.
https://doi.org/10.1007/978-3-030-53288-8_20

[25], by Graf and Saïdi [14], Henzinger *et al.* [16] and McMillan [26] in connection with abstraction like CEGAR, by Wang *et al.* [17] in connection with machine-learning based program verification.

Craig interpolant generation plays a central role in interpolation-based techniques, and therefore has drawn increasing attention. In the literature, there are various efficient algorithms proposed for automatically synthesizing interpolants for decidable fragments of first-order logic, linear arithmetic, array logic, equality logic with uninterpreted functions (EUF), etc., and their combinations, and their use in verification, e.g., [6,16,18,19,26,27,33,33,37] and the references therein. Additionally, how to compare the strength of different interpolants is investigated in [9]. However, interpolant generation for non-linear theory and its combination with the aforementioned theories is still in infancy, although non-linear polynomials inequalities are quite common in safety-critical software and embedded systems [38,39].

In [7], Dai *et al.* had a first try and gave an algorithm for generating interpolants for conjunctions of mutually contradictory nonlinear polynomial inequalities based on the existence of a witness guaranteed by Stengle's Positivstellensatz [36], which is computable using semi-definite programming (SDP). Their algorithm is incomplete in general but if all variables are bounded (called Archimedean condition), then it becomes complete. A major limitation of their work is that two mutually contradictory formulas ϕ and ψ must have the same set of variables. In [10], Gan *et al.* proposed an algorithm to generate interpolants for quadratic polynomial inequalities. The basic idea is based on the insight that for analyzing the solution space of concave quadratic polynomial inequalities, it suffices to linearize them by proving a generalization of Motzkin's transposition theorem for concave quadratic polynomial inequalities. Moreover, they also discussed how to generate interpolants for the combination of the theory of quadratic concave polynomial inequalities and *EUF* based on the hierarchical calculus proposed in [34] and used in [33]. Obviously, *quadratic concave* polynomial inequalities is a very restrictive class of polynomial formulas, although most of existing abstract domains fall within it as argued in [10]. Meanwhile, in [13], Gao and Zufferey presented an approach to extract interpolants for non-linear formulas possibly containing transcendental functions and differential equations from proofs of unsatisfiability generated by δ-decision procedure [12] based on interval constraint propagation (ICP) [1] by transforming proof traces from δ-complete decision procedures into interpolants that consist of Boolean combinations of linear constraints. Thus, their approach can only find the interpolants between two formulas whenever their conjunction is not δ-satisfiable. Similar idea was also reported in [21]. In [5], Chen *et al.* proposed an approach for synthesizing non-linear interpolants based on counterexample-guided and machine-learning, but it relies on quantifier elimination in order to guarantee the completeness and convergence, which gives rise to the low efficiency of their approach theoretically. In [35], Srikanth *et al.* presented an approach called *CAMPY* to exploit non-linear interpolant generation, which is achieved by abstracting non-linear formulas (possibly with non-polynomial expressions) to the theory of linear arithmetic with uninterpreted functions, i.e., EUFLIA, to prove and/or disprove if a given program satisfies a given property, that may contain nonlinear expressions.

Example 1. In order to compare the approach proposed in this paper and the ones aforementioned, consider

$$\phi = -2xy^2 + x^2 - 3xz - y^2 - yz + z^2 - 1 \geq 0 \wedge 100 - x^2 - y^2 \geq 0 \wedge$$

$$x^2z^2 + y^2z^2 - x^2 - y^2 + \frac{1}{6}(x^4 + 2x^2y^2 + y^4) - \frac{1}{120}(x^6 + y^6) - 4 \leq 0;$$

$$\psi = 4(x - y)^4 + (x + y)^2 + w^2 - 133.097 \leq 0 \wedge 100(x + y)^2 - w^2(x - y)^4 - 3000 \geq 0.$$

It can be checked that $\phi \wedge \psi \models \bot$.

Obviously, synthesizing interpolants for ϕ and ψ in this example is beyond the ability of the above approaches reported in [7,10]. Using the method in [13] implemented in dReal3 it would return "SAT" with $\delta = 0.001$, i.e., $\phi \wedge \psi$ is δ-satisfiable, and hence it cannot synthesize any interpolant using [12]'s approach with any precision greater than 0.001^{1}. While, using our method, an interpolant $h > 0$ with degree 10 can be found as shown in Fig. 1^{2}. Additionally, using the symbolic procedure REDUCE, it can be proved that $h > 0$ is indeed an interpolant of ϕ and ψ.

In this paper, we investigate this issue and consider how to synthesize an interpolant for two polynomial formulas $\phi(\mathbf{x}, \mathbf{y})$ and $\psi(\mathbf{x}, \mathbf{z})$ with $\phi(\mathbf{x}, \mathbf{y}) \wedge \psi(\mathbf{x}, \mathbf{z}) \models \bot$, where

$$\phi(\mathbf{x}, \mathbf{y}) : f_1(\mathbf{x}, \mathbf{y}) \geq 0 \wedge \cdots \wedge f_m(\mathbf{x}, \mathbf{y}) \geq 0,$$
$$\psi(\mathbf{x}, \mathbf{z}) : g_1(\mathbf{x}, \mathbf{z}) \geq 0 \wedge \cdots \wedge g_n(\mathbf{x}, \mathbf{z}) \geq 0,$$

$\mathbf{x} \in \mathbb{R}^r$, $\mathbf{y} \in \mathbb{R}^s$, $\mathbf{z} \in \mathbb{R}^t$ are variable vectors, $r, s, t \in \mathbb{N}$, and $f_1, \ldots, f_m, g_1, \ldots, g_n$ are polynomials. In addition, $\mathcal{M}_{\mathbf{x},\mathbf{y}}\{f_1(\mathbf{x}, \mathbf{y}), \ldots, f_m(\mathbf{x}, \mathbf{y})\}$ and $\mathcal{M}_{\mathbf{x},\mathbf{z}}\{g_1(\mathbf{x}, \mathbf{z}), \ldots, g_n(\mathbf{x}, \mathbf{z})\}$ are two Archimedean quadratic modules. Here we allow uncommon variables, that are not allowed in [7], and drop the constraint that polynomials must be concave and quadratic, which is assumed in [10]. The Archimedean condition amounts to that all the variables are bounded, which is reasonable in program verification, as only bounded numbers can be represented in computer in practice. We first prove that there exists a polynomial

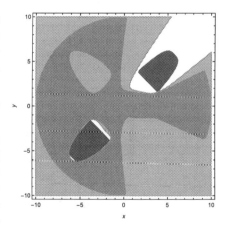

Fig. 1. Example 1. (Green region: the projection of $\phi(x, y, z)$ onto x and y; red region: the projection of $\psi(x, y, w)$ onto x and y; gray region plus the green region: the synthesized interpolant $\{(x, y) \mid h(x, y) > 0\}$.) (Color figure online)

---

[1] Alternatively, if we try the formula with the latest version of dReal4, it does not produce any output after 20 h.

[2] The mathematical representation of h is given in the full version [11].

$h(\mathbf{x})$ such that $h(\mathbf{x}) = 0$ separates the state space of $\mathbf{x}$ defined by $\phi(\mathbf{x}, \mathbf{y})$ from the one defined by $\psi(\mathbf{x}, \mathbf{z})$ theoretically, and then propose an algorithm to compute such $h(\mathbf{x})$ based on SDP. Furthermore, we propose a verification approach to assure the validity of the synthesized interpolant and consequently avoid the unsoundness caused by numerical error in SDP solving. Finally, we also discuss how to extend our results to general semi-algebraic constraints.

Another contribution of this paper is that as an application, we illustrate how to apply our approach to invariant generation in program verification by revising Lin *et al.*'s framework proposed in [22] for invariant generation based on *weakest precondition, strongest postcondition* and *interpolation* by allowing to generate nonlinear invariants.

The paper is organized as follows. Some preliminaries and the problem of interest are introduced in Sect. 2. Section 3 shows the existence of an interpolant for two mutually contradictory polynomial formulas only containing conjunction, and Sect. 4 presents SDP-based methods to compute it. In Sect. 5, we discuss how to avoid unsoundness caused by numerical error in SDP. Section 6 extends our approach to general polynomial formulas. Section 7 demonstrates how to apply our approach to invariant generation in program verification. We conclude this paper in Sect. 8.

2   Preliminaries

In this section, we first give a brief introduction on some notions used throughout this paper and then describe the problem of interest.

2.1   Quadratic Module

$\mathbb{N}$, $\mathbb{Q}$ and $\mathbb{R}$ are the sets of integers, rational numbers and real numbers, respectively. $\mathbb{Q}[\mathbf{x}]$ and $\mathbb{R}[\mathbf{x}]$ denotes the polynomial ring over rational numbers and real numbers in $r \geq 1$ indeterminates $\mathbf{x} : (x_1, \ldots, x_r)$. We use $\mathbb{R}[\mathbf{x}]^2 := \{p^2 \mid p \in \mathbb{R}[\mathbf{x}]\}$ for the set of squares and $\sum \mathbb{R}[\mathbf{x}]^2$ for the set of sums of squares of polynomials in $\mathbf{x}$. Vectors are denoted by boldface letters. $\bot$ and $\top$ stand for **false** and **true**, respectively.

Definition 1 (Quadratic Module [24]). *A subset $\mathcal{M}$ of $\mathbb{R}[\mathbf{x}]$ is called a quadratic module if it contains 1 and is closed under addition and multiplication with squares, i.e., $1 \in \mathcal{M}, \mathcal{M} + \mathcal{M} \subseteq \mathcal{M}$, and $p^2 \mathcal{M} \subseteq \mathcal{M}$ for all $p \in \mathbb{R}[\mathbf{x}]$.*

Let $\overline{p} := \{p_1, \ldots, p_s\}$ be a finite subset of $\mathbb{R}[\mathbf{x}]$, the quadratic module $\mathcal{M}_{\mathbf{x}}(\overline{p})$ or simply $\mathcal{M}(\overline{p})$ generated by $\overline{p}$ (i.e. the smallest quadratic module containing all $p_i s$) is $\mathcal{M}_{\mathbf{x}}(\overline{p}) = \{\sum_{i=0}^{s} \delta_i p_i \mid \delta_i \in \sum \mathbb{R}[\mathbf{x}]^2\}$, where $p_0 = 1$.

Archimedean condition plays a key role in the study of polynomial optimization.

Definition 2 (Archimedean). *Let $\mathcal{M}$ be a quadratic module of $\mathbb{R}[\mathbf{x}]$. $\mathcal{M}$ is said to be Archimedean if there exists some $a > 0$ such that $a - \sum_{i=1}^{r} x_i^2 \in \mathcal{M}$.*

2.2 Problem Description

Craig showed that given two formulas ϕ and ψ in a first-order theory $\mathcal{T}$, if $\phi \models \psi$, then there always exists an *interpolant* I over the common symbols of ϕ and ψ s.t. $\phi \models I$ and $I \models \psi$. In the verification literature, this terminology has been abused following [26], where a *reverse interpolant* (coined by Kovács and Voronkov in [19]) I over the common symbols of ϕ and ψ is defined by

Definition 3 (Interpolant). *Given two formulas ϕ and ψ in a theory $\mathcal{T}$ s.t. $\phi \wedge \psi \models_{\mathcal{T}} \perp$, a formula I is an* interpolant *of ϕ and ψ if (i) $\phi \models_{\mathcal{T}} I$; (ii) $I \wedge \psi \models \perp$; and (iii) I only contains common symbols and free variables shared by ϕ and ψ.*

Definition 4. *A basic semi-algebraic set $\{\mathbf{x} \in \mathbb{R}^n \mid \bigwedge_{i=1}^{s} p_i(\mathbf{x}) \geq 0\}$ is called a set of the* Archimedean form *if $\mathcal{M}_{\mathbf{x}}\{p_1(\mathbf{x}), \ldots, p_s(\mathbf{x})\}$ is Archimedean, where $p_i(\mathbf{x}) \in \mathbb{R}[\mathbf{x}]$, $i = 1, \ldots, s$.*

The interpolant synthesis problem of interest in this paper is given in Problem 1.

Problem 1. Let $\phi(\mathbf{x}, \mathbf{y})$ and $\psi(\mathbf{x}, \mathbf{z})$ be two polynomial formulas of the form

$$\phi(\mathbf{x}, \mathbf{y}) : f_1(\mathbf{x}, \mathbf{y}) \geq 0 \wedge \cdots \wedge f_m(\mathbf{x}, \mathbf{y}) \geq 0,$$
$$\psi(\mathbf{x}, \mathbf{z}) : g_1(\mathbf{x}, \mathbf{z}) \geq 0 \wedge \cdots \wedge g_n(\mathbf{x}, \mathbf{z}) \geq 0,$$

where, $\mathbf{x} \in \mathbb{R}^r$, $\mathbf{y} \in \mathbb{R}^s$, $\mathbf{z} \in \mathbb{R}^t$ are variable vectors, $r, s, t \in \mathbb{N}$, and $f_1, \ldots, f_m, g_1, \ldots, g_n$ are polynomials in the corresponding variables. Suppose $\phi \wedge \psi \models \perp$, and $\{(\mathbf{x}, \mathbf{y}) \mid \phi(\mathbf{x}, \mathbf{y})\}$ and $\{(\mathbf{x}, \mathbf{z}) \mid \psi(\mathbf{x}, \mathbf{z})\}$ are semi-algebraic sets of the Archimedean form. Find a polynomial $h(\mathbf{x})$ such that $h(\mathbf{x}) > 0$ is an interpolant for ϕ and ψ.

3 Existence of Interpolants

The basic idea and steps of proving the existence of interpolants are as follows: Because an interpolant of ϕ and ψ contains only the common symbols in ϕ and ψ, it is natural to consider the projections of the sets defined by ϕ and ψ on $\mathbf{x}$, i.e. $P_{\mathbf{x}}(\phi(\mathbf{x}, \mathbf{y})) \hat{=} \{\mathbf{x} \mid \exists \mathbf{y}. \phi(\mathbf{x}, \mathbf{y})\}$ and $P_{\mathbf{x}}(\psi(\mathbf{x}, \mathbf{z})) \hat{=} \{\mathbf{x} \mid \exists \mathbf{z}. \psi(\mathbf{x}, \mathbf{z})\}$, which are obviously disjoint. We therefore prove that, if $h(\mathbf{x}) = 0$ separates $P_{\mathbf{x}}(\phi(\mathbf{x}, \mathbf{y}))$ and $P_{\mathbf{x}}(\psi(\mathbf{x}, \mathbf{z}))$, then $h(\mathbf{x})$ solves Problem 1 (see Proposition 1). Thus, we only need to prove the existence of such $h(\mathbf{x})$ through the following steps: First, we prove that $P_{\mathbf{x}}(\phi(\mathbf{x}, \mathbf{y}))$ and $P_{\mathbf{x}}(\psi(\mathbf{x}, \mathbf{z}))$ are compact semi-algebraic sets which are unions of finitely many basic closed semi-algebraic sets (see Lemma 1). Second, using Putinar's Positivstellensatz, we prove that, for two disjoint basic closed semi-algebraic sets S_1 and S_2 of the Archimedean form, there exists a polynomial $h_1(\mathbf{x})$ such that $h_1(\mathbf{x}) = 0$ separates S_1 and S_2 (see Lemma 2). This result is then extended to the case that S_2 is a finite union of basic closed semi-algebraic sets (see Lemma 3). Finally, by generalizing Lemma 3 to the case that two compact semi-algebraic sets both are unions of finitely many basic closed semi-algebraic sets and together with Proposition 1, we prove the existence of interpolant in Theorem 2 and Corollary 1.

Proposition 1. *If $h(\mathbf{x}) \in \mathbb{R}[\mathbf{x}]$ satisfies the following constraints*

$$\forall \mathbf{x} \in P_{\mathbf{x}}(\phi(\mathbf{x}, \mathbf{y})).h(\mathbf{x}) > 0 \quad and \quad \forall \mathbf{x} \in P_{\mathbf{x}}(\psi(\mathbf{x}, \mathbf{z})).h(\mathbf{x}) < 0, \qquad (1)$$

then $h(\mathbf{x}) > 0$ is an interpolant for $\phi(\mathbf{x}, \mathbf{y})$ and $\psi(\mathbf{x}, \mathbf{z})$, where $\phi(\mathbf{x}, \mathbf{y})$ and $\psi(\mathbf{x}, \mathbf{z})$ are defined as in Problem 1.

Proof. According to Definition 3, it is enough to prove that $\phi(\mathbf{x}, \mathbf{y}) \models h(\mathbf{x}) > 0$ and $\psi(\mathbf{x}, \mathbf{z}) \models h(\mathbf{x}) \leq 0$.

Since any $(\mathbf{x}_0, \mathbf{y}_0)$ satisfying $\phi(\mathbf{x}, \mathbf{y})$ must imply $\mathbf{x}_0 \in P_{\mathbf{x}}(\phi(\mathbf{x}, \mathbf{y}))$, it follows that $h(\mathbf{x}_0) > 0$ from (1) and $\phi(\mathbf{x}, \mathbf{y}) \models h(\mathbf{x}) > 0$. Similarly, we can prove $\psi(\mathbf{x}, \mathbf{z}) \models h(\mathbf{x}) < 0$, implying that $\psi(\mathbf{x}, \mathbf{z}) \models h(\mathbf{x}) \leq 0$. Therefore, $h(\mathbf{x}) > 0$ is an interpolant for $\phi(\mathbf{x}, \mathbf{y})$ and $\psi(\mathbf{x}, \mathbf{z})$. □

In order to synthesize such $h(\mathbf{x})$ in Proposition 1, we first dig deeper into the two sets $P_{\mathbf{x}}(\phi(\mathbf{x}, \mathbf{y}))$ and $P_{\mathbf{x}}(\psi(\mathbf{x}, \mathbf{z}))$. As shown later, i.e. in Lemma 1, we will find that these two sets are compact semi-algebraic sets of the form $\{\mathbf{x} \mid \bigvee_{i=1}^{c} \bigwedge_{j=1}^{J_i} \alpha_{i,j}(\mathbf{x}) \geq 0\}$. Before this lemma, we introduce Finiteness theorem pertinent to a *basic closed semi-algebraic subset* of $\mathbb{R}^n$, which will be used in the proof of Lemma 1, where a basic closed semi-algebraic subset of $\mathbb{R}^n$ is a set of the form $\{\mathbf{x} \in \mathbb{R}^n \mid \alpha_1(\mathbf{x}) \geq 0, \ldots, \alpha_k(\mathbf{x}) \geq 0\}$ with $\alpha_1, \ldots, \alpha_k \in \mathbb{R}[\mathbf{x}]$.

Theorem 1 (Finiteness Theorem, Theorem 2.7.2 in [3]). *Let $A \subset \mathbb{R}^n$ be a closed semi-algebraic set. Then A is a finite union of basic closed semi-algebraic sets.*

Lemma 1. *The set $P_{\mathbf{x}}(\phi(\mathbf{x}, \mathbf{y}))$ is compact semi-algebraic set of the following form*

$$P_{\mathbf{x}}(\phi(\mathbf{x}, \mathbf{y})) := \{\mathbf{x} \mid \bigvee_{i=1}^{c} \bigwedge_{j=1}^{J_i} \alpha_{i,j}(\mathbf{x}) \geq 0\},$$

where $\alpha_{i,j}(\mathbf{x}) \in \mathbb{R}[\mathbf{x}]$, $i = 1, \ldots, c$, $j = 1, \ldots, J_i$. The same claim applies to the set $P_{\mathbf{x}}(\psi(\mathbf{x}, \mathbf{z}))$ as well.

Proof. For the sake of simplicity, we denote $\{(\mathbf{x}, \mathbf{y}) \mid \phi(\mathbf{x}, \mathbf{y})\}$ and $P_{\mathbf{x}}(\phi(\mathbf{x}, \mathbf{y}))$ by S and $\pi(S)$, respectively.

Because S is a compact set and π is a continuous map that maps compact set to compact set, $\pi(S)$, which is the image of a compact set under a continuous map, is compact. Moreover, as S is a semi-algebraic set and the projection of a semi-algebraic set is also a semi-algebraic set by Tarski-Seidenberg theorem [2], this implies that $\pi(S)$ is a semi-algebraic set. Thus, $\pi(S)$ is a compact semi-algebraic set.

Since $\pi(S)$ is a compact semi-algebraic set, and also a closed semi-algebraic set, we have that $\pi(S)$ is a finite union of basic closed semi-algebraic sets from Theorem 1. Hence, there exist a series of polynomials $\alpha_{1,1}(\mathbf{x}), \ldots, \alpha_{1,J_1}(\mathbf{x}), \ldots, \alpha_{c,1}(\mathbf{x}), \ldots, \alpha_{c,J_c}(\mathbf{x})$ such that $\pi(S) = \bigcup_{i=1}^{c} \{\mathbf{x} \mid \bigwedge_{j=1}^{J_i} \alpha_{i,j}(\mathbf{x}) \geq 0\} = \{\mathbf{x} \mid \bigvee_{i=1}^{c} \bigwedge_{j=1}^{J_i} \alpha_{i,j}(\mathbf{x}) \geq 0\}$. This concludes this lemma. □

After knowing the structure of $P_{\mathbf{x}}(\phi(\mathbf{x},\mathbf{y}))$ and $P_{\mathbf{x}}(\psi(\mathbf{x},\mathbf{z}))$ being a union of some basic semialgebraic sets as illustrated in Lemma 1, we next prove the existence of $h(\mathbf{x}) \in \mathbb{R}[\mathbf{x}]$ satisfying (1), as formally stated in Theorem 2.

Theorem 2. *Suppose that $\phi(\mathbf{x},\mathbf{y})$ and $\psi(\mathbf{x},\mathbf{z})$ are defined as in Problem 1, then there exists a polynomial $h(\mathbf{x})$ satisfying* (1).

As pointed out by an anonymous reviewer that Theorem 2 can be obtained by some properties of the ring of Nash functions proved in [29]. In what follows, we give a simpler and more intuitive proof. To the end, it requires some preliminaries first. The main tool in our proof is Putinar's Positivstellensatz, as formulated in Theorem 3.

Theorem 3 (Putinar's Positivstellensatz [31]). *Let $p_1, \ldots, p_k \in \mathbb{R}[\mathbf{x}]$ and $S_1 = \{\mathbf{x} \mid p_1(\mathbf{x}) \geq 0, \ldots, p_k(\mathbf{x}) \geq 0\}$. Assume that the quadratic module $\mathcal{M}(p_1, \ldots, p_k)$ is Archimedean. For $q \in \mathbb{R}[\mathbf{x}]$, if $q > 0$ on S_1 then $q \in \mathcal{M}(p_1, \ldots, p_k)$.*

With Putinar's Positivstellensatz we can draw a conclusion that there exists a polynomial such that its zero level set[3] separates two compact semi-algebraic sets of the Archimedean form, as claimed in Lemmas 2 and 3.

Lemma 2. *Let $S_1 = \{\mathbf{x} \mid p_1(\mathbf{x}) \geq 0, \ldots, p_J(\mathbf{x}) \geq 0\}$, $S_2 = \{\mathbf{x} \mid q_1(\mathbf{x}) \geq 0, \ldots, q_K(\mathbf{x}) \geq 0\}$ be semi-algebraic sets of the Archimedean form and $S_1 \cap S_2 = \emptyset$, then there exists a polynomial $h_1(\mathbf{x})$ such that*

$$\forall \mathbf{x} \in S_1.\ h_1(\mathbf{x}) > 0, \quad \forall \mathbf{x} \in S_2.\ h_1(\mathbf{x}) < 0. \tag{2}$$

Proof. Since $S_1 \cap S_2 = \emptyset$, it follows

$$p_2 \geq 0 \wedge \cdots \wedge p_J \geq 0 \wedge q_1 \geq 0 \wedge \cdots \wedge q_K \geq 0 \models -p_1 > 0.$$

Let $S_3 = \{\mathbf{x} \mid p_2 \geq 0 \wedge \cdots \wedge p_J \geq 0 \wedge q_1 \geq 0 \wedge \cdots \wedge q_K \geq 0\}$, then $-p_1 > 0$ on S_3. Since S_1 and S_2 are semi-algebraic sets of the Archimedean form, it follows $\mathcal{M}_{\mathbf{x}}(p_2(\mathbf{x}), \ldots, p_J(\mathbf{x}), q_1(\mathbf{x}), \ldots, q_K(\mathbf{x}))$ is also Archimedean. Hence, S_3 is compact. From $-p_1 > 0$ on S_3, we further have that there exists some $u_1 \in \sum \mathbb{R}[\mathbf{x}]^2$ such that $-u_1 p_1 - 1 > 0$ on S_3. Using Theorem 3, we have that

$$-u_1 p_1 - 1 \in \mathcal{M}_{\mathbf{x}}(p_2(\mathbf{x}), \ldots, p_J(\mathbf{x}), q_1(\mathbf{x}), \ldots, q_K(\mathbf{x})),$$

implying that there exists a set of sums of squares polynomials $u_2, \ldots, u_J$ and $v_0, v_1, \ldots, v_K \in \mathbb{R}[\mathbf{x}]$, such that

$$-u_1 p_1 - 1 \equiv u_2 p_2 + \cdots + u_J p_J + v_0 + v_1 q_1 + \cdots + v_K q_K.$$

Let $h_1 = \frac{1}{2} + u_1 p_1 + \cdots + u_J p_J$, i.e., $-h_1 = \frac{1}{2} + v_0 + v_1 q_1 + \cdots + v_K q_K$. It is easy to check that (2) holds. □

---

[3] The zero level set of an n-variate polynomial $h(\mathbf{x})$ is defined as $\{\mathbf{x} \in \mathbb{R}^n \mid h(\mathbf{x}) = 0\}$.

Lemma 3 generalizes the result of Lemma 2 to more general compact semi-algebraic sets of the Archimedean form, which is the union of multiple basic semi-algebraic sets.

Lemma 3. *Assume* $S_0 = \{\mathbf{x} \mid p_1(\mathbf{x}) \geq 0, \ldots, p_J(\mathbf{x}) \geq 0\}$ *and* $S_i = \{\mathbf{x} \mid q_{i,1}(\mathbf{x}) \geq 0, \ldots, q_{i,K_i}(\mathbf{x}) \geq 0\}$, $i = 1, \ldots, b$, *are semi-algebraic sets of the Archimedean form, and* $S_0 \cap \bigcup_{i=1}^{b} S_i = \emptyset$, *then there exists a polynomial* $h_0(\mathbf{x})$ *such that*

$$\forall \mathbf{x} \in S_0.\ h_0(\mathbf{x}) > 0, \quad \forall \mathbf{x} \in \bigcup_{i=1}^{b} S_i.\ h_0(\mathbf{x}) < 0. \tag{3}$$

In order to prove this lemma, we prove the following lemma first.

Lemma 4. *Let* $c, d \in \mathbb{R}$ *with* $0 < c < d$ *and* $U_0 = [c, d]^r$. *There exists a polynomial* $\hat{h}(\mathbf{x})$ *such that*

$$\mathbf{x} \in U_0 \models \hat{h}(\mathbf{x}) > 0 \models \bigwedge_{i=1}^{r} x_i > 0, \tag{4}$$

where $\mathbf{x} = (x_1, \ldots, x_r)$.

Proof. We show that there exists $k \in \mathbb{N}$ such that $\hat{h}(\mathbf{x}) = (\frac{d}{2})^{2k} - (x_1 - \frac{c+d}{2})^{2k} - \cdots - (x_r - \frac{c+d}{2})^{2k}$ satisfies (4). It is evident that $\hat{h}(\mathbf{x}) > 0 \models \bigwedge_{i=1}^{r} x_i > 0$ holds. In the following we just need to verify that $\bigwedge_{i=1}^{r} c \leq x_i \leq d \models \hat{h}(\mathbf{x}) > 0$ holds. Since $c \leq x_i \leq d$, we have $(x_i - \frac{c+d}{2})^{2k} \leq (\frac{d-c}{2})^{2k}$ and $(\frac{d}{2})^{2k} - \sum_{i=1}^{r}(x_i - \frac{c+d}{2})^{2k} \geq (\frac{d}{2})^{2k}\ r(\frac{d-c}{2})^{2k}$. Obviously, if an integer k satisfies $(\frac{d}{d-c})^{2k} > r$, then $(\frac{d}{2})^{2k} - \sum_{i=1}^{r}(x_i - \frac{c+d}{2})^{2k} > 0$. The existence of such k satisfying $(\frac{d}{d-c})^{2k} > r$ is assured by $\frac{d}{d-c} > 1$. $\qquad\square$

Now we give a proof for Lemma 3 as follows.

Proof (of Lemma 3). For any i with $1 \leq i \leq b$, according to Lemma 2, there exists a polynomial $h_i \in \mathbb{R}[\mathbf{x}]$, satisfying $\forall \mathbf{x} \in S_0.\ h_i(\mathbf{x}) > 0$ and $\forall \mathbf{x} \in S_i.\ h_i(\mathbf{x}) < 0$.

Next, we construct $h_0(\mathbf{x}) \in \mathbb{R}[\mathbf{x}]$ from $h_1(\mathbf{x}), \ldots, h_b(\mathbf{x})$. Since S_0 is a semi-algebraic set of the Archimedean form, S_0 is compact and thus $h_i(\mathbf{x})$ has minimum value and maximum value on S_0, denoted by c_i and d_i respectively. Let $c = \min(c_1, \ldots, c_b)$ and $d = \max(d_1, \ldots, d_b)$. Clearly, $0 < c < d$.

From Lemma 4 there must exist a polynomial $\hat{h}(w_1, \ldots, w_b)$ such that

$$\bigwedge_{i=1}^{b} c \leq w_i \leq d \models \hat{h}(w_1, \ldots, w_b) > 0, \tag{5}$$

$$\hat{h}(w_1, \ldots, w_b) > 0 \models \bigwedge_{i=1}^{b} w_i > 0. \tag{6}$$

Let $h_0'(\mathbf{x}) = \hat{h}(h_1(\mathbf{x}), \ldots, h_b(\mathbf{x}))$. Obviously, $h_0'(\mathbf{x}) \in \mathbb{R}[\mathbf{x}]$. We next prove that $h_0'(\mathbf{x})$ satisfies (3) in Lemma 3.

For all $\mathbf{x}_0 \in S_0$, $c \leq h_i(\mathbf{x}_0) \leq d$, $i = 1,\ldots,b$, $h'_0(\mathbf{x}_0) = \hat{h}(h_1(\mathbf{x}_0),\ldots,h_b(\mathbf{x}_0)) > 0$ by (5). Therefore, the first constraint in (3), i.e. $\forall \mathbf{x}_0 \in S_0.h_0(\mathbf{x}_0) > 0$, holds.

For any $\mathbf{x}_0 \in \bigcup_{i=1}^{b} S_i$, there must exist some i such that $\mathbf{x}_0 \in S_i$, implying that $h_i(\mathbf{x}_0) < 0$. By (6) we have $h'_0(\mathbf{x}_0) = \hat{h}(h_1(\mathbf{x}_0),\ldots,h_b(\mathbf{x}_0)) \leq 0$.

Thus, we obtain the conclusion that there exists a polynomial $h'_0(\mathbf{x})$ such that $\forall \mathbf{x} \in S_0$. $h'_0(\mathbf{x}) > 0$, and $\forall \mathbf{x} \in \bigcup_{i=1}^{b} S_i$. $h'_0(\mathbf{x}) \leq 0$. Also, since S_0 is a compact set, and $h'_0(\mathbf{x}) > 0$ on S_0, there must exist some positive number $\epsilon > 0$ such that $h'_0(\mathbf{x}) - \epsilon > 0$ over S_0. Then $h'_0(\mathbf{x}) - \epsilon < 0$ on $\bigcup_{i=1}^{b} S_i$. Therefore, setting $h_0(\mathbf{x}) := h'_0(\mathbf{x}) - \epsilon$, Lemma 3 is proved. □

In Lemma 3 we proved that there exists a polynomial $h(\mathbf{x}) \in \mathbb{R}[\mathbf{x}]$ such that its zero level set is a barrier between two semi-algebraic sets of the Archimedean form, of which one set is a union of finitely many basic semi-algebraic sets. In the following we will give a formal proof of Theorem 2, which is a generalization of Lemma 3.

Proof (of Theorem 2). According to Lemma 1 we have that $P_{\mathbf{x}}(\phi(\mathbf{x},\mathbf{y}))$ and $P_{\mathbf{x}}(\psi(\mathbf{x},\mathbf{z}))$ are compact sets, and there respectively exists a set of polynomials $p_{i,j}(\mathbf{x}) \in \mathbb{R}[\mathbf{x}]$, $i = 1,\ldots,a$, $j = 1,\ldots,J_i$, and $q_{l,k}(\mathbf{x}) \in \mathbb{R}[\mathbf{x}]$, $l = 1,\ldots,b$, $k = 1,\ldots,K_i$, such that

$$P_{\mathbf{x}}(\phi(\mathbf{x},\mathbf{y})) = \{\mathbf{x} \mid \bigvee_{i=1}^{a} \bigwedge_{j=1}^{J_i} p_{i,j}(\mathbf{x}) \geq 0\}, \quad P_{\mathbf{x}}(\psi(\mathbf{x},\mathbf{z})) = \{\mathbf{x} \mid \bigvee_{l=1}^{b} \bigwedge_{k=1}^{K_l} q_{l,k}(\mathbf{x}) \geq 0\}.$$

Since $P_{\mathbf{x}}(\phi(\mathbf{x},\mathbf{y}))$ and $P_{\mathbf{x}}(\psi(\mathbf{x},\mathbf{z}))$ are compact sets, there exists a positive $N \in \mathbb{R}$ such that $f = N - \sum_{i=1}^{r} x_i^2 \geq 0$ over $P_{\mathbf{x}}(\phi(\mathbf{x},\mathbf{y}))$ and $P_{\mathbf{x}}(\psi(\mathbf{x},\mathbf{z}))$. For each $i = 1,\ldots,a$ and each $l = 1,\ldots,b$, set $p_{i,0} = q_{l,0} = f$. Denote $\{\mathbf{x} \mid \bigvee_{i=1}^{a} \bigwedge_{j=0}^{J_i} p_{i,j}(\mathbf{x}) \geq 0\} = \bigcup_{i=1}^{a}\{\mathbf{x} \mid \bigwedge_{j=0}^{J_i} p_{i,j}(\mathbf{x}) \geq 0\}$ by P_1 and $\{\mathbf{x} \mid \bigvee_{l=1}^{b} \bigwedge_{k=0}^{K_l} q_{l,k}(\mathbf{x}) > 0\} = \bigcup_{l=1}^{b}\{\mathbf{x} \mid \bigwedge_{k=0}^{K_l} q_{l,k}(\mathbf{x}) \geq 0\}$ by P_2. It is easy to see that $P_1 = P_{\mathbf{x}}(\phi(\mathbf{x},\mathbf{y})$, $P_2 = P_{\mathbf{x}}(\psi(\mathbf{x},\mathbf{z}))$.

Since $\phi \wedge \psi \models \bot$, there does not exist $(\mathbf{x},\mathbf{y},\mathbf{z}) \in \mathbb{R}^{r+s+t}$ that satisfies $\phi \wedge \psi$, implying that $P_{\mathbf{x}}(\phi(\mathbf{x},\mathbf{y})) \cap P_{\mathbf{x}}(\psi(\mathbf{x},\mathbf{z})) = \emptyset$ and thus $P_1 \cap P_2 = \emptyset$. Also, since $\{\mathbf{x} \mid \bigwedge_{j=0}^{J_{i_1}} p_{i_1,j}(\mathbf{x}) \geq 0\} \subseteq P_1$, for each $i_1 = 1,\ldots,a$, $\{\mathbf{x} \mid \bigwedge_{j=0}^{J_{i_1}} p_{i_1,j}(\mathbf{x}) \geq 0\} \cap P_2 = \emptyset$ holds. By Lemma 3 there exists $h_{i_1}(\mathbf{x}) \in \mathbb{R}[\mathbf{x}]$ such that

$$\forall \mathbf{x} \in \{\mathbf{x} \mid \bigwedge_{j=0}^{J_{i_1}} p_{i_1,j}(\mathbf{x}) \geq 0\}.h_{i_1}(\mathbf{x}) > 0, \quad \forall \mathbf{x} \in P_2.h_{i_1}(\mathbf{x}) < 0.$$

Let $S' = \{\mathbf{x} \mid -h_1(\mathbf{x}) \geq 0,\ldots,-h_a(\mathbf{x}) \geq 0, N - \sum_{i=1}^{r} x_i^2 \geq 0\}$. Obviously, S' is a semialgebraic set of the Archimedean form, $P_2 \subset S'$ and $P_1 \cap S' = \emptyset$. Therefore, according to Lemma 2, there exists a polynomial $\overline{h}(\mathbf{x}) \in \mathbb{R}[\mathbf{x}]$ such that $\forall \mathbf{x} \in S'$. $\overline{h}(\mathbf{x}) > 0$ and $\forall \mathbf{x} \in P_1$. $\overline{h}(\mathbf{x}) < 0$. Let $h(\mathbf{x}) = -\overline{h}(\mathbf{x})$, then we have $\forall \mathbf{x} \in P_1$. $h(\mathbf{x}) > 0$ and $\forall \mathbf{x} \in P_2$. $h(\mathbf{x}) < 0$, implying that $\forall \mathbf{x} \in P_{\mathbf{x}}(\phi(\mathbf{x},\mathbf{y})).h(\mathbf{x}) > 0$ and $\forall \mathbf{x} \in P_{\mathbf{x}}(\psi(\mathbf{x},\mathbf{z})).h(\mathbf{x}) < 0$. Thus, this completes the proof of Theorem 2. □

Consequently, we immediately have the following conclusion.

Corollary 1. *Let $\phi(\mathbf{x}, \mathbf{y})$ and $\psi(\mathbf{x}, \mathbf{z})$ be defined as in Problem 1. There must exist a polynomial $h(\mathbf{x}) \in \mathbb{R}[\mathbf{x}]$ such that $h(\mathbf{x}) > 0$ is an interpolant for ϕ and ψ.*

Actually, since $P_{\mathbf{x}}(\phi(\mathbf{x}, \mathbf{y}))$ and $P_{\mathbf{x}}(\psi(\mathbf{x}, \mathbf{z}))$ both are compact set by Lemma 1, and $h(\mathbf{x}) > 0$ on $P_{\mathbf{x}}(\phi(\mathbf{x}, \mathbf{y}))$ and $h(\mathbf{x}) < 0$ on $P_{\mathbf{x}}(\psi(\mathbf{x}, \mathbf{z}))$, we can obtain $h'(\mathbf{x})$ by giving a small perturbation to the coefficients of $h(\mathbf{x})$ such that $h'(\mathbf{x})$ has the property of $h(\mathbf{x})$. Hence, there should exist a $h(\mathbf{x}) \in \mathbb{Q}[\mathbf{x}]$ such that $h(\mathbf{x}) > 0$ is an interpolant for ϕ and ψ, intuitively.

Theorem 4. *Let $\phi(\mathbf{x}, \mathbf{y})$ and $\psi(\mathbf{x}, \mathbf{z})$ be defined as in Problem 1. There must exist a polynomial $h(\mathbf{x}) \in \mathbb{Q}[\mathbf{x}]$ such that $h(\mathbf{x}) > 0$ is an interpolant for ϕ and ψ.*

Proof. We just need to prove there exists a polynomial $h(\mathbf{x}) \in \mathbb{Q}[\mathbf{x}]$ satisfying (1).

By Theorem 2, there exists a polynomial $h'(\mathbf{x}) \in \mathbb{R}[\mathbf{x}]$ satisfying (1). Since $P_{\mathbf{x}}(\phi(\mathbf{x}, \mathbf{y}))$ and $P_{\mathbf{x}}(\psi(\mathbf{x}, \mathbf{z}))$ are compact sets, $h'(\mathbf{x}) > 0$ on $P_{\mathbf{x}}(\phi(\mathbf{x}, \mathbf{y}))$ and $h'(\mathbf{x}) < 0$ on $P_{\mathbf{x}}(\psi(\mathbf{x}, \mathbf{z}))$, there exist $\eta_1 > 0$ and $\eta_2 > 0$ such that

$$\forall \mathbf{x} \in P_{\mathbf{x}}(\phi(\mathbf{x}, \mathbf{y})).h'(\mathbf{x}) - \eta_1 \geq 0, \ \forall \mathbf{x} \in P_{\mathbf{x}}(\psi(\mathbf{x}, \mathbf{z})).h'(\mathbf{x}) + \eta_2 \leq 0.$$

Let $\eta = \min(\frac{\eta_1}{2}, \frac{\eta_2}{2})$. Suppose $h'(\mathbf{x}) \in \mathbb{R}[\mathbf{x}]$ has the form $h'(\mathbf{x}) = \sum_{\alpha \in \Omega} c_\alpha \mathbf{x}^\alpha$, where $\alpha \in \mathbb{N}^r$, $\Omega \subset \mathbb{N}^r$ is a finite set of indices, r is the dimension of $\mathbf{x}$, $\mathbf{x}^\alpha$ is the monomial $\mathbf{x}_1^{\alpha_1} \cdots \mathbf{x}_r^{\alpha_r}$, and $0 \neq c_\alpha \in \mathbb{R}$ is the coefficient of monomial $\mathbf{x}^\alpha$. Let $N = |\Omega|$ be the cardinality of Ω. Since $P_{\mathbf{x}}(\phi(\mathbf{x}, \mathbf{y}))$ and $P_{\mathbf{x}}(\psi(\mathbf{x}, \mathbf{z}))$ are compact sets, for any $\alpha \in \Omega$, there exists $M_\alpha > 0$ such that $M_\alpha = \max\{|\mathbf{x}^\alpha| \mid \mathbf{x} \in P_{\mathbf{x}}(\phi(\mathbf{x}, \mathbf{y})) \cup P_{\mathbf{x}}(\psi(\mathbf{x}, \mathbf{z}))\}$. Then for any fixed polynomial $\hat{h}(\mathbf{x}) = \sum_{\alpha \in \Omega} d_\alpha \mathbf{x}^\alpha$, with $d_\alpha \in [c_\alpha - \frac{\eta}{NM_\alpha}, c_\alpha + \frac{\eta}{NM_\alpha}]$, and any $\mathbf{x} \in P_{\mathbf{x}}(\phi(\mathbf{x}, \mathbf{y})) \cup P_{\mathbf{x}}(\psi(\mathbf{x}, \mathbf{z}))$, we have

$$|\hat{h}(\mathbf{x}) - h'(\mathbf{x})| = |\sum_{\alpha \in \Omega} (d_\alpha - c_\alpha)\mathbf{x}^\alpha| \leq \sum_{\alpha \in \Omega} |(d_\alpha - c_\alpha)| \cdot |\mathbf{x}^\alpha| \leq \sum_{\alpha \in \Omega} \frac{\eta}{NM_\alpha} \cdot M_\alpha = \eta.$$

Since $\eta = \min(\frac{\eta_1}{2}, \frac{\eta_2}{2})$, hence

$$\forall \mathbf{x} \in P_{\mathbf{x}}(\phi(\mathbf{x}, \mathbf{y})).\hat{h}(\mathbf{x}) \geq \frac{\eta_1}{2} > 0, \quad \forall \mathbf{x} \in P_{\mathbf{x}}(\psi(\mathbf{x}, \mathbf{z})).\hat{h}(\mathbf{x}) \leq -\frac{\eta_2}{2} < 0. \quad (7)$$

Since for any $d_\alpha \in [c_\alpha - \frac{\eta}{NM_\alpha}, c_\alpha + \frac{\eta}{NM_\alpha}]$ (7) holds, there must exist some rational number $r_\alpha \in \mathbb{Q}$ in $[c_\alpha - \frac{\eta}{NM_\alpha}, c_\alpha + \frac{\eta}{NM_\alpha}]$ satisfying (7) because of the density of rational numbers. Thus, let $h(\mathbf{x}) = \sum_{\alpha \in \Omega} r_\alpha \mathbf{x}^\alpha$. Clearly, it follows that $h(\mathbf{x}) \in \mathbb{Q}[\mathbf{x}]$ and (1) holds. □

So, the existence of $h(\mathbf{x}) \in \mathbb{Q}[\mathbf{x}]$ is guaranteed. Moreover, from the proof of Theorem 4, we know that a small perturbation of $h(\mathbf{x})$ is permitted, which is a good property for computing $h(\mathbf{x})$ in a numeric way. In the subsequent subsection, we recast the problem of finding such $h(\mathbf{x})$ as a semi-definite programming problem.

4   SOS Formulation

Similar to [7], in this section, we discuss how to reduce the problem of finding $h(\mathbf{x})$ satisfying (1) to a sum of squares programming problem.

Theorem 5. *Let* $\phi(\mathbf{x}, \mathbf{y})$ *and* $\psi(\mathbf{x}, \mathbf{z})$ *be defined as in the Problem 1. Then there exist* $m + n + 2$ *SOS (sum of squares) polynomials* $u_i(\mathbf{x}, \mathbf{y})$ $(i = 1, \dots, m+1)$, $v_j(\mathbf{x}, \mathbf{z})$ $(j = 1, \dots, n+1)$ *and a polynomial* $h(\mathbf{x})$ *such that*

$$h - 1 = \sum_{i=1}^{m} u_i f_i + u_{m+1}, \quad -h - 1 = \sum_{j=1}^{n} v_j g_j + v_{n+1}, \tag{8}$$

and $h(\mathbf{x}) > 0$ *is an interpolant for* $\phi(\mathbf{x}, \mathbf{y})$ *and* $\psi(\mathbf{x}, \mathbf{z})$.

Proof. By Theorem 2 there exists a polynomial $\hat{h}(\mathbf{x})$ such that

$$\forall \mathbf{x} \in P_{\mathbf{x}}(\phi(\mathbf{x}, \mathbf{y})).\hat{h}(\mathbf{x}) > 0, \quad \forall \mathbf{x} \in P_{\mathbf{x}}(\psi(\mathbf{x}, \mathbf{z})).\hat{h}(\mathbf{x}) < 0.$$

Set $S_1 = \{(\mathbf{x}, \mathbf{y}) \mid f_1 \geq 0, \dots, f_m \geq 0\}$ and $S_2 = \{(\mathbf{x}, \mathbf{z}) \mid g_1 \geq 0, \dots, g_n \geq 0\}$. Since $\hat{h}(\mathbf{x}) > 0$ on S_1, which is compact, there exist $\epsilon_1 > 0$ such that $\hat{h}(\mathbf{x}) - \epsilon_1 > 0$ on S_1. Similarly, there exist $\epsilon_2 > 0$ such that $-\hat{h}(\mathbf{x}) - \epsilon_2 > 0$ on S_2. Let $\epsilon = \min(\epsilon_1, \epsilon_2)$, and $h(\mathbf{x}) = \frac{\hat{h}(\mathbf{x})}{\epsilon}$, then $h(\mathbf{x}) - 1 > 0$ on S_1 and $-h(\mathbf{x}) - 1 > 0$ on S_2. Since $\mathcal{M}_{\mathbf{x}, \mathbf{y}}(f_1(\mathbf{x}, \mathbf{y}), \dots, f_m(\mathbf{x}, \mathbf{y}))$ is Archimedean, from Theorem 3, we have $h(\mathbf{x}) - 1 \in \mathcal{M}_{\mathbf{x}, \mathbf{y}}(f_1(\mathbf{x}, \mathbf{y}), \dots, f_m(\mathbf{x}, \mathbf{y}))$. Similarly, $-h(\mathbf{x}) - 1 \in \mathcal{M}_{\mathbf{x}, \mathbf{z}}(g_1(\mathbf{x}, \mathbf{z}), \dots, g_n(\mathbf{x}, \mathbf{z}))$. That is, there exist $m + n + 2$ SOS polynomials u_i, v_j satisfying the following semi-definite constraints:

$$h(\mathbf{x}) - 1 = \sum_{i=1}^{m} u_i f_i + u_{m+1}, \quad -h(\mathbf{x}) - 1 = \sum_{j=1}^{n} v_j g_j + v_{n+1}. \qquad \square$$

According to Theorem 5, the problem of finding $h(\mathbf{x}) \in \mathbb{R}[\mathbf{x}]$ solving Problem 1 can be equivalently reformulated as the problem of searching for SOS polynomials $u_1(\mathbf{x}, \mathbf{y}), \dots, u_m(\mathbf{x}, \mathbf{y})$, $v_1(\mathbf{x}, \mathbf{z}), \dots, v_n(\mathbf{x}, \mathbf{z})$ and a polynomial $h(\mathbf{x})$ with appropriate degrees such that

$$\begin{cases} h(\mathbf{x}) - 1 - \displaystyle\sum_{i=1}^{m} u_i f_i \in \sum \mathbb{R}[\mathbf{x}, \mathbf{y}]^2, \\[2mm] -h(\mathbf{x}) - 1 - \displaystyle\sum_{j=1}^{n} v_j g_j \in \sum \mathbb{R}[\mathbf{x}, \mathbf{z}]^2, \\[2mm] u_i \in \sum \mathbb{R}[\mathbf{x}, \mathbf{y}]^2, i = 1, \dots, m, \\[1mm] v_j \in \sum \mathbb{R}[\mathbf{x}, \mathbf{z}]^2, j = 1, \dots, n. \end{cases} \tag{9}$$

(9) is SOS constraints over SOS multipliers $u_1(\mathbf{x}, \mathbf{y}), \dots, u_m(\mathbf{x}, \mathbf{y})$, $v_1(\mathbf{x}, \mathbf{z})$, $\dots, v_n(\mathbf{x}, \mathbf{z})$, polynomial $h(\mathbf{x})$, which is convex and could be solved by many existing semi-definite programming solvers such as the optimization library AiSat [7] built on CSDP [4]. Therefore, according to Theorem 5, $h(\mathbf{x}) > 0$ is an interpolant for ϕ and ψ, which is formulated in Theorem 6.

Theorem 6 (Soundness). *Suppose that $\phi(\mathbf{x}, \mathbf{y})$ and $\psi(\mathbf{x}, \mathbf{z})$ are defined as in Problem 1, and $h(\mathbf{x})$ is a feasible solution to (9), then $h(\mathbf{x})$ solves Problem 1, i.e. $h(\mathbf{x}) > 0$ is an interpolant for ϕ and ψ.*

Moreover, we have the following completeness theorem stating that if the degrees of $h(\mathbf{x}) \in \mathbb{R}[\mathbf{x}]$ and $u_i(\mathbf{x}, \mathbf{y}) \in \sum \mathbb{R}[\mathbf{x}, \mathbf{y}]^2$, $v_j(\mathbf{x}, \mathbf{z}) \in \sum \mathbb{R}[\mathbf{x}, \mathbf{z}]^2$, $i = 1, \ldots, m$, $j = 1, \ldots, n$, are large enough, $h(\mathbf{x})$ can be synthesized definitely via solving (9).

Theorem 7 (Completeness). *For Problem 1, there must be polynomials $u_i(\mathbf{x}, \mathbf{y}) \in \mathbb{R}_N[\mathbf{x}, \mathbf{y}]$ $(i = 1, \ldots, m)$, $v_j(\mathbf{x}, \mathbf{z}) \in \mathbb{R}_N[\mathbf{x}, \mathbf{z}]$ $(j = 1, \ldots, n)$ and $h(\mathbf{x}) \in \mathbb{R}_N[\mathbf{x}]$ satisfying (11) for some positive integer N, where $\mathbb{R}_k[\cdot]$ stands for the family of polynomials of degree no more than k.*

Proof. This is an immediate result of Theorem 5.   □

Example 2. Consider two contradictory formulas ϕ and ψ defined by

$$f_1(x, y, z, a_1, b_1, c_1, d_1) \geq 0 \wedge f_2(x, y, z, a_1, b_1, c_1, d_1) \geq 0 \wedge f_3(x, y, z, a_1, b_1, c_1, d_1) \geq 0,$$
$$g_1(x, y, z, a_2, b_2, c_2, d_2) \geq 0 \wedge g_2(x, y, z, a_2, b_2, c_2, d_2) \geq 0 \wedge g_3(x, y, z, a_2, b_2, c_2, d_2) \geq 0,$$

respectively, where

$$f_1 = 4 - x^2 - y^2 - z^2 - a_1^2 - b_1^2 - c_1^2 - d_1^2, \quad f_2 = -y^4 + 2x^4 - a_1^4 - 1/100,$$
$$f_3 = z^2 - b_1^2 - c_1^2 - d_1^2 - x - 1, \qquad\qquad g_1 = 4 - x^2 - y^2 - z^2 - a_2^2 - b_2^2 - c_2^2 - d_2^2,$$
$$g_2 = x^2 - y - a_2 - b_2 - d_2^2 - 3, \qquad\qquad g_3 = x.$$

It is easy to observe that ϕ and ψ satisfy the conditions in Problem 1. Since there are local variables in ϕ and ψ and the degree of f_2 is 4, the interpolant generation methods in [7] and [10] are not applicable. We get a concrete SDP problem of the form (9) by setting the degree of the polynomial $h(x, y, z)$ in (9) to be 2. Using the MATLAB package YALMIP [23] and Mosek [28], we obtain

$$h(x, y, z) = -416.7204 - 914.7840x + 472.6184y + 199.8985x^2 + 190.2252y^2$$
$$+ 690.4208z^2 - 187.1592xy.$$

Pictorially, we plot $P_{x,y,z}(\phi(x, y, z, a_1, b_1, c_1, d_1))$, $P_{x,y,z}(\psi(x, y, z, a_2, b_2, c_2, d_2))$ and $\{(x, y, z) \mid h(x, y, z) > 0\}$ in Fig. 2. It is evident that $h(x, y, z)$ as presented above for $d_h = 2$ is a real interpolant for $\phi(x, y, z, a, b, c, d)$ and $\psi(x, y, z, a, b, c, d)$.

5   Avoidance of the Unsoundness Due to Numerical Error in SDP

In this section, we discuss how to avoid the unsoundness of our approach caused by numerical error in SDP based on the work in [32].

A square matrix A is *positive semidefinite* if A is real symmetric and all its eigenvalues are nonnegative, denote by $A \succeq 0$.

In order to solve formula (9) to obtain $h(\mathbf{x})$, we first need to fix a degree bound of u_i, v_j and h, say $2d$, $d \in \mathbb{N}$. It is well-known that any $u(\mathbf{x}) \in \sum \mathbb{R}[\mathbf{x}]^2$ with degree $2d$ can be represented by

$$u(\mathbf{x}) \equiv E_d(\mathbf{x})^T C_u E_d(\mathbf{x}), \qquad (10)$$

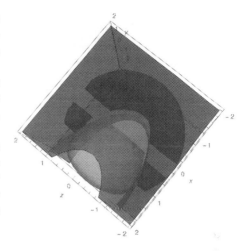

Fig. 2. Example 2. (Red region: $P_{x,y,z}$ $(\phi(x, y, z, a_1, b_1, c_1, d_1))$; green region: $P_{x,y,z}(\psi(x, y, z, a_2, b_2, c_2, d_2))$; gray region: $\{(x, y, z) \mid h(x, y, z) > 0\}$.) (Color figure online)

where $C_u \in \mathbb{R}^{\binom{r+d}{d} \times \binom{r+d}{d}}$ with $C_u \succeq 0$, $E_d(\mathbf{x})$ is a column vector with all monomials in $\mathbf{x}$, whose total degree is not greater than d, and $E_d(\mathbf{x})^T$ stands for the transposition of $E_d(\mathbf{x})$. Equaling the corresponding coefficient of each monomial whose degree is less than or equal to $2d$ at the two sides of (10), we can get a linear equation system as

$$\mathtt{tr}(A_{u,k} C_u) = b_{u,k}, \ k = 1, \ldots, K_u, \qquad (11)$$

where $A_{u,k} \in \mathbb{R}^{\binom{r+d}{d} \times \binom{r+d}{d}}$ is constant matrix, $b_{u,k} \in \mathbb{R}$ is constant, $\mathtt{tr}(A)$ stands for the trace of matrix A. Thus, searching for u_i, v_j and h satisfying (9) can be reduced to the following SDP problem:

$$
\begin{aligned}
\mathtt{find} : \ & C_{u_1}, \ldots, C_{u_m}, C_{v_1}, \ldots, C_{v_n}, C_h, \\
\mathtt{s.t.} \ & \mathtt{tr}(A_{u_i,k} C_{u_i}) = b_{u_i,k}, \ i = 1, \ldots, m, k = 1, \ldots, K_{u_i}, \\
& \mathtt{tr}(A_{v_j,k} C_{v_j}) = b_{v_j,k}, \ j = 1, \ldots, n, k = 1, \ldots, K_{v_j}, \qquad (12) \\
& \mathtt{tr}(A_{h,k} C_h) = b_{h,k}, \ k = 1, \ldots, K_h, \\
& \mathtt{diag}(C_{u_1}, \ldots, C_{u_m}, C_{v_1}, \ldots, C_{v_n}, C_{h-1-uf}, C_{-h-1-vg}) \succeq 0,
\end{aligned}
$$

where C_{h-1-uf} is the matrix corresponding to polynomial $h - 1 - \sum_{i=1}^{m} u_i f_i$, which is a linear combination of $C_{u_1}, \ldots, C_{u_m}$ and C_h; similarly, $C_{-h-1-vg}$ is the matrix corresponding to polynomial $-h - 1 - \sum_{j=1}^{n} v_j g_j$, which is a linear combination of $C_{v_1}, \ldots, C_{v_n}$ and C_h; and $\mathtt{diag}(C_1, \ldots, C_k)$ is a block-diagonal matrix of $C_1, \ldots, C_k$.

Let D be the dimension of $C = \mathtt{diag}(C_{u_1}, \ldots, C_{-h-1-vg})$, i.e., $\mathtt{diag}(C_{u_1}, \ldots, C_{-h-1-vg}) \in \mathbb{R}^{D \times D}$ and $\widehat{C}$ be the approximate solution to (12) returned by calling a numerical SDP solver, the following theorem is proved in [32].

Theorem 8 ([32], Theorem 3). $C \succeq 0$ *if there exists* $\widetilde{C} \in \mathbb{F}^{D \times D}$ *such that the following conditions hold: 1.* $\widetilde{C}_{ij} = C_{ij}$, *for any* $i \neq j$; *2.* $\widetilde{C}_{ii} \leq C_{ii} - \alpha$, *for any* i; *and 3. the Cholesky algorithm implemented in floating-point arithmetic can conclude that* $\widetilde{C}$ *is positive semi-definite, where* $\mathbb{F}$ *is a floating-point format,* $\alpha = \frac{(D+1)\kappa}{1-(2D+2)\kappa}\mathtt{tr}(C) + 4(D+1)(2(D+2) + \max_i\{C_{ii}\})\eta$, *in which* κ *is the unit roundoff of* $\mathbb{F}$ *and* η *is the underflow unit of* $\mathbb{F}$.

Corollary 2. *Let* $\widetilde{C} \in \mathbb{F}^{D \times D}$. *Suppose that* $\frac{(D+1)D\kappa}{1-(2D+2)\kappa} + 4(D+1)\eta \leq \frac{1}{2}$, $\beta = \frac{(D+1)\kappa}{1-(2D+2)\kappa}\mathtt{tr}(\widetilde{C}) + 4(D+1)(2(D+2) + \max_i\{\widetilde{C}_{ii}\})\eta > 0$, *where* $\mathbb{F}$ *is a floating-point format. Then* $\widetilde{C} + 2\beta I \succeq 0$ *if the Cholesky algorithm based on floating-point arithmetic succeeds on* $\widetilde{C}$, *i.e., concludes that* $\widetilde{C}$ *is positive semi-definite.*

According to Remark 5 in [32], for IEEE 754 binary64 format with rounding to nearest, $\kappa = 2^{-53}(\simeq 10^{-16})$ and $\eta = 2^{-1075}(\simeq 10^{-323})$. In this case, the order of magnitude of β is 10^{-10} and $\frac{(D+1)D\kappa}{1-(2D+2)\kappa} + 4(D+1)\eta$ is 10^{-13}, much less than $\frac{1}{2}$. Obviously, β becomes smaller when the length of binary format becomes longer. W.l.o.g., we suppose that the Cholesky algorithm succeed in computing $\widehat{C}$ the solution of (12), which is reasonable as if an SDP solver returns a solution $\widehat{C}$, then $\widehat{C}$ should be considered to be positive semi-definite in the sense of numeric computation.

So, by Corollary 2, we have $\widehat{C} + 2\beta I \succeq 0$ holds, where I is the identity matrix with the corresponding dimension. Then we have

$$\mathtt{diag}(\widehat{C}_{u_1}, \ldots, \widehat{C}_{u_m}, \widehat{C}_{v_1}, \ldots, \widehat{C}_{v_n}, \widehat{C}_{h-1-uf}, \widehat{C}_{-h-1-vg}) + 2\beta I \succeq 0.$$

Let $\epsilon = \max_{p \in P, 1 \leq i \leq K_p} |\mathtt{tr}(A_{p,i}\widehat{C}_p) - b_{p,i}|$, where $P = \{u_1, \ldots, u_m, v_1, \ldots, v_n, h\}$, which can be regarded as the tolerance of the SDP solver. Since $|\mathtt{tr}(A_{p,i}C_p) - b_{p,i}|$ is the error term for each monomial of p, i.e., ϵ can be considered as the error bound on the coefficients of polynomials u_i, v_j and h, for any polynomial $\widehat{u}_i$ ($\widehat{v}_j$ and $\widehat{h}$), computed from (11) by replacing C_u with the corresponding $\widehat{C_u}$, there exists a corresponding remainder term R_{u_i} (resp. R_{v_j} and R_h) with degree not greater than $2d$, whose coefficients are bounded by ϵ. Hence, we have

$$\widehat{u}_i + R_{u_i} + 2\beta E_d(\mathbf{x}, \mathbf{y})^T E_d(\mathbf{x}, \mathbf{y}) \in \sum \mathbb{R}[\mathbf{x}, \mathbf{y}]^2, i = 1, \ldots, m,$$

$$\widehat{v}_j + R_{v_j} + 2\beta E_d(\mathbf{x}, \mathbf{z})^T E_d(\mathbf{x}, \mathbf{z}) \in \sum \mathbb{R}[\mathbf{x}, \mathbf{z}]^2, j = 1, \ldots, n,$$

$$\widehat{h} + R_h - 1 - \sum_{i=1}^{m}(\widehat{u}_i + R'_{u_i})f_i + 2\beta E_d(\mathbf{x}, \mathbf{y})^T E_d(\mathbf{x}, \mathbf{y}) \in \sum \mathbb{R}[\mathbf{x}, \mathbf{y}]^2, \quad (13)$$

$$-\widehat{h} + R'_h - 1 - \sum_{j=1}^{m}(\widehat{v}_j + R'_{v_j})g_j + 2\beta E_d(\mathbf{x}, \mathbf{z})^T E_d(\mathbf{x}, \mathbf{z}) \in \sum \mathbb{R}[\mathbf{x}, \mathbf{z}]^2.$$

Now, in order to avoid unsoundness of our approach caused by the numerical issue due to SDP, we have to prove

$$f_1 \geq 0 \wedge \cdots \wedge f_m \geq 0 \Rightarrow \widehat{h} > 0, \tag{14}$$

$$g_1 \geq 0 \wedge \cdots \wedge g_n \geq 0 \Rightarrow \widehat{h} < 0. \tag{15}$$

Regarding (14), let $R_{2d,\mathbf{x}}$ be a polynomial in $\mathbb{R}[|\mathbf{x}|]$, whose total degree is $2d$, and all coefficients are 1, e.g., $R_{2,x,y} = 1 + |x| + |y| + |x^2| + |xy| + |y^2|$. Since $S = \{(\mathbf{x}, \mathbf{y}) \mid f_1 \geq 0 \wedge \cdots \wedge f_m \geq 0\}$ is a compact set, then for any polynomial $p \in \mathbb{R}[\mathbf{x}, \mathbf{y}]$, $|p|$ is bounded on S. Let M_1 be an upper bound of $R_{2d,\mathbf{x},\mathbf{y}}$ on S, M_2 an upper bound of $E_d(\mathbf{x}, \mathbf{y})^T E_d(\mathbf{x}, \mathbf{y})$, and M_{f_i} an upper bound of f_i on S. Then, $|R_{u_i}|$, $|R'_{u_i}|$ and $|R_h|$ are bounded by ϵM_1. Let $E_{\mathbf{xy}} = E_d(\mathbf{x}, \mathbf{y})^T E_d(\mathbf{x}, \mathbf{y})$. So for any $(\mathbf{x}_0, \mathbf{y}_0) \in S$, considering the polynomials below at $(\mathbf{x}_0, \mathbf{y}_0) \in S$, by the first and third line in (13),

$$\widehat{h} \geq 1 - R_h + \sum_{i=1}^{m}(\widehat{u}_i + R'_{u_i})f_i - 2\beta E_{\mathbf{xy}}$$

$$\geq 1 - \epsilon M_1 + \sum_{i=1}^{m}(\widehat{u}_i + R_{u_i} + 2\beta E_{\mathbf{xy}} + R'_{u_i} - R_{u_i} - 2\beta E_{xy})f_i - 2\beta M_2$$

$$= 1 - \epsilon M_1 - 2\beta M_2 + \sum_{i=1}^{m}(\widehat{u}_i + R_{u_i} + 2\beta E_{\mathbf{xy}})f_i + \sum_{i=1}^{m}(R'_{u_i} - R_{u_i} - 2\beta E_{\mathbf{xy}})f_i$$

$$\geq 1 - \epsilon M_1 - 2\beta M_2 + 0 - \sum_{i=1}^{m}(\epsilon M_1 + \epsilon M_1 + 2\beta M_2)M_{f_i}$$

$$= 1 - (2\sum_{i=1}^{m} M_{f_i} + 1)M_1\epsilon - 2(\sum_{i=1}^{m} M_{f_i} + 1)M_2\beta.$$

Whence,

$$f_1 \geq 0 \wedge \cdots \wedge f_m \geq 0 \Rightarrow \widehat{h} \geq 1 - (2\sum_{i=1}^{m} M_{f_i} + 1)M_1\epsilon - 2(\sum_{i=1}^{m} M_{f_i} + 1)M_2\beta.$$

Let $S' = \{(\mathbf{x}, \mathbf{z}) \mid g_1 \geq 0 \wedge \cdots \wedge g_n \geq 0\}$, M_3 be an upper bound of $R_{2d,\mathbf{x},\mathbf{z}}$ on S', M_4 an upper bound of $E_d(\mathbf{x}, \mathbf{z})^T E_d(\mathbf{x}, \mathbf{z})$ on S', and M_{g_j} an upper bound of g_j on S'. Similarly, it follows

$$g_1 \geq 0 \wedge \cdots \wedge g_n \geq 0 \Rightarrow -\widehat{h} \geq 1 - (2\sum_{j=1}^{n} M_{g_j} + 1)M_3\epsilon - 2(\sum_{j=1}^{n} M_{g_j} + 1)M_4\beta.$$

So, the following proposition is immediately.

Proposition 2. *There exist two positive constants γ_1 and γ_2 such that*

$$f_1 \geq 0 \wedge \cdots \wedge f_m \geq 0 \Rightarrow \widehat{h} \geq 1 - \gamma_1\epsilon - \gamma_2\beta, \tag{16}$$

$$g_1 \geq 0 \wedge \cdots \wedge g_n \geq 0 \Rightarrow -\widehat{h} \geq 1 - \gamma_1\epsilon - \gamma_2\beta. \tag{17}$$

Since ϵ and β heavily rely on the numerical tolerance and the floating point representation, it is easy to see that ϵ and β become small enough with $\gamma_1\epsilon < \frac{1}{2}$ and $\gamma_2\beta < \frac{1}{2}$, if the numerical tolerance is small enough and the length of the floating point representation is long enough. This implies

$$f_1 \geq 0 \wedge \cdots \wedge f_m \geq 0 \Rightarrow \widehat{h} > 0, \quad g_1 \geq 0 \wedge \cdots \wedge g_n \geq 0 \Rightarrow -\widehat{h} > 0.$$

If so, any numerical result $\widehat{h} > 0$ returned by calling an SDP solver to (12) is guaranteed to be a real interpolant for ϕ and ψ, i.e., a correct solution to Problem 1.

Example 3. Consider the numerical result for Example 2 in Sect. 4. Let M_{f_1}, M_{f_2}, M_{f_3}, M_{g_1}, M_{g_2}, M_{g_3}, M_1, M_2, M_3, M_4 are defined as above. It is easy to see that

$$f_1 \geq 0 \Rightarrow |x| \leq 2 \wedge |y| \leq 2 \wedge |z| \leq 2 \wedge |a_1| \leq 2 \wedge |b_1| \leq 2 \wedge |c_1| \leq 2 \wedge |d_1| \leq 2.$$

Then, by simple calculations, we obtain $M_{f_1} = 4, M_{f_2} = 32, M_{f_3} = 3, M_1 = 83, M_2 = 29$. Thus,

$$(2\sum_{i=1}^{m} M_{f_i} + 1)M_1 = 6557, \quad 2(\sum_{i=1}^{m} M_{f_i} + 1)M_2 = 2320.$$

Also, since

$$g_1 \geq 0 \Rightarrow |x| \leq 2 \wedge |y| \leq 2 \wedge |z| \leq 2 \wedge |a_2| \leq 2 \wedge |b_2| \leq 2 \wedge |c_2| \leq 2 \wedge |d_2| \leq 2,$$

we obtain $M_{g_1} = 4, M_{g_2} = 7, M_{g_3} = 2, M_3 = 83, M_4 = 29$. Thus,

$$(2\sum_{i=1}^{m} M_{g_i} + 1)M_3 = 2241, \quad 2(\sum_{i=1}^{m} M_{g_i} + 1)M_4 = 812.$$

Consequently, we have $\gamma_1 = 6557$ and $\gamma_2 = 2320$ in Proposition 2.

Due to the fact that the default error tolerance is 10^{-8} in the SDP solver Mosek and h is rounding to 4 decimal places, we have $\epsilon = \frac{10^{-4}}{2}$. In addition, as the absolute value of each element in $\widehat{C}$ is less than 10^3, and the dimension of D is less than 10^3, we obtain

$$\beta = \frac{(D+1)\kappa}{1 - (2D+2)\kappa}\text{tr}(\widetilde{C}) + 4(D+1)(2(D+2) + \max_i(\widetilde{C}_{ii}))\eta \leq 10^{-6}.$$

Consequently, $\gamma_1\epsilon \leq 6557 \cdot \frac{10^{-4}}{2} < \frac{1}{2}$, $\gamma_2\beta \leq 2320 \cdot 10^{-6} < \frac{1}{2}$, which imply that $h(x, y, z) > 0$ presented in Example 2 is indeed a real interpolant.

Remark 1. Besides, the result could be verified by the following symbolic computation procedure instead: computing $P_\mathbf{x}(\phi)$ and $P_\mathbf{x}(\psi)$ first by some symbolic tools, such as Redlog [8] which is a package that extends the computer algebra system REDUCE to a computer logic system; then verifying

$\mathbf{x} \in P_{\mathbf{x}}(\phi) \Rightarrow h(\mathbf{x}) > 0$ and $\mathbf{x} \in P_{\mathbf{x}}(\psi) \Rightarrow h(\mathbf{x}) < 0$. For this example, $P_{x,y,z}(\phi)$ and $P_{x,y,z}(\psi)$ obtained by Redlog are too complicated and therefore not presented here. The symbolic computation can verify that $h(x, y, z)$ in this example is exactly an interpolant, which confirms our conclusion. Alternatively, we can also solve the SDP in (9) using a SDP solver with infinite precision [15], and obtain an exact result. But this only works for problems with small size because a SDP solver with infinite precision is essentially based on symbolic computation as commented in [15].

6   Generalizing to General Polynomial Formulas

Problem 2. Let $\phi(\mathbf{x}, \mathbf{y})$ and $\psi(\mathbf{x}, \mathbf{z})$ be two polynomial formulas defined as follows,

$$\phi(\mathbf{x}, \mathbf{y}) : \bigvee_{i=1}^{m} \phi_i, \ \phi_i = \bigwedge_{k=1}^{K_i} f_{i,k}(\mathbf{x}, \mathbf{y}) \geq 0; \quad \psi(\mathbf{x}, \mathbf{z}) : \bigvee_{j=1}^{n} \psi_j, \ \psi_j = \bigwedge_{s=1}^{S_j} g_{j,s}(\mathbf{x}, \mathbf{z}) \geq 0,$$

where all $f_{i,k}$ and $g_{j,s}$ are polynomials. Suppose $\phi \wedge \psi \models \bot$, and for $i = 1, \dots, m$, $j = 1, \dots, n$, $\{(\mathbf{x}, \mathbf{y}) \mid \phi_i(\mathbf{x}, \mathbf{y})\}$ and $\{(\mathbf{x}, \mathbf{z}) \mid \psi_j(\mathbf{x}, \mathbf{z})\}$ are all semi-algebraic sets of the Archimedean form. Find a polynomial $h(\mathbf{x})$ such that $h(\mathbf{x}) > 0$ is an interpolant for ϕ and ψ.

Theorem 9. *For Problem 2, there exists a polynomial $h(\mathbf{x})$ satisfying*

$$\forall \mathbf{x} \in P_{\mathbf{x}}(\phi(\mathbf{x}, \mathbf{y})).h(\mathbf{x}) > 0, \quad \forall \mathbf{x} \in P_{\mathbf{x}}(\psi(\mathbf{x}, \mathbf{z})).h(\mathbf{x}) < 0.$$

Proof. We just need to prove that Lemma 1 holds for Problem 2 as well. Since $\{(\mathbf{x}, \mathbf{y}) \mid \phi_i(\mathbf{x}, \mathbf{y})\}$ and $\{(\mathbf{x}, \mathbf{z}) \mid \psi_j(\mathbf{x}, \mathbf{z})\}$ are all semi-algebraic sets of the Archimedean form, then $\{(\mathbf{x}, \mathbf{y}) \mid \phi(\mathbf{x}, \mathbf{y})\}$ and $\{(\mathbf{x}, \mathbf{z}) \mid \psi(\mathbf{x}, \mathbf{z})\}$ both are compact. See $\{(\mathbf{x}, \mathbf{y}) \mid \phi(\mathbf{x}, \mathbf{y})\}$ or $\{(\mathbf{x}, \mathbf{z}) \mid \psi(\mathbf{x}, \mathbf{z})\}$ as S in the proof of Lemma 1, then Lemma 1 holds for Problem 2. Thus, the rest of proof is same as that for Theorem 2.   □

Corollary 3. *Let $\phi(\mathbf{x}, \mathbf{y})$ and $\psi(\mathbf{x}, \mathbf{z})$ be defined as in Problem 2. There must exist a polynomial $h(\mathbf{x})$ such that $h(\mathbf{x}) > 0$ is an interpolant for ϕ and ψ.*

Theorem 10. *Let $\phi(\mathbf{x}, \mathbf{y})$ and $\psi(\mathbf{x}, \mathbf{z})$ be defined as in Problem 2. Then there exists a polynomial $h(\mathbf{x})$ and $\sum_{i=1}^{m}(K_i + 1) + \sum_{j=1}^{n}(S_j + 1)$ sum of squares polynomials $u_{i,k}(\mathbf{x}, \mathbf{y})$ ($i = 1, \dots, m$, $k = 1, \dots, K_i + 1$), $v_{j,s}(\mathbf{x}, \mathbf{z})$ ($j = 1, \dots, n$, $s = 1, \dots, S_j$) satisfying the following semi-definite constraints such that $h(\mathbf{x}) > 0$ is an interpolant for $\phi(\mathbf{x}, \mathbf{y})$ and $\psi(\mathbf{x}, \mathbf{z})$:*

$$h - 1 = \sum_{k=1}^{K_i} u_{i,k} f_{i,k} + u_{i,K_i+1}, \quad i = 1, \dots, m; \tag{18}$$

$$-h - 1 = \sum_{s=1}^{S_j} v_{j,s} g_{j,s} + v_{j,S_j+1}, \quad j = 1, \dots, n. \tag{19}$$

Proof. By the property of Archimedean, the proof is same as that for Theorem 5.   □

Similarly, Problem 2 can be equivalently reformulated as the problem of searching for sum of squares polynomials satisfying

$$
\begin{cases}
h(\mathbf{x}) - 1 - \displaystyle\sum_{k=1}^{K_i} u_{i,k} f_{i,k} \in \sum \mathbb{R}[\mathbf{x}, \mathbf{y}]^2, i = 1, \ldots, m; \\[2.5ex]
-h(\mathbf{x}) - 1 - \displaystyle\sum_{s=1}^{S_j} v_{j,s} g_{j,s} \in \sum \mathbb{R}[\mathbf{x}, \mathbf{z}]^2, j = 1, \ldots, n; \\[2.5ex]
u_{i,k} \in \sum \mathbb{R}[\mathbf{x}, \mathbf{y}]^2, i = 1, \ldots, m, k = 1, \ldots, K_i; \\[1.5ex]
v_{j,s} \in \sum \mathbb{R}[\mathbf{x}, \mathbf{z}]^2, j = 1, \ldots, n, s = 1, \ldots, S_j.
\end{cases}
\tag{20}
$$

Example 4. Consider

$$
\phi(x, y, a_1, a_2, b_1, b_2) : (f_1 \geq 0 \wedge f_2 \geq 0) \vee (f_3 \geq 0 \wedge f_4 \geq 0),
$$
$$
\psi(x, y, c_1, c_2, d_1, d_2) : (g_1 \geq 0 \wedge g_2 \geq 0) \vee (g_3 \geq 0 \wedge g_4 \geq 0),
$$

where

$$
\begin{aligned}
f_1 &= 16 - (x+y-4)^2 - 16(x-y)^2 - a_1^2, & f_2 &= x + y - a_2^2 - (2 - a_2)^2, \\
f_3 &= 16 - (x+y+4)^2 - 16(x-y)^2 - b_1^2, & f_4 &= -x - y - b_2^2 - (2 - b_2)^2, \\
g_1 &= 16 - 16(x+y)^2 - (x-y+4)^2 - c_1^2, & g_2 &= y - x - c_2^2 - (1 - c_2)^2, \\
g_3 &= 16 - 16(x+y)^2 - (x-y-4)^2 - d_1^2, & g_4 &= x - y - d_2^2 - (1 - d_2)^2.
\end{aligned}
$$

We get a concrete SDP problem of the form (20) by setting the degree of $h(x, y)$ in (20) to be 2. Using the MATLAB package YALMIP and Mosek, we obtain

$$
h(x, y) = -2.3238 + 0.6957x^2 + 0.6957y^2 + 7.6524xy.
$$

The result is plotted in Fig. 3, and can be verified either by numerical error analysis as in Example 2 or by a symbolic procedure like REDUCE as described in Remark 1.

Example 5 (Ultimate). Consider the following example taken from [5], which is a challenging benchmark to existing approaches for nonlinear interpolant generation.

$$
\phi = (f_1 \geq 0 \wedge f_2 \geq 0 \vee f_3 \geq 0) \wedge f_4 \geq 0 \wedge f_5 \geq 0 \vee f_6 \geq 0,
$$
$$
\psi = (g_1 \geq 0 \wedge g_2 \geq 0 \vee g_3 \geq 0) \wedge g_4 \geq 0 \wedge g_5 \geq 0 \vee g_6 \geq 0,
$$

where

$$
\begin{aligned}
f_1 &= 3.8025 - x^2 - y^2, & f_2 &= y, \\
f_3 &= 0.9025 - (x-1)^2 - y^2, & f_4 &= (x-1)^2 + y^2 - 0.09, \\
f_5 &= (x+1)^2 + y^2 - 1.1025, & f_6 &= 0.04 - (x+1)^2 - y^2, \\
g_1 &= 3.8025 - x^2 - y^2, & g_2 &= -y, \\
g_3 &= 0.9025 - (x+1)^2 - y^2, & g_4 &= (x+1)^2 + y^2 - 0.09, \\
g_5 &= (x-1)^2 + y^2 - 1.1025, & g_6 &= 0.04 - (x-1)^2 - y^2.
\end{aligned}
$$

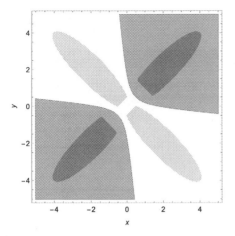

Fig. 3. Example 4. (Red region: $P_{x,y}$ ($\phi(x, y, a_1, a_2, b_1, b_2)$); green region: $P_{x,y}(\psi(x, y, c_1, c_2, d_1, d_2))$; gray region: $\{(x, y) \mid h(x, y) > 0\}$.) (Color figure online)

Fig. 4. Example 5. (Red region: $P_{x,y}$ ($\phi(x, y)$); green region: $P_{x,y}(\psi(x, y))$; gray region: $\{(x, y) \mid h(x, y) > 0\}$.) (Color figure online)

We first convert ϕ and ψ to the disjunction normal form as:

$$\phi = (f_1 \geq 0 \wedge f_2 \geq 0 \wedge f_4 \geq 0 \wedge f_5 \geq 0) \vee (f_3 \geq 0 \wedge f_4 \geq 0 \wedge f_5 \geq 0) \vee (f_6 \geq 0),$$
$$\psi = (g_1 \geq 0 \wedge g_2 \geq 0 \wedge g_4 \geq 0 \wedge g_5 \geq 0) \vee (g_3 \geq 0 \wedge g_4 \geq 0 \wedge g_5 \geq 0) \vee (g_6 \geq 0).$$

We get a concrete SDP problem of the form (20) by setting the degree of $h(x, y)$ in (20) to be 7. Using the MATLAB package YALMIP and Mosek, keeping the decimal to four, we obtain

$$\begin{aligned}
h(x, y) = {} & 1297.5980x + 191.3260y - 3172.9653x^3 + 196.5763x^2y + 2168.1739xy^2 \\
& + 1045.7373y^3 + 1885.8986x^5 - 1009.6275x^4y + 3205.3793x^3y^2 - 1403.5431x^2y^3 \\
& + 1842.0669xy^4 + 1075.2003y^5 - 222.0698x^7 + 547.9542x^6y - 704.7474x^5y^2 \\
& + 1724.7008x^4y^3 - 728.2229x^3y^4 + 1775.7548x^2y^5 - 413.3771xy^6 + 1210.2617y^7.
\end{aligned}$$

The result is plotted in Fig. 4, and can be verified either by numerical error analysis as in Example 2 or by a symbolic procedure like REDUCE as described in Remark 1.

7   Application to Invariant Generation

In this section, as an application, we sketch how to apply our approach to invariant generation in program verification, the details can be found in [11].

In [22], Lin *et al.* proposed a framework for invariant generation using *weakest precondition, strongest postcondition* and *interpolation*, which consists of two procedures, i.e., synthesizing invariants by forward interpolation based on *strongest postcondition* and *interpolant generation*, and by backward interpolation based on *weakest precondition* and *interpolant generation*. In [22], only linear invariants can be synthesized as no powerful approaches are available to synthesize nonlinear interpolants. Obviously, our results can strengthen their framework by allowing to generate nonlinear invariants. For example, we can revise the procedure Squeezing Invariant - Forward in their framework and obtain Algorithm 1. The major revisions include:

- firstly, we exploit our method to synthesize interpolants see line 4 in Algorithm 1;
- secondly, we add a conditional statement for A_{i+1} at line 7–10 in Algorithm 1 in order to make A_{i+1} to be Archimedean.

The procedure Squeezing Invariant - backward can be revised similarly.

Algorithm 1. Revised Squeezing Invariant - Forward

Input: An annotated loop: $\{P\}$ while ρ do C $\{Q\}$, where P and Q are Archimedean
Output: (yes/no, $\mathcal{I}$), where $\mathcal{I}$ is a loop invariant
1: $A_0 \leftarrow P$; $B_0 \leftarrow (\neg\rho \wedge \neg Q)$; $i \leftarrow 0$; $j \leftarrow 0$;
2: **while** $\top$ **do**
3:    **if** $(\bigvee_{k=0}^{i} A_i) \wedge B_j$ is not satisfiable, $(\bigvee_{k=0}^{i} A_i)$ and B_j are Archimedean **then**
4:       call our method to synthesize an interpolant for $(\bigvee_{k=0}^{i} A_i)$ and B_j, say $\mathcal{I}_i$;
         {Use our method to generate interpolant}
5:       **if** $\{\mathcal{I}_i \wedge \rho\} C \{\mathcal{I}_i\}$ **then**
6:          **return** (yes, $\mathcal{I}_i$);
7:       **else if** $\mathcal{I}_i$ is Archimedean **then**
8:          $A_{i+1} \leftarrow \mathsf{sp}(\mathcal{I}_i \wedge \rho, C)$;
9:       **else**
10:          $A_{i+1} \leftarrow \mathsf{sp}(A_i \wedge \rho, C)$;
11:      **end if**
         {sp: a predicate transformer to compute the strongest postcondition of C w.r.t. $\mathcal{I}_i \wedge \rho$}
12:      $i \leftarrow i + 1$; $B_{j+1} \leftarrow B_0 \vee (\rho \wedge \mathsf{wp}(C, B_j))$;
         {wp: a predicate transformer to compute the weakest precondition of C w.r.t. B_j}
13:      $j \leftarrow j + 1$;
14:   **else if** A_i is concrete **then**
15:      **return** (no, $\bot$);
16:   **else**
17:      **while** A_i is not concrete **do**
18:         $i \leftarrow i - 1$;
19:      **end while**
20:      $A_{i+1} \leftarrow \mathsf{sp}(A_i \wedge \rho, C)$; $i \leftarrow i + 1$;
21:   **end if**
22: **end while**

Example 6. Consider a loop program given in Algorithm 2 for controlling the acceleration of a car adapted from [21]. Suppose we know that vc is in $[0, 40]$ at the beginning of the loop, we would like to prove that $vc < 49.61$ holds after the loop. Since the loop guard is unknown, it means that the loop may terminate after any number of iterations.

We apply Algorithm 1 to the computation of an invariant to ensure that $vc < 49.61$ holds. Since vc is the velocity of car, $0 \leq vc < 49.61$ is required to hold in order to maintain safety. Via Algorithm 1, we have $A_0 = \{vc \mid vc(40 - vc) \geq 0\}$ and $B = \{vc \mid vc < 0\} \cup \{vc \mid vc \geq 49.61\}$. Here, we replace B with $B' = [-2, -1] \cup [49.61, 55])$, i.e., $B' = \{vc \mid (vc+2)(-1-vc) \geq 0 \vee (vc-49.61)(55-vc) \geq 0\}$, in order to make it with Archimedean form.

Firstly, it is evident that $A_0 : vc(40 - vc) \geq 0$ implies $A_0 \wedge B' \models \bot$. By applying our approach, we obtain an interpolant

$$\mathcal{I}_0 : 1.4378 + 3.3947 * vc - 0.083 * vc^2 > 0$$

for A_0 and B'. It can be verified that $\{\mathcal{I}_0\} C \{\mathcal{I}_0\}$ (line 5) does not hold, where C stands for the loop body.

Secondly, by setting $A_1 = sp(\mathcal{I}_0, C)$ (line 8) and re-calling our approach, we obtain an interpolant

$$\mathcal{I}_1 : 2.0673 + 3.0744 * vc - 0.0734 * vc^2 > 0$$

for $A_0 \cup A_1$ and B'. Likewise, it can be verified that $\{\mathcal{I}_1\} C \{\mathcal{I}_1\}$ (line 5) does not hold.

Algorithm 2. Control code for accelerating a car

```
1: /* Pre: vc ∈ [0, 40] */
2: while unknown do
3:     fa ← 0.5418 * vc * vc;
4:     fr ← 1000 - fa;
5:     ac ← 0.0005 * fr;
6:     vc ← vc + ac;
7: end while
8: /* Post: vc < 49.61 */
```

Thirdly, repeating the above procedure again, we obtain an interpolant

$$\mathcal{I}_2 : 2.2505 + 2.7267 * vc - 0.063 * vc^2 > 0,$$

and it can be verified that $\{\mathcal{I}_2\} C \{\mathcal{I}_2\}$ holds, implying that $\mathcal{I}_2$ is an invariant. Moreover, it is trivial to verify that $\mathcal{I}_2 \Rightarrow vc < 49.61$.

Consequently, we have the conclusion that $\mathcal{I}_2$ is an inductive invariant which witnesses the correctness of the loop.

8   Conclusion

In this paper we propose a sound and complete method to synthesize Craig interpolants for mutually contradictory polynomial formulas $\phi(\mathbf{x}, \mathbf{y})$ and $\psi(\mathbf{x}, \mathbf{z})$, with the form $f_1 \geq 0 \wedge \cdots \wedge f_n \geq 0$, where f_i's are polynomials in $\mathbf{x}, \mathbf{y}$ or $\mathbf{x}, \mathbf{z}$ and the quadratic module generated by f_i's is Archimedean. The interpolant is generated by solving a semi-definite programming problem, which is a generalization of the method in [7] dealing with mutually contradictory formulas with the same set of variables and the method in [10] dealing with mutually contradictory formulas with concave quadratic polynomial inequalities. As an application, we apply our approach to invariant generation in program verification.

As a future work, we would like to consider interpolant synthesizing for formulas with strict polynomial inequalities. Also, it deserves to consider how to synthesize interpolants for the combination of non-linear formulas and other theories based on our approach and other existing ones, as well as further applications to the verification of programs and hybrid systems.

Acknowledgments. We thank Dr. Sicun Gao, Dr. Damien Zufferey and Dr. Mingshuai Chen for their help on using dReal. We are indebted to anonymous reviewers for their detailed and constructive criticisms and comments on the preliminary version, which help to improve the presentation of this paper very much. This work is financially supported by NSFC under grants 61902284 (the first author), 61732001 (the second and fourth authors), 61532019 (the second author), 61836005 (the third author), 61625206 (the fourth author) and 61802318 (the fifth author), and the third author is also in part supported by Hundred Talents Program under grant No. Y8YC235015.

References

1. Benhamou, F., Granvilliers, L.: Continuous and interval constraints. In: Handbook of Constraint Programming. Foundations of Artificial Intelligence, vol. 2, pp. 571–603 (2006)
2. Bierstone, E., Milman, P.D.: Semianalytic and subanalytic sets. Publications Mathematiques de l'IHÉS **67**, 5–42 (1988)
3. Bochnak, J., Coste, M., Roy, M.: Real Algebraic Geometry. Springer, Heidelberg (1998). https://doi.org/10.1007/978-3-662-03718-8
4. Borchers, B.: CSDP, a C library for semidefinite programming. Optim. Methods Softw. **11**(1–4), 613–623 (1999). http://projects.coin-or.org/csdp/
5. Chen, M., Wang, J., An, J., Zhan, B., Kapur, D., Zhan, N.: NIL: learning nonlinear interpolants. In: Fontaine, P. (ed.) CADE 2019. LNCS (LNAI), vol. 11716, pp. 178–196. Springer, Cham (2019). https://doi.org/10.1007/978-3-030-29436-6_11
6. Cimatti, A., Griggio, A., Sebastiani, R.: Efficient interpolant generation in satisfiability modulo theories. In: Ramakrishnan, C.R., Rehof, J. (eds.) TACAS 2008. LNCS, vol. 4963, pp. 397–412. Springer, Heidelberg (2008). https://doi.org/10.1007/978-3-540-78800-3_30
7. Dai, L., Xia, B., Zhan, N.: Generating non-linear interpolants by semidefinite programming. In: Sharygina, N., Veith, H. (eds.) CAV 2013. LNCS, vol. 8044, pp. 364–380. Springer, Heidelberg (2013). https://doi.org/10.1007/978-3-642-39799-8_25

8. Dolzmann, A., Sturm, T.: REDLOG: computer algebra meets computer logic. ACM SIGSAM Bull. **31**(2), 2–9 (1997)
9. D'Silva, V., Kroening, D., Purandare, M., Weissenbacher, G.: Interpolant strength. In: Barthe, G., Hermenegildo, M. (eds.) VMCAI 2010. LNCS, vol. 5944, pp. 129–145. Springer, Heidelberg (2010). https://doi.org/10.1007/978-3-642-11319-2_12
10. Gan, T., Dai, L., Xia, B., Zhan, N., Kapur, D., Chen, M.: Interpolant synthesis for quadratic polynomial inequalities and combination with *EUF*. In: Olivetti, N., Tiwari, A. (eds.) IJCAR 2016. LNCS (LNAI), vol. 9706, pp. 195–212. Springer, Cham (2016). https://doi.org/10.1007/978-3-319-40229-1_14
11. Gan, T., Xia, B., Xue, B., Zhan, N.: Nonlinear Craig interpolant generation. CoRR, abs/1903.01297 (2019)
12. Gao, S., Kong, S., Clarke, E.: Proof generation from delta-decisions. In: SYNASC 2014, pp. 156–163 (2014)
13. Gao, S., Zufferey, D.: Interpolants in nonlinear theories over the reals. In: Chechik, M., Raskin, J.-F. (eds.) TACAS 2016. LNCS, vol. 9636, pp. 625–641. Springer, Heidelberg (2016). https://doi.org/10.1007/978-3-662-49674-9_41
14. Graf, S., Saidi, H.: Construction of abstract state graphs with PVS. In: Grumberg, O. (ed.) CAV 1997. LNCS, vol. 1254, pp. 72–83. Springer, Heidelberg (1997). https://doi.org/10.1007/3-540-63166-6_10
15. Henrion, D., Naldi, S., Safey El Din, M.: Exact algorithms for semidefinite programs with degenerate feasible set. In: ISSAC 2018, pp. 191–198 (2018)
16. Henzinger, T., Jhala, R., Majumdar, R., McMillan, K.: Abstractions from proofs. In: POPL 2004, pp. 232–244 (2004)
17. Jung, Y., Lee, W., Wang, B.-Y., Yi, K.: Predicate generation for learning-based quantifier-free loop invariant inference. In: Abdulla, P.A., Leino, K.R.M. (eds.) TACAS 2011. LNCS, vol. 6605, pp. 205–219. Springer, Heidelberg (2011). https://doi.org/10.1007/978-3-642-19835-9_17
18. Kapur, D., Majumdar, R., Zarba, C.: Interpolation for data structures. In: FSE 2006, pp. 105–116 (2006)
19. Kovács, L., Voronkov, A.: Interpolation and symbol elimination. In: Schmidt, R.A. (ed.) CADE 2009. LNCS (LNAI), vol. 5663, pp. 199–213. Springer, Heidelberg (2009). https://doi.org/10.1007/978-3-642-02959-2_17
20. Krajíček, J.: Interpolation theorems, lower bounds for proof systems, and independence results for bounded arithmetic. J. Symbol. Logic **62**(2), 457–486 (1997)
21. Kupferschmid, S., Becker, B.: Craig interpolation in the presence of non-linear constraints. In: Fahrenberg, U., Tripakis, S. (eds.) FORMATS 2011. LNCS, vol. 6919, pp. 240–255. Springer, Heidelberg (2011). https://doi.org/10.1007/978-3-642-24310-3_17
22. Lin, S., Sun, J., Xiao, H., Sanán, D., Hansen, H.: FiB: squeezing loop invariants by interpolation between forward/backward predicate transformers. In: ASE 2017, pp. 793–803 (2017)
23. Lofberg., J.: YALMIP: a toolbox for modeling and optimization in MATLAB. In: CACSD 2004, pp. 284–289. IEEE (2004)
24. Marshall, M.: Positive Polynomials and Sums of Squares. American Mathematical Society, Providence (2008)
25. McMillan, K.L.: Interpolation and SAT-based model checking. In: Hunt, W.A., Somenzi, F. (eds.) CAV 2003. LNCS, vol. 2725, pp. 1–13. Springer, Heidelberg (2003). https://doi.org/10.1007/978-3-540-45069-6_1
26. McMillan, K.: An interpolating theorem prover. Theoret. Comput. Sci. **345**(1), 101–121 (2005)

27. McMillan, K.L.: Quantified invariant generation using an interpolating saturation prover. In: Ramakrishnan, C.R., Rehof, J. (eds.) TACAS 2008. LNCS, vol. 4963, pp. 413–427. Springer, Heidelberg (2008). https://doi.org/10.1007/978-3-540-78800-3_31

28. Mosek, A.: The MOSEK optimization toolbox for MATLAB manual. Version 7.1 (Revision 28), p. 17 (2015)

29. Mostowski, T.: Some properties of the ring of nash functions. Annali della Scuola Normale Superiore di Pisa **3**(2), 245–266 (1976)

30. Pudlák, P.: Lower bounds for resolution and cutting plane proofs and monotone computations. J. Symbol. Logic **62**(3), 981–998 (1997)

31. Putinar, M.: Positive polynomials on compact semi-algebraic sets. Indiana Univ. Math. J. **42**(3), 969–984 (1993)

32. Roux, P., Voronin, Y.-L., Sankaranarayanan, S.: Validating numerical semidefinite programming solvers for polynomial invariants. Formal Methods Syst. Des. **53**(2), 286–312 (2017). https://doi.org/10.1007/s10703-017-0302-y

33. Rybalchenko, A., Sofronie-Stokkermans, V.: Constraint solving for interpolation. J. Symb. Comput. **45**(11), 1212–1233 (2010)

34. Sofronie-Stokkermans, V.: Interpolation in local theory extensions. In: Logical Methods in Computer Science, vol. 4, no. 4 (2008)

35. Srikanth, A., Sahin, B., Harris, W.: Complexity verification using guided theorem enumeration. In: POPL 2017, pp. 639–652 (2017)

36. Stengle, G.: A nullstellensatz and a positivstellensatz in semialgebraic geometry. Ann. Math. **207**, 87–97 (1974)

37. Yorsh, G., Musuvathi, M.: A combination method for generating interpolants. In: Nieuwenhuis, R. (ed.) CADE 2005. LNCS (LNAI), vol. 3632, pp. 353–368. Springer, Heidelberg (2005). https://doi.org/10.1007/11532231_26

38. Zhan, N., Wang, S., Zhao, H.: Formal Verification of Simulink/Stateflow Diagrams. Springer, Cham (2017). https://doi.org/10.1007/978-3-319-47016-0

39. Zhao, H., Zhan, N., Kapur, D., Larsen, K.G.: A "hybrid" approach for synthesizing optimal controllers of hybrid systems: a case study of the oil pump industrial example. In: Giannakopoulou, D., Méry, D. (eds.) FM 2012. LNCS, vol. 7436, pp. 471–485. Springer, Heidelberg (2012). https://doi.org/10.1007/978-3-642-32759-9_38

Approximate Counting of Minimal Unsatisfiable Subsets

Jaroslav Bendík[1](✉) and Kuldeep S. Meel[2]

[1] Masaryk University, Brno, Czech Republic
xbendik@gmail.com
[2] National University of Singapore, Singapore, Singapore

Abstract. Given an unsatisfiable formula F in CNF, i.e. a set of clauses, the problem of Minimal Unsatisfiable Subset (MUS) seeks to identify a minimal subset of clauses $N \subseteq F$ such that N is unsatisfiable. The emerging viewpoint of MUSes as the root causes of unsatisfiability has led MUSes to find applications in a wide variety of diagnostic approaches. Recent advances in identification and enumeration of MUSes have motivated researchers to discover applications that can benefit from rich information about the set of MUSes. One such extension is that of counting the number of MUSes. The current best approach for MUS counting is to employ a MUS enumeration algorithm, which often does not scale for the cases with a reasonably large number of MUSes.

Motivated by the success of hashing-based techniques in the context of model counting, we design the first approximate MUS counting procedure with (ε, δ) guarantees, called AMUSIC. Our approach avoids exhaustive MUS enumeration by combining the classical technique of universal hashing with advances in QBF solvers along with a novel usage of union and intersection of MUSes to achieve runtime efficiency. Our prototype implementation of AMUSIC is shown to scale to instances that were clearly beyond the realm of enumeration-based approaches.

1 Introduction

Given an unsatisfiable Boolean formula F as a set of clauses $\{f_1, f_2, \ldots f_n\}$, also known as conjunctive normal form (CNF), a set N of clauses is a Minimal Unsatisfiable Subset (MUS) of F iff $N \subseteq F$, N is unsatisfiable, and for each $f \in N$ the set $N \setminus \{f\}$ is satisfiable. Since MUSes can be viewed as representing the *minimal reasons* for unsatisfiability of a formula, MUSes have found applications in wide variety of domains ranging from diagnosis [45], ontologies debugging [1], spreadsheet debugging [29], formal equivalence checking [20], constrained counting and sampling [28], and the like. As the scalable techniques for identification of MUSes appeared only about decade and half ago, the earliest applications primarily focused on a reduction to the identification of a single MUS or a small set of MUSes. With an improvement in the scalability of MUS identification techniques, researchers have now sought to investigate extensions of MUSes

---

Work done in part while the first author visited National University of Singapore.

© The Author(s) 2020
S. K. Lahiri and C. Wang (Eds.): CAV 2020, LNCS 12224, pp. 439–462, 2020.
https://doi.org/10.1007/978-3-030-53288-8_21

and their corresponding applications. One such extension is MUS counting, i.e., counting the number of MUSes of F. Hunter and Konieczny [26], Mu [45], and Thimm [56] have shown that the number of MUSes can be used to compute different inconsistency metrics for general propositional knowledge bases.

In contrast to the progress in the design of efficient MUS identification techniques, the work on MUS counting is still in its nascent stages. Reminiscent of the early days of model counting, the current approach for MUS counting is to employ a complete MUS enumeration algorithm, e.g., [3,12,34,55], to explicitly identify all MUSes. As noted in Sect. 2, there can be up to exponentially many MUSes of F w.r.t. $|F|$, and thus their complete enumeration can be practically intractable. Indeed, contemporary MUS enumeration algorithms often cannot complete the enumeration within a reasonable time [10,12,34,47]. In this context, one wonders: *whether it is possible to design a scalable MUS counter without performing explicit enumeration of MUSes?*

The primary contribution of this paper is a probabilistic counter, called AMUSIC, that takes in a formula F, tolerance parameter ε, confidence parameter δ, and returns an estimate guaranteed to be within $(1 + \varepsilon)$-multiplicative factor of the exact count with confidence at least $1 - \delta$. Crucially, for F defined over n clauses, AMUSIC explicitly identifies only $\mathcal{O}(\log n \cdot \log(1/\delta) \cdot (\varepsilon)^{-2})$ many MUSes even though the number of MUSes can be exponential in n.

The design of AMUSIC is inspired by recent successes in the design of efficient XOR hashing-based techniques [15,17] for the problem of model counting, i.e., given a Boolean formula G, compute the number of models (also known as solutions) of G. We observe that both the problems are defined over a power-set structure. In MUS counting, the goal is to count MUSes in the power-set of F, whereas in model counting, the goal is to count models in the power-set that represents all valuations of variables of G. Chakraborty et al. [18,52] proposed an algorithm, called ApproxMC, for approximate model counting that also provides the (ϵ, δ) guarantees. ApproxMC is currently in its third version, ApproxMC3 [52]. The base idea of ApproxMC3 is to partition the power-set into $nCells$ small cells, then pick one of the cells, and count the number $inCell$ of models in the cell. The total model count is then estimated as $nCells \times inCell$. Our algorithm for MUS counting is based on ApproxMC3. We adopt the high-level idea to partition the power-set of F into small cells and then estimate the total MUS count based on a MUS count in a single cell. The difference between ApproxMC3 and AMUSIC lies in the way of counting the target elements (models vs. MUSes) in a single cell; we propose novel MUS specific techniques to deal with this task. In particular, our contribution is the following:

- We introduce a QBF (quantified Boolean formula) encoding for the problem of counting MUSes in a single cell and use a Σ_3^P oracle to solve it.
- Let $\mathtt{UMU}_F$ and $\mathtt{IMU}_F$ be the union and the intersection of all MUSes of F, respectively. We observe that every MUS of F (1) contains $\mathtt{IMU}_F$ and (2) is contained in $\mathtt{UMU}_F$. Consequently, if we determine the sets $\mathtt{UMU}_F$ and $\mathtt{IMU}_F$, then we can significantly speed up the identification of MUSes in a cell.

– We propose a novel approaches for computing the union UMU_F and the intersection IMU_F of all MUSes of F.
– We implement AMUSIC and conduct an extensive empirical evaluation on a set of *scalable* benchmarks. We observe that AMUSIC is able to compute estimates for problems clearly beyond the reach of existing enumeration-based techniques. We experimentally evaluate the *accuracy* of AMUSIC. In particular, we observe that the estimates computed by AMUSIC are significantly closer to true count than the theoretical guarantees provided by AMUSIC.

Our work opens up several new interesting avenues of research. From a theoretical perspective, we make polynomially many calls to a Σ_3^P oracle while the problem of finding a MUS is known to be in FP^{NP}, i.e. a MUS can be found in polynomial time by executing a polynomial number of calls to an NP-oracle [19,39]. Contrasting this to model counting techniques, where approximate counter makes polynomially many calls to an NP-oracle when the underlying problem of finding satisfying assignment is NP-complete, a natural question is to close the gap and seek to design a MUS counting algorithm with polynomially many invocations of an FP^{NP} oracle. From a practitioner perspective, our work calls for a design of MUS techniques with native support for XORs; the pursuit of native support for XOR in the context of SAT solvers have led to an exciting line of work over the past decade [52,53].

2 Preliminaries and Problem Formulation

A Boolean formula $F = \{f_1, f_2, \ldots, f_n\}$ in a conjunctive normal form (CNF) is a set of Boolean clauses over a set of Boolean variables $Vars(F)$. A Boolean clause is a set $\{l_1, l_2, \ldots, l_k\}$ of literals. A literal is either a variable $x \in Vars(F)$ or its negation $\neg x$. A truth assignment I to the variables $Vars(F)$ is a mapping $Vars(F) \rightarrow \{1,0\}$. A clause $f \in F$ is satisfied by an assignment I iff $I(l) = 1$ for some $l \in f$ or $I(k) = 0$ for some $\neg k \in f$. The formula F is satisfied by I iff I satisfies every $f \in F$; in such a case I is called a *model* of F. Finally, F is *satisfiable* if it has a model; otherwise F is *unsatisfiable*.

A QBF is a Boolean formula where each variable is either universally ($\forall$) or existentially ($\exists$) quantified. We write $Q_1 \cdots Q_k$-QBF, where $Q_1, \ldots Q_k \in \{\forall, \exists\}$, to denote the class of QBF with a particular type of alternation of the quantifiers, e.g., $\exists\forall$-QBF or $\exists\forall\exists$-QBF. Every QBF is either true (valid) or false (invalid). The problem of deciding validity of a formula in $Q_1 \cdots Q_k$-QBF where $Q_1 = \exists$ is Σ_k^P-complete [43].

When it is clear from the context, we write just *formula* to denote either a QBF or a Boolean formula in CNF. Moreover, throughout the whole text, we use F to denote the input Boolean Formula in CNF. Furthermore, we will use capital letters, e.g., S, K, N, to denote other CNF formulas, small letters, e.g., f, f_1, f_i, to denote clauses, and small letters, e.g., x, x', y, to denote variables.

Given a set X, we write $\mathcal{P}(X)$ to denote the power-set of X, and $|X|$ to denote the cardinality of X. Finally, we write $Pr[O : \mathbb{P}]$ to denote the probability of an

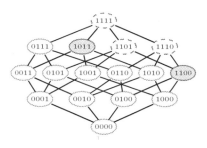

Fig. 1. Illustration of the power set of the formula F from the Example 1. We denote individual subsets of F using the bit-vector representation. The subsets with a dashed border are the unsatisfiable subsets, and the others are satisfiable subsets. The MUSes are filled with a background color. (Color figure online)

outcome O when sampling from a probability space $\mathbb{P}$. When $\mathbb{P}$ is clear from the context, we write just $Pr[O]$.

Minimal Unsatisfiability

Definition 1 (MUS). *A set N, $N \subseteq F$, is a* minimal unsatisfiable subset *(MUS) of F iff N is unsatisfiable and for all $f \in N$ the set $N \setminus \{f\}$ is satisfiable.*

Note that the minimality concept used here is set minimality, not minimum cardinality. Therefore, there can be MUSes with different cardinalities. In general, there can be up to exponentially many MUSes of F w.r.t. $|F|$ (see the Sperner's theorem [54]). We use $\texttt{AMU}_F$ to denote the set of all MUSes of F. Furthermore, we write $\texttt{UMU}_F$ and $\texttt{IMU}_F$ to denote the union and the intersection of all MUSes of F, respectively. Finally, note that every subset S of F can be expressed as a bit-vector over the alphabet $\{0, 1\}$; for example, if $F = \{f_1, f_2, f_3, f_4\}$ and $S = \{f_1, f_4\}$, then the bit-vector representation of S is 1001.

Definition 2. *Let N be an unsatisfiable subset of F and $f \in N$. The clause f is* necessary *for N iff $N \setminus \{f\}$ is satisfiable.*

The necessary clauses are sometimes also called *transition* [6] or *critical* [2] clauses. Note that a set N is a MUS iff every $f \in N$ is necessary for N. Also, note that a clause $f \in F$ is necessary for F iff $f \in \texttt{IMU}_F$.

Example 1. We demonstrate the concepts on an example, illustrated in Fig. 1. Assume that $F = \{f_1 = \{x_1\}, f_2 = \{\neg x_1\}, f_3 = \{x_2\}, f_4 = \{\neg x_1, \neg x_2\}\}$. In this case, $\texttt{AMU}_F = \{\{f_1, f_2\}, \{f_1, f_3, f_4\}\}$, $\texttt{IMU}_F = \{f_1\}$, and $\texttt{UMU}_F = F$.

Hash Functions

Let n and m be positive integers such that $m < n$. By $\{1, 0\}^n$ we denote the set of all bit-vectors of length n over the alphabet $\{1, 0\}$. Given a vector $v \in \{1, 0\}^n$

and $i \in \{1, \ldots, n\}$, we write $v[i]$ to denote the i-th bit of v. A hash function h from a family $H_{xor}(n, m)$ of hash functions maps $\{1, 0\}^n$ to $\{1, 0\}^m$. The family $H_{xor}(n, m)$ is defined as $\{h \mid h(y)[i] = a_{i,0} \oplus (\bigoplus_{k=1}^{n} (a_{i,k} \wedge y[k])) \text{ for all } 1 \leq i \leq m\}$, where $\oplus$ and $\wedge$ denote the Boolean XOR and AND operators, respectively, and $a_{i,k} \in \{1, 0\}$ for all $1 \leq i \leq m$ and $1 \leq k \leq n$.

To choose a hash function uniformly at random from $H_{xor}(n, m)$, we randomly and independently choose the values of $a_{i,k}$. It has been shown [24] that the family $H_{xor}(n, m)$ is pairwise independent, also known as strongly 2-universal. In particular, let us by $h \leftarrow H_{xor}(n, m)$ denote the probability space obtained by choosing a hash function h uniformly at random from $H_{xor}(n, m)$. The property of pairwise independence guarantees that for all $\alpha_1, \alpha_2 \in \{1, 0\}^m$ and for all distinct $y_1, y_2 \in \{1, 0\}^n$, $Pr[\bigwedge_{i=1}^{2} h(y_i) = \alpha_i : h \leftarrow H_{xor}(n, m)] = 2^{-2m}$.

We say that a hash function $h \in H_{xor}(n, m)$ *partitions* $\{0, 1\}^n$ into 2^m *cells*. Furthermore, given a hash function $h \in H_{xor}(n, m)$ and a cell $\alpha \in \{1, 0\}^m$ of h, we define their *prefix-slices*. In particular, for every $k \in \{1, \ldots, m\}$, the kth *prefix* of h, denoted $h^{(k)}$, is a map from $\{1, 0\}^n$ to $\{1, 0\}^k$ such that $h^{(k)}(y)[i] = h(y)[i]$ for all $y \in \{1, 0\}^n$ and for all $i \in \{1, \ldots, k\}$. Similarly, the kth prefix of α, denoted $\alpha^{(k)}$, is an element of $\{1, 0\}^k$ such that $\alpha^{(k)}[i] = \alpha[i]$ for all $i \in \{1, \ldots, k\}$. Intuitively, a cell $\alpha^{(k)}$ of $h^{(k)}$ originates by merging the two cells of $h^{(k+1)}$ that differ only in the last bit.

In our work, we use hash functions from the family $H_{xor}(n, m)$ to partition the power-set $\mathcal{P}(F)$ of the given Boolean formula F into 2^m cells. Furthermore, given a cell $\alpha \in \{0, 1\}^m$, let us by $\mathtt{AMU}_{\langle F, h, \alpha \rangle}$ denote the set of all MUSes in the cell α; formally, $\mathtt{AMU}_{\langle F, h, \alpha \rangle} = \{M \in \mathtt{AMU}_F \mid h(bit(M)) = \alpha\}$, where $bit(M)$ is the bit-vector representation of M. The following observation is crucial for our work.

Observation 1. *For every formula* F, $m \in \{1, \ldots, |F| - 1\}$, $h \in H_{xor}(|F|, m)$, *and* $\alpha \in \{0, 1\}^m$ *it holds that:* $\mathtt{AMU}_{\langle F, h^{(i)}, \alpha^{(i)} \rangle} \supseteq \mathtt{AMU}_{\langle F, h^{(j)}, \alpha^{(j)} \rangle}$ *for every* $i < j$.

Example 2. Assume that we are given a formula F such that $|F| = 4$ and a hash function $h \in H_{xor}(4, 2)$ that is defined via the following values of individual $a_{i,k}$:

$$a_{1,0} = 0, \quad a_{1,1} = 1, \quad a_{1,2} = 1, \quad a_{1,3} = 0, \quad a_{1,4} = 1$$
$$a_{2,0} = 0, \quad a_{2,1} = 1, \quad a_{2,2} = 0, \quad a_{2,3} = 0, \quad a_{2,4} = 1$$

The hash function partitions $\mathcal{P}(F)$ into 4 cells. For example, $h(1100) = 01$ since $h(1100)[1] = 0 \oplus (1 \wedge 1) \oplus (1 \wedge 1) \oplus (0 \wedge 0) \oplus (1 \wedge 0) = 0$ and $h(1100)[2] = 0 \oplus (1 \wedge 1) \oplus (0 \wedge 1) \oplus (0 \wedge 0) \oplus (1 \wedge 0) = 1$. Figure 2 illustrates the whole partition and also illustrates the partition given by the prefix $h^{(1)}$ of h.

2.1 Problem Definitions

In this paper, we are concerned with the following problems.

Name: (ϵ, δ)-#MUS problem
Input: A formula F, a tolerance $\epsilon > 0$, and a confidence $1 - \delta \in (0, 1]$.
Output: A number c such that $Pr[|\mathtt{AMU}_F|/(1 + \epsilon) \leq c \leq |\mathtt{AMU}_F| \cdot (1 + \epsilon)] \geq 1 - \delta$.

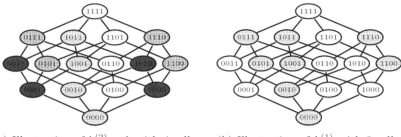

(a) Illustration of $h^{(2)} = h$ with 4 cells: $\boxed{\alpha_1 = 00}$, $\boxed{\alpha_2 = 01}$, $\boxed{\alpha_3 = 10}$, $\boxed{\alpha_4 = 11}$.

(b) Illustration of $h^{(1)}$ with 2 cells: $\boxed{\alpha_1 = 0}$, $\boxed{\alpha_2 = 1}$.

Fig. 2. Illustration of the partition of $\mathcal{P}(F)$ by $h = h^{(2)}$ and $h^{(1)}$ from Example 2. In the case of h, we use 4 colors, orange, pink, white, and blue, to highlight its four cells. In case of $h^{(1)}$, there are only two cells: the white and the blue cells are merged into a white cell, and the pink and the orange cells are merged into an orange cell. (Color figure online)

Name: MUS-membership problem
Input: A formula F and a clause $f \in F$.
Output: *True* if there is a MUS $M \in \mathrm{AMU}_F$ such that $f \in M$ and *False* otherwise.

Name: MUS-union problem
Input: A formula F.
Output: The union UMU_F of all MUSes of F.

Name: MUS-intersection problem
Input: A formula F.
Output: The intersection IMU_F of all MUSes of F.

Name: (ϵ, δ)-#SAT problem
Input: A formula F, a tolerance $\epsilon > 0$, and a confidence $1 - \delta \in (0, 1]$.
Output: A number m such that $Pr[m/(1 + \epsilon) \leq c \leq m \cdot (1 + \epsilon)] \geq 1 - \delta$, where m is the number of models of F.

The main goal of this paper is to provide a solution to the (ϵ, δ)-#MUS problem. We also deal with the MUS-membership, MUS-union and MUS-intersection problems since these problems emerge in our approach for solving the (ϵ, δ)-#MUS problem. Finally, we do not focus on solving the (ϵ, δ)-#SAT problem, however the problem is closely related to the (ϵ, δ)-#MUS problem.

3   Related Work

It is well-known (see e.g., [21,36,51]) that a clause $f \in F$ belongs to IMU_F iff f is necessary for F. Therefore, to compute IMU_F, one can simply check each $f \in F$ for being necessary for F. We are not aware of any work that has focused on the MUS-intersection problem in more detail.

The MUS-union problem was recently investigated by Mencia et al. [42]. Their algorithm is based on gradually refining an *under*-approximation of UMU_F until the exact UMU_F is computed. Unfortunately, the authors experimentally show that their algorithm often fails to find the exact UMU_F within a reasonable time even for relatively small input instances (only an under-approximation is computed). In our work, we propose an approach that works in the other way: we start with an *over-approximation* of UMU_F and gradually refine the approximation to eventually get UMU_F. Another related research was conducted by Janota and Marques-Silva [30] who proposed several QBF encodings for solving the MUS-membership problem. Although they did not focus on finding UMU_F, one can clearly identify UMU_F by solving the MUS-membership problem for each $f \in F$.

As for counting the number of MUSes of F, we are not aware of any previous work dedicated to this problem. Yet, there have been proposed plenty of algorithms and tools (e.g., [3,9,11,12,35,47]) for enumerating/identifying all MUSes of F. Clearly, if we enumerate all MUSes of F, then we obtain the exact value of $|\text{AMU}_F|$, and thus we also solve the (ϵ, δ)-#MUS problem. However, since there can be up to exponentially many of MUSes w.r.t. $|F|$, MUS enumeration algorithms are often not able to complete the enumeration in a reasonable time and thus are not able to find the value of $|\text{AMU}_F|$.

Very similar to the (ϵ, δ)-#MUS problem is the (ϵ, δ)-#SAT problem. Both problems involve the same probabilistic and approximation guarantees. Moreover, both problems are defined over a power-set structure. In MUS counting, the goal is to count MUSes in $\mathcal{P}(F)$, whereas in model counting, the goal is to count models in $\mathcal{P}(Vars(F))$. In this paper, we propose an algorithm for solving the (ϵ, δ)-#MUS problem that is based on ApproxMC3 [15,17,52]. In particular, we keep the high-level idea of ApproxMC3 for processing/exploring the power-set structure, and we propose new low-level techniques that are specific for MUS counting.

4 AMUSIC: A Hashing-Based MUS Counter

We now describe AMUSIC, a hashing-based algorithm designed to solve the (ε, δ)-#MUS problem. The name of the algorithm is an acronym for Approximate Minimal Unsatisfiable Subsets Implicit Counter. AMUSIC is based on ApproxMC3, which is a hashing-based algorithm to solve (ε, δ)-#SAT problem. As such, while the high-level structure of AMUSIC and ApproxMC3 share close similarities, the two algorithms differ significantly in the design of core technical subroutines.

We first discuss the high-level structure of AMUSIC in Sect. 4.1. We then present the key technical contributions of this paper: the design of core subroutines of AMUSIC in Sects. 4.3, 4.4 and 4.5.

4.1 Algorithmic Overview

The main procedure of AMUSIC is presented in Algorithm 1. The algorithm takes as an input a Boolean formula F in CNF, a tolerance $\epsilon\,(> 0)$, and a confidence

---

Algorithm 1: AMUSIC(F, ϵ, δ)

---

1   threshold $\leftarrow 1 + 9.84(1 + \frac{\epsilon}{1+\epsilon})(1 + \frac{1}{\epsilon})^2$
2   $Y \leftarrow$ FindMUSes(F, threshold)
3   **if** $|Y| <$ threshold **then return** $|Y|$
4   $G \leftarrow$ getUMU(F)
5   $\mathrm{I}_G \leftarrow$ getIMU(G)
6   nCells $\leftarrow 2$; $C \leftarrow$ emptyList; $iter \leftarrow 0$
7   **while** $iter < \lceil 17 \log_2(3/\delta) \rceil$ **do**
8     $iter \leftarrow iter + 1$
9   (nCells, nSols) $\leftarrow$ AMUSICCore(G, I_G, threshold, nCells)
10   **if** nCells $\neq$ null **then** AddToList(C, nCells $\times$ nSols)

11 **return** FindMedian(C)

---

parameter $\delta \in (0, 1]$, and returns an estimate of $|\mathrm{AMU}_F|$ within tolerance ϵ and with confidence at least $1 - \delta$. Similar to ApproxMC3, we first check whether $|\mathrm{AMU}_F|$ is smaller than a specific threshold that is a function of ε. This check is carried out via a MUS enumeration algorithm, denoted FindMUSes, that returns a set Y of MUSes of F such that $|Y| = \min(\text{threshold}, |\mathrm{AMU}_F|)$. If $|Y| <$ threshold, the algorithm terminates while identifying the exact value of $|\mathrm{AMU}_F|$. In a significant departure from ApproxMC3, AMUSIC subsequently computes the union (UMU_F) and the intersection (IMU_F) of all MUSes of F by invoking the subroutines GetUMU and GetIMU, respectively. Through the lens of set representation of the CNF formulas, we can view UMU_F as another CNF formula, G. Our key observation is that $\mathrm{AMU}_F = \mathrm{AMU}_G$ (see Sect. 4.2), thus instead of working with the whole F, we can focus only on G. The rest of the main procedure is similar to ApproxMC3, i.e., we repeatedly invoke the core subroutine called AMUSICCore. The subroutine attempts to find an estimate c of $|\mathrm{AMU}_G|$ within the tolerance ϵ. Briefly, to find the estimate, the subroutine partitions $\mathcal{P}(G)$ into nCells cells, then picks one of the cells, and counts the number nSols of MUSes in the cell. The pair (nCells, nSols) is returned by AMUSICCore, and the estimate c of $|\mathrm{AMU}_G|$ is then computed as nSols $\times$ nCells. There is a small chance that AMUSICCore fails to find the estimate; it such a case nCells = nSols = null. Individual estimates are stored in a list C. After the final invocation of AMUSICCore, AMUSIC computes the median of the list C and returns the median as the final estimate of $|\mathrm{AMU}_G|$. The total number of invocations of AMUSICCore is in $\mathcal{O}(\log(1/\delta))$ which is enough to ensure the required confidence $1 - \delta$ (details on assurance of the (ϵ, δ) guarantees are provided in Sect. 4.2).

    We now turn to AMUSICCore which is described in Algorithm 2. The partition of $\mathcal{P}(G)$ into nCells cells is made via a hash function h from $H_{xor}(|G|, m)$, i.e. nCells $= 2^m$. The choice of m is a crucial part of the algorithm as it regulates the size of the cells. Intuitively, it is easier to identify all MUSes of a small cell; however, on the contrary, the use of small cells does not allow to achieve a reasonable tolerance. Based on ApproxMC3, we choose m such that a cell given by a hash function $h \in H_{xor}(|G|, m)$ contains almost threshold many MUSes. In

---

Algorithm 2: AMUSICCore(G, I_G, threshold, $prevNCells$)

---

1 Choose h at random from $H_{xor}(|G|, |G| - 1)$
2 Choose α at random from $\{0, 1\}^{|G|-1}$
3 nSols $\leftarrow$ CountInCell(G, I_G, h, α, threshold)
4 **if** nSols $=$ threshold **then return** (null, null)
5 $mPrev \leftarrow \log_2 prevNCells$
6 (nCells, nSols) $\leftarrow$ LogMUSSearch(G, I_G, h, α, threshold, $mPrev$)
7 **return** (nCells, nSols)

---

particular, the computation of AMUSICCore starts by choosing at random a hash function h from $H_{xor}(|G|, |G| - 1)$ and a cell α at random from $\{0, 1\}^{|G|-1}$. Subsequently, the algorithm tends to identify m^{th} prefixes $h^{(m)}$ and $\alpha^{(m)}$ of h and α, respectively, such that $|\text{AMU}_{\langle G, h^{(m)}, \alpha^{(m)}\rangle}| <$ threshold and $|\text{AMU}_{\langle G, h^{(m-1)}, \alpha^{(m-1)}\rangle}| \geq$ threshold. Recall that $\text{AMU}_{\langle G, h^{(1)}, \alpha^{(1)}\rangle} \supseteq \cdots \supseteq \text{AMU}_{\langle G, h^{(|G|-1)}, \alpha^{(|G|-1)}\rangle}$ (Observation 1, Sect. 2). We also know that the cell $\alpha^{(0)}$, i.e. the whole $\mathcal{P}(G)$, contains at least threshold MUSes (see Algorithm 1, line 3). Consequently, there can exist at most one such m, and it exists if and only if $|\text{AMU}_{\langle G, h^{(|G|-1)}, \alpha^{(|G|-1)}\rangle}| <$ threshold. Therefore, the algorithm first checks whether $|\text{AMU}_{\langle G, h^{(|G|-1)}, \alpha^{(|G|-1)}\rangle}| <$ threshold. The check is carried via a procedure CountInCell that returns the number nSols $= \min(|\text{AMU}_{\langle G, h^{(|G|-1)}, \alpha^{(|G|-1)}\rangle}|, \text{threshold})$. If nSols $=$ threshold, then AMUSICCore fails to find the estimate of $|\text{AMU}_G|$ and terminates. Otherwise, a procedure LogMUSSearch is used to find the required value of m together with the number nSols of MUSes in $\alpha^{(m)}$. The implementation of LogMUSSearch is directly adopted from ApproxMC3 and thus we do not provide its pseudocode here (note that in ApproxMC3 the procedure is called LogSATSearch). We only briefly summarize two main ingredients of the procedure. First, it has been observed that the required value of m is often similar for repeated calls of AMUSICCore. Therefore, the algorithm keeps the value $mPrev$ of m from previous iteration and first test values near $mPrev$. If none of the near values is the required one, the algorithm exploits that $\text{AMU}_{\langle G, h^{(1)}, \alpha^{(1)}\rangle} \supseteq \cdots \supseteq \text{AMU}_{\langle G, h^{(|G|-1)}, \alpha^{(|G|-1)}\rangle}$, which allows it to find the required value of m via the galloping search (variation of binary search) while performing only $\log |G|$ calls of CountInCell.

   Note that in ApproxMC3, the procedure CountInCell is called BSAT and it is implemented via an NP oracle, whereas we use a Σ_3^P oracle to implement the procedure (see Sect. 4.3). The high-level functionality is the same: the procedures use up to threshold calls of the oracle to check whether the number of the target elements (models vs. MUSes) in a cell is lower than threshold.

4.2   Analysis and Comparison with ApproxMC3

Following from the discussion above, there are three crucial technical differences between AMUSIC and ApproxMC3: (1) the implementation of the subroutine CountInCell in the context of MUS, (2) computation of the intersection IMU_F of all MUSes of F and its usage in CountInCell, and (3) computation of the union

UMU_F of all MUSes of F and invocation of the underlying subroutines with G (i.e., UMU_F) instead of F. The usage of CountInCell can be viewed as domain-specific instantiation of BSAT in the context of MUSes. Furthermore, we use the computed intersection of MUSes to improve the runtime efficiency of CountInCell. It is perhaps worth mentioning that prior studies have observed that over 99% of the runtime of ApproxMC3 is spent inside the subroutine BSAT [52]. Therefore, the runtime efficiency of CountInCell is crucial for the runtime performance of AMUSIC, and we discuss in detail, in Sect. 4.3, algorithmic contributions in the context of CountInCell including usage of IMU_F. We now argue that the replacement of F with G in line 4 in Algorithm 1 does not affect correctness guarantees, which is stated formally below:

Lemma 1. *For every G' such that $\mathsf{UMU}_F \subseteq G' \subseteq F$, the following hold:*

$$\mathsf{AMU}_F = \mathsf{AMU}_{G'} \tag{1}$$

$$\mathsf{IMU}_F = \mathsf{IMU}_{G'} \tag{2}$$

Proof. (1) Since $G' \subseteq F$ then every MUS of G' is also a MUS of F. In the other direction, every MUS of F is contained in the union UMU_F of all MUSes of F, and thus every MUS of F is also a MUS of G' ($\supseteq \mathsf{UMU}_F$).

(2) $\mathsf{IMU}_F = \bigcap_{M \in \mathsf{AMU}_F} = \bigcap_{M \in \mathsf{AMU}_{G'}} = \mathsf{IMU}_{G'}$.

Equipped with Lemma 1, we now argue that each run of AMUSIC can be simulated by a run of ApproxMC3 for an appropriately chosen formula. Given an unsatisfiable formula $F = \{f_1, \ldots, f_{|F|}\}$, let us by B_F denote a satisfiable formula such that: (1) $Vars(B_F) = \{x_1, \ldots, x_{|F|}\}$ and (2) an assignment $I : Vars(B_F) \rightarrow \{1, 0\}$ is a model of B_F iff $\{f_i | I(x_i) = 1\}$ is a MUS of F. Informally, models of B_F one-to-one map to MUSes of F. Hence, the size of sets returned by CountInCell for F is identical to the corresponding BSAT for B_F. Since the analysis of ApproxMC3 only depends on the correctness of the size of the set returned by BSAT, we conclude that the answer computed by AMUSIC would satisfy (ε, δ) guarantees. Furthermore, observing that CountInCell makes threshold many queries to Σ_3^P-oracle, we can bound the time complexity. Formally,

Theorem 1. *Given a formula F, a tolerance $\varepsilon > 0$, and a confidence $1 - \delta \in (0, 1]$, let AMUSIC(F, ε, δ) return c. Then $Pr[|\mathsf{AMU}_F|/(1+\epsilon) \le c \le |\mathsf{AMU}_F| \cdot (1+\epsilon)] \ge 1 - \delta$. Furthermore, AMUSIC makes $\mathcal{O}(\log |F| \cdot \frac{1}{\varepsilon^2} \cdot \log(1/\delta))$ calls to Σ_3^P oracle.*

Few words are in order concerning the complexity of AMUSIC. As noted in Sect. 1, for a formula on n variables, approximate model counters make $\mathcal{O}(\log n \cdot \frac{1}{\varepsilon^2} \cdot \log(1/\delta))$ calls to an NP oracle, whereas the complexity of finding a satisfying assignment is NP-complete. In our case, we make calls to a Σ_3^P oracle while the problem of finding a MUS is in FP^{NP}. Therefore, a natural direction of future work is to investigate the design of a hashing-based technique that employs an FP^{NP} oracle.

Algorithm 3: CountInCell(G, $\mathtt{I}_G$, h, α, threshold)

---

1 $c \leftarrow 0$; $\mathcal{M} \leftarrow \{\}$
2 **while** $c <$ threshold **do**
3      $M \leftarrow \mathtt{GetMUS}(G, \mathtt{I}_G, \mathcal{M}, h, \alpha)$
4   **if** $M = $ null **then return** c
5      $\mathcal{M} \leftarrow \mathcal{M} \cup \{M\}$
6      $c \leftarrow c + 1$

7 **return** c

4.3 Counting MUSes in a Cell: CountInCell

In this section, we describe the procedure $\mathtt{CountInCell}$. The input of the procedure is the formula G (i.e., $\mathtt{UMU}_F$), the set $\mathtt{I}_G = \mathtt{IMU}_G$, a hash function $h \in H_{xor}(|G|, m)$, a cell $\alpha \in \{0,1\}^m$, and the threshold value. The output is $c = min(\mathsf{threshold}, |\mathtt{AMU}_{\langle G, h, \alpha \rangle}|)$.

The description is provided in Algorithm 3. The algorithm iteratively calls a procedure $\mathtt{GetMUS}$ that returns either a MUS M such that $M \in (\mathtt{AMU}_{\langle G, h, \alpha \rangle} \setminus \mathcal{M})$ or null if there is no such MUS. For each M, the value of c is increased and M is added to $\mathcal{M}$. The loop terminates either when c reaches the value of threshold or when $\mathtt{GetMUS}$ fails to find a new MUS (i.e., returns null). Finally, the algorithm returns c.

GetMUS. To implement the procedure $\mathtt{GetMUS}$, we build an $\exists\forall\exists$-QBF formula $\mathtt{MUSInCell}$ such that each witness of the formula corresponds to a MUS from $\mathtt{AMU}_{\langle G, h, \alpha \rangle} \setminus \mathcal{M}$. The formula consists of several parts and uses several sets of variables that are described in the following.

The main part of the formula, shown in Eq. (3), introduces the first existential quantifier and a set $P = \{p_1, \ldots, p_{|G|}\}$ of variables that are quantified by the quantifier. Note that each valuation I of P corresponds to a subset S of G; in particular let us by $I_{P,G}$ denote the set $\{f_i \in G \mid I(p_i) = 1\}$. The formula is build in such a way that a valuation I is a witness of the formula if and only if $I_{P,G}$ is a MUS from $\mathtt{AMU}_{\langle G, h, \alpha \rangle} \setminus \mathcal{M}$. This property is expressed via three conjuncts, denoted $\mathtt{inCell}(P)$, $\mathtt{unexplored}(P)$, and $\mathtt{isMUS}(P)$, encoding that (i) $I_{P,G}$ is in the cell α, (ii) $I_{P,G}$ is not in $\mathcal{M}$, and (iii) $I_{P,G}$ is a MUS, respectively.

$$\mathtt{MUSInCell} = \exists P.\, \mathtt{inCell}(P) \wedge \mathtt{unexplored}(P) \wedge \mathtt{isMUS}(P) \tag{3}$$

Recall that the family $H_{xor}(n, m)$ of hash functions is defined as $\{h \mid h(y)[i] = a_{i,0} \oplus (\bigoplus_{k=1}^{n} a_{i,k} \wedge y[k])$ for all $1 \leq i \leq m\}$, where $a_{i,k} \in \{0,1\}$ (Sect. 2). A hash function $h \in H_{xor}(n, m)$ is given by fixing the values of individual $a_{i,k}$ and a cell α of h is a bit-vector from $\{0,1\}^m$. The formula $\mathtt{inCell}(P)$ encoding that the set $I_{P,G}$ is in the cell α of h is shown in Eq. (4).

$$\mathtt{inCell}(P) = \bigwedge_{i=1}^{m} (a_{i,0} \oplus (\bigoplus_{p \in \{p_k \mid a_{i,k}=1\}} p) \oplus \neg\alpha[i]) \tag{4}$$

To encode that we are not interested in MUSes from $\mathcal{M}$, we can simply block all the valuations of P that correspond to these MUSes. However, we can do better. In particular, recall that if M is a MUS, then no proper subset and no proper superset of M can be a MUS; thus, we prune away all these sets from the search space. The corresponding formula is shown in Eq. (5).

$$\texttt{unexplored}(P) = \bigwedge_{M \in \mathcal{M}} ((\bigvee_{f_i \in M} \neg p_i) \wedge (\bigvee_{f_i \notin M} p_i)) \tag{5}$$

The formula $\texttt{isMUS}(P)$ encoding that $I_{P,G}$ is a MUS is shown in Eq. (6). Recall that $I_{P,G}$ is a MUS if and only if $I_{P,G}$ is unsatisfiable and for every *closest subset* S of $I_{P,G}$ it holds that S is satisfiable, where *closest subset* means that $|I_{P,G} \setminus S| = 1$. We encode these two conditions using two subformulas denoted by $\texttt{unsat}(P)$ and $\texttt{noUnsatSubset}(P)$.

$$\texttt{isMUS}(P) = \texttt{unsat}(P) \wedge \texttt{noUnsatSubset}(P) \tag{6}$$

The formula $\texttt{unsat}(P)$, shown in Eq. (7), introduces the set $Vars(G)$ of variables that appear in G and states that every valuation of $Vars(G)$ falsifies at least one clause contained in $I_{P,G}$.

$$\texttt{unsat}(P) = \forall\, Vars(G). \bigvee_{f_i \in G} (p_i \wedge \neg f_i) \tag{7}$$

The formula $\texttt{noUnsatSubset}(P)$, shown in Eq. (8), introduces another set of variables: $Q = \{q_1, \ldots, q_{|G|}\}$. Similarly as in the case of P, each valuation I of Q corresponds to a subset of G defined as $I_{Q,G} = \{f_i \in G \,|\, I(q_i) = 1\}$. The formula expresses that for every valuation I of Q it holds that $I_{Q,G}$ is satisfiable or $I_{Q,G}$ is not a closest subset of $I_{P,G}$.

$$\texttt{noUnsatSubset}(P) = \forall Q.\, \texttt{sat}(Q) \vee \neg \texttt{subset}(Q, P) \tag{8}$$

The requirement that $I_{Q,G}$ is satisfiable is encoded in Eq. (9). Since we are already reasoning about the satisfiability of G's clauses in Eq. (7), we introduce here a copy G' of G where each variable x_i of G is substituted by its primed copy x_i'. Equation (9) states that there exists a valuation of $Vars(G')$ that satisfies $I_{Q,G}$.

$$\texttt{sat}(Q) = \exists\, Vars(G'). \bigwedge_{f_i \in G'} (\neg q_i \vee f_i) \tag{9}$$

Equation (10) encodes that $I_{Q,G}$ is a closest subset of $I_{P,G}$. To ensure that $I_{Q,G}$ is a *subset* of $I_{P,G}$, we add the clauses $q_i \rightarrow p_i$. To ensure the *closeness*, we use cardinality constraints. In particular, we introduce another set $R = \{r_1, \ldots, r_{|G|}\}$ of variables and enforce their values via $r_i \leftrightarrow (p_i \wedge \neg q_i)$. Intuitively, the number of variables from R that are set to 1 equals to $|I_{P,G} \setminus I_{Q,G}|$. Finally, we add cardinality constraints, denoted by $\texttt{exactlyOne}(R)$, ensuring that exactly one r_i is set to 1.

$$\texttt{subset}(Q, P) = \exists R. \bigwedge_{p_i \in P} ((q_i \to p_i) \land (r_i \leftrightarrow (p_i \land \neg q_i))) \land \texttt{exactlyOne}(R) \quad (10)$$

Note that instead of encoding a *closest subset* in Eq. 10, we could just encode that $I_{Q,G}$ is an arbitrary proper subset of $I_{P,G}$ as it would still preserve the meaning of Eq. 6 that $I_{P,G}$ is a MUS. Such an encoding would not require introducing the set R of variables and also, at the first glance, would save a use of one existential quantifier. The thing is that the whole formula would still be in the form of $\exists\forall\exists$-QBF due to Eq. 9 (which introduces the second existential quantifier). The advantage of using a closet subset is that we significantly prune the search space of the QBF solver. It is thus matter of contemporary QBF solvers whether it is more beneficial to reduce the number of variables (by removing R) or to prune the searchspace via R.

For the sake of lucidity, we have not exploited the knowledge of $\texttt{IMU}_G$ (I_G) while presenting the above equations. Since we know that every clause $f \in \texttt{IMU}_G$ has to be contained in every MUS of G, we can fix the values of the variables $\{p_i \mid f_i \in \texttt{IMU}_G\}$ to 1. This, in turn, significantly simplifies the equations and prunes away exponentially many (w.r.t. $|\texttt{IMU}_G|$) valuations of P, Q, and R, that need to be assumed. To solve the final formula, we employ a $\exists\forall\exists$-QBF solver, i.e., a Σ_3^P oracle.

Finally, one might wonder why we use our custom solution for identifying MUSes in a cell instead of employing one of existing MUS extraction techniques. Conventional MUS extraction algorithms cannot be used to identify MUSes that are in a cell since the cell is not "continuous" w.r.t. the set containment. In particular, assume that we have three sets of clauses, K, L, M, such that $K \subset L \subset M$. It can be the case that K and M are in the cell, but L is not in the cell. Contemporary MUS extraction techniques require the search space to be continuous w.r.t. the set containment and thus cannot be used in our case.

4.4   Computing $\texttt{UMU}_F$

We now turn our attention to computing the union $\texttt{UMU}_F$ (i.e., G) of all MUSes of F. Let us start by describing well-known concepts of *autark variables* and a *lean kernel*. A set $A \subseteq Vars(F)$ of variables is an *autark* of F iff there exists a truth assignment to A such that every clause of F that contains a variable from A is satisfied by the assignment [44]. It holds that the union of two autark sets is also an autark set, thus there exists a unique largest autark set (see, e.g., [31,32]). The *lean kernel* of F is the set of all clauses that do not contain any variable from the largest autark set. It is known that the *lean kernel* of F is an over-approximation of $\texttt{UMU}_F$ (see e.g., [31,32]), and there were proposed several algorithms, e.g., [33,38], for computing the lean kernel.

Algorithm. Our approach for computing $\texttt{UMU}_F$ consists of two parts. First, we compute the lean kernel K of F to get an over-approximation of $\texttt{UMU}_F$, and

---

Algorithm 4: getUMU(F)

---

1 $K \leftarrow$ the lean kernel of F; $\mathcal{M} \leftarrow \{\}$
2 **for** $f \in K \setminus \{f \in M \mid M \in \mathcal{M}\}$ **do**
3 $\quad$ | $\quad W \leftarrow$ checkNecessity(f, K)
4 $\quad$ | $\quad$ **if** $W \neq$ **null then** $\mathcal{M} \leftarrow \mathcal{M} \cup \{$ a MUS of $W\}$
5 $\quad$ | $\quad$ **else** $K \leftarrow K \setminus \{f\}$
6 **return** K

---

then we gradually refine the over-approximation K until K is exactly the set UMU_F. The refinement is done by solving the MUS-membership problem for each $f \in K$. To solve the MUS-membership problem efficiently, we reveal a connection to necessary clauses, as stated in the following lemma.

Lemma 2. *A clause $f \in F$ belongs to UMU_F iff there is a subset W of F such that W is unsatisfiable and f is necessary for W (i.e., $W \setminus \{f\}$ is satisfiable).*

Proof. $\Rightarrow$: Let $f \in \text{UMU}_F$ and $M \in \text{AMU}_F$ such that $f \in M$. Since M is a MUS then $M \setminus \{f\}$ is satisfiable; thus f is necessary for M.
$\Leftarrow$: If W is a subset of F and $f \in W$ a necessary clause for W then f has to be contained in every MUS of W. Moreover, W has at least one MUS and since $W \subseteq F$, then every MUS of W is also a MUS of F.

Our approach for computing UMU_F is shown in Algorithm 4. It takes as an input the formula F and outputs UMU_F (denoted K). Moreover, the algorithm maintains a set $\mathcal{M}$ of MUSes of F. Initially, $\mathcal{M} = \emptyset$ and K is set to the lean kernel of F; we use an approach by Marques-Silva et al. [38] to compute the lean kernel. At this point, we know that $K \supseteq \text{UMU}_F \supseteq \{f \in M \mid M \in \mathcal{M}\}$. To find UMU_F, the algorithm iteratively determines for each $f \in K \setminus \{f \in M \mid M \in \mathcal{M}\}$ if $f \in \text{UMU}_F$. In particular, for each f, the algorithm checks whether there exists a subset W of K such that f is necessary for W (Lemma 2). The task of finding W is carried out by a procedure checkNecessity(f, K). If there is no such W, then the algorithm removes f from K. In the other case, if W exists, the algorithm finds a MUS of W and adds the MUS to the set $\mathcal{M}$. Any available single MUS extraction approach, e.g., [2,5,7,46], can be used to find the MUS.

To implement the procedure checkNecessity(f, K) we build a QBF formula that is true iff there exists a set $W \subseteq K$ such that W is unsatisfiable and f is necessary for W. To represent W we introduce a set $S = \{s_g \mid g \in K\}$ of Boolean variables; each valuation I of S corresponds to a subset $I_{S,K}$ of K defined as $I_{S,K} = \{g \in K \mid I(s_g) = 1\}$. Our encoding is shown in Eq. 11.

$$\exists S, \textit{Vars}(K). \forall \textit{Vars}(K'). s_f \wedge (\bigwedge_{g \in K \setminus \{f\}} (g \vee \neg s_g)) \wedge (\bigvee_{g \in K'} (\neg g \wedge s_g)) \qquad (11)$$

The formula consists of three main conjuncts. The first conjunct ensures that f is present in $I_{S,K}$. The second conjunct states that $I_{S,K} \setminus \{f\}$ is satisfiable, i.e., that there exists a valuation of $Vars(K)$ that satisfies $I_{S,K} \setminus \{f\}$. Finally, the last conjunct express that $I_{S,K}$ is unsatisfiable, i.e., that every valuation of $Vars(K)$ falsifies at least one clause of $I_{S,K}$. Since we are already reasoning about variables of K in the second conjunct, in the third conjunct, we use a primed version (a copy) K' of K.

Alternative QBF Encodings. Janota and Marques-Silva [30] proposed three other QBF encodings for the MUS-membership problem, i.e., for deciding whether a given $f \in F$ belongs to UMU_F. Two of the three proposed encodings are typically inefficient; thus, we focus on the third encoding, which is the most concise among the three. The encoding, referred to as JM encoding (after the initials of the authors), uses only two quantifiers in the form of $\exists\forall$-QBF and it is only linear in size w.r.t. $|F|$. The underlying ideas by JM encoding and our encoding differ significantly. Our encoding is based on necessary clauses (Lemma 2), whereas JM exploits a connection to so-called *Maximal Satisfiable Subsets*. Both the encodings use the same quantifiers; however, our encoding is smaller. In particular, the JM uses $2 \times (Vars(F) + |F|)$ variables whereas our encoding uses only $|F| + 2 \times Vars(F)$ variables, and leads to smaller formulas.

Implementation. Recall that we compute UMU_F to reduce the search space, i.e. instead of working with the whole F, we work only with $G = \text{UMU}_F$. The soundness of this reduction is witnessed in Lemma 1 (Sect. 4.2). In fact, Lemma 1 shows that it is sound to reduce the search space to any G' such that $\text{UMU}_F \subseteq G' \subseteq F$. Since our algorithm for computing UMU_F subsumes repeatedly solving a Σ_2^P-complete problem, it can be very time-consuming. Therefore, instead of computing the exact UMU_F, we optionally compute only an over-approximation G' of UMU_F. In particular, we set a (user-defined) time limit for computing the lean kernel K of F. Moreover, we use a time limit for executing the procedure checkNecessity(f, K); if the time limit is exceeded for a clause $f \in K$, we conservatively assume that $f \in \text{UMU}_F$, i.e., we over-approximate.

Sparse Hashing and UMU_F. The approach of computation of UMU_F is similar to, in spirit, computation of independent support of a formula to design sparse hash functions [16,28]. Briefly, given a Boolean formula H, an *independent support* of H is a set $\mathcal{I} \subseteq Vars(H)$ such that in every model of H, the truth assignment to $\mathcal{I}$ uniquely determines the truth assignment to $Vars(H) \setminus \mathcal{I}$. Practically, independent support can be used to reduce the search space where a model counting algorithm searches for models of H. It is interesting to note that the state of the art technique reduces the computation of independent support of a formula in the context of model counting to that of computing (Group) Minimal Unsatisfiable Subset (GMUS). Thus, a formal study of computation of independent support in the context of MUSes is an interesting direction of future work.

Algorithm 5: getIMU(G)

---

1 $C \leftarrow G$
2 $K \leftarrow \emptyset$
3 **while** $C \neq \emptyset$ **do**
4       $f \leftarrow$ choose $f \in C$
5       $(sat?,\ I,\ core) \leftarrow$ checkSAT($G \setminus \{f\}$)
6   **if** $sat?$ **then**
7           $R \leftarrow$ RMR($G,\ f,\ I$)
8           $K \leftarrow K \cup \{f\} \cup R$
9           $C \leftarrow C \setminus (\{f\} \cup R)$
10   **else**
11          $C \leftarrow C \cap core$

12 **return** K

4.5 Computing IMU_G

Our approach to compute the intersection IMU_G (i.e., I_G) of all MUSes of G is composed of several ingredients. First, recall that a clause $f \in G$ belongs to IMU_G iff f is necessary for G. Another ingredient is the ability of contemporary SAT solvers to provide either a model or an *unsat core* of a given unsatisfiable formula $N \subseteq G$, i.e., a small, yet not necessarily minimal, unsatisfiable subset of N. The final ingredient is a technique called *model rotation*. The technique was originally proposed by Marques-Silva and Lynce [40], and it serves to explore necessary clauses based on other already known necessary clauses. In particular, let f be a necessary clause for G and $I : Vars(G) \rightarrow \{0,1\}$ a model of $G \setminus \{f\}$. Since G is unsatisfiable, the model I does not satisfy f. The model rotation attempts to alter I by switching, one by one, the Boolean assignment to the variables $Vars(\{f\})$. Each variable assignment I' that originates from such an alternation of I necessarily satisfies f and does not satisfy at least one $f' \in G$. If it is the case that there is exactly one such f', then f' is necessary for G. An improved version of model rotation, called *recursive model rotation*, was later proposed by Belov and Marques-Silva [6] who noted that the model rotation could be recursively performed on the newly identified necessary clauses.

Our approach for computing IMU_G is shown in Algorithm 5. To find IMU_G, the algorithm decides for each f whether f is necessary for G. In particular, the algorithm maintains two sets: a set C of *candidates* on necessary clauses and a set K of already known necessary clauses. Initially, K is empty and $C = G$. At the end of computation, C is empty and K equals to IMU_G. The algorithm works iteratively. In each iteration, the algorithm picks a clause $f \in C$ and checks $G \setminus \{f\}$ for satisfiability via a procedure checkSAT. Moreover, checkSAT returns either a model I or an unsat core *core* of $G \setminus \{f\}$. If $G \setminus \{f\}$ is satisfiable, i.e. f is necessary for G, the algorithm employs the recursive model rotation, denoted by RMR(G, f, I), to identify a set R of additional necessary clauses. Subsequently, all the newly identified necessary clauses are added to K and removed from C.

In the other case, when $G \setminus \{f\}$ is unsatisfiable, the set C is reduced to $C \cap core$ since every necessary clause of G has to be contained in every unsatisfiable subset of G. Note that $f \notin core$, thus at least one clause is removed from C.

5   Experimental Evaluation

We employed several external tools to implement AMUSIC. In particular, we use the QBF solver CAQE [49] for solving the QBF formula MUSInCell, the 2QBF solver CADET [50] for solving our $\exists\forall$-QBF encoding while computing UMU_F, and the QBF preprocessor QRATPre+ [37] for preprocessing/simplifying our QBF encodings. Moreover, we employ muser2 [7] for a single MUS extraction while computing UMU_F, a MaxSAT solver UWrMaxSat [48] to implement the algorithm by Marques-Silva et al. [38] for computing the lean kernel of F, and finally, we use a toolkit called pysat [27] for encoding cardinality constraints used in the formula MUSInCell. The tool along with all benchmarks that we used is available at https://github.com/jar-ben/amusic.

Objectives. As noted earlier, AMUSIC is the first technique to (approximately) count MUSes without explicit enumeration. We demonstrate the efficacy of our approach via a comparison with two state of the art techniques for MUS enumeration: MARCO [35] and MCSMUS [3]. Within a given time limit, a MUS enumeration algorithm either identifies the whole AMU_F, i.e., provides the exact value of $|AMU_F|$, or identifies just a subset of AMU_F, i.e., provides an under-approximation of $|AMU_F|$ with no approximation guarantees.

The objective of our empirical evaluation was two-fold: First, we experimentally examine the scalability of AMUSIC, MARCO, and MCSMUS w.r.t. $|AMU_F|$. Second, we examine the *empirical accuracy* of AMUSIC.

Benchmarks and Experimental Setup. Given the lack of dedicated counting techniques, there is no sufficiently large set of publicly available benchmarks to perform critical analysis of counting techniques. To this end, we focused on a recently emerging theme of evaluation of SAT-related techniques on *scalable benchmarks*[1]. In keeping with prior studies employing empirical methodology based on scalable benchmarks [22,41], we generated a custom collection of CNF benchmarks. The benchmarks mimic requirements on multiprocessing systems. Assume that we are given a system with two groups (kinds) of processes, $A = \{a_1, \ldots, a_{|A|}\}$ and $B = \{b_1, \ldots, b_{|B|}\}$, such that $|A| \geq |B|$. The processes require resources of the system; however, the resources are limited. Therefore, there are restrictions on which processes can be active simultaneously. In particular, we have the following three types of mutually independent restrictions on the system:

---

[1] M. Y. Vardi, in his talk at BIRS CMO 18w5208 workshop, called on the SAT community to focus on scalable benchmarks in lieu of competition benchmarks. Also, see: https://gitlab.com/satisfiability/scalablesat (Accessed: May 10, 2020).

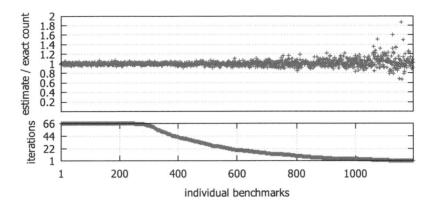

Fig. 3. The number of completed iterations and the accuracy of the final MUS count estimate for individual benchmarks.

- The first type of restriction states that "at most $k - 1$ processes from the group A can be active simultaneously", where $k \leq |A|$.
- The second type of restriction enforces that "if no process from B is active then at most $k-1$ processes from A can be active, and if at least one process from B is active then at most $l - 1$ processes from A can be active", where $k, l \leq |A|$.
- The third type of restriction includes the second restriction. Moreover, we assume that a process from B can activate a process from A. In particular, for every $b_i \in B$, we assume that when b_i is active, then a_i is also active.

We encode the three restrictions via three Boolean CNF formulas, R_1, R_2, R_3. The formulas use three sets of variables: $X = \{x_1, \ldots, x_{|A|}\}$, $Y = \{y_1, \ldots, y_{|B|}\}$, and Z. The sets X and Y represent the Boolean information about activity of processes from A and B: a_i is active iff $x_i = 1$ and b_j is active iff $y_j = 1$. The set Z contains additional auxiliary variables. Moreover, we introduce a formula $\mathtt{ACT} = (\bigwedge_{x_i \in X} x_i) \wedge (\bigwedge_{y_i \in Y} y_i)$ encoding that all processes are active. For each $i \in \{1, 2, 3\}$, the conjunction $G_i = R_i \wedge \mathtt{ACT}$ is unsatisfiable. Intuitively, every MUS of G_i represents a minimal subset of processes that need to be active to violate the restriction. The number of MUSes in G_1, G_2, and G_3 is $\binom{|A|}{k}$, $\binom{|A|}{k} + |B| \times \binom{|A|}{l}$, and $\binom{|A|}{k} + \sum_{i=1}^{|B|}(\binom{|B|}{i} \times \binom{|A|-1}{l-i})$, respectively. We generated G_1, G_2, and G_3 for these values: $10 \leq |A| \leq 30$, $2 \leq |B| \leq 6$, $\lfloor \frac{|A|}{2} \rfloor \leq k \leq \lfloor \frac{3 \times |A|}{2} \rfloor$, and $l = k - 1$. In total, we obtained 1353 benchmarks (formulas) that range in their size from 78 to 361 clauses, use from 40 to 152 variables, and contain from 120 to 1.7×10^9 MUSes.

All experiments were run using a time limit of 7200 s and computed on an AMD EPYC 7371 16-Core Processor, 1 TB memory machine running Debian Linux 4.19.67-2. The values of ϵ and δ were set to 0.8 and 0.2, respectively.

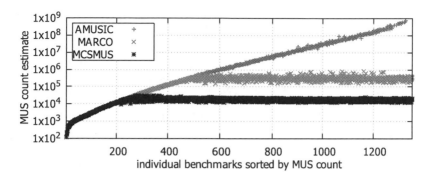

Fig. 4. Scalability of AMUSIC, MARCO, and MCSMUS w.r.t. $|AMU_F|$.

Accuracy. Recall that to compute an estimate c of $|AMU_F|$, AMUSIC performs multiple iteration of executing AMUSICCore to get a list C of multiple estimates of $|AMU_F|$, and then use the median of C as the final estimate c. The more iterations are performed, the higher is the confidence that c is within the required tolerance $\epsilon = 0.8$, i.e., that $\frac{|AMU_F|}{1.8} \leq c \leq 1.8 \cdot |AMU_F|$. To achieve the confidence $1 - \delta = 0.8$, 66 iterations need to be performed. In case of 157 benchmarks, the algorithm was not able to finish even a single iteration, and only in case of 251 benchmarks, the algorithm finished all the 66 iterations. For the remaining 945 benchmarks, at least some iterations were finished, and thus at least an estimate with a lower confidence was determined.

We illustrate the achieved results in Fig. 3. The figure consists of two plots. The plot at the bottom of the figure shows the number of finished iterations (y axis) for individual benchmarks (x-axis). The plot at the top of the figure shows how accurate were the MUS count estimates. In particular, for each benchmark (formula) Γ, we show the number $\frac{c}{|AMU_F|}$ where c is the final estimate (median of estimates from finished iterations). For benchmarks where all iterations were completed, it was always the case that the final estimate is within the required tolerance, although we had only 0.8 theoretical confidence that it would be the case. Moreover, the achieved estimate never exceeded a tolerance of 0.1, which is much better than the required tolerance of 0.8. As for the benchmarks where only some iterations were completed, there is only a single benchmark where the tolerance of 0.8 was exceeded.

Scalability. The scalability of AMUSIC, MARCO, and MCSMUS w.r.t. the number of MUSes ($|AMU_F|$) is illustrated in Fig. 4. In particular, for each benchmark (x-axis), we show in the plot the estimate of the MUS count that was achieved by the algorithms (y-axis). The benchmarks are sorted by the exact count of MUSes in the benchmarks. MARCO and MCSMUS were able to finish the MUS enumeration, and thus to provide the count, only for benchmarks that contained at most 10^6 and 10^5 MUSes, respectively. AMUSIC, on the other hand, was able to provide estimates on the MUS count even for benchmarks that contained up to

10^9 MUSes. Moreover, as we have seen in Fig. 3, the estimates are very accurate. Only in the case of 157 benchmarks where AMUSIC finished no iteration, it could not provide any estimate.

6   Summary and Future Work

We presented a probabilistic algorithm, called AMUSIC, for approximate MUS counting that needs to explicitly identify only logarithmically many MUSes and yet still provides strong theoretical guarantees. The high-level idea is adopted from a model counting algorithm ApproxMC3: we partition the search space into small cells, then count MUSes in a single cell, and estimate the total count by scaling the count from the cell. The novelty lies in the low-level algorithmic parts that are specific for MUSes. Mainly, (1) we propose QBF encoding for counting MUSes in a cell, (2) we exploit MUS intersection to speed-up localization of MUSes, and (3) we utilize MUS union to reduce the search space significantly. Our experimental evaluation showed that the scalability of AMUSIC outperforms the scalability of contemporary enumeration-based counters by several orders of magnitude. Moreover, the practical accuracy of AMUSIC is significantly better than what is guaranteed by the theoretical guarantees.

Our work opens up several questions at the intersection of theory and practice. From a theoretical perspective, the natural question is to ask if we can design a scalable algorithm that makes polynomially many calls to an *NP* oracle. From a practical perspective, our work showcases interesting applications of QBF solvers with native XOR support. Since approximate counting and sampling are known to be inter-reducible, another line of work would be to investigate the development of an almost-uniform sampler for MUSes, which can potentially benefit from the framework proposed in UniGen [14,16]. Another line of work is to extend our MUS counting approach to other constraint domains where MUSes find an application, e.g., F can be a set of SMT [25] or LTL [4,8] formulas or a set of transition predicates [13,23].

Acknowledgments. This work was supported in part by National Research Foundation Singapore under its NRF Fellowship Programme [NRF-NRFFAI1-2019-0004] and AI Singapore Programme [AISG-RP-2018-005], and NUS ODPRT Grant [R-252-000-685-13]. The computational work for this article was performed on resources of the National Supercomputing Centre, Singapore https://www.nscc.sg.

References

1. Arif, M.F., Mencía, C., Ignatiev, A., Manthey, N., Peñaloza, R., Marques-Silva, J.: BEACON: an efficient SAT-based tool for debugging $\mathcal{EL}^+$ ontologies. In: Creignou, N., Le Berre, D. (eds.) SAT 2016. LNCS, vol. 9710, pp. 521–530. Springer, Cham (2016). https://doi.org/10.1007/978-3-319-40970-2_32
2. Bacchus, F., Katsirelos, G.: Using minimal correction sets to more efficiently compute minimal unsatisfiable sets. In: Kroening, D., Păsăreanu, C.S. (eds.) CAV 2015. LNCS, vol. 9207, pp. 70–86. Springer, Cham (2015). https://doi.org/10.1007/978-3-319-21668-3_5

3. Bacchus, F., Katsirelos, G.: Finding a collection of MUSes incrementally. In: Quimper, C.-G. (ed.) CPAIOR 2016. LNCS, vol. 9676, pp. 35–44. Springer, Cham (2016). https://doi.org/10.1007/978-3-319-33954-2_3

4. Barnat, J., Bauch, P., Beneš, N., Brim, L., Beran, J., Kratochvíla, T.: Analysing sanity of requirements for avionics systems. Formal Aspects Comput. **28**(1), 45–63 (2015). https://doi.org/10.1007/s00165-015-0348-9

5. Belov, A., Heule, M.J.H., Marques-Silva, J.: MUS extraction using clausal proofs. In: Sinz, C., Egly, U. (eds.) SAT 2014. LNCS, vol. 8561, pp. 48–57. Springer, Cham (2014). https://doi.org/10.1007/978-3-319-09284-3_5

6. Belov, A., Marques-Silva, J.: Accelerating MUS extraction with recursive model rotation. In: FMCAD, pp. 37–40. FMCAD Inc. (2011)

7. Belov, A., Marques-Silva, J.: MUSer2: an efficient MUS extractor. JSAT **8**, 123–128 (2012)

8. Bendík, J.: Consistency checking in requirements analysis. In: ISSTA, pp. 408–411. ACM (2017)

9. Bendík, J., Beneš, N., Černá, I., Barnat, J.: Tunable online MUS/MSS enumeration. In: FSTTCS. LIPIcs, vol. 65, pp. 50:1–50:13. Schloss Dagstuhl - Leibniz-Zentrum fuer Informatik (2016)

10. Bendík, J., Černá, I.: Evaluation of domain agnostic approaches for enumeration of minimal unsatisfiable subsets. In: LPAR. EPiC Series in Computing, vol. 57, pp. 131–142. EasyChair (2018)

11. Bendík, J., Černá, I.: MUST: minimal unsatisfiable subsets enumeration tool. TACAS 2020. LNCS, vol. 12078, pp. 135–152. Springer, Cham (2020). https://doi.org/10.1007/978-3-030-45190-5_8

12. Bendík, J., Černá, I., Beneš, N.: Recursive online enumeration of all minimal unsatisfiable subsets. In: Lahiri, S.K., Wang, C. (eds.) ATVA 2018. LNCS, vol. 11138, pp. 143–159. Springer, Cham (2018). https://doi.org/10.1007/978-3-030-01090-4_9

13. Bendík, J., Ghassabani, E., Whalen, M., Černá, I.: Online enumeration of all minimal inductive validity cores. In: Johnsen, E.B., Schaefer, I. (eds.) SEFM 2018. LNCS, vol. 10886, pp. 189–204. Springer, Cham (2018). https://doi.org/10.1007/978-3-319-92970-5_12

14. Chakraborty, S., Fremont, D.J., Meel, K.S., Seshia, S.A., Vardi, M.Y.: On parallel scalable uniform SAT witness generation. In: Baier, C., Tinelli, C. (eds.) TACAS 2015. LNCS, vol. 9035, pp. 304–319. Springer, Heidelberg (2015). https://doi.org/10.1007/978-3-662-46681-0_25

15. Chakraborty, S., Meel, K.S., Vardi, M.Y.: A scalable approximate model counter. In: Schulte, C. (ed.) CP 2013. LNCS, vol. 8124, pp. 200–216. Springer, Heidelberg (2013). https://doi.org/10.1007/978-3-642-40627-0_18

16. Chakraborty, S., Meel, K.S., Vardi, M.Y.: Balancing scalability and uniformity in SAT witness generator. In: Proceedings of DAC (2014)

17. Chakraborty, S., Meel, K.S., Vardi, M.Y.: Algorithmic improvements in approximate counting for probabilistic inference: from linear to logarithmic SAT calls. In: Proceedings of IJCAI (2016)

18. Chakraborty, S., Meel, K.S., Vardi, M.Y.: Algorithmic improvements in approximate counting for probabilistic inference: from linear to logarithmic SAT calls. In: IJCAI, pp. 3569–3576. IJCAI/AAAI Press (2016)

19. Chen, Z.-Z., Toda, S.: The complexity of selecting maximal solutions. Inf. Comput. **119**(2), 231–239 (1995)

20. Orly, C., Moran, G., Michael, L., Alexander, N., Vadim, R.: Designers work less with quality formal equivalence checking. In: DVCon. Citeseer (2010)

21. de Kleer, J., Williams, B.C.: Diagnosing multiple faults. Artif. Intell. **32**(1), 97–130 (1987)
22. Elffers, J., Giráldez-Cru, J., Gocht, S., Nordström, J., Simon, L.: Seeking practical CDCL insights from theoretical sat benchmarks. In: IJCAI, pp. 1300–1308. International Joint Conferences on Artificial Intelligence Organization, July 2018
23. Ghassabani, E., Gacek, A., Whalen, M.W., Heimdahl, M.P.E., Wagner, L.G.: Proof-based coverage metrics for formal verification. In: ASE, pp. 194–199. IEEE Computer Society (2017)
24. Gomes, C.P., Sabharwal, A., Selman, B.: Near-uniform sampling of combinatorial spaces using XOR constraints. In: NIPS, pp. 481–488. MIT Press (2006)
25. Guthmann, O., Strichman, O., Trostanetski, A.: Minimal unsatisfiable core extraction for SMT. In: FMCAD, pp. 57–64. IEEE (2016)
26. Hunter, A., Konieczny, S.: Measuring inconsistency through minimal inconsistent sets. In: KR, pp. 358–366. AAAI Press (2008)
27. Ignatiev, A., Morgado, A., Marques-Silva, J.: PySAT: a Python toolkit for prototyping with SAT Oracles. In: Beyersdorff, O., Wintersteiger, C.M. (eds.) SAT 2018. LNCS, vol. 10929, pp. 428–437. Springer, Cham (2018). https://doi.org/10.1007/978-3-319-94144-8_26
28. Ivrii, A., Malik, S., Meel, K.S., Vardi, M.Y.: On computing minimal independent support and its applications to sampling and counting. Constraints **21**(1), 41–58 (2015). https://doi.org/10.1007/s10601-015-9204-z
29. Jannach, D., Schmitz, T.: Model-based diagnosis of spreadsheet programs: a constraint-based debugging approach. Autom. Softw. Eng. **23**(1), 105–144 (2014). https://doi.org/10.1007/s10515-014-0141-7
30. Janota, M., Marques-Silva, J.: On deciding MUS membership with QBF. In: Lee, J. (ed.) CP 2011. LNCS, vol. 6876, pp. 414–428. Springer, Heidelberg (2011). https://doi.org/10.1007/978-3-642-23786-7_32
31. Büning, H.K., Kullmann, O.: Minimal unsatisfiability and autarkies. In: Handbook of Satisfiability. FAIA, vol. 185, pp. 339–401. IOS Press (2009)
32. Kullmann, O.: Investigations on autark assignments. Discrete Appl. Math. **107**(1–3), 99–137 (2000)
33. Kullmann, O., Marques-Silva, J.: Computing maximal autarkies with few and simple Oracle queries. In: Heule, M., Weaver, S. (eds.) SAT 2015. LNCS, vol. 9340, pp. 138–155. Springer, Cham (2015). https://doi.org/10.1007/978-3-319-24318-4_11
34. Liffiton, M.H., Malik, A.: Enumerating infeasibility: finding multiple MUSes quickly. In: Gomes, C., Sellmann, M. (eds.) CPAIOR 2013. LNCS, vol. 7874, pp. 160–175. Springer, Heidelberg (2013). https://doi.org/10.1007/978-3-642-38171-3_11
35. Liffiton, M.H., Previti, A., Malik, A., Marques-Silva, J.: Fast, flexible MUS enumeration. Constraints **21**(2), 223–250 (2016). https://doi.org/10.1007/s10601-015-9183-0
36. Liffiton, M.H., Sakallah, K.A.: Algorithms for computing minimal unsatisfiable subsets of constraints. J. Autom. Reasoning **40**(1), 1–33 (2008). https://doi.org/10.1007/s10817-007-9084-z
37. Lonsing, F., Egly, U.: QRATPre+: effective QBF preprocessing via strong redundancy properties. In: Janota, M., Lynce, I. (eds.) SAT 2019. LNCS, vol. 11628, pp. 203–210. Springer, Cham (2019). https://doi.org/10.1007/978-3-030-24258-9_14
38. Marques-Silva, J., Ignatiev, A., Morgado, A., Manquinho, V.M., Lynce, I.: Efficient autarkies. In: ECAI. FAIA, vol. 263, pp. 603–608. IOS Press (2014)
39. Marques-Silva, J., Janota, M.: On the query complexity of selecting few minimal sets. Electron. Colloquium Comput. Complex. (ECCC) **21**, 31 (2014)

40. Marques-Silva, J., Lynce, I.: On improving MUS extraction algorithms. In: Sakallah, K.A., Simon, L. (eds.) SAT 2011. LNCS, vol. 6695, pp. 159–173. Springer, Heidelberg (2011). https://doi.org/10.1007/978-3-642-21581-0_14
41. Meel, K.S., Shrotri, A.A., Vardi, M.Y.: Not all FPRASs are equal: demystifying FPRASs for DNF-counting. Constraints **24**(3), 211–233 (2018). https://doi.org/10.1007/s10601-018-9301-x
42. Mencía, C., Kullmann, O., Ignatiev, A., Marques-Silva, J.: On computing the union of MUSes. In: Janota, M., Lynce, I. (eds.) SAT 2019. LNCS, vol. 11628, pp. 211–221. Springer, Cham (2019). https://doi.org/10.1007/978-3-030-24258-9_15
43. Meyer, A.R., Stockmeyer, L.J.: The equivalence problem for regular expressions with squaring requires exponential space. In: SWAT (FOCS), pp. 125–129. IEEE Computer Society (1972)
44. Monien, B., Speckenmeyer, E.: Solving satisfiability in less than 2^n steps. Discrete Appl. Math. **10**(3), 287–295 (1985)
45. Kedian, M.: Formulas free from inconsistency: an atom-centric characterization in priest's minimally inconsistent LP. J. Artif. Intell. Res. **66**, 279–296 (2019)
46. Nadel, A., Ryvchin, V., Strichman, O.: Accelerated deletion-based extraction of minimal unsatisfiable cores. JSAT **9**, 27–51 (2014)
47. Narodytska, N., Bjørner, N., Marinescu, M.-C., Sagiv, M.: Core-guided minimal correction set and core enumeration. In: IJCAI, pp. 1353–1361 (2018). ijcai.org
48. Piotrów, M.: Uwrmaxsat-a new minisat+-based solver in maxsat evaluation 2019. In: MaxSAT Evaluation 2019, p. 11 (2019)
49. Rabe, M.N., Tentrup, L.: CAQE: a certifying QBF solver. In: FMCAD, pp. 136–143. IEEE (2015)
50. Rabe, M.N., Tentrup, L., Rasmussen, C., Seshia, S.A.: Understanding and extending incremental determinization for 2QBF. In: Chockler, H., Weissenbacher, G. (eds.) CAV 2018. LNCS, vol. 10982, pp. 256–274. Springer, Cham (2018). https://doi.org/10.1007/978-3-319-96142-2_17
51. Reiter, R.: A theory of diagnosis from first principles. Artif. Intell. **32**(1), 57–95 (1987)
52. Soos, M., Meel, K.S.: BIRD: engineering an efficient CNF-XOR SAT solver and its applications to approximate model counting. In: Proceedings of the AAAI (2019)
53. Soos, M., Nohl, K., Castelluccia, C.: Extending SAT solvers to cryptographic problems. In: Kullmann, O. (ed.) SAT 2009. LNCS, vol. 5584, pp. 244–257. Springer, Heidelberg (2009). https://doi.org/10.1007/978-3-642-02777-2_24
54. Sperner, E.: Ein satz über untermengen einer endlichen menge. Math. Z. **27**(1), 544–548 (1928). https://doi.org/10.1007/BF01171114
55. Stern, R.T., Kalech, M., Feldman, A., Provan, G.M.: Exploring the duality in conflict-directed model-based diagnosis. In: AAAI. AAAI Press (2012)
56. Thimm, M.: On the evaluation of inconsistency measures. Meas. Inconsistency Inf. **73**, 19–60 (2018)

Tinted, Detached, and Lazy CNF-XOR Solving and Its Applications to Counting and Sampling

Mate Soos[1], Stephan Gocht[2], and Kuldeep S. Meel[1(✉)]

[1] School of Computing, National University of Singapore, Singapore, Singapore
meel@comp.nus.edu.sg
[2] Lund University, Lund, Sweden

Abstract. Given a Boolean formula, the problem of counting seeks to estimate the number of solutions of F while the problem of uniform sampling seeks to sample solutions uniformly at random. Counting and uniform sampling are fundamental problems in computer science with a wide range of applications ranging from constrained random simulation, probabilistic inference to network reliability and beyond. The past few years have witnessed the rise of hashing-based approaches that use XOR-based hashing and employ SAT solvers to solve the resulting CNF formulas conjuncted with XOR constraints. Since over 99% of the runtime of hashing-based techniques is spent inside the SAT queries, improving CNF-XOR solvers has emerged as a key challenge.

In this paper, we identify the key performance bottlenecks in the recently proposed BIRD architecture, and we focus on overcoming these bottlenecks by accelerating the XOR handling within the SAT solver and on improving the solver integration through a smarter use of (partial) solutions. We integrate the resulting system, called BIRD2, with the state of the art approximate model counter, ApproxMC3, and the state of the art almost-uniform model sampler UniGen2. Through an extensive evaluation over a large benchmark set of over 1896 instances, we observe that BIRD2 leads to consistent speed up for both counting and sampling, and in particular, we solve 77 and 51 more instances for counting and sampling respectively.

1 Introduction

A CNF-XOR formula φ is represented as conjunction of two Boolean formulas $\varphi_{\text{CNF}} \wedge \varphi_{\text{XOR}}$ wherein φ_{CNF} is represented in Conjunctive Normal Form (CNF) and φ_{XOR} is represented as conjunction of XOR constraints. While owing to the NP-completeness of CNF, every CNF-XOR formula can be represented as a CNF formula with only a linear increase in the size of the resulting formula, such a transformation may not be ideal in several scenarios. In particular, it is

---

The resulting tools ApproxMC4 and UniGen3 are available open source at https://github.com/meelgroup/approxmc and https://github.com/meelgroup/unigen.

© The Author(s) 2020
S. K. Lahiri and C. Wang (Eds.): CAV 2020, LNCS 12224, pp. 463–484, 2020.
https://doi.org/10.1007/978-3-030-53288-8_22

well known that modern Conflict Driven Clause Learning (CDCL) SAT solvers perform poorly on XOR formulas represented in CNF form despite the existence of efficient polynomial time decision procedures for XOR constraints. Furthermore, constraints arising from domains such as cryptanalysis and circuits can be naturally described as CNF-XOR formulas and these domains served as the early inspiration for design of SAT solvers with native support for XORs through the usage of Gaussian Elimination. These efforts lead to the development of CryptoMiniSat, a SAT solver that sought to perform Conflict Driven Clause Learning and Gaussian Elimination in tandem. The architecture of the early verisons of CryptoMiniSat sought to employ disjoint storage of CNF and XOR clauses – reminiscent to the architecture of SMT solvers.

While CryptoMiniSat was originally designed for cryptanalysis, its ability to handle XORs natively has led it to be a fundamental building block of the hashing-based techniques for approximate model counting and sampling. Model counting, also known as #SAT, and uniform sampling of solutions for Boolean formulas are two fundamental problems in computer science with a wide variety of applications [1,11,18]. The core idea of hashing-based techniques for approximate counting and almost-uniform sampling is to employ XOR-based 3-wise independent hash functions[1] to partition the solution space of F into *roughly equal small* cells of solutions. The usage of XOR-based hash functions allows us to represent a cell as conjunction of a Boolean formula in conjunctive normal form (CNF) and XOR constraints, and a SAT solver is invoked to enumerate solutions inside a randomly chosen cell. The corresponding counting and sampling algorithms typically employ the underlying solver in an incremental fashion and invoke the solver thousands of times, thereby necessitating the need for runtime efficiency. In this context, Soos and Meel [19] observed that the original architecture of CryptoMiniSat did not allow a straightforward integration of pre- and in-processing which of late has emerged to be key techniques in SAT solving. Accordingly, Soos and Meel [19] proposed a new architecture, called BIRD, that relied on the key idea of keeping the XOR constraints in both CNF form and XOR form. Soos and Meel integrated BIRD into CryptoMiniSat, and showed that state of the art approximate model counter, ApproxMC, when integrated with the new version of CryptoMiniSat achieves significant runtime improvements. The resulting version of ApproxMC was called ApproxMC3.

Motivated by the success of BIRD in achieving significant runtime performance improvements, we sought to investigate the key bottlenecks in the runtime performance of CryptoMiniSat when handling CNF+XOR formulas. Given the prominent usage of CNF-XOR formulas by the hashing based techniques, we study the runtime behavior of CryptoMiniSat for the the queries issued by the hashing-based approximate counters and samplers, ApproxMC3 and UniGen2 respectively. Our investigation leads us to make five core technical contributions. The first four contributions contribute towards architectural advances in han-

---

[1] While approximate counting techniques [10] only require 2-wise independent hash functions, hashing-based sampling techniques [6,9] require 3-wise independent hash functions.

dling of CNF-XOR formulas while the fifth contribution focuses on algorithmic improvements in the hashing-based techniques for counting and sampling:

1. **Matrix row handling improvements** for efficient propagation and conflict checking of XOR constraints
2. **XOR constraint detaching** from the standard unit propagation system for higher unit propagation speed
3. **Lazy reason clause generation** to reduce reason generation overhead for unused reasons generated from XOR constraints
4. **Allowing partial solution extraction** by the SAT solver
5. **Intelligent reuse of solutions** by hashing-based techniques to reduce the number of SAT calls

We integrate these improvements into the BIRD framework, the resulting framework is called BIRD2. The BIRD2 framework is applied to state of the art approximate model counter, ApproxMC3, and to the almost-uniform sampler UniGen2 [6,9]. The resulting counter and sampler are called ApproxMC4 and UniGen3 respectively. We conducted an extensive empirical evaluation with over 1800 benchmarks arising from diverse domains with computational effort totalling 50,000 CPU hours. With a timeout of 5000 s, ApproxMC3 and UniGen2+BIRD were able to solve only 1148 and 1012 benchmarks, while ApproxMC4 and UniGen3 solved 1225 and 1063 benchmarks respectively. Furthermore, we observe a consistent speedup for most of the benchmarks that could be solved by ApproxMC3 and UniGen2+BIRD. In particular, the PAR-2[2] score improved from 4146 with ApproxMC3 to 3701 with ApproxMC4. Similarly, the corresponding PAR-2 scores for UniGen3 and UniGen2+BIRD improved to 4574 from 4878.

2   Notations and Preliminaries

Let F be a Boolean formula in conjunctive normal form (CNF) and $\mathsf{Vars}(F)$ the set of variables in F. Unless otherwise stated, we use n to denote the number of variables in F i.e., $n = |\mathsf{Vars}(F)|$. An assignment of truth values to the variables in $\mathsf{Vars}(F)$ is called a *satisfying assignment* or *witness* of F if it makes F evaluate to true. We denote the set of all witnesses of F by $sol(F)$. If we are only interested in a subset of variables $S \subseteq \mathsf{Vars}(F)$ we will use $sol(F)_{\downarrow S}$ to indicate the projection of $sol(F)$ on S.

The problem of *propositional model counting* is to compute $|sol(F)|$ for a given CNF formula F. A *probably approximately correct* (or PAC) counter is a probabilistic algorithm $\mathsf{ApproxCount}(\cdot, \cdot, \cdot)$ that takes as inputs a formula F, a tolerance $\varepsilon > 0$, and a confidence $1 - \delta \in (0, 1]$, and returns a count c with (ε, δ)-guarantees, i.e., $\Pr\left[|sol(F)|/(1 + \varepsilon) \le c \le (1 + \varepsilon)|sol(F)|\right] \ge 1 - \delta$. Projected

---

[2] PAR-2 score, that is, penalized average runtime, assigns a runtime of two times the time limit (instead of a "not solved" status) for each benchmark not solved by a tool.

model counting is defined analogously using $sol(F)_{\downarrow S}$ instead of $sol(F)$, for a given sampling set $S \subseteq \mathsf{Vars}(F)$.

A *uniform sampler* outputs a solution $y \in sol(F)$ such that $\Pr[y$ is output$] = \frac{1}{|sol(F)|}$. An *almost-uniform sampler* relaxes the guarantee of uniformity and in particular, ensures that $\frac{1}{(1+\varepsilon)|sol(F)|} \leq \Pr[y$ is output$] \leq \frac{1+\varepsilon}{|sol(F)|}$.

Universal Hash Functions. Let $n, m \in \mathbb{N}$ and $\mathcal{H}(n, m) \triangleq \{h : \{0,1\}^n \to \{0,1\}^m\}$ be a family of hash functions mapping $\{0,1\}^n$ to $\{0,1\}^m$. We use $h \xleftarrow{R} \mathcal{H}(n, m)$ to denote the probability space obtained by choosing a function h uniformly at random from $\mathcal{H}(n, m)$. To measure the quality of a hash function we are interested in the set of elements of S mapped to α by h, denoted $\mathsf{Cell}_{\langle S, h, \alpha \rangle}$ and its cardinality, i.e., $|\mathsf{Cell}_{\langle S, h, \alpha \rangle}|$. To avoid cumbersome terminology, we abuse notation slightly and we use $\mathsf{Cell}_{\langle F, m \rangle}$ (resp. $\mathsf{Cnt}_{\langle F, m \rangle}$) as shorthand for $\mathsf{Cell}_{\langle sol(F), h, \alpha \rangle}$ (resp. $|\mathsf{Cell}_{\langle sol(F), h, \alpha \rangle}|$).

Definition 1. *A family of hash functions $\mathcal{H}(n, m)$ is k-wise independent[3] if $\forall \alpha_1, \alpha_2, \ldots \alpha_k \in \{0,1\}^m$ and for distinct $\mathbf{y}_1, \mathbf{y}_2, \ldots \mathbf{y}_k \in \{0,1\}^n$, $h \xleftarrow{R} \mathcal{H}(n, m)$,*

$$\Pr\left[(h(\mathbf{y}_1) = \alpha_1) \wedge (h(\mathbf{y}_2) = \alpha_2) \ldots \wedge (h(\mathbf{y}_k) = \alpha_k)\right] = \left(\frac{1}{2^m}\right)^k \qquad (1)$$

Note that every k-wise independent hash family is also $k-1$ wise independent.

Prefix Slicing. While universal hash families have nice concentration bounds, they are not adaptive, in the sense that one cannot build on previous queries. In several applications of hashing, the dependence between different queries can be exploited to extract improvements in theoretical complexity and runtime performance. Thus, we are typically interested in prefix slices of hash functions [10] as follows.

Definition 2. *For every $m \in \{1, \ldots n\}$, the mth prefix-slice of h, denoted $h^{(m)}$, is a map from $\{0,1\}^n$ to $\{0,1\}^m$, such that $h^{(m)}(\mathbf{y})[i] = h(\mathbf{y})[i]$, for all $y \in \{0,1\}^n$ and for all $i \in \{1, \ldots m\}$. Similarly, the mth prefix-slice of α, denoted $\alpha^{(m)}$, is an element of $\{0,1\}^m$ such that $\alpha^{(m)}[i] = \alpha[i]$ for all $i \in \{1, \ldots m\}$.*

Explicit Hash Functions. The most common explicit hash family used in state of the art sampling and counting techniques is based on random XOR constraints. Viewing $\mathsf{Vars}(F)$ as a vector $\boldsymbol{x}$ of dimension $n \times 1$, we can represent the hash family as follows: Let $\mathcal{H}_{xor}(n, m) \triangleq \{h : \{0,1\}^n \to \{0,1\}^m\}$ be the family of functions of the form $h(x) = \boldsymbol{M}\boldsymbol{x} + \boldsymbol{b}$ with $\boldsymbol{M} \in \mathbb{F}_2^{m \times n}$ and $\boldsymbol{b} \in \mathbb{F}_2^{m \times 1}$ where the entries of $\boldsymbol{M}$ and b are independently generated according to the

---

[3] The phrase *strongly 2-universal* is also used to refer to 2-wise independent as noted by Vadhan in [23], although the concept of 2-universal hashing proposed by Carter and Wegman [4] only required that $\Pr[h(x) = h(y)] \leq \frac{1}{2^m}$.

Bernoulli distribution with probability $1/2$. Observe that $h^{(m)}(x)$ can be written as $h^{(m)}(\boldsymbol{x}) = \boldsymbol{M}^{(m)}\boldsymbol{x} + \boldsymbol{b}^{(m)}$, where $\boldsymbol{M}^{(m)}$ denotes the submatrix formed by the first m rows and n columns of $\boldsymbol{M}$ and $\boldsymbol{b}^{(m)}$ is the first m entries of the vector $\boldsymbol{b}$. It is well known that $\mathcal{H}_{xor}$ is 3-wise independent [9].

3   Background

The general idea of hashing-based model counting and sampling is to use a hash function from a suitable family, e.g. $\mathcal{H}_{xor}$, to divide the solution space into cells that are sufficiently small such that all solutions within a cell can be enumerated efficiently. Given such a cell, its size can then be used to estimate the total count of solutions or we can return a random element of this small cell to produce a sample. Hence, hashing-based sampling and counting are closely related.

3.1   Hashing-Based Model Counting

The seminal work of Valiant [24] established that #SAT is #P-complete. Toda [22] showed that the entire polynomial hierarchy is contained inside the complexity class defined by a polynomial time Turing machine equipped with #P oracle. Building on Carter and Wegman's [4] seminal work of universal hash functions, Stockmeyer [21] proposed a probabilistic polynomial time procedure relative to an NP oracle to obtain an (ε, δ)-approximation of F.

The core theoretical idea of the hashing-based approximate solution counting framework proposed in ApproxMC [8], building on Stockmeyer [21], is to employ 2-universal hash functions to partition the solution space, denoted by $sol(F)$ for a formula F, into *roughly equal small* cells, wherein a cell is called *small* if it has solutions less than or equal to a pre-computed threshold, thresh. An NP oracle is employed to check if a cell is small by enumerating solutions one-by-one until either there are no more solutions or we have already enumerated thresh $+ 1$ solutions. In practice, a SAT solver is used to realize the NP oracle. To ensure polynomially many calls to the oracle, thresh is set to be polynomial in the input parameter ε. To determine the right number of cells, i.e., the value of m for $\mathcal{H}(n, m)$, a search procedure is invoked. Finally, the subroutine, called ApproxMCCore, computes the estimate as the number of solutions in the randomly chosen cell scaled by the number of cells (i.e, 2^m). To achieve probabilistic amplification of the confidence, multiple invocations of the underlying subroutine, ApproxMCCore, are performed with the final count computed as the median of estimates returned by ApproxMCCore.

Two key algorithmic improvements proposed in ApproxMC2 [10] are significant to practical performance: (1) the search for the right number of cells can be performed via galloping search, and (2) one can first perform linear search over a small enough interval (chosen to be of size 7) around the value of m found in the previous iteration of ApproxMCCore. The practical profiling of ApproxMC2 reveals that linear search is sufficient after the first invocation of ApproxMCCore. Note that the linear search seeks to identify a value of m such that $\mathsf{Cnt}_{\langle F, m-1 \rangle} \geq \mathsf{thresh}$

and $Cnt_{\langle F,m\rangle} <$ thresh for an appropriately chosen thresh. ApproxMC is currently in its third generation: ApproxMC3.

3.2   Hashing-Based Sampling

Jerrum, Valiant, and Vazirani [14] showed that the approximate counting and almost-uniform counting are polynomially inter-reducible. Building on Jerrum et al.'s result, Bellare, Goldreich, and Petrank [2] proposed a probabilistic uniform generator that makes polynomially many calls to an NP oracle where each NP query is the input formula F conjuncted with constraints encoding a degree n polynomially representing n-wise independent hash functions where n is the number of variables in F. The practical implementation of Bellare et al.'s technique did not scale beyond few tens of variables. Chakraborty, Meel, and Vardi [7,9], sought to combine the inter-reducibility and the usage of independent hashing, and proposed a hashing-based framework, called UniGen, that employs 3-wise independent hashing and makes polynomially many calls to an NP oracle.

The core theoretical idea of the hashing-based sampling framework, proposed in UniGen, exploits the close relationship between counting and sampling. UniGen first invokes ApproxMC to compute an estimate of the number of solutions of the given formula F. It then uses the count to determine the number of cells that the solution space should be partitioned into using 3-wise independent hash functions. At this point, it is worth mentioning that the state of the art hashing-based sampling employ 3-wise independent hash functions. Fortunately, the family of hash functions, $\mathcal{H}_{xor}$, is also known to be 3-wise independent. There after, similar to ApproxMC, a linear search over a small enough interval (chosen to be of size 4) is invoked to find the *right* value of m where a randomly chosen cell's size is within the desired bounds. For such a cell, all its solutions are enumerated and one of the solutions is randomly chosen. Again, similar to ApproxMC2 (and ApproxMC3), the linear search seeks to identify a value of m such that $Cnt_{\langle F,m-1\rangle} \geq$ thresh and $Cnt_{\langle F,m\rangle} <$ thresh for an appropriately chosen thresh. UniGen is currently in its second generation: UniGen2 [6].

3.3   The Underlying SAT Solver

The underlying SAT solver is invoked through subroutine BoundedSAT, which is implemented using CryptoMiniSat. Formally, BoundedSAT takes as inputs a formula F, a threshold thresh, and a sampling set S, and returns a subset Y of $sol(F)_{\downarrow S}$, such that $|Y| = \min(\text{thresh}, |sol(F)_{\downarrow S}|)$. The formula F consists of the original formula, which we want to count or sample, conjuncted with a set of XOR constraints defined through a hash function sampled from the family $\mathcal{H}_{xor}$. We henceforth denote such formulas as CNF-XOR formulas. Note that the efficient encoding of XOR constraints into CNF requires the introduction of new variables and hence the sampling set S usually does not contain all variables in F.

As is consistent with prior studies, profiling of ApproxMC3 and UniGen2 reveal that over 99% of the time is spent in the runtime of BoundedSAT. Therefore recent efforts have focused on improving BoundedSAT. Soos and Meel [19] sought to address the performance of the underlying SAT solver by proposing a new architecture, called BIRD, that allows the usage of in- and pre-processing techniques for a Gauss Jordan Elimination (GJE)-augmented SAT solver. ApproxMC2, integrated with BIRD, called ApproxMC3, gave up to three orders of magnitude runtime performance improvement. Such significant improvements are rare in the SAT community. Encouraged by Soos and Meel's observations, we seek to build on top of BIRD to achieve an even tighter integration of the underlying SAT solver and ApproxMC3/UniGen2.

BIRD: Blast, Inprocess, Recover, and Destroy. Pre- and inprocessing techniques are known to have a large impact on the runtime performance of SAT solvers. However, earlier Guassian elimination architectures were unable to perform these techniques. Motivated by this inability, Soos and Meel [19] proposed a new framework, called BIRD, that allows usage of inprocessing techniques for GJE-augmented CDCL solvers. The key idea of BIRD is to blast XOR clauses into CNF clauses so that any technique working solely on CNF clauses does not violate soundness of the solver. To perform Gauss-Jordan elimination, one needs efficient algorithms and data structures to extract XORs from CNF. The entire framework is presented as follows:

BIRD: Blast, In-process, Recover, and Destroy

Step 1 Blast XOR clauses into normal CNF clauses
Step 2 Inprocess (and pre-process) over CNF clauses
Step 3 Recover simplified XOR clauses
Step 4 Perform CDCL on CNF clauses with on-the-fly Gauss-Jordan Elimination (GJE) on XOR clauses until inprocessing is scheduled
Step 5 Destroy XOR clauses and goto **Step 2**

The above loop terminates as soon as a satisfying assignment is found or the formula is proven UNSAT. The BIRD architecture separates inprocessing from CDCL solving and therefore every sound inprocessing step can be employed.

4   Technical Contributions to CNF-XOR Solving

Inspired by the success of BIRD, we seek to further improve the underlying SAT solver's architecture based on the queries generated by the hashing-based techniques. To this end, we relied on extensive profiling of CryptoMiniSat augmented with BIRD to identify the key performance bottlenecks, and propose solutions to overcome some of the challenges.

4.1   Detaching XOR Clauses from Watch-Lists

Given a formula F in CNF, the recovery phase of BIRD attempts to construct a set of XORs, H such that $F \rightarrow H$. As detailed in [19], the core technique for recovery of an XOR of size k is to establish whether the required 2^{k-1} combinations of clauses are implied by the existing CNF clauses. For example, the XOR $x_1 \oplus x_2 \oplus x_3 = 0$ (where $k = 3$) can be recovered if the existing set of CNF clauses implies the following $4 (= 2^{3-1})$ clauses: $(x_1 \vee x_2 \vee \neg x_3) \wedge (x_1 \vee \neg x_2 \vee x_3) \wedge (\neg x_1 \vee x_2 \vee x_3) \wedge (\neg x_1 \vee \neg x_2 \vee \neg x_3)$. To this end, the first stage of the recovery phase of BIRD iterates over the CNF clauses and for a given clause, called base_cl of size k, searches whether the remaining $2^{k-1} - 1$ clauses are implied as well, in which case the resulting XOR is added. It is worth noting that a clause can imply multiple clauses over the the the set of variables of base_cl; For example if the base_cl $= (x_1 \vee \neg x_2 \vee x_3)$, then the clause $(\neg x_1)$ would imply the two clauses $(\neg x_1 \vee \neg x_2 \vee \neg x_3)$ and $(\neg x_1 \vee x_2 \vee x_3)$. Note that given a base_cl, we are only interested in clauses over the variables in base_cl.

During blasting of XORs into CNF, XORs are first cut into smaller XORs by introducing auxiliary variables. Hence, the first stage of recovery phase must recover these smaller XORs and the second phase reconstructs the larger XORs by XOR-ing two XORs together if they differ only on one variable, referred to as a *clash variable*. For example, $x_1 \oplus x_2 \oplus x_3 = 0$ and $x_3 \oplus x_4 \oplus x_5 = 1$ can be XOR-ed together over clash variable x_3 to obtain $x_1 \oplus x_2 \oplus x_4 \oplus x_5 = 1$.

Since BIRD performs CDCL in tandem with Gauss-Jordan elimination, it is worth noting that the Gauss-Jordan elimination (GJE)-based decision procedure is sound and complete, i.e., all unit propagations and conflicts implied by the given set of XORs would be discovered by a GJE-based decision procedure. For the initial formula (in CNF) F and the recovered set of XORs, H, if a set of CNF clauses G is implied by H, then presence or absence of G does not affect soundness and completeness of GJE-augmented CDCL engine. Our extensive profiling of the BIRD framework integrated in CryptoMiniSat revealed a significant time spent in examination of clauses in G during unit propagation. To this end, we sought to ask how to design an efficient technique to find all the CNF clauses implied by the recovered XORs. These clauses could be detached from unit propagation without any negative effect on correctness of execution.

A straightforward approach would be to mark all the clauses during the blasting phase of XORs into CNF. However, the incompleteness of the recovery phase of BIRD does not guarantee that all such marked clauses are indeed implied by the recovered set of XORs. Another challenge in the search for detachable clauses arises due to construction of larger XORs by combining smaller XORs. For example, while $x_1 \oplus x_2 \oplus x_3 = 0$ and $x_3 \oplus x_4 \oplus x_5 = 1$ imply $(x_1 \vee x_2 \vee \neg x_3)$ and $(x_3 \vee x_4 \vee x_5)$, the combined XOR $x_1 \oplus x_2 \oplus x_4 \oplus x_5 = 1$ does not imply $(x_1 \vee x_2 \vee \neg x_3)$ and $(x_3 \vee x_4 \vee x_5)$.

Two core insights inform our design of the modification of the recovery phase and search for detachable clauses. Firstly, given a base clause base_cl, if a clause cl participates in the recovery of XORs over the variables in base_cl, then cl is implied by the recovered XOR if the number of variables in cl is the same as that of base_cl. We call such a clause cl a *fully participating clause*. Secondly, let G_1 and G_2 be the set of CNF clauses implied by two XORs q_1 and q_2 that share exactly one variable, say x_i. Let $U = (\mathsf{Vars}(q_1) \cup \mathsf{Vars}(q_2)) \backslash x_i$. Let q_3 be the XOR obtained by XORing together q_1 and q_2, then, $sol(q_3)_{\downarrow U} \subseteq sol(G_1 \wedge G_2)_{\downarrow U}$ if x_i does not appear in the remaining clauses, i.e., $x_i \notin \mathsf{Var}\,[F \setminus (G_1 \cup G_2)]$.

The above two insights lead us to design a modified recovery and detachment phase as follows. During recovery, we add every *fully participating clause* to the set of detachable clauses D. Let $\mathcal{U} = S \cup (\mathsf{Vars}(D) \cap \mathsf{Vars}(F \backslash D))$. Then, the recovery of longer XORs is only performed over clash variables that do not belong to $\mathcal{U}$. We then detach the clauses in D from watch-lists during GJE-augmented CDCL phase, mark the clash variables as non-decision variables, perform CDCL, and only reattach the clauses and re-set the clash variables to be decision variables after the Destroy phase of BIRD.

If the formula is satisfiable, the design of the solver is such that the solution is always found during the GJE-augmented CDCL solving phase. Since clauses in D are detached and the clash variables are set to be not decided on during this phase, the clash variables are always left unassigned. As discussed below, however, we only need to extract solutions over the sampling set S, therefore the solution found is adequate as-is, without the clash variables, which are by definition not over S as they are only introduced for having short encodings of XORs into CNF.

Conceptually, this approach reconciles the overhead introduced by BIRD, i.e., that XOR constraints are also present as regular clauses, with the neatness of the original CryptoMiniSat that stored XOR and regular constraints in different data structures. This reconciliation takes the best of both worlds.

4.2   Fast Propagation/Conflict Detection and Reason Generation

We identified two key bottlenecks in the the current GJE component of BIRD framework integrated in CryptoMiniSat, which we sought to improve upon. To put our contributions in the context, we first describe the technical details of the core data structures and algorithms.

Han-Jiang's GJE. To perform Gaussian elimination on a set of XORs, the XORs are represented as a matrix where each row represents an XOR and each column represents a variable. The framework proposed by Soos et al. updates the matrix whenever a variable is assigned and removes the assigned variable from all XORs by zeroing out the corresponding column. However, using the matrix in such a way involves significant memory copying during backtracking due to having to revert the matrix to a previous version.

To avoid the overhead, Han and Jiang proposed a new framework [13] building on Simplex-like techniques that performs Gauss-Jordan elimination, i.e., using reduced row echelon form instead of row echelon form. The key data structure innovation was to employ a two-watched variable scheme for each row of the matrix wherein the watched variables are called basic and non-basic variables. Essentially, the basic variables are the variables on the diagonal of a matrix in reduced row echelon form and hence every row has exactly one basic variable and the basic variable only occurs in one row. Similar to standard CDCL solving, when a matrix row's watch is assigned, the GJE component must determine whether the row (1) propagates, (2) needs to assign a new watch, (3) is satisfied, or (4) is conflicted. It is worth recalling that a row would propagate if all except one variable has been assigned and would conflict or be satisfied if all the variables in a row have been assigned. Furthermore, we need to find a new watch if a watched variable was assigned and there is more than one unassigned variable left. If a basic variable is replaced by a new watch then the two corresponding columns are swapped and the reduced row echelon form is recomputed. In practice swapping columns is avoided by keeping track of which column is a basic variable.

For propagation, checking for conflict, and conflict clause generation Han-Jiang proposed a sequential walk through a row that eagerly computes the reason clause and stops when it encounters a new watch variable or reaches until the end of the row. At that point, the system (1) knows whether the row is satisfied, propagating, or conflicted, and (2) if not satisfied, has eagerly computed the reason clause for the propagation or the conflict.

For general benchmarks where XOR constraints do not play an influential role in determining satisfiability of the underlying problem, the GJE component can be as small as 10% of the entire solving time. However, for formulas generated generated by hashing-based techniques, our profiling demonstrated several cases where the Gaussian elimination component could be very time consuming, taking up to 90% of solving time.

While the choice of GJE combined with clever data structure maintenance led to significant improvements of the runtime of Gaussian Elimination component, our profiling identified two processes as key bottlenecks: propagation checking and reason generation. We next discuss our proposed algorithmic improvements that achieve significant runtime improvement by addressing these bottlenecks.

Tinted Fast Unit Propagation. The core idea to achieve faster propagation is based on bit-level parallelism via the different native operations supported by modern CPUs. In particular, modern CPUs provide native support for basic bitwise operations on bit fields such as AND, INVERT, hamming weight computation (i.e., the number of non-zero entries), and *find first set* (i.e., finding the index of first non-zero bit). Given the widespread support of SIMD extensions, the above operations can be performed at the rate of 128...512 bits per instruction. Therefore, the core data structure represents every 0-1 vector as a bit field.

A set of XORs over n variables $x_1, \ldots, x_n$ is represented as $\boldsymbol{M}\boldsymbol{x} = \boldsymbol{b}$ for a 0-1 matrix $\boldsymbol{M}$ of size $m \times n$, 0-1 vector b of length m and $\boldsymbol{x} = (x_1, \ldots, x_n)^T$. Consider the i−th row of $\boldsymbol{M}$, denoted by $\boldsymbol{M}[i]$. Let $\boldsymbol{a}$ be a 0-1 vector of size n such that $\boldsymbol{a}[j]=1$ if the variable x_j is assigned True or False, and 0 in case

x_j is unassigned. Let v be a 0-1 vector of size n such that $v[j] = 1$ if x_j is set to True and 0 otherwise. Let $\overline{z}$ be the bitwise inverse of a 0-1 vector z and & be the bitwise AND operation. Let $W_{unass} = \mathsf{hamming\_weight}(\overline{a}\&M[i])$ the number of unassigned variables in the XOR represented by row i, and $W_{val} = \mathsf{hamming\_weight}(v\&M[i])$ the number of satisfied variables. We view the computation of W_{unass} and W_{val} as viewing the world of M through the tinted lens of v and $\overline{a}$. Now, the following holds:

1. Row i is satisfied if and only if $W_{unass} = 0$ and $(W_{val} \mod 2) \oplus b[i] = 0$.
2. Row i causes a conflict if and only if $W_{unass} = 0$ and $(W_{val} \mod 2) \oplus b[i] = 1$.
3. Row i propagates if and only if $W_{unass} = 1$. Propagated variable is the one that corresponds to the column with the only bit set in $\overline{a}\&M[i]$. The value propagated is $(W_{val} \mod 2) \oplus b[i]$.
4. A new watch needs to be found for row i if and only if $W_{unass} \geq 2$. The new watch is any one of the variables corresponding to columns with the bits set to 1 in $\overline{a}\&M[i]$, except for the already existing watch variable.

Reason Generation. For propagation and conflict we generate the reason clauses for row i as follows. We forward-scan $M[i]$ for all set bits and insert the corresponding variable into the reason clause as a literal that evaluates to false under the current assignment. In the case of propagation, the literal added for the propagated variable, say x_j, is added as literal $\neg x_j$ if $(W_{val} \mod 2) \oplus b[i] = 0$ and x_j otherwise.

Example. For example, let $b[i] = 1$ and $M[i] = 10011$ corresponding to variables $x_1, x_2, \ldots x_5$ and assignments 1?11? respectively, where "?" indicates an unassigned variable. Then $a = 10110, \overline{a}\&M[i] = 00001, W_{unass} = 1, v = 10110, v\&M[i] = 10010, W_{val} = 2$ and $(W_{val} \mod 2) \oplus b[i] = 1$. Therefore, this row propagates (case 3 above), and the reason generated is $(\neg x_1 \vee \neg x_4 \vee x_5)$. If the assignments were 11110, then $W_{unass} = 0$ and $(W_{val} \mod 2) \oplus b[i] = 1$ so this row conflicts (case 2 above), with conflict clause $(\neg x_1 \vee \neg x_4 \vee x_5)$.

Performance. Notice that all cases only require bitwise and, inverse, hamming weight and find first set operations. To find a new watch in case 4 we first find the first bit that is set to 1 in $\overline{a}\&M$ by invoking find first set. In case the obtained index is the same as the existing watch variable, we remove the first 1-bit by left shifting and run find first set again to find the second 1-bit. Bitwise and and inverse are trivially single-assembly instructions. We use compiler intrinsics to execute find first set and hamming weight functions, which compile down to BSF and POPCNT in x86 assembly, respectively. It is worth pointing out that we keep the bit field representations of a and v synchronized when variables are assigned. During backtracking we reset these to zero and refill them as needed. For better cache efficiency, we use sequential set of bit-packed 64-bit integers to represent all bit-fields, rows, and matrices.

Although bit-packing is not a novel concept in the context of CNF-XOR solving, let us elaborate why we believe that our contribution is conceptually interesting. Soos et al. [20] used bit-packed pre- and post-evaluated matrices. Since post-evaluated matrices lose information, they have to be saved and reloaded on backtracking. Han and Jiang's code [13] changed this to using pre-evaluated matrices only, which free the system from having to save and reload. But it was slow, because bit-by-bit evaluation had to happen on every matrix row read (thanks to the missing post-evaluation matrix). Our improved approach is essentially merging the best of both worlds: fast evaluation, without having to save and reload.

4.3 Lazy Reason Clause Generation

As discussed earlier, the current BIRD performs eager reason clause generation in a spirit similar to the original proposal by Han and Jiang. At the time of proposal of eager clause generation by Han and Jiang, the state of the art SAT solver at that time could solve problems with XOR clauses of sizes in few tens to few hundreds. The improved scalability, however, highlights the overhead due to eager reason clause generation. During our profiling, we observed that for several problems, the independent support of the underlying formula ranges in thousands, and therefore, leading to generation of reason clauses involving thousands of variables. The generation of such long reason clauses is time consuming and tedious. Furthermore, a significant fraction of reason clauses are never required during conflict analysis phase as we are, often, focused only on finding a 1UIP clause. Therefore, we seek to explore lazy reason clause generation.

Let the state of a clause c indicate whether c is satisfied, conflicted or undetermined (i.e., the clause is neither satisfied nor conflicted). The core design of our lazy generation technique is based on the following invariant satisfied by CDCL-based techniques: Once a (CNF/XOR) clause is satisfied or conflicted, the assignment to the variables in the clause does not change as long the state of the clause does not change. Observe that when a clause propagates, the propagated literal changes the state of the clause to satisfied. Furthermore, as long as all variables are assigned, the row will not participate in GJE because none of the contained variables can become a basic watch. Therefore, whenever an XOR clause propagates, we keep an index of the row and the propagating literal but do not compute the reason clause. Now, whenever a reason clause is requested, we compute the reason clause as detailed above and return a pointer to the computed reason clause, and index the computed clause by the corresponding row. To ensure correctness, whenever a row causes a propagation, we delete the existing reason clause but we do not eagerly compute the new corresponding reason clause. On the other hand, if a row is conflicting, the conflict analysis requires the reason clause immediately and as such the reason clause is eagerly computed.

Lazy reason clause generation allows us to skip the majority of reason clauses to be generated. Furthermore, given that a row cannot lead to more than one reason clause, it allows us to statically allocate memory for them. This is in stark contrast to the original implementation that not only eagerly computed all reason clauses, but also dynamically allocated memory for them, freeing the memory up during backtracking.

4.4   Skipping Solution Extension of Eliminated Variables

SAT solvers aim to present a clean and uncomplicated API interface with internal behavior typically hidden to enable fast pacing development of heuristics without necessitating change in the interface for the end users. While such a design philosophy allows easier integration, it may be an hindrance to achieving efficiency for the use cases that may not be seeking a simple off-the-shelf behavior. Given the surge of projected counting and sampling as the desired formulation, BoundedSAT is invoked with a sampling set and we are interested only in the assignment to variables in the sampling set. A naive solution would be to obtain a complete assignment over the entire set of variables and then extract an assignment over the desired sampling set. In this context, we wonder if we can terminate early after the variables in the sampling set are assigned. In modern SAT solvers, once the solver has determined that the formula is satisfied, the *solution extension* subroutine is invoked that extends the current partial assignment to a complete assignment. Upon profiling, we observed that, during solution extension, a significant time is spent in computing an assignment to the variables eliminated due to Bounded Variable Elimination (BVE) [12] during pre- and inprocessing. When a solution is found, the eliminated clauses must be re-examined in reverse, linear, order to make sure the eliminated variables in the model are correctly assigned. This examination process can be time-consuming on large instances with large portions of the CNF eliminated.

BVE is widely used in modern SAT solvers owing to its ability to eliminate a large subset of the input formula and thereby allowing compact data structures. While disabling BVE would eliminate the overhead during solution extension phase, it would also significantly degrade performance during solving phase. Since we are interested in solutions only over the sampling set, we disable the invocation of bounded variable elimination for variables in the sampling set. Therefore, whenever the SAT solver determines that the current partial assignment satisfies the formula, all the variables in the sampling set are assigned and we do not invoke solution extension. The disabling of solution extension can save significant (over 20%) time on certain instances.

4.5   Putting It All Together: BIRD2

We combine improvements proposed above into our new framework, called BIRD2, a namesake to capture the primary architecture of Blast, In-process, Recover, Detach, and Destroy. For completeness, we present the core skeleton of BIRD2 in Algorithm 1. BIRD2 terminates as soon as a satisfying assignment is found or the formula is proven UNSAT. Similar to BIRD, BIRD2 architecture separates inprocessing from CDCL solving and therefore every sound inprocessing step can be employed.

Algorithm 1. BIRD2(φ) $\qquad\qquad\qquad$ $\triangleright$ φ *has a mix of CNF and XOR clauses*

1: **Blast** XOR clauses into normal CNF clauses
2: **In-process** (and pre-process) over CNF clauses
3: **Recover** XOR clauses
4: **Detach** CNF clauses implied by recovered XOR clauses
5: Perform CDCL on CNF clauses with on-the-fly *improved* GJE on XOR clauses until: (a) in-processing is scheduled, (b) a satisfying assignment is found, or (c) formula is found to be unsatisfiable.
6: **Destroy** XOR clauses and reattach detached CNF clauses. Goto line 2 if conditions (b) or (c) above don't hold. Otherwise, return satisfying assignment or report unsatisfiable.

---

5 Technical Contribution to Counting and Sampling

In this section, we discuss our primary technical contribution to hashing-based sampling and counting techniques.

5.1 Reuse of Previously Found Solutions

The usage of a prefix-slicing ensures monotonicity of the random variable, $\mathsf{Cnt}_{\langle F,i \rangle}$, since from the definition of prefix-slicing, we have that for all i, $h^{(i+1)}(x) = \alpha^{(i+1)} \implies h^{(i)}(x) = \alpha^{(i)}$. Formally,

Proposition 1. *For all* $1 \leq i < m$, $\mathsf{Cell}_{\langle F,i+1 \rangle} \subseteq \mathsf{Cell}_{\langle F,i \rangle}$

Furthermore as is evident from the analysis of ApproxMC3 [10], the pairwise independence of the family $\mathcal{H}_{xor}$ implies $\frac{\mathsf{E}[\mathsf{Cnt}_{\langle F,i \rangle}]}{\mathsf{E}[\mathsf{Cnt}_{\langle F,j \rangle}]} = 2^{j-i}$. Therefore, once we obtain the set of solutions from invocation of BoundedSAT for $F \wedge (h^i)^{-1}(\mathbf{0})$ (i.e., after putting i XORs), we can potentially reuse the returned solutions when we are interested in enumerating solutions for $F \wedge (h^j)^{-1}(\mathbf{0})$. In particular, note that if $i > j$, then Proposition 1 implies that all the solutions $F \wedge (h^i)^{-1}(\mathbf{0})$ are indeed solutions for $F \wedge (h^j)^{-1}(\mathbf{0})$ and we can invoke BoundedSAT with adjusted threshold. On the other hand, for $i < j$, we can check if the solutions of $F \wedge (h^i)^{-1}(\mathbf{0})$ also satisfy $F \wedge (h^{i+1})^{-1}(\mathbf{0})$.

On closer observation, we find that the latter case may not be always helpful when i and j differ by more than a small constant since the ratio of their expected number of solutions decreases exponentially with $j - i$. Interestingly, as discussed in Sect. 3, both ApproxMC3 and UniGen2 employ linear search over intervals of sizes 4 to 7. for the right values of m. In particular, for both ApproxMC3 and UniGen2, the linear search seeks to identify a value of m^* such that $\mathsf{Cnt}_{\langle F,m^*-1 \rangle} \geq$ thresh and $\mathsf{Cnt}_{\langle F,m^* \rangle} <$ thresh for an appropriately chosen thresh. Therefore, when invoking BoundedSAT for $i = k$ after determining that for $i = k + 1$, $\mathsf{Cnt}_{\langle F,k+1 \rangle} <$ thresh, we can replace thresh with thresh $- \mathsf{Cnt}_{\langle F,k+1 \rangle}$. Similarly, when invoking BoundedSAT for $i = k$ after determining that for $i = k - 1$, $\mathsf{Cnt}_{\langle F,k-1 \rangle} \geq$ thresh, we first check how many solutions of $F \wedge (h^{k-1})^{-1}(\mathbf{0})$ satisfy $F \wedge (h^k)^{-1}(\mathbf{0})$. As noted above, in expectation, thresh/2 out of thresh solutions of $F \wedge (h^{k-1})^{-1}(\mathbf{0})$ would satisfy $F \wedge (h^k)^{-1}(\mathbf{0})$.

5.2   ApproxMC4 and UniGen3

That said, we turn our focus to hashing-based sampling and counting techniques to showcase the impact of BIRD2. To this end, we integrate BIRD2 along with the proposed technique in Sect. 5.1 into the state of the art hashing-based counting and sampling tools: ApproxMC3 and UniGen2 respectively. We call our improved counting tool ApproxMC4 and our improved sampling tool UniGen3.

Assurance of Correctness. We believe it to be imperative to strongly verify correctness and quality of results provided by our tools, as it is not only possible but indeed easy to accidentally generate incorrect or low quality results, as demonstrated by Chakraborty and Meel [5]. To ensure the quality and correctness of our sampler and counter, we used three methods: (1) fuzzed the system as first demonstrated in SAT by Brummayer et al. [3], (2) compared the approximate counts returned by ApproxMC4 with the counts computed by a known good exact model counter as previously performed by Soos and Meel [19], and (3) compared the distribution of samples generated by UniGen4 on an example problem against that of a known good uniform sampler as previously performed by Chakraborty et al. [9]. We focus on (1), i.e. fuzzing, here and defer the discussion about (2) and (3) to the next section.

Fuzzing is a technique [17] used to find bugs in code by generating random inputs and observing crashes, invariant check fails, and other errors from the output of the system under test. CryptoMiniSat has such a built-in fuzzer generating random CNFs and verifying the output of the solver. To account for XOR constraints, we improved the built-in fuzzer of CryptoMiniSat by adding a counting- and sampling-specific XOR-CNF generator. This inserts randomly generated XORs that form distinct matrices inside the generated CNFs and adds a randomly generated sampling set over some of these matrices. We also added hundreds of lines of invariant checks to our improved Gauss-Jordan elimination algorithm, running throughout our fuzzing tests. Running this improved fuzzer for many hundreds of CPU hours has greatly helped debugging and gaining confidence in our implementation.

6   Evaluation

To evaluate the performance and quality of approximations and samples computed by ApproxMC4 and UniGen3, we conducted a comprehensive study involving 1896 benchmarks as released by Soos and Meel [16] comprising a wide range of application areas including probabilistic reasoning, plan recognition, DQMR networks, ISCAS89 combinatorial circuits, quantified information flow, program synthesis, functional synthesis, logistics, and the like.

In the context of counting, we focused on a comparison of the performance of ApproxMC4 vis-a-vis ApproxMC3. In the context of sampling, a simple methodology would have been a comparison of UniGen3 vis-a-vis the state of the art sampler, UniGen2. Such a comparison, in our view, would be unfair to UniGen2 as while ApproxMC3 builds on BIRD framework, such is not the case for UniGen2. It is worth noting that the BIRD framework, proposed by Soos and Meel [19], can work as a drop-in replacement for the SAT solver in UniGen2, as it only changes the underlying SAT solver. Therefore, we used UniGen2 augmented with BIRD, called UniGen2+BIRD henceforth, as baseline for performance comparisons in the rest of this paper, as it is significantly faster than UniGen2, and therefore, will lead to a fair comparison and showcase improvements solely due to BIRD2.

To keep in line with prior studies, we set $\varepsilon = 0.8$ and $\delta = 0.8$ for ApproxMC3 and ApproxMC4 respectively. Similarly, we set $\varepsilon = 16$ for both UniGen3 and UniGen2+BIRD respectively. The experiments were conducted on a high performance computer cluster, each node consisting of 2xE5-2690v3 CPUs with 2×12 real cores and 96 GB of RAM. We use a timeout of 5000 s for each experiment, which consisted of running a tool on a particular benchmark.

6.1 Performance

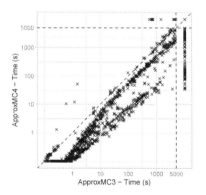

Fig. 1. Comparison of ApproxMC4 and ApproxMC3. ApproxMC4 is faster below the diagonal. Time outs are plotted behind the 5000 s mark.

ApproxMC4 vis-a-vis ApproxMC3. Figure 1 shows a scatter plot comparing ApproxMC4 and ApproxMC3. Although, there are some benchmarks that are solved faster with ApproxMC3 there is a clear trend demonstrating the speed up achieved through our improvements: ApproxMC4 can solve many benchmarks more than 10 times faster and in total solves 77 more instances than ApproxMC3. In particular, ApproxMC3 and ApproxMC4 solved 1148 and 1225 instances respectively, while achieving PAR-2 scores of 4146 and 3701 respectively.

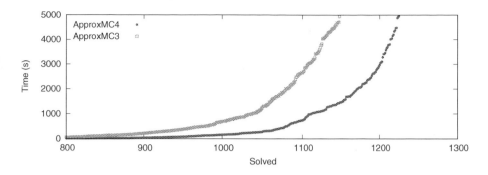

Fig. 2. Cactus plot showing behavior of ApproxMC4 and ApproxMC3

Figure 2 shows the cactus plot for ApproxMC3 and ApproxMC4. We present the number of benchmarks on the x-axis and the time taken on the y-axis. A point (x, y) implies that x benchmarks took less than or equal to y seconds to solve for the corresponding tool.

To present a detailed picture of performance gain achieved by ApproxMC4 over ApproxMC3, we present a runtime comparison of ApproxMC4 vis-a-vis ApproxMC3 in Table 1 on a subset of benchmarks. Column 1 of the table presents benchmarks names, while columns 2 and 3 list the number of variables and clauses. Column 4 and 5 list the runtime (in seconds) of ApproxMC4 and ApproxMC3, respectively.

While investigating the large improvements in performance, we observed that when both the sampling set and the number of solutions is large for a problem, the new system can be up to an order of magnitude faster. In these cases the Gauss-Jordan elimination (GJE) component of the SAT solver dominated the runtime of ApproxMC3 due to the large matrices involved in such problems. The improvements of BIRD2 has led to significant improvement in efficiency of GJE component and we observe that the runtime, in such instance, is now often dominated by the CDCL solver's propagation and conflict clause generation routines.

UniGen3 vis-a-vis UniGen2+BIRD. Similar to Fig. 2, Fig. 3 shows the cactus plot for UniGen3, UniGen2+BIRD, and UniGen2. We present the number of benchmarks on the x-axis and the time taken on the y-axis. UniGen3 and UniGen2+BIRD were able to solve 1012 and 1063 instances, respectively while achieving PAR-2 scores of 4574 and 4878, respectively. UniGen2 could solve only 360 benchmarks, thereby justifying our choice of implementing UniGen2+BIRD as a baseline for fair comparison to showcase strengths of BIRD2. We would like to highlight that the cactus plot shows that given a 2600 s timeout, UniGen can sample as many benchmarks as UniGen2+BIRD would do for a 5000 s timeout.

To present a clear picture of performance gain by UniGen3 over UniGen2+BIRD, we present runtime comparison for UniGen3 vis-a-vis UniGen2+BIRD in Table 1, where in addition to data on ApproxMC3 and

Table 1. Performance comparison of ApproxMC3 vis-a-vis ApproxMC4 and UniGen2+BIRD vis-a-vis UniGen3. TO indicates timeout after 5000 s or out of memory. Notice that on many problems that used to time out even for counting, we can now confidently sample.

Benchmark	Vars	Cls	ApproxMC3 time (s)	ApproxMC4 time (s)	UniGen2+BIRD 500 samples time (s)	UniGen3 500 samples time (s)
or-70-5-1-UC-20	140	350	6.03	2.07	14.21	6.08
prod-4	7497	37358	56.65	7.09	171.57	36.54
min-8	1545	4230	152.53	5.58	471.47	35.04
parity.sk_11_11	13116	47506	389.26	436.32	705.85	809
leader_sync4_11	205198	129149	346.4	20.55	1019.09	106.93
blasted_TR_b12_2	2426	8373	308.08	20.46	1218.01	546.62
hash-8-6	377545	1517574	462.28	266.59	1321.91	633.84
s15850a_15_7	10995	24836	1206.17	31.69	2782.96	230.17
ConcreteRole	395951	1520924	1694.19	309.07	3083.99	923.69
tire-3	577	2004	3059.19	233.28	3876.03	797.42
04B-2	19510	86961	1860.97	625.81	TO	2236.31
blasted_case138	849	2253	TO	3691.9	TO	TO
hash-11-4	518449	2082039	4602.95	4043.4	TO	TO
karatsuba.sk_7_41	19594	82417	3192.85	3410.36	TO	TO
log-3	1413	29487	TO	123.15	TO	408.25
modexp8-8-6	167793	633614	4439.21	TO	TO	TO
or-100-5-6-UC-20	200	500	TO	1689.47	TO	4898.43
prod-28	52233	261422	TO	235.02	TO	1053.9
s38417_15_7	25615	57946	TO	187.71	TO	TO
signedAvg	30335	91854	TO	114.15	TO	582.01

ApproxMC4, columns 5 and 6 lists the runtime for UniGen3 and UniGen2+BIRD respectively. Similar to the observation above, we note that UniGen3 is able to sample for instances that timed out even for ApproxMC3. It is worth to recall that UniGen3 (and UniGen2) first makes a call to an approximate counter during its parameter search phase.

Remark 1. Since the runtime improvements of ApproxMC4 and UniGen3 are primarily due to improvements in the underlying SAT solver, it is worth pointing out, to put our contribution in context, that the difference between average PAR-2 scores of the top two solvers in a SAT competition is usually less than 100.

6.2   Quality and Correctness

Quality of Counting. To evaluate the quality of approximation we follow the same approach as Soos and Meel [19] and compare the approximate counts returned by ApproxMC4 with the counts computed by an exact model counter, namely DSharp[4]. The approximate counts and the exact counts are used to compute the observed tolerance ε_{obs}, which is defined as $\max(\frac{|sol(F)_{\downarrow S}|}{\text{AprxCount}} - 1, \frac{\text{AprxCount}}{|sol(F)_{\downarrow S}|} - 1)$, where AprxCount is the estimate computed by ApproxMC4 for a formula F and a sampling set S, which are both given for each benchmark. Note that, using ε_{obs}, we can rewrite the theoretical (ε, δ)-guarantee to $\Pr[\varepsilon_{obs} \leq \varepsilon] \geq 1 - \delta$ and hence we expect that ε_{obs} is mostly below $\varepsilon = 0.8$. The observed tolerance ε_{obs} over all benchmarks is shown in Fig. 4. We observe a maximal value for ε_{obs} of 0.3333 and the the arithmetic mean of ε_{obs} across all benchmarks is 0.0411. Hence, the approximate counts are much closer to the exact counts than is theoretically guaranteed.

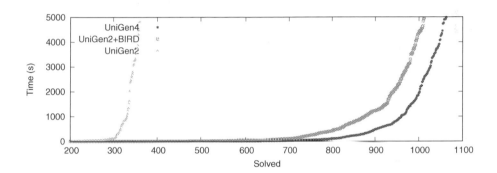

Fig. 3. Sampling performance of UniGen2 and UniGen2+BIRD versus UniGen3.

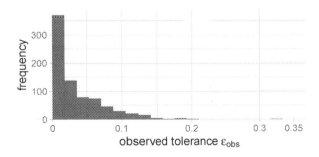

Fig. 4. The histogram of the observed tolerance ε_{obs} shows that the approximate counts are very close to the exact counts.

---

[4] DSharp is used because of its ability to handle sampling sets.

Quality of Sampling. To evaluate the quality of sampling, we employed the uniformity tester, Barbarik, proposed by Chakraborty and Meel [5]. To this end, we selected 35 benchmarks from the pool of benchmarks employed by Chakraborty and Meel in their work and we tested UniGen3 for all the 35 benchmarks. We observed that Barbarik accepts UniGen3 for all the 35 instances, thereby providing a certificate for uniformity. We refer the reader to [5] for detailed discussion of the guarantees provided by Barbarik. Keeping in line with past work on sampling that tries to demonstrate the quality of sampling on a representative benchmark where exact uniform sampling is feasible via enumeration-based techniques, we chose the CNF instance *blasted_case110* (287 variables and 16384 solutions), which has been chosen in the previous studies as well. To this end, we implemented a simple ideal uniform sampler, denoted by US henceforth, by enumerating all the solutions and then picking a solution uniformly at random. We then generate $4,039,266$ samples from both UniGen3 and US. In each case, the number of times various witnesses were generated was recorded, yielding a distribution of the counts. Fig. 5 shows the distributions of counts generated versus # of solutions. The x-axis represents counts and the y-axis represents the number of witnesses appearing the specified number of times. Thus, the point (230,212) represents the fact that each of 212 distinct witnesses were generated 230 times among the $4,039,266$ samples. While UniGen3 provides guarantees of almost-uniformity only, the two distributions are statistically indistinguishable. In particular, the KL divergence [15] of the distribution by UniGen from that of US is 0.003989.

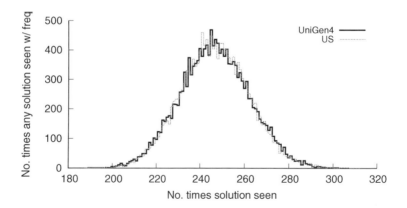

Fig. 5. Distribution of solution recurrence as generated by UniGen3 and US for the CNF `blasted_case110.cnf`.

7   Conclusions

We investigated the bottlenecks of CNF-XOR solving in the context of hashing-based approximate model counting and almost uniform sampling as implemented in ApproxMC3 and UniGen2 respectively. In this paper, we proposed five technical improvements, as follows: (1) detaching the clausal representation of XOR constraints from unit propagation, (2) lazy reason generation for XOR constraints, (3) bit-level parallelism for XOR constraint propagation, (4) partial solution extraction only covering the sampling set and (5) solution reuse. These improvements were incorporated into the new framework BIRD2, which led to the construction of improved approximate model counter ApproxMC4 and almost uniform sampler UniGen3. Experiments over a large set of benchmarks from various domains clearly show an improvement in running time and 77 more problems could be solved for counting and 51 more for sampling.

Acknowledgments. We are grateful to Yash Pote for the early discussions of solution reuse. Work done in part while the second author visited NUS.

This work was supported in part by National Research Foundation Singapore under its NRF Fellowship Programme[NRF-NRFFAI1-2019-0004] and AI Singapore Programme [AISG-RP-2018-005], and NUS ODPRT Grant [R-252-000-685-13]. The second author was funded by the Swedish Research Council (VR) grant 2016-00782. The computational work for this article was performed on resources of the National Supercomputing Centre, Singapore https://www.nscc.sg.

References

1. Baluta, T., Shen, S., Shinde, S., Meel, K.S., Saxena, P.: Quantitative verification of neural networks and its security applications. In: Proceedings of the 2019 ACM SIGSAC Conference on Computer and Communications Security, CCS 2019, pp. 1249–1264 (2019)
2. Bellare, M., Goldreich, O., Petrank, E.: Uniform generation of NP-witnesses using an NP-oracle. Inform. Comput. **163**(2), 510–526 (2000)
3. Brummayer, R., Lonsing, F., Biere, A.: Automated testing and debugging of SAT and QBF solvers. In: Strichman, O., Szeider, S. (eds.) SAT 2010. LNCS, vol. 6175, pp. 44–57. Springer, Heidelberg (2010). https://doi.org/10.1007/978-3-642-14186-7_6
4. Carter, J.L., Wegman, M.N.: Universal classes of hash functions. In: ACM Symposium on Theory of Computing, pp. 106–112. ACM (1977)
5. Chakraborty, S., Meel, K.S.: On testing of uniform samplers. In: Proceedings of AAAI Conference on Artificial Intelligence (AAAI), January 2019
6. Chakraborty, S., Fremont, D.J., Meel, K.S., Seshia, S.A., Vardi, M.Y.: On parallel scalable uniform sat witness generation. In: Proceedings of TACAS, pp. 304–319 (2015)
7. Chakraborty, S., Meel, K.S., Vardi, M.Y.: A scalable and nearly uniform generator of SAT witnesses. In: Proceedings of CAV, pp. 608–623 (2013)
8. Chakraborty, S., Meel, K.S., Vardi, M.Y.: A scalable approximate model counter. In: Proceedings of CP, pp. 200–216 (2013)
9. Chakraborty, S., Meel, K.S., Vardi, M.Y.: Balancing scalability and uniformity in SAT witness generator. In: Proceedings of DAC, pp. 1–6 (2014)
10. Chakraborty, S., Meel, K.S., Vardi, M.Y.: Algorithmic improvements in approximate counting for probabilistic inference: from linear to logarithmic SAT calls. In: Proceedings of IJCAI (2016)

11. Duenas-Osorio, L., Meel, K.S., Paredes, R., Vardi, M.Y.: Counting-based reliability estimation for power-transmission grids. In: Proceedings of AAAI (2017)
12. Eén, N., Biere, A.: Effective preprocessing in SAT through variable and clause elimination. In: Bacchus, F., Walsh, T. (eds.) Proceedings of SAT, pp. 61–75 (2005)
13. Han, C.-S., Jiang, J.-H.R.: When boolean satisfiability meets Gaussian elimination in a simplex way. In: Madhusudan, P., Seshia, S.A. (eds.) CAV 2012. LNCS, vol. 7358, pp. 410–426. Springer, Heidelberg (2012). https://doi.org/10.1007/978-3-642-31424-7_31
14. Jerrum, M.R., Valiant, L.G., Vazirani, V.V.: Random generation of combinatorial structures from a uniform distribution. Theor. Comput. Sci. 43(2–3), 169–188 (1986)
15. Kullback, S., Leibler, R.A.: On information and sufficiency. Ann. Math. Stat. 22(1), 79–86 (1951)
16. Meel, K.S.: Model counting and uniform sampling instances (May 2020). https://doi.org/10.5281/zenodo.3793090
17. Miller, B.P., et al.: Fuzz revisited: a re-examination of the reliability of UNIX utilities and services. Tech. rep. University of Wisconsin-Madison Department of Computer Sciences (1995)
18. Roth, D.: On the hardness of approximate reasoning. Artif. Intell. 82(1), 273–302 (1996)
19. Soos, M., Meel, K.S.: BIRD: engineering an efficient CNF-XOR SAT solver and its applications to approximate model counting. In: AAAI Conference on Artificial Intelligence, AAAI, pp. 1592–1599. AAAI Press (2019)
20. Soos, M., Nohl, K., Castelluccia, C.: Extending SAT solvers to cryptographic problems. In: Proceedings of SAT (2009)
21. Stockmeyer, L.: The complexity of approximate counting. In: Proceedings of STOC, pp. 118–126 (1983)
22. Toda, S.: On the computational power of PP and (+)P. In: Proceedings of FOCS, pp. 514–519. IEEE (1989)
23. Vadhan, S.P., et al.: Pseudorandomness. Found. Trends Theor. Comput. Sci. 7(1–3), 1–336 (2012)
24. Valiant, L.G.: The complexity of enumeration and reliability problems. SIAM J. Comput. 8(3), 410–421 (1979)

Automated and Scalable Verification of Integer Multipliers

Mertcan Temel[1,2(✉)], Anna Slobodova[2], and Warren A. Hunt Jr.[1]

[1] University of Texas at Austin, Austin, TX, USA
`{mert,hunt}@cs.utexas.edu`
[2] Centaur Technology, Inc., Austin, TX, USA
`anna@centtech.com`

Abstract. The automatic formal verification of multiplier designs has been pursued since the introduction of BDDs. We present a new rewriter-based method for efficient and automatic verification of signed and unsigned integer multiplier designs. We have proved the soundness of this method using the ACL2 theorem prover, and we can verify integer multiplier designs with various architectures automatically, including Wallace, Dadda, and 4-to-2 compressor trees, designed with Booth encoding and various types of final stage adders. Our experiments have shown that our approach scales well in terms of time and memory. With our method, we can confirm the correctness of 1024×1024-bit multiplier designs within minutes.

Keywords: Multipliers · Hardware verification · Formal methods · ACL2

1 Introduction

Arithmetic circuit designs may contain bugs that may not be detected through random testing. Since the Pentium FDIV bug [29], formal verification has become more prominent for validating the correctness of arithmetic circuits. Despite being a crucial part of all processors, verifying the correctness of arithmetic circuits, specifically multipliers, is still an ongoing challenge.

There have been numerous efforts to find a scalable and automated method to formally verify integer multipliers. Early methods that were based on attempts to represent hardware and its specification in various canonical forms - BDDs [6] and derivatives, have an exponential space complexity. Therefore, they were applicable only for small circuits. Similarly, SAT-based methods did not prove to be scalable [28].

There are several approaches for the verification of hardware multipliers used in the industry. One is based on writing a simple RTL multiplier design without optimizations and comparing it to the candidate multiplier design through equivalence checking [14,35]. This approach works only when the reference design is structurally close to the original under verification and relies on the correctness

© The Author(s) 2020
S. K. Lahiri and C. Wang (Eds.): CAV 2020, LNCS 12224, pp. 485–507, 2020.
https://doi.org/10.1007/978-3-030-53288-8_23

of the reference design and proof maintenance whenever designers make structural changes. Another approach is to find a suitable decomposition of a design into parts that can be verified automatically and compose those results into a top-level theorem [13,15,30]. The drawback of this method is that it requires manual intervention by the verification engineer who decides about the boundaries of the decomposition. A third approach involves guiding a mechanized proof checker manually [27].

In recent years, the search for more automatic procedures resulted in methods based on symbolic computational algebra [7,16,22,23,40] . This approach makes it possible for certain types of multipliers to be verified automatically for larger designs. However, they have limitations as to what type of multipliers they can check (see experiments in Sect. 6). They are implemented as unverified programs and, as far as we are aware, only one of them [16] produces certificates.

We have developed an automatic rewriter-based method for verification of hardware integer multipliers that is

- widely applicable,
- provably correct, and
- scalable

We implemented and verified our method with the ACL2 theorem proving system, which is a subset of the LISP programming language. Our method is not ACL2 specific and can be adapted to other platforms with suitable adjustments. In this paper, we also provide proof of its termination. Even though we have not proved the completeness of this method, our tool can verify various multiplier designs. We test our method on designs implemented with (System) Verilog where design hierarchy is maintained. We can verify various types of multipliers in a favorable time; for example, we tested our method with 8 different types of 1024×1024 multipliers and verified each of them in less than 10 min, while the other state-of-the-art tools ran for more than 3 h.

The paper is structured as follows. In Sect. 2, we present some concepts that might be necessary to understand our approach. These include the basic notion of term rewriting and the ACL2 system (Sect. 2.1), the semantics for hardware modeling (Sect. 2.2), and some basic multiplier architectures (Sect. 2.3). Preliminaries are followed by our specification and top-level correctness theorem for multiplier designs (Sect. 3). We explain our methodology to prove this top-level correctness theorem with term rewriting in Sect. 4. Section 5 describes the termination of our rewriting algorithm. Experiments with various benchmarks are given and discussed in Sect. 6.

2   Preliminaries

In this section, we describe the concepts and tools required to understand the method proposed in this paper. We review the ACL2 theorem prover and term rewriting, how Verilog designs are translated and used in proofs, and various integer multiplier architectures.

2.1   ACL2 and Term Rewriting

ACL2 is a LISP-based interactive theorem prover that can be used to model computer systems and prove properties about such models using both its internal procedures as well as appealing to external tools such as SAT and SMT solvers. ACL2 is used by the industry for both software and hardware verification [12]. Our methodology to prove multipliers correct uses ACL2-based term rewriting.

ACL2 can store proved lemmas as *rewrite rules*, and later use them when attempting to confirm other conjectures. ACL2 terms are prefix expressions and rewriting is attempted on terms such as (fnc arg1 arg2 ...). Left-hand side of a rewrite rule is unified with terms; in case of a successful unification, the matched term is replaced by a properly instantiated right-hand side if all hypotheses are satisfied. Example 1 shows two rewrite rules, the second of which can be proved using the first as a lemma. When users submit a defthm event, ACL2 attempts to confirm the conjecture by rewriting it in an inside-out manner. For the conjecture given in x-x_y-y, the rewriter replaces (+ x (- x)) and (+ y (- y)) with 0 using a-a as a lemma. Then the resulting term (+ 0 0) is replaced with 0 using the executable counterpart of the function +.

Example 1. A simple rewrite rule a-a, and a theorem x-x_y-y proved subsequently using a-a as a lemma.

```
(defthm a—a
   (implies (integerp a)
            (equal (+ a (− a)) 0)))
(defthm x—x_y—y
   (implies (and (integerp x) (integerp y))
            (equal (+ (+ x (− x)) (+ y (− y)))
                   0)))
```

The rewriting mechanism in ACL2 is much more complex and intricate than we indicate here [18]. Throughout the rest of this paper, we omit ACL2 specific implementation details whenever possible. Understanding the basics of term rewriting is sufficient to follow our methodology.

2.2   Semantics for Hardware Designs

We convert (System) Verilog designs to *SVL* netlists in ACL2 and use SVL functions for semantics and simulation of circuit designs [33]. SVL netlists preserve hierarchical information about hardware designs and they are based on the *SV* [31] and *VL* [32] tools that are also included in the ACL2 libraries. These tools have been used by several companies to confirm the correctness of various circuit designs [12]. In this section, we describe the format of SVL netlists, and how they are simulated hierarchically.

An SVL netlist is an association list where each key is a module name, and its corresponding value is the definition of the module. An SVL module is composed of input and output signals, and a list of occurrences. An occurrence can be an assignment or an instantiation of another module. Example 2 shows a simplified SVL netlist containing a half and a full-adder.

Example 2. An *SVL* netlist for half and full-adder.

```
(("ha" (inputs   x y)
       (outputs s c)
       (occs ((occ1 :assign s (bitxor x y))
              (occ2 :assign c (bitand x y)))))
 ("fa" (inputs   x y z)
       (outputs s c)
       (occs ((occ1 :module "ha" (ins x y)   (outs t1 t2))
              (occ2 :module "ha" (ins t1 z) (outs s t3))
              (occ3 :assign c    (bitor t2 t3)))))))
```

The semantics of an SVL netlist is given by a recursively defined ACL2 function, svl-run. This function traverses occurrences of a module and simulates them in order by evaluating the assignments and making a recursive call for the submodules. After each occurrence, the values of wires/signals are stored in an association list, and when finished, svl-run retrieves and returns the values of output signals from this association list. These values can be concrete (svl-run is executed), or symbolic (the rewriter processes a call of svl-run with variables for inputs), which can create ACL2 expressions representing the functionality of the design for each output. For example, we can generate expressions for the outputs of the full-adder ("fa") in Example 2: $(\oplus$ x y z) and $(\lor$ $(\land$ x y) $(\land$ $(\oplus$ x y) z)). Alternatively, since the design retains hierarchy, submodules can be replaced by their specification. For example, assume that we have specification functions s-ha and c-ha for each output of the half-adder ("ha"), and we proved a rewrite rule to replace calls of svl-run of "ha" with these functions. If we rewrite the instantiations of "ha" with this rule while expanding the definition of "fa", we can instead get (s-ha (s-ha x y) z) and $(\lor$ (c-ha x y) (c-ha (s-ha x y) z)) for each output of "fa".

2.3   Multiplier Architectures

In this section, we discuss the most commonly used algorithms to implement integer multipliers. We summarize partial-product *generation* algorithms, such as Booth encoding, and partial-product *summation* algorithms, such as Wallace-tree. Even though the applicability of our verification method is not confined to a specific set of algorithms, reviewing them is beneficial for understanding the verification problem.

We can divide multiplier designs into two main components: partial product generation and summation. Figure 1a shows these two steps on multiplication of two 3-bit two's-complement signed integers. We perform sign-extension (for signed numbers) or zero-extension (for unsigned numbers) on inputs, generate partial products, and then add them together to obtain the multiplication result in a fashion similar to grade-school multiplication. The integer multipliers we have verified implement various partial-product generation and summation algorithms for the same functionality with optimizations for better gate-delay and/or area.

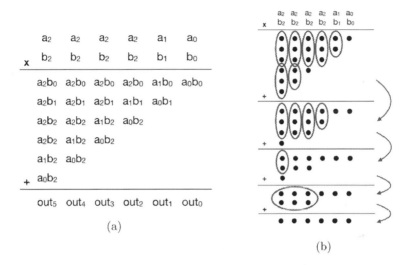

$$
\begin{array}{cccccc}
a_2 & a_2 & a_2 & a_2 & a_1 & a_0 \\
b_2 & b_2 & b_2 & b_2 & b_1 & b_0 \\
\end{array}
$$

Fig. 1. (a) Grade-school-like multiplication for two 3-bit two's-complement integers, and (b) a Wallace-tree-like multiplier performing bit-level additions on the partial products

Baugh-Wooley [1] and Booth [2] are commonly used algorithms to generate partial products. Baugh-Wooley is used for signed multiplication, and it generates partial products as shown in Fig. 1a, but with a sign-extension algorithm to prevent the repetition of generated partial product bits. A more commonly used alternative is Booth encoding, which can be used for both signed and unsigned multiplication. Instead of simply multiplying all the single bits of the two inputs with each other, Booth encoding uses more than one bit at a time from one of the operands, and it derives a more complex form for partial products. This helps reduce the number of rows for partial products, thus helping shrink the summation circuitry and allowing more parallelism. Booth encoding can be implemented with different radices, which determine the number of multiplier bits used at a time to create partial products (e.g., Booth radix-4 [21] uses 3 bits at a time). The higher the radix, the fewer the partial products; however, higher radices yield a more complex design. Booth encoding can be combined with sign-extension algorithms [38] to prevent repetition in generated partial products.

A rudimentary way to sum partial products is by using a shift-and-add algorithm. One may use an accumulator and a vector adder such as a ripple-carry adder to shift and add partial products. An array multiplier is a variation of this algorithm and it is implemented using a very similar principle with some additional optimizations. Due to their regular structure, verifying the correctness of these multipliers has not been a challenging problem [5]. However, these circuits often have very large gate delays, and Wallace-tree like multipliers are preferred over these algorithms in industrial applications.

A family of partial product summation algorithms, which are often called Wallace-tree like multipliers [36], use parallelism to obtain multiplication results with less gate-delay but produce a very irregular and complex design structure. Figure 1b shows an example of a Wallace-tree algorithm. In the first summation layer, we see the generated partial products corresponding to the ones in Fig. 1a. The Wallace-tree algorithm selects groups of bits from these partial products and passes them to full and half-adders. After these parallel bit-level additions, resulting carry and sum output bits are replaced on another layer whose summation will also yield the multiplication result. At each stage, layers are compressed, and the number of rows decreases. We repeat this process until we reach a state where we have only two rows. Then, instead of using full and half adders to finish additions, a vector adder (final stage adder), such as carry-lookahead and parallel prefix adders, is used. This method may provide a significant delay reduction over array multipliers. There exist numerous variations of Wallace-tree multipliers such as Dadda-tree [8] and 4-to-2 compressor trees [11]. Due to their highly irregular structure, reasoning about Wallace-tree like multipliers is a difficult problem, especially when combined with complex partial product generation algorithms such as Booth encoding. There is a lot of room for circuit designers to deviate from text-book algorithm definitions when creating multipliers, which increases the importance of having an automated method to verify these circuits with minimal assumptions about the structure.

3   Specification

We aim to prove the functional correctness of signed and unsigned multiplier designs. We do that by proving an ACL2 theorem demonstrating the equivalence of semantics of a multiplier circuit design to the built-in ACL2 multiplication function (*) with appropriate sign extensions and truncations.

We work with integer multiplier circuits that are designed to multiply two numbers (signed or unsigned) stored in bit-vectors and cut (truncate) the resulting number to return it as a bit-vector. If we are multiplying m-bit and n-bit numbers, then the first $m+n$ bits of the result is sufficient to represent all output values. For example, assume that we are multiplying signed numbers –4 and 3, represented with 4-bit vector 1100 and 3-bit vector 011, respectively. Then, a correct multiplier would return the 7-bit vector 1111100, which represents -12.

Listing 1.1 shows the final ACL2 theorem we prove for signed integer multipliers, where a and b are variables and *m* and *n* are concrete values[1]. This theorem states that for all integers a and b, simulating an m-by-n signed multiplier circuit returns a value that is equivalent to multiplication of sign-extended a and b, truncated at $m + n$ bits. On the left-hand side, *signed_mxn_mult*

---

[1] By convention, "*" characters surrounding variables, such as *m*, signify constants in ACL2.

is an ACL2 constant that contains the multiplier design in SVL format which is translated from (System) Verilog, and `svl-run` is the function to simulate this module with inputs a and b. On the right-hand side, $*$ is the built-in integer multiplication function, `truncate` returns first $m+n$ bits of the result, and `signext` returns a number that represents the sign-extended value of a bit-vector. Multiplier designs are implemented with fixed values of m and n; therefore, we prove such theorems for constants m and n and variables a and b. The ACL2 theorem for unsigned multiplication has the same form but in the place of `signext`, we use the `truncate` function, which performs zero-extension. The actual statement of the theorem contains more components than shown, including function calls to extract outputs and parameters for state-holding elements; we only give the essentials for brevity.

Listing 1.1. The Final Correctness Theorem for Signed Multipliers

```
(defthm multiplier_is_correct
  (implies (and (integerp a)
                (integerp b))
           (equal (svl-run (list a b) *signed_mxn_mult*)
                  (truncate (+ *m* *n*)
                            (* (signext *m* a)
                               (signext *n* b)))))))
```

4   Methodology

The correctness theorem given in Listing 1.1 is proved by rewriting both sides of the equality to two syntactically equivalent terms. In this section, we describe our methodology to rewrite both sides to a specific form through an automated rewriting mechanism.

We have a targeted final expression for each output bit of a multiplier design, the mathematical formula of which is given in Definition 2. The variables a and b are the inputs/operands of multiplication with a certain size (e.g., 64 bits for 64×64 multiplication); and in this formula, they are sign-extended for two's complement signed multiplication or zero-extended for unsigned multiplication.

Definition 1. *We define functions s and c as follows.*

$$\forall x \in \mathbb{Z} \; s(x) = mod_2(x)$$

$$\forall x \in \mathbb{Z} \; c(x) = \left\lfloor \frac{x}{2} \right\rfloor$$

Definition 2. *The targeted form for each output bit (out_j) is defined as follows.*

$$w_j = \begin{cases} (\sum_{i=0}^{j} a_i b_{j-i}) + c(w_{j-1}) & \text{if } j \geq 0 \\ 0 & \text{otherwise.} \end{cases}$$

$$out_j = s(w_j)$$

where $a_i b_{j-i}$ is logical AND of the ith and $(j-i)$th bits of operands a and b.

Table 1 shows an example of this targeted final form for the first four output bits of 3×3 two's complement signed multiplication (see Fig. 1a). Each output bit is represented with expressions composed of the s, c, and $+$ functions. In this representation, the outermost function of each expression is s, carry bits from previous columns are calculated with a single c per column, and the terms in summations are sorted lexicographically. Two's complement signed or unsigned integer multiplication implemented by our candidate designs (See Sect. 6) can be represented by an expression of this form.

Table 1. Expressions for the final form of the first four output bits from Fig. 1a

out_3	out_2	out_1	out_0
$s(a_0b_3 + a_1b_2 + a_2b_1 + a_3b_0$	$s(a_0b_2 + a_1b_1 + a_2b_0$	$s(a_1b_0 + a_0b_1$	$s(a_0b_0)$
$+c(a_0b_2 + a_1b_1 + a_2b_0$	$+c(a_1b_0 + a_0b_1$	$+c(a_0b_0))$	
$+c(a_1b_0 + a_0b_1$	$+c(a_0b_0)))$		
$+c(a_0b_0)))$			

A summary of our rewriting approach to verify multiplier designs is given in Fig. 2. Our method works with design semantics such as SVL where circuit hierarchy can be maintained and we reason about adder modules and the main multiplier module at different stages. As the first step, we work only with adder modules (e.g., half/full-adders and final stage adders) instantiated as submodules by the candidate multiplier design. We state a conjecture similar to Listing 1.1 for each adder module. We simplify their gate-level circuit description and prove them equivalent to their specification. We save these proofs as rewrite rules where *lhs* is `svl-run` of adder module and *rhs* is its specification. Having created these rewrite rules for all the adder modules, we start working on the correctness proof of the multiplier design as stated in Listing 1.1. On the LHS, as we derive ACL2 expressions from the definition of multiplier designs (see Sect. 2.2), we replace instantiated adder modules with their specification, and we apply two other sets of rewrite rules to simplify summation tree and partial product logic. On the RHS, we rewrite the multiplier specification into the targeted final form of multiplication, and we syntactically compare the two resulting terms to conclude our multiplier design proofs.

We simplify adder and multiplier modules by stating a set of lemmas in the form of equality *lhs* = *rhs*. These lemmas are used to create a term rewriting mechanism where expressions from circuit definitions are unified with *lhs* and replaced with their corresponding *rhs*. We aim to provide a set of lemmas so that such an automated system of rewriting can reduce a wide range of multiplier circuit designs to the final form as given in Table 1. In pursuit of this goal, we devised and experimented with various rewriting strategies; and we came up with a well-performing heuristic. In the subsections below, we describe these

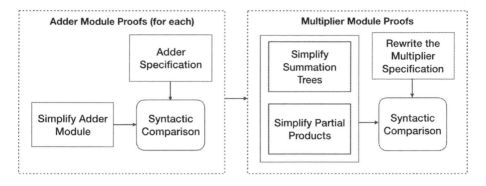

Fig. 2. Summary of the overall method

lemmas separated into two main sets for adder and multiplier modules, and the general mechanism to prove them equivalent to their specification. The lemmas we introduce are proved using ACL2, and we omit the proofs for brevity.

4.1   Adder Module Proofs

The first step of our rewriting strategy is to represent the outputs of adder modules in terms of the s, c, and $+$ functions. We first determine the modules that serve as adder components in multiplier designs, such as half-adders, full-adders, 4-to-2-compressors, and final stage adders. Then we state a conjecture similar to Listing 1.1 where lhs is svl-run of the adder module and rhs is its specification. We prove this conjecture with a library of rewrite rules, derived from the lemmas given in this section, which can simplify various types of adder modules and prove them equivalent to their specification.

For vector adders, specifications have a fixed format as shown in Table 2; however, for single-bit adders, such as full-adders and 4-to-2 compressors, specifications may vary. The format of these specifications can be of any form as long as they are composed of only the s, c, and $+$ functions as given in Table 2. For adders that are not given in this table (e.g., 4:2 compressors), users may derive their specifications by simplifying them with the lemmas introduced below.

We expect adder modules to be composed of logical AND ($\wedge$), OR ($\vee$), XOR ($\oplus$), and NOT ($\neg$) gates in certain patterns. We get expressions for these circuits' functionality in terms of these functions through SVL semantics. We rewrite these expressions with the lemmas given below to simplify them to the same form as their specification. We define the operators $\wedge$ (and), $\vee$ (or), $\oplus$ (exclusive or), and $\neg$ (negation) to work with integer-valued bits (e.g., $1 \wedge 0 = 0$, $1 \vee 1 = 1$, or $0 \oplus 1 = 1$).

Lemma 1. $\forall x, y \in \{0, 1\}\ x \oplus y = s(x + y)$

Lemma 2. $\forall x, y \in \{0, 1\}\ x \wedge y = c(x + y)$

Lemma 3. $\forall x, y, h, g \in \{0, 1\}\ c(x + y + h) \vee (s(x + y) \wedge g) = c(x + y + (h \vee g))$

Table 2. Rewritten outputs of some adders

Adder	out_3	out_2	out_1	out_0
Half-adder	–	–	$c(a_0 + a_1)$	$s(a_0 + a_1)$
Full-adder	–	–	$c(a_0 + a_1 + a_2)$	$s(a_0 + a_1 + a_2)$
Vector adders	$s(a_3 + b_3$ $+c(a_2 + b_2$ $+c(a_1 + b_1$ $+c(a_0 + b_0)))$	$s(a_2 + b_2$ $+c(a_1 + b_1$ $+c(a_0 + b_0)))$	$s(a_1 + b_1$ $+c(a_0 + b_0))$	$s(a_0 + b_0)$

We implement these lemmas as well as some corollaries as rewrite rules so that terms that can be unified with the *lhs* of equations are replaced by their respective *rhs*. An example corollary is $\forall x, y, g \in \{0, 1\}$ $(x \wedge y) \vee (s(x + y) \wedge g) = c(x + y + g)$ that can be derived from Lemmas 2 and 3. Similarly, $\forall x, y, h \in \{0, 1\}$ $c(x + y + h) \vee s(x + y) = c(x + y + 1)$ can be derived from Lemma 3. These extra lemmas help expand our coverage to match more term patterns that may occur.

We add other rewrite rules using elementary properties of $\vee$, $\wedge$ and $+$ that help facilitate simplification. Lemma 3, and some corollaries rewrite terms with repeated variables. In such cases, in order for the rewriter to match the *lhs* with an applicable term, it is necessary to flatten the terms with associativity (e.g., $((a + b) + c) = (a + b + c)$) and lexicographically sort them using commutativity (e.g., $(b + a) = (a + b)$) for every $+$, $\vee$ and $\wedge$ instance. Other examples of rewrite rules we have in our system implement identity and inverse properties of addition. Finally, we have a lemma that rewrites the definition of $\oplus$, which is $(\neg ab \vee a \neg b)$, in terms of s as given in Lemma 1.

Note that we put a restriction on the use of the rewrite rule for Lemma 2 such that it is used only when x and y are input wires of the adder module. The function c is a specification for carry, and not all AND gates may calculate carry by themselves. We have observed that only the logical AND of input signals should be rewritten to c. Rewriting the other instances of $\wedge$ in terms of c prevents application of Lemma 3 and complicates our rewriting approach. We enforce this restriction in ACL2 through a syntactic check.

Our experiments given in Sect. 6 demonstrate that the method we described in this section can automatically simplify vector adders including ripple-carry, carry-lookahead [26] and parallel-prefix adders such as Brent-Kung [4], Ladner-Fischer [20], Kogge-Stone [19], Han-Carlson [9] and others.

Reasoning about adder modules before the candidate multiplier module is a crucial step in our rewriting mechanism. The functionality of all the adder modules should be represented with the s, c, and $+$ functions when expanding the definition of the multiplier module. Then, and only then, the multiplier design can be simplified and proved correct with the lemmas described in the subsequent section.

4.2 Multiplier Module Proofs

After creating rewrite rules for adder modules, we start working with the correctness proof of our candidate multiplier design as given in Listing 1.1. Similarly, we convert multiplier modules into ACL2 expressions, replace instantiated adder modules with their specifications, and perform simplification with a rewriting mechanism derived from the lemmas introduced in this section. We first describe how we simplify complex expressions that originate from summation tree algorithms such as Wallace-tree. Secondly, we add more lemmas to simplify partial product logic that may be generated with Booth encoding. After rewriting with these lemmas, we expect to have simplified multiplier designs to our targeted final form as given in Table 1. We rewrite the multiplication specification into our final form as well and conclude verification with a syntactic equivalence check.

Simplify Summation Trees. In some integer multiplier designs, summation of partial products may be implemented with a very irregular structure, as is the case with Wallace-tree like multipliers (see Sect. 2.3), and it can be challenging to simplify them to a regular and more easily interpretable form. We describe a set of lemmas, solving this problem by providing an efficient and automated mechanism for such complex structures. Below, we discuss the simplification method for multiplier designs implemented with simple partial products.

Having rewritten the adder components in terms of the s, c, and $+$ functions, Example 3 shows the term representing the 4th LSB of a Wallace-tree multiplier output. Our goal is to reduce such terms to our final form as given in Table 1.

Example 3. The 4th LSB of the Wallace-tree multiplier output from Fig. 1b after adder submodules are rewritten in terms of the s, c and $+$ functions:

$$s(\ s(\ s(a_3b_0 + a_2b_1 + a_1b_2)$$
$$+a_0b_3$$
$$+c(a_2b_0 + a_1b_1 + a_0b_2))$$
$$+c(s(a_2b_0 + a_1b_1 + a_0b_2) + c(a_1b_0 + a_0b_1)))$$

In such summation trees, we observe many nested calls for s. These can be simplified easily by the following rule.

Lemma 4. $\forall x, y \in \mathbb{Z}\ s(s(x) + y) = s(x + y)$

Example 4. Example 3 simplified with Lemma 4:

$$s(a_3b_0 + a_2b_1 + a_1b_2 + a_0b_3$$
$$+c(a_2b_0 + a_1b_1 + a_0b_2)$$
$$+c(s(a_2b_0 + a_1b_1 + a_0b_2) + c(a_1b_0 + a_0b_1)))$$

Terms derived from summation trees may include many instances for addition of two or more calls of c. Since such instances are not present in the final form, we try to remove them. That can be done by merging such calls of c through a temporary conversion to d as implemented with the lemmas given below.

Definition 3. *We define function d as follows.*

$$\forall x \in \mathbb{Z} \; d(x) = \frac{x}{2}$$

Lemma 5. $\forall x, y \in \mathbb{Z} \; c(x) + c(y) = d(x + y - s(x) - s(y))$

Lemma 6. $\forall x, y \in \mathbb{Z} \; c(x) + d(y) = d(x + y - s(x))$

Lemma 7. $\forall x, y \in \mathbb{Z} \; d(x) + d(y) = d(x + y)$

Lemma 8. $\forall x \in \mathbb{Z} \; d(-s(x) + x) = c(x)$

Applying Lemmas 5, 6, 7, and 8 repeatedly to the term in Example 4, we obtain the term given in Example 5. Since $\forall a, b \in \{0, 1\} \; c(a \wedge b) = 0$, we have a term that matches the 4th bit of the final form for multiplication as given in Table 1. It is not required to convert certain instances of d back to c with Lemma 8; however, we can achieve better proof-time performance by shrinking terms with this rewrite.

Example 5. Example 4 simplified with Lemma 5, 6, 7, 8:

$$s(a_3 b_0 + a_2 b_1 + a_1 b_2 + a_0 b_3$$
$$+c(a_2 b_0 + a_1 b_1 + a_0 b_2$$
$$+c(a_1 b_0 + a_0 b_1)))$$

Rewriting with Lemmas 5 and 6 creates new instances of s, which may not seem preferable at first glance because terms become less similar to the final form. However, we have found that for correct designs, these extra subterms cancel out and vanish during the rewriting process. We have seen this to be the case even for very large and much more complex terms that may have millions of nodes.

We implement these lemmas as rewrite rules as well as some elementary algebraic properties in order to flatten and sort terms lexicographically in summations. Our rewrite rules do not subsume each other, and they may be applied with an arbitrary order until none of the rules are applicable.

Simplify Partial Products. Unlike the simple partial product generation method, multipliers with Booth encoding implement a more advanced algorithm to generate partial products. That results in terms that are more complex (see Example 6) than those we have addressed so far. We expand our rewriting mechanism for simplification of summation trees and add more rewrite rules for automated simplification of partial products such as the ones generated with Booth encoding and sign extension tricks.

Example 6. Below is a term for the second LSB of a multiplier output, implemented with Booth radix-4 encoding and before any simplification for partial products took place:

$$
\begin{aligned}
s([&\neg b_1 b_0 a_1 \vee b_1 \neg b_0 \neg a_0 \vee b_1 b_0 \neg a1] \\
+&c([b_1 b_0 \vee b_1 \neg b_0] \\
&+[b_1 \neg b_0 \vee \neg b_1 b_0 a_0 \vee b_1 b_0 \neg a_0]))
\end{aligned}
$$

Similar to other multiplier verification methods [25], we perform algebraic rewriting on the $\oplus$, $\vee$ and $\neg$ functions with the following lemmas.

Lemma 9. $\forall x \in \{0,1\}\ \neg x = 1 - x$

Lemma 10. $\forall x, y \in \{0,1\}\ x \vee y = x + y - xy$

Lemma 11. $\forall x, y \in \{0,1\}\ x \oplus y = x + y - xy\ - xy$

Example 7. Example 6 rewritten with Lemma 9, 10, and 11 as well as elementary algebraic properties.

$$
\begin{aligned}
s(&b_1 + b_0 a_1 - b_1 a_0 + b_1 b_0 a_0 - b_1 b_0 a_1 - b_1 b_0 a_1 \\
+&c(b_1 + b_1 + b_0 a_0 - b_1 b_0 a_0 - b_1 b_0 a_0))
\end{aligned}
$$

We would like such expressions to be simplified to our final form. When deriving our rewrite rules, we concentrate on the terms with negative and/or duplicate arguments and realize that applying the following set of lemmas is sufficient to simplify such complex expressions.

Lemma 12. $\forall x, y \in \mathbb{Z}\ s((-x) + y) = s(x + y)$

Lemma 13. $\forall x, y \in \mathbb{Z}\ c((-x) + y) = (-x) + c(x + y)$

Lemma 14. $\forall x, y \in \mathbb{Z}\ d((-x) + y) = (-x) + d(x + y)$

Lemma 15. $\forall x, y \in \mathbb{Z}\ s(x + x + y) = s(y)$

Lemma 16. $\forall x, y \in \mathbb{Z}\ c(x + x + y) = x + c(y)$

Lemma 17. $\forall x, y \in \mathbb{Z}\ d(x + x + y) = x + d(y)$

Example 8. Below is the resulting term after Example 7 is simplified using Lemma 12–17 and elementary algebraic properties. We obtain a term matching the final form in Table 1.

$$
s(b_0 a_1 + b_1 a_0 + c(b_0 a_0))
$$

We implement these lemmas as rewrite rules along with the rules for simplification of summation trees. All of these lemmas automatically work together without any user intervention.

Algebraic rewriting of logical gates can be very expensive in terms of time and memory. For this reason, we limit the application of these rules to the partial product logic only. For example, if applied indiscriminately, Lemmas 10 and 11 can cause terms to grow exponentially. Even though partial product generation logic may allocate a large area in multipliers, rewriting the adders to the s, c, and $+$ functions isolates partial products from each other and segregates them into small chunks. We expect that expressions representing partial products are composed of the $\vee$, $\wedge$, $\oplus$, and $\neg$ functions only. Therefore, we restrict Lemmas 9–11 to apply to terms that are composed of these functions only; and we restrict Lemmas 12–17 to apply to terms that are composed of minterms, and the $-$ and $+$ functions only. For instance, in Lemma 13, if we are unifying x with a term that contains an instance of s, c or d, then we prevent rewriting with a syntactic check. This heuristic helps contain this potentially expensive approach to only local and smaller terms.

Rewrite the Multiplier Specification. In our proposed rewriting scheme, we have a targeted representation for each output bit of multiplication as given in Definition 2. The rewriter cannot derive this form directly from the built-in ACL2 multiplication ($*$) function. Thus, we provide a recursively defined function *multbycol* that follows the formula in Definition 2. We prove *multbycol* to be equivalent to the $*$ function. When the rewriter works on the conjecture stating the correctness of a multiplier design as shown in Listing 1.1, (truncate size (* a b)) is rewritten to (multbycol a b size). The rewriter can then efficiently convert the specification into the targeted final form.

Using the rewriting mechanism described in this section, we can verify multipliers with Baugh-Wooley, sign/unsigned Booth radix-4, and simple partial product generation algorithms with various summation tree algorithms such as Wallace and Dadda tree. Note that Lemmas 9–17 work together with Lemmas 4–8 but contradict Lemmas 1–3. This is the reason why our method relies on semantics where the design hierarchy is maintained so that we can simplify the logic in adder modules with Lemmas 1–3 and simplify the remainder of a multiplier design with Lemmas 4–17 at a different time. When this separation is possible, multiplier designs are verified fully automatically without requiring users to designate the type of algorithm used. The complete process of proving the equivalence of semantics of a multiplier design to its specification is verified using ACL2.

5   Termination

Our rewriter does not enforce proof of termination for rewrite rules. The program terminates either when there are not any applicable rules or when a certain number of steps are taken, which may happen if that number is too small for the current conjecture, there is a loop between rules, or some rules grow some terms indefinitely. Even though it is not required by the rewriter, it is important to show that our rewriting algorithm requires a limited number of steps and does not run indefinitely.

Terms from conjectures change every time a rewrite rule is applied. Therefore, for each of our rewriting algorithms (adder and multiplier module simplification), we define a measure calculated on the term and show that it decreases every time we rewrite with one of our lemmas. We first define the measure for simplifying adder modules (Lemmas 1–3). Since carried out separately, we define another measure for the summation tree and partial product simplification algorithms (Lemmas 4–17). For brevity, we omit the discussion for termination with other lemmas pertaining to elementary algebraic properties such as commutativity and associativity.

5.1   Measure for Adder Module Simplification

The first part of our multiplier verification algorithm is simplifying the logic in adder components and rewriting them in terms of the s, c, and $+$ functions. Below, we define auxiliary functions and a measure that guarantees termination of this part of the algorithm that rewrites terms with Lemmas 1–3.

Definition 4 (f_1). *Function f_1 counts the number of symbols (constants, functions and variables) in a term.*

Definition 5 (f_2). *Function f_2 counts the occurrences of $\land$ and $\oplus$ in a term.*

For example, computing f_1 and f_2 on the term $s(x \oplus y + x \land z + c(x \oplus y))$ yields 13 and 3, respectively.

Definition 6 *We define a measure m_1 as follows, where the resulting ordered pairs are compared lexicographically.*

$$m_1(term) =< f_2(term), f_1(term) >$$

The pairs produced by m_1 are ordered lexicographically: thus, the value of m_1 decreases if f_2 decreases (no matter the value of f_1), or f_2 stays the same and f_1 decreases. Rewriting with Lemmas 1, 2, and 3 decreases f_2. Rewriting with some corollaries does not change the value of f_2 but decreases f_1 . For example, rewriting with the corollary $\forall x, y, h \in \{0, 1\}$ $c(x + y + h) \lor s(x + y) = c(x + y + 1)$ does not change f_2 but decreases f_1. In short, every step taken with these lemmas decreases the value of m_1 calculated on the resulting term. Therefore, the rewriting algorithm for adder modules terminates.

5.2   Measure for Multiplier Module Simplification

Rewriting for summation tree and partial product generation algorithms are performed together with a rewriting algorithm derived with Lemmas 4–17, excluding Lemmas 1–3. Therefore, we define a single measure to describe the termination of this part of the rewriting mechanism. Below we give definitions for some auxiliary functions and our measure.

Definition 7 (f_3). *Function f_3 sums the occurrence-depth of negative minterms, where the occurrence-depth is calculated with respect to the overall term.*

For example, computing f_3 on the term $s(x_0x_1 + c(-x_2y_0 + c(-x_3y_1)))$ yields 5 because its negative minterms $-x_2y_0$ and $-x_3y_1$ occur at depth 2 and 3, respectively. These values can be calculated by counting the unclosed parentheses from the beginning up to the occurrence of these terms.

Definition 8 (f_4). *Function f_4 computes the number of unique occurrences of functions $\{c,\ d,\ \neg,\ \oplus,\ \vee\}$.*

For example, computing f_4 for the term $c(x_0) + s(x_1 + c(x_0) + c(x_1))$ yields 2 because even though there are three instances of c, the second occurrence of $c(x_0)$ is not counted.

Definition 9. *We define measure m_2 to return ordered triples as follows, to be compared lexicographically.*

$$m_2(term) =< f_4(term), f_3(term), f_1(term) >$$

The value of m_2 decreases if f_4 decreases, or f_4 stays the same and f_3 decreases, or f_4 and f_3 stay the same and f_1 decreases. Below we discuss how rewriting with Lemmas 4–17 satisfy this measure for termination.

Rewriting with Lemmas 4 and 8 does not change the value of f_4. For both lemmas, if x is unified with a term that contains a negative minterm, then the value of f_3 decreases, otherwise, f_3 remains the same. By removing an instance of s, rewriting with both lemmas decreases f_1 and consequently m_2.

Rewriting with Lemmas 5, 6, 7, 9, 10, and 11 decreases f_4, and therefore m_2, by removing an instance of d, c, $\neg$, $\vee$ or $\oplus$. Even though rewriting with some of these lemmas creates copies of terms, the value of f_4 decreases because it does not count the same term more than once.

Rewriting with Lemmas 12–17 does not affect the value of f_4 since they are restricted to rewrite terms that contain only the $+$ and $-$ functions, and minterms. For Lemmas 12, 13, and 14, x can only be unified with a positive minterm. Therefore, rewriting with these lemmas does not change f_3. For Lemmas 15, 16, and 17, if x is unified with a negative minterm, then f_3 decreases. Otherwise, f_3 remains the same and f_1 decreases.

In short, rewriting with Lemmas 1–3 decreases the measure m_1 and rewriting with Lemmas 4-17 decreases the measure m_2. Therefore, our proposed rewriting mechanism terminates.

6   Experiments

In this section, we present our experimental results and compare them to the other state-of-the-art tools for the automated verification of multiplier designs. We have gathered a large set of multipliers from 3 different generators, and run all the experiments for other verification tools and ours on the same computer (A 2014 model iMac Intel(R) Core(TM) i7-4790K CPU @ 4.00 GHz with 32 GB system memory) for comparison. The instructions and a ready-to-run VM image to run our tool and reproduce these experimental results can be found online at http://mtemel.com/mult.html.

For benchmarking, we used 3 different generators. The tool from Homma et al. [10] generates Booth encoded sign and unsigned multipliers (input size up to 64 bits) with various summation tree and final stage adders. Designs from Homma et. al. have multiple copies of half/full-adder modules as well as some other adder modules. Since our method requires reasoning about each adder module, we wrote a function that scans the modules and automatically simplifies them as described in Sect. 4.1. Secondly, we used *SCA-genmul* [24] to generate simple unsigned and Baugh-Wooley based signed (also referred to as simple signed) multipliers. This tool does not generate Booth-encoded multipliers. Finally, we used another multiplier generator [34] that can generate large Booth-encoded multipliers.

We have measured the complete proof time for each benchmark, when available, and compared our results to the work of D. Kaufmann et al. [16] and A. Mahzoon et al. [23]. These methods are based on computer algebra, and they are the best performing tools at the time this paper is rewritten. Since we verified the correctness of our tool using ACL2, we do not generate certificates. D. Kaufmann et al. implement their method in a stand-alone C program but they generate certificates to check their proofs. We measured the total time to verify/certify and check certificates. A. Mahzoon et al. also test their method with a stand-alone C program but it does not produce any certificates. Even though it is not a complete comparison, we still include the results of their tool for the same benchmarks.

When we run our tool on these benchmarks, we only need to identify the names of the adder modules, their I/O size; multiplier I/O size, and whether they perform signed or unsigned multiplication in order to determine their specification. The proofs finish automatically, and users can see the specification explicitly to validate what is proved. The other tools are not interactive and use some heuristics to decide on the specification internally based on the design.

D. Kaufmann et al. [16] and A. Mahzoon et al. [23] both use AIGs as inputs, and we use SVL [33], all of which are translated from (System) Verilog using external tools. For the other tools, we used Yosys [39] and ABC [3] to create AIGs, without any optimization. For our tool, we created SVL netlists as described in Sect. 2.2. Since we compare the performance of different verification methods, we do not include the translation time in any of these results.

Table 3 shows the result of experiments run with a collection of circuits. The benchmarks are described with the generator, partial product generation algorithm, summation tree algorithm, and final stage adder. Generators are *tem* [34], *sca* [24], and *hom* [10]. Partial product generation algorithms are *sp* (simple unsigned/signed or Baugh-Wooley-based), and *bp* (unsigned and signed Booth radix-4 encoded). Summation tree algorithms are *dt* (Dadda tree), *wt* (Wal-

Table 3. Proof-time results in seconds for various multiplier designs

Size	Benchmark		AM [23][a]	DK [16]		Our tool	
			Unsigned	Unsigned	Signed	Unsigned	Signed
64 × 64	sca	sp-dt-bk	39	6	6	1	1
	sca	sp-wt-lf	33	6	6	1	1
	sca	sp-cwt-ks	TO	65	58	1	1
	sca	sp-ar-rc	23	5	5	1	1
	tem	sp-dt-ks	173	7	7	1	1
	tem	sp-wt-lf	33	6	6	1	1
	tem	bp-dt-hc	TO	44	49	1	1
	tem	bp-wt-rp	TO	45	49	2	2
	hom	bp-dt-ks	288	8	TE	2	2
	hom	bp-bdt-hc	TO	7	7	2	2
	hom	bp-os-bk	71	6	TO	3	3
	hom	bp-wt-cla	108	24	21	13	12
	hom	bp-4:2-lf	TE	7	7	3	3
128 × 128	sca	sp-dt-bk	643	33	36	2	3
	sca	sp-wt-lf	633	34	38	2	2
	sca	sp-cwt-ks	TO	TO	TO	3	3
	sca	sp-ar-rc	384	27	27	18	18
	tem	sp-dt-ks	TO	47	49	2	3
	tem	sp-wt-lf	650	40	40	2	2
	tem	bp-dt-hc	TO	877	1037	7	7
	tem	bp-wt-rp	TO	918	1067	12	13
256 × 256	sca	sp-dt-bk	TO	213	209	9	11
	sca	sp-wt-lf	15351	226	223	11	13
	sca	sp-cwt-ks	TO	TO	TO	13	15
	tem	sp-dt-ks	TO	234	232	10	12
	tem	sp-wt-lf	15552	220	221	10	12
	tem	bp-dt-hc	TO	11555	14043	41	47
	tem	bp-wt-rp	TO	11975	14264	54	58
512 × 512	sca	sp-dt-bk	TO	1562	1562	53	64
	sca	sp-wt-lf	TO	1588	1577	61	76
	tem	sp-dt-ks	TO	1655	1655	68	75
	tem	sp-wt-lf	TO	1604	1609	65	82
	tem	bp-dt-hc	TO	TO	TO	246	281
	tem	bp-wt-rp	TO	TO	TO	371	380
1024 × 1024	sca	sp-dt-bk	TO	13746	13247	339	397
	sca	sp-wt-lf	TO	13560	14005	322	345
	tem	sp-dt-ks	TO	14125	15198	324	392
	tem	sp-wt-lf	TO	13664	13708	327	393

[a] Does not produce certificates.
TE: Terminated with an error. **TO**: Time-out. 5400 s. (90 min) for 64 × 64 and 128 × 128, 16200 s (270 min) for the rest.

lace tree), *cwt* (counter-based Wallace tree), *ar* (array), *os* (overturned-stairs tree), *bdt* (balanced delay tree), and *4:2* (4-to-2 compressor tree). Finally, the final stage adders are *bk* (Brent-Kung), *lf* (Ladner-Fischer), *rc* (Ripple-carry), *ks* (Kogge Stone), *csk* (Carry-skip), *hc* (Han-Carlson), and *cla* (Carry-lookahead). The selection of benchmarks was arbitrary but we have concentrated on Wallace-tree-like multipliers with complex final stage adders as they have a more widespread industrial application. For experiments with 64 × 64 and 128 × 128 multipliers, we set the time limit to 1.5 h, and for larger designs, we set the limit to 4.5 h. The results are given in seconds rounded to the nearest integer.

For all the benchmarks we have tested, our tool out-performed the other tools in all cases. Our method is shown to verify benchmarks the others cannot and produce a more homogeneous timing performance across different designs. A. Mahzoon et al. [23] work only on unsigned multipliers. Both A. Mahzoon et al. and D. Kaufmann et al. [16] give fluctuating results for multipliers with different architectures and/or different generators. For some benchmarks, the other tools terminated with an error such as segmentation fault (marked with TE). Our work is more resilient to differences in designs and it scales much better (proof times increase by 4.5–6 times when circuit size grows 4 times). For Wallace-tree like multipliers with simple partial products, about 40% of the time on average is spent on simplification with the lemmas given in Sect. 4, and the rest is spent by conversion of SVL semantics to ACL2 expressions. For multipliers with Booth-encoding, over 70% of the time is spent on partial product simplification. Array multipliers are the only type of circuit for which our tool struggles to scale. We believe that is because the minimal parallelism this circuit implements causes our rewriting engine to do much more work as compared to other multiplier structures. Even though memory use is not reported here, it scales the same way as timings, and it grows as big as 30 GB for the largest (1024 × 1024) circuits we have tested.

Additionally, since integer multipliers are used to implement floating-point operations, we tested our method in a correctness proof for an implementation of a floating-point multiply-add instruction for Centaur Technology, and we got similar results.

7   Related Work and Conclusion

Having described our method, we now compare it with the related work. Well-known methods to verify multipliers include generic reasoning methods such as BDDs and SAT solvers. However, these tools do not scale well with large multipliers. For the last few years, efforts to verify large integer multipliers have explored the symbolic computer algebra approach based on Gröbner basis [7,16,22,23,28,37]. As far as we are aware, all these tools are stand-alone, unverified C programs and none of them except D. Kaufmann et al. [16] produces certificates. The soundness and completeness of this approach is shown only in theory [17]. We compared our method to the studies with the best timing performance [16,23]. The tools implementing these methods identify adder components in designs automatically and perform some rewriting. Their rewriting strategy is different than ours; their method does not rely on maintained design hierarchy and separate reasoning of adder and multiplier modules. Even though they provide a more automatic system, their application appears to be limited to some known patterns. Additionally, our tool is implemented on an interactive tool, which can enable users to carry out more complicated proofs such as the correctness of floating-point circuits. The limitation of our method is that it relies on maintaining circuit hierarchy. Should this pose a problem for some designs, it might be possible for our method to be adapted in the future to work with flattened modules and identify adder components similarly to the related work.

When a proof fails for a multiplier design, our tool does not output a user-friendly message. We will work to improve our tool to process the resulting terms from failed verification attempts and generate counterexamples for incorrect designs.

In this paper, we have presented an efficient method with a proven tool to verify large and complex integer multipliers. With maintained circuit hierarchy, we can automatically verify very irregular multiplier designs; for example, various 1024×1024 Wallace-tree like multipliers can be verified in less than 10 min. We believe that our tool can find broader applications because it can be extended to verify circuits, such as floating-point multipliers, that include an integer multiplier as a submodule.

Acknowledgments. We would like to thank the reviewers for their feedback, and Matt Kaufmann for his helpful directives when implementing this method in ACL2. This material is based upon work supported in part by DARPA under Contract No. FA8650- 17-1-7704. A part of this work was completed while M. Temel was working at Centaur Technology.

References

1. Baugh, C.R., Wooley, B.A.: A two's complement parallel array multiplication algorithm. IEEE Trans. Comput. **C–22**, 1045–1047 (1973). https://doi.org/10.1109/t-c.1973.223648
2. Booth, A.D.: A signed binary multiplication technique. Q. J. Mech. Appl. Math. **4**, 236–240 (1951). https://doi.org/10.1093/qjmam/4.2.236. Oxford University Press (OUP)
3. Brayton, R., Mishchenko, A.: ABC: an academic industrial-strength verification tool. In: Touili, T., Cook, B., Jackson, P. (eds.) CAV 2010. LNCS, vol. 6174, pp. 24–40. Springer, Heidelberg (2010). https://doi.org/10.1007/978-3-642-14295-6_5
4. Brent, K.: A regular layout for parallel adders. IEEE Trans. Comput. **C–31**(3), 260–264 (1982). https://doi.org/10.1109/tc.1982.1675982
5. Bryant, R.E., Chen, Y.A.: Verification of arithmetic functions with binary moment diagrams. In: DAC 1994 (1994). https://doi.org/10.21236/ada281028
6. Burch, J.R.: Using BDDs to verify multipliers. In: Proceedings of the 28th ACM/IEEE Design Automation Conference, DAC 1991, pp. 408–412. Association for Computing Machinery, New York (1991). https://doi.org/10.1145/127601.127703

7. Ciesielski, M., Su, T., Yasin, A., Yu, C.: Understanding algebraic rewriting for arithmetic circuit verification: a bit-flow model. IEEE Trans. Comput.-Aided Des. Integr. Circ. Syst. (2019). https://doi.org/10.1109/tcad.2019.2912944

8. Dadda, L.: Some Schemes for Parallel Multipliers (1965)

9. Han, T., Carlson, D.A.: Fast area-efficient VLSI adders. In: 1987 IEEE 8th Symposium on Computer Arithmetic, pp. 49–56 (1987). https://doi.org/10.1109/arith. 1987.6158699

10. Homma, N., Watanabe, Y., Aoki, T., Higuchi, T.: Formal design of arithmetic circuits based on arithmetic description language. IEICE Trans. **89–A**, 3500–3509 (2006). https://doi.org/10.1109/ispacs.2006.364918. https://www.ecsis.riec.tohoku.ac.jp/topics/amg/

11. Hsiao, S.F., Jiang, M.R., Yeh, J.S.: Design of high-speed low-power 3–2 counter and 4–2 compressor for fast multipliers. Electron. Lett. **34**, 341–343 (1998). https:// doi.org/10.1049/el:19980306. Institution of Engineering and Technology (IET)

12. Hunt, W.A., Kaufmann, M., Moore, J.S., Slobodova, A.: Industrial hardware and software verification with ACL2. Philos. Trans. Roy. Soc. A Math. Phys. Eng. Sci. **375**(2104), 20150399 (2017). https://doi.org/10.1098/rsta.2015.0399

13. Hunt, W.A., Swords, S., Davis, J., Slobodova, A.: Use of formal verification at centaur technology. In: Hardin, D. (ed.) Design and Verification of Microprocessor Systems for High Assurance Applications, pp. 65–88. Springer, Heidelberg (2010). https://doi.org/10.1007/978-1-4419-1539-9_3

14. Jacobi, C., Weber, K., Paruthi, V., Baumgartner, J.: Automatic formal verification of fused-multiply-add FPUS. In: Proceedings of the Conference on Design, Automation and Test in Europe, DATE 2005, vol. 2, pp. 1298–1303. IEEE Computer Society, USA (2005). https://doi.org/10.1109/DATE.2005.75

15. Kaivola, R., Narasimhan, N.: Formal verification of the pentium ® 4 floating-point multiplier. In: 2002 Design, Automation and Test in Europe Conference and Exposition (DATE 2002), Paris, France, 4–8 March 2002, pp. 20–27 (2002). https://doi.org/10.1109/DATE.2002.998245

16. Kaufmann, D., Biere, A., Kauers, M.: Verifying large multipliers by combining SAT and computer algebra. In: 2019 Formal Methods in Computer Aided Design (FMCAD), pp. 28–36 (2019). https://doi.org/10.23919/FMCAD.2019.8894250

17. Kaufmann, D., Biere, A., Kauers, M.: Incremental column-wise verification of arithmetic circuits using computer algebra. Formal Methods Syst. Des. (2019). https:// doi.org/10.1007/s10703-018-00329-2

18. Kaufmann, M., Moore, J.S.: ACL2 rule classes documentation (2019). http:// www.cs.utexas.edu/users/moore/acl2/manuals/current/manual/index-seo.php/ ACL2____RULE-CLASSES

19. Kogge, P.M., Stone, H.S.: A parallel algorithm for the efficient solution of a general class of recurrence equations. IEEE Trans. Comput. **C–22**(8), 786–793 (1973). https://doi.org/10.1109/tc.1973.5009159

20. Ladner, R.E., Fischer, M.J.: Parallel prefix computation. J. ACM (JACM) **27**(4), 831–838 (1980). https://doi.org/10.1145/322217.322232

21. MacSorley, O.L.: High-speed arithmetic in binary computers. Proc. IRE **49**, 67–91 (1961). https://doi.org/10.1109/jrproc.1961.287779

22. Mahzoon, A., Große, D., Drechsler, R.: PolyCleaner: clean your polynomials before backward rewriting to verify million-gate multipliers. In: 2018 IEEE/ACM International Conference on Computer-Aided Design (ICCAD), pp. 1–8 (2018). https:// doi.org/10.1145/3240765.3240837

23. Mahzoon, A., Große, D., Drechsler, R.: RevSCA: using reverse engineering to bring light into backward rewriting for big and dirty multipliers. In: Proceedings of the 56th Annual Design Automation Conference 2019, DAC 2019, pp. 185:1–185:6. ACM, New York (2019). https://doi.org/10.1145/3316781.3317898

24. Mahzoon, A., Große, D., Drechsler, R.: SCA multiplier generator GenMul (2019). http://www.sca-verification.org

25. Ritirc, D., Biere, A., Kauers, M.: A practical polynomial calculus for arithmetic circuit verification. In: Bigatti, A.M., Brain, M. (eds.) 3rd International Workshop on Satisfiability Checking and Symbolic Computation (SC2 2018), pp. 61–76. CEUR-WS (2018)

26. Rosenberger, G.B.: Simultaneous Carry Adder (1960)

27. Russinoff, D.M.: Formal Verification of Floating-Point Hardware Design: A Mathematical Approach. Springer, Heidelberg (2019). https://doi.org/10.1007/978-3-319-95513-1

28. Sayed-Ahmed, A., Große, D., Kühne, U., Soeken, M., Drechsler, R.: Formal verification of integer multipliers by combining Gröbner basis with logic reduction. In: Proceedings of the 2016 Design, Automation & Test in Europe Conference & Exhibition (DATE), pp. 1048–1053. Research Publishing Services (2016). https://doi.org/10.3850/9783981537079_0248

29. Sharangpani, H., Barton, M.L.: Statistical Analysis of Floating Point Flaw in the Pentium Processor (1994)

30. Slobodova, A., Davis, J., Swords, S., Hunt, W.A.: A flexible formal verification framework for industrial scale validation. In: Proceedings of the 9th IEEE/ACM International Conference on Formal Methods and Models for Codesign (MEMOCODE), pp. 89–97. IEEE/ACM, Cambridge (2011). https://doi.org/10.1109/memcod.2011.5970515

31. Swords, S.: ACL2 SV Documentation (2015). http://www.cs.utexas.edu/users/moore/acl2/manuals/current/manual/?topic=ACL2____SV

32. Swords, S.: ACL2 VL Documentation (2015). http://www.cs.utexas.edu/users/moore/acl2/manuals/current/manual/?topic=ACL2____VL

33. Temel, M.: ACL2 SVL Documentation (2019). http://www.cs.utexas.edu/users/moore/acl2/manuals/current/manual/?topic=ACL2____SVL

34. Temel, M.: Fast Multiplier Generator (2019). https://github.com/temelmertcan/multgen

35. Vasudevan, S., Viswanath, V., Sumners, R.W., Abraham, J.A.: Automatic verification of arithmetic circuits in RTL using stepwise refinement of term rewriting systems. IEEE Trans. Comput. **56**(10), 1401–1414 (2007). https://doi.org/10.1109/tc.2007.1073

36. Wallace, C.S.: A suggestion for a fast multiplier. IEEE Trans. Electron. Comput. **13**, 14–17 (1964). https://doi.org/10.1109/pgec.1964.263830

37. Watanabe, Y., Homma, N., Aoki, T., Higuchi, T.: Application of symbolic computer algebra to arithmetic circuit verification (2007). https://doi.org/10.1109/iccd.2007.4601876

38. Weste, N., Harris, D.M.: Principles of CMOS VLSI Design: a systems perspective. STIA **85**, 547–555 (1993)

39. Wolf, C., Glaser, J., Kepler, J.: Yosys-A Free Verilog Synthesis Suite (2013)

40. Yu, C., Ciesielski, M., Mishchenko, A.: Fast algebraic rewriting based on and-inverter graphs. IEEE Trans. Comput.-Aided Des. Integr. Circ. Syst. **37**(9), 1907–1911 (2018). https://doi.org/10.1109/tcad.2017.2772854

Interpolation-Based Semantic Gate Extraction and Its Applications to QBF Preprocessing

Friedrich Slivovsky[(✉)]

TU Wien, Vienna, Austria
fs@ac.tuwien.ac.at

Abstract. We present a new semantic gate extraction technique for propositional formulas based on interpolation. While known gate detection methods are incomplete and rely on pattern matching or simple semantic conditions, this approach can detect any definition entailed by an input formula.

As an application, we consider the problem of computing unique strategy functions from Quantified Boolean Formulas (QBFs) and Dependency Quantified Boolean Formulas (DQBFs). Experiments with a prototype implementation demonstrate that functions can be efficiently extracted from formulas in standard benchmark sets, and that many of these definitions remain undetected by syntactic gate detection.

We turn this into a preprocessing technique by substituting unique strategy functions for input variables and test solver performance on the resulting instances. Compared to syntactic gate detection, we see a significant increase in the number of solved QBF instances, as well as a modest increase for DQBF instances.

1 Introduction

Due to the effectiveness of modern satisfiability (SAT) solvers [20], propositional logic has become the language of choice for encoding hard combinatorial problems arising in areas such as electronic design automation [50] and AI planning. Since many of these problems are hard for levels of the polynomial hierarchy beyond NP, their propositional encodings can be exponentially larger than their original descriptions. This imposes a limit on the problem instances that can be feasibly solved even with extremely efficient SAT solvers, and has prompted research on decision procedures for more succinct logical formalisms such as Quantified Boolean Formulas (QBFs).

Quantified Boolean Formulas (QBFs) are propositional formulas combined with universal and existential quantification over truth values and offer much more succinct encodings of problems from domains such as planning and synthesis [12]. At the same time, QBF evaluation is PSPACE-complete, and in spite

This research was supported by the Vienna Science and Technology Fund (WWTF) under grant number ICT19-060.

S. K. Lahiri and C. Wang (Eds.): CAV 2020, LNCS 12224, pp. 508–528, 2020.
https://doi.org/10.1007/978-3-030-53288-8_24

of substantial progress in solver technology, many practically relevant instances remain hard to solve.

In part, this hardness appears to be a matter of encoding. The most commonly used format for QBFs is Prenex Conjunctive Normal Form (PCNF). A PCNF formula consists of a quantifier prefix and a matrix in conjunctive normal form. As in the case of propositional logic, any QBF can be converted to PCNF with linear overhead but this transformation is known to adversely affect solver performance [1]. This appears to be due to two issues: First, conversion to CNF causes a bias towards reasoning about unsatisfiability while making it difficult to reason about solutions, violating the inherent duality of QBF solving. Second, prenexing introduces spurious variable dependencies that needlessly constrain solvers [5,40]. In light of these issues, researchers have introduced two new formats for representing non-CNF (and even non-prenex) QBFs in the QCIR [30] and QAIGER standards, and solvers supporting these standards have been developed. When only a PCNF encoding is available, *gate extraction* techniques can be used to (re)construct a non-CNF QBF [21]. *Syntactic* gate extraction relies on the detection of patterns of clauses and auxiliary variables introduced when converting a propositional formula to CNF [16]. The corresponding algorithms are fast but incomplete and can only detect definitions from a pre-defined library of gates.

In this paper, we introduce a new semantic gate extraction technique based on SAT solving and interpolation. In contrast to known approaches, this method is complete: a definition ψ of a variable x can be extracted from a propositional formula φ whenever the equivalence $x \equiv \psi$ is entailed by φ. We obtain this result as a generalization of recent work that leverages definability for propositional model counting [25,33]. Owing to a result known as Padoa's Theorem, determining whether a variable x is definable in terms of X is in coNP and can be decided by a SAT call [33]. We show that a definition ψ of x in terms of X can be obtained as an *interpolant* of the formula passed to the SAT solver (Theorem 2). For SAT solvers that use a proof system with feasible interpolation—in particular, CDCL solvers that generate resolution proofs [32]—this means a definition can be efficiently extracted from a proof of definability.

We apply this new gate extraction technique to identify unique strategy functions of QBFs and Dependency QBFs. In a controller synthesis setting, a variable with a unique strategy function corresponds to a control signal with a unique (as a Boolean function) implementation. We can add such an implementation to the specification without affecting the remaining control signals.

Experiments with a prototype show that definitions can be efficiently computed for formulas from standard QBF benchmark sets, and that for many instances a large fraction of variables have unique strategy functions that cannot be identified by syntactic gate detection. We further test the performance of solvers on instances obtained by replacing input variables with their definitions. For 2QBF formulas and PCNF formulas, this significantly increases the number of instances solved by some systems compared to purely syntactic gate extraction. Our experiments further show that semantic gate detection is orthogonal to techniques implemented in state-of-the-art preprocessors.

Semantic gate detection is efficient and conceptually simple. By definition, it preserves logical equivalence and is compatible with strategy extraction. As such, we believe it is an essential addition to the state of the art in preprocessing (D)QBF.

2 Preliminaries

We assume a countably infinite set V of propositional *variables* and consider *propositional formulas* constructed from V using the connectives $\neg$ (negation), $\wedge$ (conjunction), $\vee$ (disjunction), $\rightarrow$ (implication), and $\leftrightarrow$ (the biconditional). For a propositional formula φ, we write $var(\varphi)$ to denote the set of variables occurring in φ. A *literal* is a variable v or a negated variable $\neg v$. A *clause* is a finite disjunction of literals. A clause is *tautological* if it contains both v and $\neg v$ for some variable v. A propositional formula is in *conjunctive normal form (CNF)* if it is a finite conjunction of non-tautological clauses. An *assignment* of a subset $X \subseteq V$ of variables is a function that maps X to the set $\{0,1\}$ of truth values. For a set X of variables we let $[X]$ denote the set of assignments of X. Two assignments $\sigma : X \rightarrow \{0,1\}$ and $\tau : Y \rightarrow \{0,1\}$ *agree* on a subset $W \subseteq X \cap Y$ of their common domain if $\sigma(w) = \tau(w)$ for each $w \in W$. For two assignments $\sigma : X \rightarrow \{0,1\}$ and $\tau : Y \rightarrow \{0,1\}$ that agree on the entire intersection of their domains we define the combined assignment $\sigma \cup \tau : X \cup Y \rightarrow \{0,1\}$ as $(\sigma \cup \tau)(v) = \sigma(v)$ if $v \in X$ and $(\sigma \cup \tau)(v) = \tau(v)$ otherwise.

For a propositional formula φ and an assignment $\tau : X \rightarrow \{0,1\}$ with $var(\varphi) \subseteq X$, we let $\varphi[\tau]$ denote the truth value obtained by evaluating φ under τ. The formula φ is *satisfied* by τ if $\varphi[\tau] = 1$. In this case we call τ a *satisfying assignment* of φ. Otherwise, if $\varphi[\tau] = 0$, formula φ is *falsified* by τ. A formula is *satisfiable* if it has a satisfiable assignment, otherwise it is *unsatisfiable*. A formula φ *implies* a formula ψ if $\varphi \wedge \neg\psi$ is unsatisfiable.

We consider Quantified Boolean Formulas (QBFs) in *Prenex Normal Form (PNF)*. A QBF $\Phi = Q.\varphi$ in PNF consists of a *quantifier prefix* Q and a propositional formula φ, called the *matrix* of Φ. The quantifier prefix is a sequence $Q_1 x_1 \ldots Q_n x_n$ where $Q_i \in \{\forall, \exists\}$ and the x_i are pairwise distinct variables for $1 \leq i \leq n$. The quantifier prefix defines an ordering $<_\Phi$ on its variables as $x_i <_\Phi x_j$ for $1 \leq i < j \leq n$. We assume that QBFs do not contain free variables and every variable in the quantifier prefix appears in the matrix, formally $\{x_1, \ldots, x_n\} = var(\varphi)$. Accordingly, we write $var(\Phi) = var(\varphi)$ for the set of variables appearing in the QBF Φ. We further assume that every variable of Φ occurs exactly once in its quantified prefix. The set of *existential* variables of Φ is $var_\exists(\Phi) = \{x_i \mid 1 \leq i \leq n, Q_i = \exists\}$, and the set of *universal* variables of Φ is $var_\forall(\Phi) = \{x_i \mid 1 \leq i \leq n, Q_i = \forall\}$. For a variable $x \in var(\Phi)$, we let $type_\Phi(x) = Q$ if $x \in var_Q(\Phi)$, for $Q \in \{\forall, \exists\}$, omitting Φ from the subscript if the QBF is understood.

Let Φ a QBF and let $x \in var(\Phi)$ be one of its variables with $type(x) = Q$. A *strategy function* for x is a function $f : [var(\Phi) \setminus var_Q(\Phi)] \rightarrow \{0,1\}$ such that $f(\tau) = f(\tau')$ for any two assignments τ and τ' that agree on variables in

$\{ v \in var(\Phi) \setminus var_Q(\Phi) \mid v <_\Phi x \}$.[1] Given an indexed family $F = \{f_x\}_{x \in X}$ of strategy functions such that $X \subseteq var_Q(\Phi)$ for $Q \in \{\forall, \exists\}$, the *response* of F to an assignment $\tau : (var(\Phi) \setminus var_Q(\Phi)) \to \{0,1\}$ is the assignment $F(\tau) : X \to \{0,1\}$ given by $F(\tau)(x) = f_x(\tau)$. An *existential winning strategy* (for Φ) is a family $F = \{f_u\}_{u \in var_\exists(\Phi)}$ of strategy functions such that, for any universal assignment $\tau : var_\forall(\Phi) \to \{0,1\}$, the assignment $\tau \cup F(\tau)$ satisfies the matrix of Φ. Dually, a *universal winning strategy* (for Φ) is a family $F = \{f_u\}_{u \in var_\forall(\Phi)}$ of strategy functions such that, for any existential assignment $\sigma : var_\exists(\Phi) \to \{0,1\}$, the assignment $\sigma \cup F(\sigma)$ falsifies the matrix. A QBF Φ is *true* if there is an existential winning strategy for Φ, and *false* if there exists a universal winning strategy for Φ.

3   Semantic Gate Extraction by Interpolation

This work builds on an application of propositional *definability* to the model counting problem [33]. We begin by recalling two basic concepts.

Definition 1. *Let φ be a formula, let X be a subset of its variables, and let x be a variable. Variable x is* defined *in terms of X in φ if $\sigma(x) = \tau(x)$ for any two satisfying assignments σ and τ of φ that agree on X. A* definition *of x by X in φ is a formula ψ with $var(\psi) \subseteq X$ such that $\sigma(x) = \psi[\sigma]$ for any satisfying assignment σ of φ.*

It is readily verified that there is a definition for every variable that is defined. Lagniez et al. [33] observe that the following result can be used to determine whether a variable is defined [34,39].

Theorem 1 (Padoa's Theorem). *Let φ be a formula and let $X \subseteq var(\varphi)$ be a subset of its variables. Let φ' be the propositional formula obtained by replacing every variable $y \in var(\varphi) \setminus X$ by a new variable y'. Let $x \in var(\varphi)$ be a variable. If $x \notin X$, then x is defined in φ by X if, and only if, the formula $\varphi \wedge x \wedge \varphi' \wedge \neg x'$ is unsatisfiable.*

For the purposes of preprocessing in model counting, it is sufficient to know *that* a variable x is defined by X in φ, and the above result shows that this can be decided by a SAT solver. It is not necessary to compute the corresponding definition, whose size is not polynomially bounded in the size of φ under common assumptions in computational complexity [33].

While finding definitions is harder than deciding definability in theory, the difference virtually disappears in practice. Our main theoretical contribution, stated as Theorem 2 below, says that a definition can be obtained as an *interpolant* of the formula constructed in the statement of Padoa's Theorem. Since interpolants can be efficiently (in linear time) generated from resolution proofs [22,32], the distinction between detecting definability and computing definitions

---

[1] We sometimes refer to existential strategy functions as *Skolem* functions and universal strategy functions as *Herbrand* functions.

becomes moot when a CDCL SAT solver is used to decide (un)satisfiability: once it determines that the formula is unsatisfiable it has already (implicitly or explicitly) produced a proof from which a definition can be extracted at a small overhead.[2]

Before proving Theorem 2, we recall the definition of an interpolant following McMillan [36].

Definition 2 (Interpolant). *Let ψ and χ be an formulas such that $\psi \wedge \chi$ is unsatisfiable. An* interpolant *for ψ and χ is a formula I such that*

(1) ψ implies I,
(2) $I \wedge \chi$ is unsatisfiable, and
(3) I only refers to variables common to ψ and χ.

Craig's Interpolation Theorem [9] states that every pair of jointly unsatisfiable propositional formulas have an interpolant.[3] It remains to show that an interpolant for a formula witnessing definability in fact yields a definition.

Lemma 1. *Let φ be a formula and let $X \subseteq var(\varphi)$ be a subset of its variables. Let φ' be the formula obtained by replacing every variable $y \in var(\varphi) \setminus X$ by a new variable y'. For any variable $x \in var(\varphi) \setminus X$, an interpolant for $\varphi \wedge x$ and $\varphi' \wedge \neg x'$ is a definition of x by X in φ.*

Proof. Let I be an interpolant for $\varphi \wedge x$ and $\varphi' \wedge \neg x'$. By property (3) of Definition 2, I only refers to the common variables $var(\varphi \wedge x) \cap var(\varphi' \wedge \neg x') = X$ of these formulas. To see that I defines x in φ, consider a satisfying assignment $\sigma : var(\varphi) \rightarrow \{0,1\}$ of φ. If $\sigma(x) = 1$ then $\varphi \wedge x$ is satisfied by σ. The formula $\varphi \wedge x$ implies I by property (1), so $I[\sigma] = 1$ as well. Otherwise, $\sigma(x) = 0$ and we can construct a satisfying assignment σ' of $\varphi' \wedge \neg x'$ by setting $\sigma'(v) = \sigma(v)$ for $v \in X$ along with $\sigma'(v') = \sigma(v)$ for $v \in var(\varphi) \setminus X$. By property (2), $I \wedge \varphi' \wedge \neg x'$ is unsatisfiable, so we must have $I[\sigma'] = I[\sigma] = 0$.

Theorem 2. *Let φ be a formula and let $X \subseteq var(\varphi)$ be a subset of its variables. Let φ' be the formula obtained by replacing every variable $y \in var(\varphi) \setminus X$ by a new variable y'. A variable $x \in var(\varphi) \setminus X$ is defined in terms of X in φ if, and only if, the formula $\varphi \wedge x \wedge \varphi' \wedge \neg x'$ is unsatisfiable, and a definition of x in terms of X can be obtained as an interpolant for $\varphi \wedge x$ and $\varphi' \wedge \neg x'$.*

Proof. By Theorem 1 variable $x \in var(\varphi) \setminus X$ is defined in terms of X in φ if, and only if, the formula $\varphi \wedge x \wedge \varphi' \wedge \neg x'$ is unsatisfiable. Craig's Interpolation Theorem tells us that in this case there is an interpolant for $\varphi \wedge x$ and $\varphi' \wedge \neg x'$, which defines x in terms of X by Lemma 1.

---

[2] Assuming the SAT solver does not use the full power of the DRAT proof system [51].
[3] In fact, the result holds even for first order logic, but we will confine ourselves to the propositional case.

4   Extracting Unique QBF Strategy Functions

In this section, we show how Theorem 2 can be used to extract unique strategy functions of QBFs. We say that the Skolem (Herbrand) function of an existential (universal) variable x in a QBF is *unique* if it is the same in every existential (universal) winning strategy. In particular, if x is existentially (universally) quantified and the formula is false (true), then the strategy function of x is trivially unique (there is none). In other words, the strategy function of a variable x is unique if there is *at most one* such function for x that is part of a winning strategy. The following result states that propositional definability is a sufficient condition for uniqueness of a strategy function.

Proposition 1. *Let $\Phi = Q_1 x_1 \ldots Q_n x_n . \varphi$ be a QBF. If an existential (universal) variable x_i is defined in terms of variables $X \subseteq \{ x_j \mid 1 \leq j < i, Q_j \neq Q_i \}$ in φ ($\neg \varphi$) its Skolem (Herbrand) function is unique.*

Proof. We only consider the case where x_i is an existential variable of Φ (the case where x_i is a universal variable is symmetric). Let $F = \{ f_{x_j} \}_{x_j \in var_\exists(\Phi)}$ and $G = \{ g_{x_j} \}_{x_j \in var_\exists(\Phi)}$ be existential winning strategies and $\tau : var_\forall(\Phi) \to \{0, 1\}$ an assignment to the universal variables. Since F and G are existential winning strategies both $\sigma_F = \tau \cup F(\tau)$ and $\sigma_G = \tau \cup G(\tau)$ must be satisfying assignments of φ. The assignments σ_F and σ_G agree on $X \subseteq var_\forall(\Phi)$, so we must have $f_{x_i}(\tau) = \sigma_F(x_i) = \sigma_G(x_i) = g_{x_i}(\tau)$ because x_i is defined in terms of X. Since τ was chosen arbitrarily, this identity holds for every universal assignment, so the functions f_{x_i} and g_{x_i} coincide.

To see that definability is not a *necessary* condition for a strategy function to be unique, consider the following example.

Example 1. Let $\Phi = \forall x \exists y \forall z . (x \leftrightarrow y) \vee z$. The formula $\psi = x$ represents the unique existential winning strategy (set y to the same value as x). However, variable y is not defined in terms of x: the assignments $\{x, y, z\}$ and $\{x, \neg y, z\}$ both satisfy the matrix and agree on x, but differ on y. Intuitively, the reason why the existential strategy function for y is unique in spite of y not being defined is that the universal player would never assign z true as required by one of the assignments witnessing non-definability.

4.1   An Algorithm for Computing Unique Strategy Functions

We now describe an algorithm for computing unique strategy functions of a QBF based on Proposition 1. By using an interpolating SAT solver (ITPSATSOLVER) that supports both incremental solving and assumptions [22], we can extract definitions for variables of a given quantifier type (universal or existential) using a single solver instance. Pseudocode is shown as Algorithm 1 below.

Let $\Phi = Q_1 x_1 \ldots Q_n x_n . \varphi$ be a QBF and let $Q \in \{\forall, \exists\}$ be a quantifier type. Algorithm 1 first determines the leftmost variable x_i in the prefix of Φ that has quantifier type Q (line 3). The strategy function of any variable to the right of x_i in the prefix (including x_i itself) may use the variables to its left (*shared*), so we can begin by looking for definitions of x_i in terms of *shared*. Towards constructing the formula for the corresponding unsatisfiability check according to Theorem 2, $\mathrm{COPY}(\varphi, X)$ returns a copy φ' of the matrix φ where each variable $x \in var(\varphi) \setminus shared$ has been replaced by a fresh variable x'. Next (lines 9–14), we consider each variable x_j with quantifier type Q—these are the variables we want to find definitions of—and introduce two fresh "selector" variables s_i and s'_i, while adding clauses $(\neg s_j \vee x_j)$ and $(\neg s'_j \vee \neg x'_j)$ to φ and φ', respectively. These clauses allow us to represent $\varphi \wedge x_j \wedge \varphi' \wedge \neg x'_j$ by assuming literals s_j and s'_j.[4]

After initializing the SAT solver, we consider the variables $x_1, \ldots, x_n$ in the order of the quantifier prefix (lines 18–29). If variable x_j has quantifier type Q, we want to check whether x_j is defined in φ in terms of oppositely quantified variables X_j that precede it in the prefix (Proposition 1 tells us that in this case the strategy function of x_j is unique). For the first such variable x_j, it is clear that the set of variables common to φ and φ' is precisely X. Unsatisfiability of $\varphi \wedge x_j \wedge \varphi' \wedge \neg x'_j$ is decided by calling the SAT solver under assumptions $\{s_j, s'_j\}$: the assumptions ensure that x_j and $\neg x'_j$ are set to true by propagation, and all remaining selector variables can be set to false so as to satisfy the clauses they occur in without interfering with the remaining clauses. If the solver determines unsatisfiability, an interpolant I_j is computed (line 22), which by Theorem 2 corresponds to a definition of x_j, and adds the pair (x_j, I_j) to a list of definitions. Otherwise, if x_j has the quantifier type opposite to Q, the strategy function of any variable with quantifier type Q considered later may use x_j. Accordingly (lines 26–27), we add clauses $(x_j \vee \neg x'_j)$ and $(\neg x_j \vee x'_j)$ to φ' through the incremental interface of the SAT solver. This has two effects: first, it enforces equivalence of x_j and x'_j, and second, x_j is added to the common vocabulary of φ and φ', so that it can appear in interpolants computed in later iterations.[5]

Soundness of Algorithm 1 as stated in the following proposition can be proved by a straightforward induction on the quantifier prefix using Theorem 2 and Proposition 1.

Proposition 2. *Given a quantified Boolean formula Φ and a quantifier type $Q \in \{\forall, \exists\}$, Algorithm 1 terminates with a (possibly empty) set $\{(x_1, I_1) \ldots (x_k, I_k)\}$ of pairs (x_i, I_i) such that I_i represents the unique strategy function of x_i in Φ and $var(x_i) \in var_Q(\Phi)$ for $1 \leq i \leq k$.*

Example 2. Consider the QBF $\Psi = \forall x_1 \exists y_1 \forall x_2 \exists y_2. \varphi$, where

$$\varphi = (x_1 \vee y_1) \wedge (\neg x_1 \vee \neg y_1) \wedge (x_2 \vee y_2) \wedge (\neg x_2 \vee \neg y_2).$$

---

[4] Two distinct selector variables are required to ensure that they do not belong to the common variables of φ and φ'.

[5] One could also add these clauses to φ, in which case x'_j would become part of the shared vocabulary. This has the slight disadvantage that subsequently computed definitions may use a mixture of variables from φ and φ', rather than just φ.

Algorithm 1. Extracting Unique Strategy Functions by Interpolation

```
1: procedure GETDEFINITIONSQBF(Φ, Q ∈ {∀,∃})
2:     Q₁x₁ ... Qₙxₙ.φ ← Φ
3:     i = min{ 1 ≤ i ≤ n | Qᵢ = Q }
4:     shared ← {x₁, ..., xᵢ₋₁}
5:     if Q = ∀ then
6:         φ ← ¬φ                                    ▷ ∀-strategies aim to falsify the matrix.
7:     end if
8:     φ' ← COPY(φ, shared)
9:     sametype ← { j | 1 ≤ j ≤ n and Qⱼ = Q }
10:    for j ∈ sametype do
11:        sⱼ, s'ⱼ ← fresh variables
12:        φ ← φ ∧ (¬sⱼ ∨ xⱼ)
13:        φ' ← φ' ∧ (¬s'ⱼ ∨ ¬x'ⱼ)
14:    end for
15:    solver ← ITPSATSOLVER(φ, φ')
16:    defined ← ∅
17:    k ← max{ i ≤ k ≤ n | Qₖ = Q }
18:    for j = i, ..., k do
19:        if Qⱼ = Q then
20:            result ← solver.SOLVE({sⱼ, s'ⱼ})
21:            if result = UNSAT then
22:                Iⱼ ← solver.GETINTERPOLANT()
23:                defined ← defined ∪ {(xⱼ, Iⱼ)}
24:            end if
25:        else                                       ▷ Qⱼ ≠ Q
26:            solver.ADDCLAUSE(φ', xⱼ ∨ ¬x'ⱼ)
27:            solver.ADDCLAUSE(φ', ¬xⱼ ∨ x'ⱼ)
28:        end if
29:    end for
30:    return defined
31: end procedure
```

We illustrate a run of Algorithm 1 on Ψ with $Q = \exists$. Since y_1 is the leftmost existential variable, we create a copy φ' of φ with every variable except x_1 renamed, that is,

$$\varphi' = (x_1 \vee y_1') \wedge (\neg x_1 \vee \neg y_1') \wedge (x_2' \vee y_2') \wedge (\neg x_2' \vee \neg y_2').$$

We also add the clauses $(\neg s_1 \vee y_1)$ and $(\neg s_2 \vee y_2)$ to φ and the clauses $(\neg s_1' \vee \neg y_1')$ and $(\neg s_2' \vee \neg y_2')$ to φ'. In the main loop, Algorithm 1 first checks whether $\varphi \wedge \varphi'$ is unsatisfiable under the assumptions $\{s_1, s_1'\}$. Unit propagation simplifies φ to (omitting unused selector variables and clauses)

$$(\neg x_1) \wedge (x_2 \vee y_2) \wedge (\neg x_2 \vee \neg y_2),$$

and φ' simplifies to

$$(x_1) \wedge (\neg x_2' \vee y_2') \wedge (\neg x_2' \vee \neg y_2').$$

By resolving $(\neg x_1)$ with (x_1) we obtain the empty clause, and $\neg x_1$ is the corresponding interpolant,[6] so $(y_1, \neg x_1)$ is added to the set of definitions. Next, we consider the universally quantified variable x_2 and add the clauses $(x_2 \vee \neg x_2')$ and $(\neg x_2 \vee x_2')$ to φ'. Finally, we check whether y_2 is definable by calling the SAT solver under the assumptions $\{s_2, s_2'\}$. Now, the formula φ simplifies to

$$(x_1 \vee y_1) \wedge (\neg x_1 \vee \neg y_1) \wedge (\neg x_2),$$

and φ' simplifies to

$$(x_1 \vee y_1') \wedge (\neg x_1 \vee \neg y_1') \wedge$$
$$(x_2') \wedge (x_2 \vee \neg x_2') \wedge (\neg x_2 \vee x_2').$$

Unit propagation derives the clause (x_2) from the clauses in the second line, which can be resolved with the clause $(\neg x_2)$ from φ to obtain a resolution refutation of the formula $\varphi \wedge \varphi'$, with $\neg x_2$ as an interpolant. Accordingly, $(y_2, \neg x_2)$ is added to the set of definitions. Algorithm 1 terminates with the definitions $\{(y_1, \neg x_1), (y_2, \neg x_2)\}$, and it is readily verified that $y_1 \equiv \neg x_1$, $y_2 \equiv \neg x_2$ is indeed the unique existential winning strategy of Ψ.

4.2   Improvements and Generalization to Dependency QBF

Consider a QBF $\Phi = \forall x_1, x_2 \exists y_1, y_2.(x_1 \leftrightarrow x_2) \leftrightarrow (y_1 \leftrightarrow y_2)$. It is easy to verify that Φ is true and that y_1 and y_2 do not have unique Skolem functions: for every assignment to the universal variables there are two ways of setting y_1 and y_2 so as to satisfy the matrix, so neither existential variable is defined by the universal variables alone. However, each variable is defined by all remaining variables. For instance, variable y_2 is defined by x_1, x_2, and y_1.

More generally, increasing the set of defining variables allows us to detect more definitions: if x is defined in terms of X then it is also defined in terms of any enclosing set $X' \supset X$. To exploit this, we modified Algorithm 1 so as to assume a total ordering of variables and check for definitions of a variable x in terms of all variables X which precede it in the quantifier prefix. This can be implemented by simply adding clauses encoding equivalence of x_j and x_j' (lines 26–27) regardless of quantifier type.

Technically, this leads to an alternative definition of a "winning strategy" for a QBF where each strategy function takes an assignment to all preceding variables as input. Both definitions are ultimately equivalent in the sense that a winning strategy according to one definition can be transformed into a winning strategy according to the other definition without changing its responses (cf. the work on quantifier elimination by functional composition and self-substitution [8,14,28,29]). One can prove an analogue of Proposition 1 stating that the strategy function—according to the alternative definition—of a variable x is unique whenever x is defined in terms of the variables preceding x in the quantifier prefix.

---

[6] As mentioned above, interpolants can be efficiently extracted from resolution refutations [32,36,46].

Dependency Quantified Boolean Formulas (DQBFs) generalize QBFs by allowing a non-linear quantifier prefix. More specifically, each existential variable is annotated with a set of universal variables its Skolem function may depend on. A DQBF is true if there is an existential winning strategy such that each Skolem function satisfies these restrictions [2]. Although evaluating DQBF is NEXPTIME-complete and thus believed to be much harder than evaluating QBF, the fact that problems can be concisely encoded in DQBF [12,18] has prompted the development of dedicated DQBF solvers [13,15,17,48].

Algorithm 1 can easily be extended to compute unique Skolem functions of DQBF. The standard DQDIMACS format [15] allows for the combination of a linear quantifier prefix with variables for which the dependency sets are explicitly stated. The linear quantifier prefix can be handled as before. For each existential variable x with explicit dependency set D_x we simply check whether x is defined by D_x. If multiple variables $x_1, \ldots, x_k$ have the same dependency set D_x (which is frequently the case in benchmark formulas) we check whether x_i is defined by $D_x \cup \{x_1, \ldots, x_{i-1}\}$ for each $1 \leq i \leq k$. Again, this technically requires a non-standard definition of Skolem functions for DQBF but can easily be proven sound.

5   Implementation

We implemented the algorithm described in the previous section in a prototype named UNIQUE. As a back end SAT solver we use ITPMINISAT, a modified version of MINISAT [11] bundled with the EXTAVY model checker that efficiently generates interpolants in memory and supports both assumptions and incremental solving [22,49]. UNIQUE can read PCNF formulas (QDIMACS), prenex non-CNF QBFs (QCIR), as well as DQBFs with CNF matrices (DQDIMACS).

Interpolants obtained from ITPMINISAT are represented as And-Inverter graphs (AIGs) and accessed through the AIG library of ABC [7]. To make use of the structural sharing capabilities of AIGs, we maintain a single AIG representing the interpolants computed in the main loop (lines 18–29) of Algorithm 1. Whenever a new interpolant is obtained, the corresponding AIG returned by ITP-MINISAT is merged into the existing AIG. If the number of AIG nodes exceeds a (geometrically increasing) threshold, we use the ABC macro *compress2* to reduce the size of the combined AIG. Upon termination, and assuming the AIG is not too large, this is followed up by a round of *FRAIGing* [37] and a final application of *compress2*.

While running UNIQUE on QBFs with multiple quantifier alternations we noticed that ITPMINISAT got stuck attempting to solve some of the definability queries. Further testing revealed that the corresponding instances were hard for most state-of-the-art solvers. Increasing the overall timeout would allow us to solve these instances in some cases, but naturally the corresponding interpolants (for unsatisfiable instances) were very large (and difficult to compress with ABC). This clearly defeats the purpose of detecting unique strategy functions quickly. We thus decided to impose a limit on the number of conflicts

for each call of ITPMINISAT (currently set to 1000 conflicts). This significantly
reduces the overall running time of UNIQUE for many instances and ensures that
individual interpolants are small, but only marginally decreases the total number
of definitions found.

Since the individual definability queries are independent of each other, it is
not necessary to determine for each input variable whether it is defined. Accordingly, we implemented UNIQUE as an *anytime* algorithm: upon termination, it
returns the set of variables with unique strategy functions identified up to that
point, along with the AIG representing the corresponding functions.

6   Experiments

For the experiments described below we used a cluster with Intel Xeon E5649
processors at 2.53 GHz running 64-bit Linux.

6.1   Gate Extraction

We first ran UNIQUE to compute unique strategy functions for the instances in
the 2QBF (402 instances) benchmark set from the 2018 QBF Evaluation, as
well as the PCNF (558), QCIR (341), and DQBF (333) benchmark sets from
the 2019 QBF Evaluation.[7] For each job we imposed a time limit of 600 s and a
memory limit of 1.8 GB.

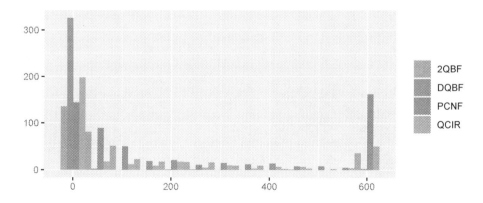

Fig. 1. Running time (s) of UNIQUE by benchmark set. For each 50-s interval within
the time limit (x-axis), the number of instances (y-axis) processed by UNIQUE with a
running time in that interval is shown.

Figure 1 shows a histogram for the running time of UNIQUE on different
benchmark sets. While most instances are processed quickly, UNIQUE runs into

---

[7] http://www.qbflib.org.

the time limit for a significant number of PCNF instances. Generally, the running time increases with the size of the matrix and the number of variables. This explains why almost all DQBF formulas are processed quickly, as these tend to be much smaller compared to formulas from the other benchmark sets.

Figure 2 shows a histogram for the fraction of existential variables with unique strategy functions in 2QBF and PCNF instances (turquoise bars). We clearly see a bimodal distribution here: there is a large number of instances where the strategy functions of most variables are unique, but also a significant number of instances where few existential strategy functions are unique. To determine how many of the corresponding definitions cannot be found by syntactic gate detection, we used the QCIR-CONV script provided by GHOSTQ [31] to convert 2QBF and PCNF instances to QCIR, and ran UNIQUE again on the resulting circuits. To do this, the circuit is translated (back) to CNF, but auxiliary variables representing gates are ignored by the definability check. Testing showed that a one-sided CNF encoding [42] works better than standard Tseitin conversion.

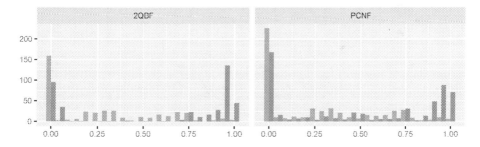

Fig. 2. Fraction of existential variables with unique strategy functions in 2QBF (left) and PCNF (right) instances before (turquoise) and after (red) syntactic gate detection. For each fraction (x-axis) we see the number of instances (y-axis) with the corresponding fraction of unique existential strategy functions. (Color figure online)

Table 1 (left) shows quartiles for the distributions of unique existential strategy functions detected by UNIQUE in each benchmark set.[8] We only show the distribution for existential variables in Table 1 and Fig. 2 since very few universal variables were found to have unique strategy functions. In fact, only 51 instances from the QCIR benchmark set encoding bounded synthesis for Petri games contained such universal variables.

The fraction of variables with unique strategy functions was smallest for QCIR instances. This is expected, since they can represent circuit structure directly and do not require auxiliary variables to encode gate definitions. By

---

[8] For instance, the left side of the first row of Table 1 says that for 75% of 2QBF instances, UNIQUE was able to identify 3% of Skolem functions as unique; for half of the instances, at least 90% of existential variables were identified as having unique Skolem functions; and for 25% of instances, at least 96%.

Table 1. Distribution (quartiles) of the fraction of unique Skolem functions identified by UNIQUE before (left) and after (right) preprocessing with HQSPRE. Rows marked by a star (*) show the distribution after syntactic gate detection.

	Original			Preprocessed		
	1st	Median	3rd	1st	Median	3rd
2QBF	0.03	0.9	0.96	0	0	0
2QBF*	0	0.22	0.54	0	0	0
PCNF	0	0.53	0.94	0	0	0.03
PCNF*	0	0.21	0.53	0	0	0.02
QCIR	0	0	0.13	–	–	–
DQBF	0.57	0.88	0.94	0	0.22	0.45

contrast, 2QBF and DQBF instances contain many variables with unique strategy functions. For about half of the instances, between roughly 90% and 95% of the existential strategy functions are unique.

On the right of Table 1 we show the distribution of unique existential strategy functions after preprocessing with HQSPRE [52]. Clearly, only very few unique Skolem functions are detected by UNIQUE. This may be in part due to the fact that preprocessing detects and removes gate definitions [27]. Another possibility is that definitions are simply lost: some of the most powerful preprocessing techniques for QBF currently used only preserve the truth value and not the set of strategies [23]. We will return to this topic at the end of the next subsection.

6.2 Solving Formulas Augmented with Definitions

Unique strategy functions of a (D)QBF can be substituted for their variables without changing the set of winning strategies. This can be used in preprocessing to reduce the number of quantified variables, typically at the cost of increasing the size of the matrix. In the following experiments, we substituted definitions found by UNIQUE for the defined variables and ran QBF and DQBF solvers on the resulting instances.

First, we considered the 2QBF benchmark set. We picked the QCIR solvers QUABS [47], QFUN [26], and GHOSTQ [31], along with the dedicated 2QBF (PCNF) solver CADET [43]. For the QCIR solvers, the performance on instances constructed by syntactic gate detection with QCIR-CONV serves as a baseline. We compare it with performance on instances obtained by UNIQUE and—since QCIR-CONV also performs circuit-level simplifications that go beyond gate extraction—with a combination of both where QCIR-CONV and UNIQUE are run in sequence.

For CADET, we compare performance on the original 2QBF instances with performance on QDIMACS instances augmented with CNF encodings of definitions extracted by UNIQUE. For each configuration, we report the number of

instances solved within a time limit of 15 min. To isolate the effect of adding definitions, the time required by UNIQUE (and QCIR-CONV) is not counted towards
the time limit.[9] The results are shown in Fig. 3 (left).

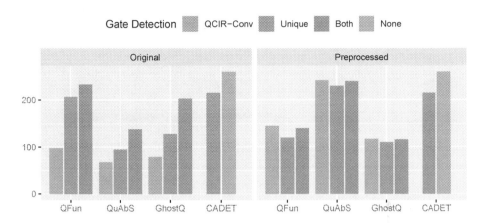

Fig. 3. Number of 2QBF instances solved (y-axis) by solvers (x-axis) using different
gate detection methods before (left) and after (right) preprocessing with HQSPRE.

QFUN, QUABS, and GHOSTQ benefit considerably from semantic gate extraction, in particular when applied on top of syntactic gate extraction. By contrast,
CADET solves *fewer* instances augmented with gate definitions than original
instances. We found this surprising, since variable definitions should be detected
by CADET's heuristic for identifying unique Skolem functions. Perhaps most
definitions found by UNIQUE are already covered in this way, so that the additional clauses simply slow down propagation. We believe that explicitly telling
CADET which variables have already been identified as determined should
result in a speedup overall.

Figure 4 takes a closer look at solving times for individual instances (for this
plot, memory outs are treated as timeouts). CADET is slower on instances
augmented by UNIQUE but fairly consistent, while the effect on the other solvers
is more erratic. We conjecture that this is because the set of existential strategies
is preserved and the instances thus "look similar" to CADET.

Next, we tested with PCNF instances and considered the QDIMACS solvers
DEPQBF [5] and CAQE [44], as well as the QCIR solvers QUABS [47],
QFUN [26], and QUTE [40]. Again, we compare the number of instances solved
in 15 min with different options for gate detection. Results are shown in Fig. 5
(left). Again all QCIR solvers benefit from gate detection with UNIQUE when performed on top of syntactic gate detection with QCIR-CONV, while performance

---

[9] The results are qualitatively the same when the running time of UNIQUE is counted
towards the time limit: the largest decrease in the number of solved instances across
all benchmark sets and configurations is 7.

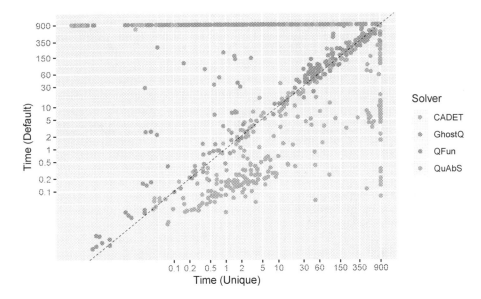

Fig. 4. Solving time (s) for 2QBF instances with (x-axis) and without UNIQUE (y-axis).

decreases for both QDIMACS solvers. The additional clauses and variables introduced by UNIQUE apparently do not help these solvers and simply result in a slowdown.

Finally, we tested the impact of UNIQUE on DQBF (DQDIMACS) instances solved by HQS [19] and DCAQE [48] within 15 min. Since DQBF solvers currently do not (yet) support non-CNF input, we translate definitions to CNF and add them to the original formulas. Note that whenever an existential variable x is defined by (a subset of) its dependency set, we can safely let x depend on additional variables. This is sound since the response of variable x is already determined by the variables in the original dependency set and cannot change depending on other inputs. In particular, we can collect all defined variables (and auxiliary variables) in an "innermost" existential quantifier block that depends on all universal variables. Since many existential variables have uniquely determined strategy functions (see Table 1), this allows us to push many variables into the innermost quantifier block and get closer to a linear quantifier prefix. For HQS, this translates into a small increase in the number of solved instances (208 vs. 189), whereas DCAQE basically solves the same number of instances (133 vs. 135).

Interaction with Preprocessing. QBF solvers for PCNF are typically paired with preprocessors such as BLOQQER [6] or HQSPRE [52]. These are highly engineered tools that batter instances with a barrage of techniques and can often solve formulas completely on their own. Most solvers benefit greatly from

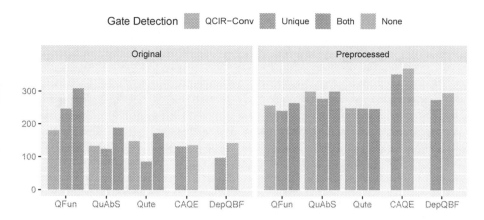

Fig. 5. PCNF instances solved (y-axis) by solver (x-axis) using different methods for gate detection before (left) and after (right) preprocessing with HQSPRE.

preprocessing. This is evident in Fig. 5 (right), which shows the number of solved PCNF instances with different forms of gate detection after preprocessing with HQSPRE (within a timeout of 600 s). Here, the number of solved instances increases significantly for almost all systems.

At the same time, preprocessing appears to obscure or destroy definitions. UNIQUE hardly finds any definitions in preprocessed instances (cf. Table 1) and accordingly has little impact on performance. For QFUN, which benefitted most from gate detection in our experiments, this translates to a substantial reduction in the number of solved instances. On the 2QBF benchmark set (Fig. 3), both QFUN and GHOSTQ solve significantly fewer instances with HQSPRE compared to the combination of UNIQUE and QCIR-CONV, whereas the number of solved instances almost doubles for QUABS. Understanding which preprocessing techniques obscure gate definitions and why certain solvers benefit more from gate detection than others are important questions for future work.[10]

7 Related Work

Our semantic gate detection technique is closely related to a method for *determinizing* Boolean relations by Jiang et al. [29], a problem that essentially corresponds to solving 2QBF. The authors show that, for a (total) relation $R(X, y)$ with a single output variable y, a functional implementation of y can be obtained as an interpolant for $\neg R(X, 0) \wedge \neg R(X, 1)$. This can be used to determinize

---

[10] We also ran experiments with QCIR-CONV and UNIQUE applied *before* preprocessing. The results were significantly worse, so we do not report them in detail. Standard preprocessing requires PCNF input, so that definitions have to be encoded using additional clauses and Tseitin variables. Just like the PCNF solvers in the other experiments, HQSPRE appears to be unable to do anything useful with these extra clauses and variables.

relations $R(X, Y)$ with a set of output variables $Y = \{y_1, \ldots, y_n\}$. First, an implementation f_n for y_n can be computed by treating R as a relation with inputs $X \cup \{y_1, \ldots, y_{n-1}\}$ and single output y_n. Subsequently, the implementation f_n can be substituted for y_n to obtain a relation $R'(X, Y \setminus \{y_n\})$. By repeating this process, a functional implementation f_1 of y_1 can eventually be obtained. Substituting f_i into f_{i+1} for $1 \leq i < n$ results in functional implementations that only depend on the original input variables X. This approach does not require for any of the output variables to be defined by X, but an implementation of y_i solely in terms of the input variables X is only available at the very end of this process. For *deterministic* relations $R(X, Y)$ (where every y is defined in terms of X), the authors show that a functional implementation of $y \in Y$ can be obtained as the interpolant of a formula that corresponds to the formula in the statement of Padoa's theorem. Our result stated as Theorem 2 is more general in that it holds for multi-output relations that are not necessarily deterministic.

Hofferek et al. use interpolation to synthesize multiple functional implementations from a single proof and thus avoid the increase in formula size incurred by repeated substitution [24]. This has an analogue in *strategy extraction* for QBF, which allows for implementations of all (existential or universal) variables to be obtained from a proof [3]. However, strategy extraction requires the input QBF has been solved, whereas our main interest is in preprocessing QBF.

There is a series of works on recovering gate definitions from CNF formulas. Li integrated rules for detecting equivalent literals in a Davis-Putnam style algorithm [35]. Ostrowski et al. represent formulas as graphs to detect patterns corresponding to and-gates, or-gates, and equivalences [38]. Roy et al. use CNF signatures to detect a richer set of gates [45]. Fu and Malik extend this to arbitrary (user-specified) gate libraries and ensure that a maximum acyclic circuit is constructed [16].

In the context of QBF, Bacchus and Goultiaeva showed that circuit reconstruction can speed up solvers by providing them with a better set of initial cubes [21]. They also extended the scope of these techniques to CNF formulas obtained from circuits by the Plaisted-Greenbaum encoding [42]. Scholl and Pigorsch developed a QBF solver that manipulates an AIG representation of the matrix to perform quantifier elimination and relies on circuit reconstruction to simplify the initial AIG [41].

Balabanov et al. proposed a SAT-based semantic gate extraction technique [4]. Their approach has the disadvantage that a subset of clauses inducing a definition has to be guessed. As a more efficient heuristic, they suggest to identify *pseudo* definitions instead. A set of clauses $(A_1 \vee x), \ldots, (A_k \vee x), (B_1 \vee \neg x), \ldots, (B_l \vee \neg x)$ is a pseudo definition of x if the formula $A_1 \wedge \cdots \wedge A_k \wedge B_1 \wedge \cdots \wedge B_l$ is unsatisfiable. Rabe and Seshia use a similar criterion in their *incremental determinization* algorithm to identify variables that are *(locally) deterministic* [43]. Checking for pseudo definitions is typically efficient but limits the range of definitions that can be detected.

8   Conclusion

Syntactic gate detection has been shown to benefit SAT solvers [10,16] and QBF solvers [21]. The underlying algorithms are fast but limited to a predefined library of gates. By contrast, our semantic gate extraction method can detect any definition entailed by an input formula but requires an interpolating SAT solver. In the context of SAT, this overhead likely outweighs any potential benefits. However—as demonstrated by our experiments—there is significant potential for application to harder problems such as QBF and DQBF evaluation. Here, preprocessing is just a first step.

At the same time, our results show that substituting unique strategy functions can slow down solvers. In some sense, this is counter-intuitive: ideally, providing solvers with unique strategy functions should give them a head start, or at least not hurt their performance. By analogy, if we give a SAT solver part of a backbone assignment, it can simply instantiate accordingly and need not consider the corresponding variables for the remainder of its run. With the exception of CADET, QBF solvers currently cannot "instantiate" variables with strategy functions in this way, since they are only equipped to reason about assignments. We believe that designing techniques for reasoning about *strategies* is a key challenge in developing the next generation of QBF solvers.

Acknowledgements. The author would like to thank Adrian Rebola-Pardo, Matthias Schlaipfer, and Georg Weissenbacher for helpful discussions.

References

1. Ansótegui, C., Gomes, C.P., Selman, B.: The Achilles' heel of QBF. In: Veloso, M.M., Kambhampati, S. (eds.) AAAI 2005, pp. 275–281. AAAI Press/The MIT Press (2005)
2. Balabanov, V., Chiang, H.J.K., Jiang, J.R.: Henkin quantifiers and Boolean formulae: a certification perspective of DQBF. Theor. Comput. Sci. **523**, 86–100 (2014)
3. Balabanov, V., Jiang, J.R.: Unified QBF certification and its applications. Formal Methods Syst. Des. **41**(1), 45–65 (2012)
4. Balabanov, V., Jiang, J.R., Mishchenko, A., Scholl, C.: Clauses versus gates in CEGAR-based 2QBF solving. In: Darwiche, A. (ed.) Beyond NP, Papers from the 2016 AAAI Workshop, AAAI Workshops, vol. WS-16-05. AAAI Press (2016)
5. Lonsing, F., Biere, A.: Integrating dependency schemes in search-based QBF solvers. In: Strichman, O., Szeider, S. (eds.) SAT 2010. LNCS, vol. 6175, pp. 158–171. Springer, Heidelberg (2010). https://doi.org/10.1007/978-3-642-14186-7_14
6. Biere, A., Lonsing, F., Seidl, M.: Blocked clause elimination for QBF. In: Bjørner, N., Sofronie-Stokkermans, V. (eds.) CADE 2011. LNCS (LNAI), vol. 6803, pp. 101–115. Springer, Heidelberg (2011). https://doi.org/10.1007/978-3-642-22438-6_10
7. Brayton, R., Mishchenko, A.: ABC: an academic industrial-strength verification tool. In: Touili, T., Cook, B., Jackson, P. (eds.) CAV 2010. LNCS, vol. 6174, pp. 24–40. Springer, Heidelberg (2010). https://doi.org/10.1007/978-3-642-14295-6_5

8. Bubeck, U., Kleine Büning, H.: Nested boolean functions as models for quantified boolean formulas. In: Järvisalo, M., Van Gelder, A. (eds.) SAT 2013. LNCS, vol. 7962, pp. 267–275. Springer, Heidelberg (2013). https://doi.org/10.1007/978-3-642-39071-5_20

9. Craig, W.: Three uses of the Herbrand-Gentzen theorem in relating model theory and proof theory. J. Symb. Log. **22**(3), 269–285 (1957)

10. Eén, N., Biere, A.: Effective preprocessing in SAT through variable and clause elimination. In: Bacchus, F., Walsh, T. (eds.) SAT 2005. LNCS, vol. 3569, pp. 61–75. Springer, Heidelberg (2005). https://doi.org/10.1007/11499107_5

11. Eén, N., Sörensson, N.: An extensible SAT-solver. In: Giunchiglia, E., Tacchella, A. (eds.) SAT 2003. LNCS, vol. 2919, pp. 502–518. Springer, Heidelberg (2004). https://doi.org/10.1007/978-3-540-24605-3_37

12. Faymonville, P., Finkbeiner, B., Rabe, M.N., Tentrup, L.: Encodings of bounded synthesis. In: Legay, A., Margaria, T. (eds.) TACAS 2017. LNCS, vol. 10205, pp. 354–370. Springer, Heidelberg (2017). https://doi.org/10.1007/978-3-662-54577-5_20

13. Finkbeiner, B., Tentrup, L.: Fast DQBF refutation. In: Sinz, C., Egly, U. (eds.) SAT 2014. LNCS, vol. 8561, pp. 243–251. Springer, Cham (2014). https://doi.org/10.1007/978-3-319-09284-3_19

14. Fried, D., Tabajara, L.M., Vardi, M.Y.: BDD-based boolean functional synthesis. In: Chaudhuri, S., Farzan, A. (eds.) CAV 2016. LNCS, vol. 9780, pp. 402–421. Springer, Cham (2016). https://doi.org/10.1007/978-3-319-41540-6_22

15. Fröhlich, A., Kovásznai, G., Biere, A., Veith, H.: iDQ: Instantiation-based DQBF solving. In: Pragmatics of SAT 2014 (2014)

16. Fu, Z., Malik, S.: Extracting logic circuit structure from conjunctive normal form descriptions. In: VLSI Design 2007, (ICES 2007), pp. 37–42. IEEE Computer Society (2007)

17. Ge-Ernst, A., Scholl, C., Wimmer, R.: Localizing quantifiers for DQBF. In: Barrett, C.W., Yang, J. (eds.) 2019 Formal Methods in Computer Aided Design, FMCAD 2019, San Jose, CA, USA, 22–25 October 2019, pp. 184–192. IEEE (2019)

18. Gitina, K., Reimer, S., Sauer, M., Wimmer, R., Scholl, C., Becker, B.: Equivalence checking of partial designs using dependency quantified Boolean formulae. In: 31st International Conference on Computer Design, ICCD 2013, pp. 396–403. IEEE (2013)

19. Gitina, K., Wimmer, R., Reimer, S., Sauer, M., Scholl, C., Becker, B.: Solving DQBF through quantifier elimination. In: Nebel, W., Atienza, D. (eds.) DATE 2015, pp. 1617–1622. ACM (2015)

20. Gomes, C.P., Kautz, H., Sabharwal, A., Selman, B.: Satisfiability solvers. In: Handbook of Knowledge Representation, Foundations of Artificial Intelligence, vol. 3, pp. 89–134. Elsevier (2008)

21. Goultiaeva, A., Bacchus, F.: Recovering and utilizing partial duality in QBF. In: Järvisalo, M., Van Gelder, A. (eds.) SAT 2013. LNCS, vol. 7962, pp. 83–99. Springer, Heidelberg (2013). https://doi.org/10.1007/978-3-642-39071-5_8

22. Gurfinkel, A., Vizel, Y.: Druping for interpolates. In: FMCAD 2014, pp. 99–106. IEEE (2014)

23. Heule, M., Järvisalo, M., Lonsing, F., Seidl, M., Biere, A.: Clause elimination for SAT and QSAT. J. Artif. Intell. Res. **53**, 127–168 (2015)

24. Hofferek, G., Gupta, A., Könighofer, B., Jiang, J.R., Bloem, R.: Synthesizing multiple Boolean functions using interpolation on a single proof. In: Formal Methods in Computer-Aided Design, FMCAD 2013, Portland, OR, USA, 20–23 October 2013, pp. 77–84. IEEE (2013)

25. Ivrii, A., Malik, S., Meel, K.S., Vardi, M.Y.: On computing minimal independent support and its applications to sampling and counting. Constraints **21**(1), 41–58 (2016)
26. Janota, M.: Towards generalization in QBF solving via machine learning. In: McIlraith, S.A., Weinberger, K.Q. (eds.) AAAI-18, pp. 6607–6614. AAAI Press (2018)
27. Järvisalo, M., Biere, A., Heule, M.: Simulating circuit-level simplifications on CNF. J. Autom. Reasoning **49**(4), 583–619 (2012)
28. Jiang, J.-H.R.: Quantifier elimination via functional composition. In: Bouajjani, A., Maler, O. (eds.) CAV 2009. LNCS, vol. 5643, pp. 383–397. Springer, Heidelberg (2009). https://doi.org/10.1007/978-3-642-02658-4_30
29. Jiang, J.R., Lin, H., Hung, W.: Interpolating functions from large Boolean relations. In: Roychowdhury, J.S. (ed.) ICCAD 2009, pp. 779–784. ACM (2009)
30. Jordan, C., Klieber, W., Seidl, M.: Non-CNF QBF solving with QCIR. In: Darwiche, A. (ed.) Beyond NP, Papers from the 2016 AAAI Workshop. AAAI Workshops, vol. WS-16-05. AAAI Press (2016)
31. Klieber, W., Sapra, S., Gao, S., Clarke, E.: A non-prenex, non-clausal QBF solver with game-state learning. In: Strichman, O., Szeider, S. (eds.) SAT 2010. LNCS, vol. 6175, pp. 128–142. Springer, Heidelberg (2010). https://doi.org/10.1007/978-3-642-14186-7_12
32. Krajícek, J.: Interpolation theorems, lower bounds for proof systems, and independence results for bounded arithmetic. J. Symb. Log. **62**(2), 457–486 (1997)
33. Lagniez, J., Lonca, E., Marquis, P.: Improving model counting by leveraging definability. In: Kambhampati, S. (ed.) IJCAI 2016, pp. 751–757. IJCAI/AAAI Press (2016)
34. Lang, J., Marquis, P.: On propositional definability. Artif. Intell. **172**(8–9), 991–1017 (2008)
35. Li, C.M.: Integrating equivalency reasoning into Davis-Putnam procedure. In: Kautz, H.A., Porter, B.W. (eds.) Proceedings of the Seventeenth National Conference on Artificial Intelligence and Twelfth Conference on on Innovative Applications of Artificial Intelligence, July 30 - August 3, 2000, Austin, Texas, USA, pp. 291–296. AAAI Press/The MIT Press (2000)
36. McMillan, K.L.: Interpolation and SAT-based model checking. In: Hunt, W.A., Somenzi, F. (eds.) CAV 2003. LNCS, vol. 2725, pp. 1–13. Springer, Heidelberg (2003). https://doi.org/10.1007/978-3-540-45069-6_1
37. Mishchenko, A., Chatterjee, S., Brayton, R.: FRAIGs: A unifying representation for logic synthesis and verification. Technical report, Berkeley (2005)
38. Ostrowski, R., Grégoire, É., Mazure, B., Saïs, L.: Recovering and exploiting structural knowledge from CNF formulas. In: Van Hentenryck, P. (ed.) CP 2002. LNCS, vol. 2470, pp. 185–199. Springer, Heidelberg (2002). https://doi.org/10.1007/3-540-46135-3_13
39. Padoa, A.: Essai d'une théorie algébrique des nombres entiers, précédé d'une Introduction logique à une théorie déductive quelconque. Bibliothèque du Congrès International de Philosophie (1903)
40. Peitl, T., Slivovsky, F., Szeider, S.: Dependency learning for QBF. J. Artif. Intell. Res. **65**, 180–208 (2019)
41. Pigorsch, F., Scholl, C.: Exploiting structure in an AIG based QBF solver. In: Benini, L., Micheli, G.D., Al-Hashimi, B.M., Müller, W. (eds.) DATE 2009, pp. 1596–1601. IEEE (2009)
42. Plaisted, D.A., Greenbaum, S.: A structure-preserving clause form translation. J. Symb. Comput. **2**(3), 293–304 (1986)

43. Rabe, M.N., Seshia, S.A.: Incremental determinization. In: Creignou, N., Le Berre, D. (eds.) SAT 2016. LNCS, vol. 9710, pp. 375–392. Springer, Cham (2016). https://doi.org/10.1007/978-3-319-40970-2_23
44. Rabe, M.N., Tentrup, L.: CAQE: A certifying QBF solver. In: Kaivola, R., Wahl, T. (eds.) FMCAD 2015, pp. 136–143. IEEE Computer Soc. (2015)
45. Roy, J., Markov, I., Bertacco, V.: Restoring circuit structure from SAT instances. In: Proceedings of International Workshop on Logic and Synthesis, pp. 663–678 (2004)
46. Schlaipfer, M., Weissenbacher, G.: Labelled interpolation systems for hyper-resolution, clausal, and local proofs. J. Autom. Reasoning **57**(1), 3–36 (2016)
47. Tentrup, L.: Non-prenex QBF solving using abstraction. In: Creignou, N., Le Berre, D. (eds.) SAT 2016. LNCS, vol. 9710, pp. 393–401. Springer, Cham (2016). https://doi.org/10.1007/978-3-319-40970-2_24
48. Tentrup, L., Rabe, M.N.: Clausal abstraction for DQBF. In: Janota, M., Lynce, I. (eds.) SAT 2019. LNCS, vol. 11628, pp. 388–405. Springer, Cham (2019). https://doi.org/10.1007/978-3-030-24258-9_27
49. Vizel, Y., Gurfinkel, A., Malik, S.: Fast interpolating BMC. In: Kroening, D., Păsăreanu, C.S. (eds.) CAV 2015. LNCS, vol. 9206, pp. 641–657. Springer, Cham (2015). https://doi.org/10.1007/978-3-319-21690-4_43
50. Vizel, Y., Weissenbacher, G., Malik, S.: Boolean satisfiability solvers and their applications in model checking. Proc. IEEE **103**(11), 2021–2035 (2015)
51. Wetzler, N., Heule, M.J.H., Hunt, W.A.: DRAT-trim: efficient checking and trimming using expressive clausal proofs. In: Sinz, C., Egly, U. (eds.) SAT 2014. LNCS, vol. 8561, pp. 422–429. Springer, Cham (2014). https://doi.org/10.1007/978-3-319-09284-3_31
52. Wimmer, R., Reimer, S., Marin, P., Becker, B.: HQSpre – an effective preprocessor for QBF and DQBF. In: Legay, A., Margaria, T. (eds.) TACAS 2017. LNCS, vol. 10205, pp. 373–390. Springer, Heidelberg (2017). https://doi.org/10.1007/978-3-662-54577-5_21

TarTar: A Timed Automata Repair Tool

Martin Kölbl[1]([✉]), Stefan Leue[1]([✉]),
and Thomas Wies[2]([✉])

[1] University of Konstanz, Konstanz, Germany
Martin.Koelbl@uni-konstanz.de, Stefan.Leue@uni-konstanz.de
[2] New York University, New York, USA
wies@cs.nyu.edu

Abstract. We present TarTar, an automatic repair analysis tool that,
given a timed diagnostic trace (TDT) obtained during the model checking of a timed automaton model, suggests possible syntactic repairs of the
analyzed model. The suggested repairs include modified values for clock
bounds in location invariants and transition guards, adding or removing
clock resets, etc. The proposed repairs guarantee that the given TDT
is no longer feasible in the repaired model, while preserving the overall
functional behavior of the system. We give insights into the design and
architecture of TarTar, and show that it can successfully repair 69%
of the seeded errors in system models taken from a diverse suite of case
studies.

1 Introduction

A reactive system with requirements pertaining to its timing behavior is often
modeled as a network of timed automata (NTA) [BY03]. Whether a timing
requirement holds in an NTA can be analyzed by timed model checkers such
as Uppaal [BLL+95] or opaal [DHJ+11]. In case of a requirement violation, a
model checker returns a timed counterexample, also called a timed diagnostic
trace (TDT). Until now, developers must manually identify and correct such
violations by analyzing the generated TDTs. It is therefore desirable to support
this process by an automated tool set that not only determines whether timing
requirements are met, but also proposes syntactic repairs of the NTA in case
they are not.

In [KLW19] we presented an automated repair analysis that analyzes a TDT
obtained from the violation of a timed safety property and returns syntactic
repair suggestions that avoid the concrete executions of the TDT violating the
property. The analysis performs an additional admissibility check ensuring that
the repaired model is functionally equivalent with the original NTA, which means
that no action traces are added or omitted by the repair.

To illustrate the repair analysis consider the NTA in Figs. 1(a) and (b). It
describes a *client* that sends a request *req* to a database *db* and expects to receive
a response *ser* within 4 time units after sending the request. The client contains a

© The Author(s) 2020
S. K. Lahiri and C. Wang (Eds.): CAV 2020, LNCS 12224, pp. 529–540, 2020.
https://doi.org/10.1007/978-3-030-53288-8_25

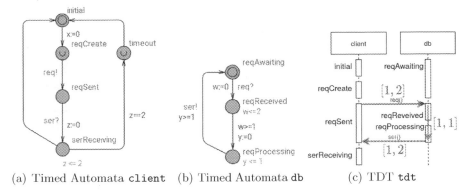

(a) Timed Automata `client`   (b) Timed Automata `db`   (c) TDT `tdt`

Fig. 1. Network of timed automata - running example

clock x that measures the time delay between the request creation and the receiving of a response in location *serReceiving*. The NTA allows to execute a TDT that violates the property, illustrated as a sequence diagram with time intervals in Fig. 1(c). A time interval in the sequence diagram denotes the minimal and maximal time delay for the message transmission and processing times in *db*, respectively. The repair computation analyzes the TDT and produces several syntactic repairs to the NTA that avoid the property violation. In [KLW19], the computed repairs aim at the modification of clock bounds in location invariants and transition guards. An example of such a repair is to reduce the bound in the time constraint $w \leq 2$ from 2 to 1. The modified bound constrains the maximal transmit time of the *req* message so that the resulting NTA receives all responses within the expected time. This repair eliminates the problematic executions of the TDT in the original NTA without changing the functional behavior of the system, which is confirmed by an admissibility test defined in [KLW19]. However, in general, it may not be possible to repair the model using only clock bound alterations.

Contributions. We present TARTAR [tar20], which extends the initial prototype implementation of the clock bound repair analysis presented in [KLW19] to a more comprehensive NTA repair tool. Specifically, the extended tool implements new analyses that can suggest a whole range of repairs in addition to clock bound variation, such as modifying comparison operators in constraints, clock references, clock resets, and location urgency. Examples of new repairs computed for the model in Fig. 1 are:

- Exchanging the comparison operator in the constraint $w \geq 1$ to $w < 1$ ensures that the time to send a request is below 1 time unit.
- An exchange of clock z in $z \leq 2$ with clock y restricts the time of processing and receiving the response to at most 2 time units.
- To reset the clock y on the previous transition instead ensures that the time for sending and processing the request is below 1 time unit.

– Making the location *serReceiving* urgent reduces the time to receive a response to 0.

We call a repair admissible if the repaired system is functionally equivalent to the unrepaired system. The repair analysis implemented in TarTar returns the complete set of admissible repairs.

The repair analysis combines concepts and algorithms from model checking, constraint solving, and automata theory. A real-time model checker is used to generate TDTs for a given NTA that violate a given timed safety property. TarTar translates the TDT into a linear real arithmetic constraint system. An SMT solver is used to compute a repair for the generated constraint system by solving a MaxSMT problem. An automata-based language equivalence test checks whether the repair is admissible in the NTA model. The collaboration between these subcomponents yields a complex tool architecture. We provide insights into the design and implementation of this architecture and the underlying infrastructure of supporting tools. We evaluate the new repair analyses by applying TarTar to a number of NTA models. We systematically inject different modifications in these correct models and compute repairs for the obtained faulty models, which results in at least one admissible repair for 69% of the TDTs.

Related Work. Other tools exist that compute repairs. The tool BugAssist [JM11] analyzes C-code by solving a MaxSMT problem. The tool ReAssert [DDG+11] checks a set of possible modification to repair broken unit tests. Angelix [MYR16], S3 [LCL+17] and SemFix [NQRC13] compute repairs by symbolic execution and constraint solving. SketchFix [HZWK18] is based on lazy candidate generation. All tools are not repairing broken time constraints. We are not aware of related work on tools for the repair of timed automata models. A more comprehensive overview of related work on automated repair is given in [LPR19]. A discussion of work related to the foundations of our repair analysis can be found in [KLW19].

2   New Types of Repair Analyses

The repair analysis presented in [KLW19] and implemented in the prototype version of TarTar encodes a TDT as a constraint system in linear real arithmetic. It computes syntactic correct modifications of the underlying NTA by introducing bound variation variables v. For example, possible bound modifications for a clock bound $x \leq 2$ are expressed by a modified clock bound $x \leq 2 + v$. The repairs are computed by solving a partial SMT problem on the TDT constraint system, involving soft-assert constraints on the bound variation variables. No repair is computed whenever the soft assertion $v = 0$ holds, otherwise the computed value of v characterizes the repair. In the following we sketch the new types of repairs implemented in TarTar. For a more comprehensive description, which space limitations do not allow us to provide here, we refer to [KLW20].

Operator Variation Repair Analysis. This analysis is motivated by the assumption that a wrong comparison operator in a location invariant or transition guard may cause a property violation. We assume for the repair encoding that the operators $\sim$ are indexed according to their order in the sequence $\langle\, <, \leq, =, \geq, > \,\rangle$. The possible repairs are encoded by a fresh variation variable v_i^{ov} where the value of v_i^{ov} is the index of the corresponding comparison operator. If $x < 4$ is computed as a repair, then $v_i^{ov} = 1$.   Using this repair analysis, TARTAR finds two admissible repairs for the example in Figs. 1(a) and (b) that replace the comparison operator in the clock constraint $w >= 1$ by $<$ or $<=$, respectively.

Clock Reference Repair Analysis. This analysis aims to repair property violations resulting from errors that stem from the unintended use of a wrong clock variable. We enumerate all the positions of clock variables in clock bound constraints using index i and all clock variables using index k. We then introduce for every position i, a fresh variation variable v_i^{cv} whose value k indicates the clock c_k to be used at that position in the repaired model. For example, if $y \leq 2$ is a repaired constraint, where the position of y in the constraint has index 3 and clock y has index 1, then $v_3^{cv} = 1$. Applying this repair analysis to the examples in Figs. 1(a) and (b), TARTAR finds 13 admissible clock reference modification repairs, each involving two modifications. Nine repairs exchange y in the constraints $y \leq 1$ and $y \geq 1$ by a selection from the set of clocks z, x and w. Four repairs exchange y in the constraint $y \leq 1$ by w or x, and w in the constraint $w \geq 1$ by y or z.

Reset Clock Repair Analysis. This analysis aims to repair a property violation by adding or removing clock resets. We introduce a variation variable $v_{i,j}^{rv}$ for each clock c_i and the transition leaving location λ_j in the TDT. The reset status in the extended constraint system is inverted when $v_{i,j}^{rv} \neq 0$: if c_i was not reset before, it will now be reset, and vice versa. Applying the reset repair analysis to the examples in Figs. 1(a) and (b), TARTAR finds four admissible repairs. One repair removes the reset of clock y, another removes the reset of clock z and two repairs add a reset of clock x either on the transitions towards the state *reqProcessing* or the transition towards the state *serReceiving*.

Urgent Location Repair Analysis. This analysis aims to repair cases where a faulty usage of urgent locations, which are always left with zero delay after entering, causes a property violation. Urgency of a location is modeled in the TDT constraint system by setting the location delay δ_j to 0. We define a fresh variation variable v_i^{uv} for a location λ_j. For $v_i^{uv} \neq 0$, the urgency for a location λ_j is inverted.   Applying the urgency location repair analysis to the examples in Figs. 1(a) and (b), TARTAR finds two inadmissible repairs. The first one makes the state *reqAwaiting* urgent, and another repair makes the state *serReceiving* urgent.

3   Usage of TarTar

We have implemented all repair analyses described in [KLW19] and in this paper in a tool named TARTAR. It provides a graphical user interface, a command-line interface and a web-interface which enables the execution of this resource intensive software on compute servers. A user selects one of these interfaces via arguments provided when invoking the Java library implementing TarTar. For real-time model checking, TarTar relies on Uppaal.

- The argument –*web* launches the web server and corresponding interface.
- Any other arguments launches the command-line mode. When using the argument –*help*, the command-line console prints some help information.
- When no arguments are given, the graphical user interface depicted in Fig. 2(a) is launched. The interface offers three tabs. *New Analysis* starts a repair analysis, *New Experiment* starts fault seeding which is described later in Sect. 5, and *Version* shows the current version number of TarTar.

All tool interfaces expect the same types of inputs in order to start a TarTar analysis run. The user specifies a file containing the Uppaal model as input and selects the kind of repair to compute. Optionally, a file with a TDT of the given Uppaal model can be specified. When no TDT is provided, TarTar automatically calls Uppaal to compute a TDT. The result of an analysis is one repaired model file for every computed repair, as well as a text file that summarizes which repairs are admissible.

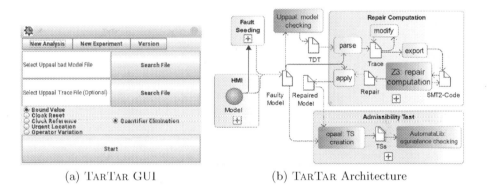

(a) TarTar GUI   (b) TarTar Architecture

Fig. 2. TarTar tool

4   Software Architecture and Implementation of TarTar

The software architecture of TarTar is depicted in Fig. 2(b). The orange rectangles in the figure represent external tools that TarTar calls in the course of the repair analysis. Uppaal is a state-of-the-art and closed-source model checking tool, which TarTar uses to compute a TDT for a given model and property. The SMT solver Z3 [dMB08] is used to solve the generated partial MaxSMT problems. To check the admissibility of a repair, TarTar uses opaal and the AutomataLib component of LearnLib [IHS15] since they conveniently provide functionality used during admissibility checking.

Data Flow Architecture. TARTAR consists of many computation steps. For example, a TDT is parsed internally and stored as a Trace. This Trace is then modified and exported as SMT-LIB2 [BFT17] code. We define a computation step of TARTAR as the computation transforming input into result artifacts. This focus on artifacts ensures a highly cohesive architecture and clear interfaces between any two computation steps. Computation steps with identical objectives are grouped into a project. This results in four projects depicted by blue rectangles in Fig. 2(b).

- *HMI* denotes the user interfaces of TARTAR. The user inputs a timed model. TARTAR then calls the project *Repair Computation* using a faulty timed model as a parameter. In case that the model is correct, TARTAR calls the project *Fault Seeding*.
- *Fault Seeding* seeds faults into a correct model and then repairs the faulty model by computing repairs using *Repair Computation*. We use this analysis in Sect. 5 in order to benchmark the *Repair Computation* analyses.
- *Repair Computation* computes candidate repairs for a faulty timed model, applies these repairs to the model and finally automatically calls the *Admissibility Test*.
- *Admissibility Test* checks for every repaired model whether the computed repair is also admissible.

Control Flow Architecture. TARTAR computes iteratively a set of repairs for a given faulty Uppaal model and a given property Π using the following steps:

0. *Counterexample Creation.* TARTAR calls Uppaal to verify the model against Π. In case Π is violated, it stores a shortest symbolic TDT witnessing the violation in XML format.
1. *Diagnostic Trace Creation.* TARTAR parses the model and the TDT into a data structure *Trace*. To add potential repairs, TARTAR copies the trace and replaces the constraints that will potentially be subject to a repair by their modified variants. The modified trace is then translated to a logic constraint system, represented in SMT-LIB2 code.
2. *Repair Computation.* Z3 [dMB08] then solves a MaxSMT problem on the modified trace constraint system, computing a repair in which the number of unmodified constraints on the variation variables of type $v = 0$ is maximized. Since Z3 can solve a MaxSMT problem only for quantifier-free linear real arithmetic, TARTAR first runs a quantifier elimination on the constraint system. It then solves the MaxSMT problem with soft constraints requiring $v = 0$ for all variation variables. For a more comprehensive presentation of this construction we refer the reader to [KLW20]. In case no solution is found, TARTAR terminates. Otherwise, TARTAR applies the repair to the faulty model and returns a repaired model.
3. *Admissibility Check.* TARTAR checks the admissibility of a repair and compares the untimed languages of the faulty and repaired models. TARTAR calls the model checker opaal in order to compute the timed transition systems (TTS) of the original and the repaired Uppaal model. We modified the

opaal model checker in such a way that it returns the TTS for a model. TarTar then checks whether the two TTS have equivalent untimed languages, in which case the repair is admissible. This check is implemented using the library AutomataLib. In case the two TTS are not equivalent, the admissibility test returns a trace as a witness for the difference.

4. *Iteration.* TarTar enumerates all repairs, i.e., all combinations of constraint modifications that correct the TDT. The repairs are iteratively enumerated starting with the ones that require the smallest number of modifications to the model. After a repair is computed, the combination of modified variables that has been found is prevented from being reconsidered for future repairs by setting these modification variables to 0 using hard asserts. TarTar then proceeds with attempting to compute further, previously unconsidered repairs.

Component Architecture. We implemented TarTar with the general infrastructure depicted in Fig. 3. The interface *Job* provides a general abstraction for an algorithm and specifies the necessary input and result values of the algorithm by the class *Description.* TarTar contains a *Job* for the projects *Fault Seeding, Repair Computations* and *Admissibility Test.*

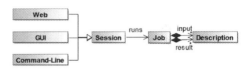

Fig. 3. TarTar component architecture

The class *Session* executes a *Job* and derivations of *Session* provide the different interfaces to the user. With this infrastructure, the analysis implementation in TarTar is independent from the implementation of the user interfaces, thus reducing coupling and improving modifiability of the code.

Implementation Details. We implemented the different projects that constitute TarTar in Java and use the build-management tool maven [Mav19] to manage the dependencies between the projects. TarTar interacts differently with the external tools that are needed for different purposes. It calls Uppaal via the command-line interface in order to generate a TDT and calls Z3 via its API to compute a repair. For the admissibility check, it calls opaal using a command-line script and the AutomataLib as an included Java library. For the implementation of the TarTar analyses the following two details are essential.

We modify constraints in an Uppaal model in order to apply a repair or to seed a fault. Since neither clock constraints nor transitions possess explicit unique identifiers in an Uppaal model, it is not obvious which constraint to change. We therefore uniquely identify a constraint by traversing the constraints in the sequence stored in the Uppaal model file and use the constraint index in this sequence as its identifier.

The complexity of the algorithms for solving quantifier elimination and the MaxSMT problem increase exponentially with the number of variables in the SMT model [KLW19]. We therefore reduce the number of variables by exploiting implied equality constraints. For example, a variable c_j is created for every clock c in every step j of the TDT. We eliminate c_j explicitly before quantifier elimination by replacing it with the term $\sum_{i \in r..j} d_i$, where d_i is the time delay at step i in the trace and r is the last step before j where c was reset.

5 Evaluation

Evaluation Strategy. In order to evaluate the repair analyses both qualitatively and quantitatively, we need to synthesize a set of faulty timed automata. To the best of our knowledge, no benchmark suite for faulty timed automata exists. We therefore create faulty models by using the fault seeding strategy from [KLW19] which is motivated by ideas from mutation testing [JH11]. Mutation testing evaluates the quality of a test suite for a given program by systematically corrupting program code and determining the ratio of corruptions that the test suite is able to detect. We apply the same principle to evaluate the quality of our repair technique. As proposed in [KLW19], fault seeding modifies a single clock constraint so that the result is a set of models that violate a given property. During the seeding, the bound of a single clock constraint is modified by an amount of $\{-10, -1, +1, +0.1M, +M\}$, where M is the maximal clock bound occurring in a given model. Our observation was that making either small modifications that are close to the bound value or modifications in the order of the maximal bound value M often introduce actual errors in the model. We have extended fault seeding to the new types of repairs. In particular, fault seeding additionally exchanges the comparison operator in a clock constraint by $\{<, \leq, =, \geq, >\}$, swap a referenced clock with all other clocks occurring in the given model, modify the reset clocks of any transition, and switch for any location whether it is urgent. TARTAR checks automatically whether a modified TA violates a given property. If this is the case, it performs all of the above defined repair analyses.

Results. We applied fault seeding to the models in [KLW19] and analyzed the obtained TDTs using the above described repair analyses implemented in TARTAR. All analyses were performed on a computer with an i7-6700K CPU (4.00 GHz), 60 GB of RAM and a 64 bit Linux operating system. We summarize the results of the experiment per considered model (Table 1) and per type of considered repair (Table 2). Column Sd contains the count of seeded faults that result in a number $\#T$ of faulty models. T_{UP} is the maximal time that Uppaal needs to create a TDT for the faulty models, and the longest TDT has a length of Ln. TARTAR computed for the TDTs overall a number $\#R$ repairs of which $\#A$ are admissible. An admissible repair is found for $\#S$ of the TDTs. The computation effort for a repair analysis is given by the time T_{QE} for successful quantifier elimination, the number of timeouts $\#O$ of quantifier eliminations after 10 min, the average time T_R to compute a repair and the memory consumption M_R. The constraint system that Z3 solves has the count $\#Vr$ of variables and $\#Cn$ of constraints. The effort for the admissibility check is given in time T_{Adm} and memory M_A. All times are given in seconds and memory consumption in MB. Notice that we omit the columns pertaining to the fault seeding and TDT computation in Table 2 as they are irrelevant here.

Table 1. Experimental results according to model.

Repair	#Sd	#T	T_{UP}	Ln	#R	#A	#S	T_{QE}	#O	T_R	M_R	#Vr	#Cn	T_{Adm}	M_A
db rep.	110	13	0.016	4	229	138	9	89.346	2	0.911	14.53	30	91	2.080	45
csma	191	10	0.012	2	70	26	8	0.049	0	0.023	0.58	16	72	1.825	75
elevator	88	5	0.011	1	7	5	4	0.049	0	0.020	0.53	6	28	1.665	17
viking	310	9	0.015	18	9	7	5	86.539	21	1.436	20.07	120	180	1.952	543
bando	1,955	40	0.111	279	4,061	209	21	31.555	46	4.922	20.86	1,156	8,144	19.57	1251
Pacemaker	1,187	12	0.022	9	62	19	10	0.663	20	0.325	2.59	116	988	1.994	206
SBR	353	50	0.027	84	751	660	31	117.057	86	2.686	37.16	765	1,211	138.004	211
FDDI	314	36	0.014	11	166	105	34	29.859	51	3.074	9.70	116	272	2.241	128

Overall, TarTar seeded 4.508 faults. This resulted in 175 TDTs in total (60 TDTs due to bound modification, 72 due to operator variation, 27 due to changing the clock reference, 8 due to complementing the reset of clocks and 8 due to the switching of urgent locations). TarTar found 5,355 repairs, out of which 1,169 were admissible. It found at least one admissible repair for 122 of the TDTs. The maximal number of modified constraints in the admissible repairs computed for a single TDT using all types of analysis was 25.

Table 2. Experimental results according to type of repair.

Repair	#R	#A	#S	T_{QE}	#O	T_R	M_R	#Vr	#Cn	T_{Adm}	M_A
Bound Modification	533	364	85	15.209	8	4.922	20.86	1,156	2,498	138.004	525
Operator Variation	3,929	96	51	117.057	44	2.686	37.16	996	8,144	59.117	543
Clock Reference	693	625	35	33.282	61	3.074	14.13	1,120	5,355	116.944	206
Reset Clock	45	37	13	89.346	113	0.911	14.53	996	2,836	2.051	45
Urgent Location	155	47	37	0.107	0	0.135	3.16	1,120	2,502	58.551	1,251

Interpretation. Few of the seeded faults resulted in a property violation. TarTar seeded 4.508 faults which led to 175 TDTs, thus only 3.9% of these faults result in a TDT. This supports the hypothesis that, in practice, often times only few time constraints have an impact on a property violation. TarTar computes at least one admissible repair by bound modification for 85 (48%) of the 175 TDTs, by operator variation for 51 (29%), by clock reference for 35 (20%), by clock reset for 13 (7%) and by urgent location for 37 (21%). Every analysis on its own computes less admissible repairs than the combination of all repair analyses, which solves 122 (69%) of the 175 TDTs. The largest number of modified constraints in all the admissible repairs for a single TDT was 25, which is less than anticipated. This low number of modified constraints infer that, for the examples that we considered, only a few constraints of each TDT combined to admissible repairs. The number of modified constraints determines the number of possible repairs that have an impact on whether a property is violated or not. Since it was observed in [KLW19] that the computational effort for the repair computation is largely determined by the quantifier elimination step, we expect that in light of the observed 226 timeouts a more efficient quantifier elimination would lead to a significantly higher number of repairs. Furthermore, the number of timeouts, and thus the computation time needed for the repair, rises with the length of the analyzed TDT. The model *SBR* has the most timeouts with 86 and the third longest trace with a length of 84 steps. The model *bando* has the third most timeouts with 46 and the longest trace. Obviously, the longer the TDT, the larger the resulting constraint system, leading to increased computational effort. The *bando* model has the largest constraint system with 1,156 variables and 8,144 constraints. The *SBR* model has the second largest constraint system with 765 variables and 1,211 constraints. The model *FDDI* has a shorter trace of length of 11 and a much smaller constraint system with 116 variables and 272 constraints. From this we conclude that the complexity of a repair depends not only on the trace length, but also on the intrinsic complexity of the model. Modifying states from urgent to non-urgent during fault seeding resulted in only 8 TDTs. This low number is due to the observation that the considered models contain only few urgent states. Modifying non-urgent states to urgent ones, however, did not lead to a single property violation resulting in a TDT. The rationale is that urgency ensures to leave a state immediately without a delay which leads to a restriction rather than a relaxation regarding the time budget spent along an execution trace. As a consequence, making a state urgent does not cause a property violation in many models since the type of the checked properties is typically time bounded reachability, and a restricted time budget does not make it more likely that the property is violated. We finally observe that the admissibility check requires more computation resources than the repair computation. The maximal memory used for the admissibility test was 1,251 MB in contrast to 37.16 MB for the repair computation. This is in line with our expectation since the admissibility test searches the state space of the full NTA, while the repair analyses only considers a single TDT.

6   Conclusion

We have presented the TARTAR tool, its architecture and implementation, and illustrated its application to a number of significant case studies. In the course of our work we have extended the repair analysis that is implemented in TAR-TAR for bound modification to modifications of comparison operators, clock references, reset of clocks and missing urgencies. The evaluation of the repair analyses showed that an admissible repair is computed for at least 69% of the analyzed TDTs. The integration of various tools with heterogeneous interfaces posed a particular challenge to the architecture of TARTAR which we addressed by the definition of intermediate artifacts.

In future work we plan to explore the interplay between different repairs that are computed for a repaired system that still violates a property, and develop refined strategies to select promising repairs from a repair set. A further generalization of the analysis is to not only compute clock constraint modifications for faulty models but also to compute possible relaxations of clock constraints for correct models in order to support design space exploration.

References

[BFT17] Barrett, C., Fontaine, P., Tinelli, C.: SMT-lib (2017). http://smtlib.cs. uiowa.edu/language.shtml

[BLL+95] Bengtsson, J., Larsen, K., Larsson, F., Pettersson, P., Yi, W.: UPPAAL— a tool suite for automatic verification of real-time systems. In: Alur, R., Henzinger, T.A., Sontag, E.D. (eds.) HS 1995. LNCS, vol. 1066, pp. 232– 243. Springer, Heidelberg (1996). https://doi.org/10.1007/BFb0020949

[BY03] Bengtsson, J., Yi, W.: Timed automata: semantics, algorithms and tools. In: Desel, J., Reisig, W., Rozenberg, G. (eds.) ACPN 2003. LNCS, vol. 3098, pp. 87–124. Springer, Heidelberg (2004). https://doi.org/10.1007/ 978-3-540-27755-2_3

[DDG+11] Daniel, B.: Reassert: a tool for repairing broken unit tests. In: ICSE, pp. 1010–1012. ACM (2011)

[DHJ+11] Dalsgaard, A.E., et al.: opaal: a lattice model checker. In: Bobaru, M., Havelund, K., Holzmann, G.J., Joshi, R. (eds.) NFM 2011. LNCS, vol. 6617, pp. 487–493. Springer, Heidelberg (2011). https://doi.org/10.1007/ 978-3-642-20398-5_37

[dMB08] de Moura, L., Bjørner, N.: Z3: an efficient SMT solver. In: Ramakrishnan, C.R., Rehof, J. (eds.) TACAS 2008. LNCS, vol. 4963, pp. 337–340. Springer, Heidelberg (2008). https://doi.org/10.1007/978-3-540-78800-3_24

[HZWK18] Hua, J., Zhang, M., Wang, K., Khurshid, S.: SketchFix: a tool for automated program repair approach using lazy candidate generation. In: ESEC/SIGSOFT FSE, pp. 888–891. ACM (2018)

[IHS15] Isberner, M., Howar, F., Steffen, B.: The open-source LearnLib. In: Kroening, D., Păsăreanu, C.S. (eds.) CAV 2015. LNCS, vol. 9206, pp. 487–495. Springer, Cham (2015). https://doi.org/10.1007/978-3-319-21690-4_32

[JH11] Jia, Y., Harman, M.: An analysis and survey of the development of mutation testing. IEEE Trans. Software Eng. **37**(5), 649–678 (2011)

[JM11] Jose, M., Majumdar, R.: Bug-assist: assisting fault localization in ANSI-C programs. In: Gopalakrishnan, G., Qadeer, S. (eds.) CAV 2011. LNCS, vol. 6806, pp. 504–509. Springer, Heidelberg (2011). https://doi.org/10.1007/ 978-3-642-22110-1_40

[KLW19] Kölbl, M., Leue, S., Wies, T.: Clock bound repair for timed systems. In: Dillig, I., Tasiran, S. (eds.) CAV 2019. LNCS, vol. 11561, pp. 79–96. Springer, Cham (2019). https://doi.org/10.1007/978-3-030-25540-4_5

[KLW20] Kölbl, M., Leue, S., Wies, T.: Tartar: a timed automata repair tool. CoRR, abs/2002.02760 (2020). https://www.sen.uni-konstanz.de/publications

[LCL+17] Le, X.-B.D., Chu, D.-H., Lo, D., Goues, C.L., Visser, W.: S3: syntax- and semantic-guided repair synthesis via programming by examples. In: ESEC/SIGSOFT FSE, pp. 593–604. ACM (2017)

[LPR19] Le Goues, C., Pradel, M., Roychoudhury, A.: Automated program repair. Commun. ACM **62**(12), 56–65 (2019)

[Mav19] Apache Software Foundation. Maven (2019). https://maven.apache.org/

[MYR16] Mechtaev, S., Yi, J., Roychoudhury, A.: Angelix: scalable multiline program patch synthesis via symbolic analysis. In ICSE, pp. 691–701. ACM (2016)

[NQRC13] Nguyen, H.D.T., Qi, D., Roychoudhury, A., Chandra, S.: Semfix: program repair via semantic analysis. In: ICSE, pp. 772–781. IEEE Computer Society (2013)

[tar20] Tartar 2019–2020. https://github.com/sen-uni-kn/tartar

Hybrid and Dynamic Systems

SAW: A Tool for Safety Analysis of Weakly-Hard Systems

Chao Huang[1]([✉])(iD), Kai-Chieh Chang[2], Chung-Wei Lin[2](iD), and Qi Zhu[1](iD)

[1] Northwestern University, Evanston, USA
{chao.huang,qzhu}@northwestern.edu
[2] National Taiwan University, Taipei, Taiwan
551100kk@gmail.com, cwlin@csie.ntu.edu.tw

Abstract. We introduce SAW, a tool for safety analysis of weakly-hard systems, in which traditional hard timing constraints are relaxed to allow bounded deadline misses for improving design flexibility and runtime resiliency. Safety verification is a key issue for weakly-hard systems, as it ensures system safety under allowed deadline misses. Previous works are either for linear systems only, or limited to a certain type of nonlinear systems (e.g., systems that satisfy exponential stability and Lipschitz continuity of the system dynamics). In this work, we propose a new technique for infinite-time safety verification of general nonlinear weakly-hard systems. Our approach first discretizes the safe state set into grids and constructs a directed graph, where nodes represent the grids and edges represent the reachability relation. Based on graph theory and dynamic programming, our approach can effectively find the safe initial set (consisting of a set of grids), from which the system can be proven safe under given weakly-hard constraints. Experimental results demonstrate the effectiveness of our approach, when compared with the state-of-the-art. An open source implementation of our tool is available at https://github.com/551100kk/SAW. The virtual machine where the tool is ready to run can be found at https://www.csie.ntu.edu.tw/~r08922054/SAW.ova.

Keywords: Weakly-hard systems · Safety verification · Graph theory

1 Introduction

Hard timing constraints, where deadlines should always been met, have been widely used in real-time systems to ensure system safety. However, with the

This work is supported by the National Science Foundation awards 1834701, 1834324, 1839511, 1724341, and the Office of Naval Research grant N00014-19-1-2496. It is also supported by the Asian Office of Aerospace Research and Development (AOARD), jointly with the Office of Naval Research Global (ONRG), award FA2386-19-1-4037, the Taiwan Ministry of Education (MOE) grants NTU-107V0901 and NTU-108V0901, the Taiwan Ministry of Science and Technology (MOST) grants MOST-108-2636-E-002-011 and MOST-109-2636-E-002-022.
C. Huang and K.-C. Chang—Contributed equally.

S. K. Lahiri and C. Wang (Eds.): CAV 2020, LNCS 12224, pp. 543–555, 2020.
https://doi.org/10.1007/978-3-030-53288-8_26

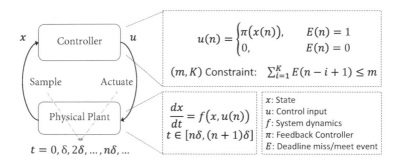

Fig. 1. A weakly-hard system with perfect sensors and actuators.

rapid increase of system functional and architectural complexity, hard deadlines have become increasingly pessimistic and often lead to infeasible designs or over provisioning of system resources [16,20,21,32]. The concept of weakly-hard systems are thus proposed to relax hard timing constraints by allowing occasional deadline misses [2,11]. This is motivated by the fact that many system functions, such as some control tasks, have certain degrees of robustness and can in fact tolerate some deadline misses, as long as those misses are bounded and dependably controlled. In recent years, considerable efforts have been made in the research of weakly-hard systems, including schedulability analysis [1,2,5,12–14,19,25,28,30], opportunistic control for energy saving [18], control stability analysis and optimization [8,10,22,23,26], and control-schedule co-design under possible deadline misses [3,6,27]. Compared with hard deadlines, weakly-hard constraints can more accurately capture the timing requirements of those system functions that tolerate deadline misses, and significantly improve system feasibility and flexibility [16,20]. Compared with soft deadlines, where any deadline miss is allowed, weakly-hard constraints could still provide deterministic guarantees on system safety, stability, performance, and other properties under formal analysis [17,29].

A common type of weakly-hard model is the (m, K) constraint, which specifies that among any K consecutive task executions, at most m instances could violate their deadlines [2]. Specifically, the high-level structure of a (m, K)-constrained weakly-hard system is presented in Fig. 1. Given a sampled-data system $\dot{x} = f(x, u)$ with a sampling period $\delta > 0$, the system samples the state x at the time $t = i\delta$ for $n = 0, 1, 2, \ldots$, and computes the control input u with function $\pi(x)$. If the computation completes within the given deadline, the system applies u to influence the plant's dynamics. Otherwise, the system stops the computation and applies zero control input. As aforementioned, the system should ensure the control input can be successfully computed and applied within the deadline for at least $K - m$ times over any K consecutive sampling periods.

For such weakly-hard systems, a natural and critical question is whether the system is safe by allowing deadline misses defined in a given (m, K) constraint.

There is only limited prior work in this area, while nominal systems have been adequately studied [4,9,15,31]. In [8], a weakly-hard system with linear dynamic is modeled as a hybrid automaton and then the reachability of the generated hybrid automaton is verified by the tool SpaceEx [9]. In [7], the behavior of a linear weakly-hard system is transformed into a program, and program verification techniques such as abstract interpretation and SMT solvers can be applied.

In our previous work [17], the safety of nonlinear weakly-hard systems are considered for the first time. Our approach tries to derive a safe initial set for any given (m, K) constraint, that is, starting from any initial state within such set, the system will always stay within the same safe state set under the given weakly-hard constraint. Specifically, we first convert the infinite-time safety problem into a finite one by finding a set satisfying both *local safety* and *inductiveness*. The computation of such valid set heavily lies on the estimation of the system state evolution, where two key assumptions are made: 1) The system is exponentially stable under nominal cases without any deadline misses, which makes the system state contract with a constant decay rate; 2) The system dynamics are Lipschitz continuous, which helps bound the expansion under a deadline miss. Based on these two assumptions, we can abstract the safety verification problem as a one dimensional problem and use linear programming (LP) to solve it, which we call *one-dimension abstraction* in the rest of the paper.

In practice, however, the assumptions in [17] are often hard to satisfy and the parameters of exponential stability are difficult to obtain. In addition, while the scalar abstraction provides high efficiency, the experiments demonstrate that the estimation is always over conservative. In this paper, we go one step further and present a new tool SAW for infinite-time safety verification of nonlinear weakly-hard systems **without any particular assumption on exponential stability and Lipschitz bound**, and try to be less conservative than the scalar abstraction. Formally, the problem solved by this tool is described as follows:

Problem 1. Given an (m, K) weakly-hard system with nonlinear dynamics $\dot{x} = f(x, u)$, sampling period δ, and safe set X, find a safe initial set X_0, such that from any state $x(0) \in X_0$, the system will always be inside X.

To solve this problem, we first discretize the safe state set X into grids. We then try to find the grid set that satisfies both local safety and inductiveness. For each property, we build a directed graph, where each node corresponds to a grid and each directed edge represents the mapping between grids with respect to reachability. We will then be able to leverage graph theory to construct the initial safe set. Experimental results demonstrate that our tool is effective for general nonlinear systems.

2   Algorithms and Tool Design

The schematic diagram of our tool SAW is shown in Fig. 2. The input is a model file that specifies the system dynamics, sampling period, safe region and other parameters, and a configuration file of Flow* [4] (which is set by default but can

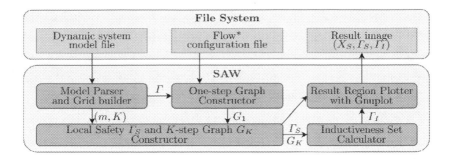

Fig. 2. The schematic diagram of SAW.

Algorithm 1: Overall algorithm of SAW

Data: Dynamic system f with safe state region X, the control law π,
          weakly-hard constraint (m, K), sampling period δ
Result: Safe initial state set X_0
1   $\Gamma = \mathbf{partition}(X, p)$;
    /* Search the grid set that satisfies local safety.   */
2   $G_1 = \mathbf{constructOneStepGraph}()$;
3   $\Gamma_S, G_K = \mathbf{calculateLocalSafety}()$;
    /* Search the grid set that satisfies inductiveness.   */
4   $\Gamma_I = \mathbf{calculateInductivenessSet}()$;
5   **return** Γ_I;

---

also be customized). After fed with the input, the tool works as follows (shown in Algorithm 1). The safe state set X is first uniformly partitioned into small grids $\Gamma = \{v_1, v_2, \ldots, v_{p^d}\}$, where $X = v_1 \cup v_2 \cup \cdots \cup v_{d^p}$, $v_i \cap v_j = \phi$ ($\forall i \neq j$), d is the dimension of the state space, and p is the number of partitions in each dimension (Line 1 in Algorithm 1). The tool then tries to find the grids that satisfy the local safety. It first invokes a reachability graph constructor to build a one-step reachability graph G_1 to describe how the system evolves in one sampling step (Line 2). Then, a dynamic programming (DP) based approach finds the largest set $\Gamma_S = \{v_{s_1}, v_{s_2}, \ldots, v_{s_n}\}$ from which the system will not go out of the safe region. The K-step reachability graph G_K is also built in the DP process based on G_1 (Line 3). After that, the tool searches the largest subset Γ_I of Γ_S that satisfies the inductiveness by using a reverse search algorithm (Line 4). The algorithm outputs Γ_I as the target set X_0 (Line 5).

The key functions of the tool are the reachability graph constructor, DP-based local safety set search, and reverse inductiveness set search. In the following sections, we introduce these three functions in detail.

2.1   Reachability Graph Construction

Integration in dynamic system equations is often the most time-consuming part to trace the variation of the states. In this function, we use Flow* to get a valid

---

Algorithm 2: Construct one-step graph: **constructOneStepGraph()**

Data: Dynamic system f, grid set Γ, the control law π, sampling period δ
Result: Directed graph $G_1(\Gamma, E_1)$
```
/* Initialize the edge set E₁ of G₁.                              */
```
1 $E_1 \longleftarrow \emptyset$;
2 **for** $v \in \Gamma$ **do**
```
      /* Consider deadline miss (e = 1)/meet (e = 0) respectively.   */
```
3   **for** $e \in \{0,1\}$ **do**
```
         /* Compute one step reachable set R₁(v) from v.              */
```
4          $R_1(v) = \mathbf{Flow^*}(v, \delta, e)$;
```
         /* v is unsafe and no edge is added if Xᶜ ∩ R₁(v) ≠ ∅.       */
```
5   **if** $X^c \cap R_1(v) \neq \emptyset$ **then Conitnue**;
```
         /* Add an edge pointing v' from v if v' ∩ R₁(v) ≠ ∅.         */
```
6   **for** $v' \in \Gamma$ **do**
7   **if** $v' \cap R_1(v) \neq \emptyset$ **then** $E_1 \longleftarrow E_1 \cup \{(v,e,v')\}$;
8 **return** $G_1(\Gamma, E_1)$;

---

overapproximation of reachable set (represented as flowpipes) starting from every grid after a sampling period δ. Given a positive integer n, the graph constructed by the reachability set after n sampling period, $n \cdot \delta$, is called a n-step graph G_n. Since the reachability for all the grids in any sampling step is independent under our grid assumption, we first build G_1 and then reuse G_1 to construct G_K later without redundant computation of reachable set.

One-step graph is built with Algorithm 2. We consider deadline miss and deadline meet separately, corresponding to two categories of edges (Line 3). For a grid v, if the one-step reachable set $R_1(v)$ intersects with unsafe state X^c, then it is considered as an unsafe grid and we let its reachable grid be $\emptyset$. Otherwise, if $R_1(v)$ intersects with another grid v' under the deadline miss/meet event e, then we add a directed edge (v, e, v') from v' to v with label e. The number of outgoing edges for each grid node v is bounded by p^d. Assuming that the complexity of Flow* to compute flowpipes for its internal clock ϵ is $O(1)$, we can get the overall time complexity as $O(|\Gamma| \cdot p^d \cdot \delta/\epsilon)$.

K-step graph G_K is built for finding the grid set that satisfies local safety and inductiveness. To avoid redundant computation on reachable set, we construct G_K based on G_1 by traversing K-length paths, as the bi-product of local safety set searching procedure.

2.2   DP-Based Local Safety Set Search

We propose a bottom-up dynamic programming for considering all the possible paths, utilizing the overlapping subproblems property (Algorithm 3). The reachable grid set at step K that is derived from a grid v at step $k \leq K$ with respect to the number of deadline misses $n \leq m$ can be defined as $\mathrm{DP}(v, n, k)$. To be consistent with Algorithm 2, this set is empty if and only if it does not satisfy the local safety. We need to derive $\mathrm{DP}(v, 0, 0)$. Initially, the zero-step reachability is

---

Algorithm 3: Search grid set for local safety: **calculateLocalSafety()**

Data: Directed graph $G_1(\Gamma, E_1)$, weakly-hard constraint (m, K)
Result: Grid set Γ_S, directed graph $G_K(\Gamma, E_K)$

1 **for** $v \in \Gamma$ **do**
2 | **for** $n \leftarrow 0$ **to** m **do**
3 | | $\mathrm{DP}(v, n, K) \longleftarrow \{v\}$;
4 **for** $k \leftarrow K - 1$ **to** 0 **do**
5 | **for** $v \in \Gamma$ **do**
6 | | **for** $n \leftarrow 0$ **to** m **do**
7 | | | isSafe $\leftarrow True$;
8 | | | **for** $e \in \{0, 1\}$ **do**
9 | | | | **if** $n + e \leq m$ **then**
10 | | | | | nextGrids$(v) \longleftarrow \{v' \mid (v, e, v') \in E_1\}$;
11 | | | | | **if** $nextGrids(v) = \emptyset$ **then** isSafe $\leftarrow False$; **break**;
12 | | | | | **for** $v' \in nextGrids(v)$ **do**
13 | | | | | | $R(v') \longleftarrow \mathrm{DP}(v, n + e, k + 1)$;
14 | | | | | | **if** $R(v) = \emptyset$ **then** isSafe $\leftarrow False$; **break**;
15 | | | | | | $\mathrm{DP}(v', n, k) \longleftarrow \mathrm{DP}(v', n, k) \cup R(v)$;
16 | | | **if** $isSafe = false$ **then**
17 | | | | $\mathrm{DP}(v, n, k) \longleftarrow \emptyset$;
18 $\Gamma_S \longleftarrow \{v \mid \mathrm{DP}(v, 0, 0) \neq \emptyset\}$;
19 $E_K \longleftarrow \{(v, v') \mid v \in \mathrm{DP}(v, 0, 0)\}$;
20 **return** $\Gamma_S, G_K(\Gamma, E_K)$;

---

straight forward, i.e., $\forall u \in \Gamma, n \in [0, m]$, $\mathrm{DP}(v, n, K) = \{v\}$. The transition is defined as:

$$\forall k \in [0, K - 1] : \mathrm{DP}(v, n, k) = \bigcup_{\forall v', e : (v, e, v') \in E_1, n + e \leq m} \mathrm{DP}(v', n + e, k + 1).$$

If there exists an empty set on the right hand side or there is no outgoing edge from v for any e such that $n + e \leq m$, we let $\mathrm{DP}(v, n, k) = \emptyset$. Finally, we have $\Gamma_S = \{v \mid \mathrm{DP}(v, 0, 0) \neq \emptyset\}$, $E_K = \{(v, v') \mid v' \in \mathrm{DP}(v, 0, 0)\}$.

We used *bitset* to implement the set union which can accelerate 64 times under the 64-bit architecture. The time complexity is $O(|\Gamma|^2 / bits \cdot p^d \cdot K^2 + |\Gamma|^2)$, where *bits* depends on the running environment. $|\Gamma|^2$ is contributed by G_K.

2.3 Reverse Inductiveness Set Search

To find the grid set $\Gamma_I \subseteq \Gamma_S$ that satisfies inductiveness, we propose a reverse search algorithm Algorithm 4. Basically, instead of directly searching Γ_I, we try to obtain Γ_I by removing any grid v within Γ_S, from which there exists a path reaching $\Gamma_U = \Gamma - \Gamma_S$. Specifically, Algorithm 4 starts with initializing $\Gamma_U = \Gamma - \Gamma_S$ (line 1). The Γ_U iteratively absorbs the grid v that can reach Γ_U in K sampling periods, until a fixed point is reached (line 2–3). Finally $\Gamma_I = \Gamma - \Gamma_U$ is the largest set that satisfies inductiveness. It is implemented as a breadth first search (BFS) on the reversed graph of G_K, and the time complexity is $O(|\Gamma|^2)$.

Algorithm 4: Search grid set for inductiveness: **calculateInductiveness-Set()**

Data: Directed graph $G_K(\Gamma, E_K)$, Grid set Γ_S
Result: Grid set Γ_I

1 $\Gamma_U \longleftarrow \Gamma - \Gamma_S$;
2 **while** $\exists (v, v') \in E_K$ *such that* $v \notin \Gamma_U, v' \in \Gamma_U$ **do**
3    $\quad \mid \quad \Gamma_U \longleftarrow \Gamma_U \cup \{v\}$;
4 $\Gamma_I = \Gamma - \Gamma_U$;
5 **return** Γ_I;

---

3 Example Usage

Example 1. Consider the following linear control system from [17]:

$$\begin{bmatrix} \dot{x}_1 \\ \dot{x}_2 \end{bmatrix} = \begin{bmatrix} 0 & 1 \\ 0 & -0.1 \end{bmatrix} \begin{bmatrix} x_1 \\ x_2 \end{bmatrix} + u, \quad \text{where} \quad u = \begin{bmatrix} 0 & 0 \\ -0.375 & -1.15 \end{bmatrix} \begin{bmatrix} x_1 \\ x_2 \end{bmatrix}.$$

$\delta = 0.2$ and *step_size* $= 0.01$. The initial state set is $x_1 \in [-1, 1]$ and $x_2 \in [-1, 1]$. The safe state set is $x_1 \in [-3, 3]$ and $x_2 \in [-3, 3]$. Following the input format shown in Listing 1.1. Thus, we prepare the model file as Listing 1.2.

```
1  <state_dim> <input_dim> <grid_count>
2  <state_var_names> <input_var_names>
3  <state_ode.1>
4  ...
5  <state_ode.state_dim>
6  <input_equa.1>
7  ...
8  <input_equa.input_dim>
9  <period> <step_size>
10 <m> <k>
11 <safe_state.1>
12 ...
13 <safe_state.state_dim>
14 <initial_state.1>
15 ...
16 <initial_state.state_dim>
```

Listing 1.1. Input format

```
1  2 1 50
2  x1 x2 u
3  x2
4  -0.1 * x2 + u
5  -0.375 * x1 - 1.15 * x2
6  0.2 0.01
7  2 5
8  -3 3
9  -3 3
10 -1 1
11 -1 1
```

Listing 1.2. example/model1.txt

Then, we run our program with the model file.

```
1 ./saw example/model1.txt
```

To further ease the use of our tool, we also pre-complied our tool for x86_64 linux environment. In such environment, users do not need to compile our tool and can directly invoke **saw_linux_x86_64** instead of **saw** (which is only available after manually compiling the tool).

```
1 ./saw_linux_x86_64 example/model1.txt
```

The program output is shown in Listing 1.3. Line 6 shows the number of edges of G_1. Lines 8–10 provide the information of G_K, including the number of edges and nodes. Line 12 prints the safe initial set X_0. Our tool then determines whether the given initial set is safe by checking if it is the subset of X_0.

```
1  [Info] Parsing model.
2  [Info] Building FLOW* configuration.
3  [Info] Building grids.
4  [Info] Building one-step graph.
5         Process: 100.00%
6  [Success] Number of edges: 19354
7  [Info] Building K-step graph.
8  [Success] Start Region Size: 1908
9             End Region: 1208
10            Number of Edges: 102436
11 [Info] Finding the largest closed subgraph.
12 [Success] Safe Initial Region Size: 1622
13 [Info] Calculating area.
14            Initial state region: 4.000000
15            Grids Intersection:   4.000000
16            Result: safe
```

Listing 1.3. Verification result

Table 1. Benchmark setting. ODE denotes the ordinary differential equation of the example, π denotes the control law, and δ is the discrete control stepsize.

#	ODE	π	δ	Safe state set	(m, K)
1	$\dot{x}_1 = x_2$ $\dot{x}_2 = -0.1x_2 + u$	$u = -0.375x_1 - 1.15x_2$	0.2	$x_1 \in [-3.0, 3.0]$ $x_2 \in [-3.0, 3.0]$	$(2, 5)$
2	$\dot{x}_1 = -2x_1 + u_1$ $\dot{x}_2 = -0.9x_2 + u_2$	$u_1 = -x_1$ $u_2 = -x_1 - x_2$	0.3	$x_1 \in [-6.0, 6.0]$ $x_2 \in [-6.0, 6.0]$	$(1, 10)$
3	$\dot{x}_1 = x_2 + u$ $\dot{x}_2 = -2x_1 - 0.1x_2 + u$	$u = x_1$	1.6	$x_1 \in [-3.0, 3.0]$ $x_2 \in [-3.0, 3.0]$	$(2, 10)$
4	$\dot{x} = x^2 - x^3 + u$	$u = -2x$	0.6	$x \in [-4.0, 4.0]$	$(2, 100)$
5	$\dot{x} = 0.2x + 0.03x^2 + u$	$u = -0.3x^3$	1.6	$x \in [-2.0, 2.0]$	$(1, 5)$
6	$\dot{x}_1 = x_2 - x_1^3 + x_1^2$ $\dot{x}_2 = u$	$u = -1.22x_1 - 0.57x_2$ $-0.129x_2^3$	0.1	$x_1 \in [-5.0, 5.0]$ $x_2 \in [-5.0, 5.0]$	$(2, 15)$

4   Experiments

We implemented a prototype of SAW that is integrated with Flow*. In this section, we first compare our tool with the one-dimension abstraction [17], on the full benchmarks from [17] (#1–#4) and also additional examples with no guarantee on exponential stability from related works (#5 and #6) [24]. Table 1 shows the benchmark settings, including the (m, K) constraint set for each benchmark. Then, we show how different parameter settings affect the verification results of our tool. All our experiments were run on a desktop, with 6-core 3.60 GHz Intel Core i7.

4.1   Comparison with One-Dimension Abstraction

Table 2 shows the experimental results. It is worth noting that the one-dimension abstraction cannot find the safe initial set in most cases from [17]. In fact, it only

Table 2. Experimental results. ExpParam denotes the parameters of the exponential stability, where "N/A" means that either the system is not exponentially stable or the parameters are not available. Initial state set denotes the set that needs to be verified. The last two columns denote the verification results of the one-dimension abstraction [17] and SAW, respectively. "—" means that no safe initial set X_0 is found by the tool. p represents the partition number for each dimension in SAW. Time (in seconds) represents the execution time of SAW.

#	ExpParam	Initial state set	One-dimension abstraction	SAW		
			Result	p	Result	Time
1	$\alpha = 1.8,$ $\lambda = 0.4$	$x_1 \in [-1.0, 1.0]$ $x_2 \in [-1.0, 1.0]$	—	50	Yes	72.913
2	$\alpha = 1.1,$ $\lambda = 1.8$	$x_1 \in [-6.0, 6.0]$ $x_2 \in [-6.0, 6.0]$	No $(X_0 : x_1^2 + x_2^2 \le 1.947^2)$	30	Yes	10.360
3	$\alpha = 2,$ $\lambda = 0.37$	$x_1 \in [-1.0, 2.0]$ $x_2 \in [-1.0, 1.0]$	—	100	Yes	183.30
4	$\alpha = 1.4,$ $\lambda = 1$	$x \in [-4.0, 4.0]$	—	30	Yes	80.613
5	N/A	$x \in [-1.56, 1.32]$	—	100	Yes	4.713
6	N/A	$x_1 \in [-5.0, 5.0]$ $x_2 \in [-5.0, 5.0]$	—	50	Yes	750.77

works effectively for a limited set of (m, K), e.g., when no consecutive deadline misses is allowed. For general (m, K) constraints, one-dimension abstraction performs much worse due to the over-conservation. Furthermore, we can see that, without exponential stability, one-dimension abstraction based approach is not applicable for the benchmarks #5 and #6. Note that for benchmark #2, one-dimension abstraction obtains a non-empty safe initial set X_0, which however, does not contain the given initial state set. Thus we use "No" instead of "—" to represent this result. Conversely, for every example, our tool computes a feasible X_0 that contains the initial state set (showing the initial state set is safe), which we denote as "Yes".

4.2   Impact of (m, K), Granularity, and Stepsize

(m, K). We take benchmark #1 (Example 1 in Sect. 3) as an example and run our tool under different (m, K) values. Figures 3a, 3b, 3c demonstrate that, for this example, the size of local safety region Γ_S shrinks when K gets larger. The size of inductiveness region Γ_I grows in contrast. Γ_S becomes the same as Γ_I when K gets larger, in which case m is the primary parameter that influences the size of Γ_I.

Granularity. We take benchmark #3 as an example, and run our tool with different partition granularities. The results (Figs. 3d, 3e, 3f) show that Γ_I grows

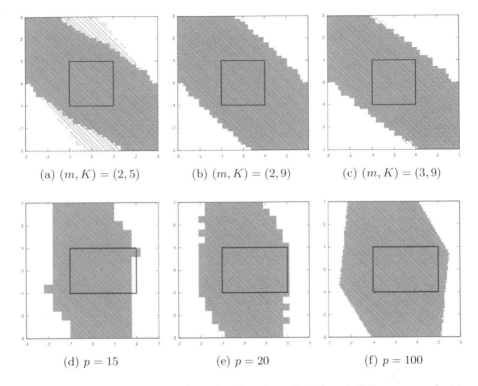

(a) $(m, K) = (2, 5)$ (b) $(m, K) = (2, 9)$ (c) $(m, K) = (3, 9)$

(d) $p = 15$ (e) $p = 20$ (f) $p = 100$

Fig. 3. Results under different (m, K) values (3a, 3b, 3c) and different granularities (3d, 3e, 3f). The green solid region is Γ_I. The slashed region is Γ_S. The blue rectangle is the initial state set that needs to be verified. (Color figure online)

when p gets larger. The choice of p has significant impact on the result (e.g., the user-defined initial state set cannot be verified when $p = 15$).

Stepsize. We take benchmark #5 as an example, and run our tool with different stepsizes of Flow*. With the same granularity $p = 100$, we get the safe initial state set $\Gamma_I = [-1.56, 1.32]$ when $step\_size = 0.1$, but Γ_I is empty when $step\_size = 0.3$. The computation times are 4.713 s and 1.835 s, respectively. Thus, we can see that there is a trade-off between the computational efficiency and the accuracy.

5   Conclusion

In this paper, we present a new tool SAW to compute a tight estimation of safe initial set for infinite-time safety verification of general nonlinear weakly-hard systems. The tool first discretizes the safe state set into grids. By constructing a reachability graph for the grids based on existing tools, the tool leverages graph theory and dynamic programming technique to compute the safe initial set. We demonstrate that our tool can significantly outperform the state-of-the-art one-dimension abstraction approach, and analyze how different constraints and parameters may affect the results of our tool. Future work includes further speedup of the reachability graph construction via parallel computing.

References

1. Ahrendts, L., Quinton, S., Boroske, T., Ernst, R.: Verifying weakly-hard real-time properties of traffic streams in switched networks. In: Altmeyer, S. (ed.) 30th Euromicro Conference on Real-Time Systems (ECRTS 2018). Leibniz International Proceedings in Informatics (LIPIcs), vol. 106, pp. 15:1–15:22. Schloss Dagstuhl-Leibniz-Zentrum fuer Informatik, Dagstuhl (2018). https://doi.org/10.4230/LIPIcs.ECRTS.2018.15. http://drops.dagstuhl.de/opus/volltexte/2018/8987
2. Bernat, G., Burns, A., Liamosi, A.: Weakly hard real-time systems. IEEE Trans. Comput. **50**(4), 308–321 (2001). https://doi.org/10.1109/12.919277
3. Bund, T., Slomka, F.: Controller/platform co-design of networked control systems based on density functions. In: ACM SIGBED International Workshop on Design, Modeling, and Evaluation of Cyber-Physical Systems, pp. 11–14. ACM (2014)
4. Chen, X., Ábrahám, E., Sankaranarayanan, S.: Flow*: an analyzer for non-linear hybrid systems. In: Sharygina, N., Veith, H. (eds.) CAV 2013. LNCS, vol. 8044, pp. 258–263. Springer, Heidelberg (2013). https://doi.org/10.1007/978-3-642-39799-8_18
5. Choi, H., Kim, H., Zhu, Q.: Job-class-level fixed priority scheduling of weakly-hard real-time systems. In: IEEE Real-Time Technology and Applications Symposium (RTAS) (2019)
6. Chwa, H.S., Shin, K.G., Lee, J.: Closing the gap between stability and schedulability: a new task model for cyber-physical systems. In: IEEE Real-Time Technology and Applications Symposium (RTAS) (2018)
7. Duggirala, P.S., Viswanathan, M.: Analyzing real time linear control systems using software verification. In: RTSS, pp. 216–226. IEEE (2015)
8. Frehse, G., Hamann, A., Quinton, S., Woehrle, M.: Formal analysis of timing effects on closed-loop properties of control software. In: 2014 IEEE Real-Time Systems Symposium, pp. 53–62, December 2014. https://doi.org/10.1109/RTSS.2014.28
9. Frehse, G., et al.: SpaceEx: scalable verification of hybrid systems. In: Gopalakrishnan, G., Qadeer, S. (eds.) CAV 2011. LNCS, vol. 6806, pp. 379–395. Springer, Heidelberg (2011). https://doi.org/10.1007/978-3-642-22110-1_30
10. Gaid, M.B., Simon, D., Sename, O.: A design methodology for weakly-hard real-time control. IFAC Proc. Vol. **41**(2), 10258–10264 (2008). https://doi.org/10.3182/20080706-5-KR-1001.01736. http://www.sciencedirect.com/science/article/pii/S1474667016406129, 17th IFAC World Congress
11. Hamdaoui, M., Ramanathan, P.: A dynamic priority assignment technique for streams with (m, k)-firm deadlines. IEEE Trans. Comput. **44**(12), 1443–1451 (1995)
12. Hammadeh, Z.A.H., Ernst, R., Quinton, S., Henia, R., Rioux, L.: Bounding deadline misses in weakly-hard real-time systems with task dependencies. In: Design, Automation Test in Europe Conference Exhibition (DATE), pp. 584–589, March 2017. https://doi.org/10.23919/DATE.2017.7927054

13. Hammadeh, Z.A.H., Quinton, S., Ernst, R.: Extending typical worst-case analysis using response-time dependencies to bound deadline misses. In: Proceedings of the 14th International Conference on Embedded Software, EMSOFT 2014, pp. 10:1–10:10. ACM, New York (2014). https://doi.org/10.1145/2656045.2656059. http://doi.acm.org/10.1145/2656045.2656059

14. Hammadeh, Z.A.H., Quinton, S., Panunzio, M., Henia, R., Rioux, L., Ernst, R.: Budgeting under-specified tasks for weakly-hard real-time systems. In: Bertogna, M. (ed.) 29th Euromicro Conference on Real-Time Systems (ECRTS 2017). Leibniz International Proceedings in Informatics (LIPIcs), vol. 76, pp. 17:1–17:22. Schloss Dagstuhl-Leibniz-Zentrum fuer Informatik, Dagstuhl (2017). https://doi.org/10.4230/LIPIcs.ECRTS.2017.17. http://drops.dagstuhl.de/opus/volltexte/2017/7163

15. Huang, C., Chen, X., Lin, W., Yang, Z., Li, X.: Probabilistic safety verification of stochastic hybrid systems using barrier certificates. TECS 16(5s), 186 (2017)

16. Huang, C., Wardega, K., Li, W., Zhu, Q.: Exploring weakly-hard paradigm for networked systems. In: Workshop on Design Automation for CPS and IoT (DESTION 2019) (2019)

17. Huang, C., Li, W., Zhu, Q.: Formal verification of weakly-hard systems. In: The 22nd ACM International Conference on Hybrid Systems: Computation and Control (HSCC) (2019)

18. Huang, C., Xu, S., Wang, Z., Lan, S., Li, W., Zhu, Q.: Opportunistic intermittent control with safety guarantees for autonomous systems. In: Design Automation Conference (DAC) (2020)

19. Li, J., Song, Y., Simonot-Lion, F.: Providing real-time applications with graceful degradation of QoS and fault tolerance according to (m, k)-firm model. IEEE Trans. Industr. Inf. 2(2), 112–119 (2006)

20. Liang, H., Wang, Z., Roy, D., Dey, S., Chakraborty, S., Zhu, Q.: Security-driven codesign with weakly-hard constraints for real-time embedded systems. In: 37th IEEE International Conference on Computer Design (ICCD 2019) (2019)

21. Lin, C., Zheng, B., Zhu, Q., Sangiovanni-Vincentelli, A.: Security-aware design methodology and optimization for automotive systems. ACM Trans. Des. Autom. Electron. Syst. (TODAES) 21(1), 18:1–18:26 (2015). https://doi.org/10.1145/2803174. http://doi.acm.org/10.1145/2803174

22. Marti, P., Camacho, A., Velasco, M., Gaid, M.E.M.B.: Runtime allocation of optional control jobs to a set of CAN-based networked control systems. IEEE Trans. Industr. Inf. 6(4), 503–520 (2010). https://doi.org/10.1109/TII.2010.2072961

23. Pazzaglia, P., Pannocchi, L., Biondi, A., Natale, M.D.: Beyond the weakly hard model: measuring the performance cost of deadline misses. In: Altmeyer, S. (ed.) 30th Euromicro Conference on Real-Time Systems (ECRTS 2018). Leibniz International Proceedings in Informatics (LIPIcs), vol. 106, pp. 10:1–10:22. Schloss Dagstuhl-Leibniz-Zentrum fuer Informatik, Dagstuhl (2018). https://doi.org/10.4230/LIPIcs.ECRTS.2018.10. http://drops.dagstuhl.de/opus/volltexte/2018/8993

24. Prajna, S., Parrilo, P.A., Rantzer, A.: Nonlinear control synthesis by convex optimization. IEEE Trans. Autom. Control 49(2), 310–314 (2004)

25. Quinton, S., Hanke, M., Ernst, R.: Formal analysis of sporadic overload in real-time systems. In: Proceedings of the Conference on Design, Automation and Test in Europe, DATE 2012, EDA Consortium, San Jose, CA, USA, pp. 515–520 (2012). http://dl.acm.org/citation.cfm?id=2492708.2492836

26. Ramanathan, P.: Overload management in real-time control applications using (m, k)-firm guarantee. IEEE Trans. Parallel Distrib. Syst. 10(6), 549–559 (1999). https://doi.org/10.1109/71.774906

27. Soudbakhsh, D., Phan, L.T., Annaswamy, A.M., Sokolsky, O.: Co-design of arbitrated network control systems with overrun strategies. IEEE Trans. Control Netw. Syst. **5**(1), 128–141 (2016)
28. Sun, Y., Natale, M.D.: Weakly hard schedulability analysis for fixed priority scheduling of periodic real-time tasks. ACM Trans. Embed. Comput. Syst. (TECS) **16**(5s), 171 (2017)
29. Wardega, K., Li, W.: Application-aware scheduling of networked applications over the low-power wireless bus. In: Design, Automation and Test in Europe Conference (DATE), March 2020
30. Xu, W., Hammadeh, Z.A.H., Kröller, A., Ernst, R., Quinton, S.: Improved deadline miss models for real-time systems using typical worst-case analysis. In: 2015 27th Euromicro Conference on Real-Time Systems, pp. 247–256, July 2015. https://doi.org/10.1109/ECRTS.2015.29
31. Yang, Z., Huang, C., Chen, X., Lin, W., Liu, Z.: A Linear programming relaxation based approach for generating barrier certificates of hybrid systems. In: Fitzgerald, J., Heitmeyer, C., Gnesi, S., Philippou, A. (eds.) FM 2016. LNCS, vol. 9995, pp. 721–738. Springer, Cham (2016). https://doi.org/10.1007/978-3-319-48989-6_44
32. Zhu, Q., Sangiovanni-Vincentelli, A.: Codesign methodologies and tools for cyber-physical systems. Proc. IEEE **106**(9), 1484–1500 (2018). https://doi.org/10.1109/JPROC.2018.2864271

PIRK: Scalable Interval Reachability Analysis for High-Dimensional Nonlinear Systems

Alex Devonport[1]([✉]), Mahmoud Khaled[2],
Murat Arcak[1], and Majid Zamani[3,4]

[1] University of California, Berkeley, Berkeley, CA, USA
{alex_devonport,arcak}@berkeley.edu
[2] Technical University of Munich, Munich, Germany
khaled.mahmoud@tum.de
[3] University of Colorado, Boulder, Boulder, CO, USA
majid.zamani@colorado.edu
[4] Ludwig Maximilian University, Munich, Germany

Abstract. Reachability analysis is a critical tool for the formal verification of dynamical systems and the synthesis of controllers for them. Due to their computational complexity, many reachability analysis methods are restricted to systems with relatively small dimensions. One significant reason for such limitation is that those approaches, and their implementations, are not designed to leverage parallelism. They use algorithms that are designed to run serially within one compute unit and they can not utilize widely-available high-performance computing (HPC) platforms such as many-core CPUs, GPUs and Cloud-computing services.

This paper presents PIRK, a tool to efficiently compute reachable sets for general nonlinear systems of extremely high dimensions. PIRK can utilize HPC platforms for computing reachable sets for general high-dimensional non-linear systems. PIRK has been tested on several systems, with state dimensions up to 4 billion. The scalability of PIRK's parallel implementations is found to be highly favorable.

Keywords: Reachability analysis · ODE integration · Runge-Kutta method · Mixed monotonicity · Monte Carlo simulation · Parallel algorithms

1 Introduction

Applications of safety-critical cyber-physical systems (CPS) are growing due to emerging IoT technologies and the increasing availability of efficient computing devices. These include smart buildings, traffic networks, autonomous vehicles, truck platooning, and drone swarms, which require reliable bug-free

---

A. Devonport and M. Khaled—Contributed equally.

© The Author(s) 2020
S. K. Lahiri and C. Wang (Eds.): CAV 2020, LNCS 12224, pp. 556–568, 2020.
https://doi.org/10.1007/978-3-030-53288-8_27

software that perform in real-time and fulfill design requirements. Traditional simulation/testing-based strategies may only find a small percentage of the software defects and the repairs become much costly as the system complexity grows. Hence, in-development verification strategies are favorable since they reveal the faults in earlier stages, and guarantee that the designs satisfy the specifications as they evolve through the development cycle. Formal methods offer an attractive alternative to testing- and simulation-based approaches, as they can verify whether the specifications for a CPS are satisfied for all possible behaviors from a set of the initial states of the system. *Reachable sets* characterize the states a system can reach in a given time range, starting from a certain initial set and subjected to certain inputs. They play an important role in several formal methods-based approaches to the verification and controller synthesis. An example of this is *abstraction-based* synthesis [1–4], in which reachable sets are used to construct a finite-state "abstraction" which is then used for formal synthesis.

Computing an exact reachable set is generally not possible. Most practical methods resort to computing over-approximations or under-approximations of the reachable set, depending on the desired guarantee. Computing these approximations to a high degree of accuracy is still a computationally intensive task, particularly for high-dimensional systems. Many software tools have been created to address the various challenges of approximating reachable sets. Each of these tools uses different methods and leverages different system assumptions to achieve different goals related to computing reachable sets. For example, CORA [5] and SpaceEx [6] tools are designed to compute reachable sets of high accuracy for very general classes of nonlinear systems, including hybrid ones. Some reachability analysis methods rely on specific features of dynamical systems, such as linearity of the dynamics or sparsity in the interconnection structure [7–9]. This allows computing the reachable sets in shorter time or for relatively high-dimensional systems. However, it limits the approach to smaller classes of applications, less practical specifications, or requires the use of less accurate (e.g., linearized) models.

Other methods attack the computational complexity problem by computing reachable set approximations from a limited class of set representations. An example of limiting the set of allowed overapproximations are *interval reachability* methods, in which reachable sets are approximated by Cartesian products of intervals. Interval reachability methods allow for computing the reachable sets of very general non-linear and high-dimensional systems in a short amount of time. They also pose mild constraints on the systems under consideration, usually only requiring some kind of boundedness constraint instead of a specific form for the system dynamics. Many reachability tools that are designed to scale well with state dimension focus on interval reachability methods: these include Flow* [10], CAPD [11], C2E2 [12], VNODE-LP [13], DynIbex [14], and TIRA [15].

Another avenue by which reachable set computation time can be reduced, which we believe has not been sufficiently explored, is the use of parallel computing. Although most reachability methods are presented as serial algorithms, many of them have some inherent parallelism that can be exploited. One example of a tool that exploits parallelism is XSpeed [16], which implements a parallelized version of a support function-based reachability method. However, this parallel method is limited to linear systems, and in some cases only linear systems with invertible dynamics. Further, the parallelization is not suitable for massively parallel hardware: only some of the work (sampling of the support functions) is offloaded to the parallel device, so only a relatively small number of parallel processing elements may be employed.

In this paper, we investigate the parallelism for three interval reachability analysis methods and introduce PIRK, the Parallel Interval Reachability Kernel. PIRK uses *simulation-based* reachability methods [17–19], which compute rigorous approximations to reachable sets by integrating one or more systems of ODEs. PIRK is developed in C++ and OpenCL as an open-source[1] *kernel* for pFaces [20], a recently introduced acceleration ecosystem. This allows PIRK to be run on a wide range of computing platforms, including CPUs clusters, GPUs, and hardware accelerators from any vendor, as well as cloud-based services like AWS.

The user looking to use a reachability analysis tool for formal verification may choose from an abundance of options, as our brief review has shown. What PIRK offers in this choice is a tool that allows for massively parallel reachability analysis of high-dimensional systems with an application programming interface (API) to easily interface with other tools. To the best of our knowledge, PIRK is the first and the only tool that can compute reachable sets of general non-linear systems with dimensions beyond the billion. As we show later in Sect. 5, PIRK computes the reachable set for a traffic network example with 4 billion dimension in only 44.7 min using a 96-core CPU in Amazon AWS Cloud.

2   Interval Reachability Analysis

Consider a nonlinear system with dynamics $\dot{x} = f(t, x, p)$ with state $x \in \mathbb{R}^n$, a set of initial states $\mathcal{X}_0$, a time interval $[t_0, t_1]$, and a set of time-varying inputs $\mathcal{P}$ defined over $[t_0, t_1]$. Let $\Phi(t; t_0, x_0, p)$ denote the state of the system, at time t, of the trajectory beginning at time t_0 at initial state x_0 under input p. We assume the systems are continuous-time.

The finite-time forward reachable set is defined as

$$R_{t_0, t_1} = \{\Phi(t_1; t_0, x, p) | x \in \mathcal{X}_0, p \in \mathcal{P}\}.$$

For the problem of *interval* reachability analysis, there are a few more constraints on the problem structure. An *interval set* is a set of the form $[\underline{a}, \overline{a}] =$

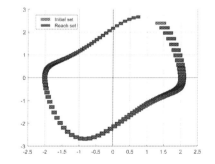

Fig. 1. An example of an Interval Reachability problem for a nonlinear system. Red rectangle: initial set. Blue rectangles: reachable sets for several final times t_1. (Color figure online)

---

[1] PIRK is publicly available at https://github.com/mkhaled87/pFaces-PIRK.

$\{a : \underline{a} \le a \le \overline{a}\}$, where $\le$ denotes the usual partial order on real vectors, that is the partial order with respect to the positive orthant cone. The vectors $\underline{a}$ and $\overline{a}$ are the lower and upper bounds respectively of the interval set. An interval set can alternatively be described by its center $a^* = \frac{1}{2}(\overline{a} + \underline{a})$ and half-width $[a] = \frac{1}{2}(\overline{a} - \underline{a})$. In interval reachability analysis, the initial set must be an interval, and inputs values restricted to an interval set, i.e. $p(t) \in [\underline{p}, \overline{p}]$, and the reachable set approximation must also be an interval (Fig. 1). Furthermore, certain methods for computing interval reachable sets require further restrictions on the system dynamics, such as the state and input Jacobian matrices being bounded or sign-stable.

2.1   Methods to Compute Interval Reachable Sets

PIRK computes interval reachable sets using three different methods, allowing for different levels of tightness and speed, and which allow for different amounts of additional problem data to be used.

The *Contraction/Growth Bound* method [4,21,22] computes the reachable set using component-wise contraction properties of the system. This method may be applied to input-affine systems of the form $\dot{x} = f(t,x) + p$. The growth and contraction properties of each component of the system are first characterized by a *contraction matrix* C. The contraction matrix is a component-wise generalization of the matrix measure of the Jacobian $J_x = \partial f / \partial x$ [19,23], satisfying $C_{ii} \ge J_{x,ii}(t,x)$ for diagonal Jacobian elements $J_{x,ii}(t,x)$, and $C_{ij} \ge |J_{x,ij}(t,x)|$ for off-diagonal Jacobian elements $J_{x,ij}(t,x)$. The method constructs a reachable set over-approximation by separately establishing its *center* and *half-width*. The center is found by simulating the trajectory of the center of the initial set, that is as $\varPhi(t_1; t_0, x^*, p^*)$. The half width is found by integrating the *growth dynamics* $\dot{r} = g(r,p) = Cr + [p]$, where $[p] = \frac{1}{2}(\overline{p} - \underline{p})$, over $[t_0, t_1]$ with initial condition $r(t_0) = [x] = \frac{1}{2}(\overline{x} - \underline{x})$.

The *Mixed-Monotonicity* method [24] computes the reachable set by separating the increasing and decreasing portions of the system dynamics in an auxiliary system called the *embedding system* whose state dimension is twice that of the original system [25]. The embedding system is constructed using a *decomposition function* $d(t, x, p, \hat{x}, \hat{p})$, which encodes the increasing and decreasing parts of the system dynamics and satisfies $d(t, x, p, x, p) = f(t, x, p)$. The evaluation of a single trajectory of the embedding system can be used to find a reachable set over-approximation for the original system.

The *Monte Carlo* method computes a probabilistic approximation to the reachable set by evaluating the trajectories of a finite number m of pairs *sample points* $(x_0^{(i)}, p^{(i)})$ in the initial set and input set, and selecting the smallest interval that contains the final points of the trajectories. Unlike the other two methods, the Monte Carlo method is restricted to constant-valued inputs, i.e. inputs of the form $p(t) = p$, where $p \in [\underline{p}, \overline{p}]$. Each sampled initial state $x_0^{(i)}$ is integrated over $[t_0, t_1]$ with its input $p^{(i)}$ to yield a final state $x_1^{(i)}$. The interval reachable set is then approximated by the elementwise minimum and maximum of the $x_1^{(i)}$. This approximation satisfies a probabilistic guarantee of correctness, provided that enough sample states are chosen [26]. Let $[\underline{R}, \overline{R}]$ be the approximated reachable set, $\epsilon, \delta \in (0, 1)$, and $m \geq \left(\frac{2n}{\epsilon}\right) \log\left(\frac{2n}{\delta}\right)$. Then, with probability $1 - \delta$, the approximation $[\underline{R}, \overline{R}]$ satisfies $P(R_{t_0, t_1} \setminus [\underline{R}, \overline{R}]) \leq \epsilon$, where $P(A)$ denotes the probability that a sampled initial state will yield a final state in the set A, and $\setminus$ denotes set difference. The probability that a sampled initial state will be sent to a state outside the estimate (the "accuracy" of the estimate) is quantified by ϵ. Improved accuracy (lower ϵ) increases the sample size as $O(1/\epsilon)$. The probability that running the algorithm will fail to give an estimate satisfying the inequality (The "confidence") is quantified by δ. Improved confidence (lower δ) increases the sample size by $O(\log(1/\delta))$.

3   Parallelization

The bulk of the computational work in each method is spent in ODE integration. Hence, the most effective approach by which to parallelize the three methods is to design a parallel ODE integration method. There are several available methods for parallelizing the task of ODE integration. Several popular methods for parallel ODE integration are parallel extensions of Runge-Kutta integration methods, which are the most popular serial methods for ODE integration.

PIRK takes advantage of the task-level parallelism in the Runge-Kutta equations by evaluating each state dimension in parallel. This parallelization scheme is called *parallelization across space* [27]. PIRK specifically uses a space-parallel version of the fourth-order Runge Kutta method, or space-parallel RK4 for brevity. In space-parallel RK4, each parallel thread is assigned a different state variable to evaluate the intermediate update equations. After each intermediate step, the threads must synchronize to construct the updated state in global memory. Space-parallel RK4 can use as many parallel computation elements as there are state variables: since PIRK's goal is to compute reachable sets for extremely high-dimensional systems, this is sufficient in most cases.

The space-parallel scheme is not hardware-specific, and may be used with any parallel computing platform. PIRK is similarly hardware-agnostic: the pFaces ecosystem, for which PIRK is a kernel, provides a common interface to run on a variety of heterogeneous parallel computing platforms. The only difference between platforms that affects PIRK is the number of available parallel processing elements (PEs).

4   Complexity of the Parallelized Methods

The parallelized implementations of the three reachability methods described in Sect. 2.1 use space-parallel RK4 to perform almost all computations other than setting up initial conditions. We can therefore find the time and memory complexity of each method by analyzing the complexity of space-parallel RK4 and counting the number of times each method uses it.

For a system with n dimensions, space-parallel RK4 scales linearly as the number of PEs (denoted by P) increases. In a computer with a single PE (i.e., $P = 1$), the algorithm reduces to the original serial algorithm. Then, suppose that a parallel computer has $P \leq n$ PEs of the same type. We assume a computational model under which instruction overhead and latency from thread synchronization are negligible, memory space has equal access time from all processing elements, and the number of parallel jobs can be evenly distributed among the P processing elements.[2] Under this *parallel random-access machine* model [28], the time complexity of space-parallel RK4 is reduced by a factor of P: each PE is responsible for computing n/P components of the state vector. Therefore, for fixed initial and final times t_0 and t_1, the time complexity of the algorithm is $O(\frac{n}{P})$.

The parallel version of the contraction/growth bound method uses space-parallel RK4 twice. First, it is used to compute the solution of the system's ODE f for the center of the initial set $\mathcal{X}_0$. Then, it is used to compute the growth/contraction of the initial set $\mathcal{X}_0$ by solving the ODE g of the growth dynamics. Since this method uses a fixed number of calls of space-parallel RK4, its time complexity is also $O(\frac{n}{P})$ for a given t_0 and t_1.

The parallelized implementation of the mixed-monotonicity method uses space-parallel RK4 only once, in order to integrate the $2n$-dimensional embedding system. This means that the mixed-monotonicity method also has a time complexity of $O(\frac{n}{P})$ for fixed t_0 and t_1. However, the mixed-monotonicity method requires twice as much memory as the growth bound method, since it runs space-parallel RK4 on a system of dimension $2n$.

The parallelized implementation of the Monte Carlo method uses space-parallel RK4 m times, once for each of the m sampled initial states. The implementation uses two levels of parallelization. The first level is a set of parallel threads over the samples used for simulations. Then, within each thread, another parallel set of threads are launched by space-parallel RK4. This is realized as one parallel job of $m \times n$ threads. Consequently, the Monte Carlo method has a complexity of $O(\frac{mn}{P})$. Since only the elementwise minima and maxima of the sampled states need to be stored, this method only requires as much memory as the growth bound method.

Remark 1. A pseudocode of each parallel algorithm and a detailed discussion of their time and space complexities are provided in an extended version of this paper [29]. The extended version also contains additional details for the case studies that will be presented in the next section.

5   Case Studies

In each of the case studies to follow, we report the time it takes PIRK to compute reachable sets for systems of varying dimension using all three of its methods on

---

[2] While these non-idealities will be present in real systems and slow down computation, they should not affect the asymptotic complexity.

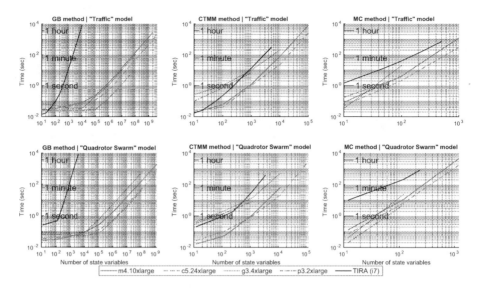

Fig. 2. Logarithmic plots of the results for speed tests of the traffic model (first row) and the quadrotor swarm (second row). Speed test results for the serial interval reachability toolbox TIRA are also shown for the traffic model.

a variety of parallel computing platforms. We perform some of the same tests using the serial tool TIRA, to measure the speedup gained by PIRK's ability to use massively parallel hardware.

We set a time limit of 1 h for all of the targeted case studies, and report the maximum dimensions that could be reached under this limit. The Monte Carlo method is given probabilistic parameters $\epsilon = \delta = 0.05$ in each case study where it is used. We use four AWS machines for the computations with PIRK: m4.10xlarge which has a CPU with 40 cores, c5.24xlarge which has a CPU with 96 cores, g3.4xlarge which has a GPU with 2048 cores, and p3.2xlarge which has a GPU with 5120 cores. For the computations with TIRA, we used a machine with a 3.6 GHz Intel i7 CPU.

5.1 n-link Road Traffic Model

We consider the road traffic analysis problem reported in [30], a proposed benchmark for formal controller synthesis. We are interested in the density of cars along a single one-way lane. The lane is divided into n segments, and the density of cars in each segment is a state variable. The continuous-time dynamics are derived from a spatially discretized version of the Cell Transmission Model [31]. This is a nonlinear system with sparse coupling between state variables.

The results of the speed test are shown in the first row of Figure 2. The machines m4.10xlarge and c5.24xlarge reach up to 2 billion and 4 billion dimensions, respectively, using the growth/contraction method, in 47.3 min and 44.7 min, respectively. Due to memory limitations of the GPUs, the machines g3.4xlarge and p3.2xlarge both reach up to 400 million in 106 s and 11 s, respectively.

The relative improvement of PIRK's computation time over TIRA's is significantly larger for the growth bound method than for the other two. This difference stems from how each tool computes the half-width of the reachable set from the radius dynamics. TIRA solves the radius dynamics by computing the full matrix exponential using MATLAB's expm, whereas PIRK directly integrates the dynamics using parallel Runge-Kutta. This caveat applies to Sect. 5.2 as well.

5.2   Quadrotor Swarm

The second test system is a swarm of K identical quadrotors with nonlinear dynamics. The system dynamics of each quadrotor model are derived in a similar way to the model used in the ARCH-COMP 18 competition [32], with the added simplification of a small angle approximation in the angular dynamics and the neglect of Coriolis force terms. A derivation of both models is available in [33]. Similar to the n-link traffic model, this system is convenient for scaling: system consisting of one quadrotor can be expressed with 12 states, so the state dimension of the swarm system is $n = 12K$. While this reachability problem could be decomposed into K separate reachability problems which can be solved separately, we solve the entire 12K-dimensional problem as a whole to demonstrate PIRK's ability to make use of sparse interconnection.

The results of the speed test are shown in Fig. 2 (second row). The machines m4.10xlarge and c5.24xlarge reach up to 1.8 billion dimensions and 3.6 billion dimensions, respectively, (using the growth/contraction method) in 48 min and 32 min, respectively. The machines g3.4xlarge and p3.2xlarge both reach up to 120 million dimensions in 10.6 min and 46 s, respectively.

5.3   Quadrotor Swarm with Artificial Potential Field

The third test system is a modification of the quadrotor swarm system which adds interactions between the quadrotors. In addition to the quadrotor dynamics described in Sect. 5.2, this model augments each quadrotor with an artificial potential field to guide it to the origin while avoiding collisions. This controller applies nonlinear force terms to the quadrotor dynamics that seek to minimize an *artificial potential U* that depends on the position of all of the quadrotors. Due to the interaction of the state variables in the force terms arising from the potential field, this system has a dense Jacobian. In particular, at least 25% of the Jacobian elements will be nonzero for any number of quadrotors.

Table 1 shows the times of running PIRK using this system on the four machines m4.10xlarge, c5.24xlarge, g3.4xlarge and p3.2xlarge in Amazon AWS. Due to the high density of this example, we focus on the memory-light growth bound and the Monte-Carlo methods. PIRK computed the reach sets of systems up to 120,000 state variables (i.e., 10,000 quadrotors). Up to 1,200 states, all machines solve the problems in less than one second. Some of the

Table 1. Results for running PIRK to compute the reach set of the quadrotors swarm with artificial potential field. "N/M" means that the machine did not have enough memory to compute the reachable set.

Method	No. of states	Memory (MB)	Time (seconds)			
			m4.10xlarge	c5.24xlarge	g3.4xlarge	p3.2xlarge
GB	1200	2.8	≤ 1.0	≤ 1.0	≤ 1.0	≤ 1.0
GB	12000	275.3	≤ 1.0	≤ 1.0	≤ 1.0	≤ 1.0
GB	120000	27,473.1	69.6	68.3	N/M	N/M
MC	1200	45.7	1.0	≤ 1.0	2.0	≤ 1.0
MC	12000	457.5	56.8	23.7	233.1	40.6
MC	120000	4577.6	$\geq$ 2h	3091.8	N/M	5081.0

machines lack the required memory to solve the problems requiring large memory (e.g., 27.7 GB of memory is required to compute the reach set of the system with 120,000 state variables using the growth bound method).

5.4 Heat Diffusion

The fourth test system is a model for the diffusion of heat in a 3-dimensional cube. The model is based on a benchmark used in [7] to test a method for numerical verification of affine systems. A model of the form $\dot{x} = f(t, x, p)$ which approximates the heat transfer through the cube according to the heat equation can be obtained by discretizing the cube into an $\ell \times \ell \times \ell$ grid, yielding a system with ℓ^3 states. The temperature at each grid point is taken as a state variable. Each spatial derivative is replaced with a finite-difference approximation. Since the heat equation is a linear PDE, the discretized system is linear.

We take a fixed state dimension of $n = 10^9$ by fixing $\ell = 1000$. Integration takes place over $[t_0, t_1] = [0, 20]$ with time step size $h = 0.02$. Using the Growth bound method, PIRK solves the problem on m4.10xlarge in 472 min, and in 350.2 min on c5.24xlarge. This is faster than the time reported in [7] (30 h) using the same machine.

5.5 Overtaking Maneuver with a Single-Track Vehicle

The remaining case studies focus on models of practical importance with low state dimension. Although PIRK is designed to perform well on high-dimensional systems, it is also effective at quickly computing reachable sets for low dimensional systems, for applications that require many reachable sets. The first such case study is single-track vehicle model with seven states, presented in [34].

We fix an input that performs a maneuver to overtake an obstacle in the middle lane of a 3-lane highway. To verify that the maneuver was safely completed, we compute reachable sets over a range of points and ensuring that the reachable set does not intersect any obstacles. We consider a step-size of 0.005 s in a time window between 0 and 6.5 s. We compute one reachable set at each time step, resulting in a "reachable tube" comprising 1300 reachable sets. PIRK

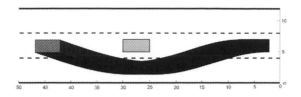

Fig. 3. Reachable tube for the single-track vehicle.

computed the reachable tube in 0.25 s using the growth bound method on an i7 CPU (Fig. 3).

5.6 Performance on ARCH Benchmarks

In order to compare PIRK's performance to existing tools, we tested PIRK's growth bound implementation on three systems from the ARCH-COMP'18 category report for systems with nonlinear dynamics [32]. This report contains benchmark data from several popular reachability analysis tools (C2E2, CORA, Flow*, Isabelle, SpaceEx, and SymReach) on nonlinear reachability problems with state dimensions between 2 and 12.

Table 2. Results from running PIRK (growth bound method) to compute the reach sets for the examples reported in the ARCH-2018 competition.

Benchmark model	PIRK	CORA	CORA/SX	C2E2	Flow*	Isabelle	SymReach
Van der Pol (2 states)	0.13	2.3	0.6	38.5	1.5	1.5	17.14
Laub-Loomis (7 states)	0.04	0.82	0.85	0.12	4.5	10	1.93
Quadrotor (12 states)	0.01	5.2	1.5	–	5.9	30	2.96

Table 2 compares the computation times for PIRK on the three systems to those reported by other tools in [32]. All times are in seconds. PIRK ran on an i9 CPU, while the others ran on i7 and i5: see [32] for more hardware details. PIRK solves each of the benchmark problems faster than the other tools. Both of the i7 and i9 processors used have 6 to 8 cores: the advantage of PIRK is its ability to utilize all available cores.

6 Conclusion

Using a simple parallelization of interval reachability analysis techniques, PIRK is able to compute reachable sets for nonlinear systems faster and at higher dimensions than many existing tools. This performance increase comes from PIRK's ability to use massively parallel hardware such as GPUs and CPU clusters, as well as the use of parallelizable simulation-based methods. Future work will focus on improving the memory-usage of the mixed monotonicity and Monte-Carlo based methods, including an investigation of adaptive sampling strategies, and on using PIRK as a helper tool to synthesize controllers for high-dimensional systems.

References

1. Zamani, M., et al.: Symbolic models for nonlinear control systems with- out stability assumptions. IEEE Trans. Autom. Control **57**(7), 1804–1809 (2012)
2. Belta, C., Yordanov, B., Ebru, G.: Formal Methods for Discrete-Time Dynamical Systems. Springer, Cham (2017). https://doi.org/10.1007/978-3-319-50763-7
3. Tabuada, P.: Verification and Control of Hybrid Systems: A Symbolic Approach. Springer, Cham (2009). https://doi.org/10.1007/978-1-4419-0224-5
4. Reißig, G., Weber, A., Rungger, M.: Feedback refinement relations for the synthesis of symbolic controllers. IEEE Trans. Autom. Control **62**(4), 1781–1796 (2017)
5. Althoff, M.: An introduction to CORA 2015. In: Proceedings of the Workshop on Applied Verification for Continuous and Hybrid Systems (2015)
6. Frehse, G., et al.: SpaceEx: scalable verification of hybrid systems. In: Gopalakrishnan, G., Qadeer, S. (eds.) CAV 2011. LNCS, vol. 6806, pp. 379–395. Springer, Heidelberg (2011). https://doi.org/10.1007/978-3-642-22110-1_30
7. Bak, S., Tran, H.-D., Johnson, T.T.: Numerical verification of affine systems with up to a billion dimensions. In: Proceedings of the 22nd ACM International Conference on Hybrid Systems: Computation and Control, pp. 23–32. ACM (2019)
8. Kurzhanskiy, A.A., Varaiya, P.: Ellipsoidal toolbox (ET). In: Proceedings of the 45th IEEE Conference on Decision and Control, pp. 1498–1503. IEEE (2006)
9. Dreossi, T.: SAPO: reachability computation and parameter synthesis of polynomial dynamical systems. In: Proceedings of the 20th International Conference on Hybrid Systems: Computation and Control, pp. 29–34. ACM (2017)
10. Chen, X., Ábrahám, E., Sankaranarayanan, S.: Flow*: an analyzer for non-linear hybrid systems. In: Sharygina, N., Veith, H. (eds.) CAV 2013. LNCS, vol. 8044, pp. 258–263. Springer, Heidelberg (2013). https://doi.org/10.1007/978-3-642-39799-8_18
11. The CAPD Group. Computer Assisted Proofs in Dynamics group, a C++ package for rigorous numerics (2019). http://capd.ii.uj.edu.pl/. Accessed 20 Oct 2019
12. Duggirala, P.S., Mitra, S., Viswanathan, M., Potok, M.: C2E2: a verification tool for stateflow models. In: Baier, C., Tinelli, C. (eds.) TACAS 2015. LNCS, vol. 9035, pp. 68–82. Springer, Heidelberg (2015). https://doi.org/10.1007/978-3-662-46681-0_5
13. Nedialkov, N.S.: Implementing a rigorous ODE solver through literate programming. In: Rauh, A., Auer, E. (eds.) Modeling, Design, and Simulation of Systems with Uncertainties. Mathematical Engineering, vol. 3. Springer, Heidelberg (2011). https://doi.org/10.1007/978-3-642-15956-5_1
14. Sandretto, J.A.D., Chapoutot, A.: Validated explicit and implicit Runge-Kutta methods (2016)
15. Meyer, P.-J., Devonport, A., Arcak, M.: TIRA: toolbox for interval reachability analysis. In: arXiv preprint arXiv:1902.05204 (2019)
16. Ray, R., et al.: XSpeed: accelerating reachability analysis on multi- core processors. In: Piterman, N. (eds.) Hardware and Software: Verification and Testing, pp. 3–18. Springer, Cham (2015). ISBN: 978-3-319-26287-1

17. Huang, Z., Mitra, S.: Computing bounded reach sets from sampled simulation traces. In: Proceedings of the 15th ACM International Conference on Hybrid Systems: Computation and Control, pp. 291–294. ACM (2012)
18. Julius, A.A., Pappas, G.J.: Trajectory based verification using local finite-time invariance. In: Majumdar, R., Tabuada, P. (eds.) HSCC 2009. LNCS, vol. 5469, pp. 223–236. Springer, Heidelberg (2009). https://doi.org/10.1007/978-3-642-00602-9_16
19. Maidens, J., Arcak, M.: Reachability analysis of nonlinear systems using matrix measures. IEEE Trans. Autom. Control **60**(1), 265–270 (2014)
20. Khaled, M., Zamani, M.: pFaces: an acceleration ecosystem for symbolic control. In: Proceedings of the 22nd ACM International Conference on Hybrid Systems: Computation and Control, pp. 252–257. ACM (2019)
21. Kapela, T., Zgliczyński, P.: A Lohner-type algorithm for control systems and ordinary differential inclusions. In: arXiv preprint arXiv:0712.0910 (2007)
22. Fan, C., et al.: Locally optimal reach set over-approximation for non-linear systems. In: 2016 International Conference on Embedded Software (EMSOFT), pp. 1–10. IEEE (2016)
23. Arcak, M., Maidens, J.: Simulation-based reachability analysis for nonlinear systems using componentwise contraction properties. In: Lohstroh, M., Derler, P., Sirjani, M. (eds.) Principles of Modeling. LNCS, vol. 10760, pp. 61–76. Springer, Cham (2018). https://doi.org/10.1007/978-3-319-95246-8_4
24. Coogan, S., Arcak, M., Belta, C.: Formal methods for control of traffic flow: Automated control synthesis from finite-state transition models. IEEE Control Syst. Mag. **37**(2), 109–128 (2017)
25. Gouzé, J.-L., Hadeler, K.P.: Monotone flows and order intervals. In: Nonlinear World 1, pp. 23–34 (1994)
26. Devonport, A., Arcak, M.: Data-Driven Reachable Set Computation using Adaptive Gaussian Process Classification and Monte Carlo Methods (2019). arXiv: 1910.02500 [eess.SY]
27. Solodushkin, S.I., Iumanova, I.F.: Parallel numerical methods for ordinary differential equations: a survey. In: CEUR Workshop Proceedings, vol. 1729. CEUR-WS, pp. 1–10 (2016)
28. Jaja, J.: An Introduction to Parallel Algorithms. Addison-Wesley, Reading (1992)
29. Devonport, A., et al.: PIRK: Scalable Interval Reachability Analysis for High-Dimensional Nonlinear Systems (2020). arXiv: 2001.10635 [eess.SY]
30. Coogan, S., Arcak, M.: A benchmark problem in transportation networks. In: arXiv preprint arXiv:1803.00367 (2018)
31. Coogan, S., Arcak, M.: A compartmental model for traffic networks and its dynamical behavior. IEEE Trans. Autom. Control **60**(10), 2698–2703 (2015)
32. Immler, F., et al.: ARCH-COMP18 category report: continuous and hybrid systems with nonlinear dynamics. In: Proceedings of the 5th International Workshop on Applied Verification for Continuous and Hybrid Systems (2018)
33. Beard, R.: Quadrotor dynamics and control rev 0.1. Technical report Brigham Young University (2008)
34. Althoff, M.: CommonRoad: vehicle models. In: Technische Universität München, Garching, pp. 1–25 (2017)

AEON: Attractor Bifurcation Analysis of Parametrised Boolean Networks

Nikola Beneš, Luboš Brim, Jakub Kadlecaj,
Samuel Pastva$^{(\boxtimes)}$, and David Šafránek

Faculty of Informatics, Masaryk University, Brno,
Czech Republic
{xbenes3,brim,xkadlec2,xpastva,
safranek}@fi.muni.cz

Abstract. Boolean networks (BNs) provide an effective modelling tool for various phenomena from science and engineering. Any long-term behaviour of a BN eventually converges to a so-called attractor. Depending on various logical parameters, the structure and quality of attractors can undergo a significant change, known as a bifurcation. We present a tool for analysing bifurcations in asynchronous parametrised Boolean networks. To fight the state-space and parameter-space explosion problem the tool uses a parallel semi-symbolic algorithm.

Keywords: Boolean networks · Attractors · Bifurcation analysis

1 Introduction

Boolean networks (BNs) provide an effective mathematical tool to model computational processes and other phenomena from science and engineering. BNs represent a generalisation of other relevant mathematical models, which appeared previously as cellular automata (CA), suggested by Wolfram [39] for computation modelling, or formal genetic nets [24] and Thomas networks [37], proposed for gene regulatory networks. This gives an idea of the versatility of BNs in different applications (mathematics, physics chemistry, biology, ecology, etc.) and engineering (computation, artificial intelligence, electronics, circuits, etc.).

The development of formal methods for analysis and synthesis of Boolean networks has recently attracted a lot of attention [11,18,20,28,36]. In this paper, we are primarily interested in BN models for computational systems biology [29]. In general, biological processes are emerging from complex inter- and intra-cellular interactions and they cannot be sufficiently understood and controlled without the help of powerful computer-aided modelling and analysis methods [38]. BNs serve an important purpose of describing overall interactions within a living cell at an appropriate level of abstraction and they provide a systematic approach to model crucial states of cell dynamics – so-called *phenotypes* [22].

Supported by the Czech Science Foundation grant No. 18-00178S.

S. K. Lahiri and C. Wang (Eds.): CAV 2020, LNCS 12224, pp. 569–581, 2020.
https://doi.org/10.1007/978-3-030-53288-8_28

The level of abstraction provided by BNs makes them an important tool for design of targetted therapeutic procedures such as cell reprogramming [36] based on changing one cell phenotype to another, allowing regeneration of tissues or neurons [21]. Since phenotypes are determined by long-term behaviour of biological systems, fully automatised identification of phenotypes by employing BN models is a necessary step towards the future of modern medicine. Owing to the fact there is a continuous lack of sufficiently detailed (mechanistic) information on biological processes, there is definitely a need to work with models involving uncertain (or insufficient) knowledge. In this paper, we present a unique tool that makes a significant contribution towards fully automatised analysis of long-term behaviour of BN models with uncertain knowledge.

We start with giving some intuition on BNs. A BN consists of a set of Boolean *variables* whose state is determined by other variables in the network through a set of Boolean *update functions* assigned to the variables (different update functions can be assigned to different variables) and *regulations* placed on them. If at each point of time all the update functions are applied simultaneously we speak about *synchronous dynamics*, if only one of the update functions is chosen non-deterministically to modify the corresponding Boolean variable, we speak of *asynchronous dynamics*. In this paper we consider asynchronous Boolean networks only.

In real-world applications, the update functions for some of the variables are typically (partially) unknown and are represented as logical *parameters* of the network. We speak of *parametrised Boolean networks* [40] in this case. If all the parameters are fixed to a concrete Boolean function, a parametrised BN turns into a (non-parametrised) BN.

The long-term behaviour of a BN, starting from an initial state, has three possible outcomes. Briefly, the first situation is when the network evolves to a single stable state. Such states are the fixed points or *point attractors* or *stable states*. The second situation is that the network periodically oscillates through a finite sequence of states—an *oscillating attractor* or *attractive cycle* (the discrete equivalent of a limit cycle in continuous systems). The third case is what we call a *disordered attractor* (or chaotic oscillation [32]), an attractor that is neither stable not periodically oscillating and in which the system may behave unpredictably, due to the nondeterminism of the asynchronous semantics of BNs. Attractors are particularly relevant in the context of biological modelling as they are used to represent differentiated cellular types or tissues (in the case of fixed points) [2] and biological rhythms or oscillations (in the case of cycles) [17].

The set of network states that converge to the same attractor forms the *basin of attraction* of that attractor [7]. Attractors (and their basins) are disjoint entities and the state space is compartmentalised by imaginary "attractor boundaries". The entire dynamics of a Boolean network can be represented as a state transition system in which the trajectories from initial states are depicted, revealing the basins of attraction and associated attractors. We call such a representation the *attractor landscape* of the network [13].

In parametrised BNs the attractor landscape changes as the parameters are varied. Some of these changes may lead to a qualitatively different landscape (defined, e.g., in the count and/or quality of attractors). Such a qualitative change is called a *bifurcation* and the values of parameters for which it occurs are called *bifurcation points*. Determining (all) bifurcation points for a network, called *attractor bifurcation analysis*, is an important task in the analysis of BNs [4].

While BN models are intuitive, mathematically simple to describe, and supported by analytical methods [12], analysis of large models appearing in real cases is severely limited by the lack of robust computational tools running efficiently on high-performance hardware. Several computational tools have been developed for construction, visualisation and analysis of attractors in non-parametrised BNs. Amongst them, the established tools include ATLANTIS [34], Bio Model Analyzer (BMA) [6], BoolNet [31], PyBoolNet [27], lnet [7], The Cell Collective [23], CellNetAnalyzer [25], and ASSA-PBN [30]. Another group of existing tools targets the parameter synthesis problem for parametrised BNs. The most prominent tools here are GRNMC [20], GINsim [10] (indirectly through NuSMV [14]), and TREMPPI [35]. In general, parameter synthesis tools can be used to identify parameters producing a specified long-term behaviour (depending on the logics employed), however, they do not provide a sufficient solution for identification and classification of all attractors in the system. Finally, it is worth noting that there have recently appeared several tools aiming at control of cell behaviour through BNs (i.e., driving a cell into the desired state). A well-known representative of these tools is ViSiBooL [33].

To the best of our knowledge, none of the existing tools is capable of performing attractor bifurcation analysis in parametrised models. Bifurcation analysis has been recently recognised as a fundamental approach that provides a new framework for understanding the behaviour of biological networks. The ability to make a dramatic change in system behaviour is often essential to organism function, and bifurcations are therefore ubiquitous in biological networks such as the switches of the cell cycle. The tool AEON is supposed to fill in the gap in the existing tools supporting analysis of Boolean network models.

AEON builds on methods and algorithms for asynchronous parametrised BNs we have introduced in our previous research [1,3 5]. To deal with the state-space and parameter-space explosion problem, the tool implements a shared-memory parallel semi-symbolic algorithm. The results the tool provides to the user can be used for example to the design of "wet" experiments, better understanding of the system's dynamics, or to control or re-program the system. As attractors model phenotypes, one of the most urgent needs for computer aided support, such as AEON can provide, is in applications in therapeutic innovations.

We believe that attractor bifurcation computed by AEON will shift the current technology toward a comprehensive method when integrated with tools aimed at control or other analysis methods.

2 Attractors in Parametrised Boolean Networks

In this section, we define precisely the problem of attractor bifurcation analysis. We also give an overview of the necessary technical background needed to describe the algorithmic solution and its implementation. More details can be found in [4].

A *Boolean network (BN)* consists of a finite set of *state variables* $\mathcal{V}$ (whose elements we denote by A, B, ...), a set of *regulations* $R \subseteq \mathcal{V} \times \mathcal{V}$, and a family of Boolean *update functions* $\mathcal{F} = \{F_A \mid A \in \mathcal{V}\}$. If $(B, A) \in R$, we say that B is a *regulator* of A. For each $A \in \mathcal{V}$, we call the set $\mathcal{C}(A) = \{B \in \mathcal{V} \mid (B, A) \in R\}$ of its regulators the *context* of A. A *state* of the BN is an assignment of Boolean values to the variables, i.e. a function $\mathcal{V} \rightarrow \{0, 1\}$. The type signature of each update function F_A is given by the context of A as $F_A : \{0, 1\}^{\mathcal{C}(A)} \rightarrow \{0, 1\}$.

In Boolean networks, one often describes various properties of the network regulations. Here, we focus on three most basic types of regulation: We say that $(A, B) \in R$ is *observable* if there exists a state where changing the value of A also changes the value of F_B. In the tool, edges that might be non-observable are drawn using dashed lines.

We say that a regulation $(A, B) \in R$ is *activating* if by increasing A, one cannot decrease the value of F_B. Symmetrically, the regulation is *inhibiting* if by increasing A, one cannot increase the value of F_B. In the tool, activating edges are denoted using green colour and sharp arrow tips, inhibiting edges are denoted using red colour and flat arrow tips, and edges that might be neither activating nor inhibiting are denoted using grey colour.

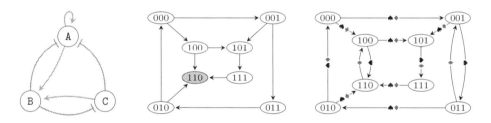

Fig. 1. Illustration of a (parametrised) BN and its state transition graph. (Color figure online)

Let us now consider an example of a BN with $\mathcal{V} = \{A, B, C\}$, the regulations R as denoted in Fig. 1 (left) and the update functions: $F_A = A \vee \neg B \vee \neg C$, $F_B = A \vee C$, $F_C = \neg B$. We can see that all regulations are observable and the colour (and shape) of the arrows respects the properties of activation and inhibition, e.g. (B, A) is an inhibition, because by increasing the value of B, we cannot increase the value of F_A.

The semantics of a Boolean network is given as a directed *state transition graph*. The state space of the graph is the set of all possible assignments of Boolean values to the variables, i.e. $\{0, 1\}^{\mathcal{V}}$. We consider the state of the Boolean network to evolve in an *asynchronous* manner, i.e. each variable is updated independently. We thus add a transition $s \rightarrow t$ if $s \neq t$ and if there exists a variable A such that $t(A) = F_A(s)$ and $t(X) = s(X)$ for all $X \in \mathcal{V} \setminus \{A\}$. We also use the notation $\to^*$ to denote the reflexive and transitive closure of $\to$, i.e. $s \to^* t$ means that the state t is reachable from the state s.

The semantics of the BN from our example is illustrated in Fig. 1 (middle). The states are represented as Boolean triples denoting the values assigned to the variables A, B, and C, respectively.

The long-term behaviour that we are interested in is captured by the notion of *attractors*. In discrete-state systems, attractors are represented by terminal strongly connected components (TSCCs) of the graph. A TSCC is a maximal set of states S such that for all $s, t \in S$, $s \to^* t$, and for all $s \in S$, $s \to t$ implies $t \in S$.

To classify the attractors of a given BN, we consider three primary kinds of long-term behaviour:

– *stability* ($\odot$) We say that an attractor is stable, if it consists of a single state, in which the network stays forever.
– *oscillation* ($\circlearrowleft$) We consider an attractor to be oscillating if it is a single cycle of states. The size of such cyclic attractor is often referred to as its *period*.
– *disorder* ($\rightleftarrows$) Finally, an attractor is said to be disordered if it is neither stable nor oscillating. This means that although the network will stay in the attractor forever, it will behave somewhat unpredictably due to nondeterminism.

The long-term behaviour of a BN is then characterised by a multi-set over the universe of the three behaviours $\{\odot, \circlearrowleft, \rightleftarrows\}$. We call such multi-set a *behaviour class* and we denote the set of all possible behaviour classes $\mathfrak{C}$. In our example, the BN has only one attractor, and this attractor is stable; it consists of the single state 110, see Fig. 1 (middle).

To deal with the fact that the update function family $\mathcal{F}$ might not be fully known, we extend the Boolean network with a set of *logical parameters* which determine the exact behaviour of each update function. These parameters have the form of uninterpreted Boolean functions, which can be used as part of the update functions' description.

Formally, we assume a finite set of *parameter names* $\mathfrak{P}$, whose elements we denote by P, Q, ...; we assume that every $P \in \mathfrak{P}$ has an associated arity a_P meaning that P is an a_P-ary uninterpreted function over Boolean values. Note that nullary uninterpreted functions are also allowed and can be seen as simply Boolean parameters. We call an interpretation that assigns to each $P \in \mathfrak{P}$ an a_P-ary Boolean function a *parametrisation*. We usually work with a subset of parametrisations, called the *valid* parametrisations and denoted by P.

A *parametrised Boolean network* consists of a set of variables $\mathcal{V}$, a set of regulations $R \subseteq \mathcal{V} \times \mathcal{V}$ as in the non-parametrised case, a set of parameter names $\mathfrak{P}$, its associated set of valid parametrisations P, and a family of *parametrised update functions* $\mathfrak{F} = \{\widehat{F}_A \mid A \in \mathcal{V}\}$. Each $\widehat{F}_A$ is written as a Boolean expression that may contain the uninterpreted functions of $\mathfrak{P}$.

Let us now modify the previous example so that we view the BN from Fig. 1 (left) as a parametrised one with the following update functions: $\widehat{F}_A = A \vee \neg B \vee \neg C$, $\widehat{F}_B = P(A, C)$, $\widehat{F}_C = \neg B$, where P is a parameter name with arity 2. The set of valid parametrisations is constrained symbolically using the description of activations and inhibitions in Fig. 1 (left). In this case, there are only two possible parametrisations p_1 (denoted by ♠) and p_2 (denoted by ♦). The parametrisation p_1 assigns to P the function $(x, y) \mapsto x \vee y$, while p_2 assigns to P the function $(x, y) \mapsto x \wedge y$. Note that other assignments would violate the description, namely that both (A, B) and (C, B) are observable and activating.

By fixing a concrete parametrisation $p \in P$, we can interpret all the parameter names and thus transform the parametrised update functions into non-parametrised ones, obtaining a (non-parametrised) BN, called the *p-instantiation* of the parametrised BN. We then generalise the definition of attractors to parametrised BNs, saying that a set of states S is an *attractor in parametrisation* $p \in P$ if S is an attractor in the p-instantiation.

The asynchronous semantics of a parametrised BN can be described using an *edge-coloured* state transition graph. The transitions of this graph are assigned a set of so-called *colours*—in our case, the colours correspond exactly to the parametrisations. The states are given as in the non-parametrised case. We then say that $s \to t$ if there exists a parametrisation p such that $s \to t$ in the p-instantiation. The set of colours of $s \to t$ is the set of all such parametrisations. In our example, the graph is depicted in Fig. 1 (right; the edges are annotated with ♠, ♦, or both).

Problem Formulation. We now formulate the problem of *attractor bifurcation analysis of parametrised BN* as follows: Given a parametrised BN with a set of valid parametrisations P, compute the *bifurcation function* $\mathcal{A} : P \to \mathfrak{C}$ that assigns to each parametrisation p the behaviour class of the p-instantiation of the given parametrised BN.

In our example, the function $\mathcal{A}$ maps p_1 (♠) to $\{\odot\}$ (one stable attractor $\{110\}$) and p_2 (♦) to $\{\circlearrowleft\}$ (one oscillating attractor $\{100, 101, 111, 110\}$).

3   Attractor Bifurcation Analysis with AEON

The workflow of our approach, as implemented in the tool, is illustrated in Fig. 2. As an input, we take a parametrised BN including a graphical description of the regulations. The tool computes its asynchronous semantics as a symbolic edge-coloured graph represented using BDDs [8]. This is then used as an input to a parallel TSCC detecting algorithm based on [1], which extracts the attractors on the fly. Each attractor is classified as one of the three above-mentioned types and this information is used to incrementally build the bifurcation function $\mathcal{A}$, also represented symbolically using BDDs. More details about the algorithm as well as the classification procedure can be found in [4].

The bifurcation function induces a partitioning of the parameter space in which two parametrisations are equivalent if their p-instantiations have the same behaviour class. This partitioning is presented to the user as a list of behaviour classes together with the cardinality of the respective parameter space partitions, see Fig. 3. The user can select one of these classes and obtain a *witness BN*,

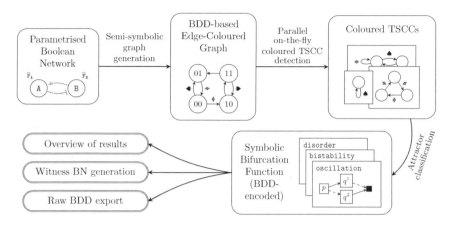

Fig. 2. The workflow of the AEON tool.

i.e. a p-instantiation of the parametrised BN where p is one of the corresponding parametrisations. Finally, the tool also provides the whole bifurcation function encoded as BDDs—this output can be used for post-processing by further tools.

4   Implementation

The tool architecture consists of two components as seen in Fig. 4: the *compute engine*, and a web-based, user-facing GUI application (*the client*). The engine is responsible for the actual computation and acts as a web server to which the client establishes a connection. Using web-based GUI enables portability across different platforms, and the separation of the user interface from the compute engine enables the user to run the computation remotely on high-performance hardware.

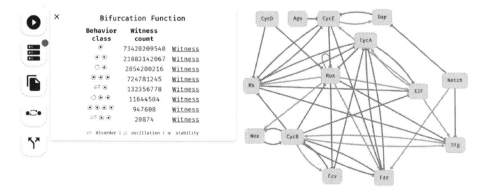

Fig. 3. Screenshot of the tool displaying a parametrised BN together with the bifurcation analysis results.

One of the responsibilities of the client is to provide a user friendly, multi-platform editor of parametrised BNs, since no popular BN editors currently support parameters. Architecturally, the client consists of several modules:

- `Live Model`: In-memory representation of the currently displayed model.
- `Compute Engine Connection` maintains the communication between the client and the compute engine.
- `Network Editor`: An interactive drag-and-drop editor for drawing the structure of the BN (variables, regulations). The implementation is based on the popular Cytoscape [19] library for graph visualisation and manipulation.
- `Parametrised BN Editor`: The update functions can be modified in a separate parametrised BN editor tab. This module is also responsible for basic integrity checks and static analysis of the BN, some of which is asynchronously deferred to the compute engine.
- `Import/Export` facilitates serialisation and transfer of the BNs to other tools. We currently provide a compact text-based format specifically designed for AEON and a universally adopted XML-based SBML level 3 qual standard [9].

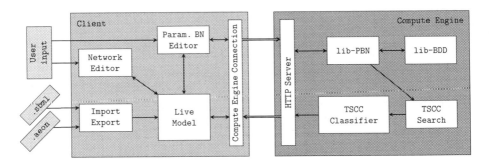

Fig. 4. Overview of the tool architecture showing the main components of the GUI client and the compute engine. Arrows represent the general flow of information between individual components.

The compute engine is written entirely in Rust to ensure fast and reliable operation (as well as easy portability). The functionality of the engine is split into separate libraries to allow later reuse:

- `lib-BDD`: Our own robust, thread-safe, scalable Rust-based implementation of BDDs.
- `lib-PBN`: A general purpose library for working with parametrised BNs. It provides serialisation to and from the AEON text format as well as SBML. Most importantly, it provides a parameter encoder that maps sets of parametrisations of the parametrised BN to BDDs. Using this encoder, the library implements an on-the-fly generation of the edge-coloured state transition graph corresponding to the asynchronous semantics of the given parametrised BN.

- TSCC Search algorithm implements the component search algorithm as presented in [1]. The algorithm uses parallel reachability procedures as well as asynchronous processing of independent parts of the state space to fully utilise available CPUs and thus speed up the computation. The algorithm is extended with appropriate cancellation points so that the user can stop the computation when needed.
- TSCC Classifier classifies and stores information about the discovered components. Specifically, for each non-empty behaviour class, we store a BDD representation of the parametrisations that result in this type of behaviour.

Aside from the general overview of the tool, we would like to highlight two additional aspects of AEON:

On-the-Fly Results: The attractors are discovered gradually. At any time during the computation the user may inspect the partial result, i.e. the bifurcation function computed so far. Although this is not the final outcome, such partial information can still prove useful, e.g. if unexpected attractor behaviour is found and the update functions of the model need to be adjusted.

SBML with Parameters: In our implementation, when dealing with fully instantiated networks, we always output valid SBML. Unfortunately, the current SBML standard does not allow parameters or uninterpreted functions inside the update function terms. In fact, the update functions in SBML are represented using MathML[1] which in general allows arbitrary mathematical expressions, but its use in SBML is restricted. To export parametrised BNs, we intentionally disregard the restriction and our tool produces MathML formulae with parameters. Note that existing SBML implementations can be easily extended to also support parametrised BNs, since they already contain MathML parsers.

Both the client[2] and the compute engine[3] are released as open source under the MIT License. Furthermore, an online version of the client is available at https://biodivine.fi.muni.cz/aeon/, including links to pre-built binaries of the computation engine for all major OSes.

5   Evaluation

We evaluated the efficiency and applicability of AEON tool on a set of real biological models taken from the GINsim model database [10], ranging from small toy examples to large real world models. The experiments were performed on a 32-core AMD Ryzen workstation with 64 GB of memory. All tested models are available in AEON source code repository (see footnote 3) as benchmark models.

---

[1] https://www.w3.org/TR/MathML3/.

[2] https://github.com/sybila/biodivine-aeon-client.

[3] https://github.com/sybila/biodivine-aeon-server.

The results are reported in Table 1. In general, the results show that the combination of symbolic representation of parametrisations and shared-memory parallel exploration of the state space allowed us to handle realistic BNs with large parameter spaces and non-trivial number of attractor bifurcations in reasonable time. Finally, let us note that the findings provided by AEON are in line with known properties of these biological models and even have a potential to provide new insights on the modelled biological processes.

Table 1. The evaluation results. Number of classes refers to the number of distinct behaviour classes discovered by the algorithm. The times in the form `minutes:seconds` refer to total runtime on 1 and two 32 CPU cores respectively.

Model name	State space size	Param. space size	No. of classes	Time (1cpu)	Time (32cpu)
Asymmetric Cell Division	2^5	$\sim 2^{18}$	11	0:05.62	0:03.39
Budding Yeast (Orlando)	2^9	$\sim 2^{18}$	6	0:35.22	0:02.93
TCR Signalisation	2^{10}	$\sim 2^{14}$	17	0:26.61	0:04.42
Drosophila Cell Cycle	2^{14}	$\sim 2^{36}$	8	27:48.1	1:42.28
Fission Yeast Cell Cycle	2^{10}	$\sim 2^{31}$	201	25:20.9	4:00.29
Mammalian Cell Cycle	2^{10}	$\sim 2^{44}$	176	38:39.6	8:02.14
Budding Yeast (Irons)	2^{18}	$\sim 2^{26}$	7	Timeout	52:28.1

In particular, in the case of the *TCR Signalisation* model, the authors have shown in [26] that their non-parametrised model produces seven possible stable states and one non-trivial attractor. By using AEON, we were able to confirm their findings as well as analyse a fully parametrised version of the model, finding sixteen other possible behaviours. Interestingly, in this model, all discovered seventeen behaviour classes consist of exactly eight attractors.

For the *Budding Yeast (Orlando)* model [16], the authors state that for several different parametrisations, the model always reaches a stable state (based on simulation). Our analysis performed with AEON has confirmed that the original instantiation of the model has indeed a single stable attractor. Moreover, we have found that in the fully parametrised version of the model, almost ninety thousand instantiations have a single stable attractor. Additionally, we have also found there is almost an equal number of instantiations producing disordered attractors and also several oscillating attractors. AEON is capable to generate witnesses for all of these situations thus opening the biological questions targeting the existence of the corresponding phenotypes in nature.

The *Fission Yeast Cell Cycle* model [15] is known to contain one primary stable attractor as well as eleven artificial attractors. It is known that various multi-valued modifications of the original model exist that remove these artificial stable attractors from the model while preserving the only single stable attractor [16]. By parametrising the model adequately and applying our method using AEON, we have discovered that a large portion of the parameter space of the model also produces a single stable attractor.

References

1. Barnat, J., et al.: Detecting attractors in biological models with uncertain parameters. In: Feret, J., Koeppl, H. (eds.) CMSB 2017. LNCS, vol. 10545, pp. 40–56. Springer, Cham (2017). https://doi.org/10.1007/978-3-319-67471-1_3
2. Baudin, A., Paul, S., Su, C., Pang, J.: Controlling large Boolean networks with single-step perturbations. Bioinformatics **35**(14), i558–i567 (2019)
3. Beneš, N., Brim, L., Demko, M., Pastva, S., Šafránek, D.: A model checking approach to discrete bifurcation analysis. In: Fitzgerald, J., Heitmeyer, C., Gnesi, S., Philippou, A. (eds.) FM 2016. LNCS, vol. 9995, pp. 85–101. Springer, Cham (2016). https://doi.org/10.1007/978-3-319-48989-6_6
4. Beneš, N., Brim, L., Pastva, S., Poláček, J., Šafránek, D.: Formal analysis of qualitative long-term behaviour in parametrised Boolean networks. In: Ait-Ameur, Y., Qin, S. (eds.) ICFEM 2019. LNCS, vol. 11852, pp. 353–369. Springer, Cham (2019). https://doi.org/10.1007/978-3-030-32409-4_22
5. Beneš, N., Brim, L., Pastva, S., Šafránek, D.: Parallel parameter synthesis algorithm for hybrid CTL. Sci. Comput. Program. **185**, 102321 (2020)
6. Benque, D., et al.: BMA: visual tool for modeling and analyzing biological networks. In: Madhusudan, P., Seshia, S.A. (eds.) CAV 2012. LNCS, vol. 7358, pp. 686–692. Springer, Heidelberg (2012). https://doi.org/10.1007/978-3-642-31424-7_50
7. Berntenis, N., Ebeling, M.: Detection of attractors of large boolean networks via exhaustive enumeration of appropriate subspaces of the state space. BMC Bioinformatics **14**, 361 (2013)
8. Bryant, R.E.: Graph-based algorithms for Boolean function manipulation. IEEE Trans. Comput. **35**(8), 677–691 (1986)
9. Chaouiya, C., et al.: SBML qualitative models: a model representation format and infrastructure to foster interactions between qualitative modelling formalisms and tools. BMC Syst. Biol. **7**(1), 135 (2013)
10. Chaouiya, C., Naldi, A., Thieffry, D.: Logical modelling of gene regulatory networks with GINsim. In: van Helden, J., Toussaint, A., Thieffry, D. (eds.) Bacterial Molecular Networks. Methods in Molecular Biology, vol. 804, pp. 463–479. Springer, New York (2012). https://doi.org/10.1007/978-1-61779-361-5_23
11. Chatain, T., Haar, S., Paulevé, L.: Boolean networks: beyond generalized asynchronicity. In: Baetens, J.M., Kutrib, M. (eds.) AUTOMATA 2018. LNCS, vol. 10875, pp. 29–42. Springer, Cham (2018). https://doi.org/10.1007/978-3-319-92675-9_3
12. Cheng, D., Qi, H., Li, Z.: Analysis and Control of Boolean Networks. CCE. Springer, London (2011). https://doi.org/10.1007/978-0-85729-097-7

13. Choi, M., Shi, J., Jung, S.H., Chen, X., Cho, K.H.: Attractor landscape analysis reveals feedback loops in the p53 network that control the cellular response to DNA damage. Sci. Signal. **5**(251), ra83 (2012)
14. Cimatti, A., et al.: NuSMV 2: an opensource tool for symbolic model checking. In: Brinksma, E., Larsen, K.G. (eds.) CAV 2002. LNCS, vol. 2404, pp. 359–364. Springer, Heidelberg (2002). https://doi.org/10.1007/3-540-45657-0_29
15. Davidich, M.I., Bornholdt, S.: Boolean network model predicts cell cycle sequence of fission yeast. PloS ONE **3**, e1672 (2008)
16. Fauré, A., Thieffry, D.: Logical modelling of cell cycle control in eukaryotes: a comparative study. Mol. BioSyst. **5**(12), 1569–1581 (2009)
17. Feillet, C., et al.: Phase locking and multiple oscillating attractors for the coupled mammalian clock and cell cycle. Proc. Natl. Acad. Sci. **111**(27), 9828–9833 (2014)
18. Fisher, J., Köksal, A.S., Piterman, N., Woodhouse, S.: Synthesising executable gene regulatory networks from single-cell gene expression data. In: Kroening, D., Păsăreanu, C.S. (eds.) CAV 2015. LNCS, vol. 9206, pp. 544–560. Springer, Cham (2015). https://doi.org/10.1007/978-3-319-21690-4_38
19. Franz, M., Lopes, C.T., Huck, G., Dong, Y., Sumer, O., Bader, G.D.: Cytoscape.js: a graph theory library for visualisation and analysis. Bioinformatics **32**(2), 309–311 (2016)
20. Giacobbe, M., Guet, C.C., Gupta, A., Henzinger, T.A., Paixão, T., Petrov, T.: Model checking the evolution of gene regulatory networks. Acta Informatica **54**(8), 765–787 (2016). https://doi.org/10.1007/s00236-016-0278-x
21. Graf, T., Enver, T.: Forcing cells to change lineages. Nature **7273**(462), 587–594 (2009)
22. Hartmann, A., Ravichandran, S., del Sol, A.: Modeling cellular differentiation and reprogramming with gene regulatory networks. In: Cahan, P. (ed.) Computational Stem Cell Biology. MMB, vol. 1975, pp. 37–51. Springer, New York (2019). https://doi.org/10.1007/978-1-4939-9224-9_2
23. Helikar, T., et al.: The cell collective: toward an open and collaborative approach to systems biology. BMC Syst. Biol. **6**(1), 96 (2012)
24. Kauffman, S.A.: Metabolic stability and epigenesis in randomly constructed genetic nets. J. Theor. Biol. **22**(3), 437–467 (1969)
25. Klamt, S., Saez-Rodriguez, J., Gilles, E.D.: Structural and functional analysis of cellular networks with CellNetAnalyzer. BMC Syst. Biol. **1**(1), 2 (2007)
26. Klamt, S., Saez-Rodriguez, J., Lindquist, J.A., Simeoni, L., Gilles, E.D.: A methodology for the structural and functional analysis of signaling and regulatory networks. BMC Bioinformatics **7**(1), 56 (2006)
27. Klarner, H., Streck, A., Siebert, H.: PyBoolNet: a Python package for the generation, analysis and visualization of Boolean networks. Bioinformatics **33**(5), 770–772 (2016)
28. Kolčák, J., Šafránek, D., Haar, S., Paulevé, L.: Parameter space abstraction and unfolding semantics of discrete regulatory networks. Theor. Comput. Sci. **765**, 120–144 (2019)
29. Le Novère, N.: Quantitative and logic modelling of molecular and gene networks. Nat. Rev. Genet. **16**, 146–158 (2015)
30. Mizera, A., Pang, J., Su, C., Yuan, Q.: ASSA-PBN: a toolbox for probabilistic Boolean networks. IEEE/ACM Trans. Comput. Biol. Bioinf. **15**(4), 1203–1216 (2018)
31. Müssel, C., Hopfensitz, M., Kestler, H.A.: BoolNet-an R package for generation, reconstruction and analysis of Boolean networks. Bioinformatics **26**(10), 1378–1380 (2010)

32. de Cavalcante, H.L.D.S., Gauthier, D.J., Socolar, J.E.S., Zhang, R.: On the origin of chaos in autonomous Boolean networks. Philos. Trans. R. Soc. A Math. Phys. Eng. Sci. **368**, 495–513 (2010)
33. Schwab, J.D., Kestler, H.A.: Automatic screening for perturbations in Boolean networks. Front. Physiol. **9**, 431 (2018)
34. Shah, O.S., et al.: ATLANTIS - attractor landscape analysis toolbox for cell fate discovery and reprogramming. Sci. Rep. **8**(1), 3554 (2018)
35. Streck, A., Thobe, K., Siebert, H.: Comparative statistical analysis of qualitative parametrization sets. In: Abate, A., Šafránek, D. (eds.) HSB 2015. LNCS, vol. 9271, pp. 20–34. Springer, Cham (2015). https://doi.org/10.1007/978-3-319-26916-0_2
36. Su, C., Paul, S., Pang, J.: Controlling large Boolean networks with temporary and permanent perturbations. In: ter Beek, M.H., McIver, A., Oliveira, J.N. (eds.) FM 2019. LNCS, vol. 11800, pp. 707–724. Springer, Cham (2019). https://doi.org/10.1007/978-3-030-30942-8_41
37. Thomas, R.: Boolean formalization of genetic control circuits. J. Theor. Biol. **42**(3), 563–585 (1973)
38. Waddington, C.H.: Towards a theoretical biology. Nature **218**, 525–527 (1968)
39. Wolfram, S.: Cellular automata as models of complexity. Nature **311**, 419–424 (1984)
40. Zou, Y.M.: Boolean networks with multiexpressions and parameters. IEEE/ACM Trans. Comput. Biol. Bioinf. **10**, 584–592 (2013)

A Novel Approach for Solving the BMI Problem in Barrier Certificates Generation

Xin Chen[1], Chao Peng[2(✉)], Wang Lin[3(✉)], Zhengfeng Yang[2(✉)],
Yifang Zhang[1], and Xuandong Li[1]

[1] State Key Laboratory for Novel Software Technology, Nanjing University,
Nanjing, China
{chenxin,zhangyifan,lxd}@nju.edu.cn
[2] Shanghai Key Lab of Trustworthy Computing, East China Normal University,
Shanghai, China
{cpeng,zfyang}@sei.ecnu.edu.cn
[3] School of Information Science and Technology, Zhejiang Sci-Tech University,
Hangzhou, China
linwang@zstu.edu.cn

Abstract. Barrier certificates generation is widely used in verifying safety properties of hybrid systems because of the relatively low computational complexity it costs. Under sum of squares (SOS) relaxation, the problem of barrier certificate generation is equivalent to that of solving a bilinear matrix inequality (BMI) with a particular type. The paper reveals the special feature of the problem, and adopts it to build a novel computational method. The proposed method introduces a sequential iterative scheme that is able to find analytical solutions, rather than the nonlinear solving procedure to produce numerical solutions used by general BMI solvers and thus is more efficient than them. In addition, different from popular LMI solving based methods, it does not make the verification conditions more conservative, and thus reduces the risk of missing feasible solutions. Benefitting from these two appealing features, it can produce barrier certificates not amenable to existing methods, which is supported by a complexity analysis as well as the experiment on some benchmarks.

Keywords: Formal verification · Hybrid systems · Barrier certificates · Bilinear matrix inequalities

This work was supported by the National Key Research and Development Program of China under Grant No. 2017YFA0700604, the National Natural Science Foundation of China under Grant 61772203, 61751210, 61632015, Scientific and Technological Innovation 2030 Major Projects under Grant 2018AAA0100902, the Shanghai Natural Science Foundation, China under Grant 17ZR1408300, Zhejiang Provincial Natural Science Foundation of China under Grant LY20F020020.

S. K. Lahiri and C. Wang (Eds.): CAV 2020, LNCS 12224, pp. 582–603, 2020.
https://doi.org/10.1007/978-3-030-53288-8_29

1   Introduction

Cyber-physical systems (CPS) consists of tightly coupled physical components such as electrical, mechanical, hydraulic, and biological components and software systems. They are deeply involved in many safety-critical systems, for example, high confidence medical devices, traffic control and safety systems, advanced automotive systems and critical infrastructure control systems. Safety verification helps to ensure them not to behave dangerously.

Hybrid systems are popular models used in the verification of Cyber-physical systems, for its ability to describe interacting discrete transitions and continuous dynamics [18]. Safety verification contributes to checking safety properties by determining whether a system can evolve to some states violating desired safety properties when it starts at some initial conditions. A successful verification of a hybrid system can raise our confidence in its corresponding Cyber-physical system.

For Cyber-physical systems with real time constraints, fast verification is a vital requirement. For example, a online verification module in a monitoring system should return the result before the deadline is reached. The paper aims at fast verification of hybrid systems to satisfy the requirement of fast verification of Cyber-physical systems.

Intuitively, safety verification of hybrid systems can be performed by computing the reachable set. Reachable set computation based approaches explicitly computes either exact or approximate reachable sets corresponding to the dynamics in the model, and then compares them with unsafe regions. It has been successfully adopted in verifying behaviors of a system within a finite horizon. However, due to their intrinsic computational difficulty, approaches of this kind can hardly scale up to complex non-linear systems.

Many research efforts have been devoted to barrier certificate generation. A barrier certificate is a function, of which the zero level set separates the unsafe region from all reachable states of a system. It requires all system trajectories starting from some initial conditions fall into one side of the barrier certificate while the unsafe region resides on the other. As the existence of a barrier certificate implies that the unsafe region is not reachable, the safety verification problem can be transformed into the problem of barrier certificate generation. Compared with reachable set computation [31], barrier certificate generation requires much less computation, since the unsafe region leads to seeking a barrier certificate. Especially, it behaves very well when a safety property concerns infinite time horizon [21, 34].

Barrier certificate generation is a computation intensive task. A set of verification conditions corresponding to a specific type of barrier certificates is given at first. Then they are encoded into some constraints on state variables and unknown coefficients of barrier certificates of a specific type. Finally, those unknown coefficients are determined by solving the constraints [27]. Thus, how to encode verification conditions and solve them in an effective way is a critical and challenging problem in barrier certificate based verification.

Acting as the barrier between reachable states and the unsafe region, a barrier certificate should always evaluate to be nonnegative or negative accordingly in spite of what type it is. To achieve this, the most popular computational method utilizes the theory of Putinar's Positivstellensatz to derive a *sum of squares* (SOS) program of the barrier certificate, which results in a *bilinear matrix inequality* (BMI) solving problem belonging to the class of NP-hard problems [20,21]. An effective and efficient BMI solver is a prerequisite for success in exploiting SOS relaxation based methods.

The general BMI problem can be solved by the commercial BMI solver PENBMI [14] at the cost of a very high computational complexity, where the (exterior) penalty and (interior) barrier method incorporates with the augmented Lagrangian method. To make it more tractable, the convex SOS relaxation based methods become popular. They transform the BMI problem (non-convex) to a *linear matrix inequality* (LMI) problem (convex) by fixing some multipliers and then solve it quickly via convex optimization such as semidefinite programming (SDP). Unfortunately, the removal of non-convexity may yield too conservative verification conditions so that the solution to the original BMI problem is invisible to the derived LMI problem.

The paper focuses on quickly solving the BMI problem derived from SOS relaxation by directly attacking the problem without relaxing it to a LMI one. Taking advantage of the special feature of the problem, that is all bilinear terms are cross ones between different parameter vectors, a sequential iterative scheme is proposed. It treats the non-convex BMI problem directly so as to avoid the loss of precision accompanied with non-convexity removing. Meanwhile, it provides much lower computational complexity than the PENBMI solver. Hence, the proposed method spends much less time in computation and has the potential to find solutions beyond the reach of existing methods.

To be specific, a feasible solution to the BMI problem can be found by a dual augmented Lagrangian iterative framework. At each iteration, the minimization over the four sets of primal variables is divided into four sequential minimization problems with respect to one set of primal variables by fixing the other three sets. On the theoretical side, we show that our method returns the feasible solution in cubic time, while the PENBMI solver in quartic time. We have developed a prototyping tool implementing the proposed method and compared it with the PENBMI solver and the LMI solver: SOSTOOLS [22] over a set of benchmarks gathered from the literature. The experiment shows that our tool is more effective than them and provides a much lower computational complexity than the PENBMI solver.

The paper is organized as follows. Section 2 describes the connection between safety verification and barrier certificate generation. Section 3 addresses how to transform the problem of barrier certificate generation into a BMI solving problem. In Sect. 4, a sequential iterative scheme is presented followed by a complexity analysis. Section 5 contains detailed examples illustrating the use of our method as well as the experiment on benchmarks. We compare with related works in Sect. 6 before concluding in Sect. 7.

2   Preliminaries

Notations. Let $\mathbb{R}$ be the field of real number. $\mathbb{R}[\mathbf{x}]$ denotes the polynomial ring with coefficients in $\mathbb{R}$ over variables $\mathbf{x} = [x_1, x_2, \cdots, x_n]^T$. Let $\Sigma[\mathbf{x}] \subset \mathbb{R}[\mathbf{x}]$ be the space of SOS polynomials. S^n denotes the set of $n \times n$ symmetric matrices, and the notation $B \succeq 0$ means that the matrix $B \in S^n$ is positive semidefinite. $\langle A, B \rangle$ denotes the inner product between A and B.

A continuous dynamical system is modeled by a finite number of first-order ordinary differential equations

$$\dot{\mathbf{x}} = \mathbf{f}(\mathbf{x}), \tag{1}$$

where $\dot{\mathbf{x}}$ denotes the derivative of $\mathbf{x}$ with respect to the time variable t, and $\mathbf{f}(\mathbf{x})$ is called vector field $\mathbf{f}(\mathbf{x}) = [f_1(\mathbf{x}), \cdots, f_n(\mathbf{x})]^T$ defined on an open set $\Psi \subseteq \mathbb{R}^n$. We assume that $\mathbf{f}$ satisfies the local Lipschitz condition, which ensures that given $\mathbf{x} = \mathbf{x}_0$, there exists a time $T > 0$ and a unique function $\tau : [0, T) \mapsto \mathbb{R}^n$ such that $\tau(0) = \mathbf{x}_0$. And $\mathbf{x}(t)$ is called a solution of (1) that starts at a certain initial state $\mathbf{x}_0$, that is, $\mathbf{x}(0) = \mathbf{x}_0$. Namely, $\mathbf{x}(t)$ is also called a trajectory of (1) from $\mathbf{x}_0$.

Definition 1 (Continuous System). *A continuous system over* $\mathbf{x}$ *consists of a tuple* $\mathbf{S} : \langle \Theta, \mathbf{f}, \Psi \rangle$*, wherein* $\Theta \subseteq \mathbb{R}^n$ *is a set of initial states,* $\mathbf{f}$ *is a vector field over the domain* $\Psi \subseteq \mathbb{R}^n$*.*

A hybrid system is a system which exhibits mixed discrete-continuous behaviors. A popular model for representing hybrid systems is hybrid automata [1], which combine finite state automata modeling the discrete dynamics, and differential equations modeling the continuous dynamics.

Definition 2 (Hybrid Automata). *A hybrid automaton is a tuple* $\mathbf{H} : \langle L, X, F, \Psi, E, \Xi, \Delta, \Theta, \ell_0 \rangle$*, where*

- *L, a finite set of locations (or models);*
- *$X \subseteq \mathbb{R}^n$ is the continuous state space. The hybrid state space of the system is defined by $\mathcal{X} = L \times X$ and a state is defined by $(\ell, \mathbf{x}) \in \mathcal{X}$;*
- *$F : L \rightarrow (\mathbb{R}^n \rightarrow \mathbb{R}^n)$, assigns to each location $\ell \in L$ a locally Lipschitz continuous vector field $\mathbf{f}_\ell$;*
- *Ψ assigns to each location $\ell \in L$ a location condition (location invariant) $\Psi(\ell) \subseteq \mathbb{R}^n$;*
- *$E \subseteq L \times L$ is a finite set of discrete transitions;*
- *Ξ assigns to each transition $e \in E$ a switching guard $\Xi_e \subseteq \mathbb{R}^n$;*
- *Δ assigns to each transition $e \in E$ a reset function $\Delta_e : \mathbb{R}^n \rightarrow \mathbb{R}^n$;*
- *$\Theta \subseteq \mathbb{R}^n$, an initial continuous state set;*
- *$\ell_0 \in L$, the initial location. The initial state space of the system is defined by $\ell_0 \times \Theta$.*

Trajectories of hybrid systems combine continuous flows and discrete transitions. Concretely, a trajectory of $\mathbf{H}$ is an infinite sequence of states $\sigma = \{s_0, s_1, s_2, \cdots\}$ such that

- **[Initiation]** $s_0 = (\ell_0, \mathbf{x}_0)$, with $\mathbf{x}_0 \in \Theta$;
  Furthermore, for each pair of consecutive state $(s_i, s_{i+1}) \in \sigma$ with $s_i = (\ell_i, \mathbf{x}_i)$ and $s_{i+1} = (\ell_{i+1}, \mathbf{x}_{i+1})$ satisfies the following one of the two *consecution* conditions:
- **[Discrete Consecution]** $e = (\ell_i, \ell_{i+1}) \in E$, $\mathbf{x}_i \in \Xi_e$ and $x_{i+1} = \Delta_e(\mathbf{x}_i)$;
- **[Continuous Consecution]** $\ell_i = \ell_{i+1}$, and there exists a time interval $\delta > 0$ such that the solution $\mathbf{x}(\mathbf{x}_i; t)$ to $\dot{\mathbf{x}} = \mathbf{f}_{\ell_i}$ evolves from $\mathbf{x}_i$ to $\mathbf{x}_{i+1}$, while satisfying the location invariant $\Psi(\ell_i)$. Formally, $\mathbf{x}(\mathbf{x}_i, \delta) = \mathbf{x}_{i+1}$ and $\forall t \in [0, \delta], \mathbf{x}(\mathbf{x}_i, t) \in \Psi(\ell_i)$.

If Σ is the set of all possible trajectories of $\mathbf{H}$, the reachable set is defined by $R = \{s | \exists \varsigma \in \Sigma : s \in \varsigma\}$, i.e., R contains all states that are elements of at least one trajectory ς.

In this paper, we focus on semi-algebraic hybrid systems, that is, the corresponding vector fields are polynomials and the sets $\Theta, \Psi(\ell), \Xi_e, \Delta_e$ in $\mathbf{H}$ are semi-algebraic, represented by polynomial equations and inequalities. The semi-algebraic sets Θ, $\Psi(\ell)$, Ξ_e, and Δ_e in Definition 2 are represented as follows:

$$
\begin{cases}
\Theta := \{\mathbf{x} \in \mathbb{R}^n \,|\, \theta(\mathbf{x}) \geq 0\}, \\
\Psi(\ell) := \{\mathbf{x} \in \mathbb{R}^n \,|\, \psi_\ell(\mathbf{x}) \geq 0\}, \\
\Xi_e := \{\mathbf{x} \in \mathbb{R}^n \,|\, \rho_e(\mathbf{x}) \geq 0\}, \\
\Delta_e := \{\mathbf{x}' \in \mathbb{R}^n \,|\, \delta_e(\mathbf{x}') \geq 0\},
\end{cases}
$$

where $\ell \in L$, $e \in E$, $\theta(\mathbf{x})$, $\psi_\ell(\mathbf{x})$, $\rho_e(\mathbf{x})$, and $\delta_e(\mathbf{x}')$ are vectors of polynomials, and the inequalities are satisfied entry-wise. Suppose that X_u assigns to each location $\ell \in L$ an unsafe region $X_u(\ell)$, defined by

$$
X_u(\ell) := \{\mathbf{x} \in \mathbb{R}^n \,|\, \zeta_\ell(\mathbf{x}) \geq 0\},
$$

where ζ_ℓ is a vector of polynomials. The safety specification is described over the trace of state $(\ell, \mathbf{x})$ w.r.t. unsafe regions $X_u(\ell)$.

Definition 3 (Safety). *Given a hybrid system* $\mathbf{H} : \langle L, X, F, \Psi, E, \Xi, \Delta, \Theta, \ell_0 \rangle$ *and unsafe regions* $X_u(\ell)$, *the safety property holds if there exist no trajectories of* $\mathbf{H}$ *starting from the initial set* $\ell_0 \times \Theta$, *can evolve to any state specified by* $X_u(\ell)$, *i.e.,* $\forall \ell \in L \,\forall \sigma \in \Sigma . s \in \sigma \models s \notin X_u(\ell)$.

For safety verification of hybrid systems, the notion of barrier certificates [21] plays an important role. A barrier certificate maps all the states in the reachable set R to non-negative reals and all the states in the unsafe region to negative reals, thus can be employed to prove safety of hybrid systems. However, the exact reachable set R is usually intractable for most hybrid systems. In [21], a sufficient inductive condition for barrier certificates is defined as follows.

Definition 4 (Barrier Certificate). *A barrier certificate of hybrid system* $\mathbf{H}$ *for safety w.r.t. unsafe regions* $X_u(\ell)$ *is a set of real functions* $\{B_\ell(\mathbf{x})\}$ *such that, for all* $\ell \in L$ *and* $e = (\ell, \ell') \in E$, *the following conditions hold:*

$$\begin{cases} \forall \mathbf{x} \in \Theta : B_{\ell_0}(\mathbf{x}) \geq 0, \\ \forall \mathbf{x} \in \Psi(\ell) : B_\ell(\mathbf{x}) = 0 \models \left\langle \frac{\partial B_\ell}{\partial \mathbf{x}}(\mathbf{x}), \mathbf{f}_\ell(\mathbf{x}) \right\rangle > 0, \\ \forall \mathbf{x} \in \Xi_e, \forall \mathbf{x}' \in \Delta_e(\mathbf{x}) : B_\ell(\mathbf{x}) \geq 0 \models B_{\ell'}(\mathbf{x}') \geq 0, \\ \forall \mathbf{x} \in X_u(\ell) : B_\ell(\mathbf{x}) < 0. \end{cases} \quad (2)$$

Note that $\left\langle \frac{\partial B_\ell}{\partial \mathbf{x}}(\mathbf{x}), \mathbf{f}_\ell(\mathbf{x}) \right\rangle$ is the Lie derivative of $B_\ell(\mathbf{x})$ with respect to the vector field $\mathbf{f}_\ell(\mathbf{x})$.

3   Transfer to BMI

The problem of generating barrier certificates in Definition 4 is an infinite-dimensional problem. In order to make it amenable to polynomial optimization, the barrier certificate $\{B_\ell(\mathbf{x})\}$ should be restricted to a set of polynomials with a priori degree bound. Putinar's Positivstellensatz provides a powerful representation for polynomial positivity on semi-algebraic sets, which helps to transform the problem of barrier certificate generation into solving a semidefinite programming via SOS relaxation.

Arising from the second and third conditions of Definition 4, where the parameters of $\{B_\ell(\mathbf{x})\}$ appear on the antecedent sides, the associated SOS representations using Putinar's Positvstellensatz form non-convex BMI constraints, yielded from the polynomial products between the barrier certificate and its polynomial multipliers.

In what follows, the procedure for transforming barrier certificate generation into BMI solving is recapped in detail. Firstly, SOS relaxation is applied to encode the entailment checking in condition (2) as an SOS program. In fact, all the conditions of Definition 4 can be expressed as a unified type, say, a polynomial is nonnegative (positive) on a semi-algebraic set, which can be characterized by Putinar's Positivstellensatz.

Let $\mathbb{K}$ be a basic semi-algebraic set defined by:

$$\mathbb{K} = \{\mathbf{x} \in \mathbb{R}^n \mid g_1(\mathbf{x}) \geq 0, \ldots, g_s(\mathbf{x}) \geq 0\}, \quad (3)$$

where $g_j \in \mathbb{R}[\mathbf{x}], 1 \leq j \leq s$. Given the finite family $\mathbf{g} = \{g_1(\mathbf{x}), \ldots, g_s(\mathbf{x})\}$, the polynomial set defined by

$$M(\mathbf{g}) =:= \left\{ \sigma_0 + \sum_{i=1}^{s} \sigma_i g_i \mid \sigma_i \in \Sigma[\mathbf{x}], 0 \leq i \leq s \right\}$$

is called the quadratic module generated by $\mathbf{g}$.

Theorem 1. *[Putinar's Positivstellensatz] Let $\mathbb{K} \subset \mathbb{R}[\mathbf{x}]$ be as in (3). Assume that the quadratic module $M(\mathbf{g})$ is archimedean, namely, there exists $u(\mathbf{x}) \in M(\mathbf{g})$ such that the set $\{\mathbf{x} \in \mathbb{R}^n | u(\mathbf{x}) \geq 0\}$ is compact. If $f(\mathbf{x})$ is strictly positive on $\mathbb{K}$, then $f(\mathbf{x})$ can be represented as*

$$f(\mathbf{x}) = \sigma_0(\mathbf{x}) + \sum_{i=1}^{s} \sigma_i(\mathbf{x}) g_i(\mathbf{x}), \quad (4)$$

where $\sigma_i \in \Sigma[\mathbf{x}], 0 \leq i \leq s$.

Following Theorem 1, the existence of the representation (4) provides a sufficient and necessary condition of polynomial positivity on a semi-algebraic set $\mathbb{K}$ [23]. Although the number of auxiliary polynomials in the representation (4) is only one more than the number of polynomials that define $\mathbb{K}$, the degree bound for $\sigma_i(\mathbf{x})$ is exponential with n and $\deg(\mathbf{f})$. From a computational point of view, the method for finding the above representation has some degree of conservativeness, say, by fixing a priori much smaller degree bound D for $\sigma_i(\mathbf{x})$. Thus, a sufficient condition for the nonnegativity of the given polynomial $f(\mathbf{x})$ on the semi-algebraic set $\mathbb{K}$ is provided as

$$f(\mathbf{x}) = \sigma_0(\mathbf{x}) + \sum_{i=1}^{s} \sigma_i(\mathbf{x})g_i, \tag{5}$$

with $\deg(\sigma_i) \leq D, \sigma_i \in \Sigma[\mathbf{x}], 1 \leq i \leq s$. The representation (5) ensures that a polynomial is nonnegative on a given semi-algebraic set. At this point, all conditions in Definition 4 can be derived as a unified type, i.e., polynomial nonnegativity on a semi-algebraic set. The representation (5) is used to characterize the conditions of barrier certificate generation, for they are more tractable.

Theorem 2. *Let the semi-algebraic hybrid system* $\mathbf{H}$ *and the unsafe regions* $X_u(\ell)$ *be defined as the above. Let D be a positive integer. Suppose there exist polynomials* $\{B_\ell(\mathbf{x})\}$ *and* $\{\nu_\ell(\mathbf{x})\}$ *with* $\deg(\nu_\ell) \leq D$, *positive numbers $\epsilon_{\ell,1}$ and $\epsilon_{\ell,2}$, and vectors of sums of squares* $\sigma(\mathbf{x}), \lambda_{e,i}(\mathbf{x}), \gamma_e(\mathbf{x}), \eta_e(\mathbf{x}), \phi_\ell(\mathbf{x}), \mu_\ell(\mathbf{x})$ *with the degree bound D, such that the following expressions:*

$$
\begin{aligned}
&B_{\ell_0}(\mathbf{x}) - \sigma(\mathbf{x})\theta(\mathbf{x}) \\
&B_{\ell'}(\mathbf{x}') - \lambda_e(\mathbf{x})\rho_e(\mathbf{x}) - \gamma_e(\mathbf{x}')\delta_e(\mathbf{x}') - \eta_e(\mathbf{x})B_\ell(\mathbf{x}) \\
&\left\langle \tfrac{\partial B_\ell}{\partial \mathbf{x}}(\mathbf{x}), \mathbf{f}_\ell(\mathbf{x}) \right\rangle - \phi_\ell(\mathbf{x})\psi_\ell(\mathbf{x}) - \nu_\ell(\mathbf{x})B_\ell(\mathbf{x}) - \epsilon_{\ell,1} \\
&-B_\ell(\mathbf{x}) - \mu_\ell(\mathbf{x})\zeta_\ell(\mathbf{x}) - \epsilon_{\ell,2}
\end{aligned}
\tag{6}
$$

are SOSes for each $\ell \in L$ and $e \in E$. Then $\{B_\ell(\mathbf{x})\}$ satisfies the conditions in Definition 4, and therefore guarantees the safety of $\mathbf{H}$.

Remark that a polynomial $f(\mathbf{x})$ with $\deg(f) = 2d$ is a sum of squares if and only if there exists a real symmetric and positive semidefinite matrix Q, called as the Gram matrix, such that $f(\mathbf{x}) = \mathbf{v}_d(\mathbf{x})^T Q \mathbf{v}_d(\mathbf{x})$, where $\mathbf{v}_d(\mathbf{x})$ is the vector consisting of all the monomials of degree less than or equal to d. In view of the conditions (6) in Theorem 2, the problem of generating the barrier certificates requires introducing the auxiliary (Gram matrices) variables. In fact, the decision variables in the SOS program (6) are the coefficients of all the unknown polynomials in (6), such as $B_\ell(\mathbf{x}), \sigma(\mathbf{x}), \lambda_e(\mathbf{x})$ and the associated Gram matrices. The polynomial products, i.e., $B_\ell(\mathbf{x})\eta_e(\mathbf{x})$ and $B_\ell(\mathbf{x})\nu_\ell(\mathbf{x})$, derive some quadratic terms of the products of these unknown coefficients, which occur in the second and third constraints of (6). As a consequence, the problem for generating barrier certificates in Theorem 2 derives a non-convex BMI problem. We now show the transformation by a simple example.

Example 1. Consider the system $\dot{x} = -x$ with location invariant $\Psi = \{x \in \mathbb{R} : x^2 - 1 \leq 0\}$. Suppose the barrier certificate $B(x)$ with $\deg(B) = 1$, we predetermine its template as $B(x) = u_0 + u_1 x$ with $u_0, u_1 \in \mathbb{R}$ and $u_1 \neq 0$. For simplicity, here we consider the second condition in Definition 4, that is, to find $B(x)$ which satisfies

$$\forall x \in \Psi : B(x) = 0 \models \frac{\partial B}{\partial x} \cdot (-x) \geq 0.$$

Following the SOS relaxation in (6), we need to find $B(x)$ such that

$$\phi_0(x) := \frac{\partial B}{\partial x} \cdot (-x) - \phi_1(x) \cdot (1 - x^2) - \phi_2(x) \cdot B(x) - \epsilon \qquad (7)$$

and $\phi_1(x)$ are SOSes, $\phi_2(x) \in \mathbb{R}[x]$, $\epsilon \in \mathbb{R}_{>0}$. We assume that $\phi_1 = u_2$ and $\phi_2 = v$, with $u_2 \in \mathbb{R}_{\geq 0}$ and $v \in \mathbb{R}$. Then (7) yields $\phi_0(x) = u_2 x^2 - (u_1 v + u_1)x - u_0 v - u_2 - \epsilon$, and its Gram matrix representation $\phi_0(x) = \mathbf{v}_1(x)^T Q \mathbf{v}_1(x)$, where

$$Q = \begin{bmatrix} u_2 & -\frac{1}{2}u_1 v - \frac{1}{2}u_1 \\ -\frac{1}{2}u_1 v - \frac{1}{2}u_1 & -u_0 v - u_2 - \epsilon \end{bmatrix} \text{ and } \mathbf{v}_1(x) = \begin{bmatrix} x \\ 1 \end{bmatrix}.$$

Since $\phi_0(x)$ and $\phi_1(x)$ must be SOSes, we have $Q \succeq 0$ and $u_2 \geq 0$, which is equivalent to

$$\mathcal{B}(u_0, u_1, u_2, v) = \begin{bmatrix} u_2 & 0 & 0 \\ 0 & u_2 & -\frac{1}{2}u_1 v - \frac{1}{2}u_1 \\ 0 & -\frac{1}{2}u_1 v - \frac{1}{2}u_1 & -u_0 v - u_2 - \epsilon \end{bmatrix} \succeq 0.$$

Therefore, the requirement that $\phi_0(x)$ and $\phi_1(x)$ are SOSes is translated into the BMI constraint of the form

$$\mathcal{B} = B_{0,0} + \sum_{i=0}^{2} u_i B_{i,0} + v B_{0,1} + \sum_{i=0}^{2} u_i v B_{i,1} \succeq 0, \qquad (8)$$

where all $B_{i,j} \in S^3$ are constant matrices.   □

As illustrated in Example 1, the problem of generating barrier certificates satisfying condition (6) can be transformed into a BMI problem of the form

Find $\mathbf{u} \in \mathbb{R}^p$, $\mathbf{v} \in \mathbb{R}^q$

$$\text{s.t. } \mathcal{B}(\mathbf{u}, \mathbf{v}) = B_{0,0} + \sum_{i=1}^{p} u_i B_{i,0} + \sum_{j=1}^{q} v_j B_{0,j} + \sum_{i=1}^{p}\sum_{j=1}^{q} u_i v_j B_{ij} \succeq 0, \qquad (9)$$

where all $B_{i,j} \in S^t$ are constant matrices, $\mathbf{u} = [u_1, \ldots, u_p]^T$, $\mathbf{v} = [v_1, \ldots, v_q]^T$ are parameter coefficients of the unknown polynomials occurring in the original SOS program. Essentially, the BMI problem (9) is NP-hard. To simplify the problem considerably, the canonical approach is to swap $\mathbf{v}$, corresponding to the polynomial multipliers $\eta_e(\mathbf{x})$ and $\nu_e(\mathbf{x})$, with the fixed vector. This strategy can reduce the BMI constraint into the associated LMI one. Unfortunately, the resulting LMI problem is considerably more conservative than the original BMI one. To be specific, the fixed $\eta_e(\mathbf{x})$ and $\nu_\ell(\mathbf{x})$ may result in too conservative verification conditions that rule out barrier certificates satisfy the non-convex conditions but not the stronger convex conditions.

By investigating (9), we can find a crucial feature of $\mathcal{B}(\mathbf{u}, \mathbf{v})$, that is, all cross terms between parameters of $\mathbf{u}$ and $\mathbf{v}$ are of the form $u_i\, v_j$. The feature motivates us to design a more efficient approach for the specific type of BMI problems.

4   A Sequential Iterative Scheme for Solving BMI Problems

The conventional approaches for solving the BMI problem typically employ the augmented Lagrangian iterative framework, wherein each iteration involves two optimization problems for primal and dual variables. Due to the existence of nonlinear terms (quartic terms) in the associated Lagrangian function, the analytical solutions to the first problem do not exist. The iterative-based nonlinear solving procedure is introduced to obtain the numerical solutions which results in a time-consuming computing process.

Observing the BMI problem (9), we can see that all nonlinear terms are the cross terms between $\mathbf{u}$ and $\mathbf{v}$. As a result, the associated dual augmented Lagrangian function is *quartic* for all variables, but is *quadratic* with respect to each single variable. Having this crucial feature, if we choose one variable as the independent variable and assign the others with fixed values, we may get the problem of minimizing the quadratic function. According to the first-order optimality condition, given a quadratic function $f(\mathbf{x})$, the sufficient and necessary condition that $\tilde{\mathbf{x}}$ is a minimizer of $f(\mathbf{x})$ requires that the gradient of $f(\mathbf{x})$ to be zero at $\tilde{\mathbf{x}}$, i.e., $\nabla f(\tilde{\mathbf{x}}) = 0$. As a consequence, the analytical solutions to our studied optimization problem can be easily formulated, since the gradient of the associated Lagrangian function is affine.

The analytical optimal solutions can be obtained by calling simple matrix computation, and thus are much more efficient than numerical solutions whose computation relies on complicated nonlinear optimization methods. The computational advantage is further demonstrated by a complexity analysis of our scheme against the existing BMI solving algorithm that combines the (exterior) penalty and (interior) barrier method with the augmented Lagrangian method, presented later in this section.

To utilize the computational advantage of analytical optimal solutions, for the first optimization problem (w.r.t primal variables) involved in each iteration of the augmented Lagrangian iterative framework, rather than using the usual joint minimization for all primal variables, we introduce a sequential minimization scheme, that is, dividing it into four sequential sub-optimization problems over one independent variable while keeping the others fixed. More concretely, the sub-optimization problem with one single primal variable is constructed by replacing the other variables with their optimal solutions obtained from the current iteration (if available) or the last iteration.

This section first introduces an iterative scheme to solve the BMI problem and then illustrates how to derive analytical solutions to the sub-problems in each iteration followed by a complexity analysis against the existing algorithm.

4.1   An Iterative Scheme

We start by presenting a straightforward reformulation of the BMI problem (9) as follows:

$$
\begin{cases}
\lambda^* = \min \lambda \\
\quad s.t.\ Z = \lambda \cdot I + \mathcal{B}(\mathbf{u}, \mathbf{v}) \\
\quad\quad Z \succeq 0.
\end{cases}
\tag{10}
$$

Clearly, there exists a feasible solution $(\mathbf{u}, \mathbf{v})$ to the BMI problem (9) if and only if the optimal value of problem (10) is non-positive, i.e., $\lambda^* \le 0$. We try to build an iterative scheme for dealing with the optimization problem (10).

The augmented Lagrangian function $\mathcal{L}$ associated with (10) is defined as:

$$
\mathcal{L}_\mu(\lambda, \mathbf{u}, \mathbf{v}, Z, U) = \lambda + \langle U, Z - \lambda I - \mathcal{B}(\mathbf{u}, \mathbf{v}) \rangle + \frac{1}{2\mu} \| Z - \lambda I - \mathcal{B}(\mathbf{u}, \mathbf{v}) \|_F^2, \tag{11}
$$

where $\mu > 0$, $\langle \cdot, \cdot \rangle$ means the inner product operator, and $\| \cdot \|_F$ denotes the Frobenius norm of a matrix. Let $U \in S^t$ be the Lagrangian multiplier associated with the equality constraint, the dual function is defined as

$$
g(U) = \inf_{(\lambda, \mathbf{u}, \mathbf{v}, Z)} \mathcal{L}_\mu(\lambda, \mathbf{u}, \mathbf{v}, Z, U),
$$

and the *Lagrange dual problem* associated with (10) is to maximize this dual function $g(U)$, i.e., $\max_U g(U)$. Clearly, the dual function yields lower bounds on the optimal value λ^* of the problem (10), that is, $g(U) \le \lambda^*$ for any U.

Applying the dual ascent [17] to the augment Lagrangian function yields the iterative scheme, consisting of the following updates

$$
\left.
\begin{aligned}
(\lambda^{k+1}, \mathbf{u}^{k+1}, \mathbf{v}^{k+1}, Z^{k+1}) &:= \operatorname*{argmin}_{\lambda, \mathbf{u}, \mathbf{v}, Z} \mathcal{L}_\mu(\lambda, \mathbf{u}, \mathbf{v}, Z, U^k), \\
s.t.\ \ Z &\succeq 0, \\
U^{k+1} &:= \operatorname*{argmax}_{U} \mathcal{L}_\mu(\lambda^{k+1}, \mathbf{u}^{k+1}, \mathbf{v}^{k+1}, Z^{k+1}, U),
\end{aligned}
\right\}
\tag{12}
$$

where the first step is the primal variables update, and the second step is the dual variable update.

The first step in (12) consists of quartic terms and is lack of analytical solution. Thus, it requires jointly minimizing $\mathcal{L}_\mu(\lambda, \mathbf{u}, \mathbf{v}, Z, U^k)$ with respect to $\lambda, \mathbf{u}, \mathbf{v}$ and Z, which can be directly solved by applying the iterative-based nonlinear optimization procedure at the cost of a high computational complexity. Instead of the usual joint minimization solving, we separate the minimization over the primal variables $\lambda, \mathbf{u}, \mathbf{v}, Z$ into four steps, that is, $\lambda, \mathbf{u}, \mathbf{v}$ and Z are updated in an alternating scheme, that is, minimizing $\mathcal{L}_\mu$ with respect to one primal variable given the others fixed. In detail, the sequential iterative scheme consists of the following new iterations:

$$\lambda^{k+1} \quad := \underset{\lambda}{\arg\min}\, \mathcal{L}_\mu(\lambda, \mathbf{u}^k, \mathbf{v}^k, Z^k, U^k), \tag{13}$$

$$\mathbf{u}^{k+1} \quad := \underset{\mathbf{u}}{\arg\min}\, \mathcal{L}_\mu(\lambda^{k+1}, \mathbf{u}, \mathbf{v}^k, Z^k, U^k), \tag{14}$$

$$\mathbf{v}^{k+1} \quad := \underset{\mathbf{v}}{\arg\min}\, \mathcal{L}_\mu(\lambda^{k+1}, \mathbf{u}^{k+1}, \mathbf{v}, Z^k, U^k), \tag{15}$$

$$Z^{k+1} := \underset{Z \succeq 0}{\arg\min}\, \mathcal{L}_\mu(\lambda^{k+1}, \mathbf{u}^{k+1}, \mathbf{v}^{k+1}, Z, U^k), \tag{16}$$

$$U^{k+1} := \underset{U}{\arg\max}\, \mathcal{L}_\mu(\lambda^{k+1}, \mathbf{u}^{k+1}, \mathbf{v}^{k+1}, Z^{k+1}, U). \tag{17}$$

The above iterative scheme introduces a sequential minimization that treats the four primal variables one by one. Benefited from the fact that the explicit formulae for the minimizer or maximizer (13–17) are available, the analytical solutions can be directly derived. Furthermore, as the computation of those analytical solutions involves only simple matrix computation, such as eigenvalue decomposition and matrix inverse, it will be very efficient.

4.2   Analytical Solutions for the Sequential Iteration

In this subsection, we focus on how to find analytical solutions to problems (13–17) in terms of the first-order optimality conditions.

Theorem 3. *The minimizer* λ^{k+1} *of (13),i.e.,*

$$\lambda^{k+1} := \underset{\lambda}{\arg\min}\, \mathcal{L}_\mu(\lambda, \mathbf{u}^k, \mathbf{v}^k, Z^k, U^k),$$

has the following analytical formula:

$$\lambda^{k+1} := \frac{1}{t}\sum_{i=1}^{t}(Z_{i,i}^k - \mathcal{B}_{i,i}(\mathbf{u}^k, \mathbf{v}^k)) + \frac{\mu}{t}\cdot(\mathrm{Tr}(U^k) - 1), \tag{18}$$

where $\mathrm{Tr}(U^k)$ *denotes the trace of* U^k.

Proof. The first-order optimality condition for (13) is

$$\nabla_\lambda \mathcal{L}_\mu = 1 - \mathrm{Tr}(U^k) + \frac{t}{\mu}\lambda - \frac{1}{\mu}\sum_{i=1}^{t}(Z_{i,i}^k - \mathcal{B}_{i,i}(\mathbf{u}^k, \mathbf{v}^k)) = 0.$$

It follows that the specified λ^{k+1} in (18) is the optimal solution of (13), which concludes the proof. $\qquad\square$

The first-order optimality condition resembling Theorem 3 can also be invoked to produce the corresponding analytical solutions to (14) and (15), respectively.

Theorem 4. Let $\mathbf{v}^k = [v_1^k, \ldots, v_q^k]^T \in \mathbb{R}^q$, and define $X^{[i]} = B_{i,0} + \sum_{\ell=1}^q v_\ell^k B_{i,\ell}$ for $0 \le i \le p$. Let $\mathbf{u}^{k+1}$ be the minimizer of (14). Then

$$\mathbf{u}^{k+1} := S^{-1} \cdot [r_1, \ldots, r_p]^T, \tag{19}$$

where $S = [s_{ij}] \in \mathbb{R}^{p \times p}$ with $s_{ij} = \frac{1}{\mu}\langle X^{[i]}, X^{[j]}\rangle$, and

$$r_i = \langle U^k + \frac{1}{\mu}(Z^k - \lambda^{k+1}I - X^{[0]}), X^{[i]}\rangle, 1 \le i \le p.$$

Proof. The first-order optimality condition for (14) is

$$\nabla_{\mathbf{u}}\mathcal{L}_\mu(\lambda^{k+1}, \mathbf{u}, \mathbf{v}^k, Z^k, U^k) = (\nabla_{\mathbf{u}_1}\mathcal{L}_\mu, \nabla_{\mathbf{u}_2}\mathcal{L}_\mu, \cdots, \nabla_{\mathbf{u}_p}\mathcal{L}_\mu)^T = 0,$$

and the i-th gradient function $\nabla_{\mathbf{u}_i}\mathcal{L}_\mu(\lambda^{k+1}, \mathbf{u}, \mathbf{v}^k, Z^k, U^k)$, $1 \le i \le p$ is

$$\langle U^k, -\sum_{\ell=1}^q v_\ell^k B_{i,\ell} - B_{i,0}\rangle + \frac{1}{\mu}\langle Z^k - \lambda^{k+1}I - \mathcal{B}(\mathbf{u}, \mathbf{v}^k), -\sum_{\ell=1}^q v_\ell^k B_{i,\ell} - B_{i,0}\rangle.$$

Then we have

$$\nabla_{\mathbf{u}_i}\mathcal{L}_\mu(\lambda^{k+1}, \mathbf{u}, \mathbf{v}^k, Z^k, U^K) = \langle U^k, -X^{[i]}\rangle + \frac{1}{\mu}\langle Z^k - \lambda^{k+1}I - \mathcal{B}(\mathbf{u}, \mathbf{v}^k), -X^{[i]}\rangle$$

for $i = 1 \ldots, p$.

Thus, $\nabla_{\mathbf{u}}\mathcal{L}_\mu(\lambda^{k+1}, \mathbf{u}, \mathbf{v}^k, Z^k, U^k) = 0$ yields (19), which proves the claim. $\square$

Theorem 5. Let $\mathbf{u}^{k+1} = [u_1^{k+1}, \ldots, u_p^{k+1}]^T \in \mathbb{R}^p$, and define $Y^{[j]} = B_{0,j} + \sum_{\ell=1}^p u_\ell^{k+1} B_{\ell,j}$, for $0 \le j \le q$. Let $\mathbf{v}^{k+1}$ be the minimizer of (15). Then

$$\mathbf{v}^{k+1} := T^{-1} \cdot [w_1, \ldots, w_q]^T, \tag{20}$$

where $T = [t_{ij}] \in \mathbb{R}^{q \times q}$ with $t_{ij} = \frac{1}{\mu}\langle Y^{[i]}, Y^{[j]}\rangle$, and

$$w_i = \langle U^k + \frac{1}{\mu}(Z^k - \lambda^{k+1}I - Y^{[0]}), Y^{[i]}\rangle, \quad 1 \le i \le q.$$

Proof. Similar to the proof of Theorem 4. $\square$

The theorems below demonstrate the analytical solutions to the Z-minimization and U-maximization, respectively.

Theorem 6. Let Z^{k+1} be the minimizer of (16), and U^{k+1} be the solution of (17). Denote by P^{k+1} the matrix $P^{k+1} := \lambda^{k+1}I + \mathcal{B}(\mathbf{u}^{k+1}, \mathbf{v}^{k+1}) - \mu U^k$. Suppose $P^{k+1} = Q\Sigma Q^T$ is a spectral decomposition, namely,

$$P^{k+1} = Q\Sigma Q^T = [Q_+ \ Q_\ddagger] \begin{bmatrix} \Sigma_+ & 0 \\ 0 & \Sigma_- \end{bmatrix} \begin{bmatrix} Q_+^T \\ Q_\ddagger^T \end{bmatrix},$$

where Σ_+ and $Q_\dagger$ are the nonnegative eigenvalues and the associated orthogonal eigenvectors, while Σ_- and $Q_\ddagger$ are the negative eigenvalues and the associated orthogonal eigenvectors. Then we have

$$Z^{k+1} := Q_\dagger \Sigma_+ Q_\dagger^T, \tag{21}$$

$$U^{k+1} := -\frac{1}{\mu} Q_\ddagger \Sigma_- Q_\ddagger^T. \tag{22}$$

Proof. The first-order optimality condition for (16) is

$$\nabla_Z \mathcal{L}_\mu(\lambda^{k+1}, \mathbf{u}^{k+1}, \mathbf{v}^{k+1}, Z, U^k) = 0. \tag{23}$$

In view of the terms of (23), the problem (16) is translated to

$$Z^{k+1} = \underset{Z \succeq 0}{\operatorname{argmin}} \| Z - \lambda^{k+1} I - \mathcal{B}(\mathbf{u}^{k+1}, \mathbf{v}^{k+1}) + \mu U^k \|_F^2, \tag{24}$$

which reads as

$$Z^{k+1} = \underset{Z \succeq 0}{\operatorname{argmin}} \| Z - P^{k+1} \|_F^2.$$

According to the spectral decomposition of P^{k+1}, the result (21) immediately follows.

From (17), we have

$$U^{k+1} = U^k + \frac{1}{\mu}(Z^{k+1} - \lambda^{k+1} I - \mathcal{B}(\mathbf{u}^{k+1}, \mathbf{v}^{k+1}))$$

$$= \frac{1}{\mu}(Z^{k+1} - P^{k+1}),$$

which yields the result (22). $\square$

4.3   Algorithm and Complexity Analysis

From the above observation in Sect. 4.1 and Sect. 4.2, the detailed procedure for the sequential iterative scheme is summarized in Algorithm 1.

Remark 1. At the beginning of Algorithm 1, $\mathbf{u}^0 \in \mathbb{R}^p$, $\mathbf{v}^0 \in \mathbb{R}^q$ are selected randomly, $Z^0 = M_0^\top \cdot M_0$ where $M_0 \in \mathbb{R}^t$ is chosen randomly, and heuristically $U^0 = \delta \cdot I_t$ with $\delta > 0$.

Remark 2. There are several options for the stopping criterion of the loop in Algorithm 1. That is, Algorithm 1 will stop and return the current result when one of the following cases occurs:

– $|\lambda^{k+1} - \lambda^k| \leq \epsilon$,
– $\| Z^{k+1} - Z^k \| \leq \epsilon$,

where ϵ is a given tolerance. A reasonable value for the stopping criterion might be $\epsilon = 10^{-6}$.

Algorithm 1: Sequential Iterative Scheme for solving a BMI (SISBMI)

Input: Problem (9); initial values $\mathbf{u}^0$, $\mathbf{v}^0$, Z^0 and U^0.
Output: A feasible solution $(\mathbf{u}^*, \mathbf{v}^*)$ of (9).

1 **while** *stopping criterion not met* **do**
2   Compute λ^{k+1} according to (18);
3   Compute $\mathbf{u}^{k+1}$ and $\mathbf{v}^{k+1}$ according to (19) and (20), respectively;
4      $\mathcal{B}^{k+1} \leftarrow \mathcal{B}(\mathbf{u}^{k+1}, \mathbf{v}^{k+1})$;
5   Get the minimal eigenvalue of $\mathcal{B}^{k+1}$, denoted by $\hat{\lambda}$;
6   **if** $\hat{\lambda} \geq 0$ **then**
7          $(\mathbf{u}^*, \mathbf{v}^*) \leftarrow (\mathbf{u}^{k+1}, \mathbf{v}^{k+1})$;
8   **return** $(\mathbf{u}^*, \mathbf{v}^*)$;
9   Compute Z^{k+1} according to (21);
10   Compute U^{k+1} according to (22).

Complexity Analysis

We analyze the complexity of Algorithm 1 and further compare it with the algorithm in PENBMI solver [14], which combines the (exterior) penalty and (interior) barrier method with the augmented Lagrangian method. The BMI problem we study corresponds to a nonconvex optimization problem with quartic terms. For the BMI problems of the special form, neither of the two algorithms can guarantee to converge. A complete complexity analysis is not available as the number of iterations is not predictable. Therefore, the computational complexity of one iteration becomes a safe baseline for performance evaluation. In this paper, we follow the same complexity analysis as that in [14], i.e. analyzing the complexity in one iteration.

Recall that the dimension of the matrix $\mathcal{B}(\mathbf{u}, \mathbf{v})$ in (9) is t, and the numbers of variables $\mathbf{u}$ and $\mathbf{v}$ are p and q, respectively. We see that each iteration in Algorithm 1 can be divided into five steps. Firstly, the step of updating λ costs $O(t)$ flops, which is carried out by $3t + 3$ adds. In the step of $\mathbf{u}$−update, the complexity is clearly dominated by the computation of the inverse of $A_{\mathbf{u}} \in \mathbb{R}^{p \times p}$, which costs $O(p^3)$ flops [5]. Analogously, $\mathbf{v}$−update can be done in $O(q^3)$ flops. In the step of Z−update, the critical issue is to compute the eigenvalue decomposition of matrix $V^{k+1} \in \mathbb{R}^{t \times t}$, at a cost of about $\frac{4}{3}t^3$ flops. So the step of Z−update requires $O(t^3)$ flops. Finally, the step of U−update requires about $O(t)$ flops by performing U^{k+1}.

Now, the complexity for the above steps in each iteration of Algorithm 1 is summarized as follows:

- Calculation of $\lambda \to O(t)$;
- Calculation of $\mathbf{u} \to O(p^3)$;
- Calculation of $\mathbf{v} \to O(q^3)$;
- Calculation of $Z \to O(t^3)$;
- Calculation of $U \to O(t)$.

The total cost of each iteration in Algorithm 1 is then $O(p^3 + q^3 + t^3)$, while the cost of the algorithm adopted in PENBMI is approximately $O((p + q)t^3 + (p + q)^2 t^2 + (p + q)^3)$, as shown in [14]. Assume that p, q and t are bounded by $T \in \mathbb{Z}$, i.e., $T = \max\{p, q, t\}$, the complexity of Algorithm 1 is approximately $O(T^3)$, whereas the complexity of PENBMI is approximately $O(T^4)$.

5   Experiments

In this section, we first show our method by verifying a nonlinear continuous system and then compare our Sequential Iterative Scheme tool: SISBMI solver with the other two solvers: PENBMI and SOSTOOLS.

Example 2. Consider the following nonlinear continuous system [28]

$$\begin{bmatrix} \dot{x}_1 \\ \dot{x}_2 \\ \dot{x}_3 \end{bmatrix} = \begin{bmatrix} 10(x_2 - x_1) \\ x_1(28 - x_3) - x_2 \\ x_1 x_2 - \frac{8}{3} x_3 \end{bmatrix}$$

with the location invariant

$$\Psi = \{\mathbf{x} \in \mathbb{R}^3 \mid -20 \le x_1, x_3 \le 20, -20 \le x_2 \le 0\}.$$

It is required to verify that all trajectories of the system starting from the initial set

$$\Theta = \{\mathbf{x} \in \mathbb{R}^3 \mid (x_1 + 14.5)^2 + (x_2 + 14.5)^2 + (x_3 - 12.5)^2 \le 16\}$$

will never enter the unsafe region

$$X_u = \{\mathbf{x} \in \mathbb{R}^3 \mid (x_1 + 16.5)^2 + (x_2 + 14.5)^2 + (x_3 - 2.5)^2 \le 38.44\}.$$

It suffices to find a barrier certificate $B(\mathbf{x})$, which satisfies all the conditions in Definition 3. Suppose that the degree of $B(\mathbf{x})$ is 4, and the degree bound $D = 6$. Firstly, we construct a bilinear SOS program (6), which is further transformed into a BMI problem of the form (9) where the dimension of $\mathcal{B}(\mathbf{u}, \mathbf{v})$ is 78, and the number of decision variables is 396. By applying our algorithm, we succeed to solve the BMI problem and obtain the following barrier certificate

$$B(\mathbf{x}) = \underbrace{-0.0020 x_1^4 - 0.0013 x_3^4 - 0.0131 x_1^2 x_3^2 - 0.0022 x_1 x_2 x_3^2 + \cdots + 0.0938 x_1 + 62.5702}_{28 \; terms}.$$

As shown in Fig. 1, the zero level set of the barrier certificate $B(\mathbf{x})$ (the steelblue surface) separates X_u (the red ball) from all trajectories starting from Θ (the green ball). Therefore, the safety of the above system is verified.

Alternatively, by applying the PENBMI solver to compute the solution of the problem (9), we cannot find barrier certificates with degree less than 6.   □

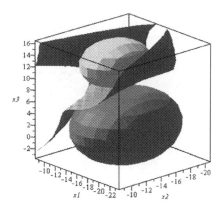

Fig. 1. Phase portrait of the system in Example 2. (Color figure online)

Example 3. Consider the following hybrid system [20] depicted in Fig. 2, where

$$\mathbf{f}_1 = \begin{bmatrix} -x_2 \\ -x_1 + x_3 \\ x_1 + (2x_2 + 3x_3)(1 + x_3^2) \end{bmatrix}, \quad \mathbf{f}_2 = \begin{bmatrix} -x_2 \\ -x_1 + x_3 \\ -x_1 - 2x_2 - 3x_3 \end{bmatrix}.$$

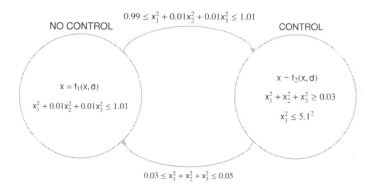

Fig. 2. The hybrid automata of the system in Example 3

The system starts in location ℓ_1 with the initial set

$$\Theta = \{\mathbf{x} \in \mathbb{R}^3 : x_1^2 + x_2^2 + x_3^2 \leq 0.01\}.$$

Our task is to verify that the system will never enter the unsafe set

$$X_u(\ell_2) = \{\mathbf{x} \in \mathbb{R}^3 : 5 < x_1 < 5.1\}.$$

Applying our SISBMI solver, we obtain the polynomial barrier certificate with degree 4:

$$B_{\ell_1}(\mathbf{x}) = \underbrace{0.0551x_1^4 + 0.0392x_2^4 + 0.0079x_3^4 + 0.0696x^2x_3^2 + \cdots - 1.1134x_1 + 2.701}_{35\ terms},$$

$$B_{\ell_2}(\mathbf{x}) = \underbrace{0.0273x_1{}^4 + 0.0541x_1^3x_2 - 1.098x_1x_2^2 - 0.521x_1x_2x_3 + \cdots - 2.725x_1 + 8.197}_{35\ terms}.$$

$\square$

Our SISBMI solver was implemented in Matlab (2018b), and was compared with two solvers PENBMI and SOSTOOLS over a set of benchmarks in the literature on barrier certificates generation. Among these benchmark examples, examples C1–C15 are semi-algebraic continuous systems and examples H1–H7 are semi-algebraic hybrid systems. The performance is reported in Table 1. All the experiments were performed on 2.6 GHz Intel i5 processor under Windows 10 with 8 GB RAM.

Table 1. Algorithm performance on benchmarks

ID	n	$|L|$	$d_{\mathbf{f}}$	BMI									LMI	
				t	N	SISBMI			PENBMI				SOSTOOLS	
						d_s	I_s	T_s	d_p	I_p	T_p		d_l	T_l
C1 from [33]	2	1	3	21	33	2	32	0.2189	2	24	0.9198		2	0.1949
C2 from [24]	2	1	1	30	58	4	73	0.5475	—				—	
C3 from [21]	2	1	3	21	39	2	29	0.2761	2	22	1.3353		—	
C4 from [30]	3	1	2	32	72	2	44	0.4126	2	23	1.8237		2	0.3245
C5 from [26]	3	1	3	32	72	2	47	0.4761	2	28	1.5435		2	0.3362
C6 from [3]	3	1	2	78	396	4	83	4.3598	—				—	
C7 from [28]	4	1	3	50	145	2	72	3.9577	2	28	21.0502		2	3.8658
C8 from [9]	3	1	2	32	72	—			2	40	2.4555		—	
C9 from [6]	4	1	2	31	86	—			2	42	4.6909		—	
C10 from [13]	7	1	2	73	394	2	112	10.7156	2	44	108.5615		2	7.2807
C11 from [13]	9	1	2	102	908	2	264	20.6856	2	30	272.4551		2	15.8167
C12 from [8]	12	1	1	70	123	2	108	3.2712	—				—	
H1 from [25]	2	2	2	38	65	2	61	0.4899	2	25	2.1499		2	0.2074
H2 from [36]	2	2	3	42	69	2	77	0.6331	2	24	2.2786		2	0.2265
H3 from [15]	2	2	2	75	138	2	115	3.7394	—				—	
H4 from [2]	2	3	1	42	89	1	70	0.5326	1	21	0.9968		2	0.1856
H5 from [1]	3	3	1	67	64	2	112	1.0864	—				—	
H6 from [7]	4	6	2	840	2736	2	616	48.0548	—				—	
H7 from [20]	3	2		3	170	899	4	219	18.7912	4	32	243.9832		—

In Table 1, n denotes the number of the system variables, and $|L|$ denotes the number of locations; d_f denotes the maximal degree of the polynomials in the vector fields; t is the dimension of the matrix $\mathcal{B}(\mathbf{u}, \mathbf{v})$, and N refers to the number of decision variables appearing in the BMI problem (9), namely, $\dim(\mathbf{u}) + \dim(\mathbf{v})$; d_s, d_p and d_l denote the degrees of the barrier certificates obtained via SISBMI, PENBMI and SOSTOOLS, respectively; I_s and I_p are the numbers of iterations used by SISBMI and PENBMI, respectively; T_s, T_p and T_l record the time spent by computation in seconds; the symbol—means that the solver was unable to return a feasible solution with the degree bound $\deg(B) \leq 6$.

Table 1 shows that for the 19 examples, our SISBMI solver can successfully handle 17 of them while the numbers of successful examples of PENBMI and SOSTOOLS are 13 and 9, respectively. Our SISBMI solver seems to provide the best solving capability. There are 10 examples that can be treated by BMI solvers (either SISBMI or PENBMI) unable to be solved by the LMI solver SOSTOOLS due to the more conservative conditions in the corresponding LMI problems. To evaluate the best performance of SOSTOOLS, we have tried some widely used multipliers [16, 20], such as $0, \pm 1, \pm(1 + x_1^2 + \cdots + x_n^2)$, as well as some polynomial multipliers with random coefficients and the prior degree bound that guarantee the degrees of the polynomials involved in the verification conditions (6) do not increase. Examples C8-C9 show the case where the solver PENBMI performs better than our SISBMI solver as a result of the fact that both SISBMI and PENBMI solvers only find local optimal solutions to the BMI problems.

The above analysis on effectiveness can also be used to support that our SISBMI solver is a necessary complement to the existing tools. As shown in Table 1, PENBMI solver can cover 13 examples. To solve the remaining 6 examples, it has to resort to the SISBMI solver.

Considering the efficiency, the solver SOSTOOLS performs the best for almost all the successful examples because of the much lower computational complexity for solving the relaxed LMI problems. The efficiency comparison between SISBMI and PENBMI solvers can be made by examining the ratio between the execution times of these two solvers in Table 1. For the 11 examples that are solved by both tools, on average, our SISBMI solver costs 3.4 times than PENBMI solver in the number of iterations while only costs 0.27 times than PENBMI solver in time. That is for all the successful examples, our SISBMI solver takes much less time than PENBMI solver even it spends more iterations, which complies with the complexity analysis of the underlying algorithms. Both the theoretical analysis and the experiments support that our SISBMI solver is more efficient than PENBMI solver.

6   Related Work

In theory, the problem of barrier certificate generation is a quantifier elimination problem. The verification conditions corresponding to a barrier certificate can be encoded into a set of constraints on state variables and coefficients where the unknown coefficients are existentially quantified and state variables are universally quantified. Hence, several symbolic computation approaches [11, 19, 29], such as cylindrical algebraic decomposition (CAD) or Grönber bases computation, have been directly applied to attack the associated quantifier elimination problems. However, due to the high computational complexity, they suffer from the scalability problem.

Due to the relatively low computational complexity, SOS relaxation based methods become popular. Rather than directly handling quantified constraints, they transform them to a non-convex bilinear matrix inequality. Z. Yang et al. [35] relied on the BMI solver PENBMI to compute exact polynomial barrier certificates. O. Bouissou et al. [3] applied interval analysis to handle the BMI problem derived from the dynamical systems whose initial and unsafe regions are restricted to the box form. G. Jessica et al. [10] presented an augmented Lagrangian framework for the special case of bilinear programs that arise from data flow constraints and correspond to the construction of numerical abstract domains aiming at safety verification.

To alleviate its computational intractability, a convex surrogate has been proposed that behaves fairly well. Specifically, once the multipliers are fixed, the BMI problem is further transformed into a LMI problem that can be quickly solved by convex optimization. S. Prajna et al. [20] had first put the idea forward. A. Sogokon et al. [34] employed the comparison principle associated with the convex verification conditions, to generate vector barrier certificates in safety verification.

Inspired by the fact that it is the non-convex feature of verification conditions prevents well-developed convex optimization to be directly applied, many convex but stronger verification conditions are studied. H. Kong et al. [16] proposed an exponential condition for semi-algebraic hybrid systems. Kapinski et al. [12] diagnosed convex verification conditions to Lyapunov-based barrier certificates. C. Sloth et al. [32] considered convex barrier certificates associated with compositional conditions for a group of interconnected hybrid systems. L. Dai et al. [4] studied how to balance the convexity of verification conditions with the expressiveness of barrier certificates. All these convex verification conditions are equivalent forms of LMI problems. They facilitate problem-solving at the risk of losing feasible solutions.

7   Conclusion

We have presented a sequential iterative scheme for solving the BMI problem derived from the barrier certificate generation of semi-algebraic hybrid systems. Taking advantage of the special feature of the bilinear terms, the proposed approach is more efficient than the existing BMI solver. Furthermore, compared with popular LMI solving based methods, the solving procedure does not make the verification condition more conservative, and thus reduces the risk of missing solutions. In virtue of the two appealing features, our approach can produce barrier certificates not amenable to existing methods, which is evidenced by a theoretical complexity analysis as well as the experiment on some benchmarks.

References

1. Alur, R., et al.: The algorithmic analysis of hybrid systems. Theoret. Comput. Sci. **138**(1), 3–34 (1995). https://doi.org/10.1016/0304-3975(94)00202-T
2. Alur, R., Dang, T., Ivančić, F.: Predicate abstraction for reachability analysis of hybrid systems. ACM Trans. Embedded Comput. Syst. (TECS) **5**(1), 152–199 (2006). https://doi.org/10.1145/1132357.1132363
3. Bouissou, O., Chapoutot, A., Djaballah, A., Kieffer, M.: Computation of parametric barrier functions for dynamical systems using interval analysis. In: Proceedings of the IEEE 53rd Annual Conference on Decision and Control (CDC), pp. 753–758. IEEE (2014). https://doi.org/10.1109/CDC.2014.7039472
4. Dai, L., Gan, T., Xia, B., Zhan, N.: Barrier certificates revisited. J. Symbol. Comput. **80**, 62–86 (2017). https://doi.org/10.1016/j.jsc.2016.07.010
5. Demmel, J.: Matrix computations. SIAM Rev. **28**(2), 252–255 (1986)
6. Ferragut, A., Gasull, A.: Seeking Darboux polynomials. Acta Applicandae Mathematicae **139**(1), 167–186 (2014). https://doi.org/10.1007/s10440-014-9974-0
7. Fisher, M.E.: A semiclosed-loop algorithm for the control of blood glucose levels in diabetics. IEEE Trans. Biomed. Eng. **38**(1), 57–61 (1991). https://doi.org/10.1109/10.68209
8. Gao, S.: Quadcopter model. https://github.com/dreal/benchmarks
9. Goubault, E., Jourdan, J.H., Putot, S., Sankaranarayanan, S.: Finding non-polynomial positive invariants and Lyapunov functions for polynomial systems through Darboux polynomials. In: Proceedings of the 2014 American Control Conference (ACC), pp. 3571–3578. IEEE (2014). https://doi.org/10.1109/ACC.2014.6859330
10. Gronski, J., Ben Sassi, M.-A., Becker, S., Sankaranarayanan, S.: Template polyhedra and bilinear optimization. Formal Methods Syst. Des. **54**(1), 27–63 (2018). https://doi.org/10.1007/s10703-018-0323-1
11. Gulwani, S., Tiwari, A.: Constraint-based approach for analysis of hybrid systems. In: Proceedings of the 20th International Conference on Computer Aided Verification (CAV), pp. 190–203 (2008). https://doi.org/10.1007/978-3-540-70545-1_18
12. Kapinski, J., Deshmukh, J.V., Sankaranarayanan, S., Aréchiga, N.: Simulation-guided Lyapunov analysis for hybrid dynamical systems. In: Proceedings of the Hybrid Systems: Computation and Control (HSCC), pp. 133–142. ACM (2014). https://doi.org/10.1145/2562059.2562139
13. Klipp, E., Herwig, R., Kowald, A., Wierling, C., Lehrach, H.: Systems Biology in Practice: Concepts, Implementation and Application. Wiley-Blackwell, Weinheim (2005)
14. Kočvara, M., Stingl, M.: PENNON: a code for convex nonlinear and semidefinite programming. Optim. Methods Softw. **18**(3), 317–333 (2003). https://doi.org/10.1080/1055678031000098773
15. Kong, H., Bogomolov, S., Schilling, C., Jiang, Y., Henzinger, T.A.: Safety verification of nonlinear hybrid systems based on invariant clusters. In: Proceedings of the 20th International Conference on Hybrid Systems: Computation and Control, pp. 163–172. ACM (2017). https://doi.org/10.1145/3049797.3049814
16. Kong, H., He, F., Song, X., Hung, W.N.N., Gu, M.: Exponential-condition-based barrier certificate generation for safety verification of hybrid systems. In: Sharygina, N., Veith, H. (eds.) CAV 2013. LNCS, vol. 8044, pp. 242–257. Springer, Heidelberg (2013). https://doi.org/10.1007/978-3-642-39799-8_17

17. Nocedal, J., Wright, S.: Numerical Optimization. Springer, Heidelberg (2006). https://doi.org/10.1007/978-0-387-40065-5
18. Platzer, A.: Virtual substitution & real arithmetic. Logical Foundations of Cyber-Physical Systems, pp. 607–628. Springer, Cham (2018). https://doi.org/10.1007/978-3-319-63588-0_21
19. Platzer, A., Clarke, E.M.: Computing differential invariants of hybrid systems as fixedpoints. Formal Methods Syst. Des. **35**(1), 98–120 (2009). https://doi.org/10.1007/s10703-009-0079-8
20. Prajna, S., Jadbabaie, A.: Safety verification of hybrid systems using barrier certificates. In: Alur, R., Pappas, G.J. (eds.) HSCC 2004. LNCS, vol. 2993, pp. 477–492. Springer, Heidelberg (2004). https://doi.org/10.1007/978-3-540-24743-2_32
21. Prajna, S., Jadbabaie, A., Pappas, G.J.: A framework for worst-case and stochastic safety verification using barrier certificates. IEEE Trans. Autom. Control **52**(8), 1415–1429 (2007). https://doi.org/10.1109/TAC.2007.902736
22. Prajna, S., Papachristodoulou, A., Parrilo, P.A.: SOSTOOLS: sum of squares optimization toolbox for MATLAB (2002). http://www.cds.caltech.edu/sostools
23. Putinar, M.: Positive polynomials on compact semi-algebraic sets. Indiana Univ. Math. J. **42**, 968–984 (1993)
24. Ratschan, S., She, Z.: Constraints for continuous reachability in the verification of hybrid systems. In: Calmet, J., Ida, T., Wang, D. (eds.) AISC 2006. LNCS (LNAI), vol. 4120, pp. 196–210. Springer, Heidelberg (2006). https://doi.org/10.1007/11856290_18
25. Ratschan, S., She, Z.: Safety verification of hybrid systems by constraint propagation-based abstraction refinement. ACM Trans. Embedded Comput. Syst. **6**(1), 573–589 (2007). https://doi.org/10.1145/1210268.1210276
26. Ratschan, S., She, Z.: Providing a basin of attraction to a target region of polynomial systems by computation of Lyapunov-like functions. SIAM J. Control Optim. **48**(7), 4377–4394 (2010). https://doi.org/10.1137/090749955
27. Roux, P., Voronin, Y.-L., Sankaranarayanan, S.: Validating numerical semidefinite programming solvers for polynomial invariants. Formal Methods Syst. Des. **53**(2), 286–312 (2017). https://doi.org/10.1007/s10703-017-0302-y
28. Sankaranarayanan, S., Chen, X., Abrahám, E.: Lyapunov function synthesis using Handelman representations. In: The 9th IFAC Symposium on Nonlinear Control Systems, pp. 576–581 (2013). https://doi.org/10.3182/20130904-3-FR-2041.00198
29. Sankaranarayanan, S., Sipma, H., Manna, Z.: Constructing invariants for hybrid systems. Formal Methods Syst. Des. **32**(1), 25–55 (2008). https://doi.org/10.1007/s10703-007-0046-1
30. Sassi, M.A.B., Sankaranarayanan, S.: Stability and stabilization of polynomial dynamical systems using bernstein polynomials. In: Proceedings of the 18th International Conference on Hybrid Systems: Computation and Control, HSCC 2015, Seattle, WA, USA, 14–16 April 2015, pp. 291–292 (2015). https://doi.org/10.1145/2728606.2728639
31. Sibai, H., Mitra, S.: State estimation of dynamical systems with unknown inputs: entropy and bit rates. In: Proceedings of the 21st International Conference on Hybrid Systems: Computation and Control, pp. 217–226 (2018). https://doi.org/10.1145/3178126.3178150
32. Sloth, C., Pappas, G.J., Wisniewski, R.: Compositional safety analysis using barrier certificates. In: Proceedings of the 15th ACM International Conference on Hybrid Systems: Computation and Control, pp. 15–24. ACM (2012). https://doi.org/10.1145/2185632.2185639

33. Sogokon, A., Ghorbal, K., Johnson, T.T.: Non-linear continuous systems for safety verification (benchmark proposal). In: Applied Verification for Continuous and Hybrid Systems Workshop (ARCH) (2016)
34. Sogokon, A., Ghorbal, K., Tan, Y.K., Platzer, A.: Vector barrier certificates and comparison systems. In: Proceedings of the 22nd International Symposium on Formal Methods, pp. 418–437 (2018). https://doi.org/10.1007/978-3-319-95582-7_25
35. Yang, Z., Lin, W., Wu, M.: Exact verification of hybrid systems based on bilinear SOS representation. ACM Trans. Embedded Comput. Syst. **14**(1), 1–19 (2015). https://doi.org/10.1145/2629424
36. Zeng, X., Lin, W., Yang, Z., Chen, X., Wang, L.: Darboux-type barrier certificates for safety verification of nonlinear hybrid systems. In: Proceedings of the 2016 International Conference on Embedded Software (EMSOFT), pp. 1–10 (2016). https://doi.org/10.1145/2968478.2968484

Reachability Analysis Using Message Passing over Tree Decompositions

Sriram Sankaranarayanan[✉]

University of Colorado, Boulder, CO, USA
srirams@colorado.edu

Abstract. In this paper, we study efficient approaches to reachability analysis for discrete-time nonlinear dynamical systems when the dependencies among the variables of the system have low treewidth. Reachability analysis over nonlinear dynamical systems asks if a given set of target states can be reached, starting from an initial set of states. This is solved by computing conservative over approximations of the reachable set using abstract domains to represent these approximations. However, most approaches must tradeoff the level of conservatism against the cost of performing analysis, especially when the number of system variables increases. This makes reachability analysis challenging for nonlinear systems with a large number of state variables. Our approach works by constructing a dependency graph among the variables of the system. The tree decomposition of this graph builds a tree wherein each node of the tree is labeled with subsets of the state variables of the system. Furthermore, the tree decomposition satisfies important structural properties. Using the tree decomposition, our approach abstracts a set of states of the high dimensional system into a tree of sets of lower dimensional projections of this state. We derive various properties of this abstract domain, including conditions under which the original high dimensional set can be fully recovered from its low dimensional projections. Next, we use ideas from message passing developed originally for belief propagation over Bayesian networks to perform reachability analysis over the full state space in an efficient manner. We illustrate our approach on some interesting nonlinear systems with low treewidth to demonstrate the advantages of our approach.

1 Introduction

Reachability analysis asks whether a target set of states is reachable over a finite or infinite time horizon, starting from an initial set for a dynamical system. This problem is fundamental to the verification of systems, and is known to be challenging for a wide variety of models. This includes cyber-physical systems, physical and biological processes. In this paper, we study reachability analysis algorithms for nonlinear, discrete-time dynamical systems. The key challenge in analyzing such systems arises from the difficulty of representing the reachable sets of these systems. As a result, we resort to over-approximations of reachable sets using tractable set representations such as intervals [16], ellipsoids,

S. K. Lahiri and C. Wang (Eds.): CAV 2020, LNCS 12224, pp. 604–628, 2020.
https://doi.org/10.1007/978-3-030-53288-8_30

polyhedra [19], and low degree semi-algebraic sets [2]. Whereas these representations are useful for reachability analysis, they also trade off the degree of overapproximation in representing various sets against the complexity of performing operations such as intersections, unions, projections and image computations over these sets. The theory of abstract interpretation allows us to design various abstract domains that serve as representations for sets of states in order explore these tradeoffs [17,18,34]. However, for nonlinear dynamical systems, these representations often become too conservative or too expensive as the number of state variables grow.

In this paper, we study reachability analysis using the idea of tree decompositions over the dependency graph of a dynamical system. Tree decompositions are a well-known idea from graph theory [37], used to study properties of various types of graphs. The treewidth of a graph is an intrinsic property of a graph that relates to how "far away" a given graph is from a tree. For instance, trees are defined to have a treewidth of 1. Many commonly occurring families of graphs such as *series-parallel graphs* have treewidth 2 and so on. Formally, a tree decomposition of a graph is a tree whose nodes are associated with subsets of vertices of the original graph along with some key conditions that will be described in Sect. 2. We use tree decompositions to build an abstract domain. The abstraction operation projects a set of states in the full system state space along each of the nodes of the tree, yielding various projections of this set. The concretization combines projections back into the high dimensional set. We study various properties of this abstract domain. First, we characterize abstract elements that can potentially be generated by projecting some concrete elements along the nodes of the tree (so called *canonical* elements, Definition 10). Next we characterize those sets which can be abstracted along the tree decomposition and reconstructed without any loss in information (tree decomposable sets, Definition 11). In this process, we also derive a *message passing* approach wherein nodes of the tree can exchange information to help refine sets of states in a sound manner. However, as we will demonstrate, the abstraction is "lossy" in general since projections of tree decomposable sets are not necessarily tree decomposable. We discuss some interesting ways in which precision can be regained by carefully analyzing this situation.

We combine these ideas together into an approach for reachability analysis of nonlinear systems using a grid domain that represents complex non convex sets as a union of fixed size cells using a gridding of the state-space. Although such a domain would be prohibitively expensive, we show that the tree decomposition abstract domain can drastically cut down on the complexity of computing reachable set overapproximations in this domain, yielding precise reachable set estimation for some nonlinear systems with low treewidth. We demonstrate our approach using a prototype implementation to show that for a restricted class of systems whose dependency graphs have low treewidth, our approach can be quite efficient and precise at the same time. Although some interesting systems have low treewidth property, it is easy to see that many systems will have treewidths that are too high for our approach. Our future work will consider how systems

S. Sankaranarayanan

whose dependency graphs do not have sufficiently low treewidth can still be tackled in a conservative manner using some ideas from this paper.

1.1   Related Work

As mentioned earlier, the concept of tree decompositions and treewidth originated in graph theory [37]. The concept of treewidth gained popularity when it was shown that many NP-complete problems on graphs such as graph coloring could be solved efficiently for graphs with small treewidths [5]. Courcelle showed that the problem of checking if a given graph satisfies a formula in the monadic second order logic of graphs can be solved in linear time on graphs with bounded treewidth [15]. Several NP-complete problems such as 3-coloring can be expressed in this logic. Tree decompositions are also used to solve inference problems over Bayesian networks leading to representations of the Bayesian networks such as junction trees that share many of the properties of a tree decomposition [29]. In fact, belief propagation over junction trees is performed by passing messages that marginalize the probability distributions at various nodes of the tree. This is analogous to the message passing approach described here.

Tree decomposition techniques have been applied to model checking problems over finite state systems. For instance, Obdržálek show that the μ-calculus model checking problem can be solved in linear time in the size of a finite-state system whose graph has a bounded treewidth [35]. However, as Ferrara et al. point out, requiring the state graph of a system to have a bounded treewidth is often restrictive [24]. Instead, they study concurrent finite state systems wherein the communication graph has a bounded tree width. However, they conclude that while it is more reasonable to assume that the communication graph has a bounded tree width, it does not confer much advantages to verification problems. For instance, they show that the unrolling of these systems over time potentially results in unbounded treewidth. In this paper, we consider a different approach wherein we study the treewidth of dependency graphs of the system. We find that many systems have small treewidth and exploit this property. At the same time, we note that some of the benchmarks studied have "sparse" dependency graphs but treewidths that are too large for our approach.

Tree decomposition techniques have also been studied in static analysis of programs. The control and data flow graphs of structured programs without goto-statements or exceptional control flow are known to have small treewidth that can be exploited to perform compiler optimizations such as register allocation quite efficiently [38]. Chatterjee et al. have shown how to exploit small treewidth property of the control flow graphs of procedures in programs to perform interprocedural dataflow analysis by modeling the execution of programs with procedures as recursive state machines [11]. However, this approach seems restricted to control dominated properties such as sequence of function calls. In a followup work, they study control and data flow analysis problems for concurrent systems, wherein each component has constant treewidth [10]. In contrast, our approach studies dynamical system and consider tree decompositions of the data dependency graph.

The use of message passing in this paper closely resembles past work by Gulwani and Jojic [27]. Therein, a program verification problem involving the verification pre/post and intermediate assertions in a program is solved by passing messages that can propagate information between assertions along program paths in a randomized fashion. The approach is shown to be similar to loopy belief propagation used in Bayesian inference. The key differences are (a) we use data dependencies and tree decompositions rather than control flow paths to pass information along; and (b) we formally prove properties of the message passing algorithm.

Our approach is conceptually related to a well-known idea of speeding up static analysis of large programs using "packing" of program variables [4,28]. This approach was used successfully in the Astreé static analyzer [3,4,21]. Therein, clusters of variables representing small sets of dependent local and global are extracted. The remaining program variables are abstracted away and the abstract interpretation process is carried out over just these variables. The usefulness of this approach has borne out in other abstract interpretation efforts, including Varvel [28]. The key idea in this paper can be seen as a formalization of the rather informal "clustering" approach using tree decompositions. We demonstrate theoretical properties as well as the ability to pass messages to improve the results of the abstract interpretation.

The use of the dependency graph structure to speed up reachability analysis approaches has been explored in the past for speeding up Hamilton-Jacobi-based approaches by Mo Chen et al. [12] as well as flowpipe based approaches by Xin Chen et al. [13]. Both approaches consider the directed dependency graph wherein x_i is connected to x_j if the former appears in the dynamical update equation of the latter variable. The approaches perform a strongly connected component (SCC) decomposition and analyze each SCC in a topological sorted order. However, this approach breaks as soon as the system has large SCCs, which is common. As a result, Xin Chen et al. show how SCCs can themselves be broken into numerous subsets at the cost of a more conservative solution. In contrast, the tree decomposition approach can be applied to exploit sparsity even when the entire dependency graph is a single SCC.

2 Preliminaries

In this section, we will describe the system model under analysis, the dependency graph structure and the basics of tree decompositions. Let $X : \{x_1, \ldots, x_n\}$ be a set of *system variables* and $\mathbf{x} : X \mapsto \mathbb{R}$ represent a valuation to these system variables. Let D be the domain of all valuations of X, that describes the *state space* of the system. For convenience let $\mathbf{x}_i$ denote $\mathbf{x}(x_i)$. Also, let $W : \{w_1, \ldots, w_m\}$ represent disturbance variables and $\mathbf{w} : W \mapsto \mathbb{R}$ represent a vector of $m \geq 0$ external disturbance inputs that take values in some compact disturbance space $\mathcal{W}$.

Definition 1 (Dynamical Model). *A model Π is a tuple $\langle X, W, D, \mathcal{W}, f, X_0, U \rangle$, wherein $X, W, D, \mathcal{W}$ are as defined above, f is an arithmetic expression* *over variables in X, W describing the dynamics, X_0 is a set of possible initial valuations (states) and U is a designated set of unsafe states.*

The dynamics are given by $\mathbf{x}(t + 1) = \mathsf{eval}(f, \mathbf{x}, \mathbf{w})$, wherein eval evaluates a given an expression f, a set of valuations to the system variables $\mathbf{x} \in D$ and disturbances $\mathbf{w} \in \mathcal{W}$, and returns a new set of valuations for each variable in X, denoted by $\mathbf{x}(t + 1)$.

For simplicity, we write $f(\mathbf{x}, \mathbf{w})$ to denote $\mathsf{eval}(f, \mathbf{x}, \mathbf{w})$ for a function expression f. A state of the system is a valuation $\mathbf{x} : X \mapsto \mathbb{R}$ such that $\mathbf{x} \in D$. Given a finite sequence of disturbance inputs $\mathbf{w}(0), \ldots, \mathbf{w}(T)$, for some $T \geq 0$ and $\mathbf{w}(i) \in \mathcal{W}$ for all $i \in [0, T]$, an execution of the system is a sequence of states $\mathbf{x}(0), \ldots, \mathbf{x}(T + 1)$, such that $\mathbf{x}(0) \in X_0$, $\mathbf{x}(t) \in D$ for $t \in [0, T + 1]$ and $\mathbf{x}(t+1) = f(\mathbf{x}(t), \mathbf{w}(t))$ for all $t \in [0, T]$. According to these semantics, the system may fail to have an execution for a given disturbance sequence $\mathbf{w}(t)$, $t \in [0, T]$ and initial state $\mathbf{x}(0)$ if for some state $\mathbf{x}(t)$, we have $f(\mathbf{x}(t), \mathbf{w}(t)) \notin D$.

A state $\mathbf{x}(t)$ is reachable (at time t) if there is an execution of the form $\mathbf{x}(0), \ldots, \mathbf{x}(t)$, satisfying the constraints above. We say that the unsafe state U is reachable iff some state $\mathbf{x} \in U$ is reachable. Furthermore, we say that U is reachable within a finite time horizon T, iff some state $\mathbf{x} \in U$ is reachable at time $t \in [0, T]$.

Example 1. Consider a nonlinear example of a dynamical model Π with state space $\mathbf{x} : (x_1, x_2, x_3)$ and $\mathbf{w} : (w_1)$. The dynamics can be written as parallel assignments to the state variables:

$$x_1 := x_1 + 0.25x_2 - 0.05x_1 sin(x_2), \quad x_2 := x_2 + w_1, \quad x_3 := x_3 - 0.2x_3x_2,$$

The assignments are all evaluated in parallel to update the current state $\mathbf{x}(t)$ to a new state $\mathbf{x}(t + 1)$. The domain D is $x_i \in [-3, 3]$ for $i = 1, 2, 3$ and the disturbance $w_1 \in [-0.1, 0.1]$. The initial set X_0 is $x_1 \in [-0.2, 0.2] \land x_2 \in [-0.3, 0] \land x_3 \in [0, 0.4]$.

We will now define the dependency (hyper)graph of the system Π. For convenience, we write the update function (expression) f of a system Π in terms of individual updates $(f_1, \ldots, f_n)$, wherein $x'_j = f_j(\mathbf{x}, \mathbf{w})$. We say that system variable x_i (or disturbance variable w_j) is a *proper input* to the expression f_k if x_i (or w_j) occurs as a subterm in f_k. Let $\mathsf{inps}(f_k)$ denote the set of all proper input variables to the function (expression) f_k.

As an example, consider $X = \{x_1, \ldots, x_4\}$ and $W = \{w_1, w_2\}$ and the expression $f : x_1x_4 - w_1$. The proper inputs to f are $\{x_1, x_4, w_1\}$. We exclude cases such as $g : \frac{sin^2(x_1) + cos^2(x_1)}{sin^2(x_2) + cos^2(x_2)}$ that has $\{x_1, x_2\}$ as proper inputs. However a simplification using elementary trigonometric rules can eliminate them. We will assume that all expressions are simplified to involve the least number of variables.

Definition 2 (Dependency Hypergraph). *A dependency hypergraph of a system Π has vertices $V : X \cup W$, given by the union of the system and disturbance variables with hyperedge set $E \subseteq 2^V$ given by $E = \{e_1, \ldots, e_n\}$,* *wherein for each update* $x_k := f_k(\mathbf{x}, \mathbf{w})$ *(k = 1, . . . , n), we have the hyperedge* $e_k : \{x_k\} \cup \mathsf{inps}(f_k)$*. In other words, each update* $x_k := f_k(\mathbf{x}, \mathbf{w})$ *yields an edge that includes* x_k *along with all the system/disturbance variables that are proper inputs to* f_k*.*

Example 2. The dependency hypergraph for the system from Example 1 has the vertices $V : \{x_1, x_2, x_3, w_1\}$ and the edges $\{e_1 : \{x_1, x_2\}, \ e_2 : \ \{x_2, w_1\}$ and $e_3 : \{x_2, x_3\}\}$.

2.1   Tree Decomposition

We will now discuss tree decompositions and the associated concept of treewidth of a hypergraph $G : (V, E)$. The tree decomposition will be applied to the dependency hypergraphs (Definition 2) for systems Π (Definition 1).

Definition 3 (Tree Decomposition and Treewidth). *Given a hypergraph* $G : (V, E)$*, a tree decomposition is a tree* $T : (N, C)$ *and a mapping* VERTS $: N \mapsto 2^V$*, wherein* N *is the set of tree nodes,* C *is the set of tree edges and* VERTS$(\cdot)$ *associates each node* $u \in N$ *with a set of graph vertices* VERTS$(n) \subseteq V$*. The tree decomposition satisfies the following conditions:*

1. *For vertex* $v \in V$ *there exists (at least one)* $n \in N$ *such that* $v \in$ VERTS(n).
2. *For each hyperedge* $e \in E$ *there exists (at least one)* $n \in N$: $e \subseteq$ VERTS(n).
3. *For each vertex* v*, for any two nodes* n_1, n_2 *such that* $v \in$ VERTS(n_1) *and* $v \in$ VERTS(n_2)*, then* $v \in$ VERTS(n) *for each node* n *along the unique path between* n_1 *and* n_2 *in the tree. Stated another way, the subset of nodes* $N_v : \{n \in N \mid v \in$ VERTS$(n)\}$ *induces a subtree of* T *(denoted* T_v*).*

The width of a tree decomposition is given by $\max\{|\text{VERTS}(n)| \mid n \in N\} - 1$*. In other words, we find the node* n *in the tree whose associated set of vertices has the largest cardinality. We subtract one from this maximal cardinality to obtain the treewidth. A tree decomposition is optimal for a graph* G *if no other tree decomposition exists with a strictly smaller width. The treewidth of a hypergraph* G *is given by width of an optimal tree decomposition.*

It is easy to show that if the graph G is a tree, it has treewidth 1. Likewise, a cycle has tree width 2.

Example 3. The tree decomposition of the hypergraph G from Example 2 has three nodes $\{n_1, n_2, n_3\}$ with edges (n_1, n_2) and (n_2, n_3). The nodes along with the associated vertex sets are as follows:

$$n_2 : \{x_2, w_1\} \!-\! n_1 : \{x_2, x_3\} \!-\! n_3 : \{x_1, x_2\}$$

Although the tree decomposition is not a rooted tree, we often designate an arbitrary node $r \in N$ as the root node, and consider the tree T as a rooted tree with root r.

Finding a Tree Decomposition: Interestingly, the problem of finding the treewidth of a graph is itself a NP-hard problem. However, many practical approaches exist for graphs with small treewidths. For instance, Bodlaender presents an algorithm that runs in time $O(k^{O(k^3)})$ to construct a tree decomposition of width at most k or conclude that the treewidth of the graph is at least $k + 1$ [6]. Such an approach can be quite useful if a given graph is suspected to have a small tree width in the first place. Besides this, many efficient algorithms exist to approximate the treewidth of a graph to some constant factor. A detailed survey of these results is available elsewhere [7,8]. Open-source packages such as HTD can compute treewidth for graphs with thousands of nodes [1]. Finally, we note that if a tree decomposition of width k can be found, then one can be found with at most $|V|$ nodes.

Lemma 1. *Let T be a tree decomposition for a (multi)graph G with vertices V and treewidth k. There exists a tree decomposition $\hat{T}$ of G with the same treewidth k, and at most $|V|$ nodes.*

A proof is provided in the extended version of the paper.

3 Abstract Domains Using Tree Decompositions

In this section, we will define abstract domains using tree decompositions of the dependency hypergraph of the system under analysis. Let Π be a transition system over system variables X. The concrete states are given by $\mathbf{x} \in D$, wherein $\mathbf{x} : X \mapsto \mathbb{R}$ maps each state variable $x_j \in X$ to its value $\mathbf{x}(x_j)$ (denoted $\mathbf{x}_j$).

Definition 4 (Projections). *The projection of a state $\mathbf{x}$ to a subset of state variables $J \subseteq X$, denoted as $\mathsf{proj}(\mathbf{x}, J)$, is a valuation $\hat{\mathbf{x}} : J \mapsto \mathbb{R}$ such that $\hat{\mathbf{x}}(x_i) = \mathbf{x}(x_i)$ for all $x_i \in J$. For a set of states $S \subseteq D$ and a subset of state variables $J \subseteq X$, we denote the projection of S along (the dimensions of) J as $\mathsf{proj}(S, J) : \{\mathsf{proj}(\mathbf{x}, J) \mid \mathbf{x} \in S\}$.*

Definition 5 (Extensions). *Let R be a set of states involving just the variables in the set $J_1 \subseteq X$, i.e, $R \subseteq \mathsf{proj}(D, J_1)$. We define the extension of R into a set of variables $J_2 \supseteq J_1$ as $\mathsf{ext}_{J_2}(R) : \{\mathbf{x} \in \mathsf{proj}(D, J_2) \mid \mathsf{proj}(\mathbf{x}, J_1) \in R\}$.*

In other words, the extension of a set embeds each element in the larger dimensional space defined by J_2 allowing "all possible values" for the dimensions in $J_2 \setminus J_1$.

We will use the notation $\mathsf{ext}(S)$ to denote the set $\mathsf{ext}_X(S)$, i.e, its extension to the entire set of state variables X. For a state $\mathbf{x}_S$, we will use $\mathsf{ext}(\mathbf{x}_S)$ denote $\mathsf{ext}(\{\mathbf{x}_S\})$.

Definition 6 (Product (Join) of Sets). *Let $R_1 \subseteq \mathsf{proj}(D, J_1)$ and $R_2 \subseteq \mathsf{proj}(D, J_2)$. We define $R_1 \otimes R_2 : \{\mathbf{x} : J_1 \cup J_2 \mapsto \mathbb{R} \mid \mathsf{proj}(\mathbf{x}, J_1) \in R_1 \text{ and } \mathsf{proj}(\mathbf{x}, J_2) \in R_2\}$.*

Let $T : (N, C)$ be a tree decomposition of the dependency hypergraph of the system. Recall that for each node $n \in N$ we associate a set of system/disturbance variables denoted by VERTS(n). Let VERTS$_X(n)$ denote the set of system variables: VERTS(n)$\cap X$. We say that an update function $x_k := f_k(\mathbf{x}, \mathbf{w})$ is associated with a node n in the tree iff $\{x_k\} \cup \mathsf{inps}(f_k) \subseteq$ VERTS(n).

Lemma 2. *For every system variable x_k, its update $x_k := f_k(\mathbf{x}, \mathbf{w})$ is associated with at least one node $n \in N$.*

Proof. This follows from those of a tree decomposition that states that every hyperedge in the dependency hypergraph must belong to VERTS(n) for at least one node $n \in N$.

3.1   Abstraction and Concretization

We consider subsets of the concrete states for the system Π, i.e, the set 2^D, ordered by set inclusion as our *concrete domain*. Given a tree decomposition, T, we define an abstract domain through projection of a concrete set along VERTS(n) for each node n of T.

Definition 7 (Abstract Domain). *Each element s of the abstract domain $\mathbb{A}_T$ is a mapping that associates each node $n \in N$ with a set $s(n) \subseteq \mathsf{proj}(D, \text{VERTS}_X(n))$.*
For $s_1, s_2 \in \mathbb{A}_T$, $s_1 \sqsubseteq s_2$ iff $s_1(n) \subseteq s_2(n)$ for each $n \in N$.

We will use the notation $\mathsf{proj}(S, n)$ for a node $n \in N$ to denote $\mathsf{proj}(S, \text{VERTS}_X(n))$.

Definition 8 (Abstraction Map). *Given a tree decomposition T, the abstraction map α_T takes a set of states $S \subseteq D$ and produces a mapping that associates tree node $n \in N$ to a projection of S along the variables VERTS$_X(n)$. Formally,*

$$\alpha_T(S) : \ \lambda n : N. \ \mathsf{proj}(S, n).$$

Thus, an abstract state s is a map that associates each node n of the tree to a set $s(n) \subseteq D_n$. We now define the concretization map γ_T.

Definition 9 (Concretization Map). *The concretization $\gamma_T(s)$ of an abstract state is defined as $\gamma_T(s) : \ \bigcap_{n \in N} \mathsf{ext}(s(n))$. In other words, we take $s(n)$ for every node $n \in N$, extend it to the full dimensional space of all system variables and intersect the result over all nodes $n \in N$.*

Example 4. Consider a simple tree decomposition T with 2 nodes n_1, n_2 and a single edge (n_1, n_2). Let VERTS(n_1) : $\{x_1, x_2\}$ and VERTS(n_2) : $\{x_2, x_3\}$. Let the domain D be the set $\mathbf{x}_i \in \{1, 2, 3\}$ for $i = 1, 2, 3$. We use the notation $(\overset{x_1}{v_1}, \overset{x_2}{v_2}, \overset{x_3}{v_3})$ to denote a state $\mathbf{x}$ that maps x_1 to the value v_1, x_2 to the value v_2 and so on.

Now consider the set $S = \{(\overset{x_1 \, x_2 \, x_3}{1,1,1}), (\overset{x_1 \, x_2 \, x_3}{1,1,2}), (\overset{x_1 \, x_2 \, x_3}{1,2,3})\}$. We have that $s : \alpha(S)$ is the mapping that projects S onto the dimensions (x_1, x_2) for node n_1 and (x_2, x_3) for node n_2:

$$n_1 \mapsto \{(\overset{x_1 \, x_2}{1,1}), (\overset{x_1 \, x_2}{1,2})\}, \quad n_2 \mapsto \{(\overset{x_1 \, x_2}{1,1}), (\overset{x_1 \, x_2}{1,2}), (\overset{x_2 \, x_3}{2,3})\}.$$

Likewise, we verify that the concretization map $\gamma(s)$ will yields us:

$$\gamma(s) : \{(\overset{x_1 \, x_2 \, x_3}{1,1,1}), (\overset{x_1 \, x_2 \, x_3}{1,1,2}), (\overset{x_1 \, x_2 \, x_3}{1,2,3})\}.$$

For convenience, if the tree T is clear from the context, we will drop the subscripts to simply write α and γ for the abstraction and concretization map, respectively.

Theorem 1. *For any tree decomposition T, the maps α and γ form a Galois connection. I.e, for all $S \subseteq D$ and $s \in \mathbb{A}_T$: $\alpha(S) \sqsubseteq s$ iff $S \subseteq \gamma(s)$.*

Proof. Let S, s be such that $\alpha(S) \sqsubseteq s$. Therefore, $\mathsf{proj}(S, n) \subseteq s(n) \; \forall n \in N$ by the definition of $\sqsubseteq$. Pick any, $\mathbf{x} \in S$. First, $\mathsf{proj}(\mathbf{x}, n) \in \mathsf{proj}(S, n)$ and therefore, $\mathsf{proj}(\mathbf{x}, n) \in s(n)$ for all $n \in N$. Thus, $\mathbf{x} \in \mathsf{ext}(s(n))$ for each node $n \in N$. Therefore, $\mathbf{x} \in \bigcap_{n \in N} \mathsf{ext}(s(n))$, and hence, $\mathbf{x} \in \gamma(s)$, by defn. of γ. Therefore, $S \subseteq \gamma(s)$.

Conversely, assume $S \subseteq \gamma(s)$. Since $\gamma(s) = \bigcap_{n \in N} \mathsf{ext}(s(n))$ (from Definition 9). Therefore, $S \subseteq \mathsf{ext}(s(n))$ forall $n \in N$. Therefore, for all $\mathbf{x} \in S$, $\mathsf{proj}(\mathbf{x}, n) \in s(n)$. Therefore, $\mathsf{proj}(S, n) \subseteq s(n)$ for every $n \in N$. Finally, this yields $\alpha(S) \sqsubseteq s$.

The meet operation is defined as $s_1 \sqcap s_2 : \lambda n. \; s_1(n) \cap s_2(n)$, and likewise, the join is defined as $s_1 \sqcup s_2 : \lambda n. \; s_1(n) \cup s_2(n)$. We recall two key facts that follow from Galois connection between α and γ.

1. For any set $S \subseteq D$, we have $S \subseteq \gamma(\alpha(S))$. Abstracting a concrete set and concretizing it back again "loses information". To see why, we start from $\alpha(S) \sqsubseteq \alpha(S)$ and apply the Galois connection to derive $S \subseteq \gamma(\alpha(S))$.
2. Likewise, for any abstract domain object $s \in \mathbb{A}$, we have $\alpha(\gamma(s)) \sqsubseteq s$. I.e, for any element s, taking its concretization and abstracting it "gains information". To prove this, we start from $\gamma(s) \subseteq \gamma(s)$ and conclude that $\alpha(\gamma(s)) \sqsubseteq s$.

Example 5. Returning back to Example 4, now consider the set

$$\hat{S} = \{(\overset{x_1 \, x_2 \, x_3}{1,1,2}), (\overset{x_1 \, x_2 \, x_3}{1,2,3}), (\overset{x_1 \, x_2 \, x_3}{2,1,2}), (\overset{x_1 \, x_2 \, x_3}{2,2,4})\}.$$

Its abstraction $\hat{s} : \alpha(\hat{S})$ is given by the mapping:

$$n_1 \mapsto \{(\overset{x_1 \, x_2}{1,1}), (\overset{x_1 \, x_2}{1,2}), (\overset{x_1 \, x_2}{2,1}), (\overset{x_1 \, x_2}{2,2})\}, \quad n_2 \mapsto \{(\overset{x_2 \, x_3}{1,2}), (\overset{x_2 \, x_3}{2,3}), (\overset{x_2 \, x_3}{2,4})\}.$$

We note that $\gamma(\hat{s})$ is the set: $\{(\overset{x_1 \, x_2 \, x_3}{1,1,2}), (\overset{x_1 \, x_2 \, x_3}{1,2,3}), (\overset{x_1 \, x_2 \, x_3}{1,2,4}), (\overset{x_1 \, x_2 \, x_3}{2,1,2}), (\overset{x_1 \, x_2 \, x_3}{2,2,3}), (\overset{x_1 \, x_2 \, x_3}{2,2,4})\}$. Thus $\hat{S} \subseteq \gamma(\hat{s})$. Notice that $(\overset{x_1 \, x_2 \, x_3}{2,2,3})$ and $(\overset{x_1 \, x_2 \, x_3}{1,2,4})$ are part of $\gamma(\hat{s})$ but not the original set $\hat{S}$. Similarly, consider the abstract element $s_1 : n_1 \mapsto \{(\overset{x_1 \, x_2}{1,1}), (\overset{x_1 \, x_2}{1,2})\}, \quad n_2 \mapsto \{(\overset{x_2 \, x_3}{1,3})\}$. We note that $\gamma(s_1) : \{(\overset{x_1 \, x_2 \, x_3}{1,1,3})\}$ and therefore $\alpha(\gamma(s_1))$ yields the abstract element $s_2 \sqsubseteq s_1 : n_1 \mapsto \{(\overset{x_1 \, x_2}{1,1})\}, \quad n_2 \mapsto \{(\overset{x_2 \, x_3}{1,3})\}$.

3.2   Canonical Elements and Message Passing

In the tree decomposition, various nodes share information about the subsets of vertices associated with each node. Since the subsets have elements in common, it is possible that a node n_1 has information about a variable x_2 that is also present in some other node n_2 of the tree. We will now see how to take an abstract element s and refine each $s(n)$ by exchanging information between nodes in a systematic manner.

For each edge $(n_1, n_2) \in C$ of the tree, define the set of variables in common as $CV(n_1, n_2)$: VERTS$(n_1) \cap$ VERTS(n_2) and $CV_X(n_1, n_2)$: VERTS$_X(n_1) \cap$ VERTS$_X(n_2)$.

Definition 10 (Canonical Elements). *An abstract element s is said to be canonical if and only if for each edge $(n_1, n_2) \in C$ in the tree:*

$$\mathsf{proj}(s(n_1), CV_X(n_1, n_2)) = \mathsf{proj}(s(n_2), CV_X(n_1, n_2)).$$

In other words, if we took the common variables VERTS$_X(n_1) \cap$ VERTS$_X(n_2)$*, the set $s(n_1)$ projected along these common variables is equal to the projection of $s(n_2)$ along the common variables.*

Example 6. Consider the abstract element s_1 from Example 5: $n_1 \mapsto \{(\overset{x_1}{\hat 1}, \overset{x_2}{\hat 1}), (\overset{x_1}{\hat 1}, \overset{x_2}{\hat 2})\}$, $n_2 \mapsto \{(\overset{x_2}{\hat 1}, \overset{x_3}{\hat 3})\}$. $\mathsf{proj}(s_1(n_1), CV(n_1, n_2))$ is the set $\{\overset{x_2}{\hat 1}, \overset{x_2}{\hat 2}\}$ whereas $\mathsf{proj}(s_1(n_2), CV(n_1, n_2))$ is simply $\{\overset{x_2}{\hat 1}\}$. Therefore, s_1 fails to be canonical.

The key theorem of tree decomposition is that a canonical element in the abstract domain can be seen as the projection of a concrete set S along VERTS$_X(n)$ for each node n of the tree. To prove that we will first establish a useful property of a canonical element s.

Lemma 3. *For every canonical element $s \in \mathbb{A}$, node $n \in N$ and element $\mathbf{x}_n \in s(n)$, we have that $\mathsf{ext}(\mathbf{x}_n) \cap \gamma(s) \neq \emptyset$.*

Stated another way, the lemma claims that for any canonical s, any $\mathbf{x}_n \in s(n)$ can be extended to form some element of $\gamma(s)$. A proof is provided in the extended version.

Theorem 2. *An element s is canonical (Definition 10) if and only if $s = \alpha(S)$ for some concrete set S.*

Ideally, in abstract interpretation, we would like to work with abstract domain objects that satisfy $s = \alpha(\gamma(s))$. One way to ensure that is to take any given domain element s_0 and simply calculate out $\alpha(\gamma(s_0))$ by applying the maps. However, $\gamma(s_0)$ in our domain takes lower dimensional projections and reconstructs a set in the full states pace. It may thus be too expensive to compute. Fortunately, canonical objects satisfy the equality $s = \alpha(\gamma(s))$. Therefore, given any object $s \in \mathbb{A}$ that is not necessarily canonical, we would like to make it canonical: I.e, we seek an object $\hat s$ such that $\gamma(\hat s) = \gamma(s)$, but $\hat s$ is canonical. As mentioned earlier, directly computing $\hat{s} = \alpha(\gamma(s))$ can be prohibitively expensive, depending on the domain. We now describe a *message passing* approach.

First, we convert the tree T to a rooted tree by designating an arbitrary node $r \in N$ as the root of the tree.

Message Passing along Edges: Let (n_1, n_2) be an edge of the tree and s be an abstract element. A message from n_1 to n_2 is defined as the set $\mathsf{msg}(s, n_1 \to n_2) : \mathsf{proj}(s(n_1), \mathrm{CV}(n_1, n_2))$. In other words, we project the set $s(n_1)$ along the dimensions that are common to (n_1, n_2).

Once a node n_2 receives $M : \mathsf{msg}(s, n_1 \to n_2)$, it processes the message by updating $s(n_2)$ as $s(n_2) := s(n_2) \cap \mathsf{ext}_{\mathrm{VERTS}(n_2)}(M)$. In other words, it intersects the message (extended to the dimensions in n_2) with the current set that is associated with n_2.

Example 7. Consider a tree decomposition with three nodes $\{n_1, n_2, n_3\}$ and the edges (n_1, n_2) and (n_2, n_3). Let $\mathrm{VERTS}(n_1) : \{x_1, x_2\}$, $\mathrm{VERTS}(n_2) : \{x_2, x_4\}$ and $\mathrm{VERTS}(n_3) : \{x_2, x_3\}$. Let D be the domain $\{1, 2, 3, 4\}^4$. Consider the abstract element s:

$$n_1 \mapsto \{\overset{x_1\ x_2}{(1,2)}, \overset{x_1\ x_2}{(3,3)}, \overset{x_1\ x_2}{(1,4)}\},\ n_2 \mapsto \{\overset{x_2\ x_4}{(1,1)}, \overset{x_2\ x_4}{(2,2)}, \overset{x_2\ x_4}{(3,3)}, \overset{x_2\ x_4}{(4,4)}\},\ n_3 \mapsto \{\overset{x_2\ x_3}{(4,4)}, \overset{x_2\ x_3}{(2,3)}\}.$$

A message $\mathsf{msg}(s, n_1 \to n_2)$ is given by the set $\mathsf{proj}(s(n_1), \{x_2\}) : \overset{x_2\ x_3\ x_4}{\{2, 3, 4\}}$. This results in the new abstract object s' wherein the element $\overset{x_2\ x_4}{(1,1)}$ is removed from $s(n_2)$:

$$n_1 \mapsto \{\overset{x_1\ x_2}{(1,2)}, \overset{x_1\ x_2}{(3,3)}, \overset{x_1\ x_2}{(1,4)}\},\ n_2 \mapsto \{\overset{x_2\ x_4}{\cancel{(1,1)}}, \overset{x_2\ x_4}{(2,2)}, \overset{x_2\ x_4}{(3,3)}, \overset{x_2\ x_4}{(4,4)}\},\ n_3 \mapsto \{\overset{x_2\ x_3}{(4,4)}, \overset{x_2\ x_3}{(2,3)}\}.$$

Upwards Message Passing: The upwards message passing works from leaves up to the root of the tree according to the following two rules:

1. First, each leaf of the tree n passes a message to its parent n_p. The parent node n_p intersects its current value $s(n_p)$ with the message to update its current set.
2. After a node has received (and processed) a message from all its children, it passes a message up to its parent, if one exists.

The upwards message passing terminates at the root since it does not have a parent to send a message to.

Example 8. Going back to Example 7, we designate n_2 as the root and the upwards pass sends the messages $\mathsf{msg}(s, n_1 \to n_2)$ and $\mathsf{msg}(s, n_3 \to n_2)$. This results in the following updated element:

$$n_1 \mapsto \{\overset{x_1\ x_2}{(1,2)}, \overset{x_1\ x_2}{(3,3)}, \overset{x_1\ x_2}{(1,4)}\},\ n_2 \mapsto \{\overset{x_2\ x_4}{\cancel{(1,1)}}, \overset{x_2\ x_4}{(2,2)}, \overset{x_2\ x_4}{\cancel{(3,3)}}, \overset{x_2\ x_4}{(4,4)}\},\ n_3 \mapsto \{\overset{x_2\ x_3}{(4,4)}, \overset{x_2\ x_3}{(2,3)}\}.$$

Downwards Message Passing: The downwards message passing works from the root down to the leaves.

1. To initialize, the root sends a message to all its children.
2. After a node has received (and processed) a message from its parent, it sends a message to all its children.

The overall procedure to make a given abstract object s canonical is as follows: (a) perform an upwards message passing phase and (b) perform a downwards message passing phase.

Example 9. Going back to Example 8, the downward message passing phase sends messages from $n_2 \to n_1$ and $n_2 \to n_3$. The resulting element $\hat{s}$ is

$$n_1 \mapsto \{\overset{x_1\ x_2}{(1,2)}, \overset{x_1\ x_2}{\cancel{(3,3)}}, \overset{x_1\ x_2}{(1,4)}\}, \; n_2 \mapsto \{\overset{x_1\ x_2}{\cancel{(1,1)}}, \overset{x_2\ x_4}{(2,2)}, \overset{x_2\ x_4}{\cancel{(3,3)}}, \overset{x_2\ x_4}{(4,4)}\}, \; n_3 \mapsto \{\overset{x_2\ x_4}{(4,4)}, \overset{x_2\ x_4}{(2,3)}\}.$$

On the other hand, it is important to perform message passing upwards first and then downwards second. Reversing this does not yield a canonical element. For instance going back to Example 7, if we first performed a downwards pass from n_2, the result is unchanged:

$$n_1 \mapsto \{\overset{x_1\ x_2}{(1,2)}, \overset{x_1\ x_2}{(3,3)}, \overset{x_1\ x_2}{(1,4)}\}, \; n_2 \mapsto \{\overset{x_1\ x_2}{(1,1)}, \overset{x_2\ x_4}{(2,2)}, \overset{x_2\ x_4}{(3,3)}, \overset{x_2\ x_4}{(4,4)}\}, \; n_3 \mapsto \{\overset{x_2\ x_4}{(4,4)}, \overset{x_2\ x_4}{(2,3)}\}.$$

Performing an upwards pass now yields the element s_2:

$$n_1 \mapsto \{\overset{x_1\ x_2}{(1,2)}, \overset{x_1\ x_2}{(3,3)}, \overset{x_1\ x_2}{(1,4)}\}, \; n_2 \mapsto \{\overset{x_2\ x_4}{\cancel{(1,1)}}, \overset{x_2\ x_4}{(2,2)}, \overset{x_2\ x_4}{\cancel{(3,3)}}, \overset{x_2\ x_4}{(4,4)}\}, \; n_3 \mapsto \{\overset{x_2\ x_4}{(4,4)}, \overset{x_2\ x_4}{(2,3)}\}.$$

However this is not canonical, since the element $\overset{x_1\ x_2}{(3,3)}$ in $s_2(n_1)$ violates the requirement over the edge (n_1, n_2).

Let $\hat{s}$ be the resulting abstract object after the message passing procedure finishes.

Theorem 3. *The result of message passing $\hat{s}$ is a canonical object, and it satisfies $\gamma(\hat{s}) = \gamma(s)$.*

Proof (Sketch). First, we note that whenever a message is passed for an abstract value s from node m to n along an edge (m, n) resulting in a new abstract value s': **(P1)** $\gamma(s') = \gamma(s)$; and **(P2)** the projection of $s'(n)$ along the dimensions $CV(m, n)$ is now contained in that of $s'(m)$ along $CV(m, n)$. Furthermore, property **(P2)** remains unchanged regardless of any future messages that are passed along the tree edges.

Next, it is shown that after each upwards pass, when a message is passed, property **(P2)** (stated above) holds for each node m and its parent node n since a message is passed from m to n. During the downwards pass, property **(P2)** holds for each node n and its child node m in the tree. Combining the two, we note that for each edge (m, n) in the tree, we have property **(P2)** in either direction guaranteeing that $\mathsf{proj}(s^*(m), CV(m, n)) = \mathsf{proj}(s^*(n), CV(m, n))$, for the final result s^*, or in other words that s^* is canonical.

3.3   Decomposable Sets and Post-conditions

We have already noted that for any concrete set over $S \subseteq D$, the process of abstracting it by projecting into nodes of a tree T, and re-concretizing it is "lossy": I.e, $S \subseteq \gamma(\alpha(S))$. In this section, we study "tree decomposable" concrete sets S for which $\gamma(\alpha(S)) = S$. Ideally, we would like to prove that if a set S is tree decomposable then so is the set $\mathsf{post}(S, \Pi)$ of next states. However, we will disprove this by showing a counterexample. Nevertheless, we will present an analysis of why this fact fails and suggest approaches that can "manage" this loss in precision.

Definition 11 (Decomposable Sets). *We say that a set S is tree decomposable given a tree T iff $\gamma(\alpha(S)) = S$.*

This is in fact a "global" definition of decomposability. In fact, a nice "local" definition can be provided that is reminiscent of the notion of conditional independence in graphical models. We will defer this discussion to an extended version of this paper due to space limitations.

Example 10. Consider set $S : \{(\overset{x_1}{1}, \overset{x_2}{2}, \overset{x_3}{1}), (\overset{x_1}{2}, \overset{x_2}{2}, \overset{x_2}{2})\}$ and tree T below:

$$\boxed{n_1 : \{x_1, x_2\}} \!-\!\!-\! \boxed{n_2 : \{x_2, x_3\}}$$

We wish to check if S is T-decomposable. We have $s : \alpha(S)$ as

$$s(n_1) : \mathsf{proj}(S, n_1) : \{(\overset{x_1}{1}, \overset{x_2}{2}), (\overset{x_1}{2}, \overset{x_2}{2})\} \quad s(n_2) : \mathsf{proj}(S, n_2)\{(\overset{x_2}{2}, \overset{x_3}{1}), (\overset{x_2}{2}, \overset{x_3}{2})\}.$$

Now, $\gamma(s):\{(\overset{x_1}{1}, \overset{x_2}{2}, \overset{x_3}{1}), (\overset{x_1}{1}, \overset{x_2}{2}, \overset{x_2}{2}), (\overset{x_1}{2}, \overset{x_2}{2}, \overset{x_3}{1}), (\overset{x_2}{2}, \overset{x_2}{2}, \overset{x_2}{2}).\}.$ We note that the set S is not tree decomposable. On the other hand, one can verify that the set $S_1:\{(\overset{x_1}{1}, \overset{x_2}{2}, \overset{x_3}{2}), (\overset{x_1}{2}, \overset{x_2}{2}, \overset{x_2}{2})\}$ is tree decomposable.

The following lemma will be quite useful.

Lemma 4. *Let S_1, S_2 be tree decomposable sets over T. Their intersection is tree decomposable.*

Let Π be a transition system over system variables in $\mathbf{x} \in D$. For a given set $S \subseteq D$, us define the post-condition $\mathsf{post}(S, \Pi)$ to be the set of states reachable in one step starting from some state in S:

$$\mathsf{post}(S, \Pi) : \{\mathbf{x}' \mid \mathbf{x} \in S, \ \mathbf{x}' = \mathsf{eval}(f, \mathbf{x})\}.$$

Let us also consider a transition relation R over pairs of states $(\mathbf{x}, \mathbf{x}') \in D \otimes D$:

$$R = \{(\mathbf{x}, \mathbf{x}') \mid \mathbf{x}, \mathbf{x}' \in D \text{ and } \mathbf{x}' = \mathsf{eval}(f, \mathbf{x})\}.$$

The relation R can be viewed as the intersection of n relations: $R : \bigcap_{x_j \in X} R_j$, wherein

$$R_j : \{(\mathbf{x}, \mathbf{x}') \mid \mathbf{x}, \mathbf{x}' \in D \text{ and } \mathbf{x}'_j = \mathsf{eval}(f_j, \mathbf{x})\}.$$

In other words, R_j is a component of R that models the update of the system variable x_j. Also for each $x_j \in X$, let e_j : $\mathsf{inps}(f_j) \cup x_j$ be the inputs to the update function f_j and the node x_j itself.

Given the tree T, we define the extended tree T' as having the same node set N and edge set C as T. However, $\mathrm{VERTS}_{T'}(n) = \mathrm{VERTS}_T(n) \cup \{x'_j \mid x_j \in \mathrm{VERTS}_T(n)\}$. Note that T' with the labeling $\mathrm{VERTS}_{T'}$ satisfies all the condition of a tree decomposition for a graph G save the addition of vertices x'_i in each node of the tree. We will write $\mathrm{VERTS}'(n)$ to denote the set $\mathrm{VERTS}_{T'}(n)$.

Lemma 5. *The transition relation R of a system Π is tree T' decomposable.*

The proof is provided in the extended version and is done by writing R as an intersection of tree decomposable relations R_j, and appealing to Lemma 4.

First, we show the negative result that the image of a tree (T) decomposable set under a tree (T') decomposable transition relation is not tree decomposable, in general.

Example 11. Let $X = \{x_1, x_2, x_3\}$ and consider again the tree decomposition from Example 10. Let S be the set $\{(\overset{x_1}{*}, \overset{x_2}{*}, \overset{x_3}{*})\}$, wherein we use the wild card character as notation that can be substituted for any element in the set $\{1, 2\}$. Therefore, we take S to be a set with 8 elements. Clearly S is tree decomposable in the tree T from Example 10.

Consider the transition relation R that will be written as the intersection of three transition relations:

$$R_1 : \{(X, X') \mid x'_1 = x_2\}, \quad R_2 : \{(X, X') \mid x'_2 \in \{1, 2\}\}, \quad R'_3 : \{(X, X') \mid x'_3 = x_2\}.$$

Clearly R is tree T' decomposable. We can now compute the post-condition of S under this relation. The reader can verify the post-condition $\hat{S}$: $\{(\overset{x_1}{1}, \overset{x_2}{*}, \overset{x_3}{1}), (\overset{x_1}{2}, \overset{x_2}{*}, \overset{x_3}{2})\}$. However, $\hat{S}$ is not tree decomposable. We note that $\hat{s}$: $\alpha(\hat{S})$ is the set $\hat{s}(n_1)$: $\{(\overset{x_1}{*}, \overset{x_2}{*})\}$ and $\hat{s}(n_2)$: $\{(\overset{x_1}{*}, \overset{x_2}{*})\}$. Therefore $\gamma(\hat{s})$ is the set $\{(\overset{x_1}{*}, \overset{x_2}{*}, \overset{x_3}{*})\}$.

As noted above, the set R is tree T' decomposable. If S is tree decomposable, we can extend S to a set S' : $\mathrm{ext}_{X'}(S)$ that is now defined over $X \cup X'$ and is also tree decomposable. As a result $S' \cap R$ is also tree decomposable. However, the postcondition of S is the set $\mathsf{proj}(S' \cap R, X')$. Thus, the key operation that failed was the projection operation involved in computing the post-condition. This suggests a possible solution to this issue albeit an expensive one: at each step, we maintain the reachable states using both current and next state variables, thus avoiding projection. In effect, the reachable states at the ith step will be entire trajectories of the system expressed over variables $X_0 \cup X_1 \cup \cdots X_i$. This is clearly not practical. However, a more efficient solution is to note that some of the current state variables can be projected out without losing the tree decomposability property. Going back to Example 11, we note that we can safely project away $\{x_1, x_3\}$, while maintaining the new reachable set in terms of (x_2, x'_1, x'_2, x'_3). In this way, we may recover the lost precision back.

In conclusion, we note that tree decompositions may lose precision over post-conditions. However, the loss in precision can be avoided if carefully selected "previous state variables" are maintained as the computation proceeds. The question of how to optimally maintain this information will be investigated in the future.

4   Grid-Based Interval Analysis

We now combine the ideas to create a disjunctive interval analysis using tree decompositions. The main idea here is to apply tree decompositions not to the concrete set of states but to an abstraction of the concrete domain by grid-based intervals.

We will now describe the interval-based abstraction of sets of states dynamical system Π in order to perform over-approximate reachability analysis. Let us fix a system $\Pi : \langle \mathbf{x}, \mathbf{w}, D, W, f, X_0, U \rangle$ as defined in Definition 1. We will assume that the domain of state variables D is a hyper-rectangle given by $D : [L(x_1), U(x_1)] \times \cdots \times [L(x_n), U(x_n)]$ for $L(x_j), U(x_j) \in \mathbb{R}$ and $L(x_j) \leq U(x_j)$ for each $j = 1, \ldots, n$. In other words, each system variable x_j lies inside the interval $[L(x_j), U(x_j)]$. Likewise, we will assume that $W : \prod_{k=1}^{m} [L(w_k), U(w_k)]$ such that $L(w_k) \leq U(w_k)$ and $L(w_k), U(w_k) \in \mathbb{R}$.

We will consider a *uniform* cell decomposition wherein each dimension is divided into some natural number $M > 0$ of equal sized subintervals. The ith *subinterval* of variable x_j is denoted as $\mathsf{subInt}(x_j, i)$, and is given by $[L(x_j) + i\delta_j, L(x_j) + (i+1)\delta_j]$ for $i = 0, \ldots, M - 1$ and $\delta_j : \frac{(U(x_j) - L(x_j))}{M}$. Similarly, we will define $\mathsf{subInt}(w_k, i)$ for disturbance variables w_k whose domains are also divided into M subdivisions. The overall domain $D \times W$ is therefore divided into M^{m+n} cells wherein each cell is indexed by a tuple of natural numbers $\mathbf{i} : \langle i_1, \ldots, i_n, i_{n+1}, \ldots, i_{n+m} \rangle$, such that $i_j \in \{0, \ldots, M - 1\}$ and the cell corresponding to $\mathbf{i}$ is given by:

$$\gamma_C(\mathbf{i}) : \prod_{j=1}^{n} \mathsf{subInt}(x_j, \mathbf{i}_j) \times \prod_{k=1}^{m} \mathsf{subInt}(w_k, \mathbf{i}_{n+k}) \tag{1}$$

Definition 12 (Grid-Based Abstract Domain). *The grid based abstract domain is defined by the set $C : \mathcal{P}(\mathbf{i} \in \{0, \ldots, M\}^{m+n})$, wherein each abstract domain element is a set of grid cells. The sets are ordered simply by set inclusion $\subseteq$ between sets of grid cells. The abstraction map $\alpha_C : \mathcal{P}(D) \to C$ is defined as follows:*

$$\alpha_C(S) : \{\mathbf{i} \in C \mid \gamma_C(\mathbf{i}) \cap S \neq \emptyset\}.$$

The concretization map γ_C is defined above in (1).

Definition 13 (Interval Propagator). *An interval propagator (IP) is a higher order function that takes in the description of a function f with k real-valued inputs and p real valued outputs, and an interval $I : [l_1, u_1] \times \cdots \times [l_k, u_k]$*

and outputs an interval (hyperrectangle over $\mathbb{R}^p$) $\textsc{IntvlProp}(f, I)$ *such that the following soundness guarantees hold:*

$$(\forall \mathbf{x} \in D) \bigwedge_{j=1}^{k} \mathbf{x}_j \in [l_j, u_j] \implies \mathsf{eval}(f, \mathbf{x}) \in \textsc{IntvlProp}(f, I).$$

In practice, interval arithmetic approaches have been used to build sound interval propagators [33]. However, they suffer from issues such as the *wrapping effect* that make their outputs too conservative. This can be remedied by either (a) performing a finer subdivision of the inputs (i.e, increasing M) to ensure that the intervals I being input into the $\textsc{IntvlProp}$ are sufficiently small to guarantee tight error bounds; or (b) using higher order arithmetics such as affine arithmetic or Taylor polynomial arithmetic [25,32].

The interval propagator serves to define an abstract post-condition operation over sets of cells $\hat{S} \subseteq \mathcal{C}$. Given such a set, $\hat{S}$, we compute the post condition in the abstract domain. Informally, the post condition is given (a) by iterating over each cell in S; and (b) computing the possible next cells using $\textsc{IntvlProp}$. Formally, we define the abstract post operation as follows:

$$\mathsf{post}_C(\hat{S}, \Pi) : \bigcup_{\mathbf{i} \in \hat{S}} \alpha_C(\textsc{IntvlProp}(f, \gamma_C(\mathbf{i}))).$$

Given this machinery, an abstract T-step reachability analysis is performed in the standard manner: (a) abstract the initial state; (b) compute post condition for T steps; and (c) check for intersections of the abstract states with the abstraction of the unsafe set. We can also define and use widening operators to make the sequence of iterates converge. The grid based abstract domain can offer some guarantees with respect to the quality of the abstraction. For instance, we can easily bound the Hausdorff distance between the underlying concrete set and the abstraction as a function of the discretization sizes δ_j. However, the desirable properties come at a high computational cost since the number of cells grows exponentially in the number of system and disturbance variables.

4.1   Tree Decomposed Analysis

We now consider a tree-decomposed approach based on the concept of nodal abstractions. The key idea here is to perform the grid-based abstraction not on the full set of system and disturbance variables, but instead on individual *nodal* abstractions over a tree decomposition T.

Definition 14 (Nodal   Abstractions).   *A   nodal   abstraction* $\textsc{Nodal}$ $\textsc{Abstraction}(\Pi, n)$ *corresponding to a node $n \in N$ is defined as follows*

1. *The set of system variables are given by X_n :* $\textsc{Verts}_X(n)$ *with domain given by D_n :* $\mathsf{proj}(D, X_n)$.
2. *The initial states are given by* $\mathsf{proj}(X_0, X_n)$.

3. *The unsafe set is given by* $\mathsf{proj}(U, X_n)$.

4. *The set of disturbance variables are* $Y_n :$ VERTS$_W(n)$ *with domain given by* $W_n : \mathsf{proj}(W, W_n)$.

5. *The updates are described by a* relation $R(X_n, X'_n)$ *that relate the possible current states* X_n *and next states* X'_n. *The relation is constructed as a conjunction of assertions over variables* x_i, x'_i *wherein* $x_i \in X_n$.

   (a) *If the update* $x_i := f_i(\mathbf{x}, \mathbf{w})$ *is associated with the node* n, *we add the conjunct* $x'_i = f_i(X_n, W_n)$, *noting that the proper inputs to* f_i *are contained in* VERTS(n).

   (b) *Otherwise,* $x'_i \in \mathsf{proj}(D, \{x_i\})$ *that simply states that the next state value of the variable* x_i *is some value in its domain.*

Given a system Π, the nodal abstraction is a conservative abstraction, and therefore, it preserves reachability properties.

Lemma 6. *For any reachable state* $\mathbf{x}$ *of* Π *at time* t, *its projection* $\mathsf{proj}(\mathbf{x}, X_n)$ *is a reachable state of* NODALABSTRACTION(Π, n) *at time* t.

Since each nodal abstraction involves at most $\omega + 1$ variables, the abstraction at each node can involve at most $M^{\omega+1}$ cells where ω is the tree width. Also, note that a tree decomposition can be found with tree width ω that has at most $|X| + |W|$ nodes. This implies that the number of nodal abstractions can be bounded by $(|X| + |W|)$.

Let $\Pi(n) :$ NODALABSTRACTION(Π, n) be the nodal abstraction for tree node $n \in N$. For each node $n \in N$, we instantiate a grid based abstract domain for $\Pi(n)$ ranging over the variables VERTS$_X(n)$. At the ith step of the reachability analysis, we maintain a map s_i each node n to a set of grid cells $s_i(n)$ defined over VERTS(n).

1. Compute $\hat{s}_i(n) : \mathsf{post}_C(s_i(n), \Pi(n))$.
2. Make $\hat{s}_i$ canonical using message passing between nodes to obtain s_{i+1}.

The message passing is performed not over projections of concrete states but over cells belonging to the grid based abstract domain. Nevertheless, we can easily extend the soundness guarantees in Theorem 3 to conclude soundness of the composition.

Once again, we can stop this process after T steps or use widening to force convergence. We now remark on a few technicalities that arise due to the way the tree decomposition is constructed.

Intersections with Unsafe Sets: Checking for a non-empty intersection with the unsafe sets may require constructing concrete cells over the full dimensional space if the unsafe sets are not tree decomposable for the tree T. However in many cases, the unsafe states are specified as intervals over individual variables, which yields a tree decomposable set. In such cases, we need to intersect the abstraction at each node with the unsafe set and perform message passing to make it canonical before checking for emptiness.

Handling Guards and Invariants: We have not discussed guards and invariants. It is assumed that such guards and invariants are tree decomposable over the tree T. In this case, we can check which abstract cells have a non-empty intersection with the guard using message passing. The handling of transition systems with guards and invariants will be discussed as part of future extensions.

5   Experimental Evaluation

In this section, we describe an experimental evaluation of our approach over a set of benchmark problems. Our evaluation is based on a C++-based prototype implementation that can read in the description of a nonlinear dynamical system over a set of system and disturbance variables. The dynamics can currently include polynomials, rational functions and trigonometric functions. Our implementation uses the MPFI library to perform interval arithmetic over the grid cells [36]. We use the HTD library to compute tree decompositions [1]. The system then computes a time-bounded reachable set over the first T steps of the system's execution. Currently, we plot the results and compare the reachable set estimates against simulation data. We also compare the reachable sets computed by the tree decomposition approach against an approach without using tree decompositions. However, we note that the latter approach timed out on systems beyond 4 state variables.

Table 1 presents the results over a small set of challenging nonlinear systems benchmarks along with a comparison to two other approaches (a) the approach without tree decomposition and (b) the tool SAPO [22] which computes time bounded reachable sets for polynomial systems using the technique of parallelotope bundles described by Dreossi et al. [23]. The benchmarks range in number of system variables from 3 to 20 state variables. We describe the sources for each benchmark where appropriate. Note that the SAPO tool does not handle nonpolynomial dynamics or time varying disturbances at the time of writing.

The treewidths range from 1 for the simplest system (Example 1) to 3 for the 7-state Laub Loomis oscillator example [30]. We note that the tree decomposition was constructed within 0.01 s for all the examples. We also note that systems with as many as 20 state variables are handled by our approach whereas the monolithic approach cannot handle systems beyond 4 state variables. We now compare the results of our approach to that of the monolithic approach on the two cases where the latter approach completed.

System # 1: Consider again the system from Example 1 with 3 state variables and 1 disturbance. We have already noted a tree decomposition of tree width 1 for this example.

System # 2: In this example, we consider a system over 4 state variables $\{x, y, z, w\}$ and one disturbance variable w_1.

$$x := 0.5x + y + 0.05xy - w_1, \ y := -0.7y - 0.03x, \ z := z - 0.4y,$$
$$w := w - 0.05xw$$

622   S. Sankaranarayanan

Table 1. Results on benchmark examples. $|X|$: Number of state variables, $|W|$: number of disturbance variables, Tree Decomp.: reachability using tree decompositions, Monolithic: reachability analysis without tree decompositions. SAPO: number of directions ($|L|$), number of bundles ($|T|$) and running time. All timings are reported in seconds on a Macbook pro laptop running MacOS 10.14 with 16 GB RAM and 3.4 GHz Intel core i7 processor. Reachability analysis was carried out for 15 time steps.

Name	$|X|$	$|W|$	Tree Width	Tree Decomp.		Monolithic		SAPO	
				Time	# Cells	Time	# Cells	$(|L|,|T|)$	Time
System # 1	3	1	1	14.4	0.22M	1047.6	7.6M	-n/a-	
System # 2	4	1	2	2.7	24K	652	3.1M	-n/a-	
SIR [23,40]	3	0	1	4.1	95K	143	2M	(3,1)	0.1
1D-Lattice-10 [39]	10	0	2	99	1.1M	TO (1.5 h)		(16,6)	679
Ebola-epidemic [14]	5	0	2	799.4	1.9M	TO (1.5 h)		(5,5)	0.02
p53-gene-reg [31]	6	0	2	135.8	98K	TO (1.5 h)		-n/a-	
Influenza-epidemic [22]	4	0	2	517.9	1.4M	TO (1.5 h)		(7,4)	0.1
Coupled-vanderpol	6	0	2	10.5	0.1M	TO (1.5 h)		(10,5)	2.5
Laub-Loomis [20,30]	7	0	3	1755.1	2.6M	TO (1.5 h)		(12,6)	1.8
Honeybee* [9,23]	6	4	3	206.1	2.1M	TO (1.5 h)		(8,4)	0.7
Phosporelay [22]	7	0	3	1566.2	7.5M	TO (1.5 h)		(10,4)	1.2
Coord. Vehicles (1)	5	1	2	150.2	0.5M	TO (1.5 h)		-n/a-	
Coord. Vehicles (2)	10	2	2	1175.2	2M	TO (1.5 h)		-n/a-	
Coord. Vehicles (4)	20	4	2	2206.7	3.9M	TO (1.5 h)		-n/a-	

The domains include $(x,y,z,w) \in [-1,1]^4$ and divided into 16×10^8 grid cells (200 for each state variable). The disturbance $w_1 \in [-0.1, 0.1]$. The initial conditions are $x \in [0.08, 0.16], y \in [-0.16, -.05], z \in [0.12, 0, 31]$ and $w \in [-0.15, -0.1]$. We obtain a tree decomposition of width 2, wherein the nodes include $n_1 : \{x, y, w_1\}$, $n_2 : \{y, z\}$ and $n_3 : \{x, w\}$ with the edges (n_1, n_2) and (n_1, n_3).

Figure 1 compares the resulting reachable sets for the tree decomposed reachability analysis versus the monolithic approach. We note differences between the two reachable sets but the loss in precision is not significant.

Coordinated Vehicles: In this example, we study nonlinear vehicle models of vehicles executing coordinated turns. Each vehicle has states $(x_i, y_i, v_{x,i}, v_{y,i}, \omega)$, representing positions, velocities and the rate of change in the yaw angle, respectively, with a disturbance w_i. The dynamics are given by

$$x_i := x_i + 0.1 v_{x,i}, \ y_i := y_i + 0.1 v_{y,i}, \ v_{x,i} = v_{x,i} + 0.1 v_{x,i} \cos(0.1\omega_i)$$
$$- 0.1 v_{y,i} \sin(0.1\omega_i) \omega_i = 0.5\omega_i + 0.5\omega_0 + 0.1 w_i$$

The vehicles are loosely coupled with ω_i representing the turn rate of the ith vehicle and ω_0 that of the "lead" vehicle. The ith vehicle tries to gradually

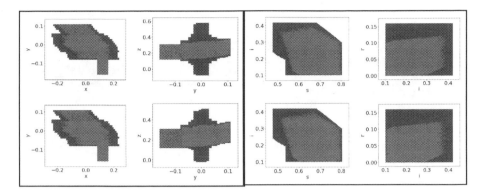

Fig. 1. Reachable set projections (shaded blue) for System# 2 (left) and the SIR model [22] (right). Top: tree decomposition approach and Bottom: monolithic approach without tree decompositions. Reachable sets are identical for the SIR model. Note the difference in range of z for the system #2. The red dots show the results of simulations. (Color figure online)

align its turn rate to that of the lead vehicle. This model represents a simple scenario of loosely coupled systems that interact using a small set of state variables. Applications including models of cardiac cells that are also loosely coupled through shared action potentials [26]. The variables x_i, y_i are set in the domain $[-15, 15]$ and subdivided into 300 parts along each dimension. Similarly, the velocities range over $[-10, 10]$ and are subdivided into 500 parts each and the yaw rate ranges over $[-0.2, 0.2]$ radians/sec and subdivided into 25 parts. The disturbance ranges over $[-0.1, 0.1]$. Table 1 reports results from models involving $1, 2$ and 4 vehicles. Since they are loosely coupled, the treewidth of these models is 2.

Laub-Loomis Model: The Laub-Loomis model is a molecular network that produces spontaneous oscillations for certain values of the model parameters. The model's description was taken from Dang et al. [20]. The system has 7 state variables each of which was subdivided into 100 cells yielding a large state space with 10^{14} cells. We note that the tree width of the graph is 3, yielding nodes with upto 4 variables in them.

Comparison with SAPO. SAPO is a state-of-the-art tool that uses polytope bundles and Bernstein polynomials to represent and propagate reachable sets for polynomial dynamical systems [22,23]. We compare our approach directly on SAPO for identical models and initial sets. Note that SAPO does not currently handle non-polynomial models or models with time-varying disturbances. Table 1 shows that SAPO is orders of magnitude faster on all the models, with the sole exception of the 1D-Lattice-10 model. Figure 2 shows the comparison of the reachable sets computed by our approach (shaded blue region) against those

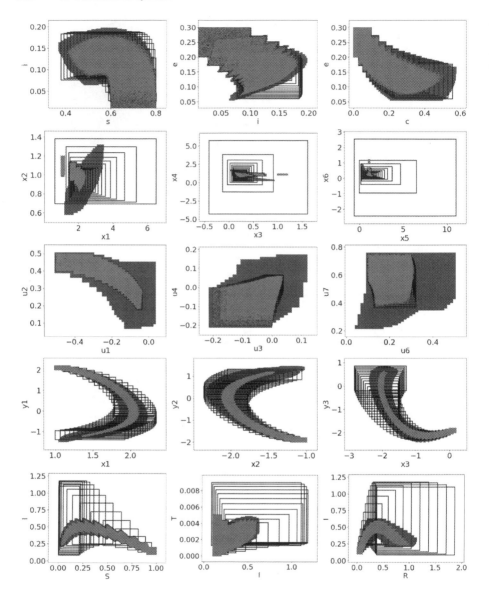

Fig. 2. Comparison of various projections of the reachable sets computed by our approach shown in blue, the reachable set computed by SAPO shown as black rectangles and states obtained through random simulation shown in red dots. Top row: ebola model, second row: phosporelay, third row: 1d-lattice-10, fourth row: vanderpol (35 steps) and bottom row: influenza model. (Color figure online)

computed by SAPO (black rectangles) for five different models. We note that for three of the models compared, neither reachable set is contained in the other. For the one dimensional lattice model, SAPO produces a better reachable set, whereas our approach is better for the influenza model. We also note that both for our approach the precision can be improved markedly by increasing the number of subdivisions, albeit at a large computational cost that depends on the treewidth of the model. The same is true for SAPO, where the number of directions and the template sizes have a non-trivial impact on running time.

Models with Large Treewidths. We briefly report on a few models that we attempted with large treewidths. For such models, our approach of decomposing the space into cells becomes infeasible due to the curse of dimensionality.

A model of how honeybees select between different sites [9,23] has 6 variables and its tree width is 5 with a single tree node containing all state variables. However, the large treewidth is due to two terms in the model which are replaced by disturbance variables that overapproximate their value. This brings down the treewidth to 3, making it tractable for our approach. Details of this transformation are discussed in our extended version. Treewidth reduction using abstractions is an interesting topic for future work.

We originally proposed to analyze a 2D grid lattice model taken from Vleck et al [39]. However, a 2D 10×10 lattice model has a dependency hypergraph that forms a 10×10 grid with treewidth 10. Likewise, the 17-state crazyflie benchmark for SAPO [22] could not be analyzed by our approach since its treewidth is too large.

6 Conclusions

We have shown how tree decompositions can define an abstract domain that projects concrete sets along the various subsets of state variables. We showed how message passing can be used to exchange information between these subsets. We analyze the completeness of our approach and show that the abstraction is lossy due to the projection operation. We show that for small tree width models, a gridding-based analysis of nonlinear system can be used whereas such approaches are too expensive when applied in a monolithic fashion. For the future, we plan to study tree decompositions for abstract domains such as disjunctions of polyhedra, parallelotope bundles and Taylor models. The process of model abstraction to reduce treewidth is another interesting future possibility.

Acknowledgments. This work was supported by US NSF under award number CPS 1836900, CCF 1815983 and the US Air Force Research Laboratory (AFRL). The author acknowledges Profs. Mohamed Amin Ben Sassi and Fabio Somenzi for helpful discussions, and the anonymous reviewers for their comments.

References

1. Abseher, M., Musliu, N., Woltran, S.: htd – a free, open-source framework for (customized) tree decompositions and beyond. In: Salvagnin, D., Lombardi, M. (eds.) CPAIOR 2017. LNCS, vol. 10335, pp. 376–386. Springer, Cham (2017). https://doi.org/10.1007/978-3-319-59776-8_30

2. Adjé, A., Gaubert, S., Goubault, E.: Coupling policy iteration with semi-definite relaxation to compute accurate numerical invariants in static analysis. In: Gordon, A.D. (ed.) ESOP 2010. LNCS, vol. 6012, pp. 23–42. Springer, Heidelberg (2010). https://doi.org/10.1007/978-3-642-11957-6_3

3. Blanchet, B., et al.: A static analyzer for large safety-critical software. In: Programming Language Design & Implementation, pp. 196–207. ACM Press (2003)

4. Blanchet, B., et al.: Design and implementation of a special-purpose static program analyzer for safety-critical real-time embedded software. In: Mogensen, T.Æ., Schmidt, D.A., Sudborough, I.H. (eds.) The Essence of Computation. LNCS, vol. 2566, pp. 85–108. Springer, Heidelberg (2002). https://doi.org/10.1007/3-540-36377-7_5

5. Bodlaender, H.L.: Dynamic programming on graphs with bounded treewidth. In: Lepistö, T., Salomaa, A. (eds.) ICALP 1988. LNCS, vol. 317, pp. 105–118. Springer, Heidelberg (1988). https://doi.org/10.1007/3-540-19488-6_110

6. Bodlaender, H.L.: A linear-time algorithm for finding tree-decompositions of small treewidth. SIAM J. Comput. **25**(6), 1305–1317 (1996)

7. Bodlaender, H.L.: Fixed-parameter tractability of treewidth and pathwidth. In: Bodlaender, H.L., Downey, R., Fomin, F.V., Marx, D. (eds.) The Multivariate Algorithmic Revolution and Beyond. LNCS, vol. 7370, pp. 196–227. Springer, Heidelberg (2012). https://doi.org/10.1007/978-3-642-30891-8_12

8. Bodlaender, H.L., Koster, A.M.: Treewidth computations I. Upper bounds. Inf. Comput. **208**(3), 259–275 (2010)

9. Britton, N.F., Franks, N.R., Pratt, S.C., Seeley, T.D.: Deciding on a new home: how do honeybees agree? Proc. R. Soc. Lond. Ser. B Biol. Sci. **269**(1498), 1383–1388 (2002)

10. Chatterjee, K., Ibsen-Jensen, R., Goharshady, A.K., Pavlogiannis, A.: Algorithms for algebraic path properties in concurrent systems of constant treewidth components. ACM Trans. Program. Lang. Syst. **40**(3), 1–43 (2018)

11. Chatterjee, K., Ibsen-Jensen, R., Pavlogiannis, A., Goyal, P.: Faster algorithms for algebraic path properties in recursive state machines with constant treewidth. In: Principles of Programming Languages (POPL), pp. 97–109. Association for Computing Machinery, New York (2015)

12. Chen, M., Herbert, S., Tomlin, C.: Exact and efficient Hamilton-Jacobi-based guaranteed safety analysis via system decomposition. In: IEEE International Conference on Robotics and Automation (ICRA) (2017, to appear). arXiv:1609.05248

13. Chen, X., Sankaranarayanan, S.: Decomposed reachability analysis for nonlinear systems. In: 2016 IEEE Real-Time Systems Symposium (RTSS), pp. 13–24, November 2016

14. Chowell, G., Hengartner, N., Castillo-Chavez, C., Fenimore, P., Hyman, J.: The basic reproductive number of Ebola and the effects of public health measures: the cases of Congo and Uganda. J. Theor. Biol. **229**(1), 119–126 (2004)

15. Courcelle, B.: The monadic second-order logic of graphs iii: treewidth, forbidden minors and complexity issues. Informatique Théorique **26**, 257–286 (1992)

16. Cousot, P., Cousot, R.: Static determination of dynamic properties of programs. In: Proceedings of the ISOP 1976, pp. 106–130. Dunod, Paris (1976)

17. Cousot, P., Cousot, R.: Comparing the Galois connection and widening/narrowing approaches to abstract interpretation. In: Bruynooghe, M., Wirsing, M. (eds.) PLILP 1992. LNCS, vol. 631, pp. 269–295. Springer, Heidelberg (1992). https://doi.org/10.1007/3-540-55844-6_142

18. Cousot, P., Cousot, R.: Abstract interpretation: a unified lattice model for static analysis of programs by construction or approximation of fixpoints. In: ACM Principles of Programming Languages, pp. 238–252 (1977)
19. Cousot, P., Halbwachs, N.: Automatic discovery of linear restraints among the variables of a program. In: POPL 1978, pp. 84–97, January 1978
20. Dang, T., Dreossi, T.: Falsifying oscillation properties of parametric biological models. In: Hybrid Systems Biology (HSB). EPTCS, vol. 125, pp. 53–67 (2013)
21. Delmas, D., Souyris, J.: Astrée: from research to industry. In: Nielson, H.R., Filé, G. (eds.) SAS 2007. LNCS, vol. 4634, pp. 437–451. Springer, Heidelberg (2007). https://doi.org/10.1007/978-3-540-74061-2_27
22. Dreossi, T.: Sapo: reachability computation and parameter synthesis of polynomial dynamical systems. In: Hybrid Systems: Computation and Control (HSCC), pp. 29–34. ACM (2017)
23. Dreossi, T., Dang, T., Piazza, C.: Parallelotope bundles for polynomial reachability. In: Hybrid Systems: Computation and Control (HSCC), pp. 297–306. ACM (2016)
24. Ferrara, A., Pan, G., Vardi, M.Y.: Treewidth in verification: local vs. global. In: Sutcliffe, G., Voronkov, A. (eds.) LPAR 2005. LNCS (LNAI), vol. 3835, pp. 489–503. Springer, Heidelberg (2005). https://doi.org/10.1007/11591191_34
25. de Figueiredo, L.H., Stolfi, J.: Self-validated numerical methods and applications. In: Brazilian Mathematics Colloquium Monograph. IMPA, Rio de Janeiro (1997)
26. Grosu, R., et al.: From cardiac cells to genetic regulatory networks. In: Gopalakrishnan, G., Qadeer, S. (eds.) CAV 2011. LNCS, vol. 6806, pp. 396–411. Springer, Heidelberg (2011). https://doi.org/10.1007/978-3-642-22110-1_31
27. Gulwani, S., Jojic, N.: Program verification as probabilistic inference. In: POPL, POPL 2007, pp. 277–289. Association for Computing Machinery (2007)
28. Ivančić, F., et al.: Scalable and scope-bounded software verification in VARVEL. Autom. Softw. Eng. **22**(4), 517–559 (2014). https://doi.org/10.1007/s10515-014-0164-0
29. Koller, D., Friedman, N.: Probabilistic Graphical Models. The MIT Press, Cambridge (2009)
30. Laub, M.T., Loomis, W.F.: A molecular network that produces spontaneous oscillations in excitable cells of dictyostelium. Mol. Biol. Cell **9**(12), 3521–3532 (1998)
31. Leenders, G., Tuszynski, J.A.: Stochastic and deterministic models of cellular p53 regulation. Front. Oncol. **3**, 64 (2013)
32. Makino, K., Berz, M.: Taylor models and other validated functional inclusion methods. Int. J. Pure Appl. Math. **4**(4), 379–456 (2003)
33. Moore, R.E., Kearfott, R.B., Cloud, M.J.: Introduction to Interval Analysis. SIAM, Philadelphia (2009)
34. Nielson, F., Nielson, H.R., Hankin, C.: Algorithms. In: Nielson, F., Nielson, H.R., Hankin, C. (eds.) Principles of Program Analysis. Springer, Heidelberg (1999). https://doi.org/10.1007/978-3-662-03811-6_6
35. Obdržálek, J.: Fast Mu-Calculus model checking when tree-width is bounded. In: Hunt, W.A., Somenzi, F. (eds.) CAV 2003. LNCS, vol. 2725, pp. 80–92. Springer, Heidelberg (2003). https://doi.org/10.1007/978-3-540-45069-6_7
36. Revol, N., Rouillier, F.: Motivations for an arbitrary precision interval arithmetic and the MPFI library. Reliable Comput. **11**, 275–290 (2005). https://doi.org/10.1007/s11155-005-6891-y
37. Robertson, N., Seymour, P.: Graph minors. III. Planar tree-width. J. Comb. Theory Ser. B **36**(1), 49–64 (1984)
38. Thorup, M.: All structured programs have small tree width and good register allocation. Inf. Comput. **142**(2), 159–181 (1998)

39. Vleck, E.S.V., Mallet-Paret, J., Cahn, J.W.: Traveling wave solutions for systems of ODEs on a two-dimensional spatial lattice. SIAM J. Appl. Math. **59**, 455–493 (1998)
40. Weisstein, E.W.: SIR model, from MathWorld-A Wolfram Web Resource. https://mathworld.wolfram.com/SIRModel.html. Accessed May 2020

Fast and Guaranteed Safe Controller Synthesis for Nonlinear Vehicle Models

Chuchu Fan[1]([✉]) [iD], Kristina Miller[2] [iD], and Sayan Mitra[2] [iD]

[1] Department of Computing and Mathematical Sciences,
California Institute of Technology, Pasadena, USA
`chuchu@caltech.edu`
[2] Department of Electrical and Computer
Engineering, University of Illinois
at Urbana-Champaign, Champaign, USA
`{kmmille2,mitras}@illinois.edu`

Abstract. We address the problem of synthesizing a controller for nonlinear systems with reach-avoid requirements. Our controller consists of a reference controller and a tracking controller which drives the actual trajectory to follow the reference trajectory. We identify a type of reference trajectory such that the tracking error between the actual trajectory of the closed-loop system and the reference trajectory can be bounded. Moreover, such a bound on the tracking error is independent of the reference trajectory. Using such bounds on the tracking error, we propose a method that can find a reference trajectory by solving a satisfiability problem over linear constraints. Our overall algorithm guarantees that the resulting controller can make sure every trajectory from the initial set of the system satisfies the given reach-avoid requirement. We also implement our technique in a tool FACTEST. We show that FACTEST can find controllers for four vehicle models (3–6 dimensional state space and 2–4 dimensional input space) across eight scenarios (with up to 22 obstacles), all with running time at the sub-second range.

1 Introduction

Design automation and safety of autonomous systems is an important research area. Controller synthesis aims to provide correct-by-construction controllers that can guarantee that the system under control meets certain requirements. Controller synthesis is a type of program synthesis problem. The synthesized program or *controller* g has to meet the given requirement R, when it is run in

The authors acknowledge support from the DARPA Assured Autonomy under contract FA8750-19-C-0089, the Air Force Office of Scientific Research under grant AFOSR FA9550-17-1-0236, and the National Science Foundation under grant NSF CCF 1918531. The views, opinions and/or findings expressed are those of the authors and should not be interpreted as representing the official views or policies of the Department of Defense or the U.S. Government.

S. K. Lahiri and C. Wang (Eds.): CAV 2020, LNCS 12224, pp. 629–652, 2020.
https://doi.org/10.1007/978-3-030-53288-8_31

(closed-loop) composition with a given physical process or *plant* $\mathcal{A}$. Therefore, a synthesis algorithm has to account for the combined behavior of g and $\mathcal{A}$.

Methods for designing controllers for asymptotic requirements like stability, robustness, and tracking, predate the algorithmic synthesis approaches for programs [3,16,30]. However, these classic control design methods normally do not provide formal guarantees in terms of handling bounded-horizon requirements like safety. Typical controller programs are small, well-structured, and at core, have a succinct logic ("bang-bang" control) or mathematical operations (PID control). This might suggest that controllers could be an attractive target for algorithmic synthesis for safety, temporal logic (TL), and bounded time requirements [1,9,18,34,38].

On the other hand, *motion planning (MP)*, which is an instance of the controller synthesis for robots is notoriously difficult (see [21] Chapter 6.5). A typical MP requirement is to make a robot $\mathcal{A}$ track certain waypoints while meeting some constraints. A popular paradigm in MP, called sampling-based MP, gives practical, *fully automatic*, randomized, solutions to hard problem instances by only considering the geometry of the vehicle and the free space [14,15,20,21]. However, they do not ensure that the dynamic behavior of the vehicle will actually follow the planed path without running into obstacles. Ergo, MP continues to be a central problem in robotics[1].

In this paper, we aim to achieve faster control synthesis with guarantees by exploiting a separation of concerns that exists in the problem: (A) how to drive a vehicle/plant to a *given waypoint?* and (B) Which *waypoints* to choose for achieving the ultimate goal? (A) can be solved using powerful control theoretic techniques—if not completely automatically, but at least in a principled fashion, with guarantees, for a broad class of $\mathcal{A}$'s. Given a solution for (A), we solve (B) algorithmically. A contribution of the paper is to identify characteristics of a solution of (A) that make solutions of (B) effective. Consider nonlinear control systems $\mathcal{A}: \frac{d}{dt}x = f(x,u)$ and reach-avoid requirements defined by a goal set G that the trajectories should reach, and obstacles $\mathbf{O}$ the trajectories should avoid. The above separation leads to a two step process: (A) Find a state feedback tracking controller g_{trk} that drives the actual trajectory of the closed-loop system ξ_g to follow a reference trajectory ξ_{ref}. (B) Design a reference controller g_{ref}, which consists of a reference trajectory ξ_{ref} and a reference input u_{ref}. The distance between ξ_g and ξ_{ref} is called the tracking error e. If we can somehow know beforehand the value of e without knowing ξ_{ref}, we can use such error to bloat $\mathbf{O}$ and shrink G, and then synthesize ξ_{ref} such that it is e away from the obstacles (inside the goal set). For linear systems, this was the approach used in [7], but for nonlinear systems, the tracking error e will generally change with ξ_{ref}, and the two steps get entangled.

For a general class of nonlinear vehicles (such as cars, drones, and underwater vehicles), the tracking controller g_{trk} is always designed to minimize the tracking

---

[1] In the most recent International Conference on Robotics and Automation, among the 3,512 submissions "Path and motion planning" was the second most popular key phrase.

error. The convergence of the error can be proved by a Lyapunov function for certain types of ξ_{ref}. We show how, under reasonable assumptions, we can use Lyapunov functions to bound the value of the tracking error *even when the waypoints changes* (Lemma 2). This error bound is independent of ξ_{ref} so long as ξ_{ref} satisfies the assumptions. For step (B) we introduce a SAT-based trajectory planning methods to find such ξ_{ref} and u_{ref} by solving a satisfiability (SAT) problem over quantifier free linear real arithmetic (Theorem 1). Moreover, the number of constraints in the SMT problem scales linearly to the increase of number of obstacles (and not with the vehicle model). Thus, our methods can scale to complex requirements and high dimensional systems.

Putting it all together, our final synthesis algorithm (Algorithm 2) guarantees that any trajectory following the synthesized reference trajectory will satisfy the reach-avoid requirements. The resulting tool FACTEST is tested with four non-linear vehicle models and on eight different scenarios, taken from MP literature, which cover a wide range of 2D and 3D environments. Experiment results show that our tool scales very well: it can find the small covers $\{\Theta_j\}_j$ and the corresponding reference trajectories and control inputs satisfying the reach-avoid requirements most often in less than a second, even with up to 22 obstacles. We have also compared our SAT-based trajectory planner to a standard RRT planner, and the results show that our SAT-based method resoundingly outperforms RRT. To summarize, our main contributions are:

1. A method (Algorithm 2) for controller synthesis separating tracking controller g_{trk} and search for reference controller g_{ref}.
2. Sufficient conditions for tracking controller error performance that makes the decomposition work (Lemma 2 and Lemma 3).
3. An SMT-based effective method for synthesizing reference controller g_{ref}.
4. The FACTEST implementation of the above and its evaluation showing very encouraging results in terms of finding controllers that make any trajectories of the closed-loop system satisfy reach-avoid requirements (Sect. 6).

Related Works. *Model Predictive Control (MPC).* MPC [4,25,45,49] has to solve a constrained, discrete-time, optimal control problem. MPC for controller synthesis typically requires model reduction for casting the optimization problem as an LP [4], QP [2,36], MILP [33,34,45]. However, when the plant model is nonlinear [8,22], it may be hard to balance speed and complex requirements as the optimization problem become nonconvex and nonlinear.

Discrete Abstractions. Discrete, finite-state, abstraction of the control system is computed, and then a discrete controller is synthesized by solving a two-player game [10,17,24,42,47]. CoSyMA [28], Pessoa [37], LTLMop [18,46], Tulip [9,48], and SCOTS [38] are based on these approaches. The discretization step often leads to a severe state space explosion for higher dimensional models.

Safe Motion Planning. The idea of bounding the tracking error through pre-computation has been used in several techniques: FastTrack [11] uses Hamilton-Jacobi reachability analysis to produce a "safety bubble" around planed paths.

Reachability based trajectory design for dynamical environments (RTD) [44] computes an offline forward reachable sets to guarantee that the robot is not-at-fault in any collision. In [40], a technique based on convex optimization is used to compute tracking error bounds. Another technique [23,43] uses motion primitives expanded by safety funnels, which defines similar ideas of safety tubes.

Sampling Based Planning. Probabilistic Road Maps (PRM) [15], Rapidly-exploring Random Trees (RRT) [19], and fast marching tree (FMT) [12] are widely used in actual robotic platforms. They can generate feasible trajectories through known or partially known environments. Compared with the deterministic guarantees provided by our proposed method, these methods come with stochastic guarantees. Also, they are not designed to be robust to model uncertainty or disturbances. MoveIT [5] is a tool designed to implement and benchmark various motion planners on robots. The motion planners in MoveIT are from the open motion planning library (OMPL) [41], which implements motion planners abstractly.

Controlled Lyapunov Function (CLF). CLF have been used to guarantee that the overall closed-loop controlled system satisfies a reach-while-stay specification [35]. Instead of asking for a CLF for the overall closed-loop system, our method only needs a Lyapunov function for the tracking error, which is a weaker local requirement. CLF is often a difficult requirement to meet for nonlinear vehicle models.

2   Preliminaries and Problem Statement

Let us denote real numbers by $\mathbb{R}$, non-negative real numbers by $\mathbb{R}_{\geq 0}$, and natural numbers by $\mathbb{N}$. The n-dimensional *Euclidean space* is $\mathbb{R}^n$. For a vector $x \in \mathbb{R}^n$, $x^{(i)}$ is the ith entry of x and $\|x\|_2$ is the 2-norm of x. For any matrix $A \in \mathbb{R}^{n \times m}$, A^T is its *transpose*; $A^{(i)}$ is the ith row of A. Given a $r \geq 0$, an *r-ball* around $x \in \mathbb{R}^n$ is defined as $B_r(x) = \{x' \in \mathbb{R}^n \mid \|x' - x\|_2 \leq r\}$. We call r the radius of the ball. Given a matrix $H \in \mathbb{R}^{r \times n}$ and a vector $b \in \mathbb{R}^r$, an (H, b)-*polytope* is denoted by $Poly(H, b) = \{x \in \mathbb{R}^n \mid Hx \leq b\}$. Each row of the inequality $H^{(i)}x \leq b^{(i)}$ defines a *halfspace*. We also call $H^{(i)}x = b^{(i)}$ the *surface* of the polytope. Let $\mathsf{dP}(H) = r$ denotes the number of rows in H. Given a set $S \subseteq \mathbb{R}^n$, the radius of S is defined as $\sup_{x,y \in S} \|x - y\|_2/2$.

State Space and Workspace. The state space of control systems will be a subspace $\mathcal{X} \subseteq \mathbb{R}^n$. The *workspace* is a subspace $\mathcal{W} \subseteq \mathbb{R}^d$, for $d \in \{2, 3\}$, which is the physical space in which the robots have to avoid obstacles and reach goals. Given a state vector $x \in \mathcal{X}$, its projection to $\mathcal{W}$ is denoted by $x \downarrow p$. That is, $x \downarrow p = [p_x, p_y]^\mathsf{T} \in \mathbb{R}^2$ for ground vehicles on the plane and $x \downarrow p = [p_x, p_y, p_z]^\mathsf{T} \in \mathbb{R}^3$ for aerial and underwater vehicles. When x is clear from context we will write $x \downarrow p$ as simply p. The vector x may include other variables like velocity, heading, pitch, etc., but p only has the position in Cartesian coordinates. We assume that the goal set $G := Poly(H_G, b_G)$ and the unsafe set $\mathbf{O}$ (obstacles) are specified by polytopes in $\mathcal{W}$; $\mathbf{O} = \cup O_i$, where $O_i := Poly(H_{o,i}, b_{o,i})$ for each obstacle i.

Trajectories and Reach-Avoid Requirements. A *trajectory* ξ over $\mathcal{X}$ of duration T is a function $\xi : [0, T] \to \mathcal{X}$, that maps each time t in the time *domain* $[0, T]$ to a point $\xi(t) \in \mathcal{X}$. The *time bound or duration* of ξ is denoted by $\xi.\mathsf{ltime} = T$. The projection of a trajectory $\xi : [0, T] \to \mathcal{X}$ to $\mathcal{W}$ is written as $\xi \downarrow p : [0, T] \to \mathcal{W}$ and defined as $(\xi \downarrow p)(t) = \xi(t) \downarrow p$. We say that a trajectory $\xi(t)$ *satisfies a reach-avoid requirement given by unsafe set* $\mathbf{O}$ *and goal set* G if $\forall t \in [0, \xi.\mathsf{ltime}], \xi(t) \downarrow p \notin \mathbf{O}$ and $\xi(\xi.\mathsf{ltime}) \downarrow p \in G$. See Fig. 1 for an example.

Given a trajectory $\xi : [0, T] \to \mathcal{X}$ and a time $t > 0$, the *time shift* of ξ is a function $(\xi + t) : [t, t + T] \to \mathcal{X}$ defined as $\forall t' \in [t, t + T], (\xi + t)(t') = \xi(t' - t)$. Strictly speaking, for $t > 0, \xi + t$ is not a trajectory. The *concatenation* of two trajectories $\xi_1 \frown \xi_2$ is a new trajectory in which ξ_1 is followed by ξ_2. That is, for each $t \in [0, \xi_1.\mathsf{ltime} + \xi_2.\mathsf{ltime}], (\xi_1 \frown \xi_2)(t) = \xi_1(t)$ when $t \leq \xi_1.\mathsf{ltime}$, and equals $\xi_2(t - \xi_1.\mathsf{ltime})$ when $t > \xi_1.\mathsf{ltime}$. Trajectories are closed under concatenation, and many trajectories can be concatenated in the same way.

2.1   Nonlinear Control System

Definition 1. *An* (n, m)-*dimensional control system* $\mathcal{A}$ *is a 4-tuple* $\langle \mathcal{X}, \Theta, \mathbf{U}, f \rangle$ *where (i)* $\mathcal{X} \subseteq \mathbb{R}^n$ *is the state space, (ii)* $\Theta \subseteq \mathcal{X}$ *is the initial set, (iii)* $\mathbf{U} \subseteq \mathbb{R}^m$ *is the input space, and (iv)* $f : \mathcal{X} \times \mathbf{U} \to \mathcal{X}$ *is the dynamic function that is Lipschitz continuous with respect to the first argument.*

A control system with no inputs $(m = 0)$ is called a *closed* system.

Let us fix a time duration $T > 0$. An *input trajectory* $u : [0, T] \to \mathbf{U}$, is a continuous trajectory over the input space $\mathbf{U}$. We denote the set of all possible input trajectories to be $\mathcal{U}$. Given an input signal $u \in \mathcal{U}$ and an initial state $x_0 \in \Theta$, a *solution* of $\mathcal{A}$ is a continuous trajectory $\xi_u : [0, T] \to \mathcal{X}$ that satisfies (i) $\xi_u(0) = x_0$ and (ii) for any $t \in [0, T]$, the time derivative of ξ_u at t satisfies the differential equation:

$$\frac{d}{dt} \xi_u(t) = f(\xi_u(t), u(t)). \tag{1}$$

For any $x_0 \in \Theta, u \in \mathcal{U}, \xi_u$ is a state trajectory and we call such a pair (ξ_u, u) a state-input trajectory pair.

A *reference state trajectory* (or *reference trajectory* for brevity) is a trajectory over $\mathcal{X}$ that the control system tries to follow. We denote reference trajectories by ξ_{ref}. Similarly, a *reference input trajectory* (or *reference input*) is a trajectory over $\mathbf{U}$ and we denote them as u_{ref}. Note these ξ_{ref} and u_{ref} are not necessarily solutions of (1). Figure 1 shows reference and actual solution trajectories.

We call a reference trajectory ξ_{ref} and a reference input u_{ref} together as a reference controller g_{ref}. Given g_{ref}, a *tracking controller* g_{trk} is a function that is used to compute the inputs for $\mathcal{A}$ so that in the resulting closed system, the state trajectories try to follow ξ_{ref}.

Definition 2. *Given an* (n, m)-*dynamical system* $\mathcal{A}$, *a reference trajectory* ξ_{ref}, *and a reference input* u_{ref}, *a tracking controller for the triple* $\langle \mathcal{A}, \xi_{\mathsf{ref}}, u_{\mathsf{ref}} \rangle$ *is a (state feedback) function* $g_{\mathsf{trk}} : \mathcal{X} \times \mathcal{X} \times \mathbf{U} \to \mathbf{U}$.

At any time t, the tracking controller g_{trk} takes in a current state of the system x, a reference trajectory state $\xi_{ref}(t)$, and a reference input $u_{ref}(t)$, and gives an input $g_{trk}(x, \xi_{ref}(t), u_{ref}(t)) \in \mathbf{U}$ for $\mathcal{A}$. The controller g for $\mathcal{A}$ is determined by both the reference controller g_{ref} and the tracking controller g_{trk}. The resulting trajectory ξ_g of the closed control system ($\mathcal{A}$ closed with g_{ref} and g_{trk}) satisfies:

$$\frac{d}{dt}\xi_g(t) = f\left(\xi_g(t), g_{trk}\left(\xi_g(t), \xi_{ref}(t), u_{ref}(t)\right)\right), \forall\, t \in [0, T] \backslash D, \qquad (2)$$

where D is the set of points in time where the second or third argument of g_{trk} is discontinuous[2].

2.2   Controller Synthesis Problem

Definition 3. *Given a (n, m)-dimensional nonlinear system $\mathcal{A} = \langle \mathcal{X}, \Theta, \mathbf{U}, f \rangle$, its workspace $\mathcal{W}$, goal set $G \subseteq \mathcal{W}$ and the unsafe set $\mathbf{O} \subseteq \mathcal{W}$, we are required to find (a) a tracking controller g_{trk}, (b) a partition $\{\Theta_j\}_j$ of Θ, and (c) for each partition Θ_j, a reference controller $g_{j,ref}$, which consists of a state trajectory $\xi_{j,ref}$ and an input trajectory $u_{j,ref}$, such that $\forall x_0 \in \Theta_j$, the unique trajectory ξ_g of the closed system as in Eq. (2) starting from x_0 reaches G and avoids $\mathbf{O}$.*

Again, $\xi_{j,ref}$ and $u_{j,ref}$ in $g_{j,ref}$ are not required to be a state-input pair, but, for each initial state $x_0 \in \Theta_j$, the closed loop trajectory ξ_g following ξ_{ref} *is* a valid state trajectory with corresponding input u generated by g_{trk} and $g_{j,ref}$. In this paper, we will decompose the controller synthesis problem: Part (a) will be delivered by design engineers with knowledge of vehicle dynamics, and parts (b) and (c) will be automatically synthesized by our algorithm. The latter being the main contribution of the paper.

Example 1. Consider a ground vehicle moving on a 2D workspace $\mathcal{W} \subseteq \mathbb{R}^2$ as shown in Fig. 1.

This scenario is called **Zigzag** and it is adopted from [32]. The red polytopes are obstacles. The blue and green polytopes are the initial set Θ and the goal set G. There are also obstacles (not shown in the figure) defining the boundaries of the entire workspace. The black line is a projection of a reference trajectory to the workspace: $\xi_{ref}(t) \downarrow p$. This would not be a feasible state trajectory for a ground vehicle that cannot make sharp turns. The purple dashed curve is a

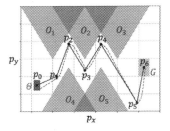

Fig. 1. Zigzag scenario for a controller synthesis problem. The initial set is blue, the goal set is green, and the unsafe sets are red. A valid reference trajectory is shown in black and a feasible trajectory is shown in purple. (Color figure online)

---

[2] ξ_g is a standard solution of ODE with piece-wise continuous right hand side.

real feasible state trajectory of the system starting from Θ with a tracking controller g_{trk}, where g_{trk} will be introduced in Example 2.

Consider the standard nonlinear bicycle model of a car [31]. The control system has 3 state variables: the position p_x, p_y, and the heading direction θ. Its motion is controlled by two inputs: linear velocity v and rotational velocity ω. The car's dynamics are given by:

$$\tfrac{d}{dt}p_x = v\cos(\theta), \tfrac{d}{dt}p_y = v\sin(\theta), \tfrac{d}{dt}\theta = \omega. \tag{3}$$

3 Constructing Reference Trajectories from Waypoints

If $\xi_{\mathsf{ref}}(t) \downarrow p$ is a PWL (PWL) curve in the workspace $\mathcal{W}$, we call $\xi_{\mathsf{ref}}(t)$ a PWL reference trajectory. In $\mathcal{W}$, a PWL curve can be determined by the endpoints of each line segment. We call such endpoints the *waypoints* of the PWL reference trajectory. In Fig. 1, the black points $p_0, \cdots, p_6$ are waypoints of $p(t) = \xi_{\mathsf{ref}}(t) \downarrow p$.

Consider any vehicle on the plane[3] with state variables p_x, p_y, θ, v (x-position, y-position, heading direction, linear velocity) and input variables a, ω (acceleration and angular velocity). Once the waypoints $\{p_i\}_{i=0}^k$ are fixed, and if we enforce constant speed $\bar{v}$ (i.e., $\xi_{\mathsf{ref}}(t) \downarrow v = \bar{v}$ for all $t \in [0, \xi_{\mathsf{ref}}.\mathsf{ltime}]$), then $\xi_{\mathsf{ref}}(t)$ can be uniquely defined by $\{p_i\}_{i=0}^k$ and $\bar{v}$ using Algorithm 1. The semantics of ξ_{ref} and u_{ref} returned by Waypoints_to_Traj is that the reference trajectory requires the vehicle to move at a constant speed $\bar{v}$ along the lines connecting the waypoints $\{p_i\}_{i=0}^k$. In Example 1, $\xi_{\mathsf{ref}}(t), u_{\mathsf{ref}}(t)$ can also be constructed using Waypoints_to_Traj moving v to input variables and dropping a.

We notice that if $k = 1$, $\xi_{\mathsf{ref}}(t), u_{\mathsf{ref}}(t)$ returned by Algorithm 1 is a valid state-input trajectory pair. However, if $k > 1$, $\xi_{\mathsf{ref}}(t), u_{\mathsf{ref}}(t)$ returned by Algorithm 1 is usually not a valid state-input trajectory pair. This is because $\theta_{\mathsf{ref}}(t)$ is discontinuous at the waypoints and no bounded inputs $u_{\mathsf{ref}}(t)$ can drive the vehicle to achieve such $\theta_{\mathsf{ref}}(t)$. Therefore, when $k > 1$, $\xi_{\mathsf{ref}}(t)$ is a PWL reference trajectory with no $u_{\mathsf{ref}}(t)$ such that $\xi_{\mathsf{ref}}, u_{\mathsf{ref}}$ are solutions of (1).

Algorithm 1: Waypoints_to_Traj($\{p_i\}_{i=0}^k, \bar{v}$)

---

   input   : $\{p_i\}_{i=0}^k, \bar{v}$

1 $\forall t \in [0, \sum_{i=1}^k \frac{\|p_j - p_{j-1}\|_2}{\bar{v}}], v_{\mathsf{ref}}(t) = \bar{v}, a_{\mathsf{ref}}(t) = 0, \omega_{\mathsf{ref}}(t) = 0;$

2 $\forall i \geq 1, \forall t \in \left[\sum_{j=1}^{i-1} \frac{\|p_j - p_{j-1}\|_2}{\bar{v}}, \sum_{j=1}^{i} \frac{\|p_j - p_{j-1}\|_2}{\bar{v}} \right),$

   $p_{\mathsf{ref}}(t) = p_{i-1} + \bar{v}t - \sum_{j=1}^{i-1} \|p_j - p_{j-1}\|_2,$

   $\theta_{\mathsf{ref}}(t) = \mathsf{mod}(\mathsf{atan2}((p_{y,i} - p_{y,i-1}), (p_{x,i} - p_{x,i-1}), 2\pi);$

3 $\xi_{\mathsf{ref}}(t) = [p_{\mathsf{ref}}(t), \theta_{\mathsf{ref}}(t), v_{\mathsf{ref}}(t)];$

4 $u_{\mathsf{ref}}(t) = [a_{\mathsf{ref}}(t), \omega_{\mathsf{ref}}(t)];$

5 **return** $\xi_{\mathsf{ref}}(t), u_{\mathsf{ref}}(t)$;

---

[3] A similar construction works for vehicles in 3D workspaces with additional variables.

Proposition 1. *Given a sequence of waypoints $\{p_i\}_{i=0}^{k}$ and a constant speed $\bar{v}$, $\xi_{ref}(t)$, $u_{ref}(t)$ produced by* Waypoints_to_Traj($\{p_i\}_{i=0}^{k}, \bar{v}$) *satisfy:*

- $p_{ref}(t) = \xi_{ref}(t) \downarrow p$ *is a piece-wise continuous function connecting* $\{p_i\}_{i=0}^{k}$.
- *At time $t_i = \sum_{j=1}^{i} \|p_j - p_{j-1}\|_2 / \bar{v}$, $p_{ref}(t_i) = p_i$. We call $\{t_i\})_{i=1}^{k}$ the concatenation time.*
- $\xi_{ref}(t) = \xi_{ref,1}(t) \frown \cdots \frown \xi_{ref,k}(t)$ *and* $u_{ref}(t) = u_{ref,1}(t) \frown \cdots \frown u_{ref,k}(t)$, *where $(\xi_{ref,i}, u_{ref,i})$ are state-input trajectory pairs returned by the function* Waypoints_to_Traj($\{p_{i-1}, p_i\}, \bar{v}$).

Outline of Synthesis Approach. In this Section, we present an Algorithm Waypoints_to_Traj for constructing reference trajectories from arbitrary sequence of waypoints. In Sect. 4, we precisely characterize the type of vehicle tracking controller our method requires from designers. On our tool's webpage [27], we show with several extra examples that indeed developing such controllers is non-trivial, far from automatic, yet bread and butter of control engineers. In Sect. 5, we present the main synthesis algorithm, which uses the tracking error bounds from the previous section, to construct waypoints, for each initial state, which when passed through Waypoints_to_Traj provide the solutions to the synthesis problem.

4   Bounding the Error of a Tracking Controller

4.1   Tracking Error and Lyapunov Functions

Given a reference controller g_{ref}, a tracking controller g_{trk}, and an initial state $x_0 \in \Theta$, the resulting trajectory ξ_g of the closed control system ($\mathcal{A}$ closed with g_{ref} and g_{trk}) is a state trajectory that starts from x_0 and follows the ODE (2). In this setting, we define the *tracking error* at time t to be a continuous function:

$$e : \mathcal{X} \times \mathcal{X} \to \mathbb{R}^n.$$

When $\xi_g(t)$ and $\xi_{ref}(t)$ are fixed, we also write $e(t) = e(\xi_g(t), \xi_{ref}(t))$ which makes it a function of time. One thing to remark here is that if $\xi_{ref}(t)$ is discontinuous, then $e(t)$ is also discontinuous. In this case, the derivative of $e(t)$ cannot be defined at the points of discontinuity. To start with, let us assume that $g_{ref} = (\xi_{ref}, u_{ref})$ is a valid state-input pair so ξ_{ref} is a continuous state trajectory. Later we will see that the analysis can be extended to cases when ξ_{ref} is discontinuous but a concatenation of continuous state trajectories.

When (ξ_{ref}, u_{ref}) is a valid state-input pair and $e(t)$ satisfy an differential equation $\frac{d}{dt}e(t) = f_e(e(t))$, we use Lyapunov functions, which is a classic technique for proving stability of an equilibrium of an ODE, to bound the tracking error $e(t)$. The Lie derivative $\frac{\partial V}{\partial e} f_e(e)$ below captures the rate of change of the function V along the trajectories of $e(t)$.

Definition 4 (Lyapunov functions [16]). *Fix a state-input reference trajectory pair (ξ_{ref}, u_{ref}), assume that the dynamics of the tracking error e for a closed control system $\mathcal{A}$ with g_{ref} and g_{trk} can be rewritten as $\frac{d}{dt}e(t) = f_e(e(t))$, where $f_e(0) = 0$. A continuously differentiable function $V : \mathbb{R}^n \to \mathbb{R}$ satisfying (i) $V(0) = 0$, (ii) $\forall e \in \mathbb{R}^n, V(e) \geq 0$, and (iii) $\forall e \in \mathbb{R}^n, \frac{\partial V}{\partial e}f_e(e) \leq 0$, is called a Lyapunov function for the tracking error.*

Example 2. For the car of Example 1, with a continuous reference trajectory $\xi_{ref}(t) = [x_{ref}(t), y_{ref}(t), \theta_{ref}(t)]^{\mathsf{T}}$, we define the tracking error in a coordinate frame fixed to the car [13]:

$$
\begin{pmatrix} e_x(t) \\ e_y(t) \\ e_\theta(t) \end{pmatrix} = \begin{pmatrix} \cos(\theta(t)) & \sin(\theta(t)) & 0 \\ -\sin(\theta(t)) & \cos(\theta(t)) & 0 \\ 0 & 0 & 1 \end{pmatrix} \begin{pmatrix} x_{ref}(t) - p_x(t) \\ y_{ref}(t) - p_y(t) \\ \theta_{ref}(t) - \theta(t) \end{pmatrix}. \tag{4}
$$

With the reference controller function g defined as:

$$
\begin{aligned}
v(t) &= v_{ref}(t)\cos(e_\theta(t)) + k_1 e_x(t), \\
\omega(t) &= \omega_{ref}(t) + v_{ref}(t)(k_2 e_y(t) + k_3 \sin(e_\theta(t))),
\end{aligned} \tag{5}
$$

it has been shown in [13] when $k_1, k_2, k_3 > 0$, $\frac{d}{dt}\omega_{ref}(t) = 0$, and $\frac{d}{dt}v_{ref}(t) = 0$,

$$
V([e_x, e_y, e_\theta]^{\mathsf{T}}) = \frac{1}{2}(e_x^2 + e_y^2) + \frac{1 - \cos(e_\theta)}{k_2} \tag{6}
$$

is a Lyapunov function with negative semi-definite time derivative $\frac{\partial V}{\partial x}f_e = -k_1 e_x^2 - \frac{v_{ref}k_3 \sin^2(e_\theta)}{k_2}$.

4.2   Bounding Tracking Error Using Lyapunov Functions: Part 1

Consider a given closed control system, $\mathcal{A}$ with g_{ref} and g_{trk}, in this section, we will derive upper bounds on the tracking error e. Later in Sect. 5, we will develop techniques that take the tracking error into consideration for computing reference trajectories ξ_{ref}.

To begin with, we consider state-input reference trajectory pairs (ξ_{ref}, u_{ref}) where u_{ref} is continuous, and therefore, ξ_{ref} and ξ_g are differentiable. Let us assume that the tracking error dynamics $(\frac{d}{dt}e(t) = f_e(e(t)))$ has a Lyapunov function $V(e(t))$. The following is a standard result that follows from the theory of Lyapunov functions for dynamical systems.

Lemma 1. *Consider any state-input trajectory pair (ξ_{ref}, u_{ref}), an initial state x_0, the corresponding trajectory ξ_g of the closed control system, and a constant $\ell > 0$. If the tracking error $e(t)$ has a Lyapunov function V, and if initially $V(e(0)) \leq \ell$, then for any $t \in [0, \xi_{ref}.ltime]$, $V(e(t)) \leq \ell$.*

This lemma is proved by showing that $V(e(t)) = V(e(0)) + \int_0^t \frac{d}{dt}V(e(\tau))d\tau \leq V(e(0))$. The last inequality holds since $\frac{d}{dt}V(e(\tau)) = \frac{\partial V}{\partial e}f_e(e) \leq 0$ for any $\tau \in [0, t]$ according the definition of Lyapunov functions (Definition 4).

Lemma 1 says that if we can bound $V(e(0)) = V(e(x_0, \xi_{\text{ref}}(0)))$, we can bound $V(e(\xi_g(t), \xi_{\text{ref}}(t)))$ at any time t within the domain of the trajectories, regardless of the value of $\xi_{\text{ref}}(t)$. This could decouple the problem of designing the tracking controller g_{trk} and synthesizing the reference controller g_{ref} as a state-input trajectory pair $(\xi_{\text{ref}}, u_{\text{ref}})$.

Example 3. Given two waypoints p_0, p_1 for the car in Example 1, take the returned value of `Waypoints_to_Traj`$(\{p_0, p_1\}, \bar{v})$, move v_{ref} to u_{ref} and drop a_{ref}. Then, the resulting $(\xi_{\text{ref}}, u_{\text{ref}})$ is a continuous and differentiable state-input reference trajectory pair. Moreover, if the robot is controlled by the tracking controller as in Eq. (5), $V(e(t)) = \frac{1}{2}(e_x(t)^2 + e_y(t)^2) + \frac{1 - \cos(e_\theta(t))}{k_2}$ is a Lyapunov function for the corresponding tracking error $e(t) = [e_x(t), e_y(t), e_\theta(t)]^\mathsf{T}$.

From Eq. (4), it is easy to check that $e_x^2(t) + e_y(t)^2 = (x_{\text{ref}}(t) - p_x(t))^2 + (y_{\text{ref}}(t) - p_y(t))^2$ for any time t. Assume that initially the position of the vehicle satisfies $[p_x(0), p_y(0)]^\mathsf{T} \in B_\ell([x_{\text{ref}}(0), y_{\text{ref}}(0)]^\mathsf{T})$. We check that $V(e(0)) = \frac{1}{2}(e_x(0)^2 + e_y(0)^2) + \frac{1 - \cos(e_\theta(0))}{k_2} \leq \frac{\ell^2}{2} + \frac{2}{k_2}$.

From Lemma 1, we know that $\forall t \in [0, \xi_{\text{ref}}.\text{ltime}]$, $V(e(t)) \leq \frac{\ell^2}{2} + \frac{2}{k_2}$. Then we have $(x_{\text{ref}}(t) - p_x(t))^2 + (y_{\text{ref}}(t) - p_y(t))^2 = (e_x(t)^2 + e_y(t)^2) \leq \ell^2 + \frac{4}{k_2}$. That is, the position of the robot at time t satisfies $[p_x(t), p_y(t)]^\mathsf{T} \in B_{\sqrt{\ell^2 + \frac{4}{k_2}}}([x_{\text{ref}}(t), y_{\text{ref}}(t)]^\mathsf{T})$.

4.3   Bounding Tracking Error Using Lyapunov Functions: Part 2

Next, let us consider the case where ξ_{ref} is discontinuous. Furthermore, let us assume that it is a concatenation of several continuous state trajectories $\xi_{\text{ref},1}$ ⌢ $\cdots$ ⌢ $\xi_{\text{ref},k}$. In this case, we call ξ_{ref} a piece-wise reference trajectory. If we have a sequence of $(\xi_{\text{ref},i}, u_{\text{ref},i})$, each is a valid state-input trajectory pair and the corresponding error $e_i(t)$ has a Lyapunov function $V_i(e_i(t))$, then we can use Lemma 1 to bound the error of $e_i(t)$ if we know the value of $e_i(0)$. However, the main challenge to glue these error bounds together is that $e(t)$ would be discontinuous with respect to the entire piece-wise $\xi_{\text{ref}}(t)$.

Without loss of generality, let us assume that the Lyapunov functions $V_i(e_i(t))$ share the same format. That is, $\forall i, V_i(e_i(t)) = V(e_i(t))$. Let t_i be the concatenation time points when $\xi_{\text{ref}}(t)$ (and therefore $e(t)$) is discontinuous. We know that $\lim_{t \to t_i^-} V(e(t)) \neq \lim_{t \to t_i^+} V(e(t))$ since $\lim_{t \to t_i^-} e(t) \neq \lim_{t \to t_i^+} e(t)$.

One insight we can get from Example 3 is that although $e(t)$ is discontinuous at time t_is, some of the variables influencing $e(t)$ are continuous. For example, $e_x(t)$ and $e_y(t)$ in Example 3, which represent the error of the positions, are continuous since both the actual and reference positions of the vehicle are continuous. If we can further bound the term in $V(e(t))$ that corresponds to the *other* variables, we could analyze the error bound for the entire piece-wise reference trajectory. With this in sight, let us write $e(t)$ as $[e_p(t), e_r(t)]$, where $e_p(t) = e(t) \downarrow p$ is the projection to $\mathcal{W}$ and $e_r(t)$ is the remaining components.

Let us further assume that the Lyapunov function can be written in the form of $V(e(t)) = \alpha(e_p(t)) + \beta(e_r(t))$. Indeed, on the tool's webpage [27] we show that four commonly used vehicle models (car, robot, underwater vehicle, and hovercraft) have Lyapunov functions for the tracking error $e(t)$ of this form. If $\beta(e_r(t))$ can be further bounded, then the tracking error for the entire trajectory can be bounded using the following lemma.

Lemma 2. *Consider $\xi_{ref} = \xi_{ref,1} \frown \cdots \frown \xi_{ref,k}$, and $u_{ref} = u_{ref,1} \frown \cdots \frown u_{ref,k}$ as a piecewise reference and input with each $(\xi_{ref,i}, u_{ref,i})$ being a state-input trajectory pair. Suppose (1) $V(e(t)) = \alpha(e_p(t)) + \beta(e_r(t))$ be a Lyapunov function for the tracking error $e(t)$ of each piece $(\xi_{ref,i}, u_{ref,i})$; (2) $e_p(t)$ is continuous and $\alpha(\cdot)$ is a continuous function; (3) $\beta(e_r(t)) \in [b_l, b_u]$, and (4) $V(e(0)) \leq \varepsilon_0$. Then, the tracking error $e(t)$ with respect to ξ_{ref} and u_{ref} can be bounded by,*

$$V(e(t)) \leq \varepsilon_i, \forall i \geq 1, \forall t \in [t_{i-1}, t_i),$$

where $\forall\, i > 1, \varepsilon_i = \varepsilon_{i-1} - b_l + b_u$, $\varepsilon_1 = \varepsilon_0$ being the bound on the initial tracking error, and t_i's are the time points of concatenation[4].

Proof. We prove this by induction on i. When $i = 1$, we know from Lemma 1 that if the initial tracking error is bounded by $V(e(0))$, then for any $t \in [0, t_1), V(e(t)) \leq V(e(0)) \leq \varepsilon_0 = \varepsilon_1$, so the lemma holds.

Fix any $i \geq 1$. If $V(e(t_{i-1})) \leq \varepsilon_i$, from Lemma 1 we have $\forall t \in [t_{i-1}, t_i)$, $V(e(t)) \leq \varepsilon_i$. Also, $\lim_{t \to t_i^-} V(e(t)) = \lim_{t \to t_i^-} \alpha(e_p(t)) + \beta(e_r(t)) \leq \varepsilon_i$. Since $\forall e_r(t) \in \mathbb{R}^{n-d}, \beta(e_r(t)) \in [b_l, b_u]$, we have $\lim_{t \to t_i^-} \alpha(e_p(t)) \leq \varepsilon_i - b_l$, and $\lim_{t \to t_i^-} \alpha(e_p(t)) = \lim_{t \to t_i^+} \alpha(e_p(t))$. Therefore,

$$\varepsilon_{i+1} = \lim_{t \to t_i^+} V(e(t)) = \lim_{t \to t_i^+} \alpha(e_p(t)) + \beta(e_r(t)) \leq \varepsilon_i - b_l + b_u.$$

Another observation we have on the four vehicle models used in this paper is that not only $V(e(t))$ can be written as $\alpha(e_p(t)) + \beta(e_r(t))$ with $\beta(e_r(t))$ being bounded, but also $\alpha(e_p(t))$ can be written as $\alpha(e_p(t)) = ce_p^\mathsf{T}(t)e_p(t) = c\|p(t) - p_{ref}(t)\|_2^2$, where $c \in \mathbb{R}$ is a scalar constant; $p(t) = \xi_g(t) \downarrow p$ and $p_{ref}(t) = \xi_{ref}(t) \downarrow p$ are the actual position and reference position of the vehicle. In this case, we can further bound the position of the vehicle $p(t)$.

Lemma 3. *In addition to the assumptions of Lemma 2, if $\alpha(e_p(t)) = ce_p^\mathsf{T}(t)e_p(t) = c\|p(t) - p_{ref}(t)\|_2^2$, where $c \in \mathbb{R}, p(t) = \xi_g(t) \downarrow p$ and $p_{ref}(t) = \xi_{ref}(t) \downarrow p$. Then we have that at time $t \in [t_{i-1}, t_i)$,*

$$e_p^\mathsf{T}(t)e_p(t) \leq \frac{\varepsilon_i - b_l}{c},$$

where ε_i and b_l are from Lemma 2, which implies that

$$p(t) \in B_{\ell_i}(p_{ref}(t)), \text{ with } \ell_i = \sqrt{\frac{\varepsilon_i - b_l}{c}}.$$

---

[4] $\forall t \in [t_{i-1}, t_i), \xi_{ref}(t) = \xi_{ref,i}(t - \sum_{j=1}^{i-1} \xi_{ref,j}.\mathrm{ltime}).$

Note that Lemma 2 and 3 does not depend on the concrete values of ξ_{ref} and u_{ref}. The lemmas hold for any piece-wise reference trajectory ξ_{ref} and reference input u_{ref} as long as the corresponding error e has a Lyapunov function (for each piece of ξ_{ref} and u_{ref}).

Example 4. Continue Example 3.

Now let us consider the case of a sequence of waypoints $\{p_i\}_{i=0}^k$. Let $(\xi_{\text{ref}}, u_{\text{ref}}) = \texttt{Waypoints\_to\_Traj}(\{p_i\}_{i=0}^k, \bar{v})$. From Example 3, we know that $V(e(t)) = \frac{1}{2}(e_x(t)^2 + e_y(t)^2) + \frac{1-\cos(e_\theta(t))}{k_2}$ is a Lyapunov function for each segment of the piecewise reference trajectory $\xi_{\text{ref}}(t)$. We also know that for any value of e_θ, the term $\frac{1-\cos(e_\theta(t))}{k_2} \in [0, \frac{2}{k}]$. From Lemma 2, we have that for $t \in [t_{i-1}, t_i)$ where t_i are the concatenation time points, we have $V(e(t)) \leq V(e(0)) + \frac{2(i-1)}{k_2}$ Therefore, following Example 3, initially $V(e(0)) \leq \frac{\ell^2}{2} + \frac{2}{k_2}$. Then $\forall t \in [t_{i-1}, t_i)$, $V(e(t)) \leq \frac{\ell^2}{2} + \frac{2i}{k_2}$, and the position of the robot satisfies $[p_x(t), p_y(t)]^\intercal \in B_{\sqrt{\ell^2+\frac{4i}{k_2}}}([x_{\text{ref}}(t), y_{\text{ref}}(t)]^\intercal)$.

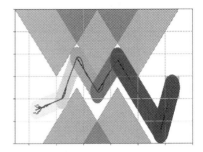

Fig. 2. Illustration of the error bounds computed from Lemma 3. The ith line segment is bloated by $\sqrt{\ell^2 + \frac{4i}{k_2}}$. The closed-loop system's trajectory $p(t)$ are purple curves and they are contained by the bloated-tube. (Color figure online)

As seen in Fig. 2, we bloat the black reference trajectory $p_{\text{ref}}(t) = \xi_{\text{ref}}(t) \downarrow p$ by $\ell_i = \sqrt{\ell^2 + \frac{4i}{k_2}}$ for the ith line segment, the bloated tube contains the real position trajectories (purple curves) $p(t)$ of the closed system.

5   Synthesizing the Reference Trajectories

In Sect. 4.3, we have seen that under certain conditions, the tracking error $e(t)$ between an actual closed-loop trajectory $\xi_g(t)$ and a piece-wise reference $\xi_{\text{ref}}(t)$ can be bounded by a piece-wise constant value, which depends on the initial tracking error $e(0)$ and the number of segments in ξ_{ref}. We have also seen an example nonlinear vehicle model with PWL ξ_{ref} for which the tracking error can be bounded.

In this section, we discuss how to utilize such bound on $e(t)$ to help find a reference controller g_{ref} consisting of a reference trajectory $\xi_{\text{ref}}(t)$ and a reference input $u_{\text{ref}}(t)$ such that closed-loop trajectories $\xi_g(t)$ from a neighborhood of $\xi_{\text{ref}}(0)$ that are trying to follow $\xi_{\text{ref}}(t)$ are guaranteed to satisfy the reach-avoid requirement. The idea of finding a g_{ref} follows a classic approach in robot motion planning. The intuition is that if we know at any time $t \in [0, \xi_{\text{ref}}.\text{ltime}]$, $\|\xi_g(t) \downarrow p - \xi_{\text{ref}}(t) \downarrow p\|_2$ will be at most ℓ, then instead of requiring $\xi_{\text{ref}}(t) \downarrow p$ to be at least ℓ away from the obstacles (inside the goal region), we will bloat the obstacles (shrink the goal set) by ℓ. Then the original problem is reduced to finding a $\xi_{\text{ref}}(t)$ such that $\xi_{\text{ref}}(t) \downarrow p$ can avoid the bloated obstacles and reach the shrunk goal set.

5.1 Use PWL Reference Trajectories for Vehicle Models

Finding a reference trajectory $\xi_{\text{ref}}(t)$ such that (a) $\xi_{\text{ref}}(t)$ satisfies the reach-avoid conditions, and (b) $\xi_{\text{ref}}(t)$ and $u_{\text{ref}}(t)$ are concatenations of state-input trajectory pairs $\{(\xi_{\text{ref},i}, u_{\text{ref},i})\}_i$ and each pair satisfies the system dynamics, is a nontrivial problem. If we were to encode the problem directly as a satisfiability or an optimization problem, the solver would have to search for over the space of continuous functions constrained by the above requirements, including the nonlinear differential constraints imposed by f. The standard tactic is to fix a reasonable template for $\xi_{\text{ref}}(t)$, $u_{\text{ref}}(t)$ and search for instantiations of this template.

From Example 4, we see that if ξ_{ref} is a PWL reference trajectory constructed from waypoints in the workspace, the tracking error can be bounded using Lemma 2. A PWL reference trajectories connecting the waypoints in the workspace have the flexibility to satisfy the reach-avoid requirement. Therefore, in this section, we fix ξ_{ref} and u_{ref} to be the reference trajectory and reference input returned by the Waypoints_to_Traj$(\cdot, \cdot)$. In Sect. 5.2, we will see that the problem of finding such PWL $\xi_{\text{ref}}(t)$ can be reduced to a satisfiability problem over quantifier-free linear real arithmetic, which can be solved effectively by off-the-shelf SMT solvers (see Sect. 6 for empirical results).

5.2 Synthesizing Waypoints for a Linear Reference Trajectory

Algorithm 1 says that $\xi_{\text{ref}}(t)$ and $u_{\text{ref}}(t)$ can be uniquely constructed given a sequence of waypoints $\{p_i\}_{i=0}^{k}$ in the workspace $\mathcal{W}$ and a constant velocity $\bar{v}$. From Proposition 1, $p_{\text{ref}}(t) = \xi_{\text{ref}}(t) \downarrow p$ connects the waypoints in $\mathcal{W}$. Also, let $t_i = \sum_{j=1}^{i} \|p_j - p_{j-1}\|_2 / \bar{v}$ be the concatenation time, $\forall t \in [t_{i-1}, t_i)$, $p(t)$ is the line segment connecting p_{i-1} and p_i. We want to ensure that $p(t) = \xi_g(t) \downarrow p$ satisfy the reach-avoid requirements. From Lemma 3, for any $t \in [t_{i-1}, t_i)$, we can bound $\|p(t) - p_{\text{ref}}(t)\|_2$ with the constant ℓ_i, then the remaining problem is to ensure that, $p_{\text{ref}}(t)$ is at least ℓ_i away from the obstacles and $p_{\text{ref}}(\xi_{\text{ref}}.\text{ltime})$ is inside the goal set with ℓ_k distance to any surface of the goal set.

Let us start with one segment $p(t)$ with $t \in [t_{i-1}, t_i)$. To enforce that $p(t)$ is ℓ_i away from a polytope obstacle, a sufficient condition is to enforce both the endpoints of the line segment to lie out at least one surface of the polytope bloated by ℓ_i.

Lemma 4. *If $p_{\text{ref}}(t)$ with $t \in [t_{i-1}, t_i)$ is a line segment connecting p_{i-1} and p_i in $\mathcal{W}$. Given a polytope obstacle $O = Poly(H_o, b_o)$ and $\ell_i > 0$, if*

$$\bigvee_{s=1}^{\text{dP}(H_O)} \left((H_o^{(s)} p_{i-1} > b_o^{(s)} + \|H_o^{(s)}\|_2 \ell_i) \wedge (H_o^{(s)} p_i > b_o^{(s)} + \|H_o^{(s)}\|_2 \ell_i) \right) = \text{True},$$

then $\forall t \in [t_{i-1}, t_i)$, $B_{\ell_i}(p_{\text{ref}}(t)) \cap O = \emptyset$.

Proof. Fix any s such that $(H_O^{(s)} p_{i-1} > b_O^{(s)} + \|H_O^{(s)}\|_2 \ell_i) \wedge (H_O^{(s)} p_i > b_O^{(s)} + \|H_O^{(s)}\|_2 \ell_i)$ holds. The set $S = \{q \in \mathbb{R}^d \mid H_O^{(s)} q > b_O^{(s)} + \|H_O^{(s)}\|_2 \ell_i\}$ defines a convex half space. Therefore, if $p_{i-1} \in S$ and $p_i \in S$, then any point on the line segment connecting p_{i-1} and p_i is in S. Therefore, for any $t \in [t_{i-1}, t_i)$, $H_O^{(s)} p_{\mathsf{ref}}(t) > b_O^{(s)} + \|H_O^{(s)}\|_2 \ell_i > b_O^{(s)}$, which means $p_{\mathsf{ref}}(t) \notin O$.

The distance between $p_{\mathsf{ref}}(t)$ and the surface $H_O^{(s)} q = b_O^{(s)}$ is $\frac{|H_O^{(s)} p_{\mathsf{ref}}(t) - b_O^{(s)}|}{\|H_O^{(s)}\|_2} >$ ℓ_i. Therefore, for any $p \in B_{\ell_i}(p_{\mathsf{ref}}(t))$ we have $\|p - p_{\mathsf{ref}}(t)\|_2 \le \ell_i$ and thus $p \notin O$.

Furthermore, $\bigwedge_{s=1}^{\mathsf{dP}(H_O)} H_O^{(s)} q \le b_O^{(s)} + \|H_O^{(s)}\|_2 \ell_i$ defines of a new polytope that we get by bloating $Poly(H_O, b_O)$ with ℓ_i. Basically, it is constructed by moving each surface of $Poly(H_O, b_O)$ along the surface's normal vector with the direction pointing outside the polytope.

Similarly, we can define the condition when $p_{\mathsf{ref}}(\xi.\mathsf{ltime}) = p_k$ is inside the goal shrunk by ℓ_k.

Lemma 5. *Given a polytope goal set $G = Poly(H_G, b_G)$ and $\ell_k > 0$, if*

$$\bigwedge_{s=1}^{\mathsf{dP}(H_G)} \left(H_G^{(s)} p_k \le b_O^{(s)} - \|H_G^{(s)}\|_2 \ell_k \right) = \mathsf{True}, \;\; then \;\; B_{\ell_k}(p_k) \subseteq G.$$

Putting them all together, we want to solve the following satisfiability problem to ensure that each line segment between p_{i-1} and p_i is at least ℓ_i away from all the obstacles and p_k is inside the goal set G with at least distance ℓ_k to the surfaces of G. In this way, $\xi_g(t)$ starting from a neighborhood of $\xi_{\mathsf{ref}}(0)$ can satisfy the reach-avoid requirement.

$$\phi_{\mathsf{waypoints}}(p_{\mathsf{ref}}(0), k, \mathbf{O}, G, \{\ell_i\}_{i=1}^k) = \exists p_0, \cdots, p_k,$$

$$p_0 == p_{\mathsf{ref}}(0)$$

$$\bigwedge_{s=1}^{\mathsf{dP}(H_G)} \left(H_G^{(s)} p_k \le b_O^{(s)} - \|H_G^{(s)}\|_2 \ell_k \right)$$

$$\bigwedge_{i=1}^{k} \left(\bigwedge_{Poly(H,b) \in \mathbf{O}} \left(\bigvee_{s=1}^{\mathsf{dP}(H)} \left(H^{(s)} p_{i-1} > b^{(s)} + \ell_i \|H^{(s)}\|_2 \wedge H^{(s)} p_i > b^{(s)} + \ell_i \|H^{(s)}\|_2 \right) \right) \right)$$

Notice that the constraints in $\phi_{\mathsf{waypoints}}$ are all linear over real arithmetic. Moreover, the number of constraints in $\phi_{\mathsf{waypoints}}$ is

$$O\left(\sum_{Poly(H,b) \in \mathbf{O}} k\mathsf{dP}(H) + \mathsf{dP}(H_G) \right).$$ That is, fixing k, the number of constraints will grow linearly with the total number of surfaces in the obstacle and goal set polytopes. Fixing $\mathbf{O}$ and G, the number of constraints will grow linear with the number of line segments k.

Theorem 1. *Fix $k \geq 1$ as the number of line segments, $p_{ref}(0) \in \mathcal{W}$ as the initial position of the reference trajectory. Assume that*

(1) $\mathcal{A}$ closed with g_{ref} and g_{trk} is such that given any sequence of $k+1$ waypoints in $\mathcal{W}$ and any $\bar{v}$, the piece-wise reference ξ_{ref} (and input u_{ref}) returned by Algorithm 1 satisfy the conditions in Lemmas 2 and 3 with Lyapunov function $V(e(t))$ for the tracking error $e(t)$.

(2) For the above ξ_{ref}, fix an ε_0 such that $V(e(0)) \leq \varepsilon_0$, let $\{\ell_i\}_{i=1}^{k}$ be error bounds for positions constructed using Lemma 2 and Lemma 3 from ε_0.

(3) $\phi_{waypoints}(p_{ref}(0), k, \mathbf{O}, G, \{\ell_i\}_{i=1}^{k})$ is satisfiable with waypoints $\{p_i\}_{i=0}^{k}$.

Let $\xi_{ref}(t), u_{ref}(t) = $ Waypoints_to_Trajectory $(\{p_i\}_{i=0}^{k}, \bar{v})$, and $p_{ref}(t) = \xi_{ref}(t) \downarrow p$. Let $\xi_g(t)$ be a trajectory of $\mathcal{A}$ closed with $g_{trk}(\cdot, \xi_{ref}, u_{ref})$ starting from $\xi_g(0)$ with $V(e(\xi_g(0), \xi_{ref}(0))) \leq \varepsilon_0$, then $\xi_g(t)$ satisfies the reach-avoid requirement.

Proof. Since $\xi_{ref}(t), u_{ref}(t)$ are a PWL reference trajectory and a reference input respectively constructed from the waypoints $\{p_i\}_{i=0}^{k}$, they satisfy Assumption (1). Moreover, $V(e(\xi_g(0), \xi_{ref}(0))) \leq \varepsilon_0$ satisfies Assumption (2). Using Lemma 2 and Lemma 3, we know that for $t \in [t_{i-1}, t_i), \|\xi_g(t) \downarrow p - \xi_{ref}(t) \downarrow p\|_2 \leq \ell_i$.

Finally, since $\{p_i\}_{i=0}^{k}$ satisfy the constraints in $\phi_{waypoints}$, using Lemma 4 and Lemma 5, we know that for any time $t \in [0, t_k]$, $\xi_g(t) \downarrow p \notin \mathbf{O}$ and $\xi_g(t_k) \in G$. Therefore the theorem holds.

5.3   Partitioning the Initial Set

Starting from the entire initial set Θ, fix $\xi_{ref}(0) \in \Theta$ and an ε_0 such that $\forall x \in \Theta, V(e(x, \xi_{ref}(0))) \leq \varepsilon_0$, then we can use Lemma 2 and Lemma 3 to construct the error bounds $\{\ell_i\}_{i=1}^{k}$ for positions, and next use $\{\ell_i\}_{i=1}^{k}$ to solve $\phi_{waypoints}$ and find the waypoints and construct the reference trajectory.

However, if the initial set Θ is too large, $\{\ell_i\}_{i=1}^{k}$ could be too conservative so $\phi_{waypoints}$ is not satisfiable. In the first two figures on the top row of Fig. 3, we could see that if we bloat the obstacle polytopes using the largest ℓ_i, then no reference trajectory is feasible. In this case, we partition the initial set Θ to several smaller covers Θ_j and repeat the above steps from each smaller cover Θ_j. In Lemma 2 and Lemma 3 we could see that the values of $\{\ell_i\}_{i=1}^{k}$ decrease if ε_0 decreases. Therefore, with the partition of Θ, we could possibly find a reference trajectory more and more easily. As shown in Fig. 3 bottom row, after several partitions, a reference trajectory for each Θ_j could be found.

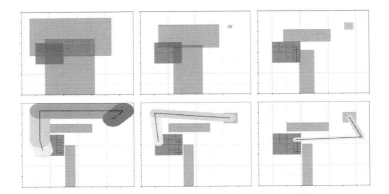

Fig. 3. Top row: each step attempting to find a reference trajectory in the space where obstacles (goal set) are bloated (shrunk) by the error bounds $\{\ell_i\}_i$. From left to right: Without partition, $\{\ell_i\}_i$ are too large so a reference trajectory cannot be found. Θ is partitioned, but $\{\ell_i\}$s for the left-top cover are still too large. With further partions, a reference trajectory could be found. Bottom row: It is shown that the bloated tubes for each cover (which contain all other trajectories from that cover) can fit between the original obstacles.

5.4 Overall Synthesis Algorithm

Taking partitioning into the overall algorithm, we have Algorithm 2 to solve the controller synthesis problem defined in Sect. 2.2. Algorithm 2 takes in as inputs (1) an (n, m)-dimensional control system $\mathcal{A}$, (2) a tracking controller g_{trk}, (3) Obstacles $\mathbf{O}$, (4) a goal set G, (5) a Lyapunov function $V(e(t))$ for the tracking error e that satisfies the conditions in Lemma 2 and Lemma 3 for any PWL reference trajectory and input, (6) the maximum number of line segments allowed $\mathsf{Seg}_{\max}$, (7) the maximum number of partitions allowed $\mathsf{Part}_{\max}$, and (8) a constant velocity $\bar{v}$. The algorithm returns a set $\mathtt{RefTrajs}$, such that for each triple $\langle \Theta_j, \xi_{j,\mathsf{ref}}, u_{j,\mathsf{ref}} \rangle \in \mathtt{RefTrajs}$, we have $\forall x_0 \in \Theta_j$, the unique trajectory ξ_g of the closed system ($\mathcal{A}$ closed with $g_{\mathsf{trk}}(\cdot, \xi_{j,\mathsf{ref}}, u_{j,\mathsf{ref}})$) starting from x_0 satisfies the reach-avoid requirement. The algorithm also returns $\langle \mathtt{Cover}, \mathbf{None} \rangle$, which means that the algorithm fails to find controllers for the portion of the initial set in $\mathtt{Cover}$ within the maximum number of partitions $\mathsf{Part}_{\max}$.

In Algorithm 2, $\mathtt{Cover}$ is the collection of covers in Θ that the corresponding ξ_{ref} and u_{ref} have not been discovered. Initially, $\mathtt{Cover}$ only contains Θ. The for-loop from Line 2 will try to find a ξ_{ref} and a u_{ref} for each $\Theta \in \mathtt{Cover}$ until the maximum allowed number for partitions is reached. At line 3, we fix the initial state of $\xi_{\mathsf{ref}}(0) = \xi_{\mathsf{init}}$ to be the center of the current cover Θ. Then at Line 4, we get the initial error bounds ε_0 after fixing ξ_{init}. Using ε_0 and the Lyapunov function $V(e)$, we can construct the error bounds $\{\ell_i\}_{i=1}^k$ for the positions of the vehicle using Lemma 2 and Lemma 3 at Line 5.

Algorithm 2: Controller synthesis algorithm

---

    input   : $\mathcal{A} = \langle \mathcal{X}, \Theta, \mathbf{U}, f \rangle, g_{\text{trk}}, \mathbf{O}, G, V(e(t)), \text{Seg}_{\text{max}}, \text{Part}_{\text{max}}, \bar{v}$
    initially: Cover $\leftarrow \{\Theta\}$, $prt \leftarrow 0, k \leftarrow 1$, RefTrajs $\leftarrow \emptyset$
1 **while** $(\text{Cover} \neq \emptyset) \wedge (prt \leq Part_{\text{max}})$ **do**
2   **for** $\Theta \in$ Cover **do**
3         $\xi_{\text{init}} \leftarrow$ Center(Θ) ;
4         $\varepsilon_0 \leftarrow a$ such that $\forall x \in \Theta, V(e(x, \xi_{\text{init}})) \leq a$;
5         $\{\ell_i\}_{i=1}^k \leftarrow$ GetBounds$(V(e(t)), \varepsilon_0)$;
6   **while** $k \leq Seg_{\text{max}}$ **do**
7   **if** CheckSAT$(\xi_{\text{init}} \downarrow p, k, \mathbf{O}, G, \{\ell_i\}_{i=1}^k)) ==$ SAT **then**
8                $p_0, \cdots, p_k \leftarrow$ GetValue$(\phi_{\text{waypoints}})$;
9                $\xi_{\text{ref}}, u_{\text{ref}} \leftarrow$ Waypoints_to_Traj$(\{p_i\}_{i=0}^k, \bar{v})$;
10   RefTrajs $\leftarrow$ RefTrajs $\cup \langle \Theta, \xi_{\text{ref}}, u_{\text{ref}} \rangle$;
11   Cover $\leftarrow$ Cover $\setminus \{\Theta\}$;
12              $k \leftarrow 1$;
13   **Break** ;
14   **else**
15              $k \leftarrow k + 1$
16   **if** $k > Seg_{\text{max}}$ **then**
17   Cover $\leftarrow$ Cover $\cup$ Partition$(\Theta) \setminus \{\Theta\}$;
18              $prt \leftarrow prt + 1$;
19              $k \leftarrow 1$;
20 **return** RefTrajs, $\langle$Cover, **None**$\rangle$;

If the **if** condition at Line 7 holds with $\{p_i\}_{i=0}^k$ being the waypoints that satisfy $\phi_{\text{waypoints}}$, then from Theorem 1 we know that the $\xi_{\text{ref}}, u_{\text{ref}}$ constructed using $\{p_i\}_{i=0}^k$ at Line 9 will be such that, the unique trajectory ξ_g of the closed system ($\mathcal{A}$ closed with $g_{\text{trk}}(\cdot, \xi_{\text{ref}}, u_{\text{ref}})$) starting from $x_0 \in \Theta$ satisfies the reach-avoid requirement. Otherwise the algorithm will increase the number of segments k in the PWL reference trajectory (Line 15). When the maximum number of line segments allowed is reached but the algorithm still could not find $\xi_{\text{ref}}, u_{\text{ref}}$ that can guarantee the satisfaction of reach-void requirement from the current cover Θ, we will partition the current Θ at Line 17 and add those partitions to Cover. At the same time, k will be reset to 1.

Theorem 2 (Soundness). *Suppose the inputs to Algorithm 2, $\mathcal{A}$, g_{trk}, $\mathbf{O}$, G, $V(e(t))$, $\bar{v}$ satisfy the conditions of Theorem 1. Let the output be* RefTrajs $= \{\langle \Theta_j, \xi_{j,ref}, u_{j,ref} \rangle\}_j$ *and* $\langle$Cover, **None**$\rangle$, *then we have (1).* $\Theta \subseteq \cup \Theta_j \cup$ Cover, *and (2). for each triple* $\langle \Theta_j, \xi_{j,ref}, u_{j,ref} \rangle$, *we have* $\forall x_0 \in \Theta_j$, *the unique trajectory* ξ_g *of the closed system ($\mathcal{A}$ closed with $g_{trk}(\cdot, \xi_{j,ref}, u_{j,ref})$) starting from x_0 satisfies the reach-avoid requirement.*

The theorem follows directly from the proof of Theorem 1.

6   Implementation and Evaluation

We have implemented our synthesis algorithm (Algorithm 2) in a prototype open source tool we call FACTEST[5] (FAst ConTrollEr SynThesis framework). Our

---

[5] All models and source code of FACTEST are available at [27].

implementation uses Pypoman[6], Yices 2.2 [6], SciPy[7] and NumPy[8] libraries. The inputs to FACTEST are the same as the inputs in Algorithm 2. FACTEST terminates in two ways. Either it finds a reference trajectory $\xi_{j,\text{ref}}$ and reference input $u_{j,\text{ref}}$ for every partition Θ_j of Θ so that Theorem 2 guarantees they solved the controller synthesis problem. Otherwise, it terminates by failing to find reference trajectories for at least one subset of Θ after partitioning Θ up to the maximum specified depth.

6.1   Benchmark Scenarios: Vehicle Models and Workspaces

We will report on evaluating FACTEST in several 2D and 3D scenarios drawn from motion planning literature (see Figs. 4). Recall, the state space $\mathcal{X}$ dimension corresponds to the vehicle model, and is separate from the dimensionality of the workspace $\mathcal{W}$. We will use four nonlinear vehicle models in these different scenarios: (a) the kinematic vehicle model (car) [31] introduced in Example 1, (b) a bijective mobile robot (robot) [13], (c) a hovering robot (hovercraft), and (d) an autonomous underwater vehicle (AUV) [29]. The dynamics and tracking controllers (g_{trk}) of the other three models are described on the FACTEST website [27]. Each of these controllers come with a Lyapunov function that meets the assumptions of Lemmas 2 and 3 so the tracking error bounds given by the lemmas $\{\ell\}_{i=1}^{k}$ can be computed.

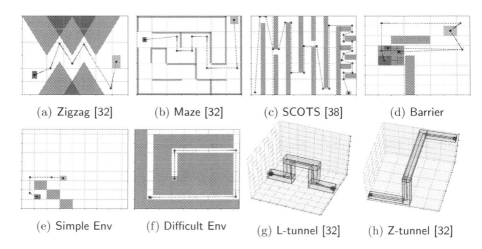

(a) Zigzag [32]   (b) Maze [32]   (c) SCOTS [38]   (d) Barrier

(e) Simple Env   (f) Difficult Env   (g) L-tunnel [32]   (h) Z-tunnel [32]

Fig. 4. 2D and 3D workspaces with initial (blue) and goal (green) sets. The scenarios run in the two-dimensional $\mathcal{W}$ use the car model. The scenarios run in the three dimensional $\mathcal{W}$ use the hovercraft model. The black lines denote ξ_{ref} and the dotted violet lines denote ξ_g. (Color figure online)

---

[6] https://pypi.org/project/pypoman/.
[7] https://www.scipy.org/.
[8] https://numpy.org/.

6.2   Synthesis Performance

Table 1 presents the performance of FACTEST on several synthesis problems. Several points are worth highlighting. (a) The absolute running time is at the sub-second range, even for 6-dimensional vehicle models with 4-inputs, operating in a 3D workspace. This is encouraging for online motion-control applications with dynamic obstacles. (b) The running time is not too sensitive to dimensions of $\mathcal{X}$ and $\mathbf{U}$ because the waypoints are only being generated in the lower dimensional workspace $\mathcal{W}$. Additionally, the construction of ξ_{ref} from the waypoints does not add significant time. However, since different models have different dynamics and Lypunov functions, they would have different error bounds for position. Such different bound could influence the final result. For example, the result for the Barrier scenario differs between the car and the robot. The car required 25 partitions to find a solution over all of Θ and the robot required 22. (c) Confirming what we have seen in Sect. 5.2, the runtime of the algorithm scales with the number of segments required to solve the scenario and the number of obstacles. (d) As expected and seen in Zigzag scenarios, all other things being the same, the running time and the number of partitions grow with larger initial set uncertainty.

Table 1. Synthesis performance on different scenarios (environment, vehicle). Dimension of state space $\mathcal{X}(n)$, input (m), radius of initial set Θ, number of obstacles $\mathbf{O}$, running time (in seconds).

Scenario	n, m	Radius of Θ	# O	Time (s)	# segments per ξ_{ref}	# partitions
Zigzag, car 1	3, 2	0.200	9	0.037	6.0	1.0
Zigzag, car 2	3, 2	0.400	9	0.212	4.0	6.0
Zigzag, car 3	3, 2	0.800	9	0.915	5.0–6.0	16.0
Zigzag, robot 1	4, 2	0.200	9	0.038	6.0	1.0
Zigzag, robot 2	4, 2	0.400	9	0.227	4.0	6.0
Zigzag, robot 3	4, 2	0.800	9	0.911	5.0–6.0	16.0
Barrier car	3, 2	0.707	6	0.697	2.0–4.0	25.0
Barrier, robot	4, 2	0.707	6	0.645	2.0–4.0	22.0
Maze, car	3, 2	0.200	22	0.174	8.0	1.0
Maze, robot	4, 2	0.200	22	0.180	8.0	1.0
SCOTS, car	3, 2	0.070	19	1.541	26.0	1.0
SCOTS, robot	4, 2	0.070	19	1.623	26.0	1.0
L-tunnel, hovercraft	4, 3	0.173	10	0.060	5.0	1.0
L-tunnel, AUV	6, 4	1.732	10	0.063	5.0	1.0
Z-tunnel, hovercraft	4, 3	0.173	5	0.029	4.0	1.0
Z-tunnel, AUV	6, 4	1.732	10	0.029	4.0	1.0

Comparison with Other Motion Controller Synthesis Tools: A Challenge. Few controller synthesis tools for nonlinear models are available for direct comparisons. We had detailed discussions with the authors of FastTrack [11], but found it difficult to plug-in new vehicle models. RTD [44] is implemented in MatLab also for specific vehicle models. Pessoa [26] and SCOTS [38] are implemented as general purpose tools. However, they are based on construction of discrete abstractions, which requires several additional user inputs. Therefore, we were only able to compare FACTEST with SCOTS and Pessoa using the scenario SCOTS. This scenario was originally built in SCOTS and is using the same car model.

The results for SCOTS and Pessoa can be found in [38]. The total runtime of SCOTS consists of the abstraction time t_{abs} and the synthesis time t_{syn}. The Pessoa tool has an abstraction time of $t_{abs} = 13509$ s and a synthesis time of $t_{syn} = 535$ s, which gives a total time of $t_{tot} = 14044$ s. The SCOTS tool has a has an abstraction time of $t_{abs} = 100$ s and a synthesis time of $t_{syn} = 413$ s, which gives a total time of $t_{tot} = 513$ s. FACTEST clearly outperforms both SCOTS and Pessoa with a total runtime of $t_{tot} = 1.541$ s. This could be attributed to the fact that FACTEST does not have to perform any abstractions, but even by looking sole at t_{syn}, FACTEST is significantly faster. However, we do note that the inputs of FACTEST and SCOTS are different. For example, SCOTS needs a growth bound function β for the dynamics but FACTEST requires Lyapunov functions for the tracking error.

6.3   RRT vs. SAT-Plan

To demonstrate the speed of our SAT-based reference trajectory synthesis algorithm (i.e. only the **while**-loop from Line 6 to Line 15 of Algorithm 2 which we call SAT-Plan), we compare it with Rapidly-exploring Random Trees (RRT) [20]. The running time, number of line segments, and number of iterations needed to find a path were compared. RRT was run using the Python Robotics library [39], which is not necessarily an optimized implementation. SAT-Plan was run using Yices 2.2. The scenarios are displayed in Fig. 4 and the results are in Fig. 5.

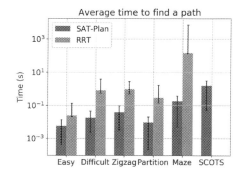 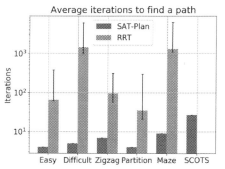

Fig. 5. Comparison of RRT and SAT-Plan. The left plot shows the runtime and the right plot shows the number of necessary iterations. Note that RRT timed out on the SCOTS scenario.

Each planner was run 100 times. The colored bars represent the average runtime and average number of iterations. The error bars represent the range of minimum and maximum. The RRT path planner was given a maximum of 5000 iterations and a path resolution of 0.01. SAT-Plan was given a maximum of 100 line segments to find a path. RRT timed out for the SCOTS scenario, unable to find a trajectory within 5000 iterations. The maze scenario timed out about 10% of the time.

Overall SAT-Plan scales in time much better as the size of the unsafe set increases. Additionally, the maximum number of iterations that RRT had to perform was far greater than the average number of line segments needed to find a safe path. This means that the maximum number of iterations that RRT must go through must be sufficiently large, or else a safe path will not be found even if one exists. SAT-Plan does not have randomness and therefore will find a reference trajectory (with k segments) in the modified space (bloated obstacles and shrunk goal) if one (with k segments) exists. Various examples of solutions found by RRT and SAT-Plan can be found on the FACTEST's website [27].

7   Conclusion and Discussion

We introduced a technique for synthesizing correct-by-construction controllers for a nonlinear vehicle models, including ground, underwater, and aerial vehicles, for reach-avoid requirements. Our tool FACTEST implementing this technique shows very encouraging performance on various vehicle models in different 2D and 3D scenarios.

There are several directions for future investigations. (1) One could explore a broader class of reference trajectories to reduce the tracking error bounds. (2) It would also be useful to extend the technique so the synthesized controller can satisfy the actuation constraints automatically. (3) Currently we require user to provide the tracking controller g_{trk} with the Lyapunov functions, it would be interesting to further automate this step.

References

1. Ames, A.D., Coogan, S., Egerstedt, M., Notomista, G., Sreenath, K., Tabuada, P.: Control barrier functions: theory and applications. In: 2019 18th European Control Conference (ECC), pp. 3420–3431. IEEE (2019)
2. Ardakani, M.M.G., Olofsson, B., Robertsson, A., Johansson, R.: Real-time trajectory generation using model predictive control. In: IEEE International Conference on Automation Science and Engineering, pp. 942–948. IEEE (2015)
3. Åström, K.J., Murray, R.M.: Feedback Systems: An Introduction for Scientists and Engineers. Princeton University Press, Princeton (2010)
4. Bemporad, A., Borrelli, F., Morari, M.: Model predictive control based on linear programming - the explicit solution. IEEE Trans. Autom. Control 47(12), 1974–1985 (2002)
5. Chitta, S., Sucan, I., Cousins, S.: Moveit![ROS topics]. IEEE Robot. Autom. Mag. 19(1), 18–19 (2012)

6. Dutertre, B.: Yices 2.2. In: Biere, A., Bloem, R. (eds.) CAV 2014. LNCS, vol. 8559, pp. 737–744. Springer, Cham (2014). https://doi.org/10.1007/978-3-319-08867-9_49

7. Fan, C., Mathur, U., Mitra, S., Viswanathan, M.: Controller synthesis made real: reach-avoid specifications and linear dynamics. In: Chockler, H., Weissenbacher, G. (eds.) CAV 2018. LNCS, vol. 10981, pp. 347–366. Springer, Cham (2018). https://doi.org/10.1007/978-3-319-96145-3_19

8. Mendes Filho, J.M., Lucet, E., Filliat, D.: Real-time distributed receding horizon motion planning and control for mobile multi-robot dynamic systems. In: International Conference on Robotics and Automation, pp. 657–663. IEEE (2017)

9. Filippidis, I., Dathathri, S., Livingston, S.C., Ozay, N., Murray, R.M.: Control design for hybrid systems with tulip: the temporal logic planning toolbox. In: IEEE Conference on Control Applications, pp. 1030–1041 (2016)

10. Girard, A.: Controller synthesis for safety and reachability via approximate bisimulation. Automatica **48**(5), 947–953 (2012)

11. Herbert, S.L., Chen, M., Han, S.J., Bansal, S., Fisac, J.F., Tomlin, C.J.: FaSTrack: a modular framework for fast and guaranteed safe motion planning. In: 2017 IEEE 56th Annual Conference on Decision and Control (CDC), pp. 1517–1522. IEEE (2017)

12. Janson, L., Schmerling, E., Clark, A., Pavone, M.: Fast marching tree: a fast marching sampling-based method for optimal motion planning in many dimensions. Int. J. Robot. Res. **34**(7), 883–921 (2015)

13. Kanayama, Y., Kimura, Y., Miyazaki, F., Noguchi, T.: A stable tracking control method for an autonomous mobile robot. In: Proceedings of the IEEE International Conference on Robotics and Automation, pp. 384–389. IEEE (1990)

14. Karaman, S., Frazzoli, E.: Incremental sampling-based algorithms for optimal motion planning. In: Robotics Science and Systems VI, vol. 104, no. 2 (2010)

15. Kavraki, L.E., Svestka, P., Latombe, J.-C., Overmars, M.H.: Probabilistic roadmaps for path planning in high-dimensional configuration spaces. IEEE Trans. Robot. Autom. **12**(4), 566–580 (1996)

16. Khalil, H.K., Grizzle, J.W.: Nonlinear Systems, vol. 3. Prentice Hall, Upper Saddle River (2002)

17. Kloetzer, M., Belta, C.: A fully automated framework for control of linear systems from temporal logic specifications. IEEE Trans. Autom. Control **53**(1), 287–297 (2008)

18. Kress-Gazit, H., Fainekos, G.E., Pappas, G.J.: Temporal logic based reactive mission and motion planning. IEEE Trans. Robot. **25**(6), 1370–1381 (2009)

19. Kuffner, J.J., LaValle, S.M.: RRT-connect: an efficient approach to single-query path planning. In: IEEE International Conference on Robotics and Automation, vol. 2, pp. 995–1001. IEEE (2000)

20. LaValle, S.M.: Rapidly-exploring random trees: a new tool for path planning (1998)

21. LaValle, S.M.: Planning Algorithms. Cambridge University Press, Cambridge (2006)

22. Liu, C., Lee, S., Varnhagen, S., Eric Tseng, H.: Path planning for autonomous vehicles using model predictive control. In: IEEE Intelligent Vehicles Symposium, pp. 174–179. IEEE (2017)

23. Majumdar, A., Tedrake, R.: Funnel libraries for real-time robust feedback motion planning. Int. J. Robot. Res. **36**(8), 947–982 (2017)

24. Mallik, K., Schmuck, A.-K., Soudjani, S., Majumdar, R.: Compositional synthesis of finite-state abstractions. IEEE Trans. Autom. Control **64**(6), 2629–2636 (2018)

25. Mayne, D.Q.: Model predictive control: recent developments and future promise. Automatica **50**, 2967–2986 (2014)
26. Mazo, M., Davitian, A., Tabuada, P.: PESSOA: a tool for embedded controller synthesis. In: Touili, T., Cook, B., Jackson, P. (eds.) CAV 2010. LNCS, vol. 6174, pp. 566–569. Springer, Heidelberg (2010). https://doi.org/10.1007/978-3-642-14295-6_49
27. Miller, K., Fan, C., Mitra, S.: Factest webpage (2020). https://kmmille.github.io/FACTEST/index.html. Accessed 13 May 2020
28. Mouelhi, S., Girard, A., Gössler, G.: CoSyMA: a tool for controller synthesis using multi-scale abstractions. In: International Conference on Hybrid Systems: Computation and Control, pp. 83–88. ACM (2013)
29. Nakamura, Y., Savant, S.: Nonlinear tracking control of autonomous underwater vehicles. In: Proceedings 1992 IEEE International Conference on Robotics and Automation, pp. A4–A9. IEEE (1992)
30. Ogata, K., Yang, Y.: Modern Control Engineering, vol. 5. Prentice Hall, Upper Saddle River (2010)
31. Paden, B., Čáp, M., Yong, S.Z., Yershov, D., Frazzoli, E.: A survey of motion planning and control techniques for self-driving urban vehicles. IEEE Trans. Intell. Veh. **1**(1), 33–55 (2016)
32. Texas A&M University Parasol MP Group, CSE Department Algorithms & applications group benchmarks
33. Raman, V., Donzé, A., Maasoumy, M., Murray, R.M., Sangiovanni-Vincentelli, A., Seshia, S.A.: Model predictive control with signal temporal logic specifications. In: 2014 IEEE 53rd Annual Conference on Decision and Control (CDC), pp. 81–87. IEEE (2014)
34. Raman, V., Donzé, A., Sadigh, D., Murray, R.M., Seshia, S.A.: Reactive synthesis from signal temporal logic specifications. In: International Conference on Hybrid Systems: Computation and Control, pp. 239–248. ACM (2015)
35. Ravanbakhsh, H., Sankaranarayanan, S.: Robust controller synthesis of switched systems using counterexample guided framework. In: 2016 International Conference on Embedded Software (EMSOFT), pp. 1–10. IEEE (2016)
36. Richter, S., Jones, C.N., Morari, M.: Computational complexity certification for real-time MPC with input constraints based on the fast gradient method. IEEE Trans. Autom. Control **57**(6), 1391–1403 (2011)
37. Roy, P., Tabuada, P., Majumdar, R.: Pessoa 2.0: a controller synthesis tool for cyber-physical systems. In: International Conference on Hybrid Systems: Computation and Control, pp. 315–316. ACM (2011)
38. Rungger, M., Zamani, M.: SCOTS: a tool for the synthesis of symbolic controllers. In: Proceedings of the 19th International Conference on Hybrid Systems: Computation and Control, pp. 99–104 (2016)
39. Sakai, A., Ingram, D., Dinius, J., Chawla, K., Raffin, A., Paques, A.: PythonRobotics: a python code collection of robotics algorithms (2018)
40. Singh, S., Majumdar, A., Slotine, J.-J., Pavone, M.: Robust online motion planning via contraction theory and convex optimization. In: 2017 IEEE International Conference on Robotics and Automation (ICRA), pp. 5883–5890. IEEE (2017)
41. Sucan, I.A., Moll, M., Kavraki, L.E.: The open motion planning library. IEEE Robot. Autom. Mag. **19**(4), 72–82 (2012)
42. Tabuada, P.: Verification and Control of Hybrid Systems - A Symbolic Approach. Springer, Heidelberg (2009). https://doi.org/10.1007/978-1-4419-0224-5
43. Tedrake, R.: LQR-trees: feedback motion planning on sparse randomized trees (2009)

44. Vaskov, S., et al.: Towards provably not-at-fault control of autonomous robots in arbitrary dynamic environments. arXiv preprint arXiv:1902.02851 (2019)
45. Vitus, M., Pradeep, V., Hoffmann, G., Waslander, S., Tomlin, C.: Tunnel-MILP: path planning with sequential convex polytopes. In: AIAA Guidance, Navigation and Control Conference and Exhibit, p. 7132 (2008)
46. Wong, K.W., Finucane, C., Kress-Gazit, H.: Provably-correct robot control with LTLMoP, OMPL and ROS. In: IEEE/RSJ International Conference on Intelligent Robots and Systems, p. 2073 (2013)
47. Wongpiromsarn, T., Topcu, U., Murray, R.M.: Receding horizon temporal logic planning. IEEE Trans. Autom. Control **57**(11), 2817–2830 (2012)
48. Wongpiromsarn, T., Topcu, U., Ozay, N., Xu, H., Murray, R.M.: Tulip: a software toolbox for receding horizon temporal logic planning. In: International Conference on Hybrid Systems: Computation and Control, pp. 313–314. ACM (2011)
49. Zeilinger, M.N., Jones, C.N., Morari, M.: Real-time suboptimal model predictive control using a combination of explicit MPC and online optimization. IEEE Trans. Autom. Control **56**(7), 1524–1534 (2011)

SeQuaiA: A Scalable Tool for Semi-Quantitative Analysis of Chemical Reaction Networks

Milan Češka[1(✉)], Calvin Chau[2], and Jan Křetínský[2]

[1] Brno University of Technology,
Brno, Czech Republic
ceskam@fit.vutbr.cz

[2] Technical University of Munich, Munich, Germany

Abstract. Chemical reaction networks (CRNs) play a fundamental role in analysis and design of biochemical systems. They induce continuous-time stochastic systems, whose analysis is a computationally intensive task. We present a tool that implements the recently proposed semi-quantitative analysis of CRN. Compared to the proposed theory, the tool implements the analysis so that it is more flexible and more precise. Further, its GUI offers a wide range of visualization procedures that facilitate the interpretation of the analysis results as well as guidance to refine the analysis. Finally, we define and implement a new notion of "mean" simulations, summarizing the typical behaviours of the system in a way directly comparable to standard simulations produced by other tools.

1 Introduction

Chemical Reaction Networks (CRNs) are a language widely used for *modelling and analysis* of biochemical systems [10] as well as for high-level programming of molecular devices [6,33]. They provide a compact formalism equivalent to Petri nets [30], vector addition systems [24] and distributed population protocols [3]. A CRN consists of a set of chemical reactions of given species, each running at a certain rate (intuitively, speed).

Example 1 (Gene expression). Our running example is the classic simple expression of a protein given by the reactions of production (p) and degradation (d) of proteins and blocking (b) the DNA, over three species: protein (P), active DNA (DNA_{on}), and blocked DNA (DNA_{off}):

$$\text{p: } D_{on} \xrightarrow{10} D_{on} + P \qquad \text{d: } P \xrightarrow{0.1} \emptyset \qquad \text{b: } D_{on} + P \xrightarrow{0.001} D_{off}$$

Using mass-action kinetics (the reaction rate is multiplied by the populations of the reactants), the CRN induces a infinite population Markov chain in Fig. 1.

This work has been partially supported by the Czech Science Foundation grant GJ20-02328Y and German Research Foundation (DFG) project 383882557 *Statistical Unbounded Verification* (KR 4890/2-1).

S. K. Lahiri and C. Wang (Eds.): CAV 2020, LNCS 12224, pp. 653–666, 2020.
https://doi.org/10.1007/978-3-030-53288-8_32

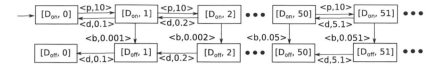

Fig. 1. The Markov chain for Gene expression, displaying the population of P. To simplify the exposition, D_{on} and D_{off} are displayed as discrete "states" of the system, but in fact the two "states" are just shorthands for 1,0 and 0,1, respectively.

In order to facilitate numerous applications in systems and synthetic biology, various techniques for simulation and formal analysis of CRNs have been proposed, e.g. [2,7,15,18,32]. We pinpoint several specifics of this setting, necessary to motivate and understand the features of the tool:

1. The analysis is notoriously difficult and **computationally expensive** due to several aspects: *state-space explosion* (exponential growth in the number of species, possibly infinite spaces due to unbounded populations as in Fig. 1, different rates for different populations, again as in Fig. 1), *stochasticity* (races between reactions), *stiffness* (rates of different magnitudes), *multimodality* (qualitatively different behaviours such as extinction of predators only, or also of preys in the predator-prey models) [17,34]. Consequently, even for small CRNs, simulations may take minutes and analyses hours.
2. We have to face **imprecise inputs**. In particular, even if all relevant reactions are known, the rates are typically not. It is then not clear what behaviours can be induced by all possible values.
3. The analysis **output need not be precise** numerically, but only qualitatively. For instance, it is important to know that initial growth is followed by extinction and what the order of magnitude of the peak population is, but not necessarily what the exact distribution at an exact time is. Unfortunately, it is hard to compute the qualitative information without the quantitative one.
4. Biologists and engineers often seek for plausible **explanations** of why the system under study features or not the discussed behaviour. In many cases, a set of system simulations/trajectories or population distributions is not sufficient and the ability to provide an accurate explanation for the temporal or steady-state behaviour is another major challenge for the existing techniques.

SeQuaiA[1] is a tool for analysis of CRN addressing these issues:

1. It features unprecedented **scalability**, analysing standard complex benchmarks within a fraction of a second.
2. It is **robust** w.r.t. concrete rates, not depending on the exact values but only on their orders of magnitude.
3. Its *semi-quantitative analysis* is **precise enough** to conclude on the qualitative behaviour of the system including rare behaviours and on rough estimates of the quantities (population sizes, times).

---

[1] Available at https://sequaia.model.in.tum.de.

4. It produces small abstract models (Markov chains) that are explicit, yet **interpretable**, making the behaviour more **explainable**.

It is based on the technique presented in [9], relying on two cornerstones. Firstly, it computes a system abstraction with **acceleration**, abstracting not only states and single transitions, but taking into account *segments* of paths. The resulting models are small enough to allow for a synoptic observation of the model dynamics. Secondly, it performs **semi-quantitative analysis**, focusing on the most probable behaviours and more qualitative, global descriptions, such as oscillation, rather than fully quantitative sequences of exact transient distributions. This yields explainable models and is a sufficient and computationally cheaper technique. While the basic theory is derived from [9], there are a number of new features and differences in our tool, not just the implementation:

Method: (i) The abstraction is *more precise* now that the tool can also compute numerical outputs, whereas [9] focuses on a manually feasible, and hence imprecise, abstraction. (ii) It suggests how to *refine the abstractions*, providing a knob for trading precision for computational resources.

Visualization: The GUI provides a number of ways to display the results, facilitating understanding the models, including (i) identification of strongly connected parts of 'iterations', corresponding to 'temporarily stable' behaviours, (ii) quantitative information on transient times and steady-state distributions, or (iii) visual qualitative explanations, such as semantic grouping of states or tracking correlations between populations.

Additional analysis instruments: (i) The new notion of *envelope* provides an explicit knob to consider not only the most probable, but also less probable behaviours. (ii) The novel concept of *mean simulation* yields summaries of most probable runs and an analysis output directly comparable to classic simulation-based tools.

Related Work. Since a direct analysis of the Markov chains induced by CRN does not scale well [19], deterministic approximations through fluid (mean-field) techniques can be applied [4,8] to large populations, but cannot adequately capture the stochasticity of CRNs caused by low population species. To this end, both can be combined in hybrid approaches [7,18,21], typically involving a computationally demanding numerical analysis. Reduction techniques such as [1,12] are based on approximate bisimulation [11], on aggregation according to the CRN-specific structure [13,27,35], or state truncation [20,28,29].

Despite the plethora of techniques, the practical analysis of CRNs often relies on the stochastic simulation [15] and its multi-scale improvements [5,14,17, 22,31,32]. The widely used tool include the platform-independent Copasi [23], DSD [25] with a convenient web-based graphical interface, or StochPy [26] easily extensible using Python scientific libraries. In contrast, our approach (i) provides a compact explanation of the system behaviour in the form of tiny models allowing for a synoptic observation (ii) can easily reveal less probable behaviours, and iii) as shown in [9], is able to analyse standard complex benchmarks in seconds and thus provides the unprecedented scalability compared to other numerical as well as simulation-based techniques.

2   Workflow and Key Functionality

In this section, we guide the reader through the workflow, discuss the key features of the tool and demonstrate them on examples. The GUI is structured into several tabs and panels reflecting the workflow of the tool. First, a CRN is either retrieved from a file in the Open model tab or a new one is created. Either way, the model can be changed in the Editor panel together with the analysis parameters. The process continues in the Analysis tab. The analysis follows in two steps. First, the *semi-quantitative abstraction* of the Markov chain for the CRN is generated; second, the *semi-quantitative* analysis is performed on the abstraction. The tool offers an explicit option to display the abstraction as a .dot file or to directly run both steps. After the complete analysis is executed, the Visualization panel offers a range of options to *display* the results, including various *quantitative properties*. Finally, the analysed model can be used to generate concrete runs on the Simulation tab, which we call *mean simulations* since they display the "average-case" behaviour. In the following we detail on these key elements.

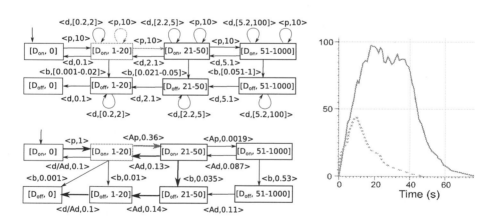

Fig. 2. Left: The abstract Markov chain for Gene expression with population discretization thresholds 20, 50 and the population bound 1000. *Top:* The classic may transition function. *Bottom:* The semi-quantitative version with accelerated transitions (denoted by prefix "A"). **Right:** The full blue line shows a typical simulation of the model (population of P), obtained using DSD tool [25]. The dotted green line corresponds to the fast variant of the model with the rate of b being 10^{-2}. (Color figure online)

2.1   Semi-quantitative Abstraction

Key Idea. The abstraction of the state space is simply given by a discretization of the population for each species into finitely many intervals, see Fig. 2 (left). The classic may abstraction of the transition function results in non-deterministic self-loops as in Fig. 2 (left top) in red, which make impossible to conclude anything useful (except for some safety properties) on the behaviour once we reach such a state, even whether it is ever left at all. Instead, [9] considers sequences of transitions: in this case, sequences of prevalently growing transitions (those increasing the population) are significantly more probable than the prevalently decreasing ones. Consequently, the self-looping transitions are *accelerated* (taken multiple times) to get a "combined" transition that brings a typical representative of this population interval into a higher interval, see Fig. 2 (left bottom) also in red. Hence the new rate reflects (i) the mass-action kinetics with the typical population in the interval and (ii) the typical number of the transition repetitions before another interval is reached. These accelerated transitions are the key idea of the semi-quantitative abstraction and are denoted by a prefix A.

Tool Inputs. Technically, the tool requires, for each species, a (possible empty) list of increasing population thresholds $t_1, t_2, \ldots t_n$ and a population bound t_b. The thresholds split the concrete population to the intervals $[0, 0], (0, t_1], (t_1, t_2], \ldots (t_{n-1}, t_n], (t_n, \infty)$. Here 0 is taken separately to reflect enabledness of actions; the representatives, used for consequent computations, are chosen to be in the middle of the intervals and derived from t_b for the last one. (For the empty list we have only one non-zero interval $(0, \infty)$). The input numbers are supposed to reflect the monitored property of interest and the required precision, the bound t_b should give a probable upper bound on the maximal population. How to obtain and iteratively improve these is discussed in Sect. 2.5 on refinement.

Example 2. Consider Gene expression, now with a 'fast' blocking where the rate of b equals 10^{-2}. A typical simulation can be seen in Fig. 2 (right, dotted green line): the number of proteins grows until several dozen, then blocking takes place until extinction. The semi-quantitative abstraction for thresholds $10, 20, 50$ yields the model in Fig. 3(a). In contrast to classic abstractions, there are no self-loops and the abstract transitions are assigned concrete rates. One can see that the blocking can in principle take place at any population and that population can decrease also when DNA is on, i.e. in states $[1, 0, \cdot]$. However, all this happens with very low probabilities and the model captures this only indirectly through the numerical labelling. This is made explicit during the semi-quantitative analysis.

2.2   Semi-quantitative Analysis

Key Idea. The aim is to prune the abstraction so that only reasonably probable behaviour is reflected, see the thick transitions in the abstraction in Fig. 2 (left bottom). To this end, we preserve in each state only the transitions with the

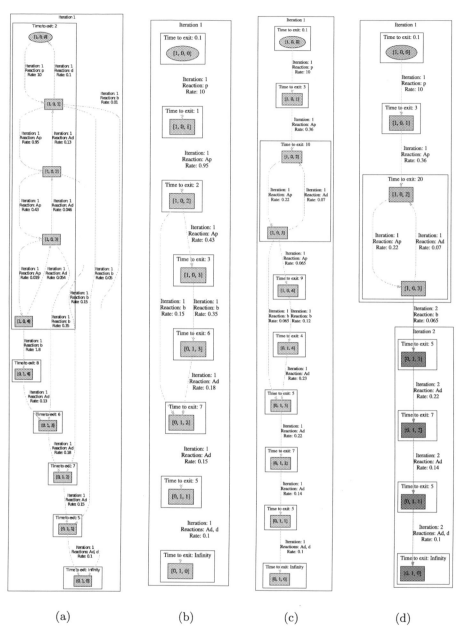

(a)   (b)   (c)   (d)

Fig. 3. (a) and (b): 'Fast' Gene expression with thresholds $10, 20, 50$. (a) depicts the full abstraction and (b) depicts *envelope* $= 3$. (c)–(e): 'Slow' Gene expression with thresholds $20, 50, 80, 150$. (d) and (e) depicts the pruned abstraction with *envelope* $= 3$ and 1, respectively.

highest rate h or almost highest rates, i.e. with $h' > h/envelope$ where $envelope > 1$ is a parameter. Parameter values in $[1, 10]$ ensure we can only look at rates of the same order of magnitude, thus the most probable events and those with e.g. only 20% chance of happening. Higher values then allow for inspection of even less probable behaviours.

Consequently, the method can naturally handle uncertainty in the reaction rates since typically only the relative magnitudes of the rates are important, actually, only their orders of magnitude. This robustness w.r.t. the input is very beneficial for biologists as the precise rates are often not known.

Example 3. The analysis of the previous 'fast' Gene expression with $envelope = 3$ is depicted in Fig. 3(b). As such it shows the most probable behaviours: the fast growth until the intervals 2 and 3 (i.e. 10–20 and 20–50) and not beyond to 4 (over 50), followed by a slower decline. The computed rates induce expected times to pass through a state, matching closely those of the simulation Fig. 2 (right, dotted green line). Moreover, we see that the blocking transition from interval 2 has a lower probability than the production, is thus less probable. As such it would not even appear as a probable one, for a stricter $envelope = 2$.

Example 4. A more complicated behaviour arises when the blocking is slow, with rate 10^{-3} as in Sect. 1. A simulation run for this case is depicted in Fig. 2 (right, full blue line). One can observe a more balanced competition between blocking and oscillation around 70–100 proteins. Similarly, while the full abstraction (not shown here) features arbitrary oscillations (also back to no proteins at all), after analysis the pruned abstraction is faithfully modelling the initial growth, subsequent oscillation only in the range of higher populations, followed by blocking and gradual extinction of proteins, see Fig. 3(c).

Technically, the analysis relies on repeated alternation of transient and steady-state analysis. First, starting from the initial state, we follow in each state only the transitions with highest rates (most probable ones), until the set of explored state reaches a fixpoint. A part of the created graph is recurrent and forms a bottom strongly connected component (BSCC) or a collection thereof. The system temporarily settles in the steady state of this BSCC. After some time has passed, also a less probable transition happens almost surely and the "BSCC" is exited. These exit points are identified by a steady-state analysis of the BSCC, taking the magnitudes of exiting and non-exiting transition rates into account. The exit points trigger a new *iteration* of the transient and then the steady-state analysis.

Example 5. Figure 3(d) illustrates a situation with two iteration using the slow variant of the model. Decreasing $envelope$ to 1 caused that the blocking reaction is explored in the second iteration – as an exit of the BSCC found in the first iteration. Before that exit happens, the "BSCC" represents a "temporary" steady state of the system.

Note on Correctness. As discussed in [9], the semi-quantitative analysis provides guarantees in the form of limit behaviour and convergence: firstly, the precision grows with the differences in the orders of magnitudes of involved rates: as their ratios tend to infinity, the error tends to zero; secondly, as the population discretization gets finer, the error in the new "accelerated" transitions is reduced, trivially being zero for complete refinement into singletons.

2.3   Visualization of Qualitative Information

A proper visualization is essential for clear presentation and easy interpretation of the results of our analysis. To this end, the tool and its GUI offer various options for visualizing the results. The basic ones, related to the graph structure, are the following. Further options, with more quantitative flavour, are discussed in the next section, followed by an example illustrating all of them.

Iterations. As the complete abstract model is typically very large and chaotic, further structuring is necessary. Therefore, the default view shows the states arranged and grouped into separate blocks, one for each iteration, additionally coloured distinctly for each iteration. Besides, we can restrict which iterations we show. This is useful to zoom in and investigate a particular part of the behaviour.

Intra-iteration SCCs (IISCCs). Additionally, the arrangement and colouring can be based on aggregating SCCs *within* each iteration (IISCCs). This helps to understand the emergence of repetitive behaviour patterns, such as oscillation or (temporary) steady state. It can be also combined with the iteration grouping.

Collapsed Views. In order to understand the system behaviour, one typically needs to have a synoptic overview of the system. For more complex systems, even the pruned abstraction could become too large and the view of the fully expanded system might not be sufficiently compact. In such cases, the aggregates discussed in the previous views, i.e., iterations and IISCCs, can be collapsed into a single nodes, hiding the complexity of the exact behaviour pattern within these areas. This allows us, for instance, to ignore the particular (temporary) oscillation or steady state in these states and to focus on more global behaviour, such as what happened before and after this behaviour and how often does it arise. In contrast to zooming in by restricting to certain iteration(s) only, the collapsed views provide a means to zoom out.

2.4   Visualization of Quantitative Information

The produced graphs are also labelled by *numerical information*. While the quantities cannot be precise due to the simplifications of the extremely scalable analysis, they match the orders of magnitudes of the observed quantities, which is often precise enough for biological purposes; for instance, the peak of protein growth happens after units vs. dozens of seconds in the fast and slow variants of Gene expression, respectively.

Transient Analysis. Firstly, each abstract transition is labelled with a rate corresponding (in the order of magnitude) to the rate of the concrete transition (or accelerated transition, i.e. a "sequence" of transitions) of a "typical" representative of the abstract state. These rates induce the expected time spent in each transient state of each iteration. Indeed, the waiting time is simply the inverse of the sum of the outgoing rates. Further, each BSCC of each iteration is labelled by an estimate of time before it is left into the next iteration. This is a key notion, which allows us to easily provide transient timing information for very stiff systems (working at different time scales). Consider the simple gene model. From Fig. 3(b) and (d) we can easily compute the expected time to the extinction (as the sum of the exit time for all SCC on the inspected path). Our analysis correctly estimates that the expected extinction time is around 24 and for the fast variant and 40 for the slow variant.

Steady State Analysis. In many biological models, the natural steady state is either extinction or unbounded explosion. Hence it does not say much about the "seemingly steady" state (the temporary steady state), i.e., behaviour that is stable for a long but finite time. Therefore, the tool provides information not only on the steady state of the whole system, but also for each iteration separately since they represent the temporary steady states discussed above. Both can be visualized as colouring of states, with higher probabilities corresponding to darker colours, immediatelly giving a synoptic view on frequent behaviours.

Correlations. Finally, correlations between population sizes can be observed as follows. The GUI can be given a set of equivalences of the form $m \sim n$ for species i, j, meaning that if a state has (abstract) population m of species i and n of j then it is regarded as satisfying the correlation in question. It is coloured accordingly and the overall colouring of the system provides further indication under which behaviour or in which phases the correlation holds.

Example 6. We demonstrate these visualization options on a more complicated gene expression model [16], widely used model for benchmarking CRN analyzers, in Fig. 4. As reported in [16,18], the behaviour oscillates between two steady states with DNA on and DNA off. Moreover, there is a correlation between high amounts of RNA present and DNA being on, and no RNA with DNA off.

The complete system and its steady state distribution is depicted in the part a) using the iteration and IISCC arrangement. This view shows immediately without seeing any details that the only interesting states are in iteration 1 including all states with a high steady-state probability (the red colouring). Therefore, in part b), we zoom in to iteration 1 and use the IISCC arrangement. In order to observe the interesting switches between the temporary steady states, we collapse the IISCCs, in the part c), and thus ignore the internal (non-interesting) behaviour of the big IISCC. Finally, in part d), we use the correlation colouring to identify states where the required correlation holds (i.e. the blue states). Comparing part c) and d) immediately reveals that the system spends the majority of the time in the states where the correlation holds.

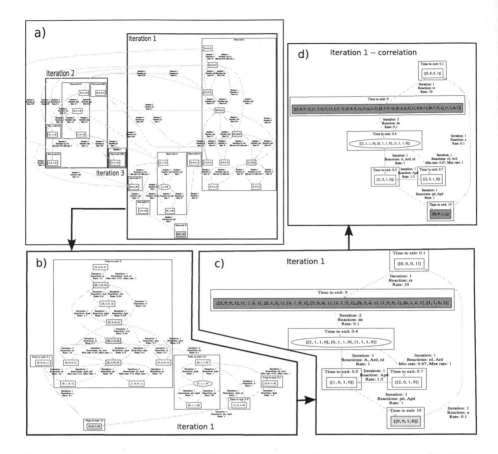

Fig. 4. A visualisation of the workflow for the extended gene expression model. (Color figure online)

2.5 Precision and Refinement

So far, we have illustrated the concepts and the functionality on models with an appropriate level of abstraction. However, it often happens that we start the investigations with a too coarse abstraction. Whenever this happens, it is important to notice this and appropriately refine the abstraction. While [9] does not discuss this issue, the tool provides support also for that.

Precision Parameters. There are several knobs for trading the size and the precision of the abstraction. They all come as input in the lower half of the Editor tab: discretization, bound, and envelope.

Example 7. Recall the initial abstraction for the Gene expression of Fig. 2 (with rate 10^{-3}). The abstraction, using thresholds 20, 50 predicts an oscillation including low populations of P (1–20) which is not correct (recall that the P oscillates on high populations before the blocking reaction occurs). Figure 3(c) and (d) show the abstraction and the consequent analysis and visualization for a refined model using thresholds $20, 50, 80, 150$ (instead of just $20, 50$). As already discussed, this abstraction already correctly predicts the system behaviour.

Discretization. The basic building block of each abstraction is the degree of details it preserves in the abstract states. Firstly, it determines how precisely we can observe the evolution of the population. For instance, whenever we want to detect whether a population typically grows beyond a bound or oscillates in a certain interval, such an interval should be present in the discretization. Secondly, the discretization should be fine enough so that in each state, the rates are reasonably (in orders of magnitude) precise. Fortunately, in our analysis their absolute precision is not vital. In contrast, we only need *relative* proportions of the rates to have the right *magnitude* to decide which behaviour is probable. Consequently, too rough abstraction is reflected in *"non-determinism"* when a state has two transitions under similar rate. In such a case, the probable behaviour cannot be determined. Therefore, the Visualization tab provides in the Colorization pane an option to provide suggestions for refinement, including highlighting non-deterministic states, pointing at the natural candidates for refinement. Note that we highlight only the states where the two transitions lead to mutually different SCCs so that a significant change in behaviour may occur.

Bounds. Similarly, for the single infinite interval (t_n, ∞), the tool inputs a *bound* which is a believed safe upper bound on the population of the species. Of course, it may be wrong. This is irrelevant in case when the population explodes beyond all bounds. However, whenever there are transitions from the highest level back to a lower one, its feasibility and rate are in question. Optimally, such states do not even occur in the pruned abstraction. If they do, we also highlight them using the Colorization for Refinement suggestions (in another colour).

Envelope. As too rough abstractions introduce too much non-determinism, dually, the degree of the non-determinism is determined (even defined) by the *envelope*, the factor between rates so that even the less probable option is still taken into account (and thus introduces non-determinism). Consequently, high values of envelope introduce non-determinism, making the analysis take also less important behaviour into account; in contrast, low values make the analyzed system deterministic, showing only the most probable behaviour. The choice of the envelope thus depends on whether such behaviours should also be reported.

2.6   Mean Simulations

Since our models, although abstract, have an operational semantics, we can even run simulations on them. Moreover, the accelerated transitions, as "sequences" of transitions, have a low variance in the expected time, by the law of large numbers. Hence their execution time can be chosen quite precisely in a deterministic way. Similarly, the time to leave an IIBSCC is quite deterministic. Thus we can generate simulation where the only random decisions are choices of transitions, but the timing follows the mean time of the respective events. Moreover, runs within the pruned abstraction reflect the most important behaviours only.

Such *mean simulations*[2], which can thus be generated from our analysis, represent groups of typical runs (modulo small time shifts and order of transitions within an SCC, which are not very relevant). Therefore, a few such simulation reflect all the present behaviours (on a level of desired significant probability) and can serve to observe multi-modalities, bifurcations, rough transient timing as well as frequencies in the steady-state and temporary steady-state. To our best knowledge, such a concept has not yet been considered for simulation of stochastic systems.

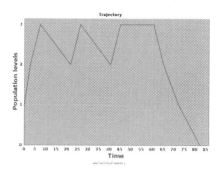

Fig. 5. Mean simulation for the slow variant of Gene expression, directly comparable to Fig. 2 (right, full line).

Example 8. Figure 5 shows an abstract simulation for our running example with discretisation thresholds $20, 50, 80, 150$. One can readily observe its validity with respect to the typical stochastic simulation in Fig. 2 (right, full blue line).

3   Conclusion

We have presented SeQuaiA, a scalable tool for robust and explainable analysis of CRNs. The analysis is precise enough as cross-validated with simulation-based results on several models widely used in the literature. One of the key contributions of the tool is the visualization, which is essential for clear presentation and easy interpretation of the results of our analysis.

References

1. Abate, A., Katoen, J.P., Lygeros, J., Prandini, M.: Approximate model checking of stochastic hybrid systems. Eur. J. Control **16**, 624–641 (2010)
2. Abate, A., Brim, L., Češka, M., Kwiatkowska, M.: Adaptive aggregation of Markov chains: quantitative analysis of chemical reaction networks. In: Kroening, D., Păsăreanu, C.S. (eds.) CAV 2015. LNCS, vol. 9206, pp. 195–213. Springer, Cham (2015). https://doi.org/10.1007/978-3-319-21690-4_12
3. Angluin, D., Aspnes, J., Eisenstat, D., Ruppert, E.: The computational power of population protocols. Distrib. Comput. **20**(4), 279–304 (2007)
4. Bortolussi, L., Hillston, J.: Fluid model checking. In: Koutny, M., Ulidowski, I. (eds.) CONCUR 2012. LNCS, vol. 7454, pp. 333–347. Springer, Heidelberg (2012). https://doi.org/10.1007/978-3-642-32940-1_24
5. Cao, Y., Gillespie, D.T., Petzold, L.R.: The slow-scale stochastic simulation algorithm. J. Chem. Phys. **122**(1), 014116 (2005)

---

[2] They are not means of values from simulations since averaging oscillating values may result in no oscillation. Rather they reflect "mean patterns".

6. Cardelli, L.: Two-domain DNA strand displacement. Math. Struct. Comput. Sci. **23**(02), 247–271 (2013)
7. Cardelli, L., Kwiatkowska, M., Laurenti, L.: A stochastic hybrid approximation for chemical kinetics based on the linear noise approximation. In: Bartocci, E., Lio, P., Paoletti, N. (eds.) CMSB 2016. LNCS, vol. 9859, pp. 147–167. Springer, Cham (2016). https://doi.org/10.1007/978-3-319-45177-0_10
8. Cardelli, L., Tribastone, M., Tschaikowski, M., Vandin, A.: Maximal aggregation of polynomial dynamical systems. Proc. Natl. Acad. Sci. **114**(38), 10029–10034 (2017)
9. Češka, M., Křetínský, J.: Semi-quantitative abstraction and analysis of chemical reaction networks. In: Dillig, I., Tasiran, S. (eds.) CAV 2019. LNCS, vol. 11561, pp. 475–496. Springer, Cham (2019). https://doi.org/10.1007/978-3-030-25540-4_28
10. Chellaboina, V., Bhat, S.P., Haddad, W.M., Bernstein, D.S.: Modeling and analysis of mass-action kinetics. IEEE Control Syst. Mag. **29**(4), 60–78 (2009)
11. Desharnais, J., Laviolette, F., Tracol, M.: Approximate analysis of probabilistic processes: logic, simulation and games. In: Quantitative Evaluation of SysTems (QEST), pp. 264–273. IEEE (2008)
12. D'Innocenzo, A., Abate, A., Katoen, J.P.: Robust PCTL model checking. In: Hybrid Systems: Computation and Control (HSCC), pp. 275–285. ACM (2012)
13. Ferm, L., Lötstedt, P.: Adaptive solution of the master equation in low dimensions. Appl. Numer. Math. **59**(1), 187–204 (2009)
14. Ganguly, A., Altintan, D., Koeppl, H.: Jump-diffusion approximation of stochastic reaction dynamics: error bounds and algorithms. Multiscale Model. Simul. **13**(4), 1390–1419 (2015)
15. Gillespie, D.T.: Exact stochastic simulation of coupled chemical reactions. J. Phys. Chem. **81**(25), 2340–2361 (1977)
16. Golding, I., Paulsson, J., Zawilski, S.M., Cox, E.C.: Real-time kinetics of gene activity in individual bacteria. Cell **123**(6), 1025–1036 (2005)
17. Goutsias, J.: Quasiequilibrium approximation of fast reaction kinetics in stochastic biochemical systems. J. Phys. Chem. **122**(18), 184102 (2005)
18. Hasenauer, J., Wolf, V., Kazeroonian, A., Theis, F.J.: Method of conditional moments (MCM) for the Chemical Master Equation. J. Math. Biol. **69**(3), 687–735 (2013). https://doi.org/10.1007/s00285-013-0711-5
19. Heath, J., Kwiatkowska, M., Norman, G., Parker, D., Tymchyshyn, O.: Probabilistic model checking of complex biological pathways. Theor. Comput. Sci. **391**(3), 239–257 (2008)
20. Henzinger, T.A., Mateescu, M., Wolf, V.: Sliding window abstraction for infinite markov chains. In: Bouajjani, A., Maler, O. (eds.) CAV 2009. LNCS, vol. 5643, pp. 337–352. Springer, Heidelberg (2009). https://doi.org/10.1007/978-3-642-02658-4_27
21. Henzinger, T.A., Mikeev, L., Mateescu, M., Wolf, V.: Hybrid numerical solution of the chemical master equation. In: Computational Methods in Systems Biology (CMSB), pp. 55–65. ACM (2010)
22. Hepp, B., Gupta, A., Khammash, M.: Adaptive hybrid simulations for multiscale stochastic reaction networks. J. Chem. Phys. **142**(3), 034118 (2015)
23. Hoops, S., et al.: COPASI - a complex pathway simulator. Bioinformatics **22**(24), 3067–3074 (2006). https://doi.org/10.1093/bioinformatics/btl485, http://bioinformatics.oxfordjournals.org/content/22/24/3067.abstract
24. Karp, R.M., Miller, R.E.: Parallel program schemata. J. Comput. Syst. Sci. **3**(2), 147–195 (1969)

25. Lakin, M.R., Youssef, S., Polo, F., Emmott, S., Phillips, A.: Visual DSD: a design and analysis tool for dna strand displacement systems. Bioinformatics **27**(22), 3211–3213 (2011)
26. Maarleveld, T.R., Olivier, B.G., Bruggeman, F.J.: StochPy: a comprehensive, user-friendly tool for simulating stochastic biological processes. PloS one **8**(11), e79345 (2013)
27. Madsen, C., Myers, C., Roehner, N., Winstead, C., Zhang, Z.: Utilizing stochastic model checking to analyze genetic circuits. In: Computational Intelligence in Bioinformatics and Computational Biology (CIBCB), pp. 379–386. IEEE (2012)
28. Mateescu, M., Wolf, V., Didier, F., Henzinger, T.A.: Fast adaptive uniformization of the chemical master equation. IET Syst. Biol. **4**(6), 441–452 (2010)
29. Munsky, B., Khammash, M.: The finite state projection algorithm for the solution of the chemical master equation. J. Chem. Phys. **124**, 044104 (2006)
30. Murata, T.: Petri nets: properties, analysis and applications. Proc. IEEE **77**(4), 541–580 (1989)
31. Rao, C.V., Arkin, A.P.: Stochastic chemical kinetics and the quasi-steady-state assumption: application to the gillespie algorithm. J. Chem. Phys. **118**(11), 4999–5010 (2003)
32. Salis, H., Kaznessis, Y.: Accurate hybrid stochastic simulation of a system of coupled chemical or biochemical reactions. J. Chem. Phys. **122**(5), 054103 (2005)
33. Soloveichik, D., Seelig, G., Winfree, E.: DNA as a universal substrate for chemical kinetics. Proc. Natl. Acad. Sci. U.S.A. **107**(12), 5393–5398 (2010)
34. Van Kampen, N.G.: Stochastic Processes in Physics and Chemistry, vol. 1. Elsevier, Amsterdam (1992)
35. Zhang, J., Watson, L.T., Cao, Y.: Adaptive aggregation method for the chemical master equation. Int. J. Comput. Biol. Drug Des. **2**(2), 134–148 (2009)

Author Index

Printed in the United States
By Bookmasters